ABBREVIATIONS

AAI	Average Age of Inventory
ABI	Active Business Income
ACP	Average Collection Period
AcSB	Accounting Standards Board
ADRs	American Depository Receipts
ANPV	Annualized Net Present Value
APP	Average Payment Period
APR	Annual Percentage Rate
ARR	Average Rate of Return
BIA	*Bankruptcy and Insolvency Act*
CAPEX	Capital Expenditures
CAPM	Capital Asset Pricing Model
CCA	Capital Cost Allowance
CCC	Cash Conversion Cycle
CCAA	Companies' Creditors Arrangement Act
CCPC	Canadian-Controlled Private Corporation
CDCC	Canadian Derivatives Clearing Corporation
CE	Certainty Equivalent
CEO	Chief Executive Officer
CFO	Chief Financial Officer
CICA	Canadian Institute of Chartered Accountants
COGS	Cost of Goods Sold
DBRS	Dominion Bond Rating Service
DFL	Degree of Financial Leverage
DOL	Degree of Operating Leverage
DRIPs	Dividend Reinvestment Plans
DRP	Default Risk Premium
DSO	Days' Sales Outstanding
DTL	Degree of Total Leverage
DVM	Dividend Valuation Model
EAC	Earnings Available for Common Shareholders
EAR	Effective Annual Rate
EBIT	Earnings Before Interest and Taxes
EBITDA	Earnings Before Interest, Taxes, Depreciation, and Amortization
EBT	Earnings Before Taxes
EFR	External Financing Required
EMH	Efficient Market Hypothesis
EOQ	Economic Order Quantity
EPS	Earnings per Share
EVA	Economic Value Added
FAT	Fixed Asset Turnover
FC	Fixed Operating Cost per Unit
FCC	Fixed Charge Coverage
FCF	Free Cash Flow
FCFO	Free Cash Flow from Operations
FDI	Foreign Direct Investment
FLM	Financial Leverage Multiplier
FTAA	Free Trade Area of the Americas
GAAP	Generally Accepted Accounting Principles
GATT	General Agreement on Tariffs and Trade
GDP	Gross Domestic Product
IOS	Investment Opportunities Schedule
IP	Inflation Premium
IPO	Initial Public Offering
IRR	Internal Rate of Return
ITC	Investment Tax Credit
IV	Intrinsic Value of a Derivative
JIT	Just-In-Time System
LIBOR	London Interbank Offered Rate
M/B	Market/Book Value Ratio
MCC	Marginal Cost of Capital
MD&A	Management's Discussion and Analysis
MNC	Multinational Company
M&P	Manufacturer and Processor
MRP	Maturity Risk Premium
NAFTA	North American Free Trade Agreement
NIAT	Net Income After Taxes
NPV	Net Present Value
OC	Operating Cycle
OCS	Optimal Capital Structure
OPEC	Organization of Petroleum Exporting Countries
P/E	Price/Earnings Ratio
PI	Profitability Index
PM	Profit Margin
POP	Prompt Offering Prospectus System
RADR	Risk-Adjusted Discount Rate
ROA	Return on Total Assets
ROE	Return on Equity
RP	Risk Premium
SCF	Statement of Cash Flows
SML	Security Market Line
SPPs	Share Purchase Plans
TAT	Total Asset Turnover
TFR	Total Financing Required
TIE	Times Interest Earned
TSOR	Term Structure of Interest Rates
TSX	Toronto Stock Exchange
UCC	Undepreciated Capital Cost
WACC	Weighted Average Cost of Capital
YTM	Yield to Maturity

PRINCIPLES OF CORPORATE FINANCE

Second Canadian Edition

PRINCIPLES OF CORPORATE FINANCE

Second Canadian Edition

Lawrence J. Gitman
San Diego State University

Sean M. Hennessey
University of Prince Edward Island

Toronto

Library and Archives Canada Cataloguing in Publication

Gitman, Lawrence J.

Principles of corporate finance / Lawrence J. Gitman, Sean M. Hennessey.—2nd Canadian ed.

Includes index.
ISBN-13: 978-0-321-45293-1

1. Corporations—Finance—Textbooks. 2. Business enterprises—Finance—Textbooks.
I. Hennessey, Sean II. Title.

HG4026.G57 2008 658.15 C2007-900118-1

ISBN-13: 978-0-321-45293-1
ISBN-10: 0-321-45293-3

Editor-in-Chief: Gary Bennett
Executive Editor: Samantha Scully
Marketing Manager: Eileen Lasswell
Developmental Editor: John Polanszky
Production Editor: Laura Neves
Copy Editor: Rodney Rawlings
Proofreader: Kelli Howey
Production Coordinator: Andrea Falkenberg
Composition: Joan M. Wilson
Photo and Permissions Research: Sandy Cooke
Art Director: Julia Hall
Cover and Interior Design: Geoff Agnew
Cover Image: Gregor Schuster/Getty Images

Photo Credits: p. 45, Jupiter; p. 111, Dick Hemingway; p. 175, © David Norton/Alamy; p. 367, Jupiter; p. 501, Jupiter; p. 551, Jupiter; p. 649, CP PHOTO/John Ulan; p. 773, CP PHOTO/Edmonton Sun–Christine Vanzella; p. 821, CP PHOTO/Paul Chiasson; p. 853, © Jim Zuckerman/CORBIS; p. 901, © Jim Zuckerman/CORBIS.

1 2 3 4 5 11 10 09 08 07

Printed and bound in the United States of America.

*Dedicated to the memory
of my mother, Dr. Edith Gitman,
who instilled in me the importance
of education and hard work.*

Lawrence J. Gitman

*To Roberta, my wife and best friend,
our son Liam,
and my parents, Aletha and Michael.*

Sean Hennessey

Brief Contents

Contents

CHAPTER 2 Financial Statements, Cash Flows, and Taxes 44

The Language of Finance

Part 2 *Financial Analysis and Planning 110*

CHAPTER 3 Financial Statement Analysis 110

Apples, Oranges, and Grapefruit!

CHAPTER 4
Financial Planning and Forecasting 174

The Best Laid Plans . . .

Part 3 *Important Financial Concepts 228*

CHAPTER 5
Financial Markets, Institutions, and Securities 228

Financial Fabric

CHAPTER 6 Time Value of Money 302

Money Time

CHAPTER 7 Risk and Return 366

"Not for a Million Bucks!"

CHAPTER 10
Leverage and Capital Structure 550

Jacking Up Owners' Wealth

CHAPTER 11
Dividend Policy 612

Paying Dividends

Part 5 *Long-Term Investment Decisions* 648

CHAPTER 12
Capital Budgeting: Principles and Techniques 648

From Dreams to Reality

CHAPTER 13
Dealing with Project Risk and Other Topics in Capital Budgeting 726

Getting a Handle on Risk

Part 6 *Working Capital Management* 772

CHAPTER 14 Working Capital and Management of Current Assets 772

Accelerating the Flow

CHAPTER 15 Management of Current Liabilities 820

Saving for a Rainy Day

Part 7 Special Topics in Corporate Finance 852

STUDENT CD-ROM

Preface

The desire to write the Canadian edition of *Principles of Corporate Finance* came out of our experiences teaching an introductory corporate finance course. When we began teaching full time, we were not very far removed from our own undergraduate studies and therefore could appreciate the difficulties some of our students were having with the textbooks they were using. They wanted a book that spoke to them in plain English. They wanted a book that tied concepts to reality. They also wanted not just descriptions, but demonstrations of financial concepts, tools, and techniques.

In writing this text, our goal was to provide students with a resource that presented the principles of Canadian corporate finance with clarity. This goal is accomplished in this text through the use of the proven teaching/learning system that is centered on clearly defined Learning Goals for each chapter and a student-focused writing style. Adding to the system are chapter-opening vignettes that provide overviews of the key ideas covered in each chapter; numerous examples of finance in practice; illustrations of how finance is integrated with other business areas; Spreadsheet Applications; links to important Web sites; and succinct end-of-chapter summaries, self-test problems, end-of-chapter problems, and cases, all tied to the chapter Learning Goals.

This text provides students with a total learning package that reduces the stress of studying corporate finance. Some readers have even suggested the text makes the learning of corporate finance "fun!" The book's conversational tone helps students to understand what can be complex concepts. In satisfying the needs of students, we believe we have satisfied the needs of instructors as well. Readers will note that the text is firmly grounded in the theory and practice of finance, but is user-friendly at the same time. From conversations with adopters, non-adopters, and practitioners, we know this is an important feature for a finance book.

The second Canadian edition of *Principles of Corporate Finance* builds upon the features and pedagogy established in the first edition. It concentrates on the concepts, techniques, and practices that students require to make corporate financial decisions in an increasingly competitive and international business environment. The strong pedagogy and generous use of examples and practical applications make the textbook an easily accessible resource for students of all abilities.

The second Canadian edition has been updated to present important current and emerging issues and techniques that affect the practice of financial management while focusing on the practical application of such concepts. The goal throughout the text is to present the material in an engaging, easy to read, and understandable style. The colourful, eye-catching design is sure to appeal to readers.

This text will become an important part of any student's reference library and will be useful in later courses in business programs, as well as in business careers. From the classroom to the office, the second Canadian edition of *Principles of Corporate Finance* will help readers get to where they want to go.

Proven Teaching/Learning System

Users of *Principles of Corporate Finance* have praised the effectiveness of the book's teaching/learning system, which is one of the book's hallmarks. The system is driven by a set of carefully developed Learning Goals that help guide and organize student reading and study. Readers will note that many of these goals have been revised and polished in the second Canadian edition to reflect changing content. The key elements of the teaching/learning system are discussed and illustrated below. Each of the features facilitates teaching and student learning to promote achievement of the Learning Goals.

Learning Goals The teaching/learning system is based on a set of Learning Goals for each chapter that are marked by special icons, like the one shown here in the margin. The Learning Goals anchor the most important concepts and techniques to be learned in the chapter. The Learning Goal icons reappear next to related text sections and again in the chapter summary, the end-of-chapter problems, and in the cases. These goals focus student attention on the most important material to learn. In addition, instructors can easily build lectures and assignments based on the Learning Goals.

Opening Vignette A photo and vignette appear opposite the title and Learning Goals of each chapter. The vignettes provide overviews of the key ideas covered in each chapter and are written in an engaging manner with the objective of bringing the chapter material to life for the reader. The photographs and vignettes are linked so the reader can immediately picture the focus of the chapter.

NEW FEATURE **Linking the Disciplines** Following the vignettes, a new feature appears that discusses how the finance topics discussed in the chapter relate to five other major business disciplines. The objectives of the Linking the Disciplines feature are to show why topics in finance matter to people working in the other functional areas of a business, to illustrate the cross-functional interactions that routinely occur in business, and to show how actions in one area of business affect other functional areas.

LINKING THE DISCIPLINES: Cross-Functional Interactions

- ***Accounting personnel*** need to know how to calculate and interpret financial ratios and the role the ratios play in decision making.
- ***Information systems analysts*** need to understand the calculation of financial ratios to design a system that quickly and easily collects and communicates the necessary data to decision makers.
- ***Management*** needs to understand how financial ratios are involved in decision making. They must also be aware of the caution that should be exercised when using ratio analysis for decision making. Management is particularly concerned with the stock market reaction to leverage and profitability ratios, as these have a major influence on how investors value a firm.
- The ***marketing department*** is particularly concerned with activity and profitability ratios. They need to understand how analysis of ratios, especially those involving sales, will affect the firm's decisions about levels of inventory, credit policies, and pricing decisions.
- Personnel in the ***operations department*** need to understand how an analysis of ratios, particularly those involving assets, cost of goods sold, inventory, and leverage, may affect requests for new equipment or facilities.

Example Method The example method is an important component of the teaching/learning system because it infuses practical demonstrations into the learning process. Seeing a financial concept or technique applied to a realistic example provides students with immediate reinforcement that helps cement their understanding of that concept or technique. Examples are provided throughout the text and, where applicable, solutions are provided in the format of timelines, financial calculator keystrokes, and spreadsheets.

Key Equations Key equations are numbered and printed in blue throughout the text to help students identify and track the most important mathematical relationships. For convenience, the symbols and variables used in these equations, as well as key abbreviations used in the book, are listed inside the front cover.

Key Terms Throughout the text, key terms and their definitions appear in the text margin when they are first introduced. This serves as an on-going glossary for the reader and makes reviewing the material much easier.

Marginal Hints Marginal hints appear in the margins and add useful pieces of information to enrich the text discussion and assist student learning.

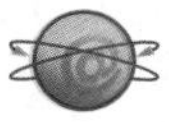

NEW FEATURE **Marginal Web Links** Links to relevant Web sites are provided in the text margins. These links augment and enrich the text discussion and assist student learning of the relevant issue. A complete list of these sites is also available on the book's Companion Website at **www.pearsoned.ca/gitman.**

Review Questions Review Questions appear at the end of each section of every chapter. As students progress through the chapter, they can test their understanding of each key concept, technique, and practice before moving on to the next section.

NEW FEATURE **Spreadsheet Applications** Spreadsheets are a widely used tool in business and it is important that students become familiar with their capabilities and power, particularly when dealing with finance. Consequently, Spreadsheet Applications, screenshots of actual Microsoft Excel® files, are a new feature in this edition and are present in most chapters. The spreadsheets provide an input area, solutions, and the formulas used to generate the solutions. In addition, the Spreadsheet Application files are available in Excel format on the Student CD-ROM that accompanies this book, as well as on the book's Companion Website (**www.pearsoned.ca/gitman**).

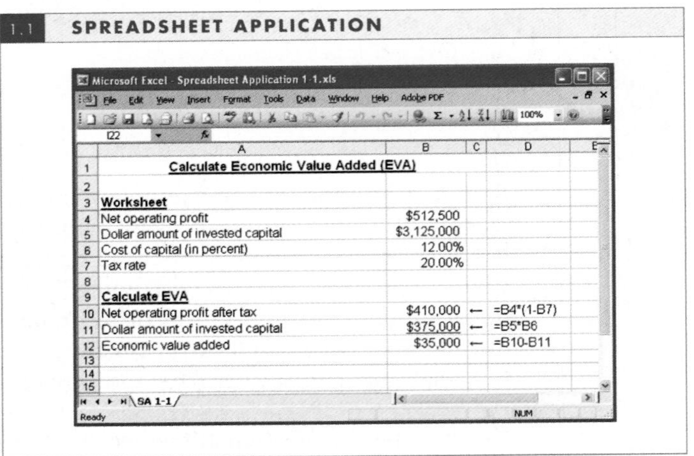

1.1 SPREADSHEET APPLICATION

	A	B	C	D
1	Calculate Economic Value Added (EVA)			
2				
3	Worksheet			
4	Net operating profit	$512,500		
5	Dollar amount of invested capital	$3,125,000		
6	Cost of capital (in percent)	12.00%		
7	Tax rate	20.00%		
8				
9	Calculate EVA			
10	Net operating profit after tax	$410,000	←	=B4*(1-B7)
11	Dollar amount of invested capital	$375,000	←	=B5*B6
12	Economic value added	$35,000	←	=B10-B11

In Practice Boxes Each chapter contains at least one In Practice box that offers insight into important financial topics through the experiences of real people and companies, both large and small. The In Practice boxes are wide-ranging in scope but share the distinction of providing practical applications of chapter concepts in a Canadian setting. They provide readers with a solid grounding in the practice of finance in the real world. Consistent exposure to real-world applications enables students to walk away from the book and onto the job well prepared with practical insight, rather than merely a conceptual grasp of the finance function.

Chapter Summaries End-of-chapter summaries are tied to the Learning Goals, which are restated for reinforcement at the beginning of each summary paragraph. The summaries facilitate students' review of the key chapter material to support mastery of the each Learning Goal.

Self-Test Problems One or more Self-Test Problems are included at the end of each chapter. Every problem is associated with appropriate Learning Goals. Appendix B, found on the Student CD-ROM that accompanies this textbook, contains solutions to all of the Self-Test Problems. These problems help to strengthen the students' understanding of the topics and the techniques presented, and prepare them to tackle real-world scenarios.

End-of-Chapter Problems A comprehensive set of Problems at the end of each chapter provides students with an additional opportunity to test their knowledge and gives professors a wealth of assignable material. Hundreds of problems are provided at three difficulty levels—basic, intermediate, and challenge. The difficulty levels indicate the amount of work that should be involved in solving the problem. All problems are associated with Learning Goals. The depth and selection of engaging problems sets this text apart from its many competitors. Guideline answers to selected Problems appear in Appendix C, found on the accompanying Student CD-ROM.

NEW FEATURE **Integrative Problems** A number of the problems in the text have been labeled "integrative" because they tie together several related topics. These are like "mini-cases" and challenge students to use multiple concepts from the chapter. These problems are associated with multiple Learning Goals, and are good preparation for the Chapter Cases.

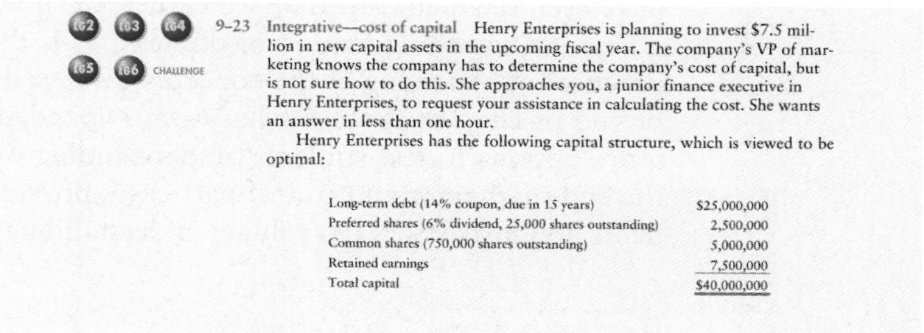

LG2 LG3 LG4 LG5 LG6 CHALLENGE

9–23 Integrative—cost of capital Henry Enterprises is planning to invest $7.5 million in new capital assets in the upcoming fiscal year. The company's VP of marketing knows the company has to determine the company's cost of capital, but is not sure how to do this. She approaches you, a junior finance executive in Henry Enterprises, to request your assistance in calculating the cost. She wants an answer in less than one hour.

Henry Enterprises has the following capital structure, which is viewed to be optimal:

Long-term debt (14% coupon, due in 15 years)	$25,000,000
Preferred shares (6% dividend, 25,000 shares outstanding)	2,500,000
Common shares (750,000 shares outstanding)	5,000,000
Retained earnings	7,500,000
Total capital	$40,000,000

Chapter Cases Cases for each chapter are available on the Student CD-ROM that accompanies the textbook. These cases enable students to apply what they've learned in each chapter to realistic situations. Each case integrates all or a number of the chapter's Learning Goals. The Chapter Cases encourage a practical understanding of financial tools and techniques without the added expense of a separate casebook. A listing of relevant cases can be found at the end of each chapter in the book.

End-of-Part Cases The Student CD-ROM also features six Integrative Cases, each associated with one of the text's Parts. The Integrative Cases challenge students to use what they have learned over several chapters in a realistic business context. The Integrative Case for Part 4, for example, requires students to apply a variety of concepts from Chapters 9 through 11 to assess and make recommendations regarding an apparel company's capital structure, cost of capital, and dividend policy.

Contemporary Design The second Canadian edition has a vibrant, contemporary design. The pedagogical use of colours in charts and graphs draws readers' attention to features of the learning system. Bars of data are highlighted with colour in tables and then graphed in the same colour so that visual learners can immediately see relationships among data.

Changes to the Second Canadian Edition

While we believe the first Canadian edition of *Principles of Corporate Finance* was a solid addition to the corporate finance texts available in Canada at the time, a number of users pointed out areas where they felt improvements could be made. In addition, as we used the book with our own students, we noted areas where the writing could be clarified and additional material added. As a result, there are changes on almost every page of this new edition of the book and a significant amount of new material has been added. Instructors can find a detailed chapter-by-chapter list of all of the changes to the second Canadian edition in the Instructor's Resource Manual. Provided below is an overview of some important changes in this new edition.

It is worthwhile to note the key features of the first Canadian edition that have been retained. As discussed earlier, the powerful Learning Goal system is still a key distinguishing feature of the text, as is the focus on examples that provide practical applications of the concepts discussed. Note that the comprehensive set of end-of-chapter Problems has been expanded, providing instructors with even more options to test students' understanding of the course material. In addition, the end-of-chapter and end-of-part cases provide additional opportunities for students and instructors to evaluate understanding of the text's key concepts.

Pedagogical Changes

- Every chapter opens with a Linking the Disciplines: Cross-Functional Interactions feature that illustrates how finance concepts relate to the other major business disciplines. This encourages students to appreciate the numerous cross-disciplinary interactions that routinely occur in business.
- Most chapters have at least one Spreadsheet Application. The spreadsheets provide an input area, solutions, and the formulas used to generate the solutions. In addition, the spreadsheet files are available on both the Student CD-ROM and the book's Companion Website (**www.pearsoned.ca/gitman**).
- Links to relevant Web sites are provided in the text margins. These links are meant to augment and enrich the text discussion and assist student learning of the relevant issue.
- New integrative Problems are provided that tie together related topics in the chapter and are associated with multiple Learning Goals.
- In Practice boxes and other time sensitive content have been updated.

New Chapter 16, Lease Financing: Concepts and Techniques

Based on reviewer feedback, the brief coverage of lease financing in the previous Chapter 16 has been replaced with an all new Chapter 16 that focuses solely on this very important topic. The chapter opens by explaining that the value of an asset is in its use, not ownership. Information regarding leasing and the leasing industry in Canada is provided. Then operating and financial leases are distinguished, and the different types of financial leases are explained. The accounting treatment of leases is presented with a focus on how leasing and purchasing an asset have similar impacts on a firm's financial position.

The cash flows and the discount rate used to evaluate whether an asset should be leased or purchased is described and the process used to answer the "lease or purchase" question is illustrated. The effects that other variables can have on the decision are explored and the advantages and disadvantages of leasing are discussed. Finally, we consider leasing from the lessor's perspective, focusing on how leasing can benefit both the lessee and the lessor due to differing discount and tax rates. We also illustrate the process that lessors use to calculate the minimum and maximum lease payment they could charge on a lease. A wide range of problems has also been written for this chapter.

Other Key Changes

Although there are far too many changes to list in this Preface (a complete listing can be found in the Instructor's Resource Manual), the addition and reorganization of some very important new topics should be highlighted here.

- We have listened and responded to requests from many instructors by adding a new section covering income trusts in Chapter 1. The controversy and debate surrounding this topic make it a particularly relevant one in the current world of Canadian corporate finance.
- Chapter 2 has been thoroughly revised and a significant amount of new content on financial statements, cash flows, and taxation has been added. In addition, the coverage of taxation issues has been updated with the most recent regulations. Overall, the discussion has been expanded to cover the implications of a variety of situations and financial decisions.
- Chapter 4 now introduces the concept of financial forecasting using a simplified approach: the percent-of-sales method. This method is also the basis for a formula that illustrates the concept of the sustainable growth rate for a firm. Also, the process used to determine external financing required when debt repayments must be made has been added.
- The chapter on financial markets, institutions, and securities (Chapter 5) now comes before the chapter on the time value of money (Chapter 6). This allows for a better flow of time value concepts to risk and return, and valuation concepts.

- The majority of references to financial tables have been replaced with references to financial calculators and spreadsheets, reflecting the widespread use of these tools in current business.
- Additional coverage on calculating risk and return variables using probabilistic data, expected return data, and actual return data has been added to Chapter 7. Both percentage and dollar data is used. Also, the discussion of the benefit of diversification in a portfolio setting has been significantly revised and more detail and examples have been added.
- In Chapter 9, the coverage of the relationship between cost of capital, the optimal capital structure, and firm value has been expanded, making this vital concept easier to understand.
- An Appendix discussing Miller and Modigliani's theory of capital structure has been added to Chapter 10. Presenting this material as an Appendix gives flexibility to instructors who may not wish to cover this material in their courses.
- A new comprehensive problem has been added to Chapter 12 that illustrates all aspects of capital budgeting analysis and better prepares students to analyze and solve the many realistic, integrative problems provided in the chapter. In addition, a new Appendix has been added that provides comprehensive coverage of Economic Value Added (EVA), an alternative way to measure a firm's ability to add value for the providers of capital.
- Chapter 13 has been thoroughly revised to present concepts more clearly, particularly the issue that risk is implicitly considered in capital budgeting, but that a particular project may have a different risk profile than the company. This means that this different risk level must be evaluated, measured, and used in project evaluation.
- Chapter 14 discusses and illustrates three strategies that can be used to finance working capital. This significantly revised section focuses on the difference between the permanent and seasonal investment in current assets.
- Chapter 17 has been thoroughly revised and reorganized to accommodate the inclusion of the new Chapter 16 dedicated to the topic of leasing. The topic of options is now covered in two sections. The first provides the basics regarding option features and pricing. The second discusses option trading. In addition, this section adds new material on the use of options by companies. Both exchange traded options and managerial options are considered.

New Student CD-ROM

Every new copy of the second Canadian edition of *Principles of Corporate Finance* comes with a Student CD-ROM that contains a wealth of valuable learning resources, including solutions to the Self-Test Problems found in the text, answers to selected end-of-chapter Problems, Chapter Cases, Integrative Cases, and files for the Spreadsheet Applications found in the textbook. Providing these resources on CD-ROM gives instructors and students greater flexibility in how they use this important material.

Other Distinguishing Features

Besides the unique and proven teaching/learning system discussed earlier, several other features distinguish this edition of *Principles of Corporate Finance* from its many competitors. These include the book's flexible organization, strong ties to practice, and the depth of material that can be used to assess student understanding.

Flexible Organization

In this edition of *Principles of Corporate Finance*, our objective was to design a text that was extremely flexible for instructors and students. The text's organization conceptually links a firm's actions and its value as determined in the securities markets. Each major decision area is presented in terms of both risk and return factors and their potential impact on owners' wealth, as reflected by share value.

In organizing each chapter, we have adhered to a managerial decision-making perspective. That is, we have described a concept such as cost of capital and have related it to the financial manager's overall goal of wealth maximization. Once a particular concept has been developed, its application is illustrated by an example. Students are not left with abstract definitions, but can truly sense the related decision-making considerations and consequences of financial concepts.

The second Canadian edition of *Principles of Corporate Finance* contains 19 chapters in seven parts. For an overview of the book's part and chapter organization, see the Brief Contents on page vii. Although the text is sequential, instructors can assign almost any chapter as a self-contained unit. Where necessary, students are directed to specific pages in earlier or later chapters where important concepts for the issue under consideration are discussed. This flexibility enables instructors to customize the text to various teaching strategies and course lengths.

In addition, this adaptability means that the content can be arranged to meet individual needs. For example, a subset of chapters and/or parts of chapters can be used for a single course in corporate or managerial finance or the total text can be used for a finance course taught over two semesters. The abundance of content, Review Questions, Problems, Chapter Cases, and Spreadsheet Applications allow an instructor to present an overview of a topic or very detailed coverage. Instructors have control over the topics covered, their sequence, and the depth of coverage.

Strong Ties to Practice

A variety of features are used in the book to anchor student understanding in the operational aspects of topics presented. Many textual discussions present practical insights and applications of concepts and techniques. In addition, a number of special features are used to both assure realism and stimulate student interest.

Cross-Disciplinary Focus The Linking the Disciplines: Cross-Functional Interactions feature helps students understand the importance of chapter material in relation to other major business disciplines. These features are placed at the beginning of each chapter, indicating the interest that other disciplines would have in the topics covered in the chapter. This feature allows students who are not finance majors to see how various finance topics relate to their chosen business field.

In Practice Each chapter contains at least one In Practice box that offers insight into important topics in finance through experiences of individuals and of real companies, both large and small. Note the long list of real companies discussed in the text provided on the inside back cover. All of the In Practice boxes provide students with a solid grounding in the practice of finance in the real world. Consistent exposure to current practical applications enables students to walk away from the book and into the workforce well-prepared with forward-looking, practical insight, rather than merely a conceptual grasp of the finance function.

International Coverage Discussions of international dimensions of chapter topics are integrated throughout the book. For example, Chapter 7 discusses the risks and returns associated with international diversification. Similarly, Chapter 13 addresses the international aspects of capital budgeting and long-term investments. Chapter 17 discusses swaps that are very useful instruments for international companies. In each chapter in which international coverage is included, the international material is integrated into chapter Learning Goals as well as the end-of-chapter Summary and Problems. Finally, Chapter 19 is devoted to international corporate finance.

Assessment Material

The text is rich in material that instructors can assign students, or that students can use to evaluate their understanding of chapter content. The variety of problems is particularly impressive in chapters where instructors and students want choice. These include Chapters 2, 3, and 4 (the review, analysis, and forecasting of financial statements), Chapter 6 (the time value of money), Chapter 8 (valuation of financial securities), Chapter 9 (cost of capital), Chapters 12 and 13 (capital budgeting), and Chapters 14 and 15 (working capital management). The impressive selection of engaging problems sets this text apart from its many competitors.

The comprehensive end-of-chapter Problems have been expanded in this edition, providing instructors with even more options to test students' understanding of the chapter material. Instructors may wish to cover certain problems in class, assign others, or use them as review questions prior to exams.

The incorporation of Excel screen captures in the Spreadsheet Applications is an important distinguishing feature of the new edition. The corresponding Excel files, provided on both the Student CD-ROM the book's Companion Website (**www.pearsoned.ca/gitman**) can be converted to other popular spreadsheet programs.

Intended Audience

This text has been designed, developed, and written for introductory courses in corporate or managerial finance at either the undergraduate or graduate level. Since the typical student will not have taken a previous course in finance, the text assumes no prior knowledge of finance. As introductory finance is part of many business programs, the text is intended for all students: finance majors and non-majors alike. The text is a self-contained resource in finance and is an ideal text for self-study or a Web-based course, given its direct style and focus on realistic examples.

Supplements to the Textbook

This edition of *Principles of Corporate Finance* provides a range of useful supplements for both instructors and students.

Teaching Tools for Instructors

Instructor's Resource CD-ROM This supplement includes the complete Instructor's Resource Manual with Solutions, the TestGen testbank, and the Microsoft PowerPoint® Presentations. Instructors can also download these supplements from Pearson Education Canada's online catalogue at **http://vig.pearsoned.ca**.

Instructor's Resource Manual with Solutions This comprehensive resource integrates the text's numerous teaching tools so that instructors can use the textbook easily and effectively in the classroom. An overview of key topics and detailed solutions to all Review Questions, end-of-chapter Problems, and Chapter Cases are provided for each chapter. Practice quizzes and solutions are also included. The manual also provides a comprehensive chapter-by-chapter listing of the changes to this new edition of the textbook.

TestGen This computerized testbank contains over 2,500 questions, including true/false, multiple choice, and essay questions. Questions can be searched and sorted by question type, Learning Goal, and level of difficulty. This software package allows instructors to custom design, generate, and save classroom tests. The test program permits instructors to edit, add, or delete questions from the test bank and organize a database of tests and student results.

PowerPoint Presentations These presentations combine lecture notes with images from the textbook. The lecture presentations for each chapter can be viewed electronically in the classroom or can be printed as black-and-white transparency masters.

Learning Tools for Students

Companion Website Beyond the book itself, students have access to the text's Companion Website at **www.pearsoned.ca/gitman**. The site contains links to valuable online resources, self-assessment quizzes, additional cases, Spreadsheet Application files, and more.

Web Exercises A number of Web Exercises are available on the Companion Website. These exercises encourage students to explore the wealth of corporate finance information available on the Web and integrates it with chapter topics. These exercises will capture student interest in using the Internet while educating them about finance-related sites. There are also practical applications of chapter concepts that complement the In Practice boxes found in every chapter.

Acknowledgments

Writing a textbook is a lengthy and complicated process that is achievable only with the co-operation and hard work of many people. We would like to thank colleagues, research assistants, editors, administrative support, students, and family for the incredible amount of help and support we received while completing this text.

First, Pearson Education Canada sought the opinion and advice of many excellent reviewers, all of whom strongly influenced various aspects of this text. We value the many comments and suggestions we received from our colleagues that helped us improve the content, organization, and flow of the book. Your efforts helped with the student-focused, user-friendly writing style of the text. The following reviewers provided extremely useful comments in preparing the second Canadian edition, and we are extremely grateful for their efforts: Walt Burton, *Okanagan University College*; Shantanu Dutta, *St. Francis Xavier University*; Raad Jassim, *Concordia University*; J. Terence Zinger, *Laurentian University*; Tom Pippy, *Conestoga College*; and Rick Nason, *Dalhousie University*.

A number of other people made important contributions to the text. Thanks to Ross Meacher for his efforts as the technical reviewer for this edition.

One person deservers special mention for her work in producing this second edition. Amanda Strongman graduated from the University of PEI in May 2006. She expressed interest in acting as a research assistant on the second Canadian edition during the summer. The summer became fall, then winter, and now, as this is written, the spring of 2007, and she is still working, helping us produce various parts of the book. Amanda helped us write the new In Practice boxes. She wrote many of the new end-of-chapter Problems and developed solutions. She updated tables and figures, and reviewed drafts of the revised material. She checked every solution in the Instructor's Resource Manual and made corrections as necessary. She helped develop the new Companion Website for the book. In short, without her assistance, this book would not have been produced in the time period it was. We sincerely thank her for the time and effort she devoted to the book.

Special thanks for the excellent administrative support provided by Edith MacLauchlan, Mollie Cooke, and Tammie Rose. Your good-natured response to my request, "I need this yesterday," is well appreciated. I am still amazed at the number of times you were able to "turn the work around" in short order. Without your cooperation and hard work, this text would not have been finished in time.

The publishing team at Pearson Education Canada deserves a tremendous amount of credit for the effort devoted to the text. The time lines were incredibly tight on this book and the top-notch group of people at Pearson helped bring it all together to produce the excellent product you are now holding. Sincere thanks to Samantha Scully, John Polanszky, Laura Neves, Andrea Falkenberg, and the many others who worked on the text. We appreciate the inspiration, team-work, and organized effort that helped pull this text together on a tight schedule. We particularly appreciated the team's ability to juggle deadlines with much grace and understanding.

Special thanks go to our many students who, over the years, helped to teach us the best way of teaching corporate finance. Individual contributions of students are too numerous to mention here.

Michael Hennessey read various drafts of chapters and provided editorial advice; I wish to thank him for his ongoing support. Finally, thanks to Roberta and Liam for patiently providing support, understanding, and good humour throughout the long writing process.

A Note to Students

In writing this text, our goal was to provide students with a resource that clearly presents the principles of Canadian corporate finance. The text is user-friendly and provides a total package that reduces the stress of learning corporate finance. We use plain English, tie concepts to reality, and demonstrate concepts, tools, and techniques in numerous examples. The book incorporates a proven learning system that integrates pedagogy with concepts and practical applications.

We have worked hard to present the most important concepts and practices of corporate finance in a clear and interesting way. Each chapter begins with a photo and short paragraph that introduce a key idea of the chapter. These brief introductions won't take long to read, but they will give you a useful preview of the chapter topic. You will also find at the beginning of each chapter a list of six Learning Goals. Marked by a special icon shown here in the margin, the Learning Goals are tied to first-level headings in the chapter and are reviewed point by point in the end-of-chapter Summary. These goals will help you focus your attention on the material you need to learn, where you can find it in the chapter, and whether you've mastered it by the end of the chapter.

Other features are included to support your learning experience. For example, Review Questions are provided at the end of each major text section. Although it may be tempting to rush past these questions, try to resist doing so. Pausing briefly to test your understanding of the key concepts, tools, techniques, and practices in the section you've just read will help cement your understanding of the material. Honestly assess your level of understanding of the material you've just read. If necessary, go back (even briefly) and review the material that seems unclear. This will allow you to proceed through each chapter, and the book, in an orderly and logical format

There are features in the body of each chapter that are intended to aid your study. In Practice boxes offer practical insights into the topic at hand through real corporate experiences. Linking the Disciplines: Cross-Functional Interactions features are placed at the beginning of each chapter to illustrate how corporate finance concepts are related to other business disciplines. After all, corporate finance is an essential component not just in the business curriculum or in professional training programs, but in your daily job activities, *regardless of your major.*

There are three types of marginalia in the chapters: hints, key terms, and Web links. Hints are just what their name implies—ideas and comments that help clarify important concepts. Key terms and their definitions also appear in the margin when they are first introduced. These glossary terms are the basic vocabulary of finance; be sure you learn them as you read the chapters. Web links supply the addresses of Web sites that provide interesting coverage of the material discussed at that point in the chapter.

Spreadsheet Applications are included in most chapters and will help you master the use of spreadsheets a business tool. It is important that students experience the capabilities and power of spreadsheets. In addition, the Spreadsheet Applications will aid you in solving the problems in the book.

Packaged with this new edition of the text, at no additional cost, is the Student CD-ROM that provides a wealth of valuable material including the Spreadsheet Applications, Chapter and Integrative Cases, and two important Appendices. These resources were specifically designed for this text and will aid your learning and understanding of the material.

As you progress through your finance course, look for (or make) opportunities to talk with classmates or friends about what you're reading and learning in the course. Being able to talk about the concepts and techniques of finance demonstrates how much you've learned, uncovers things you haven't yet fully understood, and gives you valuable practice for class and (eventually) the business world. While you're talking, don't neglect to discuss how the finance topics you've covered relate to other business courses you are taking or have taken.

While writing and revising the book, we made every effort to keep pace with your needs and interests. We value your ideas for improving the teaching and learning of finance. If you wish to write to us about anything in the book, please see the "Request for Feedback" section below.

We wish you all the best in your finance courses, and in your academic and professional careers.

Request for Feedback

As we designed and wrote this text, we took great care to present the material in a clear manner and to make the text as user-friendly as possible. One aspect of this process was to ensure that there were no errors in the content or in the solutions to problems. Our goal is to provide instructors and students with the best Canadian corporate finance textbook available on the market. If you have any comments on the text and its package of supplements, either positive or negative, please write to us.

We invite colleagues to relate their classroom experiences with the book and their students to indicate whether the book has achieved our goal of clearly presented of content. Compliments and constructive criticism alike will help us continue to improve the textbook and its teaching/learning system. Please write to: Sean Hennessey, School of Business Administration, University of Prince Edward Island, 550 University Avenue, Charlottetown, PE C1A 4P3. You are also invited to e-mail Sean at **hennessey@upei.ca**.

Sean M. Hennessey
Lawrence J. Gitman
May 2007

The Pearson Education Canada **COMPANION WEBSITE**

A Great Way to Learn and Instruct Online

The Pearson Education Canada Companion Website is easy to navigate and is organized to correspond to the chapters in this textbook. Whether you are a student in the classroom or a distance learner you will discover helpful resources for in-depth study and research that empower you in your quest for greater knowledge and maximize your potential for success in the course.

PEARSON
Addison Wesley

Jump to... http://www.pearsoned.ca/gitman

Home Search Help Profile

Companion Website

Home >

Companion Website

Principles of Corporate Finance, Second Canadian Edition, by Gitman and Hennessey

Student Resources

The modules in this section provide students with tools for learning course material. Each chapter includes:

- Web Cases
- Web Exercises
- Quizzes
- Web Destinations
- Spreadsheet Applications
- Other Resources

Instructor Resources

Instructors can click on a link on the opening page to visit our online catalogue and download the Instructor's Resource Manual, PowerPoint Slides, and TestGen computerized testbank.

CHAPTER 1

Overview of Corporate Finance

LEARNING GOALS

- LG1 Define *finance* and describe its three major areas—financial markets, financial services, and corporate finance—and the career opportunities within them.
- LG2 Review the forms of business organization and their respective strengths and weaknesses.
- LG3 Describe the corporate finance function, differentiate corporate finance from the closely related disciplines of economics and accounting, and identify the key activities of the financial manager.
- LG4 Explain why wealth maximization, rather than profit maximization, is the firm's goal and how economic value added (EVA), a focus on stakeholders, and ethical behaviour relate to its achievement.
- LG5 Discuss the agency issue as it relates to owner wealth maximization.
- LG6 Discuss some key concepts in finance and review the language of finance.

1.1 Finance as an Area of Study

The field of finance is broad and dynamic. It directly affects the lives of every person, organization, and branch of government in a country. There are many areas for study, and a large number of career opportunities are available in the field of finance.

What Is Finance?

finance
The knowledge, science, techniques, and art of managing money.

Finance is the management of money—more specifically, the knowledge, science, techniques, and art associated with the management of capital. Virtually all

The Balance of Power

Most businesses are structured like pyramids—with power to set policies concentrated at the top and spreading toward the bottom where day-to-day operations are carried out. However, the ultimate authority over all management of the organization resides in the owners of a corporation—its common shareholders. The goal of the business organization, and the goal of its financial managers, is to achieve the objectives of the firm's owners. This chapter will explain corporate organization and the managerial finance function within the organization. It also will explore the key goal of the firm's owners—to maximize shareholder wealth—and the role of the financial manager in meeting that goal.

individuals and organizations earn or raise money and spend or invest money. Finance is concerned with the process, institutions, markets, and instruments involved in the transfer of money among and between individuals, businesses, and governments. As such, it directly affects every individual, organization (public and private, for-profit and not-for-profit), and branch of government in the country. An understanding of finance will benefit most adults by allowing them to make better personal financial decisions. Those who work in financial jobs will benefit from an understanding of finance by being able to interface effectively with the firm's financial personnel, processes, and procedures.

Finance is closely related to economics and accounting. Individuals and organizations operate within the national and international economic environments,

LINKING THE DISCIPLINES: Cross-Functional Interactions

- ***Accounting personnel*** provide the financial statements needed for financial analysis and planning and for making investment and financial decisions. They need to understand the relationships between the firm's accounting and finance function, what agency costs are and how to deal with them, and the role of ethics in the firm.
- ***Information system analysts*** must understand the organization of the firm and the information finance personnel require for financial analysis and planning and to support investment and financing decisions.
- ***Management*** defines the tasks that will be performed by the finance department and how the finance function fits within the structure of the firm. Management must understand the legal forms of business organization, the ultimate goal of the firm, the role of corporate governance in dealing with the agency problem, and the importance of high ethical standards in the firm.
- Personnel in the ***marketing department*** need to provide input for the investment decisions made, and understand how their activities will be affected by the finance function, how their activities add value to the firm, and the role of ethics in promoting a sound corporate image.
- Personnel in the ***operations department*** need to provide input for the investment decisions made, and understand the organization of the firm and why maximizing profit is not the primary goal of the firm.

so broad macroeconomic variables have a major impact on business. Accounting is the language of finance. A solid and complete understanding of the language of accounting and the financial statements is vital for a student of finance.

Major Areas and Employment Opportunities in Finance

Finance is a discipline with many sub-branches and one or more of these impact most Canadians on a daily basis. There are three major but interrelated areas of finance: financial markets, financial services, and managerial or corporate finance. Each of these areas is discussed below. Often, a good way to introduce a business discipline is to discuss the types of career opportunities available in the field. A brief discussion of employment opportunities available in each of these areas of finance is provided in the following section.

Financial Markets

financial markets
Provide a forum where savers of funds and users of funds can transact business.

financial institutions
Intermediaries that allow for the efficient transfer of the savings of individuals, governments, and business for financial securities.

Financial markets is a branch in the study of macroeconomics. **Financial markets** provide a forum where *savers of funds* and *users of funds* can transact business. These two groups must be able to make an exchange that is expected to be beneficial to both parties. Individuals, governments, and business organizations are all involved in financial markets. In financial markets, cash moves from savers to users, and users provide a financial security in return. For financial markets to work, **financial institutions** are necessary. These are intermediaries that allow for the efficient and low-cost transfer of the savings of individuals, governments, and business for financial securities. Intermediaries include institutions such as banks and investment dealers. Investment management is a major part of this area of finance.

Numerous career opportunities are available in this area, including the trading of financial securities such as common and preferred shares, bonds and debentures, foreign exchange, commodities, derivatives, and treasury bills. In addition, banks, investment dealers, and other financial intermediaries offer thousands of jobs to business graduates each year. Other opportunities are available in the regulation of financial markets with organizations such as the Bank of Canada or the Ontario Securities Commission. There are a number of Web sites that provide more information regarding a career in this branch of finance.

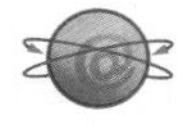

www.osc.gov.on.ca/About/ab_index.jsp
www.bankofcanada.ca/en

Financial Services

financial services
The part of finance concerned with design and delivery of advice and financial products to individuals, business, and government.

Financial services is the area of finance concerned with the design and delivery of advice and financial products to individuals, business, and government. Financial institutions such as banks, trust companies, investment dealers and brokers, personal financial planners, mutual fund companies, life and property insurance companies, mortgage brokers, and real estate companies, together with the professional organizations that support these institutions and the regulators that oversee the operation of the financial institutions, are all major participants in this sub-branch of finance. Financial services involve a variety of interesting career opportunities within the areas of banking and related institutions, personal financial planning, investments, real estate, and insurance. Career opportunities available in each of these areas are described at a number of Web sites.

www.careers-in-finance.com
www.financial-jobs.com

Corporate Finance

corporate finance
Concerns the duties of the financial manager in the business firm.

financial manager
Actively manages the financial affairs of any type of business, whether financial or nonfinancial, private or public, large or small, profit-seeking or not-for-profit.

Corporate finance is concerned with the duties of the financial manager in the business firm. **Financial managers** actively manage the financial affairs of many types of business—financial and nonfinancial, private and public, large and small, profit-seeking and not-for-profit. They perform such varied financial tasks as evaluating financial strengths and weaknesses, planning and forecasting the need for financing, managing the daily financial activities such as extending credit, collecting receivables, buying inventory, and paying suppliers to ensure sufficient cash is on hand to maintain operations, evaluating proposed large expenditures, and raising money to fund the firm's operations. In recent years, the changing economic and regulatory environments have increased the importance and complexity of the financial manager's duties. As a result, many top executives in industry and government have come from the finance area.

Another important recent trend has been the globalization of business activity. Canadian corporations have dramatically increased their sales, purchases, investments, and fund raising in other countries, and foreign corporations have likewise increased these activities in Canada. These changes have created a need for financial managers who can help a firm to manage cash flows in different currencies and protect against the risks that naturally arise from international transactions. Although this need makes the corporate finance function more

www.careers-in-finance.com
www.jobsinthemoney.com
www.higherbracket.ca

complex, it can also lead to a more rewarding and fulfilling career. Corporate finance would likely be considered the broadest area of finance, with literally millions of jobs in the area. There are numerous Web sites that provide more information regarding the possible careers in corporate finance.

The Study of Corporate Finance

An understanding of the theories, concepts, techniques, and practices presented throughout this text will fully acquaint you with the financial manager's activities and decisions. Because most business decisions are measured in financial terms, the financial manager plays a key role in the operation of the firm. People in all areas of responsibility—accounting, information technology, management, marketing, operations, and so forth—need a basic understanding of the corporate finance function.

All managers in the firm, regardless of their job descriptions, work with financial personnel to justify manpower requirements, negotiate operating budgets, deal with financial performance appraisals, and sell proposals based at least in part on their financial merits. Clearly, those managers who understand the financial decision-making process will be better able to address financial concerns and will therefore more often get the resources they need to accomplish their own goals.

At the beginning of each chapter, a feature titled "Linking the Disciplines: Cross-Functional Interactions" is provided after the list of Learning Goals. This feature discusses the link the finance topics discussed in the chapter have with five other major business disciplines: accounting, information technology, management, marketing, and operations. The objectives of the "Linking the Disciplines" feature are to show why topics in finance matter to people working in the other functional areas of a business, to illustrate the cross-functional interactions that routinely occur in business, and show how actions in one area affect and impact the other functional areas.

As you study this text, you will learn about the career opportunities in corporate finance. Some of these are briefly described in Table 1.1. Although this text focuses on profit-seeking firms, the principles presented here are equally applicable to public and not-for-profit organizations. The decision-making principles developed in this text can also be applied to personal financial decisions. We hope that this first exposure to the exciting field of finance will provide the foundation and initiative for further study and possibly even a future career.

? Review Questions

1–1 What is *finance?* Explain how this field affects the lives of everyone and every organization.

1–2 What is the *financial markets* area of finance?

1–3 What is the *financial services* area of finance?

1–4 Describe the field of *corporate finance.* Why is the study of corporate finance important regardless of the specific area of responsibility one has within the business firm?

TABLE 1.1 **Career Opportunities in Corporate Finance**

Position	Description
Financial analyst	Primarily responsible for preparing and analyzing the firm's financial plans and budgets. Other duties include financial forecasting, performing financial ratio analysis, and working closely with accounting.
Capital budgeting analyst/manager	Responsible for the evaluation and recommendation of proposed asset investments. May be involved in the financial aspects of implementation of approved investments.
Project finance manager	In large firms, arranges financing for approved asset investments. Coordinates consultants, investment bankers, and legal counsel.
Cash manager	Responsible for maintaining and controlling the firm's daily cash balances. Frequently manages the firm's cash collection, short-term investment, transfer, and disbursement activities and coordinates short-term borrowing and banking relationships.
Credit analyst/manager	Administers the firm's credit policy by analyzing or managing the evaluation of credit applications, extending credit, and monitoring and collecting accounts receivable.
Pension fund manager	In large companies, responsible for coordinating the assets and liabilities of the employees' pension fund. Either performs investment management activities or hires and oversees the performance of these activities by a third party.

LG2

1.2 Forms of Business Organization

The three basic legal forms of business organization are the *sole proprietorship*, the *partnership*, and the *corporation*. The sole proprietorship is the most common form of organization. However, the corporation is by far the dominant form with respect to sales, assets, and profits. In Canada, income trusts have become an important alternative form of business organization for **publicly traded companies**. These are companies whose common shares are listed and trade on one of the two recognized stock exchanges in Canada: the Toronto Stock Exchange (TSX) and the TSX Venture Exchange. While corporations are given primary emphasis in this textbook, it is important to recognize the growing popularity of income trusts, a very tax-efficient method of organizing a business.

publicly traded company
A company whose common shares are listed and trade on a recognized stock exchange.

www.tsx.com

Sole Proprietorships

sole proprietorship
A business owned by one person and operated for his or her own benefit.

A **sole proprietorship** is a business owned by one person who operates it for his or her own benefit. A large majority of all business firms are sole proprietorships. The typical sole proprietorship is a small business, such as a bike shop, hair salon, personal trainer, or plumber. Typically, the proprietor, along with a few employees, operates the proprietorship. He or she normally raises capital from personal resources or by borrowing and is responsible for all business decisions. The sole proprietor has **unlimited liability**, meaning that his or her total wealth, both personal and business—not merely the amount originally invested in the business—can be taken to repay creditors. The majority of sole proprietorships are found in

unlimited liability
The condition of a sole proprietorship (or general partnership) allowing the owner's total wealth to be taken to repay creditors.

TABLE 1.2 Strengths and Weaknesses of the Four Forms of Business Organization

	Legal form			
	Sole proprietorship	**Partnership**	**Corporation**	**Income Trust**
Strengths	Owner receives all profits (as well as losses) Low organizational costs Income included and taxed on proprietor's personal tax return Independence Secrecy Ease of dissolution	Can raise more funds than sole proprietorships Borrowing power enhanced by more owners More available brain power and managerial skill Income is split according to the partnership contract and taxed as personal income	Owners have *limited liability,* which guarantees that they cannot lose more than they invested Can achieve large size due to sale of common shares Ownership (shares) is readily transferable Long life of firm Can hire professional managers Has better access to financing Receives certain tax advantages	Unitholders have limited liability Can achieve large size due to sale of units Ownership (units) is readily transferable Long life of trust Can hire professional managers Has better access to financing Pays no taxes as long as all cash flows are paid to unitholders
Weaknesses	Owner has *unlimited liability* —total wealth can be taken to satisfy debts Limited fund-raising power tends to inhibit growth Proprietor must be jack-of-all-trades Difficult to give employees long-run career opportunities Lacks continuity when proprietor dies	Owners have *unlimited liability* and may have to cover debt of other partners Partnership is dissolved when a partner dies Can be difficult to liquidate or transfer partnership	Taxes generally higher, because corporate income is taxed and dividends paid to owners are also taxed More expensive to organize than other business forms Subject to greater government regulation If publicly traded, lacks secrecy, since financial and other reports must be released to the public	More expensive to organize than corporation Subject to greater government regulation If publicly traded, lacks secrecy, since financial and other reports must be released to the public Difficult to fund growth, as unitholders expect to receive much of the cash flow

the wholesale, retail, service, and construction industries. The key strengths and weaknesses of sole proprietorships are summarized in Table 1.2.

Partnerships

partnership
A business owned by two or more people and operated for profit.

A **partnership** consists of two or more owners doing business together for profit. Partnerships, which account for a small percentage of all businesses, are typically larger than sole proprietorships. Finance, insurance, accounting, and real estate firms are the most common types of partnerships, with some of these businesses often having large numbers of partners.

partnership agreement
The written contract used to formally establish a business partnership.

limited partnership
A partnership with one or more general partners with unlimited liability and one or more limited partners with limited liability.

Most partnerships are established by a written contract known as a **partnership agreement.** In a *general partnership,* all partners have unlimited liability, and each *general partner* is legally liable for all of the debts of the partnership. To avoid this disadvantage, a **limited partnership** can be formed. Under this arrangement, there are one or more general partners with unlimited liability and one or more *limited partners* with limited liability. These partners are only responsible for the funds they invested in the business. Limited partners are not allowed to be involved in the management of the business; they are passive investors. Limited partnerships are common in real estate development, with the limited partners providing the cash and the general partner(s) developing the property. Strengths and weaknesses of partnerships are summarized in Table 1.2.

Corporations

corporation
A business entity created by law (often called a "legal entity").

Hint
For many small corporations, as well as small proprietorships and partnerships, there is no access to financial markets. In addition, whenever the owners make a loan, they usually must provide a personal guarantee.

A **corporation** is an artificial entity created by law. Often called a "legal entity," a corporation has the powers of an individual in that it can sue and be sued, make and be party to contracts, and acquire property and incur debts in its own name. The corporation is the dominant form of business organization. It accounts for nearly all of the assets owned and sales and profits generated by all businesses in Canada. But the vast majority of corporations are very small businesses. For example, of the 2.3 million businesses in Canada, fewer than 3,000 have more than 500 employees. While some people in a community may know of a local electrician, law firm, store, or small manufacturer, most Canadians and many people around the world know of large Canadian corporations such as Alcan, Petro-Canada, Barrick Gold, Bell Canada Enterprises (BCE), or Royal Bank. These large corporations employ large numbers of people and are involved in all types of businesses. At one time, goods-producing corporations accounted for a majority of corporate activity in Canada. Over the last 30 years, however, the service sector has experienced tremendous growth and now accounts for a significant majority of total corporate sales, profits, and total assets. The key strengths and weaknesses of corporations are summarized in Table 1.2.

shareholders
The owners of a corporation, whose ownership or "equity" is evidenced by ***common shares.***

common shares
The purest and most basic form of corporate ownership.

dividends
Periodic distributions of earnings to the shareholders of a firm.

board of directors
Group elected by the firm's shareholders and having ultimate authority to guide corporate affairs and set corporate strategy.

The owners of a corporation are its **shareholders,** whose ownership or "equity" is evidenced by *common shares.*[1] This form of ownership is defined and discussed in Chapter 5; at this point suffice it to say that **common shares** are the purest and most basic form of corporate ownership. Shareholders expect to earn a return by receiving **dividends**—periodic distributions of earnings—or by realizing gains through increases in share price. As noted in the upper portion of Figure 1.1, every year the shareholders vote to elect the members of the board of directors, to approve the appointment of the company's auditor, and to deal with other matters affecting the company.

The **board of directors** has the ultimate authority in guiding corporate affairs and in setting corporate strategy. The board of directors is headed by the chair. For most corporations, the chair of the board is normally the company's CEO, the founding CEO, or a well-respected business person with a long association with the company. The directors include key corporate personnel as well as outside individuals who typically are successful businesspeople and executives of

1. Corporations may also have preferred shares but preferred shareholders are not owners. There are no ownership rights attached to preferred shares. Some corporations do not have shareholders but rather have "members" who often have rights similar to those of shareholders—they are entitled to vote and receive dividends. Examples include cooperatives, credit unions, mutual insurance companies, and many charitable organizations.

other major organizations. Outside directors for major corporations are typically paid an annual fee (retainer) of $10,000 to $50,000 or more, plus fees for attending board meetings, and are frequently granted options to buy a specified number of the firm's common shares at a stated—and often attractive—price.

president or chief executive officer (CEO) Corporate official responsible for managing the firm's day-to-day operations and carrying out the policies established by the board of directors.

The **president or chief executive officer (CEO)** is responsible for managing day-to-day operations and carrying out the policies established by the board. The CEO is required to report periodically to the firm's directors. It is important to note the division between owners and managers in a large corporation, as shown by the dashed horizontal line in Figure 1.1. This separation and some of the

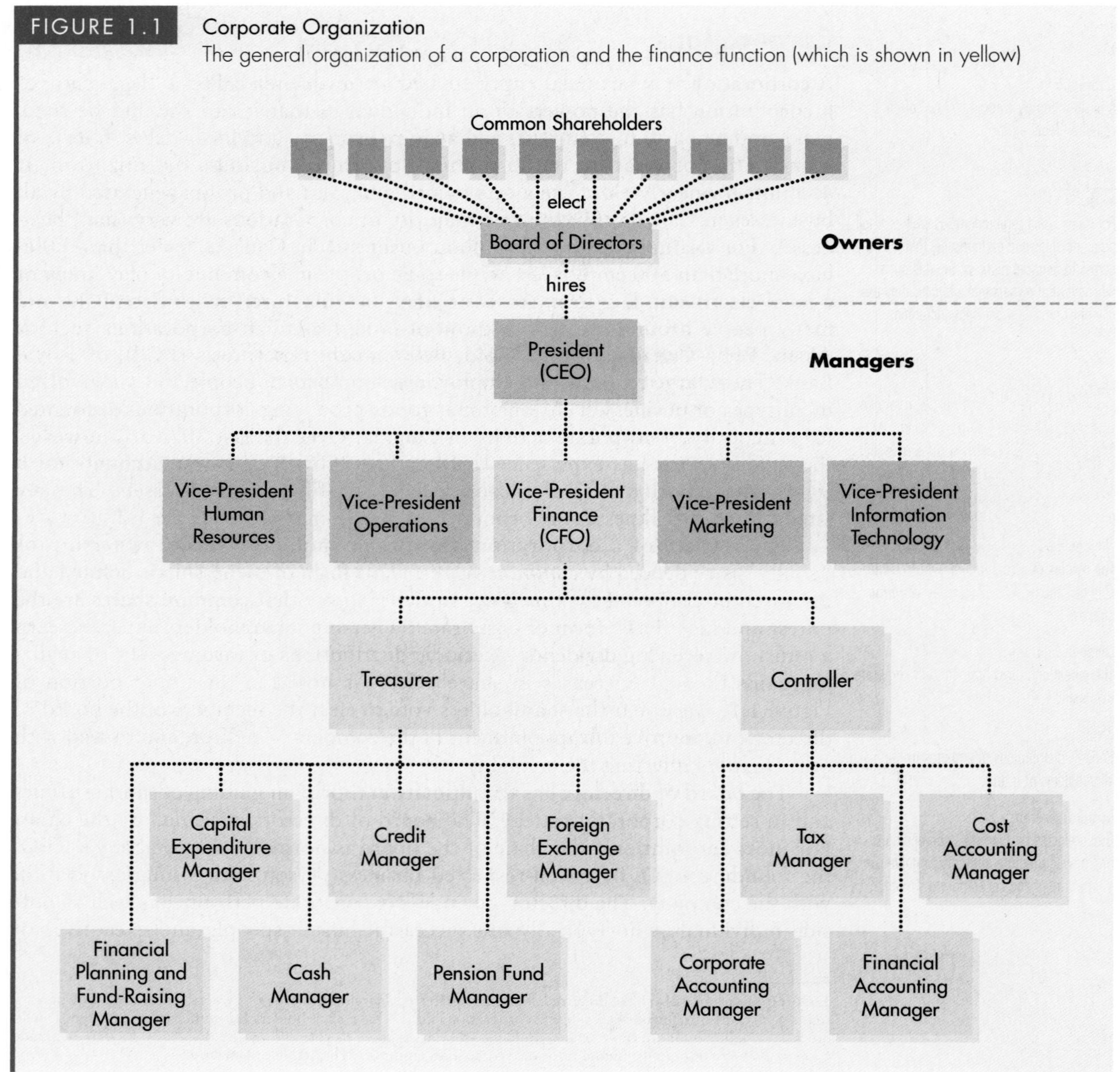

FIGURE 1.1 Corporate Organization
The general organization of a corporation and the finance function (which is shown in yellow)

issues surrounding it will be addressed in the discussion of *the agency issue* later in this chapter. Also note that while the board of directors hires the CEO and, depending on the company, possibly the various vice-presidents, these senior managers are responsible for the hiring of all other employees.

Income Trusts

To fully appreciate the concept of an income trust, we must first understand trusts. In law, a trust is a relationship in which one party (a trustee) holds property on behalf of or for the benefit of another (a beneficiary). For income tax purposes, a trust is considered a taxpayer. An income trust is created when the assets held by the trust are real property or an interest in an active business that produces a cash flow. The operating entity distributes the majority of its cash flow to the unitholders who must pay tax on that cash flow. If any of the cash flow from the operating entity is retained in the trust, the trust would be required to pay income tax on those funds.

The limited partnership trust structure is the most commonly used method of establishing an income trust. Here, the proceeds of a public offering of units are used to subscribe for the units and debt of a newly formed business trust, which in turn uses the proceeds to acquire a limited partnership interest in a newly formed limited partnership. The limited partnership then uses the proceeds to acquire the operating business. The limited partnership trust allows existing equity owners to receive limited partnership units on a tax-deferred basis that are exchangeable for units of the fund. As shown in Figure 1.2, the distributable cash generated by the operating business is distributed up the chain to the unitholders.

income trust
Created through the conversion of a regular corporation to a trust structure, where the business becomes a different type of legal entity; the benefit is a significant reduction in taxes.

An **income trust** is created through the conversion of a regular corporation to a trust structure. Essentially, the business becomes a different type of legal entity; it changes its legal structure to a trust. What is the benefit of doing this? In Canada, we have a double taxation problem when companies pay profits to shareholders as dividends. Dividends are paid out of after-tax income. So a company with before-tax earnings of $1,000,000 must first pay tax on those earnings. Assuming a tax rate of 40 percent, the company will pay $400,000 of taxes and have $600,000 of earnings remaining that can be paid as dividends. But shareholders receiving the dividends must also pay taxes. Assuming a tax rate of 20 percent, $120,000 of taxes will be paid leaving only $480,000 of after-tax income. So, of the $1,000,000 of earnings, a total of $520,000, 52 percent, is paid as taxes.

A corporation that is converted and held inside a trust structure avoids paying any tax on profits, assuming the profits are distributed to the holders of the trust (the unitholders). If, in the above example, the corporation is an income trust that pays out the $1,000,000 of earnings as distributions, only the unitholders pay tax.[2] If the average tax rate of the unitholders is 40 percent, after-tax income is $600,000, a $120,000 advantage over the corporate structure. The tax advantages enjoyed by income trusts and unitholders are significant, and a very attractive feature of this form of business organization.

---

2. For income trusts, the cash flows generated by the trust are paid to unitholders, not just the profits. The distributions often include a tax-free return of capital. This is another key difference between trusts and corporations.

FIGURE 1.2

A Model of Creating an Income Trust

SOURCE: Based on Alexandra Iliopoulos and John Vettese, "The Canadian Income Trust Market," *The 2005 Lexpert CCCA/ACCJE Corporate Counsel Directory and Yearbook* (Toronto: Cassels Brock & Blackwell LLP, 2005).

www.casselsbrock.com/publications/Lexpert_IncomeTrusts.pdf

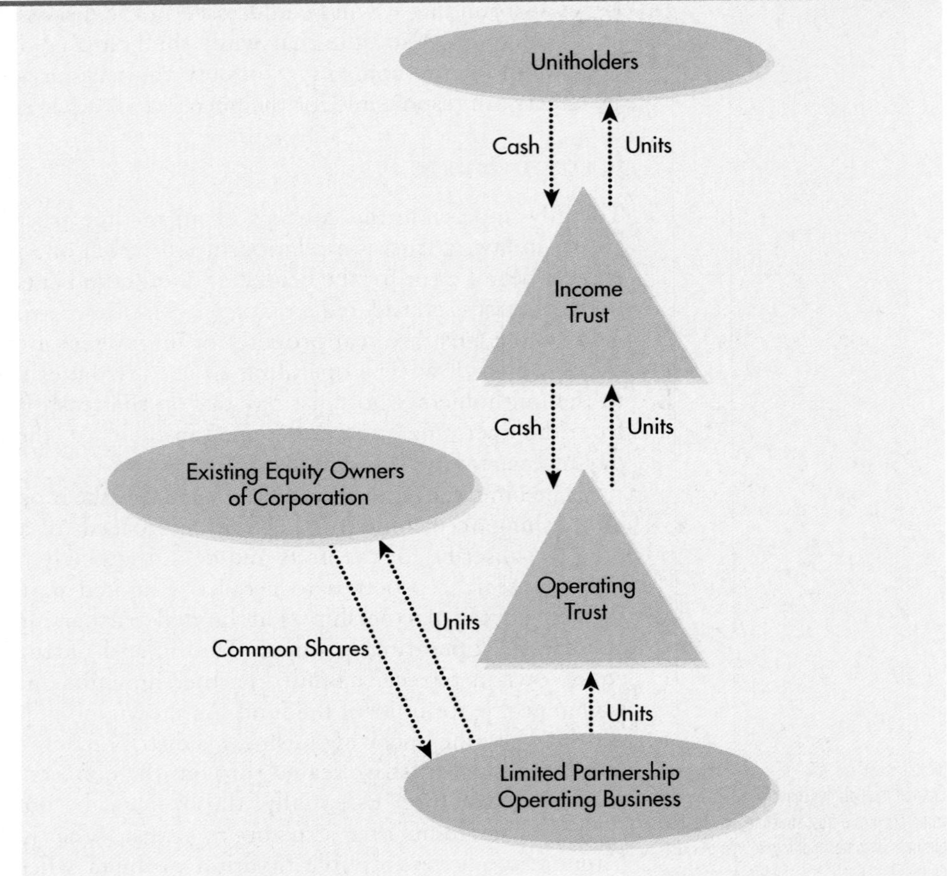

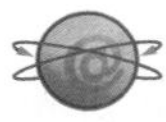

www.barclaysfunds.ca
http://research.cibcwm.com/res/Equ/ArEquIRITI.html

S&P/TSX Composite Index
The measure of how the Canadian stock market has done over a stated time period, which might be a day, a week, a month, a year, or a number of years.

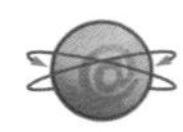

www.investcom.com/incometrust/incometrust.htm

The trust structure clearly makes financial sense. This, in part, explains the huge increase in popularity in income trusts. For example, in 1998, there were 52 income trusts listed on the TSX with a market capitalization of $17.1 billion. As of the time of the writing of this chapter (summer 2006), there were over 260 income trusts, with a market capitalization approaching $200 billion. The group became large enough to have over 70 trusts included as part of the **S&P/TSX Composite Index**, the measure of how the Canadian stock market has done over a stated time period. Various Web sites provide up-to-date data on trusts.

Another reason for the large increase in the number of income trusts is that they are very attractive to individual investors due to their high yields. The percentage yield is based on the distributions paid to the unitholders, divided by the price of the units. In the summer of 2006, yields ranged from 5 percent to over 20 percent and many trusts provided yields in the double digits. With interest rates on bank accounts between 0 and 2 percent, and yields on even long-term debt securities in the 5 percent range, income trusts became an attractive alternative for investors. Current yields on income trusts are available on various Web sites.

Given their nature, income trusts should be based on businesses that are stable, are relatively mature, and have a generous and predictable cash flow. These traits allow much of the cash flow generated by the business to be distributed rather than reinvested to fund future growth. The four basic types of income trusts, defined by the nature of their underlying assets, are: (1) resource (primarily oil and gas), (2) business, (3) real estate (REITs), and (4) utility (power and pipelines). Companies holding real estate were the original type of corporations that were converted to income trusts (REITs). Real estate is the ideal type of asset to hold in a trust structure, since it generates very predictable cash flows (assuming the property is rented). At one time, REITs were the only type of income trust available. But in the summer of 2006, the REIT category accounted for only about 12 percent of the total value of income trusts.

The decline in relative importance of REITs was due, not to a deficiency with the category, but rather to the rapid increase in other types of trusts. For example, in the summer of 2006, the resource category accounted for about half of the total value of income trusts. The boom in this category resulted from the realization that, for these companies, large tax savings were possible with a conversion. As a result, many oil and gas companies converted to trusts in the 2002 to 2005 period. In addition, the substantial increase in the price of energy in the 2003 to 2006 period resulted in a rapid rise in price of these trusts. This occurred as distributions increased and as investors expected even higher yields in the future. The combination has resulted in resource trusts dominating in terms of value.

In the summer of 2006, the business category accounted for about 30 percent of the total value of income trusts. This sector expanded and became quite diverse due to the surge in offerings in the 2003 to 2005 time period. For example, income trusts were created for companies in fast food, ice, sardine packing, financial services, jam, cold storage, beer, retirement homes, film production, pet food, mattresses, and long-distance trucking.

Like any other type of investment, income trusts have their own unique risks and rewards. It is important to recognize that income trusts are using their assets to generate cash flows that are then paid out to investors. Without additional assets, at some point the distributions will decline. Some income trusts are low-growth businesses that are essentially distributing their assets. A fundamentally sound income trust can provide an investor with stable cash flows over a long time horizon, as well as the potential for capital appreciation. But all income trusts are not equal, and without careful analysis an investor can lose money. Income trusts have a lower claim on assets than the holders of debt securities, and the distributions are not based on a legal commitment but on management projections for cash flows from the underlying assets. Even if distributions are maintained, the gains made from the distributions may be reduced by falling market prices.

In summary, the income trust structure only makes sense for publicly traded companies with high tax rates. So, in terms of the total number of corporations in Canada, income trusts are a very small percentage. But for just businesses listed on the TSX, income trusts have become a significant factor in terms of both number and size. The key strengths and weaknesses of income trusts are summarized in Table 1.2.

On October 31, 2006, as this book was going to press, the federal government changed how income trusts would be taxed. Beginning in 2011, all current income trusts other than REITs are to be taxed at the same rate as corporations. This will likely mean that very few additional corporations will convert to the income trust structure. In addition, with the tax benefit gone by 2011, some trusts may convert back to the corporate structure. The reason for this federal government action was the significant decline in corporate tax revenues at both the federal and the provincial level. It is virtually certain that this measure will pass, so it appears that the main motivating factor for trusts will soon be gone, and that therefore the importance of this business form for all but REITs will decline after 2011.

? Review Questions

1–5 What are the three basic forms of business organization? Which form is most common? Which form is dominant in terms of total sales, profits, and assets? Why?

1–6 Describe the role and basic relationship among the major parties in a corporation—common shareholders, board of directors, CEO, and all other employees. How are corporate owners compensated?

1–7 What is the major disadvantage of the sole proprietorship and partnership? Is this disadvantage truly eliminated with the corporate form of business ownership?

1–8 Briefly discuss the income trust as a form of business organization. What are the advantages and disadvantages of this form of organization compared to a corporation?

1.3 The Corporate Finance Function

As noted earlier, people in all areas of responsibility within the firm will interact with finance personnel, processes, and procedures to get their jobs done. For financial personnel to make useful forecasts and decisions, they must talk to individuals in other areas of the firm. The corporate finance function can be broadly described by considering its role within the organization, its relationship to economics and accounting, and the key activities of the financial manager.

Organization of the Finance Function

The size and importance of the corporate finance function depend on the size of the firm. In small firms, the finance function is generally performed by the accounting department. As a firm grows, the finance function typically evolves into a separate department linked directly to the company president or chief executive officer (CEO) through a vice-president of finance, commonly called the chief financial officer (CFO). The lower portion of the organizational chart in Figure 1.1 shows the structure of the finance function in a typical medium-to-large-size firm. Reporting to the vice-president of finance are the treasurer and the controller. The **treasurer** is commonly responsible for handling financial activities, such as financial planning and fund raising, making capital expenditure decisions, managing cash, managing credit activities, managing the pension fund, and managing foreign exchange. The **controller** typically handles the accounting activities, such as corporate accounting, tax management, financial

treasurer
The officer responsible for the firm's financial activities such as financial planning and fund raising, making capital expenditure decisions, and managing cash, credit, the pension fund, and foreign exchange.

controller
The officer responsible for the firm's accounting activities, such as corporate accounting, tax management, financial accounting, and cost accounting.

Hint
A ***controller*** is sometimes referred to as a ***comptroller***. Not-for-profit and governmental organizations frequently use "comptroller."

accounting, and cost accounting. The treasurer's focus tends to be more external, whereas the controller's focus is more internal. *The activities of the treasurer, or financial manager, are the primary concern of this text.*

foreign exchange manager
The manager responsible for monitoring and managing the firm's exposure to loss from currency fluctuations.

If international sales or purchases are important to a firm, it may well employ one or more finance professionals whose job is to monitor and manage the firm's exposure to loss from currency fluctuations. A trained financial manager can "hedge," or protect against, this and similar risks, at reasonable cost, using a variety of financial instruments. These **foreign exchange managers** (or traders) typically report to the firm's treasurer.

Relationship to Economics

marginal analysis
Economic principle that states that financial decisions should be made and actions taken only when the added benefits exceed the added costs.

The field of finance is closely related to economics. Financial managers must understand the economic framework and be alert to the consequences of varying levels of economic activity and changes in economic policy. They must also be able to use economic theories as guidelines for efficient business operation. Examples include supply-and-demand analysis, profit-maximizing strategies, and price theory. A primary economic principle used in corporate finance is **marginal analysis,** the principle that financial decisions should be made and actions taken only when the added benefits exceed the added costs. Nearly all financial decisions ultimately come down to an assessment of their marginal benefits and marginal costs. A basic knowledge of economics is therefore necessary to understand both the environment and the decision techniques of managerial finance.

Example Jamie Teng is a financial manager for Nord Department Stores—a large chain of upscale department stores operating primarily in western Canada. She is currently trying to decide whether to replace one of the firm's online computers with a new, more sophisticated one that would both speed processing time and handle a larger volume of transactions. The new computer would require a cash outlay of $80,000, and the old computer could be sold to net $28,000. The total benefits from the new computer (measured in today's dollars) would be $100,000, and the benefits over a similar time period from the old computer (measured in today's dollars) would be $35,000. Applying marginal analysis to this data, we get

Benefits with new computer	$100,000	
Less: Benefits with old computer	35,000	
(1) Marginal (added) benefits		$65,000
Cost of new computer	$ 80,000	
Less: Proceeds from sale of old computer	28,000	
(2) Marginal (added) costs		52,000
Net benefit [(1) − (2)]		$13,000

Because the marginal (added) benefits of $65,000 exceed the marginal (added) costs of $52,000, the purchase of the new computer to replace the old one makes good financial sense and is recommended. The firm will experience a net benefit of $13,000 as a result of this action.

Relationship to Accounting

The firm's finance (treasurer) and accounting (controller) activities, shown in the lower portion of Figure 1.1, are closely related and generally overlap. Indeed, some aspects of corporate finance and accounting overlap, as both have a focus on the financial statements. In small firms the controller often carries out the finance function, and in large firms many accountants are closely involved in various finance activities. However, there are two basic differences between finance and accounting; one relates to the emphasis on cash flows and the other to decision making.

Emphasis on Cash Flows

The accountant's primary function is to develop and provide data for measuring the performance of the firm, assessing its financial position, and paying taxes. Using certain standardized and generally accepted principles, the accountant prepares financial statements that recognize sales revenue and the expenses that were incurred to generate the sales, at the time of sale. This approach is referred to as the **accrual basis.**

accrual basis
Recognizes sales revenue at the time of sale and the expenses incurred to generate the sales.

cash basis
Recognizes revenues and expenses only with respect to actual inflows and outflows of cash.

The financial manager, on the other hand, places primary emphasis on *cash flows,* the intake and outgo of cash. He or she maintains the firm's solvency by planning the cash flows necessary to satisfy its obligations and to acquire assets needed to achieve the firm's goals. The financial manager uses this **cash basis** to recognize the revenues and expenses only with respect to actual inflows and outflows of cash. Regardless of its profit or loss, a firm must have a sufficient flow of cash to meet its obligations as they come due. It is not uncommon for profitable firms still to experience financial problems due to holding insufficient amounts of cash.

Example Peakes Quay, Inc., a small yacht dealer, in the calendar year just ended sold one yacht for $100,000; the yacht was purchased during the year at a total cost of $80,000. Although the firm paid in full for the yacht during the year, at year end it has yet to collect the $100,000 accounts receivable from the customer. The accounting view and the financial view of the firm's performance during the year are given by the following income and cash flow statements, respectively.

Accounting (accrual basis) view	
Income Statement Peakes Quay, Inc. for the year ended 12/31	
Sales revenue	$100,000
Less: Costs	80,000
Net profit	$ 20,000

Financial (cash basis) view	
Cash Flow Statement Peakes Quay, Inc. for the year ended 12/31	
Cash inflow	$ 0
Less: Cash outflow	80,000
Net cash flow	($80,000)

In an accounting sense Peakes Quay is profitable, but it is a financial failure in terms of actual cash flow. Its lack of cash flow resulted from the uncollected account receivable of $100,000. Without adequate cash inflows to meet its obligations the firm will not survive, regardless of its level of profits.

Hint
The primary emphasis of accounting is on accrual methods; the primary emphasis of financial management is on cash flow methods.

The preceding example shows that accrual accounting data do not fully describe the circumstances of a firm. Thus, the financial manager must look beyond financial statements to obtain insight into developing or existing problems. The financial manager, by concentrating on cash flows, should be able to avoid insolvency and achieve the firm's financial goals. It is also worth noting that the financial manager measures cash flow on an after-tax basis.

Decision Making

We come now to the second major difference between finance and accounting: decision making. Whereas accountants devote most of their attention to the collection and presentation of financial data, financial managers evaluate the accounting statements, develop additional data, and make decisions based on their assessment of the associated returns and risks. Accountants provide consistently developed and easily interpreted data about the firm's past, present, and future operations. Financial managers use these data, either in raw form or after adjustments and analyses, as inputs to the decision-making process. Essentially, finance takes over where accounting leaves off. Accounting focuses on information collection and generation. Finance uses information to make decisions. This is a good way to distinguish between the two disciplines.

Key Activities of the Financial Manager

The financial manager's primary activities are (1) performing financial analysis and planning, (2) making investment decisions, and (3) making financing decisions. Figure 1.3 relates each of these financial activities to the firm's balance sheet. Although investment and financing decisions can be conveniently viewed in terms of the balance sheet, these decisions are made on the basis of their cash flow effects. This focus on cash flow will become clearer in later chapters.

Performing Financial Analysis and Planning

Financial analysis and planning is concerned with (1) monitoring the firm's financial condition, (2) evaluating the need for increased (or reduced) productive

FIGURE 1.3
Financial Activities
Key activities of the financial manager

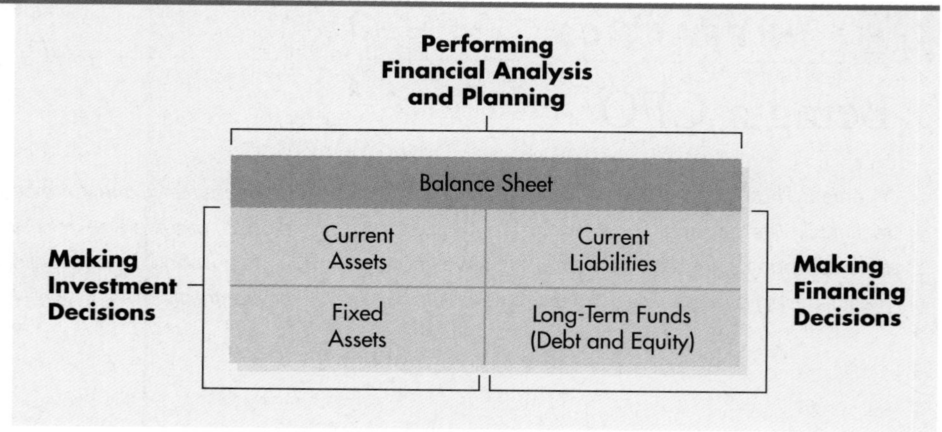

capacity, and (3) determining what financing is required. Monitoring the firm's *working capital* position is a vital aspect of financial analysis and a day-to-day activity that ensures the company survives and grows. Working capital is the firm's level of current assets, such as accounts receivable and inventory, and the use of current liabilities, such as accounts payable and short-term loans. These functions encompass the entire balance sheet as well as the firm's income statement and other financial statements. Although this activity relies heavily on accrual-based financial statements, its underlying objective is to assess the firm's cash flows and develop plans that ensure adequate cash flow to support goal achievement.

Making Investment Decisions

Investment decisions determine both the mix and the type of assets found on the left-hand side of the firm's balance sheet. *Mix* refers to the number of dollars of current and fixed assets. Once the mix is established, the financial manager attempts to maintain optimal levels of each type of current asset. The financial manager also decides which fixed assets to acquire and when existing fixed assets need to be modified, replaced, or liquidated. The process of planning and analyzing the investment in fixed assets is referred to as capital budgeting. Investment decisions are important because they affect the firm's success in achieving its goals.

Making Financing Decisions

Financing decisions deal with the right-hand side of the firm's balance sheet and involve two major areas. First, the most appropriate mix of short-term and long-term financing must be established. A second and equally important concern is which individual short-term or long-term sources of financing are best at a given point in time. The two long-term financing choices are debt and equity capital. Many of these decisions are dictated by necessity, but some require in-depth analysis of the financing alternatives, their costs, and their long-run implications. The mix of short- and long-term financing and the mix of debt and equity financing used is the company's **capital structure**. Again, it is the effect of these decisions on the firm's goal achievement that is most important.

capital structure
The mix of short- and long-term financing and the mix of debt and equity financing used by a company.

1.1 **IN PRACTICE**

Being a CFO

Wanted: Physically fit thinker with excellent operational, technical, interpersonal, and leadership skills to maintain company's infrastructure and achieve management's strategic goals. Must have extensive knowledge of accounting and finance, endurance to deal with skeptics and the stress of rising workloads, and the ability to respond to and anticipate a changing business environment.

▶

(Continued)

What does it take to be a successful chief financial officer (CFO)? Obviously, a thorough knowledge of both accounting and finance is a prerequisite, but what else is important? An undergraduate degree and often graduate education in business (MBA) are starters. An accounting designation helps, but CFOs are no longer viewed just as bean counters making sure that debits equal credits and that income exceeds expenses. These days, CFOs are expected to have a full-spectrum perspective of the nature of the company.

No longer just focused on finance, CFOs are key members of the executive team setting the company's overall financial strategy and participating in senior management activities. Successful CFOs share common abilities and responsibilities. Key abilities include: analytical thinking, strategic planning, creativity, leadership, interpersonal skills, and general management experience. CFOs are responsible for implementing management information systems, reviewing operational and acquisition strategies, raising external financing, managing cash, and communicating with investors and other members of senior management. They interact with all functional areas of a business on a daily basis.

According to a study by Robert Half International Inc., the future of the profession lies in technology, specifically, expertise in information technology and experience in the emerging technology environment. Increasingly, CFOs and their department are becoming more involved with their company's technology ventures and with e-commerce.

Due to the availability of high-tech tools, CFOs are deeply involved in what is happening with the company. Better reporting and forecasting tools are helping CFOs take a more visionary role in the firm, and become vital strategic members of the company. The right financial reporting technology means CFOs have quick access to important information and ensures they are making the best changes for the best results. It is expected that the role of the CFO will continue to change as technology continues to advance and businesses increasingly embrace new and ever-changing technologies.

Another trend in the profession is the rise of female CFOs, a trend also occurring in other management-level positions. In fact, Canada's 2006 CFO of the year was Karen Maidment, Chief Financial and Administrative Officer of BMO Financial Group. She was the first female to receive the honour since the award was first presented in 2003.

Maidment plays a vital role in the activities of BMO Financial Group. She is responsible for the company's financial strategy, financial reporting and planning, taxation, treasury, investor relations, legal and compliance, corporate communications, economics and enterprise risk, and portfolio management. Prior to joining BMO, Maidment worked at Clarkson Gordon and Clarica Life Insurance Company, where she served as CFO and played a leadership role in the demutualization of the company and in the first initial public offering in Canada for demutualized insurers. Her most recent award probably comes as no surprise to those in the business world: Ms. Maidment was named one of Canada's top 100 most powerful women in 2005 and has been included in *Financial Post's* Power 50 list of top Canadian businesswomen in 2003, 2004, and 2005.

For current job postings for chief financial officer positions, go to **www.cfo.com/cfocareers**. 

SOURCES: Stephanie Sanborn, "Technology Helps CFOs Expand Their Roles," *InfoWorld* 23(11) (March 12, 2001), p. 34; "Corporate Information—Executive Bios," Bank of Montreal site, May 2006, **www.bmo.com**; "BMO Financial Group's Karen Maidment Named Canada's CFO of the Year for 2006," PricewaterhouseCoopers site, April 18, 2006, **www.pwc.com/extweb/ncpressrelease.nsf**; Stephen Taub, "The CFO of the Future," CFO.com, June 29, 2001. See: **www.cfo.com/article.cfm/2997645**.

? Review Questions

1–9 What financial activities does the treasurer, or financial manager, perform in the mature firm?

1–10 Explain why the financial manager should possess a basic knowledge of economics. What is the primary economic principle used in managerial finance?

1–11 What are the major differences between accounting and finance with respect to: (**a**) emphasis on cash flows; (**b**) decision making?

1–12 What are the three key activities of the financial manager? Relate them to the firm's balance sheet.

1.4 Goal of the Financial Manager

As noted earlier, the owners of a corporation are normally distinct from its managers. Actions of the financial manager should be taken to achieve the objectives of the firm's owners, its common shareholders. In most cases, if financial managers are successful in this endeavour, they will also achieve their own financial and professional objectives. So, financial managers need to know the objectives of the firm's owners. Many people believe that the owners' objective is always to maximize profit. Let's begin by looking at that goal.

Maximize Profit?

To achieve the goal of profit maximization, the financial manager takes only those actions that are expected to contribute to the firm's overall profits. For each alternative being considered, the financial manager would select the one that is expected to result in the highest monetary return. Corporations commonly measure profits in terms of **earnings per share (EPS)**, which represent the amount earned during the accounting period on each outstanding common share of the corporation. EPS are calculated by dividing the period's total earnings available for the firm's common shareholders by the number of common shares outstanding.

earnings per share (EPS)
The amount earned during the accounting period on each outstanding common share, calculated by dividing the period's total earnings available for the firm's common shareholders by the number of common shares outstanding.

Example Nick Dukakis, the financial manager of Neptune Manufacturing, a producer of marine engine components, is attempting to choose between two major investments, X and Y. Each is expected to have the following earnings per share effects over its 3-year life.

	Earnings per share (EPS)			
Investment	Year 1	Year 2	Year 3	Total for years 1, 2, and 3
X	$1.40	$1.00	$0.40	$2.80
Y	0.60	1.00	1.40	3.00

Based on the profit-maximization goal, investment Y would be preferred over investment X, because it results in higher total earnings per share over the 3-year period.

But profit maximization is not a reasonable goal. It fails for a number of reasons: it ignores (1) the timing of returns, (2) cash flows available to common shareholders, and (3) risk.[3]

Timing

Because the firm can earn a return on funds it receives, *the receipt of funds sooner rather than later is preferred.* In our example, in spite of the fact that the total earnings from investment X are smaller than those from Y, investment X provides much greater earnings per share in the first year. The larger returns in year 1 could be reinvested to provide greater future earnings. Timing issues are considered through time-value-of-money calculators. Chapter 6 is devoted to time value calculation.

Cash Flows

Profits do *not* necessarily result in cash flows available to the common shareholders. Owners receive cash flow either in the form of cash dividends paid them or the proceeds from selling their shares for a higher price than initially paid. A greater EPS does not necessarily mean that a firm's board of directors will vote to increase dividend payments.

Furthermore, a higher EPS does not necessarily translate into a higher share price. Firms sometimes experience earnings increases without any correspondingly favourable change in share price. Only when earnings increases are accompanied by increased future cash flows would a higher share price be expected. For example, a firm in a highly competitive technology-driven business could increase its earnings by significantly reducing its research and development expenditures. As a result the firm's expenses would be reduced, thereby increasing its profits. But because of its now poorer competitive position, the firm's share price would drop, as many well-informed investors sell their shares in anticipation of lower future cash flows. In this case, the earnings increase was accompanied by lower future cash flows and therefore a lower share price.

Risk

risk
The chance that actual outcomes may differ from those expected.

Hint
This is one of the most important concepts in the book. Investors who seek to avoid risk will always require a bigger reward for taking bigger risks.

Profit maximization also disregards **risk**—the chance that actual outcomes may differ from those expected. A basic premise in corporate finance is that a tradeoff exists between return (cash flow) and risk. *Return and risk are in fact the key determinants of share price, which represents the wealth of the owners in the firm.*

Cash flow and risk affect share price differently: higher cash flow is generally associated with a higher share price. Higher risk tends to result in a lower share price, because the shareholders must be compensated for the greater risk. For example, if a lawsuit claiming significant damages is filed against a company, its share price typically will immediately drop. This occurs not because of any near-term cash flow reduction, but rather in response to the firm's increased risk—

3. Another criticism of profit maximization is the potential for profit manipulation through the creative use of elective accounting practices. This has become a widespread complaint of common shareholders in both Canada and the United States.

there's a chance that the firm will have to pay out a large amount of cash some time in the future to eliminate or fully satisfy the claim. Simply put, the increased risk reduces the firm's share price. In general, individuals are risk-averse—that is, they want to avoid risk. When risk is involved, they expect to earn higher rates of return on investments of higher risk and lower rates on lower-risk investments. The key point, which will be fully developed in Chapter 7, is that differences in risk can significantly affect the value of an investment.

Because profit maximization does not achieve the objectives of the firm's owners, it should *not* be the goal of the financial manager.

Maximize Shareholder Wealth

The goal of the firm, and therefore of all managers and employees, is *to maximize the wealth of the owners for whom it is being operated.* The wealth of corporate owners is measured by the price of the common shares, which in turn is based on the timing of returns (cash flows), their magnitude, and their risk. The goal is to maximize the value of the common shareholders' total interest in the company. This is measured by multiplying the total number of common shares outstanding by the common share price.

When considering each financial decision alternative or possible action in terms of its impact on the firm's share price, *financial managers should accept only those actions that are expected to increase share price.* Figure 1.4 depicts this process. Because share price represents the owners' wealth in the firm, share-price maximization is consistent with owner-wealth maximization. Note that *return (cash flows) and risk are the key decision variables in the wealth maximization process.* It is important to recognize that earnings per share (EPS), because they are viewed as an indicator of the firm's future returns (cash flows), often appear to affect share price. Two important issues related to share-price maximization are economic value added (EVA) and the focus on stakeholders.

Economic Value Added (EVA)

economic value added (EVA)
EVA, a way to measure the value of a company, is the difference between a company's net operating profit after tax and the total cost of invested capital.

Economic value added (EVA) is a performance measure that focuses on economic profit rather than accounting profit. It allows for a look beyond headline earnings, and concentrates on free cash flow as a way to measure the value of a company. EVA captures a firm's true economic profit by recognizing that the

FIGURE 1.4
Share Price Maximization
Financial decisions and share price

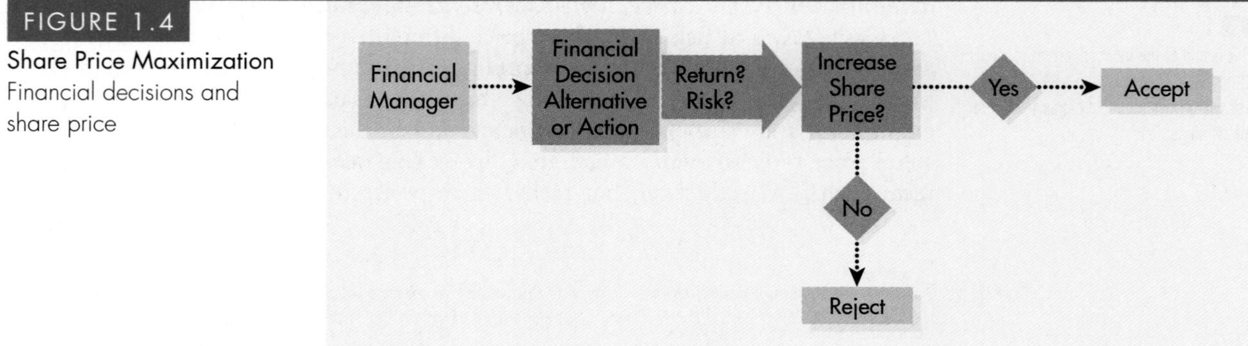

capital used by a firm has a cost. This cost, called the *cost of capital* or *capital charge*, includes the cost of both debt and equity. EVA, over a given time period, is defined as the difference between a company's net operating profit after tax and the total cost of invested capital.

EVA is based on three concepts. The first is that cash flows are the best indicators of performance. Accounting distortions must therefore be corrected when calculating EVA. As a result, the accrual-based operating profit is translated into a cash-based operating profit. Second, some expenses are really investments and should be capitalized on the balance sheet. The calculation of EVA therefore involves the reclassification of some current expenses as balance sheet items. The combination of items 1 and 2, on an after-tax basis, is net operating profit after tax (NOPAT). Third, the capital invested in the business is not free, and this cost must be accounted for. The EVA calculation therefore deducts a charge for the invested capital. This cost is the firm's weighted average cost of capital (WACC). Using these inputs, the EVA of a company can be determined as follows:

$$\text{EVA} = \text{NOPAT} - (\text{Dollar amount of invested capital} \times \text{WACC\%}) \tag{1.1}$$

A positive EVA means the company has created value above the minimum required rate of return, whereas a negative EVA means the company has fallen short of the minimum required rate of return and has thus destroyed wealth. An EVA of zero means the company is generating a return equal to the investor's required rate of return. This is acceptable, but a high positive EVA is always preferred, because this is a sign of a very effective management team.

For example, the EVA of a company with after-tax operating earnings of \$410,000 for the year and associated financing costs of \$375,000 would be \$35,000 for the year (i.e., \$410,000 − \$375,000). Because this EVA is positive, the company has created additional value for the providers of the capital to the firm during the year. Since it is the shareholders who take the ultimate risk when investing in companies, the positive EVA flows to them. Of course, in practice numerous accounting and financial issues would be involved in estimating the net operating profit after tax for the company, the company's invested capital, and the costs of the individual sources of capital. Spreadsheet Application 1.1 provides the EVA analysis for the above example.

The growing popularity of EVA is due to both the relative simplicity of the value added concept and its strong link to owner wealth maximization. Advocates of EVA believe it exhibits a strong link to share prices—positive EVAs are associated with increasing share prices, and vice versa. While EVA analysis is very popular in the United States, only a handful of companies in Canada have attempted to implement the technique. Two of these companies are Domtar, the third-largest manufacturer of business, printing and publishing, and technical and specialty paper in North America, and Alcan, the second-largest aluminum company in the world. Coca-Cola is a long-time user of EVA. A former CEO of the company has stated: "You only get rich if you invest money at a higher rate of return than the cost of that money to you." This comment clearly illustrates the concept.

Given that highly successful firms such as Coca-Cola use and widely tout the effectiveness of EVA as a method that helps the company focus on creating shareholder value, it is surprising that more Canadian companies are not using the technique to help make investment decisions. While EVA is popular among some companies, it is important to note that it shares some similarities with other

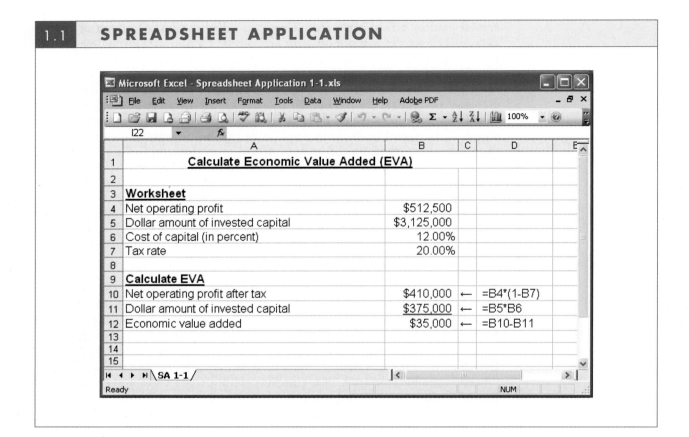

1.1 SPREADSHEET APPLICATION

Microsoft Excel - Spreadsheet Application 1-1.xls

	A	B	C	D
1	**Calculate Economic Value Added (EVA)**			
2				
3	**Worksheet**			
4	Net operating profit	$512,500		
5	Dollar amount of invested capital	$3,125,000		
6	Cost of capital (in percent)	12.00%		
7	Tax rate	20.00%		
8				
9	**Calculate EVA**			
10	Net operating profit after tax	$410,000	←	=B4*(1-B7)
11	Dollar amount of invested capital	$375,000	←	=B5*B6
12	Economic value added	$35,000	←	=B10-B11
13				
14				
15				

SA 1-1

valuation techniques such as *net present value (NPV)*, which is described in detail in Chapter 12. What's important at this point is to recognize that useful tools, such as EVA, are available for operationalizing the owners' wealth-maximization goal.[4]

What About Stakeholders?

stakeholders
Groups such as employees, customers, suppliers, creditors, owners, communities, and others who have a direct economic link to the firm.

Although shareholder-wealth maximization is the primary goal, in recent years many firms have broadened their focus to include the interests of *stakeholders* as well as shareholders. **Stakeholders** are groups such as employees, customers, suppliers, creditors, owners, communities, and others who have a direct economic link to the firm. Employees are paid for their labour, customers purchase the firm's products or services, suppliers are paid for the materials and services they provide, creditors provide debt financing that is to be repaid subject to specified terms, owners provide equity financing for which they expect to be compensated, and communities provide the environment the company and many of the

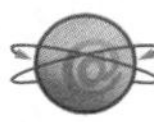

4. For a good overview of EVA (including a video on the concept), see Stern Stewart & Co.'s Web site at: **www.sternstewart.com** or Brian A. Schofield, "EVAluating Stocks," *Canadian Investment Review*, Spring, 2000; available at: **www.investmentreview.com/archives/2000/spring/stocks.html**.

stakeholders operate within. A firm with a *stakeholder focus* consciously avoids actions that would prove detrimental to stakeholders. The goal is not to maximize stakeholder well-being but to preserve it.

The stakeholder view does not alter the shareholder wealth maximization goal. Such a view is often considered part of the firm's "social responsibility" and is expected to provide maximum long-run benefit to shareholders by maintaining positive stakeholder relationships. Such relationships should minimize stakeholder turnover, conflicts, and litigation. Clearly, the firm can better achieve its goal of shareholder wealth maximization with the cooperation of—rather than conflict with—its other stakeholders.

The Role of Ethics

In recent years, the ethics of actions taken by certain businesses have received major media attention. While the negative actions of businesses often make the headlines, the vast majority of businesses act in an ethical manner when making decisions. For example, Fraser Papers is one of North America's largest producers of specialized paper products, and paper production is an area in which numerous environmental problems have occurred over the years. Recognizing this issue, Fraser has integrated environmental protection into its business processes and decisions, making it a key part of the company's identity. The company works on regularly improving its environmental performance and management of forest land. For Fraser Papers, sustainable development means creating economic growth while caring for society and the environment.

The company has implemented an environmental management system that: (1) ensures the company fully complies with all applicable environmental legislation and regulations, (2) consistently operates with the principles of sustainable forestry, (3) reduces the environmental impact of its activities, (4) has risk management procedures in place to prevent and respond to emergencies, (5) communicates with stakeholders, including employees, shareholders, the communities in which the company operates, and the government, (6) supports environmental research and implements findings, and (7) audits the environmental impact of its operations. In addition, the company assigns appropriate human and financial resources to support the environmental management system. Fraser Papers requires its operations to develop policies, systems, organizations, and competencies, and to embrace an environmental commitment consistent with these principles. The company requires all employees to take responsibility for environmental protection in their jobs.

Bombardier, a world-leading manufacturer of transportation products including regional and amphibious aircraft, business jets, passenger railcars, and light rail vehicles, meets its social and humanitarian responsibilities primarily through the J. Armand Bombardier Foundation (named after the founder of the company). Since 1965, the non-profit Foundation has served as an instrument for giving back to the communities in which the company operates. It receives funding equivalent to 3 percent of the company's income before income taxes. In its history, the Foundation has donated millions of dollars to a significant number of social welfare organizations and provides major funding for education, health, culture, social development, and humanitarian causes. In the 2006 fiscal year, the foundation made donations worth nearly $5 million to various causes.

These are just two examples of how Canadian publicly traded companies attempt to ensure they act in an ethical manner. If one were to read the information released by most Canadian companies, one would find similar types of actions described. Clearly, these and other similar actions have raised the question of **ethics**—standards of conduct or moral judgment. Today, the business community in general and the financial community in particular are developing and enforcing ethical standards. Credit for this is primarily due to the increased public awareness resulting from the widespread publicity surrounding major ethical violations and their perpetrators. The goal of these ethical standards is to motivate business and market participants to adhere to both the letter and the spirit of laws and regulations concerned with business and professional practice.

ethics
Standards of conduct or moral judgment.

It can be argued that a business enterprise actually strengthens its competitive position by maintaining high ethical standards. A logical way to encourage ethical business behaviour is for firms to adopt a business code of ethics. Many Canadian companies have done this, and highlights of the ethical code are often included in the company's *annual report*, the report to common shareholders that summarizes and documents the firm's financial activities during the past year. In addition, it is now common to see advertisements in newspapers and magazines or on television that explain what a company is doing to be a "good corporate citizen."

These initiatives may have been motivated by the downfall of numerous companies and individuals starting in 2001 over ethical violations. Companies such as Enron, WorldCom, Tyco, ImClone, Dynegy, Global Crossing, Parmalat, Adelphia Communications, Arthur Andersen, HealthSouth, Hollinger International, and Nortel Networks, among others, have all exhibited questionable, and in a few cases illegal, behaviour. As a consequence, all suffered huge financial losses and, in some cases, bankruptcy over corrupt actions. Many other companies were tarnished over claims of unethical accounting practices. Business ethics is associated with the struggle to curtail corporate power, particularly the power of the CEO. Ethical behaviour helps balance the two major pulls of capitalism: efficiency and greed.

Considering Ethics

Robert A. Cooke, a noted ethicist, suggests that the following questions be used to assess the ethical viability of a proposed action.[5]

1. Is the action or anticipated action arbitrary or capricious? Does it unfairly single out an individual or group?
2. Does the action or anticipated action violate the moral or legal rights of any individual or group?
3. Does the action or anticipated action conform to accepted moral standards?
4. Are there alternative courses of action that are less likely to cause actual or potential harm?

5. Robert A. Cooke, "Business Ethics: A Perspective," in *Arthur Andersen Cases on Business Ethics* (Chicago: Arthur Andersen, September 1991), pp. 2 and 5.

Clearly, considering such questions before taking an action can help to ensure its ethical viability. Specifically, Cooke suggests the impact of a proposed decision should be evaluated from a number of perspectives before it is finalized:

1. Are the rights of any stakeholder being violated?
2. Does the firm have any overriding duties to any stakeholder?
3. Will the decision benefit any stakeholder to the detriment of another stakeholder?
4. If there is detriment to any stakeholder, how should this be remedied, if at all?
5. What is the relationship between shareholders and other stakeholders?

Today, more and more firms are directly addressing the issue of ethics by establishing corporate ethics policies and guidelines and by requiring employee compliance with them. Frequently, employees are required to sign a formal pledge to uphold the firm's ethics policies. Such policies typically apply to employee actions in dealing with all corporate stakeholders, including the public at large. Many companies require employees to participate in ethics seminars and training programs that convey and demonstrate corporate ethics policy.

Ethics and Share Price

The implementation of a proactive ethics program is believed to enhance corporate value. An ethics program can produce a number of positive benefits: reduce potential litigation and judgment costs; maintain a positive corporate image; build shareholder confidence; and gain the loyalty, commitment, and respect of all of the firm's stakeholders. Such actions, by maintaining and enhancing cash flow and reducing perceived risk (as a result of greater investor confidence), are expected to positively affect the firm's share price. *Ethical behaviour is therefore viewed as necessary for achievement of the firm's goal of owner-wealth maximization.*[6]

Triple Bottom Line

When setting goals, is there a direct way of ensuring the interests of stakeholders are considered and that the firm is acting ethically? An approach that has been suggested is to implement *triple bottom line reporting*, a term coined by John Elkington, co-founder of the business consultancy SustainAbility. This goal looks beyond just financial results to measure a firm's success. Its advocates encourage companies to think not just in terms of the financial bottom line but also in terms of the "social bottom line" and the "environmental bottom line." It is a means of expanding the traditional reporting framework by taking into consideration social and environmental performance in addition to financial performance.

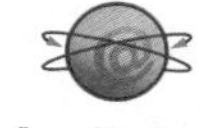

www.web-miner.com/busethics.htm

6. For an excellent discussion of how corporations can maximize wealth in an ethical manner, see Donald R. Chambers and Nelson J. Lacey, "Corporate Ethics and Shareholder Wealth Maximization," *Financial Practice and Education* (Spring/Summer), 1996, pp. 93–96, and Mark Schacter, "Boards Face New Social Responsibility," *CA Magazine*, May 2005. In addition, there are numerous Web sites and news and journal articles devoted to the concept of business ethics and ethical leadership.

Even though it is a relatively new practice, and even though a firm's social and environmental performance cannot be easily measured and quantified, triple bottom line reporting is gaining popularity, being used by such companies as AT&T, Dow Chemicals, Shell, British Telecom, and BC Hydro.

So, What Is the Financial Goal of a Company?

This section of the chapter considers the financial goal of a company. When you think about possible financial goals a company could pursue, items such as the following may come to mind:

- maximize sales
- maximize cash flow
- maximize market share
- maximize profits
- minimize costs
- maximize number of customers
- maximize return on sales, investment, or shareholders' equity
- ensure earnings stability
- achieve a certain level of sales, profits, market share, or return

The major financial goal a company should be concerned with is to maximize shareholder wealth. This is the value of the company to the owners—the common shareholders. Shareholder wealth is a function of the number of common shares outstanding multiplied by the price of the common shares. The goal of financial management should be to maximize this value, but not at the expense of other stakeholders, society, or the environment. Companies that try to maximize the wealth of their shareholders, without due consideration of others, will not achieve the goal. For those attempting this, there will be plenty of costs in terms of lost reputation and sales, increased costs, and significant litigation that will distract management from running the company.

Therefore, the sole financial goal of the company is to maximize the value of the company in an ethical manner by treating all stakeholders equitably. This is depicted in Figure 1.5.

FIGURE 1.5

The Financial Goal

Maximize shareholder wealth

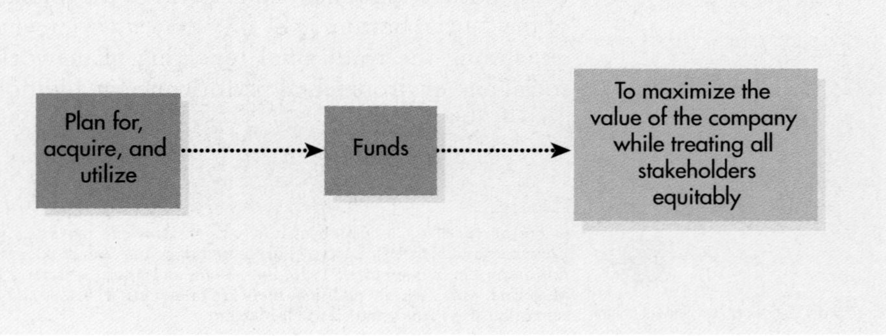

? Review Questions

1–13 For what three basic reasons is profit maximization inconsistent with wealth maximization?

1–14 What is *risk?* Why must risk as well as return be considered by the financial manager when evaluating a decision alternative or action?

1–15 What is the goal of the firm and therefore of all managers and employees? Discuss how one measures achievement of this goal.

1–16 What is *economic value added (EVA)*? How is it used? Why is it currently quite popular?

1–17 Describe the role of corporate ethics policies and guidelines, and discuss the relationship that is believed to exist between ethics and share price.

1.5 The Agency Issue[7]

We have seen that the goal of the financial manager should be to maximize the wealth of the owners of the firm. Thus management can be viewed as *agents* of the owners who have hired them and given them decision-making authority to manage the firm for the owners' benefit. Technically, any manager who owns less than 100 percent of the firm is, to some degree, an agent of the other owners. This separation of owners and managers is shown by the dashed horizontal line in Figure 1.1.

In theory, most financial managers would agree with the goal of owner-wealth maximization. In practice, however, managers are also concerned with their personal wealth, job security, lifestyle, and fringe benefits, such as posh offices, country club memberships, limousines, and private jets, all provided at company expense. Choosing to spend scarce company resources in such ways will likely not lead to the maximization of shareholder wealth, but rather the maximization of senior managers' lifestyle and enjoyment. In addition, such concerns may make managers reluctant or unwilling to take more than moderate risk if they perceive that too much risk might result in a loss of job and damage to personal wealth. The result of such a "satisficing" approach (a compromise between satisfaction and maximization) is a less-than-maximum return and, in all likelihood, loss of wealth for the owners.

Hint
An investment advisor (stockbroker) has the same issue. If she gets you to buy and sell more stock, it's good for ***her,*** but it may ***not*** be good for you.

agency problem
The likelihood that managers may place personal goals ahead of corporate goals.

So, for the modern corporation, the separation of ownership and control creates an **agency problem**. Professional managers act as agents for the owners (common shareholders) in running the corporation. The decisions made and actions taken by management impact shareholders and other stakeholders, but also the wealth, tenure, and reputation of management. Consequently, the senior managers of a company may pursue their own goals for personal gain at the expense of shareholders, and measures must be taken to prevent or minimize this

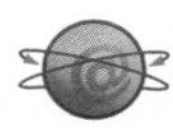

www.upei.ca/~sbusines/faculty/hennessey/research.html

7. This section of the chapter is based on the paper "Corporate Governance and Publicly-Traded Companies," by Sean M. Hennessey. The complete paper is available online.

and resolve the conflicts between the owners and managers at minimal cost.[8] This is the goal of corporate governance.

Corporate Governance

corporate governance
The set of actions and procedures common shareholders use to ensure they receive a reasonable return on their investment in the company.

agency costs
The reduction in shareholders' wealth due to the agency problem.

Corporate governance is the set of actions and procedures used to ensure a company is managed so shareholders receive a return on their investment in the company that is reasonable, given the risks involved. These measures are meant to minimize **agency costs**, the reduction in shareholders' wealth due to the agency problem. In many public companies, ownership is fragmented across many investors, giving full control of the company to management with no or a very small ownership position. In such cases there can be significant agency problems, and corporate governance is vital to ensure management's actions serve shareholders and not management. The objective of corporate governance is to ensure acceptable performance. For managers who are not creating shareholder wealth, who are behaving in their own interests, or who are simply incompetent, shareholder and market mechanisms should serve to check the inefficiency and penalize any poor performance.[9]

There are four approaches to corporate governance: (1) the board of directors, who monitor management, (2) management compensation plans, including options, (3) the mechanism of the market that evaluates management's performance (through the market price of the common shares), and (4) takeovers. The first two are internal corporate governance mechanisms, the latter two external. Each is considered below.

Board of Directors

An obvious form of corporate governance is the board of directors, whose mandate is to monitor management on behalf of shareholders. Most large companies whose common shares are publicly traded have millions, or in some cases billions, of common shares outstanding, and tens of thousands of common shareholders. Some of these shareholders are large, owning tens of thousands of shares; some are very small, owning 100 or fewer shares. For example, Manulife Financial, based in Toronto, is the largest life insurance company in Canada and the fourth-largest life insurance company in the world. In October 2006, the company had a market value of $57 billion, and over 1.5 billion common shares outstanding, with over 900,000 common shareholders. Obviously, the individual shareholders of Manulife cannot be actively involved in the affairs of the company.

www.manulife.com

The shareholders elect a small group of people, the board of directors, to represent their interests to senior management. The board hires the CEO and

8. The agency problem and related issues are addressed in the following papers: Michael C. Jensen and William H. Meckling, "Theory of the Firm: Managerial Behavior, Agency Costs and Ownership Structure," *Journal of Financial Economics*, 3 (1976), pp. 305–360 and Michael C. Jensen, "Agency Cost of Free Cash Flow, Corporate Finance, and Takeovers," *American Economic Review*, 76 (1986), pp. 323–329. For a detailed discussion and practical application of agency issues in Canada, see: Sean Hennessey, "Corporate Governance Mechanisms in Action: The Case of Air Canada," Chapter 7 in *Corporate Governance: A Global Perspective, Advances in Financial Economics*, Vol. 11, eds. Mark Hirschey, John Kose, and Anil K Makhija (Greenwich, CT: JAI Press 2005), pp. 127–166, or "A Remarkably Futile Record," *National Post*, December 15, 2001, both available at: **www.upei.ca/~sbusines/faculty/hennessey/research.html**.

9. For excellent practical discussions of corporate governance, including ways to improve standards and practices, see: Carol Hansell, "The Road to Good Governance," *CA Magazine*, December 2003, or A. Atkinson and S. Salterio, "Shaping Good Conduct: The Search for More Effective Systems of Corporate Governance," *CMA Management*, February 2002, pp. 19–23.

other senior managers. The board's role is to directly represent shareholders' interests to management. They are responsible for ensuring that the senior managers act in the best interests of the owners. This implies the maximization of shareholder value, not of management's income or job tenure. If a company's financial performance is poor, the ultimate power of the board is to decrease the compensation paid to the senior management team, or replace underperforming managers.

For publicly traded companies in Canada, a document detailing the duties and responsibilities of the board must be in place. Each year, companies are required to disclose this information to shareholders. The disclosure generally includes a statement to the effect that the company's approach to corporate governance is to ensure that the business affairs of the company are managed to enhance shareholder value. Usually, a lengthy list of guidelines is provided that indicate the governance process. An all-inclusive statement to the effect that the board assumes responsibility for the stewardship of the company usually heads the list. Boards directly represent shareholders' interests to management and *should* afford excellent protection for shareholders. While boards are meant to help solve the agency problem in managing public companies, agency issues may also affect the performance of the board of directors.

Perhaps the first person to recognize the agency problem and to draw attention to the problems of boards was Adam Smith in 1776. In his landmark book *The Wealth of Nations*, Smith argued that directors are negligent and profuse, not as vigilant with other people's money as with their own. Boards often include the very managers the board supposedly monitors. While these inside directors may be a minority on the board, their positions in and knowledge of the company afford them powerful voices. Furthermore, the outside or non-management board members are selected by and may be sympathetic to management.

For example, in Canada, corporate boards seem to be drawn from the same small subset of people. Boards have been described as: "a close-knit fraternity of perhaps 100 peripatetic directors, each serving on between five and 15 boards. It's still a fairly closed network, you might call it stacking the deck."[10] Board memberships are lucrative and membership is often tied to the ability to work with the CEO. The CEO often serves on other companies' boards. It's a system where being critical of senior management may be very difficult. There may be an element of people helping each other to "get cookies out of the jar."

The effectiveness of corporate boards may be hampered by a "culture of seduction." Directors are wooed by high retainer fees, fees for attending each meeting, and with perks such as access to corporate jets, first-class travel, contributions to their favourite charities, and consulting contracts. It may be that for some companies, the board of directors puts management's interest ahead of the goal of maximizing shareholder wealth.

Compensation Plans

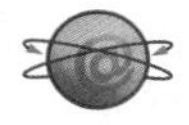

www.theglobeandmail.com/robmagazine

A second corporate governance mechanism is management compensation plans. The senior managers of publicly traded corporations in Canada are well paid. For example, every year the *Globe and Mail*'s Report on Business completes a

10. See: David Olive, "CEOs Not Sharing Investors' Pain: Compliant Boards Find a Way to Prop Up Executive Pay," *National Post*, May 22, 2001.

survey of CEO compensation. The survey includes all the companies included in the S&P/TSX Composite Index. In 2005, Canada's CEOs saw their total compensation soar an average of 39 percent from 2004 (itself a year of huge compensation increases) as stock markets and commodity prices continued to increase. The average CEO in Canada earned about $4.3 million in 2005. This was a significant increase from 2003, when the average CEO took home about $3.2 million. The pay leader for 2005 was Hank Swartout, CEO of Precision Drilling Trust, who received almost $75 million. Hunter Harrison of Canadian National Railway was second with total compensation of over $56 million.

Most would agree that compensation levels like these would be more than enough to motivate managers to do a good job for shareholders. This is particularly the case when it is realized that very little of the huge pay packages senior managers receive is salary. One part of the compensation package offered to the managers of most publicly traded companies is **incentive plans** that tie part of management's compensation to the price of the company's common shares. The most popular incentive plan is the granting of **stock options** to management. These options allow managers to purchase common shares at the market price set at the time of the grant. If the market price of the common shares increases, managers will be rewarded by being able to sell the shares at the higher market price.

incentive plans
Management compensation plans that tend to tie management compensation to share price; most popular incentive plan involves the grant of *stock options.*

stock options
An incentive allowing managers to purchase common shares at the market price set at the time of the grant.

The premise underlying the granting of stock options is that tying compensation to the value of the company's common shares should align the interests of shareholders and management. Greater overlap between ownership and control reduces the conflicts between owners and managers. Too little ownership may lead to inefficient use of a company's free cash flow, or outright theft; too much, to management entrenchment and empire-building. It has been suggested that there is some optimal level of ownership by management that fully aligns the interest of shareholders and managers. Both managers and shareholders have incentives to avoid management ownership stakes that do not align the interests of the two parties.

Although in theory these options should motivate, they are sometimes criticized because positive management performance can be masked in a poor stock market in which share prices in general have declined due to economic and behavioural "market forces" outside of management's control. The reverse is also true. In addition, the share option component is just an additional part of the pay package; it does not replace the manager's salary. Compounding the problem is that the options are often exercisable in the short run, encouraging short-term, not long-term, planning. This can result in management actions that seek to maximize short-term earnings at the expense of long-term performance. Finally, there is no real cost to managers if the market price of the shares does not reach the exercise price; the managers received their salary anyway. Will this process make managers feel like owners?

In response to these issues with options, the use of **performance plans** has grown in popularity in recent years due to their relative independence from market forces. These plans compensate managers on the basis of their proven performance measured by earnings per share (EPS), growth in EPS, and other ratios of return. **Performance shares,** common shares granted to management as a result of meeting the stated performance goals, are often used in these plans. These shares should replace all or a large part of a manager's salary, and the plans should require managers to hold the shares for many years before being allowed to sell. This would be an effective corporate governance measure;

performance plans
Plans that compensate managers on the basis of proven performance measured by EPS, growth in EPS, and other ratios of return. *Performance shares* and/or *cash bonuses* are used as compensation under these plans.

performance shares
Common shares granted to management for meeting stated performance goals.

unfortunately, only a few publicly traded companies have adopted this compensation method.

cash bonuses
Cash paid to management for achieving certain performance goals.

Another form of performance-based compensation is **cash bonuses,** cash payments tied to the achievement of certain performance goals. Under performance plans, management understands in advance the formula used to determine the amount of performance shares or cash bonus it can earn during the period. In addition, the minimum benefit (typically, $0) and maximum benefit available under the plan are specified.

To illustrate each of these components of the compensation paid to managers, reconsider the Report on Business CEO compensation survey for 2005. We have already seen that in 2005 Canada's CEOs saw their total compensation soar an average of 39 percent to an average of $4.3 million. But the combination of salaries and bonuses climbed only 6 percent. The real driver of the pay increase was stock option gains which soared 47 percent over 2004. CEOs, on average, earned $1.8 million each from exercising stock options—a number that climbs to $4.5 million if only those CEOs who cashed out options are included. Of the top 25 CEOs in terms of the value of options exercised, the average amount received was a staggering $12.4 million. And the big paydays will continue. By the end of 2005, the CEOs of these publicly traded companies held a total of $2.2 billion of in-the-money stock options, an average of $9 million for each CEO.

At almost $75 million, Hank Swartout, CEO of Precision Drilling Trust, topped the pay list in 2005. It is interesting to note that of this amount, only $840,000 was salary. He received a bonus of $3.4 million and other compensation of $15.6 million. But, also in 2005, Mr. Swartout cashed out all his stock options when Precision Drilling converted into an income trust. This generated a $55 million gain. Hunter Harrison of Canadian National Railway was second on the pay list, with total compensation of over $56 million. His salary was $1.7 million, bonus $4.7 million, and other compensation $1.7 million. But he also received performance shares worth $20.9 million and gained $27.2 million from options.

Although experts agree that an effective way to motivate management is to tie compensation to performance, the execution of many compensation plans has been closely scrutinized in recent years. Shareholders, both individuals and institutions, have publicly questioned the appropriateness of the multimillion-dollar compensation packages (including salary, bonus, and long-term compensation) that many corporate executives receive.

Although the sizable compensation packages provided to managers may be justified by significant increases in shareholder wealth, recent studies have failed to find a strong relationship between CEO compensation and share price. The publicity surrounding these large compensation packages (without corresponding share price performance) has had little impact to date in reducing the level of executive compensation. New compensation plans that better link management compensation with increases in shareholder wealth are expected to be developed and implemented.

Market Forces

A corporate governance mechanism external to the company is the stock market. It has been long argued that when shareholders can freely trade their common shares in efficiently operated markets, the mechanism of market pricing allows shareholders to "vote" on managements' actions, thereby minimizing agency costs and encouraging acceptable performance. If a company's financial performance is poor, shareholder "voting" in the stock market will result in the common share price declining. When this happens, shareholder wealth will be reduced, not maximized, and the board of directors should question the poor corporate performance. In addition, stock options provided to managers will lose value or become worthless. With this series of events, changes should occur, either with the strategic direction of the company, the tactics the company is using to meet their goals, or with senior management. The ultimate power of the board (shareholders) is to fire underperforming managers.

In addition, in Canada, institutional investors, such as mutual funds, pension funds, and life insurance companies, often own a majority of the common shares of publicly traded companies. These professional money managers, who hold large blocks of common shares in many companies, would be expected to watch the performance of these companies very closely. Poor company performance, leading to declining share prices, may provoke these large shareholders to attempt to gain control of the board and fire underperforming managers, replacing them with more competent managers. Note that the formal mechanism through which these shareholders act is by voting their shares in the election of directors, who are empowered to hire and fire operating management. In addition to their legal voting rights, large shareholders are able to communicate with and exert pressure on management to perform or be fired.

While good and bad company performance is reflected in the market price of a company's common shares, the external mechanism of market pricing itself does not lead to better company results. A falling share price, on its own, does not discipline managers; shareholders and others must act. When institutional shareholders act, this behaviour is referred to as *shareholder activism*. In the United States, large shareholders are very active in ensuring acceptable company performance. In Canada, shareholder activism is very rare, even in cases where institutional investors own a large majority (more than 70 percent) of the common shares of a company and company performance is poor. The reason for the lack of shareholder activism in Canada is not clear.

Hostile Takeovers

Another external market force that has in recent years threatened management to perform in the best interests of shareholders is the possibility of a *hostile takeover*. A **hostile takeover** is the acquisition of the firm (the *target*) by another firm or group (the *acquirer*) that is not supported by management. Hostile takeovers typically occur when the acquirer feels that the target firm is being poorly managed and, as a result, is undervalued in the marketplace. The acquirer believes that by acquiring the target at its current low price and restructuring its management, operations, and financing, it can enhance the firm's value—that is, its share price. If the hostile takeover succeeds, often the first move the acquiring company makes is to replace the current management team and the board. Although techniques are available for defending against hostile takeovers, the constant threat of a takeover often motivates management to perform so the company's share price remains high and does not attract the attention of potential acquirers.

hostile takeover
The acquisition of the firm (the *target*) by another firm or group (the *acquirer*) that is not supported by management.

Research on takeovers suggests that the shareholders of target firms benefit, since the takeover price is generally at a significant premium to the market price prior to the takeover. However, the returns to the acquiring firm's shareholders are at best zero, and are often negative. In addition, takeovers are an extreme and expensive corporate governance mechanism that require access to large amounts of capital and are open to political interference. Takeovers can create agency problems for the bidding firm's shareholders when empire-building is the motivation and the acquirer overpays.

In addition, while a company may be acquired, that doesn't mean the company's shareholders received a fair price for their shares. For an acquisition to make sense to an acquiring company, less than full price has to be paid. By implication, the target company's shareholders may not receive full value. Finally, it seems strange that shareholders have to rely on another company's management to discipline their own management. The poor company performance should have been recognized by the board prior to any hostile takeover action.

Summary

There is little question that agency problems exist for publicly traded companies and that the associated costs can be very high for shareholders. The goals of management may be in conflict with and even supercede those of shareholders. When managers hold little equity in the firm and shareholders are too dispersed or unable to enforce value maximization, corporate assets may be deployed to benefit managers rather than shareholders.

The shareholders of both well and poorly managed companies must be able to rely on their representatives, the board of directors. Board members must be independent and financially literate. They must have a broad understanding of the economic and industrial environment and of the business. They must understand and be able to contribute to the strategic direction of the business, ask questions, and act if management is not achieving specified targets. They must have the ability to absorb and process complex information with integrity and discipline. They must feel free to offer different points of view. They must hold an equity position in the company purchased with their own money.

In short, all board members must be viewed by management and stakeholders as credible representatives of shareholders. If not, shareholders will be left to the mercy of the agents. Companies with good managers need good boards. The shareholders and stakeholders of companies with poor managers need better boards.

? Review Questions

1–18 What is the *agency problem* and what are *agency costs*?

1–19 What is *corporate governance*? Discuss the four corporate governance mechanisms.

1–20 Describe and differentiate between *incentive* and *performance* compensation plans.

1–21 Discuss the importance of the board of directors' corporate governance mechanism.

1.6 Key Financial Concepts: The Language of Finance

For many introductory courses in functional areas like finance, marketing, or operations management, learning the language of the discipline is a vital step to understanding the topics discussed. Imagine a mathematics student not understanding words and concepts like model, probability, factors, functions, matrices, calculus, or logarithms. Without knowledge of some of the basic concepts of a subject, it would be impossible to understand applications of the concepts or advanced material based on the concepts. A foundation level of understanding in a discipline must be formed that can then be built upon. This section of the chapter provides a brief overview of some key financial concepts and introduces some key words in the language of finance. These concepts are covered in much greater detail later in the book. Interested readers can also visit various sites on the Web for additional readings on many topics in corporate finance.

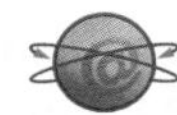

www.teachmefinance.com

http://en.wikipedia.org/wiki/Corporate_finance

www.duke.edu/~charvey/Classes/wpg/glossary.htm

Basic Accounting

A complete understanding of basic accounting and the four key financial statements (income statement, balance sheet, statement of retained earnings, and statement of cash flows) is vital in order to become comfortable with corporate finance. Students should know the characteristics of each statement and all of the major items that appear on them, understand the relationships between the statements, and be able to work with the statements to determine missing data. Readers have likely been exposed to these statements; however, Chapter 2 provides a refresher.

Financial Forecasting

financial forecasting
The process used to estimate a company's requirement for financing for a future time period.

Financial forecasting is the process used to estimate a company's requirement for financing for a future time period. Financing is required to invest in assets. Assets are necessary to support increases in sales and profits. Generally, financial forecasting is associated with expected sales growth. A key part of the process is to forecast the company's financial statements. The future time period may be short-term, for example, the next quarter or next year, or long-term, forecasts for the next five to ten years. The key outputs of the financial forecasting process are the amount of funds the company will require to operate over the forecast period and the forecasted financial statements.

Financial Markets

Financial markets provide a forum where *savers of funds* and *users of funds* can transact business. These two groups must be able to make an exchange that is expected to be beneficial to both parties. Individuals, governments, and business organizations are all involved in the financial markets. In the financial markets, cash moves from savers to users, and users provide a financial security in return. The financial security indicates the compensation the saver will receive in return for providing the funds. The compensation may be a rate of return on the funds, a promise to repay the funds at some point in the future, and/or a right of ownership. For financial markets to work, financial institutions, intermediaries that allow for the efficient and low-cost transfer of the savings of individuals, governments, and business for financial securities, are necessary. These intermediaries include institutions like banks and investment dealers.

money market
The market where debt securities that will mature within one year are traded.

capital market
The market that trades long-term debt securities and common and preferred equity securities.

There are two distinct financial markets: the money market and the capital market. Debt securities that will mature within one year are traded in the **money market.** The principal money market security is Government of Canada treasury bills, or t-bills as they are more commonly known. In the **capital market,** long-term debt securities, like bonds and debentures, and preferred and common shares are traded. The term "market" may be misleading to describe this trading. There is no physical market for much of the trading of financial securities that occur in the financial markets. The "market" for all debt securities is the communication system that exists between the traders of these financial securities. All trading of these securities occurs in cyberspace, the networks that connect computers.

primary market
The market where financial securities are initially issued and where the issuer receives the proceeds from the sale of the financial security.

A second way to subdivide financial markets is by the nature of the transaction. A financial security must be "created," and this occurs in the primary market. The **primary market** is the market where a financial security is initially issued and where the issuer (the organization selling the financial security) receives the proceeds from the sale of the security to savers (investors). Again, there is no physical location for the primary market; the market exists in cyberspace. Once the security is created, a second market must exist to allow the initial purchaser of the security an opportunity to trade this and other securities.

secondary market
The market that allows the owner of a previously created financial security to sell this security or to buy more of this or other securities, or allows a buyer to express an interest in acquiring a financial security.

This is the secondary market. The **secondary market** allows the owner of a previously created financial security to sell the security or to buy more of this or other securities, or allows a buyer to express an interest in acquiring a financial security. This interaction between interested buyers and sellers in the secondary market sets the price of financial securities. As demand for a particular financial security increases, so too will the price. As more holders of a particular financial security wish to sell, prices will decline. The secondary market for all debt securities is in cyberspace.

stock exchange
An actual, physical secondary market that allows investors to buy and sell preferred and common shares.

For preferred and common shares, however, there is an actual, physical market. This is the stock market, which is also referred to as a stock exchange. A **stock exchange** allows investors to buy and sell preferred and common shares. The largest stock exchange in Canada is the Toronto Stock Exchange (TSX). The various stock exchanges in a country constitute the stock market. Millions of shares are traded each day on the various stock exchanges around the world. The company whose shares are being traded is not involved. All of these trades are between investors.

Risk–Return Tradeoff

risk–return tradeoff
The return expected depends on the amount of risk taken.

risk-averse
The attitude toward risk in which a higher return would be expected if risk increased.

required rate of return
The minimum return required given the risk of an investment; the greater the risk of loss, the greater the required return.

Most financial decisions entail a **risk–return tradeoff;** that is, the return expected depends on the amount of risk taken. To receive a high rate of return, a high degree of risk must be taken. Those wishing to take less risk must be satisfied with a lower return. Individuals are assumed to be **risk-averse.** To be encouraged to take more risk, a higher return must be offered or expected. A risk–return tradeoff is associated with all financial decisions a company must make. For example, decisions regarding a company's production capacity, the level of investment in assets, and the mix of short-term debt, long-term debt, and equity financing used in the business all involve a risk–return tradeoff. The **required rate of return** on an investment is based on a minimum acceptable return plus a premium for the level of risk taken. The greater the risk of loss, the greater the required risk premium and thus return.

interest
The return paid on debt financing.

interest rate
The cost of money. The greater the risk of the debt security, the higher the interest rate.

Interest is the return paid on debt financing. The **interest rate** is the cost of money. Investors lending money to the Canadian government in the form of short-term debt (treasury bills) or long-term debt (bonds) will expect to receive a lower rate of interest (lower return) than if they lent their money to a corporation regardless of its size or perceived level of safety. A corporation is always more risky than the federal government. Therefore, the expected return is always higher. The greater the risk, the higher the expected return.

Cost of Capital

A company raises financing using a certain mix of debt and common equity financing. This is the company's capital structure. Investors providing the financing require a specific rate of return that compensates for the risk of the financial security. When lending money, various conditions are stated, one of which is the cost of the money: the interest rate on the loan. The providers of debt financing must be paid the stated rate of interest or they are entitled to force the firm into bankruptcy. This right reduces the risk of debt for the lender and thus the return required. On the other hand, the return expected on common equity is based on net income after tax. Common shareholders are entitled to receive the residual income of the company. Since there is no guarantee that a company will generate a profit, the risk of common equity is much higher than debt and so too is the return required.

Therefore, a company will be financed with a certain mix of lower cost debt and higher cost common equity. The percentage of debt multiplied by its cost is added to the percentage of equity multiplied by its cost to determine the company's overall cost of financing. This is the **cost of capital**, the cost to the company of raising additional financing in the percentages that are considered best for it.

cost of capital
The overall cost to a company of a mix of debt and common equity financing.

Capital Budgeting

Companies raise financing from both internal and external sources. Internal sources include reinvested profits and amortization. This was considered in the discussion of the statement of cash flows. External sources are debt, both short- and long-term, and preferred-share and common-share financing. With the combined financing, the company will invest in assets. **Capital budgeting** is the process of analyzing the investment in assets with an expected life greater than one year. These assets may be a new piece of equipment, a new manufacturing facility, or a new product. These assets must be expected to provide a return that compensates for the cost of the financing that was used to acquire them. This is the basis of capital budgeting, ensuring that the return expected from the acquisition of an asset compensates for the cost of the funds invested in the asset. The cost of the funds, of course, is based on the risk of the financial security.

capital budgeting
The process of analyzing the investment in assets with an expected life greater than one year.

? Review Question

1–22 Define each of the following key financial concepts.
   a. financial forecasting
   b. financial markets including their main function and types

c. stock exchange
d. risk–return tradeoff
e. required rate of return
f. interest rates
g. cost of capital
h. cost of debt and equity financing
i. capital budgeting

1.7 Using This Text

The text's organization links the firm's activities to its value, as determined in the securities markets. The activities of the financial manager are described in seven parts:

Part 1: Introduction to Corporate Finance
Part 2: Financial Analysis and Planning
Part 3: Important Financial Concepts
Part 4: Long-Term Financing Decisions
Part 5: Long-Term Investment Decisions
Part 6: Working Capital Management
Part 7: Special Topics in Corporate Finance

Each major decision area is presented in terms of both return and risk factors and their potential impact on the owners' wealth. Coverage of international events and topics is integrated into the chapter discussions. A separate international corporate finance chapter is also included.

The text has been developed around a group of 114 learning goals—six per chapter. Mastery of these goals results in a broad understanding of the theories, concepts, techniques, and practices of corporate finance. These goals have been carefully integrated into a learning system. Each chapter begins with a numbered list of learning goals. Next to each major text heading is a *toolbox,* which notes by number the specific learning goal(s) addressed in that section. At the end of each section of the chapter (positioned before the next major heading) are review questions that test your understanding of key theories, concepts, techniques, and practices in that section. At the end of each chapter, the chapter summaries, self-test problems, and problems are also keyed by number to each chapter's learning goals. By linking all elements to the learning goals, the integrated learning system facilitates the mastery of those goals.

Each chapter has a corresponding Case on the Student CD-ROM that integrates the chapter materials. Integrative Cases that tie together the key topics covered in each Part are also provided on the Student CD-ROM. All of the cases can be used to synthesize and apply related concepts and techniques.

SUMMARY

LG1 **Define *finance* and describe its three major areas—financial markets, financial services, and corporate finance—and the career opportunities within them.** Finance, the art and science of managing money, affects the lives of every person and every organization. Financial markets provide a forum where savers of funds and users of funds transact business. Career opportunities available include the trading of financial securities and work with the financial intermediaries that allow the markets to function and the organizations that regulate the markets. Financial services involve the design and delivery of financial products. Major opportunities in financial services exist within banking and related institutions, personal financial planning, investments, real estate, and insurance. Managerial finance, concerned with the duties of the financial manager in the business firm, offers numerous career opportunities such as financial analyst, capital budgeting analyst/manager, project finance manager, cash manager, credit analyst/manager, and pension fund manager. The recent trend toward globalization of business activity has created new demands and opportunities in managerial finance.

LG2 **Review the forms of business organization and their respective strengths and weaknesses.** The basic forms of business organization are the sole proprietorship, the partnership, and the corporation. In Canada, income trusts have become an important alternative form of business organization for publicly traded companies. Although there are more sole proprietorships than any other form of business organization, the corporation is dominant in terms of business sales, profits, and assets. The owners of a corporation are its common shareholders. Shareholders expect to earn a return by receiving dividends or by realizing gains through increases in share price. An income trust is created through the conversion of a regular corporation to a trust structure, where the business becomes a different type of legal entity; the benefit is a significant reduction in taxes. Given their nature, income trusts should be based on businesses that are stable and relatively mature, and have a generous and predictable cash flow. The key strengths and weaknesses of each form of business organization are summarized in Table 1.2.

LG3 **Describe the corporate finance function, differentiate corporate finance from the closely related disciplines of economics and accounting, and identify the key activities of the financial manager.** All areas of responsibility within a firm interact with finance personnel, processes, and procedures. In large firms, the managerial finance function might be handled by a separate department headed by the vice president of finance (CFO), to whom the treasurer and controller report; in small firms, the finance function is generally performed by the accounting department. The financial manager must understand the economic environment and relies heavily on the economic principle of marginal analysis when making decisions. Financial managers use accounting data but differ from accountants, who devote primary attention to accrual methods and to gathering and presenting data, by concentrating on cash flows and decision making. The three key activities of the financial manager are (1) performing financial analysis and planning, (2) making investment decisions, and (3) making financing decisions.

LG4 **Explain why wealth maximization, rather than profit maximization, is the firm's goal and how economic value added (EVA), a focus on stakeholders, and ethical behaviour relate to its achievement.** The goal of the financial manager is to maximize the owners' wealth (dependent on share price) rather than profits, because profit maximization ignores the timing of returns, does not directly consider cash flows, and ignores risk. Because return and risk are the key determinants of share price, both must be assessed by the financial manager when evaluating decision alternatives or actions. EVA is a measure used to determine whether the company is being managed in a way that positively contributes to the owners' wealth. The wealth maximizing actions of financial managers should be consistent with the preservation of the wealth of *stakeholders*, groups such as employees, customers, suppliers, creditors, owners, communities, and others who have a direct economic link to the firm. Positive ethical practices by the firm and its managers are believed to be necessary for achievement of the firm's goal of owner-wealth maximization. A triple bottom line may help focus management and the organization on their financial, societal, and environmental obligations.

LG5 **Discuss the agency issue as it relates to owner-wealth maximization.** For the modern corporation, the separation of ownership and control creates an agency problem. Professional managers act as agents for the owners (common shareholders) in running the corporation. The decisions made and actions taken by management impact not only shareholders and other stakeholders but also the wealth, tenure, and reputation of management. Consequently, the senior managers of a company may pursue their own goals for personal gain. Corporate governance is the set of actions and procedures used to ensure a company is managed so that shareholders receive a return on their investment in the company that is reasonable given the risks. These measures are meant to minimize agency costs, the reduction in shareholders' wealth due to the agency problem. There are four approaches to corporate governance, mechanisms that shareholders rely upon to ensure managers do not act in their own self-interest at the expense of investors: (1) the board of directors, who monitor management, (2) management compensation plans, including options, (3) the mechanism of the market, which both evaluates management's performance (through the market price of the common shares) and allows individual shareholders to become holders of large voting blocks of shares concentrating ownership and control, and (4) takeovers. The first two are internal corporate governance mechanisms, the latter two external.

Discuss some key concepts in finance and review the language of finance. For many introductory courses in functional areas such as corporate finance, learning the language of the discipline is vital in order to understand the topics discussed. Without knowledge of some of the basic concepts in a subject, it is very difficult to understand applications of the concepts or advanced material based on the concepts. Some of the key financial concepts and terms in the language of finance to know are: basic accounting and the four key financial statements, financial forecasting, financial markets, risk–return tradeoff, cost of capital, and capital budgeting.

SELF-TEST PROBLEM

(Solution in Appendix B)

ST 1–1 Goals of a company Liam Murphy, financial analyst with Doyle Power Supply, is evaluating two different projects that the firm could implement. Doyle Power Supply's current earnings per share are $1.63, the company has 10,000,000 common shares outstanding, and the company's common shares are trading for $19.50 per share.

If Doyle implements project 1, the firm will issue 1,000,000 common shares, the total increase in EPS will be $1.32 (in today's dollars), and the firm's share price will increase to $28. If project 2 is implemented, the firm will issue 1,800,000 common shares, the total increase in EPS will be $1.19 (in today's dollars), and Doyle's common share price will increase to $26.50.

a. If profit maximization was Doyle Power Supply's goal, which project should Liam Murphy recommend? Why?

b. If share price maximization was Doyle Power Supply's goal, which project should Liam Murphy recommend? Why?

c. If the maximization of common shareholder wealth was Doyle Power Supply's goal, which project should Liam Murphy recommend? Why?

d. As Liam Murphy, which project would you recommend? Why?

e. Why might project 2 be the better project, even though it results in lower EPS and a lower share price? Explain.

PROBLEMS

BASIC 

1–1 Liability comparisons Meredith Harper has invested $25,000 in Southwest Development Company. The firm has recently declared bankruptcy and has $60,000 in unpaid debts. Explain the nature of payments, if any, by Ms. Harper in each of the following situations.

a. Southwest Development Company is a sole proprietorship owned by Ms. Harper.

b. Southwest Development Company is a 50–50 partnership of Ms. Harper and Christopher Black.

c. Southwest Development Company is a corporation.

INTERMEDIATE

1–2 Marginal analysis and economic value added (EVA) Ken Allen, capital budgeting analyst for Bally Gears, Inc., has been asked to evaluate a proposal. The manager of the automotive division believes that replacing the robotics used on the heavy truck gear line will produce total benefits of $560,000 (in today's dollars) over the next 5 years. The existing robotics would produce benefits of $400,000 (also in today's dollars) over that same time period. An initial cash investment of $220,000 would be required to install the new equipment. The manager estimates that the existing robotics can be sold for $70,000. Show how Ken will apply marginal analysis techniques to determine the following:

a. The marginal (added) benefits of the proposed new robotics.

b. The marginal (added) cost of the proposed new robotics.

c. The net benefit of the proposed new robotics.

d. What Ken Allen should recommend that the company do, and why.

e. The factors besides the costs and benefits that should be considered before the final decision is made.

f. Now assume that Bally Gears acquired the robotics equipment. During the next fiscal year the company generated before-tax operating profits of $345,000. The company's tax rate is 25 percent. The total capital invested in the business is $1,500,000. Bally's cost of financing (the cost of the capital) is 13.6 percent. What was Bally's economic value added (EVA) for the year? What does your answer for EVA mean?

BASIC 

1–3 Incremental analysis Alden Ltd. is evaluating the purchase of a new machine that will cost $422,000. The existing machine is worth $110,000. The total number of units the firm can produce with the old machine is 200,000. The new machine will result in production increasing by 75,000 units. All production is sold at a price of $6 per unit. The total costs of production with the old machine are $3.50 per unit. With the new machine costs will decline by $0.40 per unit. Using marginal analysis, does it make sense for Alden to replace the current machine?

BASIC 

1–4 Accrual income versus cash flow for a period Thomas Book Sales, Inc. supplies textbooks to college and university bookstores. The books are shipped with a proviso that they must be paid for within 30 days, but can be returned for a full refund credit within 90 days. In the current year, Thomas shipped and billed book titles totalling $760,000. Collections during the year totalled $690,000. Thomas Book's finance manager knows that the difference between shipments and collections is books that will be returned sometime early in the new year. The cost to the company of all the books that were shipped during the year was $300,000. The cost to the company of the books that were kept was $272,400.

a. Based on the above information, develop Thomas Book's simplified income statement based on accrual accounting.

b. Based on the above information, develop Thomas Book's simplified income statement based on cash accounting.

c. Which of these statements is more useful to the financial manager? Why?

BASIC  **1–5 Economic value added** The CFO of Laidlaw Inc. is wondering how the company is doing in terms of creating value for the company's common shareholders. To answer the question, the CFO wishes to calculate the company's economic value added (EVA) for the most recent fiscal year. The total amount of capital Laidlaw has invested in the business is $5,840,000. Laidlaw's cost of capital is 15.3 percent. During the year, the company's before-tax operating profits were $1,185,000. The firm's tax rate is 32 percent. How has the company done in terms of creating value for the company's shareholders? Comment on the implications of your findings.

INTERMEDIATE  **1–6 Identifying agency problems, costs, and resolutions** Explain why each of the following situations is an agency problem and what costs to the firm might result from it. Suggest how the problem might be dealt with short of firing the individual(s) involved.

a. The front desk receptionist routinely takes an extra 20 minutes of lunch to take care of her personal errands.

b. Division managers are padding cost estimates in order to show short-term efficiency gains when the costs come in lower than the estimates.

c. The firm's chief executive officer has secret talks with a competitor about the possibility of a merger in which (s)he would become the CEO of the combined firms.

d. A branch manager lays off experienced full-time employees and staffs customer service positions with part-time or temporary workers to lower employment costs and raise this year's branch profit. The manager's bonus is based on profitability.

CASE CHAPTER 1 Assessing the Goal of Sports Products, Inc.

See the enclosed Student CD-ROM for cases that help you put theories and concepts from the text into practice.

Be sure to visit the Companion Website for this book at **www.pearsoned.ca/gitman** for a wealth of additional learning tools including self-test quizzes, Web exercises, and additional cases.

CHAPTER 2

Financial Statements, Cash Flows, and Taxes

LEARNING GOALS

LG1 Review the characteristics, format, key components, and relationships between the income statement, balance sheet, statement of retained earnings, and statement of cash flows.

LG2 Analyze a company's cash flows and develop and interpret the statement of cash flows.

LG3 Introduce the basics of corporate taxation in Canada, including an understanding of how the tax-deductibility of expenses reduces their actual, after-tax cost to a profitable company.

LG4 Discuss and illustrate capital cost allowance (CCA), the tax version of amortization, and how CCA increases a company's cash flows.

LG5 Explain and illustrate how a corporation determines and uses tax rates to calculate taxes payable.

LG6 Review the information provided in a publicly traded company's annual report to shareholders.

2.1 The Four Principal Financial Statements

One of the chief objectives of this chapter is to provide an understanding of the information presented in the financial statements developed by companies. The Canadian Institute of Chartered Accountants (CICA) has developed a set of accounting standards that specify the four financial statements that companies

The Language of Finance

The language of, and many concepts studied in, finance logically flow from an understanding of accounting. It is often said that accounting provides the basis for the language of finance. Financial statements provide the foundation data for many topics in finance. To avoid difficulties in corporate finance, it is important to know the "language" of the discipline. You must understand and be able to apply concepts such as reinvested profits, earnings available for common shareholders, dividends, shareholders' equity, cash flow, working capital, amortization, and earnings per share. The purpose of this chapter is to review the content and format of the four basic financial statements and the relationships between the statements, to examine a company's cash flow, to discuss corporate taxation, and to introduce some key terms and concepts in finance.

must develop and how information is to be presented and disclosed in the financial statements. The CICA's objective is to ensure companies provide information that meets the needs of users of financial statements. The four financial statements that companies normally produce are the income statement, balance sheet, statement of retained earnings, and cash flow statement. For regulatory reasons, companies must produce these statements yearly. A well-run firm would want to produce these statements at least quarterly, if not monthly or even weekly, for internal control purposes.

LINKING THE DISCIPLINES: Cross-Functional Interactions

- ***Accounting personnel*** prepare the financial statements and set up systems so that the financial records and reports conform to generally accepted accounting principles (GAAP). They need to understand the rules regarding the taxation of corporations and the tax implications of capital losses, non-capital losses, recaptured amortization, and terminal losses.
- ***Information systems analysts*** need to understand what data are included in the firm's financial statements to design systems that will supply such data to those who prepare and use the statements.
- ***Management*** must perform a thorough interpretation of the financial statements and understand how the statements will be analyzed by those inside and outside the firm to assess various aspects of performance. Management must consider the statements from the viewpoint of their various stakeholders and keep a dual focus on both the firm's cash flow and its profitability.
- The ***marketing department*** must understand the effects their decisions will have on the financial statements, particularly the income statement and the statement of cash flows.
- Personnel in the ***operations department*** must understand how the costs of production are reflected in the firm's financial statements and the importance of cash flow from operations. The cash flow from operations must be positive (operating cash inflows greater than operating cash outflows) for the firm to survive in the long run.

Canadian Institute of Chartered Accountants (CICA)
Sets accounting, auditing, and assurance standards for business, not-for-profit organizations, and government, and represents the CA profession in Canada.

generally accepted accounting principles (GAAP)
The accounting practices, procedures, and standards used to maintain financial records, reports, and statements.

Accounting Standards Board (AcSB)
The accounting profession's rule-setting body, part of the CICA, that authorizes the generally accepted accounting principles (GAAP) used in Canada.

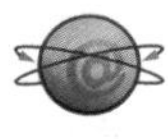

www.cica.ca

www.investopedia.com/university/financialstatements

The **Canadian Institute of Chartered Accountants (CICA)** sets accounting, auditing, and assurance standards for business, not-for-profit organizations, and government. It also issues guidance on control and governance, and represents the CA profession in Canada, which has approximately 70,000 CAs and 8,500 students. The guidelines used to prepare and maintain financial records, reports, and statements are known as **generally accepted accounting principles (GAAP).** These accounting practices, procedures, and standards specify how transactions and other events are to be recognized, measured, presented, and disclosed in financial statements. The objective of such standards is to meet the needs of users of financial statements by providing the information required to make informed decisions. The **Accounting Standards Board (AcSB)**, part of the CICA, is the accounting profession's rule-setting body that authorizes accounting practices and principles.

In this chapter, we use the four financial statements from the 2008 annual report of a hypothetical company, Baker Corporation, to illustrate and describe the statements. This chapter also discusses the relationships between the four financial statements. For additional information on the financial statements, there are many good sites on the Web.

Income Statement

The **income statement** provides a financial summary of the firm's operating results for a specified period. Most common are income statements covering a 1-year period ending at a specified date, ordinarily December 31 of the calendar year. Many large firms, however, operate on a 12-month financial cycle, or *fiscal year,* that ends at a time other than December 31. Monthly income statements are typically prepared for use by management, and quarterly statements must be made available to the shareholders of publicly owned corporations.

Hint
Some firms, such as retailers and agricultural firms, end their fiscal year at the end of their operating cycle rather than at the end of the calendar year—for example, retailers at the end of January and agricultural firms at the end of September.

Table 2.1 presents Baker Corporation's income statement for the year ended December 31, 2008. The statement begins with *sales revenue*—the total dollar amount of sales during the period—from which the *cost of goods sold* is deducted. Cost of goods sold (COGS) is the total direct cost of producing or purchasing the product sold. COGS is normally the total of direct materials, direct labour, and direct factory overhead. The difference between sales revenue and COGS is gross margin. For Baker Corporation, the resulting gross margin of $700,000 represents the amount remaining to satisfy operating, financial, and tax costs after meeting the costs of producing or purchasing the products sold. Next, *operating expenses,* which include selling expense, general and administrative expense, lease expense, and amortization expense, are deducted from gross margin.

Companies can purchase and own assets, or use and lease assets. The lease expense is associated with a contract for the use of an asset and, as such, could be considered a financial expense. However, this expense is often shown as an operating expense on the income statement, as in this case.

amortization
The systematic expensing of a portion of the cost of a fixed asset against sales.

Amortization is the systematic expensing of a portion of the cost of a fixed asset against sales. This expense is associated with capital assets, assets that are expected to have a life greater than one year. Expenditures on these assets are not expensed; rather, they are capitalized and the expenditure is written off over time via the amortization expense.[1] The resulting *operating earnings* of $370,000 represent the profits earned from producing and selling products; this amount does not consider financial and tax costs. (Operating earnings are often called *earnings before interest and taxes,* or *EBIT.*)[2] Next, the financial cost—*interest expense*—is subtracted from operating earnings to find *earnings before taxes (EBT).* After subtracting $70,000 in 2008 interest, Baker Corporation had $300,000 of earnings before taxes.

After the appropriate tax rates have been applied to before-tax earnings, taxes are calculated and deducted to determine *net income* (or *earnings*) *after taxes* (NIAT). Baker Corporation's net income after taxes for the 2008 fiscal year was $180,000. With the NIAT, Baker Corporation may pay dividends to shareholders or reinvest the profits back into the company. A company can have two types of shareholders: preferred and common. Dividends must be paid to preferred shareholders before common shareholders receive any income. Baker Corporation has preferred shareholders so the dividends due on the preferred shares must be subtracted from NIAT to arrive at *earnings available for common shareholders (EAC).* All income after all expenses and preferred share dividends have been paid belongs to the common shareholders. Shareholders can receive the benefit of the EAC in two ways. First, the company can directly pay the EAC as *common share dividends.* In this way, the EAC provides a direct cash payment to common shareholders. Second, any EAC not paid to shareholders, by default, is reinvested back into the company.

1. *Amortization* is the term used in this book to describe this expense. This is the case since in 1990, the CICA recommended that "amortization" replace the term "depreciation." In practice, amortization is sometimes included within COGS. In this book, however, amortization will be shown as an operating expense in order to be able to highlight its impact on cash flows.

2. In practice, EBITDA is often used to measure operating earnings. This means earnings before interest, taxes, depreciation, and amortization.

TABLE 2.1 Baker Corporation Income Statement ($000) for the Year Ended December 31, 2008

Sales revenue		$1,700
Less: Cost of goods sold		1,000
Gross margin		$ 700
Less: Operating expenses		
Selling expense	$ 75	
General and administrative expense	130	
Lease expense[a]	25	
Amortization expense	100	
Total operating expenses		330
Operating earnings (EBIT)		$ 370
Less: Interest expense		70
Earnings before taxes (EBT)		$ 300
Less: Taxes (rate = 40%)		120
Net income after taxes (NIAT)		$ 180
Less: Preferred share dividends		10
Earnings available for common shareholders (EAC)		$ 170
Earnings per share (EPS)[b]		$ 1.70

[a]Since this expense is associated with a contract for the use of an asset, it could be considered a financial expense, although it is often shown as an operating expense on the income statement, as in this case.

[b]Calculated by dividing the earnings available for common shareholders by the number of shares of common shares outstanding ($170,000 ÷ 100,000 shares = $1.70 per share).

After reading the previous paragraph, you may be wondering how reinvesting a portion of the profits is a benefit to common shareholders. Since the EAC belong to the common shareholders, why doesn't the company pay all of it to common shareholders as dividends? It is easy to see the benefit of receiving a cash payment to common shareholders, but how are *reinvested profits* a benefit? A company will grow over time. In order to support growth, a company requires money. Some, or all, of the EAC is retained by all companies to provide money needed to support current and future growth. A growing company should have higher net income (and EAC) in future years. If so, the value of the company will increase and so too will shareholder wealth.

A key financial item reported by corporations is *earnings per share (EPS)*. EPS is calculated by dividing EAC by the number of common shares outstanding. EPS represents the amount earned on each outstanding common share during the period of time covered by the income statement. For the 2008 fiscal year, Baker Corporation's EAC was $170,000. Assuming Baker had 100,000 common shares outstanding, this EAC represents earnings of $1.70 for each common share. Note that the income statement does not indicate whether Baker Corporation paid common share dividends. To determine the dollar amount of dividends paid, the balance sheet can be used.

Example Auto Corp's net income after tax for the 2008 fiscal year was \$68,400,000. Auto Corp has 85,942,000 common shares outstanding. The company paid \$9,100,000 of preferred share dividends and \$23,200,000 of common share dividends. Earnings available for common shareholders were \$59,300,000 (\$68,400,000 − \$9,100,000), EPS were \$0.69 (\$59,300,000 ÷ 85,942,000), and reinvested profits were \$36,100,000 (\$59,300,000 − \$23,200,000). The reinvested profits are a source of financing that is used to invest in assets. The assets are required to support increasing sales. When sales increase, so too should profits. When profits increase, the value of common shares increases.

Balance Sheet

balance sheet
Summary statement of the firm's financial position at a given point in time.

Hint
The balance sheet identity or equation is A = L + E, Assets = Liabilities + Equity.

The **balance sheet** presents a summary statement of the firm's financial position at a given point in time. The statement balances the firm's *assets* (what it owns) against its financing, which can be either *debt* (what it owes) or *equity* (what was provided by owners). Baker Corporation's balance sheets on December 31 of 2007 and 2008 are presented in Table 2.2. They show a variety of asset, liability (debt), and equity accounts. The basic balance sheet identity or equation is:

$$\underset{\text{Assets}}{(A)} = \underset{\text{Liabilities}}{(L)} + \underset{\text{Equity}}{(E)} \qquad (2.1)$$

This concept is depicted in Figure 2.1.

current assets
Short-term assets, expected to be converted into cash within 1 year or less.

current liabilities
Short-term liabilities, expected to be paid within 1 year or less.

An important distinction is made between short-term and long-term assets and liabilities. The **current assets** and **current liabilities** are *short-term* assets and liabilities. This means that they are expected to be converted into cash (current assets) or paid (current liabilities) within 1 year or less. Managing the level of current assets and the use of current liabilities is termed *working capital management*. All other assets and liabilities, along with shareholders' equity, which is assumed to have an infinite life, are considered *long-term*, or *fixed*, because they are expected to remain on the firm's books for 1 year or more.

As is customary, the assets are listed beginning with the most liquid down to the least liquid. Current assets therefore precede fixed assets. Cash is listed first since it is the most liquid asset—it is cash! *Marketable securities* held by the company represent very liquid short-term investments, such as Government of Canada treasury bills or term deposits issued by a chartered bank or trust company. Because of their highly liquid nature, marketable securities are frequently viewed as a form of cash. *Accounts receivable* are the total credit sales made by the company that are uncollected as of the date of the balance sheet. *Inventories*

FIGURE 2.1
Basic Balance Sheet Equation
A = L + E

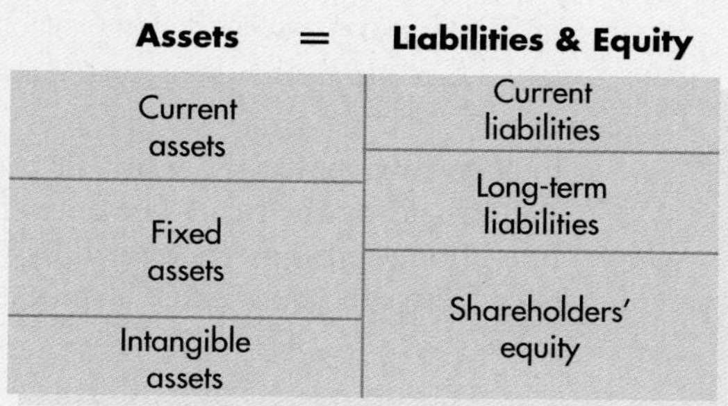

Assets	=	Liabilities & Equity
Current assets		Current liabilities
		Long-term liabilities
Fixed assets		
		Shareholders' equity
Intangible assets		

TABLE 2.2 Baker Corporation Balance Sheets ($000)

	December 31	
Assets	**2007**	**2008**
Current assets		
Cash	$ 300	$ 400
Marketable securities	200	600
Accounts receivable	500	400
Inventories	900	600
Total current assets	$1,900	$2,000
Gross fixed assets (at cost)		
Land and buildings	$1,050	$1,200
Machinery and equipment	800	850
Furniture and fixtures	220	300
Vehicles	80	100
Other (includes certain leases)	50	50
Total gross fixed assets (at cost)	$2,200	$2,500
Less: Accumulated amortization	1,200	1,300
Net fixed assets	$1,000	$1,200
Total assets	$2,900	$3,200
Liabilities and shareholders' equity		
Current liabilities		
Accounts payable	$ 500	$ 700
Accruals	200	100
Line of credit	650	525
Current portion of long-term debt	50	75
Total current liabilities	$1,400	$1,400
Long-term debt	$ 400	$ 540
Total liabilities	$1,800	$1,940
Shareholders' equity		
Preferred shares (4,000 shares outstanding)	$ 100	$ 100
Common shares (95,000 shares outstanding in 2007, 100,000 in 2008)	500	560
Retained earnings	500	600
Total shareholders' equity	$1,100	$1,260
Total liabilities and shareholders' equity	$2,900	$3,200

include raw materials, work in process (partially finished goods), and finished goods held by the firm. The entry for *gross fixed assets* is the original cost of all fixed (long-term) assets owned by the firm.[3] *Net fixed assets* represent the difference between gross fixed assets and *accumulated amortization*—the running

3. For convenience the term *fixed assets* is used throughout this text to refer to what, in a strict accounting sense, is captioned "property, plant, and equipment." This simplification of terminology permits certain financial concepts to be more easily developed.

total of the amortization expense recorded each year. For example, the amortization expense recorded by Baker Corporation for the 2008 fiscal year was $100,000 (see Table 2.1). The accumulated amortization as of the beginning of the 2008 fiscal year was $1,200,000 (the same as the end of the 2007 fiscal year). The $100,000 expense for 2008 is added to this amount to calculate accumulated amortization as of the end of the 2008 fiscal year.

intangible assets
Assets that cannot be seen or touched, but are valuable to a company. Examples include the value of trademarks, patents, franchise rights, and goodwill.

goodwill
The amount paid for a business in excess of the value of the assets acquired.

Hint
Another interpretation of the balance sheet is that on one side are the assets that have been purchased to be used to increase the profit of the firm. The other side indicates how these assets were acquired, either by borrowing or by investing the owners' money.

Although not shown in Table 2.2, it is common to also see **intangible assets** on a balance sheet. Intangible assets cannot be seen or touched, but are valuable. In some cases, they are some of the most valuable assets owned by a company. Examples of intangibles include the value of trademarks, patents, franchise rights, and goodwill. **Goodwill** is created only when a business is purchased and the amount paid for the business is greater than the value of the assets acquired. The premium paid is an asset termed goodwill. Chapter 18 provides more details and examples of how goodwill is calculated and expensed over time. All intangible assets except goodwill are amortized over time as their value declines.

Like assets, the liabilities and equity accounts are listed on the balance sheet from short-term to long-term. Current liabilities are amounts the company must repay within the year. *Accounts payable* are credit purchases made by the company that are unpaid as of the date of the balance sheet. A *line of credit* is a borrowing arrangement between a chartered bank and a company that allows the company to borrow up to a maximum amount at any time. The line of credit is generally repayable on the demand of the bank.

Accruals are amounts the company owes for a service received or an obligation incurred, but for which payment has not yet been made. Essentially, they are payables other than accounts payable. Examples of accruals include taxes due the government, wages due employees, or rent due a landlord. These might all be termed "payables," as in taxes payable, wages payable, or rent payable. Sometimes, all of these payables are grouped and simply termed "*accruals*."

A *line of credit* is a borrowing arrangement between a chartered bank and a company that allows the company to borrow up to a maximum amount (termed the *credit limit*) at any time. The line of credit is generally repayable on the demand of the bank. The interest rate charged on the line of credit is based on the *prime rate* plus a premium that accounts for the risk of the borrower. The riskier the borrower, the higher the premium the bank will charge. The difference between the interest rate on a loan and the bank's cost of funds is the *spread* on the loan. *Notes payable* is another form of short-term loan that may be seen on a balance sheet.

It is standard practice to also include as a current liability the amount of long-term debt the company must repay during the coming year. This is termed the *current portion of long-term debt*, and is the amount of loan principal that the company must repay the lender at some point over the next 12 months. This amount does not include the interest owed. For example, on December 31, 2007, Baker was required to repay $50,000 of principal on their long-term debt at some point during the 2008 fiscal year. By the end of the 2008 fiscal year, this payment would have been made. The $75,000 that appears for 2008 must be repaid during the 2009 fiscal year. The "current portion" amount flows from the long-term amount of debt.

Long-term debt represents debt for which payment is not due in the current year. Common examples of long-term debt are term loans, bonds, and debentures. These are amounts the firm has borrowed from financial institutions and institutional and individual investors. These concepts are fully discussed ion Chapter 5.

Shareholders' equity represents the amount of money invested in the company by the shareholders. The *preferred share entry* shows the total amount raised from the

stated value
The actual value of preferred shares when originally sold to investors.

sale of preferred shares ($100,000 for Baker Corporation). Preferred shares are sold for a certain amount, which is referred to as the "stated value." The **stated value** is an arbitrary amount set by the company when the preferred shares are initially sold to investors. Usual values are $10, $20, $25, and $50 per share. The stated value indicates the actual value of the shares when they are sold. For Baker Corporation, $100,000 of preferred share financing was raised, and from the balance sheet we know 4,000 shares are outstanding. The stated value of the preferred shares was $25 per share ($100,000 ÷ 4,000 shares). Recall from the income statement that Baker Corporation paid preferred share dividends of $10,000. This is $2.50 per share ($10,000 ÷ 4,000 shares). Therefore, the preferred share dividend was 10 percent of the stated value. Preferred shareholders have no ownership interest in the firm. These shareholders are "preferred" in two ways: first, they are entitled to receive dividends before common shareholders; second, if the company goes bankrupt, preferred shareholders receive any payments prior to common shareholders.

common equity
The total investment made by the company's owners consisting of the value of common shares plus retained earnings.

common shares
The total proceeds received from the sale of common shares since the company was formed.

Common equity indicates the total investment made by the company's owners. **Common equity** consists of two components: the value of common shares and retained earnings. The entry for **common shares** reflects the total proceeds received from the sale of common shares since the company was formed. This is the amount common shareholders paid when the common shares were sold. As of December 31, 2007, Baker Corporation had sold 95,000 common shares, raising $500,000 of financing. On average, common shareholders paid $5.26 per common share. This does not mean that all of the common shares were sold at the same time, simply that since Baker Corporation was formed, 95,000 common shares have been sold and that $500,000 of financing has been received by the company. During the 2008 fiscal year, Baker Corporation sold 5,000 additional common shares, raising $60,000 of financing. The shares were sold for an average of $12 per share. In Canada, common shares generally have no par value.

retained earnings
The running total of all earnings, net of dividends, that have been retained and reinvested in the firm since its inception.

Retained earnings represent the running total of all earnings, net of dividends, that have been retained and reinvested in the firm since its inception. It is important to recognize that retained earnings *are not cash* and cannot be used to pay expenses or purchase assets. Rather, the retained earnings account represents the dollar amount of profits that have been retained and used by the company over its complete operating history to finance the purchase of assets. The current year's contribution to retained earnings is termed *reinvested profits*. It should also be noted that both reinvested profits and the retained earnings account can be negative. This is the case since instead of making profits, the firm can lose money. Losses, as well as profits, flow to retained earnings.

book value
The total value of common equity at the date of the balance sheet. Book value per share is book value divided by the number of common shares outstanding.

Book value is the total value of common equity as of the date of the balance sheet. Common equity normally consists of the value of common shares plus retained earnings. Book value is sometimes referred to as *net worth*. It can be calculated as E = A − L. Instead of total book value, book value per share is often used. Book value per share is total book value divided by the number of common shares outstanding. For Baker Corporation, *book value per share* as of December 31, 2008 is $11.60 ($560,000 + $600,000) / (100,000 common shares).

Baker Corporation's balance sheets show that the firm's total assets increased from $2,900,000 in 2007 to $3,200,000 in 2008. The $300,000 increase was due primarily to the $200,000 increase in net fixed assets. The asset increase in turn appears to have been financed primarily by an increase in long-term debt and common equity, both common shares and reinvested profits. Better insight into these changes can be derived from the statement of cash flows, which we will discuss shortly.

Refer again to Figure 2.1, the basic balance sheet equality. Note that the respective percentages of the various accounts will vary by type of company. Companies in the retail or service sectors carry large amounts of current assets and relatively low investment in fixed assets. Industrial companies have a large investment in fixed assets. Technology companies often have large amounts of intangible assets on their balance sheets. How companies finance their assets (the combination of current and long-term liabilities and equity) also varies by company.

Example Viat Corporation has current assets of $321,000, fixed assets of $78,000, and intangible assets of $14,000. Viat's long-term debt is $41,000, the value of their common shares is $22,000, while retained earnings total $111,000. What are Viat Corporation's current liabilities?

Since total assets are $413,000, liabilities and equity must also total this amount. Long-term debt is $41,000, while total common equity is $133,000. Therefore, current liabilities must be $239,000. Note that the majority of Viat Corporation's assets are current. The company also uses a large amount of current liabilities to finance assets.

Statement of Retained Earnings

statement of retained earnings
Details the change in retained earnings from the beginning to the end of the fiscal year.

The **statement of retained earnings** details the change in retained earnings from the beginning to the end of the fiscal year. Changes in retained earnings is based on net income after tax. Recall, with NIAT, a company can pay dividends (preferred and/or common) and/or reinvest the net income back into the company. Profits reinvested flow to retained earnings. For Baker Corporation, retained earnings at the beginning of the 2008 fiscal year (which is the same as the end of the 2007 fiscal year) was $500,000. By the end of 2008, the balance was $600,000. What happened?

Table 2.3 presents the statement for Baker Corporation for the year ended December 31, 2008. A review of the statement shows that the company began the year with $500,000 in retained earnings and had net income after taxes of $180,000, from which it paid a total of $80,000 in dividends, resulting in year-end retained earnings of $600,000. Thus, the net increase in retained earnings for Baker Corporation was $100,000 ($180,000 net income after taxes minus $80,000 in dividends) during 2008. This is the dollar amount of profits the company reinvested.

TABLE 2.3 Baker Corporation Statement of Retained Earnings ($000) for the Year Ended December 31, 2008

Retained earnings balance (January 1, 2008)		$500
Plus: Net income after taxes (for 2008)		180
Less: Cash dividends (paid during 2008)		
Preferred shares	($10)	
Common shares	(70)	
Total dividends paid		(80)
Retained earnings balance (December 31, 2008)		$600

Statement of Cash Flows

statement of cash flows (SCF)
Provides a summary of the firm's operating, investment, and financing cash flows and reconciles them with changes in its cash and marketable securities during the period of concern.

The fourth financial statement companies must complete is the **statement of cash flows (SCF)**. The SCF provides a summary of inflows and outflows of cash over the same period of time as the balance sheet, typically the fiscal year. The SCF, which prior to 1998 was termed the statement of changes in financial position (SCFP), provides insight into the firm's operating, investment, and financing cash flows and reconciles them with changes in its cash and marketable securities during the period of concern. Since understanding cash flows is vital, the following section fully discusses the concept and presents the process used to develop and analyze a statement of cash flows.

? Review Questions

2–1 What are the characteristics of and what are the main items shown on the (**a**) income statement; (**b**) balance sheet; and (**c**) statement of retained earnings? Describe each of the statements.

2–2 Discuss the relationships between the four financial statements discussed in this section of the chapter.

2.2 Completing and Analyzing a Statement of Cash Flows

The statement of cash flows (SCF) documents and details the change in a company's cash and marketable securities over an accounting period, normally a fiscal year. Therefore, as you prepare a SCF, keep in mind that you know the correct answer before you complete the statement. The correct answer is simply the change in cash (and marketable securities), as shown on the balance sheet, from one fiscal year (e.g., 2007) to the next (e.g., 2008).

Example Consider Table 2.2. Here we see that from the 2007 to the 2008 fiscal year for Baker Corporation, cash increased by $100,000 while marketable securities increased by $400,000, a total change of $500,000. Therefore, the SCF for Baker Corporation for the 2008 fiscal year *must* show cash and marketable securities increasing by $500,000.

Before completing the statement of cash flows for Baker Corporation, however, we will discuss how cash flows through a firm and the classification of cash inflows and outflows.

Hint
Remember that, in finance, cash is king. Income statement profits are good, but they do not pay the bills, nor do asset owners accept them in place of cash.

The Firm's Cash Flows

operating flows
Cash flows directly related to production and sale of the firm's products and services.

Figure 2.2 illustrates the firm's cash flows. Note that marketable securities, because of their highly liquid nature, are considered the same as cash. Both cash and marketable securities represent a reservoir of liquidity that is *increased by cash inflows* and *decreased by cash outflows*. Also note that the firm's cash flows have been divided into (1) operating flows, (2) investment flows, and (3) financing flows. The **operating flows** are cash inflows and outflows directly related to

FIGURE 2.2 The Flow of Cash Through a Firm

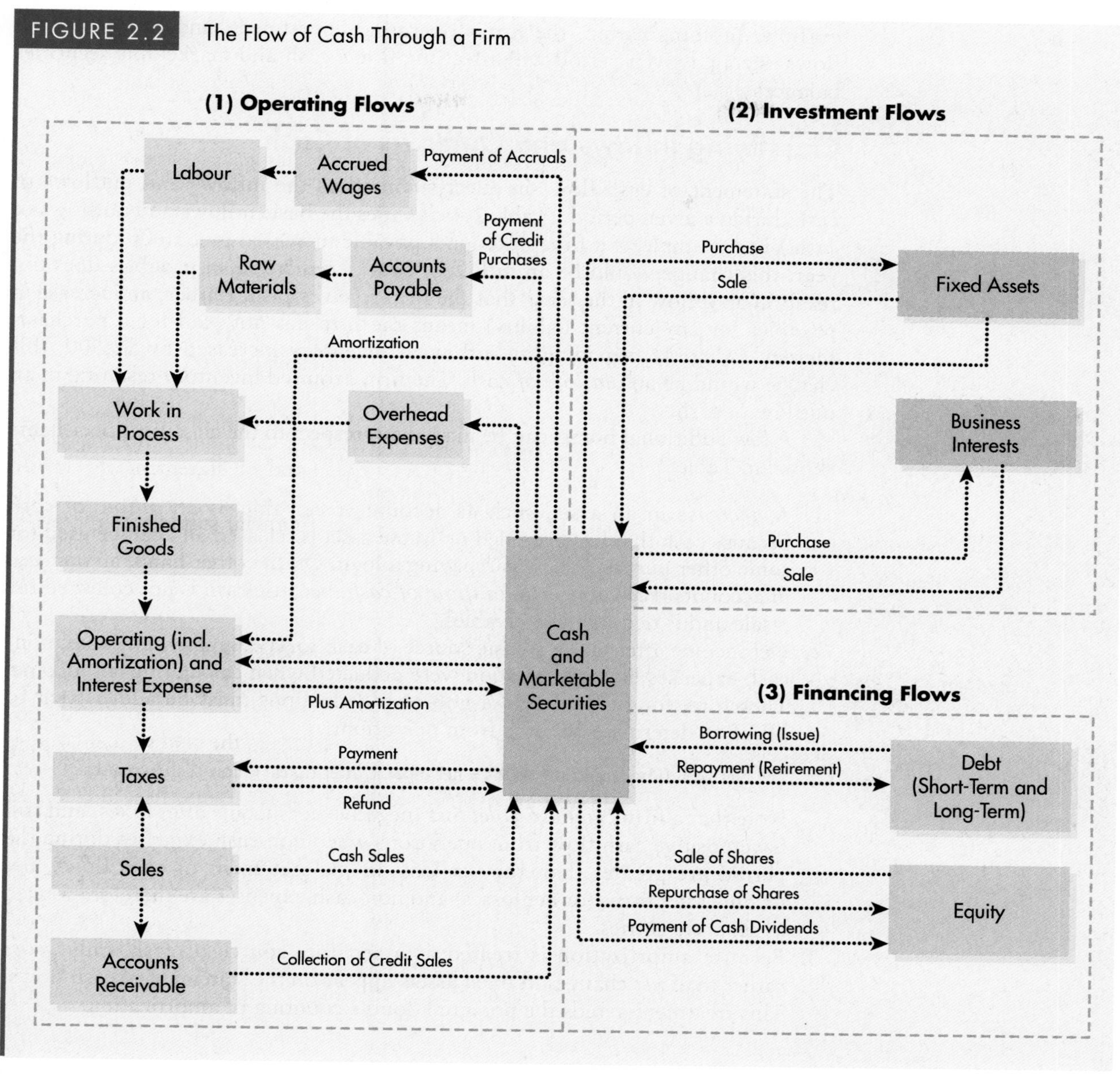

investment flows
Cash flows associated with purchase and sale of both fixed assets and business interests.

financing flows
Cash flows that result from debt and equity financing transactions; include issue and repayment of debt, cash inflow from the sale of stock, and cash outflows to pay cash dividends or repurchase stock.

production and sale of the firm's products and services. These flows capture the income statement and changes in current assets and current liabilities (excluding cash and the line of credit) that occurred during the period. **Investment flows** are cash flows associated with purchase and sale of both fixed assets and business interests. Clearly, purchase transactions would result in cash outflows, whereas sales transactions would generate cash inflows. The **financing flows** result from debt and equity financing transactions. Incurring and repaying either short-term debt (line of credit) or long-term debt would result in a corresponding cash inflow or outflow. Similarly, the sale of stock would result in a cash inflow; the payment of cash dividends or repurchase of stock would result in a financing outflow. In combination, the firm's operating, investment, and financing cash flows during a given period will affect the firm's cash and marketable securities balances.

Classifying Inflows and Outflows of Cash

The statement of cash flows in effect summarizes the inflows and outflows of cash during a given period. (Table 2.4 classifies the basic inflows and outflows of cash.) For example, if a firm's accounts payable increased by $1,000 during the year, this change would be an *inflow of cash*. An increase in payables does not result in an inflow in the sense that the firm receives cash. Rather, an increase in payables (or any current liability) means the firm has not paid for a purchase, thereby indirectly providing an inflow. If inventory increased by $2,500, this change would be an *outflow of cash*. The firm acquired inventory resulting in an outflow of cash.

A few additional points can be made with respect to the classification scheme shown in Table 2.4:

1. A *decrease* in an asset, such as accounts receivable, is an *inflow of cash* because cash that has been tied up in the asset is released and can be used for some other purpose, such as repaying a loan. On the other hand, an *increase* in accounts receivable is an *outflow of cash,* because cash is not collected for a sale and is tied up in receivables.
2. Net income after tax is a basic source of cash for a company. But note, non-cash expenses like amortization were deducted when calculating net income. Therefore, for the SCF, these non-cash deductions must be added back to NIAT to determine net cash from operations:

   Net cash flow from operations = net income after taxes + non-cash expenses

   Note that a firm can have a *net loss* (negative net income after taxes) and still have positive cash flow from operations when non-cash expenses during the period are greater than the net loss. In the statement of cash flows, net income after taxes (or net losses) and non-cash expenses are therefore treated as separate entries.
3. Because amortization is treated as a separate source of cash, only *gross* rather than *net* changes in fixed assets appear on the statement of cash flows. This treatment avoids the potential double counting of amortization.

TABLE 2.4 The Inflows and Outflows of Cash

Inflows	Outflows
Decrease in any asset	Increase in any asset
Increase in any liability	Decrease in any liability
Net income after taxes	Net loss
Amortization and other non-cash expenses	Dividends paid
Sale of shares	Repurchase or retirement of shares

4. Direct entries of changes in retained earnings are not included on the statement of cash flows. Instead, entries for items that affect retained earnings appear as net income or losses after taxes and dividends paid.

Developing the Statement of Cash Flows

The statement of cash flows (SCF) can be developed by following a six-step process.

Step 1 is to note the correct answer. Remember, when preparing a SCF, you always know the final answer before you begin the process. The bottom line answer is the change in cash (and marketable securities) from the previous year's to the current year's balance sheet. As noted on page 54, for Baker Corporation for the 2008 fiscal year, the SCF *must* show cash and marketable securities increasing by $500,000. The real question that is being answered with the SCF is, *What happened to cash*? Overall, cash changed by a certain amount. The SCF illustrates the inflows and outflows that resulted in the change. The SCF takes information from the income statement and balance sheet and puts it in a format that explains the change in cash.

Step 2 is to calculate net cash from operations. This is based on the income statement. Start with net income after tax. Add to that amortization, the non-cash expense that was deducted from sales to determine net income. This equals net cash from operations.

Example ▼ Baker Corporation's income statement for the 2008 fiscal year (Table 2.1) indicates that NIAT was $180,000 while amortization was $100,000. Net cash from operations is the sum of these two amounts, or $280,000. This is illustrated in Table 2.5, Baker Corporation's statement of cash flows for the 2008 fiscal year. ▲

Step 3 is to determine the total changes in non-cash working capital accounts. Recall, working capital refers to current assets and current liabilities. For this step, exclude cash (and marketable securities) and current liabilities with a direct cost of financing, accounts such as a line of credit or current portion of long-term debt. Start with the first non-cash current asset. Refer to Table 2.4. If a current asset increases, this is a use of cash. A decrease is a source. The opposite holds for current liabilities.

Example ▼ Review Baker Corporation's balance sheets. Receivables decreased by $100,000 from 2007 to 2008. The company is collecting cash for credit sales in a more timely manner, therefore providing a source of cash. Inventories decrease by $300,000. Baker is selling inventory more rapidly, providing a source of cash. Move on to current liabilities. Accounts payable increase. Baker is making purchases, but not paying for them. This is an indirect source of cash. Accruals decrease: Baker is paying off expenses. This is a use of cash. The line of credit and current portion of long-term debt are costly forms of financing and will be considered elsewhere in the SCF. These four items constitute changes in non-cash working capital items. The net impact is a $500,000 source of cash (see Table 2.5). ▲

Cash from operating activities is the combination of the net cash from operations and the changes in non-cash working capital items. For Baker Corporation, this is $780,000 (see Table 2.5).

Remember that for the SCF both of the main financial statements, the income statement and the balance sheet, are analyzed. This section of the statement has considered most of the income statement, the current assets, and the current liabilities. The remaining sections of the SCF must consider changes in the other items: fixed assets, liabilities with a direct cost, and equity.

Step 4 is to determine cash flow from investing activities. For this step, focus on the gross amount of fixed assets on the balance sheet. Note that the accumulated amortization account is not considered. This is the case since the change in accumulated amortization is the current year's amortization expense and this amount was already considered in Step 2.

TABLE 2.5 Baker Corporation Statement of Cash Flows ($000) for the Year Ended December 31, 2008

A.	**Cash flow from operating activities**			
Step 2	NIAT[a]		$180	
	Plus: Non-cash expense (amortization)		100	
	Net cash from operations		280	
	Plus: Changes in non-cash working capital accounts			
Step 3	Decrease in accounts receivable	$100		
	Decrease in inventory	300		
	Increase in accounts payable	200		
	Decrease in accruals	(100)[b]	500	
	Cash flow from operating activities			$780
B.	**Cash flow from investing activities**			
Step 4	Increase in land and buildings		(150)	
	Increase in machinery and equipment		(50)	
	Increase in furniture and fixtures		(80)	
	Increase in vehicles		(20)	
	Cash flow from investing activities			(300)
C.	**Cash flow from financing activities**			
Step 5	Decrease in line of credit		(125)	
	Increase in current portion of long-term debt		25	
	Increase in long-tem debt		140	
	Increase in common shares		60	
	Payment of preferred dividend[a]		(10)	
	Payment of common dividend[a]		(70)	
	Cash flow from financing activities			20
	Increase in cash and marketable securities during year			500
Steps 1 and 6	Cash and marketable securities at beginning of year			500
	Cash and marketable securities at end of year			$1,000

[a]Note that the change in retained earnings is excluded from the SCF. This change is indirectly considered through the combination of net income after tax and the preferred and common share dividends.

[b]It is customary to use parentheses to denote negative numbers, which in this case is a cash outflow.

Example Review Baker Corporation's balance sheets (Table 2.2). The gross value of each of the assets with the exception of "other" increased. Each of these changes is a use of cash. The total increase in assets is $300,000. Each of the changes are reflected on Baker Corporation's SCF for the 2008 fiscal year.

As is clear from the above, when the gross fixed assets and accumulated amortization accounts are provided on the balance sheet, it is very easy to determine the investment in fixed assets. However, many firms just report their net fixed assets on the balance sheet, and this can somewhat complicate the calculation of the investment in fixed assets. If only the net fixed assets amount was provided on Baker Corporation's balance sheet, how would the investment in fixed assets be calculated? In 2008, net fixed assets increased by $200,000. This reflects two changes: gross fixed assets increased by $300,000, accumulated amortization by $100,000. The net change was $200,000. Therefore, to calculate the investment in gross fixed assets, add the amortization expense for the year to the change in net fixed assets. For Baker, this is $300,000.

Example The following information for Duncan Inc. was taken from their 2007 and 2008 financial statements:

	2007	2008
Amortization expense (from income statements)		$ 32,100
Net fixed assets (from balance sheet)	$157,200	$211,800

To calculate the investment made in fixed assets in 2008, first determine the change in net fixed assets. It is $54,600 ($211,800 – $157,200). Is this the investment made in fixed assets? No, because the firm also expensed some of the previous investment in fixed assets through the amortization expense. So, the investment in fixed assets was actually $86,700 ($54,600 + $32,100). To fully see this, consider the additional information from Duncan Inc. financial statements for 2007 and 2008:

	2007	2008
Amortization expense		$ 32,100
Gross fixed assets	$361,500	448,200
Less: Accumulated amortization	204,300	236,400
Net fixed assets	$157,200	$211,800

Note that the investment in fixed assets was actually $86,700, as calculated above.

Step 5 is to determine cash flow from financing activities. For this step, focus on the changes in liabilities with a direct cost (both short- and long-term) and equity.

Example Consider Baker Corporation's balance sheets (Table 2.2). The line of credit decreased by $125,000. Baker repaid a portion of the short-term debt and this is a use of cash. The current portion of long-term debt increased from $50,000 to $75,000 between 2007 and 2008. The $25,000 difference is a source of cash. Long-term debt increased by $140,000. The company issued long-term debt raising capital, a source of cash. Preferred equity did not change. Common shares increased by $60,000. As previously discussed, Baker Corporation sold 5,000 common shares to raise financing. Obviously, this is a source of cash. In 2008, retained earnings increased by $100,000. Baker reinvested a portion of their NIAT. This appears to be a source of cash, but remember—profits have already been considered in Step 2.

Baker Corporation's NIAT was the first item considered on the SCF. Baker's NIAT in 2008 was $180,000, yet the change in retained earnings was only $100,000. What happened? Remember, with NIAT a company can pay dividends (both preferred and common) or reinvest. Baker Corporation paid dividends of $80,000 ($10,000 preferred plus $70,000 common) and reinvested the difference. Since the $180,000 was considered in cash flows from operations, dividends must be considered cash outflows from financing activities. This analysis is reflected on Baker Corporation's SCF for 2008. To determine total dividends paid, use the following equation:

$$\text{Total dividends} = \text{NIAT} - \text{change in retained earnings}$$

Step 6 is to combine the cash flows from the three sources to determine the change in cash (and marketable securities). In this case, cash and marketable securities increased by $500,000. Compare this with the answer reached in Step 1 of the analysis. Here we noted that cash and marketable securities increased by $500,000. Therefore, we know the SCF is correct. To complete the statement, it is usual to also show cash (and marketable securities) at the beginning and end of the period on the SCF. These are the amounts of cash on the balance sheet. This is included on Baker Corporation's SCF for the 2008 fiscal year.

Interpreting the Statement

The statement of cash flows allows the financial manager and other interested parties to analyze the firm's cash flow. The manager should pay special attention to both the major categories of cash flow and the individual items of cash inflow and outflow, to assess whether any developments have occurred that are contrary to the company's financial policies. In addition, the statement can be used to evaluate progress toward projected goals. This statement does not match specific cash inflows with specific cash outflows, but it can be used to isolate inefficiencies. For example, increases in accounts receivable and inventories resulting in major cash outflows may signal credit or inventory problems, respectively.

In addition, the financial manager can prepare a statement of cash flows developed from projected, or pro forma, financial statements. This approach can be used to determine whether planned actions are desirable in view of the resulting cash flows.

2.1 SPREADSHEET APPLICATION

Microsoft Excel - Spreadsheet Application 2-1.xls

File Edit View Insert Format Tools Data Window Help Adobe PDF

G75

	A	B	C	D	E	F	G
79	**Baker Corporation**						
80	**Cash Flow Statement**						
81	**For the Year Ended December 31, 2008 (in $000)**						
82							
83	**Cash Flow from Operating Activities**						
84						**Formulas**	
85	NIAT		$180		←	=C22	
86	plus: Non-cash expenses		100		←	=C14	
87	Net cash from operations			$280	←	=C85+C86	
88							
89	Plus: Changes in Non-Cash Working Capital Accounts						
90	Decrease in accts receivable		100		←	=B38-C38	
91	Decrease in inventory		300		←	=B39-C39	
92	Increase in accts payable		200		←	=C58-B58	
93	Decrease in accruals		-100		←	=C59-B59	
94	Cash from Non-Cash Working Capital			500	←	=sum(C90:C93)	
95							
96	*Cash from Operating Activities*			*780*	←	=D87+D94	
97							
98	**Cash Flow from Investing Activities**						
99							
100	Increase in land and buildings		-150		←	=B44-C44	
101	Increase in machinery and equipment		-50		←	=B45-C45	
102	Increase in furniture and fixtures		-80		←	=B46-C46	
103	Increase in vehicles		-20		←	=B47-C47	
104							
105	*Cash from Investing Activities*			*-300*	←	=sum(C100:C103)	
106							
107	**Cash Flow from Financing Activities**						
108							
109	Decrease in line of credit		-125		←	=C60-B60	
110	Increase in current portion of long-term debt		25		←	=C61-B61	
111	Increase in long-term debt		140		←	=C64-B64	
112	Sale of common shares		60		←	=C69-B69	
113	Payment of preferred dividends		-10				
114	Payment of common dividends		-70				
115							
116	*Cash from Financing Activities*			*20*	←	=sum(C109:C114)	
117							
118	Increase in Cash during year			500	←	=sum(D96:D116)	
119							
120	Cash at beginning of year			500	←	=B36+B37	
121							
122	Cash at end of year			$1,000	←	=C36+C37	
123							

SA 2-1

Ready NUM

Example Analysis of Baker Corporation's statement of cash flows in Table 2.5 does not seem to indicate the existence of any major problems for the company. Its $780,000 of cash provided by operating activities plus the $20,000 provided by financing activities were used to invest an additional $300,000 in fixed assets and to increase cash and marketable securities by $500,000. The individual items of cash inflow and outflow seem to be distributed in a fashion consistent with prudent financial management. The firm seems to be growing: less than half of its earnings ($80,000 out of $180,000) was paid to shareholders as dividends, and gross fixed assets increased by three times the amount of historic cost written off through amortization expense ($300,000 increase in gross fixed assets versus $100,000 in amortization expense).

Major cash inflows were realized by decreasing accounts receivable and inventories (suggesting good management of current assets) and increasing accounts payable, providing a free source of financing. The major outflows of cash were to increase cash and marketable securities by $500,000 and thereby improve liquidity and increase fixed assets by $300,000. Note that this latter investment was financed with $100,000 of reinvested profits, $100,000 of long-term debt and common share financing, and $100,000 of amortization. Financing fixed assets with long-term sources of financing is good financial practice. Overall, Baker Corporation's SCF tends to support the fact that the firm was well managed financially during the period.

A complete understanding of the income statement, balance sheet, and statement of retained earnings, and the relationships that exist between them, is a prerequisite to the effective interpretation of the statement of cash flows.

Importance of the Cash Flow Statement

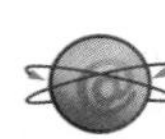

www.crfonline.org/orc/cro/cro-10.html#2

The cash flow statement is vitally important, so it is ironic that the cash flow statement is the one least scrutinized by investors and financial analysts. Investors and analysts seem to obsess over a company's income statement and its earnings per share, and to pay much less attention to the balance sheet and cash flow statement.

This is wrong. Income statements may not provide a clear picture of a company's results. They can be clouded by various one-time events, and possibly some distorting accounting treatments of revenues and/or costs. While GAAP arguably standardize accounting practices, accountants still have a great deal of latitude in how GAAP are reflected in the accounts. How revenues and costs are recognized can dramatically affect a firm's net income.

Nortel Networks is a classic Canadian example of a company that took extreme liberty in reporting income. As a consequence, the firm went through three years of upheaval between 2003 and 2006. The company incurred over $100 million of accounting fees in order to restate their financial results for the period 2000 to 2005. As well, many senior executives, including the CEO, the CFO, and the controller, were fired and a number of board members replaced. The company was also subjected to a number of class action lawsuits relating to accounting and other financial issues dating back to 2000, which were settled for $2.5 billion in 2006. While such problems are rare in Canada, they can happen and will affect the income statement. By contrast, the cash flow statement gives investors a much clearer view of a company's cash-generating (and keeping!) capabilities. And that's what's important.

Free Cash Flow

Free cash flow (FCF) is the cash available to make payments to the creditors and investors that supplied capital to the company. As we have already seen in this chapter, the basic source of cash to a company is from their operational activities. A company generates revenue by selling its products and services. In generating revenue, the company incurs operational expenses like cost of goods sold, salaries, selling and general administrative expenses, and amortization. The difference between revenues and operating expenses is operating earnings (EBIT).

The company must pay tax on its earnings, so from a cash perspective the after-tax operating earnings is the source of cash.[4] But, since we are calculating free cash flow, the non-cash expense, amortization, must be added back in, as we did with the statement of cash flows. These two amounts are used to determine free cash flow from operations (FCFO) as follows, where T is the firm's tax rate:

$$\text{FCFO} = \text{EBIT} \times (1 - \text{T}) + \text{amortization} \tag{2.2}$$

To produce revenue, the company must also invest cash in fixed assets, like real estate, buildings, and equipment, as well as in other long-term assets. We will term this total outlay *capital expenditures*, or CAPEX. Finally, the company must also invest in working capital to support its business activities. The amount of cash that is left over after these items are considered is the company's free cash flow for the period. The process to calculate FCF is provided below:

$$\text{FCF} = \text{FCFO} - \text{CAPEX} - \text{change in non-cash working capital} \tag{2.3}$$

The numbers needed to calculate FCF can be found on the company's income statement, balance sheet, and/or the statement of cash flows. FCF is an important measure. This is the cash left over after the payment of all cash expenses and the investments required by the firm—the hard cash available to pay the company's various providers of capital. Recognize, as well, that this is the cash the company's management might use to fund additional investments in assets or the acquisition of other companies. FCF can give the management of a company much leeway for activities that can compound the agency problem discussed in Chapter 1.

Example ▼ Suppose we were asked to calculate Baker Corporation's free cash flow for the December 31, 2008 fiscal year. By reviewing the income statement, we can determine FCFO as follows:

$$\begin{aligned}\text{FCFO} &= \$370{,}000 \times (1 - 0.40) + \$100{,}000 \\ &= \$222{,}000 + \$100{,}000 \\ &= \$322{,}000\end{aligned}$$

Then, by reviewing the statement of cash flows (or the balance sheet), we can determine Baker Company's free cash flow as follows:

$$\begin{aligned}\text{FCF} &= \$322{,}000 - \$300{,}000 - (-\$500{,}000) \\ &= \$322{,}000 - \$300{,}000 + \$500{,}000 \\ &= \$522{,}000\end{aligned}$$

4. Note that this would also be NIAT if the firm were financed entirely by equity.

Note that in the above example, Baker Corporation's non-cash working capital declined between 2007 and 2008. Consider the company's balance sheet in 2007. Non-cash current assets total $1,400,000 while non-financing current liabilities total $700,000. The difference is $700,000. In 2008, non-cash current assets total $1,000,000 while non-financing current liabilities total $800,000. The difference is $200,000. Non-cash working capital declined by $500,000 from 2007 to 2008, which is a source of cash. (Note that this is also the result on the statement of cash flows.)

Since in the FCF formula we subtract the change in non-cash working capital, when we subtract a minus it becomes a plus. Therefore, Baker Company's free cash flow for the December 31, 2008 fiscal year is $522,000. This is very different from the $170,000 of NIAT reported on the income statement. Baker Company has a great deal of cash that can be used to make interest and/or principal payments on debt, to pay dividends to shareholders, to buy back preferred or common shares, or for other purposes as decided by management.

A final consideration: There is nothing "free" about free cash flow. Remember that it is simply the cash not needed to invest in either current or fixed assets, and so "free" to distribute to creditors or shareholders as interest, principal repayments, dividends, or share repurchases. Readers should also note that there is some debate on how free cash flow should be calculated. Some users calculate it in different ways. For our purposes we will always use the method discussed above.

2.1 IN PRACTICE

It's the Cash Flow That Matters

As individuals, we need cash to live; without cash it would be impossible to live a full and satisfying life. Like individuals, cash is the lifeline of a business. Without it, a business would not exist, as it would have no means to pay expenses or finance the purchase of assets such as inventory, land, buildings, and equipment. It could not market its products or services to potential customers or pay employees to help run the organization.

Since cash is so important to a company, one wonders why it is so often ignored when assessing a company's performance. But this has traditionally been the case. The evaluation of a company's performance is most commonly reported in terms of accounting measures such as profits and earnings per share. A more useful measure of performance, however, is free cash flow. Free cash flow gives investors and analysts a sense of how company cash is deployed. For example, it allows analysts to see how much cash is tied up in receivables and inventory, and shows a clear picture of the firm's liquidity position. It has been said, "Profit is a concept, cash flow is reality."

Free cash flow signals a company's ability to make interest or principal payments on debt, pay dividends to shareholders, buy back shares, and/or invest in other assets. One of the most important features of free cash flow is that it tracks all money within the company, regardless of whether the cash outlay is counted as an expense in the calculation of income or turned into an asset on the balance sheet. It also removes the "guesstimates" involved in reported earnings by establishing how much cash a company has after paying its bills for ongoing activities and growth. As the CFO of a

(Continued)

large food production company states, "Cash flow is the real barometer for business. Profit numbers can be more easily manipulated."

Many companies are starting to recognize the importance of free cash flow in the valuation of a company. A statement in Bell Canada Enterprise's 2005 annual report reads, "We consider free cash flow to be an important indicator of the financial strengths and performance of our business because it shows how much cash is available to repay debt and reinvest in our company. We present free cash flow consistently from period to period, which allows us to compare our financial performance on a consistent basis. We believe that certain investors and analysts use free cash flow to value a business and its underlying assets." When running or analyzing a business, it is vital to recognize the importance of cash flow.

SOURCES: "Going with the Flow," from **CFO.com**, September 2003; Bell Canada Enterprises 2005 annual report, available on SEDAR, **www.sedar.com**; "Free Cash Flow—Sound Good?" KeyStone Financial Publishing Corp, available at **www3.keystocks.com/small-cap-market-buzz/earnings-picture-exorcizes-scary-October-nov-4-2005.68.html**.

? Review Questions

2–3 Describe the overall cash flow through the firm in terms of: (**a**) operating flows; (**b**) investment flows; and (**c**) financing flows.

2–4 Consider changes in specific asset, liability, and equity accounts. Is the change a cash inflow or outflow? Discuss.

2–5 Describe the first four steps in developing the statement of cash flows. How are changes in fixed assets and accumulated amortization treated on this statement?

2–6 What inputs to the statement of cash flows are obtained from the income statement? Explain how the income statement and balance sheet can be used to determine dividends for the period of concern. What other methods can be used to obtain the value of dividends?

2–7 Why are cash and marketable securities the only current assets, and short-term debt with a direct cost the only current liabilities excluded from the change in the non-cash working capital items section on the SCF?

2–8 How can the accuracy of the final statement balance, "net increase (decrease) in cash and marketable securities," be conveniently verified on the SCF?

2–9 How is the statement of cash flows interpreted and used by the financial manager and other interested parties?

2–10 Explain why the cash flow statement is important.

2–11 Why is the income statement not a good indicator of a company's performance?

2–12 How is free cash flow calculated, and is it really "free?"

2–13 Explain what a firm can do with their free cash flow. Why is it an important measure to shareholders?

2.3 The Basics of Corporate Taxation

Taxes have a major impact on many types of financial decisions made by both individuals and businesses. Knowing how businesses are taxed is vital for a full understanding of the financial actions they take. But note that the tax system in Canada is incredibly complex and ever-changing. New tax rates and regulations are released every year in the Budgets released by both federal and provincial governments. Even though in this Section we have provided the most recent tax rates and regulations at the time of writing (summer 2006), by the time you read this changes will certainly have been made. After reading this Section you will not be a tax expert, but you will have the big picture on how corporations are taxed.

Businesses, like individuals, must pay taxes on income. Before calculating taxes, businesses can deduct all direct operating and financial expenses from sales to arrive at earnings before taxes (EBT). The EBT of sole proprietorships and partnerships is taxed as the income of the individual owners, whereas corporations are viewed as separate legal entities and their EBT is subject to corporate taxes. The Canada Revenue Agency (CRA) administers tax laws for the Government of Canada and for most provinces and territories. The remainder of this Section is devoted to corporate taxation. Tax terminology and glossaries of tax terms relevant to Canada are available on the Web.

www.cra-arc.gc.ca/tax/business/topics/corporations/menu-e.html
www.taxtips.ca/glossary.htm#N

Types of Business Income

Corporations can earn four types of income: active business income, passive income, dividends from other corporations, and capital gains. **Active business income** is income derived from normal business activities. The corporation is in business to sell a product or a service. In doing so, the business will incur expenses that can then be deducted from sales. The difference is earnings before taxes (taxable income) generated from the normal operation of the business. Active business income also includes any income that is incidental to the business—income that is only a small portion of total income.

active business income
Income derived from normal business activities of a corporation; the difference between sales and expenses.

Active business income does not include income from a specified investment business or from a personal services business. A specified investment business is a business whose principal purpose is to derive income from the property of the corporation such as interest, dividends, rents, or royalties. A personal services business is a business that a corporation carries on to provide services to another entity (such as a person or a partnership) that an officer or employee of that entity would usually perform. If the corporation is considered one of these types of business, and employs fewer than six people, the income generated is considered **passive income** and is taxed at higher corporate tax rates.

passive income
Income from a specified investment business or from a personal services business that is taxed at higher corporate tax rates.

A company will often hold the preferred and common shares of other corporations for investment purposes. If the companies whose shares are held pay dividends, this income, in the hands of the receiving company, is termed **intercorporate dividends**. These payments are included as income, but if the dividends are received from a taxable Canadian corporation, the full amount of the dividend is not taxable. This is because the income that generated the dividend was already taxed in the hands of the corporation that paid the dividend. Therefore, the net tax impact of such dividends on taxes owed is nil. But the dividends will increase NIAT.

intercorporate dividends
Dividends received by a corporation from investments in preferred and common shares held in other corporations.

capital gains
The positive difference between the selling price of a capital asset and the asset's original cost plus the costs incurred to sell the asset.

capital assets
A fixed asset that is amortized, land, or financial assets (common shares, preferred shares, and fixed income securities like bonds) held by a corporation.

taxable capital gain
The portion of the capital gain that is taxable; currently the taxable portion is 50 percent.

Capital Gains and Losses

The fourth source of business income is capital gains. **Capital gains** are generated when a company sells a capital asset for more than its initial purchase price. **Capital assets** include fixed assets that are amortized, land, and financial assets such as common shares, preferred shares, and fixed income securities like bonds. The capital gain is the difference between the selling price and the purchase price. As well, any costs incurred to sell the asset may also be deducted. Only 50 percent of capital gains are taxable. This amount is termed the **taxable capital gain** and is included as income. This capital gains inclusion rate, like all tax regulations, is subject to change, and in fact has been changed a number of times over the past 20 years.

Example During the current tax year, Greengage Inc. sells 5,000 common shares that it holds in an affiliated company. The shares originally cost Greengage $5,000 when they were purchased 20 years ago. In the meantime the affiliated company has done very well and has listed its shares on the Toronto Stock Exchange. The 5,000 common shares are now worth $517,000. To sell the shares, Greengage must pay a $2,100 transaction expense.

The shares are sold for much more than their cost, so there is a capital gain on the transaction. How much is it? It is the proceeds from sale, less the original cost of the shares and the expenses incurred to sell the shares, as follows:

$$\$517{,}000 - \$5{,}000 - \$2{,}100 = \$509{,}900$$

The taxable capital gain is 50 percent of the gain, so it is $254,950. Greengage Inc. will have to include that amount in income for tax purposes for the current tax year.

net capital gains
The difference between capital gains and losses for a tax year; 50 percent of this amount is taxable.

Capital losses are the opposite of capital gains. If a firm sells an asset for less than its original cost, it incurs a capital loss. Note, though, that a company cannot claim a capital loss on fixed assets that are amortized. This is because it is expected that depreciable assets will decline in value with use. In addition, capital losses cannot be used to reduce a company's operating income. So capital losses are netted against capital gains to determine the **net capital gains**, and 50 percent of this amount is taxable. If capital losses are greater than capital gains, they can be used in other years. This issue is discussed later in this Section.

Tax-Deductible Expenses

In calculating their taxes, corporations are allowed to deduct operating expenses, as well as interest expense. The tax-deductibility of these expenses reduces their after-tax cost. The following example illustrates the benefit of tax deductibility.

Example Companies X and Y each expect in the coming year to have earnings before interest and taxes of $200,000. Company X during the year will have to pay $30,000 in interest; company Y has no debt and therefore will have no interest expense. Calculations of the earnings after taxes for these two firms are as follows:

	Company X	Company Y
Earnings before interest and taxes	$200,000	$200,000
Less: Interest expense	30,000	0
Earnings before taxes	$170,000	$200,000
Less: Taxes (40%)	68,000	80,000
Net income after taxes	$102,000	$120,000
Difference in earnings after taxes	$18,000	

The data demonstrate that whereas company X had $30,000 more interest expense than company Y, company X's net income after taxes are only $18,000 less than those of company Y ($102,000 for company X versus $120,000 for Company Y). This difference is attributable to the fact that company X's $30,000 interest expense deduction provided a tax savings of $12,000 ($68,000 for company X versus $80,000 for company Y). This amount can be calculated directly by multiplying the tax rate by the amount of interest expense (0.40 × $30,000 = $12,000). Similarly, the $18,000 *after-tax cost* of the interest expense can be calculated directly by multiplying one minus the tax rate by the amount of interest expense [$30,000 × (1 – 0.40) = $18,000]. ▲

The tax-deductibility of certain expenses reduces their actual (after-tax) cost to the profitable firm. This is a key point that is used throughout the text. After-tax amounts are used when making financial decisions, so understanding that there are tax savings associated with expenses is important. Note that for both accounting and tax purposes *interest is a tax-deductible expense, whereas dividends are not.* Because dividends are not tax deductible, their after-tax cost is equal to the amount of the dividend. Thus, a $30,000 cash dividend would have an after-tax cost of $30,000.

Amortization

Other types of tax-deductible expenses also provide a benefit to a company. Recall the statement of cash flows. One of the major components of cash flows from operations was the non-cash expense amortization. Amortization is the systematic expensing of a portion of the cost of a fixed asset against sales. This expense is associated with capital assets, assets that are expected to have a life greater than one year and whose value is expected to decline through use and/or obsolescence. Expenditures on these assets are not expensed, rather they are capitalized and the expenditure is written off over time via the amortization expense. This yearly expense: (1) allocates the cost of the asset over its useful life; and (2) recognizes that the asset has declined in value.

Example ▼ Ratheson Ltd. purchases a new machine for $100,000 that has an expected life of 10 years. A simple way to calculate amortization is the straight-line method. With this method, amortization is based on the cost of the asset divided by the expected life of the asset (in years). For Ratheson Ltd., the yearly amortization would be $10,000 ($100,000 ÷ 10 years). This expense allocates the cost of the asset over its useful life and recognizes that the asset has declined in value.

The difference between a company's sales and the allowable tax-deductible operating and financial expenses is the active business income that is taxed. This amount can be termed *earnings before taxes (EBT)* or *taxable income.*

Tax Loss Carryforward and Carryback

While it is never the goal of a company to incur losses, losses from investments in assets and from operations can be used to reduce taxes in other time periods. A capital loss occurs when a company sells a non-depreciable asset for less than its original cost. An operating loss occurs when, instead of making a profit for a year, a company loses money. In other words, the company would have negative earnings before taxes. For tax purposes, this is termed a *non-capital loss* and is the difference between the operating loss and any net capital gains. The income tax system allows firms to "carry back" and "carry forward" losses in order to reduce the impact of fluctuations in income from year to year on their tax liability.

Non-Capital Losses

Companies can carry their non-capital losses back up to three years to reduce taxable income in those years. The loss will be used as a deduction for tax purposes and will reduce taxable income in the year(s) applied. The company's taxes are recalculated on the basis of the new taxable income, and a tax refund (the difference between the original taxes paid and the new total taxes) will be issued to the company. If the non-capital loss cannot be completely used in the previous three years, the loss can be carried forward for 20 years. Until 2004, non-capital losses could only be carried forward for seven years. Since some businesses could not use these losses within this carryover period, the 2006 Budget extended the carryforward period to 20 years. This increases the likelihood that firms will be able to apply the losses against future tax liabilities.

www.cra-arc.gc.ca/tax/individuals/topics/income-tax/return/completing/deductions/lines248-260/252-e.html

Example

The earnings before taxes for Atlantic Tours Ltd. for the 2005–2008 tax years is shown below. In 2008, the company recorded an operating (non-capital) loss of $600,000. Atlantic Tours can use this operating loss to recalculate its taxes for 2005, 2006, and 2007. The operating loss is first applied to reduce the taxable income to zero for the 2005 tax year. Atlantic will then apply any remaining loss to 2006, and then to 2007. This enables the company to receive a tax refund to recover the taxes it previously paid. For Atlantic Tours, this can be done for all three years, resulting in a total tax refund of $171,185. Atlantic Tours will have $110,900 of unused losses to carry forward until 2028.

Atlantic Tours: Application of Non-capital Losses

	2005	2006	2007	2008
Original earnings before taxes	$148,900	$152,700	$187,500	–$600,000
Loss carried back	–148,900	–152,700	–187,500	
Adjusted taxable income	0	0	0	
Taxes previously paid (35%)	52,115	53,445	65,625	
Tax refund	$52,115	$53,445	$65,625	

Amount of operating loss that can be carried forward for use in 2009–2028

2008 operating loss	$600,000
Losses carried back	489,100
Losses to carry forward	$110,900

If Atlantic Tours' tax rate is 35 percent for the complete period, the real cost of the $600,000 operating loss is "only" $390,000 [$600,000 × (1 – 0.35)]. By being able to apply the loss against previous and future profits, the company reduces the true cost of the loss by $210,000 ($600,000 × 0.35). Note that in this example, Atlantic Tours had the choice of applying the loss to 2005, or 2006, or 2007. They applied the loss to the oldest tax year first, in this case 2005. This is done because, if the company loses money again in 2009, they would no longer have the option of applying the loss to the 2005 tax year, since it is no longer within the three-year carryback period. So always apply the loss to the oldest tax year first.

Capital Losses

If a firm sells a non-depreciable asset for less than its original cost, it incurs a capital loss. As previously discussed, capital losses can only be used to reduce capital gains. Therefore, if a company also sold an asset for more than its cost, the capital loss would offset all or part of the gain. Capital losses cannot be used to reduce a company's operating income. Thus, if in the year of the capital loss there are no capital gains, or more losses than gains, the remaining capital loss can be carried back three years or carried forward indefinitely until fully used. But only 50 percent of the loss will be used to offset the taxable capital gain that the loss is applied against.

Example The capital gains and losses for Music Galaxy for the 2005 to 2008 fiscal years are shown below. The company's tax rate is 35 percent. The taxable capital loss of $12,000 in 2008 can be applied to the net taxable capital gains in 2005, 2006, and 2007 to reduce the amounts to zero. The company will receive a total tax refund of $3,150. Music Galaxy will have $3,000 of taxable capital losses to carry forward indefinitely.

Music Galaxy: Application of Capital Losses

	2005	2006	2007	2008
Capital gains	$24,000	$18,000	$20,000	$2,000
Capital losses	16,000	14,000	14,000	26,000
Net capital gain (loss)	8,000	4,000	6,000	(24,000)

continued

	2005	2006	2007	2008
Taxable capital gain (loss) –50%	4,000	2,000	3,000	(12,000)
Carryback loss	−4,000	−2,000	−3,000	
Adjusted taxable capital gain (loss)	0	0	0	
Tax refund (35% tax rate)	$1,400	$700	$1,050	

Amount of taxable capital loss carryforward for use in later years

2008 taxable capital loss	$12,000
Losses carried back	9,000
Taxable capital loss to carry forward	$3,000

If given the choice, it is of much greater benefit to carry losses back rather than forward for three reasons. First, the company receives the tax refund now, rather than needing to wait for a future tax year. Second, the losses may need to be carried forward for many years into the future if operating profits or capital gains are not generated. Third, cash now is better than cash later. If losses are carried forward, the tax refund is worth much less than it would be today.

? Review Questions

2–14 Discuss the differences between active and passive income and capital gains.

2–15 Why does the federal government allow a corporation to exclude from taxable income dividends received from taxable Canadian corporations?

2–16 What benefit results from the tax deductibility of certain corporate expenses? Consider items such as amortization, interest, and dividend payments.

2–17 Distinguish between a non-capital loss and a capital loss. What are the tax rules relating to non-capital and capital losses?

2–18 If given a choice, should a firm carry losses forward or back? Explain.

2–19 On the basis of your answer above, devise and explain a strategy you would use to apply a non-capital loss of $465,000.

LG4

2.4 Capital Cost Allowance (CCA)

The amortization expense may be used for financial reporting purposes; however, for tax purposes, the Canada Revenue Agency (CRA) requires companies to use **capital cost allowance** (CCA). CCA is simply the tax version of amortization. Because the objectives of financial reporting are sometimes different from those of tax legislation, a firm often will use different amortization methods for financial reporting than those required for tax purposes. Tax laws are used to accomplish economic goals such as providing incentives for business investment in certain types of assets, whereas the objectives of financial reporting are quite different. Keeping two different sets of records for these two different purposes is legal and is a practice of all corporations.

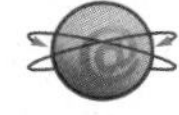

www.parl.gc.ca/information/library/PRBpubs/prb0606-e.htm

www.drtax.ca/eng/kb/new/index.html?page=keywords/t2/g516.htm

CCA is not claimed on assets, but rather on asset classes. The CRA has allocated all assets into various asset classes. All assets in the same class are

CCA rates
Rates set by the Canada Revenue Agency (CRA) that are used to calculate the CCA on an asset class; the rates range from 4 to 100 percent.

undepreciated capital cost (UCC)
The undepreciated value of an asset or asset class that is the basis for the amount of CCA that is claimed; also referred to as the *book value* of an asset.

considered in total for CCA calculation purposes. Table 2.6 provides some examples of asset classes, the applicable CCA rate, and examples of assets that are included in the class. The **CCA rates** range from 4 to 100 percent. One condition that the CRA imposes is that in the year an asset is acquired, only one-half of the allowable CCA can be claimed. This is termed the *half-year rule.*

The dollar amount of CCA that can be claimed in any year is based on the **undepreciated capital cost (UCC)** in the asset class at year-end. The UCC is the undepreciated value of an asset or asset class on which CCA is charged. It is also referred to as the *book value* of an asset. To calculate CCA, the UCC is multiplied by the applicable CCA rate. Each year, the UCC of the asset class declines as CCA is claimed. CCA is based on the declining balance of the UCC in the asset class.

TABLE 2.6 Capital Cost Allowance Rates

Class	Rate	Examples of assets
Class 1	4%	Buildings acquired after 1987, bridges, dams, airplane runways, canals, culverts, parking areas
Class 2	6%	Electrical generating equipment, pipelines
Class 3	5%	Buildings acquired before 1988, cement, steel, or stone wharves or breakwaters
Class 6	10%	Wood buildings, greenhouses, hangars, wood wharves or breakwaters, oil storage tanks, fences, water towers
Class 7	15%	Canoes, boats, fittings (for ships), engines (for ships), marine railways, scows
Class 8	20%	Furniture, office equipment, radio equipment, billboards, electric motors, engines, fishing nets and traps, tools over $500, pumps, welding equipment, milking machines
Class 9	25%	Aircraft, including furniture, fittings, or equipment attached
Class 10	30%	Automobile equipment, trailers, tractors, combines, computer hardware and systems software, buses, chain saws, outboard motors, timber equipment
Class 12	100%	Cutlery, television commercials, computer software, tableware, uniforms, tools under $500, cash registers
Class 13	SL*	Property that is leasehold interest (CCA depends on type/terms of lease)
Class 14	SL*	Patents, franchises, concessions, and licences for a limited period
Class 16	40%	Taxicabs, autos for short-term rental, freight trucks, video games, pinball machines
Class 17	8%	Roads, storage area, sidewalks, telephone or telegraph systems
Class 30	40%	Telecommunications spacecraft
Class 33	15%	Timber resource property
Class 38	30%	Power-generating movable equipment (construction)
Class 39	25%	Machinery and equipment in Class 43 acquired before February 26, 1992
Class 42	12%	Fibre optic cable
Class 43	30%	Manufacturing and processing machinery, equipment
Class 43.2	50%	Solar, wind, and other energy-saving systems acquired after February 22, 2005
Class 44	25%	Patents, licences to use patents acquired after April 26,1993
Class 45	45%	Computer hardware and systems software acquired after March 22, 2004
Class 46	30%	Data network infrastructure equipment acquired after March 22, 2004
Class 47	8%	Electrical energy transmission and distribution equipment acquired after February 22, 2005

*SL: Amortized, on a straight-line basis, over the life of the asset.

Example Tiger Beer has just acquired a new delivery truck costing $100,000. Based on Table 2.6, this is a Class 10 asset with a CCA rate of 30 percent. The dollar amount of CCA that can be claimed on this asset for the first four years is:

Year	UCC—beginning of year	CCA	UCC—end of year[a]
1	$100,000	$15,000[b]	$85,000
2	$ 85,000	$25,500	$59,500
3	$ 59,500	$17,850	$41,650
4	$ 41,650	$12,495	$29,155

[a]The undepreciated capital cost (UCC) is the asset's book value.
[b]Note that in the year an asset is acquired, only one-half of the allowable CCA can be claimed. This is termed the *half-year rule*. So, for this example, use 15%, half of the 30% CCA rate.

The calculated amount of CCA is the maximum that can be claimed in that class for the year. A company may elect to not claim the full CCA deduction available. This might be done if there is insufficient income to claim the complete deduction, or to create a sufficient level of income to claim previous year's losses, or to claim an investment tax credit. It is also important to note that the half-year rule applies to net additions to the class. To calculate net additions, first subtract the lesser of the original cost or proceeds of the asset(s) disposed of during the year from the cost of the assets acquired during the year. Now add one-half of this net amount to the UCC balance at the beginning of the year. This becomes the UCC used to calculate CCA for the year of the addition and disposal of assets.

Example For the Tiger Beer example discussed above, assume that during the fifth year Tiger sells the delivery truck for $20,000. In addition, the company acquires a new truck costing $135,000. The UCC in asset Class 10 at the beginning of the fifth year is $500,000. To calculate the CCA that could be claimed on the asset class in the fifth year, first subtract $20,000 (the lesser of the original cost or proceeds of the delivery truck) from the $135,000 cost of the new truck. This equals $115,000.

Then add half of this, $57,500, to the $500,000 of UCC in the asset class at the beginning of the year. This is $557,500. If these are the only changes to the asset class, the CCA that can be claimed on the asset class is $167,250 ($557,500 × 30%). The UCC in the asset class at the beginning of the following year is $447,750 ($557,500 − $167,250 + $57,500). Remember to add the other half of the net addition back to the asset class after calculating the CCA for the year.

Benefit of Claiming CCA

The benefit to a company of amortization (CCA) is associated with the concept of cash flows discussed in this chapter and in Chapter 1. Recall from Chapter 1 that the primary emphasis of financial management is on cash flows, not profits. Amortization (CCA) is deducted from sales when calculating taxable income. *But*, as a **non-cash expense**, the deduction does not involve an actual outlay of cash during the period; it reduces taxes but no cash has actually been used. Amortization (CCA) reduces net income (profits) but increases cash flow.

Example Consider two companies A and B, with the same earnings before amortization and taxes. Company A has an amortization (CCA) expense of $80,000; Company B does not. What are the two companies' NIAT and cash flows, assuming a tax rate of 32 percent?

	Company A	Company B
Earnings before amortization and taxes	$400,000	$400,000
Amortization	80,000	0
Earnings before taxes	$320,000	$400,000
Taxes (32%)	102,400	128,000
Net income after taxes	$217,600	$272,000
Cash flow	$297,600	$272,000

What is the benefit of amortization (CCA)? Since Company A has lower NIAT than does B, isn't B in a better financial position? It depends on what is being measured. Company A has a lower NIAT *but only because* the company was able to deduct the non-cash expense. The benefit of the non-cash expense is the reduction in taxes. Note that Company A pays $25,600 less in taxes than does Company B. Company A's ability to claim the non-cash expense actually benefited the company—the company paid lower taxes. These lower taxes provide a benefit in terms of higher cash flows. The amortization (CCA) expense provides a **tax shield**, tax savings associated with being able to claim non-cash expenses, that adds to a company's cash flow. The tax shield is calculated as: (non-cash expense × tax rate). Cash flows can be calculated in two ways:

(1) NIAT + non-cash expense;

(2) (earnings before amortization and taxes) × (1 − T) + (Amortization × T), where T is the company's tax rate.

For Company B, the cash flow is the same as NIAT, since there was no non-cash expense. For Company A, the cash flow was $297,600. This could be calculated as:

(1) $217,600 + $80,000 = $297,600;

(2) $400,000 × (1 − 0.32) + $80,000 (0.32) = $272,000 + $25,600 = $297,600.

For Baker Corporation, discussed earlier in this chapter, net cash from operations for 2008 totalled $280,000. Using the above equations, this is calculated as:

(1) Cash flows = $180,000 + $100,000 = $280,000;
(2) Cash flows = ($300,000 + $100,000) × (1 − 0.40) + $100,000 (0.40) = $240,000 + $40,000 = $280,000.

Recapture and Terminal Loss

In order to be able to claim CCA on an asset class, there must be assets in the class. So what happens if, during the year, a company sells all of the assets in a class? To evaluate the impact, two calculations must be made. First, it must be determined whether there was a capital gain on the asset. This will occur if the asset was sold for more than its original cost. As discussed earlier, there will never be a capital loss on the sale of depreciable assets.

Second, the lesser of the original cost of the asset or the proceeds from the sale are subtracted from the UCC in the asset class prior to the sale. The most likely result will be a positive or negative number. A positive number means that there is still UCC in the asset class. But, with the sale, there are no assets in the class. Since CCA must be claimed on an asset, the CRA allows the company to deduct the remaining UCC in the asset class from income. This is called a *terminal loss*. A terminal loss is like a one-time deduction of CCA. If the result is negative, the company has essentially claimed "too much" CCA and has recaptured some of the previously deducted CCA. A recapture is treated as income for tax purposes.

A final point: A terminal loss or recapture is formally recognized at year-end, and only if no other assets enter the asset pool before year-end.

Example A company with a December 31 year-end sells an asset that originally cost \$150,000 for \$10,000. Prior to the sale, the UCC in the asset class was \$17,000 (UCC_{BS}). The asset sold was the last asset in an asset pool. What happens? The two calculations described above must be made as follows:

UCC_{BS}	\$17,000	
Asset sold		
Original cost	\$150,000	No capital gain
Proceeds	\$ 10,000	
UCC_{AS}	\$7,000	Terminal loss

There is no capital gain, but there is a positive balance of UCC of \$7,000 (UCC_{AS}). This is a terminal loss, and it will be deducted from income for tax purposes. If instead the asset was sold for \$29,000, what happens?

UCC_{BS}	\$17,000	
Asset sold		
Original cost	\$150,000	No capital gain
Proceeds	\$ 29,000	
UCC_{AS}	–\$12,000	Recapture

As before, there is no capital gain, but there is a \$12,000 negative balance of UCC. This is a recapture, and it will be treated as income for tax purposes. A terminal loss or recapture occurs because, at the end of an asset's life, the market value of the asset is different from the UCC in the asset class at the time of the sale.

To determine whether a terminal loss or recapture occurs, the UCC of the asset class must be available. If there is only one asset in the class, we can calculate the UCC of an asset at any point in time by using the CCA table. But note that numerous calculations are required. If you wished to calculate the book value of a \$10 million asset with a 20 percent CCA rate at the beginning of year 25, a large number of calculations are required. Luckily, Equation 2.4 provides an easier method to calculate this value. Here d is the CCA rate for the asset.

$$\text{UCC (book value)}_{\text{Beg Yr } N} = \text{UCC} \times (1 - d/2) \times (1 - d)^{N-2} \tag{2.4}$$

For the asset discussed above, the UCC or book value of the asset at the beginning of year 25 will be:

$$\begin{aligned} \text{UCC (book value)}_{\text{Beg Yr 25}} &= \$10{,}000{,}000 \times (1 - 0.20/2) \times (1 - 0.20)^{25-2} \\ &= \$10{,}000{,}000 \times 0.90 \times 0.0059029581 \\ &= \$53{,}126.62 \text{ or } \$53{,}127 \text{ (rounded)} \end{aligned}$$

Now we can calculate the CCA that could be claimed in year 25, or determine the impact of an asset sale or purchase in the class.[5]

Example Ten years ago, E&B Enterprises purchased a $100,000 asset that had a CCA rate of 25 percent. The asset's useful life is ten years. At the beginning of year 10, what is the remaining UCC of the asset? We can calculate the UCC (book value) of the asset by using the CCA table. Or we can save time (and many calculations) by using Equation 2.4, where N is 10, since we wish to calculate the UCC before CCA was claimed in year 10, and d is 25 percent:

$$\begin{aligned} \text{UCC (book value)}_{\text{Beg Yr 10}} &= \$100{,}000 \times (1 - 0.25/2) \times (1 - 0.25)^{10-2} \\ &= \$100{,}000 \times 0.875 \times 0.100112915 \\ &= \$8{,}759.88 \text{ or } \$8{,}760 \text{ (rounded)} \end{aligned}$$

So the book value of the asset at the beginning of year 10 is $8,760 (assuming no other assets were purchased in this asset class). This is the UCC before sale (UCC_{BS}). At this point the asset is no longer useful to the firm, but it might be sold for scrap for $8,760. If this is the only asset in the class, what is the impact of the sale? By the end of year 9, E&B Enterprises would have claimed $91,240 ($100,000 – $8,760) of CCA on the asset. On the basis of the asset's fair market value, the company should have claimed $91,240 ($100,000 – $8,760) of CCA. The company claimed exactly the correct amount of CCA; therefore, the UCC after sale (UCC_{AS}) is zero and there is no recapture or terminal loss, as shown below:

UCC_{BS}	$8,760	
Asset sold		
Original cost	$100,000	No capital gain
Proceeds	$8,760	
UCC_{AS}	$0	No impact

In reality, the probability of the UCC and market value of the asset being equal at the end of the asset's life is very remote. If they are not equal, then either a recapture or a terminal loss will occur. If this happens, does it mean that the company amortized the asset at an improper CCA rate? Not at all. It simply means that the market value of the asset is different than its book value. This outcome will almost certainly occur for the vast majority of, if not all, asset sales.

5. The beginning of year N is the same as the end of year $N - 1$; it is the point after the CCA for year $N - 1$ has been claimed.

This is because the CCA rate used to amortize the asset is an estimated rate. It is almost certain that the asset will *not* amortize at exactly that rate.

Returning to the E&B Enterprises example, now assume that the asset could be sold for scrap for $12,000. If this is the only asset in the class, what is the impact of the sale?

UCC_{BS}	$8,760	
Asset sold		
Original cost	$100,000	No capital gain
Proceeds	$12,000	
UCC_{AS}	–$3,240	Recapture

By the end of year 9, E&B Enterprises would have claimed $91,240 ($100,000 – $8,760) of CCA on the asset. But, on the basis of the fair market value, the company should have claimed $88,000 ($100,000 – $12,000) of CCA. This implies that the company claimed "too much" CCA and, as of the end of year 10, has recaptured previously deducted CCA. The UCC_{AS} is –$3,240 ($88,000 – $91,240, or $8,760 – $12,000) which is the recaptured amount. Recaptured CCA is income for tax purposes, so the firm will have to pay additional taxes on this amount. The additional tax owing on the recapture will be based on: (the recapture × firm's tax rate). Again, this only occurs if the UCC_{AS} doesn't change by the company's fiscal year-end. In this example, the UCC could only change if other assets were purchased before year-end.

Returning to the E&B Enterprises example one more time, now assume that the asset could be sold for scrap for $2,000. If this is the only asset in the class, what is the impact of the sale?

UCC_{BS}	$8,760	
Asset sold		
Original cost	$100,000	No capital gain
Proceeds	$2,000	
UCC_{AS}	$6,760	Terminal loss

Now the UCC_{AS} is positive, so there is a terminal loss. On the basis of the market value of the asset, the company claimed "too little" CCA and, as of the end of year 10, has extra UCC that cannot be claimed via CCA since there are no assets left in the class. This extra is treated as an expense for tax purposes, so E&B Enterprises will claim the full amount of $6,760 in year 10 and will save taxes. The tax saving will be based on the terminal loss × firm's tax rate.

Investment Tax Credit (ITC)

investment tax credit (ITC)
An incentive for businesses in various regions of the country to purchase certain types of fixed assets or undertake certain types of research and development activities; results in a reduction in federal taxes payable.

The **investment tax credit (ITC)** is an incentive for businesses in various regions of the country to purchase certain types of fixed assets or undertake certain types of research and development activities. In 2006, the ITC rate for buildings, machinery, and equipment used in manufacturing and processing, mining, oil and gas, logging, farming, or fishing was 10 percent. This credit only applied for corporations located in the Atlantic provinces and in the Gaspé region of Quebec. For Canadian-controlled private corporations (CCPC) located throughout Canada, an ITC of 35 percent was allowed on the first $2 million of qualified scientific research and experimental development (SR&ED) expenditures. For expenditures above $2 million and for non-CCPCs, the ITC rate was 20 percent. In addition, eight of the ten provinces offer ITCs against provincial taxes payable (the two exceptions are Alberta and Prince Edward Island). The rates vary between 10 and 35 percent. These will not be considered here, as our focus is on the federal ITC.

The dollar amount of ITC can be deducted from *federal taxes payable*. The dollar amount of ITC is based on the amount of the qualifying expenditure times the ITC rate. So assuming the expenditure is $100,000 and it qualifies for a 10 percent ITC, the dollar amount of ITC is $10,000 ($100,000 × 10%). This is a direct benefit of the project and is recognized as a cash flow occurring in year 1. If the ITC cannot be used in the year the asset is acquired, it can be carried back three years and forward 20 years to reduce federal taxes payable in those years.

One minor drawback associated with ITC, is that the dollar amount of ITC must be deducted from the UCC of the asset for CCA purposes. Therefore, *a company can only claim CCA on the difference between the cost of the asset and the ITC*. So, in the previous example, the UCC for CCA purposes would be $100,000 cost of the asset minus the $10,000 ITC, making the UCC $90,000. The company would then compute CCA on the basis of the $90,000 and the CCA rate.

Example Ritter Tools has just purchased new production equipment costing $352,000. This Class 43 asset has a CCA rate of 30 percent and qualifies for a 10 percent ITC. The ITC is $35,200 meaning the UCC for the machine is $316,800 ($352,000 – $35,200). This is the UCC at the beginning of year 1, and the CCA that could be claimed on the equipment for the next three years are:

Year	UCC—beginning of year	CCA	UCC—end of year
1	$316,800	$47,520	$269,280
2	$269,280	$80,784	$188,496
3	$188,496	$56,549	$131,947

? Review Questions

2–20 Discuss what is meant by an "asset class," and why it is important.
2–21 What is the half-year rule and how is the rule applied?
2–22 What happens when a company both sells and buys assets that are in the same asset class?
2–23 In what sense does amortization act as a cash inflow? How can NIAT be adjusted to determine net cash from operations?
2–24 What is a recapture and a terminal loss, and why do they occur?
2–25 When an asset is sold from an asset class, what two calculations must be made? What are the possible outcomes?
2–26 What is an investment tax credit (ITC) and how does it impact CCA?

2.5 Corporate Tax Rates

Canadian-controlled private corporation (CCPC)
A small, private business majority-owned by Canadian residents.

For corporate tax purposes in Canada, a corporation must be classified on the basis of two characteristics. The first is whether the company is a **Canadian-controlled private corporation** (**CCPC**), which essentially is a small, private business majority-owned by Canadian residents. If the business is a CCPC, it will be subject to lower taxes on its active business income (ABI), as defined earlier in the chapter. Second is whether the company is engaged in manufacturing and processing. If so, it will pay lower provincial taxes in some provinces. If the company is not considered a manufacturer or processor, it is a general (*non-manufacturer/processor* or *non-M&P*) for tax purposes.

Federal and Provincial Rates

general rate reduction
The deduction that most corporations are allowed from the net federal tax rate of 28 percent.

In this Section, we have provided the tax rates for the 2008 calendar year on the basis of the announcements made by all levels of government as at the time of writing (summer 2006). For the 2008 calendar year, the basic federal tax rate is 38 percent, the rate that has been in effect for many years. The federal government then allows a 10 percent tax rate reduction for all income earned in a province. The net federal rate is 28 percent. A **general rate reduction** of 7.5 percent is then allowed, reducing the federal rate to 20.5 percent.[6] Each province in Canada then levies its own tax on the corporation to arrive at the general (non-M&P) corporate tax rate.

Table 2.7 provides the federal tax rate, the provincial tax rates for the ten provinces and three territories, and the combined federal and provincial tax rates for the two classifications for corporations for the 2008 calendar year. The first numeric column in Table 2.7 provides the rate for general corporations. The combined tax rates range from a low of 30.5 percent in Alberta to a high of 36.5 percent in Nova Scotia and PEI.

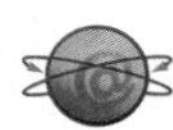

www.cra-arc.gc.ca/tax/business/topics/corporations/rates-e.html

Note that these are the rates that had been announced as of the time of the writing (summer 2006). Federal and provincial governments regularly change corporate tax rates, and the rates will most certainly have changed by the time you read this Section. For the most up-to-date corporate tax rates, see the CRA Web site.

The next numeric column in Table 2.7 provides the rate for M&P corporations. Note that only three provinces and one territory provide a lower rate for M&P corporations. This is a dramatic change when compared to the years prior to 2004. In previous years the federal government and almost every province taxed M&Ps at much lower rates than general corporations. This change in taxation may reflect the gradual reduction in the importance of the manufacturing sector in the Canadian economy; the service sector now accounts for about 60 percent of Canada's gross domestic product (GDP). To be effective, the tax system must respond to the changing nature of the economy, and this seems to have occurred starting in 2002.

6. For many years, a 4 percent federal tax surtax was applied to the 28 percent net federal rate, effectively increasing the federal rate by 1.12 percent. This surtax was eliminated in 2006. The general rate reduction is scheduled to increase to 9 percent by 2010, reducing the net federal rate to 19 percent.

TABLE 2.7 Corporate Tax Rate Schedule for the 2008 Calendar Year[a]

			Canadian–Controlled Private Corporation	
	General (non-M&P)	Manufacturing and processing	ABI up to $400,000	Investment income
Panel A: Federal Rate	20.5%	20.5%	11.5%	28.0%
Panel B: Provincial Rates				
British Columbia	12.0%	12.0%	4.5%	12.0%
Alberta	10.0%	10.0%	3.0%	10.0%
Saskatchewan	12.5%	10.0%	5.0%	12.5%
Manitoba	13.5%	13.5%	3.0%	13.5%
Ontario	14.0%	12.0%	5.5%	14.0%
Quebec	11.4%	11.4%	8.0%	16.25%
New Brunswick	12.0%	12.0%	1.0%	12.0%
Nova Scotia	16.0%	16.0%	5.0%	16.0%
Prince Edward Island	16.0%	16.0%	3.2%	16.0%
Newfoundland and Labrador	14.0%	5.0%	5.0%	14.0%
Northwest Territories	11.5%	11.5%	4.0%	11.5%
Nunavut	12.0%	12.0%	4.0%	12.0%
Yukon	15.0%	2.5%	2.5%	15.0%
Panel C: Combined Rates				
British Columbia	32.5%	32.5%	16.0%	40.0%
Alberta	30.5%	30.5%	14.5%	38.0%
Saskatchewan	33.0%	30.5%	16.5%	40.5%
Manitoba	34.0%	34.0%	14.5%	41.5%
Ontario	34.5%	32.5%	17.0%	42.0%
Quebec	31.9%	31.9%	19.5%	44.25%
New Brunswick	32.5%	32.5%	12.5%	40.0%
Nova Scotia	36.5%	36.5%	16.5%	44.0%
Prince Edward Island	36.5%	36.5%	14.7%	44.0%
Newfoundland and Labrador	34.5%	25.5%	16.5%	42.0%
Northwest Territories	32.0%	32.0%	15.5%	39.5%
Nunavut	32.5%	32.5%	15.5%	40.0%
Yukon	35.5%	23.0%	14.0%	43.0%

[a]Panel A provides the federal tax rate, Panel B the provincial tax rates, Panel C the combined tax rates. Panel C is the overall tax rate for a corporation located in each province. These are the rates that will be in effect for the 2008 calendar year, according to the announcements made by the federal and various provincial governments, up to the summer of 2006.

SOURCES: (1) PricewaterhouseCoopers, "Tax Facts and Figures for Individuals and Corporations," June 2006, available at **www.pwcglobal.com/extweb/service.nsf/docid/6fe0781f832b907f852570ca0017765e**. Used by permission. (2) Canada Revenue Agency Corporate Tax Web site, available at **www.cra-arc.gc.ca/tax/business/topics/corporations/menu-e.html**.

small business deduction
A 16.5 percent reduction in the net federal tax rate that the federal government allows CCPCs.

If the corporation is a CCPC, the federal government allows the business to claim the **small business deduction (SBD)** of 16.5 percent. This deduction is from the net federal tax rate of 28 percent. So a CCPC does not receive both the general rate reduction and the small business deduction. The 16.5 percent reduction applies to the first $400,000 of active business income and is reduced for corporations with taxable capital of more than $10 million. The third numeric column in Table 2.7 provides the tax rate for the first $400,000 of taxable income earned by CCPCs. The combined tax rates for CCPCs range from a low of 12.5 percent in New Brunswick to a high of 19.5 percent in Quebec. If the CCPC's taxable income is greater than $400,000, the tax rate applied on the excess amount of income is based on the rates in columns 1 or 2, again depending on whether the company is a M&P.

It is also important to note that active business income does not include investment income, income from a specified investment business, or income from a personal services business. Investment income, which is excluded from active business income, includes taxable capital gains less allowable capital losses, property income less property losses, and foreign business income. The tax rates on investment income are provided in the final numeric column in Table 2.7. The net federal rate of 28 percent applies, so there are no tax breaks allowed on this income.[7] Obviously, the combined tax rates on this type of income for a CCPC are much higher than on active business income. The rates range from a low of 38 percent in Alberta to a high of 44.25 percent in Quebec.

So a CCPC with active business income greater than $400,000 and investment income would have three different tax rates for various parts of its taxable income. A non-CCPC will only have one tax rate on all taxable income.[8]

As mentioned earlier, corporate taxation is a very complex topic, and our coverage has provided just an overview of the system. However, at this point you can calculate taxable income and taxes payable with the general data provided.

Example ▼ Webster Manufacturing's total sales for the fiscal year ended December 31, 2008, were $1,943,200. Direct costs of sales were $1,035,300. Operating costs were $339,400, but this included amortization expense of $95,600 and excluded Webster's allowable CCA claim of $145,800. The company made interest payments on their outstanding debt of $22,800 and paid common share dividends of $95,000. Webster Manufacturing is a CCPC based in Manitoba. The total amount of taxes Webster will pay for the 2008 fiscal year is based on the level of active business income and the company's tax rate. The active business income is based on sales less the appropriate expenses. Since amortization cannot be claimed for tax purposes, this amount must be deducted from the operating costs of $339,400. But CCA can be claimed, so this is added to the operating costs. The operating costs that Webster can claim for tax purposes is $389,600 ($339,400 – $95,600 + $145,800). Now the amount of active business income can be calculated.

7. The 28 percent rate excludes an extra $6^2/_3$ percent tax that is refundable when the CCPC pays taxable dividends. It is assumed that the corporation will pay dividends to gain the refund.

8. In addition, almost all of the provinces provide various types of tax incentives for various corporations. These are not included in the discussion, being beyond the scope of this book.

	Calculations
Sales	$1,943,200
COGS	1,035,300
Gross margin	907,900
Operating expenses	389,600
EBIT	518,300
Interest	22,800
EBT (active business income)	$ 495,500
Combined taxes	
On first $400,000 (14.5%)	$ 58,000
On remaining $95,500 (34%)	32,470
Total taxes	$ 90,470
NIAT	$ 405,030

Now assume that Webster Manufacturing's controller has just realized that the company had also received $31,210 of dividends from Rogers Industries, a taxable Canadian company, on December 27, 2008. Also, on March 31, 2008, Webster sold land that was originally purchased for $32,500 for $86,900. Real estate fees associated with the sale were $3,400. Do these transactions affect the above calculations? The dividends have no impact on the calculation of tax since they were received from a taxable Canadian corporation; they can be ignored for tax purposes. But they should be included in NIAT as they are part of income. The sale of land results in a capital gain of $51,000 ($86,900 – $32,500 – $3,400). As discussed earlier, only 50 percent of this gain is taxable. This is $25,500 and this income is taxed at the CCPC rates. But, since the company is above the $400,000 SBD limit, a rate of 34 percent is applied. So the taxes owing on the capital gain are $8,670 ($25,500 × 34%). So Webster Manufacturing's total taxes owing are now $99,140 ($90,470 + $8,670), while net income after taxes is:

Original net income after taxes	$405,030
Add: Dividends received	31,210
Add: Capital gain	51,000
Less: Taxes on capital gain	8,670
Adjusted net income	$478,570

? Review Questions

2–27 Discuss the variables used to classify a corporation for tax purposes.

2–28 What is the general rate reduction, and why is it important?

2–29 Why might certain provinces have lower corporate tax rates than others?

2–30 Discuss the deduction from the net federal tax rate the federal government provides small businesses. Why would the government provide this deduction to a small business?

2–31 Why is it important that a CCPC earn active business income?

2.6 The Annual Report

Every corporation has many and varied uses for the standardized records and reports of its financial activities. On a regular basis, financial statements are prepared for internal purposes. Management uses these statements to monitor the company's performance looking for ways to build on strengths and reduce weaknesses. Ensuring the company is generating sufficient cash flow to meet ongoing obligations is a key task for the financial managers. Periodically, reports must be prepared for regulators, creditors (lenders), and owners.

Regulators, such as provincial securities commissions and stock exchanges, enforce the accurate disclosure of corporate financial data. Creditors use financial data to evaluate the firm's creditworthiness or ability to meet scheduled debt payments. Owners use financial data to judge whether management is running the company to benefit shareholders and to decide whether to buy, sell, or hold its shares. Management must be concerned with regulatory compliance and ensure the company's creditors and owners are satisfied with the financial performance of the company.

As discussed earlier in the chapter, the guidelines used to prepare and maintain financial records, reports, and statements are known as generally accepted accounting principles (GAAP). The *Canada Business Corporations Act* and provincial corporations and securities legislation generally require companies to prepare financial statements for their shareholders in accordance with GAAP. Companies must provide a report to shareholders each year that summarizes and documents for shareholders the company's financial activities during the year. This official report is known as the **annual report.**

annual report
The report that corporations must provide to common shareholders that summarizes and documents the firm's financial activities during the past year.

Annual reports for Canadian companies that are publicly traded are often lengthy documents providing many photos together with comments from management and, of course, the companies' financial statements. Publicly traded companies are those whose common shares are listed and traded on a stock exchange. The best-known stock exchange in Canada is the Toronto Stock Exchange (TSX). All publicly traded companies are required to file their annual reports on the System for Electronic Document Analysis and Retrieval (SEDAR), a database that is easy to search. A typical annual report provides the following types of information to shareholders.

www.sedar.com

Letter to Shareholders

letter to shareholders
Typically, the first element of the annual report following a summary of the company's financial performance for the year, and the direct communication from senior management to the firm's owners.

The **letter to shareholders,** typically found after a summary of the company's financial performance for the year, provides direct communication from senior management to the company's common shareholders. Generally, the letter is from the company's CEO or the chair of the company's board of directors, the group that represents the shareholders to senior management. The letter describes the events that senior management considers to have had the greatest impact on the firm during the year. In addition, the letter generally discusses management philosophy, strategies, and actions as well as plans for the coming year and their anticipated effects on the firm's financial condition. The letter could be viewed as a summary of the annual report, providing an overview of the company's performance and key actions taken during the previous fiscal year as well as the organization's overall plans for the future. It generally tries to present a positive image for the company, putting the previous fiscal year's performance in as positive a light as possible.

Management's Discussion and Analysis

Management's Discussion and Analysis (MD&A)
MD&A is a supplemental report that allows the reader to look at the company through the eyes of management by providing a current and historical analysis of the business of the company.

Since 1989, all Canadian annual reports must contain a section termed **Management's Discussion and Analysis (MD&A)** of financial performance. MD&A is a supplemental section that analyzes and explains the company's financial results. The intent of the MD&A disclosure requirement is to give the reader the opportunity to look at the company through the eyes of management by providing a current and historical analysis of the business of the company. For the report, management is required to discuss recent financial results and the dynamics of the business and to analyze the financial statements. The report also reviews significant developments that affected the company's performance. Coupled with the financial statements, this information enables readers to better assess the company's performance, position, and future prospects.

MD&A must provide an analysis of the company's financial condition, cash flows, and results of operations for the most recently completed fiscal year, and a comparison to the previous year. The company is expected to describe trends, discuss results for separate business units, consider internal factors and external economic and industry factors affecting the company, explain changes in the company's financial condition and results of operations, and discuss and explain major changes in the direction of the business.

For financial condition, the focus of MD&A is on material information on operations with particular emphasis on liquidity, capital resources, and known trends, commitments, and events. MD&A discusses the ability of the company to generate adequate amounts of cash needed to support planned growth. Qualitative and quantitative risk factors that are expected to affect the company's business, financial condition, or results of operations must be considered. Planned capital expenditures for the upcoming fiscal year must be described and the anticipated cost and source of the funds indicated.

Financial statements are a necessary but insufficient means for measuring and reporting on overall performance. MD&A provides management the opportunity to flesh out and explain the nature of the company, its financial performance, research and development activities, and plans for the future. The report is an opportunity for the company to communicate with those who assess the company's value in the financial markets and is a critical component of a company's annual report. Essentially, this section of the annual report gives management the opportunity to present any type of relevant information they wish.

Financial Statements

Following the first two sections will be the four key financial statements required by regulators and discussed in Section 2.1 of this chapter: the income statement, balance sheet, statement of retained earnings, and statement of cash flows. Annual reports must contain the four financial statements for at least the two most recent years of operation, although many companies provide up to ten years of historical results. Prior to the financial statements are two short reports. The first is "Management's Report" outlining management's responsibility for preparing the annual report. Following this is the "Auditors' Report" describing how the auditor completed the audit of the company's financial records. The auditor must also indicate whether the financial statements presented are "free of material misstatement" and fairly present the financial position of the company.

Following the financial statements are the "Notes to Financial Statements," an important source of information on the accounting policies, procedures, calculations, and transactions underlying entries in the financial statements. The notes to the financial statements are an integral part of the financial statements. After the notes, selected financial data for the most recent eight quarters are also included, as are historical financial data for the past five to ten years. The historical data are often a summary of key operating statistics and financial ratios (discussed in Chapter 3). Graphs of key variables and ratios are also commonly included in this section of the annual report.

Summary

In Canada, there are about 2,100 companies with shares listed on one of the two Canadian stock exchanges: the Toronto Stock Exchange (TSX) and the TSX Venture Exchange. Each of these companies must produce an annual report to shareholders. Aside from providing the four principal financial statements, all annual reports must provide insight into the company's operation, management procedures, and industry position. Many of today's reports are packed with concise information, attention-grabbing graphics and colours, and interactive CD-ROMs, a welcome departure from the blandness of reports of the past. But even with all the jazz, the reports don't, or shouldn't, deviate from their main purpose: to communicate to shareholders clear, understandable, and useful company information.

Companies should view their annual report not as a requirement, but as an important vehicle for influencing readers' perceptions of the company. Good reports provide the basic information but also discuss areas such as new product development, market share, the workforce, and prospects for the future. They discuss the performance of the company's business units, providing analysis of the key issues facing the company. Operational and financial goals linked to the company's mission and strategic plan are included. Good reports provide an overview of actual performance compared to the company's stated goals and strategic initiatives.

Overall, an excellent annual report must be sophisticated and professional, yet friendly and straightforward in delivering an understanding of the company and industry.

? Review Questions

2–32 What are generally accepted accounting principles (GAAP), and who authorizes them? What role do regulators play in the financial reporting of Canadian companies?

2–33 List and describe the contents of a typical annual report for a publicly traded corporation.

2–34 What is the purpose of management's discussion and analysis (MD&A) in an annual report? Why would regulators require companies to include MD&A in the annual report?

2–35 What does the term "publicly traded corporation" mean?

SUMMARY

Review the characteristics, format, key components, and relationships between the income statement, balance sheet, statement of retained earnings, and statement of cash flows. The Canadian Institute of Chartered Accountants (CICA) has developed a set of accounting standards that specify the four financial statements that companies must develop and how information is to be presented and disclosed in the financial statements. The CICA's objective is to ensure companies provide information that meets the needs of users of financial statements.The income statement summarizes operating results for a period of time by subtracting direct costs, operating and financial expenses, and taxes from the flow of sales revenues to determine net income. The balance sheet summarizes a company's financial position at a point in time by balancing the firm's assets (what it owns) against its liabilities (what it owes) and shareholders' equity (what was provided by the owners). The statement of retained earnings illustrates what a company did with the NIAT earned during the fiscal year, reconciling the change in retained earnings from the beginning to the end of the fiscal year. NIAT not paid as dividends is reinvested and this amount flows to retained earnings on the balance sheet. The statement of cash flows summarizes the change in the cash balance from one period to the next.

Analyze a company's cash flows and develop and interpret the statement of cash flows. The SCF provides a summary of inflows and outflows of cash over the same time period as the balance sheet, typically the fiscal year. The statement is divided into operating, investment, and financing cash flows. The statement of cash flows can be developed by following a six-step process. The first step is to note the correct answer: the change in cash (and marketable securities) from the previous year's to the current year's balance sheet. The next five steps determine the cash flows from the three categories—operating, investment, and financing—and the net overall change in cash. Free cash flow (FCF) is the cash available to make payments to the creditors and investors that supplied capital to the company. It is based on after-tax operating earnings plus amortization, less total outlay capital expenditures, less change in non-cash working capital. FCF is the cash "free" to distribute to creditors or shareholders as interest, principal repayments, dividends, or share repurchases.

Introduce the basics of corporate taxation in Canada, including an understanding of how the tax-deductibility of expenses reduces their actual, after-tax cost to a profitable company. Taxes have a major impact on many types of financial decisions made by businesses, so knowing how they are taxed is vital for a full understanding of the financial actions they take. The tax system in Canada is incredibly complex and ever-changing, with new tax rates and regulations released every year by both the federal and the provincial governments. Corporations can earn four types of income: active business income, passive income, dividends from other corporations, and capital gains. Active business income is income derived from normal business activities. Businesses can deduct all direct, operating, and financial expenses from sales to arrive at earnings before taxes. Passive income is taxed at higher corporate tax rates. Dividends received from investments in taxable Canadian corporations are tax-exempt while only one-half of capital gains are subject to tax. An expense of \$100,000 for a company with a 30 percent tax rate has an actual cost of only \$70,000. This is because the expense is deductible from income; therefore, the tax system reduces the actual, after-tax cost by the amount of the expense multiplied by the tax rate, in this example \$30,000. Corporations can also use capital and non-capital operating losses to reduce the taxes they pay. These losses can be applied to prior earnings in which the corporation will receive a tax refund, or they can be carried forward and applied to reduce future taxes payable.

Discuss and illustrate capital cost allowance (CCA), the tax version of amortization, and how CCA increases a company's cash flows. Amortization, or the allocation of the cost of an asset over its useful life, is the most common type of non-cash expense. For tax purposes, however, companies are required to use **capital cost allowance** (CCA). CCA is simply the tax version of amortization. CCA is not claimed on assets, but rather on asset classes. The CRA has allocated all assets into various asset classes. All assets in the same class are considered in total for CCA calculation purposes. The dollar amount of CCA that can be claimed in any year is based on the undepreciated capital cost (UCC) in the asset class at year-end. Given the half-year rule, in the year an asset is acquired, only one-half of the allowable CCA can be claimed. Since amortization (or CCA) is a non-cash expense, the effect is to increase a company's cash flows. Amortization, and other non-cash expenses, are added back to the company's net income after tax to determine cash flows from operations. Since non-cash expenses reduce taxable income without an actual cash outflow, they are a source of cash to the company. If a company sells all of the assets in a class during a year, two calculations must be made. First, it must be determined whether there was a capital gain on the asset. Second, the lesser of the original cost of the asset or the proceeds from the sale are subtracted from the UCC in the asset class prior to the sale. If the result is positive, this is a terminal loss, which may be deducted for tax purposes. If the result is negative, the company has recaptured some of the previously deducted CCA. A recapture is treated as income for tax purposes. The outcome is formally recognized at year-end, and only if no other assets enter the asset pool before year-end. Businesses in certain regions of the country that purchase certain types of fixed assets or undertake certain types of research and development activities qualify for the investment tax credit (ITC). The dollar amount of ITC can be deducted from federal taxes payable, but the dollar amount of ITC must be deducted from the UCC of the asset for CCA purposes.

Explain and illustrate how a corporation determines and uses tax rates to calculate taxes payable. For corporate tax purposes in Canada, there are two distinct types of corporations: non-manufacturing (general) companies and companies engaged in manufacturing and processing. In addition, a company can be a Canadian-controlled private corporation (CCPC). The federal government allows CCPCs to claim the small business deduction of 16.5 percent on the first $400,000 of active business income. Active business income does not include investment income. This income is taxed at a higher rate than active business income. Corporate tax rates vary by type of organization and province of operation, but for the 2008 calendar year, rates range from 12.5 percent to 44 percent. (For many examples in this book, tax rates of between 18 percent and 40 percent are assumed.)

Review the information provided in a publicly traded company's annual report to shareholders. Companies must provide a report to shareholders each year that summarizes and documents for shareholders the company's financial activities during the year. This official report is known as the annual report. Annual reports for many large Canadian companies are lengthy documents providing a large quantity of information. A typical annual report provides valuable information to shareholders including: a summary of financial results, the letter to shareholders, management's discussion and analysis (MD&A) of financial performance, and the four key financial statements: income statement, balance sheet, statement of retained earnings, and statement of cash flows. Following the statements are notes that are an integral part of and provide more details regarding the financial statements.

SELF-TEST PROBLEMS

(Solutions in Appendix B)

ST 2–1 Understanding financial statements and free cash flow The most recent financial statements for Mick's Sporting Goods for the fiscal year ended June 30, 2008 are shown below. In 2007, the company reported net income after taxes of $202,400. Also in 2007, the company paid preferred share dividends of $9,000, or $0.90 per share, and common share dividends of $43,750, or $1.25 per share. At the end of the 2008 fiscal year, there were 11,000 preferred shares outstanding and 39,800 common shares outstanding. A dividend of $0.92 per share was paid to preferred shareholders in 2008.

Mick's Sporting Goods
Income Statement
for the year ended June 30, 2008

Sales	$2,400,000
Cost of goods sold	1,632,000
Gross margin	768,000
Operating expenses	
Selling and administrative	272,000
Amortization	112,000
Operating earnings	384,000
Interest	20,000
Earnings before tax	364,000
Taxes (35%)	127,400
Net income after tax	$ 236,600

Mick's Sporting Goods
Balance Sheet
as at June 30, 2008

	2007	2008
Current assets		
Cash	$ 40,000	$ 52,000
Accounts receivable	198,000	265,500
Inventory	302,000	424,300
Total current assets	540,000	741,800
Gross fixed assets	370,000	620,000
Less: Accumulated amortization	120,000	232,000
Net fixed assets	250,000	388,000
Total assets	$790,000	$1,129,800
Current liabilities		
Accounts payable	$114,000	$ 104,160
Line of credit	100,000	125,000
Total current liabilities	214,000	229,160
Long-term debt	125,000	?
Equity		
Preferred shares	80,000	92,000
Common shares	300,000	378,000
Retained earnings	71,000	165,640
Total liabilities and equity	$790,000	$1,129,800

Determine the following for Mick's Sporting Goods:

a. The amount of long-term debt outstanding in 2008.

b. The number of preferred and common shares sold in 2008.

c. The company's book value per share in 2007 and 2008.
d. Total dividends paid and dividends per share in 2008.
e. Earnings per share in 2007 and 2008.
f. The amount of reinvested profits in 2008.
g. Retained earnings at the beginning of 2007.
h. The average amount Mick's received from the sale of all of the preferred and common shares outstanding at the end of 2007 and those sold in 2008.
i. Mick's free cash flow for the 2008 fiscal year.

ST 2–2 **UCC, CCA, and asset sales** During 2008, Regis Company purchased a Class 7 asset, with a CCA rate of 15 percent, costing $350,000. The company's tax rate is 18.5 percent.

a. Calculate the maximum CCA Regis could claim in 2015.
b. Calculate the tax benefit of claiming the CCA in 2015.
c. Calculate the book value of the asset at the beginning of 2016.
d. Calculate the total amount of CCA the company claimed from 2008 through to the beginning of 2016.
e. Now assume that in 2016 the company purchases a new Class 7 asset costing $125,000. Calculate the maximum CCA Regis Company could claim on this asset class in 2016, and the UCC in the asset class at the beginning of 2017.
f. In 2017, the company sold the asset purchased in 2008 for $34,000. They also purchased another Class 7 asset for $186,000. Calculate the maximum CCA Regis Company could claim on this asset class in 2018, and the UCC in the asset class at the beginning of 2018.
g. In 2018, the company sells the two remaining assets in the class for $100,000. What are the tax implications of the sale?

  LG5

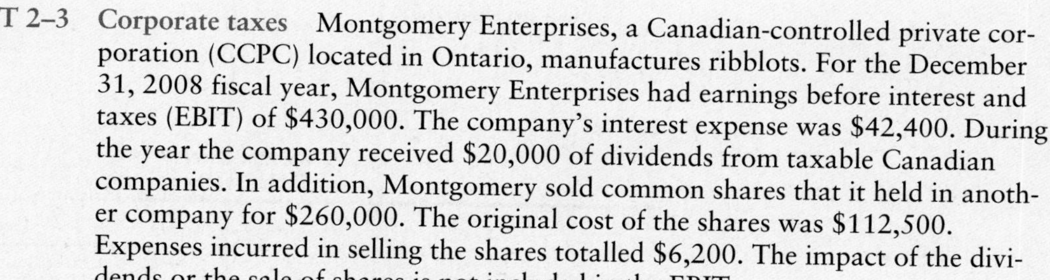

ST 2–3 **Corporate taxes** Montgomery Enterprises, a Canadian-controlled private corporation (CCPC) located in Ontario, manufactures ribblots. For the December 31, 2008 fiscal year, Montgomery Enterprises had earnings before interest and taxes (EBIT) of $430,000. The company's interest expense was $42,400. During the year the company received $20,000 of dividends from taxable Canadian companies. In addition, Montgomery sold common shares that it held in another company for $260,000. The original cost of the shares was $112,500. Expenses incurred in selling the shares totalled $6,200. The impact of the dividends or the sale of shares is not included in the EBIT.

a. Did Montgomery Enterprises realize a capital gain during the year? If so, what was the amount? What is the amount of the taxable capital gain?
b. What was Montgomery Enterprises' total taxable income for the year?
c. Using Table 2.7, calculate the company's total taxes payable and NIAT for 2008.
d. If Montgomery Enterprises was not a CCPC, what would be the total taxes payable and NIAT for 2008?
e. For part **d**, what is the after-tax cost of the interest payments Montgomery Enterprises made in 2008 (for this calculation assume they are not a CCPC)?
f. Now assume that the EBIT provided above was calculated using an amortization expense of $42,820. The firm's allowable CCA claim is $111,180. Does this impact the calculation of taxes and, if so, what is Montgomery's correct taxable income and taxes owing?

PROBLEMS

2–1 Reviewing basic financial statements The income statement for the year ended December 31, 2008, and the balance sheets for December 31, 2007 and 2008, for Technica, Inc., are given on this and the following page. Develop Technica's statement of retained earnings for the year ended December 31, 2008. Briefly discuss the form and informational content of each of these statements.

Income Statement
Technica, Inc.
for the year ended December 31, 2008

Sales revenue		$600,000
Less: Cost of goods sold		460,000
Gross margin		$140,000
Less: Operating expenses		
General and administrative expense	$30,000	
Amortization expense	30,000	
Total operating expenses		60,000
Operating earnings (EBIT)		$ 80,000
Less: Interest expense		10,000
Earnings before taxes		$ 70,000
Less: Taxes		27,100
Earnings available for common shareholders (EAC)		$ 42,900
Earnings per share (EPS)		$2.15

Balance Sheets
Technica, Inc.

	December 31	
Assets	**2007**	**2008**
Cash	$ 16,000	$ 15,000
Marketable securities	8,000	7,200
Accounts receivable	42,200	34,100
Inventories	50,000	82,000
Total current assets	$116,200	$138,300
Land and buildings	$150,000	$150,000
Machinery and equipment	190,000	200,000
Furniture and fixtures	50,000	54,000
Other	10,000	11,000
Total gross fixed assets	$400,000	$415,000

continued

Assets	2007	2008
Less: Accumulated amortization	115,000	145,000
Net fixed assets	$285,000	$270,000
Total assets	$401,200	$408,300
Liabilities and shareholders' equity		
Accounts payable	$ 49,000	$ 57,000
Line of credit	16,000	13,000
Accruals	6,000	5,000
Total current liabilities	$ 71,000	$ 75,000
Long-term debt	$160,000	$150,000
Shareholders' equity		
Common shares (20,000 shares outstanding in 2007, 19,500 in 2008)	$120,000	$110,200
Retained earnings	50,200	73,100
Total shareholders' equity	$170,200	$183,300
Total liabilities and shareholders' equity	$401,200	$408,300

BASIC LG1 **2–2 Financial statement account identification** Mark each of the accounts listed in the following table as follows:

a. In column 1, indicate in which statement—income statement (IS) or balance sheet (BS)—the account belongs.

b. In column 2, indicate whether the account is a current asset (CA), current liability (CL), expense (E), fixed asset (FA), long-term debt (LTD), revenue (R), or shareholders' equity (SE).

Account name	(1) Statement	(2) Type of account
Accounts payable	_____	_____
Accounts receivable	_____	_____
Accruals	_____	_____
Accumulated amortization	_____	_____
Administrative expense	_____	_____
Buildings	_____	_____
Cash	_____	_____
Common shares	_____	_____
Cost of goods sold	_____	_____
Amortization	_____	_____
Equipment	_____	_____
General expense	_____	_____
Interest expense	_____	_____

continued

Account name	(1) Statement	(2) Type of account
Inventories	_____	_____
Land	_____	_____
Long-term debts	_____	_____
Machinery	_____	_____
Marketable securities	_____	_____
Line of credit	_____	_____
Operating expense	_____	_____
Preferred shares	_____	_____
Preferred share dividends	_____	_____
Retained earnings	_____	_____
Sales revenue	_____	_____
Selling expense	_____	_____
Taxes	_____	_____
Vehicles	_____	_____

INTERMEDIATE 

2–3 Income statement preparation Use the *appropriate items* from the following list to prepare in good form Perry Corporation's income statement for the year ended July 31, 2009.

Item	Values ($000) at or for year ended July 31, 2009
Accounts receivable	$350
Accumulated amortization	205
Cost of goods sold	285
Amortization expense	55
General and administrative expense	60
Interest expense	25
Preferred share dividends	10
Sales revenue	525
Selling expense	35
Common shares	265
Retained earnings	325
Tax rate	40%

INTERMEDIATE

2–4 Income statement preparation On December 31, 2008, Cathy Chen, a self-employed chartered accountant (CA), completed her first full year in business. During the year, she billed $180,000 for her accounting services. She had two employees: a bookkeeper and a clerical assistant. In addition to her *monthly* salary of $4,000, Ms. Chen paid *annual* salaries of $24,000 and $18,000 to the bookkeeper and the clerical assistant, respectively. Income taxes and other deductions for Ms. Chen and her employees totalled $17,300 for the year. Expenses for office supplies, including postage, totalled $5,200 for the year. In addition, Ms. Chen spent $8,500 during the year on tax-deductible travel and entertainment associated with client visits and new business development. Lease payments for the office space rented (a tax-deductible expense) were $1,350 *per month*. Amortization expense on the office furniture and fixtures was $7,800 for the year. During the year, Ms. Chen paid interest of $7,500 on the $60,000 borrowed to start the business. The tax rate for her business is 30 percent.

a. Prepare an income statement for Cathy Chen, CA, for the year ended December 31, 2008.
b. How much *cash flow from operations* did Cathy realize during 2008? How much free cash flow from operations was generated?
c. Evaluate her 2008 financial performance.

BASIC  **2–5 Calculation of EPS and retained earnings** Philagem, Inc., ended the 2008 fiscal year with earnings *before* taxes of $218,000. The company is subject to a 40 percent tax rate and must pay $32,000 in preferred share dividends before distributing any earnings on the 85,000 common shares currently outstanding.

a. Calculate Philagem's 2008 earnings per share (EPS).
b. If the firm paid common share dividends of $0.80 per share, how many dollars would go to retained earnings?

BASIC LG1 **2–6 Balance sheet preparation** Use the *appropriate items* from the following list to prepare in good form Owen Davis Company's balance sheet at July 31, 2009.

Item	Value ($000) at July 31, 2009
Accounts payable	$ 220
Accounts receivable	450
Accruals	55
Accumulated amortization	265
Buildings	225
Cash	215
Common shares	290
Cost of goods sold	2,500
Amortization expense	45
Equipment	140
Furniture and fixtures	170
General expense	320
Inventories	375
Land	100
Long-term debt	420
Machinery	420
Marketable securities	75
Line of credit	475
Preferred shares	100
Retained earnings	370
Sales revenue	3,600
Vehicles	25

2–7 **Impact of net income on a firm's balance sheet** Conrad Air, Inc., reported net income *after tax* of $1,365,000 for the year ended August 31, 2009. Show the effect of these funds on the firm's balance sheet (given below for the previous year) in each of the following scenarios.

Balance Sheet
Conrad Air, Inc.
as of August 31, 2008

Assets		**Liabilities and shareholders' equity**	
Cash	$ 120,000	Accounts payable	$ 70,000
Marketable securities	35,000	Line of credit	55,000
Accounts receivable	45,000	Current liabilities	$ 125,000
Inventories	130,000	Long-term debt	2,700,000
Current assets	$ 330,000	Total liabilities	$2,825,000
Net equipment	$2,970,000	Common shares	$ 500,000
Net buildings	1,600,000	Retained earnings	1,575,000
Fixed assets	$4,570,000	Shareholders' equity	$2,075,000
Total assets	$4,900,000	Total liabilities and equity	$4,900,000

a. Conrad paid no dividends during the 2009 fiscal year and invested all profits in marketable securities.
b. Conrad paid dividends totalling $500,000 during the 2009 fiscal year and used the balance of the net income to retire (pay off) long-term debt.
c. Conrad paid dividends totalling $500,000 during the 2009 fiscal year and invested the balance of the net income in building a new hangar.
d. Conrad paid out all $1,365,000 as dividends to its shareholders during the 2009 fiscal year.

2–8 **Initial sale price of common shares** Beck Corporation issued 6,250 preferred shares and only sold common shares to investors once. Given Beck's shareholders' equity account that follows, determine the original price per share at which the firm sold the preferred and common shares.

Shareholders' equity ($000)	
Preferred shares	$ 125
Common shares (300,000 shares outstanding)	2,850
Retained earnings	900
Total shareholders' equity	$3,875

2–9 **Financial statement preparation** The balance sheet for Rogers Industries for March 31, 2008, appears below. Information relevant to Rogers Industries' operations for the 2009 fiscal year is given following the balance sheet. Using the data presented:

a. Prepare in good form an income statement for Rogers Industries for the year ended March 31, 2009. Be sure to show earnings per share (EPS).
b. Prepare in good form a balance sheet for Rogers Industries for March 31, 2009.
c. Determine Rogers' free cash flow from operations (FCFO) for the 2009 fiscal year.

Balance Sheet ($000)
Rogers Industries
March 31, 2008

Assets		**Liabilities and shareholders' equity**	
Cash	$ 40	Accounts payable	$ 50
Marketable securities	10	Line of credit	80
Accounts receivable	80	Accruals	10
Inventories	100	Total current liabilities	$140
Total current assets	$230	Long-term debt	$270
Gross fixed assets	$890	Preferred shares	$ 40
Less: Accumulated amortization	240	Common shares (119,000 shares outstanding)	320
Net fixed assets	$650		
Total assets	$880	Retained earnings	110
		Total shareholders' equity	$470
		Total liabilities and shareholders' equity	$880

Rogers Industries
Relevant information for the 2009 fiscal year

1. Sales were $1,200,000.
2. Cost of goods sold equals 60 percent of sales.
3. Operating expenses equal 15 percent of sales; amortization expense of $20,000 is included in this percentage.
4. Interest expense is 10 percent of the total beginning balance of the line of credit and long-term debt.
5. The firm pays 40 percent taxes on taxable income.
6. Preferred share dividends of $4,000 were paid.
7. Cash and marketable securities are unchanged.
8. Accounts receivable equal 8 percent of sales.
9. Inventory equals 10 percent of sales.
10. The firm acquired $30,000 of additional fixed assets in 2009.
11. Accounts payable equal 5 percent of sales.
12. Line of credit, long-term debt, preferred shares, and common shares remain unchanged.
13. Accruals are unchanged.
14. Cash dividends of $1 per common share were paid to common shareholders.

BASIC LG1 **2–10** **Statement of retained earnings** Hayes Enterprises began the 2008 fiscal year with a retained earnings balance of $928,000. During 2008, the firm earned $377,000 after taxes. From this amount, preferred shareholders were paid

$47,000 in dividends. At year-end 2008, the firm's retained earnings totalled $1,048,000. The firm had 140,000 common shares outstanding during 2008.

a. Prepare a statement of retained earnings for the year ended December 31, 2008, for Hayes Enterprises.

b. Calculate the firm's 2008 earnings per share (EPS).

c. How large a per-share cash dividend did the firm pay to common shareholders during 2008?

CHALLENGE  **2–11 Understanding financial statements** The financial statements for Barrie Corporation for the fiscal years ended August 31, 2008 and 2009 are provided below. In fiscal 2008, Barrie's NIAT was $162,500 and the company paid preferred share dividends of $10,000 and common share dividends of $22,250. In 2009, Barrie paid $12,500 in preferred share dividends. The number of common shares outstanding was 20,000 in 2008 and 21,000 in 2009. No new common shares were issued in 2007 or 2008.

Barrie Corporation
Income Statement
for the year ended August 31, 2009

Sales	$4,135,000
Cost of goods sold	3,308,000
Gross margin	$ 827,000
General administrative and selling expense	318,000
Amortization	117,000
Miscellaneous	54,000
Earnings before taxes	$ 338,000
Taxes (40%)	135,200
Net income after taxes	$ 202,800

Barrie Corporation
Balance Sheets
as of August 31

	2008	2009
Cash	$ 65,000	$ 76,250
Accounts receivable	284,000	401,600
Inventory	306,000	493,000
Total current assets	655,000	970,850
Land and building	95,000	126,150
Machinery	128,000	169,000
Other fixed assets	57,000	74,600
Total assets	**$935,000**	**$1,340,600**

Barrie Corporation Balance Sheets as of August 31		
	2008	2009
Accounts payable	$160,000	$ 152,700
Accruals	78,000	78,500
Total current liabilities	$238,000	$ 231,200
Long-term debt	126,000	?
Preferred equity	100,000	125,000
Common shares	410,000	500,000
Retained earnings	61,000	230,150
Total liabilities and equity	$935,000	$1,340,600

Determine the following for Barrie Corporation:

a. The amount of long-term debt outstanding in 2009.
b. The total dollar investment in assets made during 2009 and the sources of the funds invested.
c. Barrie's earnings per share (EPS) in 2008 and 2009.
d. The total dividends paid in 2009 and dividends per share (DPS) in 2008 and 2009.
e. The average amount Barrie received from the sale of all of the common shares outstanding at the end of 2008 and those sold in 2009.
f. Retained earnings as of the beginning of the 2008 fiscal year.
g. Barrie's book value and book value per share at the end of fiscal 2007, 2008, and 2009.

INTERMEDIATE  2–12 **Determining free cash flow** Using the financial statements in Problem 2–11, determine:

a. Barrie Corporation's free cash flow from operations in 2009.
b. Barrie Corporation's investment in gross fixed assets in 2009.
c. Barrie Corporation's investment in non-cash working capital in 2009.
d. Barrie Corporation's free cash flow in 2009.

INTERMEDIATE  2–13 **Understanding financial statements** Montague Corporation's financial statements are provided below. Use these statements to determine the following:

a. The total investment in assets made during 2008.
b. The sources of the funds invested.
c. Total investment in *fixed assets* during 2008.
d. The total dividends paid in 2008.
e. The average issue price per common share during 2008.
f. The book value per common share in 2007 and 2008.

Montague Corporation Income Statement for the year ended December 31, 2008	
Sales	$8,750,000
Cost of goods sold	6,200,000
Gross margin	2,550,000
General and administrative expense	830,000
Amortization	550,000
EBIT	1,170,000
Interest	300,000
Earnings before taxes	870,000
Taxes	304,500
Net income after taxes	$ 565,500

Montague Corporation Balance Sheet as at December 31	2007	2008
Cash	$ 300,000	$ 350,000
Accounts receivable	690,000	560,000
Inventory	1,020,000	1,400,000
Total current assets	2,010,000	2,310,000
Net fixed assets	5,600,000	6,200,000
Total assets	$7,610,000	$8,510,000
Accounts payable	$ 500,000	$ 450,000
Accruals	130,000	175,000
Total current liabilities	630,000	625,000
Long-term debt	4,600,000	5,100,000
Preferred equity	550,000	575,000
Common shares*	1,400,000	1,450,000
Retained earnings	430,000	760,000
Total liabilities and shareholders' equity	$7,610,000	$8,510,000

*There were 40,000 shares outstanding at the end of 2007 and 41,250 outstanding at the end of 2008.

INTERMEDIATE

2–14 **Free cash flow versus net income** Refer to the financial statements in Problem 2–13. Determine Montague Corporation's free cash flow for the 2008 fiscal year. How does this compare with the company's net income after tax for 2008? Which presents a truer picture of the firm's financial situation? Discuss.

BASIC 

2–15 **Changes in shareholders' equity** Provided below are the equity sections from the balance sheets for the 2007 and 2008 fiscal years as reported by Mountain Air Ski Resorts, Inc. The overall value of shareholders' equity has risen from $2,000,000 to $7,500,000. Use the statements to discover how this happened.

Mountain Air Ski Resorts, Inc.			2007	2008
Shareholders' equity				
Common shares				
Authorized:	5,000,000	shares		
Outstanding:	500,000	shares 2007		
	1,500,000	shares 2008	$1,000,000	$6,000,000
Retained earnings			1,000,000	1,500,000
Total shareholders' equity			$2,000,000	$7,500,000

The company paid total dividends of $200,000 during fiscal 2008.

a. What was Mountain Air's net income for fiscal 2008?

b. How many new common shares did the corporation issue and sell during 2008?

c. For the new common shares sold during 2008, what was the average price per share?

d. At what price per share did Mountain Air's original 500,000 shares sell?

INTERMEDIATE 

2–16 Reviewing the balance sheet For the 2008 fiscal year, Alpha Company had current assets of $200,000, fixed assets of $525,000, intangible assets of $65,000, long-term debt of $250,000, and $175,000 of total common equity.

a. What balance sheet account is missing from Alpha Company's balance sheet? What is the missing amount?

b. During the 2009 fiscal year, Alpha Company sold 5,000 common shares for $8 each, earned NIAT of $105,000, and paid common share dividends of $22,500. What changes would this make to the balance sheet?

c. If Alpha Company also repaid $25,000 of long-term debt during 2009, what change would this make to the balance sheet?

d. Given the changes in parts **b** and **c**, what other changes would have to occur to the balance sheet for the 2009 fiscal year?

CHALLENGE 

2–17 Understanding financial statements Selected financial information for S.D. Snack Foods, a publicly traded company, for the years ended December 31, 2007 and 2008, are shown on the next page. For the 2007 fiscal year, the company reported EPS of $1.80 and had 27,850 common shares outstanding. For the 2008 fiscal year, S.D. Snack Foods reported net income after tax of $182,300. The company typically pays out 40 percent of its earnings as dividends to preferred and common shareholders. Of the total dividends paid, 30 percent was paid to preferred shareholders in 2008. At the end of the 2008 fiscal year, there were 10,000 and 85,332 preferred and common shares outstanding, respectively. S.D. Snack Foods recorded an amortization expense of $125,000 in 2008. The common shares of the company are currently trading at $56.40.

	2007	2008
Net fixed assets	$2,450,000	$3,200,000
Preferred shares	$65,000	$65,000
Common shares	$185,000	$346,000
Retained earnings	$214,000	?

Using the above information, determine the following:

a. Retained earnings for 2008.
b. S.D.'s book value per share for 2007 and 2008.
c. The total investment made in fixed assets in 2008.
d. The earnings available for common shareholders in 2007 and 2008.
e. The average amount S.D. Snack Foods received from the sale of all the shares outstanding at the end of 2007 and the price of those sold in 2008.
f. The amount of common share dividends paid and dividends per share (DPS) in 2008.
g. S.D.'s price-to-earnings ratio in 2008.
h. The market to book value of the company in 2008.

BASIC 

2–18 **Classifying inflows and outflows** Classify each of the following items as a cash inflow (I), a cash outflow (O), or as neither (N).

Item	Change ($)	Item	Change ($)
Cash	+100	Accounts receivable	−700
Accounts payable	−1,000	NIAT	+600
Line of credit	+500	Amortization	+100
Long-term debt	−2,000	Repurchase of common shares	+600
Inventory	+200	Cash dividends	+800
Fixed assets	+400	Sale of common shares	+1,000

  BASIC

2–19 **Finding dividends paid** Colonial Paint's net income after taxes in 2008 totalled $186,000. The firm's year-end 2007 and 2008 retained earnings on its balance sheet totalled $736,000 and $812,000, respectively. Did Colonial pay dividends in 2008 and, if so, how much was paid?

CHALLENGE 

2–20 **Preparing a statement of cash flows** Given the balance sheets and selected data from the income statement of Keith Corporation that follow:

a. Prepare the firm's statement of cash flows for the year ended December 31, 2008.
b. Interpret the statement prepared above.
c. What is Keith Corporation's free cash flow from operations and free cash flow for the 2008 fiscal year?

Balance Sheets
Keith Corporation (in $000)

Assets	December 31 2007	2008
Cash	$ 1,000	$ 1,500
Marketable securities	1,200	1,800
Accounts receivable	1,800	2,000
Inventories	2,800	2,900
Total current assets	$ 6,800	$ 8,200
Gross fixed assets	$28,100	$29,500
Less: Accumulated amortization	13,100	14,700
Net fixed assets	$15,000	$14,800
Total assets	$21,800	$23,000
Liabilities and shareholders' equity		
Accounts payable	$ 1,500	$ 1,600
Line of credit	2,200	2,800
Accruals	300	200
Total current liabilities	$ 4,000	$ 4,600
Long-term debt	$ 5,000	$ 4,000
Common shares	$10,000	$11,000
Retained earnings	2,800	3,400
Total shareholders' equity	$12,800	$14,400
Total liabilities and shareholders' equity	$21,800	$23,000

Income statement data (2008)	
Total sales	$26,340
Amortization expense	1,600
Interest expense	610
Net income before tax	2,110
Net income after tax	1,400

CHALLENGE  2–21 **Preparing a statement of cash flows** Using the 2008 income statement and the 2007 and 2008 balance sheets for Technica, Inc., given in Problem 2–1, do the following:

a. Prepare the firm's statement of cash flows for the year ended December 31, 2008.

b. Interpret the statement prepared in **a.**

c. Determine Technica's free cash flow from operations and free cash flow for 2008.

BASIC  2–22 **Capital gains** Perkins Manufacturing is considering the sale of two assets, X and Y, that are not amortized. Asset X was purchased for $2,000 and will be sold today for $2,250. Asset Y was purchased for $30,000 and will be sold today for $35,000. The firm's tax rate is 20.6 percent.

a. Calculate the amount of capital gain, if any, realized on each of the assets.

b. Calculate the tax on the sale of each asset.

BASIC  2–23 **Capital gains** The following table contains purchase and sale prices and costs incurred in selling the assets for the nonamortizable capital assets of a major corporation. The firm's tax rate is 26.1 percent.

Asset	Purchase price	Sale price	Costs incurred
A	$ 3,000	$ 3,800	$ 400
B	12,000	12,360	360
C	62,000	81,000	1,000
D	41,000	45,460	460
E	16,500	18,125	125

a. Determine the amount of capital gain realized on each of the five assets.

b. Calculate the amount of tax paid on each of the assets.

INTERMEDIATE  2–24 **Loss carryforward/carryback** Prout Manufacturing Company Ltd. has items registered in its books relating to corporate taxes. The earnings before taxes excludes dividends and capital gains (losses). The company's accountant did not know how to treat the dividends and capital gains (losses), so he filed taxes only on the basis of the earnings before taxes for the year. The dividends were received from a taxable Canadian company.

	Earnings before taxes	Dividends received	Capital gains (losses)
Year 1	$ 25,000	$3,000	$ 4,000
Year 2	80,000	3,500	5,000
Year 3	45,000	4,000	8,000
Year 4	70,000	4,500	3,000
Year 5	75,000	5,000	(25,000)
Year 6	(224,000)	5,500	17,000

Assuming Prout Manufacturing's corporate tax rate is 28 percent, calculate the annual taxes the company should have paid each year, and then the amount of taxes after taking into account loss carryback and carryforward adjustments.

INTERMEDIATE  2–25 **Loss carryforward/carryback** Fred Stanley, founder and President of Stanley's Inc., smiled as he reviewed the company's most recent financial results. The company's taxable income for the 2008 fiscal year, which included a taxable capital gain of $15,000, was $521,000. This was an 8 percent increase over last year, and a substantial improvement over the results for 2005 and 2006 which recorded operating losses of $497,000 and $430,000, respectively. It looked like the financial situation of Stanley's Inc., now in its fourth year of operation, was starting to meet expectations.

a. Determine Stanley's Inc.'s total taxes payable for 2007 and 2008 assuming a tax rate of 35 percent. Be sure to consider any loss carryforward or carryback adjustments that the company is allowed to use.
b. If Stanley's Inc. incurs an operating loss of $80,000 in 2009, what impact could this have on Stanley's total taxes paid in 2007 and/or 2008?
c. Now assume that Stanley's Inc. incurred a net capital loss of $20,000 in 2009. If Stanley's Inc. reported its first capital gain of $15,000 in 2007, what impact, if any, does this have on Stanley's Inc.'s taxes paid in 2007 and 2008?

BASIC LG4

2–26 **Calculate UCC and CCA** During 2008, Q Corp purchased a Class 10 asset costing $200,000. Calculate the maximum CCA Q Corp could claim on this asset for 2008 to 2012 given that the CCA rate on the class is 30 percent. Calculate the amount of CCA the company could claim in 2027 (year 20).

BASIC LG4

2–27 **Calculate UCC and CCA** A depreciable asset's original cost was $500,000. What will be the UCC for this asset in the tenth year if the CCA rate is (a) 10 percent, (b) 20 percent, and (c) 30 percent? Calculate the maximum amount of CCA that could be claimed on this asset in the 10th year for each of the CCA rates above. What can you learn from this analysis?

BASIC LG4

2–28 **Impact of asset transactions** The current undepreciated capital cost of a specific pool of assets is $1,300,000. The firm has just sold an asset from the pool that originally cost $1,500,000. Calculate the impact of the sale, if any, on the asset class using the following assumed proceeds from sale:
i. $1 million
ii. $1.3 million
iii. $1.5 million
iv. $1.8 million

INTERMEDIATE LG4

2–29 **Impact of asset transactions** At the beginning of 2008, A Corp. had undepreciated capital cost (UCC) of $850,000 in asset Class 9 that has a CCA rate of 25 percent. On March 10, 2008, the company sold an asset costing $80,000 for $108,000. On November 11, 2008, the company purchased an asset costing $128,000.

a. Calculate the maximum CCA A Corp. could claim on this asset class for 2008.
b. Assuming no other changes occur in the asset class, calculate:
i. the UCC in the asset class at the beginning of 2009.
ii. the CCA A Corp. could claim for 2009.
iii. the UCC in the asset class at the beginning of 2019.

BASIC LG4

2–30 **Calculating CCA and tax shield** It is March, and Asto Company has just purchased a Class 17 asset at a cost of $175,000. Asto's tax rate is 26 percent.
a. Calculate the amount of CCA Asto could claim for the first four years of the asset's life.
b. What would the tax savings (shield) be for each year?
c. Explain what is meant by the term "tax shield."

INTERMEDIATE 

2–31 **Calculating UCC, ITC, and CCA** For Asto Company in the above question, assume the Class 17 asset being purchased at a cost of $175,000 is replacing another Class 17 asset that was purchased 10 years ago for $233,000. CCA has not been claimed for year 10. These were the only transactions for this asset class. The current asset can be sold for $22,000. The new asset qualifies for an ITC of 10 percent.

a. What is the incremental cost of the new asset?

b. What is the current UCC of the asset that was purchased 10 years ago?

c. Calculate the amount of CCA that Asto could claim on Class 17 for the next four years.

BASIC LG5 **2–32 Calculating taxes** Top Notch Textiles and Anderson Auto Parts both have taxable income of $457,400 for the 2008 fiscal year. Top Notch Textiles is a manufacturer located in Ontario. Anderson Auto Parts is a manufacturing CCPC, also located in Ontario. Using the tax rates provided in Table 2.7, calculate the total taxes each company must pay. Explain the difference in taxes paid, if any.

BASIC LG5 **2–33 Calculating taxes** Tantor Supply, Inc., is a small Canadian-controlled corporation based in Nova Scotia acting as the exclusive distributor of a major line of sporting goods. During 2008 the firm earned $92,500 before taxes.

a. Calculate the firm's tax liability using the corporate tax rate schedule given in Table 2.7.

b. How much is Tantor Supply's 2008 after-tax income?

BASIC LG5 **2–34 Calculating taxes** Using the corporate tax rate schedule given in Table 2.7, calculate the total taxes and after-tax earnings for the following levels of corporate earnings before taxes: $10,000; $80,000; $300,000; $500,000; $1.5 million; and $10 million. Assume the company is a non-manufacturing CCPC based in Ontario.

BASIC LG5 **2–35 Calculating taxes** For the year ended December 31, 2008, Cavendish Enterprises had taxable income of $465,000. The company is a Canadian-controlled private corporation. Calculate the taxes payable and NIAT under each of the following scenarios:

a. The company manufactures windows and is based in British Columbia.

b. The company is a tourism operator in Prince Edward Island.

BASIC  **2–36 Calculating taxes** For the year ended August 31, 2008, Collins Corporation had taxable income of $1,238,000. The company is a publicly traded corporation. Calculate the taxes payable and NIAT under each of the following scenarios:

a. The company is an oil and gas producer in Saskatchewan.

b. The company is a dry goods wholesaler in New Brunswick.

LG3  INTERMEDIATE **2–37 Calculating taxes** The bookkeeper for Wabush Inc., a Canadian-controlled private corporation, compiled the following information for the 2008 fiscal year. Sales were $3,200,000, while expenses totalled $2,500,000. Wabush received $120,000 in dividends from taxable Canadian corporations. The company also earned a capital gain on investments in the common shares of other companies of $148,600. Using this information and the tax rates provided in Table 2.7, calculate Wabush Inc.'s total taxes payable, NIAT, and average tax rate under the following conditions.

a. The company is a manufacturing corporation in Ontario.

b. The company is a non-manufacturing corporation in Newfoundland.

c. The company is not a CCPC in both parts **a** and **b**.

INTERMEDIATE  2–38 **Interest versus dividend expense** Michaels Corporation expects earnings before interest and taxes to be $40,000 for the coming year. Assuming a tax rate of 38 percent, compute the firm's earnings after taxes and earnings available for common shareholders under the following conditions:

a. The firm pays $10,000 in interest.
b. The firm pays $10,000 in preferred share dividends.
c. Explain why there is a difference in the answers, given that the amount paid is the same in the two cases.

BASIC  2–39 **Cash flow** A firm had net income after taxes of $50,000 in 2008. Amortization expenses of $30,000 were incurred. What was the firm's net *cash flow from operations* during 2008?

BASIC  2–40 **Tax deductibility of expenses** AX Company's salary expense for the current fiscal year was $475,000. AX's tax rate is 44.1 percent. What was the actual, after-tax cost of the salary expense to AX Company for the fiscal year?

BASIC  2–41 **Tax deductibility of expenses** Laytin Lumber recently finished replanting 5,000 acres of forest land at a cost of $3,675,000. Laytin's tax rate is 38.6 percent.

a. What is the percentage and dollar-tax break associated with the total cost of replanting?
b. What was the actual, after-tax cost of the replanting to Laytin?

   INTERMEDIATE 2–42 **Amortization, cash flow, and taxes** A firm is in the third year of ownership of its only asset, which originally cost $180,000. Amortization has not yet been claimed for the third year. The asset has a ten-year expected life and the firm is amortizing the asset using the straight-line method. The CCA rate on the asset is 30 percent.The following data is relative to the current year's operations.

Accruals	$ 15,000
Current assets	120,000
Interest expense	15,000
Sales revenue	400,000
Inventory	70,000
Total costs before amortization, interest, and taxes	290,000
Tax rate	18.1%

a. Use the *relevant data* to determine the *cash flow from operations* for the current year.
b. Explain the impact that amortization, as well as any other non-cash charges, has on a firm's cash flows.
c. Calculate the company's free cash flow from operations for the year.
d. Calculate the company's taxable income for tax purposes for the year.
e. If the company were a CCPC located in British Columbia, calculate the taxes owing for tax purposes.

BASIC  2–43 **Calculate taxes** XYZ Corp. purchased an asset for $1.3 million on January 11, 2008. It was added to a pool of assets that on January 11, 2008, had an UCC of $3 million. The firm's taxable income as of December 31, 2008, before the deduction of CCA, was $2.2 million. The CCA rate applicable to this pool of assets is 30 percent. If the firm is a CCPC operating in Quebec and is a manufacturer, and the asset is eligible for a 10 percent investment tax credit, calculate the company's total corporate tax payable.

INTERMEDIATE  2–44 **Impact of asset sales** Lethbridge Electricals Ltd., located in Hamilton, Ontario, acquired a piece of equipment on July 1, 2008, for $100,000. The equipment, a Class 8 asset, was the only asset in its class on the company's books. The maximum CCA rate permitted for Class 8 is 20 percent.

a. Calculate the maximum amount of CCA that the company could claim for Class 8 for 2008 and 2009.

b. Suppose the company sells the equipment on December 29, 2010 and no other assets are in Class 8. What will be the result in each of the following cases?

i. Proceeds of sale = $ 60,000
ii. Proceeds of sale = $ 95,000
iii. Proceeds of sale = $120,000

INTERMEDIATE  2–45 **Calculate taxes** The Laiken Company Ltd. acquired manufacturing equipment in 2008 for $140,000. The equipment, a Class 8 asset, is to be used in the company's plant located in Antigonish, Nova Scotia, and is eligible for an investment tax credit of 10 percent. Prior to 2008, the company did not own any Class 8 assets. The CCA rate applicable to the class is 20 percent. The company's federal tax payable for 2008, before the purchase of the manufacturing equipment, was $17,000.

a. Calculate the maximum possible tax savings that were available to the company for 2008 as a result of the purchase of the manufacturing equipment. Assume that the company claims the maximum CCA charges permitted each year and is not a CCPC but is considered a manufacturer.

b. If the company's net income for the year, before the purchase of the equipment, was $427,000, calculate the tax savings possible. Now assume the company is a manufacturer and a CCPC.

BASIC  2–46 **Calculate taxes** In January 2008, Varity Company purchased a special-purpose machine for $30,000. The machine was a Class 43 asset with a CCA rate of 30 percent. Assume that this is the only asset in the class and no replacement is contemplated. On March 30, 2011, the machine is sold. Varity's tax rate is 22 percent.

a. If the sale price is $35,000, what is the tax implication of the asset sale?

b. If the sale price is $5,000, what is the tax implication of the asset sale?

  LG5 CHALLENGE 2-47 **Capital gains and taxes** For the 2008 fiscal year, Logan Company, a non-manufacturing CCPC located in Alberta, had sales of $2.2 million. During the year, Logan Company spent $250,000 on the purchase of a new Class 43 machine that has a CCA rate of 30 percent. Upon the acquisition of the new machine, the company sold their old Class 43 machine for $125,000 less selling expenses of $2,500. The company originally paid $80,000 for the old machine in 2000. This is the only asset class the company owns. During the year, Logan

Company received $35,000 of common share dividends from a taxable Canadian corporation. In 2008, the company's earnings before taxes before the Class 43 transactions was $456,000. This included an amortization expense of $41,000. The company's policy is to amortize the Class 43 assets on a straight-line basis assuming a life of 20 years.

a. Was there a capital gain associated with the sale of the machinery? If so, what is the taxable amount?
b. Calculate Logan Company's taxable income.
c. Using the tax rates provided in Table 2.7, determine the total taxes.
d. What is Logan Company's net income after tax for 2008?

CHALLENGE

2-48 **Comprehensive tax problem** Murray Corp. operates in Saint John, New Brunswick. The company has provided you with the following information relating to the 2008 tax year. Murray owns two classes of assets: Class 3 with a CCA rate of 5 percent and Class 10 with a CCA rate of 30 percent. For the Class 3 assets, the following information is available:

The UCC on January 1, 2008, was $65,000.
On March 30, the company purchased an asset costing $20,000.
On December 5, it sold an asset that had cost $93,000 for $127,000.

For the Class 10 assets, the following information is available:

The UCC on January 1, 2008, was $280,000.
On June 25, the company sold an asset that had cost $48,000 for $75,000.
On October 15, it bought an asset for $92,000.

Other information is the following:

Sales for the 2008 tax year were $1,260,000 while all operating expenses were $820,000. Of this total, $84,500 was amortization. The company is a Canadian-controlled private manufacturing corporation that is eligible for a 10 percent ITC on the assets purchased. They paid dividends of $80,000 while their interest expense was $109,100. Murray Corp. received dividends of $375,000, and this amount was not included in sales. $280,000 of the dividends were from a taxable Canadian company.

a. Calculate the company's taxable income, total taxes payable, and net income after tax for the tax year ended December 31, 2008. Assume the tax rates provided in Table 2.7 apply.

CHALLENGE

2-49 **Understanding financial statements and cash flows** Darrin Cline, formerly an internationally renowned professional bicycle racer, owns and operates Cline Custom Bicycles—a firm that builds and markets custom bicycles to shops throughout Canada and the western United States. Darrin has just received his firm's 2008 income statement and balance sheet. These statements are provided below. Also included is the balance sheet for the 2007 fiscal year. Although he is quite pleased to have achieved record earnings of $106,000 in 2008, Darrin is concerned about the firm's cash flows. Specifically, he is finding it more and more difficult to pay the firm's bills in a timely manner. To gain insight into the firm's cash flow problems, Darrin is planning to have the firm's 2008 statement of cash flows prepared and evaluated.

Income Statement
Cline Custom Bicycles
for the year ended March 31, 2008 (in $000)

Sales revenue		$2,200
Less: Cost of goods sold		1,420
Gross margin		$ 780
Less: Operating expenses		
Selling expense	$300	
General and administrative expense	270	
Amortization expenses	30	
Total operating expense		600
Operating earnings (EBIT)		$ 180
Less: Interest expense		29
Earnings before taxes		$ 151
Less: Taxes (30%)		45
Net income after taxes		$ 106

Balance Sheets
Cline Custom Bicycles (in $000)

	March 31	
Assets	2007	2008
Current assets		
Cash	$ 50	$ 30
Marketable securities	20	10
Accounts receivable	350	320
Inventories	320	460
Total current assets	$ 740	$ 820
Gross fixed assets	$ 520	$ 560
Less: Accumulated amortization	150	180
Net fixed assets	$ 370	$ 380
Total assets	$1,110	$1,200
Liabilities and shareholders' equity		
Current liabilities		
Accounts payable	$ 320	$ 390
Line of credit	90	110
Accruals	20	20
Total current liabilities	$ 430	$ 520
Long-term debt	$ 350	$ 320
Total liabilities	$ 780	$ 840
Shareholders' equity		
Common shares	$ 250	$ 250
Retained earnings	80	110
Total shareholders' equity	$ 330	$ 360
Total liabilities and shareholders' equity	$1,110	$1,200

a. Use the financial data presented to prepare Cline's statement of retained earnings for the fiscal year ended March 31, 2008.
b. Use the financial data presented to prepare Cline Custom Bicycles' statement of cash flows for the fiscal year ended March 31, 2008.
c. Evaluate the statement prepared in **b** in light of Cline's current cash flow difficulties.
d. Calculate Cline's free cash flow for 2008.
e. On the basis of the analysis completed above, what recommendations might you offer Darrin Cline?

CASE CHAPTER 2 Analyzing Sample Company

See the enclosed Student CD-ROM for cases that help you put theories and concepts from the text into practice.

Be sure to visit the Companion Website for this book at **www.pearsoned.ca/gitman** for a wealth of additional learning tools including self-test quizzes, Web exercises, and additional cases.

CHAPTER 3

Financial Statement Analysis

LEARNING GOALS

LG1 Introduce the parties interested in completing a financial ratio analysis, the three types of ratio comparisons, and the four categories of ratios.

LG2 Analyze a company's liquidity,a measure of a company's ability to pay its short-term debt as it comes due.

LG3 Analyze a company's activity ratios, a measure of a company's effectiveness at managing accounts receivable, inventory, accounts payable, fixed assets, and total assets. Also, explore the link between the liquidity and activity ratios.

LG4 Discuss financial leverage and the ratios used to assess how the firm has financed assets, and the company's ability to cover the financing charges associated with the financing used.

LG5 Evaluate a company's profitability using common-size analysis and relative to the company's sales, total assets, common equity, and common share price. Also, introduce the DuPont model and explore the link between the leverage and profitability ratios.

LG6 Fully discuss the three types of ratio comparisons, illustrate how a complete ratio analysis of a company should be performed, and consider some cautions concerning ratio analysis.

3.1 Using Financial Ratios

In the preceding chapter, we reviewed the firm's four basic financial statements. The information contained in these statements is of major significance to various interested parties who regularly need to have relative measures of the company's operating efficiency. *Relative* is the key word here, because the analysis of financial statements is based on the knowledge and use of *ratios* or *relative values.*

Apples, Oranges, and Grapefruit!

You've been told many times that you can't compare apples and oranges. Does that adage mean you can't compare the financial performance of different companies? The answer depends on how you define apples and oranges. Look at the financial statements of two companies. The differences in figures can be staggering—one is an apple, one is an orange. Comparisons at this level are very difficult, if not impossible. To compare two companies, you must convert the raw numbers from the financial statements into comparable data—make the orange and apple a grapefruit! You can compare individual financial items for two companies, say the amount of debt, even though the two amounts are vastly different. The way to do it is to convert the apple and orange into a grapefruit by dividing each company's total debt by the total assets. This chapter will show you how to transform apples and oranges into grapefruit: how to use financial ratios to compare the financial performance of different firms at a point in time, and over time.

ratio analysis
Involves the methods of calculating and interpreting financial ratios to assess the firm's performance.

Ratio analysis involves methods of calculating and interpreting financial ratios to assess the firm's performance. A ratio is simply a numerator divided by a denominator, with the resulting calculation being a ratio of one of three types: (1) a percent (e.g., 19.6%); (2) a multiplier (e.g., 1.96 ×); or (3) a number of days (e.g., 19.6 days). You must understand the ratio to know the unit of the answer. You do not want to calculate a ratio of 0.8573 and convert it to a percent when it is supposed to be a multiplier. The basic inputs to ratio analysis are the firm's

LINKING THE DISCIPLINES: Cross-Functional Interactions

- *Accounting personnel* need to know how to calculate and interpret financial ratios and the role the ratios play in decision making.
- *Information systems analysts* need to understand the calculation of financial ratios to design a system that quickly and easily collects and communicates the necessary data to decision makers.
- *Management* needs to understand how financial ratios are involved in decision making. They must also be aware of the caution that should be exercised when using ratio analysis for decision making. Management is particularly concerned with the stock market reaction to leverage and profitability ratios, as these have a major influence on how investors value a firm.
- The ***marketing department*** is particularly concerned with activity and profitability ratios. They need to understand how analysis of ratios, especially those involving sales, will affect the firm's decisions about levels of inventory, credit policies, and pricing decisions.
- Personnel in the ***operations department*** need to understand how an analysis of ratios, particularly those involving assets, cost of goods sold, inventory, and leverage, may affect requests for new equipment or facilities.

income statement and balance sheet. The statement of cash flows is not used in a ratio analysis since it is an analytical statement based on the balance sheet and income statement. Before we look at those inputs, though, we need to consider why a ratio analysis is completed, describe the parties interested in financial ratios, explain the general types of ratio comparisons, and introduce the four categories of ratios.

Why Complete a Ratio Analysis?

There are three reasons for completing a ratio analysis. First, as was discussed in Chapter 1, one of the tasks of financial managers is planning. To plan, you must be familiar with the company's current financial position, know the company's strengths and weaknesses. A ratio analysis provides this detail. Second, the financial statement provides raw data that is difficult to analyze. A ratio analysis puts the raw numbers in perspective. Consider four years of income statements and balance sheets for a single company. Trying to determine what happened, what improved, what got worse, over these four years would be very difficult if all we could do was try to compare the raw numbers. It would be much easier to look at a sequence of ratios by category than to look at all of the numbers on the underlying financial statements. When analyzing the ratios, however, it is often useful to refer to individual accounts on the statements.

Third, from management's perspective, a ratio analysis is important in order to be able to anticipate the reaction of potential creditors and investors to a request for funds. Management must be able to anticipate the reaction of both creditors and shareholders to the most recent financial results and be able to explain the company's performance. A ratio analysis can provide the answers.

Interested Parties

Hint
Management should be the most interested party of this group. They not only have to worry about the financial situation of the firm, but they are also critically interested in what these other interest groups think about the firm.

Ratio analysis of a firm's financial statements is of interest to shareholders, creditors, and the firm's own management. Both present and prospective shareholders are interested in the firm's current and future level of risk and return, which directly affect share price. The firm's current and prospective creditors are primarily interested in the liquidity of the company, the current amount of debt, and the firm's ability to make interest and principal payments. A secondary concern of creditors is the firm's profitability; they want assurance that the business is healthy and will continue to be successful.

Management, like shareholders, is concerned with all aspects of the firm's financial situation. Thus, it attempts to produce financial results that will be considered favourable by both owners and creditors. In addition, management uses ratios to monitor the firm's performance from period to period. Any unexpected changes are examined, to isolate developing problems. Note, however, that the ratio analyses completed in this book are not for real companies. The book provides very little information about the sample companies. In reality, much more will be known about the situation than the information provided in even detailed textbook problems. The more that is known about the company, the more detailed and useful the ratio analysis.

Ratio Comparisons

Ratio analysis is not merely the application of a formula to financial data to calculate a given ratio. More important is the *interpretation* of the ratio value. To answer such questions as, Is it too high or too low? Is it good or bad?, a meaningful basis for comparison is needed. Three types of ratio comparisons can be made: cross-sectional, time-series, or a combination of the two.

For a cross-sectional ratio analysis, we compare one company's ratios to another company's or group of companies' ratios. To be valid, the ratios must be calculated for the same time period—the same year or quarter. For example, if we had the ratios for X Corporation for the 2008 fiscal year, we could compare them to the industry average ratios also for the 2008 fiscal year.

Time-series analysis evaluates performance over time. Comparing ratios for the most recent fiscal year to the previous three fiscal years allows the firm to determine whether it is progressing as planned. Such an analysis allows the company to evaluate what is happening with the company's financial performance over time. Developing trends can be seen by using multiyear comparisons, and knowledge of these trends can assist the firm in planning future operations.

Arguably, the most informative approach to ratio analysis is one that combines cross-sectional and time-series analyses. A combined view means the firm can evaluate its performance over time as well as assess its performance against the industry average. The industry average data could be only for the most recent year, or for each year company data is available. The three types of ratio comparisons are discussed in much more detail later in this chapter.

Categories of Financial Ratios

Financial ratios are grouped into four basic categories: liquidity ratios, activity ratios, leverage ratios, and profitability ratios. Liquidity, activity, and leverage ratios primarily measure risk; profitability ratios measure return. Both the short-

and the long-term survival of the firm are dependent on all four categories of ratios. One or two of the categories of ratios can be poorer than industry averages for a short period of time, but for the company to survive and prosper and for the company to meet the goal of maximizing shareholder wealth, none of the categories can consistently be below average.

As a rule, the necessary inputs required to complete an effective financial analysis include, at minimum, the income statement and the balance sheet. We will use these statements for Bartlett Company for the fiscal years ended December 31, 2007 and 2008 to illustrate ratio analysis. Bartlett is a manufacturer of patio furniture located in the Ottawa area. The company sells their products throughout Canada. The income statements and balance sheets are provided in Tables 3.1 and 3.2. The ratios presented in the remainder of this chapter can be applied to nearly any company. Of course, many companies in different industries use ratios that are particularly focused on aspects peculiar to their industry. In addition, there are many variations of these ratios and, in other sources you may read, you may see a different formula provided for the same ratio. This is not unusual; the writer discussing the ratio might wish to focus on a slightly different aspect of the firm's financial position.

TABLE 3.1 Bartlett Company Income Statements ($000)

	December 31	
	2007	**2008**
Sales revenue (all on credit)	$2,567	$3,074
Less: Cost of goods sold[a]	1,711	2,088
Gross margin	$ 856	$ 986
Less: Operating expenses		
Selling expense	$ 108	$ 100
General and administrative expenses	187	194
Lease expense	35	35
Amortization expense	223	239
Total operating expense	$ 553	$ 568
Operating earnings (EBIT)	$ 303	$ 418
Less: Interest expense	91	93
Earnings before taxes (EBT)	$ 212	$ 325
Less: Taxes	64	94
Net income after taxes (NIAT)	$ 148	$ 231
Less: Preferred share dividends	10	10
Earnings available for common shareholders	$ 138	$ 221
Earnings per share (EPS)[b]	$ 1.81	$ 2.88

[a]Credit purchases are 68% and 70% of cost of goods sold in 2007 and 2008, respectively.

[b]Calculated by dividing the earnings available for common shareholders by the number of shares of common shares outstanding.

TABLE 3.2 Bartlett Company Balance Sheets ($000)

	December 31	
Assets	**2007**	**2008**
Current assets		
Cash	$ 288	$ 363
Marketable securities	51	68
Accounts receivable	365	503
Inventories	300	289
Total current assets	$1,004	$1,223
Gross fixed assets (at cost)		
Land and buildings	$1,903	$2,072
Machinery and equipment	1,693	1,866
Furniture and fixtures	316	358
Vehicles	314	275
Other (includes financial leases)[a]	96	98
Total gross fixed assets (at cost)	$4,322	$4,669
Less: Accumulated amortization	2,056	2,295
Net fixed assets	$2,266	$2,374
Total assets	$3,270	$3,597
Liabilities and shareholders' equity		
Current liabilities		
Accounts payable	$ 270	$ 382
Accruals	114	159
Line of credit	99	79
Total current liabilities	$ 483	$ 620
Long-term debt (includes financial leases)[b]	$ 967	$1,023
Total liabilities	$1,450	$1,643
Shareholders' equity		
Preferred shares[c]	$ 200	$ 200
Common shares[d]	608	619
Retained earnings	1,012	1,135
Total shareholders' equity	$1,820	$1,954
Total liabilities and shareholders' equity	$3,270	$3,597

[a]The firm has a 6-year financial lease requiring annual beginning-of-year payments of $35,000. Four years of the lease still remain.

[b]Annual principal repayments on a portion of the firm's total outstanding debt amount to $71,000.

[c]The firm had 2,000 preferred shares outstanding in both years. The preferred shares have a $100 stated value and a 5% dividend, or $5.00 per share.

[d]The firm had 76,244 and 76,744 common shares outstanding in 2007 and 2008, respectively.

? Review Questions

3–1 Why should a ratio analysis be completed? For a ratio analysis of a firm, how do the viewpoints held by the firm's present and prospective shareholders, creditors, and management differ? How can these viewpoints be related to the firm's fund-raising ability?

3–2 What types of ratio comparisons can be completed by an analyst? What type of ratio comparison would be more common for internal analysis?

3.2 Analyzing Liquidity

liquidity
A firm's ability to satisfy its short-term obligations ***as they come due.***

The **liquidity** of a business firm is measured by its ability to satisfy its short-term obligations *as they come due*. Liquidity refers to the solvency of the firm's *overall* financial position—the ease with which it can pay its bills. Note that at the end of the 2008 fiscal year, Bartlett has current liabilities of $620,000 (see Table 3.2). The firm must repay this amount over the upcoming two months or, in the case of the line of credit, on demand. Liquidity ratios consider the firm's ability to repay these current liabilities within a short time period. It also recognizes that the funds required to make the payments will come from current assets: cash, receivables that are collected, and/or inventory that is sold and eventually converted to cash. The three basic measures of liquidity are (1) net working capital, (2) the current ratio, and (3) the quick (acid-test) ratio.

Net Working Capital

net working capital
A measure of liquidity calculated by subtracting current liabilities from current assets.

Net working capital, although not actually a ratio, is a common measure of a firm's overall liquidity. It is calculated as follows:

$$\text{Net working capital} = \text{current assets} - \text{current liabilities} \quad (3.1)$$

The net working capital for Bartlett Company in 2008 is:

$$\text{Net working capital} = \$1{,}223{,}000 - \$620{,}000 = \$603{,}000$$

This figure is *not* useful for comparing the performance of different firms, but it is quite useful for internal control.[1] Often the contract under which a long-term debt is incurred specifically states a minimum level of net working capital that the firm must maintain. This requirement protects creditors by forcing the firm to maintain sufficient operating liquidity. A time-series comparison of the firm's net working capital is often helpful in evaluating its operations.

Current Ratio

current ratio
A measure of liquidity calculated by dividing the firm's current assets by its current liabilities.

The **current ratio,** one of the most commonly cited financial ratios, measures the firm's ability to meet its short-term obligations. It is expressed as follows:

$$\text{Current ratio} = \frac{\text{current assets}}{\text{current liabilities}} \quad (3.2)$$

The current ratio for Bartlett Company in 2008 is:[2]

$$\frac{\$1{,}223{,}000}{\$620{,}000} = 1.97$$

1. To further analyze liquidity, some analysts calculate *net working capital as a percent of sales*. For Bartlett Company in 2008, this ratio would be 19.6 percent ($603,000 ÷ $3,074,000). In general, the larger this value, the greater the firm's liquidity, and the smaller this value, the lesser the firm's liquidity. Because of the relative nature of this measure, it is often used to make liquidity comparisons.

2. For the calculation of ratios, we will be using financial data as of the end of the fiscal year. In practice, average data are sometimes used. The average is calculated by dividing the sum of the beginning-of-year and end-of-year account balances by 2. Users of this approach feel that the resulting average ratio better reflects the firm's financial position.

The current ratio indicates the dollar amount of current assets the firm has for every dollar of current liabilities. The rule of thumb is 2. This means that for every dollar of current liabilities, the firm has $2 of current assets. Bartlett's current ratio meets the rule of thumb almost exactly. The evaluation of a ratio, however, depends on the industry in which the firm operates. For example, a current ratio of 1.0 would be considered acceptable for a utility but might be unacceptable for a manufacturing firm. The more predictable a firm's cash flows, the lower the acceptable current ratio. If Bartlett Company had a relatively predictable annual cash flow, its current ratio of 1.97 would be quite acceptable.

The current ratio can also be used to determine the percentage by which the firm's current assets might shrink, but still allow the firm to repay their current liabilities. This is calculated as follows where CR is the current ratio:[3]

$$\text{Percentage shrink} = \left[1 - \frac{1}{\text{CR}}\right] \times 100 \qquad (3.3)$$

For example, a current ratio of 1.85 means that the firm can still cover its current liabilities even if its current assets shrink by 45.9 percent ([1.0 − (1.0 ÷ 1.85)] × 100). This assumes that the firm will be able to convert all of their current assets to cash on a dollar-for-dollar basis within a reasonable time period.

It is useful to note that whenever a firm's current ratio is 1.0, net working capital is zero. If a firm has a current ratio of less than 1.0, it will have negative net working capital. Net working capital is useful only in comparing the liquidity of the same firm over time. It should not be used to compare the liquidity of different firms; the current ratio should be used instead.

Quick (Acid-Test) Ratio

quick (acid-test) ratio
A measure of liquidity calculated by dividing the firm's current assets minus inventory by current liabilities.

The **quick (acid-test) ratio** is similar to the current ratio except that it includes only the most liquid current assets: cash, marketable securities, and accounts receivable. Illiquid current assets such as inventory, prepaid expenses, and others are excluded. The generally low liquidity of inventory results from two primary factors. First, many types of inventory cannot be easily sold because they are partially completed items, special-purpose items, and the like. Second, inventory is typically sold on credit, which means that it becomes an account receivable before being converted into cash. Inventory is two steps away from cash. The quick ratio acknowledges that the cash required to repay current liabilities will come from the most liquid current assets. The quick ratio considers whether Bartlett can repay the $620,000 of current liabilities over the upcoming two months with the most liquid current assets. The quick ratio is calculated as follows:[4]

$$\text{Quick ratio} = \frac{\text{cash + marketable securities + accounts receivable}}{\text{current liabilities}} \qquad (3.4)$$

3. This transformation actually results in the ratio of net working capital to current assets. Clearly, current assets can shrink by the amount of net working capital (i.e., their excess over current liabilities) while still retaining adequate current assets to just meet current liabilities.

4. Sometimes the quick ratio is defined as (current assets − inventory) ÷ current liabilities. If a firm were to show as current assets items other than cash, marketable securities, accounts receivable, and inventories, its quick ratio would vary, depending on the method of calculation.

The quick ratio for Bartlett Company in 2008 is:

$$\frac{\$363{,}000 + \$68{,}000 + \$503{,}000}{\$620{,}000} = \frac{\$934{,}000}{\$620{,}000} = 1.51$$

This means that for every dollar of current liabilities, Bartlett has $1.51 of liquid current assets. This seems reasonable considering that the rule of thumb for the quick ratio is 1, meaning that for every dollar of current liabilities, the firm has $1 of the most liquid current assets. But, as with the current ratio, an acceptable value depends largely on the industry. The quick ratio provides a better measure of overall liquidity only when a firm's inventory cannot be easily converted into cash. If inventory is liquid, the current ratio is a preferred measure of overall liquidity. The inventory for a food retailer like, for example, Tim Hortons would be very liquid. For such companies, the current and quick ratios would give almost identical results.

Note that for all three liquidity measures—net working capital, current ratio, and quick (acid-test) ratio—the higher their value, the more liquid the firm is typically considered to be. As will be explained in Chapter 14, high liquidity presents a risk–return tradeoff for the firm. It reduces a firm's risk, since its ability to satisfy short-term obligations *as they come due* is high. But it sacrifices profitability because (1) current assets are less profitable than fixed assets and (2) current liabilities are a less expensive financing source than long-term funds. For now, suffice it to say that there is a cost of increased liquidity—a trade-off exists between profitability and liquidity (risk).

? Review Questions

3–3 What do liquidity ratios measure? Define the three liquidity ratios. What are their formulas? In what units are the output of the calculation? What do the answers mean?

3–4 Why is net working capital useful only in time-series comparisons of overall liquidity, whereas the current and quick ratios can be used for both cross-sectional and time-series analysis?

3.3 Analyzing Activity

activity ratios
Measure the company's effectiveness at managing accounts receivable, inventory, accounts payable, fixed assets, and total assets.

While the liquidity ratios consider the overall level of current assets and liabilities, the actual mix between the accounts can significantly affect the firm's "true" liquidity. **Activity ratios** measure the company's effectiveness at managing accounts receivable, inventory, accounts payable, fixed assets, and total assets. Activity ratios should be considered as a way to further analyze a company's liquidity. A company may have what is considered to be a good current ratio, which may suggest adequate liquidity. But there may be major problems with individual current assets or liabilities that will not be obvious when liquidity ratios are considered in isolation. Activity ratios are a way to uncover problems with individual current accounts. For example, consider the current assets and liabilities on the balance sheets for Firms A and B below:

Firm A			
Cash	$ 0	Accounts payable	$ 0
Marketable securities	0	Line of credit	10,000
Accounts receivable	0	Accruals	0
Inventories	20,000	Total current liabilities	$10,000
Total current assets	$20,000		

Firm B			
Cash	$ 5,000	Accounts payable	$ 5,000
Marketable securities	5,000	Line of credit	3,000
Accounts receivable	5,000	Accruals	2,000
Inventories	5,000	Total current liabilities	$10,000
Total current assets	$20,000		

The firms appear to be equally liquid, because their current ratios are both 2.0 ($20,000 ÷ $10,000). However, a closer look at the differences in the composition of current assets and liabilities suggests that *Firm B is more liquid than Firm A*. This is true for two reasons. First, Firm B has more liquid assets in the form of cash and marketable securities than Firm A, which has only a single, relatively illiquid asset in the form of inventories. Second, Firm B's current liabilities are in general more flexible than the single current liability—line of credit—of Firm A. The quick ratio confirms this. The quick ratio for Firm A is zero, but 1.5 for Firm B. This analysis, though, is still not adequate to uncover problems with individual accounts.

It is important to look beyond measures of overall liquidity to assess the effectiveness of the management of specific current accounts. A number of ratios are available for measuring the activity of the most important current accounts, which include inventory, accounts receivable, and accounts payable.[5] The activity (efficiency of utilization) of both fixed and total assets should also be assessed.

Average Age of Inventory

To calculate the average age of inventory, you can first calculate the inventory turnover ratio as follows:

$$\text{Inventory turnover} = \frac{\text{Cost of Goods Sold (COGS)}}{\text{inventory}} \qquad (3.5)$$

inventory turnover
The average number of times a company turns over (sells) their complete stock of inventory in a year.

The **inventory turnover** ratio indicates the average number of times a company turns over (sells) their complete stock of inventory in a year. Another interpretation is that the ratio reveals the number of times in a year that a company sells an average item of inventory. Clearly, this is not the same average item. Rather, in an ongoing process, a company regularly purchases or manufactures items for sale, and then sells these items. The inventory turnover ratio indicates the

5. Internal users of ratios may calculate the three current account ratios monthly. The management of net working capital is vital for all businesses, but particularly small businesses and businesses involved in the service sector and retailers. Timely analysis of the company's effectiveness at managing these three current accounts is vital.

number of times an average item is sold in a year. The inventory turnover ratio for Bartlett for the 2008 fiscal year is:

$$\text{Inventory turnover} = \frac{\$2,088,000}{\$289,000} = 7.225$$

This means that Bartlett turned over their complete stock of inventory 7.225 times in 2008. Bartlett sold an average item of inventory 7.225 times per year. Which is better, a low or a high inventory turnover? Clearly, a high inventory turnover is better, as it means a company is selling its inventory more quickly. But, if the turnover ratio is extremely high, this might suggest that the company is holding insufficient inventory and that there is a risk of stockouts and lost sales.

The inventory turnover ratio can be used to calculate the average age of inventory. The **average age of inventory** is the period of time, measured in days, that an average item of inventory is held in stock by the company. With the inventory turnover ratio, the average age of inventory can be calculated as follows:

average age of inventory
Measures the effectiveness of the company's management of inventory; it is the average length of time inventory is held by the company.

$$\text{Average age of inventory} = \frac{365}{\text{Inventory turnover}} \quad (3.6)$$

Note that the higher the inventory turnover, the lower the average age of inventory.

Example Companies 1 and 2 are both retailers of general merchandise. The following information is available for company 1 and company 2:

	Company 1	Company 2
Cost of goods sold	$15,975,301	$10,391,963
Inventory	$ 2,301,916	$ 973,942

Using this information, we can calculate the inventory turnover and the average age of inventory ratios for the two companies as follows:

	Company 1	Company 2
Inventory turnover	$= \frac{\$15,975,301}{\$2,301,916}$	$\frac{\$10,391,963}{\$973,942}$
	= 6.94	10.67
Average age of inventory	$= \frac{365}{6.94}$	$\frac{365}{10.67}$
	= 52.6 days	34.2 days

While company 1 is much larger than company 2, company 2 is much more effective at managing their inventory. Company 2 turns over their inventory much faster than 1 and, as a result, Company 2's average age of inventory is much lower. A high turnover leads to a lower average age of inventory and thus lower costs. The efficient management of inventory is vital for all firms, but especially for manufacturers and retailers. For these firms, a high inventory turnover (a low average age of inventory) leads to a lower cost of carrying inventory, and thus higher profits, and a lower risk of product obsolescence, damage, and theft.

It is clear from the above example that the turnover ratio and the average age ratio are inversely related. That is, a high (low) turnover leads to a low (high) average age. Both ratios measure the effectiveness of inventory management; however, the days-based measure is an easier concept to understand. It is also consistent with the other two working-capital-based activity ratios. An alternative approach to calculating a company's average age of inventory is with one ratio, as follows:

$$\text{Average age of inventory} = \frac{\text{inventory}}{\text{daily COGS}} = \frac{\text{inventory}}{\frac{\text{COGS}}{365}} \quad (3.7)$$

This approach can be used to calculate the average age of inventory for companies 1 and 2 as follows:

	Company 1	Company 2
Average age of inventory =	$\frac{\$2,301,916}{\frac{\$15,975,301}{365}}$	$\frac{\$973,942}{\frac{\$10,391,963}{365}}$
=	52.6 days	34.2 days

There are two items to note regarding this ratio. First, to calculate the number of days, two calculations are required, as in the first method shown. Second, the same three variables are used for the two methods. So one method can be easily derived from the other.

Since in the remainder of this chapter and book, the days-based ratios are used to evaluate the management of working capital, the second calculation method will be used. But either method could be used when calculating the average age of the three working capital accounts.

The average age of inventory for Bartlett for the 2008 fiscal year is:

$$\text{Average age of inventory} = \frac{\$289,000}{\frac{\$2,088,000}{365}} = \frac{\$289,000}{\$5,721} = 50.5 \text{ days}$$

Bartlett manufactures the patio furniture and it flows to inventory. In 2008, it took Bartlett 50.5 days to sell an average item of inventory. To analyze this answer, it must be compared to that of other firms in the same industry and to Bartlett's past average age of inventory. It would not be appropriate to compare Bartlett's result to the average age of inventory for grocery stores or airline manufacturers. An average age of inventory of 18 days would be usual for a grocery store, whereas for an airline manufacturer, the average age might be 143 days.

Average Collection Period

The **average collection period,** or average age of accounts receivable, is useful in evaluating credit and collection policies. It is arrived at by dividing the average daily credit sales into the accounts receivable balance:[6]

average collection period
The average amount of time needed to collect accounts receivable.

$$\text{Average collection period} = \frac{\text{accounts receivable}}{\text{average credit sales per day}} = \frac{\text{accounts receivable}}{\frac{\text{annual credit sales}}{365}} \quad (3.8)$$

6. The average collection period is sometimes called the *days' sales outstanding (DSO)*. A discussion of the evaluation and establishment of credit and collection policies is presented in Chapter 14.

If credit sales were not provided, total sales would be used. Also, as with the average age of inventory, the accounts receivable turnover ratio could first be calculated and then this would be used to calculate the average collection period. The average collection period for Bartlett Company in 2008 is:

$$\frac{\$503{,}000}{\frac{\$3{,}074{,}000}{365}} = \frac{\$503{,}000}{\$8{,}422} = 59.7 \text{ days}$$

On average, it takes the firm 59.7 days to collect an account receivable.

The average collection period is meaningful only in relation to the firm's credit terms, industry averages, and past experience. If Bartlett Company extends 30-day credit terms to customers, an average collection period of 59.7 days may indicate a poorly managed credit or collection department, or both. Or the lengthened collection period could be the result of an intentional relaxation of credit-term enforcement in response to competitive pressures. If the firm had extended 60-day credit terms, the 59.7-day average collection period would be a sign of excellent management of receivables. If the industry average was 35.4 days, Bartlett's result may be a sign of a major receivable problem. Or perhaps Bartlett is extending different credit terms or is using the credit policy as a way to differentiate themselves from the competition. Clearly, additional information would be required to draw definitive conclusions about the effectiveness of the firm's credit and collection policies.

It is worthwhile noting that in most industries where credit is granted to customers, the usual credit terms are net 30. That is, the seller grants the buyer a 30-day period in which to pay for the purchase. The seller expects to receive payment 30 days (or less) following the sale. It is common, however, for purchasers to "stretch" the payment period past the allowed credit period. Therefore, for a company which grants credit terms of net 30, it is not unusual to observe an average collection period of 40 or more days.

Average Payment Period

average payment period
The average amount of time needed to pay accounts payable.

The **average payment period,** or average age of accounts payable, is calculated using the same basic procedure as is used for the previous two activity ratios:

$$\text{Average payment period} = \frac{\text{accounts payable}}{\text{average credit purchases per day}} \tag{3.9}$$

$$= \frac{\text{accounts payable}}{\frac{\text{annual credit purchases}}{365}}$$

If credit purchases are not provided, total purchases would be used. However, in many cases where ratios are calculated, information about purchases is not available. While analysts inside the company may have access to purchase data, it is not normally available in published financial statements. In such cases, cost of goods sold would be used for the ratio. Also, as with the previous two ratios, the accounts payable turnover ratio could first be calculated and then this would be used to calculate the average payment period.

As indicated on the income statement (Table 3.1), Bartlett's credit purchases in 2008 were 70 percent of cost of goods sold. As such, the average payment period for Bartlett for 2008 is:

$$\frac{\$382{,}000}{\frac{0.70 \times \$2{,}088{,}000}{365}} = \frac{\$382{,}000}{\$4{,}004} = 95.4 \text{ days}$$

Again, this figure is meaningful only in relation to the average credit terms extended to the firm, industry averages, and past experience. If Bartlett Company's suppliers, on average, have extended 30-day credit terms, an analyst would conclude that Bartlett pays very late. As such the company would have a lower credit rating. If the firm has been extended 90-day credit terms, an analyst would conclude that Bartlett pays on time and would have a favourable credit rating. Prospective lenders and suppliers of trade credit are especially interested in the average payment period, because it provides them with a sense of the bill-paying patterns of the firm. Again, it is not unusual to observe average payment periods that are longer than the credit terms granted by the company to customers. Companies will "stretch" their payables, trying to match their average collection period and thus avoid the need to finance their accounts receivable. This issue is discussed in more detail in Chapters 4 and 14.

Fixed and Total Asset Turnover

fixed asset turnover Indicates the efficiency with which the firm uses its net fixed assets to generate sales.

The **fixed asset turnover** indicates the efficiency with which the firm uses its net fixed assets to generate sales. Generally, the higher a firm's fixed asset turnover, the more efficiently its fixed assets have been used to do what they have been acquired to do—generate sales. This ratio is of greatest interest to companies with a large investment in fixed assets. For retailers and service providers, the fixed asset turnover is less important since, in most cases, the investment in fixed assets is quite modest. Fixed asset turnover is calculated as follows:

$$\text{Fixed asset turnover} = \frac{\text{sales}}{\text{net fixed assets}} \tag{3.10}$$

Bartlett's fixed asset turnover for 2008 is:

$$\frac{\$3{,}074{,}000}{\$2{,}374{,}000} = 1.29$$

The fixed asset turnover indicates the dollar amount of sales generated by each dollar of net fixed assets. Bartlett generates $1.29 of sales for every dollar of net fixed assets. Note that for this ratio, only productive fixed assets are considered. Items like investments in other companies or intangibles are ignored.

total asset turnover Indicates the efficiency with which the firm uses its assets to generate sales.

The **total asset turnover** indicates the efficiency with which the firm uses its total assets to generate sales. It is calculated as follows:

$$\text{Total asset turnover} = \frac{\text{sales}}{\text{total assets}} \tag{3.11}$$

Bartlett Company's total asset turnover in 2008 is:

$$\frac{\$3{,}074{,}000}{\$3{,}597{,}000} = 0.85$$

Therefore, Bartlett generates $0.85 of sales with every dollar of total assets. The total asset turnover measures a company's overall efficiency at doing what it is supposed to do with assets—generate sales. This ratio is used later in the chapter as part of an analysis that measures the return the company generates on the overall investment in the company. As with other ratios, the fixed and total asset turnovers are only meaningful when compared to previous values for the company or to an industry average. Generally, higher values are preferable to lower values, but it is also possible for these ratios to be too high. Very high turnovers, together with declining assets, may suggest a company is not reinvesting in (overextending) their assets. In addition, these ratios can indicate the type of company being analyzed.

A company with a very high fixed asset turnover and low total asset turnover has a low level of fixed assets in relation to current assets. Retailers and service-oriented companies display this pattern. For such companies, the management of current assets is vital. For industrial and resource companies (e.g., steel, oil and gas, aircraft, automotive, utility, telephone, durable goods, and mining), a much larger percentage of assets are fixed and therefore the fixed and total asset turnover ratios will likely be low and in a similar range. Bartlett manufactures patio furniture. A glance at the company's 2008 balance sheet indicates that a large percentage of the company's assets are fixed. Bartlett's fixed and total asset turnovers are low and in a similar range.

Hint

The higher the cost of the new assets, the larger the denominator and therefore the smaller the turnover ratio.

One caution with respect to use of these ratios: they use the *historical costs* of assets. Because some firms have significantly newer or older assets than others, comparing asset turnovers of those firms can be misleading. Because of inflation and the use of historical costs, firms with newer assets will tend to have lower turnovers than those with older assets. The differences in these turnovers could therefore result from more costly assets rather than from differing operating efficiencies. The financial manager should be cautious when using this ratio for cross-sectional comparisons.

In addition, if a ratio analysis is being used as part of the process used to evaluate the purchase of a company, the acquired company's total asset turnover will likely be much higher before the purchase, if the acquired company's assets have low historical costs in relation to current market values. Once the company is purchased, the acquired assets will be valued on the balance sheet closer to their current market values. As a result, the asset turnover ratios will be much lower after the purchase.

? Review Questions

3–5 What do activity ratios measure? Define the five activity ratios. What are their formulas and in what units are their output? What do the answers mean?

3–6 To assess the reasonableness of the firm's average collection period and average payment period ratios, what additional information is needed? Explain.

3–7 A company has a fixed asset turnover of 8.37 and a total asset turnover of 1.53. What does this data suggest? Develop a simple example displaying this concept.

3–8 Develop a simple example illustrating how the fixed and total asset turnovers might decline after a company is purchased, if the acquired company's assets have low historical costs in relation to current market values.

3.4 Analyzing Leverage

Leverage indicates the amount of borrowed money (debt) that has been used to finance the acquisition of the firm's assets. A firm can acquire assets in two ways—debt or equity financing. The leverage ratio focuses on the amount of debt used. In general, the financial analyst is most concerned with long-term debt, since it commits the firm to paying interest, and eventually the principal, over the long run. Because creditors' claims must be satisfied before earnings can be distributed to shareholders, present and prospective shareholders pay close attention to the amount of leverage used by the company and the company's ability to make payments on the debt. Current and prospective creditors are also concerned about the firm's indebtedness, because the more indebted the firm, the more likely it will be unable to satisfy the creditors' claims. Management obviously must be concerned with leverage.

capitalization ratios
Show how a firm has financed the investment in assets. There are three alternatives: debt, preferred equity, and common equity.

coverage ratios
Measure the firm's ability to service the sources of financing.

There are two types of leverage ratios: capitalization and coverage. **Capitalization ratios** show how a firm has financed the investment in assets. Recall that there are three alternatives: debt, preferred equity, and common equity. The greater the use of debt as a percent of total assets, the greater the financial leverage. Later in this chapter, financial leverage is discussed in greater detail. We discuss three capitalization ratios.

Coverage ratios assess the firm's ability to service the sources of financing. This includes making the contractual interest payments and principal repayments on debt, lease payments on financial leases, and dividend payments on preferred shares. These required payments are referred to as fixed financial charges. Typically, higher coverage ratios are preferred, but too high a ratio (above industry norms) may indicate unnecessarily low risk and returns. Alternatively, the lower the firm's coverage ratios, the more risky the firm is considered to be. "Riskiness" here refers to the firm's ability to pay fixed obligations. If a firm is unable to pay these obligations, it will be in default, and its creditors may seek immediate repayment. In most instances this would force a firm into bankruptcy. Two coverage ratios—the times interest earned ratio and the fixed-charge coverage ratio—are discussed in this section.

Debt Ratio

debt ratio
Measures the proportion of total assets financed by the firm's creditors.

The **debt ratio** measures the proportion of total assets financed by the firm's creditors. The higher this ratio, the greater the amount of other people's money being used to acquire assets in an attempt to generate sales and profits. The ratio is calculated as follows:

$$\text{Debt ratio} = \frac{\text{total liabilities}}{\text{total assets}} \tag{3.12}$$

The debt ratio for Bartlett Company in 2008 is

$$\frac{\$1,643,000}{\$3,597,000} = 0.457 = 45.7\%$$

Higher ratios indicate greater reliance on debt financing, meaning higher risk and more financial leverage. For Bartlett, 45.7 percent of the assets have been financed by debt. By reviewing the 2008 balance sheet, the sources of the remaining financing can also be observed. Bartlett has preferred equity and common equity financing. The **preferred equity ratio** shows the proportion of total assets financed by preferred shareholders. For Bartlett for 2008, this ratio is 5.6 percent (\$200,000 ÷ \$3,597,000). The **common equity ratio** shows the percentage of assets financed by common shareholders. The total investment made by common shareholders includes the direct investment made when purchasing the common shares and the indirect investment made by reinvesting profits. For Bartlett for 2008, this totals \$1,754,000, \$619,000 of common shares plus \$1,135,000 of retained earnings, the running total of the profits reinvested to the end of 2008. Therefore, the common equity ratio is 48.8 percent (\$1,754,000 ÷ \$3,597,000). These three ratios display the capital structure of Bartlett and must, by definition, sum to 100 percent (excluding rounding). Companies must carefully monitor their capital structure (capitalization). Debt leads to major financial obligations—the company must make interest and principal payments or else they risk being forced into bankruptcy by creditors. Too much debt can lead to major financial problems. There are literally millions of companies that have gone bankrupt because they used too much debt financing.

preferred equity ratio
Measures the proportion of total assets financed by preferred shareholders.

common equity ratio
Measures the proportion of total assets financed by common shareholders.

Costly Debt Ratio

This ratio focuses on the debt that actually has a financing cost. Since the debt ratio considers all debt, the result can be affected by liabilities such as accounts payable, accruals, deferrals, and amounts due to shareholders. Because these forms of debt have no direct financing cost, the debt ratio can provide a misleading picture of the true debt situation. Since costly debt requires the payment of both interest and principal, it may be a better measure of the use of debt financing. The **costly debt ratio** is calculated as follows:

costly debt ratio
Measures the proportion of total assets financed by costly forms of debt financing.

$$\text{Costly debt ratio} = \frac{\text{costly debt}}{\text{total assets}} \tag{3.13}$$

The costly debt ratio for Bartlett Company in 2008 is:

$$\frac{\$1,102,000}{\$3,597,000} = 0.306 = 30.6\%$$

The costly debt ratio for Bartlett is significantly lower than the debt ratio, since payables and accruals, the two no-cost sources of debt financing, are a significant amount. Note that while the firm must pay these amounts to their creditors, as long as they do so within a reasonable period of time there are no financing costs associated with the use of this debt. They are said to be "free forms of financing." For some firms that have many no-cost liabilities on their balance sheet, this ratio can provide a much clearer picture of their true debt position.

Debt/Equity Ratio

debt/equity ratio
Measures the proportion of long-term debt to common equity.

All companies have two main sources of long-term financing: long-term debt and common equity. The **debt/equity ratio** measures the proportion of long-term debt to common equity—it focuses on the respective uses of each of the long-term sources of financing. Since the debt ratio considers all debt, the result can be affected by large amounts of current liabilities. Since long-term debt requires long-term payment of both interest and principal, it may be a better measure of the use of debt financing. The debt/equity ratio is calculated as follows:

$$\text{Debt/equity ratio} = \frac{\text{long-term debt}}{\text{common equity}} \tag{3.14}$$

The debt/equity ratio for Bartlett Company in 2008 is:

$$\frac{\$1{,}023{,}000}{\$1{,}754{,}000} = 0.583 = 58.3\%$$

For every dollar of common equity financing, Bartlett is using $0.583 of long-term debt. A suggested maximum for the debt/equity ratio is 100 percent, meaning for $1 of common equity financing, the company has $1 of long-term debt. Bartlett is well below this level. But, as with all of the ratios, the result should be compared to the previous years' ratios and to an industry average. How a company chooses to finance assets (capitalization decisions) can differ significantly across the companies in an industry. Some firms use conservative strategies, others aggressive.

The key question regarding the financing used is "Can the firm meet their required financial payments?" This is considered by the two coverage ratios. The coverage ratios link the leverage ratios to the profitability ratios. An analysis of the coverage ratios provide hints regarding the profitability of the company.

Times Interest Earned Ratio

times interest earned ratio
Sometimes called the ***interest coverage ratio,*** it measures the firm's ability to make contractual interest payments.

The **times interest earned ratio,** sometimes called the *interest coverage ratio,* measures the firm's ability to make contractual interest payments. The higher the value of this ratio, the better able the firm is to fulfill its interest obligations. The times interest earned ratio is calculated as follows:

$$\text{Times interest earned} = \frac{\text{earnings before interest and taxes (EBIT)}}{\text{interest}} \tag{3.15}$$

Applying this ratio to Bartlett Company yields the following value for 2008:

$$\text{Times interest earned} = \frac{\$418{,}000}{\$93{,}000} = 4.49$$

Earnings before interest and taxes is the same as *operating earnings.* The times interest earned ratio indicates the dollar amount of earnings available to make interest payments, for every dollar of interest. In 2008, Bartlett has $4.49 of earnings for every dollar of interest. The firm's times interest earned ratio seems acceptable. As a rule, a value of at least 3.0—and preferably closer to 5.0—is suggested. If the firm's earnings before interest and taxes were to shrink by 78 percent [(4.49 − 1.0) ÷ 4.49], the firm would still be able to pay the $93,000 in interest it owes. Thus, it has a good margin of safety. The lowest acceptable times interest earned ratio is 1. A value of 1 indicates the company would have just enough EBIT to cover the required interest payments. In such a case, the company's earnings before taxes would be zero. A times interest earned ratio less than 1 indicates the company is losing money (has negative earnings before taxes) and must raise financing to cover the interest payments.

A higher times interest earned ratio (above the industry average) is preferred, since this indicates that the company's profitability is higher than the industry's. Too high a ratio (well above the industry norms) may indicate the company has very little debt and little risk, but lower returns since the company is not benefiting from financial leverage. If the company's debt ratio is comparable to the industry, but the times interest earned ratio is higher, the company's profitability is well above industry averages. A low times interest earned ratio implies high risk and a questionable ability to service the required payments on debt. If a company is unable to pay these obligations, bankruptcy is a real possibility.

Fixed-Charge Coverage Ratio

fixed-charge coverage ratio
Measures the firm's ability to meet all fixed-payment obligations.

The **fixed-charge coverage ratio** measures the firm's ability to meet all fixed financial payments. Like the times interest earned ratio, the higher this value the better. There are four fixed financial payments: interest on debt, principal repayments on debt, lease payments, and preferred share dividends.[7] The formula for the fixed-charge coverage ratio is as follows:

$$\frac{\text{earnings before interest and taxes} + \text{lease payments}}{\text{interest} + \text{lease payments} + \dfrac{\text{principal payments}}{1 - \text{T}} + \dfrac{\text{preferred share dividends}}{1 - \text{T}}} \qquad (3.16)$$

where T is the corporate tax rate applicable to the firm's income. Principal payments and preferred share dividends must be divided by (1 − T) to adjust for the fact that these payments are made out of after-tax income. Interest and lease payments are deductible for tax purposes, so no adjustment is necessary. To put principal repayments and preferred dividends on a before-tax basis, divide them by (1 − T).

Example J & K Inc. must repay $140,000 of principal on their long-term debt and pay $70,000 of preferred share dividends this year. If J & K's tax rate is 30 percent, what must the firm's earnings before tax be in order to make these required payments? Since the required payments are made out of after-tax income, J & K needs substantially more before-tax income to make the required payments. The amount of before-tax income for the principal requirement is:

$$\frac{\$140{,}000}{1 - 0.30} = \frac{\$140{,}000}{0.70} = \$200{,}000$$

7. Although preferred share dividends, which are stated at the time of issue, can be "passed" (not paid) at the option of the firm's directors, it is generally believed that the payment of such dividends is necessary. *This text therefore treats preferred share dividends as a contractual obligation, to be paid as a fixed amount, as scheduled.*

With \$200,000 of earnings before taxes, J & K will pay \$60,000 of taxes (\$200,000 × 0.30) and will have the necessary \$140,000 of after-tax income to make the principal repayment. For the preferred share dividends, J & K requires \$100,000 of before-tax income (\$70,000 ÷ 0.70). So to make the two required payments, J & K requires \$300,000 of before-tax income.

Applying the formula to Bartlett Company for 2008 yields the following fixed-charge coverage ratio:

$$\frac{\$418{,}000 + \$35{,}000}{\$93{,}000 + \$35{,}000 + \dfrac{\$71{,}000}{1 - 0.29} + \dfrac{\$10{,}000}{1 - 0.29}}$$

$$= \frac{\$453{,}000}{\$93{,}000 + \$35{,}000 + \$100{,}000 + \$14{,}085} = \frac{\$453{,}000}{\$242{,}085} = 1.87$$

Note that the lease payment amount is taken from the income statement, while the principal and preferred share dividend payments are provided in the notes below the balance sheet. The ratio indicates that for every dollar of fixed financial charges, Bartlett has \$1.87 of earnings available to make the payments. Thus, the firm appears able to safely meet its fixed payments.

Like the times interest earned ratio, the fixed-charge coverage ratio measures the risk of the firm being unable to meet scheduled fixed payments and thus be forced into bankruptcy. The lower the ratio, the greater the risk to both lenders and owners, and the greater the ratio, the lower the risk. Higher ratios also imply the company may be more profitable than the industry, on average. This ratio therefore allows owners, creditors, and managers to assess the firm's ability to handle fixed financial obligations.

? Review Questions

3–9 What do leverage ratios measure? What are the two types of leverage ratios? What are the formulas for the various leverage ratios? In what units are the output? What do the answers mean?

3–10 A company has a times interest earned ratio of 28.63, while the industry average is 12.31. Why might the company's ratio be so much higher than the industry average?

LG5

3.5 Analyzing Profitability

There are many measures of profitability. As a group, these measures evaluate the firm's earnings with respect to a given level of sales, a certain level of assets, the owners' investment, or share value. Without profits, a firm could not attract outside capital. Moreover, present owners and creditors would become concerned about the company's future and attempt to recover their funds. Owners, creditors, and management pay close attention to boosting profits due to the great importance placed on earnings in the marketplace.

Common-Size Income Statements

common-size income statement
An income statement in which each item is expressed as a percentage of sales.

A popular tool for evaluating profitability in relation to sales is the **common-size income statement.**[8] On this statement, each item is expressed as a percentage of sales, thus highlighting the relationship between sales and each of the costs, and measures of earnings. Common-size income statements are especially useful in comparing performance across years. Three frequently cited ratios of profitability that can be read directly from the common-size income statement are (1) the gross margin, (2) the operating margin, and (3) the profit margin.

Common-size income statements for 2007 and 2008 for Bartlett Company are presented and evaluated in Table 3.3. The statements reveal that the firm's cost of goods sold increased from 66.7 percent of sales in 2007 to 67.9 percent in 2008, resulting in the gross margin declining. The **gross margin** measures the percent of each sales dollar remaining after the company has paid the direct costs of the products sold (the COGS). The higher the gross margin, the better. The lower the gross margin, the higher the relative cost of the products sold.

gross margin
Measures the percentage of each sales dollar remaining after the firm has paid the direct costs of the products sold (COGS).

Hint
This is a very significant ratio for manufacturers and retailers, especially during times of high inflation. If a company does not raise prices when the cost of the goods sold is rising, the gross margin will decline.

Table 3.3 also reveals that, as a percent of sales, all four operating expenses declined. Overall, operating expenses declined by 3 percent of sales, a very positive trend that more than offsets the increasing COGS as a percent of sales. As a result, the operating margin (EBIT) as a percent of sales increases 1.8 percent, to 13.6 percent. The **operating margin** measures the percent of each sales dollar remaining after all expenses associated with producing and selling the product and operating the company are deducted. Obviously, the higher the operating margin, the better.

operating margin
Measures the percent of each sales dollar remaining after all expenses associated with producing and selling the product and operating the company are deducted.

profit margin
Measures the percentage of each sales dollar remaining after all expenses, including financing expenses and taxes, have been deducted.

The **profit margin** measures the percentage of each sales dollar remaining after all expenses, including financing expenses and taxes, have been deducted. For Bartlett for 2008, interest expenses as a percent of sales declined by 0.5 percent even though the dollar amount of total debt and interest expense increased. Sales increased faster than the interest expense, meaning interest expense as a percent of sales declined. Taxes as a percent of sales increased significantly even though the tax rate itself declined by about 1 percent. Bartlett's earnings before taxes were much higher in 2008 than in 2007, accounting for much higher taxes. On a bottom-line basis, the profit margin as a percent of sales increased 1.7 percent to 7.5 percent, a positive trend. "Good" profit margins vary across industries. For a grocery store, a profit margin of 3 percent would be considered normal (grocery stores make money on volume) while for a jewellery store a profit margin of 12 percent would be low (most jewellery stores make money through high mark-ups but relatively low inventory turnover).

To complete the analysis of profitability, four other measures should also be calculated and added to the end of the common-size income statement. Table 3.3 provides these four measures; the sections below provide details regarding each.

Return on Total Assets (ROA)

return on total assets (ROA)
Measures the firm's overall effectiveness in generating profits with its available assets; also called the ***return on investment (ROI).***

The **return on total assets (ROA)**, also called the *return on investment (ROI)*, measures the firm's overall effectiveness in generating profits with its available

8. This statement is sometimes called a *percent income statement* or a *vertical analysis*. The same treatment is often applied to the firm's balance sheet to make it easier to evaluate changes in the asset and financial structures of the firm. In addition to measuring profitability, these statements in effect can be used as an alternative or supplement to liquidity, activity, and debt-ratio analysis.

TABLE 3.3 Bartlett Company Common-Size Income Statements

	For the years ended December 31		Trend[a]
	2007	2008	2007–2008
Sales revenue	100.0%	100.0%	N/A
Less: Cost of goods sold	66.6	67.9	worse
(1) Gross margin	33.4%	32.1%	worse
Less: Operating expenses			
Selling expense	4.2%	3.3%	better
General and administrative expenses	7.3	6.3	better
Lease expense	1.4	1.1	better
Amortization expense	8.7	7.8	better
Total operating expense	21.6%	18.5%	better
(2) Operating margin (EBIT)	11.8%	13.6%	better
Less: Interest expense	3.5	3.0	better
Earnings before taxes	8.3%	10.6%	better
Less: Taxes	2.5	3.1	worse[b]
(3) Profit margin (NIAT)	5.8%	7.5%	better
(4) Return on assets (ROA)	4.5%	6.4%	better
(5) Return on equity (ROE)	8.5%	12.6%	better
(6) Earnings per share (EPS)	$1.81	$2.88	better
(7) Price/earnings ratio (P/E)	10.0	11.1	better

[a]Simple assessment based on the trends in the percentages.

[b]Taxes as a percent of sales increased noticeably between 2007 and 2008 due to differing costs and expenses, whereas the average tax rates (taxes ÷ earnings before taxes) for 2007 and 2008 remained about the same—30% and 29%, respectively.

assets. The higher the firm's return on total assets, the better. The return on total assets is calculated as follows:

$$\text{Return on total assets} = \frac{\text{net income after taxes}}{\text{total assets}} \tag{3.17}$$

Bartlett Company's return on total assets in 2008 is

$$\frac{\$231{,}000}{\$3{,}597{,}000} = 6.4\%$$

For every $100 of assets, Bartlett generates a return of $6.42. To assess Bartlett's 6.4 percent return on total assets, appropriate cross-sectional and time-series data would be needed.

Return on Equity (ROE)

return on equity (ROE)
Measures the return earned on the owners' investment in the firm.

The **return on equity (ROE)** measures the return earned on the owners' investment in the firm. Generally, the higher this return, the better off are the owners. Return on equity is calculated as follows:

$$\text{Return on equity} = \frac{\text{earnings available for common shareholders (EAC)}}{\text{common equity}} \tag{3.18}$$

For this formula, sometimes you may see net income after tax (NIAT) as the numerator. For companies that have not issued preferred shares, NIAT and EAC will be the same. For companies with preferred shares outstanding, EAC will be less than NIAT, assuming the company has paid preferred share dividends. As well, common equity will be less than the total value of shareholders' equity, as the latter will include the value of the preferred shares issued. For companies that have preferred shares, it is important to adjust the ROE formula to just focus on the common equity components.

This ratio for Bartlett Company for 2008 is:

$$\frac{\$221{,}000}{\$1{,}754{,}000} = 12.6\%$$

Note that Bartlett has preferred shares outstanding and therefore EAC, not NIAT, is used in the formula. As well the value of common equity, not total shareholders' equity is used. For Bartlett, the result indicates that for every $100 of common equity financing, the company generates a return of $12.60 to the owners, the common shareholders. To evaluate Bartlett's 12.6 percent return on equity, appropriate cross-sectional and time-series data would be needed. Note, though, that ROE is always higher than ROA, assuming EAC is positive and the firm is not financed 100 percent by equity. As will be described shortly, this is due to financial leverage.

Earnings per Share (EPS)

Hint
EPS represents the dollar amount earned *on behalf of* each share—not the amount of earnings *actually distributed* to shareholders.

The firm's *earnings per share (EPS)* is generally of interest to present or prospective shareholders and to management. The earnings per share represents the number of dollars earned on each common share outstanding. Earnings per share is calculated as follows:

$$\text{Earnings per share} = \frac{\text{earnings available for common shareholders (EAC)}}{\text{number of common shares outstanding}} \tag{3.19}$$

Bartlett Company's earnings per share in 2008 is:

$$\frac{\$221{,}000}{76{,}744} = \$2.88$$

The earnings generated for the owners are $2.88 per share. This measure is closely watched by investors and is considered an important indicator of corporate success. In practice, companies release their EPS each quarter of the fiscal year, and the market reaction to the figure released can be very positive or negative depending on whether the reported EPS is higher or lower than the amount expected by investors. Major swings in share price can occur around the earnings release.

Price/Earnings (P/E) Ratio

price/earnings (P/E) ratio
Measures the amount investors are willing to pay for each dollar of the firm's earnings; the higher the P/E ratio, the greater the investor confidence.

Though not a true measure of profitability, the **price/earnings (P/E) ratio**, or P/E multiple, is commonly used to assess the owners' appraisal of share value.[9] The P/E ratio measures the amount investors are willing to pay for each dollar of the firm's earnings. This ratio indicates the degree of confidence that investors have in the firm's future performance. The higher the P/E ratio, the greater the investor confidence.[10] The P/E ratio is calculated as follows:

$$\text{Price/earnings (P/E) ratio} = \frac{\text{market price per common share}}{\text{earnings per share}} \tag{3.20}$$

If Bartlett Company's common shares at the end of 2008 were selling for \$33.40, using the *earnings per share (EPS)* of \$2.88 from the previous page, the P/E ratio at year-end 2008 is:

$$\frac{\$33.40}{\$2.88} = 11.60$$

Thus, investors were willing to pay \$11.60 for each \$1 of Bartlett's earnings. The P/E ratio reflects investors' expectations concerning the company's future prospects. Higher P/E ratios reflect investor optimism and confidence in the company. Lower P/E ratios reflect investor pessimism and concern. Companies that are consistently able to grow their cash flow and EPS over time will attract investor interest and have higher P/E ratios.

It is vital that the P/E ratio for a company be compared to the P/E ratios in previous years and to the P/E ratios of other companies in the industry. Only a comparison will indicate how the company is viewed by investors as a whole. For example, if a company's P/E ratio was 22.4 but the P/E ratio for the industry was 14.1, it could be said the investors have a much more positive view of the company than of the average firm in the industry. This more favourable opinion is likely because the company has been able to grow, or is expected to grow, sales, profits, and cash flow faster than the average firm in the industry. Investors are willing to pay more for each dollar of earnings of a more rapidly growing company. But, as soon as expectations concerning growth decline, so too will the share price, and with it the P/E ratio.

The DuPont Model

The DuPont model of financial analysis is named for the E. I. du Pont de Nemours and Co., more commonly known as the DuPont Corporation, where the model was originally developed and used. The model was developed in 1919 by Donaldson Brown, an electrical engineer hired by the giant chemical company in 1914. A few years later DuPont bought 23 percent of General Motors. By that time Brown, having impressed his superiors, had moved into a senior role in the finance department of DuPont. Brown was given the task of cleaning up GM's

9. Use of the price/earnings ratio to estimate the value of the firm is part of the discussion of "Other approaches to common share valuation" in Chapter 8.

10. Another popular measure of investor confidence is the *market/book (M/B) ratio*, calculated by dividing the current common shares price per share by the per share book (accounting) value of shareholders' equity. The M/B ratio reflects the level of return on equity and the degree of investor confidence. Typically, relatively high M/B ratios are associated with good equity returns and investor optimism. Relatively low M/B ratios are associated with generally poor equity returns and investor pessimism. This ratio is of greatest interest to investors.

tangled finances. This was perhaps the first large-scale financial reengineering job in the world. According to Alfred Sloan, GM's most successful CEO, much of the credit for GM's dominance of the auto industry through to the 1980s was due to the planning and control models and systems developed by Brown. One of these models was the DuPont model. From that time, the model became widely used in the analysis of a company's financial position.

DuPont model
A method used to analyze the key measure of profitability from a shareholder's perspective: return on equity (ROE). It is based on profit margin, total asset turnover, and the financial leverage multiplier.

The **DuPont model** is a very important and widely used method to analyze the sources of a company's profits, more specifically, the key measure of profitability from a shareholder's perspective: return on equity (ROE). While ROE can be calculated as shown earlier, to truly analyze and understand why a company's ROE changes over time or is different from an industry average, the DuPont model must be used. As shown in Figure 3.1, the model integrates information from the income statement and the balance sheet, and helps visualize the critical building blocks that determine the company's ROE. As illustrated, a company's ROE is based on three variables:

1. Profit margin, which measures the company's efficiency of cost control and profit generation
2. Total asset turnover, which measures the company's efficiency at using assets to generate sales
3. The financial leverage multiplier, which measures the amount of leverage the company employs

These three variables are combined in a formula to calculate ROE as follows:[11]

$$\text{ROE} = \frac{\text{EAC (NIAT)}}{\text{Sales}} \times \frac{\text{Sales}}{\text{Total Assets}} \times \frac{\text{Total assets}}{\text{Common equity}} \tag{3.21}$$

$$\text{ROE} = \text{profit margin} \times \text{total asset turnover} \times \text{FLM}$$

As shown below, the three ratios are important measures of company performance and this further illustrates the importance of using the DuPont model when analyzing ROE:

$$\text{ROE} = \begin{matrix}\text{Measures cost control} \\ \text{efficiency}\end{matrix} \times \begin{matrix}\text{Measures efficiency in using} \\ \text{assets to generate sales}\end{matrix} \times \begin{matrix}\text{Measures the use of debt} \\ \text{financing}\end{matrix}$$

It is also important to note that the first two variables in the model can be used to calculate ROA. This is illustrated in Figure 3.1. So the DuPont model can be used to analyze two of the most important summary measures of the profitability of a company. And again, this is accomplished by merging elements of the income statement with those of the balance sheet.

Example Norboard Inc. is a manufacturer of building products. The company's CFO wishes to measure the return the company is providing to the owners, the common shareholders. The CFO has collected the following information for the most recent three years. He plans on using the DuPont model to determine the

11. EAC is used to calculate profit margin when the company has paid preferred share dividends.This is because the focus of ROE is on the return earned by the common shareholders, and this is measured by EAC. The FLM can also be calculated as follows: [1 ÷ (1 − debt ratio)] which is equal to (1 ÷ equity ratio).

FIGURE 3.1 DuPont Model

An example of the DuPont model using 2008 financial statement data for Norboard Inc.[a]

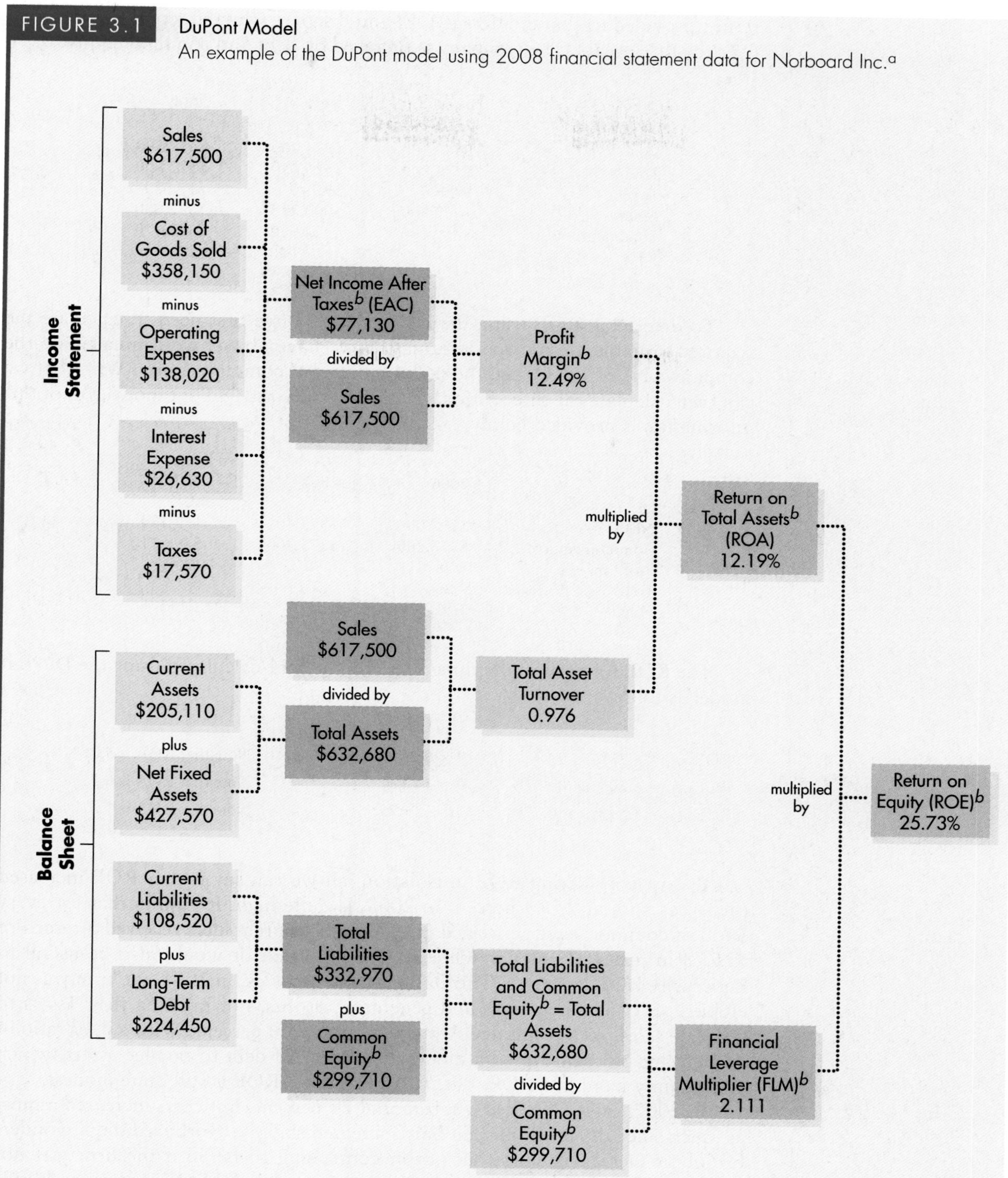

[a] This analysis uses detailed data from Norboard's financial statements for 2008. Only summary data is provided in the discussion within the chapter.
[b] Be sure to read footnote 11 regarding using the DuPont model for firms with preferred shares outstanding.

return provided to shareholders (ROE) and discover why the return has changed over the three years. The company is financed by debt and common equity.

	2006	2007	2008
Sales	\$463,200	\$574,400	\$617,500
Total expenses	\$426,800	\$525,650	\$522,800
Taxes	\$7,300	\$9,710	\$17,570
Assets	\$575,300	\$600,210	\$632,680
Total debt	\$259,100	\$324,910	\$332,970

To determine ROE using the DuPont model, we first need to calculate the required variables. From the information we have above, we can calculate the company's NIAT (EAC) and the dollar amount of common equity. With that we can then calculate the three ratios we require to use the DuPont model. All of this information is provided below:

	2006	2007	2008
NIAT	\$29,100	\$39,040	\$77,130
Common equity	\$316,200	\$275,300	\$299,710
Profit margin	6.28%	6.80%	12.49%
Total asset turnover	0.805	0.957	0.976
FLM	1.819	2.180	2.111

The ROE for each of the three years can now be calculated using the DuPont model as follows:

$ROE_{2006} = 6.28\% \times 0.805 \times 1.819 = 9.20\%$ Note that ROA is 5.06%

$ROE_{2007} = 6.80\% \times 0.957 \times 2.180 = 14.19\%$ Note that ROA is 6.51%

$ROE_{2008} = 12.49\% \times 0.976 \times 2.111 = 25.73\%$ Note that ROA is 12.19%

By just considering ROE in isolation, all we can say is that ROE increased each year and, at 25.73 percent in 2008, is quite high. It implies that for every \$100 of common equity invested in Norboard, shareholders received a return of \$25.73 in just 2008 alone. While this is important, it would also be useful to know why ROE increased. The DuPont model tells us. In 2006, the firm was not efficient at controlling costs and generating profits, nor in using their assets to generate sales. As a result, ROA was a modest 5.06 percent. With a debt ratio of 45 percent, Norboard used a moderate amount of debt to finance assets, which significantly increased ROE. But, at 9.20 percent, ROE is still quite modest.

In 2007, sales increased a substantial 24 percent. But costs increased almost as much since the profit margin only increased slightly. Norboard did a wonderful job at increasing sales, but not at controlling costs. So if the firm was not much more profitable in terms of profit margin, why did ROE increase in 2007? It increased because the company was able to generate more sales with their assets. The company's sales increased much faster than assets and so the total asset turnover increased. In turn, ROA increased to 6.51 percent. The ROE for 2007 was further affected by leverage. The company took on more debt in 2007 (the debt ratio increased to 54.1 percent) so the FLM also increased. Therefore, the higher ROE in 2007 was due to more efficient use of assets and more debt.

In 2008, the company's ROA and ROE soared. Why? Sales increased by only 7.5 percent, but the company was able to gain control of their expenses and, as a result, the profit margin almost doubled. The company's efficiency at using their assets to generate sales and their use of leverage remained relatively constant.

The strength of the DuPont model is that it allows the analyst to determine which of the three variables—profit margin, total asset turnover, or the FLM—accounts for the ROE, or changes in the ROE. It is a powerful analytical tool that should be part of every ratio analysis.

After reading the above example, reconsider Figure 3.1. Note that the data used in the figure are the more detailed results for Norboard for 2008. Be sure you recognize the key point regarding the DuPont model—it is based on the relationships between the data provided in a company's income statement and balance sheet.

Now, returning to Bartlett Company, let's apply the DuPont model. As we have already seen, Bartlett has preferred shares outstanding and, as already discussed, this somewhat changes the way the DuPont model is applied. Rather than NIAT and total shareholders' equity, we use EAC and common equity. This is because the focus is on the return to the common shareholders. Therefore, for the profit margin, EAC, not NIAT, is used. The relevant figures for Bartlett for 2007 and 2008, from Tables 3.1 and 3.2, are:

	2007	2008
EAC	$138,000	$221,000
Sales	$2,567,000	$3,074,000
Total assets	$3,270,000	$3,597,000
Common equity	$1,620,000	$1,754,000
Profit margin	5.376%	7.189%
Total asset turnover	0.785	0.855
FLM	2.019	2.051
ROE	8.52%	12.61%

Note that ROE has significantly increased from 2007 to 2008. Why? Because all three of the relevant ratios have increased. While none of the three increased significantly, the combination of the three modest increases compounds, resulting in a major increase in ROE. So even minor increases in the three underlying ratios can lead to large increases in ROE—the return provided to the owners of the company, the common shareholders.

leverage
The advantage gained by using a lever.

financial leverage
The use of debt financing to acquire assets.

Financial Leverage and Measures of Profitability

Leverage is the advantage gained by using a lever. For example, to move a large boulder, the lever might be a smaller rock and a long piece of wood. By leveraging the piece of wood between the small rock and large boulder, the boulder can be moved. Applying this concept to finance, the boulder is the maximization of the return to shareholders. The lever is debt financing. As discussed in Section 3.4, **financial leverage** is the use of debt financing to acquire assets. A company that uses financial leverage does so to reduce the amount of funds the owners must invest, to decrease the overall cost of the mix of financing used, and to maximize shareholder returns and wealth.

Hint
Financial leverage is used to reduce the amount of funds the owners must invest and to magnify the returns generated by the business on behalf of the owners. Financial leverage is a method used to maximize shareholder returns and wealth, but, with leverage, the risk of the company also increases.

3.1 IN PRACTICE

DuPont Model: Still Useful After All These Years

Even though it is around 90 years old, the DuPont model is still used to evaluate return on equity. Heavy equipment manufacturer Caterpillar Inc. and steel manufacturer Nucor both use the DuPont model to improve financial performance. A manager at Caterpillar states, "DuPont is a good tool for getting people started in understanding how they can have an impact on results." Nucor's CFO says, "It's simple. All of our people understand it. It has worked for us."

To illustrate the DuPont model, consider the following financial results for three Canadian companies for the 2005 fiscal year. Hart Stores Inc. is a value-priced chain of department stores that was started in 1955 and now has 73 stores located across Ontario, Quebec, New Brunswick, Nova Scotia, and Newfoundland. Indigo Books & Music, the corporation formed upon the merger of Indigo and Chapters, is Canada's largest book retail chain and the first to add music, gifts, and licensed cafes to its store locations. Indigo Books & Music has locations in every province across Canada. Hanfeng Evergreen is a Canadian company that is a leader in providing value-added fertilizers for China's agricultural and urban markets.

What does a DuPont analysis reveal about the three companies? The components of the DuPont analysis for the three companies are provided in the following table. The formulas used to calculate the numbers were discussed earlier.

The ROEs for these companies are similar, but for very different reasons. Hart Stores' ROE, at 18.46 percent, is the highest of the three. Hart uses low pricing to drive sales, so the profit margin is low. To reduce risk, the company uses very little financial leverage. Driving the high ROE is the very rapid total asset turnover. Given the nature of the business, Hart has high inventory turnover, no accounts receivables, and low investment in fixed assets, resulting in high total asset turnover.

Indigo Books & Music, on the other hand, relies on leverage for its ROE of 13.17 percent. Profit margin is very low, the lowest of the three, and total asset turnover is moderate. Indigo has used little common equity to finance its assets, resulting in an FLM of 4.42, and this results in the high ROE.

Hanfeng Evergreen's ROE is driven entirely by a high profit margin of 24.37 percent. The total asset turnover is very low due to the large investment in fixed assets, land and manufacturing plants and equipment, and relatively low sales. Hanfeng uses very little debt financing: its FLM is the lowest of the three at 1.11.

The DuPont model is a powerful way for management, creditors, shareholders, and other interested parties to examine overall company performance and

Company	Sales	NIAT (EAC)	Total assets	Common equity
Hart Stores Inc.	$147,970,000	$7,024,000	$48,356,000	$38,075,600
Indigo Books & Music	$787,527,000	$11,702,000	$393,085,000	$88,868,000
Hanfeng Evergreen	$40,339,460	$9,831,519	$70,091,313	$63,118,064

Company	Profit margin	×	Total asset turnover	×	FLM	=	ROE
Hart Stores Inc.	4.75%	×	3.06	×	1.27	=	18.46%
Indigo Books & Music	1.49%	×	2.00	×	4.42	=	13.17%
Hanfeng Evergreen	24.37%	×	0.58	×	1.11	=	15.58%

▶

(Continued)

risk as measured by ROA and ROE. It is a relatively simple tool that can be used to track down reasons for poor returns and lead to major insights concerning a company's operations.

SOURCES: Robin Goldwyn Blumenthal, "'Tis the Gift to Be Simple," *CFO*, January 1998, downloaded from **www.cfonet.com**; Peter C. Eisemann, "Return on Equity and Systematic Ratio Analysis," *Commercial Lending Review*, July 1, 1997; 2005 annual reports of Hart Stores Inc., Indigo Books & Music, and Hanfeng Evergreen, all available at **www.sedar.com**.

Example Rose Fitzpatrick is heading a group of investors that plan to start a new high-tech business. To begin the business, a total investment of $1,000,000 is required. To finance the business, Rose has developed two plans that she will present to the investors. Plan A requires the group to invest $800,000 of equity and the company to borrow the remaining $200,000 at a 10 percent interest rate. Plan B is to invest $200,000 of equity and borrow the remaining $800,000 at a 14 percent interest rate. Regardless of the choice, sales are expected to average $1,700,000, total operating expenses are expected to average $1,380,000, and the company's tax rate will be 22 percent. Rose wonders which alternative she should recommend to her group of investors.

The partial financial statements for the two alternatives are presented in Table 3.4. While both plans use financial leverage, Plan B uses a much greater level of leverage. One of the benefits of leverage is that the owners fully control

TABLE 3.4 Rose Fitzpatrick's Financing Plans for the New Business (in $000)

	Plan A	Plan B
Financial structure		
Debt (cost: 10% for A, 14% for B)	$ 200	$ 800
Equity	800	200
Total assets	$1,000	$ 1,000
Simplified income statement		
Sales	$1,700	$ 1,700
Total operating expenses	1,380	1,380
Earnings before interest and taxes (EBIT)	320	320
Interest expense	20	112
Earnings before taxes (EBT)	300	208
Taxes (22%)	66	45.76
Net income after taxes (NIAT)	$ 234	$162.24
ROA	23.4%	16.22%
ROE	29.25%	81.12%

the company regardless of the dollar amount of their investment. Therefore, under Plan B, the owners fully control the company, but they have only contributed 20 percent of the required financing. A partial disadvantage to this is that the potential creditors have recognized this fact and have charged a higher interest rate than in Plan A. To illustrate the second advantage of leverage, ratios must be calculated. At the bottom of Table 3.4, two profitability ratios are provided: ROA and ROE.

The return on assets suggests that Plan A is superior to Plan B. The respective ROAs are 23.4 percent versus 16.22 percent. Should Rose recommend Plan A? No. ROA considers the return on the total funds invested in the company. The owners are not concerned with the return provided on all of the funds invested in the company, only the funds they invest. Return on equity focuses on the return to the common shareholders. For Plan A, the owners are entitled to the $234,000 of profits on a total investment of $800,000, a ROE of 29.25 percent, a very attractive return. For Plan B, the owners are entitled to $162,240 on an investment of $200,000; the ROE is an impressive, and very enticing, 81.12 percent. Obviously, if the estimates for sales and expenses are accurate, Rose should recommend Plan B to her investors. The investors contribute only 20 percent of the funds required to start the company, yet fully control the company and receive a return of 81 percent on the funds invested. The use of leverage has magnified the return on the invested capital.

The above example focused on the advantages of financial leverage. As discussed in Chapter 1, however, all financial decisions entail a risk/return tradeoff. The return associated with the use of leverage has been considered but if there were only advantages, all companies would have leverage ratios of 90 percent or more. This is not the case; there are major risks associated with financial leverage. Consider that if sales decline and costs increase, EBIT is squeezed. If, in the above example, EBIT falls to $110,000, Plan A still generates NIAT of $70,200. For Plan B, however, the company will lose money. The danger of financial leverage is associated with the company's ability to service the debt. If the company is unable to make the required payments, bankruptcy will occur. More discussion concerning leverage and the factors that influence the capital structure decisions made by companies is provided in Chapter 10.

? Review Questions

3–11 What is a *common-size income statement*? What three key profitability ratios are found on this statement?

3–12 What would explain a firm's having a high gross margin and a low profit margin?

3–13 Define and differentiate between return on total assets (ROA), return on equity (ROE), and earnings per share (EPS). Which measure is probably of greatest interest to owners? Why?

3–14 What is the *price/earnings (P/E) ratio*? How does it relate to investor confidence in the firm's future? Is the P/E ratio a true measure of profitability?

3–15 What is financial leverage? What are the advantages and disadvantages of financial leverage? What are the potential advantages and disadvantages if a company has: (**a**) a 5 percent debt ratio; (**b**) a 90 percent debt ratio?

3–16 Discuss the DuPont model, indicating which variables are used in the calculation process. What does the model measure and how? How is risk captured in the model?

3.6 A Complete Ratio Analysis

With all the ratios calculated, the analyst will then want to take a global look at a firm's financial performance. As noted earlier, no single ratio is adequate for assessing all aspects of a firm's financial condition. All of the ratios calculated should be put into a table and the detailed analysis then completed. The purpose of the analysis is to determine the company's financial strengths and weaknesses. But, to perform an analysis, the calculated ratios must be compared to something. As briefly discussed earlier in the chapter, there are three types of comparisons that can be made. The comparison allows the analyst to consider all aspects of the firm's financial position to isolate areas of strength and weakness. The company will then formulate plans to build on strengths and improve areas of weakness. Prior to illustrating a complete ratio analysis, the types of ratio comparisons that can be used are discussed.

Types of Ratio Comparisons

As discussed earlier in the chapter, ratios in isolation are not very useful. Is a debt ratio of 40 percent good? It is impossible to say if that is all the information we have. If the average debt ratio for the industry is 20 percent, we can comment on the ratio. If the company has reduced the debt ratio from 60 percent to 50 percent to 40 percent, we can comment. So, to be useful, ratios must be compared to something, either industry average ratios (a cross-sectional analysis), past ratios for the company (a time-series analysis), or, and preferably, a combination of the two. Remember, the ultimate objective of a ratio analysis is not the relatively simple calculation procedure. The key is the analysis of the ratios, and to do this a meaningful basis for comparison is needed.

Cross-Sectional Analysis

cross-sectional ratio analysis Comparison of one company's ratios to another company's or group of companies' ratios calculated for the same time period; industry average ratios are often used.

For a **cross-sectional ratio analysis,** we compare one company's ratios to another company or group of companies' ratios. To be valid, the ratios must be calculated for the same time period—in other words, the same year or quarter. So, for a cross-sectional analysis, we compare ratios at a specific point in time, not across time.

The typical business is interested in how well it has performed in relation to other firms in its industry. Often, the reported financial statements of competing firms will be available for analysis.[12] Frequently, a firm will compare its ratio values to those of a key competitor or group of competitors that it wishes to

12. Cross-sectional comparisons of firms operating in several lines of business are difficult to perform. The use of weighted-average industry ratios based on the firm's product-line mix or, if data are available, analysis of the firm on a product-line basis can be performed to evaluate a multiproduct firm.

benchmarking
A type of *cross-sectional analysis* in which the firm's ratio values are compared to those of a key competitor or group of competitors, primarily to identify areas for improvement.

Hint
Industry averages are not particularly useful when analyzing firms with multiproduct lines. In the case of multiproduct firms, it is difficult to select the appropriate benchmark industry.

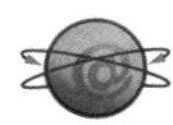

www.statscan.ca
www.canada.com/nationalpost/npb/500/index.html
www.theglobeandmail.com/top1000
www.theglobeandmail.com/business
http://today.reuters.com/investing
www.valuationresources.com
www.ventureline.com/FinAnal.asp

emulate. This type of cross-sectional analysis, called **benchmarking,** has become very popular. By comparing the firm's ratios to those of the *benchmark company* (or *companies*), it can identify areas in which it excels and, more importantly, areas for improvement.

The most popular type of comparison is to industry averages. These figures can be found in D&B's (formerly Dun & Bradstreet) *Industry Norms and Key Business Ratios*, the *Canada Company Handbook* published by Report on Business, Statistics Canada's *Financial Performance Indicators for Canadian Business*, and *The Canadian Corporate Financial Performance Survey* and *The Canadian Small Business Financial Performance Survey*, both published by the Canadian Institute of Chartered Accountants.

In addition, Statistics Canada conducts an annual survey of manufacturers (ASM) and collects a great deal of financial statistics. The data is available on the Statistics Canada Web site and is reported by the North American Industry Classification System (NAICS). A huge amount of ratio and other financial data are also available for purchase in computerized database format from *Stock Guide*, *Globe and Mail*, and *Financial Post*. Ratios for publicly traded companies in Canada and the United States, and for private companies, are also available for free on the Web at various sites.

A sample of the industry ratio data available from D&B's Industry Norms and Key Business Ratios is provided in Tables 3.5 and 3.6. Table 3.5 provides

TABLE 3.5 Median Values for Selected Ratios for Selected Industries: Assets > $1,000,000[a]

Industry	Current Ratio	Quick Ratio	Avg. Age Inventory (on Sales)	Avg. Coll. Period	Avg. Pay Period (on Sales)	Total Asset Turnover	Debt-to-Equity Ratio	Profit Margin	ROA	ROE
Nondurable goods wholesaler	1.6	0.9	37.2	39.9	29.6	2.41	231.2%	1.9%	5.4%	13.7%
Metal mining	5	3	40.6	78.1	148.9	0.40	108.3%	−28.0%	−10.0%	−21.7%
Printing and publishing	1.3	0.9	17.2	55.5	35.0	1.58	225.5%	3.8%	6.0%	15.5%
Banks	1.1	0.1	n/a	35.7	39.4	0.47	344.1%	14.4%	0.8%	11.0%
Computer and data processing	1.6	1.1	19.6	73.6	46.7	1.25	178.3%	3.1%	4.8%	12.0%
Trucking	1	0.9	2.4	49.4	25.2	2.15	305.0%	2.3%	4.8%	15.5%
Computer programming	1.7	1.2	16.2	73.8	45.3	1.20	173.1%	3.1%	4.5%	11.9%
Furniture stores	1.5	0.5	68.9	23.9	33.2	2.43	223.4%	2.1%	5.3%	11.5%
Lumber materials	1.5	0.8	35.1	38.7	20.4	2.99	282.5%	1.6%	4.3%	13.5%
Management/consulting services	1.4	1	14.1	57.3	40.2	1.93	233.0%	2.0%	3.6%	11.9%
Motor vehicle sales (retail)	1.2	0.2	77.7	11.7	8.4	3.05	419.4%	0.9%	2.9%	10.9%
Grocery stores	2.1	0.7	38.0	13.1	19.3	1.98	134.5%	2.9%	5.4%	9.6%
Residential building contractors	1.2	0.3	114.1	16.7	35.0	1.50	340.4%	2.9%	5.3%	28.2%
Hospitals	0.7	0.4	3.9	23.3	43.4	1.25	215.7%	−1.2%	−1.2%	−2.7%
Hotels/motels	0.7	0.3	9.5	17.8	39.8	0.51	267.1%	4.2%	2.8%	6.3%
Credit agencies	1.2	0.2	5.8	42.5	44.9	0.33	792.8%	16.2%	0.9%	11.5%
Service stations	1.2	0.3	81.1	16.2	19.3	2.50	359.5%	1.5%	3.6%	13.2%
Lumber products manufacturer	1.5	0.7	46.8	37.2	29.2	1.77	238.0%	2.6%	5.7%	14.0%
General building contractors	1.2	1	14.3	60.4	55.1	2.54	338.0%	1.9%	4.6%	19.9%

[a]This is the median ratio for companies in the industry with total assets of $1 million or more. D&B also provides the upper and lower quartile for each of the ratios. An example of this information is provided in Table 3.6.

Source: "Industry Norms and Key Business Ratios," D&B Canada, 2006. Reprinted with permission.

ten important ratios for a number of industries for 2004. The wide range of values for these ratios across industries and across years should be noted, particularly for the liquidity and activity ratios. A few similarities across almost all of the industries also stand out. Most particularly, note the generally very high debt/equity ratios, the quite low profit margins, and the much higher ROEs due to the high amount of leverage used.

Table 3.6 provides the range of ratio outcomes for three additional industries for 2004. Here, note the major differences in values for the upper 25 percent of firms in the respective industries versus those in the lower 25 percent. The best-performing quartile of firms in these three industries are clearly superior on all measures of financial performance than the worst-performing quartile of firms. Again, this reinforces the view that companies should not strive to be average, rather they should attempt to be in the upper portion of firms. The benefits of doing so in terms of the measures of liquidity, activity, leverage, and profitability are obvious when reviewing this table.

This type of analysis makes it clear that comparing a particular ratio to an industry standard should uncover any deviations from the norm. While a firm may have a ratio that is "better than" the industry average, this does not necessarily imply that all is fine; this "better than average" viewpoint can be misleading. Quite often a ratio value that is far better than the norm can indicate problems. These may, on more careful analysis, be more severe than had the ratio been worse than the industry average. It is therefore important to investigate *significant deviations to either side* of the industry standard. There may be "bad" reasons for what appears to be a positive ratio and "good" reasons for what appears to be a negative ratio.

The analyst must also recognize that ratios with large deviations from the norm are only the *symptoms* of a problem. Further analysis is typically required to isolate the *causes* of the problem. Once the reason for the problem is known,

TABLE 3.6 Distribution of Selected Ratios for Three Selected Industries

	Business services: 710 companies[a]			Machinery and equipment sales: 396 companies[a]			Oil and gas development: 324 companies[a]		
	Upper	**Median[b]**	**Lower**	**Upper**	**Median[b]**	**Lower**	**Upper**	**Median[b]**	**Lower**
Currrent ratio	2.5	1.5	1.0	2.2	1.6	1.2	2.0	0.9	0.4
Quick ratio	1.7	1.0	0.6	1.2	0.7	0.5	1.8	0.7	0.3
AAI (based on sales)	6.0	19.9	45.6	35.1	62.9	101.4	4.5	8.6	16.9
ACP (based on sales)	41.2	61.5	93.1	34.7	52.2	69.1	62.9	87.5	136.9
APP (based on sales)	25.6	43.4	74.5	23.0	36.9	60.2	51.1	107.7	225.6
Total asset turnover	2.38	1.38	0.75	2.86	2.14	1.47	0.83	0.36	0.25
Debt-to-equity	131.6%	195.7%	304.5%	161.3%	238.1%	361.9%	127.0%	163.8%	211.1%
Profit margin	8.1%	2.5%	−1.1%	4.3%	2.3%	0.6%	16.7%	6.1%	−5.3%
Return on assets	10.0%	3.5%	−5.5%	8.8%	4.8%	1.4%	7.3%	2.2%	−3.2%
Return on equity	29.7%	10.1%	−5.2%	26.0%	12.2%	5.4%	16.0%	4.6%	−5.0%

[a]Indicates the number of companies on which the data is based.

[b]The median is the middle value for a ratio listed from lowest to highest.
The upper quartile is the median of the upper half of the list of ratios while the lower quartile is the median of the lower half.

Source: "Industry Norms and Key Business Ratios," D&B Canada, 2006. Reprinted with permission.

management must develop prescriptive actions for eliminating it. The fundamental point is this: *Ratio analysis merely directs attention to potential areas of concern; it does not provide conclusive evidence as to the existence of a problem.*

Example In early August, Mary Boyle, the chief financial analyst at Caldwell Manufacturing, a producer of heat exchangers, gathered data on the firm's financial performance for the most recent fiscal year ended June 30. She calculated a variety of ratios and obtained industry averages. She was especially interested in average age of inventory, which reflects the speed with which the firm moves its inventory from raw materials through production into finished goods and to the customer as a completed sale. Generally, lower values of this ratio are preferred, because they indicate a quicker sale of inventory. The average age of inventory for Caldwell Manufacturing and for the industry for June 30 are provided below.

	Average age of inventory, June 30
Caldwell Manufacturing	24.7 days
Industry average	43.4 days

Mary's initial reaction to these data was that the firm had managed its inventory significantly *better than* the average firm in the industry. The average age was almost 19 days faster than the industry average. Upon reflection, however, she realized that a very low average age of inventory could also mean very low levels of inventory. The consequence of low inventory could be excessive stockouts (insufficient inventory). Discussions with people in the manufacturing and marketing departments did in fact uncover such a problem: inventories during the year were extremely low, the result of numerous production delays that hindered the firm's ability to meet demand and resulted in lost sales. What had initially appeared to reflect extremely efficient inventory management was actually the symptom of a major problem. There were, in fact, "bad" reasons for what appeared to be a positive ratio.

Time-Series Analysis

time-series analysis
Evaluation of the firm's financial performance over time using financial ratio analysis.

Time-series analysis evaluates performance over time. Comparison of current to past performance, using ratios, allows the firm to determine whether it is progressing as planned. Developing trends can be seen by using multiyear comparisons, and knowledge of these trends can assist the firm in planning future operations. As in cross-sectional analysis, any significant year-to-year changes should be evaluated to assess whether they are symptomatic of a major problem. Additionally, time-series analysis is often helpful in checking the reasonableness of a firm's projected (pro forma) financial statements. Financial forecasting is covered in the following chapter. A comparison of *current* and *past* ratios to those resulting from an analysis of *projected* statements may reveal discrepancies or overoptimism.

Combined Analysis

The most informative approach to ratio analysis is one that combines cross-sectional and time-series analyses. A combined view permits assessment of the trend in the behaviour of the ratio in relation to the trend for the industry. Figure 3.2 depicts this type of approach using the average collection period ratio over the years 2005–2008 for Compton's Drinks, a bottler of specialty soft drinks. This ratio reflects the average amount of time it takes the firm to collect credit sales. Lower values of this ratio generally are preferred. The figure quickly discloses that Compton's average collection period: (1) is now much higher than the industry's, (2) has gone from being better than the industry's to much worse, and (3) has consistently increased over the four years, while the industry's has remained relatively constant. Clearly, Compton's Drinks must become more effective in collecting accounts receivable.

Analyzing Bartlett's Ratios

Table 3.7 provides a ratio schedule for Bartlett Company. Ratios for three years, 2006 to 2008, are provided. The same data is also provided as in Spreadsheet Application 3.1 (page 150). Note that the financial statements provided in Tables 3.1 and 3.2 were used to calculate the ratios for 2007 and 2008. The 2006 ratios and the industry averages were provided separately. The table also shows the formula used to calculate each of the ratios. This is provided only for reference, and the formulas would normally not be included in the table. Using the table we can discuss Bartlett's financial performance in four areas: liquidity, activity, leverage, and profitability; note that it is possible to complete both cross-sectional and a time-series ratio analysis with the dates available.

Liquidity

As of December 31, 2008, Bartlett has $620,000 of current liabilities. Does the company have the ability to repay this debt? An analysis of the liquidity ratios should provide an answer. The current ratio has been relatively stable in the 2 range over the three years. At 1.97 in 2008, it is slightly lower than the industry average and the rule of thumb of 2. The difference is so minor that it is not a concern. The reason the ratio declined in 2008 is that between 2007 and 2008, current liabilities increased more rapidly than current assets (28.4 percent compared to 21.8 percent).

The quick ratio increases over the three years and at 1.51, is well above the rule of thumb of 1, and slightly above the industry average. Between 2007 and

FIGURE 3.2

Combined Analysis

Combined cross-sectional and time-series view of Compton Drinks' average collection period, 2005–2008

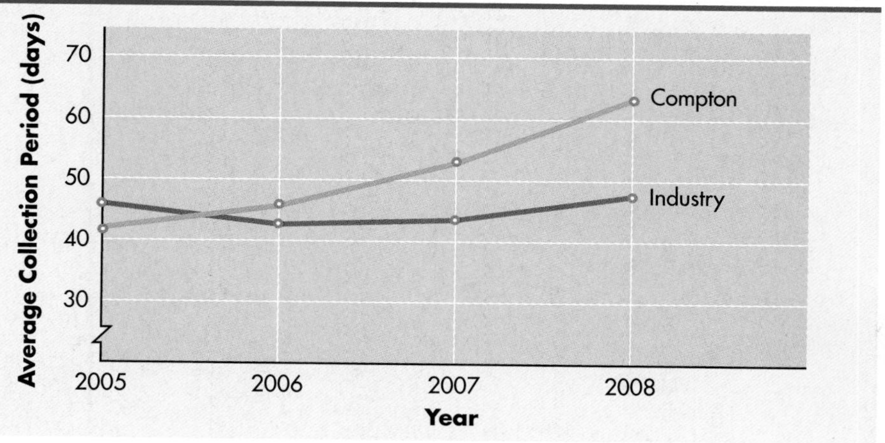

TABLE 3.7 Summary of Bartlett Company Ratios (2006–2008, including 2008 industry averages)

Ratio[a]	Formula	Year 2006	Year 2007	Year 2008	Industry average 2008	Summary Evaluation: Cross-sectional 2008	Summary Evaluation: Time series 2006–2008	Summary Evaluation: Overall
Liquidity								
Net working capital	current assets − current liabilities	$583,000	$521,000	$603,000	N/A		good	good
Current ratio	$\frac{\text{current assets}}{\text{current liabilities}}$	2.04	2.08	1.97	2.05	OK	OK	OK
Quick (acid-test) ratio	$\frac{\text{cash + marketable securities + accounts receivable}}{\text{current liabilities}}$	1.32	1.46	1.51	1.43	good	excellent	good
Activity								
Average age of inventory (AAI)	$\frac{\text{inventory}}{\text{average COGS per day}}$	71.6 days	64 days	50.5 days	55.3 days	excellent	excellent	excellent
Average collection period (ACP)	$\frac{\text{accounts receivable}}{\text{average credit sales per day}}$	44.5 days	51.9 days	59.7 days	44.9 days	very poor	very poor	very poor
Average payment period (APP)	$\frac{\text{accounts payable}}{\text{average credit purchases per day}}$	76.9 days	84.7 days	95.4 days	67.4 days	very poor	very poor	very poor
Fixed asset turnover (FAT)	$\frac{\text{sales}}{\text{net fixed assets}}$	1.38	1.13	1.29	1.15	good	OK	good
Total asset turnover (TAT)	$\frac{\text{sales}}{\text{total assets}}$	0.94	0.79	0.85	0.75	good	OK	good
Leverage								
Capitalization:								
Debt ratio	$\frac{\text{total liabilities}}{\text{total assets}}$	36.8%	44.3%	45.7%	40.0%	higher	increasing	questionable
Preferred equity ratio	$\frac{\text{preferred equity}}{\text{total assets}}$	6.8%	6.1%	5.6%	0%	OK	OK	OK
Common equity ratio	$\frac{\text{common equity}}{\text{total assets}}$	56.4%	49.5%	48.8%	60%	lower	decreasing	questionable
Costly debt ratio	$\frac{\text{costly debt}}{\text{total assets}}$	27.8%	32.6%	30.6%	28.1%	higher	mixed	good
Debt/equity ratio	$\frac{\text{long-term debt}}{\text{common equity}}$	43.5%	59.7%	58.3%	47.4%	higher	slight decrease	questionable

Ratio[a]	Formula	2006	2007	2008	Industry average 2008	Evaluation: Cross-sectional 2008	Evaluation: Time series 2006–2008	Evaluation: Overall
		Year						
Leverage (continued)								
Coverage:								
Times interest earned (TIE)	$\frac{\text{earnings before interest and taxes}}{\text{interest}}$	5.6	3.3	4.5	4.3	good	OK	OK
Fixed-charge coverage (FCC)	$\frac{\text{earnings before interest and taxes + lease payments}}{\text{int. + lease pay.} + \frac{\text{prin.}}{1 - T} + \frac{\text{pref. div.}}{1 - T}}$	2.4	1.4	1.9	1.5	good	OK	good
Profitability **(For the common-size analysis, each account is simply divided by sales)**								
Sales		100.0%	100.0%	100.0%	100.0%			
Cost of goods sold		68.6%	66.7%	67.9%	70.0%			
Gross margin		31.4%	33.3%	32.1%	30.0%	very good	mixed	good
Operating expenses								
Selling expense		3.1%	4.2%	3.3%		very good	mixed	good
General and administrative		6.4%	7.3%	6.3%				
Lease expense		1.0%	1.4%	1.1%				
Amortization		6.3%	8.7%	7.8%				
Total operating expenses		16.8%	21.5%	18.5%	19.0%			
Operating earnings (EBIT)		14.6%	11.8%	13.6%	11.0%	very good	mixed	good
Less: Interest expense		2.9%	3.5%	3.0%				
Earnings before tax		11.7%	8.3%	10.6%				
Less: Taxes		2.9%	2.5%	3.1%				
NIAT		8.8%	5.8%	7.5%	6.4%			
Return on total assets (ROA)	$\frac{\text{net income after taxes}}{\text{total assets}}$	8.3%	4.5%	6.4%	4.8%	very good	mixed	good
Return on equity (ROE)	$\frac{\text{earnings available for common shareholders}}{\text{common equity}}$	14.1%	8.5%	12.6%	8.0%	excellent	mixed	good
Earnings per share (EPS)	$\frac{\text{earnings available for common shareholders}}{\text{number of common shares outstanding}}$	$3.26	$1.81	$2.88	$2.26	N/A	mixed	N/A
Price/earnings (P/E) ratio	$\frac{\text{market price per common share}}{\text{earnings per share}}$	10.5	10.0	11.6	12.8	Poor	mixed	OK

[a]The 2006 ratios and the industry average ratios were provided. The 2007 and 2008 ratios were calculated using the financial statements presented in Tables 3.1 and 3.2.

3.1 SPREADSHEET APPLICATION

Microsoft Excel - Spreadsheet Application 3-1.xls

	A	B	C	D	E
76	Bartlett Company				
77	Ratio Analysis				
78	for the years ended December 31				
79		2007	2008		Formulas
80	Current ratio	2.08	1.97	←	=C39/C58
81	Quick ratio	1.46	1.51	←	=(C35+C36+C37)/C58
82					
83	Average age of inventory (in days)	64.00	50.52	←	=365/(C8/C38)
84	Average collection period (in days)	51.90	59.73	←	=365/(C7/C37)
85	Average payment period (in days)	84.70	95.40	←	=365/((C8*CP%)/C55)
86	Fixed asset turnover	1.13	1.29	←	=C7/C49
87	Total asset turnover	0.79	0.85	←	=C7/C51
88					
89	Debt ratio	44.34%	45.68%	←	=C61/C69
90	Debt/equity ratio	59.69%	58.32%	←	=C60/(C65+C66)
91	Times interest earned	3.33	4.49	←	=C17/C18
92	Fixed-charge coverage	1.40	1.87	←	=(C17+35)/(C18+35+(71/0.71)+(10/0.71))
93	Financial leverage multiplier	2.02	2.05	←	= C51/(C65+C66)
94					
95	Sales	100.00%	100.00%	←	=C7/C7
96	COGS	66.65%	67.92%	←	=C8/C7
97	Gross margin	33.35%	32.08%	←	=C95-C96
98	Operating expenses				
99	Selling expense	4.21%	3.25%	←	=C11/C7
100	General and administrative expenses	7.28%	6.31%	←	=C12/C7
101	Lease expense	1.36%	1.14%	←	=C13/C7
102	Amortization	8.69%	7.77%	←	=C14/C7
103	Total fixed expenses	21.54%	18.48%	←	=sum(C99:C102)
104					
105	EBIT	11.80%	13.60%	←	=C97-C103
106	Interest expense	3.54%	3.03%	←	=C18/C7
107	Earnings before taxes	8.26%	10.57%	←	=C105-C106
108	Taxes	2.48%	3.06%	←	=C20/C7
109	NIAT	5.78%	7.51%	←	=C107-C108
110					
111	ROA	4.54%	6.42%	←	=C22/C51
112	ROE	8.54%	12.60%	←	=(C22-10)/(C65+C66)
113	EPS	$1.82	$2.90	←	=(C22-10)/76.262
114					
115					
116					
117	Growth in:				
118	Sales		19.75%	←	=C7/B7-1
119	Gross margin		15.19%	←	=C9/B9-1
120	Operating costs		2.71%	←	=C15/B15-1
121	NIAT		55.66%	←	=C22/B22-1
122	Assets		10.00%	←	=C51/B51-1
123	Inventory		-3.67%	←	=C38/B38-1
124	Fixed assets		4.77%	←	=C49/B49-1
125	Total debt		13.31%	←	=C61/B61-1
126	Accounts payable		41.48%	←	=C55/B55-1
127	Equity		7.36%	←	=C67/B67-1
128					
129					

SA 3-1

Ready

2008, liquid current assets increased by 32.7 percent, more rapidly than the increase in current liabilities. Inventory declined by 3.7 percent in the same period. Therefore, while the current ratio has declined, Bartlett is actually becoming more liquid. The very large increase in accounts receivable and accounts payable should also be noted. These accounts increased 37.8 percent and 41.5 percent, respectively. Since the increase in sales was 19.8 percent, the implication is that the activity ratios for these two accounts will deteriorate.

Finally note that cash is 35.2 percent of current assets and 12 percent of total assets. Cash increased by $92,000 in 2008 to $431,000 (this is both cash and marketable securities). On January 1, 2009, Bartlett could repay all of their accounts payable and over 62 percent of their outstanding line of credit. Perhaps the firm is too liquid—cash provides a very low return. Overall, the company is very liquid; there should be no problem repaying short-term debt.

Activity

The trends discussed above are reflected in the activity ratios. The management of inventory is excellent. As indicated above, in 2008 inventory declined while sales increased resulting in the average age of inventory (AAI) declining by 13.5 days. This is in addition to the 7.6-day decrease in 2007. Over the three years, the company's AAI declined by 21 days and is now almost five days lower than the industry average. In 2006, Bartlett recognized they had an inventory problem and they have taken measures to fix the problem. Inventory management has greatly improved. This is a very positive sign.

Unfortunately, the average collection period (ACP) has moved in the opposite direction. As discussed above, receivables have grown faster than sales, so the ACP has increased from a level similar to the industry average to one that is now 15 days longer than the industry average. Assuming credit terms of net 30, at almost 60 days Bartlett's ACP is likely double the firm's credit terms. Receivables are, on average, 30 days overdue. Bartlett must improve their collection procedures, as carrying excessive receivables is costly and can lead to bad debts.

Bartlett also appears to be slow in paying its bills. The average payment period (APP) has increased by almost 20 days, and at 95 days is 28 days longer than the quite high industry average and 65 more than net 30 credit terms. Payment procedures should be examined to ensure that the company's credit standing is not adversely affected. It appears Bartlett is stretching their payables to finance the increasing investment in accounts receivable. Bartlett's suppliers may soon refuse to ship on credit. A question Bartlett should consider is: Why sit on all that cash while letting payables build? Such a policy can hurt Bartlett's credit rating.

Bartlett's fixed and total asset turnover are similar, with both increasing above the industry average after declining in 2007. It appears the company made a large investment in assets in 2007 that resulted in these ratios declining. The increase in the turnovers in 2008 is positive. But note that Bartlett is only generating $85 of sales with every $100 of total assets. The substantial investments in assets are not resulting in high sales. This, while a problem, seems to be a characteristic of the industry. Also, with both turnovers in a similar range, it is clear that Bartlett is a manufacturer. A final point: on the basis of the DuPont model, the increasing total asset turnover will have a positive impact on ROE for 2008. Overall, the activity ratios are acceptable; however, Bartlett must improve both their average collection period and the average payment period.

Leverage

Bartlett's capital structure has significantly changed over the three years and is now quite different from the industry average. Debt and preferred equity financing both require fixed payments. The combination of these two sources is 51.3 percent, over 11 percent higher than the industry average. Common equity is a comparable amount below the industry average. This implies Bartlett is using a great deal of financial leverage and thus has higher risk. But the costly debt ratio declined in 2008 and is only slightly higher than the industry average. This means that while Bartlett has more debt than the average firm, more of it is debt such as payables—debt without a financing cost.

The debt/equity ratio indicates that for every $100 of common equity financing used, Bartlett uses $58.30 of long-term debt. While the ratio is higher than the industry average, it declined in 2008, and is much lower than the accepted maximum of 100 percent. The reason for the decline in 2008 was that Bartlett's common equity grew at a faster rate than long-term debt. The growth in equity came from selling common shares plus reinvesting profits. Of the $221,000 of earnings available for common shareholders, Bartlett reinvested $123,000 in 2008. The company paid $98,000 in common dividends (see the change in retained earnings).

Bartlett's mix of financing (their capital structure) could be positive or negative depending on the company's ability to meet the required payments on the financing. Both coverage ratios increased in 2008 after a significant decline in 2007. Increasing debt in 2007, to finance the increasing assets, caused a deterioration in Bartlett's ability to service their financial obligations. The coverage ratios improved in 2008 and are now above the industry average. These ratios suggest that in 2008 Bartlett is more profitable than the average firm in the industry. So, in 2008, it does not appear that Bartlett is having difficulty meeting the financial obligations associated with the higher fixed cost forms of financing.

While Bartlett uses more financial leverage than the average firm in the industry, the company is able to service their obligations.

Profitability

A quick review of the profitability ratios in Table 3.7 indicates that after a very good 2006, total costs increased in 2007, but by 2008 Bartlett is returning to a higher level of profitability. In 2008, Bartlett's cost of goods sold, as a percent of sales, increased by 1.271 percent, after declining in 2007. While 1.271 percent may not seem like a large increase, remember that it is based on sales. With sales in 2008 of $3,074,000, the impact of the increase is that EBT is $39,071 less than it might have been if cost of goods sold, as a percent of sales, had remained the same as in 2007. This is 12 percent of the amount of EBT actually earned by the company. Controlling COGS as a percent of sales is vital for a company. Decreasing gross margins are never a good sign for a company. But, even with the increase in cost of goods sold, Bartlett's gross margin is still 2.1 percent higher than the industry average, a very positive sign.

In addition, as shown in Table 3.7, Bartlett's operating expenses as a percent of sales declined by 3 percent in 2008, after an almost 5 percent increase in 2007. This is a very positive sign of cost control. This ability to control costs resulted in

Bartlett reducing operating costs as a percent of sales to a level slightly better than the industry average of 19 percent. As a result, Bartlett's operating margin (EBIT) as a percent of sales is now 2.6 percent greater than the industry average and almost back to the level recorded in 2006. Since Bartlett uses much more financial leverage, however, Bartlett's profit margin is only 1.1 percent higher than the industry. This is likely due to the higher interest expense and possibly a higher tax rate for Bartlett.

The firm's ROA, ROE, and EPS behaved similar to its profit margin over the 2006–2008 period. Bartlett appears to have experienced a rapid expansion in assets between 2006 and 2007. The owners' return, as evidenced by the high 2008 ROE, suggests that the firm is performing well. Of course, as noted in the discussion of the DuPont model for Bartlett, the higher ROE for 2008 is due to higher levels for all three of the relevant ratios. For 2006, the higher ROE is due to the higher profit margin and total asset turnover. The FLM for 2006 would be lower than in either 2007 or 2008. A comparison of the DuPont model for Bartlett and the industry averages for 2008 reveals the following:

	Profit Margin		TA Turnover		FLM		ROE
Bartlett	7.19%	×	0.855	×	2.05	=	12.6%
Industry	6.4%	×	0.75	×	1.667	=	8.0%

The debt ratio for the industry is 40 percent. Therefore, the equity ratio is 60 percent and the FLM is 1/0.6 or 1.667. Bartlett's higher ROE is based on better cost control, more efficient use of assets to generate sales, and more debt.

Surprisingly, Bartlett's price/earnings (P/E) ratio is below the industry average. This is surprising, because Bartlett is more profitable than the average firm in the industry on all measures. While Bartlett's price/earnings (P/E) ratio did increase in 2008, perhaps the company's higher debt load, and thus higher risk, accounts for the lower P/E. If Bartlett continues to generate higher returns than the industry, the P/E ratio will continue to increase and become greater than the industry average.

In summary, the firm appears to be growing and has recently expanded its assets, primarily through the use of debt (see Table 3.7). The 2006–2008 period seems to reflect a phase of adjustment and recovery from the rapid growth in assets. Bartlett's sales, profits, and other performance factors seem to be growing with the increase in the size of the operation. The main problem areas are with the management of receivables and payables. High levels of receivables seem to be squeezing the firm's ability to pay their accounts payables in a timely manner. The company must also refrain from using more debt financing and perhaps should try to reduce the level of debt. Bartlett's common shareholders will want the P/E ratio to improve. A company with higher profitability than the industry average should also have a P/E ratio that is higher. This should occur as the company continues to adjust to the rapid growth that occurred in 2007. Major financial strengths for Bartlett are liquidity, management of inventory, the fixed and total asset turnovers, and the management of operating expenses. Areas the company should try to improve on are the management of receivables and payables, use of leverage, COGS, and valuation. In short, Bartlett appears to have recovered quite nicely in 2008 and, if this trend continues, investors will be rewarded.

Cautions About Ratio Analysis

To conclude the discussion of ratios, we should consider the following cautions:

1. A single ratio does not generally provide sufficient information from which to judge the *overall* performance of the firm. Only when a group of ratios is used can reasonable judgments be made. However, if an analysis is concerned only with certain *specific* aspects of a firm's financial position, one or two ratios may be sufficient. Remember, when analyzing ratios, it is useful to refer to the appropriate accounts on the financial statements. The combination of considering both the ratio and the underlying numbers on the financial statements will allow for a more complete analysis.
2. The financial statements being compared should be dated at the same point in time during the year. If they are not, the effects of *seasonality* may produce erroneous conclusions and decisions. For example, comparison of the average age of inventory of a toy manufacturer at the end of June with its end-of-December value can be misleading. Clearly the seasonal impact of the December holiday selling season would skew any conclusions about the firm's inventory management drawn from such a comparison. Erroneous conclusions can be avoided by comparing results for June of the current year to June of the prior year, December to December, and so forth, to eliminate the effects of seasonality.
3. It is preferable to use audited financial statements for ratio analysis. If the statements have not been audited, the data contained in them may not reflect the firm's true financial condition. For smaller, private companies a review engagement often takes the place of an audit.
4. The financial data being compared should have been developed in the same way. The use of differing accounting treatments—especially relative to inventory, profitability, and amortization—can distort the results of ratio analysis, regardless of whether cross-sectional or time-series analysis is used.
5. When industry averages are available, the analyst can consider how the subject company compares to the average firm in the industry. If all of the ratios were calculated, and the firm was average on all of them, this might be viewed as positive. But should a company strive to be average? If a result is average, it means that half of the companies in the industry have done better. While it might be considered "safe" to be average, a firm should strive to be well above average on all of the ratios. A simple analogy may drive this point home. In a course, would you rather have an average mark or one in the top 10 percent of the class? When it comes to financial performance, a company should think the same way.
6. When the ratios of one firm are compared with those of another or with those of the firm itself over time, results can be distorted due to inflation. Inflation can cause the book values of inventory and depreciable assets to differ greatly from their true (replacement) values. Additionally, inventory costs and amortization of fixed assets can differ from their true values, thereby distorting profits. These inflationary effects typically have greater impact the larger the differences in the ages of the assets of the firms being compared. Without adjustment, inflation tends to cause older firms (older assets) to appear more efficient and profitable than newer firms (newer assets). Clearly, care must be taken in comparing ratios of older to newer firms or a firm to itself over a long period of time.

7. It is sometimes very difficult to define what is a good and a bad ratio. This can be the case due to the type of industry or due to specific company policies. A current ratio of 2 meets the rule of thumb and is generally considered satisfactory. If the company carries little inventory and all sales are for cash, the implication is that current assets are primarily cash and marketable securities. While carrying such a large amount of cash provides safety, cash is an unproductive asset—the rate of return on cash is very low. Therefore is the current ratio of 2 good or bad? It depends on the company's plans for the cash and their tolerance for risk. The industry average is really a secondary consideration. Without knowing more details, it is almost impossible to say the ratio is good or bad. It is important, however, for the analyst to note the very high levels of cash. Many ratios are subject to these kinds of interpretation complexities. This is particularly the case for ratios such as fixed and total asset turnover, debt/equity ratio, average payment period, fixed-charge coverage, and the price/earnings ratio. Numerous factors influence these ratios and it is not a simple task to conclude that a particular value is good or bad. Calculating ratios is straightforward; analyzing ratios can be quite complex.

? Review Questions

3–17 Financial ratio analysis is often divided into four areas: *liquidity, activity, leverage,* and *profitability* ratios. Differentiate each of these areas of analysis from the others. Which is of the greatest relative concern to creditors?

3–18 Discuss the three types of ratio comparisons that can be completed by an analyst. To what types of deviations from the norm should the analyst devote primary attention when performing cross-sectional ratio analysis? Why?

3–19 Describe how you would approach a complete ratio analysis of the firm by summarizing a large number of ratios.

3–20 Why is it preferable to compare financial statements that are dated at the same point in time during the year?

SUMMARY

Introduce the parties interested in completing a financial ratio analysis, the three types of ratio comparisons, and the four categories of ratios. Ratio analysis allows present and prospective shareholders and lenders and the firm's management to evaluate the firm's financial performance. To be useful, the calculated ratios must be compared to something. There are three types of ratio comparisons: cross-sectional, time series, or a combination of the two. There are four categories of ratios: liquidity, activity, leverage, and profitability.

Analyze a company's liquidity, a measure of a company's ability to pay its short-term debt as it comes due. The liquidity, or ability of the firm to pay its bills as they come due, can be measured by net working capital, the current ratio, or the quick (acid-test) ratio. These ratios recognize that the funds required to repay current liabilities within a short time period will come from current assets: cash, receivables that are collected, and/or inventory that is sold and eventually converted to cash. While the liquidity ratios consider the overall level of current assets and liabilities, the actual mix between the accounts can significantly affect the firm's "true" liquidity.

LG3 **Analyze a company's activity ratios, a measure of a company's effectiveness at managing accounts receivable, inventory, accounts payable, fixed assets, and total assets. Also, explore the link between the liquidity and activity ratios.** Activity ratios measure a company's effectiveness at managing current accounts and fixed and total assets. Inventory activity is measured by average age of inventory, accounts receivable by the average collection period, and accounts payable by the average payment period. Fixed and total asset turnovers measure the efficiency with which the firm uses its assets to generate sales. The total asset turnover ratio is used as part of the DuPont model that measures the return the company generates on the equity investment in the company. The activity ratios depict the three major current accounts on which liquidity is based. The liquidity ratios should provide hints regarding the levels of the activity ratios.

LG4 **Discuss financial leverage and the ratios used to assess how the firm has financed assets, and the company's ability to cover the financing charges associated with the financing used.** The more debt a firm uses, the greater its financial leverage, which magnifies both risk and return. Leverage ratios measure both the capitalization of the company and the ability to service debts. Common measures of leverage include the debt ratio, costly debt ratio, and the debt/equity ratio. The debt/equity ratio focuses on the long-term sources of financing and considers the relative amount of long-term debt financing used. The ability to pay fixed financial charges can be measured by times interest earned and fixed-charge coverage ratios. These ratios evaluate the firm's ability to make the fixed financial charges required on the forms of financing used. Coverage ratios provide an indication of the profitability of the company. Financial leverage directly impacts the return the company generates on the equity investment in the company.

LG5 **Evaluate a company's profitability using common-size analysis and relative to the company's sales, total assets, common equity, and common share price. Also, introduce the DuPont model and explore the link between the leverage and profitability ratios.** The common-size income statement shows all items as a percentage of sales. It is used to evaluate why the firm's profitability, measured as a percent of sales, changes over time or is different from the industry average. It is a vital part of a ratio analysis. Other measures of profitability include return on total assets, return on equity, earnings per share, and the price/earnings ratio. The DuPont model is a very important and widely used method to analyze the sources of a company's profits, more specifically, the key measure of profitability from a shareholder's perspective: return on equity (ROE). The model integrates information from the income statement and balance sheet, and is based on three variables: profit margin, total asset turnover, and the financial leverage multiplier.

LG6 **Fully discuss the three types of ratio comparisons, illustrate how a complete ratio analysis of a company should be performed, and consider some cautions concerning ratio analysis.** To be useful, ratios must be compared to something, either industry average ratios (a cross-sectional analysis), past ratios for the company (a time-series analysis), or, preferably, a combination of the two. Remember, the ultimate objective of a ratio analysis is not the relatively simple calculation procedure. The key is the analysis of the ratios and, to do this, a meaningful basis for comparison is needed. Once all of the ratios are calculated, they should be put into a table, like Table 3.7, and a detailed analysis completed. The purpose of the analysis is to determine the company's financial strengths and weaknesses. Comparing the calculated ratios using a cross-sectional and/or time-series analysis allows the analyst to consider all aspects of the firm's financial position to isolate areas of strength and weakness. The company will then formulate plans to build on strengths and improve areas of weakness. There are seven cautions to recognize regarding ratio analysis.

SELF-TEST PROBLEMS

(Solutions in Appendix B)

ST 3–1 **Ratio formulas and interpretations** Without referring to the text, indicate for each of the following ratios the formula for its calculation and the kinds of problems, if any, the firm is likely to have if these ratios are too high relative to the industry average. What if they are too low relative to the industry? Create a table similar to the one that follows and fill in the empty blocks.

Ratio	Very high	Very low
Current ratio =		
Average age of inventory =		
Times interest earned =		
Gross margin percentage =		
Return on total assets =		

LG4

ST 3–2 **Balance sheet completion using ratios** Complete the 2008 balance sheet for O'Keefe Industries using the information that follows it.

Balance Sheet
O'Keefe Industries
December 31, 2008

Cash	$ 30,000	Accounts payable	$120,000
Marketable securities	25,000	Line of credit	
Accounts receivable		Accruals	20,000
Inventories		Total current liabilities	
Total current assets		Long-term debt	
Net fixed assets		Shareholders' equity	
Total assets		Total liabilities and shareholders' equity	

The following financial data for 2008 are also available:

(1) Sales totalled $1,825,000.
(2) The gross margin was 25 percent.
(3) Average age of inventory was 60 days.
(4) The average collection period was 40 days.
(5) The current ratio was 1.60.
(6) The total asset turnover ratio was 1.25.
(7) The debt ratio was 60 percent.

PROBLEMS

BASIC

3–1 Ratio comparisons Robert Arias recently inherited a stock portfolio from his uncle. Wishing to learn more about the companies that he is now invested in, Robert performs a ratio analysis on each one and decides to compare them to each other. Some of his ratios are listed.

	Island Electric Utility	Burger Heaven	Fink Software	Roland Motors
Current ratio	1.10	1.3	6.8	4.5
Quick ratio	.90	.82	5.2	3.7
Debt ratio	68.2%	46.1%	0%	34.9%
Profit margin	6.2%	14.3%	28.5%	8.4%

Assuming that his uncle was a wise investor who assembled the portfolio with care, Robert finds the wide differences in these ratios confusing. Help him out.

a. What problems might Robert encounter in comparing these companies to one another on the basis of their ratios?

b. Why might the current and quick ratios for the electric utility and the fast-food stock be so much lower than the same ratios for the other companies?

c. Why might it be all right for the electric utility to carry a large amount of debt, but the same is not true for the software company?

d. Why wouldn't investors invest all of their money in software companies instead of less profitable companies? (Focus on risk and reward.)

BASIC

3–2 Liquidity management Bauman Company's total current assets, net working capital, and inventory for each of the past four years follow:

Item	2005	2006	2007	2008
Total current assets	$16,950	$17,450	$18,230	$20,165
Net working capital	7,950	8,760	9,765	12,035
Inventory	7,000	8,150	9,600	8,130

a. Calculate the firm's current and quick ratios for each year. Compare the resulting time series of each measure of liquidity (i.e., net working capital, the current ratio, and the quick ratio).

b. Comment on the firm's liquidity over the 2005–2008 period.

c. If you were told that Bauman Company's average age of inventory for each year in the 2005–2008 period and the industry averages were as follows, would this support or conflict with your evaluation in **b**? Explain.

Average age of inventory (in days)	2005	2006	2007	2008
Bauman Company	52.1	53.7	57.9	61.4
Industry average	34.4	32.6	33.8	33.2

BASIC 

3–3 Inventory management Wilkins Manufacturing has sales of $4 million split equally over the year, and a gross margin of 40 percent. Its *end-of-quarter inventories* are as follows:

Quarter	Inventory
1	$ 400,000
2	800,000
3	1,200,000
4	200,000

a. Find the average quarterly inventory and use it to calculate the firm's average age of inventory.
b. Assuming that the company is in an industry with an inventory turnover of 2.0, how would you evaluate the management of Wilkins' inventory?

BASIC 

3–4 Accounts receivable management An evaluation of the books of Blair Supply, shown in the following table, gives the end-of-year accounts receivable balance, which is believed to consist of amounts originating in the months indicated. The company had annual sales of $2.4 million. The firm extends 30-day credit terms.

Month of origin	Amounts receivable
July	$ 3,875
August	2,000
September	34,025
October	15,100
November	52,000
December	193,000
Year-end accounts receivable	$300,000

a. Use the year-end total to evaluate the firm's collection system.
b. If 70 percent of the firm's sales occur between July and December, would this affect the validity of your conclusion in **a**? Explain.

INTERMEDIATE

3–5 Interpreting liquidity and activity ratios The new owners of Bluegrass Natural Foods, Inc., have hired you to help them diagnose and cure problems that the company has had in maintaining enough working capital. As a first step, you perform a liquidity analysis. You then do an analysis of the company's short-term activity ratios. Your calculations and appropriate industry norms are listed.

	Bluegrass	Industry norm
Current ratio	4.5	4.0
Quick ratio	2.0	3.1
Average age of inventory	60.8 days	35.1 days
Average collection period	73 days	52 days
Average payment period	31 days	40 days

a. Analyze and provide a detailed discussion of the ratios listed above. What recommendations would you make to the new owners of Bluegrass that will help them deal with any problems you uncovered?

b. Are there any issues the new owners should watch for as they implement your recommendations? Discuss.

BASIC 

3–6 **Debt analysis** Springfield Bank is evaluating Creek Enterprises, which has requested a $4,000,000 loan, to assess the firm's financial leverage and financial risk. On the basis of the leverage ratios for Creek, along with the industry averages and Creek's recent financial statements (which follow), evaluate and recommend appropriate action on the loan request.

Income Statement
Creek Enterprises
for the year ended August 31, 2008

Sales revenue		$30,000,000
Less: Cost of goods sold		21,000,000
Gross margin		$ 9,000,000
Less: Operating expenses		
Selling expense	$3,000,000	
General and administrative expenses	1,800,000	
Lease expense	200,000	
Amortization expense	1,000,000	
Total operating expense		6,000,000
Operating earnings (EBIT)		$ 3,000,000
Less: Interest expense		1,000,000
Earnings before taxes		$ 2,000,000
Less: Taxes (rate = 40%)		800,000
Net income after taxes		$ 1,200,000

Balance Sheet
Creek Enterprises
August 31, 2008

Assets		Liabilities and shareholders' equity	
Current assets		Current liabilities	
Cash	$ 1,000,000	Accounts payable	$ 8,000,000
Marketable securities	3,000,000	Line of credit	8,000,000
Accounts receivable	12,000,000	Accruals	500,000
Inventories	7,500,000	Total current liabilities	$16,500,000
Total current assets	$23,500,000	Long-term debt (includes financial leases)[b]	$20,000,000
Gross fixed assets (at cost)[a]		Shareholders' equity	
Land and buildings	$11,000,000	Preferred shares (25,000 shares, $4 dividend)	$ 2,500,000
Machinery and equipment	20,500,000	Common shares (1 million shares)	9,000,000
Furniture and fixtures	8,000,000	Retained earnings	2,000,000
Gross fixed assets	$39,500,000	Total shareholders' equity	$13,500,000
Less: Accumulated amortization	13,000,000	Total liabilities and shareholder' equity	$50,000,000
	$26,500,000		
Total assets	$50,000,000		

[a]The firm has a 4-year financial lease requiring annual beginning-of-year payments of $200,000. Three years of the lease have yet to run.
[b]Required annual principal payments are $800,000.

Industry averages	
Debt ratio	51%
Debt/equity ratio	92%
Times interest earned ratio	7.30
Fixed-charge coverage ratio	1.85

CHALLENGE

3–7 **The relationship between financial leverage and profitability** Pelican Paper, Inc., and Timberland Forest, Inc., are rivals in the manufacture of craft papers. Some financial statement values for each company for the most recent fiscal year are listed below. Use them in a ratio analysis that compares their financial leverage and profitability.

	Pelican Paper, Inc.	Timberland Forest, Inc.
Total assets	$10,000,000	$10,000,000
Total equity	9,000,000	5,000,000
Total debt	1,000,000	5,000,000
Annual interest	100,000	500,000
Total sales	$25,000,000	$25,000,000
EBIT	6,250,000	6,250,000
Net income	3,690,000	3,450,000

a. Calculate the following leverage and coverage ratios for the two companies. Discuss their financial risk and ability to cover the costs in relation to each other.
   (1) Debt ratio.
   (2) Times interest earned.

b. Calculate the following profitability ratios for the two companies. Discuss their profitability relative to each other.
   (1) Operating margin.
   (2) Profit margin.
   (3) Return on assets.
   (4) Return on equity.

c. In what way has the larger debt of Timberland Forest made it more profitable than Pelican Paper? What are the risks that Timberland's investors undertake when they choose to purchase its stock instead of Pelican's?

3–8 Leverage ratios The following information was taken from the balance sheet of Rambo Construction for the most recent fiscal year.

Rambo Construction
Portion of the Balance Sheet

Liabilities and Shareholders' Equity	
Accounts payable	$266,896
Deferred taxes	21,965
Line of credit	125,000
Total current liabilities	$413,861
Amounts due to shareholders[a]	$ 15,300
Long-term debt[b]	265,600
Total liabilities	$694,761
Preferred shares (1,000 shares, $3 dividend)	$ 25,000
Common shares	130,000
Retained earnings	274,297
Total shareholders' equity	$429,297

[a]This amount is due on demand without interest. The shareholders have indicated they will not demand repayment within the next year. As a result, the amount has not been classified as current.

[b]Annual principal repayments required on the firm's long-term debt are $24,000 per year.

In addition, during the year, Rambo reported an operating margin of 14 percent and a profit margin of 7.71 percent on sales of $1,380,670. The firm's operating expenses included a lease payment of $13,750. Rambo also paid interest on its long-term debt and line of credit of $15,780. The following industry average ratios are available:

	Industry average
Debt ratio	47.3%
Costly debt ratio	36.9%
Debt/equity	62.1%
Times interest earned	7.13
Fixed-charge coverage	3.02

Using this data, calculate all of the leverage ratios for the firm and discuss the firm's position in relation to the industry averages.

INTERMEDIATE 

3–9 Common-size statement analysis A common-size income statement of Creek Enterprises' for 2008 follows. Using the firm's 2008 income statement presented in Problem 3–6, develop the 2008 common-size income statement and compare it to the 2008 statement. Which areas require further analysis and investigation? Discuss.

Common-Size Income Statement
Creek Enterprises
for the year ended August 31, 2007

Sales revenue ($35,000,000)		100.0%
Less: Cost of goods sold		65.9
Gross margin		34.1%
Less: Operating expenses		
Selling expense	12.7%	
General and administrative expenses	6.3	
Lease expense	.6	
Amortization expense	3.6	
Total operating expense		23.2
Operating earnings		10.9%
Less: Interest expense		1.5
Earnings before taxes		9.4%
Less: Taxes (rate = 40%)		3.8
Net income after taxes		5.6%

INTERMEDIATE

3–10 Coverage and profitability ratios Gould Ltd. is attempting to calculate some of their ratios for their most recent fiscal year. The following information is available:

Net income after tax	$74,100
Interest payments	$22,000
Lease payments	$33,000
Preferred share dividends	$16,300
Common share dividends	$12,704
Principal repayments	$20,400
Common shares outstanding	31,760
Tax rate	22%

Calculate Gould's earnings per share (EPS), dividends per share (DPS), reinvested profits, and times interest earned and fixed-charge coverage ratios, and discuss the results.

3–11 Ratio proficiency MacDougal Printing, Inc., had sales totalling $40,000,000 for the most recent fiscal year. Some ratios for the company are listed. Use this information to determine the dollar values of various income statement and balance sheet accounts as requested.

MacDougal Printing, Inc. year ended June 30, 2008	
Sales	$40,000,000
Gross margin	80%
Operating margin	35%
Profit margin	8%
Return on total assets	16%
Annual credit purchases	72% of cost of goods sold
Return on equity	20%
Total asset turnover	2
Average collection period	62.2 days
Average payment period	43.4 days

Calculate values for the following:

a. Gross margin.
b. Cost of goods sold.
c. Operating earnings.
d. Operating expenses.
e. Net income after taxes.
f. Total assets.
g. Total equity.
h. Accounts receivable.
i. Accounts payable.

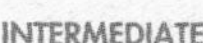 

3–12 DuPont model The following information is available for Johnson International. Industry averages are also provided.

a. Use the DuPont model to calculate ROE for both Johnson and the industry.
b. Evaluate the changes in ROE for both Johnson and the industry over the 3-year period. Comment on your findings. Are there any areas of concern for Johnson?

Johnson	**2006**	**2007**	**2008**
Financial leverage multiplier	1.75	1.75	1.85
Profit margin	5.9%	5.8%	4.9%
Total asset turnover	2.11	2.18	2.34
Industry averages			
Financial leverage multiplier	1.67	1.69	1.64
Profit margin	5.4%	4.7%	4.1%
Total asset turnover	2.05	2.13	2.15

CHALLENGE 

3–13 **Cross-sectional ratio analysis** The financial statements for Fox Manufacturing Company for the year ended March 31, 2008, along with the industry average ratios, are provided below.

a. Calculate all of the ratios for Fox for the 2008 fiscal year and include them in a ratio table together with the industry averages.

b. Analyze the table and discuss the company's financial strengths and weaknesses by category of ratio.

Income Statement **Fox Manufacturing Company** **for the year ended March 31, 2008**		
Sales revenue		$600,000
Less: Cost of goods sold		460,000
Gross margin		$140,000
Less: Operating expenses		
General and administrative expenses	$30,000	
Amortization expense	30,000	
Total operating expense		60,000
Operating earnings		$ 80,000
Less: Interest expense		10,000
Earnings before taxes		$ 70,000
Less: Taxes		27,100
Net income after taxes		$ 42,900
Earnings per share (EPS)		$ 2.15

Balance Sheet **Fox Manufacturing Company** **March 31, 2008**	
Assets	
Cash	$ 15,000
Marketable securities	7,200
Accounts receivable	34,100
Inventories	82,000
Total current assets	$138,300
Net fixed assets	$270,000
Total assets	$408,300
Liabilities and shareholders' equity	
Accounts payable	$ 57,000
Line of credit	13,000
Accruals	5,000
Total current liabilities	$ 75,000
Long-term debt	$150,000
Shareholders' equity	
Common shares (20,000 shares outstanding)	$110,200
Retained earnings	73,100
Total shareholders' equity	$183,300
Total liabilities and shareholders' equity	$408,300

Ratio	Industry averages, 2008
Net working capital	$125,000
Current ratio	2.35
Quick ratio	.87
Average age of inventory[a]	80.2 days
Average collection period[a]	35.3 days
Average payment period	47.8 days
Fixed asset turnover	1.59
Total asset turnover	1.09
Debt ratio	33.9%
Costly debt ratio	16.4%
Debt/equity ratio	46.1%
Times interest earned ratio	12.3
Gross margin	20.2%
Operating margin	13.5%
Profit margin	9.1%
Return on total assets (ROA)	9.9%
Return on equity (ROE)	16.7%
Earnings per share (EPS)	$3.10

[a]Based on end-of-year figures.

INTERMEDIATE

3–14 **Financial statement analysis** The financial statements of Zach Industries for the year ended December 31, 2008, follow.

Income Statement
Zach Industries
for the year ended December 31, 2008

Sales revenue	$160,000
Less: Cost of goods sold	106,000
Gross margin	$ 54,000
Less: Operating expenses	
Selling expense	$ 16,000
General and administrative expenses	10,000
Lease expense	1,000
Amortization expense	10,000
Total operating expense	$ 37,000
Operating earnings	$ 17,000
Less: Interest expense	6,100
Earnings before taxes	$ 10,900
Less: Taxes	4,360
Net income after taxes	$ 6,540

Balance Sheet Zach Industries December 31, 2008	
Assets	
Cash	$ 500
Marketable securities	1,000
Accounts receivable	25,000
Inventories	45,500
Total current assets	$ 72,000
Land	$ 26,000
Buildings and equipment	90,000
Less: Accumulated amortization	38,000
Net fixed assets	$ 78,000
Total assets	$150,000
Liabilities and shareholders' equity	
Accounts payable	$ 22,000
Line of credit	47,000
Total current liabilities	$ 69,000
Long-term debt	$ 22,950
Common shares	$ 31,500
Retained earnings	$ 26,550
Total liabilities and shareholders' equity	$150,000

a. Use the preceding financial statements to complete the following table. Assume that the industry averages given in the table are applicable for both 2007 and 2008.

b. Analyze Zach Industries' financial condition as it relates to (1) liquidity, (2) activity, (3) leverage, and (4) profitability. Discuss the company's overall financial condition, focusing on the strengths and weaknesses by ratio category.

Ratio	Industry average	Actual 2007	Actual 2008
Current ratio	1.80	1.84	_____
Quick ratio	.70	.78	_____
Average age of inventory[a]	146 days	140.9 days	_____
Average collection period[a]	37 days	36 days	_____
Average payment period	62 days	63.8 days	_____
Debt ratio	65%	67%	_____
Times interest earned ratio	3.8	4.0	_____
Gross margin	38%	40%	_____
Profit margin	3.5%	3.6%	_____
Return on total assets	4.0%	4.0%	_____
Return on equity	9.5%	8.0%	_____

[a]Based on end-of-year figures.

CHALLENGE 

3–15 Integrative—Complete ratio analysis Given the following financial statements, historical ratios, and industry averages, calculate the Sterling Company's financial ratios for the most recent year. Analyze its overall financial situation from both a cross-sectional and a time-series viewpoint. Break your analysis into an evaluation of the firm's liquidity, activity, leverage, and profitability. Use a common-size analysis for profitability. Use the DuPont system to analyze ROE. Comment on the company's financial strengths and weaknesses.

Income Statement
Sterling Company
for the year ended December 31, 2008

Sales revenue		$10,000,000
Less: Cost of goods sold		7,500,000
Gross margin		$ 2,500,000
Less: Operating expenses		
Selling expense	$300,000	
General and administrative expenses	650,000	
Lease expense	50,000	
Amortization expense	200,000	
Total operating expense		1,200,000
Operating earnings (EBIT)		$ 1,300,000
Less: Interest expense		200,000
Earnings before taxes		$ 1,100,000
Less: Taxes (rate = 40%)		440,000
Net income after taxes		$ 660,000
Less: Preferred share dividends		50,000
Earnings available for common shareholders		$ 610,000
Earnings per share (EPS)		$3.05

Balance Sheet
Sterling Company
December 31, 2008

Assets			Liabilities and shareholders' equity	
Current assets			Current liabilities	
Cash		$ 200,000	Accounts payable[b]	$ 900,000
Marketable securities		50,000	Line of credit	200,000
Accounts receivable		800,000	Accruals	100,000
Inventories		950,000	Total current liabilities	$ 1,200,000
Total current assets		$ 2,000,000	Long-term debt (includes financial leases)[c]	$ 3,000,000
Gross fixed assets (at cost)[a]	$12,000,000		Shareholders' equity	
Less: Accumulated amortization	3,000,000		Preferred shares (25,000 shares, $2 dividend)	$ 1,000,000
Net fixed assets		$ 9,000,000	Common shares (200,000 shares)[d]	5,800,000
Other assets		$ 1,000,000	Retained earnings	1,000,000
Total assets		$12,000,000	Total shareholders' equity	$ 7,800,000
			Total liabilities and shareholders' equity	$12,000,000

[a]The firm has an 8-year financial lease requiring annual beginning-of-year payments of $50,000. Five years of the lease have yet to run.
[b]Annual credit purchases of $6,200,000 were made during the year.
[c]The annual principal payment on the long-term debt is $100,000.
[d]On December 31, 2008, the firm's common shares closed at $27.50.

Historical and Industry Average Ratios for Sterling Company			
Ratio	Actual 2006	Actual 2007	Industry average, 2008
Net working capital	$760,000	$720,000	$1,600,000
Current ratio	1.40	1.55	1.85
Quick ratio	1.00	.92	1.05
Average age of inventory	38.3 days	39.6 days	42.4 days
Average collection period	45.0 days	36.4 days	35.0 days
Average payment period	58.5 days	60.8 days	45.8 days
Total asset turnover	0.74	0.80	0.74
Debt ratio	20%	20%	30%
Costly debt ratio	10%	14%	23.9%
Debt/equity ratio	24.8%	25.2%	36.9%
Times interest earned ratio	8.2	7.3	8.0
Fixed-charge coverage ratio	4.5	4.2	4.2
Gross margin	28%	27%	27.5%
Operating margin	10%	12%	15.1%
Profit margin	7.2%	6.7%	8.9%
Return on total assets (ROA)	5.33%	5.36%	6.59%
Return on equity (ROE)	6.66%	6.7%	9.1%
Earnings per share (EPS)	$1.75	$2.20	$1.50
Price/earnings (P/E) ratio	12.0	10.5	11.2

INTERMEDIATE 

3–16 Complete ratio analysis, recognizing significant differences Home Health, Inc., has come to Jane Ross for a yearly financial checkup. As a first step, Jane has prepared a complete set of ratios for fiscal years 2007 and 2008. She will use them to look for significant changes in the company's situation from one year to the next.

Home Health, Inc.		
	2007	2008
Net working capital	$55,000	$58,000
Current ratio	3.25	3.00
Quick ratio	2.50	2.20
Average age of inventory days	28.5 days	35.4
Average collection period	42 days	31 days
Total asset turnover	1.40	2.00
Debt ratio	45.3%	62.5%
Times interest earned	4.00	3.85
Gross margin	68%	65%
Operating margin	14%	16%
Profit margin	8.3%	8.1%
Return on total assets	11.6%	16.2%
Return on equity	21.1%	42.6%

a. In order to focus on the degree of change, calculate the year-to-year proportional change by dividing the 2008 ratio by the 2007 ratio, subtracting 1, and multiplying the result by 100. Preserve the positive or negative sign. The result is the percentage change in the ratio from 2007 to 2008. Calculate the proportional change for the ratios shown here.

b. For any ratio that shows a year-to-year difference of 10 percent or more, state whether the difference is in the company's favour or not.

c. For the most significant changes (25 percent or more), look at the other ratios and name at least one other change that may have contributed to the change in the ratio that you are discussing.

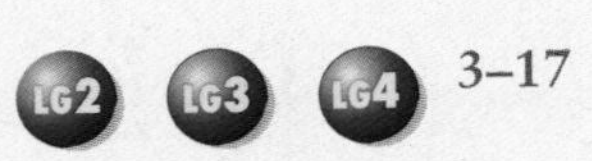

CHALLENGE

3–17 **Comprehensive ratio analysis** As Ian Morse was getting ready to leave the office one beautiful afternoon in late September, Kathy Ferguson walked into his office with a credit application from O'Leary Industrial Supply. Kathy was the commercial account sales manager of Thompson Equipment, and one of her salespeople had recently convinced the purchasing manager of O'Leary Industrial Supply to start buying industrial equipment from Thompson. Ian was the manager of Thompson's customer credit department, and all new accounts had to be approved by him and his team of account analysts.

Thompson's sales team was able to convince O'Leary Industrial Supply to provide their most recent three years of financial statements. In an accompanying note to the file, Kathy had written that the sales department was eager to see credit be granted to O'Leary, as the firm had been able to grow sales over the last two years and were taking a more aggressive approach to selling. O'Leary felt that they were just approaching a very high-growth phase in their evolution.

Prior to leaving the office, Ian had collected some industry ratios that could be used for O'Leary Industrial Supply. Ian had also completed the statement of cash flows (SCF) for the company for 2007 and calculated the ratios for 2006 and 2007. He then placed all of this information on your desk with a note stating he wanted a recommendation from you concerning the account on Tuesday morning.

You know that you will have to develop the SCF and calculate the ratios for 2008. You will then have to complete a detailed analysis of the two years of SCFs and the three years of ratios for O'Leary Industrial Supply to determine the company's financial strengths and weaknesses. You must then make and be able to justify a recommendation.

That trip to the golf course you were planning would have to wait; you were in for a few hours of work.

Industry average ratios	
Current ratio	1.6
Quick ratio	1.1
Average age of inventory (days)	85.1
Average collection period (days)	58.4
Average payment period (days)	38.8
Fixed asset turnover	8.0
Total asset turnover	1.7
Debt ratio	58.5%
Costly debt ratio	32.7%
Debt/equity ratio	41.3%
Times interest earned	4.6X
Fixed-charge coverage	2.52X
Gross profit margin	25.8%
Operating profit (EBIT)	9.9%
Profit margin	5.8%
Return on assets	8.1%
Return on equity	20.3%

O'Leary Industrial Supply
Income Statement
for the years ended December 31

	2006	2007	2008
Sales	$1,542,700	$1,841,300	$1,605,100
Cost of goods sold	1,174,800	1,397,400	1,258,900
Gross margin	367,900	443,900	346,200
Operating expenses			
Administrative expenses	187,900	141,270	146,950
Selling expense	106,300	115,580	118,700
Amortization	16,000	14,400	14,000
Total operating expenses	310,200	271,250	279,650
Operating income (EBIT)	57,700	172,650	66,550
Less: Interest expense	50,100	50,550	65,100
Earnings before tax	7,600	122,100	1,450
Income taxes	2,200	27,100	350
NIAT	$ 5,400	$ 95,000	$ 1,100

Note: Lease payments are included in the administrative expenses. The lease payments were $8,500, $10,000, and $11,500 in 2006, 2007, and 2008, respectively.

O'Leary Industrial Supply
Balance Sheets
as at December 31

	2006	2007	2008
Current assets			
Cash	$ 11,500	$ 24,700	$ 14,900
Marketable securities	7,000	7,000	7,000
Accounts receivable	297,300	361,800	410,800
Inventories	289,900	330,000	256,600
Prepaid expenses	5,500	800	5,200
Total current assets	611,200	724,300	694,500
Net plant and equipment	184,300	172,900	162,000
Goodwill	30,600	28,200	25,400
Total assets	$826,100	$925,400	$881,900
Current liabilities			
Accounts payable	$209,700	$196,700	$145,900
Line of credit	169,000	202,000	254,000
Accruals	14,400	23,700	3,700
Total current liabilities	393,100	422,400	403,600
Long-term debt	141,000	181,600	225,800
Total liabilities	$534,100	$604,000	$629,400
Equity			
Common shares	14,000	14,000	14,000
Retained earnings	278,000	307,400	238,500
Total equity	292,000	321,400	252,500
Total liabilities and equity	$826,100	$925,400	$881,900

Notes:

1. Starting in 2008, O'Leary was required to make principal repayment on their long-term debt of $15,000.
2. Retained earnings at the beginning of the 2006 fiscal year were $332,600.
3. Throughout this period, there have been 32,456 common shares outstanding.

O'Leary Industrial Supply
Cash Flow Statement
as at December 31

	2007	2008
Cash Flow from Operating Activities		
NIAT	$ 95,000	
Plus: Non-cash expenses	14,400	
Net cash from operations	$109,400	
Plus: Changes in Non-cash Working Capital Accounts		
Change in accounts receivable	–64,500	
Change in inventory	–40,100	
Change in prepaids	4,700	
Change in accounts payable	–13,000	
Change in accruals	9,300	
Cash from non-cash working capital	–103,600	
Cash from operating activities	*5,800*	
Cash Flow from Investing Activities		
Change in fixed assets	–3,000	
Change in goodwill	2,400	
Cash from investing activities	*–600*	
Cash Flow from Financing Activities		
Change in long-term debt	40,600	
Change in line of credit	33,000	
Payment of common dividend	–65,600	
Cash from financing activities	*8,000*	
Change in cash and cash equivalents during year	13,200	
Cash and cash equivalents at beginning of year	18,500	
Cash and cash equivalents at end of year	$ 31,700	

O'Leary Industrial Supply				
	2006	**2007**	**2008**	**Industry**
Liquidity Ratios				
Current ratio	1.55	1.71		1.6
Quick ratio	0.82	0.93		1.1
Activity Ratios				
Average age of inventory	90.1	86.2		85.1
Average collection period	70.3	71.7		58.4
Average payment period	65.2	51.4		38.8
Fixed asset turnover	8.37	10.65		8.0
Total asset turnover	1.86	1.99		1.7
Leverage Ratios				
Debt ratio	64.7%	65.3%		58.5%
Costly debt ratio	37.5%	41.5%		32.7%
Debt/equity ratio	48.3%	56.5%		41.3%
Times interest earned	1.15	3.42		4.6x
Fixed charge coverage	1.13	3.02		2.52
Vertical Analysis and Profitability Ratios				
Sales	100.00%	100.00%		
COGS	76.15%	75.89%		
Gross margin	23.85%	24.11%		25.8%
Administrative expenses	12.18%	7.67%		
Selling expense	6.89%	6.28%		
Amortization	1.04%	0.78%		
Total operating expenses	20.11%	14.73%		
Operating profit (EBIT)	3.74%	9.37%		9.9%
Interest expense	3.25%	2.74%		
EBT	0.49%	6.63%		
Taxes	0.14%	1.47%		
Profit margin	0.35%	5.16%		5.8%
Return on assets	0.65%	10.27%		8.1%
Return on equity	1.85%	29.56%		20.3%
DuPont model	0.35% × 1.86 × 2.829 ...	5.16% × 1.99 × 2.879 ...		
Growth Ratios				
Sales		19.4%		
Gross margin		20.7%		
NIAT		1659%		
Total assets		12.0%		
Total debt		13.1%		

CASE CHAPTER 3

Assessing Martin Manufacturing's Current Financial Position

See the enclosed Student CD-ROM for cases that help you put theories and concepts from the text into practice.

Be sure to visit the Companion Website for this book at **www.pearsoned.ca/gitman** for a wealth of additional learning tools including self-test quizzes, Web exercises, and additional cases.

CHAPTER 4

Financial Planning and Forecasting

LEARNING GOALS

LG1 Understand the financial planning process, including long-term (strategic) financial plans and short-term (operating) plans.

LG2 Discuss the cash budget, the importance of sales forecasts, procedures for preparing a cash budget, and how to cope with uncertainty when preparing a cash budget.

LG3 Discuss the fundamentals associated with preparing the pro forma income statement and balance sheet.

LG4 Discuss and illustrate the percent-of-sales forecasting method, a simplified approach to forecasting a firm's income statement and balance sheet, and determine the amount of external financing a company requires to operate during the forecast year.

LG5 Discuss the weaknesses of the percent-of-sales forecasting method, and illustrate two other approaches to preparing a pro forma income statement.

LG6 Discuss and illustrate the judgmental approach to preparing a pro forma balance sheet for a company, and develop a statement of external financing required for the company for the forecast year.

4.1 The Financial Planning Process

Financial planning is an important aspect of the firm's operations because it provides road maps for guiding, coordinating, and controlling the firm's actions to achieve its objectives. Three key aspects of the financial planning process are *cash planning (forecasting the need for cash)*, *forecasting future profitability*, and

The Best-Laid Plans . . .

We all plan for the future. Some of our plans are realized, some are not. Even though a particular event may not turn out as you expected, you still go through the process of planning. Companies are pretty much in the same position. Because there is much in the business and financial environments that is beyond their control, they try to control their future by careful and extensive planning and then forecasting, for both the long term and the short term. Even though, as the great Scottish poet Robert Burns might have said, the best-laid plans of mice and men often go astray, planning is still an essential part of business life. This chapter outlines the financial planning process, with particular attention to planning focused on the firm's cash and its future financial position as depicted in a forecasted income statement and balance sheet.

forecasting the need for financing. Cash forecasting involves the preparation of the firm's cash budget. Profits are forecast by developing a pro forma or projected income statement. Financing needs are forecasted through the use of the forecasted income statement, and by projecting the firm's balance sheet for the forecast period. In addition, the projected statement of external financing required determines the total, the internal, and the external financing the firm

LINKING THE DISCIPLINES: Cross-Functional Interactions

- ***Accounting personnel*** need to provide the data required to prepare the cash budget and accurate pro forma financial statements so the amount of financing the firm requires to support future growth can be determined.
- ***Information systems analysts*** will design financial planning and budgeting modules within the financial information system. They will also help design forecasting systems that will allow management to simulate their forecasts in the form of a sensitivity analysis.
- ***Management*** needs to understand the process used to prepare the cash budget and pro forma financial statements, and how they can be used in the decision-making process to prevent financial problems within the firm.
- The ***marketing department*** will provide the finance department with the sales forecast. Forecasting is dependent on an accurate estimate for sales. Marketing personnel will need to inform the financial planners of new-product introduction and the significant changes in promotion that will occur and that may impact sales and costs.
- Personnel in the ***operations department*** will provide production costing information that will be used to complete the pro forma income statement. In addition, any new assets that will be required in production must be costed so these asset acquisitions can be reflected in the forecasted statements, and in the calculation of the financing required for the forecast year.

pro forma statements
Projected, or forecasted, financial statements: the income statement and the balance sheet.

financial planning process
Planning that begins with long-term (strategic) financial plans that in turn guide the formulation of short-term (operating) plans and budgets.

will require for the forecast period. The **pro forma statements** are not only useful for internal financial planning, but also are routinely required by existing and prospective lenders.

The **financial planning process** begins with long-term, or strategic, financial plans that in turn guide the formulation of short-term, or operating, plans and budgets. Generally, the short-term plans and budgets implement the firm's long-term strategic objectives. The major emphasis in this chapter is on short-term financial plans and budgets, though a few comments on long-term financial plans are provided below.

Long-Term (Strategic) Financial Plans

long-term (strategic) financial plans
Planned financial actions and the anticipated financial impact of those actions over periods ranging from 2 to 10 years.

Long-term (strategic) financial plans lay out a company's planned financial actions and the anticipated financial impact of those actions over periods ranging from 2 to 10 years. The use of 5-year strategic plans, which are revised as significant new information becomes available, is common. Generally, firms that are subject to relatively short production cycles tend to use shorter planning horizons.

Long-term financial plans are part of an integrated strategy that, along with production and marketing plans, guides the firm toward achievement of its strategic goals. Those long-term plans consider proposed fixed asset outlays, research and development activities, marketing and product development actions, capital structure, and major sources of financing. Also included would be termination of existing projects, product lines, or lines of business; repayment or retirement of outstanding debts; and any planned acquisitions. Such plans tend to be supported by a series of annual budgets and profit plans. Given the long-term nature of strategic plans, they are subject to regular revision. As the operating environment and the firm's own circumstances change, so too should the plans.

Short-Term (Operating) Financial Plans

short-term (operating) financial plans
Planned short-term financial actions and the anticipated impact of those actions.

Short-term (operating) financial plans specify short-term financial actions and the anticipated impact of those actions. These plans most often cover a 1-to-2-year period. Key inputs include the sales forecast and various forms of operating and financial data. Key outputs include a number of operating budgets, the cash budget, and pro forma financial statements. The entire short-term financial planning process is outlined in the flow diagram of Figure 4.1.

Hint
Electronic spreadsheets such as Excel and QuattroPro are widely used to streamline the process of preparing and evaluating these short-term financial planning statements.

Short-term financial planning begins with the sales forecast. The sales forecast will be based, in part, on historic sales. From it, production plans are developed that take into account lead (preparation) times and include estimates of the required types and quantities of raw materials. Using the production plans, the firm can estimate direct labour requirements, factory overhead outlays, and operating expenses. Once these estimates have been made, the firm's pro forma income statement and cash budget can be prepared. These two statements are also based, in part, on income statements from previous year(s). With the income statements and balance sheets from previous years, pro forma income statement, cash budget, fixed asset outlay plan, and long-term financing plan, the pro forma balance sheet can finally be developed. Throughout the remainder of this chapter, we will concentrate on the key outputs of the short-term financial planning process: the cash budget, the pro forma income statement, and the pro forma balance sheet.

FIGURE 4.1 Short-Term Financial Planning
The short-term (operating) financial planning process

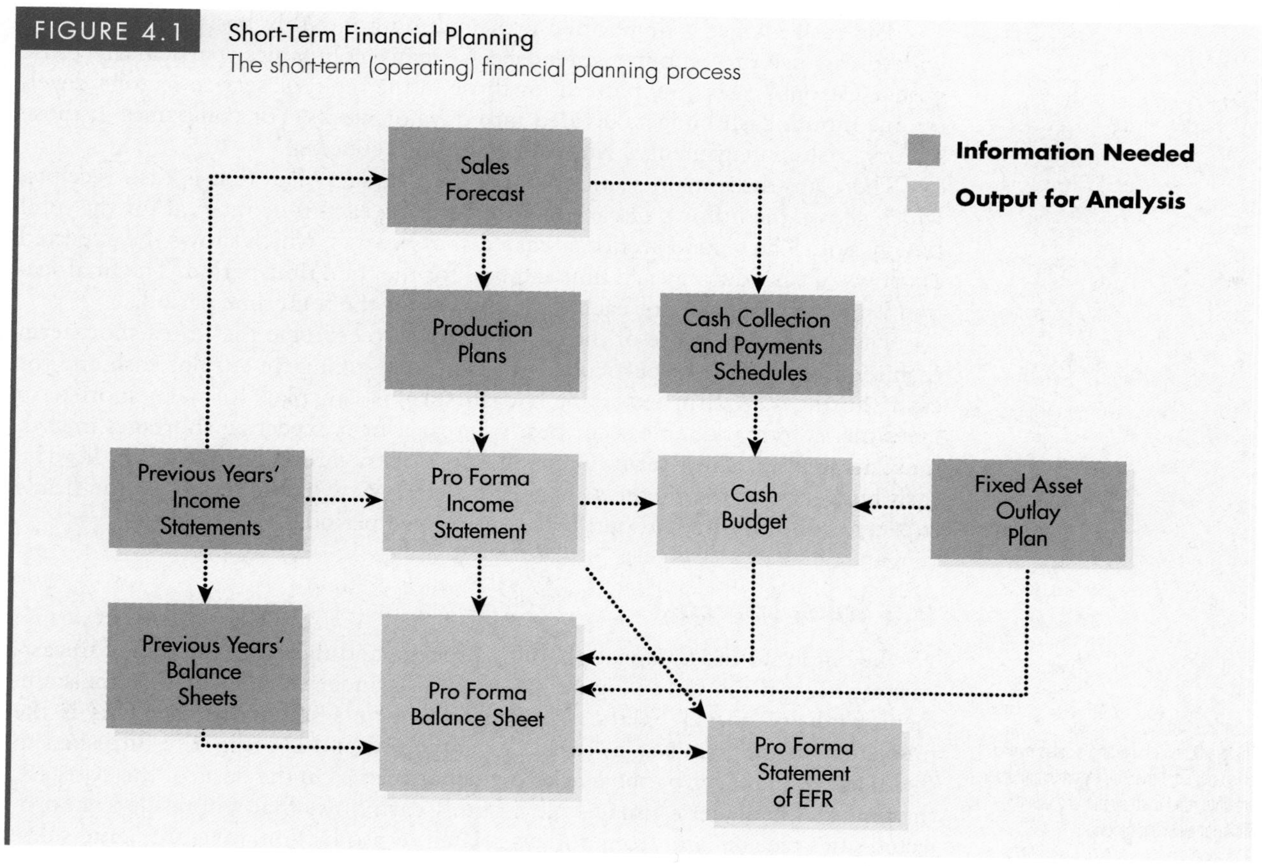

? Review Questions

4–1 What is the *financial planning process?* Define and contrast *long-term (strategic) financial plans* and *short-term (operating) financial plans.*

4–2 Which three statements result as part of the short-term (operating) financial planning process? Describe the flow of information from the sales forecast through the preparation of these statements.

4.2 Cash Planning: The Cash Budget

cash budget (cash forecast)
A statement of the firm's planned inflows and outflows of cash that is used to estimate its short-term cash requirements.

The **cash budget**, or **cash forecast**, is an estimate of the inflows and outflows of cash, and the cash balance (surplus or shortage) for a forecast period. A cash budget is important to ensure a company will have a sufficient amount of cash to operate over the forecast period. Typically, the cash budget is designed to cover a 6-month or 1-year period, divided into shorter time intervals. The number and type of intervals depend on the nature of the business. For example, a company may develop a cash budget for a total period of six months, but focus on cash flows in monthly intervals. Another company may use a total period of three months, but focus on weekly intervals. The more seasonal and uncertain a firm's cash flows, the greater the number of intervals.

The cash budget is quite often presented on a monthly basis. But, given the widespread use of computer spreadsheets, many companies, particularly those with a seasonal cash flow pattern, or those in the retail or service sectors, develop one-month cash budgets divided into days or weeks. For companies in those sectors, cash management is vital and a constant concern.

There are three main sections to the cash budget. The first is cash receipts, which shows the inflows of cash expected during each time interval for the total time period. The second section is cash disbursements, which shows the expected outflows of cash during each time interval for the total time period. The final section is the cash balance for each time interval for the total time period.

The ultimate purpose of the cash budget is to estimate the firm's short-term cash requirements, with particular attention to planning for surplus cash and for cash shortages. A firm expecting a cash surplus can plan to make short-term investments in marketable securities, whereas a firm expecting shortages in cash must arrange for short-term financing, most often through a line of credit. The cash budget gives the financial manager a clear view of the timing of the firm's expected cash inflows and outflows over a given period.

The Sales Forecast

sales forecast
The prediction of the firm's sales over a given period, based on external and internal data, and used as the key input to the financial planning process.

The key input to the financial planning process, and therefore the three forecasted statements displayed in Figure 4.1—the cash budget, pro forma income statement, and pro forma balance sheet—is the firm's **sales forecast**. This is the prediction of the firm's sales over a given period and is ordinarily furnished to the financial manager by the marketing department. On the basis of this forecast, the financial manager estimates the monthly cash flows that will result from projected sales receipts and from outlays related to production, inventory, and sales.

The manager also determines the level of fixed assets required and the amount of financing, if any, needed to support the forecast level of production and sales. In practice, obtaining good data is the most difficult aspect of forecasting.[1] The sales forecast is normally based on an analysis of external and internal data.

external forecast
A sales forecast based on the relationships observed between the firm's sales and certain key external economic indicators.

An **external forecast** is based on the relationships observed between the firm's sales and certain key external economic indicators such as the gross domestic product (GDP), disposable personal income, and/or monetary indicators such as interest rates and growth in the money supply. Forecasts containing these indicators are readily available. The rationale for this approach is that because the firm's sales are often closely related to some aspect of overall national economic activity, a forecast of economic activity should provide insight into future sales.

internal forecast
A sales forecast based on a buildup, or consensus, of forecasts through the firm's own sales channels.

Internal forecasts are based on a buildup, or consensus, of sales forecasts through the firm's own sales channels. Typically, the firm's salespeople in the field are asked to estimate the number of units of each type of product that they expect to sell in the coming year. These forecasts are collected and totalled by the sales manager, who may adjust the figures using knowledge of specific markets or of the salesperson's forecasting ability. Finally, adjustments may be made for additional internal factors, such as production capabilities.

Hint
The firm needs to spend a great deal of time and effort to make the sales forecast as precise as possible. An "after the fact" analysis of the prior year's forecast will help the firm determine which approach or combination of approaches will give it the most accurate forecasts.

Firms generally use a combination of external and internal forecast data to make the final sales forecast. The internal data provide insight into sales expectations, and the external data provide a means of adjusting these expectations to take into account general economic factors. The nature of the firm's product also often affects the mix and types of forecasting methods used.

Preparing the Cash Budget

The general format of the cash budget is presented in Table 4.1. We will discuss each of its components individually.

TABLE 4.1 The General Format of the Cash Budget

	Jan.	Feb.	...	Nov.	Dec.
Cash receipts	$XXX	$XXG		$XXM	$XXT
Less: Cash disbursements	XXA	XXH	...	XXN	XXU
Net cash flow	XXB	XXI		XXO	XXV
Add: Beginning cash	XXC	XXD	XXJ	XXP	XXQ
Ending cash	XXD	XXJ		XXQ	XXW
Less: Minimum cash balance	XXE	XXK	...	XXR	XXY
Required total financing	$	$XXL		$XXS	$
Excess cash balance	$XXF				$XXZ

1. A discussion of the calculation of the various forecasting techniques, such as regression, moving averages, and exponential smoothing, is not included in this text. For a description of the technical side of forecasting, refer to a basic statistics, econometrics, or management science text.

Cash Receipts

cash receipts
All of a firm's inflows of cash in a given financial period.

Cash receipts include all of a firm's inflows of cash in a given financial period. The most common components of cash receipts are cash sales, collections of accounts receivable, and other cash receipts.

Example Coulson Industries, a defence contractor, is developing a cash budget for the final quarter (three months) of the fiscal year, on a monthly basis. So a cash budget for October, November, and December must be developed. Coulson's sales in August and September were \$100,000 and \$200,000, respectively. Sales of \$400,000, \$300,000, and \$200,000 have been forecast for October, November, and December, respectively. Historically, 20 percent of the firm's sales have been for cash, 50 percent have generated accounts receivable collected after 1 month, and the remaining 30 percent have generated accounts receivable collected after 2 months. Bad debt expenses (uncollectible accounts) have been negligible.[2]

In December, the firm will receive a \$30,000 dividend from common shares held in a subsidiary. The schedule of expected cash receipts for the company is presented in Table 4.2. Note that it contains five main parts: forecast sales by time interval, portion of sales that are for cash, collections of accounts receivable (A/R), other cash receipts, and total cash receipts. Each of these is discussed below and illustrated using the information for Coulson Industries.

Forecast sales Sales forecasts are the beginning point for any financial forecasting exercise. Sales forecasts are needed to develop the cash budget and pro forma income statement and balance sheet. For the cash budget, collections of cash are based on sales forecasts. As well, purchases are often based on projected sales. Sales forecasts can be on a daily, weekly, or monthly basis. In Table 4.2, the (A) and (F) signify that the sales amount is either the actual figure reported (A), or is a forecasted sales amount (F). In this case, the August and September sales figures are the actual figures reported.

TABLE 4.2 A Schedule of Projected Cash Receipts for Coulson Industries ($000)

Forecast sales	Aug. (A*) \$100	Sept. (A*) \$200	Oct. (F*) \$400	Nov. (F*) \$300	Dec. (F*) \$200
Cash sales (20%)	\$ 20	\$ 40	\$ 80	\$ 60	\$ 40
Collections of accounts receivable					
Lagged 1 month (50%)		50	100	200	150
Lagged 2 months (30%)			30	60	120
Cash dividend received					30
Total cash receipts			\$210	\$320	\$340

*A is actual sales, F is forecasted sales

2. Normally, it would be expected that the collection percentages would total slightly less than 100 percent, because some of the accounts receivable would be uncollectible. In this example, the sum of the collection percentages is 100 percent (20% + 50% + 30%), which reflects the fact that all sales are assumed to be collected.

Cash sales The cash sales shown for each month represent 20 percent of the total sales forecast for that month.

Collections of accounts receivable These entries represent the collection of accounts receivable resulting from sales in earlier months.

Lagged 1 month These figures represent sales made in the preceding month that generated accounts receivable collected in the current month. Because 50 percent of the current month's sales are collected 1 month later, the collections of A/R with a 1-month lag shown for September represent 50 percent of the sales in August, collections for October represent 50 percent of September sales, and so on.

Lagged 2 months These figures represent sales made 2 months earlier that generated accounts receivable collected in the current month. Because 30 percent of sales are collected 2 months later, the collections with a 2-month lag shown for October represent 30 percent of the sales in August, and so on.

Other cash receipts These are cash receipts expected from sources other than sales. The most common cash receipts are

- Interest received
- Dividends received
- Proceeds from the sale of equipment
- Proceeds from a bank or other loan
- Proceeds from the sale of common or preferred shares
- Lease receipts

For Coulson Industries, the only other cash receipt is the $30,000 cash dividend that will be received in December.

Total cash receipts This figure represents the total of all the cash receipts listed for each month. For Coulson Industries, we are concerned only with the forecast period of October, November, and December, as shown in Table 4.2.

Cash Disbursements

cash disbursements
All outlays of cash by the firm during a given financial period.

Cash disbursements include all outlays of cash by the firm during a given financial period. The most common cash disbursements are

- Cash purchases
- Payments of accounts payable
- Rent (and lease) payments
- Wages and salaries
- Tax payments
- Fixed asset outlays
- Interest payments
- Cash dividend payments
- Principal payments on loans
- Repurchases or retirements of common or preferred shares

It is important to recognize that *amortization and other non-cash charges are NOT included in the cash budget,* because they merely represent a scheduled writeoff of an earlier cash outflow. The impact of amortization, as noted in Chapter 2, is reflected in the cash outflow for the tax payments.

Example Coulson Industries has gathered the following data needed for the preparation of a cash disbursements schedule for October, November, and December.

Purchases The firm's purchases from suppliers are 70 percent of sales. Of the purchases, 10 percent are for cash, 70 percent are on credit becoming payables that are paid the month following purchase, while 20 percent are on credit that are paid two months following the purchase.[3]

Rent payments Rent of $5,000 will be paid each month.

Wages and salaries The firm's wages and salaries are estimated by adding 10 percent of its monthly sales to the $8,000 fixed cost figure.

Tax payments Taxes of $25,000 must be paid in December.

Fixed asset outlays New machinery costing $130,000 will be purchased in September and paid for in November.

Interest payments An interest payment of $10,000 is due in December.

Cash dividend payments Cash dividends of $20,000 will be paid in October.

Principal payments (loans) A $20,000 principal payment is due in December.

Repurchases or retirements of common shares No repurchase or retirement of common shares is expected during the October–December period.

The firm's cash disbursements schedule is presented in Table 4.3. Some items in the table are explained in greater detail below.

TABLE 4.3 A Schedule of Projected Cash Disbursements for Coulson Industries ($000)

Purchases (70% of sales)	Aug. $70	Sept. $140	Oct. $280	Nov. $210	Dec. $140
Cash purchases (10%)	$ 7	$ 14	$ 28	$ 21	$ 14
Payments of accounts payable					
Lagged 1 month (70%)		49	98	196	147
Lagged 2 months (20%)			14	28	56
Rent payments			5	5	5
Wages and salaries			48	38	28
Tax payments					25
Fixed asset outlays				130	
Interest payments					10
Cash dividend payments			20		
Principal payments					20
Total cash disbursements			$213	$418	$305

3. Unlike the collection percentages for sales, the total of the payment percentages should equal 100 percent, because it is expected that the firm will pay off all of its accounts payable.

Purchases Purchases from suppliers are 70 percent of the forecast sales for each month. Purchases are included to facilitate the calculation of the cash purchases and related payments.

Cash purchases The cash purchases represent 10 percent of each month's purchases.

Payments of accounts payable These entries represent the payment of accounts payable (A/P) resulting from purchases in earlier months.

Lagged 1 month These figures represent purchases made in the preceding month that are paid for in the current month. Because 70 percent of the firm's purchases are paid for 1 month later, the payments with a 1-month lag shown for September represent 70 percent of the August purchases, payments for October represent 70 percent of September purchases, and so on.

Lagged 2 months These figures represent purchases made 2 months earlier that are paid for in the current month. Because 20 percent of the firm's purchases are paid for 2 months later, the payments with a 2-month lag for October represent 20 percent of the August purchases, and so on.

Wages and salaries These amounts were obtained by adding $8,000 to 10 percent of the *sales* in each month. The $8,000 represents the salary component; the rest represents wages.

The remaining items on the cash disbursements schedule are self-explanatory.

Net Cash Flow, Ending Cash, Financing, and Excess Cash

net cash flow
The mathematical difference between the firm's cash receipts and its cash disbursements in each period.

ending cash
The sum of the firm's beginning cash and its net cash flow for the period.

required total financing
Amount of funds needed by the firm if the ending cash for the period is less than the desired minimum cash balance; typically represented by a line of credit.

excess cash balance
The (excess) amount available for investment by the firm if the period's ending cash is greater than the desired minimum cash balance; assumed to be invested in marketable securities.

Now look back at the general-format cash budget in Table 4.1. For our example, we now have inputs for the first two items and are now able to calculate the net cash flow for each time interval. The firm's **net cash flow** is found by subtracting the cash disbursements from cash receipts in each period. Then, by adding beginning cash to the firm's net cash flow, the **ending cash** for each period can be found. Finally, subtracting the desired minimum cash balance from ending cash yields the **required total financing** or the **excess cash balance.**

Note that only one of these results can occur. Either the firm will require cash or it will have excess cash. If the ending cash is less than the minimum cash balance, *financing* is required. Such financing is typically viewed as short-term and therefore will be raised by using a line of credit. If the ending cash is greater than the minimum cash balance, *excess cash* exists. Any excess cash is assumed to be invested in a liquid, short-term, interest-paying vehicle—that is, in marketable securities.

Example Table 4.4 presents Coulson Industries' cash budget, based on the cash receipt and cash disbursement data already developed. At the end of September, Coulson's cash balance was $50,000 and its line of credit and marketable securities equalled $0.[4] The company wishes to maintain a minimum cash balance of

4. If Coulson had either an outstanding line of credit or held marketable securities at the end of September, this information would have to be provided so the relevant amount could be included in the cash budget for September.

TABLE 4.4 A Cash Budget for Coulson Industries ($000)

	Oct.	Nov.	Dec.
Total cash receipts[a]	$210	$320	$340
Less: Total cash disbursements[b]	213	418	305
Net cash flow	$ (3)	$ (98)	$ 35
Add: Beginning cash	50	47	(51)
Ending cash	$ 47	$ (51)	$ (16)
Less: Minimum cash balance	25	25	25
Required total financing (line of credit)[c]	—	$ 76	$ 41
Excess cash balance (marketable securities)[d]	$ 22	—	—

[a]From Table 4.2.
[b]From Table 4.3.
[c]Values are placed in this line when the ending cash is less than the desired minimum cash balance. These amounts are typically financed short-term and are most often raised using a line of credit.
[d]Values are placed in this line when the ending cash is greater than the desired minimum cash balance. These amounts are typically assumed to be invested short-term in marketable securities.

$25,000 in their bank account. Most firms like to maintain a certain minimum amount of cash for liquidity purposes and to deal with unexpected events.

Table 4.4 indicates that Coulson will have excess cash that can be invested in marketable securities for a certain period of time. This investment will earn a small amount of interest in that period, but this is not included in the cash budget. The interest may be viewed as a cushion in case some of the cash receipts are overstated, or cash disbursements understated. Note that the excess cash for October was not due to a positive cash flow in October, but rather to the $50,000 of cash the firm had on hand at the end of September.

For November, Coulson is expecting a large negative cash flow, primarily due to the purchase of the new machinery. Therefore, the marketable securities will have to be cashed sometime in October and the proceeds used to pay for the purchase. In addition, the cash budget indicates that the company will also have to be able to access $76,000 from their line of credit in November. Finally in December, Coulson is expecting a positive cash flow of $35,000. This amount is used to repay the line of credit. This leads to an important point. Note that the required total financing figures in the cash budget refer to *how much will be owed at the end of the month;* they do *not* represent the monthly changes in borrowing.

The monthly changes in borrowing and in excess cash can be found by further analyzing the cash budget. In October, the $50,000 beginning cash, which becomes $47,000 after the $3,000 net cash outflow, results in a $22,000 excess cash balance once the $25,000 minimum cash is deducted. In November, the $76,000 of required total financing resulted from the $98,000 net cash outflow less the $22,000 of excess cash from October. The $41,000 of required total financing in December resulted from reducing November's $76,000 of required total financing by the $35,000 of net cash inflow during December. Summarizing, the financial actions for each month would be as follows:

October:	Invest $22,000 of excess cash in marketable securities.
November:	Liquidate the $22,000 of marketable securities and borrow $76,000 using the line of credit.
December:	Repay $35,000 on the line of credit.

Evaluating the Cash Budget

Hint

The cash budget is not only a great tool to let management know when it has cash shortages or excesses, but it is usually a document required by potential creditors. It communicates to them what the money lent is going to be used for, and how and when they will get their loan paid back.

The cash budget provides the firm with figures indicating whether a cash shortage or surplus is expected to result in each of the time intervals covered by the forecast. Each interval's figure is based on the internally imposed requirement of a minimum cash balance and *represents the total balance at the end of the month.*

At the end of each of the 3 months, Coulson expects the following balances in cash, marketable securities, and notes payable:

	End-of-month balance ($000)		
Account	**Oct.**	**Nov.**	**Dec.**
Cash	$25	$25	$25
Marketable securities	22	0	0
Line of credit	0	76	41

Note that the firm is assumed to first liquidate its marketable securities to meet deficits and then borrow using a line of credit if additional financing is needed. As a result, a firm will not have marketable securities and a line of credit outstanding on its cash budget at the same time. Note, though, that it is possible for both items to appear on the balance sheet. A company may hold marketable securities and have a line of credit outstanding as at a point in time. The expectation is that this situation would not be in effect for a long period of time.

Hint

The manager will usually arrange to borrow more than the maximum financing indicated in the cash budget, because of the uncertainty of the ending cash values, which are derived from various forecasts.

Because it may be necessary for the firm to borrow up to $76,000 for the 3-month period, the financial manager should be sure that a line of credit is established or some other arrangement made to ensure the availability of these funds.

Coping with Uncertainty in the Cash Budget

Aside from careful estimating of the inputs to the cash budget, there are two ways of coping with the uncertainty of the cash budget.[5] One is to prepare several cash budgets—based on pessimistic, most likely, and optimistic forecasts. From this range of cash flows, the financial manager can determine the amount of financing needed to cover the most adverse situation. The use of several cash budgets based on differing assumptions also should give the financial manager a

5. The term *uncertainty* is used here to refer to the variability of the cash flow outcomes that may actually occur in the forecast period.

sense of the riskiness of alternatives so that he or she can make more intelligent short-term financial decisions. This sensitivity analysis, or "what if" approach, is often used to analyze cash flows under a variety of possible circumstances. Computers and electronic spreadsheets are commonly used to simplify the process of sensitivity analysis.

Example Table 4.5 presents the summary of Coulson Industries' cash budget prepared for each month of concern using pessimistic, most likely, and optimistic estimates of cash receipts and disbursements. The most likely estimate is based on the expected outcomes presented earlier in Tables 4.2 through 4.4.

During October, Coulson will at worst need a maximum of $15,000 of financing, and at best it will have a $62,000 excess cash balance available for short-term investment. During November, Coulson could have excess cash of $5,000, or need financing of as much as $185,000. The December projections show maximum borrowing of $190,000 with a possible excess cash balance of $107,000. By considering the extreme values reflected in the pessimistic and optimistic outcomes, Coulson Industries should be better able to plan cash requirements. For the 3-month period, the peak borrowing requirement under the most pessimistic circumstances would be $190,000, which is considerably greater than the most likely estimate of $76,000 for this period. On the other hand, if the optimistic outcome occurs, Coulson would not have to borrow any funds in the quarter and by the end of December would have $107,000 in marketable securities.

TABLE 4.5 A Sensitivity Analysis of Coulson Industries' Cash Budget ($000)

	October			November			December		
	Pessimistic	Most likely	Optimistic	Pessimistic	Most likely	Optimistic	Pessimistic	Most likely	Optimistic
Total cash receipts	$160	$210	$285	$ 210	$320	$ 410	$ 275	$340	$422
Less: Total cash disbursements	200	213	248	380	418	467	280	305	320
Net cash flow	$(40)	$ (3)	$ 37	$(170)	$ (98)	$ (57)	$ (5)	$ 35	$102
Add: Beginning cash	50	50	50	10	47	87	(160)	(51)	30
Ending cash	$ 10	$ 47	$ 87	$(160)	$ (51)	$ 30	$(165)	$(16)	$132
Less: Minimum cash balance	25	25	25	25	25	25	25	25	25
Required total financing	$ 15	—	—	$ 185	$ 76	—	$ 190	$ 41	—
Excess cash balance	—	$ 22	$ 62	—	—	$ 5	—	—	$107

A second and much more sophisticated way of coping with uncertainty in the cash budget is *simulation*.[6] By simulating the occurrence of sales and other uncertain events, the firm can develop a probability distribution of its ending cash flows for each month. The financial decision maker can then use the probability distribution to determine the amount of financing necessary to provide a desired degree of protection against a cash shortage.

Cash Flow Within the Month

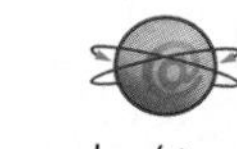

www.pearsoned.ca/gitman

Because the cash budget shows cash flows only on a total monthly basis, the information provided by the cash budget is not necessarily adequate for ensuring solvency. A firm must look more closely at its pattern of daily cash receipts and cash disbursements to ensure that adequate cash is available for paying bills as they come due. For an example related to this topic, see the book's Web site.

The synchronization of cash flows in the cash budget at month-end does not ensure that the firm will be able to meet daily cash requirements. Because a firm's cash flows are generally quite variable when viewed on a daily basis, effective cash planning requires a look *beyond* the cash budget. The financial manager must therefore plan and monitor cash flow more frequently than on a monthly basis. The greater the variability of cash flows from day to day, the greater the attention required.

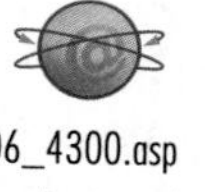

www.toolkit.cch.com/text/P06_4300.asp

www.tutor2u.net/business/presentations/accounts/cashbudget/default.html

That is why most well-managed firms use at most a weekly time interval for a cash budget. Many firms that generate high amounts of sales (and cash) use a daily time interval. With the widespread use of computer spreadsheets, many companies have developed inexpensive and easily used spreadsheet-based cash budgets that track the balance of cash held by the firm on a daily basis. More information regarding cash budgets and spreadsheet templates is available on various Web sites.

? Review Questions

4–3 What is the purpose of the *cash budget?* The key input to the cash budget is the sales forecast. What is the difference between *external* and *internal* forecast data?

4–4 Briefly describe the basic format of the cash budget, beginning with forecast sales and ending with *required total financing* or *excess cash balance.*

4–5 How can the two "bottom lines" of the cash budget be used to determine the firm's short-term borrowing and investment requirements?

4–6 What is the cause of uncertainty in the cash budget? What two techniques can be used to cope with this uncertainty?

4–7 What actions or analysis beyond preparation of the cash budget should the financial manager undertake to ensure that cash is available when needed? Why?

6. A more detailed discussion of the use of simulation is included among the approaches for dealing with risk in capital budgeting in Chapter 13.

4.1 **IN PRACTICE**

Financial Forecasting: Predicting the Unknown

Meteorologists and financial planners have a common problem: difficulty in making accurate forecasts. Like the weather, a company's financial results are very difficult to accurately predict. But accurate forecasting is a critical part of financial management. In the past, financial forecasting was often overlooked, but now it is recognized as an essential part of financial management and control. In fact, in a recent survey of 200 companies, forecasting was identified as the most important issue currently facing companies.

This should come as no surprise, given that accurate forecasting brings with it significant financial benefits. Such benefits include the ability of the firm to: identify its key value and cost drivers and develop appropriate performance measures, effectively plan and budget the firm's performance, simulate its aspired or expected performance using driver-based scenarios, and understand how operating or leading drivers impact its financial outcomes. Accurate forecasting can also lead to an increased return on investment. For example, companies that forecast their cash requirements for more than three months in the future generate an extra 30 basis points' return on their cash holdings.

The key to realizing benefits is to ensure that the forecasts are based on clear, reliable, and accurate information. As the saying goes, "Garbage in, garbage out." While companies may recognize the importance of financial forecasting, they are still facing difficulties in making accurate forecasts. The primary reason is that companies are not ensuring that the information they use to forecast is reliable. As a financial consultant says, "Up-front, solid, accurate data collection and research is one of the keys to accurate forecasting. A lot of people don't envision going through the process of really ensuring that data is reflective of historical trends. They don't prepare the data and build the framework of the forecasting model effectively. So that is one of the downfalls—they are starting with a weak foundation and ultimately they end in failure."

It is important to note that as forecasts are made farther into the future, the accuracy and certainty of the forecasts is reduced. This may lead one to wonder why companies should even bother forecasting beyond the immediate future. The reason such forecasting is important is that it forces the company to recognize the economic and market factors that might influence the operation. For example, an analysis of these factors might reveal that the purchase or sale of an asset or business would not be wise.

▶

4.3 Fundamentals of Preparing the Pro Forma Financial Statements

The cash budget focuses on forecasting the flow of cash to ensure the firm has access to sufficient cash to operate and remain solvent. The cash may be generated by operations, by liquidating marketable securities, or from utilizing a line of credit or another source of financing. A cash budget is not the only statement that must be forecasted. Figure 4.1 indicates that a company must also forecast prof-

(Continued)

While all the components of the financial forecast are important, the most important forecast, and the starting point of the process, is the sales forecast. After an accurate estimate for sales has been established, the rest of the process is easier. Sales forecasts are the basis on which companies estimate their cash budgets, profitability, investment in assets, and the amount of financing required to support the forecasted level of sales.

There are no specific, formal guidelines, but good financial forecasting is based on seven key principles:

- Forecasting is not an afterthought to be tacked onto the end of the period-end reporting process, but is a critical process in its own right. In turn, business units must be given time to consider and submit high-quality forecasts.
- Forecasting should be carried out frequently. Many companies have now positioned forecasting as a critical business process that is repeated at least on a monthly basis.
- Forecasts should "roll" by setting an objective and realistic assessment of performance up to 15–18 months ahead of time.
- Forecasts should start with the main business drivers, which in most businesses revolve around sales.
- Forecasts should be stated in terms of the company's complete business performance management framework, including both leading indicators and lagging financials.
- Forecast accuracy must be measured, and should become one of the key business indicators for which business unit general managers are held accountable.
- Actual outcomes must be compared to the forecast, as this forms the basis for building the following year's budget. The comparison also highlights the gap between actual results and the budget, and therefore forewarns management of either financing shortfalls or surpluses.

SOURCES: "Determining the Value of a Business," Business and Entrepreneurship Resource Center, March 1, 2005, **www.zeromillion.com/business/buying/business-valuation.html**; "Cash Flow Forecasting," The Treasury and Finance Network, April 13, 2005, **www.gtnews.com/feature/77.cfm**; Tony Vadasz, "Accurate Forecasting as a Fundamental Part of Financial Management," Parson Consulting, April 11, 2005, **www.gtnews.com/article/5874.cfm**; Bruce Lynn, "Forecasting: If It Is So Important Why Can't Companies Get It Right?" The Financial Executives Consulting Group, April 11, 2005, **www.gtnews.com/article/5877.cfm**.

itability by preparing a pro forma income statement and determine their future financial position and need for financing by preparing a pro forma balance sheet.

Pro forma statements are vital for management to evaluate the future expected financial position and for current and prospective investors (shareholders) and creditors to evaluate the firm's ability to provide a return on the funds invested. The preparation of these statements requires a careful blending of a number of procedures to account for the revenues, expenses, assets, liabilities, and equity resulting from the firm's anticipated level of operations. The basic steps in this process were shown in the flow diagram of Figure 4.1.

The financial forecasting process considers expected profitability and estimates the amount of financing the firm requires to operate over the forecast period. There are three key outputs of the financial forecasting process: (1) a pro forma income statement; (2) a pro forma balance sheet; and (3) a statement of external financing required. Financing is required to invest in assets. Assets are required to support increasing sales and profits. Therefore, financial forecasting is associated with increasing sales. As stated earlier in the chapter, an accurate sales forecast is the starting point for financial planning and forecasting.

Example For the 2008 fiscal year, Franklin Inc.'s sales were $800,000 and the company's total assets were $510,000. Obviously, Franklin must also have $510,000 of liabilities and shareholders' equity, which indicates the financing the firm used to acquire the assets. For 2009, Franklin expects sales will increase by 25 percent or by $200,000 to $1,000,000. Franklin estimates that in order to generate and support the increased sales, assets must increase by $130,000. Therefore, total assets will increase to $640,000.

The implication is that Franklin must raise $130,000 of financing as debt, equity, or a combination of the two. Note that a portion of the $130,000 may come from reinvested profits, so some of the financing may be generated internally. The expected amount of reinvested profits is based on the pro forma income statement. In addition, some of the required financing will come from increases in current liabilities such as accounts payable and accruals. Recall from Chapter 2 that, for the statement of cash flows, if a current liability increases, this is a source of cash. This is an internal source of financing for financial forecasting purposes. So, while Franklin must raise $130,000 of financing to support increasing assets and sales, a portion of this will come from the two internal sources.

Items Required for Forecasting the Pro Forma Statements

To prepare a pro forma statement, three inputs are required: (1) financial statements for the previous year, (2) sales forecast for the forecast year, and (3) forecasts for all other financial statement accounts. When forecasting, a large number of assumptions (forecasts) must be made. An important point to note is that financial forecasting simply reflects a set of assumptions regarding a company's financial situation for the forecast period. The first assumption (or forecast) is expected sales. Other assumptions are then made and these are reflected in the pro forma financial statements.

? Review Questions

4–8 What is the purpose of preparing pro forma statements? What inputs are required?

4–9 What are the outputs of the financial forecasting process? What is reflected in these outputs?

4.4 A Simple Approach to Financial Forecasting

Hint
A key point in understanding pro forma statements is that these are the goals and objectives of the firm for the planning period. In order for these goals and objectives to be achieved, operational plans will have to be developed. Financial plans can be realized only if the correct actions are implemented.

To illustrate the basic concepts associated with financial forecasting, consider Vectra Manufacturing, which manufactures and sells one product. It has two basic models—model X and model Y—which are produced by the same process but require different amounts of raw material and labour. The income statement for the firm's 2008 fiscal year is provided in Table 4.6. It indicates that Vectra had sales of $100,000, total cost of goods sold of $80,000, earnings before taxes of $9,000, and net income after taxes of $7,650. The firm paid $3,060 in cash dividends, leaving $4,590 to be reinvested and transferred to retained earnings. The firm's balance sheet for 2008 is provided in Table 4.7.

TABLE 4.6 Vectra Manufacturing Income Statement for the Year Ended December 31, 2008

Total sales	$100,000
Less: Cost of goods sold	80,000
Gross margin	$ 20,000
Less: Operating expenses	10,000
Operating earnings	$ 10,000
Less: Interest expense	1,000
Earnings before taxes	$ 9,000
Less: Taxes (15%)	1,350
Net income after taxes (profit margin)	$ 7,650 (7.65%)
Less: Common share dividends	3,060
Reinvested profits (to retained earnings)	$ 4,590

TABLE 4.7 Vectra Manufacturing Balance Sheet as at December 31, 2008

Assets		Liabilities and equities	
Cash	$ 6,000	Accounts payable	$ 7,000
Marketable securities	4,000	Accruals	2,300
Accounts receivable	13,000	Line of credit	8,300
Inventory	16,000	Other current liabilities	1,400
Total current assets	$ 39,000	Total current liabilities	$ 19,000
Net fixed assets	$ 61,000	Long-term debt	$ 18,000
Total assets	$100,000	Shareholders' equity	
		Common shares	$ 30,000
		Retained earnings	$ 33,000
		Total liabilities and shareholders' equity	$100,000

Like the cash budget, the key input for the development of pro forma statements is the sales forecast. Based on both external and internal data, sales for Vectra for the 2009 fiscal year are expected to increase by 40 percent. This implies sales will increase by $40,000 to $140,000. The large increase is due, in part, to selling more units, plus increasing the selling price of the product by 18 percent. Vectra Manufacturing's marketing department has indicated that the majority of the company's customers are willing to pay a higher price given the product's high quality and perceived value. In addition, since labour and materials costs are expected to increase, the finance department feels the selling price should increase to cover the higher costs.

Tables 4.6 and 4.7, and the marketing department's sales forecast, provide the first two inputs required to project the financial statements for Vectra. To prepare the pro forma income statement, assumptions regarding the various expenses are required. An assumption that can be made to simplify the process is that all expenses remain the same percent of sales in the forecast year as they were in the previous fiscal year. This approach to financial forecasting is called the **percent-of-sales method.** For Vectra, the expenses as a percent of sales for the 2008 fiscal year were:

percent-of-sales method
A method of developing the pro forma income statement that assumes all expenses remain the same percent of sales in the forecast year as they were in the most recent fiscal year.

$$\frac{\text{cost of goods sold}}{\text{sales}} = \frac{\$80{,}000}{\$100{,}000} = 80.0\%$$

$$\frac{\text{operating expenses}}{\text{sales}} = \frac{\$10{,}000}{\$100{,}000} = 10.0\%$$

$$\frac{\text{interest expense}}{\text{sales}} = \frac{\$1{,}000}{\$100{,}000} = 1.0\%$$

$$\frac{\text{taxes}}{\text{sales}} = \frac{\$1{,}350}{\$100{,}000} = 1.35\%$$

Note that the dollar amounts used in the above calculations are taken from the 2008 income statement (Table 4.6). The percent-of-sales approach assumes that the relationship that existed between each of the expenses and sales in the previous fiscal year will also apply in the forecast year. In other words, while the scale of the numbers on the income statement will change, the percentage relationship with sales will remain the same. This is a simple assumption, but one that illustrates the basics of financial forecasting.

To project the income statement for 2009, use the previously calculated expense percentages. In other words, reflect the percent-of-sales assumption in the pro forma income statement. Vectra's sales for 2009 are forecasted to be $140,000. Applying the percent-of-sales assumption results in the pro forma income statement provided in Table 4.8. Note that in Table 4.8, the **dividend payout ratio**, the percent of NIAT (or earnings available to common shareholders) that is paid out to common shareholders as dividends during the year, is 40 percent. This is the same percentage of earnings that was paid out in 2008. So the percent-of-sales method also assumes the payout ratio remains the same.

dividend payout ratio
The percent of NIAT (or earnings available to common shareholders) that is paid out to common shareholders as dividends during the year.

With the percent-of-sales approach, all costs increase with sales. So, with sales increasing 40 percent, so too will cost of goods sold, all operating expenses, interest expense, and taxes. The net effect is that net income after tax (NIAT) will also increase 40 percent. This is exactly what occurs. Note in 2008 that NIAT was $7,650. The forecast for NIAT for 2009 is $10,710. This is a 40 percent increase. (See the highlighted number on Table 4.8.) This also means that

TABLE 4.8 Vectro Manufacturing: Actual and Pro Forma Income Statements (Prepared Using the Percent-of-Sales Method) for Years Ended December 31

	2008 Actual	2009 Pro Forma
Sales revenue	$100,000	$140,000
Less: Cost of goods sold (80%)	80,000	112,000
Gross margin	$ 20,000	$ 28,000
Less: Operating expenses (10%)	10,000	14,000
Operating earnings	$ 10,000	$ 14,000
Less: Interest expense (1%)	1,000	1,400
Earnings before taxes	$ 9,000	$ 12,600
Less: Taxes (15% of EBT or 1.35% of sales)	1,350	1,890
Net income after taxes (profit margin)	$ 7,650	$ 10,710 (7.65% of sales)
Less: Common share dividends (40% payout)	3,060	4,284
Reinvested profits (to retained earnings)	$ 4,590	$ 6,426

the profit margin will be the same in 2009 as it was in 2008. In addition, the portion of the profits reinvested are also the same.

Projecting the Balance Sheet

With the pro forma income statement prepared, the next step is to develop the balance sheet for 2009 using the percent-of-sales method. The same assumption that was used for the income statement will also be used for the balance sheet. That is, we assume certain items will vary directly with sales. The items that are assumed to vary directly with sales are all of the asset accounts, with the exception of marketable securities, and accounts payable, and accruals. The implication of the asset accounts varying directly with sales is that the firm is operating at peak capacity. Therefore, to support any sales increase, the firm's assets must also increase.

As discussed earlier in the chapter, accounts payable and accruals will also increase with sales. The reason for this is that these current liabilities are associated with the purchase of inventory and other direct costs of production. Since these items are increasing with sales, so too will accounts payable and accruals. For financial forecasting, the increases in accounts payable and accruals are termed **spontaneous sources of financing**—because the company is not deliberately increasing these accounts, rather they increase spontaneously as sales increase. This increase is an internal source of financing for the company.

spontaneous sources of financing
The increases in accounts payable and accruals that will occur as inventory and other direct costs of production increase with sales, an internal source of financing for the company.

The remaining items on the balance sheet—marketable securities, other liabilities, and equity—will only change if management acts to change them. The amount of the line of credit, long-term debt, common shares, and retained earnings will only change if the company pays off or acquires debt, issues or repurchases common shares, or reinvests profits. These factors are directly in the control of management, so you will have to be told something about these accounts before changing them on the pro forma balance sheet. Applying these concepts to Vectra, we first determine the relationships between the relevant balance sheet accounts and sales for the 2008 fiscal year. The percentage relationships are provided below:

Vectra Manufacturing
Balance Sheet as a Percent of Sales
as at December 31, 2008

Cash	6%	Accounts payable	7%
Marketable securities	N/A	Accruals	2.3%
Accounts receivable	13%	Line of credit	N/A
Inventories	16%	Other current liabilities	N/A
Total current assets	35%	Total current liabilities	9.3%
Net fixed assets	61%	*Other liability and equity accounts must be changed by management actions.*	
Total assets	96%		

This analysis suggests that if Vectra's sales increased by $1,000 in 2009, Vectra would require $960 more in assets, structured in the percentages indicated above. As we know, to acquire assets, a company needs funds. Therefore, Vectra will require $960 of financing to acquire the assets. Some of this financing will come from internal sources. Note that the above analysis also indicates that if sales increased by $1,000 in 2009, accounts payable and accruals will increase by a combined $93. As discussed earlier, this spontaneous increase in the two current liabilities provides a source of financing.

So, with the spontaneous increase in the two current liabilities considered, Vectra requires $867 of financing ($960 − $93) for every $1,000 increase in sales. In addition, the income statement forecasted earlier provides another internal source of financing. The forecast indicated that the company will pay out 40 percent of the profits as dividends to common shareholders. The remainder will be reinvested. These reinvested profits are an internal source of financing that will flow to retained earnings on the balance sheet. Based on the increase in assets, we have a total requirement for financing. The change in assets from the latest fiscal year to the forecast year determines the **total financing required** (TFR). An increase in total assets reflects the need for financing. A portion of the TFR may be generated internally. We have two internal sources of financing, the spontaneous increase in payables and accruals and the reinvested profits. This can be seen when comparing the 2008 actual and the first pro forma balance sheets provided in Table 4.9.

total financing required
The change in total assets from the latest fiscal year to the forecast year.

A review of the first pro forma balance sheet for Vectra results in six findings. First, each of the assets (except marketable securities) have increased by 40 percent. This makes perfect sense, since it is the assumption of the percent-of-sales forecasting method. Second, total assets have increased by $38,400. Sales increased by $40,000, and since the assets that will increase with sales are 96 percent of sales ($40,000 × 96%) this too makes sense. Third, accounts payable and accruals also increased by 40 percent, which is also consistent with the forecasting method.

Fourth, retained earnings increase, since, as we have already seen in the income statement, Vectra reinvested $6,426 of profits. Fifth, none of the other accounts change, since as yet no information is provided that would result in these accounts changing. Sixth, the balance sheet does not balance. This will always be the case when forecasting. For the forecast year, either the firm will

TABLE 4.9 **Vectra Manufacturing: Actual and Pro Forma Balance Sheets (Percent-of-Sales Method) as of December 31**

Assets	2008 Actual	2009 Pro forma 1	2009 Pro forma 2
Cash	$ 6,000	$ 8,400	$ 8,400
Marketable securities	4,000	4,000	0
Accounts receivable	13,000	18,200	18,200
Inventory	16,000	22,400	22,400
Total current assets	39,000	53,000	49,000
Net fixed assets	61,000	85,400	85,400
Total assets	$100,000	$138,400	$134,400
Liabilities and Equity			
Accounts payable	$ 7,000	$ 9,800	$ 9,800
Accruals	2,300	3,220	3,220
Line of credit	8,300	8,300	32,554
Other current liabilities	1,400	1,400	1,400
Total current liabilities	19,000	22,720	46,974
Long-term debt	18,000	18,000	18,000
Shareholders' Equity			
Common shares	30,000	30,000	30,000
Retained earnings	33,000	39,426	39,426
Total liabilities and equity	$100,000	$110,146	$134,400

require financing, or they will generate excess financing. Determining which will occur is the main objective of forecasting.

So at this point we have a pro forma balance sheet that doesn't balance. When comparing the total assets to the total liabilities and equity for the 2009 forecast year, it is clear that the firm requires more on the liabilities and equity side—the firm requires financing. How much? To answer, one can simply subtract the total liabilities and equity from the total assets. The answer is $28,254, and this would be the external financing required (EFR). But there are two concerns.

First, note that on the 2009 balance sheet, marketable securities of $4,000 are included. Generally, marketable securities provide a much lower rate of return than the cost of financing to a company. It makes no sense for Vectra to raise $28,254 of financing when they hold $4,000 of low-return marketable securities. Therefore, prior to raising financing, the expectation is that Vectra will liquidate the marketable securities, thereby reducing EFR by $4,000 to $24,254. When this assumption is reflected in the second pro forma balance sheet, total assets declines by the $4,000.

statement of external financing required The forecasted statement that shows the difference between total financing required and the two internal sources of financing, providing the amount of external financing required.

Second, the analyst should always calculate EFR separately. To do this, calculate total financing required and then subtract the two internal sources of financing. This is best done by developing the **statement of external financing required.** Table 4.10 provides this statement for Vectra for the 2009 forecast. Following this approach also ensures that your calculations in the pro forma balance sheet are correct.

As discussed above, the difference between the total assets and the total liabilities and equity on the second pro forma balance sheet is $24,254. This is also

TABLE 4.10 Vectra Manufacturing: Calculation of External Financing Required (Percent-of-Sales Method) for the Forecast Year Ended December 31, 2009

Total financing required (TFR) (based on change in total assets)		\$34,400
Less: Internal sources		
Increase in accounts payable	\$2,800	
Increase in accruals	920	
Reinvested profits	6,426	
Total internal sources		10,146
External financing required (EFR)		\$24,254

the amount calculated in Table 4.10. Therefore, Vectra must raise this amount of debt and/or equity financing. For this example, we will assume that the funds are raised using the line of credit. This assumption is reflected in the second pro forma balance sheet. The complete forecast is also provided as Spreadsheet Application 1.

At this point the forecasting process is complete. Given the forecasts for the 2009 fiscal year, we have developed the three forecasted statements and determined the amount of EFR that the company must raise. The company must then attempt to raise this amount of funds in order to have the money available to invest in assets and support the increasing sales.

Before concluding this section, note that a *positive* value for "external financing required," like that shown in Table 4.10, means that to support the forecast level of operation, the firm must raise funds externally using debt and/or equity financing. Once the form of financing is determined, the pro forma balance sheet is modified to reflect the external financing required in the debt and/or equity accounts.

A *negative* value for external financing required indicates that the firm's forecast financing is in excess of its needs. In this case, funds would be available for use in repaying debt, repurchasing common shares, increasing dividends, or investing in assets. Once the specific actions are determined, the external financing required is reflected in the pro forma balance sheet with the planned reductions in the debt and/or equity accounts, increases in assets, or increased dividends.

Formula Approach for the Percent-of-Sales Forecasting Method

As seen above, with the percent-of-sales forecasting method, EFR can be calculated by developing the pro forma balance sheet and statement of EFR. But it is also possible to determine EFR by using the following formula:

$$\text{EFR}_1 = \frac{A_v}{S_0}(S_0 \times g) - \frac{L_v}{S_0}(S_0 \times g) - [S_0(1 + g) \times \text{PM}_1 \times b_1] \tag{4.1}$$

where
EFR_1 = external financing required for the forecast year (year 1)
A_v = assets that vary directly with sales for the most recently completed fiscal year (year 0)
S_0 = sales for the most recently completed fiscal year (year 0)
L_v = liabilities that vary directly with sales for the most recently completed fiscal year (year 0)
g = growth rate in sales, in percent, for the forecast year
PM_1 = profit margin as a percentage for the forecast year
b_1 = earnings retention ratio (1 − dividend payout ratio) for the forecast year

4.1 SPREADSHEET APPLICATION

Microsoft Excel - Spreadsheet Application 4-1.xls

	A	B	C	D	E
2	**Vectra Manufacturing**				
3	**Actual and Pro Forma Income Statements**				
4	**Prepared Using the Percent-of-Sales Method**				
5	**For the Years Ended December 31**				
6					
7		2008(A)	2009(F)		
8	Sales Revenue	$100,000	$140,000	←	=B8*(1.4)
9	Cost of Goods Sold	80,000	112,000	←	=B9*(1.4)
10	Gross Profit Margin	$20,000	$28,000	←	=C8-C9
11	Less: Operating expenses	10,000	14,000	←	=B11*(1.4)
12	Operating earnings	10,000	14,000	←	=C10-C11
13	Less: Interest expenses	1,000	1,400	←	=B13*(1.4)
14	Earnings Before Taxes (EBT)	9,000	12,600	←	=C12-C13
15	Taxes (15%)	1,350	1,890	←	=B15*(1.4)
16	Net income after tax (NIAT)	7,650	10,710	←	=C14-C15
17	Less: Common share dividends (40%)	3,060	4,284	←	=C16*(0.4)
18	Reinvested Profits	$4,590	$6,426	←	=C16-C17
19					
20					
21	**Vectra Manufacturing**				
22	**Actual and Pro Forma Balance Sheets**				
23	**Prepared Using the Percent-of-Sales Method**				
24	**As at December 31**				
25					
26	**Assets**	2008(A)	2009(F)		Formulas
27	Current Assets				
28	Cash	$6,000	$8,400	←	=(B28/B34)*C8
29	Marketable Securities	4,000	0	←	=IF((C28+C30+C31+C33)>B34,0,B29)
30	Accounts Receivable	13,000	18,200	←	=(B30/B34)*C8
31	Inventory	16,000	22,400	←	=(B31/B34)*C8
32	Total Current Assets	39,000	49,000	←	=sum(C28:C31)
33	Net Fixed Assets	61,000	85,400	←	=(B33/B34)*C8
34	Total Assets	$100,000	$134,400	←	=C32+C33
35					
36	**Liabilities and Shareholder's Equity**				
37	Current Liabilities				
38	Account Payable	$7,000	$9,800	←	=(B38/B49)*C8
39	Accruals	2,300	3,220	←	=(B39/B49)*C8
40	Line of Credit	8,300	32,554	←	=B40+C64
41	Other current liabilities	1,400	1,400	←	=B41
42	Total current liabilities	$19,000	$46,974	←	=sum(C38:C41)
43					
44	Long-term debt	18,000	18,000	←	=B44
45					
46	Shareholders' equity				
47	Common shares	30,000	30,000	←	=B47
48	Retained earnings	33,000	39,426	←	=B48+C18
49	Total liabilities and equity	$100,000	$134,400	←	=sum(C42:C48)
50					
51					

SA 4-1

Ready NUM

continued

4.1 SPREADSHEET APPLICATION (continued)

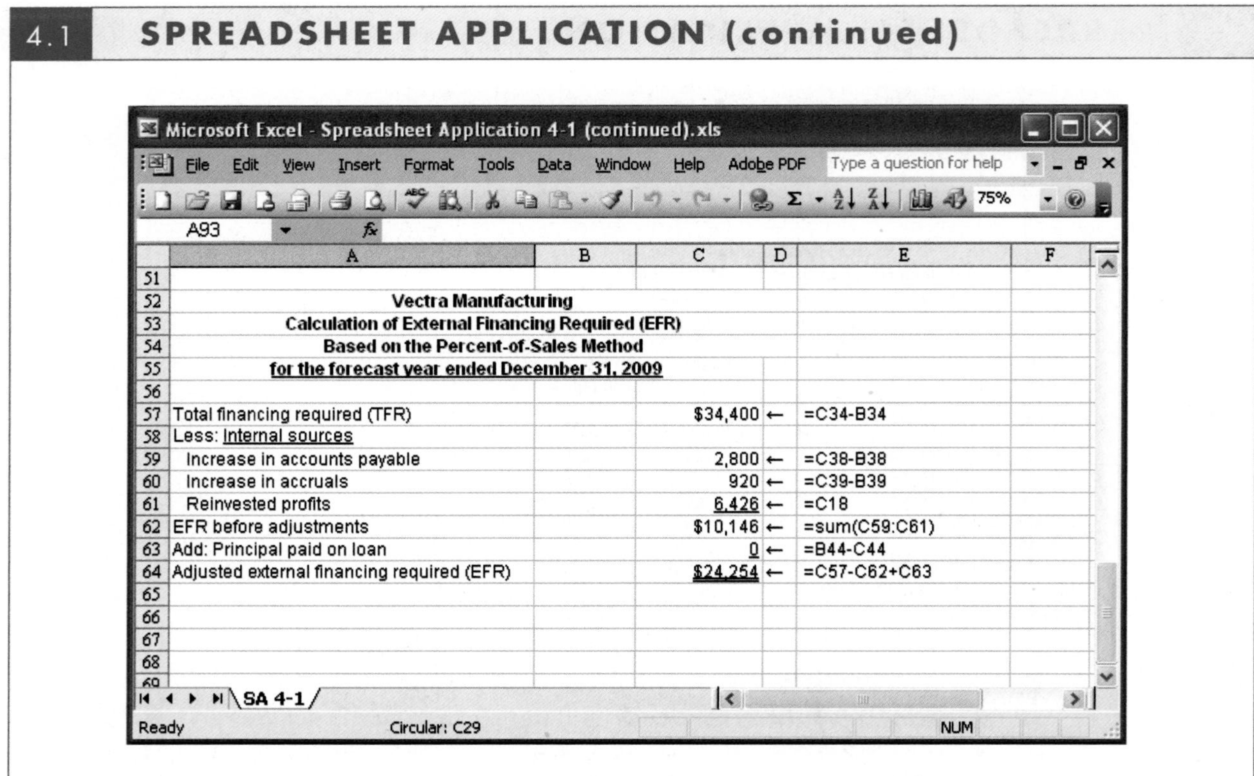

Microsoft Excel - Spreadsheet Application 4-1 (continued).xls

	A	B	C	D	E	F
51						
52	Vectra Manufacturing					
53	Calculation of External Financing Required (EFR)					
54	Based on the Percent-of-Sales Method					
55	for the forecast year ended December 31, 2009					
56						
57	Total financing required (TFR)		$34,400	←	=C34-B34	
58	Less: Internal sources					
59	Increase in accounts payable		2,800	←	=C38-B38	
60	Increase in accruals		920	←	=C39-B39	
61	Reinvested profits		6,426	←	=C18	
62	EFR before adjustments		$10,146	←	=sum(C59:C61)	
63	Add: Principal paid on loan		0	←	=B44-C44	
64	Adjusted external financing required (EFR)		$24,254	←	=C57-C62+C63	
65						
66						
67						
68						

SA 4-1

Ready Circular: C29 NUM

capital intensity ratio
The dollar amount of assets needed for each $1 increase in sales; the larger the number, the more capital-intensive the company, and therefore the higher the amount of financing required.

The A_v/S_0 variable is called the **capital intensity ratio.** It indicates the dollar amount of assets needed for each $1 increase in sales. The larger the number, the more capital-intensive the company and the higher the assets required for a given increase in sales. This also means the company will require higher amounts of financing for the forecast year. Some companies are very capital-intensive, some less so.

Example We have two companies each with $1,000 of sales. Assets that vary directly with sales for company 1 are $3,000, but are only $800 for company 2. What happens if the sales for each company are forecasted to increase by 70 percent or $700? The capital intensity ratio for company 1 is 3 ($3,000/$1,000). For company 2, the ratio is 0.80 ($800/$1,000). Therefore, for each $1 increase in sales, company 1 will require $3 of assets (and financing). For each $1 increase in sales, company 2 will require $0.80 of assets (and financing). For the $700 increase in sales, company 1 will require $2,100 of assets (and financing), while company 2 only requires $560. Company 1 must be able to access large amounts of financing when sales increase; it is much more capital-intensive than company 2.

Applying the formula approach for Vectra Manufacturing using the information provided in the previous section, we can find the EFR as follows. Note that for this example, the $(S_0 \times g)$ variable is $40,000, since g, the growth rate in sales, is 40 percent.

$$
\begin{aligned}
\text{EFR}_1 &= \frac{\$96{,}000}{\$100{,}000}(\$40{,}000) - \frac{\$9{,}300}{\$100{,}000}(40{,}000) - [\$140{,}000 \times (7.65\%) \times (1 - 0.40)] \\
&= 96\%(\$40{,}000) - 9.3\%(\$40{,}000) - \$10{,}710(60\%) \\
&= \$38{,}400 - \$3{,}720 - \$6{,}426 \\
&= \$28{,}254
\end{aligned}
$$

This, of course, is exactly the same amount as in Table 4.9. The formula approach is simply another way to calculate EFR given the simplified assumptions implicit with the percent-of-sales forecasting method. But, again, note that the correct amount of EFR is $4,000 less than that calculated, since it makes no sense for Vectra to raise $28,254 of financing when they hold $4,000 of low-return marketable securities. Therefore, as before, the amount of EFR Vectra will attempt to raise is $24,254.

If Vectra was expected to experience a very high growth in sales in the year, what impact will that have on EFR? If the growth rate in sales was 80 percent, what would be the amount of EFR? Inserting 80 percent into the formula and adjusting for the sale of the marketable securities results in the following:

$$
\begin{aligned}
\text{EFR} &= (\$76{,}800 - \$7{,}440 - \$8{,}262) - \$4{,}000 \\
&= \$61{,}098 - \$4{,}000 \\
&= \$57{,}098
\end{aligned}
$$

For a company with only $100,000 of assets, raising an additional $57,098 of external financing would be a real challenge. A lesson that can be learned from this analysis is that high rates of sales growth mean a company must raise large amounts of external financing to support the higher sales growth. This can be difficult and very time-consuming for many firms. Convincing creditors to lend money and/or investors to purchase additional equity can be challenging.

Sustainable Growth Rate

If a company feels that it is not possible to raise financing from external sources, a question that is reasonable to ask is: What rate of sales growth can be financed with only internal sources of financing? This would be the point where EFR is zero. By making a modified Equation 4.1 equal to zero, we can solve for g. In this format, g will be the rate of sales growth that can be financed completely with internal sources of financing. We can calculate this for Vectra as follows:

$$
\begin{aligned}
\text{EFR}_1 &= 0 = \frac{A_v}{S_0}(S_0 \times g) - \frac{L_v}{S_0}(S_0 \times g) - [S_0(1 + g) \times \text{PM}_1 \times b_1] - \text{sale of marketable securities} \\
&= (96\% \times \$100{,}000 \times g) - (9.3\% \times \$100{,}000 \times g) - [\$100{,}000 \times (1 + g) \times 7.65\% \times (0.60)] - \\
&\quad \$4{,}000 \\
&= \$96{,}000g - \$9{,}300g - [(\$100{,}000 \times 7.65\% \times 0.60) + (\$100{,}000g \times 7.65\% \times 0.60)] - \\
&\quad \$4{,}000 \\
&= \$96{,}000g - \$9{,}300g - (\$4{,}590 + \$4{,}590g) - \$4{,}000 \\
&= \$96{,}000g - \$9{,}300g - \$4{,}590 - \$4{,}590g - \$4{,}000 \\
&= \$82{,}110g - \$8{,}590 \\
\$8{,}590 &= \$82{,}110g \\
g &= 10.46\%
\end{aligned}
$$

So, if sales grow less than 10.5 percent, Vectra will be able to finance the required investment in assets with the combination of the internal sources of financing, plus the sale of the marketable securities.

? Review Questions

4–10 What is the basic assumption used for the percent-of-sales forecasting method? What is the basic forecasting lesson you learn from using this simplified forecasting approach?
4–11 What is meant by the term *spontaneous sources of financing*?
4–12 How are the pro forma balance sheet and statement of external financing required related?
4–13 If a company has marketable securities, how might this impact the calculation of external financing required?
4–14 Discuss the formula approach that can be used for the percent-of-sales forecasting method.
4–15 What is the capital intensity ratio, and why is it important in financial forecasting?
4–16 What is meant by the term *sustainable growth rate*? Why might it be useful to know this rate for a company?

4.5 Other Methods to Forecast the Income Statement

The previous section fully discussed the percent-of-sales forecasting method. The strength of this approach to forecasting is that there are very few assumptions that must be reflected in the forecasted financial statements. Essentially, all accounts on the statements remain the same percent of sales or do not change. The strength of this simplified forecasting technique is that it fully illustrates the concepts associated with forecasting, without getting bogged down in a whole set of assumptions.

The approach allows the focus to be on the concept that, since sales are forecasted to increase, the firm requires assets to support increasing sales, meaning that the firm requires financing (debt and/or equity), while recognizing that some of the financing will be generated internally, some externally. But, as a simplified forecasting technique, it is not a realistic approach to forecasting. This section discusses the weaknesses associated with the percent-of-sales forecasting method and illustrates two other approaches to forecasting the income statement.

Weaknesses of the Percent-of-Sales Approach

There are three weaknesses with the percent-of-sales approach to financial forecasting. First, it is unrealistic to assume that all expenses will remain exactly the same percent of sales from one fiscal year to the next. This will never occur in reality and therefore it is illogical to assume it will when preparing a pro forma income statement. Second, with the percent-of-sales method, a company is essentially locked into a given profit margin. Note that for the 2008 actual and 2009 pro forma income statements, the profit margin is 7.65 percent. The percent-of-sales approach rules out the idea that a company may reduce costs and therefore increase profit margins. An alternative method of forecasting is the judgmental approach, where values of individual accounts are estimated based on an analysis of the current situation.

Example Vectra Manufacturing's actual income statement for the fiscal year ended December 31, 2008, is provided in Table 4.11. As discussed earlier for 2008, cost of goods sold is very high at 80 percent of sales. The profit margin is low at 7.65 percent. Assume that a ratio analysis revealed that the industry average was 28 percent for gross margin and 12.6 percent for profit margin. With these comparative figures, perhaps Vectra would want to attempt to gain better control of costs and increase profits.

For the 2009 forecast year, Vectra plans to reduce cost of goods sold to 76 percent of sales as a first step in trying to achieve the industry standard for profitability. In addition, operating expenses are expected to increase slightly to 11 percent of sales while interest expense will increase to $1,100. Vectra's tax rate is expected to remain at 15 percent of earnings before taxes. The company plans to reduce common share dividends to $1,000 in order to increase the amount of reinvested profits (increase internal sources of financing).

These assumptions are reflected in the pro forma income statement provided in the second column of Table 4.11. Note, the assumption used to generate the forecast is shown to the right of the number. Using these assumptions, all of the expense figures are a different percent of sales from those recorded in 2008. As well, the profit margin increases to 10.38 percent, which now approaches the industry average. The judgmental approach is a more realistic approach to financial forecasting.

TABLE 4.11 **Vectra Manufacturing: Actual and Pro Forma Income Statements (Prepared Using the Judgmental Approach) for Years Ended December 31**

	2008 Actual		2009 Pro forma	
Sales revenue	$100,000		$140,000	
Less: Cost of goods sold	80,000		106,400	(76% of sales)
Gross margin	$ 20,000		33,600	
Less: Operating expenses	10,000		15,400	(11% of sales)
Operating earnings	$ 10,000		18,200	
Less: Interest expenses	1,000		1,100	(stated dollar amount)
Earnings before taxes	$ 9,000		17,100	
Less: Taxes (15%)	1,350		2,565	(15% of EBT)
Net income after tax (profit margin)	$ 7,650	(7.65%)	14,535	(10.38%)
Less: Common share dividends	4,000		1,000	(stated dollar amount)
Reinvested profits (to retained earnings)	$ 3,650		$ 13,535	

The third weakness of the percent-of-sales approach is that it assumes that all of the firm's costs are variable. If a firm has no fixed costs, it will not receive the benefits that often result from them.[7] Therefore, the use of past cost and expense ratios generally *tends to understate profits when sales are increasing and overstate profits when sales are decreasing.* Clearly, if a firm has fixed costs and these costs do not change when sales increase, the result is increased profits. But if some costs are fixed and do not change when sales decline, this will tend to lower profits. The best way to adjust for the presence of fixed costs in pro forma income statement preparation is to break the firm's historical costs and expenses into *fixed* and *variable components.*[8]

Example Vectra Manufacturing's 2008 actual and 2009 pro forma income statements, broken into fixed and variable cost components, are provided in Table 4.12.

Breaking Vectra's expenses into fixed and variable components may provide a more accurate projection of its pro forma profit. Had the firm treated all costs as variable, its pro forma NIAT would equal 7.65% of sales, just as was the case in 2008 ($7,650 NIAT ÷ $100,000 sales). As shown in Table 4.8, by assuming that *all* costs are variable, the NIAT would have been $10,710 (7.65% × $140,000 projected sales) instead of the $26,350 of NIAT obtained above by using the firm's fixed cost/variable cost breakdown.

TABLE 4.12 Vectra Manufacturing: Actual and Pro Forma Income Statements (Prepared Assuming Some Costs Are Fixed) for Years Ended December 31

	2008 Actual	2009 Pro forma
Sales revenue	$100,000	$140,000
Less: Cost of goods sold		
Fixed cost	40,000	40,000
Variable cost (40% × sales)	40,000	56,000
Gross margin	$ 20,000	$ 44,000
Less: Operating expenses		
Fixed expense	5,000	5,000
Variable expense (5% × sales)	5,000	7,000
Operating earnings	$ 10,000	$ 32,000
Less: Interest expense (all fixed)	1,000	1,000
Earnings before taxes	$ 9,000	$ 31,000
Less: Taxes (15%)	1,350	4,650
Net income after taxes (profit margin)	$ 7,650 (7.65%)	$ 26,350 (18.82%)

7. The potential returns as well as risks resulting from use of fixed (operating and financial) costs to create "leverage" are discussed in Chapter 10. The key point to recognize here is that when the firm's revenue is *increasing*, fixed costs can magnify returns.

8. The application of *regression analysis*—a statistically based technique for measuring the relationship between variables—to past cost data as they relate to past sales could be used to develop equations that recognize the fixed and variable nature of each cost. Such equations could be employed when preparing the pro forma income statement from the sales forecast. The use of the regression approach in pro forma income statement preparation is wide spread, and many computer software packages for use in pro forma preparation rely on this technique. Expanded discussions of the application of this technique can be found in most management science texts.

This example should make it clear that ignoring fixed costs in the pro forma income statement preparation process may result in the misstatement of the firm's forecast profit. Therefore, when preparing the pro forma income statement, break expenses down into their fixed and variable components if the information is available.

? Review Questions

4–17 Instead of the percent-of-sales approach, what other methods can be used to develop the pro forma income statement? What are the advantages of these other methods in comparison to the percent-of-sales approach?

4–18 Comment on the following statement: "Because nearly all firms have fixed costs, ignoring them in the pro forma income statement preparation process typically results in misstatement of the firm's forecast profit." How can such a "misstatement" be avoided?

4.6 Judgmental Approach to Forecasting the Balance Sheet

judgmental approach
A method for developing the pro forma balance sheet in which the values of certain balance sheet accounts are estimated, and others are calculated, based on a ratio analysis.

A number of other approaches can be used to prepare the pro forma balance sheet for a company. Probably the best and most popular is the judgmental approach. Under the **judgmental approach,** stated assumptions for the balance sheet accounts are reflected in the pro forma balance sheet. These assumptions may be a value or may be a stated objective based on a ratio analysis. Recall that the purpose of a ratio analysis is to uncover a company's financial strengths and weaknesses. Therefore, when forecasting the financial results for an upcoming time period, it makes sense for the firm to plan to build on the financial strengths and correct the financial weaknesses. The judgmental approach to forecasting allows for this and explains why this technique is widely used in reality.

For example, a ratio analysis may reveal that a company's average collection period is 73.2 days. If the industry average were 42.6 days, the firm's objective might be to reduce the average collection period to the industry average over a three-year period. For the upcoming year, the firm's goal may be to reduce the average collection period to 63 days. This target is used to forecast the firm's accounts receivable for the forecast year. A similar procedure can be used for inventory and accounts payable.

Reflecting each of the stated assumptions in the pro forma balance sheet generates values for each account. As discussed earlier, the change in assets from the latest fiscal year (i.e., 2008) to the forecast year (i.e., 2009) determines the total financing required (TFR). A portion of the TFR may be generated internally. The most obvious source of internal financing is reinvested profits.

Reinvested profits will provide a portion, and in some cases, all of the TFR. A second internal source is changes in accounts payable and accruals (items such as taxes payable or wage payables). Accounts payable and accruals are amounts a company owes but for which there is no obvious direct financing cost. For example, taxes payable is an amount owed by the firm but as long as the company pays the amount owed by the due date, there is no financing cost. As discussed earlier, these types of current liabilities provide a spontaneous source of financing.

Therefore, the difference between the TFR and the two internal sources of financing is the amount of external financing the firm requires to operate during the forecast year. The external financing required (EFR) is the figure that makes the balance sheet balance.

To illustrate the judgmental approach to forecasting a company's balance sheet, we will prepare the pro forma balance sheet for Vectra Manufacturing for the 2009 fiscal year. Returning to Table 4.7, Vectra's balance sheet for 2008, we can see that we must forecast five asset accounts, five liability accounts, and one equity account. Note that there are two equity accounts; however, the forecast for retained earnings has essentially already been made. Since we have already forecasted the 2009 income statement, we have estimated the amount of profits Vectra will reinvest in 2009. To develop Vectra's pro forma balance sheet, we will use the pro forma income statement prepared using the judgmental approach. The assumptions we will be using are listed below. Note, as well, that the process used to estimate each of the accounts is also included. Table 4.13 presents the 2008 actual and the 2009 pro forma balance sheet for Vectra.

TABLE 4.13 **Vectra Manufacturing: Actual and Pro Forma Balance Sheets (Prepared Using the Judgemental Approach) as of December 31**

	2008 Actual	2009 Pro forma 1	2009 Pro forma 2
Assets			
Cash	$ 6,000	$ 8,000	$ 8,000
Marketable securities	4,000	4,000	0
Accounts receivable	13,000	15,726	15,726
Inventory	16,000	21,280	21,280
Total current assets	$ 39,000	$ 49,006	$ 45,006
Net fixed assets	61,000	89,000	89,000
Total assets	$100,000	$138,006	$134,006
Liabilities and equity			
Accounts payable	$ 7,000	$ 8,133	$ 8,133
Accruals	2,300	575	575
Line of credit	8,300	8,300	20,938
Other current liabilities	1,400	1,400	1,400
Total current liabilities	$ 19,000	$ 18,408	$ 31,046
Long-term debt	$ 18,000	$ 18,000	$ 26,425
Shareholders' equity			
Common shares	$ 30,000	$ 30,000	$ 30,000
Retained earnings	33,000	46,535	46,535
Total liabilities and equity	$100,000	$112,943	$134,006

1. A minimum cash balance of $8,000 is desired. This implies that the firm always wants to hold at least this amount of cash. The cash is used for unexpected costs and for liquidity purposes. Therefore, on December 31, it is assumed that Vectra will have $8,000 of cash in their current account at the bank.
2. Marketable securities are assumed to remain unchanged from their current level of $4,000, unless the funds are needed for financing purposes.
3. For the 2008 fiscal year, the average collection period was 47.45 days ($13,000/($100,000 ÷ 365)). Assuming that this is 10 days higher than the industry average, Vectra plans to target a 41-day average collection period for 2009. Therefore, accounts receivable for 2009 is $15,726 (($140,000 ÷ 365) × 41 days), where the $140,000 is the sales forecast for the 2009 forecast year. The concept reflected in this calculation is that accounts receivable are uncollected sales. Since sales average $383.56 per day, and it will take 41 days to collect these credit sales, receivables will average $15,726.
4. For the 2008 fiscal year, days in inventory was 73 days ($16,000/($80,000 ÷ 365)). Assuming that this is comparable to the industry average, Vectra is planning to target the same number of days for the 2009 forecast year. To complete the pro forma balance sheet, the pro forma income statement developed in Table 4.11 will be used. Therefore, the forecast for inventory for 2009 is $21,280 (($106,400 ÷ 365) × 73 days). The concept reflected in this calculation is that inventory is unsold production. Since COGS averages $291.51 per day, and it will take 73 days to sell this production, inventory will average $21,280.
5. In 2009, Vectra plans to acquire a new machine costing $35,000. Total amortization in 2009 will be $7,000. (Note that the increase in operating expenses to 11 percent of sales in Table 4.11 reflects the increased amortization.) Adding the $35,000 to net fixed assets of $61,000 and subtracting the amortization of $7,000 results in net fixed assets of $89,000 in 2009.
6. Purchases are 45 percent of cost of goods sold. Vectra's average payment period in 2008 was 71 days [$7,000/(($80,000 × 45%) ÷ 365)]. Vectra's suppliers have been requesting more rapid payment so the company plans to reduce the average payment period to 62 days in 2009. Therefore, accounts payable in 2009 is $8,133 [(($106,400 × 45%) ÷ 365) × 62 days]. The concept reflected in this calculation is that payables are unpaid for purchases. Since purchases average $131.18 per day, and it will take 62 days to pay for these purchases, payables will average $8,133.
7. Accruals are primarily taxes payable, and Vectra expects to have them fully paid by March 1, 2009. Therefore, accruals are expected to decline by 75 percent for 2009. This means accruals will be $575 on the forecasted balance sheet.
8. The line of credit is assumed to remain unchanged from the current level of $8,300. This is the usual assumption for any liability or equity account with an obvious cost of financing (e.g., line of credit, long-term debt, preferred equity, and common shares). This assumption is usually made since the objective of preparing the pro forma balance sheet is to determine the amount of financing the company requires for the forecast year. So, unless different information is provided, always assume that items with an obvious cost of financing remain unchanged.
9. No change in other current liabilities is expected. They are expected to remain at the level of the previous year: $1,400.

10. The firm's long-term debt and its common shares are expected to remain unchanged at $18,000 and $30,000, respectively; no issues, retirements, or repurchases of bonds or stocks are planned. Again, this is the usual assumption.
11. Retained earnings will increase from the beginning level of $33,000 (from the balance sheet dated December 31, 2008, in Table 4.7) to $46,535. The increase of $13,535 represents the amount of reinvested profits calculated in the 2009 pro forma income statement in Table 4.11.
12. If external financing is required, the marketable securities will be sold. Any remaining financing will be raised as follows: the line of credit will be used for 60 percent, the remaining 40 percent will be raised as long-term debt.

The second numeric column in Table 4.13 presents the 2009 pro forma balance sheet for Vectra. Note that the first 11 assumptions discussed above are reflected in the statement. But, as with the balance sheet forecasted earlier using the percent-of-sales method, the initial pro forma balance sheet doesn't balance. When comparing the total assets to the total liabilities and equity for the 2009 forecast year, it is clear that the firm requires more on the liabilities and equity side—the firm requires financing. But before any financing is raised the $4,000 of marketable securities will be sold, as it makes no sense to hold an asset that provides a return lower than the cost of financing to a company. In addition, we will raise the remaining financing in the assumed percentages: 60 percent line of credit, 40 percent long-term debt. These assumptions are reflected in the second pro forma balance sheet.

Table 4.14 provides the statement of external financing required for Vectra for the 2009 forecast based on the two forecasted statements. Vectra requires $21,063 of external financing in 2009. Note that, while there are two spontaneous sources of financing, one of them declines between 2008 and 2009. So the accruals do not provide a source of financing; rather, the forecasted change will be a use of financing. Since this use is greater than the increase in payables, the total internal sources of financing are $12,943. The resulting EFR of $21,063 is assumed to be raised using two sources: 60 percent, or $12,638, will come from the line of credit, and 40 percent, or $8,425, will be long-term debt. This assumption is reflected in the second pro forma balance sheet.

TABLE 4.14 Vectra Manufacturing: Calculation of External Financing Required (EFR) for the Forecast Year Ended December 31, 2009

Total financing required (TFR) (change in total assets)		$34,006
Less: Internal sources		
Increase in payables	$ 1,133	
Decrease in accruals	−1,725	
Reinvested profits	13,535	
Total internal sources		12,943
External financing required		$21,063

Adjustments to EFR

In some cases, adjustments will have to be made to the EFR figure calculated in the statement of EFR. Reconsider Table 4.14. Note that the statement of EFR reflects all changes in the assets accounts, and in payables, accruals, and retained earnings from the 2008 to the 2009 fiscal year. But, if any of the other accounts change due to actions taken by management, these changes must also be reflected in the statement of EFR. Some changes that may occur would be the scheduled repayment of principal on short-term or long-term debt or the repurchase of preferred or common shares. If changes such as these occurred during the forecast year, the statement of EFR would have to be adjusted accordingly.

For example, assume that on July 22, 2009, Vectra must make a $5,000 principal repayment on their long-term debt. On the 2009 pro forma 1 forecast, long-term debt will be reduced to $13,000. This will reduce the total liabilities and equity amount to $107,943. The implication is that EFR will increase by $5,000. To illustrate this increase, the statement of EFR will be modified as follows:

EFR before adjustments	$21,063 (as shown in Table 4.14)
Plus: Long-term debt repayment	$ 5,000
Adjusted EFR	$26,063

The impact is that Vectra will now require $26,063 of external financing in 2009. As before, this is assumed to be raised using two sources: 60 percent, or $15,638, will come from the line of credit, and 40 percent, or $10,425, will be long-term debt. These additional amounts would be shown in the second pro forma balance sheet. The complete forecast is also provided as Spreadsheet Application 2.

4.2 SPREADSHEET APPLICATION

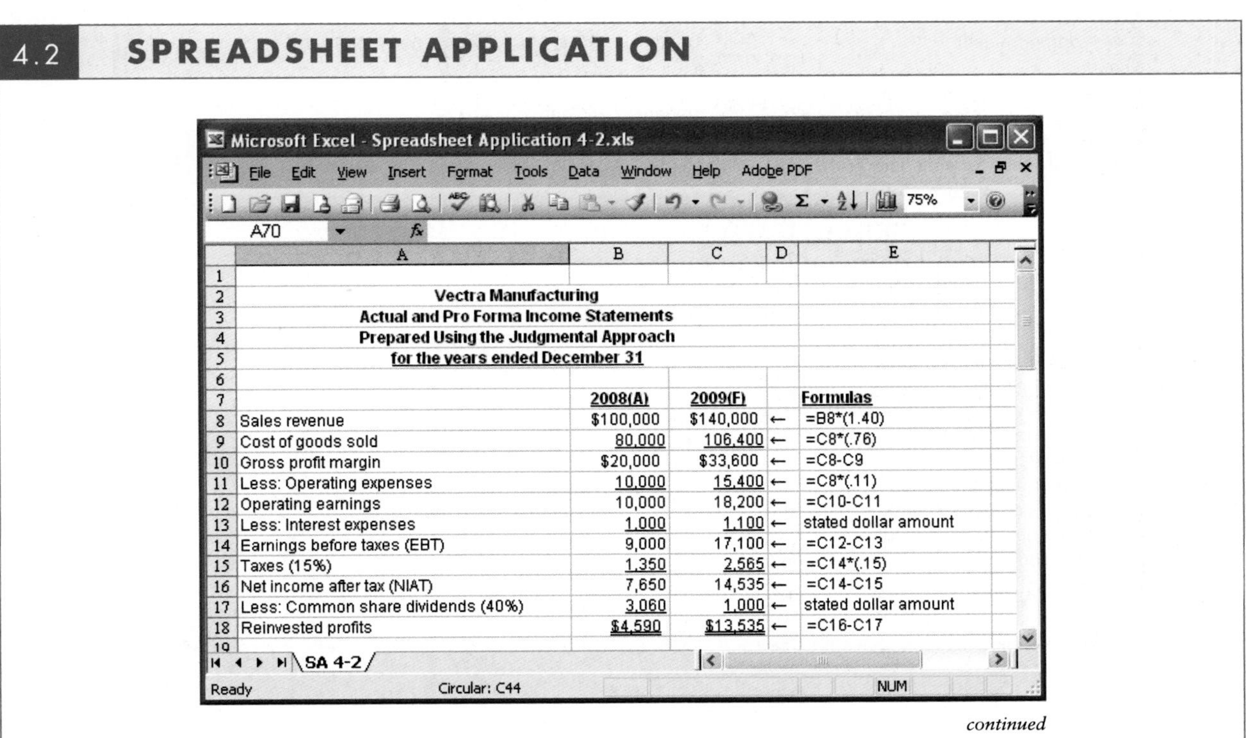

Microsoft Excel - Spreadsheet Application 4-2.xls

Vectra Manufacturing
Actual and Pro Forma Income Statements
Prepared Using the Judgmental Approach
for the years ended December 31

	2008(A)	2009(F)		Formulas
Sales revenue	$100,000	$140,000	←	=B8*(1.40)
Cost of goods sold	80,000	106,400	←	=C8*(.76)
Gross profit margin	$20,000	$33,600	←	=C8-C9
Less: Operating expenses	10,000	15,400	←	=C8*(.11)
Operating earnings	10,000	18,200	←	=C10-C11
Less: Interest expenses	1,000	1,100	←	stated dollar amount
Earnings before taxes (EBT)	9,000	17,100	←	=C12-C13
Taxes (15%)	1,350	2,565	←	=C14*(.15)
Net income after tax (NIAT)	7,650	14,535	←	=C14-C15
Less: Common share dividends (40%)	3,060	1,000	←	stated dollar amount
Reinvested profits	$4,590	$13,535	←	=C16-C17

continued

4.2 SPREADSHEET APPLICATION (continued)

Microsoft Excel - Spreadsheet Application 4-2 (continued).xls

	A	B	C	D	E
21	Vectra Manufacturing				
22	Actual and Pro Forma Balance Sheets				
23	Prepared Using the Judgmental Approach				
24	As at December 31				
25					
26	**Assets**	2008(A)	2009(F)		**Formulas**
27	Current Assets				
28	Cash	$6,000	$8,000	←	stated dollar amount
29	Marketable Securities	4,000	0	←	=IF((C28+C30+C31+C33)>B34,0,B29)
30	Accounts Receivable	13,000	15,726	←	=(C8/365)*41
31	Inventory	16,000	21,280	←	=(C9/365)*73
32	Total Current Assets	39,000	45,006	←	=sum(C28:C31)
33	Net Fixed Assets	61,000	89,000	←	=(B33+35,000)-7,000
34	Total Assets	$100,000	$134,006	←	=C32+C33
35					
36	**Liabilities and Shareholder's Equity**				
37	Current Liabilities				
38	Account Payable	$7,000	$8,133	←	=((C9*0.45)/365)*62
39	Accruals	2,300	575	←	=B39*(1-0.75)
40	Line of Credit	8,300	23,938	←	=B40+(C65*.60)
41	Other current liabilities	1,400	1,400	←	=B41
42	Total current liabilities	$19,000	$34,046	←	=sum(C38:C41)
43					
44	Long-term debt	18,000	23,425	←	=B44-5,000+(C65*.40)
45					
46	Shareholders' equity				
47	Common shares	30,000	30,000	←	=B47
48	Retained earnings	33,000	46,535	←	=B48+C18
49	Total liabilities and equity	$100,000	$134,006	←	=sum(C42:C48)
50					
51					
52	Vectra Manufacturing				
53	Calculation of External Financing Required (EFR)				
54	Based on the Judgmental Approach				
55	For the Forecast Year Ended December 31, 2009				
56					**Formulas**
57	Total Financing Required (TFR)		$34,006	←	=C34-B34
58	Less: Internal Sources				
59	Increase in accounts payable		1,133	←	=C38-B38
60	Decrease in accruals		-1,725	←	=C39-B39
61	Reinvested Profits		13,535	←	=C18
62	Total internal sources		12,943		=sum(C59:C61)
63	EFR before adjustments		21,063	←	=C57-C62
64	Add: Principal paid on loan		5,000	←	=5,000
65	Adjusted external financing required (EFR)		$26,063	←	=C57-C62+C64

SA 4-2

Ready NUM

Using Pro Forma Statements

In addition to estimating the amount of external financing that is required to support a given level of sales, pro forma statements also provide a basis for analyzing in advance the level of profitability and overall financial performance of the firm in the coming year. Using pro forma statements, both financial managers and lenders can analyze the firm's expected financial performance. Sources and uses of cash can be evaluated by preparing a pro forma statement of cash flows. Various ratios can be calculated from the pro forma income statement and balance sheet to evaluate performance.

After analyzing the pro forma statements, the financial manager can take steps to adjust planned operations to achieve short-term financial goals. For example, if profits on the pro forma income statement are too low, a variety of pricing or cost-cutting actions, or both, might be initiated. If the projected level of accounts receivable on the pro forma balance sheet is too high, changes in credit policy or collection policy may be called for. Pro forma statements are therefore of key importance in solidifying the firm's financial plans for the coming year.

Pro forma statements are a tool that should be used to evaluate the impact various planned scenarios might have on a company's future financial position. The purpose of the plan is not to lock the company's management into a particular position, but rather to indicate to management the impact a particular set of actions might have on the company's financial position. Plans can be altered, and should be, as the fiscal year unfolds. Pro forma statements should not be completed and then filed away never to be looked at again. As actual results are realized, the plan should be adjusted and the differences between the plan and the actual results used as the basis for improving financial forecasting in the future.

? Review Questions

4–19 Describe the *judgmental approach* for forecasting the pro forma balance sheet. Contrast this with the more detailed approach shown in Figure 4.1.

4–20 Discuss the process used to calculate *external financing required.* Differentiate between the interpretation and strategy associated with positive and negative values for *external financing required.*

4–21 What is the financial manager's objective in evaluating pro forma statements?

SUMMARY

LG1 **Understand the financial planning process, including long-term (strategic) financial plans and short-term (operating) plans.** The three key aspects of the financial planning process are cash planning, forecasting future profitability, and forecasting the need for financing. To forecast cash requirements, a cash budget must be prepared. Forecasting profitability requires a pro forma income statement, while both an income statement and balance sheet must be forecast to estimate the amount of financing required. Long-term (strategic) financial plans act as a guide for preparing short-term (operating) financial plans. Long-term plans tend to cover periods ranging from 2 to 10 years and are updated regularly. Short-term plans most often cover a 1-to-2-year period.

LG2 **Discuss the cash budget, the importance of sales forecasts, procedures for preparing a cash budget, and how to cope with uncertainty when preparing a cash budget.** The cash planning process uses the cash budget, based on a sales forecast, to estimate short-term cash surpluses and shortages. The sales forecast is based on external and internal data. The cash budget shows the expected inflows and outflows of cash for a specific time interval (i.e., 1 day, 1 week, or 1 month) and a total time period (i.e., 1 month, 13 weeks, or 6 months). So the cash budget might be daily for a month, weekly for 13 weeks, or monthly for six months. The purpose of the cash budget is to estimate cash receipts, cash disbursements, net cash flow, and cash balance for each time period, and total interval of time. Ending cash is estimated by adding beginning cash to the net cash flow. By subtracting the desired minimum cash balance from the ending cash, the financial manager can determine required total financing (typically a line of credit) or the excess cash balance (typically held as marketable securities). To cope with uncertainty in the cash budget, sensitivity analysis (preparation of several cash budgets) or computer simulation can be used.

LG3 **Discuss the fundamentals associated with preparing the pro forma income statement and balance sheet.** There are three required inputs for financial forecasting: previous years' financial statements, sales forecasts, and forecasts for all other financial statement accounts. There are three outputs: a pro forma income statement, a pro forma balance sheet, and a statement of external financing required (EFR). Financial forecasting simply reflects a set of assumptions regarding a company's financial position for a forecast period.

LG4 **Discuss and illustrate the percent-of-sales forecasting method, a simplified approach to forecasting a firm's income statement and balance sheet, and determine the amount of external financing a company requires to operate during the forecast year.** The percent-of-sales forecasting method assumes that all income statement items remain the same percent of sales for the forecast year as for the previous fiscal year. This means that the relationship that existed between each of the expenses and sales in the previous fiscal year, will also apply in the forecast year. To prepare the pro forma balance sheet using the percent-of-sales method, we assume that most of the asset accounts, accounts payable, and accruals will vary directly with sales. The implication is that the firm is operating at peak capacity. With both statements developed, total financing required and the internal sources of financing can be determined. With these, we can calculate external financing required (EFR) using a statement of EFR. EFR can also be calculated using the formula approach. EFR is the difference between total financing required, which is based on the change in total assets from the previous fiscal year to the forecast year, and internal sources, the combination of reinvested profits and the change in spontaneous liabilities between years. A positive value for EFR means that the firm must raise funds externally; a negative value indicates that funds are available for use in repaying debt, repurchasing stock, increasing dividends, or acquiring assets.

LG5 **Discuss the weaknesses of the percent-of-sales forecasting method, and illustrate two other approaches to preparing a pro forma income statement.** The strength of the percent-of-sales method is that it fully illustrates the concepts associated with forecasting, without getting bogged down in a whole set of assumptions. But it is not a realistic approach to forecasting. The method has three weaknesses: it is unrealistic, it locks a company into a given level of profitability, and it assumes that all costs are variable. The second method is the judgmental approach, where values of individual accounts are estimated based on an analysis of the current situation. The third approach is to break historical expenses into fixed and variable components. The latter two methods are superior approaches to preparing the pro forma income statement.

LG6 **Discuss and illustrate the judgmental approach to preparing a pro forma balance sheet for a company, and develop a statement of external financing required for the company for the forecast year.** With the judgmental approach, stated assumptions for the balance sheet accounts are reflected in the pro forma balance sheet. These assumptions may be a value or a stated objective based on a ratio analysis. With this approach we can build on the financial strengths and attempt to correct the financial weaknesses that were uncovered in a ratio analysis. As before, the ultimate goal is to determine the amount of external financing the firm requires to operate during the forecast year. In some cases, adjustments will have to be made to the EFR figure calculated in the statement of EFR. The statement of EFR reflects all changes in the asset accounts, payables, accruals, and retained earnings from the previous to the forecast year. But, if the company repays principal on short-term or long-term debt, or repurchases preferred or common shares, the statement of EFR would have to be adjusted accordingly. Pro forma statements are commonly used to analyze the firm's level of profitability and overall financial performance so that adjustments can be made to planned operations to achieve short-term financial goals.

SELF-TEST PROBLEMS

(Solutions in Appendix B)

ST 4–1 **Cash budget and pro forma balance sheet inputs** Jane McDonald, a financial analyst for Carroll Company, has prepared the following sales and cash disbursement estimates for the period February to June of the current year.

Month	Sales	Cash disbursements
February	$500,000	$400,000
March	600,000	300,000
April	400,000	600,000
May	200,000	500,000
June	200,000	200,000

Ms. McDonald notes that historically, 30 percent of sales have been for cash. Of the *credit sales,* 70 percent are collected 1 month after the sale, and the remaining 30 percent are collected 2 months after the sale. The firm wishes to maintain a minimum ending balance in its cash account of $25,000. Balances above this amount would be invested in short-term government securities (marketable securities), whereas any deficits would be financed through short-term bank borrowing (line of credit). The beginning cash balance at April 1 is $115,000.

a. Prepare a cash budget for the period April to June.

b. How much financing, if any, at a maximum would Carroll Company need to meet its obligations during this 3-month period?

c. If a pro forma balance sheet dated at the end of June were prepared from the information presented, give the value of each of the following: cash, line of credit, marketable securities, and accounts receivable.

ST 4–2 Pro forma income statement Euro Designs, Inc., expects sales during 2009 to increase from the 2008 level of $3.5 million to $3.9 million. Due to a scheduled large loan payment, the interest expense in 2009 is expected to drop to $325,000. The tax rate will remain 40 percent. The firm plans to increase its cash dividend payments during 2009 to $320,000. The company's year-end 2008 income statement follows.

Income Statement Euro Designs, Inc. for the year ended December 31, 2008	
Sales revenue	$3,500,000
Less: Cost of goods sold	1,925,000
Gross margin	$1,575,000
Less: Operating expenses	420,000
Operating earnings	$1,155,000
Less: Interest expense	400,000
Earnings before taxes	$ 755,000
Less: Taxes (40%)	302,000
Net income after taxes	$ 453,000
Less: Cash dividends	250,000
To retained earnings	$ 203,000

a. Assuming cost of goods sold and operating expenses remain the same percent of sales in 2009 as they were in 2008, prepare the 2009 pro forma income statement for Euro Designs.

b. Explain why the forecasted statement may underestimate the company's actual profitability in 2009.

PROBLEMS

4–1 Cash receipts A firm has actual sales of $65,000 in April and $60,000 in May. It expects sales of $70,000 in June and $100,000 in July and in August. Assuming that sales are the only source of cash inflows and that half of these are for cash and the remainder are collected evenly over the following 2 months, what are the firm's expected cash receipts for June, July, and August?

BASIC

4–2 Cash disbursements schedule Maris Brothers, Inc., needs a cash disbursements schedule for the months of April, May, and June. Use the format of Table 4.3 and the following information in its preparation.

Sales: February = $500,000; March = $500,000; April = $560,000; May = $610,000; June = $650,000; July = $650,000

Purchases: Purchases are calculated as 60 percent of the next month's sales, 10 percent of purchases are made in cash, 50 percent of purchases are paid for 1 month after purchase, and the remaining 40 percent of purchases are paid for 2 months after purchase.

Rent: The firm pays rent of $8,000 per month.

Wages and salaries: Base wage and salary costs are fixed at $6,000 per month plus a variable cost of 7 percent of the current month's sales.

Taxes: A tax payment of $54,500 is due in June.

Fixed asset outlays: New equipment costing $75,000 will be bought and paid for in April.

Interest payments: An interest payment of $30,000 is due in June.

Cash dividends: Dividends of $12,500 will be paid in April.

Principal repayments and retirements: No principal repayments or retirements are due during these months.

INTERMEDIATE 

4–3 **Cash budget** Grenoble Enterprises had sales of $50,000 in March and $60,000 in April. Forecast sales for May, June, and July are $70,000, $80,000, and $100,000, respectively. The firm has a cash balance of $5,000 on May 1 and wishes to maintain a minimum cash balance of $5,000. Given the following data, prepare and interpret a cash budget for the months of May, June, and July.

(1) The firm makes 20 percent of sales for cash, 60 percent are collected in the next month, and the remaining 20 percent are collected in the second month following sale.
(2) The firm receives other income of $2,000 per month.
(3) The firm's actual or expected purchases, all made for cash, are $50,000, $70,000, and $80,000 for the months of May through July, respectively.
(4) Rent is $3,000 per month.
(5) Wages and salaries are 10 percent of the previous month's sales.
(6) Cash dividends of $3,000 will be paid in June.
(7) Payment of principal and interest of $4,000 is due in June.
(8) A cash purchase of equipment costing $6,000 is scheduled in July.
(9) Taxes of $6,000 are due in June.

CHALLENGE 

4–4 **Cash budget** The actual sales and purchases for Xenocore, Inc., for September and October 2008, along with its forecast sales and purchases for the period November 2008 through April 2009, follow.

Year	Month	Sales	Purchases
2008	September (A)	$210,000	$120,000
2008	October (A)	250,000	150,000
2008	November (F)	170,000	140,000
2008	December (F)	160,000	100,000
2009	January (F)	140,000	80,000
2009	February (F)	180,000	110,000
2009	March (F)	200,000	100,000
2009	April (F)	250,000	90,000

The firm makes 20 percent of all sales for cash and collects on 40 percent of its sales in each of the 2 months following the sale. Other cash inflows are expected to be $12,000 in September and April, $15,000 in January and March, and $27,000 in February. The firm pays cash for 10 percent of its purchases. It pays for 50 percent of its purchases in the following month and for 40 percent of its purchases 2 months later.

Wages and salaries amount to 20 percent of the preceding month's sales. Rent of $20,000 per month must be paid. Interest payments of $10,000 are due in January and April. A principal payment of $30,000 is also due in April. The firm expects to pay cash dividends of $20,000 in January and April. Taxes of $80,000 are due in April. The firm also intends to make a $25,000 cash purchase of fixed assets in December. At the beginning of November, Xenocore has $22,000 of cash. The company wishes to maintain a minimum cash balance of $15,000.

a. Develop a cash budget for Xenocore for the six-month period November to April. Does the firm need to arrange for financing during this period? If so, how should the firm secure financing and how much should it request?

BASIC 

4–5 Cash flow concepts The following represent financial transactions that Johnsfield & Co. will be undertaking in the next planning period. For each transaction, check the statement or statements that will be affected immediately.

	Statement		
Transaction	**Cash budget**	**Pro forma income statement**	**Pro forma balance sheet**
Cash sale			
Credit sale			
Accounts receivable are collected			
Asset with 5-year life is purchased			
Amortization is taken			
Amortization of goodwill is taken			
Sale of common shares			
Retirement of outstanding bonds			
Fire insurance premium is paid for the next 3 years			

CHALLENGE 

4–6 Cash budget Tracy Company has been operating for years without a line of credit. It is July 2, and the company's finance manager, Dick Pound, realizes this cannot continue. He has scheduled a meeting with the account manager at the Royal Toronto Bank to request a line of credit. Dick wonders what maximum limit he should request from the bank to see Tracy through the next six months of the year. Dick knows that if he can show the account manager that Tracy can manage the line of credit over this six-month period, he will be able to secure a higher maximum limit for the final six months of the year. The following sales data is available. As is indicated, the figures for April to June are actual, those for the remaining months are forecasts.

April (A)	$225,000	October (F)	$500,000
May (A)	250,000	November (F)	450,000
June (A)	350,000	December (F)	175,000
July (F)	400,000	January (F)	225,000
August (F)	550,000	February (F)	250,000
September (F)	900,000		

Historically, 5 percent of Tracy's sales are for cash, 6 percent are credit sales that are collected within the month of sale, 50 percent are credit sales collected the month following the sale, 28 percent are credit sales collected the second month following the sale, and 11 percent are credit sales collected the third month following the sale. Bad debts are negligible.

In the manufacturing process, the company has three direct costs. Raw materials are 36 percent of sales. Raw materials are ordered and received two months prior to the month of the sale, and are paid for in the month following receipt. Direct labour costs are 19 percent of sales while direct factory overhead is 8 percent of sales. Both are paid in the month the expense is incurred.

General and administrative expenses are $32,500 a month, lease payments under long-term contracts are $12,500 a month, depreciation expenses are $30,000 a month, and miscellaneous expenses are $10,250 a month. An income tax payment of $82,500 is due in August, another for $62,000 is due in December. A payment of $350,000 on a new research laboratory that is being built is due in October. Cash on hand on July 1 is $20,000, and the company wishes to maintain a minimum cash balance of $50,000 at all times.

a. Prepare a monthly cash budget for the six months July to December for Tracy Company. Assuming these forecasts are accurate, as Dick Pound, how large a limit on the line of credit would you request from the account manager at the Royal Toronto Bank?

b. Now assume that cash inflows are received uniformly during the month (cash receipts come in at the rate of $^1/_{30}$ each day), but that all cash outflows are paid on the fifth of the month. Will this have an effect on the cash budget? Will the cash budget you have prepared be valid under these assumptions? If not, what can be done to make a valid estimate of financing requirements?

INTERMEDIATE LG2

4–7 Cash budget—Sensitivity analysis Trotter Enterprises, Inc., has gathered the following data in order to plan for its cash requirements and short-term investment opportunities for October, November, and December. All amounts are shown in thousands of dollars.

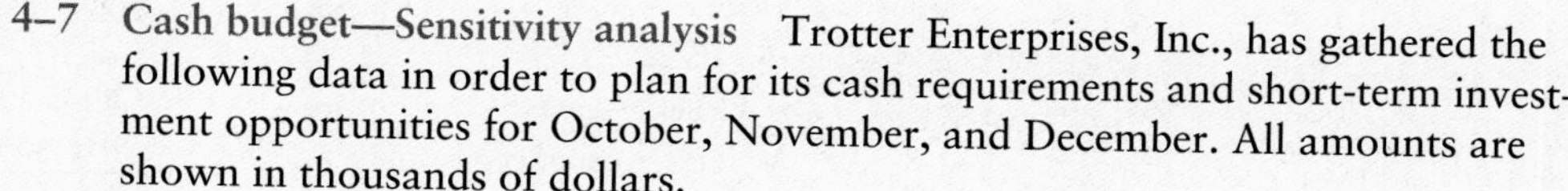

	October			November			December		
	Pessimistic	Most likely	Optimistic	Pessimistic	Most likely	Optimistic	Pessimistic	Most likely	Optimistic
Total cash receipts	$260	$342	$462	$200	$287	$366	$191	$294	$353
Total cash disbursements	285	326	421	203	261	313	287	332	315

a. Prepare a sensitivity analysis of Trotter's cash budget using −$20,000 as the beginning cash balance for October and a minimum required cash balance of $18,000.

b. Use the analysis prepared in part **a** to predict Trotter's financing needs and investment opportunities over the months of October, November, and December. Discuss how the knowledge of the timing and amounts involved can aid the planning process.

INTERMEDIATE 

4–8 Multiple cash budgets—Sensitivity analysis Brownstein, Inc., expects sales of $100,000 during each of the next 3 months. It will make monthly purchases of $60,000 during this time. Wages and salaries are $10,000 per month plus 5 percent of sales. Brownstein expects to make a tax payment of $20,000 in the next month and a $15,000 purchase of fixed assets in the second month and to receive $8,000 in cash from the sale of an asset in the third month. All sales and purchases are for cash. Beginning cash and the minimum cash balance are assumed to be zero.

a. Construct a cash budget for the next 3 months.

b. Brownstein is unsure of the sales levels, but all other figures are certain. If the most pessimistic sales figure is $80,000 per month and the most optimistic is $120,000 per month, what are the monthly minimum and maximum ending cash balances that the firm can expect for each of the 1-month periods?

c. Briefly discuss how the financial manager can use the data in parts **a** and **b** to plan for financing needs.

BASIC

4–9 Pro forma income statement The income statement for the 2008 fiscal year for Metroline Manufacturing is provided below. The company wishes to forecast their 2009 income statement. The marketing department estimates that sales will increase by $100,000 in 2009. Cost of goods sold (COGS) and operating expenses are expected to remain the same percent of sales in 2009 as they were in 2008. Interest expense is expected to increase to $42,000 in 2009 while the tax rate will decline to 36 percent. The company plans to maintain the same dividend payout ratio in 2009 as in 2008.

Income Statement
Metroline Manufacturing
for the year ended December 31, 2008

Sales revenue	$1,400,000
Less: Cost of goods sold	910,000
Gross margin	$ 490,000
Less: Operating expenses	120,000
Operating earnings	$ 370,000
Less: Interest expense	35,000
Earnings before taxes	$ 335,000
Less: Taxes (40%)	134,000
Net income after taxes	$ 201,000
Less: Cash dividends	60,300
To retained earnings	$ 140,700

a. Using this data, prepare a pro forma income statement for the year ended December 31, 2009.

b. The finance department has estimated that in 2008, $210,000 of the COGS was a fixed expense. The remainder was variable and will change with sales. For the operating expenses, $36,000 was fixed, while variable was 6 percent of sales. This split is expected to remain the same for 2009. For all other items, the previous forecasts will remain the same. Given this data, prepare a pro forma income statement for December 31, 2009.

INTERMEDIATE

4–10 Pro forma income statement—Sensitivity analysis Allen Products, Inc., wants to do a sensitivity analysis for the coming year. The pessimistic prediction for sales is $900,000; the most likely amount of sales is $1,125,000; and the optimistic prediction is $1,280,000. Allen's income statement for the most recent year is as follows.

Income Statement **Allen Products, Inc.** **for the year ended July 31, 2009**	
Sales revenue	$937,500
Less: Cost of goods sold	421,875
Gross margin	$515,625
Less: Operating expenses	234,375
Operating earnings	$281,250
Less: Interest expense	30,000
Earnings before taxes	$251,250
Less: Taxes (25%)	62,813
Net income after taxes	$188,437

a. Use the *percent-of-sales method,* the income statement for July 31, 2009, and the sales revenue estimates to develop pessimistic, most likely, and optimistic pro forma income statements for the coming year.

b. Explain how the percent-of-sales method could result in an overstatement of profits for the pessimistic case and an understatement of profits for the most likely and optimistic cases.

c. Restate the pro forma income statements prepared in part **a** to incorporate the following assumptions about costs:

$250,000 of the cost of goods sold is fixed; the rest is variable.
$180,000 of the operating expenses is fixed; the rest is variable.
All of the interest expense is fixed.

d. Compare your findings in part **c** to your findings in part **a.** Do your observations confirm your explanation in part **b**?

BASIC LG6

4–11 Pro forma balance sheet Leonard Industries wishes to prepare a pro forma balance sheet for December 31, 2009. The firm expects 2009 sales to total $3,000,000. The following information has been gathered.

(1) A minimum cash balance of $50,000 is desired.
(2) Marketable securities are expected to remain unchanged.
(3) Accounts receivable represent 10% of sales.
(4) Inventories represent 12% of sales.

(5) A new machine costing $90,000 will be acquired in 2009. Total amortization for the year will be $32,000.
(6) Accounts payable represent 14% of sales.
(7) Accruals, other current liabilities, long-term debt, and common shares are expected to remain unchanged.
(8) The firm's profit margin is 4%, and it expects to pay out $70,000 in cash dividends during 2009.
(9) The December 31, 2008 balance sheet follows.

Balance Sheet
Leonard Industries
December 31, 2008

Assets		**Liabilities and equity**	
Cash	$ 45,000	Accounts payable	$ 395,000
Marketable securities	15,000	Accruals	60,000
Accounts receivable	255,000	Other current liabilities	30,000
Inventories	340,000	Total current liabilities	$ 485,000
Total current assets	$ 655,000	Long-term debt	$ 350,000
Net fixed assets	$ 600,000	Common shares	$ 200,000
Total assets	$1,255,000	Retained earnings	$ 220,000
		Total liabilities and shareholders' equity	$1,255,000

a. Using the *judgmental approach*, prepare a pro forma balance sheet and statement of EFR for Leonard Industries for December 31, 2009. If external financing is required, it will be raised by using long-term debt.
b. Other than increasing profitability or changing payables or accruals, what could Leonard Industries do in 2009 to reduce the external financing required to zero? Discuss at least three options open to the company.

4–12 **Pro forma balance sheet** Peabody & Peabody has 2008 sales of $10 million. It wishes to analyze expected performance and financing needs for 2010—2 years ahead. Given the following information, answer questions **a** and **b.**
(1) The percent of sales for items that vary directly with sales are as follows:
Profit margin, 3%
Accounts receivable, 12%
Inventory, 18%
Accounts payable, 14%
(2) Marketable securities and other current liabilities are expected to remain unchanged.
(3) A minimum cash balance of $480,000 is desired.
(4) A new machine costing $650,000 will be acquired in 2009, and equipment costing $850,000 will be purchased in 2010. Total amortization in 2009 is forecast as $290,000, and in 2010 $390,000 of amortization will be charged.
(5) Accruals are expected to rise to $500,000 by the end of 2010.
(6) No sale or retirement of long-term debt is expected.

(7) No sale or repurchase of common shares is expected.
(8) The dividend payout of 40 percent of net income after taxes is expected to continue.
(9) Sales are expected to be $11 million in 2009 and $12 million in 2010.
(10) The December 31, 2008 balance sheet follows.

Balance Sheet
Peabody & Peabody
December 31, 2008
($000)

Assets		Liabilities and equity	
Cash	$ 400	Accounts payable	$1,400
Marketable securities	200	Accruals	400
Accounts receivable	1,200	Other current liabilities	80
Inventories	1,800	Total current liabilities	$1,880
Total current assets	$3,600	Long-term debt	$2,000
Net fixed assets	$4,000	Common equity	$3,720
Total assets	$7,600	Total liabilities and shareholders' equity	$7,600

a. Prepare a pro forma balance sheet and a statement of EFR for the year ended December 31, 2010 for Peabody & Peabody. Assume any required financing will be long-term debt.

b. Prior to arranging for the amount of external financing required calculated above, what should Peabody & Peabody do? Reflect this change in your forecasts.

INTERMEDIATE  **4–13** **Percent-of-sales technique** The financial statements for the 2008 fiscal year for Red Queen Restaurants are provided below. For 2009, sales are expected to increase by 20 percent. The company wishes to develop pro forma financial statements for the 2009 fiscal year using the percent-of-sales forecasting method. Red Queen feels that all income statement items will remain the same percent of sales in 2009 as they were in 2008. The company is operating at full capacity with their assets.

Income Statement
Red Queen Restaurants
for the year ended December 31, 2008

Sales revenue	$800,000
Less: Cost of goods sold	600,000
Gross margin	$200,000
Less: Operating expenses	100,000
Earnings before taxes	$100,000
Less: Taxes (40%)	40,000
Net income after taxes	$ 60,000
Less: Cash dividends	20,000
Reinvested profits (to retained earnings)	$ 40,000

Balance Sheet
Red Queen Restaurants
December 31, 2008

Assets		Liabilities and equity	
Cash	$ 32,000	Accounts payable	$100,000
Marketable securities	18,000	Taxes payable	20,000
Accounts receivable	150,000	Other current liabilities	5,000
Inventories	100,000	Total current liabilities	$125,000
Total current assets	$300,000	Long-term debt	$200,000
Net fixed assets	$350,000	Common shares	$150,000
Total assets	$650,000	Retained earnings	$175,000
		Total liabilities and shareholders' equity	$650,000

a. Given the above data, prepare the pro forma financial statements for Red Queen Restaurants for December 31, 2009. Include a statement of external financing required and reflect the results from this statement in the balance sheet. Be sure to consider marketable securities in your analysis. Assume that Red Queen will sell common shares to raise any external financing that is required. If surplus financing is generated, the funds will be used to repay the long-term debt.

b. Calculate external financing required for Red Queen Restaurants for 2009 using the formula approach for the percent-of-sales method. Be sure to consider marketable securities in your answer.

c. What rate of sales growth could Red Queen Restaurants sustain using just internal sources of financing? Be sure to include marketable securities in your analysis.

INTERMEDIATE  4–14 **Forecast balance sheet** Return again to the Red Queen Restaurants data from Problem 4–13. Now for 2009, sales are expected to increase by 30 percent and net income after tax will be $95,000. Use this and the following data to develop a pro forma balance sheet and a statement of external financing required for December 31, 2009. Reflect the results from the statement of EFR on the balance sheet. Assume that Red Queen will sell common shares to raise any external financing that is required. If surplus financing is generated, the funds will be used to repay the long-term debt. The following forecasts are available:

(1) The firm expects to pay $35,000 in cash dividends in 2009.
(2) The firm wishes to maintain a minimum cash balance of $30,000.
(3) Accounts receivable represent approximately 18 percent of annual sales.
(4) The firm's ending inventory will change at the same percentage rate as sales in 2009.
(5) A new machine costing $42,000 will be purchased in 2009. Total amortization for 2009 will be $17,000.
(6) Accounts payable will change at the same percentage rate as sales in 2009.
(7) Taxes payable will decline by $8,000 in 2009.
(8) Marketable securities, other current liabilities, long-term debt, and common shares will remain unchanged.

INTERMEDIATE  **4–15 Formula approach and sustainable growth rate** Horizon Ltd. reported net income of $32,418 on sales of $720,400 for the 2008 fiscal year. The company has $1,116,620 of assets, all of which vary directly with sales. Accounts payable and accruals account for 25 percent of the $669,972 the firm holds in total liabilities. The company's policy is to pay out 32 percent of profits as dividends to common shareholders.

a. If sales increase by 10 percent in 2009, what will be the external financing required? To answer this question, use the formula approach for the percent-of-sales method.

b. If sales increase by 50 percent in 2009, what will be the external financing required? To answer this question, use the formula approach for the percent-of-sales method.

c. What lesson can be learned from this analysis?

d. What is Horizon's sustainable growth rate?

e. If $12,640 of total assets are marketable securities and these do not vary with sales, what is the sustainable growth rate? Explain.

CHALLENGE  **4–16 Pro forma forecasts** It is January 12, 2009, and the VP finance of Novelty Books has assigned you the task of doing some long-term planning. The VP wishes to determine financing requirements for the next three years, 2009 to 2011. To do this, he has asked you to forecast the level of net income for each of the next three years and to develop a balance sheet for the 2011 fiscal year. The balance sheet for the 2008 fiscal year is provided below.

Sales in 2009 are expected to be $1,500,000, a 14 percent increase over 2008. Sales are expected to increase by 10 percent in each of 2010 and 2011. The company's gross margin in 2008 was 25 percent, and the VP of finance feels it is possible to increase it by 1 percent in each of the next three years. In 2008, the company's profit margin was a meagre 3.9 percent, and the VP of finance is forecasting it to increase to 4.6 percent in 2009, 5.9 percent in 2010, and 7.1 percent in 2011. The firm will maintain a dividend payout ratio of 30 percent indefinitely. The firm calculates its amortization expense for a year by multiplying the previous year's net fixed assets by 11 percent.

By 2011, the company wishes to have a minimum cash balance equal to 25 percent of accounts payable. To control the required investment in working capital accounts, management has set a 2011 target of 46.2 days for the average collection period, 47.9 days for the average payment period, and an inventory turnover of 5.5. Novelty Books is planning to renovate some stores in 2009 and 2010 with the expected investment in fixed assets being $184,900 and $147,870, respectively. In 2011, a new central warehouse will be built at a cost of $337,800.

Accruals are expected to increase at the same rate as sales in 2009, 2010, and 2011. Novelty is required to make annual principal payments of $34,500 per year on their long-term debt. The firm will not repurchase any shares over the next three years.

Novelty Books Pro Forma Balance Sheet as at December 31, 2008			
Assets		**Liabilities and Shareholders' Equity**	
Cash	$ 25,000	Accounts payable	$ 158,137
Accounts receivable	202,589	Accruals	11,389
Inventory	267,500	Total current liabilities	169,526
Total current assets	495,089	Long-term debt	385,000
Net fixed assets	763,470	Common shares	315,000
		Retained earnings	389,033
Total assets	$1,258,559	Total liabilities and equity	$1,258,559

a. Given the above information, develop the pro forma balance sheet and statement of EFR for the 2011 fiscal year. How much external financing will Novelty Books require for the next three years? Assume that any external financing required will be split equally between long-term debt and the sale of new common shares.

INTERMEDIATE  **4–17 Percent-of-sales technique** The financial statements for B2B Supplies Inc. for the 2008 fiscal year are provided below. The company is attempting to determine the amount of financing they must raise to operate for the 2009 fiscal year. Currently, B2B Supplies is operating at full capacity with all assets. Therefore, all assets will fluctuate directly with any increase in sales. The only liabilities that will fluctuate directly with sales are accounts payable and accruals. For the 2009 fiscal year, sales are forecasted to increase by 30 percent. The company expects their profit margin and dividend payout ratio to remain the same in 2009. B2B Supplies plans to raise any external financing required through the company's line of credit.

B2B Supplies Inc. Income Statement for the year ended December 31, 2008	
Sales	$2,800,000
Cost of goods sold	1,764,000
Gross margin	1,036,000
Selling and administrative expenses	560,000
Amortization	77,000
Earnings before interest and taxes	$ 399,000
Interest	70,000
Earnings before taxes	$ 329,000
Taxes	85,400
Net income after taxes	$ 243,600
Dividends paid to common shareholders	$ 145,600

B2B Supplies Inc.
Balance Sheet
as at December 31, 2008

Assets		Liabilities and Shareholders' Equity	
Cash	$ 42,000	Accounts payable	$ 280,000
Accounts receivable	364,000	Accruals	112,000
Inventory	294,000	Line of credit	315,000
Total current assets	$ 700,000	Total current liabilities	$ 707,000
Net fixed assets	$1,610,000	Long-term debt	483,000
		Common shares	427,000
		Retained earnings	693,000
Total assets	$2,310,000	Total liabilities and equity	$2,310,000

a. Given the above information, what forecasting method would be used to develop the forecasts for the 2009 fiscal year? Discuss why you would use this method.
b. Now develop pro forma financial statements and a statement of EFR for B2B Supplies for the 2009 fiscal year.
c. Calculate EFR for B2B Supplies for 2009 using the formula approach for the forecasting method used.
d. What rate of sales growth could B2B Supplies sustain without requiring any external financing?
e. Now, based on the original information, if B2B Supplies were not operating at full capacity with fixed assets but expected to purchase $165,000 of fixed assets, how much external financing is required? For this part you do not have to develop new pro forma statements, simply provide an answer for EFR. What can you learn from this analysis?
f. Now, based on the original information, if B2B Supplies' profit margin is 11 percent and the dividend payout ratio 25 percent, how much external financing is required? For this part you do not have to develop new pro forma statements, simply provide an answer for EFR. What can you learn from this analysis?

INTERMEDIATE  4–18 **Judgmental technique** Return again to the 2008 financial statements for B2B Supplies. For 2009, sales are forecasted to increase by 30 percent. With this increase, the company's financial director expects many accounts will be affected. Cash will increase by $7,000. The company plans to target an average collection period of 43.5 days and an inventory turnover of 6.4. The company plans to acquire new equipment at a cost of $175,000. Accounts payable will increase by 14 percent, but accruals will remain unchanged. The company must repay $65,000 of its long-term debt. Lower materials costs will result in the gross margin increasing to 40 percent. Selling and administrative expense will increase by $70,000 while the amortization expense will increase by $17,500. The repayment of a portion of long-term debt will reduce the interest expense by $14,000. The company expects to pay dividends of $168,000 in 2009. B2B Supplies' tax rate will be 32 percent for the forecast year.

a. Given this information, develop pro forma financial statements and a statement of EFR for B2B Supplies for the 2009 fiscal year. Assume that the first $75,000 of required funds will be financed with long-term debt. Any remaining required funds will be financed by selling common shares. Any surplus financing will be used to repay the line of credit.

b. If B2B Supplies reduces the company's average payment period to 49 days, while the average collection period and average age of inventory remain at the level recorded in 2008, how much external financing is required? For this part you do not have to develop new pro forma statements, simply provide an answer for EFR. What can you learn from this analysis?

CHALLENGE  **4–19 Percent-of-sales technique** Elite Auto, a luxury car dealer, is planning to use the percent-of-sales forecasting method to prepare pro forma financial statements and to determine the need for financing. The balance sheet for Elite Auto as of December 31, 2008, is shown below. In 2008, Elite Auto reported net income after taxes of $12,687,500 on sales of $200 million. The company paid dividends of $3,806,250 to common shareholders. Elite Auto expects the relationship between sales and all income statement items to remain the same in the future. Elite is operating at full capacity with all assets. For 2009, sales are projected to increase by 30 percent.

Elite Auto
Balance Sheet
as at December 31, 2008 (in $000)

Assets		**Liabilities and Shareholders' Equity**	
Cash	$ 2,500	Accounts payable	$ 9,250
Accounts receivable	18,750	Accruals	4,500
Inventory	41,250	Line of credit	13,250
Total current assets	$62,500	Total current liabilities	$27,000
Net fixed assets	25,250	Mortgage loan	19,250
		Common shares	14,200
		Retained earnings	27,300
Total assets	$87,750	Total liabilities and equity	$87,750

a. Develop Elite Auto's pro forma balance sheet and statement of EFR for December 31, 2009. Assume that any external financing will be raised by using the line of credit.

b. Calculate the following ratios on the basis of your projections for 2009. Elite Auto's 2008 ratios and industry average ratios, applicable for all time periods, are provided for comparison. Comment on the ratios.

	Elite Auto December 31, 2008	**Elite Auto December 31, 2009**	**Industry Averages**
Current ratio	2.31	?	3
Debt ratio	52.71%	?	30%
ROE	30.57%	?	12%

c. Now assume that the 30 percent growth in sales is spread over three years; that is, sales grow by 10 percent each year. Develop Elite Auto's pro forma balance sheet and statement of EFR at the end of the three-year period, as of December 31, 2011. Assume that any external financing required will be financed by using the line of credit. Now calculate the three ratios in part **b** and comment on the differences between the 2009 and 2011 values and with the industry averages.

d. Which of the two options for sales growth would be the most feasible for Elite Auto to manage? Would it be easier to manage 30 percent sales growth in one year, or 10 percent per year over three years? Fully discuss and indicate any lessons you can learn from this problem.

CHALLENGE

4–20 **Integrative—Pro forma statements** Provincial Imports, Inc., has assembled the following financial statements and other information for you to use to prepare financial plans for the coming year.

Income Statement
Provincial Imports, Inc.
for the year ended December 31, 2008

Sales revenue	$5,000,000
Less: Cost of goods sold	2,750,000
Gross margin	$2,250,000
Less: Operating expenses	862,000
Less: Amortization	88,000
Operating earnings	$1,300,000
Less: Interest expense	100,000
Earnings before taxes	$1,200,000
Less: Taxes (40%)	480,000
Net income after taxes	$ 720,000
Paid: Cash dividends	288,000

Balance Sheet
Provincial Imports, Inc.
December 31, 2008

Assets		Liabilities and equity	
Cash	$ 200,000	Accounts payable	$ 700,000
Marketable securities	275,000	Taxes payable	95,000
Accounts receivable	625,000	Line of credit	200,000
Inventories	500,000	Other current liabilities	5,000
Total current assets	$1,600,000	Total current liabilities	$1,000,000
Net fixed assets	1,400,000	Long-term debt	550,000
		Common shares	75,000
Total assets	$3,000,000	Retained earnings	1,375,000
		Total liabilities and equity	$3,000,000

Information related to financial projections for the 2009 fiscal year is provided below:

(1) Sales are projected to increase by 20 percent.
(2) The industry average for gross margin is 46.5 percent and the company plans to attain that level in 2009.
(3) The industry average for operating expenses is 18.2 percent of sales. This includes amortization. Excluding amortization, Provincial Imports expects operating expenses to be 17.1 percent of sales in 2009. Amortization expense for 2009 will be $110,000. The increase in amortization is due to a new computer system costing $486,000 that will be purchased in 2009.
(4) Interest expense is based on the amount of debt outstanding. The interest rate on the long-term debt is 12 percent and the amount of long-term debt outstanding did not change during the 2008 fiscal year. The interest rate on the line of credit averaged 13.6 percent in 2008 and the average line of credit outstanding was $250,000. The company expects the interest rate on the line of credit will average 13 percent in 2009. Total interest expense is expected to be $92,000 in 2009.
(5) Due to changes in tax legislation, the company expects the tax rate in 2009 will fall to 36 percent. Provincial's goal is to pay 40 percent of NIAT as dividends to the common shareholders.
(6) Cash, marketable securities, and other current liabilities will remain unchanged for 2009.
(7) For the 2009 forecast year, the company is planning for an average collection period of 44 days, an average age of inventory of 65 days, and average payment period, based on COGS, of 85 days.
(8) Taxes payable will be 30 percent of the total estimated taxes owing from the 2009 income statement.
(9) If the company requires external financing, they will first sell their marketable securities. Any remaining financing will be raised by using the line of credit. If surplus financing is generated internally, Provincial Imports will repay the line of credit.

a. Prepare a pro forma income statement and balance sheet and a statement of EFR for Provincial Imports, Inc., for the 2009 fiscal year. Which approach to financial forecasting will you use?

b. Reconsider the forecasted statements. Based on the information available, which estimates, if any, do you believe are incorrect? Explain.

c. Calculate Provincial Imports' current ratio, total asset turnover, debt ratio, times interest earned, profit margin, and return on equity ratios for 2008 and 2009. Comment on the trends.

d. This will be forecast 2 for Provincial Imports. Now assume that the cost of goods sold will be 55.6 percent of sales, operating expenses excluding amortization will be 18 percent of sales, and amortization expense will increase to $144,500. In addition to the new computer system, the company also plans to invest an additional $225,000 in fixed assets. As well, the average age of inventory will be 74 days, while the average payment period will fall to 71 days. The firm must also make a $150,000 principal repayment on their long-term debt. All other forecasts as previously stated in the problem will remain unchanged. Now prepare the pro forma income statement, balance sheet, and statement of EFR.

e. For the forecasts in part **d**, if the average age of inventory were 84 days and not 74 days, what impact would this have on EFR? Show your work, but do not complete a whole new forecast.

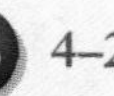

CHALLENGE

4–21 Comprehensive financial forecasting O'Leary Industrial Supply (see Problem 3–17 in Chapter 3) is attempting to forecast their financial statements for the 2009 fiscal year. First, the company is planning to use three forecasting techniques to prepare the pro forma income statement. Sales are expected to increase by 20 percent in 2009.

a. Prepare the pro forma income statement for O'Leary Industrial for 2009 using the percent-of-sales forecasting technique.

b. Now, using the following split between fixed and variable direct and operating costs, prepare the pro forma income statement for O'Leary Industrial for 2009.
   - COGS: fixed—$225,000; variable—64% of sales.
   - Administrative expenses: fixed—$150,000; variable—1% of sales.
   - Selling expenses: fixed—$20,000; variable—6.25% of sales.
   - Amortization: fixed—$16,250.
   - Interest expense: flat $25,000 plus an interest rate of 13.5% applies to the line of credit outstanding at the beginning of the year.
   - Tax rate: 20.6%.
   - The company will pay 40% of their profits as dividends in 2009.

c. Now, based on the following estimates for the individual income statement accounts, prepare the pro forma income statement for O'Leary Industrial for 2009.

   Sales will increase by 20 percent. COGS will fall to 76.5 percent of sales. Administrative expenses will be $150,000 while selling expense will be 7.2 percent of sales. Amortization will be 10 percent of the beginning net plant and equipment. Interest expense will fall by $5,000, since the company is required to repay $25,000 of their long-term debt (a principal repayment). The tax rate will be 20.6 percent. O'Leary Industrial expects to pay $40,000 in dividends in 2009.

d. Why are the results different for the three approaches? Which method would you place the most faith in? Explain.

e. O'Leary Industrial Supply will now forecast their balance sheet for the 2009 fiscal year. Use the income statement forecasted in part **c** above in order to forecast the balance sheet. Given the following estimates for the individual accounts, prepare the pro forma balance sheet and statement of EFR for O'Leary Industrial for 2009.

   O'Leary wants a minimum cash balance of $25,000, and the company will attempt to reduce the average age of inventory to 70 days and the average collection period to 75 days, while the average payment period will increase slightly to 44 days. Prepaid expenses and accruals will change with sales. O'Leary expects to invest $150,000 in fixed assets in 2009 while goodwill will decline by $2,500. The company is required to repay $25,000 of their long-term debt (a principal repayment).

   Any financing required will be raised by first liquidating marketable securities. If funds are still required, then O'Leary will use a line of credit for 25 percent of the funds, 25 percent will be raised by selling preferred shares, and the remainder will come from the sale of common shares.

f. Discuss the implications of your forecasts. As an advisor to O'Leary, what changes would you recommend, and what is the impact of these changes on EFR?

g. Using your forecasts developed in parts **c** and **e** above, what is the impact on the results if the ACP only fell to 90 days rather than the 75 days assumed? What does this indicate about the sensitivity of the results of financial forecasting?

CASE CHAPTER 4 Preparing Martin Manufacturing's 2009 Pro Forma Financial Statements

See the enclosed Student CD-ROM for cases that help you put theories and concepts from the text into practice.

Be sure to visit the Companion Website for this book at **www.pearsoned.ca/gitman** for a wealth of additional learning tools including self-test quizzes, Web exercises, and additional cases.

CHAPTER 5

Financial Markets, Institutions, and Securities

LEARNING GOALS

LG1 Introduce the types of financial markets and how the markets operate, the important role played by financial institutions, the major types of financial securities, and the importance of trust to the operation of the financial markets.

LG2 Describe the money market and the major instruments traded in the market, particularly treasury bills.

LG3 Describe the key characteristics of long-term debt, one of the major capital market securities.

LG4 Describe the key characteristics of common and preferred shares, two additional capital market securities.

LG5 Differentiate among debt, preferred equity, and common equity capital.

LG6 Review the process of how financial securities are created and issued, and the important role played by the investment banker.

5.1 Financial Markets and Institutions

For a country's economy to develop and economic wealth to be created, four key features must be present. The country must be democratic so that no one person or party stays in power for an extended time period resulting in political and economic power being concentrated in the hands of a few. The country must follow the capitalistic economic model that rewards initiative and risk taking. The coun-

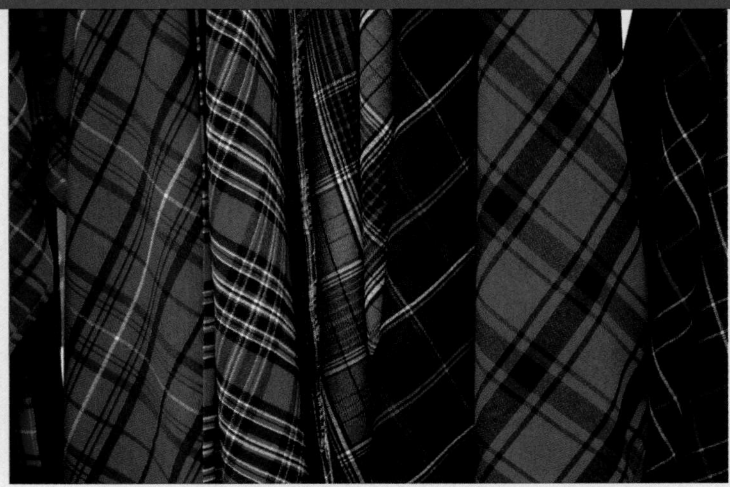

Financial Fabric

The financial environment is like a fabric woven from many different threads—savers (suppliers) and users (demanders) of funds, financial institutions like banks, financial markets such as the money market and stock exchanges, and the federal government and its regulatory agencies. The common thread running through the entire fabric is money. Those who have excess money are willing to put it to use in ways that make it possible for those who need money to obtain it, for a cost. This chapter describes the prominent threads in the fabric of the financial environment: the participants, the institutions and markets that channel money from savers to users, and the types of debt and equity securities created when the transaction occurs. For a financial market to exist, the participants must have a great deal of trust in the strength of the fabric.

try must have a well-established and functioning system of laws that protects the population from unlawful acts of others or the state. And the country must have well-developed financial markets.

Unfortunately, in most of the 193 countries in the world, one or more of these four key features is missing. As a result, much of the world's population live in non- or underdeveloped countries. These countries do not have a functioning economy, so wealth is not created. As a consequence, the vast majority of the

LINKING THE DISCIPLINES: Cross-Functional Interactions

- ***Accounting personnel*** need to understand the various types of financial securities to be able to properly account for new issues, retirements, or redemptions, and must also participate in the underwriting process and help in the preparation of the preliminary prospectus.
- ***Information systems analysts*** need to have an understanding of the types of financing sources to develop systems that support the company's debt management program, and maintain the relationships with the financial institutions the company must deal with.
- ***Management*** needs to develop and manage relationships with the company's banker and investment banker, and understand the differences between debt and equity capital and the process that is used to create and issue securities to raise funds.
- The ***marketing department*** needs to understand the role the financial markets play in the firm's ability to raise capital to fund marketing initiatives.
- Personnel in the ***operations department*** need to understand the role financial institutions and markets play in raising the funds necessary to maintain and invest in the firm's production assets.

population lives in poverty. In these countries, the nation's wealth is usually concentrated in the hands of a small number of the country's political and military leaders.

For the countries in the world that have the four key features, the path to economic wealth was similar. As democracy, capitalism, and a system of laws became entrenched in the fabric of the country, effective and organized financial markets developed. As this occurred, an opportunity was created for those with savings to interact with those requiring money. Those acquiring the money could then acquire assets, or start or expand a business. As this happened, more assets and workers were demanded eventually leading to a middle class evolving and flourishing. As the middle class became the largest percentage of the population, the economy further expanded, leading to increased opportunities for all members of society.

The benefits of this process to a country include consistent economic growth, industrialization, increasing living standards, better jobs, higher incomes, more leisure time, and increased access to quality education and health care. Every member of society has the opportunity to improve their situation. While all four features are vital for economic wealth creation, in this book we focus on the creation of effective and organized financial markets. For a country to develop economically, financial markets are a necessity.

An Overview of Financial Markets

Financial markets provide a forum where suppliers of funds (savers) and demanders of funds (users) can transact business. Financial markets exist to facilitate the transfer of funds between savers and users of funds. Savers and users of funds must be able to interact and to make an exchange that is beneficial to both parties. Financial markets exist for one purpose: to bring savers and users of funds together to make a fair exchange, one that provides value to both parties.

In the financial markets, cash moves from savers to users, and users provide a financial security in return. The financial security indicates the compensation the saver will receive in return for providing the funds. The compensation may be a rate of return on the funds, a promise to repay the funds at some point in the future, and/or a right of ownership. For financial markets to function efficiently, financial institutions, intermediaries that allow for the efficient and low-cost transfer of the savings of individuals, governments, and business for financial securities, are necessary.

There are many types of financial intermediaries, institutions like banks and investment dealers, but they all serve the same purpose: to channel funds from those who wish to save to those who wish to spend or invest. Economic markets match the demand and supply of valuable items. Financial markets perform the same function with money, but they are special in one critical way: They link the present and the future. Financial markets allow savers to convert current cash into future spending, and users to convert future cash into current spending. By acting as a channel through which savings can finance investment, the financial system helps drive growth.

Participants in the Financial Markets

Savers and users of funds in the financial markets include individuals, business organizations (profit and not-for-profit), the various levels of government (federal, provincial, and municipal), and international participants. In an advanced economy like Canada's, almost everyone is part of the financial markets, whether they know it or not. Individuals regularly save and invest money and, in so doing, use the financial markets. Individuals also purchase high-cost items like cars, houses, appliances, and travel, for which they may not have the available cash. To make these purchases, individuals must access the financial markets. As we saw in Chapter 4, companies require cash from external sources to support increasing assets and sales. Governments regularly raise cash in the financial markets when expenditures are not matched by tax revenues and other sources of income.

Individuals are large net suppliers of funds while businesses and governments have historically been large net demanders of funds. While some businesses can be savers, with large cash balances invested in financial securities, overall the business sector is a net demander of funds. At best, the government sector is in balance, neither a net demander or supplier of funds. Since the mid-1970s, however, the government sector in Canada has been a large net demander of funds. While the various levels of government in Canada, particularly the federal government, have eliminated operating deficits in the last few years, when all government expenditures are considered, the government sector in Canada is a net demander of funds.

Since the early 1990s, a growing trend is the internationalization of financial markets. In Canada, it is relatively easy for individuals to purchase financial securities in most developed countries throughout the world. Businesses and governments regularly raise cash in foreign markets. For example, it is not unusual for a Canadian company to raise cash in the European financial markets or for the federal government of Canada to borrow money in the American financial markets. There are domestic and international participants in the financial markets of all developed economies. The international sector can be a net supplier or demander of funds in a particular country. In Canada, for example, the international sector is a net demander of funds. More money flows out of the Canadian economy to international participants than flows in from international participants.

Classifying Financial Markets

There are two distinct financial markets: the *money market* and the *capital market*. Debt securities that will mature within one year are traded in the money market. The principal money market security is Government of Canada treasury bills, or t-bills, as they are more commonly known. The capital market involves the trading of long-term debt securities, like bonds and debentures, and preferred and common shares.

A second way to classify financial markets is by the nature of the transaction. A financial security must be "created" and this occurs in the *primary market*. With the security created, a *secondary market* must exist that allows the owner of a previously created financial security to sell the security, to buy more of this or other securities, or for a buyer to acquire a financial security. Both the money and capital markets have a primary and secondary market. The primary market creates and places an initial value on financial securities. Savers now own financial securities that they may, at some point, want to sell for cash. This is the function of the secondary market: it allows for the subsequent trading of previously created financial securities.

Figure 5.1 presents this classification of financial markets. Note that the life of the security created is a distinguishing feature of the money and capital markets. While long-term debt may be outstanding for 25 or more years and common shares for 50 or more years, money market securities may exist for only 90 days.

Flow of Funds in the Financial Markets

Figure 5.2 depicts the financial markets as they exist in most developed countries. There are three distinct flow of funds channels shown. For the first channel, labelled ①, cash flows from savers through financial intermediaries to users. For example, consider a simple transaction like depositing $500 in a bank account. This creates a simple financial security, a "loan" to the bank. You have agreed to lend the bank your $500 and by accepting the deposit, the bank agrees to give you access to your money at any time and pay you a modest rate of interest while the funds remain deposited. The bank then pools your $500 with other deposits and lends them out to users in the form of loans and mortgages. Each of these transactions creates additional financial securities.

FIGURE 5.1

Classification of Financial Markets

Money market	Capital market
Trades debt securities that will mature within one year.	Trades long-term debt securities, like bonds and debentures, and preferred and common shares.

Both markets have a primary market that creates and places an initial value on financial securities and a secondary market that allows for the subsequent trading of previously created financial securities.

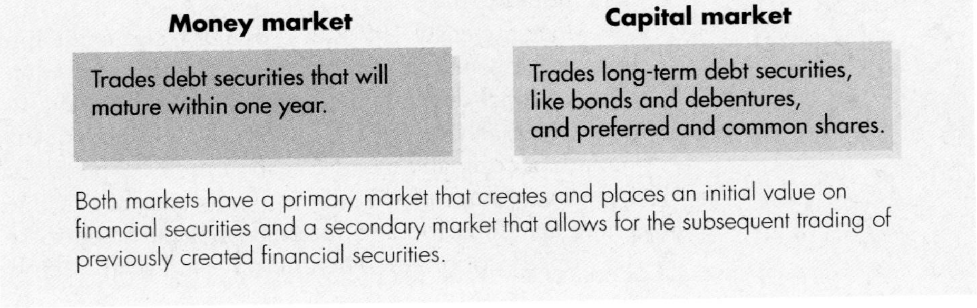

FIGURE 5.2

Flow of Funds in the Financial Markets

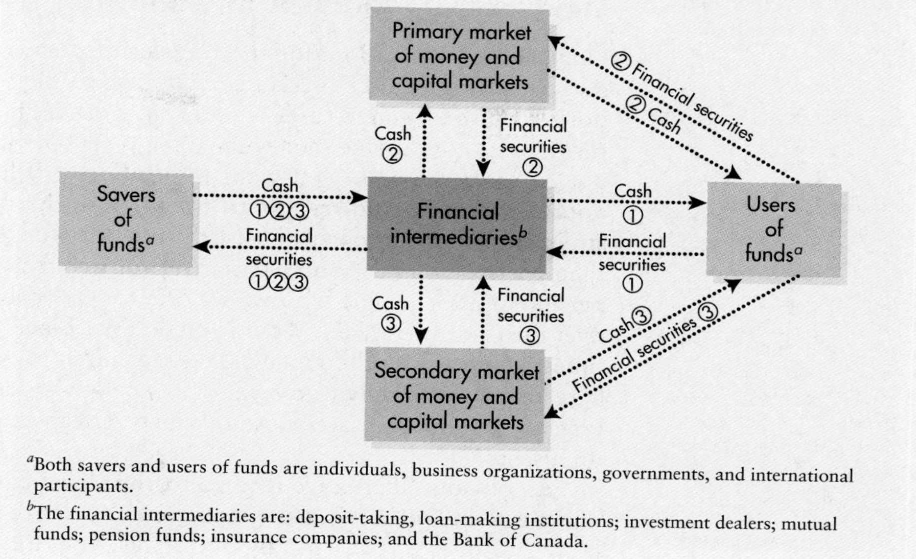

[a]Both savers and users of funds are individuals, business organizations, governments, and international participants.

[b]The financial intermediaries are: deposit-taking, loan-making institutions; investment dealers; mutual funds; pension funds; insurance companies; and the Bank of Canada.

For the second channel, labelled ② in Figure 5.2, cash flows from savers to financial intermediaries, who then provide funds to users via the money or capital markets. These are primary market transactions. For example, assume a company needs to build a new production plant costing $500 million. To raise the required financing, the company decides to sell common shares. The company creates the common shares, uses a financial intermediary (an investment banker) to sell the shares, and then receives the cash from savers. The transaction occurs in the primary market within the capital market. In the primary market, financial securities are created and demanders of funds receive cash from savers.

For the third channel, labelled ③ in Figure 5.2, cash flows from savers to financial intermediaries who buy and sell financial securities on behalf of savers in the money or capital markets. These are secondary market transactions. As an example, consider the primary market sale of common shares discussed above. With this transaction complete, the primary market has "done its job." Savers now own the common shares. Assuming the savers wish to sell the shares at some point, a secondary market must exist that allows for the subsequent trading of financial securities. Note that for this third channel, the company whose securities are being traded is not involved. All of these trades are between investors. In this case, investors who sell the shares are the users, since they are receiving cash. Investors buying the shares are the savers, since they are paying the cash and receiving the shares.

For both the second and third channels described above, the financial intermediary may hold the security on behalf of the savers or the savers may directly receive the security. Also, for these two channels, the term "market" may be misleading. Many think of markets as physical locations where buyers and sellers meet. The only physical market where financial securities are traded is the secondary market for preferred and common shares—the stock market or stock exchange. All primary market transactions and the secondary market trading of debt securities (in both the money and capital markets) occur in the computer networks between financial intermediaries.

The Financial Markets in Operation

Financial markets allow for the transfer of cash for financial securities. How does this transfer occur? Assume you wish to buy a car costing $25,000. You don't have the required cash, but you are working full time and would be able to buy the car after saving money for three years. Obviously, this alternative would not be ideal for you. You want the car now! What can you do? You could approach family and friends to try to raise the money but this can lead to strained relations, broken friendships, and the word "no" being used more often than you would like. As an alternative, you could advertise in your local newspaper looking for people who would like to lend you money that you will repay over the next three years. Would you do this? Likely not. First, it will take a long time to try to raise the money. And second, you may end up with 25 different agreements in place with the various people who lent you money. In short, this type of financial transaction is not timely, effective, or efficient. What could you do instead?

An obvious alternative is to go to your local bank (or trust company, credit union or—in Quebec—caisse populaire) to arrange for a $25,000 loan that will be repaid over three years. By doing this, you are using the financial markets. Review Figure 5.2. You, the car buyer, are a demander of funds. You will use a financial intermediary (a bank) to acquire the money needed to buy the car. The cash the bank lends you was obtained from savers, the suppliers of funds. The savers may be your friends, family, or the people who might have responded to your newspaper ad seeking money: in short, people who have "lent" the financial institution money through a savings (or chequing) account or another type of financial security.

You, the car buyer, may end up receiving the money from the very people you originally thought of approaching. Instead of directly receiving the money, however, you have used a financial intermediary and created a financial security, a car loan. This type of transaction happens thousands of times a day in the Canadian financial market and takes 30 minutes or less. It is an organized and efficient way to having money move from savers to users.

If we didn't have financial markets in Canada, think of the alternative scenario of raising money. Would you buy a car, or house, or that 54-inch plasma television that you always wanted if you had to approach family and friends or strangers every time you wished to buy a product or service for which you didn't have the required amount of cash? Would these people lend you money, *if* they had money? Think of the impact this would have on the Canadian economy. Very few high-cost items would be sold and the economy would become subsistence-based. Items that allowed for basic living would be available, but little else. The importance of the financial markets and financial intermediaries to an advanced economy cannot be overstated; they are key factors enabling an economy to operate and grow. The various types of financial intermediaries are discussed in the following section.

Financial Intermediaries

There are six principal financial intermediaries in Canada: (1) deposit-taking, loan-making institutions; (2) investment dealers; (3) mutual funds; (4) pension funds; (5) life insurance companies; and (6) the Bank of Canada. Table 5.1

TABLE 5.1 **Total Assets of the Major Financial Intermediaries in Canada for Four Years: 1991, 1996, 2001, and 2006 (millions)**

Financial Intermediary	1991	1996	2001	2006
Deposit-taking, loan-making:				
Chartered banks	$ 634,340	$1,104,828	$1,710,432	$2,384,917
Trust and mortgage loan	135,055	72,301	$9,701	17,553
Credit unions and caisses populaires	79,858	104,441	134,955	192,141
Other	41,866	51,763	85,933	144,144
Total deposit-taking, loan-making	891,119	1,333,333	1,941,021	2,738,755
Life insurance companies	156,046	208,098	282,414	415,928
Mutual funds	53,700	216,745	438,179	660,247
Pension funds	225,762	419,665	576,933	833,317
Investment dealers*	2,898	7,158	12,454	21,132
Bank of Canada	27,045	30,584	41,804	51,635
Total assets of all financial intermediaries	$1,356,570	$2,215,583	$3,292,805	$4,721,014

*For investment dealers, the amount shown is regulatory capital.

SOURCES: Bank of Canada, "Banking and Financial Statistics," June 2002 and February 2007, Tables B1, C3, and D1–D4; Statistics Canada, "Quarterly Estimates of Trusteed Pension Funds," Catalogue No. 74-001, Table 2800003, CANSIM II Series V15219043, Market Value of Total Assets; Investment Industry Association of Canada, "Securities Industry Performance," available at **www.iiac.ca/en/research/publications.php**; Investment Funds Institute of Canada, "Industry Statistics," available at **www.ific.ca/eng/frames.asp?l1=Statistics.**

details the total assets managed by these financial intermediaries in 1991, 1996, 2001, and 2006. Two items should be noted from a review of this table. First, the scale of the numbers is immense and difficult to fathom. In 2006, the total assets of the six intermediaries totalled over $4.7 trillion. Every dollar of this was provided by savers and flowed through the financial markets to demanders of funds. The financial intermediaries handle tremendous volumes of cash. Second, the flow of cash in the Canadian financial system has grown by 228.6 percent over the 16 years (15 growth periods). This is an average yearly growth rate of 8.67 percent, much higher than growth in the overall economy.

The largest and most visible financial intermediaries in any economy are deposit-taking, loan-making institutions. These institutions account for about 58 percent of the total assets managed by the financial intermediaries in 2006. Almost every individual in Canada, from the very young to the old, deals with at least one of these institutions. These include the big six Canadian chartered banks (and 12 other domestic banks), trust companies, credit unions (caisses populaires in Quebec), finance companies, and sales finance companies. The first three institutions provide most of the financial services required by individuals. Savings and chequing accounts, all types of loans, and even access to financial securities like common shares, preferred shares, and bonds and debentures are available at these institutions.

www.cba.ca/en

Finance companies raise funds in the money market that they then lend to individuals at very high interest rates. Finance companies in Canada include

http://financial.wellsfargo.com/canada/en/index.html

CitiFinancial, Wells Fargo Financial Corporation, and Associate Financial Services. Sales finance companies also raise funds in the money market for subsequent loan to consumers for the purchase of goods. Canadian Tire, Sears, major car manufacturers, and major retailers all either have their own sales finance companies or use the services of one.

The second financial intermediary, investment dealers, perform two basic functions that ensure the smooth operation of the money and capital markets. First, they act as agents for financial security transactions completed by both individual and institutional investors in the secondary markets of the money and capital markets. The current owner of a financial security may wish to sell a security, while another individual may wish to buy. Investors must use an investment dealer, acting as an agent, to buy or sell financial securities. The investment dealer receives a fee, termed a commission, for providing this service. The second function performed by investment dealers is the underwriting or investment banking function. This is discussed in more detail in Section 5.6.

www.ida.ca
www.iiac.ca

Example Tom Driscoll wishes to sell the 500 common shares of Dire Corp. that he owns. Tom approaches an investment dealer and places the order to sell. The investment dealer, acting as Tom's agent, sends the order to the Toronto Stock Exchange (TSX). Another investment dealer has an order to buy 500 shares of Dire Corp. The two orders are crossed on the TSX and a financial market transaction occurs. The investment dealer, as the financial intermediary, used the capital market to raise cash for Tom, the user of funds. A saver of funds provided the cash and received Tom's 500 common shares. This is an example of a secondary market transaction in the capital market. Thousands of these transactions, involving millions of common shares, happen each trading day on the TSX.

The next three financial intermediaries all perform the same basic function: They invest money for the future benefit of savers (primarily individuals) and are very large holders of financial securities. These three intermediaries—mutual funds, pension funds, and life insurance companies—are termed **institutional investors. Mutual funds** are investment companies that receive cash from individuals for investment in both money and capital market securities. The individuals providing the funds are the owners of the mutual fund. The money is managed by investment professionals to achieve a specific investment objective such as safety, growth, income, high risk, liquidity, or some combination of objectives. The money could be invested in Canada, the United States, or any international market.

institutional investors
Financial intermediaries such as mutual funds, pension funds, and life insurance companies.

mutual funds
Investment companies that receive cash from individuals for investment in both money and capital market securities.

Thousands of mutual funds, with a wide variety of investment objectives and mandates, are available to individuals in Canada. The returns earned on the securities purchased by the fund managers flow back to the owners. A mutual fund is similar in nature to a corporation. Professional managers act on behalf of owners to generate a return on the money invested by the owners. But note that, while the managers are termed professionals, this does not mean they achieve high rates of return on the money invested. As in all occupations, there are good and bad managers. Just because mutual fund managers are termed "professional" does not mean they are good investors. Note the tremendous rate of growth in mutual fund assets in Table 5.1. Between 1991 and 2006, mutual fund assets increased by about 1,130 percent, or an average of 18.2 percent per year.

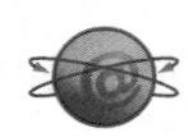

www.globefund.com
www.ific.ca/eng

pension funds
Investment entities established by employers to provide a pension to employees during retirement.

Pension funds are investment entities established by employers to provide a pension to employees during retirement. Each pay period a certain dollar amount is withheld from each employee's pay. Employers often match this contribution. The total contributions are then forwarded to the pension fund for investment in money and capital market securities. The funds are invested to ensure sufficient funds are available to pay retired employees their pensions. Over the 15 years, pension plan assets increased an average of 9.1 percent per year.

life insurance companies
Invest premiums from life insurance policyholders to ensure sufficient funds are available to pay out the stated value of the life insurance policy upon the death of the policyholder.

Life insurance companies receive premiums from life insurance policyholders. The premiums are invested to ensure sufficient funds are available to pay out the stated value of the life insurance policy upon the death of the policyholder. Over the 15 years, life insurance assets increased an average of 6.75 percent per year.

Bank of Canada
The central bank in Canada whose main function is to manage monetary policy.

The sixth financial intermediary is a country's central bank. In Canada, this institution is the **Bank of Canada.** The main function of the central bank is to manage monetary policy. Monetary policy consists of two components: the level of short-term interest rates and the exchange rate for the Canadian dollar. The combined effect of these two variables is termed *monetary conditions*. The goal of the bank is to keep inflation low, which keeps interest rates low. Low inflation results in productive long-term investment leading to long-lasting economic growth and job creation.

http://bankofcanada.ca/en/index.html

A second function of the Bank of Canada is to raise funds on behalf of the federal government. The Bank of Canada may sell treasury bills or bonds of various maturities. The choice made will depend on the planned use and cost of the money in the market. This function is similar to that performed by the finance department for a company. Essentially the Bank of Canada is the fiscal and monetary agent for the government of Canada.

Table 5.2 provides a balance sheet for all of the Canadian chartered banks. Note that loans are a major asset for the banks while the deposits of customers are a major liability. From the table, it is clear that the banks are major

TABLE 5.2 Assets and Liabilities of the Chartered Banks as of July 31, 2006 (millions)

Assets		Liabilities and equity	
Cash	$ 6,818	Individual savings accounts	$ 437,692
T-bills	30,661	Business savings accounts	294,160
Government of Canada bonds	84,637	Demand deposits	158,409
Loans to:		Government deposits	2,902
Individuals	222,211	Bankers' acceptances	49,091
Businesses	257,606	Non-deposit liabilities	311,235
Governments	2,795	Subordinated debentures	25,072
Mortgages	430,941	Preferred shares	5,981
Provincial and municipal securities	26,436	Common shares	31,848
Corporate securities	164,776	Retained earnings	68,519
Other Canadian assets	195,971	International liabilities	807,749
International loans and investments	769,806		
Total assets	$2,192,658	Total liabilities and equity	$2,192,658

SOURCE: Bank of Canada, "Banking and Financial Statistics," September 2006, Table C3-C4. Copyright © 1995–2007, Bank of Canada.

participants in the international financial markets. Also note the low amount of equity on the balance sheet. Banks operate with very little equity and make money on the difference in the interest rates they pay on their liabilities (deposits) and charge on their assets (loans). This is termed "making money on the spread," the difference between the two rates.

To put these numbers for the Canadian chartered banks in context, consider Table 5.3. Here we see the ten largest banks in the world by country of origin and by total assets. This table is part of a listing of the top 1,000 banks in the world as compiled by the magazine *The Banker*. The listing indicates that each of the top six banks is almost as large as the whole Canadian banking industry combined. The top 25 banks account for 41.6 percent of total assets of the top 1,000 banks. The largest Canadian bank is the Royal Bank, with assets of about US$425 billion. Royal is only the 37th-largest bank in the world. While the numbers for the Canadian banks and for the Canadian financial markets are large, Table 5.3 makes it clear that the financial institutions and markets in other developed countries are gargantuan and much larger than the "large" Canadian banks.

www.thebanker.com

Table 5.1 also indicates that the three institutional investors managed a total of $1.85 trillion on behalf of individuals in 2006. Obviously, based on these numbers, the level of individual savings in Canada is substantial. In comparison, the remaining two financial intermediaries appear to be very minor players in the Canadian financial markets. The assets of investment dealers and the Bank of Canada are very modest, a very small fraction of the assets of the other intermediaries. The importance of these two intermediaries is measured not in terms of assets, but in terms of the key functions performed. Without investment dealers or the Bank of Canada, the financial markets would not operate efficiently. For example, investment dealers handle every dollar invested by the three large institutional investors. The Bank of Canada raises all financing required by the Government of Canada and manages monetary policy, which determines the cost of money.

TABLE 5.3 Top Ten Banks in the World by Assets, 2006 (millions of US$)

Rank	Bank	Country	Total assets
1	Barclays Bank	U.K.	$1,591,524
2	UBS	Switzerland	1,567,564
3	Mitsubishi UFJ Financial Group	Japan	1,508,541
4	HSBC Holdings	U.K.	1,501,970
5	Citigroup	U.S.A.	1,493,987
6	BNP Paribas	France	1,484,109
7	Crédit Agricole Groupe	France	1,380,617
8	Royal Bank of Scotland	U.K.	1,337,512
9	Bank of America Corp.	U.S.A.	1,291,795
10	Mizuho Financial Group	Japan	$1,226,627

SOURCE: "The Top 1000 World Banks: 2006," *The Banker*, July 3, 2006, available at **www.thebanker.com**.

Trust and Financial Markets

A key but often overlooked concept associated with financial markets is "trust." In order for financial markets to function efficiently, the participants in the market must have trust in the system. When individuals deposit money in a bank, invest in the debt securities of a company or government, or buy common or preferred shares, they are displaying trust in the system. They believe their money will be available when they require it. For example consider Maureen, who deposits $5,000 in a savings account. She is giving up possession of the money. Maureen would do this only if she believed she would receive an appropriate rate of return on the deposited funds, and have instant access to the money. If she lacked trust in the system, if she did not believe that both of these conditions would be met, then she would not deposit the money. If individuals do not deposit their money, then financial markets will not exist. The same concept applies to investments in all other financial securities.

In non-democratic, non-capitalistic countries, there is no trust in the financial markets. This is the case since the country's currency is often worthless and the financial system is often corrupt. In these cases, another medium of exchange is used. Sometimes real assets like gold or diamonds might be used, but most often a hard currency like the U.S. dollar becomes the medium of exchange. In these economies there is no trust in the country's currency, so a substitute is used. Residents keep their wealth in paper form: the currency of another country.

Countries in this situation will remain underdeveloped, since substantive financial markets do not exist or are underdeveloped. Trust in the country's financial system is lacking, so money is never provided to financial intermediaries. The exchange between savers and users never occurs. The black market in U.S. dollars becomes the country's *de facto* financial market. There is no faith that the country's currency will retain its value, or that money deposited in a bank will be returned. So even very modest individual wealth is kept close at hand, and financial markets do not develop.

? Review Questions

5–1 Why are financial markets important?

5–2 What basic function do the financial markets perform?

5–3 Who are the main participants in the financial markets? Are they net suppliers or demanders of funds?

5–4 How can financial markets be classified?

5–5 Discuss the three flow-of-funds channels that exist in the financial markets.

5–6 List and briefly discuss the key function performed by the various financial intermediaries in the Canadian financial markets.

5–7 Why is trust an important concept when dealing with financial markets?

5.2 The Money Market

The money market involves the trading of debt securities that will mature within one year. Note, though, that Government of Canada bonds with up to three years to run until maturity are also considered money market instruments because of their very high level of safety and liquidity. There is no physical location for the money market. It is an artificial market—the computer networks between investment dealers. In Canada, the money market came into existence in March 1935 when the federal government established the Bank of Canada. The money market developed as an important part of the financial markets during 1953–1954 when a number of changes were made to the operation of the Bank of Canada. These changes led to and encouraged the trading of money market instruments between financial institutions. Since that period, the money market has substantially increased in size and the Bank of Canada has maintained its position as the central and most prominent financial institution within the market.

Money Market Instruments

http://bankofcanada.ca/en/wfsgen.html

The single largest issuer of money market securities is the Government of Canada. The Bank of Canada, on behalf of the federal government, regularly sells promissory notes in the money market. Essentially, the federal government is borrowing money from savers using an unsecured loan. These promissory notes are called *treasury bills* or, more commonly, *t-bills*. As of October 2006, there were approximately $120 billion of t-bills outstanding. Other types of money market instruments traded are short-term government bonds, commercial paper, bankers' acceptances, and finance company paper. As of October 2006, there were approximately $206 billion of corporate money market securities outstanding. Of this amount, commercial paper is by far the largest component, with about $156.6 billion outstanding. Statistics regarding the value of money market securities outstanding are available at the Bank of Canada's Web site. Each of the money market securities are discussed individually in the sections that follow.

Treasury Bills

Due to the large quantity of treasury bills outstanding, they occupy a key position in the money market. Treasury bills were originally issued in March 1934, but were rarely traded. As the market evolved and the federal government's need for financing increased, t-bills were issued every week and huge volumes traded in the secondary market. Today, t-bills are auctioned every second Tuesday and previously issued t-bills mature. T-bills are promissory notes issued by the federal government, and sold by the Bank of Canada, which acts as the federal government's banker. Sales are made to the distributors of Government of Canada securities. The government securities distributors are specified chartered banks, investment dealers, and the Bank of Canada. A current list of government securities distributors is available on the Bank of Canada's Web site.

http://bankofcanada.ca/en/markets/markets_auct.html

The eligible distributors purchase the bills through a competitive bidding process. Two weeks before each auction, the Bank of Canada makes a "preliminary call for tenders" informing the financial community about the size and maturities of the upcoming t-bill auction. One week before the auction, the Bank of Canada finalizes the amounts and maturities of the bills to be offered. The value of t-bills auctioned varies by week, but is usually in the $6-to-$12-billion range. The maturities offered are those that best meet the federal government's requirement for financing, but the maximum is always 364 days. An example of an actual auction announcement is provided as Table 5.4.

The table indicates that $10.5 billion of t-bills were auctioned in three maturities: 98 days or 14 weeks, 182 days or 26 weeks, and 364 days or 52 weeks. The

TABLE 5.4 **A Call for Tenders for a Treasury Bill Auction**

Bank of Canada, Ottawa
For Release: October 24, 2006, 10:40 E.T.
Treasury Bills—Final Call for Tenders

On behalf of the Minister of Finance, final details of the upcoming Government of Canada treasury bill auction were announced today. This auction will be conducted by the Bank of Canada on behalf of the Government of Canada, subject to the "Standard Terms for Auctions of Government of Canada Treasury Bills."

Auction Date:	2006.10.31
Bidding Deadline:	10:30:00 E.T.
Total Amount:	$10,500,000,000

Amount	Issue	Term	Maturity	Outstanding prior to auction
$5,900,000,000	2006.11.02	98 days	2007.02.08	$3,500,000,000
2,300,000,000	2006.11.02	182 days	2007.05.03	0
2,300,000,000	2006.11.02	364 days	2007.11.01	0
Total amount maturing on 2006.11.02:	$9,700,000,000			
Of which held by Bank of Canada and clients:	$1,375,000,000			

SOURCE: Bank of Canada, **http://bankofcanada.ca/en/cars/cars.htm**.

largest amount auctioned were 98-day t-bills. This is usual. Note that this auction occurred on October 31, a Tuesday, but the t-bills were dated November 2, a Thursday. Finally, as shown at the bottom of the table, $9.7 billion of t-bills were maturing on the issue date. As discussed in Chapter 4, it is normal for large organizations to have a debt management program whereby as some debt matures additional debt is issued. Since the federal government has a very large amount of debt, with maturities that could range from 1 day to 30 years, the debt must be closely managed. Note that the net impact of the t-bills auctioned and those maturing is that the federal debt increased by $800 million. More recent t-bill auction announcements are available on the Bank of Canada's Web site.

http://bankofcanada.ca/en/cars/cars.html

On the Tuesday of the auction, the distributors submit their bids to the Bank of Canada by computer. Since the money markets are ever-changing, the bidders will wait until just a few seconds before the 10:30 a.m. EST deadline to make their bid. The highest bidder receives all of the bills for the maturity for which they bid (subject to limits). Succeeding high bids are then allocated bills. If there are a number of bids at the lowest successful price, then the remainder of the bills are allotted on a *pro rata* basis. The bills are dated the Thursday of the week of the auction and will mature on a Thursday a number of weeks in the future.

An average, high, and low bid are announced together with the corresponding yields. It is usual for bidders to submit several bids at varying prices and amounts in order that at least one bid will be successful. The Bank of Canada usually submits two bids: one for the bills it seeks for its own portfolio and another as a reserve bid to acquire the entire issue. This latter bid has two objectives. First, it will guarantee that the entire issue will be sold, avoiding any embarrassment to the government. Second, it prevents collusion on the part of other bidders to artificially lower the price of the minimum successful bid. The Bank also has the right to refuse all bids and leave the issue of t-bills unsold.

TABLE 5.5 **The Results of a Treasury Bill Auction**

Treasury Bills—Auction Results

On behalf of the Minister of Finance, it was announced today that tenders for Government of Canada treasury bills have been accepted as follows:

Auction Date: 2006.10.31
Bidding Deadline: 10:30:00 EST
Total Amount: $10,500,000,000

Amount	Issue	Maturity	Outstanding after auction	Yield and price	Allotment ratio	Bank of Canada purchase
$5,900,000,000	2006.11.02	2007.02.08	$9,400,000,000	Avg.: 4.169 98.89304	70.68571	$600,000,000
				Low: 4.163 98.89462		
				High: 4.173 98.89199		
2,300,000,000	2006.11.02	2007.05.03	2,300,000,000	Avg.: 4.183 97.95685	72.94118	300,000,000
				Low: 4.177 97.95972		
				High: 4.190 97.95350		
2,300,000,000	2006.11.02	2007.11.01	2,300,000,000	Avg.: 4.172 96.00562	53.06849	300,000,000
				Low: 4.169 96.00838		
				High: 4.174 96.00378		

Value of bids submitted by distributors:

Maturity	Total	Non-competitive
2007.02.08	$11,201,500,000	$6,500,000
2007.05.03	4,546,000,000	6,000,000
2007.11.01	4,702,600,000	7,600,000

SOURCE: Bank of Canada, **http://bankofcanada.ca/en/cars/cars.htm**. Copyright © 1995–2007, Bank of Canada.

An example of the results of a t-bill auction is provided as Table 5.5. Note that the average, high, and low bids are provided. To understand these bids, it is important to note that t-bills are sold at a discount and, at maturity, return the par value. The par value is always some multiple of $1,000. The return earned by the purchaser is the difference between the two amounts. All debt securities are priced like those shown in Table 5.5. The price shown is a percent of par. For the 98-day t-bills in Table 5.5, the average price was 98.89304 percent of par. So, to buy $100,000,000 of par, the purchaser would pay $98,893,040. The difference between the price paid and the par value purchased is $1,106,960. This is the dollar yield. Over the 98-day holding period, this is a 4.169 percent yield. The lowest bid provides the purchaser with the lowest yield, and thus the government with the highest proceeds. Note as well that there is great demand for t-bills from the eligible distributors. The value of the bids submitted are double the amounts offered for the three maturities. More recent t-bill auction results are available on the Bank of Canada's Web site.

http://bankofcanada.ca/en/cars/cars.html

After the t-bill auction, the government securities distributors begin to sell t-bills to other financial institutions, business organizations, and individuals. The regularity of the issue process means that t-bills with maturities ranging from 1 day to 364 days will be outstanding and available to the market. Thus, investors may choose the particular maturity that best coincides with the period of time they wish to invest funds. The yield on the bills sold in the secondary market is less than that received by the distributors. The difference is the return the distributor earns on the t-bill transaction. While t-bill transactions for amounts as low as $5,000 of par value can occur, most secondary market transactions are usually in multiples of $1,000,000.

T-bills are sold on a discount basis at both the auction and the subsequent trading in the secondary market. The yield the purchaser receives is the difference between the price paid and the par value. For example, assume that a $1,000,000 par value t-bill with 98 days to maturity is priced at 98.868653. What yield would an investor purchasing this t-bill receive? Remember, all debt securities are quoted as a percent of par. So the investor would pay $988,686.53 for the t-bill, wait 98 days until maturity, and then receive the $1,000,000 of par value. The dollar yield on the t-bill is $11,313.47 over the 98 days. To determine the percentage yield, the following formula can be used. Note that the formula provides the yield on a yearly basis, so it annualizes the return for the particular maturity.

$$V = P_0 \times \left[1 + \frac{i \times n}{365}\right] \tag{5.1}$$

where:

V = par value of the t-bill, is always a multiple of $1,000
P_0 = price paid for the t-bill now
i = yield on t-bills
n = number of days to maturity

For the example discussed above, the following process is used to solve for i, the yield on the t-bill. This is also provided in Spreadsheet Application 5.1.

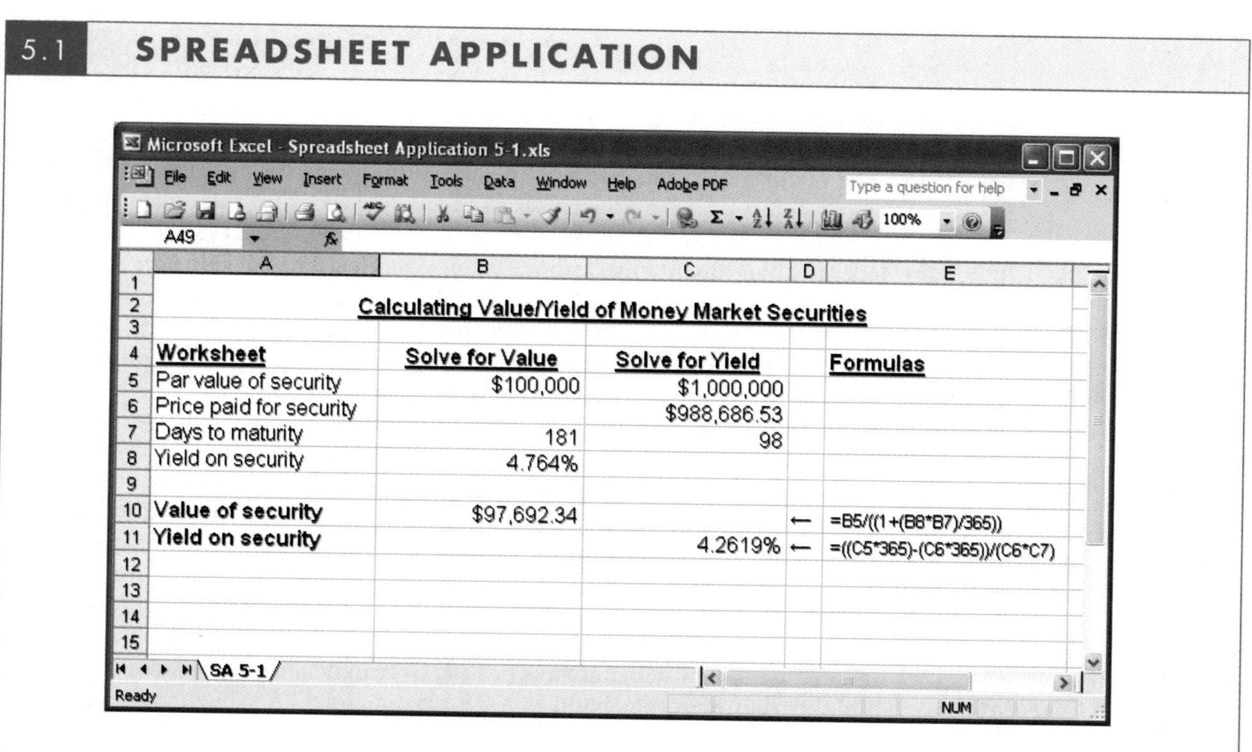

5.1 SPREADSHEET APPLICATION

Microsoft Excel - Spreadsheet Application 5-1.xls

Calculating Value/Yield of Money Market Securities

Worksheet	Solve for Value	Solve for Yield		Formulas
Par value of security	$100,000	$1,000,000		
Price paid for security		$988,686.53		
Days to maturity	181	98		
Yield on security	4.764%			
Value of security	$97,692.34		←	=B5/((1+(B8*B7)/365))
Yield on security		4.2619%	←	=((C5*365)-(C6*365))/(C6*C7)

$$\$1{,}000{,}000 = \$988{,}686.53\left[1 + \frac{i \times 98}{365}\right]$$

$$\$1{,}000{,}000 = \$988{,}686.53 + \left[\frac{\$988{,}686.53 \times i \times 98}{365}\right]$$

$$\$1{,}000{,}000 - \$988{,}686.53 = \$265{,}455.5615i$$

$$\$11{,}313.47 = \$265{,}455.5615i$$

$$i = \frac{\$11{,}313.47}{\$265{,}455.5615}$$

$$i = 4.2619\%$$

So, to solve the problem, the first step is to multiply the price paid by the figures in the brackets. Doing this results in one known and one unknown, the yield (i). Solving for i indicates that an investor purchasing and holding this t-bill for the 98 days to maturity would receive a return of 4.2619 percent, quoted on an annual basis.

Instead of the price being provided, information regarding the yield may be available, in which case the price of the t-bill must be calculated. For example, how much should be paid for a \$100,000 par value t-bill that matures in 181 days if the yield is 4.7635 percent? By using Equation 5.1 provided above, we can solve for P_0, the amount an investor should pay for this t-bill.

$$\$100{,}000 = P_0 \times \left[1 + \frac{0.047635 \times 181}{365}\right]$$

$$\$100{,}000 = 1.02362174\ P_0$$

$$P_0 = \$97{,}692.34$$

An investor purchasing this \$100,000 t-bill for \$97,692.34 and holding it for 181 days would receive a yield of 4.7635 percent. This result is also provided in Spreadsheet Application 5.1.

The auction of t-bills has two purposes. First, the funds raised will be used to repay holders of the maturing series of t-bills. Second, if the dollar amount of t-bills offered is greater than the amount maturing, the funds raised will be used by federal government operations. From March 1980 to February 1996, the weekly t-bill auction also was used to set the **Bank Rate**, the interest rate the Bank of Canada charges on one-day loans to financial institutions (chartered banks and investment dealers) as the lender of last resort. The procedure used to set the Bank Rate has significantly changed since 1996.

Bank Rate
The interest rate the Bank of Canada charges on one-day loans to financial institutions (chartered banks and investment dealers) as the lender of last resort.

Now the Bank Rate is based on the **overnight rate**, the average interest rate the Bank of Canada wants financial institutions to use when they lend each other money for one day, or "overnight." The overnight rate is the main tool used by the Bank of Canada to conduct monetary policy. The overnight rate is also the foundation for other interest rates in the economy. When the overnight rate changes, all financial institutions adjust their interest rate for both savings and lending.

overnight rate
The average interest rate the Bank of Canada wants financial institutions to use when they lend each other money for one day, or "overnight."

The Bank of Canada operates the system to make sure trading in the overnight market stays within its **operating band**. This band, which is one-half of a percentage point wide, always has the overnight rate target at its centre. For example, if the operating band is 4.25 percent to 4.75 percent, the overnight rate target is 4.50 percent. The Bank Rate is the upper limit of the operating band, so it is 25 basis points (0.25%) above the overnight rate. Since financial

operating band
A band, one-half of a percentage point wide, with the overnight rate at the centre and the bank rate at the top.

institutions know that the Bank of Canada will always lend money at the Bank Rate, and pay interest on deposits at the bottom, it makes no sense for the institutions to trade overnight funds at rates outside the band. The Bank of Canada can also intervene in the overnight market, if the market rate is moving away from the target rate. Through this system, the Bank of Canada controls the level of interest rates prevalent in the economy. Additional information regarding how the Bank of Canada influences interest rates in Canada is available on the Bank of Canada's Web site.

www.bankofcanada.ca/en/backgrounders/bg-p2.html

Short-Term and Short-Dated Government Bonds

short-dated bonds
Long-term government bonds that are approaching maturity.

Long-term government bonds that are approaching maturity, known as **short-dated bonds**, are also traded in the money market. Generally, the one- to three-year bonds will have higher yields than treasury bills because of the longer period of time to maturity and thus the greater risk of price fluctuations if interest rates change. There has been a large increase in the use of short-term bonds by the federal government since 1980. For example, in October 2006, there were $88.6 billion of federal government bonds outstanding with maturities of less than three years.

Commercial Paper

commercial paper
Short-term, unsecured promissory notes issued by corporations; sometimes referred to as *corporate paper.*

Commercial paper, sometimes referred to as *corporate paper*, is short-term, unsecured promissory notes issued primarily by financial and industrial corporations with excellent credit reputations. Corporate paper is usually supported by a stand-by line of credit from a bank or a guarantee from a parent or affiliate company. Like t-bills, commercial paper is sold at a discount to yield the par value at maturity. Issued in large denominations, normally of no less than $500,000, the maturities can vary from 1 day to 365 days. Most common, however, are maturities of 30, 60, or 90 days.

Since 1996, the market for commercial paper has exploded in Canada. At one time, the amount of commercial paper outstanding in the money market was a small fraction of the dollar amount of t-bills outstanding. Now, there is *more* commercial paper issued in the Canadian money market than t-bills. Since 1996, the amount of commercial paper outstanding has increased at an annual rate of 12.6 percent. In the same period, the dollar amount of t-bills outstanding has declined at an annual rate of about 1 percent.

Finance Company Paper

finance company paper
Short-term secured promissory notes issued by sales finance companies.

Short-term secured promissory notes issued by sales finance companies are known as **finance company paper**. These notes are usually secured by a pledge of installment obligations due to the company in amounts providing a reasonable margin or cushion of protection to the lender. Minimum amounts offered are $50,000 with maturities ranging from 30 to 365 days. To issue finance company paper, the sales finance company purchases installment debt (conditional sales contracts) from retail organizations that deal in consumer durables (e.g., furniture stores). The contracts have been signed by purchasers of these durables. The contracts are then packaged according to maturity. The "packages" are used as collateral for promissory notes issued by the finance companies and sold to financial institutions. These notes are called finance company or "acceptance paper."

Bankers' Acceptances

bankers' acceptances Created when a chartered bank adds its guarantee of payment to the promissory note of a corporate borrower.

Bankers' acceptances are corporate paper with an additional guarantee. A bankers' acceptance is created when a chartered bank adds its guarantee of payment to the promissory note of a corporate borrower. The borrowing company receives the money from the bank. The bank then sells the bankers' acceptances, through an investment dealer, in the money market. As with most other money market securities, bankers' acceptances are traded on a discount basis to yield the par value. Bankers' acceptances usually trade to yield a rate slightly lower than corporate paper, given the greater security offered by the bank's guarantee. Bankers' acceptances are issued in multiples of $100,000 and have a term of 180 days or less. The usual terms are 30, 60, or 90 days. At maturity, the banker repays the holder the face value and the borrowing company repays the bank.

Bankers' acceptances were introduced in 1962 but were very slow to develop as a method for raising funds. The principal reason was the high "stamping fee" the banks charged in order to add their guarantee to the paper. Beginning in the late 1970s, competition between banks resulted in the stamping fee being reduced to between 0.35 percent and 1.5 percent of the face value of the bankers' acceptance. This resulted in a dramatic increase in the use of this form of short-term financing. In October 2006, there were about $49.3 billion of bankers' acceptances outstanding in the money market.

Day Loans

day loans Made by chartered banks to investment dealers who are major holders of treasury bills.

Day loans are made by chartered banks to investment dealers who are major holders of treasury bills. These loans are not made for any fixed period, but the banks can demand repayment at any time. If the demand is made before noon, repayment must be made by 3:00 p.m. the same day. The dealers pledge their inventories of securities as collateral for the loan. The immediate repayment provision makes these loans the most liquid asset next to cash itself, held by the banks. Therefore, the banks are willing to make day-to-day loans at much lower interest rates than ordinary commercial loans. The day-to-day loan rate is marginally less than the current yield on treasury bills and, hence, the dealers can earn a small profit on the securities they have pledged as collateral. The rate can be adjusted daily.

For this system to work, the investment dealers must be able to pay, within hours, loans totalling millions of dollars. This works because the Bank of Canada has extended special purchase and resale agreements (repos) to these investment dealers. The Bank stands ready to buy treasury bills and short-term government bonds from the dealers, subject to an agreement whereby the dealers must repurchase these securities within a certain period at a price to net the Bank a return equal to the bank rate. While day-to-day loans and repos are not large in terms of amounts outstanding, they are fundamental to the effective operation of the overnight money market. Without these two instruments, the money market would not operate as effectively as it does.

The Eurocurrency Market

Eurocurrency market The market for short-term bank deposits denominated in U.S. dollars or other easily convertible currencies.

The international equivalent of the domestic money market is called the **Eurocurrency market**. This is a market for short-term loans and deposits denominated in U.S. dollars or other easily convertible currencies. Historically, the Eurocurrency market has been centred in London, but it has evolved into a large, global market. A Eurocurrency deposit arises when funds are deposited in a bank in a currency other than the local currency of the country where the bank is located. For example, if a Canadian corporation deposited U.S. dollars in a London bank, this would create a Eurodollar deposit (a dollar deposit at a bank in Europe). About two-thirds of Eurocurrency deposits are Eurodollars, deposits of U.S. dollars. Almost all Eurodeposits are *time deposits*, meaning that the bank promises to repay the deposit, with interest, at a fixed date in the future—say, 6 months.

The bank then loans these deposits to creditworthy corporate or government borrowers. Eurocurrency loans are usually unsecured, made in multiples of $1 million, and for between one day and one year. The interest rate on Eurocurrency loans is based on the **London Interbank Offered Rate (LIBOR).** This is the rate charged on Eurocurrency loans made between banks. In other words, one bank can borrow from another bank at LIBOR.

London Interbank Offered Rate (LIBOR)
The base interest rate on all Eurocurrency loans.

The LIBOR is set on a daily basis by the British Bankers' Association and will vary depending on the currency used and the term of the loan. In other words, the LIBOR for a one-month loan for U.S. dollars will be different from the LIBOR for a one-month loan for Euros. In addition, the LIBOR for a one-month loan for U.S. dollars will be different from the LIBOR for a six-month loan for U.S. dollars.

The LIBOR is derived from a filtered average of the world's most creditworthy banks' interbank deposit rates for very large loans with maturities between overnight and one full year. It is the most widely used reference rate for short-term interest rates worldwide. Current and historic LIBORs are available at the British Bankers' Association Web site.

www.bba.org.uk/public/libor

Corporate borrowers are also active in the Eurocurrency market. Non-bank borrowers will pay a premium over the LIBOR. The premium is based on the risk of the borrower. For example, the borrowing rate for a multinational corporation may be quoted as LIBOR plus 62. The 62 refers to basis points of interest where 1 basis point is 1/100th of a percent. Therefore, 62 basis points is 0.62 percent. If LIBOR were 4.79 percent, the multinational corporation would be able to borrow at 5.41 percent (4.79% + 0.62%). Another, more secure multinational corporation might be able to borrow at LIBOR plus 12.

The Eurocurrency market has grown rapidly, primarily because it is an unregulated, wholesale, and a truly global market that fills the needs of both borrowers and lenders. Those with excess cash are able to make large, short-term, and safe deposits at attractive interest rates. Borrowers are able to arrange large loans quickly, confidentially, and at attractive interest rates. For Eurodollar loans, interest is accumulated and repaid with the principal as a lump sum.

Example

A Canadian company deposits US$100 million in a bank located in London. This creates a Eurocurrency deposit that the bank will then lend. Assume that a corporation approaches the bank for a US$100 million loan for seven months. The bank quotes the borrower an interest rate of the LIBOR plus 129 basis points. The premium charged reflects the risk of the borrower. The LIBOR for U.S. dollars for a maturity of seven months is 4.128 percent. To determine the amount the borrowing company has to repay the bank located in London, the first step is to determine the borrowing rate. It is 5.418 percent (4.128% + 1.29%). The company will borrow the US$100 million for seven months; therefore, the interest owed is based on the following analysis:

$$\text{Interest owed} = \$100{,}000{,}000 \times 5.418\% \times \frac{7}{12} = \$3{,}160{,}500$$

So, at the end of the seven months, the borrowing company will have to repay the bank $103,160,500.

There are a number of other types of instruments issued in the money market. These include certificates of deposit, foreign exchange swaps, interbank deposits, swapped deposits, bearer deposit notes, provincial and municipal paper, and foreign short-term securities. The money market continually changes and develops, and new instruments appear to fill perceived needs of the market. The items discussed here are those of major importance. They provide an adequate cross-section of money market instruments. An understanding of their features and diversity will go far towards explaining what contributes to the myriad interest rates in evidence in the Canadian economy.

? Review Questions

5–8 What is the money market, and what is the principal security traded?

5–9 What are treasury bills? Who issues them and why, and how are they issued?

5–10 Money market securities are said to be "sold at a discount." What does this mean? What is the general equation used to determine the price or yield on money market securities?

5–11 What is the bank rate? Overnight rate? Operating band?

5–12 List and briefly discuss the other principal money market securities that trade in Canada.

5–13 What is the Eurocurrency market? What is the London Interbank Offered Rate (LIBOR), and how is it used in the Eurocurrency market?

5.3 Capital Market Securities: Long-Term Debt

There are three major capital market securities: (1) debt with a maturity greater than one year (long-term debt), (2) common shares, and (3) preferred shares. Each of these is a source of long-term financing for a corporation. In Chapter 4 we saw that the objective of financial forecasting is to determine the amount of external financing the firm requires to operate over a coming time period. One, or a combination, of these securities may be the source of the long-term financing required.

When most people think of financial securities, these are the ones that are top of mind. This is the case since these securities, particularly common shares, are very visible. Common shares are the subject of a great deal of media attention. Both television and newspapers provide details on a daily basis regarding stock market trading and information on how the common shares of major companies have fared in the day's trading. Also, the majority of adult Canadians are owners of common shares, either directly through purchases on the stock market, or indirectly through pension plans or mutual funds. Events in the capital market have a pronounced impact on many Canadians. The first capital market security, long-term debt, is discussed in this section.

Long-Term Debt: Term Loans

term loan
A borrowing arrangement, usually with a bank, for a certain amount at a stated interest rate for a specific time period.

There are two major types of long-term debt. The first is bank-supplied financing like a term loan. With a **term loan**, a certain amount is borrowed at a stated interest rate for a specific time period. It is similar in nature to a long-term loan made by an individual when purchasing a high-cost item like a car or house. A term loan is usually secured by a fixed asset and is generally not callable by the bank, assuming the borrower makes the regular payment. In addition to the asset pledged as security for the loan, the lender may request additional security. This can be provided as a floating charge on all assets which, in case of default, allows the lender to claim all assets necessary to recoup the remaining principal on the loan.

Term loans are usually provided by banks, but can also come from governments or government-funded organizations like the Business Development Bank of Canada (BDC), and through the Canada Small Business Financing Program. With this latter program the small business arranges to borrow up to $250,000 from their lending institution and the federal government guarantees the repayment of 85 percent of the amount borrowed. Domestic banks provide more than half of the debt financing used by businesses in Canada. For example, in November 2006, Canadian chartered banks had over $202.6 billion of loans outstanding to Canadian businesses.

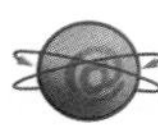

http://strategis.ic.gc.ca/epic/internet/incsbfp-pfpec.nsf/en/Home

The interest rate charged on term loans may float with the prime rate or it may be fixed for a stated number of years. Payments are usually on a monthly basis and consist of both principal and interest. These payments will retire the loan over the period of time the loan is outstanding (the amortization period). As an example, assume a company arranges for a $200,000 term loan from their bank. The interest rate on the loan is 7.5 percent and the company will repay the loan over five years. The required monthly payments on the loan are $4,007.59.

Each payment will consist of some interest and some principal. As payments are made, the dollar amount of interest will fall and the amount of principal will increase. Therefore, the loan is paid off over the five-year amortization period. This type of loan is termed an installment loan, which is discussed in more detail in Chapter 6. Some term loans may just require interest payments on a periodic basis, usually monthly. For these interest-only loans, the monthly payments do not reduce the principal amount borrowed; the payments are interest only. The borrower would then repay the principal at some future date or dates.

Long-Term Debt: Bonds and Debentures

While term loans are used by many corporations, the real focus of this chapter is on long-term debt securities issued by borrowers, not on term loans from financial institutions like banks. This second type of long-term debt is raised in the capital market by both governments and corporations. There are two general categories: bonds and debentures. The major distinction is that a **bond** is secured by a specific asset or assets pledged as collateral. A mortgage on a property is a concept equivalent to a bond. The property is the collateral for the mortgage.

bond
A long-term debt security that has a specific asset or assets pledged as collateral.

debenture
An unsecured long-term debt security that is backed by the general earnings potential of the corporation.

long-term debt
A contractual liability between the two parties, the borrower (issuer) and the lender (saver).

A **debenture** is an unsecured loan. The general earnings potential of the issuer is the only backing for the issue. The term "bond" is often used as the general descriptor for long-term debt. For example, government debt is referred to as bonds. Note, though, that governments do not pledge collateral for long-term debt financing so this description is incorrect. Governments issue debentures.

Long-term debt is a contractual liability between the two parties: the borrower (issuer) and the lender (saver). The agreement specifies that the issuer has borrowed a stated amount of money, termed the par value, and promises to repay it in the future under clearly defined terms. Also, while the debt is outstanding, the issuer will pay the investor a stated rate of interest. Long-term debt is usually issued for between 10 and 30 years. The basic par value denomination used is $1,000. For long-term debt, the interest rate is termed the **coupon rate** and it is set at the time of the issue and is constant for the full term of the issue. The coupon rate is quoted on a yearly basis, but is paid semiannually, or every six months.

coupon rate
The interest rate on a long-term debt issue which is set at the time of the issue and is constant for the full term of the issue.

Example

Today, the federal government issued $850 million of long-term debt with a coupon rate of 7.5 percent and a term of 20 years. This is a debenture that will mature 20 years from today, when the government will repay the holders of the debenture the $850 million of par value. In the meantime, the government will pay the debenture holders interest of 7.5 percent per year. So, for a single $1,000 denomination of debentures, the government will pay $75 of interest each year.

Since interest is paid twice a year, not monthly or yearly, investors will receive $37.50 every six months. Six months from today, the first coupon payment will be made. Six months later, on the anniversary of the issue, the second $37.50 is paid. In total, 40 coupon payments will be made. In addition, a 41st payment, the par value borrowed, will be repaid when the debenture matures. A key fact to remember about long-term debt is that the par value and the coupon rate remain constant for the life of the issue. The par value is always $1,000, and the coupon rate is fixed and does not change. In this case it will be 7.5 percent for the full 20 years.

Coupon rates are set at the time of the issue and are based on interest rate levels in the economy for debt of similar risk. The coupon rate and par value are fixed for the term of the debt issue and will not change regardless of what happens to interest rates in the economy. Once issued in the primary market, the bonds will then start to trade in the secondary market. Here, bonds trade on yield, which means that as yields on debt securities of similar risk change, market prices of the bonds will also change. The relationship is inverse. That is, as interest rates increase (decrease), the value of debt securities currently outstanding decreases (increases). This characteristic of long-term debt is discussed in much greater detail in Chapter 8.

Types of Bonds and Debentures

Table 5.6 lists and discusses the characteristics of the various types of long-term debt securities that may be issued by borrowers in Canada. There are two categories of debt securities discussed in the table: traditional and contemporary. Traditional securities include *mortgage bonds, debentures,* and *subordinated debentures*. Contemporary securities include *income bonds, zero-coupon bonds, junk bonds, floating-rate bonds, extendible notes, retractable bonds, convertible bonds,* and *real return bonds*. Note that these are all referred to as bonds, but in many cases they are really debentures since they are unsecured.

In recent years, changing market conditions and investor preferences have spurred innovations in debt financing. Designing new financial securities or processes is referred to as **financial engineering**. Investment dealers, who underwrite the risks of financing for issuers, are usually responsible for these innovations. Successful financial engineering reduces the costs of financing and minimizes taxes, while meeting market needs and all regulatory requirements. Financial engineering in the long-term debt market will likely continue into the future.

financial engineering
Designing new financial securities or processes due to changing market conditions and investor preferences.

TABLE 5.6 Major Types and Characteristics of Long-Term Debt Securities

Type of debt security	Characteristics
	Traditional Debt Securities
Mortgage bonds	Long-term debt financing secured by real estate, buildings, manufacturing facilities, or other fixed assets. Borrowers have pledged specific asset(s) as collateral for the financing and, in case the borrower defaults on the bond, lenders have claim on the proceeds from the sale of mortgaged assets. If the claim is not fully satisfied, the lender becomes a general creditor. The *first-mortgage* claim must be fully satisfied before distribution of proceeds to *second-mortgage* holders, and so on. A number of mortgages can be issued against the same collateral. In the event of bankruptcy, secured debtholders normally receive most of the financing they provided.
Debentures	Unsecured bonds that only creditworthy firms can issue. The lenders' claims are the same as those of any general creditor. May have other unsecured bonds subordinated to them.
Subordinated debentures	Claims are not satisfied until those of the creditors holding senior debts have been fully satisfied. The lender's claim is that of a general creditor but not as good as a senior debt claim.
	Contemporary Debt Securities
Income bonds	Payment of interest is required only when earnings are available. Commonly issued in the reorganization of a failing firm. The lender's claim is that of a general creditor. The "bonds" are not in default when interest payments are missed, because they are contingent only on earnings being available. If missed, coupons often accumulate. Income bonds prohibit the payment of dividends to shareholders if coupon payments are missed. In many respects, income bonds resemble preferred shares.
Zero (or low) coupon bonds	Issued with no (zero) or a very low coupon rate and sold at a large discount from par. A significant portion (or all) of the investor's return comes from gain in value (i.e., par value minus purchase price). They are valued like long-term money market securities.
Junk bonds	Debt rated below investment grade by one of the major debt rating agencies in either Canada or the United States. Investment-grade debt is rated BBB or above. Since the 1980s, junk bonds have been regularly used by rapidly growing firms to obtain growth capital or as a way to finance mergers and takeovers. These are high-risk bonds with high yields—typically yielding between 3 percent and 10 percent more than the best-quality corporate debt.
Floating-rate bonds	Stated interest rate is adjusted periodically within stated limits in response to changes in specified money or capital market rates. Popular when future inflation and interest rates are uncertain. Tend to sell at close to par due to the automatic adjustment to changing market conditions. Some issues provide for annual redemption at par at the option of the bondholder.
Extendible bonds (notes)	Short maturities, typically 1 to 5 years, that can be renewed for a similar period at the option of holders. An issue might be a series of 3-year renewable notes over a period of 15 years. Every 3 years, the holders could extend the notes for another 3 years, at a new rate competitive with market interest rates at the time of renewal.
Retractable bonds	Gives the bondholder the option to sell the bond back to the company at par ($1,000) either on a specific date, and every 1 to 5 years thereafter, or if the firm is acquired, acquires another company, or issues a large amount of additional debt. In return for the retraction privilege, the bond's yield is lower than that of a non-retractable bond.
Convertible bonds	A bond that at the option of the holder can be converted into a predetermined number of common shares of the issuer on a specified date. There may be multiple opportunities to convert. Convertible bonds are termed a *hybrid security*, since the holder receives guaranteed coupon payments but also benefits if the company's share price increases. The coupon rate on convertibles is lower than on regular bonds but offers the opportunity of a large gain if the company's common share price increases.
Real return bonds (RRB)	Bonds that adjust the semiannual coupon payments and the par value for inflation. This feature ensures that investors' purchasing power is maintained regardless of the future rate of inflation. The coupon payment on RRB is based on the inflation-adjusted principal and, at maturity, the principal is repaid in inflation-adjusted dollars. Real return bonds are primarily issued by governments but were used to finance the construction of two major mega-projects: the 108-kilometre 407 Express Toll Route which connects major centres in the greater Toronto area, and the 12.9-kilometre Confederation Bridge between New Brunswick and Prince Edward Island.

Trust Indenture

trust indenture (trust deed)
The legal document that details the contractual relationship between the borrower and lender.

trustee
A third party who acts on behalf of the purchasers of the debt securities.

The **trust indenture** or **trust deed** is the legal document that details the contractual relationship between the borrower and lender. It is a very long and complex document. The indenture specifies a **trustee** who acts as a third party on behalf of the purchasers of the debt securities. The trustee is usually a commercial trust company, with most of these companies now being divisions of the chartered banks. The trustee is paid to act as a watchdog on behalf of the debtholders and is empowered to take action if the terms of the indenture are violated.

The trustee ensures that the issuer does not default on its contractual obligations to the debtholders. The indenture specifies the rights of the debtholders and the duties of the issuer. Included in the indenture are all financial information regarding the issue and the issuer, a description of any collateral pledged, restrictive covenants on the operation of the company, call provision (redemption clause), and, possibly, a sinking-fund provision.

Financial Information

Obviously, all financial information regarding the issue such as the amount of funding raised, the coupon rate, the maturity date, and the firm's plans for the money would be included in the information provided to investors. In addition, all financial statements and certain key ratios of the issuer would be included in the document.

Collateral

The indenture will include a detailed description of the collateral pledged for a bond issue. For example, if a manufacturing plant were used as collateral, all details of the plant, its location, and the equipment and materials inside that plant would be provided. If the company defaulted on the loan, the lenders of the funds would know exactly what the collateral was and where it was located. Usually, the disposition of the collateral in various circumstances is specified.

Restrictive Covenants

restrictive covenants
Contractual clauses that place operating and financial constraints on the borrower.

Trust indentures normally include certain **restrictive covenants**—contractual clauses that place operating and financial constraints on the borrower. Restrictive covenants, coupled with standard debt provisions, help protect bondholders against increasing borrower risk. Without these provisions, the borrower could increase the firm's risk but not have to pay an increased return (interest). The most common restrictive covenants are:

1. Require that the borrower *maintain minimum ratio positions*, particularly regarding liquidity, leverage, and profitability. These requirements ensure against loan default and the ultimate failure of the company. Key ratios usually included in the indenture are a minimum times interest earned ratio, a maximum debt ratio, and a minimum current ratio.
2. *Prohibit borrowers from selling accounts receivable* to generate cash. Doing so could cause a long-run cash shortage if proceeds are used to meet current obligations.

3. Impose *restrictions on the purchase and sale of fixed assets* by the borrower. The sale of fixed assets could damage the firm's ability to repay the bonds. The purchase of fixed assets may lead to excess levels of unproductive assets or of capital.
4. *Constrain subsequent borrowing.* Additional long-term debt may be prohibited, or additional borrowing may be subordinated to the original loan. **Subordination** means that subsequent creditors agree to wait until all claims of the *senior debt* are satisfied.
5. *Limit the firm's annual cash dividend payments* to a specified percentage or amount or restrict payment if the firm does not meet a certain profit level.
6. *Protect against a reduction in value of collateral pledged* against the debt issue. The protection of bond collateral is crucial to increase the safety of a bond issue.

subordination
A stipulation that subsequent creditors agree to wait until all claims of the *senior debt* are satisfied.

Other restrictive covenants may sometimes be included in bond indentures. All restrictive covenants are intended to protect bondholders against increased risk. The violation of any provision by the borrower gives the bondholders the right to demand immediate repayment of the debt. Generally, the trustee, acting for the bondholders, will evaluate any violation to determine whether it is serious enough to jeopardize the loan. The bondholders may then decide to demand immediate repayment, continue the loan, or alter the terms of the bond indenture.

Sinking-Fund Requirements

sinking-fund requirement
A provision providing for the gradual retirement of long-term debt prior to the original term of the issue.

An additional provision often included in a bond indenture is a **sinking-fund requirement.** A sinking fund results in the gradual retirement of all or a portion of a long-term debt issue prior to the original term of the issue. Usually, a mandatory fixed amount of the bond issue is purchased and retired every year. To exercise this requirement, the corporation makes semiannual or annual payments to a *trustee*, who then uses these funds, on behalf of the company, to purchase and retire the relevant amount of bonds. For a sinking fund, the company has to pay, at most, the par value of the bonds purchased, plus any accrued interest.

The sinking fund is exercised in one of two ways: either in the open market or through a lottery process. The trustee would purchase the bonds in the open market when yields on comparable-risk bonds have increased, when the market price of the debt is less than the par value at the time that the sinking fund must be exercised. The bonds would be purchased using the lottery system when yields on comparable risk bonds have decreased, when the market price of the bonds is higher than the par of $1,000. The lottery system works because all bonds have a serial number that is associated with a particular purchaser of the bonds. For a $500 million bond issue, there might be 500,000 serial numbers, one for each $1,000 of par. If $20 million of the bond issue were to be purchased, the trustee would draw 20,000 serial numbers and the owners would be contacted and the bonds purchased and retired.

The sinking fund can be viewed as a benefit for both the issuer and the investor. The company does not need to worry about repaying the entire principal of a bond issue on the maturity date. This reduces the risk of not being able to access a large amount of money at the maturity. In addition, if the market price of the bonds is over $1,000, this means interest rates have decreased since the issue date. Therefore, the company can retire a portion of the higher-cost debt and raise additional debt financing at a lower cost. For the investor, a sinking fund provides a demand for the issue in the secondary market, plus reduces the risk of the issuer defaulting on the repayment of the remaining principal upon maturity.

Example A number of years ago, Magna Corporation issued a $500 million bond with an 8.25 percent coupon rate and a term of 25 years. The issue has a sinking fund that requires the company purchase and retire 1/20th of the issue. The sinking fund will be first exercised on the 11th anniversary of the issue. This means that Magna will retire 1/20th ($25 million) of the bond issue each year over the final 15 years of the bond's life. If the 11th anniversary is tomorrow, the trustee for the issue will purchase the bonds in the open market if they are trading for less than the $1,000 par value. This will occur when the yield in the market has increased since the date of issue. For each year this occurs, the sinking fund requirement will cost less than $25 million.

The lottery process will be used when the value of the bond in the market is greater than the $1,000 par value. This will occur when the yield in the market has decreased since the date of issue. For each year this occurs, the sinking fund requirement will cost $25 million plus accrued interest. This also means that some investors will have their bonds purchased when the market price is greater than the par value. Essentially some investors will lose when the lottery process is used to exercise a sinking fund. In contrast, the company will be able to issue new debt financing at a lower cost.

Call Feature

call price (bond)
The stated price at which bonds may be repurchased prior to maturity by using the call feature.

call premium
The amount by which the call price exceeds the bond's par value.

This provision is included in almost all long-term debt issues. It gives the issuer the opportunity to repurchase bonds prior to maturity. The **call price** is the stated price at which bonds may be repurchased prior to maturity. Sometimes the call feature can be exercised only during a certain period. The call price is always par plus a **call premium**, the amount by which the call price exceeds the bond's par value, that is quoted as a percent of par. For example, if the call premium were 4 percent, the call price would be $1,040 [$1,000 + (4% × $1,000)]. The premium compensates bondholders for having the bond called away from them, and it is the cost to the issuer of calling the bonds.

The call feature enables the issuer to retire outstanding debt prior to maturity. Thus, when interest rates fall, an issuer can call an outstanding bond and reissue a new bond at a lower interest rate. When interest rates rise, the call privilege will not be exercised—it would not make financial sense. Of course, to sell a callable bond, the issuer must pay a higher interest rate than on non-callable bonds of equal risk to compensate bondholders for the risk of having the bonds called away from them.

Example Assume Magna's $500 million bond issue from the above example also has a call provision that allows the company to call the bond issue in for retirement starting on the 19th anniversary of the issue, and each year thereafter. The 19th anniversary is tomorrow and the call price is par plus 4 percent. What will Magna do to decide if the issue should be called in for retirement?

Magna will exercise the call feature if bonds of comparable risk and time to maturity were trading to yield less than 8.25 percent. In this case the bonds will be trading for more than $1,000. If exercised, Magna would have to pay bondholders the call price, which is par ($1,000) plus the call premium of $40, or $1,040 per $1,000 of par value. Magna could then issue new bonds with a lower coupon rate and benefit from the savings on the remaining coupon payments. The yield on the comparable-risk bonds would have to be sufficiently low to compensate Magna for the call premium as well.

If the coupon that Magna would have to pay on the new issue were 7.5 percent, Magna would save 0.75 percent, or $7.50 per year on the coupon payments, per $1,000 of par. For the six years remaining to maturity, this would imply a total saving of $45. Given that the $40 call premium would have to be paid now, while the $45 saving would be realized over six years, this savings may not be sufficient to justify calling the bond in for retirement. The process used to make the call decision that adjusts for the different timing of the cash flows will be provided in Chapter 12.

Bond Ratings

A bond rating is an independent and objective assessment of the investment quality of a long-term debt issue. A rating is a basic measure of the default risk of the issuer and the issue. Rating agencies judge the default risk of the borrower. There is one major debt rating agency in Canada, the Dominion Bond Rating Service (DBRS), and three in the United States: Standard & Poor's (S&P), Moody's, and Fitch Ratings. The issuer, either a government or corporate borrower, pays one or more of the bond rating services to provide a rating for their debt issue. The debt rating agency rates the issue and provides ongoing coverage for the complete term of the issue. Debt issuers pay the agencies for a bond rating in order to send a message to the market of the quality of their issue.

The rating assigned to an issue is based on both quantitative and qualitative factors. For quantitative factors, a comprehensive financial profile of the company is completed. Financial ratio and cash flow analyses are used to assess the likely payment of interest and principal. For long-tem debt, all categories of ratios are important, but the leverage and profitability ratios may be the most important categories. Qualitative factors include items such as the record and quality of management, future developments in the industry, market potential, nature and diversification of product lines, changes in the government regulations, social changes, and the company's market share, expansion record, accounting policies, and level of development in comparison to competitors. Qualitative factors may be at least as important as quantitative analysis in rating a debt security. Table 5.7 provides the rating system used by DBRS.

For DBRS, the top rating is AAA and the ratings decline to D, meaning the debt issue is in default. Either the issuer has missed a scheduled payment of interest or principal, or will miss such a payment in the near future. The eight rating categories, other than AAA or D, are further denoted by the sub-ratings "high," "middle," and "low." Therefore, there are 26 possible ratings that DBRS might use to measure the default risk of a particular issue. For example, a bond might be rated *AA (high)*, *AA*, which implies average, or *AA (low)*.

The higher the rating, the lower the risk; the lower the risk, the lower the required yield. So at the time of issue, a AAA-rated bond, of a given maturity, would provide the lowest coupon rate to investors, and the bond would trade in

TABLE 5.7 The Long-Term Debt Rating Scale Used by the Dominion Bond Rating Service[a]

Rating	Brief description[b]	
AAA	Highest credit quality	
AA	Superior credit quality	
A	Satisfactory credit quality	
BBB	Adequate credit quality	
BB	Speculative	
B	Highly speculative	
CCC	Very highly speculative	In practice, there is little difference among these three categories.
CC	Very highly speculative	
C	Very highly speculative	
D	Bonds in default of either interest or principal	

[a]Note that "high" and "low" qualifiers are used to indicate the relative standing of a credit within a particular rating category. The lack of one of these designations indicates a rating which is essentially in the middle of the category. The high and low qualifiers are not used for the AAA or the D category.

[b]For a more detailed description, see DBRS's Web site at the address provided below.

SOURCE: Dominion Bond Rating Service Limited; and Web site, **www.dbrs.com/intnlweb/jsp/common/infoPage.faces.**

the market at the lowest yields. This is the basic risk–return tradeoff. The lower the risk the investor takes as measured by a bond rating, the lower the expected return.

In all developed countries the federal government is the least risky borrower. Therefore, the federal government will pay the lowest coupon rate on a new debt issue and federal government debt will trade at the lowest yields. All other borrowers (both government and corporate) pay some premium over the federal government rate. The premium is measured in a certain number of basis points. A basis point is 1/100 of a percent, so 50 basis points is 0.50 percent.

Maintaining a rating of BBB or above is vital for issuers of long-term debt. This is the case since institutional investors, particularly life insurance companies and pension plans, are restricted by law from investing in debt with less than a BBB rating. So a bond or debenture rated BBB (low) could be purchased by a pension plan or life insurance company, but if it were rated BB (high) it could not. Most mutual funds also adhere to this rule. A debt security with a rating less than BBB is referred to as a junk bond. A junk bond is a long-term debt security of low quality expected to provide a high rate of return. Based on the risk–return tradeoff, however, the higher the return, the greater the default risk.

Bond rating agencies continually review the companies which they rate and ratings of outstanding issues are often either downgraded or upgraded. The change in rating can be quite large or quite small, but most often it is one or two rating notches. For example, a downgrade from AA (high) to AA is a one rating notch downgrade. A change in rating from AA (high) to AA (low) is a two rating notch downgrade. If a rating is downgraded, it is because the rating agency believes the default risk of the issue has increased. As a result, the market price of the debt issue will decline. Downgrades lead to decreasing market prices for the long-term debt issue, and thus increasing yields. The reverse is true for upgrades.

Note that these changes in market prices *are not related to changes in interest rates in the market*, but rather to changes in the risk of the issue or issuer.

Note, however, that immediately after a change in ratings, the organization issuing the debt is unaffected. Investors are affected since the price of all of the organization's outstanding financial securities will change. The organization is only affected when it issues new debt securities. A downgrade will result in higher interest rates being required on new loans, while an upgrade will result in lower interest rates on new issues of debt securities.

Setting Coupon Rates

floor rate
The yield on federal government debt for any maturity.

As discussed earlier, the coupon rate on a long-term debt issue is set at the time of the issue and is constant for the term of the issue. The coupon rate is based on two factors. The first is the floor rate. The **floor rate** for debt of any maturity is the yield provided on federal government debt. The federal government is the least risky issuer of long-term debt securities in any developed economy. At any point in time, the federal government will have debt outstanding for very short to very long maturities. To set the coupon rate on a 20-year debenture issue, for example, the beginning point is to determine the yield on 20-year government of Canada debt. Bond prices and yields are available from newspapers, financial intermediaries, such as investment dealers, and on the Internet.

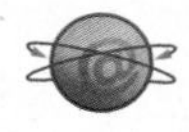

www.canada.com/nationalpost/financialpost/fpmarketdata/index.html

Table 5.8 provides bond quotations for a variety of issuers for trading that occurred on October 31, 2006. This data was taken from the *National Post* Market Data Web site. More recent trading data is easily accessible through this site. For each bond, the table provides the issuer, the coupon rate on the issue, the maturity date by month, day, and year, the price as a percent of par, and the yield based on the previous items. (The process used to calculate yield is covered in Chapter 8.) For the federal government, there is data provided for issues that mature between 1 and about 30 years from the date of the quotes.

Consider the second highlighted issue for the federal government in Table 5.8. The issue carries a coupon rate of 9.75 percent, matures in about 15 years from the date of the quote, is trading for 161.94 percent of par, or $1,619.40 per $1,000 of par, and provides a yield of 4.07 percent. As discussed earlier, debt securities trade on yield. Since this federal government debt security was issued, interest rates, and thus yields, *have fallen substantially*. As a result, the market price of the issue *has increased substantially*. Note the inverse relationship between market yields and prices. This quote also indicates that on October 31, 2006, in Canada, the floor rate for 15-year debt was 4.07 percent, the minimum rate acceptable to investors. The same analysis might be applied to any of the federal debt securities included in the table. Information about current yields is available on the Web.

http://bankofcanada.ca/en/rates/bonds.html

risk premium
The additional coupon investors will require based on the risk of the issuer and of the debt issue.

For any other issuer, the yield on debt securities of any maturity will be higher than the federal government yield. The additional return is based on the second factor determining coupon rates: the risk premium. The **risk premium** is the additional return investors will require on the basis of the risk of the issuer and of the debt issue. Issuer risk is based on a bond rating, while issue risk is based on the specifics of the debt issue. The market will rationally evaluate both aspects and demand an appropriate premium.

For example, consider the third highlighted issue for the federal government in Table 5.8. The issue matures in about 30 years from the date of the quote, and is yielding 4.03 percent. Compare that to the three highlighted provincial bond

TABLE 5.8 Selected Bond Quotations for October 31, 2006

Federal

Issuer	Coupon	Maturity Date	Price	Yield	Issuer	Coupon	Maturity Date	Price	Yield
Canada	2.750	Dec 01/07	98.66	4.03	Canada	4.000	Jun 01/16	100.06	3.99
Canada	4.250	Dec 01/08	100.66	3.91	Canada	4.000	Jun 01/17	99.81	4.02
Canada	10.750	Oct 01/09	118.62	3.91	Canada	9.750	Jun 01/21	161.94	4.07
Canada	4.000	Sep 01/10	100.39	3.89	Canada	9.250	Jun 01/22	159.16	4.08
Canada	3.750	Sep 01/11	99.38	3.89	Canada	8.000	Jun 01/27	153.69	4.11
Canada	5.250	Jun 01/12	106.65	3.91	Canada	5.750	Jun 01/33	127.18	4.07
Canada	5.250	Jun 01/13	107.58	3.93	Canada	5.000	Jun 01/37	116.92	4.03
Canada	5.000	Jun 01/14	106.73	3.96					
Canada	11.250	Jun 01/15	152.51	3.96					

Provincial

Issuer	Coupon	Maturity Date	Price	Yield	Issuer	Coupon	Maturity Date	Price	Yield
BC	6.375	Aug 23/10	108.05	4.07	Ontario	7.600	Jun 02/27	141.16	4.51
BC	5.400	Jun 18/35	115.09	4.46	Ontario	4.700	Jun 02/37	103.18	4.51
Manitoba	5.750	Jun 02/08	102.44	4.14	Quebec	6.250	Dec 01/10	107.88	4.13
NewBr	6.000	Dec 27/17	114.32	4.36	Quebec	4.500	Dec 01/16	100.55	4.43
Newfld	5.250	June 4/14	106.11	4.30	Quebec	5.750	Dec 01/36	116.94	4.69
NovaSc	6.600	Jun 01/27	127.92	4.50	Saskat	5.500	Jun 02/08	102.06	4.14
Ontario	5.700	Dec 01/08	103.17	4.09					
Ontario	4.400	Mar 08/16	100.85	4.29					

Corporate

Issuer	Coupon	Maturity Date	Price	Yield	Issuer	Coupon	Maturity Date	Price	Yield
BCE	6.750	Oct 30/07	101.93	4.72	GM Accep	6.550	Jun 11/08	99.30	7.01
BC Gas	6.95	Sept 21/29	120.18	5.40	GToAA	4.70	Feb 15/16	99.87	4.72
Bell	6.550	May 01/29	109.77	5.77	GW Life	6.670	Mar 21/33	122.64	5.10
BellAlt	4.720	Sep 26/11	100.31	4.65	Hydro One	4.64	Mar 3/16	100.94	4.51
BMO	6.903	Jun 30/10	108.46	4.37	IPL	8.200	Feb 15/24	137.20	4.97
BNS	7.310	Dec 31/10	110.93	4.40	Loblaw	6.650	Nov 08/27	113.56	5.55
Domtar	10.00	Apr 15/11	110.56	7.18	Westcoast	6.750	Dec 15/27	117.87	5.33
Ford Credit	6.50	Jul 10/08	97.31	8.24	Ypg Holdings	5.25	Feb 15/16	98.63	5.44
Ford Credit	5.35	Feb 10/10	91.30	8.46					
GE Capital	3.650	Jun 07/10	98.08	4.23					

SOURCE: "FP Market Data," *National Post*, available at **www.canada.com/nationalpost/financialpost/fpmarketdata/index.html.**

issues. All three mature in about 30 years from the date of the quote. But the respective yields are 4.46 percent, 4.51 percent, and 4.69 percent. Since all government debt has the same features, the different yields are based on additional risk. While all of the ten provinces are good credit risks, they are not as secure as the federal government.

TABLE 5.9 **Bond Ratings for the Canadian Provinces**

Province	DBRS rating
Newfoundland and Labrador	A (low)
New Brunswick	A (high)
Nova Scotia	A
Prince Edward Island	A (low)
Quebec	A (high)
Ontario	AA
Manitoba	A (high)
Saskatchewan	A (high)
Alberta	AAA
British Columbia	AA

SOURCE: Dominion Bond Rating Service, available at **www.dbrs.com/intnlweb/jsp/common/menu.faces.**

Therefore, bonds issued by the provinces must provide a premium for investors. The floor rate for 30-year debt was 4.03 percent. Table 5.9 provides the DBRS bond rating for the ten Canadian provinces. They range from AAA for Alberta to A (low) for Newfoundland and PEI. The provinces of British Columbia and Ontario are rated AA, so the risk is slightly higher than for the federal government. The risk premiums were 43 and 48 basis points, respectively. Quebec is rated A (high), meaning higher risk. The risk premium is 66 basis points. At the time of this example, these issuers would have to provide these coupon rates on any new 30-year debt issue.

The premium for corporate issuers will be even greater. This is clear from looking at the difference in yields between the first highlighted federal government issue, the one that matures on June 1, 2016, and the three highlighted corporate issues in Table 5.8. All four issues mature about 9.5 years from the date of the quote, but the yields are very different. The risk premiums are 73, 52, and 145 basis points for the GToAA, Hydro One, and Yellow Pages issues, respectively. These are very high premiums given the 3.99 percent floor rate on the federal issue. Obviously, the debt issues of even large, very secure corporations carry much higher levels of default risk than the federal government and the provinces.

International Bond Issues

Eurobond
Long-term debt issued by an international borrower in a currency other than that of the country in which it is sold.

Companies and governments borrow internationally using Eurobonds and foreign bonds. Both of these provide creditworthy borrowers the opportunity to obtain large amounts of long-term debt financing quickly, in their choice of currency, with flexible repayment terms, and with less regulation. A **Eurobond** is issued by an international borrower in a currency other than that of the country in which it is sold. For example, a Canadian company could sell a Eurobond denominated in Japanese yen in Germany. From the founding of the Eurobond market in the 1960s until the mid-1980s, "blue chip" U.S. corporations were the largest single class of Eurobond issuers. Many of these companies were able to borrow in this market at interest rates below those paid by the U.S. government.

As the market matured, issuers were able to choose the currency in which they borrowed, and European, Canadian, and Japanese borrowers became major participants. In recent years, the Eurobond market has become much more balanced in terms of the mix of borrowers, total issue volume, and currency of denomination. Only large, internationally known, very secure companies can issue Eurobonds. For such companies the use of Eurobonds can result in significantly lower debt costs. The Canadian dollar segment of the Eurobond market is relatively small.

foreign bond
Long-term debt issued in a country's financial market, in that country's currency, by a foreign borrower.

A **foreign bond** is issued in a country's financial market, in that country's currency, by a foreign borrower. A yen-denominated bond issued in Japan by a Canadian company is an example of a foreign bond. The largest foreign bond market is in the United States. Most foreign bonds issued by Canadian companies are issued in U.S. dollars in the United States. The federal and provincial governments and corporations with high sales in the United States are major issuers of U.S. foreign bonds.

? Review Questions

5–14 What is the difference between a term loan and long-term debt? What is the difference between a bond and a debenture?

5–15 What are the basic characteristics of long-term debt financing?

5–16 List and briefly describe the various types of bonds and debentures.

5–17 What is the trust indenture, and what provisions are usually included in the document? What role does the trustee play for a long-term debt issue?

5–18 What is a bond rating and what role does it have for a debt issue? Who are the major bond rating agencies in North America?

5–19 What is a high rating, and what is the benefit of having a high rating for an issuer? What happens when an organization's debt is downgraded?

5–20 How are coupon rates set on new debt issues? Why is the floor rate an important concept in this process?

5–21 What are the basic characteristics of and differences between Eurobonds and foreign bonds?

5.4 Capital Market Securities: Common and Preferred Shares

The previous section examined the first capital market security: long-term debt. This section discusses the two remaining capital market securities: common shares and preferred shares. Common shares signify ownership of the company. Corporations are separate legal entities that must issue shares and be owned by others, either individual, corporate, or institutional investors. The sale of the shares to the owners also raises common equity capital for the firm. This direct investment is in addition to the regular reinvestment of profits that is also part of the equity investment made by the common shareholders.

In addition, some firms may later issue a second class of equity, preferred shares, to raise additional equity capital. Although both common and preferred shares are forms of equity capital, the characteristics of preferred shares make them more similar to debt than common equity. Here we consider the key features and behaviours of both common and preferred shares.

Common Shares

Common shareholders, the owners of corporations, are sometimes referred to as residual owners. They have no guarantee of receiving any cash inflows, but receive what is left—the residual—after all other claims on the firm's income and assets have been satisfied. They are assured of only one thing: that they cannot lose any more than they have invested in the firm. This important feature of common equity is referred to as **limited liability**. As a result of their generally uncertain position, common shareholders expect to be compensated with adequate dividends and, ultimately, capital gains. The fundamental characteristics of common shares are discussed below.

limited liability
A feature of common equity meaning that investors cannot lose more than they have invested in the firm.

Ownership

The common shares of a firm can be **privately owned** by a single individual, **closely owned** by a small group of investors (such as a family), or **publicly owned** by a broad group of unrelated individual or institutional investors. Typically, small corporations are privately owned, and if their shares are traded, this occurs very infrequently and in small amounts. Large, publicly owned corporations, whose shares are generally actively traded on a stock exchange, are emphasized in the following discussions.

privately owned (company)
All common shares of a firm are owned by a single individual.

closely owned (company)
All common shares of a firm are owned by a small group of investors (such as a family).

publicly owned (company)
Common shares of a firm are owned by a broad group of unrelated individual or institutional investors.

Preemptive Rights

Preemptive rights allow common shareholders to maintain their proportionate ownership in the corporation when new shares are issued. They allow existing shareholders to maintain the same percentage of the vote and protect against the dilution of their ownership. **Dilution of ownership** may result in a reduction in the total earnings accruing to current shareholders as each shareholder has a claim on a *smaller* portion of the firm's earnings than previously.

preemptive rights
Allow common shareholders to maintain their proportionate ownership in the corporation when new shares are issued.

dilution of ownership
Occurs when a new share issue results in each present shareholder having a claim on a smaller part of the firm's earnings than previously.

Example You own 10,000 shares of a company with 1 million shares outstanding. This means you own 1 percent of the company. If the company issued an additional 250,000 shares, you must purchase 1 percent of these, 2,500 shares, to maintain your ownership stake in the company. If you do not exercise any preemptive rights that may be associated with the issue and do not buy any shares, your ownership interest will fall to 0.8 percent (10,000/1,250,000). If this occurs, your right to the earnings of the company will fall from 1 to 0.8 percent.

One way that companies attempt to provide preemptive rights to shareholders is through a *rights offering*. **Rights** are financial instruments that give shareholders the option of purchasing additional shares at a stated price, termed the *subscription price*, in direct proportion to the number of shares currently owned. The subscription price of the right is always less than the current market price of the share.

rights
Financial instruments that give shareholders the option of purchasing additional shares at a subscription price in direct proportion to the number of shares owned; the purchase price is always less than the current market price of the shares.

Note that while the rights give shareholders the *option* to purchase shares, current shareholders do not *have* to exercise the right. But, since the right allows the holder to purchase shares at a price less than the current market price, the rights are valuable. Consequently, the rights trade in the same market as the company's common shares. Rights are very short-term in nature and usually only have a life of 60 days at most. Most rights must be exercised within 30 days of the rights announcement.

Example Lobo Enterprises wishes to raise capital and is planning on using a rights offering. The company has 5 million common shares outstanding and will issue 1 right to shareholders for each share owned. The company's shares are trading for \$25 on the Toronto Stock Exchange. The subscription price for the rights offering is \$20 per share and the investor will require 4 rights to buy one share. Therefore, through this offering, Lobo will issue 1,250,000 new common shares and raise \$25 million of financing, less the costs of the rights issue. Are the rights valuable? They certainly are! An investor could go to the market, buy 4 shares costing \$100, and receive the right to buy one more share for \$20. So, for a total investment of \$120, the investor ends up with five shares worth \$125 (5 shares × \$25). You receive a "free" \$5 or \$1 per share. The rights are worth \$1 each.

This answer can also be calculated using the equation for the value of a right (V_R) as follows:

$$V_R = \frac{P_0 - S}{N + 1} \qquad (5.2)$$

where:

P_0 = market price of the shares at the time of the rights offering
S = the subscription price for the rights offering
N = number of rights required to buy the new share

Using Equation 5.2 and the data in the above example, we can determine the value of the right as:

$$V_R = \frac{\$25 - \$20}{4 + 1} = \$1.00$$

As calculated above, when the rights offering is announced, the rights will be worth \$1 each, and will trade on the Toronto Stock Exchange. Shareholders of Lobo Enterprises who do not wish to purchase more shares of the company will be able to sell the rights, and still receive the value of the rights. Until the early 1980s in Canada, rights were widely used by companies to raise financing from current shareholders. These seasoned issuers (companies with shares already trading on the TSX) used rights, since selling shares through other means was very expensive and time-consuming. As will be discussed later in the chapter, this changed with the advent of the bought deal and the Prompt Offering Prospectus System. Now, rights offerings are very rare in Canada.

Dilution of Earnings

Dilution of earnings occurs when the number of common shares a firm has outstanding increases, while the earnings available to common shareholders either stays the same or does not increase by the same percentage amount as the number of shares. Dilution means earnings per share (EPS) decline. Earnings may be diluted when companies issue new common shares. This will occur if the same amount of earnings available to common shareholders are allocated across a larger number of shares.

Example Johnson Electronics' earnings available for common shareholders (EAC) for the fiscal year ended December 31, 2008, are expected to be $35,250,000. The company has 14.1 million common shares outstanding. Therefore, the company's EPS are expected to be $2.50 ($35,250,000/14,100,000). If on July 22, 2008, Johnson sold an additional 3 million shares in the primary market for $34.50 each, will earnings be diluted? If EAC is not expected to change, then with the sale of shares Johnson will have 17.1 million common shares outstanding rather than 14.1 million. Now EPS will be $2.06 ($35,250,000/17,100,000), resulting in earnings dilution of $0.44 per share. So, with the new share issue, dilution of earnings occurs.

Can dilution be prevented? Consider that with the new share issue, Johnson Electronics will raise an additional $103,500,000 of financing. Assuming that this is invested in assets, what amount of profit must be generated to prevent dilution? If the company generates $7.5 million of additional EAC (3M shares × $2.50/share) with the $103,500,000 of financing raised, the company's EPS will not be diluted. Each new share generates the required EPS, so no dilution occurs. This implies that a return of 7.246 percent must be generated on the financing raised. If the company generates a return less than this, some dilution will still occur. If they generate a return of more than this, EPS will actually increase. These results are also provided in Spreadsheet Application 5.2.

Authorized, Outstanding, and Issued Shares

A company's *articles of incorporation* define the type and number of common shares it may issue. Most large companies and most publicly traded companies in Canada are incorporated under the *Canada Business Corporations Act*. Under the Act, companies must issue common shares *without* a par value. In the *articles of incorporation*, a company may be authorized to issue a certain number of common shares and/or a certain value of common share. Or, the company could be authorized to issue an unlimited number of common shares.

If a limited number or value of shares is authorized, and the company later realizes that more shares must be issued, the company must obtain approval from shareholders to amend the articles of incorporation. On the balance sheet, common shares are valued at the price sold. For example, if a company sold 240,000 common shares to investors for $10 per share, the common share account on the balance sheet would increase by $2,400,000 (240,000 common shares × $10).

Authorized shares become issued and outstanding when they are sold to investors. If the firm repurchases any of their outstanding shares, these shares are

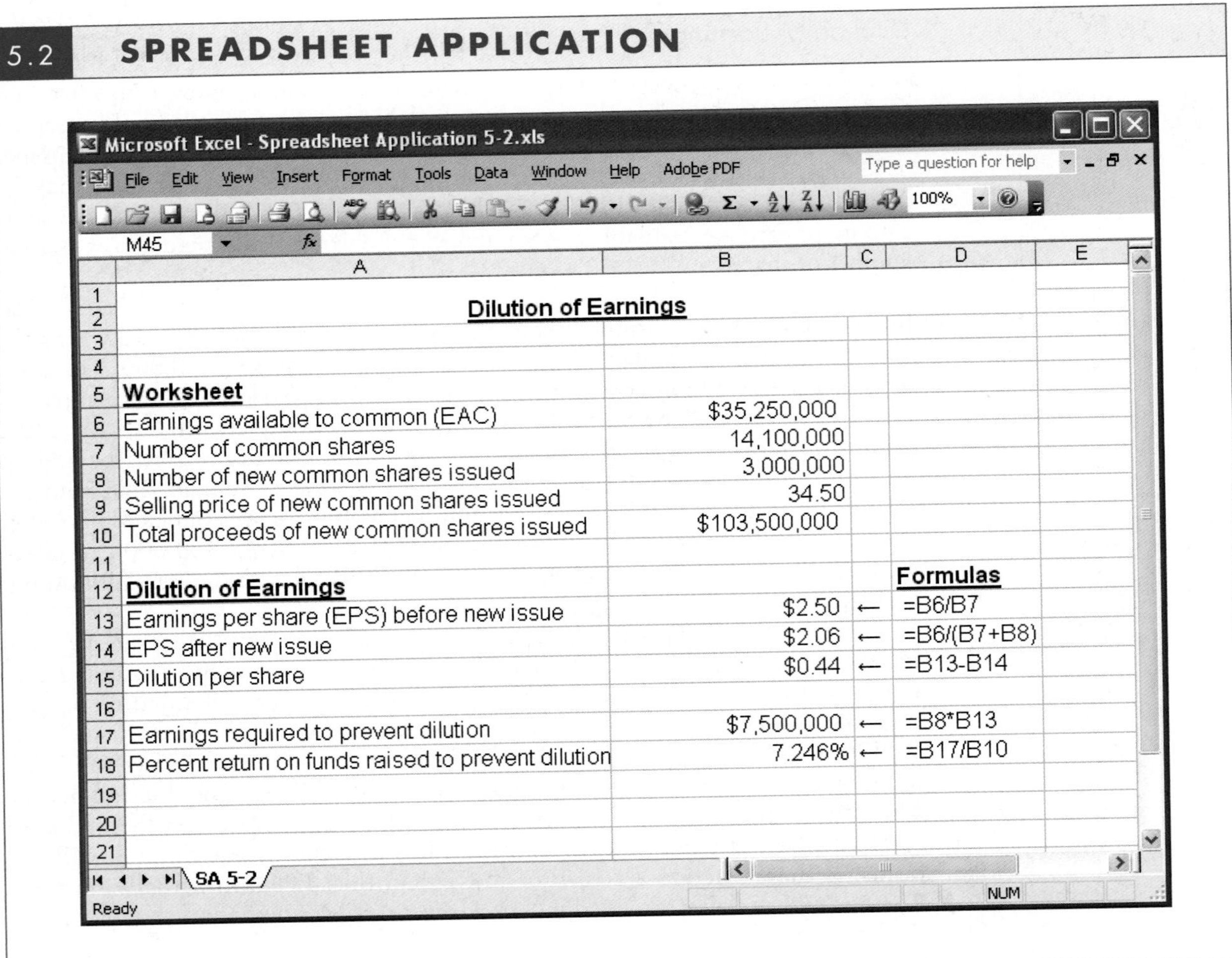

5.2 SPREADSHEET APPLICATION

Microsoft Excel - Spreadsheet Application 5-2.xls

Dilution of Earnings

	A	B	C	D
5	**Worksheet**			
6	Earnings available to common (EAC)	$35,250,000		
7	Number of common shares	14,100,000		
8	Number of new common shares issued	3,000,000		
9	Selling price of new common shares issued	34.50		
10	Total proceeds of new common shares issued	$103,500,000		
11				
12	**Dilution of Earnings**			**Formulas**
13	Earnings per share (EPS) before new issue	$2.50	←	=B6/B7
14	EPS after new issue	$2.06	←	=B6/(B7+B8)
15	Dilution per share	$0.44	←	=B13-B14
16				
17	Earnings required to prevent dilution	$7,500,000	←	=B8*B13
18	Percent return on funds raised to prevent dilution	7.246%	←	=B17/B10

deducted from shareholders' equity on the balance sheet. A company repurchases common shares from investors when they feel their common shares are undervalued in the market. The company must obtain approval from the stock exchange that lists the shares (the TSX, in Canada) for the repurchase. After gaining approval for the repurchase and making this public, the company must wait two trading days before they can begin to repurchase their own shares.

When the shares are repurchased, they are cancelled by the company and the number of issued and outstanding shares fall. The amount paid by the company when repurchasing is first deducted from the value of common shares, but if the amount paid is more than the proceeds received when the shares were originally sold, the excess is deducted from retained earnings.

Example ▼ Golden Enterprise, a producer of medical pumps, is authorized to issue 55 million common shares. Over its operating history, the company has sold 25 million shares to investors for $8.50 per share. On October 28, 2008, Golden received permission from the TSX to repurchase up to 1 million common shares. This information is made public, and in two trading days Golden can begin to repurchase their own shares. By December 31, 2008, Golden was able to repurchase all 1 million common shares on the TSX paying an average of $19.25 per share, and then cancelled the shares. What impact will the repurchase have on the company's shareholders' equity accounts? How many additional common shares can Golden sell without gaining approval from its shareholders?

The firm has 55 million authorized shares, 25 million issued shares, and 1 million repurchased and cancelled shares. Thus, 24 million shares are outstanding (25 million issued shares – 1 million repurchased shares), and Golden can issue 31 million additional shares (55 million authorized shares – 24 million outstanding shares) without seeking shareholder approval. This total includes the repurchased shares since these were cancelled.

For the dollar impact of the repurchase, consider that the repurchased shares were originally sold for $8,500,000 (1 million shares × $8.50) and the shares were repurchased for $19,250,000 (1 million shares × $19.25). Of this amount, $8,500,000 would be deducted from the value of the common shares while the difference, $10,750,000, would be deducted from retained earnings on Golden's balance sheet. But if the company was correct and the share subsequently increased in price to $30 per share, Golden can reissue 1 million shares and essentially make money on the transaction.

Voting Rights

Generally, each common share entitles the holder to one vote at the company's annual meeting of shareholders, where the board of directors is elected and other matters voted upon, and on special issues like a takeover offer. In Canada, however, many companies have issued another class of common shares with different voting rights. These might be either **non-voting** or **subordinate voting common shares.** The benefit of being able to sell these types of shares to the public is that the individual or family who founded the company can raise equity capital through the sale of common shares, but not give up control of the company.

non-voting common shares
Common shares that carry no right to vote on issues affecting the company.

subordinate voting common shares
Common shares that carry a right to vote on issues affecting the company but the vote is inferior to the votes of other shares.

voting (or superior voting) shares
Common shares that carry superior voting privileges to other common shares.

dual-class share structure
A company that has both non-voting (or subordinate) and voting (or superior voting) shares outstanding.

The company founders hold all or most of the **voting (or superior voting) shares.** In this way, the founders will likely own a small minority of the total number of common shares outstanding. Also, they will have provided a small fraction of the total funds generated by the sale of common shares, but they will *fully* control the affairs of the company through the superior voting privileges. This type of structure is termed a **dual-class share structure.**

When different classes of common shares are issued on the basis of unequal voting rights, there is no general convention regarding the designation of the voting and non-voting or restricted-voting common shares. In some cases, the shares are designated as class A or B, with either being the superior voting shares. In other cases, a designation is not used. But in all cases, a bit of background reading will make it clear which class carries the superior voting privileges. Table 5.10 provides a listing of some Canadian companies that have a dual-class share structure. Note there are some very major, well-known companies included on this list. For additional discussion of the benefits and drawbacks of dual-class share structures, there are many readings available on the Web.

www.share.ca/files/Second%20Class%20Investors.pdf

www.parl.gc.ca/information/library/PRBpubs/prb0526-e.htm

www.nupge.ca/publications/dual%20class%20WP.pdf

In most cases, the superiority of the voting shares is limited to the vote. Both classes of shares are entitled to receive the same dividend (in some cases the subordinate shares may receive a higher dividend) and share on a *pro rata* basis in

TABLE 5.10 Canadian Companies with Dual-Class Share Structures, October 2006

ACE Aviation Holdings	Gildan Activewear
AGF Management Ltd.	Guardian Capital Group Ltd.
Alimentation Couche Tard Inc.	International Forest Products Ltd.
Alliance Atlantis Communications Inc.	Jean Coutu Group (PJC) Inc.
Arbor Memorial Services Inc.	La Senza Corporation
Astral Media Inc.	M8 Entertainment Inc.
Atco Ltd.	Magna Entertainment Corp.
Becker Milk Co. Ltd.	Magna International Inc.
Bombardier Inc.	Maple Leaf Foods
Brampton Brick Ltd.	Metro Inc.
Caldwell Partners International Inc.	MI Developments Inc.
Canadian Tire Corp. Ltd.	Newfoundland Capital Corp.
Canadian Utilities Ltd.	Onex Corporation
Canwest Global Communications Corp.	Power Corporation of Canada
CCL Industries Inc.	Prometic Life Sciences Inc.
Celestica Inc.	Quebecor Inc.
Le Chateau Inc.	Quebecor World Inc.
CHC Helicopter Corp.	Reitmans (Canada) Ltd.
Chum Ltd.	Rogers Communications Inc.
Cogeco Cable Inc.	Royal Group Technologies Limited
Cogeco Inc.	Score Media
Corby Distilleries Ltd.	Shaw Communications Inc.
Corus Entertainment Inc.	Shawcor Ltd.
Cossette Communication Group	Spectra Group of Great Restaurants
Danier Leather Inc.	St. Lawrence Cement Group Inc.
Diaz Resources Ltd.	Teck Cominco Ltd.
Dorel Industries Inc.	Telus Corporation
Dundee Bancorp Inc.	Torstar Corporation
Electrohome Limited	Transcontinental Inc.
Empire Company Ltd.	TVA Group Inc.
Fairfax Financial Holdings Ltd.	Van Houtte Inc.
FirstService Corporation	Viceroy Homes Ltd.
Four Seasons Hotels Inc.	Wescast Industries Inc.

the event of the company's liquidation. As well, in the event of a takeover offer for the company, the **coattail provision** gives the holders of the non-voting or restricted-voting shares the right to convert their shares into an equal number of the superior voting shares.

coattail provision
In the event of a takeover offer for the company, this provision allows the holders of the non-voting or restricted-voting shares the right to convert their shares into an equal number of the superior voting shares.

The coattail provision is vital to protect the interests of the subordinate voting shares in the event of a takeover offer for the company. Since in a takeover the number of votes decides the outcome, the possibility exists that a small number of superior voting shares could be acquired by the bidder at a large premium to their current value. This would allow the bidder to acquire the majority of the votes in the company while ignoring the interests of the large majority of the common shareholders. Such an event would not be fair, so in all cases where two classes of shares are outstanding a coattail provision exists.[1]

proxy statement
A statement giving the votes of a shareholder to another party.

proxy battle
The attempt by a non-management group to gain control of the management of a firm by soliciting a sufficient number of proxy votes.

Because most small shareholders do not attend the annual meeting to vote, they may sign a **proxy statement** giving their votes to another party. The solicitation of the proxies from shareholders is closely controlled by regulatory bodies to protect against proxies being solicited on the basis of misleading information. Existing management generally receives the shareholders' proxies, because it is able to solicit them at company expense. Occasionally, when the firm is widely owned, outsiders may wage a **proxy battle** to unseat the existing management and gain control. To win a corporate election, a simple majority of the shares voted, 50 percent plus 1, is all that is required. However, the odds of a non-management group winning a proxy battle are generally slim.

Dividends

The payment of dividends is at the discretion of the board of directors, and the large majority of companies listed on the TSX do not pay dividends on common shares. Those that do, normally pay dividends quarterly. For example, on August 31, 2006, the board of directors of CIBC declared a quarterly common share dividend of $0.70 per share for the quarter ending October 31, 2006. The dividend was payable on October 27, 2006 to shareholders of record at the close of business on September 28, 2006. To receive this dividend, an investor had to own the shares on September 25, three trading days before the record date. The share starts to trade ex-dividend (without the dividend) two trading days before the record date, in this case, September 26, 2006. This dividend announcement indicated that the annual dividend paid by the Bank was $2.80 ($0.70 × 4)per share. Once the dividend is declared by the board, the company is legally obliged to pay it. Dividends may be paid in cash or additional common shares. Cash dividends are the most common.

Common shareholders are not promised a dividend, but once a company starts to pay dividends, shareholders come to expect certain payments based on the historical payment pattern. The board, however, can increase, decrease, or completely eliminate the dividend at any time. Before dividends are paid to common shareholders, the claims of the government, all creditors, and preferred shareholders must be satisfied. Because of the importance of the dividend decision to the growth and valuation of the firm, detailed discussion of dividends on common shares is included in Chapter 11.

International Share Issues

international equity market
A vibrant equity market that emerged in the past 20 years to allow corporations to sell blocks of shares in several different countries simultaneously.

Although the international market for common shares is not as large as the international market for debt securities, a vibrant **international equity market** has emerged in the past 20 years. Much of this increase is due to a growing desire on the part of investors to diversify their investment portfolios internationally.

1. The dual-class common share structure is widespread among Canadian publicly traded corporations and is a complicating issue for corporate governance and valuation issues. See the following papers for discussion: C. Robinson, J. Rumsey, and A. White (1996), "Market Efficiently in the Valuation of Corporate Control: Evidence from Dual Class Equity," *Canadian Journal of Administrative Sciences*, 13, 251–263, and B. Smith and B. Amoako-Adu (1995), "Relative Prices of Dual Class Shares," *Journal of Financial and Quantitative Analysis*, 30, 223–239.

5.1 **IN PRACTICE**

Benefits of Two Classes

One of the key characteristics of common shares is that one share equals one vote. Therefore, a shareholder owning 50,000 common shares of a company where 1 million common shares are outstanding owns 5 percent of the company and is entitled to 5 percent of the votes. (This shareholder is also entitled to 5 percent of the earnings available for common shareholders.) In Canada, there are a large number of public companies with two classes of common shares: one class with superior voting privileges, one with subordinate. For the company's founders, this situation is highly attractive. By selling subordinate voting shares, the founders enjoy the advantage of raising financing using common shares without the disadvantage of losing control.

For example, Toronto-based Canadian Tire is Canada's most-shopped general merchandise retailer with 462 stores. Over 80 percent of Canadians visit one of their stores each year and their flyers and catalogues reach over 10 million households. For the fiscal year ended December 31, 2005, the company had sales of almost $7.8 billion, assets of $6 billion, and cash generated from operations of $721.2 million. The company has two classes of common shares. As of June 30, 2006, there were 3,423,366 voting common shares and 78,117,571 class A non-voting shares outstanding.

The total capital provided by the shareholders owning the voting common shares was $200,000; the A shareholders provided $709.1 million. A child and grandchild of A. J. Billes, one of the cofounders of Canadian Tire, owned 61.5 percent of the voting shares, while the owners of the Canadian Tire stores owned a further 20.5 percent. Therefore, this inside group owned 3.44 percent of the total number of shares, and provided 0.028 percent of the direct common share financing. But they possessed 82 percent of the voting rights.

The opportunity to be able to sell non-voting shares has greatly benefited the Billes family and the store owners. They have been able to retain full control of the company while providing a very tiny minority of the common equity financing. But they have not been the only ones to benefit from this arrangement—the non-voting shareholders have profited also.

Over the five years ending December 31, 2005, the non-voting shares increased in value by 297 percent, an annual return of 31.8 percent. In the same period, the overall market, as measured by the TSX Index, increased at an annual rate of 6.6 percent, while the consumer discretionary spending index only increased by 3.7 percent. In this case, allowing very concentrated ownership of the voting shares benefited all shareholders.

SOURCES: Canadian Tire. *2005 Annual Report and Management Proxy Circular.*

Many corporations have discovered that they can sell blocks of shares to investors in a number of different countries simultaneously.

For example, many large Canadian multinational companies have listed their shares on multiple stock markets. The New York, Nasdaq, London, Frankfurt, and Tokyo markets are the most popular. Some of the better-known Canadian companies that have done this include BCE, Alcan, the Big 5 banks, Canadian Natural Resources, Research in Motion, Barrick Gold, Celestica, Petro-Canada, Magna International, Potash Corp of Saskatchewan, Suncor Energy, Intrawest Corp, Brookfield Asset Management, Agnico-Eagle Mines, and Four Seasons Hotels.

Issuing shares internationally broadens the ownership base and helps a company integrate itself into the local business scene. It also enables corporations to raise far larger amounts of capital than they could have raised in any single national market. A listing on a foreign stock exchange both increases local business press coverage and serves as effective corporate advertising. Having locally traded shares can also facilitate corporate acquisitions because shares can be used as an acceptable method of payment. International equity sales have also proven to be indispensable to governments that have sold state-owned companies to private investors in recent years.

American Depository Receipts (ADRs)
Claims issued by U.S. banks that represent ownership of a foreign company's common shares held by the bank in the foreign market.

http://invest-faq.com/articles/stock-adrs.html
www.site-by-site.com/adr/toc.htm

American Depository Receipts (ADRs) have become a popular way for foreign companies to tap the North American capital market. ADRs are issued by U.S. banks and represent ownership of a foreign company's common shares held by the bank in the foreign market. Because ADRs are issued in U.S. dollars and are often for multiple numbers of shares, they often trade at prices very different from what the common shares of the underlying company trade for in the home market. ADRs give investors the opportunity to diversify their portfolios internationally. Additional information regarding ADRs and a complete listing of all ADRs available for companies around the world is available on the Web.

Preferred Shares

preferred equity
The third major source of long-term financing for corporations that broadens the firm's capital structure, raising financing without giving up ownership or incurring obligations.

Preferred equity is the third major source of long-term financing for corporations. Preferred equity is an attractive long-term source of financing as it broadens the firm's capital structure, raising financing without giving up ownership (like common stock) or incurring obligations (like debt), thus reducing the risk of the company. Preferred equity is a second class of equity that is preferred in terms of the payment of dividends and at the dissolution of the corporation.

The firm must pay preferred dividends prior to common, and preferred shareholders receive payments prior to common shareholders at liquidation. Each preferred share issue is unique and creates a new preferred share series. Some companies who rely on preferred share financing have 10 or more different series of preferred shares outstanding. For example, as of October 31, 2006, CIBC had ten preferred share issues outstanding. The latest is the Series 30 preferred. This implies that since they started to issue preferred shares, CIBC has made 30 issues and has retired 20 of these. A current listing of CIBC's preferred shares is available on their Web site. The fundamental characteristics of preferred shares are discussed below.

www.cibc.com/ca/investor-relations/share-info/preferred-shares.html

Stated Values and Dividends

stated value
The value of the preferred share on the issue date.

Preferred shares are issued with a **stated value**, which is the value of the preferred share on the issue date. The usual stated values are $10, $20, $25, $50, or $100, with $25 being the most common. Preferred shareholders receive a dividend that is based on the stated value and is constant for as long as the preferred share issue is outstanding. For example, CIBC has a Series 29 preferred share outstanding with a stated value of $25 paying a dividend of $1.35. If the dividend in dollars is known, the dividend in percent can be calculated. The dividend in percent is equal to the dollar dividend divided by the stated value, in this case $1.35 divided by $25, or 5.4 percent.

The dividend can also be quoted as a percent. For example, CIBC has a Series 30 preferred share outstanding with a stated value of $25 paying a dividend of 4.80 percent. The dividend in dollars is \$1.20 per year (\$25 × 4.8%). Dividends are quoted yearly but paid quarterly. For the CIBC Series 29 preferred, the yearly dividend is \$1.35, paid quarterly, so the holder of the preferred share would receive \$0.3375 per share every three months. For the Series 30 preferred, the quarterly dividend will be \$0.30 per share.

There is no guarantee the investor will receive preferred share dividends. As with common shares, the payment of dividends is at the discretion of the board. If a company fails to pay the dividends, preferred shareholders do not have the ability to put the firm into bankruptcy. Alleviating that problem is the **cumulative feature** associated with preferred shares. If a company misses a dividend payment, dividends are said to be in arrears. In this case, the dividends accumulate; the company would owe two dividend payments the following quarter. Referring to the CIBC Series 29 preferred, if CIBC failed to pay the dividend one quarter, then on the next quarterly dividend date, they would be required to make a dividend payment of \$0.6750. This payment would have to be made before the company could pay common share dividends.

cumulative feature
Missed dividend payments on preferred shares accumulate, meaning that dividends in arrears must be paid with the current dividend prior to the payment of dividends to common shareholders.

In theory this seems to be a positive aspect that minimizes the non-guarantee of dividend payments for preferred shareholders. In reality, however, if a company misses a preferred dividend payment the message being sent to the market is that the firm is having major financial problems. The likelihood is that the firm will end up restructuring its finances and preferred shareholders will lose a major portion of their invested capital.

Preferred Share Ratings

Given the danger associated with missed dividend payments, it makes sense for potential investors to evaluate the risk of this happening. As with long-term debt, the same rating agencies rate the default risk of preferred shares. Table 5.11 provides the preferred share rating used by DBRS. The preferred

TABLE 5.11 The Preferred Share Rating Scale Used by the Dominion Bond Rating Service[a]

Rating	Brief description[b]
Pfd-1	Superior credit quality
Pfd-2	Satisfactory credit quality
Pfd-3	Adequate credit quality
Pfd-4	Speculative
Pfd-5	Highly speculative
D	Preferred in default of either dividend or stated value

[a]Note that "high" and "low" qualifiers are used to indicate the relative standing of an issuer within a particular rating category. The lack of one of these designations indicates a rating which is essentially in the middle of the category. The high and low qualifiers are used for all categories.

[b]For a more detailed description, see DBRS's Web site at the address provided below.

SOURCES: Dominion Bond Rating Service Limited; and Web site: **www.dbrs.com/intnlweb/jsp/common/infoPage.faces**

share ratings are meant to give an indication of the risk that the borrower will not make the dividend payments. The ratings do not take factors such as pricing or market risk into consideration. They are based on quantitative and qualitative considerations that are relevant for the company.

For preferred shares there are 16 rating possibilities, three for each of the categories and one for D. As with debt, the higher the rating, the lower the risk, and, therefore, the lower the required dividend payment on a new issue of preferreds. The rating can be downgraded or upgraded with similar repercussions for both the investor and the issuer as discussed under long-term debt.

Call Feature

This provision is included in almost all preferred share issues and is often referred to as the redemption provision. This provision gives the company the option to purchase and retire the total preferred share issue on a specific date. For many issues, there are multiple call dates. The repurchase price is termed the **call price** and is generally the stated value plus a call premium. The call premium is often quoted as a percent that is based on the stated value, but on some issues just the call price is provided. For example, of the ten issues that CIBC has outstanding, the call premiums range from a low of 0 percent to a high of 4 percent. On these issues, the call price is stated and the call premium is the difference between the call price and stated value.

call price (preferred)
The repurchase price for a preferred share issue; generally the stated value plus a call premium.

If a company were redeeming a preferred share with a $100 stated value and a call premium of 4 percent, then the company would pay investors $104: $100 for the stated value and $4 for the call premium. For issues with multiple call dates, it is normal for the call premium to decline if the issue is not called. This may happen over three to four call dates and the premium is gradually reduced to zero. For example, CIBC has a Series 30 preferred share issue with a $25 stated value for which the first redemption date is April 30, 2010. The call price is $26, implying a call premium of 4% or $1. If the company does not call the issue, the next call date is April 30, 2011, and the call price is $25.75. The final call date is April 30, 2014, and the call price is the stated value: $25.

A company will exercise the redemption feature when the required dividend rate on a new preferred share issue is lower than the dividend on the current issue. For example, if a company had a preferred share outstanding with an 8 percent dividend but the preferred shares of companies with a similar risk rating were trading to yield 6 percent, it makes sense for the company to redeem the 8 percent issue. The implication is that the company could then issue new preferred shares with a 6 percent dividend rate. The company could save 2 percent dividend on the stated value. When dividend rates decline between the original date of the preferred share issue and the time the redemption feature is exercisable, the company will redeem the issue.

Types of Preferred Shares

One area where financial engineering has had a tremendous impact in Canada is preferred shares. There are numerous varieties of preferred shares in Canada. Arguably, Canada has the most developed market for preferred shares in the world. There are two reasons for this. First, as discussed in Chapter 2, for corporations, dividends received from a taxable Canadian company are exempt from taxes. This is an attractive opportunity for corporations to earn a tax-free, low-risk return (based on the rating) on excess cash balances. Second, as will be discussed in Chapter 8, for individuals, the taxes paid on dividend income are much lower than on interest income. This tax advantage reduces the attraction of debt securities and encourages individuals to invest in preferred shares, thus broadening the market for potential issuers. In this section, four types of preferred shares are discussed. This is an introductory discussion meant to give the reader a taste of the topic, not provide a full-course meal.

retractable preferreds
A type of preferred share whose holder has the right to force the issuer to repurchase the preferred share at the stated value.

Retractable preferred shares: These are similar to retractable bonds—the redemption provision in reverse. With **retractable preferreds**, the holder has the right to request that the issuer repurchase the preferred shares. The retraction price is always the stated value and there may be multiple retraction dates. The retraction provision will be exercised by investors if dividend rates increased between the time of issue and the time the retraction provision is exercisable. For example, if you owned a preferred share that had an 8 percent dividend, but the preferred shares of companies with a similar risk rating were trading to yield 10 percent, it makes sense for you to retract the issue. You could then go to the market and purchase preferred shares that provided a 10 percent rate of return.

floating rate preferreds
A type of preferred share whose quarterly dividend paid is based on interest rates in the market and will float with these rates.

Floating rate preferred shares: For most preferred share issues, the dividend is fixed at the time of issue. Each quarter, the same dollar amount of dividend is paid. **Floating rate preferreds** are structured differently: the dividend rate floats along with interest rates in the market. The dividend rate is most often based on the prime rate at chartered banks. For floating rate preferreds, as interest rates fluctuate in the market, the quarterly dividend paid changes as well. Since the dividend rate changes, the market price will remain very close to the stated value of the preferred share.

convertible preferreds
A type of preferred share whose holders have the option of converting them into a predetermined number of common shares on a specific date.

Convertible preferred shares: With **convertible preferreds**, the holder has the option of converting the preferred share into a predetermined number of common shares on a specific date. With convertible preferreds the market price is based partially on the dividend rate, but also on the changing price of the common shares. This is a hybrid security, since the holder receives dividend payments but also benefits if the company's common share price increases. The dividend rate on convertibles is lower than on regular preferreds but offers the opportunity of a large gain if the company's common share price increases.

Dutch Auction preferred shares
Preferred shares similar to money market securities with no stated maturity; the dividend rate is reset on a regular basis through a Dutch auction process.

Dutch Auction preferred shares: These are termed "preferred shares," though they are similar to money market securities. **Dutch Auction preferred shares** have no stated maturity and can be viewed as a perpetuity. The dividend rate is reset on a regular basis through a Dutch auction process. These auctions can occur on any regular schedule, though every seven weeks or quarterly are the most popular schedules. Institutional investors are the principal participants in the bidding, with the institution willing to accept the lowest dividend rate (pay the highest amount) winning the portion of the offering sought. Succeeding bids are then allotted shares. The frequent repricing provides a mechanism for the shares to accurately reflect prevailing yields in the market, and therefore they trade at the stated value. The yields are comparable to commercial paper.

When reviewing the characteristics of preferred shares, it is clear that even though they are termed an equity, they share more similarities with long-term debt than with common equity. This will be an important point when it comes time to value these shares in Chapter 8.

Trading Preferred and Common Shares

securities exchanges
The secondary marketplace that allows for the subsequent trading of financial securities created in the primary market.

When financial securities are created in the primary market transaction, a secondary marketplace must exist that allows for the subsequent trading of these financial securities. These marketplaces are the **securities exchanges**. There are two types: physical, tangible exchanges and artificial exchanges. The trading of many equity securities occurs on a physical exchange, which is often referred to as the stock market. The largest and most important stock market in Canada is the Toronto Stock Exchange (TSX). Artificial exchanges trade all debt securities and some equities. There is no physical location for the trading of these securities; rather, the trading takes place in the communication system that exists between financial intermediaries. The market is, in essence, cyberspace, the computer networks between investment dealers.

The Role of Securities Exchanges

efficient market
A market that allocates funds to their most productive uses due to competition among wealth-maximizing investors; it determines and publicizes prices that are believed to be close to their true value.

Securities exchanges create continuous liquid markets where trading can occur efficiently. **Efficient markets** allocate funds to their most productive uses. This is especially true for securities that are actively traded on major exchanges where competition among wealth-maximizing investors determines and publicizes prices that are believed to be close to their true value. The price of the individual security is determined by the demand for and supply of the security. Figure 5.3 depicts the interaction of forces of demand (represented by line D_0) and supply (represented by line S) for a given security currently selling at an equilibrium price P_0. At that price, Q_0 shares of the stock are traded.

FIGURE 5.3

Supply and Demand
Supply and demand for a security

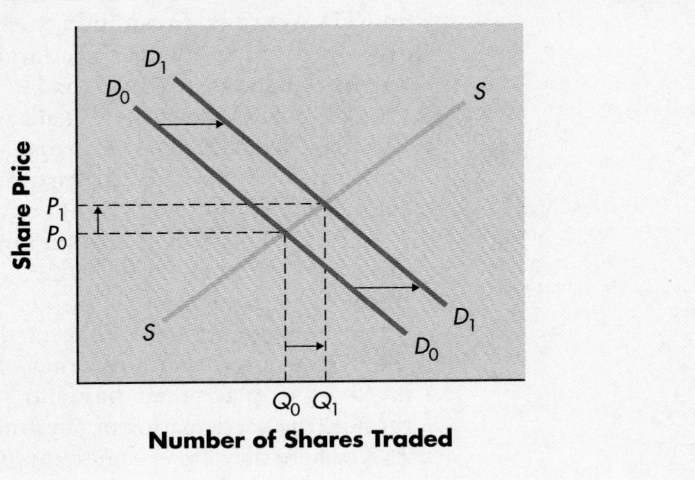

Changing evaluations of a firm's prospects will change the demand for and supply of a security and ultimately result in a new price for the security. Suppose, for example, that the firm shown in Figure 5.3 successfully launches a new product. When this information is released to the market, investors will rationally conclude that the firm's earnings and cash flows will increase. This will increase the demand for the shares from D_0 to D_1. The changing evaluation results in a higher quantity of shares traded, Q_1, at a higher equilibrium price, P_1.

The competitive market created by the major securities exchanges provides a forum in which investors continually adjust their views of the company as new information is released to the market. These changed views result in changes in the demand for and supply of shares, and therefore price. As the demand for a security increases without a corresponding increase in supply, prices increase. As the supply of a security increases without a corresponding increase in demand, prices decline. This occurs every trading day on security exchanges.

The Toronto Stock Exchange

The Toronto Stock Exchange (TSX) is one of only two stock markets in Canada. The other is the TSX Venture Exchange, which trades the common shares of early-stage, smaller companies. The TSX is where the common shares of most large Canadian companies trade. Companies like Alcan, Loblaws, BCE, Canadian Tire, Barrick Gold, the Big 5 banks, and numerous others that are household names have their shares listed on the TSX. Note, though, that other large Canadian companies are still privately owned and their common shares are not listed on an exchange. Companies like Irvings, McCain Foods, the Jim Pattison Group, AIC Mutual Funds, and Roots are still owned by the founding families.

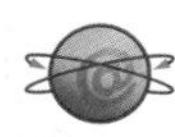

www.tsx.com/en/listings/listing_with_us/index.html

www.tsx.com/en/listings/venture_issuer_resources/

Both the TSX and the TSX Venture Exchange operate as automated, continuous auction markets where buy and sell orders of the listed securities are queued and matched in price-time priority sequence. To make transactions on the "floor" of the TSX, a firm must be a "participating organization" of the exchange. There are over 110 participating organizations, the major Canadian investment dealers being the largest. These include BMO Nesbitt Burns, CIBC World Markets, National Bank Financial, RBC Capital Markets, Scotia Capital, and TD Securities. In addition, some of the big international investment bankers also operate in Canada. The largest are Citigroup Global Markets Canada, Credit Suisse Securities Canada, Deutsche Bank Securities, Goldman Sachs Canada, HSBC Securities Canada, JPMorgan Securities Canada, Merrill Lynch Canada, Morgan Stanley Canada, and State Street Global Markets Canada. The broker-dealers who are participating organizations employ approved traders to enter orders into the system by computer in their brokerage offices.

The goal of trading is to fill buy orders (orders to purchase securities) at the lowest price and to fill sell orders (orders to sell securities) at the highest price, thereby giving both purchasers and sellers the best possible deal. Once placed, an order to buy or sell can be executed in seconds, thanks to the sophisticated trading system used. New Internet-based brokerage systems enable individual investors to place their buy and sell orders electronically. These orders flow through the participating organization's trading system and on to the floor of the TSX, where they are executed. An individual can place a buy order at the current market price and in seconds receive confirmation that the order was filled.

The Over-the-Counter Exchange

over-the-counter exchange
An intangible market for the purchase and sale of securities not listed on organized exchanges.

Nasdaq
The National Association of Securities Dealers Automated Quotation System, the best-known OTC market in the world, which rivals the New York Stock Exchange in trading volumes.

The **over-the-counter (OTC) exchange** is an intangible market for the trading of common and preferred shares not listed on an organized exchange. OTC traders, known as dealers, are linked through a networked trading system. In the United States, the major OTC exchange is the National Association of Securities Dealers Automated Quotation (Nasdaq) System. **Nasdaq** is the best-known OTC market in the world and rivals the New York Stock Exchange in trading volumes. Some of the best-known technology companies in the world trade on Nasdaq, including Microsoft, Intel, Dell, Cisco, Yahoo, and Oracle. This sophisticated communications network provides current bid and ask prices on thousands of actively traded OTC securities. The bid price is the highest price offered by the dealer to purchase a given security, and the ask price is the lowest price at which the dealer is willing to sell the security. The dealer in effect adds securities to his or her inventory by purchasing them at a bid price and sells securities from the inventory at the ask price, hoping to profit from the spread between the bid and ask price.

In Canada, the major OTC market for equities was the Canadian Dealing Network. In October 2000, this network ceased operations and all quoted securities were moved to Tier 3 of the TSX Venture Exchange. A new OTC market was created, the Canadian Unlisted Board (CUB), but listings are few and trading light. In November 2000, Nasdaq established an OTC operation in Canada, but the exchange has been slow to attract new listings. By October 2006, only a handful of companies are trading on NASDAQ Canada, and these are companies whose shares trade on the NASDAQ exchange in the United States but are claimed by NASDAQ Canada because they are Canadian companies. These companies include Research in Motion, Ballard Power Systems, and QLT Inc.

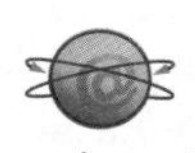

www.nasdaq-canada.com/

In June 2001, the Canadian Trading and Quotation System (CNQ) launched an electronic OTC market in Canada. CNQ is a stock exchange alternative to traditional stock exchanges where high costs and large capitalization requirements are often barriers to a stock market listing. CNQ is meant to be a low-cost, streamlined stock exchange with a high standard of disclosure. At the time of writing, only 46 companies were listed on CNQ, and trading is very light. In September 2006, only 1,100 trades occurred for a total value of $3,629,111. Many single trades on the TSX are for more than this.

www.cnq.ca

Stock Price Quotations

The financial manager needs to stay abreast of the market values of the firm's outstanding securities, particularly the common shares, whether they are traded on an organized exchange, over the counter, or in international markets. Similarly, existing shareholders need to monitor the prices of the securities they own. Information on shares and other securities is provided in quotations, which include price data along with other statistics on recent price behaviour and are widely published in news media. Security price quotations are readily available for actively traded securities.

www.globeinvestor.com
www.tsx.com
http://ca.finance.yahoo.com
www.canada.com/nationalpost/financialpost/fpmarketdata/index.html

A summary of the previous day's trading including price and volume statistics is reported in various media, including major newspapers like the *Globe and Mail* and *National Post* and the business sections of daily general newspapers. Trading information is also available on numerous Web sites.

The most timely stock quotes are available directly from investment dealers (often referred to as stockbrokers for the trading function they perform for investors) or over the Internet at the sites mentioned above, but also at many others. On these sites, quotes are often delayed by 15 to 20 minutes. For real-time quotes over the Internet, investors must pay a fee or have an investment account with an investment dealer.

Table 5.12 provides summary trading data for transactions that occurred on the TSX on October 31, 2006. This data was taken from the *National Post* Market Data Web site referred to on page 275. More recent trading data is easily accessible through this and other Web sites. Reviewing the table indicates that there is data available for common shares, preferred shares, and income trusts. For a refresher on income trusts, see Chapter 1. We will look at the quotations for CIBC that are highlighted in Table 5.12. The quotations show that most share prices are quoted in multiples of 1 cent. If shares trade for under $1.00, they can be traded in multiples of one-half cent.

The first column is the name of the company, followed by the ticker symbol for the security that is the subject for the quote. For CIBC, the symbol is CM. For companies with a dual-class share structure, there are two quotes provided, one for each of the classes of common shares. Both Canadian Tire and Canadian Utilities have dual-class share structures. For preferred shares, the trading symbols include the letters "PR," and another letter indicating the series. For income trusts, the trading symbol includes the letters "UN." Knowing the stock symbol is important, as the trading systems that provide share quotes are based on ticker symbols and these must be used in order to obtain current price data and make trades.

board lot
A trade of 100 shares, the usual multiple for most share transactions.

odd lots
Share transactions that are not for a multiple of 100 shares.

The next column, "Vol," provides the daily trading volume. Most share transactions are in multiples of 100 shares, which is termed a **board lot**. We can see that for some stocks, such as Canada Bread, very few shares traded. For others, such as Canadian Natural, almost 2.4 million shares traded. Note that according to the reported volume, some trades were not for a full board lot. These trades are termed **odd lots**. For example, a transaction for 50 shares would be an odd lot, while a transaction for 150 shares would be one board lot and an odd lot. Some sources of trading data show the number of board lots traded, so to determine the trading volume this must be multiplied by 100 to determine actual trading volume.

The "High," "Low," and "Close" columns contain the highest, lowest, and closing (last) price, respectively, at which the share traded on the given day. These values for CIBC were a high of $88.99, a low of $86.72, and a closing price of $88.96, very near its high. The next column, "Net chg," indicates the change in the closing price from that of the previous trading day. CIBC closed up $1.36 from October 30, which means the closing price on that day was $87.60.

The next two columns, labelled "52W high" and "52W low," are the highest and lowest price at which the shares sold during the preceding 52 weeks. CIBC's common share traded between $88.99 and $72.51 during the 52-week period ending October 31, 2006. Note that the 52-week high was reached on this trading day. Next is the column labelled "Div," which is the indicated annual cash dividend. This is based on the most recent quarterly dividend paid on each common share. The indicated dividend for CIBC is $2.80 per share, so CIBC's most recent quarterly dividend was $0.70 per common share. This was discussed earlier in the chapter. The next item, labelled "Yield %," is the dividend yield, which is found by dividing the indicated dividend by the closing share price. The dividend yield for CIBC is 3.1 percent ($2.80/$88.96 = 0.03147 ≈ 3.1%).

TABLE 5.12 Summary Trading Data for Transactions That Occurred on the TSX on October 31, 2006

Company	Ticker	Vol	High	Low	Close	Net chg	52W high	52W low	Div	Yield %	P/E
Canada Bread	CBY	7,225	52.50	52.00	52.00	−1.00	66.10	48.95	0.24	0.5	22.6
Canada Life Fin	CL.PR.B	1,425	26.31	26.25	26.25	−0.05	28.15	26.00	1.5625	6.0	—
Cdn Gen Invmt	CGI	4,675	26.85	26.25	26.60	+0.30	30.99	19.75	1.24	4.7	3.7
Cdn Gen Invmt	CGI.PR.B	1,500	27.66	26.60	26.60	−0.01	27.84	26.20	1.1625	4.4	—
Cdn Helicopter IT	CHL.UN	13,650	9.20	9.01	9.13	−0.07	9.70	7.00	1.05	11.5	14.4
Cdn Hotel REIT	HOT.UN	60,822	14.04	13.75	14.04	+0.29	14.04	10.65	0.9396	6.7	18.0
Cdn Hydro Devel	KHD	232,512	5.83	5.71	5.73	−0.09	6.45	4.60	—	—	NA
CIBC	CM	2,293,317	88.99	86.72	88.96	+1.36	88.99	72.51	2.80	3.1	12.4
CIBC	CM.PR.A	7,284	26.85	26.72	26.72	+0.03	27.98	26.22	1.325	5.0	—
CIBC	CM.PR.B	8,475	26.18	26.08	26.15	+0.07	27.15	25.96	1.50	5.7	—
CIBC	CM.PR.C	2,715	26.42	26.37	26.41	+0.08	27.20	25.90	1.50	5.7	—
CIBC	CM.PR.D	3,460	27.20	27.15	27.18	+0.04	27.39	26.00	1.4375	5.3	—
CIBC	CM.PR.E	5,960	27.00	26.87	26.90	—	27.39	25.77	1.40	5.2	
CIBC	CM.PR.G	4,025	27.02	26.96	26.96	—	27.61	25.75	1.35	5.0	—
CIBC	CM.PR.H	8,185	25.74	25.61	25.61	—	26.00	24.42	1.20	4.7	—
CIBC	CM.PR.P	7,150	27.43	27.28	27.39	+0.13	27.46	25.75	1.375	5.0	—
CIBC	CM.PR.R	1,000	26.86	26.56	26.79	+0.24	27.62	25.88	1.2375	4.6	—
Cdn Nat RR	CNR	1,439,029	54.15	53.15	53.50	−0.18	55.95	43.15	0.65	1.2	14.1
Cdn Natural Res	CNQ	2,374,745	58.76	56.89	58.45	+0.35	73.91	45.49	0.30	0.5	13.3
Cdn Oil Sands IT	COS.UN	1,980,305	30.63	29.63	30.42	+0.09	38.75	20.802	1.20	3.9	16.0
Cdn Pacific	CP	494,427	64.00	63.18	63.40	−0.13	65.17	45.55	0.75	1.2	12.7
Cdn REIT	REF.UN	148,183	28.21	27.17	27.24	−0.95	29.10	20.03	1.2996	4.8	26.4
Cdn Satellite	XSR	5,450	6.85	6.75	6.75	−0.10	16.00	6.26	—	—	NA
Cdn Sup Energy	SNG	32,610	2.26	2.20	2.20	−0.06	3.11	2.01	—	—	73.3
Cdn Tire	CTC	605	106.75	104.00	104.00	−0.05	135.00	95.00	0.66	0.6	24.0
Cdn Tire A	CTC.A	370,538	72.43	71.40	72.34	+0.49	?72.43	59.81	0.66	0.9	16.7
Cdn Utilities A	CU	160,770	42.75	41.86	42.10	−0.74	46.20	35.15	1.16	2.8	17.0
Cdn Utilities A	CU.X	4,500	42.30	41.72	42.23	−0.62	45.82	35.72	1.16	2.7	17.1

SOURCE: "FP Market Data," *National Post*, available at **www.canada.com/nationalpost/financialpost/fpmarketdata/index.html.**

price/earnings (P/E) ratio
Measures the amount investors are willing to pay for each dollar of the firm's earnings.

The final column is "P/E," the price/earnings (P/E) ratio, calculated by dividing the closing market price by the firm's most recent annual earnings per share (EPS). The **price/earnings (P/E) ratio** measures the amount investors are willing to pay for each dollar of the firm's earnings. CIBC's P/E ratio was 12.4: the share was trading at 12.4 times its earnings. The P/E ratio reflects investor expectations concerning the firm's future prospects. Higher P/E ratios reflect investor optimism and confidence, lower P/E ratios reflect investor pessimism and concern. Note that the trading summary provides the P/E ratio and the closing share price. Therefore, we can estimate the company's EPS. CIBC's EPS was $7.17 ($88.96/12.4) for the most recent four quarters. Note that the quotes round all answers off to the nearest decimal. CIBC's actual EPS for the most recent four quarters was $7.20. Using this number results in a P/E ratio of 12.36, 12.4 rounded.

The listings for income trusts and preferred shares are essentially identical to those of common shares, except that for preferred shares there is no value for the P/E ratio because it is not relevant. Preferred shares are only entitled to the quoted dividend. For preferred shares, the dividend yield is an important figure, since investors buy preferred shares primarily for the dividend. It should also be noted that when a share is not traded on a given day, it generally is not quoted in the trading report.

Value of Trading in the Money and Capital Markets

Table 5.13 provides the dollar value of trading that occurred in the money and capital markets for four years: 1991, 1996, 2001, and 2006. A review of this table reveals a number of interesting results. First, note the sheer volume of trading in the three markets. In 2006, over $5.1 trillion of financial market securities were traded in Canada. This excludes all of the banking and currency market trading that also occurred. Second, until 2006, the value of the securities traded on the stock market was a fraction of the value of the trading that occurred in the money and bond markets. The money market still leads in trading, but the three markets are getting to be very similar in terms of the volume of trading. The money market is a very large and important component of the Canadian financial system but is "hidden" to most observers; the stock market "gets all the press."

The reason money market securities have such high trading volumes is that a single money market security may trade seven, eight, or ten times in its very short-term life. For example, for an issue of 98-day federal government treasury bills, the first purchaser of the treasury bill in the secondary market may only hold it for 34 days. After 34 days, the holder will sell it. The next buyer may only want to hold it for 15 days, while the next buyer may want to hold it for 8 days, etc. This type of trading inflates the trading statistics for money market securities.

Third, the value of the securities traded in the money and bond markets remained relatively flat over the 1991 to 2001 period, but then increased in the period to 2006. But, over the 16 years to 2006, the value of money market trading increased at an average annual rate of only 2.3 percent. A similar trend

TABLE 5.13 Annual Dollar Value of Trading in the Canadian Financial Markets: 1991, 1996, 2001, and 2006 (in billions of dollars)

	1991	1996	2001	2006
Money market	$1,339.7	$1,548.2	$1,490.9	$1,883.8
Bond market	942.0	1,138.0	997.9	1,817.3
Stock market	90.1	331.3	712.5	1,416.1
Total value of trading	$2,371.8	$3,017.5	$3,201.3	$5,117.2

occurred in the bond market with trading increasing at an average annual rate of 4.5 percent. For the stock market, however, trading exploded, growing at an average annual rate of 20.2 percent. The value of stock market trading is now about 75 percent of the value of money market and bond market trading. The patterns of financial market trading greatly changed between 1991 and 2006.

? Review Questions

5–22 Why are common shareholders referred to as residual owners? What is meant by the term *limited liability*?

5–23 What is *dilution of ownership*? Provide an example. How can dilution of ownership be prevented?

5–24 Distinguish between *authorized, issued*, and *outstanding* common shares. Is *par value* a useful term when referring to common shares?

5–25 What is the benefit to the original owners of issuing subordinate voting shares? What is the *coattail provision* and why is it important?

5–26 Are common share dividends guaranteed? Discuss.

5–27 Discuss the characteristics of preferred shares in terms of risk for the issuing company and the investor, stated values, dividends, ratings, and call features. What various types of preferred shares can be issued?

5–28 What is the purpose of a securities exchange? What is the difference between a physical and an artificial securities exchange?

5–29 What is meant by the term *efficient markets*?

5–30 What information is provided in the stock trading reports provided in newspapers? Are there other sources of more timely stock price data? Where?

5–31 What does the price/earnings (P/E) ratio indicate?

5–32 How are preferred share quotes different from those of common shares?

5–33 Discuss the changing pattern of the dollar value of trading that occurred in the money and capital markets over the 1991 to 2006 time period.

LG5

5.5 Differences Between Debt and Equity Capital

The term *capital* denotes the long-term funds of the firm. All items on the right-hand side of the firm's balance sheet *with an obvious financing cost* (this excludes current liabilities like payables and accruals) are sources of capital. *Debt* capital includes all loans made by the firm, both short- and long-term. *Equity* capital consists of long-term funds provided by preferred and common shareholders. *Preferred* equity capital is raised by selling preferred shares. *Common* equity capital are funds provided by the firm's owners and can be raised *internally*, through reinvested profits, or externally, by selling common shares. The key differences between debt, preferred, and common equity are summarized in Table 5.14. These differences relate to voice in management, claims on the firm's income and assets, maturity, and tax treatment.

TABLE 5.14 Key Differences Among Debt, Preferred, and Common Equity Capital

	Type of capital		
Characteristic	**Debt**	**Preferred**	**Common**
Voice in management[a]	No, but power to bankrupt company	No, and no bankruptcy power	Yes, through the board of of directors
Claims on income	Senior to equity and less risky, but limited to interest	Subordinate to debt, preference over common equity	Subordinate to debt and preferred, but unlimited with increasing profits
Claims on assets	First claim, secured then unsecured	Second claim preference over common equity	Residual claim
Maturity	Stated with a finite life	None, but callable	None, but can be repurchased
Tax treatment	Interest deducted from income	No deduction; dividends paid from after-tax income	No deduction; dividends paid from after-tax income

[a]In the event the issuer violates its stated contractual obligations, debtholders and preferred shareholders *may* receive a voice in management; otherwise, only common shareholders have voting rights.

Voice in Management

Unlike creditors (lenders), the common shareholders are the owners of the firm. Holders of common shares have voting rights that permit them to select the firm's board of directors and to vote at the company's annual meeting of shareholders and on special issues. Debtholders and preferred shareholders may receive voting privileges only when the firm has violated its stated contractual obligations to them. The power of debtholders is to put the firm into bankruptcy if the company fails to meet the conditions of the loan. Arguably, this provides creditors with more real power than common shareholders.

While common shareholders vote at the company's annual meeting to elect the board of directors and on other major matters affecting the company (such as takeovers), their real power is severely limited in cases where there is no dominant shareholder. In such cases, management can fully control the company through proxy voting, regardless of the number of shares management own. This is the agency issue that we discussed in Chapter 1. In such cases, management has the power, unless the board of directors steps in and acts on behalf of the common shareholders.

Claims on Income and Assets

With income, the company must pay interest owed to creditors or face the risk of bankruptcy. The creditors are entitled to the interest owed and the principal repaid at the maturity of the loan. Regardless of how profitable the firm becomes, this is all creditors are entitled to receive. Preferred shareholders are entitled to receive dividends. If the firm fails to pay dividends, they accumulate. Common shareholders have claim on all residual income after the two previous payments are made. Their claim on income is unlimited given increasing profits, but the risk of receiving a benefit is greater given that the company's profits may decline or turn negative. Common shareholders receive the benefit of increasing profits through the payment of dividends, which is at the discretion of the board of directors, and through increasing share prices, the ultimate goal of the firm.

The equity holders' *claims on assets* of the firm also are secondary to the claims of creditors. If the firm fails, assets are sold, and the proceeds are distributed in this order: the government, employees, customers, secured creditors, unsecured creditors, preferred shareholders, and finally common shareholders. Because equity holders are the last to receive any distribution of assets in the event of bankruptcy, they expect greater returns from dividends and/or increases in share price. As is explained in Chapter 8, the cost to the firm of the various forms of equity financing are generally higher than debt. This is the case since the suppliers of equity capital take more risk because of their subordinate claims on income and assets. Despite being more costly, equity capital is necessary for the firm to grow. All firms must initially be financed with common equity and this financing continues through the reinvestment of profits, assuming the firm is profitable.

Maturity

Unlike debt, both preferred and common equity are *permanent forms* of financing. Equity does not mature and therefore repayment is not required. Although a ready market may exist for the firm's preferred and common shareholders, the price that can be realized may fluctuate. This potential fluctuation of the market price of equity makes the overall returns more risky. Note that although preferred and common shares do not mature, preferred shares can be redeemed by the firm in certain circumstances. Common shares may be repurchased and cancelled by the company. This is regularly done by companies in Canada for various reasons, but often because the firm's management believes the shares are undervalued in the market.

Tax Treatment

Interest payments to debtholders are treated as tax-deductible expenses on the firm's income statement, whereas dividend payments to common and preferred shareholders are not tax-deductible. As discussed in Chapter 3, the repayment of the principal borrowed is made from after-tax income. When a company borrows money, this is not considered taxable income, so the repayment of the borrowed funds is not deducted for tax purposes. Only the interest paid on the borrowed funds is tax-deductible. The tax-deductibility of interest lowers the cost of debt financing, thereby increasing the cost advantage of debt financing over equity financing.

? Review Questions

5–34 What are debt and equity capital? What are the key differences between them with respect to voice in management, claims on income and assets, maturity, and tax treatment?

5–35 Debtholders are only entitled to receive the promised coupon payment. How is this a benefit? How is this a potential "cost" to debtholders?

5.6 How Financial Securities Are Created and Issued

underwriting
The means by which new financial securities are created in the primary market, the basic financial market transaction.

investment banker
A term for investment dealers when performing the underwriting function.

Underwriting is the means by which new financial securities are created in the primary market. This is the basic financial market transaction. The user raises cash, the saver receives a financial security: long-term debt, preferred shares, or common shares. Money market securities are created in a similar manner; however, the focus of this discussion is on long-term securities. The issuer could be a government or corporation. The underwriter is the financial intermediary, who acts as the agent for the organization raising the funds. Investment dealers perform this function, and in this role are often referred to as **investment bankers**.

Types of Underwriting Transactions

private placements
The sale of the security directly to a group of investors or an institutional investor; these securities will not trade on financial markets after issue.

public offerings
The sale of securities that will be traded on secondary financial markets.

initial public offering (IPO)
Referred to as *going public*, the process of offering common shares of a privately owned company to the general public for the first time.

new issue
An issue of long-term debt, preferred shares, or common shares where the funds raised flow to the company.

seasoned offering
A new issue of common shares; the shares sold add to the existing pool of common shares.

secondary offering
The sale to the public of a large block of common shares held by the founding owners or a controlling company.

There are two types of primary market transactions: private placements and public financing. **Private placements** are the sale of a security directly to a group of investors or an institutional investor. These securities will not be traded on secondary financial markets, but the original investor may be able to arrange for a sale to another investor. **Public offerings** are the sale of securities that will be traded on secondary financial markets, the bond and stock markets, after issue. This discussion will focus on public financing.

Offering of securities can also be classified by title. Securities could be a new issue, a secondary offering, or the initial public offering. The **initial public offering (IPO)** title only applies to common shares and is referred to as *going public*. Going public is the process of offering common shares of a privately owned company to the general public for the first time. A **new issue** refers to long-term debt, preferred share, or common share issue. As discussed earlier, each issue of long-term debt and preferred shares is unique and does not add to the existing pool of securities. Each issue creates a new series of securities.

A new issue of common shares is referred to as a **seasoned offering,** with these shares adding to the existing pool of common shares. New issues of common shares are sold by the company. Through multiple seasoned offerings, a company will increase the number of common shares outstanding over time. A **secondary offering** occurs when a large block of previously unissued common shares held by the founding owners or a controlling company is sold to the public. The funds raised go to the sellers, not to the company whose shares are sold. These types of offering are very common in Canada.

Steps in the Underwriting Process

The underwriting process is a seven-step procedure as described below.

Step 1 The organization decides to raise long-term financing.

The process by which the organization would have realized funds were required was covered in Chapter 4. This external financing would be required to invest in assets, either current or fixed.

Step 2 Select a lead underwriter and hold discussions (the pre-underwriting conference).

The organization chooses the lead underwriter, the investment dealer ultimately responsible for selling the issue and receiving the largest percentage of the fees paid. Often organizations (both governments and companies) will deal with the same investment dealer for many years. For companies, it may be the underwriter who was associated with the companies' initial public offering (IPO) of shares.

The first item considered in the discussions is whether the firm really needs to raise additional external financing. If so, then a broad range of topics is discussed, including the firm's current financial position; current and projected economic and financial market conditions; the future outlook for the company and its industry; the amount, purpose, and type of the financing; coupon or dividend rate (if applicable); tax consequences of the issue; the timing of issue; and the area of distribution. Preliminary decisions will be made concerning each of these issues and the underwriting process will continue.

Step 3 Decide on the details of the issue and prepare and issue the preliminary prospectus.

At this point, the economic, financial market, and organization-specific factors have been analyzed and the organization and underwriter have decided to proceed with the issue. Decisions regarding all aspects of the issue will have been made, but not finalized. The **preliminary prospectus** is the document that provides all the information investors require to make a decision regarding the investment merits of the security issue.

preliminary prospectus
The document that provides all information investors require to make a decision regarding the investment merits of the security issue.

The prospectus is required for all national issues of securities and must be filed with the appropriate securities commissions for approval.[2] In Canada, each province has its own securities commission that must approve the sale of all securities in the province. The preliminary prospectus is often referred to as the **red herring**, because on the first page a statement in red ink appears stating that the securities have not been approved for sale by the provincial securities commission and sale must await the approval of the final prospectus. The preliminary prospectus will include the following types of information:

red herring
Another term for the preliminary prospectus, so called due to the statement on the first page printed in red ink stating that the securities have not been approved for sale.

1. A one-to-four-page summary of the information provided.
2. Legal opinions as to the eligibility of the security for investment purposes. (For example, in RRSPs, for pension plans, mutual funds, and so on.)
3. History of the company and industry and full description of the business of the company, including any significant changes over the previous two to five years.
4. Audited financial statements for the company for the past three to five years and management's discussion and analysis (MD&A) of the financial and operational results.
5. Description of how the proceeds of issue will be used by the organization.
6. Management's projections of future financial results.
7. Financial statement after giving effect to the offering.
8. Full disclosure of all risks associated with the issue. This clause is important in order to limit the liability of all involved in the process: the organization, underwriters, and law firms. This clause is the result of **due diligence**, the process completed by the underwriter to ensure there are no misrepresentations and that the prospectus contains full and true disclosure.
9. Discussion of tax considerations for the investor.

due diligence
The process completed by the underwriter to ensure there is no misrepresentation and that the prospectus contains full and true disclosure.

2. A number of provinces, including Ontario, require a preliminary prospectus. Since most organizations issuing securities in Canada wish to sell their securities in Ontario, most issues have a preliminary prospectus.

10. The area the issue will be sold: regional, national, and/or international.
11. Compensation of executive officers.
12. Conditions or covenants associated with the issue, especially for a long-term debt issue.

The preliminary prospectus is rigorously reviewed for compliance by all provincial securities commissions to which it is submitted. The review process can take up to 4 weeks, at which time the commissions will issue a *comment letter* that indicates required changes, seeks clarification, requests other information, and asks questions. While some issuers have decided not to proceed with an offering of securities once the process has reached this stage, it is highly unusual for the issue not to proceed.

Some important information is missing from the preliminary prospectus. The price of the issue, the number of securities to be issued, the dollar amount of the issue, the interest rate or dividend on the issue, and the underwriting fees are not included. These items are omitted since one of the purposes of the preliminary prospectus is for the underwriter to identify the extent of public interest in the issue. Once the underwriter has a better read on the market's response to the issue, these details are finalized. This occurs in the final days of the offering period and the details are included in the final prospectus. At this point, a range (low to high) in issue size will be suggested.

Step 4 Assemble the underwriting syndicate.

underwriting syndicate
The group of investment dealers who buy the security issue from the company and then resell it to investors (savers).

banking group
Includes the lead underwriter and, in most larger deals, a number of other large investment dealers.

selling group
Smaller, regional investment dealers who do not assume any of the risks of underwriting, but only attempt to sell a certain portion of the issue.

firm agreement
An underwriting agreement where the syndicate agrees to buy all of the securities at the stated price, guaranteeing the organization receives the amount of money.

best efforts agreement
An underwriting agreement where the syndicate agrees to *try* to sell the issue, but the sale is not guaranteed.

escape clauses
Provisions in the underwriting agreement that allow the syndicate to not buy the issue from the organization if specific conditions exist.

The **underwriting syndicate** is the group of investment dealers who buy the security issue from the company and then resell it to investors (savers). There are two groups in the syndicate: the banking group and the selling group. The **banking group** includes the lead underwriter and, in most larger deals, a number of other large investment dealers. The **selling group** is made up of other investment dealers (usually regional) who do not assume any of the risks of underwriting, but only attempt to sell a certain portion of the issue on a commission basis. For very large issues, there may be up to five investment dealers in the banking group, with many of the remaining investment dealers operating in Canada in the selling group.

There are two types of underwriting agreements: firm and best efforts. With a **firm agreement**, the syndicate agrees to buy all of the securities at the stated price, guaranteeing the organization selling the securities receives the implied amount of money. With a **best efforts agreement**, the syndicate agrees to *try* to sell the issue, but the sale is not guaranteed. Most underwriting agreements in Canada are firm. The risks of underwriting are associated with firm offering. The banking group purchases the security from the issuer at the stated price, less fees. The syndicate then attempts to sell the security at the issue price. If the lead underwriter's read of the market was incorrect and the issue does not sell, or sells below the specified price, the banking group could lose money on the deal. The possibility of less money being raised than given to the organization is the risk associated with underwriting. The banking group underwrites price risk for the organization, thus providing an insurance function.

To protect the syndicate, many agreements include **escape clauses**. These allow the syndicate to opt out of the deal and not buy the issue from the organization if specific conditions exist. Examples include an order that restricts the trading of the organization's securities, incorrect statements in the prospectus, or events that have a significant impact on the company or the financial markets.

For example, the stock market declining by a large percentage in a very short time period would likely trigger this clause for an issue of common shares.

Step 5 Market the issue.

Once the company addresses the concerns the securities commissions have regarding the preliminary prospectus, the company can market the issue. This is usually done by having people from the company and lead underwriter make presentations to financial analysts and institutional investors across Canada. This is referred to as the **road show**, and it may take up to two weeks. The presentations revolve around the information provided in the preliminary prospectus and the **green sheet**, a document prepared by the underwriter that summarizes key information in the prospectus. The greater the interest in the offering, the higher the proceeds to the organization.

road show
Presentations, by the company and lead underwriter, regarding the issue made to financial analysts and institutional investors across Canada.

green sheet
A document prepared by the underwriter that summarizes key information in the prospectus.

Step 6 Prepare and distribute the final prospectus.

The final prospectus contains all the information that was in the preliminary prospectus, but also includes the missing pricing information on both a total and per share basis. Decisions regarding these variables will be made based on the market response to the issue and the road show. Once finalized, all of this data is included in the final prospectus, which is then submitted to the securities commission in each province in which the issue is to be sold.

Occasionally, a base post-receipt pricing (PREP) prospectus may be filed in lieu of the final prospectus. The PREP prospectus may omit certain details concerning the issue including dollar size, pricing, fees, dividends or coupon rate, the closing date, and whether the issue is a bought deal. A supplemented PREP prospectus providing the omitted information must be filed within two days of the missing details being finalized.

Note that for a firm underwriting agreement, the banking group does not commit to the offering and is not obliged to purchase the security issue from the organization until the final prospectus is submitted for approval. The syndicate only underwrites known risk; that is, when the dollar amount of the offering is finalized. Approval of the final prospectus, referred to as **blue skying** it, normally only takes 1 to 2 days, at which time the sale of the issue can proceed.

blue skying
An investment industry term referring to the approval of the final prospectus by provincial securities commissions.

At this point, the issue may be advertised in the financial press. The advertising format used is referred to as a tombstone, due to the rectangular shape of the notice. The tombstone will provide the name of the company, the type of issue, the size, price, and date of the issue, and the investment dealers in both the banking and selling groups. The tombstone appears twice—once when the new issue is approved and again after it is sold. The only change in the two printings is the fine print at the top of the advertisement. The initial tombstone states that the securities are offered by means of a prospectus which is available from one of the investment dealers named on the tombstone. The second printing states that the securities have been sold.

While in theory the issue cannot be sold until the final prospectus is approved, in practice the underwriting syndicate began selling the issue when the decision to proceed was made by the company. These sales would have been made on the condition that the company proceed with the issue, and pending approval of the final prospectus by the securities commissions. A sale is not finalized until an investor receives the final prospectus and 48 hours elapse. In this period the investor can opt out of the purchase. Examples of both preliminary and final prospectuses are available at the Web site for the System for Electronic

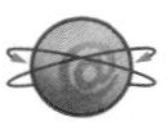

http://sedar.com/homepage_en.htm

Document Analysis and Retrieval (SEDAR). SEDAR is a filing system that provides access to almost all documents and information filed by publicly traded companies in Canada.

Step 7 Close the issue.

The closing of the deal will normally occur 2 to 3 weeks after the initial offering date. On this date, the investors who purchased the issue will be required to pay for the securities purchased. The lead underwriter, representing the banking group, will present the company issuing the securities a cheque for the issue amount less the underwriting commission. Also, the investors will receive a certificate for the amount of the issue purchased. For example, this certificate could be for 100 shares of a preferred or common share issue, or for $5,000 of par value of a bond issue.

At this point the formal underwriting process has been finalized. The primary market transaction has been completed. Cash was transferred from savers to users with a security outlining a financial position in the company flowing in the opposite direction. An intermediary (underwriting syndicate) was used to allow the transaction to be completed in the most efficient manner possible.

Time Required to Issue Securities

The seven-step underwriting process described above can take a great deal of time. A large amount of data must be brought together and presented in a logical and direct manner. For a new issue or secondary offering, the process could take 10 to 11 weeks. To complete an IPO, the average time required is about 100 days, although it often takes longer. Regardless, time is of the essence as the prospectus is prepared, approval sought from securities regulators, and interest generated from potential investors.

The POP System

prompt offering prospectus (POP) system
A filing process for firms meeting certain requirements that allows companies to raise financing within five days of filing.

short-form prospectus
The document filed for the POP system that omits much of the information that is in a "regular" prospectus.

For large, established companies, waiting 70 days to raise financing is an unnecessary impediment to growth. For companies like BCE, the big banks, Loblaws, or Magna, all information concerning their operations is freely available and easily accessible by investors. Consequently, it seems pointless to make issuers like these wait 70 days before they can raise capital. As recognition of this fact, most provincial securities commissions allow issuers to use the **prompt offering prospectus (POP) system.** Firms that meet certain size and reporting requirements can simply file a **short-form prospectus** as an addendum to current filing with the securities commissions. Much of the information that is in a "regular" prospectus can be omitted. This is allowed since all of this information is widely available in other reports the company must file. The short-form prospectus is usually approved within a week.

The POP, short-form prospectus system has reduced costs for issuers and increased flexibility to respond to market opportunities for security issues. It is not unusual for companies to regularly file short-term prospectuses in anticipation of an opportunity to raise capital in the most opportune environment. By allowing for increased flexibility, securities commissions have recognized the changing nature of financial markets and the requirement that companies be able to act quickly to changing conditions. In Canada, the large majority of the financing raised in the capital markets is done through the POP system.

Issue Costs

For most organizations, the cost of issuing securities is reasonable. For high-risk organizations or for small issues, however, the costs can be substantial. The main cost is the commission paid to the underwriting syndicate. It is normal for commissions to be stated as a percent of the gross proceeds raised through the underwriting process. The second cost is fees and expenses such as accounting, legal, travel (particularly for the road show), printing, and regulatory fees.

The commission paid will vary depending on the type of security, the size of the issue, and the main purchasers of the issue. Long-term debt securities have the lowest commission, followed by preferred shares, and then common shares. The larger the issue, the lower the percentage commission. If the securities are sold primarily to institutional investors, the commission will be lower than if the primary purchasers are individual investors.

Commissions can be less than 1 percent or greater than 10 percent. The lower end applies to large issues of long-term debt and preferred shares sold to institutional investors; the high end to a small issue of common shares sold primarily to individual investors. The commission is split three ways—among the lead underwriter, the other members of the banking group, and the members of the selling group—with the allocation based on the functions performed. Consider the following example.

Example ▼ Raynor Plastics recently issued 10 million common shares at a price of $22 per share, raising $220 million. The commission on the issue was 6 percent while fees and expenses totalled $1.2 million. Therefore, while investors paid $22 per share, the commission consumed 6 percent or $1.32 per share of this, netting Raynor $20.68. On a total dollar basis, Raynor received $206.8 million, less the $1.2 million of fees and expenses, or $205.6 million from the issue. Total issue costs were $14.4 million, or 6.55 percent of the gross proceeds. The underwriting syndicate splits the $1.32 per share, a total of $13.2 million. How is the commission split? Assume the deal between the members of the underwriting syndicate was as follows:

		Commission			
	Per share	Per share	Cumulative	Percent	Cumulative
Lead underwriter purchases common shares from Raynor: Pays	$20.68				
		$0.33	$0.33	1.5%	1.5%
Sells common shares to banking group	$21.01				
		$0.55	$0.88	2.5%	4%
Sells common shares to selling group	$21.56				
		$0.44	$1.32	2%	6%
Sells common shares to client	$22.00				

The lead underwriter makes money on every common share purchased, in this case a minimum of $0.33 per share or 1.5 percent of the total 6 percent commission. If the lead underwriter sold all 10 million shares to the other members of the banking group, the lead would make $3.3 million in total (10 million shares × $0.33). Assuming the lead sells 5 million shares to the banking group, 3 million shares to the selling group, and 2 million shares to their own clients, they would make $6.93 million (5 million × $0.33 + 3 million × $0.88 + 2 million × $1.32), or 52.5 percent of the total commission. If the members of the banking group sold 3 million of these shares to their own customers and 2 million shares to the selling group, their commission would be $4.07 million (3 million × $0.99 + 2 million × $0.55), or 30.83 percent of the total commission.

The selling group sells 5 million shares to their clients, making $0.44 per share, a total of $2.2 million or 16.67 percent of the total commission. The lead underwriter and the other members of the banking group are guaranteed to make money by selling shares to the members of the selling group. They can maximize their commissions by selling shares to their own clients. A member of the syndicate is said to be "flat" when they have sold all of their allotted shares. Based on this example, it is clear that underwriting is a very profitable activity for investment dealers.

Commissions account for the large majority of the total issue costs of new financial securities; however, fees and expenses are also a significant cost. Depending on issue size, fees can range from $100,000 to over $1,500,000. Total issue costs can range from less than 1 percent to 20 percent, depending on the particulars of the issue and issuer. For common share issues for many companies, total issue costs are in the 4 percent to 6 percent range.

For example, in November 2006, Air Canada had their IPO. This occurred 26 months after the company exited bankruptcy protection. They issued 25 million shares at $21 per share. Air Canada only received proceeds of $200 million from the issue, as they only sold 9,523,810 of the shares. The remainder of the shares were sold by ACE Aviation Holdings, the holding company of Air Canada. ACE collected $325 million from the secondary offering. The commission on the issue was 5.25 percent, while fees and expenses were $6,000,000. The IPO and secondary offering raised $525 million, but total issue costs were $33,562,500, or a quite high 6.39 percent of the gross proceeds.

In November 2006, CIBC issued 18,000,000 series 31 preferred shares with a $25 stated value. The dividend rate on the issue was 4.7 percent. The commission on the issue was 1 percent for shares sold to institutional investors and 3 percent for shares sold to others. Fees and expenses were $325,000. Therefore, gross proceeds of the issue were $450 million and CIBC netted $443,375,000 (assuming 80% of the shares were sold to institutions). Total issue costs were $6,625,000 or 1.47 percent of the gross proceeds.

In November 2006, Clarke Inc., a diversified investment holding company, raised $100 million through convertible unsecured subordinated debentures, due 2013, with a 6 percent coupon rate. The commission was 3 percent on the debentures ($3,000,000), while fees and expenses were $415,000. Total issue costs were $3,415,000 or 3.42 percent of the gross proceeds. The net amount raised was $96,585,000.

In September 2006, Atrium Biotechnologies, a developer of products for the pharmaceutical industry, announced a secondary offering of 3,930,000 subordinate voting shares at $15.80 per share. The selling shareholders were the parent company and senior management. The commission on the issue was 4 percent, while fees and expenses were $350,000. Therefore, gross proceeds of the issue were $62,094,000, and the selling shareholders netted $59,260,240. Total issue costs were $2,833,760 or 4.56 percent of the gross proceeds.

In October 2006, Enterra Energy Trust, an oil and gas unit trust, announced a new issue (a seasoned offering) of 4,125,000 trust units at $8.50 per share and $120,000,000 of 8.0 percent convertible unsecured subordinated debentures. The commission was 5 percent on the trust units (a total of $1,753,125), and 4 percent on the debentures (a total of $4,800,000), while fees and expenses were $1.5 million. The new issue raised $155,062,500, but total issue costs were $8,053,125 or 5.19 percent of the gross proceeds. The net amount raised was $147,009,375.

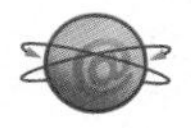

http://sedar.com/new_docs/new_en.htm

Visit the SEDAR Web site discussed earlier and read the first page of a number of final prospectuses to determine the issue costs associated with some recent financings.

Bought Deals

bought deal
The lead underwriter(s) purchases the total amount of a new security issue from the issuing company with the intention of quickly selling the issue to investors.

An important development affecting the underwriting process in Canada is the **bought deal**. The bought deal originated in Canada in early 1983 with Gordon Capital Corp., a maverick investment dealer whose actions helped reform the investment industry in Canada in the early 1980s. In a bought deal the lead underwriter(s) purchases the total amount of a new security issue from the issuing company. They then attempt to quickly sell the issue at its face value to institutional and, in some cases, individual investors. The POP system has allowed bought deals to flourish in Canada and it is now a very common way for companies to issue securities.

This is because the underwriting commissions are lower than a public offering, usually a flat 4 percent for common shares. Also, the issuer receives its funds much faster and there are no escape clauses: The underwriter completely assumes the risk of the issue not selling. If the price of the security declines within the time of the agreement but before the new issue is sold, then the underwriter can incur a loss on the issue. This is not likely to occur, however, given the short time frame between the decision to proceed with the issue and the actual sale of the issue. In fact, most bought deals are sold to institutional investors well before the underwriter agrees to the deal.

But occasionally a bought deal does turn sour, leading to a major loss for the underwriters. For example, in June 2006, Cineplex Galaxy Income Fund announced a seasoned offering of 5,250,000 trust units at a time when the units were trading for $16.10 on the TSX. A group of nine investment dealers formed an underwriting syndicate and agreed to buy the units from Cineplex and then sell them to investors for $15.90 each. After the bought deal was formalized, a major downturn occurred in the income trust market and the Cineplex unit trusts sold off to $13.40 per unit.

Obviously, no investor would now pay the $15.90 that the underwriting syndicate was asking. In order to move the units, the syndicate was forced to sell them for $13.40 each. After factoring in the commission of 5 percent, or $0.795 per unit, the members of the syndicate lost about $1.70 per unit or $8.9 million on the bought deal. While unusual, this type of situation can occur with a bought deal. But that is the risk of underwriting: there is a chance that the price of the security purchased from the issuer will quickly and significantly decline in value before the issue can be moved to investors. In such a case, the syndicate can take a real financial hit.

TABLE 5.15 **Type and Dollar Amount of Equity Underwriting on the Toronto Stock Exchange (TSX), 2001–2006 (millions)**

Type of Offering	2001	2002	2003	2004	2005	2006
Initial public offerings (IPO)	$ 9,260.1	$ 9,120.7	$11,271.5	$15,633.2	$15,226.0	$ 9,927.2
Public offerings	10,132.7	75,835.8	21,464.2	27,473.5	25,916.3	26,683.2
Private placements	1,698.4	3,267.5	4,847.8	3,408.9	5,020.5	5,183.0
Total value of equity offerings	$21,091.2	$88,224.0	$37,583.5	$46,515.6	$46,162.8	$41,793.4

SOURCE: "Summary of New Equity Financing," *The Toronto Stock Exchange Review*, various issues, ch. 1, p. 8.

Underwriting Values

Table 5.15 provides a summary of the total value of equity underwritings that occurred on the TSX for the six years 2001 to 2006. The table also details the amount raised by the type of offering: IPOs, public offerings, and private placements. As is clear from the table, a significant increase in the amount of equity financing raised occurred in 2002, and since that time an average of about $32 billion per year has been raised. In general, equity offerings are dependent on market conditions, and between 2002 and 2006 the Canadian stock market has performed very well. From the table it is clear that a sizeable equity market exists for Canadian corporations and underwriters.

? Review Questions

5–36 What is meant by *underwriting*? What is being underwritten?

5–37 What are the various types of underwriting transactions? What titles are used for underwriting offerings?

5–38 What are the major steps in the underwriting process? List and discuss each of the steps.

5–39 Discuss the following terms associated with underwriting: preliminary prospectus, red herring, due diligence, comment letter, underwriting syndicate, types of underwriting agreements, green sheet, blue skying, the closing.

5–40 What is the POP system, and why is it important for issuers of securities?

5–41 What issue costs are incurred when securities are offered? Are these a large cost item for issuers of securities?

5–42 What is a bought deal, and how does it differ from a public offering of securities?

SUMMARY

LG1 **Introduce the types of financial markets and how the markets operate, the important role played by financial institutions, the major types of financial securities, and the importance of trust to the operation of the financial markets.** For an economy to develop and economic wealth to be created, a country needs efficient and well-developed financial markets. Financial markets provide a forum where suppliers of funds (savers) and demanders of funds (users) can transact business. They bring savers and users of funds together to make a fair exchange, one that provides value to both parties. Savers and users of funds include individuals, business organizations, and the various levels of government. There are two distinct financial markets: the money market and the capital market. Both of these markets have primary and secondary markets. There are six principal financial intermediaries in Canada: (1) deposit-taking, loan-making institutions; (2) investment dealers; (3) mutual funds; (4) pension funds; (5) life insurance companies; and (6) the Bank of Canada. These institutions facilitate the transfer of funds from savers to users. There are three distinct flow of funds channels shown in Figure 5.2. For the first channel, cash flows from savers through financial intermediaries to users. In the second channel, cash flows from savers to financial intermediaries, who then provide funds to users via the money or capital markets. In the third channel, cash flows from savers to financial intermediaries who buy and sell financial securities on behalf of savers in the money or capital markets. In order for financial markets to function efficiently, the participants in the market must trust in the system.

LG2 **Describe the money market and the major instruments traded in the market, particularly treasury bills.** The money market involves the trading of debt securities that will mature within one year. There is no physical location for the money market: it is an artificial market, the computer networks between investment dealers. The principal money market security is Government of Canada treasury bills, or t-bills as they are more commonly known. T-bills are auctioned every second Tuesday by the Bank of Canada through a competitive bidding process. The Bank of Canada uses the overnight rate as the main tool to conduct monetary policy. Other money market securities include short-dated government bonds, commercial paper, finance company paper, bankers' acceptances, and day loans. All money market securities are sold on a discount basis in both the primary and secondary markets. This means that the price paid for the bill is less than its par value. The yield is the difference between the two amounts. The international equivalent of the domestic money market is called the Eurocurrency market.

LG3 **Describe the key characteristics of long-term debt, one of the major capital market securities.** Long-term debt is a contractual liability between the two parties: the borrower (issuer) and the lender (saver). The agreement specifies that the issuer has borrowed a stated amount of money, termed the par value, and promises to repay it in the future under clearly defined terms. Also, while the debt is outstanding, the issuer will pay the investor a stated rate of interest, the coupon rate. There are various types of long-term debt, but the two general categories are bonds and debentures. The trust indenture is the legal document that details the contractual relationship between the borrower and lender. It specifies a trustee who acts as a watchdog on behalf of the debtholders. The default risk of long-term debt is measured by means of a bond rating, an independent and objective assessment of the investment quality of a long-term debt issue. Ratings are used to help determine the coupon rates on debt issues. Companies and governments borrow internationally using Eurobonds and foreign bonds.

Describe the key characteristics of common and preferred shares, two additional capital market securities. Common shares signify ownership of the company. All corporations must issue common shares and be owned by shareholders. The sale also raises equity capital. Generally, each common share entitles the holder to one vote on issues affecting the company; but many companies in Canada have issued another class of common shares with restricted voting rights. Common shareholders may receive a dividend, but this payment is at the discretion of the board of directors and the large majority of companies listed on the Toronto Stock Exchange (TSX) do not pay dividends on common shares. Some firms issue a second class of equity, preferred shares, to raise additional equity capital. Preferred equity broadens the firm's capital structure, raising financing without giving up ownership (like common shares) or incurring obligations (like debt), thus reducing the risk of the company. Preferred shares are issued with a stated value and pay dividends which accumulate if the firm misses a payment. Preferred shares are rated also for the risk of default and there are many different varieties of preferreds in Canada. Although both common and preferred shares are forms of equity capital, the characteristics of preferred shares make them more similar to debt than common equity. Secondary markets exist that allow for the trading of financial securities. These marketplaces are the securities exchanges. There are two types: physical, tangible exchanges and artificial exchanges. Securities exchanges create continuous liquid markets where trading can occur efficiently. The common and preferred shares of most large Canadian companies trade on the TSX. A summary of daily trading appears in many publications and on the Internet.

Differentiate between debt, preferred equity, and common equity capital. The key differences between debt, preferred, and common equity relate to voice in management, claims on the firm's income and assets, maturity, and tax treatment. Typically, only common shareholders have voting rights. Equity holders have claims on income and assets that are secondary to the claims of creditors. There is no maturity date associated with most common and preferred shares, while all long-term debt is repaid at some point in the future. For a company, interest payments are a tax-deductible expense whereas dividend payments are paid out of after-tax income.

Review the process of how financial securities are created and issued, and the important role played by the investment banker. Underwriting is the means by which new financial securities are created in the primary market. The underwriter is the financial intermediary who acts as the agent for the organization raising the funds. Investment dealers perform this function, and are often referred to collectively as an investment banker. Underwriting is a seven-step process: the organization (1) decides to raise long-term financing; (2) selects a lead underwriter and holds discussions; (3) decides on the details of the issue and prepares and issues the preliminary prospectus; (4) assembles the underwriting syndicate; (5) markets the issue; (6) prepares and distributes the final prospectus; and (7) closes the deal. While the time to complete an underwriting deal can be quite lengthy, the prompt offering prospectus (POP) system has greatly decreased the time needed to raise cash. For most organizations, the cost of issuing securities is reasonable. The main cost is the commission paid to the underwriting syndicate; the second cost is fees and expenses. Bought deals reduce costs and increase the flexibility of issuers.

SELF-TEST PROBLEMS

(Solutions in Appendix B)

ST 5–1 **Valuing t-bills** A $1,000 par value Government of Canada treasury bill is trading for $985.84. It will mature in 126 days. What percentage rate of return (yield) would an investor buying this t-bill receive?

LG2

ST 5–2 **Valuing commercial paper** Ferris Chemicals has surplus cash that they wish to invest for 21 days. Their investment dealer indicates that a $75 million par value issue of commercial paper is available that would provide a yield of 2.94 percent over the 21 days. How much would Ferris have to pay for the issue, and what would be their dollar return on the investment?

PROBLEMS

BASIC  5–1 **Valuing t-bills** A treasury bill issued by the Canadian government with 86 days to maturity is trading to yield 3.69 percent. For $1,000 of par value, what is the maximum amount you should pay for the t-bill? Why?

INTERMEDIATE  5–2 **Valuing t-bills** A major investment dealer just purchased $300 million of 364-day treasury bills from the Bank of Canada. The investment dealer paid $287,631,317.50 for the bills.

a. What is the yield on these t-bills?

b. If the investment dealer can sell these t-bills to other investors in the secondary market at an average yield of 4.11 percent, how much money will the investment dealer make on their purchase of $300 million of t-bills from the Bank of Canada?

INTERMEDIATE  5–3 **Valuing t-bills** The Bank of Canada recently issued $1.3 billion of 98-day treasury bills on behalf of the federal government. The average bid received for the auction implied a yield of 3.114 percent.

a. How much money was raised for the federal government?

b. The high bid received implied a yield of 2.919 percent. If this were the average bid, how much *more* money would the Bank of Canada have raised?

c. The low bid received implied a yield of 3.254 percent. If this were the average bid, how much *less* money would the Bank of Canada have raised?

d. Based on the above analysis, what is the direct impact on the federal government when the Bank of Canada changes the overnight rate?

BASIC  5–4 **Invest surplus cash** Garrett Machinery must make a $42 million dividend payment in 9 days. The company currently has the cash available. Assuming they could invest the full amount in a certificate of deposit yielding 3.02 percent, would it make sense for them to make the investment? How much money would they make?

BASIC  5–5 **Valuing bankers' acceptances** AIX, a mutual fund company, plans to buy a bankers' acceptance issue that is about to be sold by NoTel, a large high tech company. The par value of the issue is $100 million and AIX's investment dealer indicates AIX would have to pay $99,062,031.83 for the issue. If the issue matures in 90 days, what rate of return would AIX receive on the issue?

BASIC  5–6 **T-bill auction** An investment dealer submits a bid of 97.8178 for $100 million of 182-day t-bills at a recent Bank of Canada auction.

a. What must the investment dealer be in order to be able to submit the bid? What will happen with the bid?

b. Assuming the investment dealer's bid is successful, how much will they be required to pay the Bank of Canada? What day(s) will all of this occur?

INTERMEDIATE  5–7 **Commercial paper** Morgan Financial Group is using the money market to raise short-term financing. The financial institution wishes to issue commercial paper with a face value of $50,000,000. The paper will be sold for $49,351,565 and will mature in 90 days at which time the investor will receive the face value.

a. What rate of return will the investor receive?
b. If Morgan Financial Group wishes to provide investors a return of 5.85 percent, at what price will they issue the commercial paper? What will be the investor's dollar return?
c. "If the commercial paper had a maturity of 30 days, the investor would receive a lower percentage return." Do you agree with this statement? Why or why not?

CHALLENGE 

5–8 Valuing bankers' acceptances For Problem 5–5, assume AIX purchased the bankers' acceptance issue. After 24 days, AIX realizes they require money to meet redemption requests from the holders of the mutual funds. AIX approaches their investment dealers, who indicate to them that yields on bankers' acceptances in the secondary market have increased to 4.025 percent.

a. How much would AIX receive if they sold the full issue of bankers' acceptances? How much did they make on the original purchase of the paper?
b. How much would AIX have made if yields did not change between the date of purchase and sale?
c. How much would AIX have made if yields declined to 3.61 percent between the date of purchase and sale?
d. Based on the above, discuss the possible risks and rewards of trading money market securities in the secondary market.
e. What would cause yields on money market securities to change?

INTERMEDIATE 

5–9 Eurocurrency market To develop a property in Malaysia, Zane Oil and Gas, based in Calgary, requires US$35 million. Zane is considering using the Eurocurrency market to raise the funds. Zane requires the money for 11 months, and they have been quoted an interest rate of LIBOR + 178.

a. What is the Eurocurrency market and how could a company based in Calgary access this market?
b. What does LIBOR + 178 mean?
c. If LIBOR was 2.73 percent, what would Zane's borrowing rate be?
d. If Zane went ahead with the loan, how much would they owe the lender in 11 months?

INTERMEDIATE 

5–10 Eurocurrency market Borden Enterprises, a Canadian company with offshore operations, deposited US$150 million in the Bank of London. Wendy's, a London, Ontario-based manufacturing company, has approached the bank for a US$150 million loan. The company requires the loan for nine months, after which time it will repay the interest and principal. The Bank of London quotes an interest rate of the LIBOR plus 89 basis points. The LIBOR is currently 4.62 percent.

a. If the Bank of London loaned the money to another bank, what interest rate would they charge? How much money would they make on the loan?
b. If the Bank of London loaned the money to Wendy's, what interest rate would they charge?
c. Explain why the interest rates the Bank of London will charge are different in parts **a** and **b**.
d. At the end of the nine months, how much will Wendy's be required to repay the Bank of London?

BASIC

5–11 Bond interest payments before and after taxes Zylex Corp. has issued 2,500 bonds with a total principal value of $2,500,000. The bonds have a coupon rate of 9.25 percent.

a. What dollar amount of interest per bond can an investor expect to receive each year from Zylex Corp.?
b. What is Zylex's total interest expense per year associated with this bond issue?
c. Assuming that Zylex is in a 35 percent corporate tax bracket, what is the company's net after-tax interest cost associated with this bond issue?

BASIC

5–12 Characteristics of long-term debt On August 31, 2008, Charter Corp. issued 25,000 debentures with a total principal value of $25 million. The term of the issue was 25 years and the coupon rate was 7 percent.

a. What was the par value of each debenture?
b. When will the debentures mature?
c. When will Charter make the first coupon payment? How much will it be per debenture certificate and in total?
d. When will Charter make the second coupon payment?
e. When will Charter make the final coupon payment? How many coupon payments will be made in total?
f. If Charter's tax rate in 2008 is 30 percent, what is the after-tax interest cost associated with this debenture issue? What is the implication of this calculation?
g. What is the effective after-tax interest rate on this issue?

INTERMEDIATE 

5–13 Sinking fund Refer to Problem 5–12. Charter's debenture issue has a sinking-fund requirement that becomes exercisable on the 16th anniversary of the issue. The sinking fund will then retire the issue over the remaining time to maturity. The sinking fund can be exercised in the open market, whereby the company will purchase and retire the debenture, or through the lottery process, whereby the company's trustee draws debentures by number for retirement.

a. What is the maximum amount Charter will contribute to the sinking fund each year once it becomes exercisable?
b. Under what circumstance will Charter exercise the sinking fund: (i) in the open market; (ii) using the lottery process? Provide examples.
c. At the beginning of the 20th year of the term of the debenture, how much of the issue is still outstanding? During the 20th year, what will Charter's total coupon payments be?

BASIC 

5–14 Call feature Rockaway Entertainment has a $300 million bond issue outstanding with a coupon rate of 6.75 percent. The bond issue has a call feature that can be exercised in six months' time. The call price is par + 5.6 percent.

a. In what circumstances would Rockaway exercise the call feature?
b. If the company does exercise the call feature, how much would they have to pay bondholders per $1,000 certificate and in total?

INTERMEDIATE 

5–15 Bond ratings The yields on corporate long-term debt securities with different bond ratings but all with the same features, maturing in 15 years, are provided below.

Rating	Yield	Rating	Yield
AAA	6%	BBB	7.08%
AA (H)	6.12%	BBB (L)	7.26%
AA	6.23%	BB	8.05%
AA (L)	6.38%	B	8.92%
A (H)	6.51%	CCC	9.81%
A	6.63%	CC	10.23%
A (L)	6.71%	C	11.65%
BBB (H)	6.90%		

a. Where do the biggest differences in yields for the different bond ratings begin? Why is this the case?

b. The yields provided are for corporate debt issues that mature in 15 years. In what range would be the yield on federal government debt that matures in 15 years? Why?

c. What is the premium in yield and as a percentage difference: (i) between AAA and A; (ii) between AAA and BBB (L); (iii) between AAA and CCC; (iv) between AAA and C? What does this analysis suggest?

BASIC  5–16 **Zero-coupon bond** A zero-coupon bond matures for $1,000 in exactly 12 years' time. If you paid $385.63 today for the bond, what average yearly rate of return will you earn?

INTERMEDIATE  5–17 **Zero-coupon bond** Assume you bought the bond in the problem above. Four years go by and you wish to sell the bond in the secondary market. If yields in the market for bonds of this risk level are 6.2 percent, how much money will you receive when you sell the bond? If yields were 10.8 percent, how much would you receive?

BASIC  5–18 **Bond quotation** Assume that the following quote for the Financial Management Corporation's $1,000-par-value bond was found in the Wednesday, November 8, 2008 issue of the *National Post*. Using the quote, answer the questions.

Fin Mgmt	8.75	June 05/14	102.46	8.42

a. On what day did the trading occur?

b. When does the bond mature?

c. What is the bond's coupon rate?

d. Assuming you bought the bond on November 8, when will you receive your first coupon payment?

e. What is the bond's *current yield*?

f. If you wished to buy $20,000 of par value of this bond, how much would it cost?

g. Why is the yield different than the coupon rate?

BASIC  5–19 **Authorized and available shares** Aspin Corporation's charter authorizes issuance of 2,000,000 shares of common stock. Currently, 1,400,000 shares are issued and outstanding. The firm wishes to raise $48,000,000 for a plant expansion. The sale of new common stock will net the firm $60 per share.

a. What is the maximum number of new shares of common stock the firm can sell without receiving further authorization from shareholders?
b. Based on the data given and your finding in **a**, will the firm be able to raise the needed funds without receiving further authorization?
c. What must the firm do to obtain authorization to issue more than the number of shares found in **a**?

INTERMEDIATE  5–20 **Restricted voting shares** In 1962, Frank Hughes established Hughes Machine Parts in rural Ontario. In 1975, Frank decided to go public and held an IPO. But, for the IPO Frank decided to issue subordinate voting shares, the B share. The B shares were entitled to one vote each. Frank and his family would hold the A shares which were entitled to 200 votes per share. After a number of secondary issues of shares, there were a total of 32,463,412 common shares outstanding; 265,000 of these were Class A shares.

a. Of the total shares issued, what percent are Class B shares?
b. What percent of the votes do the Class B shares hold?
c. What type of share is the Class A? The Class B?
d. Based on the above analysis, what possible danger exists for the Class B shareholders? Is there a protection for these shareholders?

BASIC  5–21 **Preemptive rights and the issuance of new common shares** Scarloti Pizza, Inc., has 10,000,000 authorized shares. The firm currently has 5,000,000 shares issued and outstanding. Anna Scarloti owns 500,000 shares. The firm's board of directors wishes to raise additional capital by selling 1,000,000 new shares. Anna is concerned that her ownership interest is going to be diluted by the proposed sale. Her uncle, Frank Scarloti, chairperson of the board, explains to her that she is protected by preemptive rights.

a. If the firm issues one right per share, how many rights will Anna receive?
b. How many rights will be required to purchase one of the new shares?
c. How many shares must Anna purchase to maintain her percentage of the firm's ownership?
d. If each new share is sold for $10, how much must Anna spend to maintain her percentage of the firm's ownership?

BASIC  5–22 **Rights offering** To raise the financing required for the expansion of its production facilities, Mercury Corporation just announced a rights offering. The firm currently has 15 million common shares outstanding which are trading for $18.75 on the Toronto Stock Exchange. The rights offering will see the company issue 0.5 rights for each share owned. The subscription price for the rights offering is $15 and the investor will require 5 rights to buy one share.

a. How many new common shares will the company issue assuming all shareholders take advantage of the rights offering?
b. How much financing will be raised through the rights offering?
c. Once the rights offering is announced, what will happen with the rights?
d. On the day the rights offering is announced, what is the value of one of Mercury Corporation's rights?

INTERMEDIATE 

5–23 Rights offering Larkin International, a company whose common shares trade on the TSX, has just announced a rights offering that will see shareholders receive two rights for each share owned. Three rights will be required to purchase one share. Shareholders will have 45 days from the rights announcement to exercise the rights. The subscription price for the rights offering is $12. Ben McCoy owns 100,000 shares of Larkin International, which represents a 2.5 percent stake in the company. Ben paid an average of $2.26 for the 100,000 shares he owns. Larkin's share price has fluctuated significantly in the last few months but the shares are currently trading for $14.85 on the TSX.

a. How much financing is Larkin International hoping to raise through the rights offering?

b. On the day the rights offering is announced, what is the value of a single right?

c. What should Ben do with the rights he will receive? Explain.

d. If Ben did not exercise his rights, what should he do? Assuming he does this, what will happen to his ownership position in Larkin if all the rights the company issued were exercised?

e. If on the date of the rights announcement Larkin's shares were trading for $16.74, what would be the value of the rights?

f. If 45 days after the rights announcement Larkin's shares were trading for $10.85, what will happen?

INTERMEDIATE 

5–24 Dilution of earnings Goodwood Golfing's earnings available for common shareholders (EAC) for this fiscal year is $6.5 million. Goodwood has 5 million common shares outstanding. The current share price is $24. Goodwood is considering issuing 500,000 common shares that will net the company 95 percent of the current share price when all issue costs are considered.

a. Prior to the share issue, what is Goodwood's earnings per share (EPS)?

b. Assuming Goodwood issues the share this fiscal year, what is the immediate dilution of the new share issue?

c. Assume that the proceeds from the share issue are invested and provide a 12 percent return that flows to EAC. Is there a dilutive effect of the new share issue?

INTERMEDIATE 

5–25 Dividends in arrears QTL Tech has an issue of preferred shares outstanding with a $50 stated value that pays a dividend of 7.5 percent. There are 325,000 shares outstanding. QTL has not paid preferred share dividends for 3.5 years. The company's CEO wishes to retire the preferred share issue by paying the preferred shareholders 50 percent of the dividends in arrears plus 10 percent of the stated value of the preferred.

a. What is the total amount of dividends in arrears? Provide the per share and total dollar amounts.

b. If the preferred shareholders accepted the CEO's offer, what would be the total payment QTL Tech would have to make to the preferred shareholders on a per share and total dollar basis?

c. QTL Tech common shares are trading for $1.22 on the market. If the CEO offered to convert each preferred share into 5 common shares, would this be a better deal for the preferred shareholders?

CHALLENGE  **5–26** **Convertible preferred stock** Valerian Corp. has a preferred share issue outstanding that is convertible into common shares. Each preferred share can be converted into five common shares at the option of the holder. The preferred stock pays a dividend of $10 per share per year. The common stock currently sells for $20 per share and pays a dividend of $1 per share per year.

a. Based on the conversion ratio and the price of the common shares, what is the minimum value of each preferred share?

b. If the preferred shares are selling at $96 each, should an investor convert the preferred shares to common shares?

c. What factors might cause an investor not to convert from preferred to common?

BASIC  **5–27** **Common share** Assume that the following quote for the Advanced Business Machines stock, which is traded on the TSX, was found in the Thursday, December 14 issue of the *National Post*. Using the quote, answer the questions.

AdvBusMach	ABM	1,256,432	52.90	51.75	52.43	+0.33	64.99	40.61	0.80	1.5	17.0

a. On what day did the trading activity occur?

b. What are the highest and lowest prices at which the stock sold on the day quoted?

c. What is the firm's price/earnings ratio? What does it indicate? What were ABM's most recent EPS?

d. What is the last price at which the stock traded on the day quoted?

e. What was the most recent quarterly dividend? What is the indicated dividend for ABM?

f. What is the highest and lowest price at which the stock traded during the latest 52-week period?

g. How many shares in total were traded on the day quoted? Based on this, how many board and odd lots of common shares were traded?

h. Did the common share price change from the previous trading day? If so, by how much? What did the share close at on the previous trading day?

BASIC  **5–28** **Issue costs** Blaine Lumber requires $25 million of financing and is considering a bond issue. The commission on the issue is expected to be 1.25 percent while issue costs are $325,000. What are the total issue costs on the bond issue in dollars and on a percentage basis? How much money will Blaine Lumber receive?

INTERMEDIATE  **5–29** **Issue costs** MacDonald Technology is about to go public through an IPO of their common shares. The company will sell 30 million common shares to the public for $44 per share. RDC Imperial Securities is the lead underwriter of the IPO and the total underwriting commission on the issue will be 4.5% of the total proceeds. The fees and expenses of the issue are expected to be $1.75 million. As lead underwriter, RDC will receive the full 4.5 percent commission for all shares sold to the public. Members of the banking group selling shares to the public will receive 3.5 percent, while members of the selling group selling shares to the public will receive 1.5 percent.

a. What is an IPO? Briefly discuss the process MacDonald Technology would use for the IPO. Limit your discussion of each step to two or three sentences.

b. What is the total commission MacDonald Technology will pay on the IPO?
c. What are the total issue costs on a total dollar and percentage basis? What is the net amount the company will receive?
d. RDC, as the lead underwriter, sells 15 million shares to the members of the banking group, 10 million shares to the members of the selling group, and the remaining 5 million shares directly to investors. Based on this distribution of shares, how much commission revenue will RDC Imperial Securities make on the IPO? What percentage of the total commission will the lead underwriter make?

INTERMEDIATE  5–30 **Bond ratings** Visit the Dominion Bond Rating Service Web site (www.dbrs.com). In the upper right-hand corner there is a "Quick Search" box allowing the user to search for the ratings on all of the available financial securities for a particular company. Find and report on the rating for two different types of financial securities for three different companies. Comment on the risks to an investor of buying the company's financial securities. Does DBRS discuss any recent events for the company? If so, summarize their findings in a report in the following format:

Company	Financial security	Rating action	Rating	Trend

Discussion of recent events

CASE CHAPTER 5 Financing Lobo Enterprises' Expansion Program

See the enclosed Student CD-ROM for cases that help you put theories and concepts from the text into practice.

Be sure to visit the Companion Website for this book at **www.pearsoned.ca/gitman** for a wealth of additional learning tools including self-test quizzes, Web exercises, and additional cases.

CHAPTER 6

Time Value of Money

LEARNING GOALS

LG1 Discuss the role of time value of money in finance and the use of computational aids to simplify its application.

LG2 Understand the concept of future value, its calculation for a single amount, and the effects of compounding interest more frequently than annually.

LG3 Find the future value of an ordinary annuity and an annuity due and compare these two types of annuities.

LG4 Understand the concept of present value, its calculation for a single amount, and the relationship of present to future value.

LG5 Calculate the present value of a mixed stream of cash flows, an annuity, a mixed stream with an embedded annuity, and a perpetuity.

LG6 Describe the procedures involved in (1) determining the periodic investments required to accumulate a future sum, (2) loan amortization, and (3) determining growth and interest rates.

6.1 The Role of Time Value in Finance

Firms are regularly presented with opportunities to earn positive rates of return on their funds, either through investment in real assets or in financial securities such as treasury bills, bonds, preferred shares, or common shares or deposits in a bank. Therefore, the timing of cash flows—both outflows and inflows—has important economic consequences, which financial managers explicitly recognize

Money Time

Time and money are inextricably related. We regularly pay for time, from parking meters, to video rentals, to overnight package delivery services, to visits with our lawyer or accountant. One of the principal ideas in finance is the relationship between time and money. Called the *time value of money,* this economic principle recognizes that the passage of time affects the value of money. It advises you that if offered a dollar either today or next month, you'd be better off to take the dollar today. You'll have the use of the dollar now, which you can put to some productive use for the whole month. (Also, you're more likely to *get* the dollar today; the person making the offer may not actually come through with the payment next month!) The time value concept is well reflected by the old saying "Time is money." Receiving $1,000 today is very different from receiving it in five years' time. By waiting, we incur the high cost of time, and this can translate into a major financial cost. This chapter explores the concept and various applications of the time value of money.

as the *time value of money*. Time value is based on the fact that a dollar today is worth more than a dollar that will be received tomorrow or at some future date.

The *time value of money* is a concept used in most of the remaining chapters of this book. Students of finance need to recognize that if cash inflows and/or outflows occur at different points in time, they must be adjusted to the same point in time using time value concepts. This is one of the building blocks of corporate finance. The timing of cash flows (when they will be received or paid) is

LINKING THE DISCIPLINES: Cross-Functional Interactions

- *Accounting personnel* will frequently use time value techniques to develop loan amortization schedules and to calculate bond discount and premium values. They must recognize that forecasts of cash inflows and outflows will be discounted using time value concepts.
- *Information systems analysts* need to understand time value of money calculations to design systems that accurately measure the size and timing of the firm's cash flows.
- *Management* needs to understand time value of money techniques, and how it impacts the planning of the firm's cash inflows and outflows, in order to achieve the maximum benefit from its money. They must recognize that the funds used have a cost and that this cost is used in time value calculations.
- The *marketing department* must have a complete understanding of present value, because they will need to justify funding for new marketing programs and products by using present value techniques.
- Personnel in the *operations department* need to understand time value of money, because proposed investments in production assets will be evaluated using time value of money concepts.

almost as important as the size of the cash flow. For example, if you were told that you would receive $1 million, you would likely be quite happy. But if you were then told that the $1 million will be given to you in 50 years, your joy would likely be subdued. The timing issue has a major impact on the real value of the $1 million to you. We begin our study of time value in finance by considering two views of time value—future value and present value—and the computational aids used to streamline time value calculations.

Future Versus Present Value

Financial values and decisions can be assessed by using either future value or present value techniques. Although these techniques will result in the same decisions, they view the decision differently. Future values are cash flows that occur at some point in the future: next month, next year, each year over the next 25 years, or in five years' time. As well, cash flows that occur now can be deemed to occur at a single point in time in the future, and converted to future values. Present values convert cash flows that will occur in the future to their equivalent value today, in the present. For time value, "today" or "the present" is referred to as time zero (0). A *future value* is money you will pay or receive at a given future date, while present value is the equivalent amount of money today. The future value will always be greater than the present value.

time line
A horizontal line on which time zero appears at the leftmost end and future periods are marked from left to right; can be used to depict investment cash flows.

A **time line** can be used to depict the cash flows associated with a given investment. It is a horizontal line on which time zero appears at the leftmost end and future periods are marked from left to right. A time line covering five periods (in this case, years) is given in Figure 6.1. So, time 0 is now, which is the beginning of year 1. Time 1 is the end of year 1. It is also the beginning of year 2. Time 2 is the end of year 2. It is also the beginning of year 3. This terminology continues for the full time line. Therefore, "now," "the present," "year or time

FIGURE 6.1

Time Line

Time line depicting an investment's cash flows

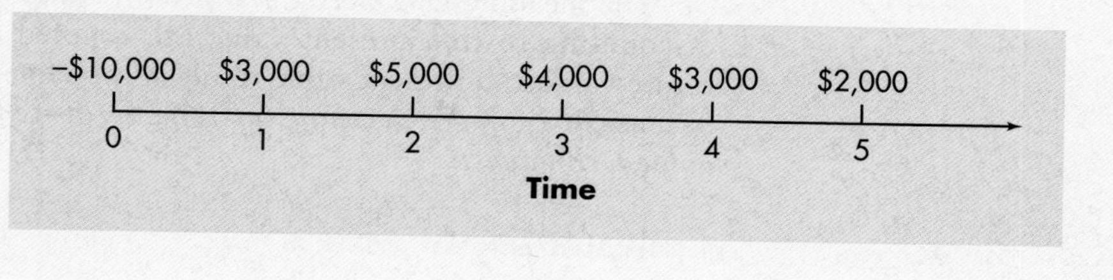

0," or the "beginning of year 1" are all synonymous; they all refer to the same point in time.

As another example, the "4" in Figure 6.1 refers to the end of year 4 and the beginning of year 5. This is a key concept throughout this book. Be sure you understand how time lines work before proceeding with your reading. The cash flow occurring at time zero and at the end of each year is shown above the line; the negative values represent *cash outflows* ($10,000 at time zero) and the positive values represent *cash inflows* ($3,000 inflow at the end of year 1, $5,000 inflow at the end of year 2, and so on). Time lines allow the analyst to fully understand the cash flows associated with a given investment.

Because money has a time value, all of the cash flows associated with an investment, such as those in Figure 6.1, must be measured at the same point in time. Typically, that point is either the end or the beginning of the investment's life. The future value technique uses *compounding* to find the future value of each cash flow at the end of the investment's life and then sums those values to find the investment's future value. This approach is depicted above the time line in Figure 6.2, which shows that the future value of each cash flow is measured at the end of the investment's 5-year life. Alternatively, the present value technique uses *discounting* to find the present value of each cash flow at time zero and then sums these values to find the investment's value today. Application of this approach is depicted below the time line in Figure 6.2.

FIGURE 6.2

Compounding and Discounting

Time line showing compounding to find future value and discounting to find present value

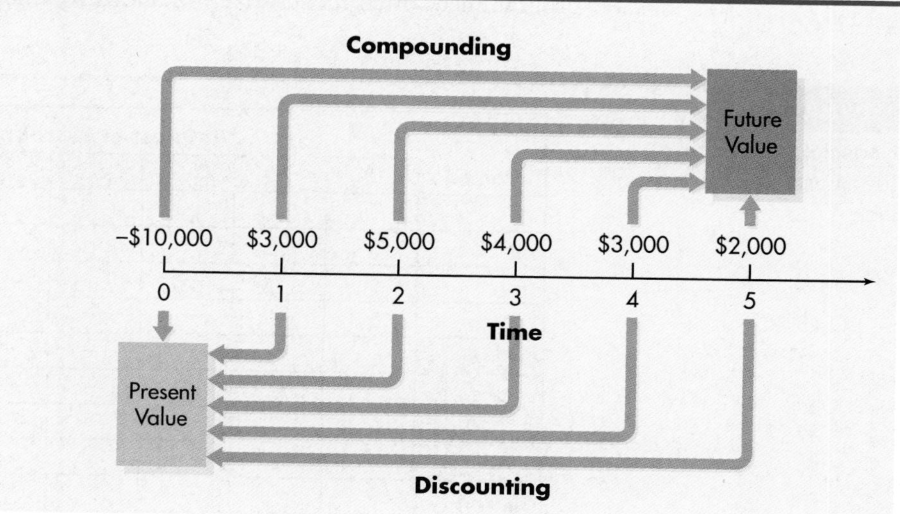

The meaning and mechanics of both compounding to find future value and discounting to find present value are covered later in this chapter. Although future value and present value result in the same decisions, *financial managers—because they make decisions at time zero—tend to rely primarily on present value techniques.*

Computational Aids

Time-consuming calculations are often involved in finding future and present values. Although you should understand the concepts and mathematics underlying these calculations, the practical application of these important time value techniques can be streamlined. Here we focus on the use of financial tables and hand-held financial calculators as computational aids. Various computer software packages can also be used to simplify time value calculations.

Financial Tables

Financial tables, easily developed from formulas, include various future and present value interest factors that simplify time value calculations. Although the degree of decimal precision (rounding) varies, the tables are typically indexed by the interest or discount rate (in columns) and the number of periods (in rows). Figure 6.3 shows this general layout. If we wished to find the time value factor at a 20 percent interest rate for 10 years, its value would be found at the intersection of the 20 percent column and the 10-year row as shown by the dark blue box. A full set of the four basic financial tables is included in Appendix A at the end of this book. These tables are described more fully later in the chapter and are used to demonstrate the application of time value techniques.

Financial Calculators

During the past 15 years, the power of financial calculators has improved dramatically, while their cost has declined. Today, a powerful financial calculator can be purchased for $20 to $30. Generally, *financial calculators* include numerous preprogrammed, often menu-driven financial routines. This chapter and those that

FIGURE 6.3

Financial Tables

Layout and use of a financial table

	Interest or Discount Rate ↓							
Period	1%	2%	...	10%	...	**20%**	...	50%
1			...		...	⋮	...	
2			...		...	⋮	...	
3			...		...	⋮	...	
⋮	⋮	⋮	...	⋮	...	⋮	...	⋮
→ 10	...	...	...	...	...	**X.XXX**	...	...
⋮	⋮	⋮	...	⋮	...	⋮	...	⋮
20			...		...		...	
⋮	⋮	⋮	...	⋮	...	⋮	...	⋮
50			...		...		...	

follow show the keystrokes for calculating time value factors and making other financial computations. For convenience, we use the important financial keys, labelled in a fashion consistent with most major financial calculators.

We focus primary attention on the keys pictured and defined in Figure 6.4. We typically use the compute (CPT) key and four of the five keys in the second row, with one of the four keys representing the unknown value being calculated. (Occasionally, all five of the keys, with one representing the unknown value, are used.) The keystrokes on some of the more sophisticated calculators are menu-driven, so that after you select the appropriate routine, the calculator prompts you to input each value; on these calculators, a compute key is not needed to obtain a solution. Regardless, any calculator with the basic future and present value functions, like those shown below, can be used in lieu of financial tables.

The process of using other financial calculators is explained in the guides that accompany them. In addition, a *Financial Calculator Guide* that discusses all financial calculators is provided on this book's Web site. It is strongly recommended that those readers who have just purchased a financial calculator read the portion of the *Guide* that refers to their financial calculator.

www.pearsoned.ca/gitman

Spreadsheets

Time value calculations can also be completed using spreadsheet programs such as Excel, Quattro Pro, and Lotus. There are preprogrammed functions that can do this, or simple mathematical equations can be written that will perform time value calculations. Both methods will be discussed and illustrated in this chapter.

Summary

Even though financial calculators or spreadsheets can complete the calculations very quickly, the key to time value is to *understand the basic underlying concepts*. Understanding what a problem is asking is the key to using the correct time value process to derive the answer. For most of the basic problems considered in this book, a financial calculator should be all you need to solve the problem, assuming you understand the situation described. With a little practice, both the speed and accuracy of financial computations using a calculator can be greatly enhanced. Note that because of a calculator's greater precision, slight differences are likely to exist between values calculated by using financial tables and

FIGURE 6.4

Calculator Keys

Important financial keys on the typical financial calculator

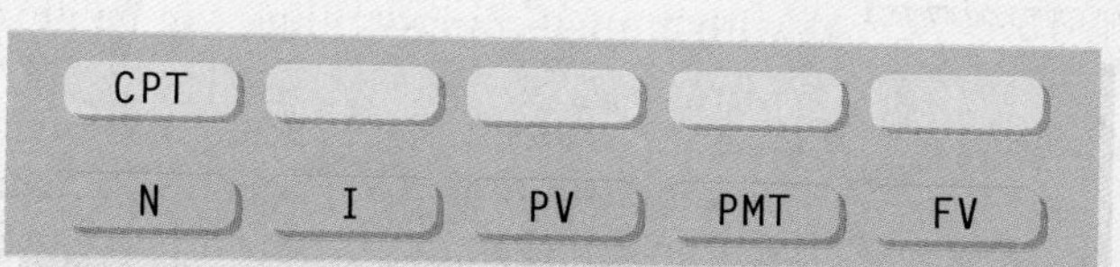

CPT — Compute Key Used to Initiate Financial Calculation Once All Values Are Input
N — Number of Periods
I — Interest or Discount Rate per Period
PV — Present Value
PMT — Amount of Payment; Used Only for Annuities
FV — Future Value

those found with a financial calculator or spreadsheet. Remember, conceptual understanding of the material is the objective. An ability to solve problems with the aid of a calculator does not necessarily reflect such an understanding, so don't settle just for answers. Work with the material until you are sure you also understand the concepts.

? Review Questions

6–1 Why does the timing of cash flows have economic consequences? What is a *time line,* and how does it depict cash flows?

6–2 What is the difference between *future value* and *present value?* Which approach is preferred by financial managers? Why?

6–3 How are financial tables laid out and accessed? Does an ability to solve problems on a financial calculator reflect conceptual understanding?

6.2 Future Value of a Single Amount

Imagine that at age 25 you begin making annual cash deposits of $2,000 into a savings plan that provides an 8 percent annual rate of return. At the end of 40 years, at age 65, you would have made deposits totalling $80,000 (40 years × $2,000 per year). Assuming that you have made no withdrawals, what do you think your account balance would be? $100,000? $200,000? $300,000? No, your $2,000 per year will have grown to $518,113! Why? Because the time value of money allowed the deposits to earn interest, and interest on interest, over the 40 years.

The Concept of Future Value

compound interest
Interest earned on a given deposit that has become part of the principal at the end of a specified period.

principal
The amount of money on which interest is paid.

future value
The value of a present amount at a future date found by applying *compound interest* over a specified period of time.

We speak of **compound interest** to indicate that the amount of interest earned on a given deposit has become part of the principal at the end of a specified period. The term **principal** refers to the amount of money on which the interest is paid. Annual compounding is the most common type, although for savings accounts at all financial institutions in Canada daily compounding of balances is the norm. The impact that different compounding periods have on future values is discussed in a few pages. The **future value** of a present amount is found by applying *compound interest* over a specified period of time. The concept of future value with annual compounding can be illustrated by a simple example.

Example If Fred Moreno places $100 in a savings account paying 8 percent interest compounded annually, at the end of 1 year he will have $108 in the account—the initial principal of $100 plus 8 percent ($8) in interest. The future value at the end of the first year is calculated as follows:

$$\text{Future value at end of year 1} = \$100 \times (1 + 0.08) = \$108$$

If Fred were to leave this money in the account for another year, he would be paid interest at the rate of 8 percent on the new principal of $108. At the end of this second year there would be $116.64 in the account—the principal at the beginning of year 2 ($108) plus 8 percent of the $108 ($8.64) in interest. The future value at the end of the second year is calculated as follows:

$$\text{Future value at end of year 2} = \$108 \times (1 + 0.08) = \$116.64$$

Substituting the expression between the equal signs in the first calculation for the $108 figure in the second calculation results in:

$$\begin{aligned}\text{Future value at end of year 2} &= \$100 \times (1 + 0.08) \times (1 + 0.08)\\ &= \$100 \times (1 + 0.08)^2\\ &= \$116.64\end{aligned}$$

This analysis leads to a more general equation for calculating future value.

The Equation for Future Value

The basic relationship above can be generalized to find the future value after any number of periods. Let

FV_n = future value at the end of period n
PV = initial principal, or present value
k = annual rate of return, generally termed the discount rate (*Note:* On financial calculators, I, i%, or I/Y is typically used to represent this rate.)
n = number of periods—typically years—the money is left on deposit

By using this notation, a general equation for the future value at the end of period n can be formulated:

$$FV_n = PV \times (1 + k)^n \tag{6.1}$$

The application of Equation 6.1 can be illustrated by a simple example.

Example Jane Farber placed $800 in an investment account paying 8 percent interest compounded annually and wonders how much money will be in the account at the end of 5 years. Substituting $PV = \$800$, $k = 0.08$, and $n = 5$ into Equation 6.1 gives the amount at the end of year 5:

$$FV_5 = \$800 \times (1 + 0.08)^5 = \$800 \times (1.46932808) = \$1{,}175.46$$

Jane will have $1,175.46 in the account at the end of the fifth year. Note, to raise 1.08 to the fifth power, key 1.08 in your calculator, press the y^x key, key in 5 for the power, and press the equal sign. This calculation provides the time value factor. Then multiply this time value factor by the initial investment.

Time Line This analysis can be depicted on a time line as shown:

Time line for future value of a single amount ($800 initial principal, earning 8%, at the end of 5 years)

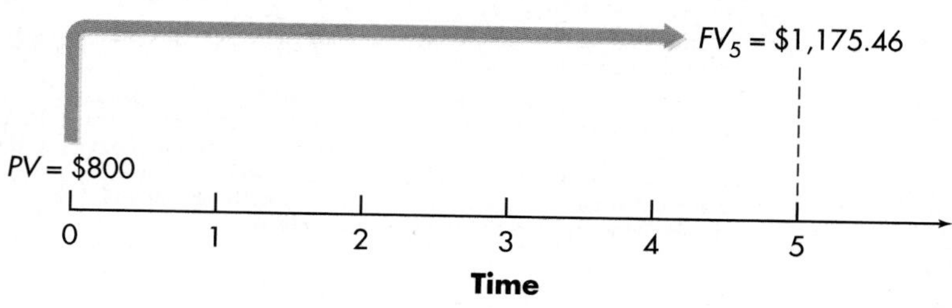

Using Tables, Calculators, and Spreadsheets to Find Future Value

Solving the equation in the preceding example is very straightforward and the equation can be easily used by students. Students can also use financial tables or a financial calculator to solve the problem, however. A table that provides values for $(1 + k)^n$ in Equation 6.1 is included in Appendix A, Table A-1.[1] The value in each cell of the table is called the **future value interest factor.** This factor is the multiplier used to calculate at a specified interest rate the future value of a present amount as of a given time. The future value interest factor for an initial principal of $1 compounded at k percent for n periods is referred to as *FVIF (k%, n per)*:

future value interest factor
The multiplier used to calculate at a specified interest rate the future value of a present amount as of a given time.

$$\text{Future value interest factor} = FVIF\ (k\%, n\ per) = (1 + k)^n \tag{6.2}$$

By finding the intersection of the annual interest rate, k, and the appropriate periods, n, you will find the future value interest factor relevant to a particular problem.[2] By letting *FVIF* (k%, n per) represent the appropriate factor, we can rewrite Equation 6.1 as follows:

$$FV_n = PV \times FVIF\ (k\%, n\ per) \tag{6.3}$$

This expression indicates that to find the future value at the end of period n of an initial deposit, we have merely to multiply the initial deposit, *PV*, by the appropriate future value interest factor.[3]

Example In the preceding example, Jane Farber placed $800 in her savings account at 8 percent interest compounded annually and wishes to find out how much will be in the account at the end of 5 years.

Table The future value interest factor for an initial principal of $1 on deposit for 5 years at 8 percent interest compounded annually, *FVIF (*8%, 5 per), found in Table A-1, is 1.469. Multiplying the initial principal of $800 by this factor results in a future value at the end of year 5 of $1,175.20. Note this is slightly less than the amount calculated on the previous page using the formula, and the amount calculated below using the financial calculator and the spreadsheet. Since the tables use rounded-off time value factors, the answers calculated with these factors will result in rounding errors. For small amounts like the ones discussed to this point, the rounding errors are quite modest. As the amount become larger, so too will the rounding errors.

1. This table is commonly referred to as a "compound interest table" or a "table of the future value of one dollar." As long as you understand the source of the table values, the various names attached to it should not create confusion; you can always make a trial calculation of a value for one factor, as a check.

2. Although we commonly deal with years rather than periods, financial tables are frequently presented in terms of periods to provide maximum flexibility.

3. Occasionally, you may want to roughly estimate how long a given sum must earn at a given annual rate to double the amount. The *Rule of* 72 is used to make this estimate; dividing the annual rate of interest into 72 results in the approximate number of periods it will take to double one's money at the given rate. For example, to double one's money at a 10 percent annual rate of interest will take about 7.2 years (72 ÷ 10 = 7.2). Looking at Table A-1, we can see that the future value interest factor for 10 percent and 7 years is slightly below 2 (1.949); this approximation therefore appears to be reasonably accurate.

Calculator[4] The preprogrammed financial functions in the financial calculator can be used to calculate the future value directly. First, key in 800 and press **PV**; next, key in 5 and press **N**; then, key in 8 and press **I** (or **I/Y** or **i%**) (which is equivalent to "k" in our notation)[5]; finally, to calculate the future value, press **CPT** and then **FV**.[6] The future value of $1,175.46 should appear on the calculator display. On some calculators, this value will be preceded by a minus sign (i.e., as −1,175.46). *Note: If a minus sign appears on your calculator, ignore it here, as well as in all other "Calculator" illustrations in this text.*[7]

Inputs:	800	5	8	0		
Functions:	PV	N	I	PMT	CPT	FV
Output:						1,175.46

Because the calculator is more accurate than the factors from the tables, a slight difference—in this case, $0.26—will frequently exist between the values found by using the tables and the financial calculator. Clearly, the improved accuracy and ease of calculation tend to favour the use of the calculator. *Note: In future examples of calculator use, we will use only a display similar to that shown above. If you need a reminder of the procedures involved, go back and review the above discussion and its footnotes.*

Spreadsheet With a spreadsheet, one could use Equation 6.1 to calculate a future value, or one could use the preprogrammed Excel future value function. Both are illustrated in Spreadsheet Application 6.1. Note that in this Application, we have provided future value calculations for five interest rates (k%) from 0% to 16%. The general format for the Excel future value function is: =FV(k%, per, PMT, PV, Type). For this function, either *PMT* or *PV* must have a value provided. For the variable not used, simply input ,, (two commas). The "Type" variable only needs to be used only if a *PMT* was made at the beginning of the period. This issue is discussed later in the chapter.

---

4. Many calculators allow the user to set the number of payments per year. Most of these calculators are preset for monthly payments—12 payments per year. Because we work primarily with annual payments—one payment per year—it is important to *make sure that your calculator is set for one payment per year.* Although most calculators are preset to recognize that all payments occur at the end of the period, it is also important to *make sure that your calculator is correctly set on the* END *mode.* Consult the reference guide that accompanies your calculator for instructions for setting these functions. You can also refer to the previously mentioned Financial Calculator Guide that is freely available on the book's Web site.

5. The known values *can be keyed into the calculator in any order;* the order specified in this as well as other calculator use demonstrations included in this text results merely from convenience and personal preference.

6. Note that the PMT function is not used in this example. If a value was inputted into this function the last time the calculator was used, the value is still in the calculator and will be used in this calculation. Therefore, to avoid calculating incorrect answers, follow *one* of the following two procedures when using financial functions. First, key in zero (0) and press the function that is not being used, in this example PMT. This clears any previous value in the function, meaning the function will not be used. *Or*, clear the financial function register *before* inputting values and making computations. The first method is easier and is the preferred approach to dealing with this potential problem. Users of financial calculators *must* get into the habit of using one of the above procedures or else incorrect answers will result.

7. The calculator differentiates inflows from the outflows by preceding outflows with a negative sign. For example, in the problem just demonstrated, the $800 present value (PV), because it was keyed as a positive number (i.e., 800) is considered an inflow or deposit. Therefore, the calculated future value (FV) of −1,175.46 is preceded by a minus sign to show that it is the resulting outflow or withdrawal. Had the $800 present value been keyed in as a negative number (i.e., −800), the future value of $1,175.46 would be displayed as a positive number (i.e., 1175.46). Simply stated, *the cash flows—present value (PV) and future value (FV)—will have opposite signs.*

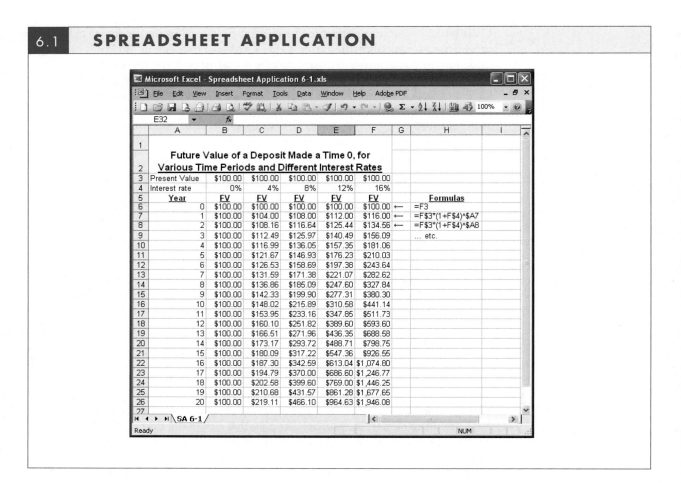

6.1 SPREADSHEET APPLICATION

Microsoft Excel - Spreadsheet Application 6-1.xls

Future Value of a Deposit Made a Time 0, for Various Time Periods and Different Interest Rates

	A	B	C	D	E	F	G	H
3	Present Value	$100.00	$100.00	$100.00	$100.00	$100.00		
4	Interest rate	0%	4%	8%	12%	16%		
5	Year	FV	FV	FV	FV	FV		Formulas
6	0	$100.00	$100.00	$100.00	$100.00	$100.00	←	=F3
7	1	$100.00	$104.00	$108.00	$112.00	$116.00	←	=F$3*(1+F$4)^$A7
8	2	$100.00	$108.16	$116.64	$125.44	$134.56	←	=F$3*(1+F$4)^$A8
9	3	$100.00	$112.49	$125.97	$140.49	$156.09		... etc.
10	4	$100.00	$116.99	$136.05	$157.35	$181.06		
11	5	$100.00	$121.67	$146.93	$176.23	$210.03		
12	6	$100.00	$126.53	$158.69	$197.38	$243.64		
13	7	$100.00	$131.59	$171.38	$221.07	$282.62		
14	8	$100.00	$136.86	$185.09	$247.60	$327.84		
15	9	$100.00	$142.33	$199.90	$277.31	$380.30		
16	10	$100.00	$148.02	$215.89	$310.58	$441.14		
17	11	$100.00	$153.95	$233.16	$347.85	$511.73		
18	12	$100.00	$160.10	$251.82	$389.60	$593.60		
19	13	$100.00	$166.51	$271.96	$436.35	$688.58		
20	14	$100.00	$173.17	$293.72	$488.71	$798.75		
21	15	$100.00	$180.09	$317.22	$547.36	$926.55		
22	16	$100.00	$187.30	$342.59	$613.04	$1,074.80		
23	17	$100.00	$194.79	$370.00	$686.60	$1,246.77		
24	18	$100.00	$202.58	$399.60	$769.00	$1,446.25		
25	19	$100.00	$210.68	$431.57	$861.28	$1,677.65		
26	20	$100.00	$219.11	$466.10	$964.63	$1,946.08		

SA 6-1

A Graphic View of Future Value

Remember that we measure future value at the *end* of the given period. The relationship between various interest or discount rates, the number of periods, and the future value of $100 is illustrated in Figure 6.5. It clearly shows that (1) the higher the interest rate, the higher the future value and (2) the longer the period of time, the higher the future value. Note that for an interest rate of 0 percent, the future value always equals the present value ($100). But for any interest rate greater than zero, the future value is greater than the present value of $100. Also note that at higher interest rates, the future value line is exponential. At very high interest rates, the effect that compounding has on the future values is quite pronounced.

Compounding More Frequently Than Annually

Rates of return are often compounded more frequently than once a year. Savings can be compounded semiannually, quarterly, monthly, weekly, daily, or even continuously. This section discusses various issues and techniques related to compounding more frequently than annually.

FIGURE 6.5

Future Value Relationship

Interest rates, time periods, and future value of $100

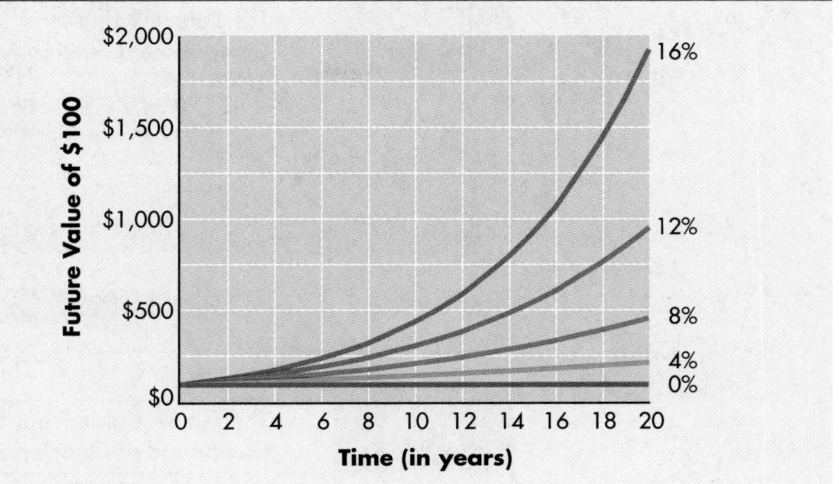

Semiannual Compounding

semiannual compounding
Compounding of interest over two periods within the year.

Semiannual compounding of interest involves two compounding periods within the year. Instead of the stated interest rate being paid once a year, one-half of the stated interest rate is paid twice a year.

Example Fred Moreno has decided to invest $100 in a savings account paying 8 percent interest *compounded semiannually.* If he leaves his money in the account for 2 years, he will be paid 4 percent interest compounded over four periods, each of which is 6 months long. Table 6.1 uses interest factors to show that at the end of 1 year, with 8 percent semiannual compounding, Fred will have $108.16; at the end of 2 years, he will have $116.99.

Quarterly Compounding

quarterly compounding
Compounding of interest over four periods within the year.

Quarterly compounding of interest involves four compounding periods within the year. One-fourth of the stated interest rate is paid four times a year.

Example Fred Moreno has found an institution that will pay him 8 percent interest *compounded quarterly.* If he leaves his money in this account for 2 years, he will be paid 2 percent interest compounded over eight periods, each of which is 3 months long. Table 6.2 uses interest factors to show the amount Fred will have at the end of 2 years. At the end of 1 year, with 8 percent quarterly compounding, Fred will have $108.24; at the end of 2 years, he will have $117.17.

Table 6.3 compares values for Fred Moreno's $100 at the end of years 1 and 2 given annual, semiannual, and quarterly compounding at the 8 percent rate. As shown, *the more frequently interest is compounded, the greater the amount of money accumulated.* This is true for any interest rate for any period of time.

TABLE 6.1 The Future Value from Investing $100 at 8% Interest Compounded Semiannually over 2 Years

Period	Beginning principal (1)	Future value interest factor (2)	Future value at end of period [(1) × (2)] (3)
6 months	$100.00	1.04	$104.00
1 year	104.00	1.04	108.16
18 months	108.16	1.04	112.49
2 years	112.49	1.04	116.99

TABLE 6.2 The Future Value from Investing $100 at 8% Interest Compounded Quarterly over 2 Years

Period	Beginning principal (1)	Future value interest factor (2)	Future value at end of period [(1) × (2)] (3)
3 months	$100.00	1.02	$102.00
6 months	102.00	1.02	104.04
9 months	104.04	1.02	106.12
1 year	106.12	1.02	108.24
15 months	108.24	1.02	110.41
18 months	110.41	1.02	112.62
21 months	112.62	1.02	114.87
2 years	114.87	1.02	117.17

A General Equation for Compounding More Frequently Than Annually

It should be clear from the preceding examples that if m equals the number of times per year interest is compounded, Equation 6.1 (our formula for annual compounding) can be rewritten as

$$FV_n = PV \times \left(1 + \frac{k}{m}\right)^{m \times n} \tag{6.4}$$

Hint If $m = 1$, Equation 6.4 reduces to Equation 6.1. Thus, if interest is compounded annually, Equation 6.4 will provide the same result as Equation 6.1.

The general use of Equation 6.4 can be illustrated with a simple example.

Example The preceding examples calculated the amount that Fred Moreno would have at the end of 2 years if he deposited $100 at 8 percent interest compounded semiannually and quarterly. For semiannual compounding, m would equal 2 in Equation 6.4; for quarterly compounding, m would equal 4. Substituting the appropriate values for semiannual and quarterly compounding into Equation 6.4:

1. *For semiannual compounding:*

$$FV_2 = \$100 \times \left(1 + \frac{0.08}{2}\right)^{2 \times 2} = \$100 \times (1 + 0.04)^4 = \$116.99$$

TABLE 6.3 The Future Value from Investing $100 at 8% Interest for Years 1 and 2 Given Various Compounding Periods

	Compounding period		
End of year	Annual	Semiannual	Quarterly
1	$108.00	$108.16	$108.24
2	116.64	116.99	117.17

2. *For quarterly compounding:*

$$FV_2 = \$100 \times \left(1 + \frac{0.08}{4}\right)^{4 \times 2} = \$100 \times (1 + 0.02)^8 = \$117.17$$

Remember, to raise a number by a power greater than 2, use the **y**^{x} key, where y is the number you wish to raise and x is the power. These results agree with the values for FV_2 in Tables 6.1 and 6.2.

If the interest were compounded monthly, weekly, or daily, m would equal 12, 52, or 365, respectively. The resulting answers are $117.29, $117.34, and $117.35.

Using Tables, Calculators, and Spreadsheets

We can use the future value interest factors for one dollar, given in Table A-1, when interest is compounded m times each year. Instead of indexing the table for k percent and n years, as we do when interest is compounded annually, we index it for $(k \div m)$ percent and $(m \times n)$ periods. However, the table is less useful, because it includes only selected rates for a limited number of periods. Instead, a financial calculator or computer software package is typically required.

Example Fred Moreno wished to find the future value of $100 invested at 8 percent compounded both semiannually and quarterly for 2 years. The number of compounding periods, m, the interest rate, and number of periods used in each case, along with the future value interest factor, are:

Compounding period	m	Interest rate $(k \div m)$	Periods $(m \times n)$	Future value interest factor from Table A-1
Semiannual	2	$8\% \div 2 = 4\%$	$2 \times 2 = 4$	1.170
Quarterly	4	$8\% \div 4 = 2\%$	$4 \times 2 = 8$	1.172

Table Multiplying each of the factors by the initial $100 deposit results in a value of $117 (1.170 × $100) for semiannual compounding and a value of $117.20 (1.172 × $100) for quarterly compounding.

Calculator If the calculator were used for the semiannual compounding calculation, the number of periods would be 4 and the interest rate would be 4 percent. The future value of $116.99 should appear on the calculator display.

Inputs: 100 | 4 | 4 | 0

Functions: PV | N | I | PMT | CPT | FV

Output: 116.99

For the quarterly compounding case, the number of periods would be 8 and the interest rate would be 2 percent. The future value of $117.17 should appear on the calculator display.

Inputs: 100 | 8 | 2 | 0

Functions: PV | N | I | PMT | CPT | FV

Output: 117.17

Comparing the calculator and table values, we can see that the calculator values generally agree with those values given in Table 6.3, but are more precise because the table factors have been rounded.

Spreadsheet For a spreadsheet, we would simply change the interest rate used in the formula or FV function in Spreadsheet Application 6.1, and add more rows to allow for increased number of periods.

Continuous Compounding

continuous compounding
Compounding of interest an infinite number of times per year at intervals of microseconds.

In the extreme case, interest can be compounded continuously. **Continuous compounding** involves compounding over every microsecond—the smallest time period imaginable. In this case, m in Equation 6.4 would approach infinity, and through the use of calculus, the equation would become:

$$FV_n \text{ (continuous compounding)} = PV \times (e^{k \times n}) \tag{6.5}$$

where e is a constant, which has a value of 2.7183.[8] The future value interest factor for continuous compounding is therefore

$$FVIF\ (k\%, n \text{ per}) \text{ (continuous compounding)} = e^{k \times n} \tag{6.6}$$

Example To find the value at the end of 2 years ($n = 2$) of Fred Moreno's $100 deposit ($PV = \$100$) in an account paying 8 percent annual interest ($k = 0.08$), compounded continuously, we can substitute into Equation 6.5:

$$FV_2 \text{ (continuous compounding)} = \$100 \times e^{.08 \times 2} = \$100 \times 2.7183^{.16}$$
$$= \$100 \times 1.1735 = \$117.35$$

Calculator To find this value using the calculator, first find the value of $e^{.16}$ by keying in .16 and then pressing **2nd**, and then e^x to get 1.1735. Next multiply this value by $100 to get the future value of $117.35.

Inputs: .16 | 2nd | e^x

Outputs: 1.1735109 | X | 100 | = | 117.35

8. Most calculators have the exponential function, typically noted by e^x, built into them. On some calculators, you may have to press the **2nd** key to access the e^x function. This is illustrated in the following example. (On some calculators, **2nd** may not have to be pressed before pressing e^x.)

The future value with continuous compounding therefore equals \$117.35, which, as expected, is larger than the future value of interest compounded semiannually (\$116.99) or quarterly (\$117.17). As was noted earlier, \$117.35 is the largest amount that would result from compounding the 8 percent interest more frequently than annually, given an initial deposit of \$100 and a 2-year time horizon. But, unless the amount invested is very large, the differences between monthly, weekly, daily, or continuous compounding are slight. Note that for Fred Moreno, the difference between weekly, daily, and continuous compounding is just one penny after two years! ▲

Nominal and Effective Annual Rates of Interest

nominal (stated) annual rate
Contractual annual rate of interest charged by a lender or promised by a borrower.

effective (true) annual rate (EAR)
The annual rate of interest actually paid or earned.

Both consumers and businesses need to make objective comparisons of loan costs or investment returns over different compounding periods. In order to put interest rates on a common basis, to allow comparison, we distinguish between nominal and effective annual rates. The **nominal,** or **stated, annual rate** is the contractual annual rate charged by a lender or promised by a borrower. The **effective,** or **true, annual rate (EAR)** is the annual rate of interest actually paid or earned.

The effective annual rate reflects the impact of compounding frequency, whereas the nominal annual rate does not. In terms of interest earnings, the EAR is probably best viewed as the *annual* interest rate that would result in the same future value as that resulting from application of the nominal annual rate using the stated compounding frequency. It increases with increased compounding frequency.

Using the notation introduced earlier, we can calculate the effective annual rate, EAR, by substituting values for the nominal annual rate, k, and the compounding frequency, m, into Equation 6.7.

$$\text{EAR} = \left(1 + \frac{k}{m}\right)^m - 1 \qquad (6.7)$$

We can apply this equation using data from preceding examples.

Example ▼ Fred Moreno wishes to find the effective annual rate associated with an 8 percent nominal annual rate ($k = 0.08$) when interest is compounded (1) annually ($m = 1$); (2) semiannually ($m = 2$); (3) quarterly ($m = 4$); and (4) daily ($m = 365$). Substituting these values into Equation 6.7, we get the following:

1. *For annual compounding:*

$$\text{EAR} = \left(1 + \frac{0.08}{1}\right)^1 - 1 = (1 + 0.08)^1 - 1 = 1 + 0.08 - 1 = 0.08 = 8\%$$

2. *For semiannual compounding:*

$$\text{EAR} = \left(1 + \frac{0.08}{2}\right)^2 - 1 = (1 + 0.04)^2 - 1 = 1.0816 - 1 = 0.0816 = 8.16\%$$

3. *For quarterly compounding:*

$$\text{EAR} = \left(1 + \frac{0.08}{4}\right)^4 - 1 = (1 + 0.02)^4 - 1 = 1.082432158 - 1 = 0.0824322 = 8.24322\%$$

4. *For daily compounding:*

$$\text{EAR} = \left(1 + \frac{0.08}{365}\right)^{365} - 1 = (1.000219178)^{365} - 1 = 8.327757\%$$

These values demonstrate two important points: (1) The nominal and effective rates are equivalent for annual compounding, and (2) the effective annual rate increases with increasing compounding frequency.[9]

When dealing with interest rates, consumers should be aware of the effect compounding has on the effective annual rate. For example, the interest rate on credit cards is often quoted on a monthly basis. The **annual percentage rate (APR)** is the *nominal annual rate* found by multiplying the periodic rate by the number of periods in 1 year. For example, a bank credit card that charges 1½ percent per month would have an APR of 18 percent (1.5% per month × 12 months per year). The effective interest rate, however, is a much higher 19.56 percent $[(1.015)^{12} - 1]$. This is the effective rate paid when a consumer carries credit card balances from one month to the next.

annual percentage rate (APR)
The *nominal annual rate* of interest, found by multiplying the periodic rate by the number of periods in 1 year.

? Review Questions

6–4 How is the *compounding process* related to the payment of interest on savings? What is the general equation for the future value, FV_n, in period n if PV dollars are deposited in an account paying k percent annual interest?

6–5 What effect would (**a**) a *decrease* in the interest rate or (**b**) an *increase* in the holding period of a deposit have on its future value? Why?

6–6 What effect does compounding interest more frequently than annually have on (**a**) the future value generated by a beginning principal and (**b**) the *effective annual rate (EAR)*? Why?

6–7 What is *continuous compounding*? How does the magnitude of the future value of a given deposit at a given rate of interest obtained by using continuous compounding compare to the value obtained by using annual or any other compounding period?

6–8 Differentiate between a *nominal annual rate* and an *effective annual rate (EAR)*. Define *annual percentage rate* (APR). Under what compounding period are the APR and the EAR equivalent?

---

9. The *maximum* effective annual rate for a given nominal annual rate occurs when interest is compounded *continuously*. The effective annual rate for this extreme case can be found by using the following equation:

$$\text{EAR (continuous compounding)} = e^{k} - 1 \qquad (6.7a)$$

For the 8 percent nominal annual rate ($k = 0.08$), substitution into Equation 6.7a results in an effective annual rate of

$$e^{.08} - 1 = 1.083287065 - 1 = 0.0832871 = 8.32871\%$$

in the case of continuous compounding. This is the highest effective annual rate attainable with an 8 percent nominal rate.

6.3 Future Value of an Annuity

annuity
A stream of equal annual cash flows. These cash flows can be *inflows* of returns earned on investments or *outflows* of funds invested to earn future returns.

ordinary annuity
An annuity for which the cash flow occurs at the *end* of each period.

annuity due
An annuity for which the cash flow occurs at the *beginning* of each period.

An **annuity** is a stream of equal annual cash flows. These cash flows can be *inflows* of returns earned on investments or *outflows* of funds invested to earn future returns. Before looking at how to calculate the future value of annuities, we should distinguish between the two basic types of annuities.

Types of Annuities

The two basic types of annuities are the *ordinary annuity* and the *annuity due.* For an **ordinary annuity,** the *cash flow occurs at the end of each period.* For an **annuity due,** the *cash flow occurs at the beginning of each period.*

Example

Fran Abrams is wondering how much money she will have if she saves the same amount each year for the next five years. She can choose between two annuities: A and B. Both are 5-year, $1,000 annuities; annuity A is an ordinary annuity, and annuity B is an annuity due. To better understand the difference between these annuities, she has illustrated the cash flow streams in Table 6.4 and in the time line below the table. Note that the amount of each annuity totals $5,000, but the two annuities differ in the timing of their cash flows: the cash flows are received sooner with the annuity due than with the ordinary annuity.

Hint
The most common occurrences of annuities in business are fixed loan payments, the interest on corporate bonds, and the dividends paid to preferred shareholders. In all three of these examples, the amount of payment at the end of each time period is the same.

Although the cash flows of both annuities in Table 6.4 total $5,000, the annuity due would have a higher future value than the ordinary annuity because each of its five annual cash flows can earn a return for one year more than each of the ordinary annuity's cash flows. In general, as is demonstrated below, *the future value of an annuity due is always greater than the future value of an otherwise identical ordinary annuity.*

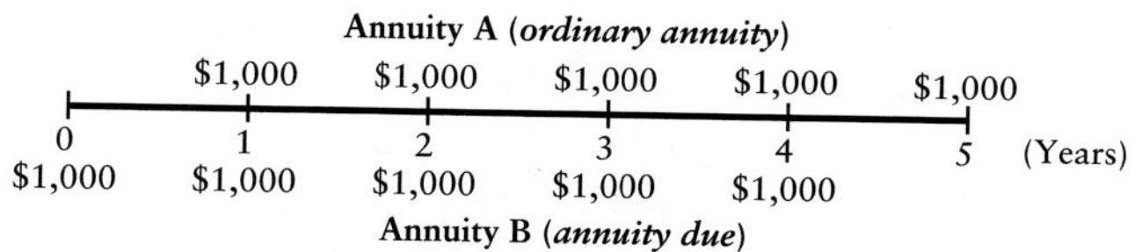

TABLE 6.4 Comparison of Ordinary Annuity and Annuity Due Cash Flows ($1,000, 5 Years)

	Annual cash flows	
Time[a]	Annuity A (ordinary)	Annuity B (annuity due)
0	$ 0	$1,000
1	1,000	1,000
2	1,000	1,000
3	1,000	1,000
4	1,000	1,000
5	1,000	0
Totals	$5,000	$5,000

[a]Time 0 is now, at the beginning of year 1. Time 1 is the end of year 1. It is also the beginning of year 2. So for the ordinary annuity, we wait one full year for the first $1,000 payment. For the annuity due, we receive the first $1,000 payment now, and another at the end of year 1, the beginning of year 2.

Because ordinary annuities are more frequently used in finance, *unless otherwise specified, the term "annuity" is used throughout this book to refer to ordinary annuities.*

Finding the Future Value of an Ordinary Annuity

The calculations required to find the future value of an ordinary annuity can be illustrated by the following example.

Example Fran Abrams wishes to determine how much money she will have at the end of 5 years if she deposits $1,000 annually at the *end of each* of the next 5 years into an investment account with a 7 percent annual return. (Her cash flows are represented by annuity A—the ordinary annuity—in Table 6.4.) Table 6.5 presents the calculations required to find the future value of this annuity at the end of year 5 using Table A-1, the future value interest factors.

Time Line This situation is depicted on the following time line:

Time line for future value of an ordinary annuity ($1,000 end-of-year deposit, earning 7%, at the end of 5 years)

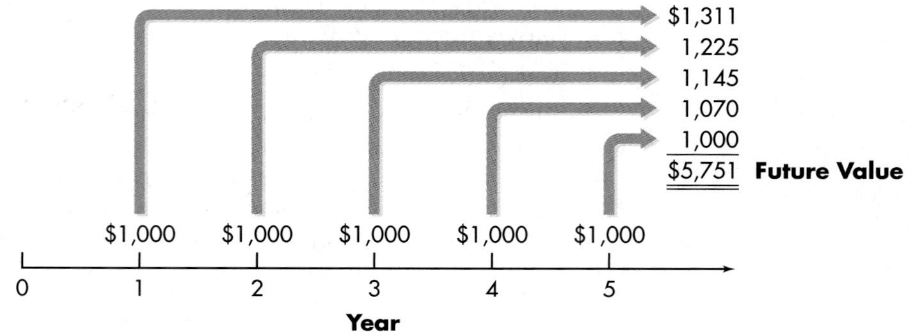

As the table and figure show, at the end of year 5, Fran will have $5,751 in her account. Column 2 of the table indicates that because the deposits are made at the end of the year, the first deposit will earn interest for 4 years, the second for 3 years, and so on. The future value interest factors in column 3 correspond to these interest-earning periods and the 7 percent rate of interest.

TABLE 6.5 The Future Value of a $1,000 5-Year Ordinary Annuity Compounded at 7%

Year	Amount deposited (1)	Number of years compounded (2)	Future value interest factors from Table A-1 (3)	Future value at end of year [(1) × (3)] (4)
1	$1,000	4	1.311	$1,311
2	1,000	3	1.225	1,225
3	1,000	2	1.145	1,145
4	1,000	1	1.070	1,070
5	1,000	0	1.000	1,000
		Future value of ordinary annuity at end of year 5		$5,751

Simplifying the Future Value of an Annuity Calculation

Hint
This is true only in the case of an annuity, because only with an annuity are the payments equal.

The calculations in the preceding example can be simplified somewhat, because each of the factors is multiplied by the same dollar amount. The calculations can be expressed as follows:

$$\begin{aligned}\text{Future value of annuity at end of year 5} &= [\$1{,}000 \times (1.311)] \\ &+ [\$1{,}000 \times (1.225)] \\ &+ [\$1{,}000 \times (1.145)] \\ &+ [\$1{,}000 \times (1.070)] \\ &+ [\$1{,}000 \times (1.000)] \\ &= \$5{,}751\end{aligned}$$

Factoring out the $1,000, we can rewrite the above expression as:

$$\begin{aligned}\text{Future value of annuity at end of year 5} &= \$1{,}000 \times (1.311 + 1.225 \\ &+ 1.145 + 1.070 + 1.000) = \$5{,}751\end{aligned}$$

This analysis indicates that to find the future value of the annuity, the annual cash flow must be multiplied by the sum of the appropriate future value interest factors, and it leads to a more general formula presented below.

Using Tables, Calculators, and Spreadsheets to Find Future Value of an Annuity

Annuity calculations can be simplified by using future value interest factors for annuities, a financial calculator, or a spreadsheet. A table for the future value of a $1 *ordinary annuity* is given in Appendix Table A-2. The factors in the table are derived by summing the future value interest factors for the appropriate number of years. In the expression above, summing these factors (the terms in parentheses) results in:

$$\begin{aligned}\text{Future value of annuity at end of year 5} &= \$1{,}000 \times (5.751) \\ &= \$5{,}751\end{aligned}$$

future value interest factor for an annuity (*FVIFa*)
The multiplier used to calculate the future value of an *ordinary annuity* at a specified interest rate over a given period of time.

The formula for the **future value interest factor for an annuity** when interest is compounded annually at k percent for n periods, $FVIFa$ (k%, n per), is:

$$FVIFa\ (k\%, n \text{ per}) = \sum_{t=1}^{n} (1 + k)^{t-1} \tag{6.8}$$

The mathematical expression used to calculate the future value interest factor for an ordinary annuity is:

$$FVIFa\ (k\%, n \text{ per}) = \left[\frac{(1 + k)^n - 1}{k}\right] \tag{6.9}$$

This expression is especially useful in the absence of the appropriate financial tables, a financial calculator, or a spreadsheet.

Now that we know how $FVIFa$ (k%, n per) is calculated, let's put it to use to find the future value of an annuity. Using FVA_n for the future value of an n-year annuity, PMT for the amount to be deposited annually at the end of each year, and $FVIFa$ (k%, n per) for the appropriate *future value interest factor for a one-*

dollar annuity compounded at k *percent for* n *years,* the relationship among these variables can be expressed as follows:

$$FVA_n = PMT \times FVIFa\,(k\%, n \text{ per}) \qquad (6.10)$$

An example will illustrate this calculation using the table, a financial calculator, and a spreadsheet.

Example As noted earlier, Fran Abrams wishes to find the future value (FVA_n) at the end of 5 years (n) of an annual *end-of-year deposit* of \$1,000 (PMT) into an account providing a 7 percent annual return (k) during the next 5 years.

Table The appropriate future value interest factor for an ordinary 5-year annuity at 7 percent found in Table A-2, is 5.751. Using Equation 6.10, the \$1,000 deposit × 5.751 results in a future value for the annuity of \$5,751.

Calculator Using the calculator inputs shown, you should find the future value of the ordinary annuity to be \$5,750.74—a more precise answer than that found using the table.

Inputs:	1000	5	7	0		
Functions:	PMT	N	I	PV	CPT	FV
Output:						5750.74

Spreadsheet With a spreadsheet, we can use the series of annual deposits and interest rate to calculate the dollar returns earned on the deposits and thus the future value. Or one could use the preprogrammed Excel future value function. Both are illustrated in Spreadsheet Application 6.2. The general format for the Excel FV function is: =FV(k%, per, PMT, PV, Type). For this function, either the *PMT* or *PV* must have a value provided. For the variable not used, simply input ,,. The "Type" variable needs to be used only if a *PMT* was made at the beginning of the period, as discussed below.

Finding the Future Value of an Annuity Due

The calculations to find the future value of the less common form of an annuity—an annuity due—can be demonstrated by the following example.

Example Fran Abrams wishes to find out how much money she would have at the end of 5 years if she deposits \$1,000 annually at the *beginning of each* of the next 5 years into an investment account providing a 7 percent annual return. Her cash flows in this case are represented by annuity B—the annuity due—in Table 6.4. Table 6.6 demonstrates the calculations required.

TABLE 6.6 The Future Value of a $1,000 5-Year Annuity Due Compounded at 7%

Year[a]	Amount deposited (1)	Number of years compounded (2)	Future value interest factors from Table A-1 (3)	Future value at end of year [(1) × (3)] (4)
0	$1,000	5	1.403	$1,403
1	1,000	4	1.311	1,311
2	1,000	3	1.225	1,225
3	1,000	2	1.145	1,145
4	1,000	1	1.070	1,070
		Future value of annuity due at end of year		$6,154

[a]Years 0, 1, 2, 3, and 4 are equivalent to the beginnings of years 1, 2, 3, 4, and 5, respectively.

Time Line This situation is depicted on the following time line:

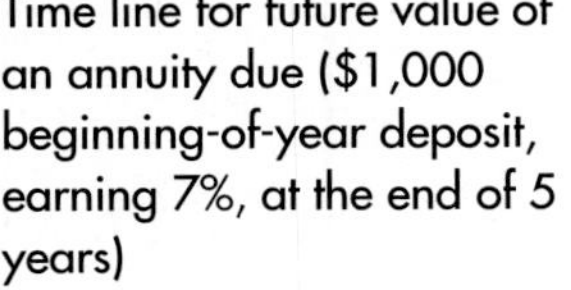

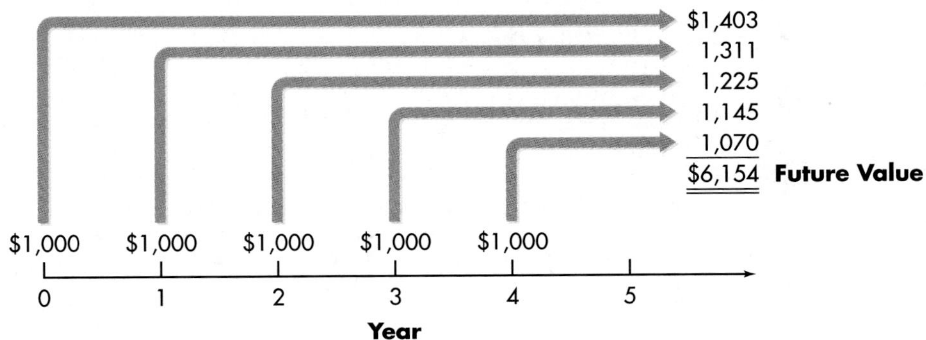

As the table and figure show, at the end of year 5, Fran will have $6,154 in her account. Column 2 of the table indicates that because the deposits are made at the beginning of each year, the first deposit earns interest for 5 years, the second for 4 years, and so on. The future value interest factors in column 3 correspond to those interest-earning periods and the 7 percent rate of interest.

Using Tables, Calculators, and Spreadsheets to Find Future Value of an Annuity Due

A simple conversion can be applied to use the future value interest factors for an ordinary annuity in Table A-2 with annuities due. Equation 6.11 presents this conversion:

$$FVIFad\,(k\%, n \text{ per}) = FVIFa\,(k\%, n \text{ per}) \times (1 + k) \quad (6.11)$$

This equation says that the future value interest factor for an n-year annuity due at k percent can be found merely by multiplying the future value interest factor

6.2 SPREADSHEET APPLICATION

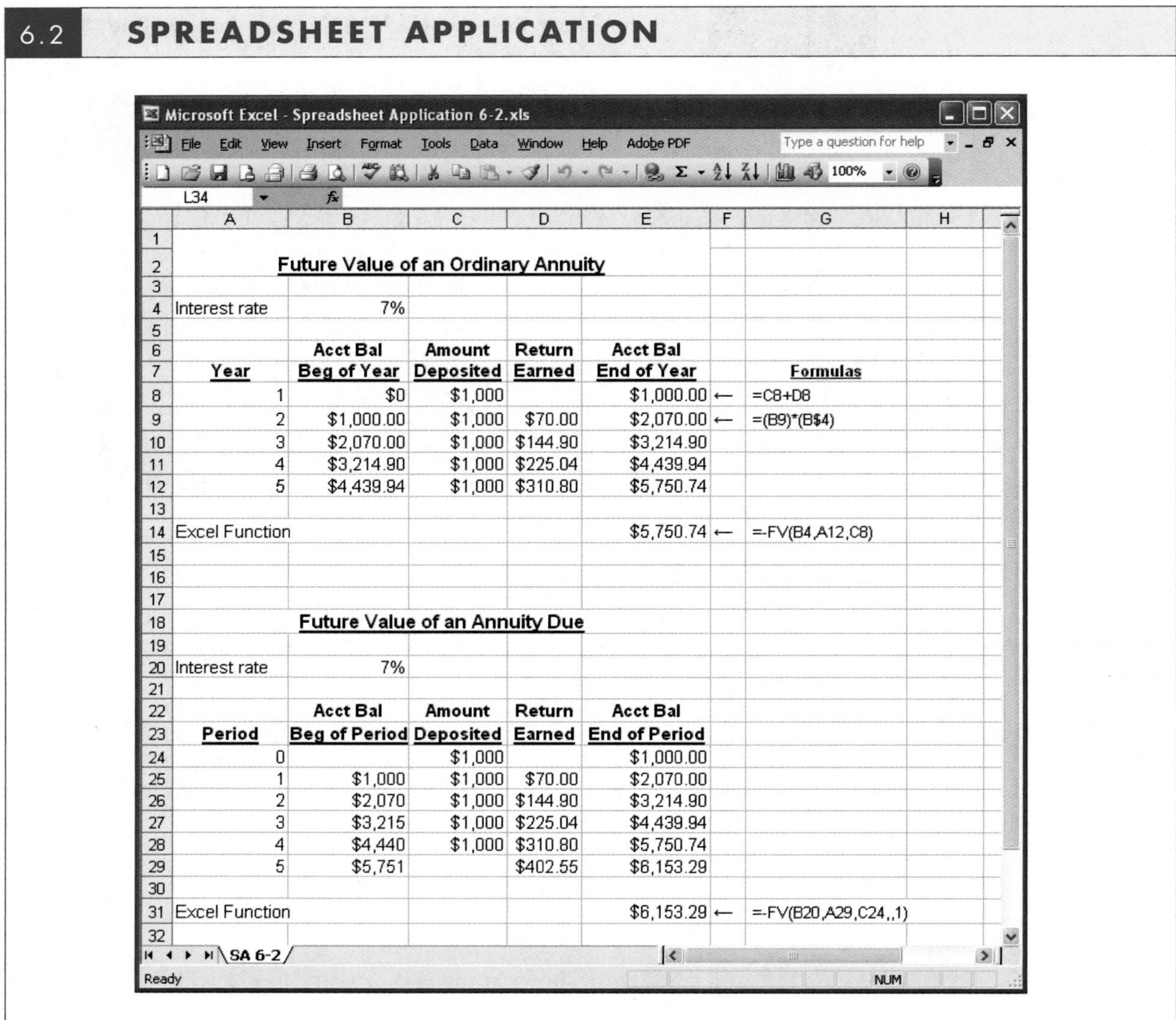

Microsoft Excel - Spreadsheet Application 6-2.xls

	A	B	C	D	E	F	G
1							
2		**Future Value of an Ordinary Annuity**					
3							
4	Interest rate	7%					
5							
6		Acct Bal	Amount	Return	Acct Bal		
7	Year	Beg of Year	Deposited	Earned	End of Year		Formulas
8	1	$0	$1,000		$1,000.00	←	=C8+D8
9	2	$1,000.00	$1,000	$70.00	$2,070.00	←	=(B9)*(B$4)
10	3	$2,070.00	$1,000	$144.90	$3,214.90		
11	4	$3,214.90	$1,000	$225.04	$4,439.94		
12	5	$4,439.94	$1,000	$310.80	$5,750.74		
13							
14	Excel Function				$5,750.74	←	=-FV(B4,A12,C8)
15							
16							
17							
18		**Future Value of an Annuity Due**					
19							
20	Interest rate	7%					
21							
22		Acct Bal	Amount	Return	Acct Bal		
23	Period	Beg of Period	Deposited	Earned	End of Period		
24	0		$1,000		$1,000.00		
25	1	$1,000	$1,000	$70.00	$2,070.00		
26	2	$2,070	$1,000	$144.90	$3,214.90		
27	3	$3,215	$1,000	$225.04	$4,439.94		
28	4	$4,440	$1,000	$310.80	$5,750.74		
29	5	$5,751		$402.55	$6,153.29		
30							
31	Excel Function				$6,153.29	←	=-FV(B20,A29,C24,,1)
32							

SA 6-2

for an ordinary annuity at k percent for n years by $(1 + k)$. Why is this adjustment necessary? Because each cash flow of an annuity due earns interest for 1 year more than an ordinary annuity (from the start to the end of the year). Multiplying $FVIFa(k\%, n \text{ per})$ by $(1 + k)$ simply adds an additional year's return to *each* annuity cash flow. An example will demonstrate how to use Equation 6.11, financial calculator, and a spreadsheet to find the future value of an annuity due.

Example As noted, Fran Abrams wishes to find the future value (FVA_n) at the end of 5 years (n) of an annual *beginning-of-year deposit* of $1,000 (PMT) into an account providing a 7 percent annual return (k) during the next 5 years.

Table Substituting $k = 7\%$ and $n = 5$ years into Equation 6.11, with the aid of the appropriate interest factor from Table A-2, we get:

$$FVIFad\ (7\%, 5\ \text{per}) = FVIFa\ (7\%, 5\text{yrs}) \times (1 + 0.07) = 5.751 \times 1.07 = 6.154$$

Then, substituting $PMT = \$1{,}000$ and $FVIFad$ (7%, 5 per) = 6.154 into Equation 6.10, we get a future value for the annuity due:

$$FVad_5 = \$1{,}000 \times 6.154 = \$6{,}154$$

Calculator Before using your calculator to find the future value of an annuity due, depending upon the specific calculator, you must either switch it to BEGIN mode or use the DUE key. Then, using the inputs shown, you should find the future value of the annuity due to be $6,153.29.

Inputs:	1000	5	7	0		
Functions:	PMT	N	I	PV	CPT	FV
Output:						6153.29

Note: Because we almost always assume end of period cash flows, *be sure to switch your calculator back to* END *mode when you have completed your annuity due calculations.*

Spreadsheet With a spreadsheet, we can modify the ordinary annuity example to calculate one more year of returns and then determine the future value, or we could use the preprogrammed Excel future value function. Both are illustrated in Spreadsheet Application 6.2. Note that in this case, the "Type" variable is set at 1, to indicate that we are dealing with an annuity due and that the *PMT* is made at the beginning of the period.

Comparison with an Ordinary Annuity

As noted earlier, the future value of an annuity due is always greater than the future value of an otherwise identical ordinary annuity. We saw this in comparing the future values at the end of year 5 of Fran Abrams' two annuities:

Ordinary annuity	$5,750.74
Annuity due	$6,153.29

Because the annuity due's cash flow occurs at the beginning of the period rather than at the end, its future value is greater. In the example, Fran would earn $402.55 more with the annuity due.

In spite of their superior earning power, annuities due are much less frequently encountered. Throughout the remainder of this text we therefore emphasize ordinary annuities. To reiterate, *unless otherwise specified, the term "annuity" refers to ordinary annuities, to which the* FVIFa *factors in Table A-2 apply.* Also, the annuity function (the PMT key) on financial calculators is preprogrammed to assume the inputted amount is an ordinary annuity.

? Review Questions

6–9 Differentiate between (**a**) an *ordinary annuity* and (**b**) an *annuity due*. Which always has greater future value for otherwise identical annuities and interest rates? Why? Which form is more common?

6–10 Explain how to conveniently determine the future value of an ordinary annuity. How can the future value interest factors for an ordinary annuity be conveniently modified to find the future value of an annuity due?

6.4 Present Value of a Single Amount

present value
The current dollar value of a future amount; the amount of money that would have to be invested today at a given rate of return over a specified period to equal the future amount.

The present value is used to determine the value today of a future amount of money. **Present value** is the current dollar value of a future amount—the amount of money that would have to be invested today at a given rate of return over a specified period to equal the future amount. Present value depends largely on the investment opportunities of the recipient and the point in time at which the amount is to be received. This section explores the present value of a single amount.

The Concept of Present Value

discounting cash flows
The process of finding present values; the inverse of compounding interest.

The process of finding present values is often referred to as **discounting cash flows.** It is concerned with answering the question: "If I can earn k percent on my money, what is the most I would be willing to pay now for an opportunity to receive some future amount of dollars, n periods from today?" This process is actually the inverse of compounding interest. Instead of finding the future value of present dollars invested at a given rate, discounting determines the present value of a future amount, assuming the opportunity to earn a certain return, k, on the money. This annual rate of return is variously referred to as the *discount rate, required return, cost of capital,* or *opportunity cost.*[10] These terms will be used interchangeably in this text.

Example ▼ Paul Shorter has an opportunity to receive \$300 one year from now. If he can earn 6 percent on his investments in the normal course of events, what is the most he should pay now for this opportunity? To answer this question, he must determine how many dollars would have to be invested at 6 percent today to have \$300 one year from now. By letting PV equal this unknown amount and using the same notation as in the future value discussion:

$$PV \times (1 + 0.06) = \$300$$

Solving this equation for PV gives us:

$$PV = \frac{\$300}{(1+0.06)}$$
$$= \$283.02$$

10. The theoretical underpinning of this "required return" is introduced in Chapter 7 and further refined in subsequent chapters.

The "present value" of \$300 received one year from today, given an opportunity cost of 6 percent, is \$283.02. That is, the investment of \$283.02 today at a 6 percent rate of return would result in \$300 at the end of one year.

The Equation for Present Value

The present value of a future amount can be found mathematically by solving Equation 6.1 for PV. In other words, the present value, PV, of some future amount, FV_n, to be received n periods from now, assuming an opportunity cost of k, is calculated as:

$$PV = \frac{FV_n}{(1+k)^n} = FV_n \times \left[\frac{1}{(1+k)^n}\right] \quad (6.12)$$

Note that the general equation for present value and the equation used in the above example are the same. The use of this equation can be illustrated by a simple example.

Example Pam Valenti wishes to find the present value of \$1,700 that will be received 8 years from now. Pam's opportunity cost is 8%. Substituting FV_8 = \$1,700, n = 8, and k = 0.08 into Equation 6.12 yields:

$$PV = \frac{\$1{,}700}{(1+.08)^8} = \frac{\$1{,}700}{1.8509302} = \$918.46$$

Time Line This analysis can be depicted on the following time line:

Time line for present value of a single amount (\$1,700 future amount, discounted at 8%, from the end of 8 years)

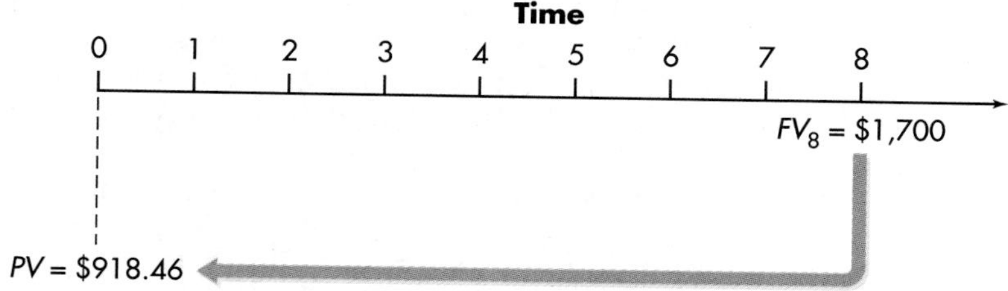

Using Tables, Calculators, and Spreadsheets to Find Present Value

present value interest factor
The multiplier used to calculate at a specified discount rate the present value of an amount to be received in a future period.

The present value calculation can be simplified by using a **present value interest factor.** This factor is the multiplier used to calculate at a specified discount rate the present value of an amount to be received in a future period. The present value interest factor for the present value of \$1 discounted at k percent for n periods is referred to as $PVIF$ (k%, n per):

$$\text{Present value interest factor} = PVIF\,(k\%, n \text{ per}) = \frac{1}{(1+k)^n} \quad (6.13)$$

Appendix Table A-3 presents present value interest factors for \$1. By letting $PVIF(k\%, n \text{ per})$ represent the appropriate factor, we can rewrite Equation 6.12:

$$PV = FV_n \times PVIF\,(k\%, n \text{ per}) \quad (6.14)$$

This expression indicates that to find the present value of an amount to be received in a future period, n, we have merely to multiply the future amount, FV_n, by the appropriate present value interest factor.

Example As noted, Pam Valenti wishes to find the present value of \$1,700 to be received 8 years from now, assuming an 8 percent rate of return.

Table The present value interest factor for 8 percent and 8 years, *PVIF*(8%, 8 per), found in Table A-3, is 0.540. Multiplying the \$1,700 future value by this factor results in a present value of \$918.

Calculator Using the calculator's financial functions and the inputs shown below, you should find the present value to be \$918.46.

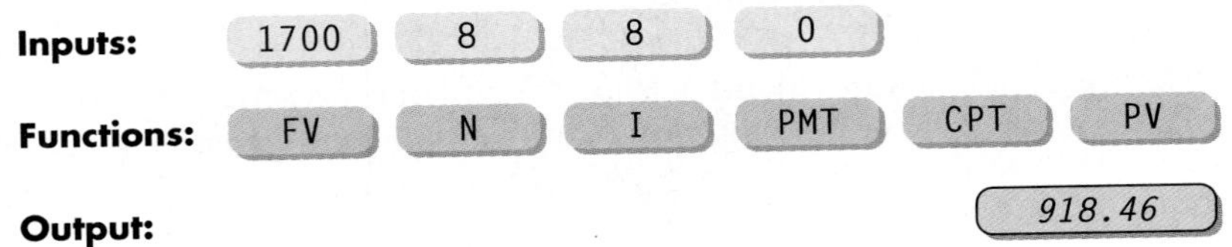

The value obtained with the equation and calculator—\$918.46—is more accurate than the values found using the table.

Spreadsheet With a spreadsheet, one could use Equation 6.12 to calculate present values, or one could use the preprogrammed Excel present value function. Both are illustrated in Spreadsheet Application 6.3. Note that in this Application, we have provided present value calculations for five discount rates (k%) from 0% to 16%. The general format for the Excel present value function is: =PV(k%, per, PMT, FV, Type). For this function, either the *PMT* or *FV* must have a value provided. For the function not used, simply input ,,. As already discussed, the "Type" variable is used only if we are dealing with an annuity due.

A Graphic View of Present Value

Remember that present value calculations assume that the future values are measured at the *end* of the given period. The relationship among various discount rates, time periods, and the present value of \$1,000 is illustrated in Figure 6.6. Everything else being equal, the figure clearly shows that: (1) the higher the discount rate, the lower the present value, and (2) the longer the period of time, the lower the present value. Also note that given a discount rate of 0 percent, the present value always equals the future value (\$1,000). But for any discount rate greater than zero, the present value is less than the future value of \$1,000.

6.3 SPREADSHEET APPLICATION

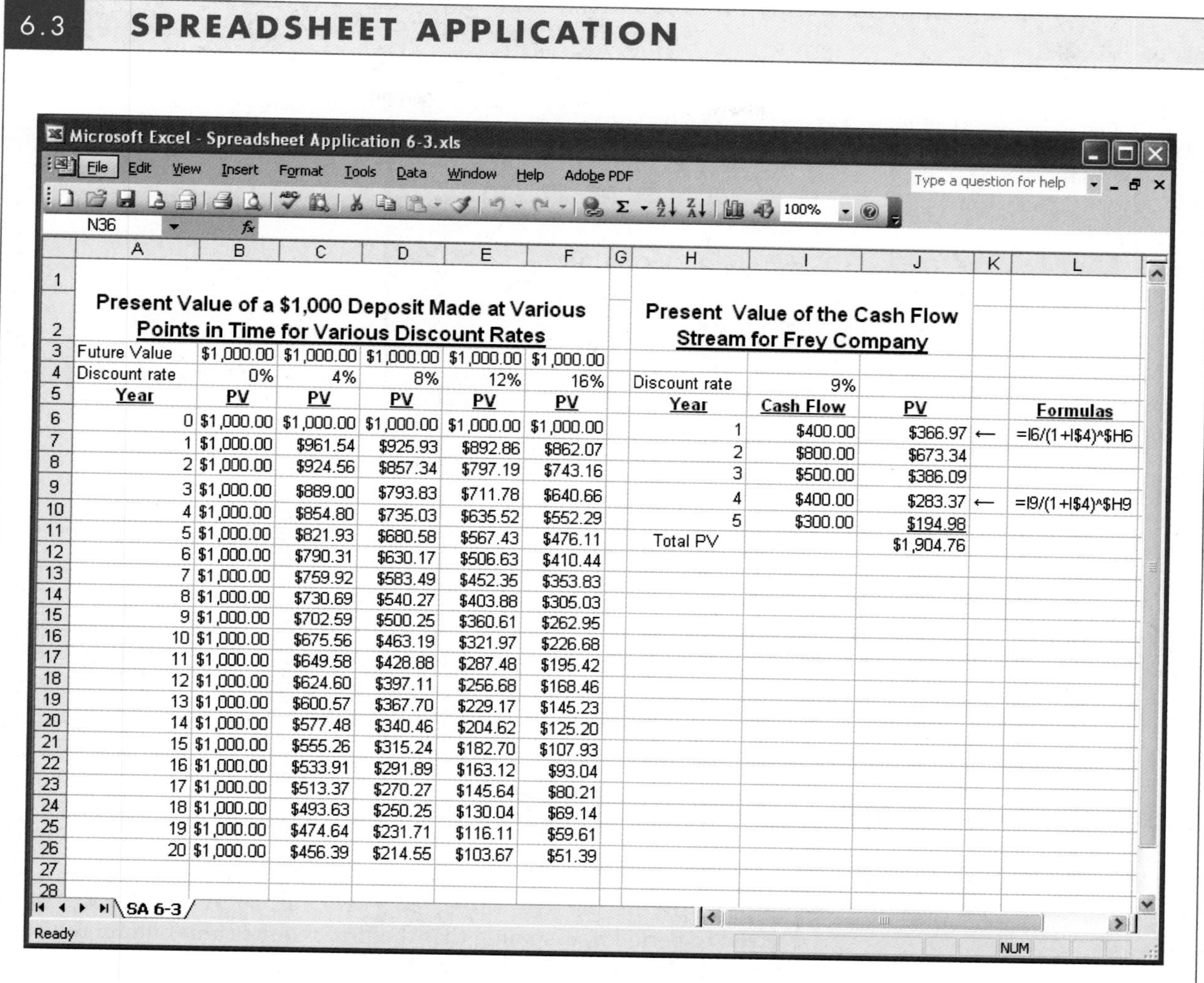

Present Value of a $1,000 Deposit Made at Various Points in Time for Various Discount Rates

Future Value	$1,000.00	$1,000.00	$1,000.00	$1,000.00	$1,000.00
Discount rate	0%	4%	8%	12%	16%
Year	**PV**	**PV**	**PV**	**PV**	**PV**
0	$1,000.00	$1,000.00	$1,000.00	$1,000.00	$1,000.00
1	$1,000.00	$961.54	$925.93	$892.86	$862.07
2	$1,000.00	$924.56	$857.34	$797.19	$743.16
3	$1,000.00	$889.00	$793.83	$711.78	$640.66
4	$1,000.00	$854.80	$735.03	$635.52	$552.29
5	$1,000.00	$821.93	$680.58	$567.43	$476.11
6	$1,000.00	$790.31	$630.17	$506.63	$410.44
7	$1,000.00	$759.92	$583.49	$452.35	$353.83
8	$1,000.00	$730.69	$540.27	$403.88	$305.03
9	$1,000.00	$702.59	$500.25	$360.61	$262.95
10	$1,000.00	$675.56	$463.19	$321.97	$226.68
11	$1,000.00	$649.58	$428.88	$287.48	$195.42
12	$1,000.00	$624.60	$397.11	$256.68	$168.46
13	$1,000.00	$600.57	$367.70	$229.17	$145.23
14	$1,000.00	$577.48	$340.46	$204.62	$125.20
15	$1,000.00	$555.26	$315.24	$182.70	$107.93
16	$1,000.00	$533.91	$291.89	$163.12	$93.04
17	$1,000.00	$513.37	$270.27	$145.64	$80.21
18	$1,000.00	$493.63	$250.25	$130.04	$69.14
19	$1,000.00	$474.64	$231.71	$116.11	$59.61
20	$1,000.00	$456.39	$214.55	$103.67	$51.39

Present Value of the Cash Flow Stream for Frey Company

Discount rate	9%			
Year	**Cash Flow**	**PV**		**Formulas**
1	$400.00	$366.97	←	=I6/(1+I$4)^$H6
2	$800.00	$673.34		
3	$500.00	$386.09		
4	$400.00	$283.37	←	=I9/(1+I$4)^$H9
5	$300.00	$194.98		
Total PV		$1,904.76		

Comparing Present Value and Future Value

We will close this section with a couple of important observations about present values. One is that the expression for the present value interest factor for k percent and n periods, $1/(1 + k)^n$, is the inverse of the future value interest factor for k percent and n periods, $(1 + k)^n$. This fact can be confirmed by dividing a present value interest factor for k percent and n periods, $PVIF(k\%, n \text{ per})$, into 1.0 and comparing the resulting value to the future value interest factor given in Table A-1 for k percent and n periods, $FVIF(k\%, n \text{ per})$. The two values will be equivalent.

Second, because of the relationship between present value interest factors and future value interest factors, we can find the present value interest factors given

FIGURE 6.6

Present Value Relationship

Discount rates, time periods, and present value of $1,000

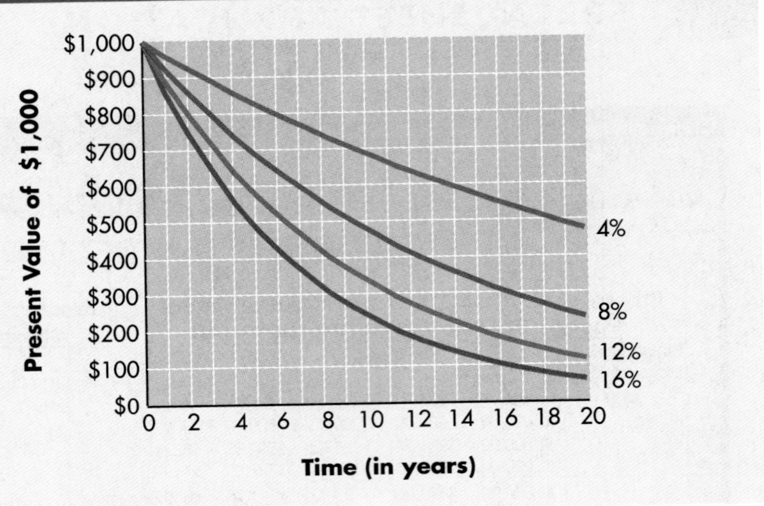

a table of future value interest factors, and vice versa. For example, the future value interest factor from Table A-1 for 10 percent and 5 periods is 1.611. Dividing this value into 1.0 yields 0.621, which is the present value interest factor given in Table A-3 for 10 percent and 5 periods.

? Review Questions

6–11 What is meant by "the present value of a future amount"? What is the equation for the present value, PV, of a future amount, FV_n, to be received in period n, assuming that the firm requires a minimum return of k percent? How are present value and future value calculations related?

6–12 What effect does *increasing* (**a**) the required return and (**b**) the time period have on the present value of a future amount? Why?

6.5 Present Value of Cash Flow Streams

mixed stream
A stream of cash flows of different amounts at various future points in time.

Quite often in finance there is a need to find the present value of a *stream* of cash flows that will be received in various future periods. Two basic types of cash flow streams are possible: the mixed stream and the annuity. A **mixed stream** is cash flows of different amounts at various future points in time. An *annuity*, as stated earlier, is a stream of cash flows of the same amount at various future points in time. Because certain shortcuts are possible in finding the present value of an annuity, we will discuss mixed streams and annuities separately. In addition, the present value of mixed streams with embedded annuities and perpetuities is considered in this section.

Present Value of a Mixed Stream

To find the present value of a mixed stream of cash flows, we determine the present value of each future amount, as described in the preceding section, and then add together all the individual present values.

Example ▼ Frey Company, a shoe manufacturer, has the opportunity to invest in a project that will provide the following mixed stream of cash flows over the next 5 years:

Year	Cash flow
1	$400
2	800
3	500
4	400
5	300

If the firm must earn at least 9 percent on its investments, what is the most it should pay for this opportunity?

Time Line This situation is depicted on the following time line. The present values shown are those calculated using a financial calculator.

Time line for present value of a mixed stream (end-of-year cash flows, discounted at 9%, over the corresponding number of years)

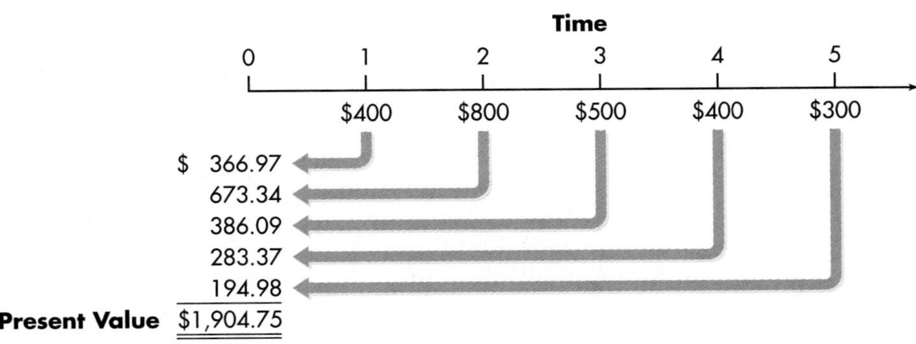

Table To solve this problem, determine the present value of each cash flow discounted at 9 percent for the appropriate number of years. The sum of these individual values is the present value of the total stream. The present value interest factors required are those shown in Table A-3. Table 6.7 presents the calculations needed to find the present value of the cash flow stream, which turns out to be $1,904.60.

Calculator You can use a calculator to find the present value of each individual cash flow, as demonstrated earlier; then add the present values to get the present value of the stream. However, most financial calculators have a function that allows you to punch in *all cash flows,* specify the discount rate, and then directly calculate the present value of the entire cash flow stream. Because calculators

TABLE 6.7 The Present Value of a Mixed Stream of Cash Flows

Year (n)	Cash flow (1)	*PVIF* (9%,*n* per)[a] (2)	Present value [(1) × (2)] (3)
1	$400	0.917	$ 366.80
2	800	0.842	673.60
3	500	0.772	386.00
4	400	0.708	283.20
5	300	0.650	195.00
		Present value of mixed stream	$1,904.60

[a]Present value interest factors at 9% are from Table A-3.

provide more precise solutions than those based on rounded table factors, the present value of Frey Company's cash flow stream found using a calculator is $1,904.75.

Spreadsheet By modifying Spreadsheet Application 6.3, the same figures as those shown in the time line can be determined. The modified spreadsheet is provided as part of Spreadsheet Application 6.3. Note that the present value equation, Equation 6.12, is used to calculate the values. All that has been done is that the discount rate is changed to 9 percent and cash flow values for the first five years have been changed.

Based on the analysis completed, it is clear that this investment project is worth, at most, $1,904.76 to Frey Company. If they paid this amount for the project, the company would receive exactly their 9 percent return. Frey should not pay more than that amount for the opportunity to receive these cash flows.

Present Value of an Annuity[11]

The method for finding the present value of an annuity is similar to that used for a mixed stream, but it can be simplified somewhat.

Example Braden Company, a small producer of plastic toys, wants to determine the value of an annuity that provides cash flows of $700 per year for 5 years. The firm requires a minimum return of 8 percent on all investments. Table 6.8 shows the long method for finding the present value of the annuity—which is the same as the method used for the mixed stream. This procedure yields a present value of $2,795.10.

11. Consistent with the discussions of future value, our concern here is only with *ordinary annuities*—those with cash flows occurring at the *end* of each period.

Time Line Similarly, this situation is depicted on the following time line. The present values shown are those calculated using a financial calculator.

Time line for present value of an annuity ($700 end-of-year cash flows, discounted at 8%, over 5 years)

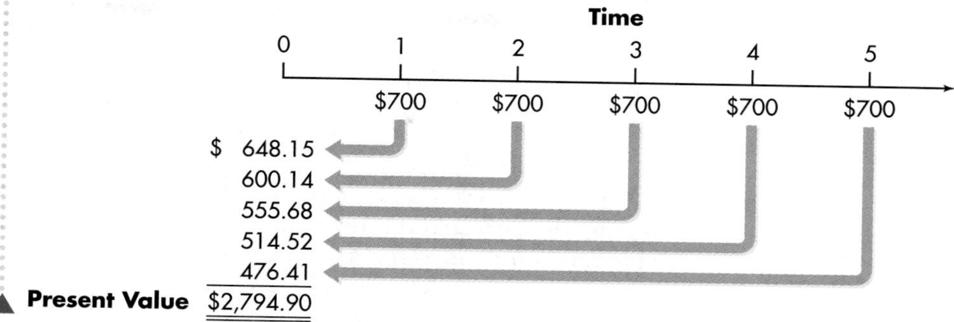

Simplifying the Present Value of an Annuity Calculation

The calculations in the preceding example can be simplified by recognizing that each of the five present value interest factors was multiplied by the same annual amount ($700). This calculation can be expressed as follows:

$$\begin{aligned}\text{Present value of annuity} &= [\$700 \times (0.926)] + [\$700 \times (0.857)] \\ &\quad + [\$700 \times (0.794)] + [\$700 \times (0.735)] \\ &\quad + [\$700 \times (0.681)] = \$2{,}795.10\end{aligned}$$

Hint
The simplification in the present value of an annuity calculation here is similar to that made earlier for the future value of an annuity.

Simplifying this equation by factoring out the $700 yields:

$$\begin{aligned}\text{Present value of annuity} &= \$700 \times (0.926 + 0.857 + 0.794 + 0.735 + 0.681) \\ &= \$2{,}795.10\end{aligned}$$

Thus, the present value of an annuity can be found by multiplying the annual cash flow by the sum of the appropriate present value interest factors. This equation leads to a more general formula introduced below.

Using Tables, Calculators, and Spreadsheets to Find the Present Value of an Annuity

Annuity calculations can be simplified by using an interest table for the present value of an annuity or a financial calculator. The values for the present value of a $1 annuity are given in Appendix Table A-4. The factors in the table are derived by summing the present value interest factors for the appropriate number of years. In the case of the above example, summing these factors results in:

$$\text{Present value of annuity} = \$700 \times (3.993) = \$2{,}795.10$$

present value interest factor for an annuity
The multiplier used to calculate the present value of an annuity at a specified discount rate over a given period of time.

The interest factors in Table A-4 actually represent the sum of the first n present value interest factors in Table A-3 for a given discount rate. The formula for the **present value interest factor for an annuity** with end-of-year cash flows that are discounted at k percent for n periods, $PVIFa(k\%, n \text{ per})$ is:[12]

$$PVIFa\ (k\%, n \text{ per}) = \sum_{t=1}^{n} \frac{1}{(1 + k)^t} \tag{6.15}$$

12. The present value interest factor for an annuity due can be found by multiplying the present value interest factor for an ordinary annuity, $PVIFa\ (k\%, n \text{ per})$, by $(1 + k)$.

The mathematical expression used to calculate the present value interest factor for an ordinary annuity is:

$$PVIFa\ (k\%, n \text{ per}) = \left[\frac{1 - \dfrac{1}{(1+k)^n}}{k}\right] \qquad (6.16)$$

This expression is especially useful in the absence of the appropriate financial tables, a financial calculator, or a spreadsheet.

By letting PVA_n equal the present value of an n-year annuity, PMT equal the amount to be received annually at the end of each year, and $PVIFa\ (k\%, n \text{ per})$ represent the appropriate value for the *present value interest factor for a one-dollar annuity discounted at* k *percent for* n *years,* the relationship among these variables can be expressed as follows:

$$PVA_n = PMT \times PVIFa\ (k\%, n \text{ per}) \qquad (6.17)$$

An example will illustrate this calculation using the table, a financial calculator, and a spreadsheet.

Example Braden Company, as noted, wants to find the present value of a 5-year annuity of \$700 assuming an 8 percent opportunity cost.

Table The present value interest factor for an annuity at 8 percent for 5 years ($PVIFa(8\%, 5 \text{ per})$) found in Table A-4, is 3.993. Using Equation 6.17, \$700 × 3.993 results in a present value of \$2,795.10, as shown in Table 6.8.

Calculator Using the calculator's financial functions and the inputs shown below, you should find the present value of the annuity to be \$2,794.90.

Inputs:	700	5	8	0		
Functions:	PMT	N	I	FV	CPT	PV
Output:						2794.90

TABLE 6.8 The Long Method for Finding the Present Value of an Annuity

Year (*n*)	Cash flow (1)	*PVIF* (8%,*n* per)[a] (2)	Present value [(1) × (2)] (3)
1	\$700	0.926	\$ 648.20
2	700	0.857	599.90
3	700	0.794	555.80
4	700	0.735	514.50
5	700	0.681	476.70
		Present value of annuity	\$2,795.10

[a]Present value interest factors at 8% are from Table A-3.

The value obtained with the calculator—$2,794.90—is more accurate than that found using the table.

Spreadsheet With a spreadsheet, we can use the series of annual cash flows and the discount rate to calculate the present value, or one could use the preprogrammed Excel present value function. Both are illustrated in Spreadsheet Application 6.4. The general format for the Excel PV function is: =PV(k%, per, PMT, FV, Type). For this function, either the *PMT* or *FV* must have a value provided. For the variable not used, simply input ,,. The "Type" variable needs to be used only if a *PMT* was made at the beginning of the period, as discussed previously in the chapter.

6.4 SPREADSHEET APPLICATION

Microsoft Excel - Spreadsheet Application 6-4.xls

	A	B	C	D	E
1					
2	**Present Value of an Ordinary Annuity**				
3					
4	Discount rate	8%			
5	**Year**	**Cash Flow**	**PV**		**Formulas**
6	1	$700.00	$648.15	←	=B6/(1+B$4)^$A6
7	2	$700.00	$600.14		
8	3	$700.00	$555.68		
9	4	$700.00	$514.52		
10	5	$700.00	$476.41		
11	Total PV		$2,794.90		
12					
13	Excel Function		$2,794.90	←	=-PV(B4,A10,B6)
14					
15					
16	**Present Value of a Mixed Stream with an Embedded Annuity**				
17					
18	Discount rate	9%			
19	**Year**	**Cash Flow**	**PV**		
20	1	$5,000.00	$4,587.16	←	=B20/(1+B$18)^$A20
21	2	$6,000.00	$5,050.08		
22	3	$7,000.00	$5,405.28		
23	4	$7,000.00	$4,958.98		
24	5	$7,000.00	$4,549.52		
25	6	$7,000.00	$4,173.87		
26	7	$8,000.00	$4,376.27		
27	8	$9,000.00	$4,516.80		
28	Total PV		$37,617.96	←	=SUM(C20:C27)
29					
30					

SA 6-4

Present Value of a Mixed Stream with an Embedded Annuity

Occasionally, a mixed stream of cash flows will have an annuity embedded within it. In such a case, the computations can be streamlined by the following three-step procedure:

Step 1 Find the present value of the annuity at the specified discount rate using the regular procedure. (*Note:* The resulting present value is measured at the beginning of the annuity, which is equivalent to the end of the period immediately preceding the start of the annuity.)

Step 2 Add the present value calculated in Step 1 to any other cash flow occurring in the period just before the start of that annuity, and eliminate the individual annuity cash flows, to determine the revised cash flows.

Step 3 Discount the revised cash flows found in Step 2 back to time zero in the normal fashion at the specified discount rate.

An example will illustrate this three-step procedure.

Example Powell Products expects an investment to generate the cash flows shown in column 1 of Table 6.9. If the firm must earn 9 percent on its investments, what is the present value of the expected cash flow stream?

Time Line The computation used in this situation is presented on the following time line. The present values shown are those calculated using a financial calculator.

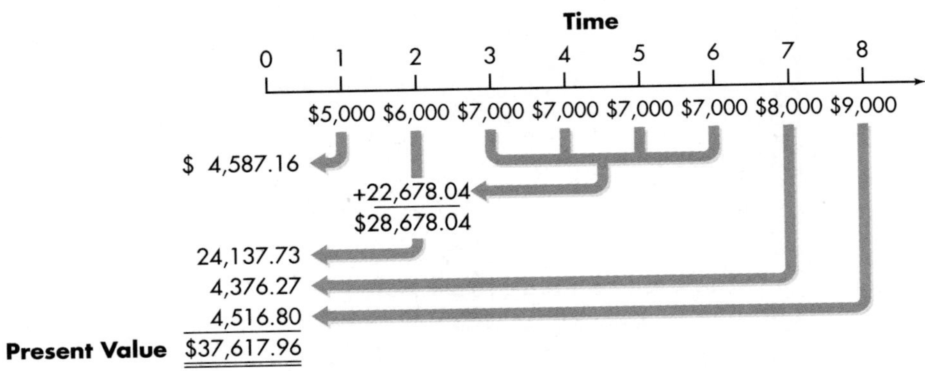

Time line for present value of a mixed stream with an embedded annuity (end-of-year cash flows, discounted at 9%, over the corresponding number of years)

Table The three-step procedure is applied to Powell's cash flows in Table 6.9, because it has a 4-year $7,000 annuity embedded in its cash flows.

Step 1 As noted in column 2 of Table 6.9, the present value of the embedded $7,000 annuity is calculated by multiplying the $7,000 by the present value of an annuity interest factor at 9 percent for 4 years (*PVIFa*(9%, 4 per)). Its present value at the beginning of year 3 (which is the same as the end of year 2) is $22,680.

Step 2 The end-of-year-2 value of the annuity, from Step 1, is added to the end-of-year-2 cash flow of $6,000 to determine the revised cash flow noted in column 3 of Table 6.9. This results in total cash flow of $28,680 in year 2 and the elimination of the annuity cash flow for years 3 through 6.

TABLE 6.9 **The Present Value of a Mixed Stream with an Embedded Annuity**

		Step 1	Step 2	Step 3	
Year (n)	Cash flow (1)	Present value of annuity (2)	Revised cash flow [(1) + (2)] (3)	*PVIF* (9%, *n* per) (4)	Present value [(3) × (4)] (5)
1	$5,000		$ 5,000	0.917	$ 4,585.00
2	6,000	22,680	28,680	0.842	24,148.56
3	7,000	↑	0	0.772	0
4	7,000	*PVIFa*(9%,4 per)	0	0.708	0
5	7,000	× 3.240	0	0.650	0
6	7,000		0	0.596	0
7	8,000		8,000	0.547	4,376.00
8	9,000		9,000	0.502	4,518.00
			Present value of mixed stream		$37,627.56

Step 3 Multiplying the revised cash flows in column 3 of Table 6.9 by the appropriate present value interest factors at 9 percent in column 4 results in the present values shown in column 5 of the table. The present value of this mixed stream, found by summing column 5, is $37,627.56.

So, the process of calculating the present value of this stream of cash flows has been simplified by first calculating the present value of the embedded annuity, and then adding the resulting value to the year 2 cash flow.

Calculator A similar procedure to that just demonstrated would be applied when using a calculator. The resulting answer would be $37,617.96, as shown on the time line.[13]

Spreadsheet With a spreadsheet, we can input the series of annual cash flows and the discount rate to calculate the present value. This is illustrated in Spreadsheet Application 6.4. As with the calculator approach, we determine the present value of this series of cash flows. Therefore, the value of this investment to Powell is $37,617.96. By paying this amount and receiving the series of cash flows provided, Powell will receive a 9 percent return on the investment. ▲

Present Value of a Perpetuity

perpetuity
An annuity with an infinite life, providing an identical cash flow every year.

A **perpetuity** is an annuity with an infinite life—in other words, an annuity that never stops providing its holder with an identical cash flow at the end of each

13. Most financial calculators have a frequency function that allows easy input of cash flow streams that have annuities embedded in them. The use of this feature, if it is available, is explained in the calculator's reference guide.

year. It is sometimes necessary to find the present value of a perpetuity. The present value interest factor for a perpetuity discounted at the rate k is

$$PVIFa(k\%, \infty) = \frac{1}{k} \tag{6.18}$$

As the equation shows, the appropriate factor, $PVIFa(k\%,\infty)$, is found merely by dividing the discount rate, k (stated as a decimal), into 1. The validity of this method can be seen by looking at the factors in Table A-4 for 8, 10, 20, and 40 percent: as the number of periods (typically years) approaches 50, the values of these factors approach 12.500 (1 ÷ 0.08), 10.000 (1 ÷ 0.10), 5.000 (1 ÷ 0.20), and 2.500 (1 ÷ 0.40), respectively. To calculate the present value of the perpetuity (PV_P), the yearly payment (PMT) is divided by the appropriate discount rate as shown in the following equation:

$$PV_P = \frac{PMT}{k\%} \tag{6.19}$$

Example Ross Clark wishes to determine the present value of an investment that is expected to provide a $1,000 cash flow each year for an indefinite time period. Ross requires a 10 percent return on the investment. Inserting the appropriate values into Equation 6.19 results in a value of $10,000 ($1,000/0.10). The same result could be obtained by using Equation 6.17. In this case we would multiply the yearly payment ($1,000) by the present value interest factor for the perpetuity, in this case 10 (1/0.10). Again, the present value of this perpetuity would be $10,000.

So the receipt of $1,000 every year for an indefinite period is worth $10,000 today if Ross can earn 10 percent on his investments. If he had $10,000 and earned 10 percent interest on it each year, $1,000 a year could be withdrawn indefinitely without touching the initial $10,000, which would never be drawn upon.

? Review Questions

6–13 How is the present value of a mixed stream of cash flows calculated? How can the calculations required to find the present value of an annuity be simplified? How can the calculation of the present value of a mixed stream with an embedded annuity be streamlined?

6–14 What is a *perpetuity*? How might the present value interest factor for such a stream of cash flows be determined?

6.6 Special Applications of Time Value

Future value and present value techniques have a number of important applications. We'll study three of them in this section: (1) the calculation of the periodic investments required to accumulate a future sum, (2) the calculation of amortization on loans, and (3) the determination of growth rates.

Investments Required to Accumulate a Future Sum

Suppose you want to buy a house 5 years from now and estimate that an initial down payment of $20,000 will be required at that time. You wish to make equal annual end-of-year investments in an account providing an annual return of 6 percent, so you must determine the annuity that will result in a lump sum equal to $20,000 at the end of year 5. The solution to this problem is closely related to the process of finding the future value of an annuity.

Earlier in the chapter, we found the future value of an n-year annuity, FVA_n, by multiplying the annual deposit, PMT, by the appropriate interest factor, $FVIFa(k\%, n \text{ per})$. The relationship of the three variables has been defined by Equation 6.10, which is rewritten below:

$$FVA_n = PMT \times FVIFa(k\%, n \text{ per})$$

We can find the annual deposit required to accumulate FVA_n dollars, given a specified interest rate, k, and a certain number of years, n, by solving the above equation for PMT. Isolating PMT on the left side of the equation gives us:

$$PMT = \frac{FVAn}{FVIFa(k\%, n \text{ per})} \qquad (6.20)$$

Once this is done, we have only to substitute the known values of FVA_n and $FVIFa(k\%, n \text{ per})$ into the right side of the equation to find the annual deposit required.

Example As just stated, you want to determine the equal annual end-of-year deposits required to accumulate $20,000 at the end of 5 years given a rate of return of 6 percent.

Table Table A-2 indicates that the future value interest factor for an annuity at 6 percent for 5 years, $FVIFa(6\%, 5 \text{ per})$, is 5.637. Substituting $FVA_5 = \$20,000$ and $FVIFa(6\%, 5 \text{ per}) = 5.637$ into Equation 6.20 yields an annual required deposit, PMT, of $3,547.99. Thus, if that amount is deposited at the end of each year for 5 years, at 6 percent interest, there will be $20,000 in the account at the end of the 5 years.

Calculator Using the calculator inputs shown, you should find the annual deposit amount to be $3,547.93.

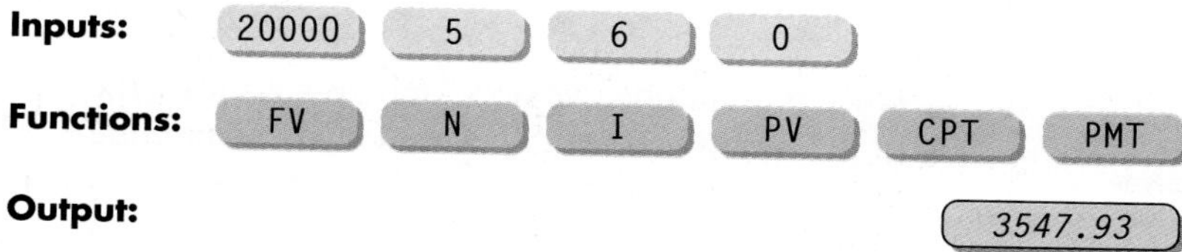

Loan Payments and the Amortization Schedule

interest-only loans
Loans that only require the periodic payment of interest and the separate repayment of principal at some future date or dates.

When individuals or companies borrow money, there are two ways the borrower can repay the loan. For the first, the borrower makes interest payments on a periodic basis, usually monthly, quarterly, semiannually, or yearly, and then repays the borrowed principal at some future date or dates. The periodic payments do not reduce the principal amount borrowed; the payments are interest only. We have already seen these **interest-only loans** a number of times in this book.

installment loan
A loan where each payment made is an equal amount, and consists of some interest and some principal; as payments are made, the amount of interest paid falls, while the amount of principal paid increases.

The second type of borrowing arrangement is referred to as an **installment loan**. Here, each loan payment is an equal amount, and consists of some interest and some principal. The payments are most often made on a monthly basis, but could be yearly as well. As payments are made, the amount of interest paid falls, while the amount of principal paid increases. This occurs because with each payment, the outstanding principal declines so the interest cost declines as well. The key to this is to remember that each loan payment is the same amount. The present value of the loan payments, discounted at the borrowing rate, will equal the amount borrowed. This implies that the lender's return on the loan will be the lending rate, while the borrower's cost will be the borrowing rate.

Calculating the payment on an installment loan involves creating an annuity out of a present amount. For example, say you borrow $6,000 at 10 percent as an installment loan, and agree to repay the loan over four years. To determine the equal payments required to repay the loan and generate a return of 10 percent, the lender views the $6,000 as a present value and then determines the future payments required that, when discounted at 10 percent, will equal $6,000. Instead of finding the present value of an annuity, we find the payment required that results in the present value.

Earlier in this chapter, we found the present value, PVA_n, of an n-year annuity by multiplying the annual amount, PMT, by the present value interest factor for an annuity, $PVIFa(k\%, n \text{ per})$. This relationship, which was originally expressed as Equation 6.17, is rewritten here:

$$PVA_n = PMT \times PVIFa(k\%, n \text{ per})$$

To find the equal annual payment required to amortize the loan, PVA_n, over a certain number of years at a specified interest rate, we need to rearrange the equation to solve for PMT. Isolating PMT on the left side of the equation gives

$$PMT = \frac{PVAn}{PVIFa(k\%, n \text{ per})} \tag{6.21}$$

loan amortization schedule
A table that allocates each loan payment to interest and principal, so that over the amortization period of the loan, the principal outstanding is reduced to 0.

Once this is done, we have only to substitute the known values into the right side of the equation to find the annual payment required. With the payment calculated, we can then develop a **loan amortization schedule** that allocates each loan payment to interest and principal. The length of the amortization period is the term of the loan multiplied by the payment frequency. Over the term of the loan, the principal outstanding will be reduced until it reaches 0 with the last loan payment.

Example As just stated, you want to determine the equal annual end-of-year payments necessary to amortize fully a \$6,000, 10 percent loan over 4 years.

Table Table A-4 indicates that the present value interest factor for an annuity corresponding to 10 percent and 4 years ($PVIFa(10\%, 4\ \text{per})$) is 3.170. Substituting PVA_4 = \$6,000 and $PVIFa(10\%, 4\ \text{per}) = 3.170$ into Equation 6.29 and solving for PMT yields an annual loan payment of \$1,892.74. Thus, to repay the interest and principal on a \$6,000, 10 percent, 4-year loan, equal annual end-of-year payments of \$1,892.74 are necessary.

Calculator Using the calculator inputs shown, you should find the annual payment amount to be \$1,892.82.

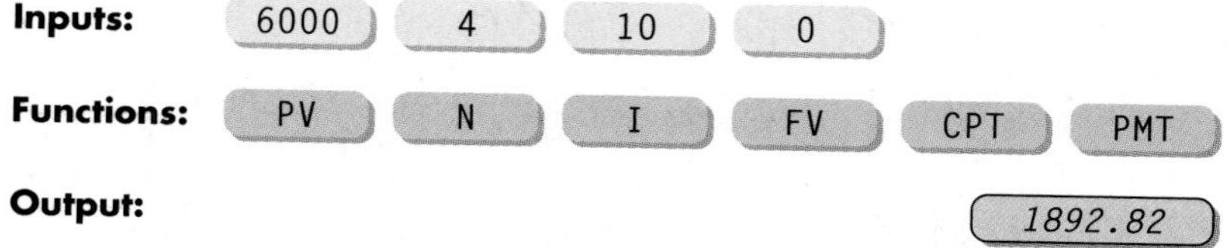

Spreadsheet With a spreadsheet, we can set up a worksheet area that provides the loan principal, interest rate, and repayment frequency. This then becomes the basis for calculating the loan payment and to develop the loan amortization schedule. This is illustrated in Spreadsheet Application 6.5. Note that the Excel PMT function has been used to calculate the loan payment. For loans with longer amortization periods, additional periods can easily be added as rows to the schedule.

The allocation of each loan payment to interest and principal can be seen in columns 3 and 4 of the *loan amortization schedule* in Table 6.10 and in Spreadsheet Application 6.5. The portion of each payment representing interest (column 3) declines over the repayment period, and the portion going to principal repayment (column 4) increases. This pattern is typical of amortized loans; with level payments, as the principal is reduced, the interest component declines, leaving a larger portion of each subsequent payment to repay principal.[14]

Growth or Interest Rates

It is often necessary to calculate the compound average annual *growth rate* (i.e., annual rate of change in values) of a series of cash flows. In doing this, either future value or present value interest factors can be used. The approach using present value interest factors is described in this section. The simplest situation is where you wish to find the rate of growth in a *series of cash flows*.

14. Most financial calculators have a function that allows the user to determine the breakdown of principal and interest for every loan payment made over the amortization period.

TABLE 6.10 Loan Amortization Schedule ($6,000 Principal, 10% Interest, 4-Year Repayment Period)

End of year	Beginning-of-year principal (1)	Loan payment (2)	Payments: Interest [0.10 × (1)] (3)	Payments: Principal [(2) − (3)] (4)	End-of-year principal [(1) − (4)] (5)
1	$6,000.00	$1,892.82	$600.00	$1,292.82	$4,707.18
2	4,707.18	1,892.82	470.72	1,422.11	3,285.07
3	3,285.07	1,892.82	328.51	1,564.32	1,720.75
4	1,720.75	1,892.82	172.07	1,720.75	0

6.5 SPREADSHEET APPLICATION

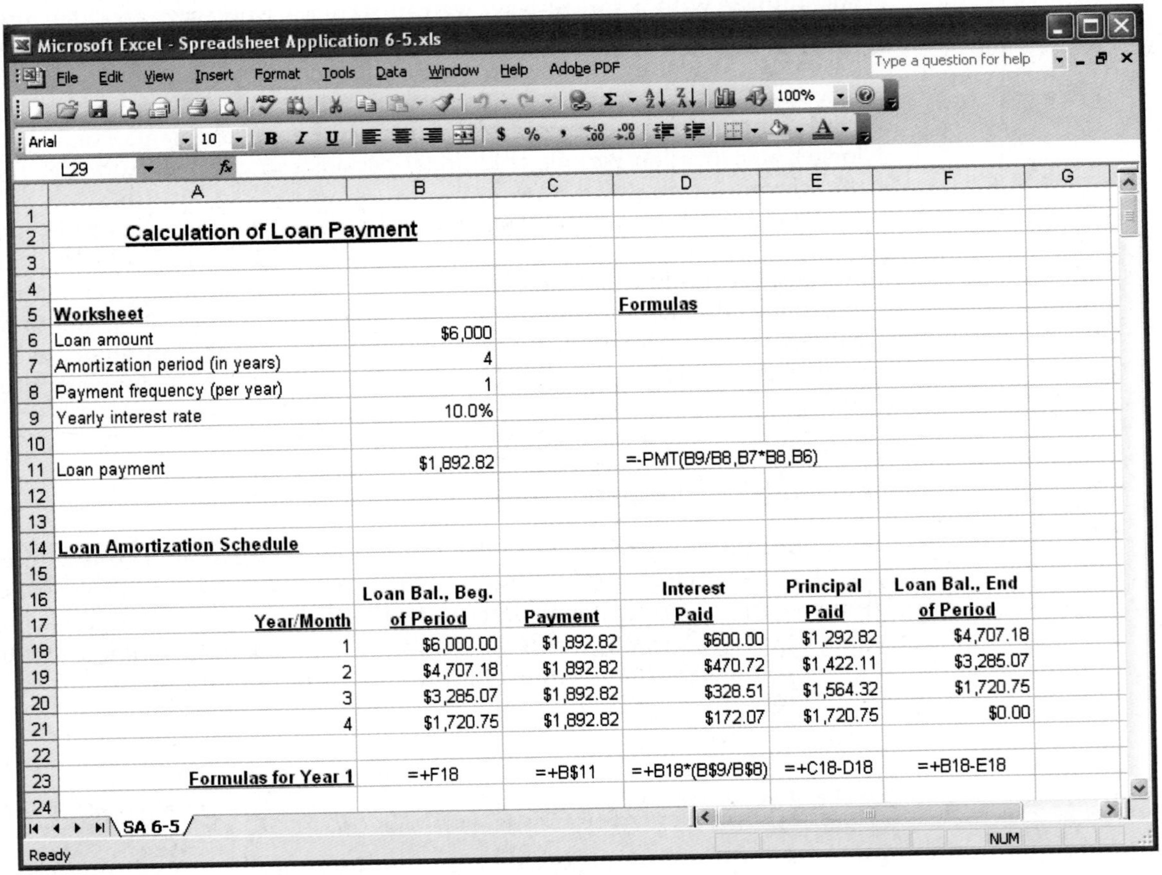

Microsoft Excel - Spreadsheet Application 6-5.xls

Calculation of Loan Payment

	A	B	C	D	E	F
5	**Worksheet**			**Formulas**		
6	Loan amount	$6,000				
7	Amortization period (in years)	4				
8	Payment frequency (per year)	1				
9	Yearly interest rate	10.0%				
11	Loan payment	$1,892.82		=-PMT(B9/B8,B7*B8,B6)		
14	**Loan Amortization Schedule**					
16–17	**Year/Month**	**Loan Bal., Beg. of Period**	**Payment**	**Interest Paid**	**Principal Paid**	**Loan Bal., End of Period**
18	1	$6,000.00	$1,892.82	$600.00	$1,292.82	$4,707.18
19	2	$4,707.18	$1,892.82	$470.72	$1,422.11	$3,285.07
20	3	$3,285.07	$1,892.82	$328.51	$1,564.32	$1,720.75
21	4	$1,720.75	$1,892.82	$172.07	$1,720.75	$0.00
23	**Formulas for Year 1**	=+F18	=+B$11	=+B18*(B$9/B$8)	=+C18-D18	=+B18-E18

SA 6-5

Example Ray Noble wishes to find the rate of growth in the following series of cash flows:

Year	Cash flow	
2004	1,250	
		1
2005	1,300	
		2
2006	1,370	
		3
2007	1,440	
		4
2008	$1,520	

By using the first year (2004) as a base year, we see that the cash flows have had four opportunities to grow. There are 5 years but four growth periods.

Table The first step in finding the growth rate is to divide the amount received in the earliest year by the amount received in the latest year. This gives the present value interest factor for a *single amount* for 4 years, *PVIF*(k%, 4 per), which is 0.822 ($1,250 ÷ $1,520). The interest rate in Table A-3 associated with the factor closest to 0.822 for 4 years is the growth rate of Ray's cash flows. In the row for year 4 in Table A-3, the factor for 5 percent is 0.823—almost exactly the 0.822 value. Therefore, the growth rate of the given cash flows is approximately (to the nearest whole percent) 5 percent.[15]

Calculator Using the calculator, we treat the earliest value as a present value, *PV*, and the latest value as a future value, FV_n. (*Note:* Most calculators require *either* the *PV* or *FV* value to be inputted as a negative number in order to calculate an unknown growth rate. Experiment with your calculator to determine which process you should follow.) Using the inputs shown below, you should find the growth rate to be 5.01 percent, which is consistent with, but more precise than, the value found using Table A-3.

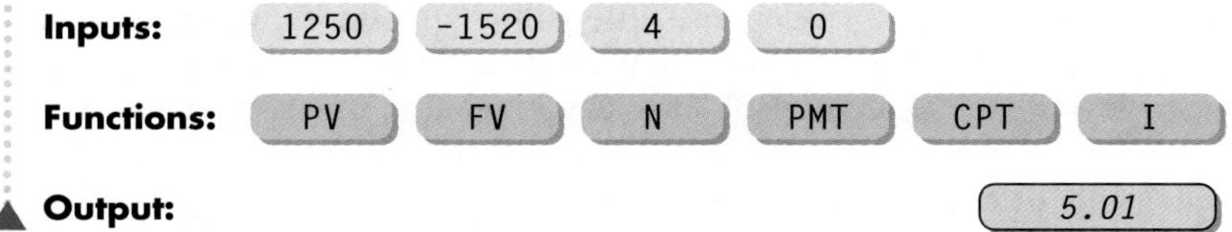

Another type of problem involves finding the interest rate associated with an *annuity*, or equal-payment loan.

Example Jan Jacobs can borrow $2,000 to be repaid in equal annual end-of-year amounts of $514.14 for the next 5 years. She wants to find the interest rate on this loan.

15. To obtain more precise estimates of growth rates, *interpolation*—a mathematical technique for estimating unknown intermediate values—can be applied. For information on how to interpolate a more precise answer in this example, see the book's home page at **www.pearsoned.ca/gitman**.

Table Substituting PVA_5 = \$2,000 and PMT = \$514.14 into Equation 6.17 and rearranging the equation to solve for $PVIFa(k\%, 5 \text{ per})$, we get

$$PVIFa(k\%, 5 \text{ per}) = \frac{PVA_5}{PMT} = \frac{\$2{,}000}{\$514.14} = 3.890$$

The interest rate for 5 years associated with the annuity factor closest to 3.890 in Table A-4 is 9 percent. Therefore, the interest rate on the loan is approximately (to the nearest whole percent) 9 percent.

Calculator (*Note:* Most calculators require *either* the *PMT* or *PV* value to be input as a negative number in order to calculate an unknown interest rate on an equal-payment loan. Experiment with your calculator to determine which process you should follow.) Using the inputs shown, you should find the interest rate to be 9 percent.

Inputs:	514.14	-2000	5	0		
Functions:	PMT	PV	N	FV	CPT	I
Output:						9.00

A final type of interest-rate problem involves finding the interest rate associated with a mixed stream of payments expected to result from a given initial investment. For example, assume that in exchange for an initial \$1,000 investment, you will receive annual cash flows over years 1 through 5 of \$200, \$400, \$300, \$500, and \$200, respectively. What interest rate would you earn on this investment? This rate is called the *internal rate of return (IRR)*. Because of the relatively complex nature of this computation, which can be greatly simplified using a financial calculator, we will defer discussion of it until it is applied in Chapter 12.

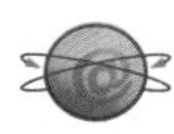

www.busadm.mu.edu/mandell/dq.html#DQ

www-ec.njit.edu/~mathis/interactive/FCBase3.html

www.studyfinance.com/lessons/timevalue/index.html

There are numerous sites on the Web that provide additional readings on time value, free time value calculators, discussion questions on time value, and time value problems. Visit as many of these sites and do as much extra reading or as many problems as you feel are useful to ensure you learn time value concepts.

6.1 **IN PRACTICE**

Really, Time Is on Your Side

For those saving money, to paraphrase Mick Jagger, "Time is on your side." Those in debt, to quote W. B. Yeats, "have no enemy but time." To illustrate the ideas associated with these quotes, consider the following examples.

Upon graduation from university, 24-year-old Early Emily Edenhurst starts work and decides to start investing \$150 per month in the common shares of some large Canadian companies. The shares will be held in a registered retirement savings account (RRSP) and are

(Continued)

expected to generate a return of 12 percent per year. Early Emily arranges to have $150 withdrawn from her savings account and deposited to her investment account every month that will then be used to buy the shares. Early Emily then immediately forgets about the plan. She works for 36 years, retiring at age 60. At this point in time, Early Emily receives a letter from the investment company indicating the amount of money that is in the RRSP. How much is there? Way back 36 years ago, Emily set up an annuity of $150 per month, that provided a return of 1 percent (12%/12 months) per month. Over the 432 months (36 years × 12) the plan was set up, Emily invested a total of $64,800. The future value of this annuity, however, is $1,088,887. Emily can begin to enjoy her retirement!

On the other hand, Late Larry Linton, who graduated with Early Emily, delayed planning for retirement. Larry only thought about retirement when he turned 50. Larry also wants to retire when he turns 60 and he wants the same amount of money as Emily. If his investment also earns 12 percent per year, how much must Larry save each month between now and retirement? Larry wants a future value of $1,088,887 in 120 months, and he expects a return of 1 percent per month. Larry must save $4,733.50 per month or $568,020 in total to have the same amount of money as Emily. Mick didn't lie; time really is on your side.

A common type of debt most individuals have at some point in their lives is a car loan. Assume you buy a car that has a sticker price of $24,500. After all other charges and taxes, the cost of the car is $28,890. You need to borrow the total amount so you visit your financial institution and negotiate a loan. The loans officer indicates that the borrowing rate is 10 percent, with monthly payments required, and she suggests an amortization period of 12 years. What are the monthly payments on the loan? The present value is the amount borrowed or $28,890, there are 144 (12 years × 12) periods, and the monthly borrowing rate is 0.833 percent (10%/12 months). Compute PMT. The monthly payment is $345.26.

Over the 12 years the loan is outstanding, the total interest paid on the loan is $20,827, or 72.1 percent of the amount borrowed. If instead of 12 years, you choose a 6-year amortization period, what is the impact? The monthly payment increases to $535.21. *But* the amount of interest paid falls to $9,645, about one-third of the amount borrowed. For those in debt, time is an enemy, since it increases the cost of debt.

Time value teaches us that the longer the period of time you save and the shorter the period of time you borrow, the better.

? Review Questions

6–15 How can you determine the size of the equal annual end-of-year deposits necessary to accumulate a certain future sum in a specified future period?

6–16 Describe the procedure used to amortize a loan into a series of equal annual payments. What is a *loan amortization schedule?*

6–17 Which present value interest factors would be used to find (**a**) the growth rate associated with a series of cash flows and (**b**) the interest rate associated with an equal-payment loan?

SUMMARY

LG1 **Discuss the role of time value of money in finance and the use of computational aids to simplify its application.** Time value of money is a concept that is used in most of the remaining chapters in the book. Financial managers use time value of money techniques when assessing the value of the expected cash flow streams associated with decision alternatives. Alternatives can be assessed by either compounding to find future value or discounting to find present value. Because they are at time zero when making decisions, financial managers rely primarily on present value techniques. Financial tables, financial calculators, and spreadsheets can streamline the application of time value techniques.

LG2 **Understand the concept of future value, its calculation for a single amount, and the effects of compounding interest more frequently than annually.** Future value relies on compound interest to measure future amounts: The initial principal or deposit in one period, along with the interest earned on it, becomes the beginning principal of the following period. Interest can be compounded at intervals ranging from annually to daily, and even continuously. The more frequently interest is compounded, the larger the future amount that will be accumulated and the higher the effective annual rate (EAR). The annual percentage rate (APR)—a nominal annual rate—is quoted on credit cards and loans. The interest factor formulas and basic equation for the future value of a single amount are given in Table 6.11.

LG3 **Find the future value of an ordinary annuity and an annuity due and compare these two types of annuities.** An annuity is a pattern of equal annual cash flows. For an ordinary annuity, cash flows occur at the end of the period. For an annuity due, cash flows occur at the beginning of the period. The future value of an ordinary annuity can be found by using the future value interest factor for an annuity; an adjustment is required to find the future value of an annuity due. The interest factor formulas and basic equation for the future value of an annuity are given in Table 6.11.

LG4 **Understand the concept of present value, its calculation for a single amount, and the relationship of present to future value.** Present value is the inverse of future value. The present value of a future amount is the amount of money today that is equivalent to the given future amount, considering the return that can be earned on the current money. The interest factor formula and basic equation for the present value of a single amount are given in Table 6.11.

LG5 **Calculate the present value of a mixed stream of cash flows, an annuity, a mixed stream with an embedded annuity, and a perpetuity.** The present value of a mixed stream of cash flows is the sum of the present values of each individual cash flow in the stream. The present value of an annuity can be found by using the present value interest factor for an annuity. For a mixed stream with an embedded annuity, the present value of the annuity is found, then used to replace the annuity flows, and the new mixed stream's present value is calculated. The present value of a perpetuity—an infinite-lived annuity—is found by dividing the yearly payment (*PMT*) by the appropriate discount rate. The interest factor formulas and basic equation for the present value of an annuity are given in Table 6.11.

LG6 **Describe the procedures involved in (1) determining the periodic investments required to accumulate a future sum, (2) loan amortization, and (3) determining growth and interest rates.** The annual deposit to accumulate a given future sum can be found by solving the equation for the future value of an annuity for the annual payment. For an installment loan, the equal payments required can be calculated and split between interest and principal. As payments are made, the amount of interest paid falls, while the amount of principal paid increases. This is illustrated in a loan amortization schedule. Growth or interest rates can be estimated by finding the unknown rate in the equation for the present value of a single amount, an annuity, or a mixed stream.

TABLE 6.11 Summary of Key Definitions, Formulas, and Equations for Time Value of Money

Variable definitions

e = exponential constant = 2.7183
EAR = effective annual rate
FV_n = future value or amount at the end of period n
FVA_n = future value of an n-year annuity
k = annual rate of return
m = number of times per year interest is compounded
n = number of periods—typically, years—over which money earns a return
PMT = amount deposited or received annually at the end of each year
PV = initial principal or present value
PVA_n = present value of an n-year annuity
t = period number index

Interest factor formulas

Future value of a single amount:

$$FVIF(k\%, n \text{ per}) = \left(1 + \frac{k}{m}\right)^{m\times n}$$ [Eq. 6.4]

for annual compounding, $m = 1$,

$$FVIF(k\%, n \text{ per}) = (1 + k)^n$$ [Eq. 6.2; factors in Table A-1]

for continuous compounding, $m = \infty$,

$$FVIF(k\%, n \text{ per}) = e^{k\times n}$$ [Eq. 6.6]

to find the effective annual rate,

$$\text{EAR} = \left(1 + \frac{k}{m}\right)^m - 1$$ [Eq. 6.7]

Future value of an (ordinary) annuity:

$$FVIFa(k\%, n \text{ per}) = \left[\frac{(1 + k)^n - 1}{k}\right]$$ [Eq. 6.9; factors in Table A-2]

Future value of an annuity due:

$$FVIFad(k\%, n \text{ per}) \text{ (annuity due)} = FVIFa_{(k\%,\, n \text{ per})} \times (1 + k)$$ [Eq. 6.11]

Present value of a single amount:

$$PVIF(k\%, n \text{ per}) = \frac{1}{(1 + k)^n}$$ [Eq. 6.13; factors in Table A-3]

Present value of an annuity:

$$PVIFa(k\%, n \text{ per}) = \left[\frac{1 - \frac{1}{(1 + k)^n}}{k}\right]$$ [Eq. 6.16; factors in Table A-4]

Present value of a perpetuity:

$$PV_P = \frac{PMT}{k\%}$$ [Eq. 6.19]

Basic equations

Future value (single amount):	$FV_n = PV \times [FVIF(k\%, n \text{ per})]$	[Eq. 6.3]
Future value (annuity):	$FVA_n = PMT \times [FVIFa(k\%, n \text{ per})]$	[Eq. 6.10]
Present value (single amount):	$PV = FV_n \times [PVIF(k\%, n \text{ per})]$	[Eq. 6.14]
Present value (annuity):	$PVA_n = PMT \times [PVIFa(k\%, n \text{ per})]$	[Eq. 6.17]

SELF-TEST PROBLEMS

(Solutions in Appendix B)

ST 6–1 **Future values** Delia Martin has $10,000 that she can deposit in any of three savings accounts for a 3-year period. Bank A compounds interest on an annual basis, bank B compounds interest twice each year, and bank C compounds interest each quarter. All three banks have a stated annual interest rate of 4%.

a. What amount would Ms. Martin have at the end of the third year, leaving all interest paid on deposit, in each bank?

b. What effective annual rate (EAR) would she earn in each of the banks?

c. On the basis of your findings in **a** and **b**, which bank should Ms. Martin deal with? Why?

d. If a fourth bank—Bank D, also with a 4 percent stated interest rate—compounds interest continuously, how much would Ms. Martin have at the end of the third year? Does this alternative change your recommendation in **c**? Explain why or why not.

ST 6–2 **Future values of annuities** Ramesh Abdul wishes to choose the better of two cash flow streams, annuity X and annuity Y, that both have the same cost. X is an *annuity due* with a cash inflow of $9,000 for each of 6 years. Y is an *ordinary annuity* with a cash inflow of $10,000 for each of 6 years. Assume that Ramesh can earn 15 percent on his investments.

a. On a purely intuitive basis, which annuity do you think is more attractive? Why?

b. Find the value of each annuity at the end of year 6.

c. Use your finding in **b** to indicate which annuity is more attractive. Why? Compare your finding to your intuitive response in **a**.

ST 6–3 **Present values** You have a choice of accepting either of two 5-year cash flow streams or lump-sum amounts. One cash flow stream is an annuity, and the other is a mixed stream. You may accept alternative A or B—either as a cash flow stream or as a lump sum. Given the cash flow stream and lump-sum amounts associated with each, and assuming you can earn a 9 percent return, which alternative (A or B) and in which form (cash flow stream or lump-sum amount) would you prefer?

	Cash flow stream	
End of year	Alternative A	Alternative B
1	$700	$1,100
2	700	900
3	700	700
4	700	500
5	700	300
	Lump-sum amount	
Now	$2,825	$2,800

 ST 6–4 **Investments required to accumulate a future sum** Judi Jordan wishes to accumulate $8,000 by the end of 5 years by making equal annual end-of-year deposits over the next 5 years. If Judi can earn 7 percent on her investments, how much must she deposit at the *end of each year* to meet this goal?

PROBLEMS

  6–1 **Using a time line** The financial manager at Starbuck Industries is considering an investment that requires an initial outlay of $25,000 and is expected to result in cash inflows of $3,000 at the end of year 1, $6,000 at the end of years 2 and 3, $10,000 at the end of year 4, $8,000 at the end of year 5, and $7,000 at the end of year 6.

a. Draw and label a time line depicting the cash flows associated with Starbuck Industries' proposed investment.
b. Use arrows to demonstrate, on the time line in **a**, how compounding to find future value can be used to measure all cash flows at the end of year 6.
c. Use arrows to demonstrate, on the same time line, how discounting to find present value can be used to measure all cash flows at time zero.
d. Which of the approaches—future value or present value—is most often relied on by the financial manager for decision-making purposes? Why?

BASIC  6–2 **Future value calculation** *Without referring to tables or the preprogrammed function on your financial calculator,* use the basic formula for future value along with the given interest rate, *k,* and number of periods, *n,* to calculate the future value interest factor in each of the cases shown in the following table. Compare the calculated value to the table value in Appendix Table A-1.

Case	Interest rate, k	Number of periods, n
A	12%	2
B	6	3
C	9	2
D	3	4

BASIC  6–3 **Future value tables** Using the appropriate equations or a financial calculator, for each of the cases shown in the following table estimate, to the exact year, how long it would take an initial deposit, assuming no withdrawals, to

a. double.
b. quadruple.

Case	Interest rate
A	7%
B	40
C	20
D	10

INTERMEDIATE 

6–4 Future values For each of the cases shown in the table below, calculate the future value of the single cash flow deposited today that will be available at the end of the deposit period if the interest is compounded annually at the rate specified over the given period.

Case	Single cash flow	Interest rate	Deposit period (years)
A	$ 200	5%	20
B	4,500	8	7
C	10,000	9	10
D	25,000	10	12
E	37,000	11	5
F	40,000	12	9

INTERMEDIATE 

6–5 Future value You have $1,500 to invest today at 7 percent interest compounded annually.

a. How much will you have accumulated in the account at the end of
(1) 3 years?
(2) 6 years?
(3) 9 years?

b. Use your findings in **a** to calculate the amount of interest earned in
(1) the first 3 years (years 1 to 3).
(2) the second 3 years (years 4 to 6).
(3) the third 3 years (years 7 to 9).

c. Compare and contrast your findings in **b**. Explain why the amount of interest earned increases in each succeeding 3-year period.

INTERMEDIATE 

6–6 Inflation and future value As part of your financial planning, you wish to purchase a new car exactly 5 years from today. The car you wish to purchase costs $14,000 today, and your research indicates that its price will increase by 2 percent to 6 percent per year over the next 5 years.

a. Estimate the price of the car at the end of 5 years if inflation is
(1) 2 percent per year.
(2) 6 percent per year.

b. How much more expensive will the car be if the rate of inflation is 6 percent rather than 2 percent?

INTERMEDIATE 

6–7 Future value and time You can invest $10,000 in a company's common shares that are expected to provide a 9 percent annual rate of return. You will make the investment either today or exactly 10 years from today. How much better off will you be at the end of 40 years if you decide to make the investment today rather than 10 years from today?

INTERMEDIATE 

6–8 Future value calculation Misty needs to have $15,000 at the end of 5 years in order to fulfill her goal of purchasing a small sailboat. She is willing to invest the funds as a single amount today but wonders what sort of investment return she will need to earn. What annual compounded rate of return will Misty need to earn in each of the following cases?

a. Misty can invest $10,200 today.
b. Misty can invest $8,150 today.
c. Misty can invest $7,150 today.

6–9 Single-payment loan repayment You plan to borrow $20,000 for a maximum period of 8 years. The interest rate on the loan will be 14 percent compounded annually. When you repay the loan, you will repay the principal and total interest owing. The loan can be repaid at the end of any earlier year with no prepayment penalty.

a. What amount would be due if the loan is repaid at the end of year 1?
b. What is the repayment at the end of year 4?
c. What amount is due at the end of year 8?
d. What can you learn from this analysis?

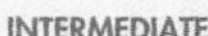

6–10 Changing compounding frequency Using annual, semiannual, quarterly, monthly, and daily compounding periods, for each of the following: (1) calculate the future value if $5,000 is initially deposited, and (2) determine the effective annual rate (EAR):

a. at 12 percent annual interest for 5 years.
b. at 16 percent annual interest for 6 years.
c. at 20 percent annual interest for 10 years.

INTERMEDIATE

6–11 Compounding frequency, future value, and effective annual rates For each of the following cases:

Case	Amount of initial deposit	Nominal annual rate, k	Compounding frequency, m (times/year)	Deposit period (years)
A	$ 2,500	6%	2	5
B	50,000	12	12	3
C	1,000	5	1	10
D	20,000	16	4	6
E	100,000	5	365	4

a. Calculate the future value at the end of the specified deposit period.
b. Determine the effective annual rate, EAR.
c. Compare the nominal annual rate, k, to the effective annual rate, EAR. What relationship exists between compounding frequency and the nominal and effective annual rates?

INTERMEDIATE

6–12 Continuous compounding For each of the following cases, find the future value at the end of the deposit period, assuming that interest is compounded continuously at the given nominal annual rate.

Case	Amount of initial deposit	Nominal annual rate, k	Deposit period (years)
A	$ 1,000	9%	2
B	25,600	10	10
C	4,000	8	7
D	2,500	12	4
E	100,000	5	4

INTERMEDIATE  **6–13 Compounding frequency and future value** You plan to invest $20,000 in an investment account today and you expect a *nominal annual rate of return* of 8 percent, which is expected to apply to all future years.

a. How much will you have in the account at the end of 10 years if interest is compounded
(1) annually?
(2) semiannually?
(3) daily?
(4) continuously?

b. What is the *effective annual rate, EAR*, for each compounding period in **a**?

c. How much greater will your account balance be at the end of 10 years if interest is compounded continuously rather than annually?

d. How does the compounding frequency affect the future value and effective annual rate for a given deposit? Explain in terms of your findings in **a** through **c**.

INTERMEDIATE  **6–14 Comparing compounding periods** René Levin wishes to determine the future value at the end of 2 years of a $15,000 investment made today into an account providing an annual rate of return of 12 percent.

a. Find the future value of René's investment assuming that interest is compounded
(1) annually.
(2) quarterly.
(3) monthly.
(4) continuously.

b. Compare your findings in **a**, and use them to demonstrate the relationship between compounding frequency and future value.

c. What is the maximum future value obtainable given the $15,000 investment, 2-year time period, and 12 percent nominal annual rate?

BASIC  **6–15 Future value of an annuity** For each of the following cases:

Case	Amount of annuity	Rate of return	Deposit period (years)
A	$ 12,500	8%	10
B	5,000	12	6
C	30,000	20	5
D	11,500	9	8
E	106,000	14	30

a. Calculate the future value of the annuity assuming that it is an
(1) ordinary annuity.
(2) annuity due.

b. Compare your findings in **a**(1) and **a**(2). All else being identical, which type of annuity—ordinary or annuity due—is preferable? Explain why.

INTERMEDIATE 

6–16 Ordinary annuity versus annuity due Marian Kirk wishes to select the better of two 10-year annuities—C and D—as described.

Annuity C	An ordinary annuity of $2,500 per year for 10 years.
Annuity D	An annuity due of $2,200 per year for 10 years.

a. Find the future value of both annuities at the end of year 10 assuming that Marian can earn:
(1) 10 percent annual return.
(2) 20 percent annual return.

b. For each return, which annuity option should Marian select? Explain.

CHALLENGE 

6–17 Future value of a retirement annuity Cal Thomas, a 25-year-old college graduate, wishes to retire at age 65. To supplement other sources of retirement income, he plans to deposit $2,000 each year into a tax-deferred registered retirement savings plan (RRSP). The RRSP will be invested to earn an annual return of 10 percent over the next 40 years.

a. If Cal makes annual end-of-year $2,000 deposits into the RRSP, how much would he have accumulated by the end of his 65th year?

b. If Cal decides to wait until age 35 to begin making annual end-of-year $2,000 deposits into the RRSP, how much would he have accumulated by the end of his 65th year?

c. Using your findings in **a** and **b,** discuss the impact of delaying making deposits into the RRSP for 10 years (age 25 to age 35) on the amount accumulated by the end of Cal's 65th year.

d. Rework parts **a, b,** and **c** assuming that Cal makes all deposits at the beginning rather than at the end of each year. Discuss the effect of beginning-of-year deposits on the future value accumulated by the end of Cal's 65th year.

INTERMEDIATE

6–18 Annuities and compounding Janet Boyle intends to deposit $3,000 per year in an account at a credit union for the next 10 years. The credit union pays an annual interest rate of 8 percent.

a. Determine the future value that Janet will have at the end of 10 years given that end-of-period deposits are made and no interest is withdrawn if
(1) $3,000 is deposited annually and the credit union pays interest annually.
(2) $1,500 is deposited semiannually and the credit union pays interest semiannually.
(3) $750 is deposited quarterly and the credit union pays interest quarterly.

b. Use your finding in **a** to discuss the effect of more frequent deposits and compounding of interest on the future value of an annuity.

BASIC  

6–19 Future value of a mixed stream For each of the mixed streams of cash flows shown in the following table, determine the future value at the end of the final year if deposits are made at the *beginning of each year* into an account providing an annual return of 12 percent, assuming that no withdrawals are made during the period.

	Cash flow stream		
Year	A	B	C
1	$ 900	$30,000	$1,200
2	1,000	25,000	1,200
3	1,200	20,000	1,000
4		10,000	1,900
5		5,000	

INTERMEDIATE  6–20 **Future value of lump sum versus a mixed stream** Gina Trembly has just contracted to sell a small parcel of land that she inherited a few years ago. The buyer is willing to pay $26,000 at closing of the transaction or will pay the amounts shown in the following table at the *beginning* of each of the next 5 years. Gina doesn't really need the money today, so she plans to let it accumulate in an account that earns 7 percent annual interest.

Mixed stream	
Beginning of year	Cash flow
1	$ 2,000
2	4,000
3	6,000
4	8,000
5	10,000

a. What is the future value of the lump sum at the end of year 5?
b. What is the future value of the mixed stream at the end of year 5?
c. Based on your findings in **a** and **b**, which alternative should Gina take?
d. If the cash flow sequence were reversed—that is, if the $10,000 was received in year 1, the $8,000 in year 2, etc.—which option would be preferred?
e. If Gina could earn 10 percent rather than 7 percent on the funds, would your recommendation in **c** change? Explain.

  6–21 **Present value** Use the basic formula for present value along with the given opportunity cost, *k*, and number of periods, *n*, to calculate the present value interest factor in each of the cases shown in the following table.

Case	Opportunity cost, k	Number of periods, n
A	2%	4
B	10	2
C	5	3
D	13	2

BASIC LG4 **6–22 Present values** For each of the cases shown in the following table, calculate the present value of the single cash flow that is to be received based on the data provided.

Case	Single cash flow	Discount rate	End of period (years)
A	$ 7,000	12%	4
B	28,000	8	20
C	10,000	14	12
D	150,000	11	6
E	45,000	20	8

BASIC LG4 **6–23 Present value concept** Answer each of the following questions.

a. What single investment, made today, earning a 12 percent annual return, will be worth $6,000 at the end of 6 years?

b. What is the present value of $6,000 to be received at the end of 6 years if the discount rate is 12 percent?

c. What is the most you would pay today for a promise to repay you $6,000 at the end of 6 years if your opportunity cost is 12 percent?

d. Briefly discuss your findings in **a** through **c**.

BASIC LG4 **6–24 Present value** Jim Nance has been offered a future payment of $50,000, 3 years from today. Jim believes he can earn a 7 percent annual return on investment opportunities over the next 3 years. What amount should Jim accept today, instead of waiting 3 years for the $50,000?

CHALLENGE

6–25 Present value and finding interest rates Today, you can buy a Province of Ontario savings bond with a 6 percent return that will mature in 6 years. The value at maturity will be $100,000. The bond will not provide any payments between now and maturity.

a. What is the most you would pay for this bond?

b. If you could find a willing seller who would sell you the bond for $68,129.55 today, what return would you earn on the savings bond?

c. If you bought the bond for the amount determined in part **a**, held the bond for 4 years, and then sold it for $86,967.45, what return did you earn over the holding period?

d. For part **c**, what return would the buyer receive if she bought the savings bond from you and held it to maturity?

INTERMEDIATE 

6–26 Present value and discount rates You just won a lottery that promises to pay you $1,000,000 exactly 10 years from today. Because the $1,000,000 payment is guaranteed by the government, opportunities exist to sell the claim today for an immediate cash payment.

a. What is the least you will sell your claim for if you could earn the following rates of return during the 10-year period?

(1) 6 percent
(2) 9 percent
(3) 12 percent

b. Rework **a** under the assumption that the $1,000,000 payment will be received in 15 years rather than 10.

c. Based on your findings in **a** and **b**, discuss the effect of both the size of the rate of return and the time until receipt of payment on the present value of a future sum.

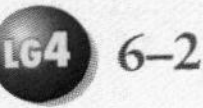

BASIC LG4 6–27 **Present value comparisons of lump sums** In exchange for a $20,000 payment today, a well-known financial institution will allow you to choose *one* of the alternatives shown in the following table. You can earn 11 percent on investments.

Alternative	Lump-sum amount
A	$28,500 at end of 3 years
B	$54,000 at end of 9 years
C	$160,000 at end of 20 years

Which of the alternatives is acceptable? Which would you take?

BASIC LG4 6–28 **Rates of return** Tom Alexander has an opportunity to purchase as many of the investments shown in the following table as he wishes. Tom requires a rate of return of at least 10 percent on any investment. The required initial investment, the value of the investment at maturity, and the term of the investment are shown below for each investment. Calculate the rate of return for each investment. Considering only the rate of return, which of the four investment opportunities should Tom choose? What other considerations may impact the decision?

Investment	Amount invested	Value at maturity
A	$18,000	$30,000 in year 5
B	600	3,000 in year 20
C	3,500	10,000 in year 10
D	1,000	15,000 in year 40

LG4 LG5 6–29 **Relationship between future value and present value** Using *only* the information in the following table:

BASIC

Year (n)	Cash flow	Future value interest factor at 5% [$FVIF(5\%, n \text{ per})$]
1	$ 800	1.050
2	900	1.103
3	1,000	1.158
4	1,500	1.216
5	2,000	1.276

a. Determine the *present value* of the mixed stream of cash flows.
b. How much would you be willing to pay for an opportunity to buy this stream, assuming that you can at best earn 5 percent on your investments?
c. What effect, if any, would a 7 percent rather than a 5 percent opportunity cost have on your analysis? Would you pay more, less, or the same for this cash flow stream? Explain.

INTERMEDIATE 

6–30 Present value of an annuity Anna Doyle was seriously injured in an industrial accident. She sued the responsible parties and was awarded a judgment of \$2,000,000. Today, she and her lawyer are attending a settlement conference with the defendants. The defendants have made an initial offer of \$156,000 per year for 25 years. Anna plans to counteroffer at \$255,000 per year for 25 years. Both offer and counteroffer have a present value of \$2,000,000, the amount of the judgment. Both assume payments at the end of each year.
a. What interest rate assumption have the defendants used in their offer?
b. What interest rate assumption have Anna and her lawyer used in their counteroffer?
c. Anna is willing to settle for an annuity that will provide her a return of 9 percent. What annual payment would be acceptable to her?

INTERMEDIATE 

6–31 Loan payments Tim Smith is shopping for a used car. He has found one priced at \$4,500. If Tim can make a \$500 down payment, the dealer will finance the balance of the car's cost at an interest rate of 12 percent over the 2 years.
a. Assuming that Tim accepts the dealer's offer, what will his *monthly* (end-of-month) payments be?
b. What would Tim's *monthly* payment be if the dealer was willing to finance the balance of the car's cost at a 9 percent interest rate?
c. What can you learn from the above answers?

INTERMEDIATE 

6–32 Present value—Mixed streams Find the present value of the streams of cash flows shown in the following table. Assume that the firm's discount rate is 12%.

A		B		C	
Year	Cash flow	Year	Cash flow	Year	Cash flow
1	−\$2,000	1	\$10,000	1–5	\$10,000/year
2	3,000	2–5	5,000/year	6–10	8,000/year
3	4,000	6	7,000		
4	6,000				
5	8,000				

INTERMEDIATE 

6–33 Present value—Mixed streams A firm has two investment opportunities, A and B, that will provide the cash flows shown in the following table:

	Cash flow stream	
Year	A	B
1	$ 50,000	$ 10,000
2	40,000	20,000
3	30,000	30,000
4	20,000	40,000
5	10,000	50,000
Totals	$150,000	$150,000

a. Find the present value of each stream using a 15 percent discount rate.
b. Compare the calculated present values and discuss them in light of the fact that the undiscounted total cash flows total $150,000 in each case.

  INTERMEDIATE

6–34 **Present value of a mixed stream** Harte Systems, Inc., a maker of electronic surveillance equipment, is considering selling the rights to market its home security system to a well-known hardware chain. The proposed deal calls for Harte to receive payments of $30,000 and $25,000 at the end of years 1 and 2 and annual year-end payments of $15,000 in years 3 through 9. A final payment of $10,000 would be due at the end of year 10.
a. Show the cash flows involved in the offer on a time line.
b. If Harte's required rate of return is 12 percent, what is the present value of this series of payments?
c. For the rights to market the home security system, a second company has offered Harte $100,000, to be paid now. Which offer should Harte accept?

INTERMEDIATE 

6–35 **Funding cash shortfalls** As part of your personal budgeting process, you have determined that in each of the next 5 years you will need the cash amounts shown in the following table, at the end of the given year, to balance your budget. You expect to be able to earn 8 percent on investments during the next 5 years and wish to fund the expected cash shortfalls over the next 5 years with a single lump-sum investment made today.

End of year	Cash shortfall
1	$ 5,000
2	4,000
3	6,000
4	10,000
5	3,000

a. What amount must you invest today to cover the expected cash shortfalls over the next 5 years?
b. What effect would an increase in your expected rate of return have on the amount calculated in **a**? Provide an example.

BASIC 

6–36 Present value of an annuity For each of the cases shown in the following table, calculate the present value of the annuity, assuming that the annuity cash flows occur at the end of each year.

Case	Amount of annuity	Interest rate	Period (years)
A	$ 12,000	7%	3
B	55,000	12	15
C	700	20	9
D	140,000	5	7
E	22,500	10	5

6–37 Present value of an annuity An insurance agent is trying to sell you a retirement annuity that will provide you with $12,000 per year for the next 25 years. You can earn 9 percent on investments. What is the most you should pay for this annuity?

CHALLENGE 

6–38 Funding your retirement You plan to retire in exactly 20 years. Your goal is to create a fund that will allow you to receive $20,000 per year for the 30 years between retirement and death (a psychic said you would die after 30 years). You know that you will be able to earn 8 percent per year during the 30-year retirement period.

a. How large a fund will you need *when you retire* in 20 years to provide the 30-year, $20,000 retirement annuity?

b. How much would you need *today* as a lump sum to provide the amount calculated in **a** if you earn 10 percent per year during the 20 years preceding retirement?

c. What effect would an increase in the rate you can earn both during and prior to retirement have on the values found in **a** and **b**? Provide an example.

INTERMEDIATE 

6–39 Present value of an annuity versus a lump sum Assume that you just won the lottery. Your prize can be taken either in the form of $40,000 at the end of each of the next 25 years (i.e., $1,000,000 over 25 years) or as a lump sum of $500,000 paid immediately.

a. If you expect to be able to earn 5 percent annually on your investments over the next 25 years, ignoring taxes and other considerations, which alternative should you take? Why?

b. Would your decision in **a** be altered if you could earn 7 percent rather than 5 percent on your investments over the next 25 years? Why?

c. On a strict economic basis, at what rate of return would you be indifferent in choosing between the two plans?

INTERMEDIATE 

6–40 Present value of a mixed stream with an embedded annuity In each of the cases shown in the following table, the mixed cash flow stream has an annuity embedded within it. Use the three-step procedure presented in the text to streamline the calculation of the present value of each of these streams, assuming a 12 percent discount rate in each case.

A		B		C	
Year	Cash flow	Year	Cash flow	Year	Cash flow
1	$12,000	1	$15,000	1–5	$ 1,000/year
2	10,000	2–10	20,000/year	6	6,000
3	8,000	11–30	25,000/year	7	7,000
4	8,000			8	8,000
5	8,000			9–15	10,000/year
6	8,000				
7	8,000				
8	5,000				

BASIC LG5

6–41 **Perpetuities** For each of the perpetuities in the following table, determine the appropriate present value interest factor to use to value the perpetuity. What is the value of each perpetuity?

Perpetuity	Annual amount	Discount rate
A	$ 20,000	8%
B	100,000	10
C	3,000	6
D	60,000	5

INTERMEDIATE

6–42 **Creating an endowment** On completion of her introductory finance course, Kieran was so pleased with the amount of useful and interesting knowledge she gained that she convinced her parents, who were wealthy alums of the university she was attending, to create an endowment. The endowment would allow three needy students to take the introductory finance course each year into perpetuity. The guaranteed annual cost of tuition and books for the course was $600 per student. The endowment would be created by making a lump-sum payment to the university. The university expected to earn exactly 6 percent per year on these funds.

a. How large an initial lump-sum payment must Kieran's parents make to the university to fund the endowment?

b. What amount would be needed to fund the endowment if the university could earn 9 percent rather than 6 percent per year on the funds?

BASIC

6–43 **Investments to accumulate future sums** For each of the cases shown in the following table, determine the amount of the equal annual end-of-year investments required to accumulate the given sum at the end of the specified period, assuming the stated annual rate of return.

Case	Sum to be accumulated	Accumulation period (years)	Rate of return
A	$ 50,000	3	12%
B	100,000	20	7
C	30,000	8	10
D	1,500,000	12	8

CHALLENGE  6–44 **Creating a retirement fund** To supplement your planned retirement in exactly 42 years, you estimate that you need to accumulate $2,200,000 by that time. You plan to make equal annual end-of-year investments into an account providing an 8 percent annual rate of return.

a. How much must the annual investments be to create the $2,200,000 fund by the end of 42 years?
b. If you can earn a 10 percent return, rather than an 8 percent return, does this have a significant impact on the yearly amount you must invest? What is the amount you must invest? Explain what has happened.
c. If you can only afford to invest $4,000 per year and will receive a 9 percent return, how much will you have in 42 years' time?
d. If you can invest $5,000 per year and still want to have $2,200,000 in 42 years' time, what rate of return must you earn on the investments?

CHALLENGE  6–45 **Accumulating a growing future sum** A retirement home at Deer Trail Estates now costs $85,000. Inflation is expected to cause this price to increase at 6 percent per year over the 20 years before C. L. Donovan retires. How much must Donovan invest each year to have the cash required to purchase a home at retirement if he can earn a 10 percent return?

   INTERMEDIATE 6–46 **Investment required** You are about to graduate from university and, since you enjoyed your time so much, you plan to make a donation to the university. But, to give you time to build up the funds necessary, you plan to make the required donation to the university in ten years' time. Your plan is to create a scholarship for $8,000 that will be granted to a deserving student each year in perpetuity. The university invests their scholarship funds and earns a return of 5.5 percent. You expect to be able to make yearly investments into an investment account that will generate an 8.5 percent return. At the end of the ten years, you plan to have the total funds required to make the donation. You will start to save for the scholarship fund now.

a. How much money will the university require in ten years to set up your planned scholarship?
b. How much will you have to save every year to have the required funds available in ten years to endow the scholarship?
c. If you started the savings plan at the end of the year, rather than at the beginning, how much will you have to save every year to have the required funds available?

  INTERMEDIATE 6–47 **Inflation, future value, and annual deposits** While vacationing in Florida, John Kelley saw the vacation home of his dreams. It was listed with a sale price of $200,000. The only catch is that John is 40 years old and plans to continue working until he is 65. John believes that he can earn 9 percent annually after taxes on his investments. He is willing to invest a fixed amount at the end of each of the next 25 years to fund the cash purchase of such a house when he retires.

a. The house price is expected to increase 5 percent a year for the next 25 years. What will John's dream house cost when he retires?
b. How much must John invest at the end of each of the next 25 years in order to have the cash purchase price of the house when he retires?
c. If John invests at the beginning instead of at the end of each of the next 25 years, how much must he invest each year?

INTERMEDIATE  **6–48 Loan payment** You have the following information about four installment loans:

Loan	Principal	Interest rate	Term of loan (years)
A	$12,000	8%	3
B	60,000	12	10
C	75,000	10	30
D	4,000	15	5

a. If the loans were to be repaid on a yearly basis, determine the required loan payments.
b. If the loans were to be repaid on a monthly basis, determine the required loan payments.
c. For the loan payments in both parts **a** and **b**, determine the total amount of interest that would be paid over the total repayment period. Explain why your answers differ between parts **a** and **b**.

INTERMEDIATE  **6–49 Loan amortization schedule** Joan Messineo borrowed $15,000 at a 14 percent annual rate of interest. This installment loan must be repaid over 3 years.
a. Calculate the yearly payment required.
b. Prepare a loan amortization schedule showing the interest and principal breakdown of each of the three loan payments.
c. Explain why the interest portion of each payment declines over time.

INTERMEDIATE  **6–50 Loan payments and amortization schedule** For each of the installment loans shown in the following table, calculate the annual payment that would be required to amortize the loan over its term. Also, develop a loan amortization table showing the split between the interest and principal paid each year over the term of the loan. Assume that the payments are made at the end of each year.

Loan	Amount	Interest rate	Term
A	$14,000	10 %	3 years
B	17,500	12.4	4 years
C	92,400	13	7 years
D	49,000	14	5 years
E	26,500	16.8	6 years

INTERMEDIATE  **6–51 Loan payments and amortization schedule** Schuyler Company wishes to purchase an asset costing $197,000. The full amount needed to finance the asset can be borrowed as an installment loan at a cost of 14 percent and must be repaid over a term of six years.
a. Determine the annual loan payment required, assuming that the payments are made at the end of each year.
b. Now develop a loan amortization schedule showing the split between the interest and principal paid each year over the term of the loan.

CHALLENGE 

6–52 Monthly loan payments and amortization schedule Franklin Company has just purchased a new machine costing $510,000. Shipping and installation costs will be $26,000. Franklin will provide 20 percent of the total cost of the machine as cash and borrow the remainder as an installment loan. The company's borrowing rate is 9.5 percent and the loan must be repaid on a monthly basis over a term of 5 years.

a. Determine the monthly loan payment required, assuming that the payments are made at the end of each month.

b. Now develop a monthly loan amortization schedule showing the split between the interest and principal paid each month over the term of the loan. Use a spreadsheet for this. How much interest is paid in the first year of the loan? If Franklin Company's tax rate is 30 percent, what is the actual cost of the interest expense?

c. If the company decides to repay the loan over 10 years rather than 5, what happens to the monthly loan payment and the total interest paid over the full term of the loan? Discuss the implications of your answer. Do not complete another loan amortization schedule.

INTERMEDIATE 

6–53 Loan interest deductions Liz Rogers just borrowed $10,000 for her business using an installment loan that is to be repaid over 3 years. The interest rate on the loan is 13 percent. As part of her firm's detailed financial planning, Liz wishes to determine the annual interest deduction attributable to the loan.

a. Determine the annual loan payment required on the loan.

b. Prepare an amortization schedule for the loan.

c. How much interest expense will Liz's firm have in *each* of the next 3 years as a result of this loan?

d. If the company's tax rate is 30 percent, what is the actual, after-tax amount of interest the company pays each year?

BASIC 

6–54 Growth and interest rates Three investments, A, B, and C, have the following series of cash flows:

	Cash flows		
Year	A	B	C
1	$500	$1,500	$2,500
2	560	1,550	2,600
3	640	1,610	2,650
4	720	1,680	2,650
5	800	1,760	2,800
6		1,850	2,850
7		1,950	2,900
8		2,060	
9		2,170	
10		2,280	

a. For each of the investments, calculate:
(i) the rate of growth in the cash flows for each year
(ii) the total rate of growth in the cash flows over the full life of the investment
(iii) the compound average annual growth rate in the cash flows

b. For each of the investments, if year 1 represents an initial deposit in an investment account paying annual interest, while the final-year value is the amount the initial deposit increases to, calculate the compound average annual rate of return on each investment.

c. Compare your answers for parts **a**(iii) and **b**. What can you conclude?

BASIC 

6–55 **Rate of return** Rishi Singh has $1,500 to invest. His investment counsellor suggests an investment that pays no stated interest but will return $2,000 at the end of 3 years.

a. What compounded annual rate of return will Mr. Singh earn with this investment?

b. Mr. Singh is considering another investment, of equal risk, which earns an annual return of 8 percent. Which investment should he take, and why?

BASIC 

6–56 **Rate of return and investment choice** Clare Jaccard has $5,000 to invest. Because she is only 25 years old, she is not concerned about the length of the investment's life. What she is sensitive to is the rate of return she will earn on the investment. With the help of her financial advisor Clare has isolated four equally risky investments, each providing a lump-sum return, shown in the following table. All of the investments require an initial $5,000 payment.

Investment	Lump-sum return	Investment life (years)
A	$ 8,400	6
B	15,900	15
C	7,600	4
D	13,000	10

a. Calculate the compounded annual rate of return on each of the four investments available to Clare.

b. Which investment would you recommend to Clare given her goal of maximizing the rate of return?

BASIC 

6–57 **Rate of return** What is your annual percentage rate of return on an investment of $10,606 if you expect to receive $2,000 each year for the next 10 years?

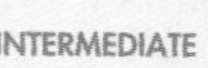 

6–58 **Choosing the best annuity** Raina Rashad wishes to choose the best of four retirement annuities available to her. In each case, in exchange for paying a single premium today, she will receive equal annual end-of-year cash benefits for a specified number of years. She considers the annuities to be equally risky and is not concerned about their differing lives. Her decision will be based solely on the rate of return she will earn on each annuity. The key characteristics of each of the four annuities are shown in the following table.

Annuity	Premium paid today	Annual benefit	Life (years)
A	$30,000	$3,100	20
B	25,000	3,900	10
C	40,000	4,200	15
D	35,000	4,000	12

a. Calculate the rate of return on each of the four annuities being considered by Raina.
b. Given Raina's stated decision criterion, which annuity should she select?

INTERMEDIATE LG6 6–59 Loan rates of interest John Fleming has been shopping for a loan to finance the purchase of a used car. He has found three possibilities that seem attractive and wishes to select the one having the lowest interest rate. The information available with respect to each of the three $5,000 loans is shown in the following table:

Loan	Principal	Annual payment	Term (years)
A	$5,000	$1,352.81	5
B	5,000	1,543.21	4
C	5,000	2,010.45	3

a. Determine the interest rate associated with each of the loans.
b. Which loan should Mr. Fleming take?

CASE CHAPTER 6 Funding Jill Moran's Retirement Annuity

See the enclosed Student CD-ROM for cases that help you put theories and concepts from the text into practice.

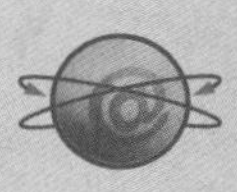

Be sure to visit the Companion Website for this book at **www.pearsoned.ca/gitman** for a wealth of additional learning tools including self-test quizzes, Web exercises, and additional cases.

CHAPTER 7

Risk and Return

LEARNING GOALS

LG1 Understand the meaning of risk, how returns are calculated for a single period and over multiple holding periods, and the concept of risk preferences.

LG2 Describe procedures for measuring the risk of a single asset, and the risk associated with a past series of returns.

LG3 Illustrate the returns and risk on different types of financial assets over the period 1938 to 2006, and discuss the lessons we can learn from this data.

LG4 Discuss the measurement of return and standard deviation for a portfolio, the various types of correlation that can exist between series of numbers, the benefits of diversification, and the impact of international assets on a portfolio.

LG5 Review the two types of risk for portfolio of assets, and the derivation and role of beta in measuring the relevant risk of both an individual security and a portfolio.

LG6 Explain the capital asset pricing model (CAPM), its relationship to the security market line (SML), and shifts in the SML caused by changes in inflationary expectations and risk aversion.

7.1 Risk and Return Fundamentals

As we have discussed earlier in the book, the principal financial goal of the company is to maximize the value of the company to their shareholders in an ethical manner. This is achieved by maximizing the price of the company's common shares.To maximize share price, the financial manager must learn to assess two key determinants: risk and return.[1]

"Not for a Million Bucks!"

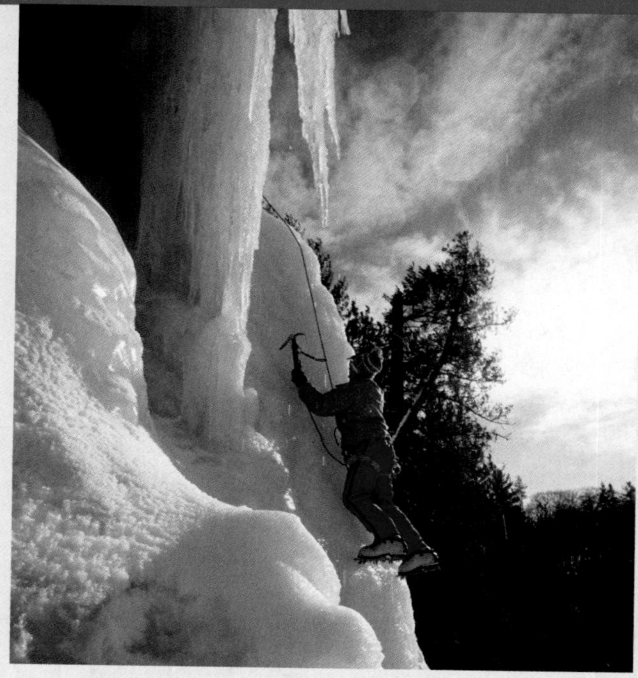

Expressions like this one and "Make it worth my while" touch on one of the key concepts of finance—that risk and return are linked. The idea that return should increase if risk increases is a fundamental concept in finance. Of course, people, as well as firms, have different views of risk, depending on who they are and what they do. Also, some people and some firms are simply more willing to take risks than are others—and for some, the mere thrill of risk is almost enough return in itself. Generally, though, most financial managers, like most people, shy away from undue risk and so must be compensated for taking on risk. As this chapter will show, firms can quantify and assess the risk and return for individual assets and for groups of assets, using various tools and techniques.

portfolio
A collection, or group, of assets.

Each financial decision presents certain risk and return characteristics, and the unique combination of these characteristics has an impact on share price. Risk can be viewed as it relates either to a single asset or to a **portfolio**—a collection, or group, of assets. We will look at both, beginning with the risk of a single

1. Two important points should be recognized here: (1) Although for convenience the publicly traded corporation is being discussed, the risk and return concepts presented apply equally well to all firms; and (2) concern centres only on the wealth of common shareholders, because they are the "residual owners" whose returns are in no way specified in advance.

LINKING THE DISCIPLINES: Cross-Functional Interactions

- ***Accounting personnel*** need to understand the relationship between risk and return to be able to determine the effect that diversification decisions have on the firm's expected streams of cash flow.
- ***Information systems analysts*** will design programs to calculate statistical measures of risk such as standard deviation and coefficient of variation, and will also create systems that develop charts and probability distributions to help management assess the risk–return tradeoff of assets.
- ***Management*** must learn to correctly assess risk and return, two key determinants in maximizing share price. They must understand the risk–return tradeoff of projects and how to evaluate and translate this data into decisions that impact the firm. Management must also understand how the addition or disposal of assets affects the risk and return of the firm's portfolio of assets.
- The ***marketing department*** considers standard deviation when deciding to add or delete product lines. The personnel must understand that even though higher-risk projects may produce higher returns, they may not be the best choice for the firm if they produce erratic cash flow patterns and fail to control risk and optimize the value of the firm.
- Personnel in the ***operations department*** need to understand why investments in plant, equipment, and systems need to be evaluated in light of their impact on the firm's overall risk and return, and therefore the value of the firm. The operations department can also influence standard deviation by entering into long-term contracts with suppliers that will reduce the fluctuations in raw materials prices, and subsequently in earnings.

asset. First, though, it is important to introduce some fundamental concepts about risk, return, and risk preferences.

Risk Defined

risk
The chance of financial loss or, more formally, the variability of returns associated with a given asset.

In the most basic sense, **risk** is the chance of financial loss. Assets having greater chances of loss are viewed as more risky than those with lesser chances of loss. More formally, the term *risk* is used interchangeably with *uncertainty* to refer to the *variability of returns associated with a given asset.* A government bond that guarantees its holder $100 interest after 30 days has virtually no risk, because there is no variability associated with the return. A $100 investment in a firm's common stock, which over the same period may earn anywhere from –$150 to $200, is very risky due to the high variability of return. The more certain the return from an asset, the less variability and therefore the less risk.

Return Defined

Obviously, if we are going to assess risk based on variability of return, we need to be certain we know what *return* is, and how to measure it. The return could be termed the actual, expected, or required return. In the discussion below, we are dealing with actual returns. This is an *ex post* value; that is, we make an investment decision, wait, and then calculate the return that was earned on the investment over the time period. Later in this chapter, and throughout the remainder of the book, we will also discuss the concept of required and expected returns. These are *ex ante* values; that is, we are estimating returns at the time we are making an investment decision.

The required return is the yearly return an investor requires given the risk of the asset. The expected return is the yearly return an investor expects to receive on the basis of an analysis of the fundamentals of the asset and its ability to generate cash flows in the future. In an efficient market, we would expect the expected and required returns to be equal. But in reality they may not be. These issues are discussed later in the chapter.

return
The total gain or loss experienced on an investment asset over a given period of time; calculated by dividing the asset's change in price plus any cash distributions during the period by its price at the beginning of the period.

For now, we will view **return** as the total gain or loss experienced on an investment asset over a given period of time. It is commonly measured as the change in the price of the asset over time plus any cash distributions received during the period, expressed as a percentage of the price of the asset at the beginning of the period. The rate of return earned on asset j over a time period, k_j, is calculated as:

$$k_j = \frac{P_{j,t} - P_{j,t-1} + C_{j,t}}{P_{j,t-1}} \tag{7.1}$$

where

k_j = the rate of return on asset j over the period $t - 1$ to t
$P_{j,t}$ = price of asset j at time t
$P_{j,t-1}$ = price of asset j at time $t - 1$
$C_{j,t}$ = cash distribution received from the investment in asset j over the time period $t - 1$ to t

The return, k_j, reflects the combined effect of changes in price, $P_{j,t} - P_{j,t-1}$, and the cash flow, $C_{j,t}$, over period $t - 1$ to t.[2]

Equation 7.1 is used to determine the rate of return over a time period as short as 1 day or as long as 20 years or more. However, in most cases, t is 1 year, and k_j therefore represents an annual rate of return.

Example Robin's Gameroom, a high-traffic video arcade, wishes to determine the return on two of its video machines, Conqueror and Demolition. Conqueror was purchased 4 years ago for \$20,000 and currently has a market value of \$21,500. During the year, it generated \$800 of after-tax cash receipts. Demolition was purchased 7 years ago; its value in the year just completed declined from \$12,000 to \$11,800. During the year, it generated \$1,700 of after-tax cash receipts. Substituting this data into Equation 7.1, we can calculate the annual rate of return, k_j, for each video machine:

Conqueror (C):

$$k_C = \frac{\$21{,}500 - \$20{,}000 + \$800}{\$20{,}000} = \frac{\$2{,}300}{\$20{,}000} = \underline{\underline{11.5\%}}$$

Demolition (D):

$$k_D = \frac{\$11{,}800 - \$12{,}000 + \$1{,}700}{\$12{,}000} = \frac{\$1{,}500}{\$12{,}000} = \underline{\underline{12.5\%}}$$

2. The beginning-of-period price, $P_{j,t-1}$, and the end-of-period price, $P_{j,t}$, are not necessarily *realized values*. They are often *unrealized*, which means that although the asset was *not* actually purchased at time $t - 1$ and sold at time t, values $P_{j,t-1}$ and $P_{j,t}$ *could* have been realized had those transactions been made.

Although the market value of Demolition declined during the year, its cash flow caused it to earn a higher rate of return than that earned by Conqueror during the same period. Clearly, the combined impact of changes in price and the cash flow generated by the asset are important when measuring the rate of return on investment.

Calculating Average Returns over Multiple Periods

The previous section provided the method to use to calculate returns on an asset for a single holding period. What happens if we invest in an asset for multiple periods; for example, we invest in the common shares of a company for five years? We can calculate returns for each year, but how is the average (mean) yearly return on the investment calculated? There are two ways to calculate the average return over a number of holding periods: the arithmetic mean return and the geometric mean return.

Arithmetic Mean Return

arithmetic mean
The sum of the periodic returns divided by the total number of periods for which returns are available.

The arithmetic mean return for an asset is calculated by adding the various periodic returns together (e.g., returns for a year) and dividing by the number of periods of returns available (for example, the number of years of returns). In other words, the **arithmetic mean** is the sum of the periodic returns divided by the total number of periods for which returns are available. It is calculated using Equation 7.2, as follows:

$$\bar{k}_j = \frac{\sum_{t=1}^{n} k_{j,t}}{n} \tag{7.2}$$

where

$\bar{k}_j$ = the arithmetic mean return over n time periods for asset j
$k_{j,t}$ = the return on asset j for holding period t
n = the number of periods of returns available

Example Let's say we have the following series of yearly returns for the Demolition video machine from the previous example: year 1: 8.6 percent, year 2: –10.8 percent, year 3: 16.1 percent, year 4: –0.6 percent, year 5: 12.5 percent. To calculate the arithmetic mean return for this period, add the five yearly returns. This equals 25.8 percent. Then divide by 5 since there are returns for 5 years. The arithmetic mean over this period is 5.16 percent. Over these five years, the Demolition video machine provided an average yearly return of 5.16 percent.

Geometric Mean Return

geometric mean
The average compound rate of return earned on the investment in an asset per holding period.

The **geometric mean** is the average compound rate of return earned on the investment in an asset per holding period. It measures the actual realized change in the value of an investment, per period, over multiple periods. The process to calculate the geometric mean is provided below.

$$k(G)_j = \sqrt[n]{(1 + k_1)(1 + k_2) \ldots (1 + k_n)} - 1 \tag{7.3}$$

where

$k(G)_j$ = the geometric mean return on asset j over n periods
k_1 = the return on asset j in period 1
k_n = the return on asset j in period n
n = the number of periods of returns available

Example Calculate the geometric mean return for the Demolition video machine using the same five years of returns as was used for the arithmetic mean. The geometric mean for the Demolition video machine is calculated as follows:

$$k(G)_D = \sqrt[5]{(1.086)\,(0.892)\,(1.161)\,(0.994)\,(1.125)} - 1$$
$$= \sqrt[5]{(1.25766741)} - 1$$
$$= 1.0469192 - 1$$
$$= 0.0469192 \text{ or } 4.69192\%$$

The geometric mean is the compound return per period over multiple periods. It shows the rate at which a sum of money grows per period. For example, assume that the geometric mean return on a portfolio of Canadian common shares was 12.5 percent over the ten-year period from January 1, 1999, to December 31, 2008. An investor purchasing the portfolio on January 1, 1999, would see their wealth compound by 12.5 percent each year over the ten years to December 31, 2008. To calculate the value of an investment at the end of multiple holding periods using the geometric mean, Equation 7.4 is used.

$$V_{EOP} = V_{BOP} \times [1 + k(G)_j]^n \quad (7.4)$$

where

V_{EOP} = the value of asset j at the end of the investment period
V_{BOP} = the value of asset j at the beginning of the investment period
$k(G)_j$ = the geometric mean yearly return on asset j
n = the number of years in the investment period

Example Assume an investment of $1,000 was made in the portfolio of Canadian common shares, from the above example, at the beginning of 1999. What would be the value of this investment at the end of 2008? The investment of $1,000 in this portfolio would compound and grow to:

$$V_{EOP} = \$1{,}000 \times [1 + 0.125]^{10}$$
$$= \$1{,}000 \times 3.24732$$
$$= \$3{,}247.32$$

This could also be solved using your financial calculator, where $1,000 is the *PV*, *n* is 10, and I/Y is 12.5. Solve for *FV*. The answer is $3,247.32.

Differences in the Two Measures: Which Is Better?

Note the difference in the two measures of average performance for the five years of returns for the Demolition video machine. The arithmetic mean is 5.16 percent; the geometric mean is 4.69 percent. One of the characteristics of the two measures is that the arithmetic mean will always be greater than the geometric mean, unless the yearly returns in a series are all the same. In such a case, the two measures would provide the same answer. The wider the distribution of returns over the holding periods, the greater the difference between the two means.

Which is the better measure of average returns? The answer depends on what you wish to measure. The arithmetic mean is a better measure of typical performance. It is a good estimate of expected yearly return on an asset in the future, assuming the past time period is representative of the future. The geometric mean is a better measure of past performance. It indicates the change in wealth over a holding period of multiple periods. In the following sections, both measures will be used and illustrated using actual yearly return data for various types of financial securities.

Risk Preferences

Feelings about risk differ among managers (and firms).[3] Thus, it is important to specify a generally acceptable level of risk. The three basic risk preference behaviours—risk-averse, risk-indifferent, and risk-seeking—are depicted graphically in Figure 7.1.

risk-indifferent
The attitude toward risk in which no change in return would be required for an increase in risk.

- For the **risk-indifferent** manager, the required return does not change as the level of risk increases from x_1 to x_2. In essence, no change in return would be required for the increase in risk. Clearly, this attitude is nonsensical in almost any business context.

FIGURE 7.1

Risk Preferences

Risk preference behaviours

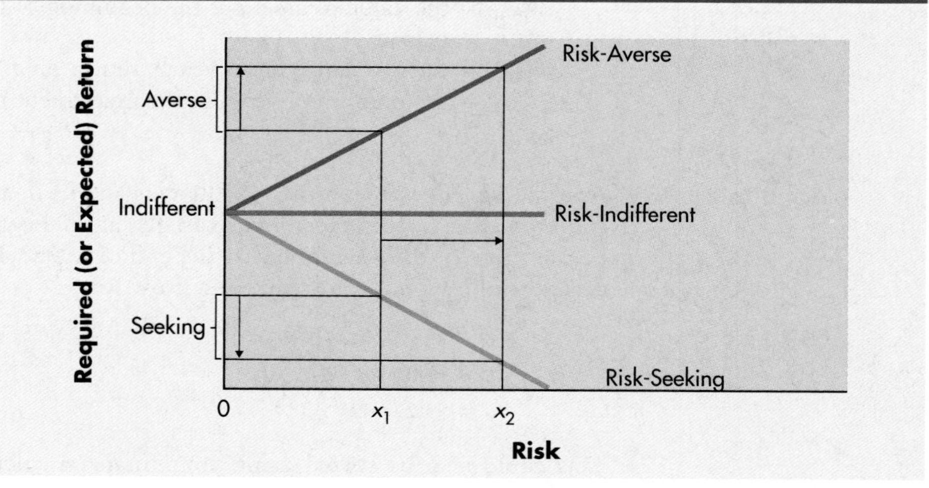

3. The risk preferences of the managers in theory should be consistent with the risk preferences of the firm. Although the *agency problem* suggests that in practice managers may not behave in a manner consistent with the firm's risk preferences, it is assumed here that they do. Therefore, the managers' risk preferences and those of the firm are assumed to be the same.

risk-averse
The attitude toward risk in which an increased return would be required for an increase in risk.

risk-seeking
The attitude toward risk in which a decreased return would be accepted for an increase in risk.

Hint
Remember that most investors are also risk-averse. Like risk-averse managers, for a given increase in risk, they also require an increase in return for their investment in that firm.

- For the **risk-averse** manager, the required return *increases* for an increase in risk. Because they shy away from risk, these managers require higher expected returns to compensate them for taking greater risk.
- For the **risk-seeking** manager, the required return *decreases* for an increase in risk. Theoretically, because they enjoy risk, these managers are willing to give up some return to take more risk. Such behaviour would be considered irrational and would negatively affect the firm and the manager's job!

It is generally assumed that people are risk-averse; for a given increase in risk, they require an increase in return. They generally tend to be conservative rather than aggressive when considering the risk they are willing to accept. Accordingly, in this text, *we assume that all financial managers are risk-averse, meaning they require higher returns when investing in assets that have higher risk.*

? Review Questions

7–1 Define *risk* as it relates to financial decision making. Do any assets have perfectly certain returns?

7–2 Define *return*. Describe the basic calculation involved in finding the return on an investment.

7–3 Discuss the two methods that can be used to calculate average returns over multiple holding periods. What is the equation for each method? Which method provides the better estimate for average return?

7–4 Compare the following risk preferences: (**a**) risk-averse, (**b**) risk-indifferent, and (**c**) risk-seeking. Which is most common among financial managers?

7.2 Risk of a Single Asset

The concept of risk is best developed by first considering a single asset held in isolation. Although you will later see that the risk of a portfolio of assets is measured in much the same way as the risk of a single asset, certain benefits accrue to holders of portfolios. For both single assets and for portfolios of assets, we can assess risk by looking at the variability of the returns earned on the asset. We then measure risk using statistical concepts. Risk can be calculated for both actual return data and expected return data. Examples using both types of return data are provided in the following discussion.

Risk Assessment

Risk can be assessed using sensitivity analysis and probability distributions, which provide a feel for the level of risk embodied in a given asset.

Sensitivity Analysis

sensitivity analysis
An approach for assessing risk that uses a number of possible return estimates to obtain a sense of the variability among outcomes.

Sensitivity analysis uses a number of possible return estimates to obtain a sense of the variability among outcomes.[4] One common method involves estimating

4. The term "sensitivity analysis" is intentionally used in a general rather than technically correct fashion here to simplify this discussion. A more technical and precise definition and discussion of this technique and "scenario analysis" is presented in Chapter 13.

TABLE 7.1 Assets A and B

	Asset A	Asset B
Initial investment	$10,000	$10,000
Annual rate of return		
Pessimistic	13%	7%
Most likely	15%	15%
Optimistic	17%	23%
Range	4%	16%

range
A measure of an asset's risk, which is found by subtracting the pessimistic (worst) outcome from the optimistic (best) outcome.

the pessimistic (worst), the most likely (expected), and the optimistic (best) returns associated with a given asset. In this case, the asset's risk can be measured by the **range,** which is found by subtracting the pessimistic outcome from the optimistic outcome. The greater the range for a given asset, the more variability, or risk, it is said to have.

Example Norman Company, a custom golf equipment manufacturer, wants to choose the better of two investments, A and B. Each requires an initial outlay of $10,000 and each has a *most likely* annual rate of return of 15 percent. Management has also made *pessimistic* and *optimistic* estimates of the returns associated with each. The three estimates for each asset, along with its range, are given in Table 7.1. Asset A appears to be less risky than asset B; its range of 4 percent (17% − 13%) is less than the range of 16 percent (23% − 7%) for asset B. The risk-averse decision maker would prefer asset A over asset B, because A offers the same most likely return as B (15%) but with lower risk (smaller range).

Note that in the above example, expected return data was used. If actual data regarding return is available, the range can be calculated to get a "feel" for the risk of an asset.

Example Liam Wagner invested in the common shares of two companies four years ago. The percentage rates of return Liam received in each of the four years is provided below:

Year	Company X	Company Y
1	10%	16%
2	-2%	-8%
3	6%	-5%
4	12%	29%

Which was the riskier investment? The range in returns for X is 14 percent [12% − (−2%)], while for Y it is 37 percent [29% − (−8%)]. The spread or distribution of returns for company Y are much wider than for company X. Company Y is riskier than X.

Although the use of sensitivity analysis and the range is rather crude, it does provide the decision maker with a feel for the behaviour of returns that can be used to roughly assess the risk involved.

Probability Distributions

probability
The *chance* that a given outcome will occur.

Probability distributions provide a more quantitative insight into an asset's risk. The **probability** of a given outcome is its *chance* of occurring. If an outcome has an 80 percent probability of occurrence, the given outcome would be expected to occur 8 out of 10 times. If an outcome has a probability of 100 percent, it is certain to occur. Outcomes having a probability of zero will never occur.

Example Norman Company's past estimates indicate that the probabilities of the pessimistic, most likely, and optimistic outcomes are 25 percent, 50 percent, and 25 percent, respectively. The sum of these probabilities must equal 100 percent; that is, they must be based on all the alternatives considered.

probability distribution
A model that relates probabilities to the associated outcomes.

bar chart
The simplest type of probability distribution; shows only a limited number of outcomes and associated probabilities for a given event.

continuous probability distribution
A probability distribution showing all the possible outcomes and associated probabilities for a given event.

A **probability distribution** is a model that relates probabilities to the associated outcomes. The simplest type of probability distribution is the **bar chart,** which shows only a limited number of outcome–probability coordinates. The bar charts for Norman Company's assets A and B are shown in Figure 7.2. Although both assets have the same most likely return, the range of return is much more dispersed for asset B than for asset A—16 versus 4 percent.

If we knew all the possible outcomes and associated probabilities, we could develop a **continuous probability distribution.** This type of distribution can be thought of as a bar chart for a very large number of outcomes.[5] Figure 7.3 presents continuous probability distributions for assets A and B.[6] Note in the figure that although A and B have the same most likely return (15 percent), the distribution of returns for asset B has much greater *dispersion* than the distribution for asset A. Clearly, asset B is more risky than asset A.

FIGURE 7.2

Bar Charts

Bar charts for asset A's and asset B's returns

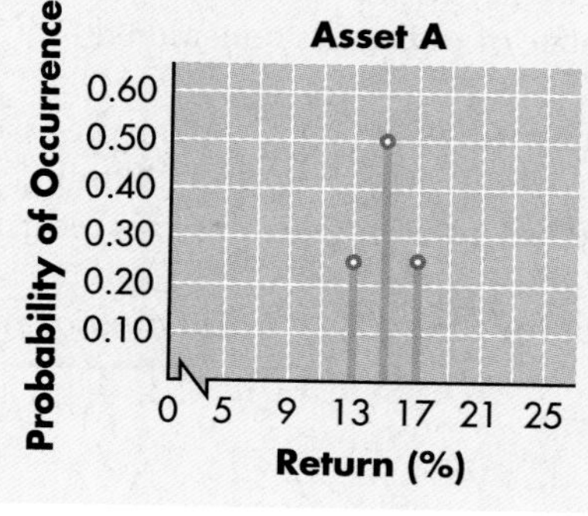

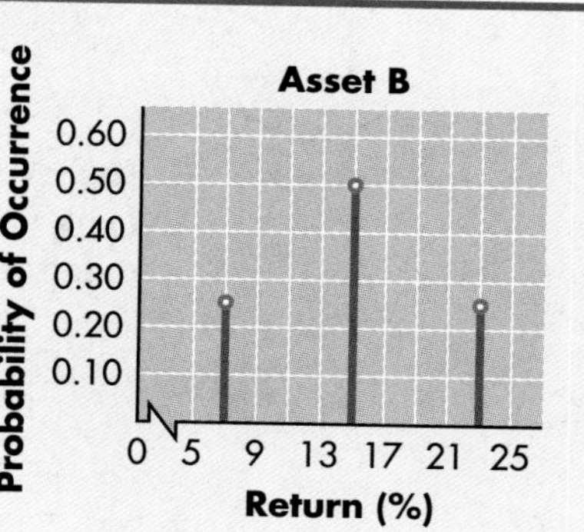

5. To develop a continuous probability distribution, one must have data on a large number of historical occurrences for a given event. Then, by developing a frequency distribution indicating how many times each outcome has occurred over the given time horizon, one can convert these data into a probability distribution. Probability distributions for risky events can also be developed by using *simulation*—a process discussed briefly in Chapter 13.

6. The continuous distribution's probabilities change due to the large number of additional outcomes considered. The area under each of the curves is equal to 1, which means that 100 percent of the outcomes, or all the possible outcomes, are considered.

FIGURE 7.3

Continuous Probability Distributions

Continuous probability distributions for asset A's and asset B's returns

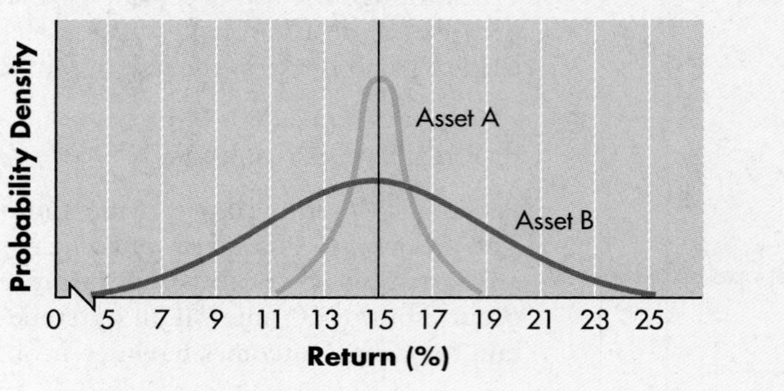

Risk Measurement

In addition to its *range,* the risk of an asset can be quantitatively measured using two statistics—the standard deviation and the coefficient of variation. Both measure the variability of asset returns.

Standard Deviation

standard deviation (σ_k) The most common statistical indicator of an asset's risk; it measures the dispersion around the *expected value.*

expected return $\hat{k}_j$ The most likely return on asset *j* over a stated period.

The most common statistical indicator of an asset's risk is the **standard deviation,** σ_k, which measures the dispersion around the *expected value.*[7] The **expected return,** $\hat{k}_j$ (termed "k-hat for asset *j*"), is the most likely return on an asset over a stated period. It is calculated as

$$\hat{k}_j = \sum_{i=1}^{n} k_{j,i} \times Pr_i \tag{7.5}$$

where

$k_{j,i}$ = return on asset *j* for the *i*th outcome
Pr_i = probability of the *i*th outcome occurring for asset *j*
n = number of outcomes considered

Example The expected values for Norman Company's assets A and B are presented in Table 7.2. Column 1 gives the Pr_i's and column 2 gives the $k_{j,i}$'s. In each case n equals 3. The expected value for each asset's return is 15 percent.

The expression for the *standard deviation of returns,* σ_j, is:

$$\sigma_j = \sqrt{\sum_{t=1}^{n} (k_{j,i} - \hat{k}_j)^2 \times Pr_i} \tag{7.6}$$

In general, the higher the standard deviation, the greater the risk.

7. Although risk is typically viewed as determined by the dispersion of outcomes around an expected value, many people believe that risk exists only when outcomes are below the expected value, because only returns below the expected value are considered bad. Nevertheless, the common approach is to view risk as determined by the variability on either side of the expected value, because the greater this variability, the less confident one can be of the outcomes associated with an investment.

TABLE 7.2 Expected Values of Returns for Assets A and B

Possible outcomes	Probability (1)	Returns (2)	Weighted value [(1) × (2)] (3)
		Asset A	
Pessimistic	0.25	13%	3.25%
Most likely	0.50	15	7.50
Optimistic	0.25	17	4.25
Total	1.00	Expected return ($\hat{k}_A$)	15.00%
		Asset B	
Pessimistic	0.25	7%	1.75%
Most likely	0.50	15	7.50
Optimistic	0.25	23	5.75
Total	1.00	Expected return ($\hat{k}_B$)	15.00%

Example Table 7.3 presents the standard deviations for Norman Company's assets A and B, based on the earlier data. The standard deviation for asset A is 1.41 percent, and the standard deviation for asset B is 5.66 percent. The higher risk of asset B is clearly reflected in its higher standard deviation.

normal probability distribution
A symmetrical probability distribution whose shape resembles a "bell-shaped" curve.

A **normal probability distribution,** depicted in Figure 7.4, always resembles a "bell-shaped" curve. It is symmetrical: from the peak of the graph, the curve's extensions are mirror images (reflections) of each other. The peak is the mean of the variable being considered. The symmetry of the curve means that half the probability is associated with the values to the left of the peak and half with values to the right. As noted on the figure, for normal probability distributions, 68.3 percent of the possible outcomes will lie between ±1 standard deviation from the mean, 95.4 percent of all outcomes will lie between ±2 standard devi-

FIGURE 7.4
Bell-Shaped Curve
Normal probability distribution, described by the mean and the standard deviation.

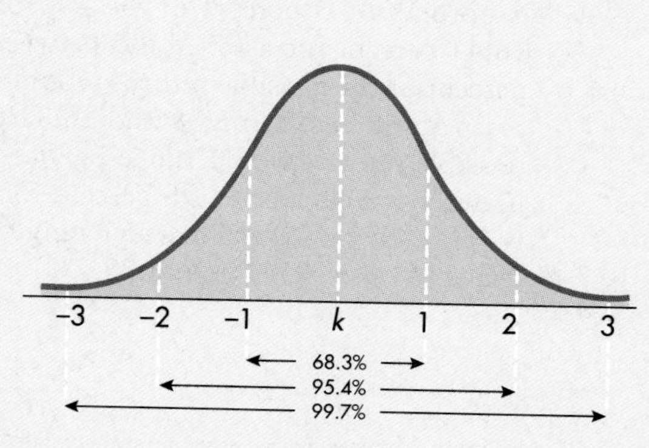

TABLE 7.3 **The Calculation of the Standard Deviation of the Returns for Assets A and B**[a]

Asset A

i	$k_{A,i}$	$\hat{k}_A$	$k_{A,i} - \hat{k}_A$	$(k_{A,i} - \hat{k}_A)^2$	Pr_i	$(k_{A,i} - \hat{k}_A)^2 \times Pr_i$
1	13%	15%	−2%	4%	0.25	1%
2	15	15	0	0	0.50	0
3	17	15	2	4	0.25	1
						= 2%

$$\sigma_A = \sqrt{\sum_{t=1}^{3} (k_{A,i} - \hat{k}_A)^2 \times Pr_i} = \sqrt{2\%} = \underline{\underline{1.41\%}}$$

Asset B

i	$k_{B,i}$	$\hat{k}_B$	$k_{B,i} - \hat{k}_B$	$(k_{B,i} - \hat{k}_B)^2$	Pr_i	$(k_{B,i} - \hat{k}_A)^2 \times Pr_i$
1	7%	15%	−8%	64%	0.25	16%
2	15	15	0	0	0.50	0
3	23	15	8	64	0.25	16
						= 32%

$$\sigma_B = \sqrt{\sum_{t=1}^{3} (k_{B,i} - \hat{k}_B)^2 \times Pr_i} = \sqrt{32\%} = \underline{\underline{5.66\%}}$$

[a]Calculations in this table are made in percentage form rather than decimal form—for example, 13% rather than 0.13. As a result, some of the intermediate computations may appear to be inconsistent with those that would result from using decimal form. Regardless, the resulting standard deviations are correct and identical to those that would result from using decimal rather than percentage form.

ations from the mean, and 99.7 percent of all outcomes will lie between ±3 standard deviations from the mean.[8]

Example If we assume that the probability distribution of returns for the Norman Company is normal, 68.3 percent of the possible returns would range between 13.59 and 16.41 percent for asset A and between 9.34 and 20.66 percent for asset B; 95.4 percent of the possible returns would range between 12.18 and 17.82 percent for asset A and between 3.68 and 26.32 percent for asset B; and 99.7 percent of the possible returns would range between 10.77 and 19.23 percent for asset A and between −1.98 and 31.98 percent for asset B. The greater risk of asset B is clearly reflected by its much wider range of possible returns for each level of confidence (68.3%, 95.4%, and 99.7%).

8. Tables of values indicating the probabilities associated with various deviations from the expected value of a normal distribution can be found in any basic statistics text. These values can be used to establish confidence limits and make inferences about possible outcomes. This is illustrated later in this chapter.

Calculating the Standard Deviation of a Past Series of Returns

In a situation where we have a past series of returns, a different approach is taken to calculating the standard deviation. Essentially each of the historic returns is allocated equal probability and the formula for standard deviation of returns, σ_j, becomes:

$$\sigma_j = \sqrt{\frac{\sum_{t=1}^{n}(k_{j,t} - \bar{k}_j)^2}{n-1}} \quad (7.7)$$

where

$k_{j,t}$ = return on asset j for period t

$\bar{k}_j$ = arithmetic mean for the series of n returns for asset j

n = number of periodic returns

Example

www.beyondtechnology.com/tips016.shtml

Assume Karen purchases the common shares in Barrick Manufacturing and holds the shares for ten years. She calculates her yearly returns as shown in the second column of Table 7.4. Based on this information, she wishes to calculate the arithmetic mean and standard deviation of these returns. The arithmetic mean is calculated by adding the ten yearly returns and dividing by 10, resulting in 12.49 percent. The process used to calculate the standard deviation is provided in Table 7.4 and Spreadsheet Application 7.1. There are also numerous Web sites that provide solution methods.

TABLE 7.4 Calculation of the Standard Deviation for a Series of Historic Returns

Year	Yearly return	Arithmetic mean	Difference	Difference squared
1	2.15%	12.49%	−10.34%	106.92%
2	39.05	12.49	26.56	705.43
3	27.80	12.49	15.31	234.40
4	13.22	12.49	0.73	000.53
5	−20.58	12.49	−33.07	1,093.62
6	31.25	12.49	18.76	351.94
7	4.59	12.49	−7.90	062.41
8	1.78	12.49	−10.71	114.70
9	32.75	12.49	20.26	410.47
10	−7.09	12.49	−19.58	383.38

Sum of the squared differences = 3,463.80

Variance[a] = $\frac{3,463.80}{10 - 1}$ = 384.87%

Standard deviation (square root of variance) 19.62%

[a]The variance is the standard deviation squared. Both the variance and standard deviation can be used as measures of risk. The variance must be calculated before the standard deviation.

7.1 SPREADSHEET APPLICATION

Microsoft Excel - Spreadsheet Application 7-1.xls

Calculating Arithmetic Mean and Standard Deviation

	A	B	C	D	E	F	G
4		Yearly	Arithmetic		Difference		
5	Year	Return	Mean	Difference	Squared		
6	1	2.15%	12.49%	-10.34%	1.0696%	←	=(B6-b17)^2
7	2	39.05%	12.49%	26.56%	7.0533%	←	=(B7-b17)^2
8	3	27.80%	12.49%	15.31%	2.3433%	←	=(B8-b17)^2
9	4	13.22%	12.49%	0.73%	0.0053%	←	=(B9-b17)^2
10	5	-20.58%	12.49%	-33.07%	10.9376%	←	=(B10-b17)^2
11	6	31.25%	12.49%	18.76%	3.5186%	←	=(B11-b17)^2
12	7	4.59%	12.49%	-7.90%	0.6244%	←	=(B12-b17)^2
13	8	1.78%	12.49%	-10.71%	1.1475%	←	=(B13-b17)^2
14	9	32.75%	12.49%	20.26%	4.1039%	←	=(B14-b17)^2
15	10	-7.09%	12.49%	-19.58%	3.8345%	←	=(B15-b17)^2
16	Sum	124.92%			34.6380%	←	=SUM(E6:E15)
17	Arithmetic mean	12.49%	← =B16/10				
18	Variance				3.8487%	←	=E16/9
19	Standard deviation				19.62%	←	=E18^0.5
22	**Arithmetic mean**	12.49%	← =AVERAGE(B6:B15)				
23	**Standard deviation**	19.62%	← =STDEV(B6:B15)				

Therefore, over these ten years, the common shares in Barrick Manufacturing provided an average yearly return of 12.49 percent. The total risk of the portfolio over these ten years, the dispersion of returns around the average, was 19.62 percent. If it was assumed that these results for the ten years were representative of what might occur with the returns on Barrick Manufacturing's common shares in the future, what could be said about the probability of the range of returns an investor might receive in a future time period? To determine this, it must be assumed that the returns on the common shares are normally distributed—an assumption that is generally accepted. If so, given the results in Table 7.4, it could be claimed that there is a:

- 68.3% probability that actual returns in the future will be between 12.49% ± 19.62%, or –7.13% to 32.11%

- 95.4% probability that actual returns in the future will be between 12.49% ± (2 × 19.62%), or –26.75% to 51.73%
- 99.7% probability that actual returns in the future will be between 12.49% ± (3 × 19.62%), or −46.37% to 71.35%.

In summary, the standard deviation of returns measures the total risk of one asset, a portfolio of assets, or a historic series of returns for an asset or portfolio. Determining risk is useful in trying to determine whether the expected return is worth the risk. This issue is discussed in more detail in Section 7.3.

Coefficient of Variation

coefficient of variation (CV) A measure of relative dispersion that is useful in comparing the risk of assets with differing expected returns.

The **coefficient of variation, *CV*,** is a measure of relative dispersion that is useful in comparing the risk of assets with differing expected or actual returns. Equation 7.8 gives the expression for the coefficient of variation:

$$CV_j = \frac{\text{standard deviation } j}{\text{average return } j} = \frac{\sigma_j}{\hat{k}_j \text{ or } \bar{k}_j} \tag{7.8}$$

The higher the coefficient of variation, the greater the risk.

Example When the standard deviation (from Table 7.3) and the expected returns (from Table 7.2) for assets A and B are substituted into Equation 7.8, the coefficients of variation for A and B are 0.094 (1.41% ÷ 15%) and 0.377 (5.66% ÷ 15%), respectively. Asset B has the higher coefficient of variation and therefore has more risk than asset A—which we already know from the standard deviation. Because both assets have the same expected return, the coefficient of variation has not provided any new information.

The real utility of the coefficient of variation comes in comparing the risk of assets that have *different* expected returns.

Example A firm wants to select the less risky of two alternative assets—X and Y. The expected return, standard deviation, and coefficient of variation for each of these assets are:

Statistics	Asset X	Asset Y
(1) Expected return	12%	20%
(2) Standard deviation	9%[a]	12%
(3) Coefficient of variation [(2) ÷ (1)]	0.75	0.60[a]

[a]Preferred asset using the given risk measure.

Based solely on their standard deviations, the firm would prefer asset X since it has a lower standard deviation than asset Y (9% versus 12%). However, management would be making a serious error in choosing asset X over asset Y since the relative risk of the assets, as reflected in the coefficient of variation, is lower for Y than for X (0.60 versus 0.75). Clearly, the use of the coefficient of variation to compare asset risk is effective because it also considers the return of the asset.

We can also calculate the coefficient of variation for the ten years of returns on Barrick Manufacturing's common shares. The coefficient of variation is equal to 1.57 (19.62% ÷ 12.49%). This means that for every unit of return, there is 1.57 units of risk. As was clear from our discussion in Chapter 5, investing in common shares can entail a significant amount of risk. The mean return, standard deviation, and coefficient of variation could also be calculated if data in dollars is available.

Example Assume that over the ten years between 1999 and 2008, a company received the following dollar returns from two investments.

Year	Dollar return	
	Investment F	**Investment G**
1999	$6,000	–$3,200
2000	4,800	–1,800
2001	–5,200	2,900
2002	9,700	3,400
2003	8,600	3,800
2004	–3,100	4,600
2005	–1,000	5,600
2006	7,400	6,100
2007	8,200	6,400
2008	9,900	5,000

The company's finance manager wonders which of the two projects was the better investment. To answer the question, she wishes to calculate the coefficient of variation for each investment. To do this, the mean return and standard deviation of returns must be calculated. This can be done by using Equations 7.2 and 7.7. Also, Spreadsheet Application 7.1, which used percentage data, can be easily modified for dollar amounts by adjusting the format of the cells. The calculations indicate that the arithmetic mean returns are $4,530 and $3,280, for investments F and G, respectively.

The standard deviation is calculated by using the same process used in Table 7.4, except dollar amounts are used, not percentage amounts. The standard deviations are $5,573.16 and $3,265.92 for investments F and G, respectively. Which was the better investment for the company? Investment F generated a higher return than G, but it was also riskier. To more accurately evaluate the two investments, the coefficient of variation can be used, as shown below:

		Investment F	**Investment G**
Coefficient of variation	=	$\frac{\$5,573.16}{\$4,530}$	$\frac{\$3,265.92}{\$3,280}$
	=	1.230	0.996

These numbers indicate that for every $100 of return on investment F, there was $1.230 of risk. For G, for every $100 of return, there was only $0.996 of risk. In terms of balancing risk and return, investment G did a better job than F. But investment F still generated a higher average return than G. Investment F generated a high return but at a higher level of risk. In contrast, G generated a more moderate return with lower risk. Which combination is better? It depends on the risk tolerance of the company. Some companies are willing to take higher risk for higher returns. Others wish to take more measured risk for slightly lower returns.

? Review Questions

7–5 How can *sensitivity analysis* be used to assess asset risk? Define and describe the role of the *range* in sensitivity analysis.

7–6 What does a plot of the *probability distribution* of outcomes show a decision maker about an asset's risk? What is the difference between a *bar chart* and a *continuous probability distribution?*

7–7 What does the *standard deviation* of asset returns indicate? What relationship exists between the size of the standard deviation and the degree of asset risk?

7–8 How does calculating the standard deviation of a single asset where the probabilities of different returns are available differ from calculating the standard deviation of a past series of returns for an asset? What is the equation for each method?

7–9 What is the *coefficient of variation?* How is it calculated? When is it preferred over the standard deviation for comparing asset risk?

LG3

7.3 Risk and Return of Financial Securities

Table 7.5 provides the yearly rates of return on four important types of financial securities and the level of inflation for Canada for the 69-year period from 1938 to 2006. The data provided includes the following:

- The rate of change in the consumer price index, the commonly used measure of inflation in the economy.
- The annualized yield on 91-day Government of Canada treasury bills (t-bills).
- The returns on an investment in a portfolio of long-term bonds issued by the Government of Canada. The minimum maturity of bonds in this portfolio is 10 years.
- The return on an index of Canadian common shares. The index of common shares trading on the Toronto Stock Exchange (TSX) is used. The S&P/TSX Composite Index is the measure of stock market performance for Canada. The yearly returns in the table include both increases in the value of the index as well as any dividends received, which are assumed to be reinvested back into the common shares.
- The return on an index of U.S. common shares including both changes in the value of the index and reinvested dividends. The index used is Standard & Poor's 500 (S&P 500), an index of 500 of the largest companies trading on

TABLE 7.5 Annual Percentage Rates of Return on Selected Financial Securities for the Period 1938 to 2006

Year	CPI	91-day t-bills	Canada long bonds	Canadian common shares	U.S. common shares In Canadian $	U.S. common shares In U.S. $
1938	–2.15	0.62	5.63	9.13	34.42	33.23
1939	2.20	0.70	–2.98	0.19	8.46	–0.89
1940	5.38	0.73	8.69	–19.13	–9.98	–9.98
1941	6.12	0.59	3.80	1.93	–11.70	–11.70
1942	2.88	0.54	3.08	13.99	21.08	21.08
1943	1.87	0.49	3.88	19.67	25.59	25.59
1944	–1.83	0.39	3.16	13.47	19.60	19.60
1945	1.87	0.37	5.18	36.05	36.09	36.39
1946	5.50	0.39	6.02	–1.50	–16.45	–8.12
1947	14.78	0.41	3.17	0.34	5.27	5.27
1948	9.09	0.41	–2.38	12.13	5.08	5.08
1949	0.69	0.48	4.85	22.61	29.78	18.00
1950	6.21	0.54	–0.12	48.43	24.63	30.47
1951	10.39	0.77	–3.13	24.04	21.35	24.61
1952	–1.18	1.05	1.99	–0.42	11.96	18.31
1953	0.00	1.65	3.64	2.15	–0.75	–1.01
1954	0.00	1.53	9.99	39.05	51.37	52.16
1955	0.60	1.45	–0.34	27.80	35.64	31.37
1956	2.96	2.90	–3.63	13.22	2.43	6.59
1957	1.72	3.86	5.89	–20.58	–9.20	–10.77
1958	2.82	2.16	–5.69	31.25	41.33	43.21
1959	1.10	4.77	–4.43	4.59	10.36	11.92
1960	1.63	3.53	7.10	1.78	3.76	0.46
1961	0.00	2.89	9.78	32.75	34.58	26.79
1962	1.60	4.04	3.05	–7.09	–5.81	–8.72
1963	2.11	3.66	4.26	15.60	23.05	22.67
1964	2.06	3.80	6.97	25.43	15.82	16.33
1965	3.03	4.03	0.96	6.68	12.50	12.37
1966	3.43	5.14	1.55	–7.07	–9.43	–10.04
1967	3.79	4.62	–2.20	18.09	23.56	23.89
1968	4.11	6.47	–0.80	22.45	10.26	10.99
1969	4.82	7.43	–2.01	–0.81	–8.33	–8.42
1970	1.26	6.58	21.98	–3.57	–1.55	3.95
1971	4.96	3.80	11.55	8.01	12.22	14.26
1972	5.12	3.59	1.11	27.38	18.62	18.91
1973	9.36	5.45	1.71	0.27	–14.53	–14.76
1974	12.33	8.22	–1.69	–25.93	–27.20	–26.37
1975	9.45	7.55	2.82	18.48	40.76	37.19
1976	5.85	9.43	19.02	11.02	24.18	23.59
1977	9.47	7.87	5.97	10.71	–0.25	–7.39
1978	8.41	8.93	1.29	29.72	14.41	6.43

continued

TABLE 7.5 continued

Year	CPI	91-day t-bills	Canada long bonds	Canadian common shares	U.S. common shares In Canadian $	U.S. common shares In U.S. $
1979	9.76	12.53	–2.62	44.77	17.25	18.24
1980	11.11	13.73	2.06	30.13	35.39	32.31
1981	12.18	20.37	–3.02	–10.25	–5.91	–4.98
1982	9.24	15.25	42.98	5.54	26.93	21.49
1983	4.60	9.86	9.60	35.49	23.26	22.41
1984	3.69	11.94	15.09	–2.39	12.37	6.13
1985	4.38	9.77	25.26	25.07	38.65	31.22
1986	4.19	9.48	17.54	8.95	17.63	18.91
1987	4.15	8.45	0.45	5.88	–0.40	5.11
1988	3.99	9.76	10.45	11.08	6.44	16.35
1989	5.23	12.91	16.29	21.37	27.57	31.39
1990	4.97	13.98	3.34	–14.80	–3.20	–3.10
1991	3.79	9.58	24.43	12.02	28.86	30.47
1992	2.13	6.50	13.07	–1.43	19.55	7.62
1993	1.69	5.28	22.88	32.55	15.10	10.08
1994	0.20	5.33	–10.46	–0.18	5.71	1.32
1995	1.75	7.44	26.28	14.53	35.71	37.58
1996	2.20	4.49	14.29	28.35	22.27	22.96
1997	0.75	3.30	17.45	14.98	39.72	33.36
1998	1.02	4.81	14.13	–1.58	38.99	28.58
1999	2.58	4.83	–7.15	31.71	15.63	21.04
2000	3.23	5.63	13.64	7.41	–6.07	–9.10
2001	0.70	4.14	3.92	–12.57	–8.70	–11.89
2002	3.88	2.55	10.09	–12.44	–23.00	–22.10
2003	1.99	2.93	8.06	26.72	8.34	28.69
2004	2.12	2.25	8.46	14.48	2.97	10.88
2005	2.15	2.67	15.05	24.13	–0.09	4.91
2006	1.63	4.04	4.15	17.26	14.99	15.79

SOURCE: Based on Table 1A from "Report on Canadian Economic Statistics 1924–2005," July 2006, Canadian Institute of Actuaries. See the report at **www.actuaries.ca/members/publications/2006/206022e-t.xls**. Used by permission. 2006 data from Bank of Canada, TSX Review, and Standard & Poor.

stock markets in the United States. Companies that are traded on both the New York and the NASDAQ stock exchange are included in the index. Two series of returns are provided, one in Canadian dollars and one in U.S. dollars. The former series is useful for a Canadian converting Canadian dollars into U.S. dollars to invest in the S&P 500. The latter series is the return earned by an American investing in the index.

To calculate the returns for a particular year, it is assumed that the relevant index is purchased on December 31 of the previous year, any income received from the index (dividends or interest) is reinvested, and that the index is sold on

December 31 of the year for which the return is calculated. So the returns for 1938, the first year returns are available for all return series, is calculated assuming the purchase of the index on December 31, 1937, the reinvestment of income received in 1938, and the sale of the index on December 31, 1938.

The 69 years from 1938 to 2006 span a period of remarkable change in the world. Numerous wars, including World War II, have been fought; communism became a widespread political system in the world but receded with the collapse of the Soviet Union; numerous countries have been formed; China has evolved from a feudal state to become an economic and military powerhouse; tremendous social changes have occurred around the world; the growth of the middle class in many countries has resulted in expanding economies and increased opportunities; the pace of technological change has been breathtaking—the list could go on. Economically, this period in Canada spans the economic boom of the early 1940s and 1950s, the period of extreme inflation of the late 1970s to early 1980s, the tech market boom in 1999 to 2000 and the subsequent bust in 2001 and 2002, and the large increase in resource prices leading a boom in the Canadian economy and stock income from 2003 through to 2006.

Over this period, significant changes have occurred. But the opportunity to invest in financial assets in order to receive a return, while recognizing the risks of such investments, has been consistent. The data in Table 7.5 provides returns on the types of investment assets that are normally purchased by individual and institutional investors, and which were discussed in Chapter 5. The major money market and capital market securities are included in the table. Note that returns on preferred shares are not provided, since an index of the returns on preferred shares is not readily available. The following sections discuss what we can learn from an analysis of this data.

Average Return and Risk

What can we learn? First, we can calculate the average yearly returns and the level of risk associated with these financial securities over the 69 years for which returns are available. Table 7.6 provides both the arithmetic and geometric mean yearly returns, the range of returns, the standard deviation of returns, and the risk premiums for the financial securities. What do these summary statistics tell us?

1. In all cases, the geometric return is less than the arithmetic return. Also, the difference between the arithmetic and geometric means is the smallest for t-bills and the greatest for the common share indexes.
2. The level of inflation over the 69 years averaged about 4 percent. The return on the Government of Canada treasury bills was slightly higher than this, followed by long-term Government of Canada bonds. The returns on the common share indexes generated by far the highest returns. Based on our understanding of the characteristics of these financial securities from Chapter 5, this result is not surprising. Common shares carry a higher level of risk than do long-term bonds or treasury bills; the returns should also be higher.
3. The higher risk is clearly displayed by the ranges and the standard deviations of the various financial securities. The range for a series of returns is the difference between the highest return and the lowest return. The range varies from a low of 20 percent for t-bills to a high of 78.5 percent for the returns on U.S. common shares. The same pattern is seen with the standard deviation. The standard deviation increases as the analysis moves from t-bills to the common share indexes.

TABLE 7.6 **Summary Return and Risk Statistics for CPI and Selected Financial Securities for the Period 1938 to 2006**

	Summary statistics				
	Geometric mean	Arithmetic mean	Standard deviation	Range	Risk premium
Inflation (CPI)	3.90%	3.96%	3.57%	16.93%	N/A
91-day t-bills	5.10	5.18	4.29	20.00	0.00
Canada long bonds	6.21	6.59	9.25	53.44	1.41
Canadian common shares	10.70	11.87	16.11	74.36	6.69
U.S. common shares (C$)	11.81	13.17	17.40	78.57	7.99
U.S. common shares (US$)	11.58	12.87	16.88	78.53	7.69

SOURCE: Based on Table 1A from "Report on Canadian Economic Statistics 1924–2005," July 2006, Canadian Institute of Actuaries. See the report at **www.actuaries.ca/members/publications/2006/206022e-t.xls**. Used by permission.

4. Since the variability of the returns is greatest for the common share indexes, the differences between the arithmetic and geometric mean will be greater for these indexes as well. For example, for t-bills, the arithmetic mean is only 0.08 percent greater than the geometric mean. But, for Canadian common shares, the arithmetic mean is 1.17 percent greater. This difference is due to the much wider distribution of returns for the common share index.
5. As discussed in Chapter 5, Government of Canada t-bills are very low risk securities; they are often viewed as being risk-free since they are very short term in nature and are guaranteed by the federal government. When comparing the return on t-bills to other financial securities, the difference is termed a risk premium. The **risk premium** is the extra return required to invest in a risky asset rather than the risk-free asset (t-bills). The risk premium for the various financial securities is also provided in Table 7.6. Note that the risk premium for Canadian common shares has averaged almost 6.7 percent over the past 69 years. Obviously common shares are riskier than alternative investments, but investors in the Canadian stock market index have been well rewarded over time for taking this risk.

risk premium
The extra return required to invest in a risky asset rather than a risk-free asset (t-bills).

Further Analysis

The evaluation of risk and return can also be seen in Figures 7.5 and 7.6. Figure 7.5 indicates what would have happened to $1 over the 69 years if it were invested in a security that provided a return equal to inflation (CPI), in t-bills, in bonds, in Canadian common shares, and in U.S. common shares denominated in Canadian dollars. The results are striking.

While t-bills grew to $30.93 and bonds to $63.94, these returns are very low when considering the results for common shares and for inflation. To just have the same purchasing power as the original $1.00 that was invested at the beginning of 1938, an investment would have had to grow to $14.00 by the end of 2006. The extra return t-bills and bonds provide over inflation is quite modest. On the other hand, the returns on common shares is much higher. The Canadian common shares increased in value to $1,109.41, while the U.S. common shares increased in value to $2,214.22, over twice that of the Canadian common shares. This value is well off the much higher levels reached in 1999.

The magnitude of the difference between the ending wealth for the Canadian and the U.S. common shares is difficult to understand when the geometric means are considered. The geometric mean of 10.70 percent for Canadian common shares is only 1.11 percent lower than the 11.81 percent for U.S. common shares. The huge difference in ending wealth is due to the effects of compounding. An extra return of 1.11 percent per year over 69 years compounds to become a very large difference in ending wealth.

After reviewing Figure 7.5, it may be logical to wonder why an investor would hold t-bills or bonds. The answer is apparent in Table 7.6, Figure 7.5, and most strongly in Figure 7.6: common shares are much riskier. The greater volatility of common shares is apparent in the ranges and standard deviations in Table 7.6 and in the erratic growth of common shares shown in Figure 7.5. In contrast, the growth in t-bills, shown in Figure 7.5, is fairly consistent; there are no violent moves either up or down.

The much greater volatility of common shares is very obvious in Figure 7.6. This figure shows the yearly returns on t-bills and Canadian common shares over the 69 years. The wide swings in yearly common share returns dramatically depict the risk associated with this financial security. In contrast, the returns on t-bills hover around 4 percent for much of the period.

It should also be noted that in 25 of the 69 years, t-bills provide a higher return than Canadian common shares. While over long time periods common shares provide an average yearly return that is greater than that of t-bills, there is no guarantee that in any specific year common shares will do so. To illustrate, consider the return earned on common shares in 1940, 1957, 1974, 2001, or 2002. Major declines in share prices occurred. Significant risk exists for investors in common shares.

FIGURE 7.5

Value of $1.00 Invested in Financial Securities: 1938 to 2006

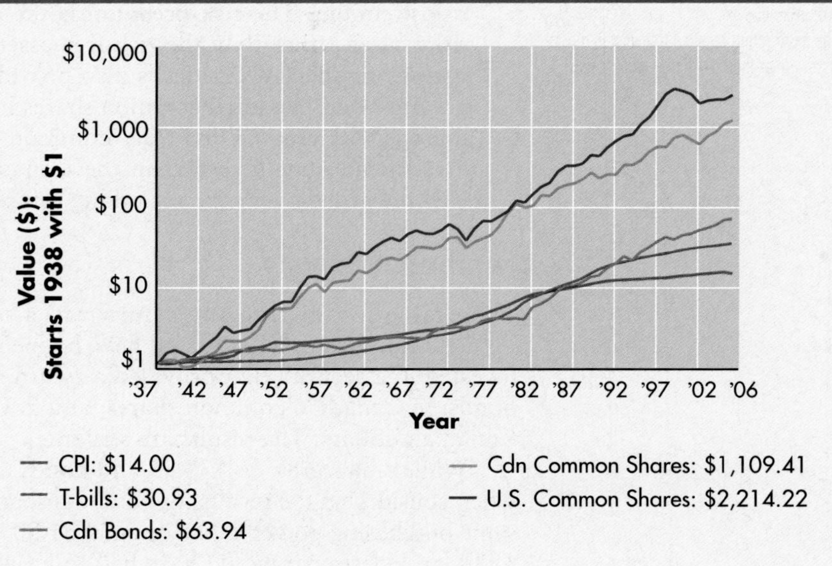

SOURCE: Based on Table 1A from "Report on Canadian Economic Statistics 1924–2005," July 2006, Canadian Institute of Actuaries. See the report at **www.actuaries.ca/members/publications/2006/206022e-t.xls**. Used by permission.

FIGURE 7.6

Volatility of Returns on T-Bills and Canadian Common Shares: 1938 to 2006

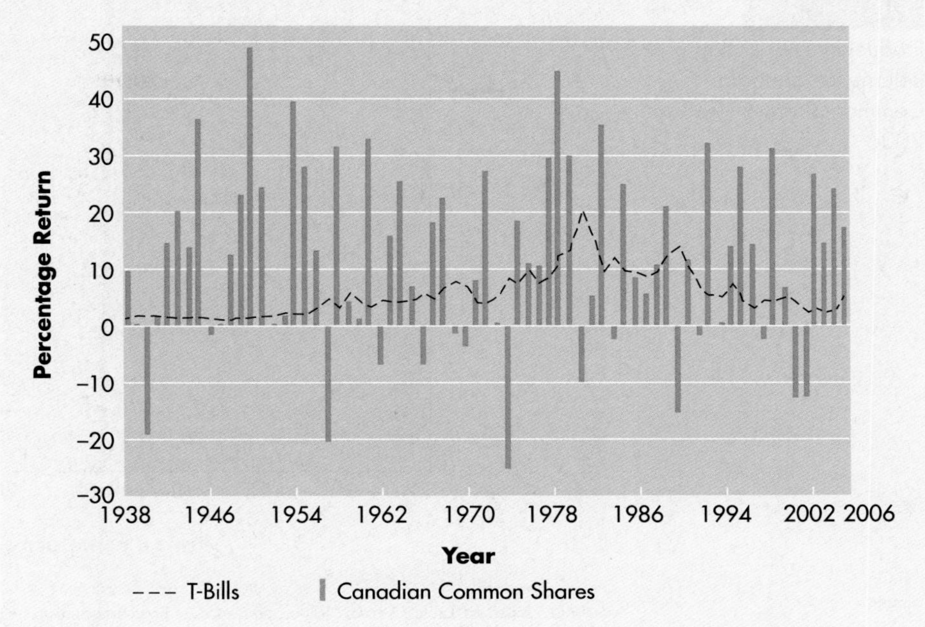

SOURCE: Based on Table 1A from "Report on Canadian Economic Statistics 1924–2005," July 2006, Canadian Institute of Actuaries. See the report at **www.actuaries.ca/members/publications/2006/206022e-t.xls**. Used by permission.

Distribution of Returns

A further lesson to learn from our analysis of historic returns is provided in Figure 7.7, which provides a frequency distribution of returns for Canadian common shares over the 69 years. It shows the number of years that returns fell in the indicated range. For example, in 14 years, returns on Canadian common shares fell in the range of between 0 and 10 percent. In an additional 16 years, returns fell in the range of between 10 and 20 percent. Note the similarity of Figure 7.7 to Figure 7.4, the normal distribution. Many random events can be described by a normal curve, including returns on financial securities. The normal curve can be completely described by the mean and the standard deviation. In the case of Canadian common shares, the average is the arithmetic mean of 11.87 percent. The standard deviation is 16.11 percent. How is this information useful?

Recall that the arithmetic mean is a good indicator of expected return in the future. Therefore, given the mean and standard deviation of the historic returns on Canadian common shares, and based on the characteristic of a normal distribution, we can say that for any given year:

- There is a 68.3 percent probability that the actual return on the index of Canadian common shares will fall in the range of 11.87 percent ± (1 × 16.11%), or −4.24 to 27.98 percent.

FIGURE 7.7

Frequency Distribution of Returns for Canadian Common Shares: 1938 to 2006

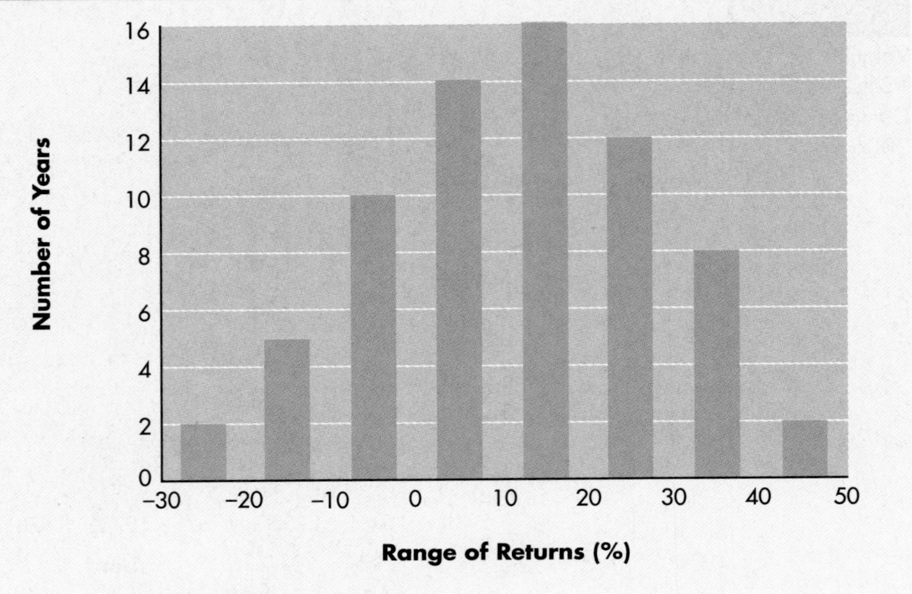

SOURCE: Based on Table 1A from "Report on Canadian Economic Statistics 1924–2005," July 2006, Canadian Institute of Actuaries. See the report at **www.actuaries.ca/members/publications/2006/206022e-t.xls**. Used by permission.

- There is a 95.4 percent probability that the actual return on the index of Canadian common shares will fall in the range of 11.87 percent ± (2 × 16.11%) or –20.35 to 44.09 percent.
- There is a 99.7 percent + probability that the actual return on the index of Canadian common shares will fall in the range of 11.87 percent ± (3 × 16.11%) or –36.46 to 60.20 percent.

Note that the positive range of possible returns is much larger than the negative. Why? This is due to the underlying yearly returns. There is a much greater probability that the returns on common shares will be positive rather than negative. This is clear from reviewing Table 7.5, and Figures 7.5 and 7.6. For example, the returns on Canadian common shares were positive for 52 of the 69 years. This is about 75 percent of the time. An investor in the common share index is more likely to receive a positive than a negative return. This is because the economy generally grows, and this growth creates the opportunity for companies to generate higher profits. Higher profits lead to high prices for common shares. This has certainly been the trend over these 69 years.

Using Historic Return Data

Suppose you have the opportunity to invest in a company that has the same level of risk as the S&P 500 Index as measured in Canadian dollars. What is the lowest return that you would accept before making this investment? To answer this question, we must first recognize that the returns on a portfolio of large U.S. common shares are risky. While we are able to say that we would like to earn a certain rate of return, there is no guarantee that the return will actually be received—that is the nature of risk. For this reason, we refer to the return as the required rate of return. Therefore, we must expect that we will receive at least this rate of return before making the investment. So, what is the lowest acceptable rate of return on the proposed investment?

Review Table 7.6. We can see that the arithmetic mean return on U.S. common shares measured in Canadian dollars is about 13.2 percent over the 69-year period. Is that our minimum acceptable rate of return? As discussed earlier, the arithmetic mean is a good estimate of the yearly return we could expect on an asset in the future. So, should we use 13.2 percent as our required return? It depends. If Government of Canada t-bills were providing a 7.2 percent return, would we be happy with a 6 percent (13.2% – 7.2%) risk premium? Consider Table 7.6 again. The historic risk premium on U.S. common shares measured in Canadian dollars was about 8 percent. If the risk premium over the 69-year study period averaged 8 percent, are we now willing to accept a risk premium of only 6 percent? We shouldn't be, based on the historic risk and returns on U.S. common shares measured in Canadian dollars. So what should we do?

Our estimate for the minimum acceptable rate of return should be based on the risk-free rate of return available at the time we are analyzing an investment opportunity, plus the appropriate risk premium. In this example, that would be 15.2 percent (7.2% + 8%). Does that seem to be a very high minimum return? Based on the historic record provided in Table 7.6, it isn't. Investing in financial assets can be risky. Investing in assets that have similar or higher risks than the portfolios of common shares used in Table 7.5 means we should expect high rates of return before making the investment. That is the most important lesson we can learn from the analysis of historic returns on securities that trade in the financial markets.

? Review Questions

7–10 What can we learn from an analysis of the historic returns on financial securities?

7–11 Based on Table 7.5, in how many years did investors in long-term bonds issued by the federal government lose money? Explain how it is possible to lose money on long-term bonds issued by the federal government.

7–12 Which financial security has the highest level of risk? How do you know this?

7–13 Using the information provided in this section, what is the approximate probability of earning a return of more than 16 percent on long-term bonds issued by the federal government? What is the probability of earning a return of less than –3 percent? What is the probability of earning a return between –3 and 16 percent?

7–14 Using the information provided in this section, what is the approximate probability of earning a return of more than 13.76 percent on Government of Canada t-bills?

7.4 Risk of a Portfolio

efficient portfolio
A portfolio that maximizes return for a given level of risk or minimizes risk for a given level of return.

Investment assets can be held individually or in portfolios. When a number of assets are held in a portfolio, the risk and return of the portfolio must be calculated. In addition, new investments must be considered in light of the risk and return of the current *portfolio of* assets.[9] The financial manager's goal is to create an **efficient portfolio,** one that maximizes return for a given level of risk or minimizes risk for a given level of return. We therefore need a way to measure the return of a portfolio of assets. Once we can do that, we will look at the statistical concept of *correlation,* which underlies the process of diversification that is used to develop an efficient portfolio.

Portfolio Return and Standard Deviation

The *return on a portfolio* is a weighted average of the returns on the individual assets from which it is formed. We can use Equation 7.9 to find the portfolio return, k_p:

$$k_p = (w_1 \times k_1) + (w_2 \times k_2) + \cdots + (w_n \times k_n) = \sum_{j=1}^{n} w_j \times k_j \quad (7.9)$$

where

w_j = proportion of the portfolio invested in asset *j*
k_j = return on asset *j*

Of course, the sum of w_j's must equal 1 indicating that all of the portfolio's assets were included in the calculation.

The *standard deviation of a portfolio's returns* is found by applying the formula for the standard deviation of a single asset. Specifically, Equation 7.6 would be used when the probabilities of the returns are known, and Equation 7.7 would be used when the outcomes are known and their related probabilities of occurrence are assumed to be equal.

Example Assume that we wish to determine the expected return and standard deviation of returns for portfolio XZ, created by combining equal portions (50%) of assets X and Z. The expected returns of assets X and Z for each of the next 5 years (2008–2012) are given in columns 1 and 2, respectively, in part A of Table 7.7. In column 3, the weights of 50 percent for both assets X and Z along with their respective returns from columns 1 and 2 are substituted into Equation 7.9. Column 4 shows the results of the calculation—an expected portfolio return of 12 percent for each year, 2008 to 2012.

Furthermore, as shown in part B of the table, the expected return on the portfolio over the 5-year period is also 12 percent (calculated by using Equation 7.2.)[10] In part C of the table, portfolio XZ's standard deviation is calculated to be 0 percent (using Equation 7.7). This value should not be surprising because the expected return each year is the same—12 percent. No variability is exhibited in the expected returns from year to year.

9. The assets might be financial, such as t-bills, bonds, preferred shares, or common shares, or real, such as land, buildings, or equipment. Theoretically, all of the concepts discussed in this chapter apply equally to financial or real assets.

10. Since the five yearly returns are all the same, the geometric mean return would also be 12 percent.

TABLE 7.7 **Expected Yearly Return, Expected Portfolio Return, and Standard Deviation of Returns for Portfolio XZ**

A. Expected yearly returns on the portfolio

	Expected return			
Year	Asset X (1)	Asset Z (2)	Portfolio return calculation[a] (3)	Expected portfolio return, $\hat{k}_p$ (4)
2008	8%	16%	$(0.50 \times 8\%) + (0.50 \times 16\%) =$	12%
2009	10	14	$(0.50 \times 10\%) + (0.50 \times 14\%) =$	12
2010	12	12	$(0.50 \times 12\%) + (0.50 \times 12\%) =$	12
2011	14	10	$(0.50 \times 14\%) + (0.50 \times 10\%) =$	12
2012	16	8	$(0.50 \times 16\%) + (0.50 \times 8\%) =$	12

B. Expected return on the portfolio, 2008–2012[b]

$$\hat{k}_p = \frac{12\% + 12\% + 12\% + 12\% + 12\%}{5} = \frac{60\%}{5} = \underline{\underline{12\%}}$$

C. Standard deviation of the portfolio's expected return[c]

$$\sigma_p = \sqrt{\frac{(12\% - 12\%)^2 + (12\% - 12\%)^2 + (12\% - 12\%)^2 + (12\% - 12\%)^2 + (12\% - 12\%)^2}{5-1}}$$

$$= \sqrt{\frac{0\% + 0\% + 0\% + 0\% + 0\%}{4}} = \sqrt{\frac{0}{4}}\% = \underline{\underline{0\%}}$$

[a]Using Equation 7.9.
[b]Using Equation 7.2.
[c]Using Equation 7.7.

correlation
A statistical measure of the relationship, if any, between series of numbers representing data of any kind.

positively correlated
Descriptive of two series that move in the same direction.

negatively correlated
Descriptive of two series that move in opposite directions.

correlation coefficient
A measure of the degree of correlation between two series.

perfectly positively correlated
Describes two *positively correlated* series that have a *correlation coefficient* of +1.

perfectly negatively correlated
Describes two *negatively correlated* series that have a *correlation coefficient* of −1.

Correlation

Correlation is a statistical measure of the relationship, if any, between series of numbers representing data of any kind, from returns to test scores. If two series move in the same direction, they are **positively correlated;** if the series move in opposite directions, they are **negatively correlated.**[11]

The degree of correlation is measured by the **correlation coefficient,** which ranges from +1 for **perfectly positively correlated** series to −1 for **perfectly negatively correlated** series. These two extremes are depicted for assets M and N in Figure 7.8. In Panel A, the returns on assets M and N move exactly together. In Panel B, the returns on assets M and N move exactly in the opposite direction. In both cases, by knowing the next return on asset M, we will be able to estimate, with certainty, the return on asset N, assuming the historic relationship does not

11. The general *long-term trend* of two series could be the same (both increasing or both decreasing) or different (one increasing, the other decreasing), and the correlation of their *short-term (point-to-point) movements* in both situations could be either positive or negative. In other words, the pattern of movement around the trends could be correlated independent of the actual relationship between the trends. Further clarification of this seemingly inconsistent behaviour can be found in most basic statistics texts.

FIGURE 7.8 Correlations
The correlation of returns between assets M and N

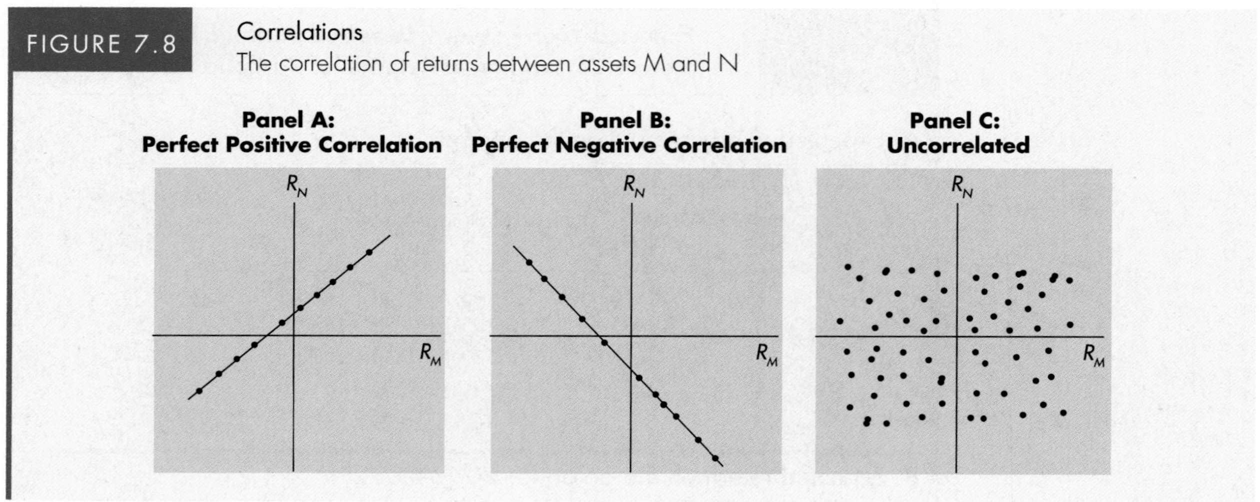

uncorrelated
Two series of data that lack any relationship; this is represented by a correlation coefficient of 0.

change. Panel C in Figure 7.8 provides a very different picture of correlation. Here, the returns are **uncorrelated.** There is no relationship between the returns on assets M and N. Knowing the next return on asset M tells us nothing about the return on asset N. In this example, the correlation coefficient on the returns of assets M and N will be 0. Correlation coefficients range from +1 to −1.

Diversification

To develop efficient portfolios, and benefit from diversification, knowing the degree of correlation that exists between the returns on assets is essential. The concept of diversification is depicted in the old saying "Don't put all your eggs in one basket," meaning don't take a great deal of undue risk by only considering one alternative. Diversification can reduce risk, *but only if* the returns on the assets are not perfectly positively correlated. The risk of a portfolio of assets whose returns are perfectly positively correlated will be based on a simple weighting of the risks of the individual assets. In such a case, there is no benefit from diversification.

For example, assume that you manufacture machine tools. The business is very cyclical, with high sales when the economy is expanding and low sales during a recession. If you acquired another machine-tool company, with sales positively correlated with those of your firm, the combined sales would still be cyclical, and risk would remain the same. Alternatively, you could acquire a sewing-machine manufacturer, which is *countercyclical.* It typically has low sales during economic expansion and high sales during recession (when consumers are more likely to make their own clothes). Combining these two companies will result in a lower level of risk than a simple weighting of the risks of the individual assets. Two additional examples of this concept are provided below.

Example An investor can purchase asset A or B, or any combination of A and B. The expected returns and standard deviations of the two assets are provided below and are illustrated in Panel A of Figure 7.9:

	A	B
Expected return	6%	16%
Standard deviation	8%	18%

FIGURE 7.9

Risk and Return of a Portfolio Consisting of Asset A and B

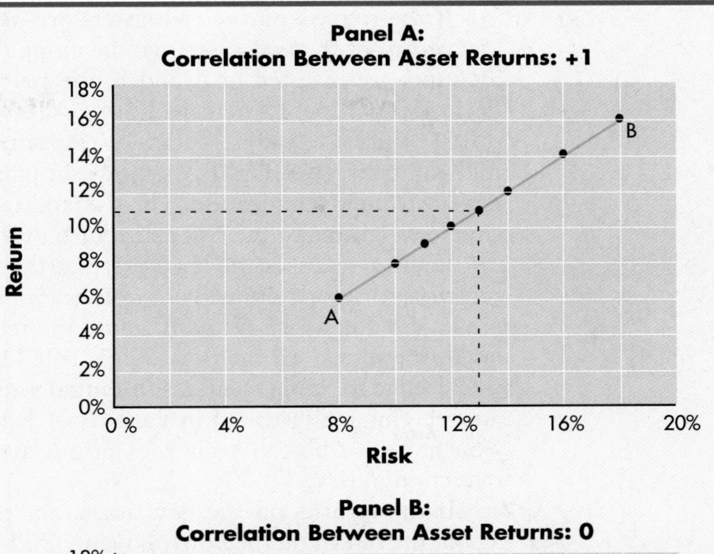

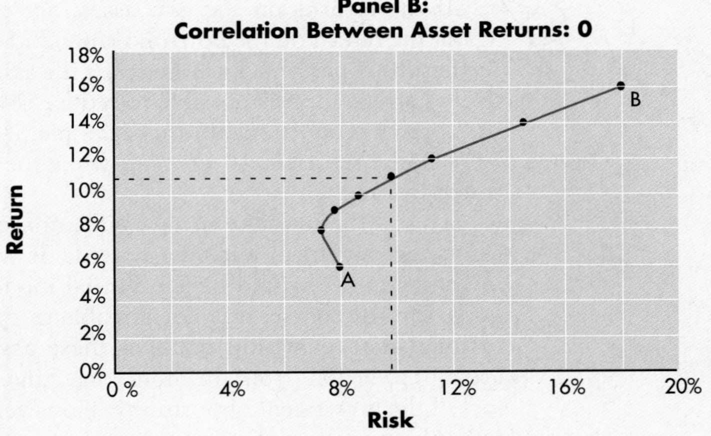

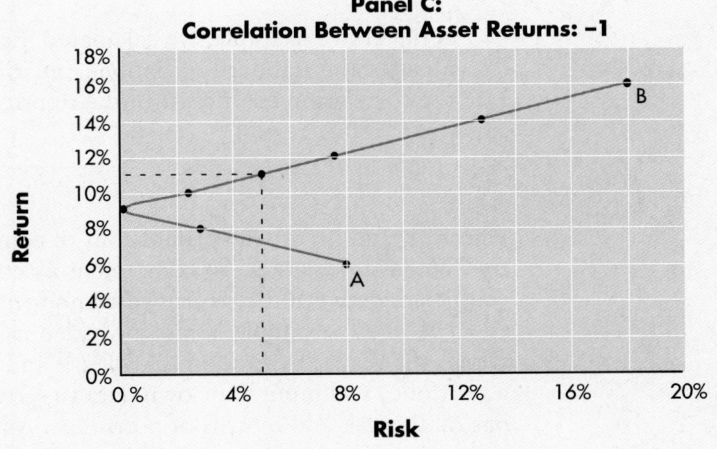

If the returns on the two assets are perfectly positively correlated, the risk and return of the two assets will lie along the line joining the assets. So, if equal amounts are invested in A and B, the portfolio's expected return and standard deviation will be 11 percent [(50% × 6%) + (50% × 16%)] and 13 percent [(50% × 8%) + (50% × 18%)], respectively. This will lie exactly on the line, midway between A and B, as shown in panel A. So, in this example, there is no benefit from diversification. The risk and return of the portfolio are based on the simple weighting of the risk and return of the two assets.

If the returns on the two assets are not perfectly positively correlated, the return on the portfolio will not change, *but the risk will decline*. If equal amounts are invested in assets A and B, and if the returns on the two assets were uncorrelated, the return on the portfolio is still 11 percent, but the standard deviation will decline to 9.8 percent, a substantial reduction from the 13 percent calculated above. This is illustrated in Panel B of Figure 7.9. Diversification has worked. You have not put all your eggs in one basket and you have benefited from a reduction in risk.

If the returns on the two assets are perfectly negatively correlated, then, again, the return on the portfolio will be 11 percent, but the risk will decline even further, to 5 percent. Even better, with assets whose returns are perfectly negatively correlated, it is possible to reduce risk to zero, when the assets are held in the correct proportions. In this example, if the portfolio consists of 69% A and 31% B, the return is 9.1 percent, while the standard deviation is 0. This is illustrated in Panel C.

This is the ultimate in diversification. It means that we can invest in risky assets, get a return, but take no risk. If we could find such a combination of investments, we would have a virtual money machine, and we could make billions. But, of course, it is not possible to find two such assets. If they existed, a rational market would uncover these assets and numerous investors would attempt to benefit from the money machine. This very activity would result in the loss of the investment opportunity. However, the point remains that while we are not able to find a money machine, we can still benefit from diversification. ▲

In the above example, we calculated the expected return using Equation 7.9. To calculate the standard deviation, Equation 7.7 must be modified to incorporate the correlation coefficient of the returns between the two assets as shown in Equation 7.10:

$$\sigma_p = \sqrt{w_1^2\sigma_1^2 + w_2^2\sigma_2^2 + 2w_1w_2r_{1,2}\sigma_1\sigma_2} \tag{7.10}$$

where w_1 and w_2 are the proportions of component assets 1 and 2, σ_1 and σ_2 are the standard deviations of component assets 1 and 2, and $r_{1,2}$ is the correlation coefficient between the returns of component assets 1 and 2.

The above example is also provided as Spreadsheet Application 7.2, which allows the reader to view a table of risk and returns, graph the risk and return of a portfolio, and input their own data to see the impact the correlation coefficient has on the risk and returns of portfolios. Another example illustrating these concepts is provided below.

Example ▼ Table 7.8 presents the expected yearly returns for three different assets—X, Y, and Z—for the next 5 years, along with their expected returns and standard deviations over the five years. Each of the assets has an expected average return of

7.2 SPREADSHEET APPLICATION

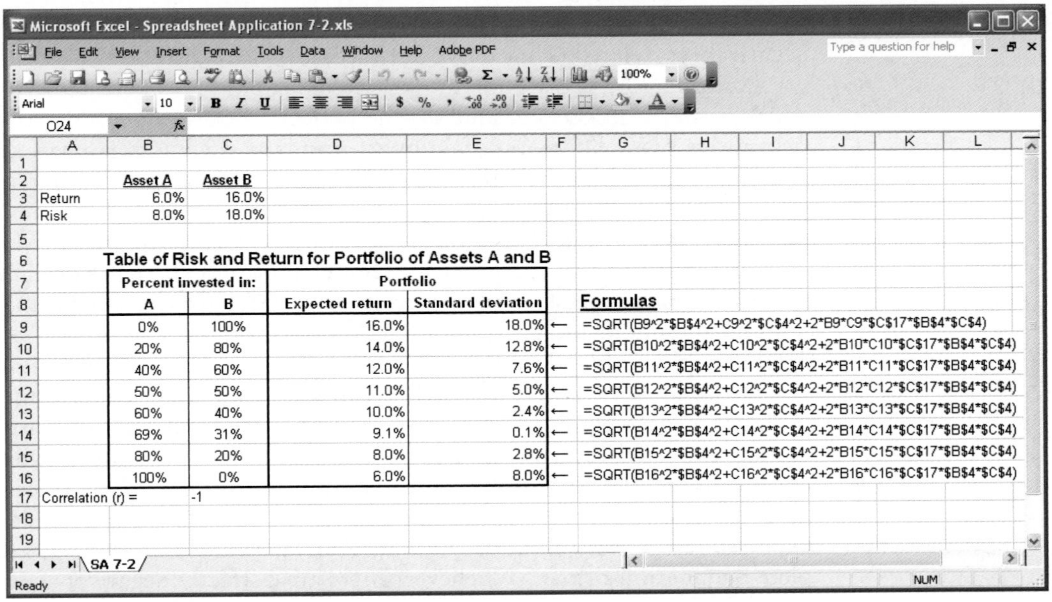

Microsoft Excel - Spreadsheet Application 7-2.xls

	Asset A	Asset B
Return	6.0%	16.0%
Risk	8.0%	18.0%

Table of Risk and Return for Portfolio of Assets A and B

Percent invested in:		Portfolio		
A	B	Expected return	Standard deviation	Formulas
0%	100%	16.0%	18.0%	← =SQRT(B9^2*$B$4^2+C9^2*$C$4^2+2*B9*C9*$C$17*$B$4*$C$4)
20%	80%	14.0%	12.8%	← =SQRT(B10^2*$B$4^2+C10^2*$C$4^2+2*B10*C10*$C$17*$B$4*$C$4)
40%	60%	12.0%	7.6%	← =SQRT(B11^2*$B$4^2+C11^2*$C$4^2+2*B11*C11*$C$17*$B$4*$C$4)
50%	50%	11.0%	5.0%	← =SQRT(B12^2*$B$4^2+C12^2*$C$4^2+2*B12*C12*$C$17*$B$4*$C$4)
60%	40%	10.0%	2.4%	← =SQRT(B13^2*$B$4^2+C13^2*$C$4^2+2*B13*C13*$C$17*$B$4*$C$4)
69%	31%	9.1%	0.1%	← =SQRT(B14^2*$B$4^2+C14^2*$C$4^2+2*B14*C14*$C$17*$B$4*$C$4)
80%	20%	8.0%	2.8%	← =SQRT(B15^2*$B$4^2+C15^2*$C$4^2+2*B15*C15*$C$17*$B$4*$C$4)
100%	0%	6.0%	8.0%	← =SQRT(B16^2*$B$4^2+C16^2*$C$4^2+2*B16*C16*$C$17*$B$4*$C$4)

Correlation (r) = -1

SA 7-2

TABLE 7.8 Yearly Returns, Expected Returns, and Standard Deviations for Assets X, Y, and Z and Portfolios XY and XZ

	Assets[a]			Portfolios[b]	
Year	X	Y	Z	XY (50%X + 50%Y)	XZ (50%X + 50%Z)
2008	8%	8%	16%	8%	12%
2009	10	10	14	10	12
2010	12	12	12	12	12
2011	14	14	10	14	12
2012	16	16	8	16	12
Statistics:					
Expected return[b]	12%	12%	12%	12%	12%
Standard deviation[c]	3.16%	3.16%	3.16%	3.16%	0%

[a] Portfolio XY consists of 50% of asset X and 50% of asset Y. Note that the two return streams are identical over the 5-year period; the returns are perfectly positively correlated. Therefore, there is no benefit when these two assets are used to create a portfolio. Portfolio XZ consists of 50% of asset X and 50% of asset Z, two perfectly negatively correlated assets. When these two assets are used to create a portfolio, risk can be eliminated.

[b] The expected returns for each asset and each portfolio over the 5 years were calculated using Equation 7.2.

[c] The standard deviation for each asset over the 5 years was calculated using Equation 7.7. The standard deviations for the portfolios over the 5 years were calculated using Equation 7.10.

12 percent and a standard deviation of 3.16 percent. The assets therefore have equal return and equal risk. The return patterns of assets X and Y are perfectly positively correlated. They move in precisely the same direction. (*Note:* The returns for X and Y are identical.)[12] The returns of assets X and Z are perfectly negatively correlated. They move in exactly opposite directions over time.

Portfolio XY Portfolio XY (shown in Table 7.8) is created by combining equal portions of assets X and Y—the perfectly positively correlated assets. The risk in this portfolio, as reflected by its standard deviation, is unaffected by this combination. Risk remains at 3.16 percent, and the expected return remains at 12 percent. Whenever perfectly positively correlated assets such as X and Y are combined, the standard deviation of the resulting portfolio cannot be reduced *below that of the least risky asset;* the maximum portfolio standard deviation will be that of the riskiest asset. Because assets X and Y have the same standard deviation, the minimum and maximum standard deviations are the same (3.16%). This result can be attributed to the unlikely situation that X and Y are identical assets.

Portfolio XZ Portfolio XZ is created by combining equal portions of the perfectly negatively correlated asets X and Z. (Calculation of portfolio XZ's annual expected returns, their expected value, and the standard deviation of expected portfolio returns was demonstrated in Table 7.7.) The risk in this portfolio, as reflected by its standard deviation, is reduced to 0 percent, while the expected return remains at 12 percent. Thus, the combination results in the complete elimination of risk. Whenever assets are perfectly negatively correlated, an optimum combination (similar to the 50–50 mix in the case of assets X and Z) exists for which the resulting standard deviation will equal 0.

To illustrate the use of Equation 7.10, the standard deviation for portfolio XZ is calculated below.

$$\sigma_{XZ} = \sqrt{[(0.50)^2 \times (3.16228)^2] + [(0.50)^2 \times (3.16228)^2] + [2 \times (0.50) \times (0.50) \times (3.16228) \times (3.16228) \times -1]}$$

$$\sigma_{XZ} = \sqrt{(0.25 \times 10) + (0.25 \times 10) + (-5)}$$

$$\sigma_{XZ} = \sqrt{2.5 + 2.5 - 5}$$

$$\sigma_{XZ} = \sqrt{0} = 0$$

Hint
Remember, low correlation between two series of numbers indicates dissimilar behaviour of the two series.

So, in general, the lower the correlation between asset returns, the greater the potential benefit of diversification. This should be clear from the two examples provided above. For each pair of assets, there is a combination that will result in the lowest risk (standard deviation) possible. How much risk can be reduced by this combination depends on the degree of correlation that exists between the returns on the assets.

Three possible correlations—perfect positive, uncorrelated, and perfect negative—illustrate the effect of correlation on the diversification of risk and return. Table 7.9 summarizes the impact of correlation on the range of return and risk for various two-asset portfolio combinations. Note that the return on the portfolio will always range between the returns on the two assets. The risk of the portfolio will range between 0 and the standard deviation of the riskiest asset. The result is dependent on how the assets are combined to form the portfolio.

12. Identical return streams are used in this example to permit clear illustration of the concepts, but it is *not* necessary for return streams to be identical for them to be perfectly positively correlated. Any return streams that move (i.e., vary) exactly together—regardless of the relative magnitude of the returns—are perfectly positively correlated.

TABLE 7.9 Correlation, Return, and Risk for Various Two-Asset Portfolio Combinations

Correlation coefficient	Range of return	Range of risk
+1 (perfect positive)	Between returns of two assets held in isolation	Between risk of two assets held in isolation
0 (uncorrelated)	Between returns of two assets held in isolation	Between risk of most risky asset and an amount less than risk of least risky asset but greater than 0
−1 (perfect negative)	Between returns of two assets held in isolation	Between risk of most risky asset and 0

This is also illustrated in Figure 7.10 where we have two assets, R and S, with expected returns of 6 and 8 percent and standard deviations of 3 and 8 percent, respectively. Depending on how the assets are combined to form a portfolio, the return on the portfolio will range between 6 and 8 percent. Depending on the correlation between the returns on R and S, the standard deviation of the portfolio will range between 0 and 8 percent. For any two-asset combination, Spreadsheet Application 7.2 can be used to determine the portfolio's risk and return.

International Diversification

The ultimate example of portfolio diversification involves including foreign assets in a portfolio. The inclusion of assets from countries that are less sensitive to the Canadian business cycle (i.e., that have lower or negative correlations) reduces the portfolio's responsiveness to market movements and to foreign currency fluctuations.

FIGURE 7.10

Possible Correlations Range of portfolio return ($\hat{k}_p$) and risk (σ_p) for combinations of assets R and S for various correlation coefficients

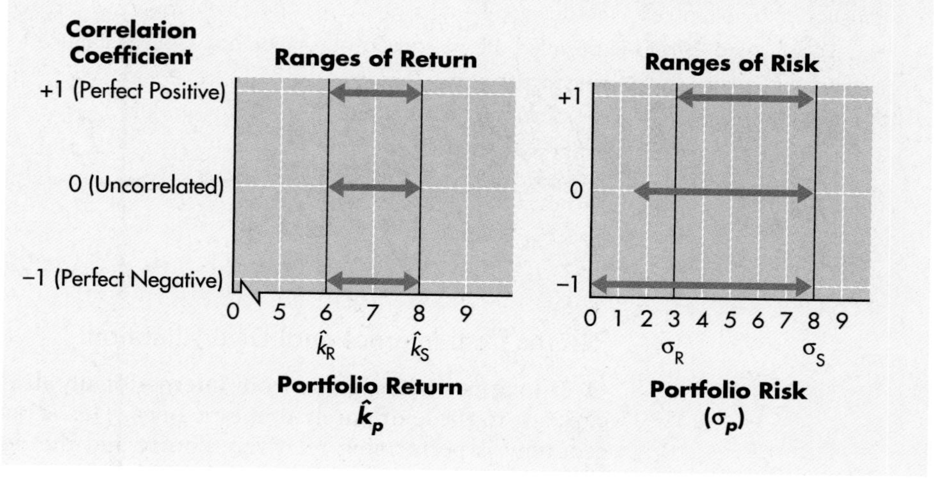

7.1 **IN PRACTICE**

Less Risk Through Diversification?

"Don't put all your eggs in one basket." That old saying is a good description of diversification. Don't put all your eggs in one basket because if the basket falls, all of your eggs break, not just a few. Does the adage also apply to companies? There are different views on the issue. In Canada, numerous companies have followed diversification strategies, some with great success, others with less.

In 1946, Atco, builders of the world's first portable industrial housing, started life in the Southern family garage. Atco's housing is now found around the world wherever there are construction or development projects. From oil developments in the far north to dam construction in Asia, Atco has provided housing from a single trailer to whole camps, really small towns, for projects in more than 100 countries.

By 1980, Atco was flourishing, driven by the boom in oil exploration. But the founder's son, Ron Southern, decided to take Atco in a different direction. Against all advice and perceived wisdom, he paid $350 million for controlling interest in a stodgy, regulated power utility in northern Alberta named Canadian Utilities. Explains Ron: "I wanted a non-cyclical business to build a stable future." He wanted to diversify Atco's cash flows from being totally dependent on construction and natural resource development.

Today Atco Group is an international group of companies, a truly diversified conglomerate. The company still engages in their two original businesses, which are manufacturing temporary housing and generating, transmitting, and distributing electricity in Alberta. But they also generate power in Europe and Australia, build and operate gas pipelines and gas storage facilities, operate water pipelines, provide site support services, cost control, and facilities management to the resource, telecommunications, and defence sectors, provide utility billing and customer care services, operate a large independent travel management company, manufacture a line of wood preservatives, market coal combustion products, and engineer and manufacture noise abatement technology for industrial facilities worldwide.

While some might consider Atco's business combinations "strange," the company spreads risk through diversification, looking for growth in one area to compensate for slower growth in others. Atco blends riskier companies, whose performance is directly tied to the economy, with ones that will perform consistently, regardless of economic conditions.

Has the strategy worked for Atco? For the fiscal year ended December 31, 2005, Atco had total assets of $7.5 billion and sales of almost $3 billion, while cash flow from operations was $735 million. The company employs 7,000 people. In October 2006, Atco's market capitalization was $2.6 billion, and in the years between 2000 and 2006, the share price increased by an average of 14 percent per year. Not bad for a company founded in the family garage.

SOURCES: Atco Group, 2005 *Annual Report and Management Proxy Circular*, available at **www.atco.com**; Diane Francis, "The Making of an Energy Empire," *National Post*, June 15, 2002.

Returns from International Diversification

Over long periods, returns from internationally diversified portfolios tend to be superior to those of purely domestic ones. This is particularly so if the Canadian economy is performing relatively poorly and the dollar is depreciating in value against most foreign currencies. At such times the dollar returns to Canadian investors on a portfolio of foreign assets can be very attractive indeed.

This is clearly shown in Table 7.5 for the returns on a portfolio of U.S. common shares measured in Canadian dollars. The average return on the S&P 500 Index (measured in U.S. dollars) is significantly higher than the returns on the Canadian Index of common shares. This is the case since the U.S. economy has generally outperformed the Canadian economy over the 1938 to 2006 period. The return on the S&P 500 Index (measured in Canadian dollars) is superior to that for the return on the S&P 500 Index (measured in U.S. dollars). This is the case since the Canadian dollar fell in relation to the U.S. dollar during this period.

However, over any single short or intermediate period, international diversification can yield subpar returns—particularly during periods when the Canadian dollar is appreciating in value relative to other currencies. When the Canadian currency gains in value, the dollar value of a foreign-currency-denominated portfolio of assets declines. Even if this portfolio yields a satisfactory return in local currency, the return to Canadian investors will be reduced when translated into dollars. Subpar local currency portfolio returns, coupled with an appreciating dollar, can yield truly dismal dollar returns to Canadian investors.

Overall, though, the logic of international portfolio diversification assumes that these fluctuations in currency values and relative performance will average out over long periods and that an internationally diversified portfolio will tend to yield a comparable return at a lower level of risk than will similar purely domestic portfolios.

Risks of International Diversification

Canadian investors should, however, also be aware of the potential dangers of international investing. In addition to the risk induced by currency fluctuations, several other financial risks are unique to international investing. The most important of these fall in the category of political risk. **Political risk** arises from the possibility that a host government might take actions harmful to foreign investors or that political turmoil in a country might endanger investments made in that country by foreign nationals. Political risks are particularly acute in developing countries, where unstable or ideologically motivated governments may attempt to block return of profits by foreign investors or even seize (nationalize) their assets in the host country.

political risk
Risk that arises from the possibility that a host government might take actions harmful to foreign investors or that political turmoil in a country might endanger investments made in that country by foreign nationals.

Even where governments do not impose exchange controls or seize assets, international investors may suffer if a shortage of hard currency prevents payment of dividends or interest to foreigners. When governments are forced to allocate scarce foreign exchange, they rarely give top priority to the interests of foreign investors. Instead, hard currency reserves are typically used to pay for necessary imports such as food and industrial materials and to pay interest on the government's own debts. Because most of the debt of developing countries is held by banks rather than individuals, foreign investors are often badly harmed when a country experiences political or economic problems. If a country does not have well developed financial markets, the possibility of political risk can be high.

? Review Questions

7–15 Why must assets be evaluated in a portfolio context? What is an *efficient portfolio?* How can the return and standard deviation of a portfolio be determined?

7–16 Why is the *correlation* between asset returns important? How does diversification allow risky assets to be combined so that the risk of the portfolio is less than the risk of the individual assets in it?

7–17 How does international diversification enhance risk reduction? When might international diversification result in subpar returns? What are *political risks,* and how do they affect international diversification?

7.5 Risk and Return: The Capital Asset Pricing Model (CAPM)

capital asset pricing model (CAPM)
The basic theory that links together risk and return for all assets.

The most important aspect of risk is the *overall risk* of the firm as viewed by investors in the marketplace. Overall risk significantly affects investment opportunities—and even more important, the owners' wealth. The basic theory that links risk and return for all assets is the **capital asset pricing model (CAPM).**[13] We will use CAPM to understand the basic risk–return tradeoffs involved in all types of financial decisions.

Types of Risk

As we saw in the previous section, if individual assets are combined to form a portfolio, the risk of the portfolio is less than the risk of either of the two underlying assets. As more assets are added to the portfolio, the standard deviation of the portfolio (σ_P) will decline further due to the effects of diversification. This concept is illustrated in Figure 7.11. Note that as more assets are added to the portfolio, σ_P declines, but at a decreasing rate. At a certain point, the effect stops completely. Research has shown that, on average, most of the risk-reduction benefits of diversification can be gained by forming portfolios containing 15 to 20 randomly selected securities.

total risk
The combination of a security's nondiversifiable and diversifiable risk.

Therefore, if an investor chose to hold seven securities in a portfolio, as shown in Figure 7.11, she would incur the level of risk as shown (σ_{P1}). Note that a portion of this risk can be eliminated by simply adding more assets to the portfolio. This leads to a very important concept: the **total risk** of a security, as measured by the standard deviation (σ_j), can be viewed as consisting of two parts:

$$\text{Total security risk } (\sigma_j) = \text{nondiversifiable risk} + \text{diversifiable risk} \qquad (7.11)$$

diversifiable risk
The portion of an asset's risk that is attributable to firm-specific, random causes; can be eliminated through diversification.

nondiversifiable risk
The relevant portion of an asset's risk attributable to market factors that affect all firms; cannot be eliminated through diversification.

Diversifiable risk, sometimes called *unsystematic risk,* represents the portion of an asset's risk that is associated with random causes that can be eliminated through diversification. It is attributable to firm-specific events, such as strikes, lawsuits, regulatory actions, and loss of a key account. **Nondiversifiable risk,** also called *systematic risk,* is attributable to market factors that affect all firms; it cannot be eliminated through diversification. Factors such as war, inflation, social trends, international incidents, and political events account for nondiversifiable risk.

---

13. The initial development of this theory is generally attributed to William F. Sharpe, "Capital Asset Prices: A Theory of Market Equilibrium Under Conditions of Risk," *Journal of Finance* 19 (September 1964), pp. 425–442, and John Lintner, "The Valuation of Risk Assets and the Selection of Risky Investments in Stock Portfolios and Capital Budgets," *Review of Economics and Statistics* 47 (February 1965), pp. 13–37. A number of authors subsequently advanced, refined, and tested this now widely accepted theory.

FIGURE 7.11

Risk Reduction

Portfolio risk and diversification

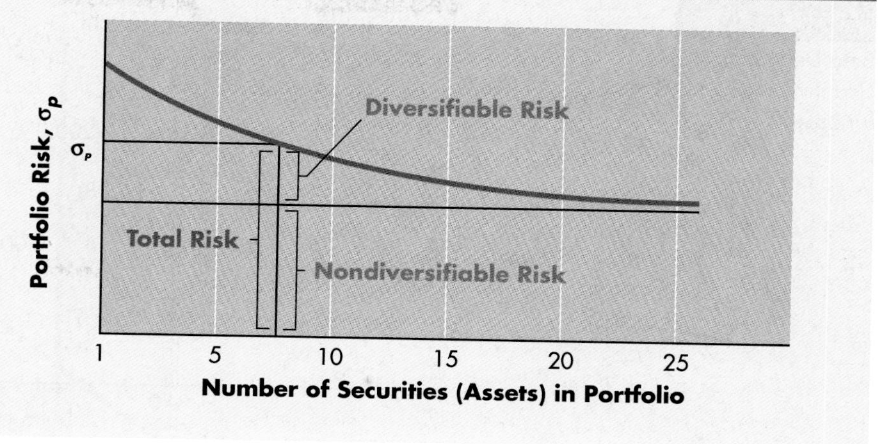

Because any investor can create a portfolio of assets that will eliminate virtually all diversifiable risk, *the only relevant risk is nondiversifiable risk*. Any investor or firm therefore must be concerned solely with nondiversifiable risk. The measurement of nondiversifiable risk is thus of primary importance in selecting assets with the most desired risk–return characteristics.

The Model: CAPM

The capital asset pricing model (CAPM) links nondiversifiable risk and return for all assets. We will discuss the model in five sections. The first defines, derives, and describes the beta coefficient, which is a measure of nondiversifiable risk. The second section presents an equation of the model itself, and the third graphically describes the relationship between risk and return. The fourth section discusses the effects of changes in inflationary expectations and risk aversion on the relationship between risk and return. The final section offers some general comments on CAPM.

Beta Coefficient

beta coefficient (β)
A measure of nondiversifiable risk. An *index* of the degree of movement of an asset's return in response to a change in the *market return*.

market return
The return on the market portfolio of all traded securities.

The **beta coefficient, β,** measures nondiversifiable risk. It is an *index* of the degree of movement of an asset's return in response to a change in the *market return*. An asset's historical returns are used in finding the asset's beta coefficient. The **market return** is the return on the market portfolio of all traded securities. In Canada, the *S&P/TSX Composite Index* is used as the market return. Although betas for actively traded stocks can be obtained from a variety of sources, you should understand how they are derived, interpreted, and applied to portfolios.

Deriving Beta from Return Data The relationship between an asset's return and the market return and its use in deriving beta can be demonstrated graphically. Figure 7.12 plots the relationship between the returns of two assets—R and S—and the market return. Note that the horizontal (x) axis measures the market returns and the vertical (y) axis measures the individual asset's

FIGURE 7.12

Beta Derivation[a]

Graphic derivation of beta for assets R and S

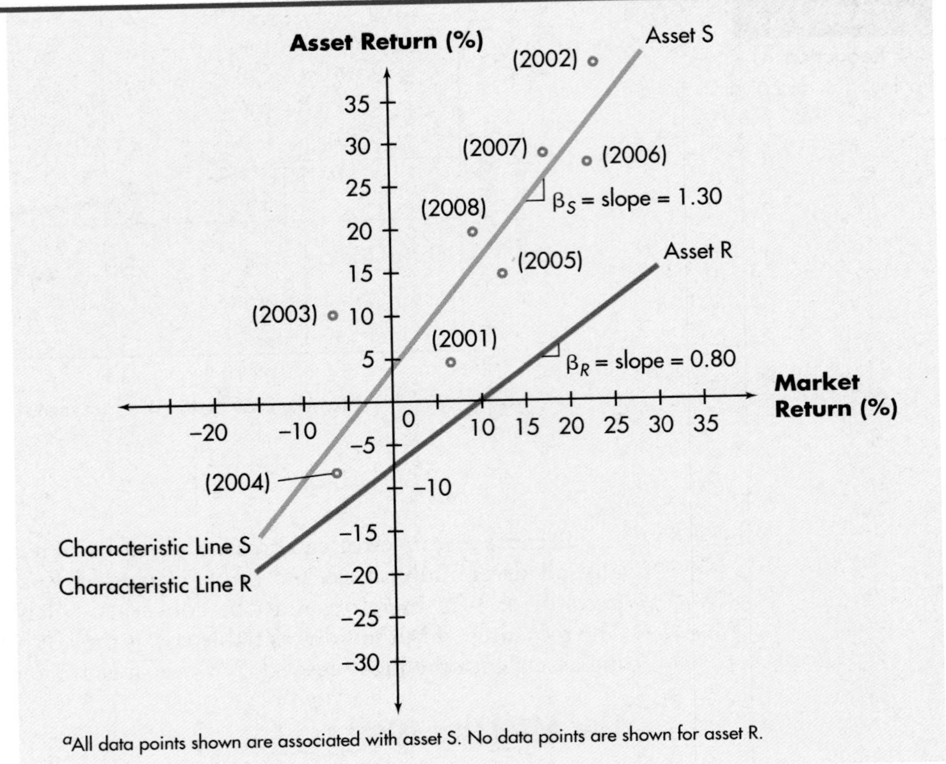

returns. The first step in deriving beta involves plotting the coordinates for the market return and asset returns from various points in time.

Such annual market return–asset return coordinates are shown *for asset S only* for the years 2001 through 2008. For example, in 2008, asset S's return was 20 percent when the market return was 10 percent. By using linear regression, a line is plotted and calculated that "best fits" the series of data points representing the returns on the asset and market. In this application, the line is called the *characteristic line*. The slope of this line is beta (β_j).[14]

---

14. The empirical measurement of beta is approached by using *least-squares regression analysis* to find the regression coefficient (β_j) in the equation for the "characteristic line":

$$k_j = a_j + \beta_j k_m + e_j$$

where

k_j = return on asset j

a_j = intercept

β_j = beta coefficient, which equals $\dfrac{Cov\,(k_j, k_m)}{\sigma_m^2}$

k_m = required rate of return on the market portfolio of securities

e_j = random error term, which reflects the diversifiable, or unsystematic, risk of asset j

where

$Cov\,(k_j, k_m)$ = covariance of the return on asset j, k_j, and the market portfolio, k_m

σ_m^2 = variance of the return on the market portfolio

The calculations involved in finding betas are somewhat rigorous. If you want to know more about these calculations, consult an advanced managerial finance or investments text.

The beta for asset R is about 0.80 and that for asset S is about 1.30. Clearly, asset S's higher beta (steeper characteristic line slope) indicates that its return is more responsive to changing market returns. Therefore it is more risky than asset R.[15] To calculate beta, it is normal to use many more than 10 data points and to use returns calculated on a more frequent basis. If monthly data were used, the minimum number of months of data an analyst would like to use is 60. For weekly (or daily data), at least 104 weeks (520 business days) would be required.

Hint
Remember that published and calculated betas are based on historical data. When investors use beta for decision making, they should recognize that past performance relative to the market average may not predict future performance.

Interpreting Betas By default, the beta of the market index is 1. This is because regressing the market return on the market return will form a straight line at 45 degrees through the origin. The slope of the line will be 1. All other betas are viewed in relation to this value. Asset betas may take on values that are either positive or negative, but positive betas are the norm. The majority of beta coefficients fall between 0.3 and 2.8. A security with a beta of 0.5 is half as risky as the market, and is viewed as "low-risk." A security with a beta of 1.0 is as risky as the market and is viewed as "average-risk." A security with a beta of 2.0 is twice as risky as the market and is viewed as "high-risk."

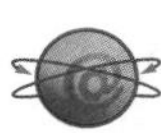

http://today.reuters.com/investing
www.theglobeandmail.com/business
http://finance.yahoo.com

Table 7.10 provides some selected beta values and their interpretations. Beta coefficients for actively traded common shares can be obtained from investment dealers, in publications such as *Financial Post Corporate Reports* or *The Investment Reporter*, and on the Internet. Betas for the common shares of selected companies are provided in Table 7.11.

Portfolio Betas The beta of a portfolio can be easily estimated using the betas of the individual assets it includes. Letting w_j represent the proportion of the portfolio's total dollar value represented by asset j and β_j equal the beta of asset j, we can use Equation 7.12 to find the portfolio beta, β_p:

$$\beta_p = (w_1 \times \beta_1) + (w_2 \times \beta_2) + \ldots + (w_n \times \beta_n) = \sum_{j=1}^{n} w_j \times \beta_j \tag{7.12}$$

For this calculation, the beta of all assets in the portfolio must be available.

TABLE 7.10 Selected Beta Coefficients and Their Interpretations

Beta	Comment	Interpretation
2.0	Move in same direction as market	Twice as responsive, or risky, as the market
1.0		Same response or risk as the market (i.e., average risk)
0.5		Only half as responsive, or risky, as the market
0		Unaffected by market movement
−0.5	Move in opposite direction to market	Only half as responsive, or risky, as the market
−1.0		Same response or risk as the market (i.e., average risk)
−2.0		Twice as responsive, or risky, as the market

15. The values of beta also depend on the time interval used for return calculations and the number of returns used in the regression analysis. In other words, betas calculated using monthly returns would not necessarily be comparable to those calculated using daily returns over the same time period.

TABLE 7.11 Beta Coefficients for the Common Shares of Selected Companies (November, 2006)

Stock	Beta	Stock	Beta
Abitibi-Consolidated	1.79	Inco	1.63
Alcan	1.48	Loblaws Companies	0.34
Bank of Montreal	0.49	Magna International	1.61
BCE Inc.	0.81	Manulife Financial	0.90
Bombardier	2.22	Maple Leaf Foods	0.59
CAE Inc.	2.00	Nortel Networks	2.48
Canadian National Railway	0.87	Onex Corp.	0.38
Canadian Natural Resources	1.28	Petro-Canada	0.81
Canadian Pacific Railway	0.98	Potash Corp. of Saskatchewan	0.77
Canadian Tire	0.68	Rogers Communications	1.43
CIBC	0.85	Royal Bank	0.58
EnCana Corp.	0.94	Sobeys	0.42
Fortis Inc.	0.46	Thompson Corp.	0.83
Forzani Group	1.37	Toronto-Dominion Bank	1.01
Four Seasons Hotels	1.00	Van Houtte	1.10
Imperial Oil	0.29	WestJet Airlines	1.11

SOURCES: Financial Post Corporate Reports, November 2006, Reuters, available at **http://today.reuters.com/investing**; *Globe and Mail Business*, available at **www.theglobeandmail.com/business.**

Hint
Mutual fund managers are key users of the portfolio beta and return concepts. They are continually evaluating what would happen to the fund's beta and return if the securities of a particular firm are added to or deleted from the fund's portfolio.

Portfolio betas are interpreted in the same way as individual asset betas. They indicate the degree of risk of the portfolio. Clearly, a portfolio containing mostly low-beta assets will have a low beta, and one containing mostly high-beta assets will have a high beta.

Example The Austin Fund, a large investment company, wishes to assess the risk of two portfolios—V and W. Both portfolios contain the common shares of five companies. The percentage of the portfolio invested in each company and the share's betas are provided in Table 7.12. The betas for the two portfolios, β_V and β_W, can be calculated by substituting data from the table into Equation 7.12:

$$\beta_V = (0.10 \times 1.65) + (0.30 \times 1.00) + (0.20 \times 1.30) + (0.20 \times 1.10) + (0.20 \times 1.25)$$
$$= 0.165 + 0.300 + 0.260 + 0.220 + 0.250 = 1.195 = \underline{\underline{1.20}}$$

$$\beta_W = (0.10 \times 0.80) + (0.10 \times 1.00) + (0.20 \times 0.65) + (0.10 \times 0.75) + (0.50 \times 1.05)$$
$$= 0.080 + 0.100 + 0.130 + 0.075 + 0.525 = \underline{\underline{0.91}}$$

Portfolio V's beta is 1.20, and portfolio W's is 0.91. These values make sense, because portfolio V contains relatively high-beta assets and portfolio W contains relatively low-beta assets. Clearly, portfolio V is more risky than portfolio W.

TABLE 7.12 Austin Fund's Portfolios V and W

Common share	Portfolio V: Proportion of portfolio	Portfolio V: Beta	Portfolio W: Proportion of portfolio	Portfolio W: Beta
1	10%	1.65	10%	0.80
2	30	1.00	10	1.00
3	20	1.30	20	0.65
4	20	1.10	10	0.75
5	20	1.25	50	1.05
Totals	100%		100%	

The Equation

By using the beta coefficient to measure nondiversifiable risk, the *capital asset pricing model (CAPM)* is given in Equation 7.13:

$$k_j = R_F + [\beta_j \times (k_m - R_F)] \tag{7.13}$$

where

k_j = required rate of return on asset j
R_F = risk-free rate of return, commonly measured by the return on short-term Government of Canada treasury bills
β_i = beta coefficient or index of nondiversifiable risk for asset j
k_m = market return; return on the market portfolio of assets

The required return on an asset, k_j, is an increasing function of beta, β_j, which measures nondiversifiable risk. In other words, *the higher the risk, the higher the required return, and the lower the risk, the lower the required return.*[16]

The model can be divided into two parts: (1) the *risk-free rate,* and (2) the *risk premium.* These are, respectively, the two elements on either side of the addition sign in Equation 7.13. The $(k_m - R_F)$ portion of the risk premium is called the *market risk premium,* because it represents the premium the investor must receive for taking the average amount of risk associated with holding the market portfolio of assets.[17]

16. Note that Equation 7.13 implicitly provides the formula for beta as follows:

$$\beta_j = \frac{(k_j - R_F)}{(k_m - R_F)}$$

17. Although CAPM has been widely accepted, a broader theory, *arbitrage pricing theory (APT),* first described by Stephen A. Ross, "The Arbitrage Theory of Capital Asset Pricing," *Journal of Economic Theory* (December 1976), pp. 341–360, has in recent years received a great deal of attention in the financial literature. The theory suggests that the risk premium on securities may be better explained by a number of factors underlying and in place of the market return used in CAPM. The CAPM in effect can be viewed as being derived from APT. Although testing of APT theory confirms the importance of the market return, it has thus far failed to clearly identify other risk factors. As a result of this failure as well as APT's lack of practical acceptance and usage, we concentrate our attention here on CAPM.

Example Benjamin Corporation, a growing computer-software developer, wishes to determine the required return on an asset Z, which has a beta of 1.5. The risk-free rate of return is estimated to be 7 percent; the return on the market portfolio of assets is 11 percent. Substituting $\beta_Z = 1.5$, $R_F = 7\%$, and $k_m = 11\%$ into the capital asset pricing model given in Equation 7.13 yields a required return:

$$k_Z = 7\% + [1.5 \times (11\% - 7\%)] = 7\% + 6\% = \underline{\underline{13\%}}$$

The market risk premium of 4 percent (11% − 7%), when adjusted for the asset's asset risk (beta) of 1.5, results in a risk premium of 6 percent (1.5 × 4%). That risk premium, when added to the 7 percent risk-free rate, results in a 13 percent required return. Other things being equal, the higher the beta, the higher the required return, and the lower the beta, the lower the required return.

To use the CAPM in practice, information regarding the expected market return and risk-free rate is required. Rather than estimating the market return, however, an estimate for the market risk premium is often used. A reasonable way to estimate the market risk premium is to base it on the average market risk premium over a long period of time. In Canada, the proxy for the market portfolio is the S&P/TSX Composite Index. Table 7.6 indicated that the average risk premium on this index over the 69 years to 2006 was about 6.7 percent.

Based on this result, a reasonable estimate of the premium investors would demand to invest in the risky market portfolio of Canadian common shares would be about 6.7 percent. Recognize, however, that this is just an estimate and is subject to change based on the expectations of the user of the CAPM. The risk-free rate used in the model is usually based on current expectations regarding the expected yield on Government of Canada treasury bills.

In their papers "Global Evidence on the Equity Risk Premium" and "The Worldwide Equity Premium: A Smaller Puzzle," Elroy Dimson, Paul Marsh, and Mike Staunton provide data on the returns earned on common shares, bonds, and treasury bills, over the 106-year period from 1900 to 2005, in the United States and 16 other countries including Canada. In their research, they develop a database of returns in these 17 countries, and estimate that the historical equity premium for the 17 countries in their sample has averaged 6.1 percent over this very long 106-year period. This is very similar to the result from Table 7.6. For the interested reader, this research is freely available on the Web.

The Graph: The Security Market Line (SML)

security market line (SML)
The depiction of the capital asset pricing model (CAPM) as a graph that reflects the required return in the marketplace for each level of nondiversifiable risk (beta).

When the capital asset pricing model (Equation 7.13) is depicted graphically, it is called the **security market line (SML)**. The SML reflects the required return in the marketplace for each level of nondiversifiable risk (beta). In the graph, risk as measured by beta (β_j) is plotted on the x axis, and required returns, k_j, are plotted on the y axis. The risk–return tradeoff is clearly illustrated by the SML.

Example In the preceding example for Benjamin Corporation, the risk-free rate, R_F, was 7 percent, and the market return, k_m, was 11 percent. The SML can be plotted by recognizing that the risk-free rate has no risk and thus has a beta of 0. Thus the SML starts at 7 percent on the y axis. The market has a beta of 1, and a required return of 11 percent. By joining these two data points, we create the SML for this set of data. Note that the slope of the SML is the market risk premium, in this case 4.

FIGURE 7.13

Security Market Line
Security market line (SML) with Benjamin Corporation's asset Z data shown

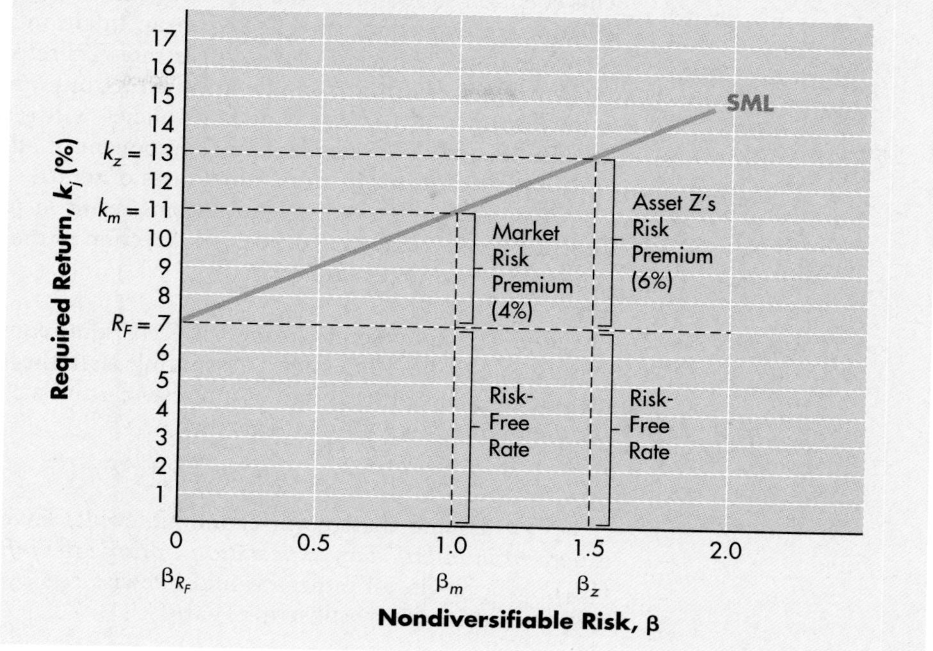

Figure 7.13 presents the resulting security market line. As traditionally shown, the security market line in the figure presents the required return associated with all positive betas. The market risk premium of 4 percent has been highlighted. For a beta for asset Z (β_z), of 1.5, its corresponding required return, k_z, is 13 percent. Also shown in the figure is asset Z's risk premium of 6 percent. It should be clear that for assets with betas greater than 1, the risk premium is greater than that for the market; for assets with betas less than 1, the risk premium is less than that for the market.

Again, note that the general equation for the required rate of return on asset j (k_j) is the risk-free rate (R_F) plus the risk premium (RP). This means that on any investment, investors will always expect to receive, at minimum, the R_F. Since the investment is risky, investors will also require a risk premium.

Shifts in the Security Market Line

The security market line is not stable over time, and shifts in the security market line can result in a change in required return. The position and the slope of the SML are affected by two major forces—inflationary expectations and risk aversion—which are separately analyzed next.[18]

Changes in Inflationary Expectations Changes in inflationary expectations affect the risk-free rate of return, R_F. The equation for the risk-free rate of return is:

$$R_F = k^* + IP \tag{7.14}$$

18. A firm's beta can change over time as a result of changes in the firm's asset mix, in its financing mix, or in external factors not within management's control, such as competitors' actions, economic activity, social and political changes, and so on. The impacts of changes in beta on required return are discussed in Chapter 8.

This equation shows that assuming a constant real rate of interest, k^*, changes in inflationary expectations, reflected in an inflation premium, *IP*, will result in corresponding changes in the risk-free rate. Therefore, a change in inflationary expectations resulting from events such as international trade embargoes or major changes in Bank of Canada policies will result in a shift in the SML. Because the risk-free rate is a basic component of all rates of return, any change in R_F will be reflected in *all* required rates of return.

Changes in inflationary expectations result in parallel shifts in the SML in direct response to the magnitude and direction of the change. This effect can best be illustrated by an example.

Example In the preceding example, using the SML, the required return for asset Z, k_Z, was found to be 13 percent. Assuming that the risk-free rate of 7 percent includes a 2 percent real rate of interest, k^*, and a 5 percent inflation premium, *IP*, then Equation 7.14 confirms that

$$R_F = 2\% + 5\% = 7\%$$

Now assume that recent economic events have resulted in an *increase of 3 percent in inflationary expectations, raising the inflation premium* to 8 percent (IP_1). As a result, all returns would likewise rise by 3 percent. In this case, the new returns (noted by subscript 1) are

$$R_{F_1} = 10\% \text{ (rises from 7\% to 10\%)}$$
$$k_{m_1} = 14\% \text{ (rises from 11\% to 14\%)}$$

Substituting these values, along with asset Z's beta (β_Z) of 1.5, into the CAPM (Equation 7.13), we find that asset Z's new required return (k_{Z_1}) can be calculated:

$$k_{Z_1} = 10\% + [1.5 \times (14\% - 10\%)] = 10\% + 6\% = \underline{\underline{16\%}}$$

Comparing k_{Z_1} of 16 percent to k_Z of 13 percent, we see that the change of 3 percent in asset Z's required return exactly equals the change in the inflation premium. The same 3% increase would result for all assets.

Figure 7.14 depicts the situation just described. It shows that the 3 percent increase in inflationary expectations results in a parallel shift upward of 3 percent in the SML. Clearly, the required returns on all assets rise by 3 percent. Note that the rise in the inflation premium from 5 to 8 percent (*IP* to IP_1) causes the risk-free rate to rise from 7 to 10 percent (R_F to R_{F1}) and the market return to increase from 11 to 14 percent (k_m to k_{m_1}). Note that the market risk premium remains 4 percent.

Therefore, the security market line shifts upward by 3 percent (SML to SML_1), causing the required return on all risky assets, such as asset Z, to rise by 3 percent. It should now be clear that *a given change in inflationary expectations will be fully reflected in a corresponding change in the returns of all assets, as reflected graphically in a parallel shift of the SML.*

Changes in Risk Aversion The slope of the security market line reflects the general risk preferences of investors in the marketplace. As discussed earlier and shown in Figure 7.1, most investors are risk-averse—they require increased returns for increased risk. This positive relationship between risk and return is graphically represented by the SML, which depicts the relationship between nondiversifiable risk as measured by beta (*x* axis), and the required return (*y* axis).

FIGURE 7.14

Inflation Shifts SML

Impact of increased inflationary expectations on the SML

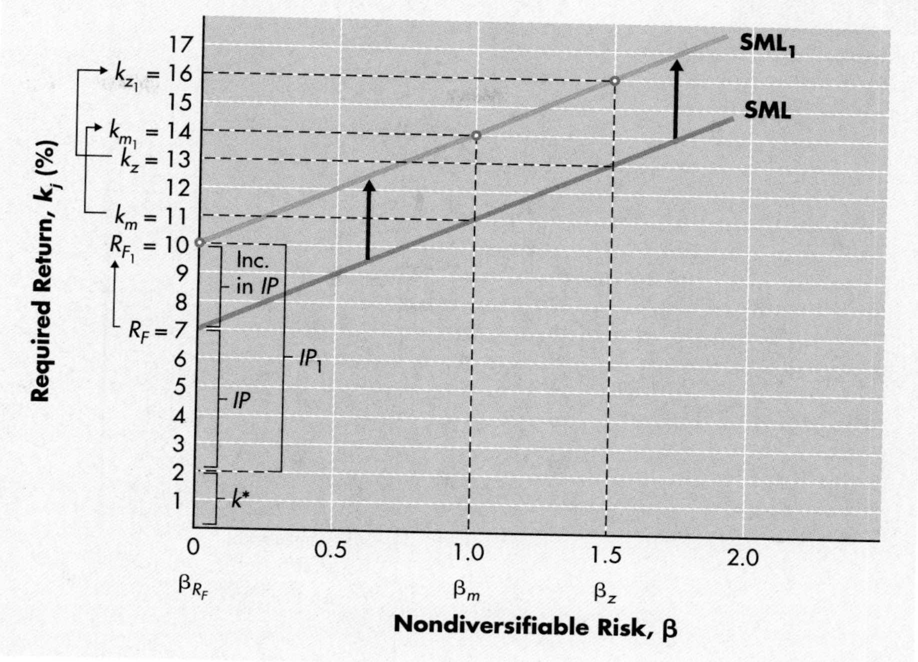

The slope of the SML reflects the degree of risk aversion: *the steeper its slope, the greater the degree of risk aversion,* because a higher level of return would be required for each level of risk as measured by beta.

Changes in risk aversion, and therefore shifts in the SML, result from changing preferences of investors, which generally result from economic, political, and social events. Examples of events that *increase* risk aversion would be a stock market crash, political uncertainty, the outbreak of war, and so forth. In general, widely accepted expectations of hard times ahead tend to cause investors to become more risk-averse, requiring higher returns as compensation for accepting a given level of risk. The impact of increased risk aversion on the SML can best be demonstrated by an example.

Example In the preceding examples, the SML in Figure 7.13 reflected a risk-free rate (R_F) of 7 percent, a market return (k_m) of 11 percent, a market risk premium ($k_m - R_F$) of 4 percent, and a required return on asset Z (k_Z) of 13 percent with a beta (β_Z) of 1.5. Assume that recent economic events have made investors more risk-averse, resulting in the market risk premium increasing to 7 percent. This means the market return (k_{m_1}) will increase to 14 percent. Graphically, this change would cause the SML to shift upward as shown in Figure 7.15. As a result, the required return on all risky assets will increase. For asset Z, with a beta of 1.5, the new required return (k_{Z_1}) will be:

$$k_{Z_1} = 7\% + [1.5 \times (14\% - 7\%)] = 7\% + 10.5\% = \underline{\underline{17.5\%}}$$

This value can be seen on the new security market line (SML_1) in Figure 7.15. Note that although asset Z's risk, as measured by beta, did not change, its

FIGURE 7.15

Risk Aversion Shifts SML

Impact of increased risk aversion on the SML

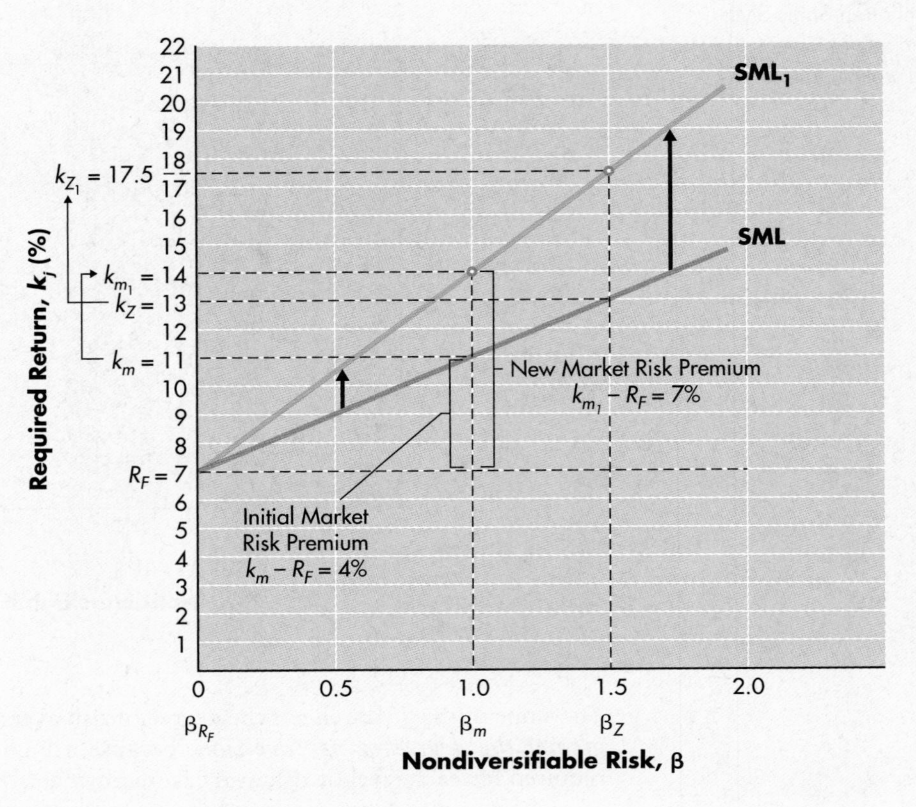

required return has increased due to the increased risk aversion reflected in the market risk premium. It should now be clear that *greater risk aversion results in higher required returns for each level of risk. Similarly, a reduction in risk aversion would cause the required return for each level of risk to decline.*

Some Comments on CAPM

The capital asset pricing model generally relies on historical data to estimate required returns. The betas, which are developed using data for the given asset as well as for the market, may or may not actually reflect the *future* variability of returns. Therefore the required returns specified by the model can be viewed only as rough approximations. Users of betas commonly make subjective adjustments to reflect their expectations of the future when such expectations differ from the actual risk–return behaviours of the past.

The CAPM was actually developed to explain the behaviour of security prices and provide a mechanism whereby investors could assess the impact of a

efficient market
An assumed "perfect" market in which there are many small investors, each having the same information and expectations with respect to securities; there are no restrictions on investment, no taxes, and no transaction costs; and all investors are rational, view securities similarly, and are risk-averse, preferring higher returns and lower risk.

proposed security investment on their portfolio's overall risk and return. It is based on an assumed **efficient market**—a market in which there are many small investors, each having the same information and expectations with respect to securities; there are no restrictions on investment, no taxes, and no transaction costs; and all investors are rational, view securities similarly, and are risk-averse, preferring higher returns and lower risk.

Although the perfect world of the efficient market appears to be unrealistic, empirical studies have provided some support for the existence of the expectational relationship described by CAPM in major markets such as the Toronto and New York Stock Exchanges.[19] In the case of real corporate assets, such as plant and equipment, research thus far has failed to prove the general applicability of CAPM because of indivisibility, relatively large size, limited number of transactions, and absence of an efficient market for such assets.

In spite of the fact that the risk–return tradeoff described by CAPM is not generally applicable to all assets, it provides a useful conceptual framework for evaluating and linking risk and required return. An awareness of this tradeoff and an attempt to consider risk as well as return in financial decision making should aid the financial manager in achieving the goal of owner wealth maximization.

? Review Questions

7–18 What is the relationship of total risk, nondiversifiable risk, and diversifiable risk? Why is nondiversifiable risk the *only relevant risk*?

7–19 What is *beta* and what does it measure? How are asset betas derived, and where can they be obtained? How can you find the beta of a portfolio?

7–20 What is the equation for the *capital asset pricing model (CAPM)*? Explain the meaning of each variable. Assuming a risk-free rate of 8 percent and a market return of 12 percent, draw the *security market line (SML)*.

7–21 What impact would the following changes have on the security market line and therefore on the required return for a given level of risk? **(a)** An increase in inflationary expectations. **(b)** Investors become less risk-averse.

7–22 Why do financial managers have difficulty applying CAPM in decision making? Generally, what benefit does CAPM provide them?

19. A large number of academic studies have raised serious questions regarding the validity of the CAPM in securities markets around the world. These studies fail to find a significant relationship between *historic* betas and *historic* returns on portfolios of large numbers of common shares over long periods of time. In other words, the *historic* beta and *historic* returns of common shares do not seem to be linked. Although these studies lead investors and researchers to question the validity of the CAPM, the theory has not been abandoned because of its logic and ease of understanding. As well, the theory's rejection as a *historical* model fails to reject its validity as an *expectational* model. Therefore, in spite of this challenge, CAPM continues to be viewed as a logical and useful framework—both conceptually and operationally—for linking *expected* nondiversifiable risk and return.

SUMMARY

LG1 **Understand the meaning of risk, how returns are calculated for a single period and over multiple holding periods, and the concept of risk preferences.** Risk is the variability of returns, or the possibility that bad or good things may happen. Return is the change in price plus any cash distributions expressed as a percentage of the initial price of the asset. To calculate returns over multiple holding periods, the arithmetic mean or the geometric mean can be used. The arithmetic mean is a better measure of typical performance. The geometric mean is a better measure of past performance. The variable definitions and equations used to calculate the rate of return are given in Table 7.13. The three basic risk preference behaviours are risk-neutral, risk-averse, and risk-seeking. Most financial decision makers are risk-averse because they require higher expected returns as compensation for taking greater risk.

LG2 **Describe procedures for measuring the risk of a single asset, and the risk associated with a past series of returns.** The risk of a single asset is measured in much the same way as the risk of a portfolio, or collection, of assets. Sensitivity analysis and probability distributions can be used to assess risk. In addition to the range, the standard deviation and the coefficient of variation are statistics that can be used to measure risk quantitatively. The standard deviation of a past series of returns can also be calculated. The key variable definitions and equations for the expected return, standard deviation of return, and the coefficient of variation are summarized in Table 7.13.

LG3 **Illustrate the returns and risk on different types of financial assets over the period 1938 to 2006, and discuss the lessons we can learn from this data.** Table 7.5 provides the yearly rates of return on four important types of financial securities and the level of inflation for Canada for the 69-year period from 1938 to 2006. The lessons we can learn from analyzing this data include: (1) the geometric return is less than the arithmetic return; (2) the returns on the common share indexes generated, by far, the highest returns; (3) the risk of common shares as measured by the range and the standard deviation is also much higher; (4) over long time periods common shares provide an average yearly return that is greater than t-bills but there is no guarantee that in any specific year common shares will do so; (5) the risk premium on the common share indexes reflects the greater risk and return, and (6) the distribution of returns on financial securities are normally distributed, meaning their possible returns can be completely described by the mean return and the standard deviation of returns.

LG4 **Discuss the measurement of return and standard deviation for a portfolio, the various types of correlation that can exist between series of numbers, the benefits of diversification, and the impact of international assets on a portfolio.** The return of a portfolio is calculated as the weighted average of returns on the individual assets from which it is formed. The variable definitions and equation for portfolio return are given in Table 7.13. The portfolio standard deviation is found by using the formula for the standard deviation of a single asset. Correlation, the statistical relationship between series of numbers, can be positive (the series move in the same direction), negative (the series move in opposite directions), or uncorrelated (the series exhibit no discernible relationship). At the extremes, the series can be perfectly positively correlated (have a correlation coefficient of +1) or perfectly negatively correlated (have a correlation coefficient of −1).

Diversification involves combining assets with low (less positive and more negative) correlation to reduce the risk of the portfolio. Although the return on a two-asset portfolio will lie between the returns of the two assets held in isolation, the range of risk depends on the correlation between the two assets. If they are perfectly positively correlated, the portfolio's risk will be between the individual asset's risks. If uncorrelated, the portfolio's risk will be between the risk of the most risky asset and an amount less than the risk of the least risky asset but greater than zero. If negatively correlated, the portfolio's risk will be between the risk of the most risky asset and zero. International diversification, which involves including foreign assets in a portfolio, can be used to further reduce a portfolio's risk.

LG5 **Review the two types of risk for a portfolio of assets, and the derivation and role of beta in measuring the relevant risk of both an individual security and a portfolio.** The total risk of a security consists of nondiversifiable and diversifiable risk. Nondiversifiable risk is the only relevant risk because diversifiable risk can be easily eliminated through diversification. Nondiversifiable risk can be measured by the beta coefficient, which reflects the relationship between an asset's return and the market return. Beta is derived by using statistical techniques to find the slope of the "characteristic line" that best explains the historic relationship between the asset's return and the market return. The beta of a portfolio is a weighted average of the betas of the individual assets that it includes.

Explain the capital asset pricing model (CAPM), its relationship to the security market line (SML), and shifts in the SML caused by changes in inflationary expectations and risk aversion. The capital asset pricing model (CAPM) uses beta to relate an asset's risk relative to the market to the asset's required return. The variable definitions and equation for CAPM are given in Table 7.13. The graphic depiction of CAPM is the security market line (SML), which shifts over time in response to changing inflationary expectations and/or changes in investor risk aversion. Changes in inflationary expectations result in parallel shifts in the SML in direct response to the magnitude and direction of change. Increasing risk aversion results in a steepening in the slope of the SML, and decreasing risk aversion reduces the slope of the SML.

TABLE 7.13 Summary of Key Definitions and Formulas for Risk and Return

Variable definitions

β_j = beta coefficient or index of nondiversifiable risk for asset j

β_p = portfolio beta

$C_{j,t}$ = cash distribution received from the investment in asset j in the time period $t - 1$ to t

CV_j = coefficient of variation of asset j

k_j = rate of return on asset j over a stated time period

$\bar{k}_j$ = arithmetic mean return for asset j over n periods

$k(G)_j$ = geometric mean return on asset j over n periods

$\hat{k}_j$ = expected return on asset j over a stated period, termed "k-hat for asset j"

k_i = return for the ith outcome

V_{EOP} = value of investment at end of holding period

V_{BOP} = value of investment at beginning of holding period

R_F = risk-free rate of return

k_m = market return; the return on the market portfolio of assets

k_p = portfolio return

n = number of outcomes considered

$P_{j,t}$ = price of asset j at time t

$P_{j,t-1}$ = price of asset j at time $t - 1$

Pr_i = probability of occurrence of the ith outcome

R_F = risk-free rate of return

σ_j = standard deviation of returns for asset j

w_j = proportion of total portfolio dollar value invested in asset j

continued

TABLE 7.13 continued

Risk and return formulas

Rate of return during period t:

$$k_j = \frac{P_{j,t} - P_{j,t-1} + C_{j,t}}{P_{j,t-1}} \quad \text{[Eq. 7.1]}$$

Arithmetic mean:

$$\bar{k}_j = \frac{\sum_{t=1}^{n} k_{j,t}}{n} \quad \text{[Eq. 7.2]}$$

Geometric mean:

$$k(G)_j = \sqrt[n]{(1 + k_1)(1 + k_2) \ldots (1 + k_n)} - 1 \quad \text{[Eq. 7.3]}$$

Value of investment:

$$V_{EOP} = V_{BOP} \times [1 + k(G)_j]^n \quad \text{[Eq. 7.4]}$$

Expected value of a return:
for probabilistic data,

$$\hat{k}_j = \sum_{i=1}^{n} k_{j,i} \times Pr_i \quad \text{[Eq. 7.5]}$$

Standard deviation of return:
for probabilistic data,

$$\sigma_j = \sqrt{\sum_{i=1}^{n} (k_{j,i} - \hat{k}_j)^2 \times Pr_i} \quad \text{[Eq. 7.6]}$$

Standard deviation of actual or expected returns, using arithmetic mean

$$\sigma_j = \sqrt{\frac{\sum_{t=1}^{n} (k_{j,t} - \bar{k}_j)^2}{n - 1}} \quad \text{[Eq. 7.7]}$$

Coefficient of variation:

$$CV_j = \frac{\sigma_j}{\hat{k}_j \text{ or } \bar{k}_j} \quad \text{[Eq. 7.8]}$$

Portfolio return:

$$k_p = \sum_{j=1}^{n} w_j \times k_j \quad \text{[Eq. 7.9]}$$

Portfolio standard deviation:

$$\sigma_p = \sqrt{w_1^2\sigma_1^2 + w_2^2\sigma_2^2 + 2w_1w_2r_{1,2}\sigma_1\sigma_2} \quad \text{[Eq. 7.10]}$$

Total security risk (σ_j) = nondiversifiable risk + diversifiable risk [Eq. 7.11]

Portfolio beta:

$$\beta_p = \sum_{j=1}^{n} w_j \times \beta_j \quad \text{[Eq. 7.12]}$$

Capital asset pricing model (CAPM):

$$k_j = R_F + [\beta_j \times (k_m - R_F)] \quad \text{[Eq. 7.13]}$$

Risk-free rate of return:

$$R_F = k^* + IP \quad \text{[Eq. 7.14]}$$

SELF-TEST PROBLEMS

(Solutions in Appendix B)

ST7–1 **Calculating the arithmetic and geometric mean** On January 1, 2007, you purchased 500 common shares of Kieran's Klubs, a golf club manufacturer. The following information regarding the price of the common shares is available:

Share price: January 1, 2007	$15.00
Share price: December 31, 2007	$30.00
Share price: December 31, 2008	$15.00

a. Using Equation 7.1, calculate the returns earned on the investment in Kieran's Klubs during 2007 and 2008.
b. Now with the returns on a single asset for two periods, calculate the average return received on the investment in Kieran's Klubs over the two years. Determine both the arithmetic and geometric mean.
c. Calculate the dollar return on the investment for 2007 and 2008.
d. Discuss the implications of the results in parts **b** and **c**.

LG4 ST 7–2 **Portfolio analysis** You have been asked for your advice in selecting a portfolio of assets and have been supplied with the following data:

	Expected return		
Year	Asset A	Asset B	Asset C
2008	12%	16%	12%
2009	14	14	14
2010	16	12	16

You have been told that you can create two portfolios—one consisting of assets A and B and the other consisting of assets A and C—by investing equal proportions (i.e., 50%) in each of the two component assets.
a. What is the expected return for each asset over the 3-year period?
b. What is the standard deviation for each asset's return?
c. What is the expected return for each portfolio per year and on average?
d. How would you characterize the correlations of returns of the two assets making up each of the two portfolios identified in **c**?
e. What is the standard deviation for each portfolio?
f. Which portfolio do you recommend? Why?

ST 7–3 **Beta and CAPM** A company's common shares have a beta, β, of 1.50. At this time, the risk-free rate of return, R_F, is 7 percent, and the return on the market portfolio of assets, k_m, is 10 percent. The common shares are *expected* to earn an annual return of 11 percent.
a. Use the capital asset pricing model (CAPM) to find the *required return* on the common shares.
b. On the basis of your calculation in **a**, would you recommend these common shares be purchased as an investment? Why or why not?
c. Assume that as a result of investors becoming less risk-averse, the market risk premium drops by 1 percent. What impact would this change have on your responses in **a** and **b**?

PROBLEMS

BASIC  7–1 **Rate of return** Douglas Keel, a financial analyst for Orange Industries, wishes to estimate the rate of return for two similar-risk investments—X and Y. Keel's research indicates that the immediate past returns will act as reasonable estimates of future returns. A year earlier, investment X had a market value of $20,000 and investment Y, of $55,000. During the year, investment X generated cash flow of $1,500 and investment Y generated cash flow of $6,800. The current market values of investments X and Y are $21,000 and $55,000, respectively.

a. What were the actual rates of return earned on investments X and Y during the most recent year?

b. What are the expected rates of return on investments X and Y for the upcoming year?

c. Assuming that the two investments are equally risky, which one should Keel recommend? Why?

BASIC  7–2 **Return calculations** For each of the investments shown in the following table, calculate the rate of return earned over the time period.

Investment	Beginning-of-period value	End-of-period value	Cash flow during period
A	$ 800	$ 1,100	$ −100
B	120,000	118,000	15,000
C	45,000	48,000	7,000
D	600	500	80
E	12,500	12,400	1,500

BASIC  7–3 **Calculating mean returns** An investor is considering buying shares of a Canadian common stock with the following returns in the past 5 years.

Year	Rate of return
1	1.13%
2	19.65
3	31.90
4	17.12
5	−19.99

a. What are the arithmetic mean and geometric mean rates of return for this stock over the past 5 years?

b. Which of the two rates of return should the investor use as an estimate of this stock's future rate of return? Why?

c. The investor has $25,000 to invest in this stock today, and she expects an average rate of return on the investment of 8.4 percent per year over the next five years. What will be the value of her investment at the end of the five-year period if her expectation about future rates of returns is correct?

BASIC LG1

7–4 Risk preferences Sharon Smith, the financial manager for Barnett Corporation, wishes to evaluate three prospective investments—X, Y, and Z. Currently, the firm earns 12 percent on its investments, which have risk of 6 percent. The expected return and expected risk of the investments are as follows:

Investment	Expected return	Expected risk
X	14%	7%
Y	12	8
Z	10	9

a. If Sharon Smith were *risk-indifferent,* which investments would she select? Explain why.
b. If she were *risk-averse,* which investments would she select? Why?
c. If she were *risk-seeking,* which investments would she select? Why?
d. Given the traditional risk preference behaviour exhibited by financial managers, which investment would be preferred? Why?

INTERMEDIATE 

7–5 Calculating returns Today you purchased 1,000 common shares of CIBC for $27.75 per share. CIBC currently pays a dividend of $1.34, which you expect to grow by 5 percent next year. You expect the share price will be $31 in one year's time.
a. What is your expected dollar and percentage return?
b. Now assume that investors' required rate of return on an investment in CIBC's stock is 13.2 percent. Using the above data, should an investor buy CIBC's common shares? Explain.

BASIC LG1

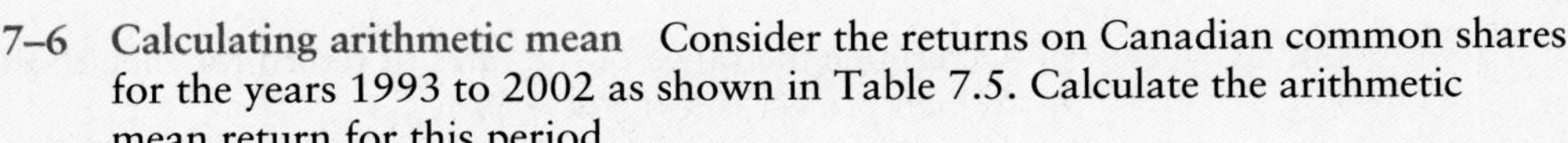

7–6 Calculating arithmetic mean Consider the returns on Canadian common shares for the years 1993 to 2002 as shown in Table 7.5. Calculate the arithmetic mean return for this period.

BASIC LG1

7–7 Calculating geometric mean Consider the returns on Canadian common shares for the years 1993 to 2002 as shown in Table 7.5.
a. Calculate the geometric mean return for this period.
b. Assume an investment of $100 was made in the portfolio of Canadian common shares at the beginning of 1993. What would be the value of this investment at the end of 2002?

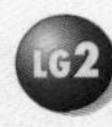
INTERMEDIATE

7-8 **Variance and standard deviation** An index of Canadian common stocks generated the following rates of return over the previous 8 years:

Year	Rate of return
1	12.56%
2	25.58
3	14.12
4	–2.58
5	28.41
6	4.05
7	–13.18
8	–15.71

a. What is the variance for the rate of return over the 8-year period covered by the table?
b. What is the standard deviation?
c. What is the coefficient of variation?
d. Discuss the implications of each of your answers.

7–9 **Risk analysis** Solar Designs is considering two possible types of expansion to its product line. After investigating the possible outcomes, the company developed the estimates shown in the following table:

	Expansion A	Expansion B
Initial investment	$12,000	$12,000
Annual rate of return		
Pessimistic	16%	10%
Most likely	20%	20%
Optimistic	24%	30%

a. Determine the range of the rates of return for each of the two projects.
b. Which project is less risky? Why?
c. If you were making the investment decision, which one would you choose? Why? What does this imply about your feelings toward risk?
d. Assume that the most likely expected return for expansion B is 21 percent per year and all other facts remain the same. Does this change your answer to part c? Why?

7–10 **Risk and probability** Micro-Pub, Inc., is considering the purchase of one of two microfilm cameras—R or S. Both should provide benefits over a 10-year period, and each requires an initial investment of $4,000. Management has constructed the following table of estimates of probabilities and rates of return for pessimistic, most likely, and optimistic results:

	Camera R		Camera S	
	Amount	Probability	Amount	Probability
Initial investment	$4,000	1.00	$4,000	1.00
Annual rate of return				
Pessimistic	20%	0.25	15%	0.20
Most likely	25%	0.50	25%	0.55
Optimistic	30%	0.25	35%	0.25

a. Determine the range of returns for each of the two cameras.
b. Determine the expected return for each camera.
c. Determine the standard deviation of returns for each camera.
d. Which camera is riskier? Why?

INTERMEDIATE  7–11 **Bar charts and risk** Swan's Sportswear is considering bringing out a line of designer jeans. Currently, it is negotiating with two different well-known designers. Because of the highly competitive nature of the industry, the two designs have been given code names J and K. After market research, the firm has established the expectations shown in the following table about the annual rates of return:

		Annual rate of return	
Market acceptance	Probability	Line J	Line K
Very poor	0.05	0.0075	0.010
Poor	0.15	0.0125	0.025
Average	0.60	0.0850	0.080
Good	0.15	0.1475	0.135
Excellent	0.05	0.1625	0.150

Use the table to:
a. Construct a bar chart for each line's annual rate of return.
b. Calculate the expected return for each line.
c. Evaluate the relative riskiness for each jean line's expected return using the bar charts.
d. Calculate the standard deviation of the returns for each line.
e. Calculate the coefficient of variation for each line.

BASIC  7–12 **Coefficient of variation** Metal Manufacturing has isolated four alternatives for meeting its need for increased production capacity. The data gathered relative to each of these alternatives is summarized in the following table.

Alternative	Expected return	Standard deviation of return
A	20%	7.0%
B	22	9.5
C	19	6.0
D	16	5.5

a. Calculate the coefficient of variation for each alternative.
b. If the firm wishes to minimize risk, which alternative do you recommend? Why?

BASIC  7–13 **Standard deviation versus coefficient of variation as measures of risk** Greengage, Inc., a successful nursery, is considering several expansion opportunities. Each of the alternatives promises to produce an acceptable return. The owners are extremely risk-averse; therefore, they will choose the least risky of the alternatives. Data on four possible projects are as follows.

Project	Expected return	Range	Standard deviation
A	12.0%	0.040	0.029
B	12.5	0.050	0.032
C	13.0	0.060	0.035
D	12.8	0.045	0.030

a. Which alternative is least risky based on range?
b. Which alternative has the lowest standard deviation? Explain why standard deviation is not an appropriate measure of risk for purposes of this comparison.
c. Calculate the coefficient of variation for each alternative. What alternative will Greengage's owners choose? Explain why this may be the better measure of risk for comparing this set of opportunities.

INTERMEDIATE  7–14 **Standard deviation** Consider the returns on Canadian common shares for the years 1993 to 2002 as shown in Table 7.5.
a. Calculate the standard deviation of these returns over this period. Interpret the answer.
b. Calculate and interpret the coefficient of variation for these returns.

CHALLENGE  7–15 **Assessing return and risk** Swift Manufacturing must choose between two asset purchases. The annual rate of return and the related probabilities given in the following table summarize the firm's analysis to this point.

Project 257		Project 432	
Rate of return	Probability	Rate of return	Probability
−10%	0.01	10%	0.05
10	0.04	15	0.10
20	0.05	20	0.10
30	0.10	25	0.15
40	0.15	30	0.20
45	0.30	35	0.15
50	0.15	40	0.10
60	0.10	45	0.10
70	0.05	50	0.05
80	0.04		
100	0.01		

a. For each project, compute:
   (1) The range of possible rates of return.
   (2) The expected return.
   (3) The standard deviation of the returns.
   (4) The coefficient of variation.

b. Construct a bar chart of each distribution of rates of return.

c. Which project would you consider less risky? Why?

CHALLENGE

7–16 Calculating returns and risk On January 2, 2001, you purchased 500 shares of Loewen Group for $9.60 per share. The following information is available concerning the yearly dividend the company paid and the year-end share price for the eight years to 2008.

Date	Dividends paid during year	Stock price at year-end
Dec. 31, 2001	$0.00	$10.65
Dec. 31, 2002	$0.12	$15.23
Dec. 31, 2003	$0.16	$12.25
Dec. 31, 2004	$0.40	$ 9.25
Dec. 31, 2005	$0.48	$14.50
Dec. 31, 2006	$0.62	$21.75
Dec. 31, 2007	$0.75	$30.35
Dec. 31, 2008	$1.00	$38.00

a. Calculate your dollar and percentage return on the investment in Loewen for each year.

b. Calculate your dollar return on the investment.

c. Calculate your arithmetic and geometric mean returns for this period. Why are the arithmetic and geometric means different?

d. Calculate the standard deviation of returns for this period. Interpret the answer.

e. Calculate and interpret the coefficient of variation for your investment in Loewen over this period.

CHALLENGE  7–17 **Integrative—Expected return, standard deviation, and coefficient of variation** Three assets—F, G, and H—are currently being considered by Perth Industries. The probability distributions of expected returns for these assets are shown in the following table.

	Asset F		Asset G		Asset H	
i	Pr_i	Return, k_i	Pr_i	Return, k_i	Pr_i	Return, k_i
1	0.10	40%	0.40	35%	0.10	40%
2	0.20	10	0.30	10	0.20	20
3	0.40	0	0.30	−20	0.40	10
4	0.20	−5			0.20	0
5	0.10	−10			0.10	−20

a. Calculate the expected return, $\hat{k}$, for each of the three assets. Which provides the largest expected return?
b. Calculate the standard deviation, σ, for each of the three assets' returns. Which appears to have the greatest risk?
c. Calculate the coefficient of variation, CV, for each of the three assets. Which appears to have the largest *relative* risk?

INTERMEDIATE  7–18 **Normal probability distribution** Assuming that the rates of return associated with a given asset investment are normally distributed and that the expected return, $\hat{k}$, is 18.9 percent and the coefficient of variation, CV, is 0.75, answer the following questions.
a. Find the standard deviation of returns, σ.
b. Calculate the range of expected return outcomes associated with the following probabilities of occurrence.
(1) 68.3 percent
(2) 95.4 percent
(3) 99.7 percent
c. Draw the probability distribution associated with your findings in **a** and **b**.

BASIC  7–19 **Distribution of returns** The annual rate of return on a Canadian common share is normally distributed with a mean of 7.4 percent and a standard deviation of 14.5 percent.

a. In what range would you expect actual future returns for common shares to be if they were:
i) one standard deviation from the mean? What is the probability that the returns will fall in the calculated range?
ii) two standard deviations from the mean? What is the probability that the returns will fall in the calculated range?

  LG4 INTERMEDIATE 7-20 **Calculation of risk premium** The rate of return on Government of Canada t-bills is commonly used as the risk-free rate of return. The following table below shows the annual rate of return on Government of Canada t-bills and on Canadian common shares over a 6-year period.

Year	T-bills	Canadian common shares
1	5.22%	32.04%
2	5.32	–0.18
3	7.34	14.31
4	4.44	–7.78
5	3.28	14.87
6	4.77	–1.56

a. What is the risk premium on the common shares in each of the 6 years in the table above?
b. What is the mean risk premium for these shares over the whole 6-year period?
c. Calculate and interpret the coefficient of variation for both the t-bills and the common shares.
d. In what range would you expect the actual future returns for both the t-bills and the common shares to be if they were two standard deviations from the mean? What is the probability that the returns will fall in the calculated range?
e. Assume you invested 30 percent of your funds in t-bills and 70 percent in the common shares. What is the standard deviation of the portfolio's return, assuming that the correlation coefficient between the returns on the two investments is +1? What is the standard deviation if the correlation coefficient is 0.10?

INTERMEDIATE  7–21 **Using historic return data** Based on Table 7.6, if you invest in a company that has 20 percent more risk than the portfolio of Canadian common shares when t-bills are providing a 7 percent return, what is the minimum rate of return you should expect?

INTERMEDIATE  7–22 **Portfolio return and standard deviation** Jamie Wong is considering investing in two assets, L and M. Asset L will represent 40 percent of the dollar value of the portfolio, and asset M will account for the other 60 percent. The expected returns over the next 6 years for each of these assets are shown in the following table.

	Expected return	
Year	Asset L	Asset M
1	14%	20%
2	14	18
3	16	16
4	17	14
5	17	12
6	19	10

a. Calculate the expected portfolio return, k_p, for *each* of the 6 years.
b. Calculate the expected value of portfolio returns, $\hat{k}_p$, over the 6-year period.
c. How would you characterize the correlation of returns of the two assets L and M?

d. Calculate the standard deviation of expected portfolio returns, σ_p, over the 6-year period if the correlation coefficient was -0.65.
e. Discuss any benefits of diversification achieved through creation of the portfolio.

INTERMEDIATE  7–23 **Portfolio analysis** You have been given the expected return data in the following table for three assets—F, G, and H—for four years.

	Expected return		
Year	**Asset F**	**Asset G**	**Asset H**
1	16%	17%	14%
2	17	16	15
3	18	15	16
4	19	14	17

For these three assets, you have isolated the three investment alternatives shown below:

Alternative	Investment
1	100% of asset F
2	50% of asset F and 50% of asset G
3	50% of asset F and 50% of asset H

The correlation coefficient of the returns between assets F and G is 0.25, and between F and H is –0.25.
a. Calculate the expected return over the 4-year period for each of the three alternatives.
b. Calculate the standard deviation of returns over the 4-year period for each of the three alternatives.
c. Use your findings in **a** and **b** to calculate the coefficient of variation for each of the three alternatives.
d. On the basis of your findings, which of the three investment alternatives do you recommend? Why?

  CHALLENGE 7–24 **Calculating portfolio returns and risk** Reconsider the Liam Wagner example on page 374 of the chapter. Using the data from this example, do the following:
a. Calculate the arithmetic and geometric mean returns for both companies. Explain why the arithmetic and geometric means are different for company Y.
b. Calculate the standard deviation of returns for both companies. Interpret the answer.
c. Calculate the coefficient of variation for both companies. Which company has the highest risk? Does your answer agree with the conclusion reached in the example?
d. Assuming Liam invested 60 percent of his funds in company X and 40 percent in Y, calculate the return on the portfolio.

e. Using the data from your answer to **d**, calculate the standard deviation of the portfolio's return, assuming that:
  i) The correlation coefficient between the returns on the two companies is +1.
  ii) The correlation coefficient between the returns on the two companies is +0.50.
  iii) The correlation coefficient between the returns on the two companies is 0.
  iv) The correlation coefficient between the returns on the two companies is −0.40.

What can you learn from this analysis?

INTERMEDIATE  7–25 **Correlation, risk, and return** Matt Peters wishes to evaluate the risk and return behaviours associated with various combinations of assets V and W under three assumed degrees of correlation—perfect positive, uncorrelated, and perfect negative. The expected return and risk values calculated for each of the assets are shown in the following table:

Asset	Expected return, $\hat{k}$	Risk (standard deviation), σ
V	8%	5%
W	13	10

a. If the returns of assets V and W are *perfectly positively correlated* (correlation coefficient = +1), describe the *range* of (1) expected return and (2) risk associated with all possible portfolio combinations.

b. If the returns of assets V and W are *uncorrelated* (correlation coefficient = 0), describe the *approximate range* of (1) expected return and (2) risk associated with all possible portfolio combinations.

c. If the returns of assets V and W are *perfectly negatively correlated* (correlation coefficient = −1), describe the *range* of (1) expected return and (2) risk associated with all possible portfolio combinations.

d. Now assume that Matt invests 70 percent of his funds in asset V and 30 percent in asset W. Calculate the standard deviation of the portfolio's return, assuming that:
  i) The correlation coefficient between the returns on the two companies is +0.46.
  ii) The correlation coefficient between the returns on the two companies is 0.
  iii) The correlation coefficient between the returns on the two companies is −0.72.

  CHALLENGE 7–26 **Calculating portfolio returns and risk** Reconsider the investment F and G example on page 382 of the chapter. Using the data from this example, do the following:

a. Assuming that the company invests 50 percent of its funds in investment F and 50 percent in investment G, calculate the return on the portfolio.

b. Given your answer to **a**, calculate the standard deviation of the portfolio's return, assuming that:
  i) The correlation coefficient between the returns on the two companies is +0.75.

ii) The correlation coefficient between the returns on the two companies is +0.10.
iii) The correlation coefficient between the returns on the two companies is –0.35.
iv) The correlation coefficient between the returns on the two companies is –0.90.

What can you learn from this analysis?

  INTERMEDIATE

7–27 International investment returns Joe Martinez, a Canadian citizen living in Toronto, invested in the common stock of Telmex, a Mexican corporation. He purchased 1,000 shares at 20.50 pesos per share. Twelve months later, he sold them at 24.75 pesos per share. He received no dividends during that time.

a. What was Joe's investment return (in total pesos and percentage terms) for the year, based on the peso value of the shares?
b. The exchange rate for pesos was 9.21 pesos per C$1 at the time of the purchase. At the time of the sale, the exchange rate was 9.85 pesos per C$1. Translate the purchase and sale prices into Canadian dollars.
c. Calculate Joe's investment return based on the Canadian dollar value of the shares.
d. Explain why the two returns are different. Which one is more important to Joe? Why?

INTERMEDIATE 

7–28 Total, nondiversifiable, and diversifiable risk David Talbot randomly selected securities from all those listed on the Toronto Stock Exchange for his portfolio. He began with one security and added securities one by one until a total of 20 securities were held in the portfolio. After each security was added, David calculated the portfolio standard deviation, σ_p. The calculated values are shown in the following table:

Number of securities	Portfolio risk, σ_p	Number of securities	Portfolio risk, σ_p
1	14.50%	11	7.00%
2	13.30	12	6.80
3	12.20	13	6.70
4	11.20	14	6.65
5	10.30	15	6.60
6	9.50	16	6.56
7	8.80	17	6.52
8	8.20	18	6.50
9	7.70	19	6.48
10	7.30	20	6.47

a. On a graph, where the number of securities in the portfolio is the x axis and the portfolio risk is the y axis, plot what happens to portfolio risk as the number of securities increases.
b. Divide the total portfolio risk in the graph into its *nondiversifiable* and *diversifiable* risk components and label each of these on the graph.

c. Describe which of the two risk components is the *relevant risk,* and explain why it is relevant. How much of this risk exists in David Talbot's portfolio?

INTERMEDIATE  **7–29 Graphic derivation of beta** A firm wishes to graphically estimate the betas for two assets—A and B. It has gathered the following return data for the market portfolio and both assets over ten years:

	Actual return		
Year	Market portfolio	Asset A	Asset B
1	6%	11%	16%
2	2	8	11
3	−13	−4	−10
4	−4	3	3
5	−8	0	−3
6	16	19	30
7	10	14	22
8	15	18	29
9	8	12	19
10	13	17	26

a. On a graph, where the x axis is market return and the y axis is asset return, plot the data points and draw the characteristic lines for assets A and B. Use two graphs.

b. Use the characteristic lines from **a** to estimate the betas for assets A and B.

c. Use the betas found in **b** to comment on the relative risks of assets A and B.

INTERMEDIATE  **7–30 Market returns** A firm wishes to assess the impact of changes in the market return on an asset that has a beta of 1.20. Assume the risk-free rate is 3 percent and the market risk premium is estimated to be 8 percent.

a. What is the estimated market return and required rate of return on the asset?

b. If the market return was expected to increase by 2.6 percent, what impact would this change be expected to have on the asset's required return?

c. If the market return was expected to decrease by 1.2 percent, what impact would this change be expected to have on the asset's required return?

d. Would this asset be considered more or less risky than the market? Explain.

INTERMEDIATE  **7–31 Required returns** Answer the following questions for assets A to D shown in the table. Assume the risk-free rate is 4 percent and the market risk premium is estimated to be 6 percent.

Asset	Beta
A	0.50
B	1.60
C	−0.20
D	0.90

a. What impact would a *10 percent increase* in the market return be expected to have on each asset's required return?
b. What impact would a *4 percent decrease* in the market return be expected to have on each asset's required return?
c. If you were certain that the market return would *increase* in the near future, which asset would you prefer? Why?
d. If you were certain that the market return would *decrease* in the near future, which asset would you prefer? Why?

INTERMEDIATE  7–32 **Required returns** Stock A has a beta of 0.80, stock B has a beta of 1.40, and stock C has a beta of −0.30. Assume the risk-free rate is 6 percent and the market return is estimated to be 14 percent.

a. Rank these stocks from the most risky to the least risky.
b. If the return on the market portfolio increases to 17 percent, what change would you expect in the required return for each of the stocks?
c. If the return on the market portfolio declines by 5 percent, what change would you expect in the required return for each of the stocks?
d. If you felt that the stock market was just ready to experience a significant decline, which stock would you likely add to your portfolio? Why?
e. If you anticipated a major stock market rally, which stock would you add to your portfolio? Why?

BASIC  7–33 **Portfolio betas** Sherry Berry is attempting to evaluate two possible portfolios—both consisting of the same five assets, but held in different proportions. She wishes to use beta to compare the risk of the portfolios and she has gathered the data shown in the following table.

		Portfolio weights	
Asset	Asset beta	Portfolio A	Portfolio B
1	1.30	10%	30%
2	0.70	30	10
3	1.25	10	20
4	1.10	10	20
5	0.90	40	20
Totals		100%	100%

a. Calculate the betas for portfolios A and B.
b. Compare the risk of each portfolio to the market as well as to each other.
c. Including the market portfolio, rank the three portfolios from lowest risk to highest risk.

BASIC  7–34 **Capital asset pricing model (CAPM)** For each of the cases shown in the following table, use the capital asset pricing model to find the required return.

Case	Risk-free rate, R_F	Market return, k_m	Beta, β
A	5%	8%	1.30
B	8	13	0.90
C	9	12	−0.20
D	10	15	1.00
E	6	10	0.60

INTERMEDIATE

7–35 **Beta coefficients** Katherine Wilson is wondering how much risk she must accept in order to generate a reasonable return on her portfolio. The risk-free return currently is 5 percent. The return on the market portfolio is 16 percent. Use the CAPM to calculate the beta coefficient associated with each of the following portfolio returns.

a. 10 percent
b. 15 percent
c. 18 percent
d. 20 percent
e. Draw a security market line (SML) based on the above data. Katherine is risk-averse. What is the highest return she can expect if she is unwilling to take more than an average risk?

INTERMEDIATE 

7–36 **Manipulating CAPM** Use the basic equation for the capital asset pricing model (CAPM) to work each of the following:

a. Find the *required return* for an asset with a beta of 0.90 when the risk-free rate and market return are 8 and 12 percent, respectively.
b. Find the *risk-free rate* for a firm with a required return of 15 percent and a beta of 1.25 when the market risk premium is 7 percent. What is the market return?
c. Find the *market return* for an asset with a required return of 16 percent and a beta of 1.10 when the risk-free rate is 9 percent.
d. Find the *beta* for an asset with a required return of 15 percent when the risk-free rate is 5 percent and the market risk premium is 6.25 percent.

LG6 CHALLENGE

7–37 **Portfolio return and beta** Jamie Peters invested $100,000 to set up the following portfolio one year ago:

Common share	Amount Invested	Beta at purchase	Yearly income	Value today
A	$20,000	0.80	$1,600	$20,000
B	35,000	0.95	1,400	36,000
C	30,000	1.50	—	34,500
D	15,000	1.25	375	16,500

a. Calculate the portfolio beta based on the original amounts invested.
b. Calculate the percentage return for each common share in the portfolio for the year.

c. Calculate the percentage return earned on the portfolio for the year.
d. At the time Jamie made his investments, investors were estimating that the market return for the coming year would be 10 percent. The estimate of the risk-free rate of return averaged 4 percent for the coming year. Calculate the required return for each stock based on its beta and the expectations of market and risk-free returns.
e. Based on your answers in parts **c** and **d**, explain how each stock in the portfolio performed relative to its required return. What factors could explain these differences?
f. Now calculate the arithmetic and geometric mean returns for the portfolio for the year, assuming equal amounts were invested in each of the shares.

INTERMEDIATE  **7–38 Security market line, SML** Assume that the risk-free rate, R_F, is currently 9 percent and that the market return, k_m, is currently 13 percent.
a. Draw and label the security market line (SML).
b. Calculate and label the *market risk premium* on the axes in **a.**
c. Given the previous data, calculate the required return on asset A having a beta of 0.80 and asset B having a beta of 1.30.
d. Draw in the betas and required returns from **c** for assets A and B on the axes in **a.** Label the *risk premiums* associated with each of these assets, and discuss them.

INTERMEDIATE  **7–39 Shifts in the security market line** Assume that the risk-free rate, R_F, is currently 8 percent, the market risk premium is 6.6 percent, and asset A has a beta, β_A, of 1.10.
a. Draw and label the security market line (SML).
b. Use the CAPM to calculate the required return, k_A, on asset A, and depict asset A's beta and required return on the SML drawn in **a.**
c. Assume that as a result of recent economic events, inflationary expectations have declined by 2 percent, lowering both the risk-free rate and market return by 2 percent. Draw the new SML on the axes in **a,** and calculate and show the new required return for asset A.
d. Assume that as a result of recent events, investors have become more risk averse, causing the market return to rise by 1 percent. Ignoring the shift in part **c,** draw the new SML on the same set of axes as used before, and calculate and show the new required return for asset A.
e. From the previous changes, what conclusions can be drawn about the impact of (1) decreased inflationary expectations and (2) increased risk aversion on the required returns of risky assets?

  INTERMEDIATE **7–40 Integrative—Risk, return, and CAPM** Wolff Enterprises must consider several investment projects, A through E, using the capital asset pricing model. Relevant information is presented in the following table.

Item	Rate of return	Beta, β
Risk-free asset	9%	0
Market portfolio	14	1.00
Project A	—	1.50
Project B	—	0.75
Project C	—	2.00
Project D	—	0
Project E	—	−0.50

a. Calculate the required return and risk premium for each project, given its level of nondiversifiable risk.
b. Use your findings in **a** to draw the security market line.
c. Discuss the relative systematic (nondiversifiable) risk of projects A through E. Rank the projects in terms of risk.
d. Assume that recent economic events have caused investors to become less risk averse, causing the market return to decline by 2 percent. Calculate the new required returns for assets A through E, and draw the new security market line on the same set of axes as used in **b.**
e. Compare your findings in **a** and **b** with those in **d.** What conclusion can you draw about the impact of a decline in investor risk aversion on the required returns of risky assets?

CASE CHAPTER 7 Analyzing Risk and Return on Wings Products' Investments

See the enclosed Student CD-ROM for cases that help you put theories and concepts from the text into practice.

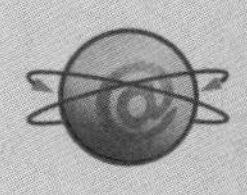

Be sure to visit the Companion Website for this book at **www.pearsoned.ca/gitman** for a wealth of additional learning tools including self-test quizzes, Web exercises, and additional cases.

CHAPTER 8

Valuation of Financial Securities

LEARNING GOALS

LG1 Describe interest rate fundamentals and the factors that affect required rates of return.

LG2 Describe the key inputs and basic model used in the valuation process.

LG3 Apply the basic valuation model to long-term debt to determine value and yield to maturity (YTM) and describe the impact that changes in required rates of return and time to maturity have on bond values.

LG4 Understand the concept of market efficiency and four techniques used to determine the value of common shares: (1) the dividend valuation model (DVM), (2) book value, (3) liquidation value, and (4) the price/earnings (P/E) multiple.

LG5 Understand the relationships among financial decisions, return, risk, and the firm's value.

LG6 Discuss valuation concepts and the techniques used to determine the value and required returns on preferred shares.

8.1 Interest Rates and Required Returns

Chapter 5 detailed the role that financial markets and institutions play in ensuring that cash is transferred from savers of funds to users of funds. The level of funds that flow between suppliers and demanders can significantly affect economic growth. Growth results from the interaction of a variety of economic factors (such as the money supply, the exchange rate of the dollar, trade balances,

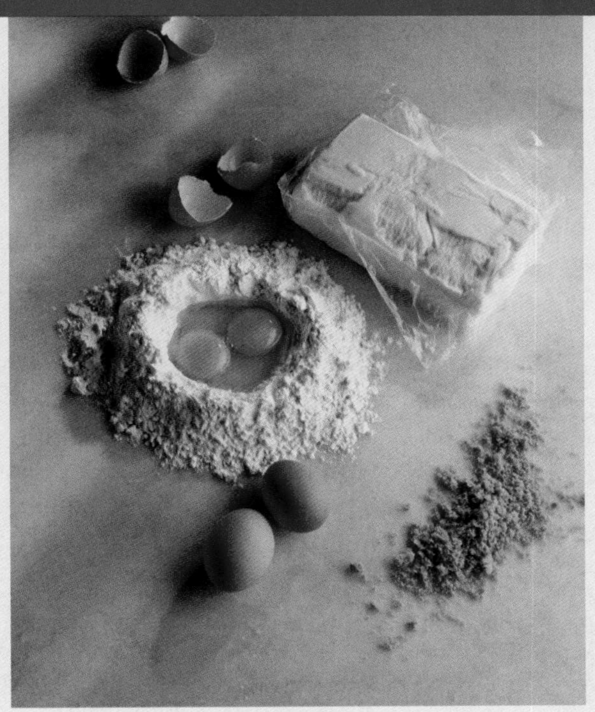

What's Baking?

With just three basic ingredients—flour, butter, and eggs—an experienced baker can create a variety of treats. The proportions used, plus the choice of other ingredients, give each creation its particular character. So, too, do three basic ingredients—returns, timing, and risk—determine the value of both real and financial assets. The choice of the other ingredients, and the market's taste for those other ingredients, determine the value of a firm's financial securities, the financial outcome of a firm's investments in real assets, and the value of a firm itself. Just as nutritionists have found ways to measure the nutritional value of food, so, too, have financial analysts devised ways, broadly called *valuation,* to measure the value of any asset. This chapter explains valuation and how the value of a firm's financial assets, such as long-term debt and common and preferred shares, is determined.

and economic policies) that affect the cost of money—the interest rate or required rate of return on the financing used by the business.

For the overall economy, the interest rate level acts as a regulating device that controls the flow of funds between suppliers and demanders. The Bank of Canada regularly assesses economic conditions and, when necessary, initiates actions to raise or lower interest rates to control inflation, the exchange rate, and economic growth. Generally, the lower the interest rate, the greater the flow of

LINKING THE DISCIPLINES: Cross-Functional Interactions

- ***Accounting personnel*** need to understand interest rates, how to properly value a firm's long-term debt and equity, and why book value per share is not an accurate basis for common stock valuation.
- ***Information systems analysts*** need to understand the sources and types of information that affect stock value and how such information can be used in stock valuation models to link proposed actions to share price.
- ***Management*** needs to understand the behaviour of interest rates and how they will affect the types of funds the firm can raise, and the timing and cost of bond issues and retirements. Management must be very conscious of the relationship between their dividend policy and the market price of the firm. Investors' expectations that a firm's dividend will be low or unpredictable will reduce the value of the firm's common shares.
- The ***marketing department*** can greatly influence the value of a firm. Through product development, promotion, and sales strategies, marketing personnel can influence investors' expectations of cash flows, risks, and consequently value.
- Personnel in the ***operations department*** need to understand that the amount of capital the firm has to invest in fixed assets and inventory will depend on the evaluations of the company by potential investors. They also need to understand how the interest rate level may affect the firm's ability to raise funds to maintain and grow the firm's production capacity.

funds and therefore the greater the economic growth; the higher the interest rate, the lower the flow of funds and economic growth.

Interest Rate Fundamentals

interest rate
The compensation paid by the borrower of funds to the lender; from the borrower's point of view, the cost of borrowing funds.

required return
The cost of funds obtained by selling equity; it is based on the return investors require given the risk of the investment.

The interest rate or required return represents the cost of money. It is the compensation that a demander of funds must pay a supplier. When funds are lent, the cost of borrowing the funds is the **interest rate.** When funds are obtained by selling equity—as in the sale of common or preferred shares—the cost to the issuer (demander) is commonly called the **required return.** This is the return investors require based on the risk of the equity position. As we learned in Chapter 7, the greater the risk of the investment, the higher the required return. For all investments, the provider of the funds must be compensated for taking risk. The required rate of return is based on the *real rate of interest*, adjusted for inflationary expectations, and risk.

The Real Rate of Interest

Assume a *perfect world* in which there is no inflation and in which funds suppliers and demanders are indifferent to the term of loans or investments because there is no risk and all outcomes are certain.[1] At any given point in time in that

1. These assumptions are made to describe the most basic interest rate, the *real rate of interest*. Subsequent discussions relax these assumptions to develop the broader concept of the interest rate and required return.

FIGURE 8.1

Supply–Demand Relationship

Supply of savings and demand for investment funds

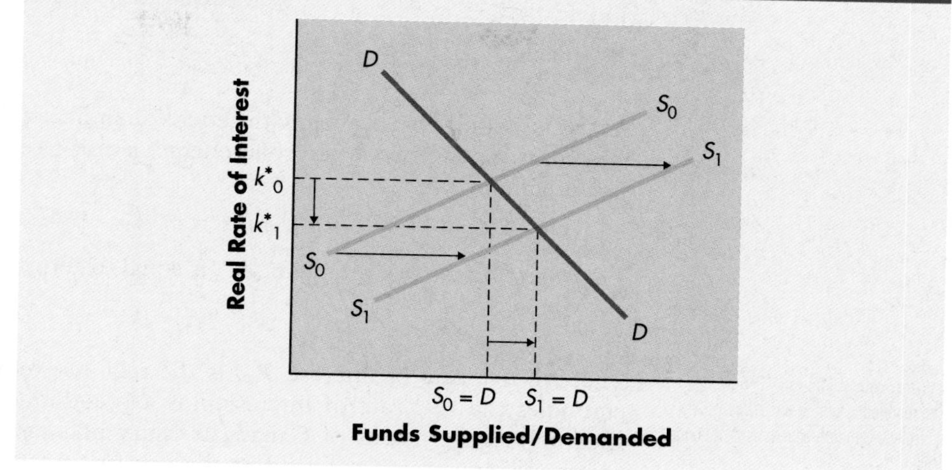

real rate of interest
The rate that creates an equilibrium between the supply of savings and the demand for investment funds in a perfect world, without inflation, where funds suppliers and demanders have no liquidity preference and all outcomes are certain.

perfect world, there would be one cost of money—the **real rate of interest.** The real rate of interest creates an equilibrium between the supply of savings and the demand for investment funds. It represents the most basic cost of money. This supply–demand relationship is shown in Figure 8.1 by the supply function (labelled S_0) and the demand function (labelled D). An equilibrium between the supply of funds and the demand for funds ($S_0 = D$) occurs at a rate of interest k_0^*, the real rate of interest.

Clearly, the real rate of interest changes with changing economic conditions, tastes, and preferences. Actions taken by the Bank of Canada could result in an increased supply of funds, causing the supply function in Figure 8.1 to shift to, say, S_1. This could result in a lower real rate of interest, k_1^*, at equilibrium ($S_1 = D$). Likewise, a change in tax laws or other factors could affect the demand for funds, causing the real rate of interest to rise or fall to a new equilibrium level. In Canada, the real rate of interest is expected to average around 2 percent over a complete economic cycle.

Nominal or Actual Rate of Interest (Return)

nominal rate of interest
The actual rate of interest charged by the supplier of funds and paid by the demander.

The **nominal rate of interest** is the actual rate of interest charged by the supplier of funds and paid by the demander. *Throughout this book, interest rates and required rates of return are nominal rates unless otherwise noted.* The nominal rate of interest differs from the real rate of interest, k^*, as a result of two factors: (1) inflationary expectations reflected in an inflation premium (IP), and (2) issuer and issue characteristics, reflected in a risk premium (RP). The risk premium could be based on differing levels of default risk, on contractual provisions of the financial security, or on the type of financial security. Since the risk profile of long-term debt, preferred shares, and common shares is very different, so too will be the required rates of return. By using this notation, the nominal rate of interest for security j, k_j, is given in Equation 8.1:

$$k_j = \underbrace{k^* + IP}_{\substack{\text{risk-free} \\ \text{rate, } R_F}} + \underbrace{RP}_{\substack{\text{risk} \\ \text{premium}}} \quad (8.1)$$

As the horizontal braces below the equation indicate, the nominal rate, k_j, can be viewed as having two basic components: a risk-free rate of interest, R_F, and a risk premium, RP:

$$k_j = R_F + RP \quad (8.2)$$

Assuming the risk premium, RP, is equal to zero, the risk-free rate equals:

$$R_F = k^* + IP \quad (8.3)^2$$

risk-free rate of interest, R_F
The required return on a risk-free asset, typically a 3-month government of Canada t-bill.

The **risk-free rate of interest, R_F,** is the required return on a risk-free asset. It embodies the real rate of interest plus a premium for inflation. The yield on short-term government of Canada treasury bills, as discussed in Chapter 5, is commonly considered the yield on the risk-free asset. The usual maturity used is 98-day or 3-month t-bills. *The real rate of interest can be estimated by subtracting the inflation premium from the nominal rate of interest.* For the risk-free asset in Equation 8.3, the real rate of interest, k^*, would equal $R_F - IP$. A simple example can demonstrate the practical distinction between nominal and real rates of interest.

Example Marilyn Carbo has $10 that she can spend on candy costing $0.25 per piece. She could therefore buy 40 pieces of candy ($10/$0.25) today. The nominal rate of interest on a 1-year deposit is currently 7 percent and the expected rate of inflation over the coming year is 4 percent. Instead of buying the 40 pieces of candy today, Marilyn can invest the $10 in a 1-year deposit account now. At the end of 1 year she would have $10.70 because she would have earned 7 percent interest—an additional $0.70 (0.07 × $10)—on her $10 deposit. The 4 percent inflation rate would over the 1-year period increase the cost of the candy by 4 percent—an additional $0.01 (0.04 × $0.25)—to $0.26 per piece. As a result, at the end of the 1-year period Marilyn would be able to buy about 41.2 pieces of candy ($10.70/$0.26), or roughly 3 percent more (41.2/40.0 = 1.03). The increase in the amount of money available to Marilyn at the end of 1 year is merely her nominal rate of return (7%), which must be reduced by the rate of inflation (4%) during the period to determine her real rate of return of 3 percent. Marilyn's increased buying power therefore equals her 3 percent real rate of return.

The premium for *inflationary expectations* in Equation 8.3 represents the average rate of *inflation* expected over the life of a loan or investment. It is *not* the rate of inflation experienced over the immediate past; rather, it reflects the forecasted rate. Take, for example, the risk-free asset. In November 2006, 3-month t-bills provided a 4.18 percent rate of return. Assuming an approximate 2 percent real rate of interest, funds suppliers were forecasting a 2.18 percent (annual) rate of inflation (4.18% – 2.00%) over the next 3 months. This was dramatically different from the expected rate of inflation 25 years earlier in 1981. At that time the 3-month t-bill rate averaged 19.1 percent, which meant an expected (annual)

2. This equation is commonly called the *Fisher equation*, named for the renowned economist Irving Fisher, who first presented this approximate relationship between nominal interest and the rate of inflation. See Irving Fisher, *The Theory of Interest* (New York: Macmillan, 1930).

inflation rate of 17.1 percent (19.1% − 2.00%). The inflationary expectation premium changes over time in response to many factors, including economic activity in the United States and other parts of the world, commodity prices, wages settlements, government policies, and international events.

Figure 8.2 illustrates the movement of the rate of inflation and the risk-free rate of interest during the 57 years from 1950 to 2006. During this period the two rates clearly moved in a similar fashion. With the exception of the temporary blip in 1951 and most of the 1970s, inflation was 4 percent or less for most of the period. T-bill returns were generally higher than inflation. Beginning in 1972, inflation started to increase, and for six of the next seven years exceeded the average yield on t-bills. From 1973 to 1982, the rate of inflation in Canada exceeded 7.5 percent, peaking at 12.4 percent in 1981. Beginning in 1983, inflation declined, and by 1992 returned to the level recorded in much of the 1950s and 1960s. T-bill returns followed the trend set by inflation. Over the complete 57-year period, inflation averaged about 4 percent and t-bill returns 5.9 percent, implying a real rate of interest of about 2 percent, as discussed earlier, over this very long economic cycle. The data clearly illustrates the significant impact inflation has on the nominal level of interest rates prevalent in the economy.

Term Structure of Interest Rates

In Chapter 5 we discussed how default risk is measured for long-term debt securities. We saw that rating agencies evaluate the potential for the issuer to default on the payment of interest and principal. The rating assigned to a particular issuer can vary from a high of AAA to a low of D (in default). There are 24

FIGURE 8.2

Impact of Inflation

Relationship between annual rate of inflation and 3-month government of Canada t-bill average annual returns, 1950–2006

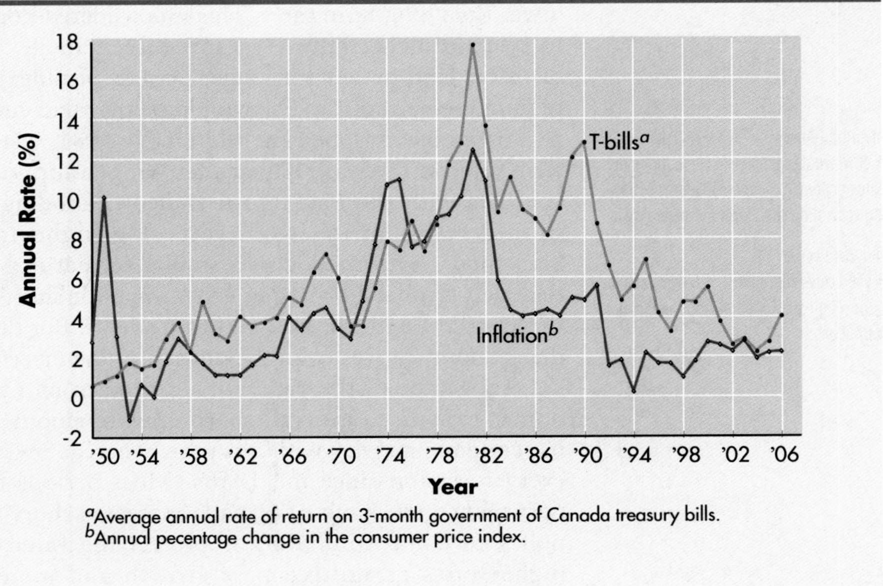

SOURCE: Statistics Canada, Consumer Price Index, Table 326-0002, Series v737344, and Average Yield on Auction of 3-Month Treasury Bills, Table 176-0043, Series v122541 [B14007].

possible ratings in between. The most secure issuer of debt securities in all developed economies is the federal government. In Canada, the federal government is rated AAA, and it will provide the lowest yield on any maturity of debt.

term structure of interest rates (TSIR)
The relationship between the yield (rate of return) and the time to maturity for debt securities with similar default risk.

For any class of debt securities with similar default risk, the **term structure of interest rates (TSIR)** relates the yield (or rate of return) to the time to maturity. Many participants in the debt market, both issuers and investors, find it useful to see how the rate of return provided on debt securities changes for different times to maturity. When constructing a TSIR, the norm is to use federal government securities, since they have very little default risk. As such, they are the ideal issuer of debt securities to use to develop the term structure prevailing in a country at a point in time.

Yield Curves

yield to maturity
Annual rate of interest earned on a security purchased on a given day and held to maturity.

yield curve
A graph of the *term structure of interest rates* that depicts the relationship between the *yield to maturity* of a security (*y* axis) and the time to maturity (*x* axis); it shows the pattern of interest rates on securities of equal quality and different maturity.

normal (upward-sloping) yield curve
An upward-sloping yield curve that indicates generally cheaper short-term borrowing costs than long-term borrowing costs.

The annual rate of interest earned on a security purchased on a given day and held to maturity is its **yield to maturity.** At any point in time, the relationship between yield to maturity and the remaining time to maturity can be represented by a graph called the **yield curve.** This is a graphic depiction of the term structure of interest rates. The yield curve shows the relationship between the yields on debt securities of similar risk (as measured by a bond rating), but different maturities. It is usual to use about ten maturities ranging from 1 month to 30 years.

At any point in time in a country, three possible yield curves might exist. The TSIR most commonly observed is the **normal** or **upward-sloping yield curve.** However, a flat or inverted (downward-sloping) yield curve might also be observed. Figure 8.3 shows three yield curves that existed in Canada at three different points in time: March 25, 1981; March 6, 1991; and May 15, 2002. Note that both the position and the shape of the yield curves change significantly over time.

inverted (downward-sloping) yield curve
A downward-sloping yield curve that indicates generally cheaper long-term borrowing costs than short-term borrowing costs.

flat yield curve
A yield curve that reflects relatively similar borrowing costs for both short- and longer-term loans.

The May 15, 2002, curve is the norm. Here, short-term interest rates are lower than long-term rates. This is considered normal, since investors would have to be paid higher returns to invest their money for longer time periods. When investors lend money for longer periods of time, they take on more risk and thus require higher returns. This would be the yield curve one would expect to observe at most points in time. The March 25, 1981, yield curve is **inverted.** Here, short-term interest rates are higher than long-term rates. This is very unusual, since it conflicts with the risk–return tradeoff. Lending funds for longer time periods should result in investors receiving higher returns; here we have lower. Sometimes, a **flat yield curve**, similar to that of March 6, 1991, exists. It reflects relatively similar borrowing costs for both short- and longer-term loans. Again, this conflicts with the risk–return tradeoff. But the flat curve is often observed as the economy moves from the normal to the inverted curve, or vice versa.

The shape of the yield curve has been an excellent predictor of future economic growth. In general, sharp upward-sloping curves signal a substantial rise in economic activity within a year, whereas inverted yield curves have preceded every recession since the 1950s. Most periods of flat or inverted yield curves occur when the Bank of Canada increases short-term rates, tightening monetary policy to control inflation or protect the value of the Canadian dollar. These higher rates curtail business growth and increase international demand for Canadian dollars.

FIGURE 8.3

Treasury Yield Curves
Yield curves for government of Canada securities: March 25, 1981; March 6, 1991; and May 15, 2002

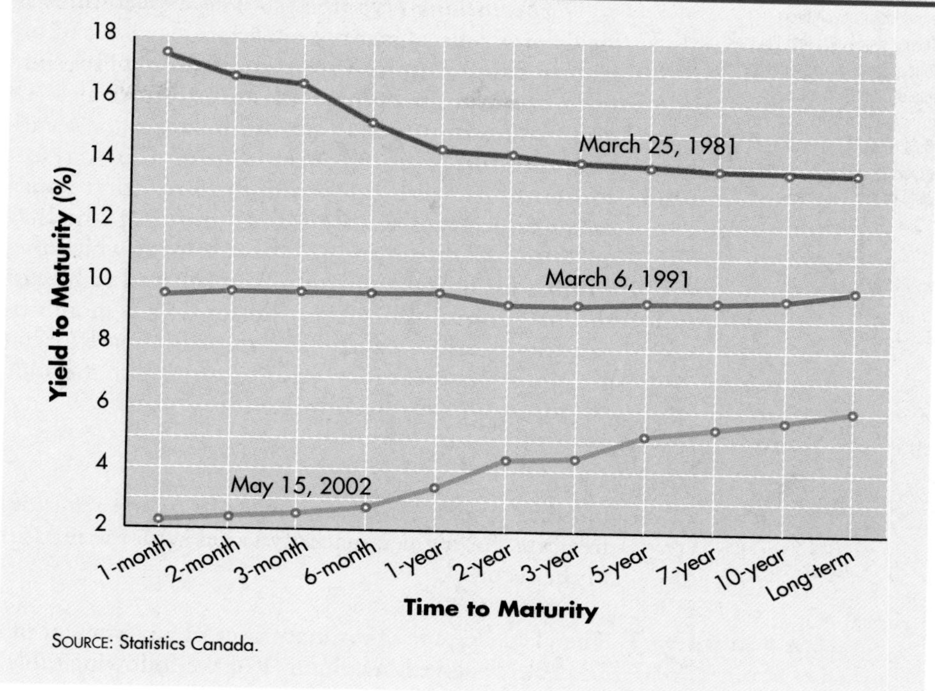

SOURCE: Statistics Canada.

Some inverted yield curves, however, result from falling long-term interest rates in the global economy. Deflationary fears can push investors toward high-quality, long-term bonds both in Canada and abroad. This increased demand for longer-term debt securities will increase their price, resulting in falling yields. Decreasing demand for short-term debt securities will result in falling prices and increasing yields. This combination will lead to a flat yield curve, and may result in an inverted yield curve.

www.globeinvestor.com
http://bankofcanada.ca/en/rates/index.html
www.bloomberg.com/markets/rates/index.html

The shape of the yield curve also affects the firm's financing decisions. A financial manager who faces a downward-sloping yield curve is likely to rely more heavily on cheaper, long-term financing; when the yield curve is upward-sloping, the manager is more likely to use cheaper, short-term financing. Although a variety of other factors also influence the choice of loan maturity, the shape of the yield curve provides useful insights into future interest-rate expectations. There are a number of Web sites that provide the current term structure of interest rates in Canada.

Theories of Term Structure

The dominance of the upward-sloping yield curve can be simply explained: Short-term securities are less risky than long-term securities because near-term events are more certain than future events, and therefore they have lower returns. However, this explanation fails to explain why yield curves often take on different shapes, such as those shown in Figure 8.3. Three theories are frequently cited to better explain the general shape of the yield curve: the expectations hypothesis, liquidity preference theory, and market segmentation theory.

expectations hypothesis
Theory suggesting that the yield curve reflects investor expectations about future interest rates; an increasing inflation expectation results in an upward-sloping yield curve and a decreasing inflation expectation results in a downward-sloping yield curve.

Expectations Hypothesis The **expectations hypothesis** suggests that the yield curve reflects investor expectations about future interest rates and inflation. Higher future rates of expected inflation will result in higher long-term interest rates; the opposite occurs with lower future rates. This widely accepted explanation of the term structure can be applied to the securities of any issuer. For example, take the case of government of Canada securities. Thus far, we have concerned ourselves solely with the 3-month treasury bill. In fact, all federal government securities are *riskless* in terms of (1) the chance that the government will default on the issue and (2) the ease with which they can be liquidated for cash without losing value. Because it is believed to be easier to forecast inflation over shorter periods of time, the shorter-term 3-month treasury bill is considered the risk-free asset. Of course, differing inflation expectations associated with different maturities will cause yields to vary. With the addition of a maturity subscript, t, Equation 8.3 can be rewritten as:

$$R_{F_t} = k^* + IP_t \tag{8.4}$$

In other words, for government of Canada securities the nominal yield, or risk-free rate, for a given maturity varies with the inflation expectation over the term of the security.[3]

Example The yield (R_{F_t}) for four maturities of government of Canada securities on March 23, 2007, is given in column 1 of the following table. Assuming that the real rate of interest is 2 percent, as noted in column 2, the inflation expectation for each maturity in column 3 is found by solving Equation 8.4 for IP_t. Although a 0.91 percent rate of inflation was expected over the 3-month period, beginning March 24, 2007, a 1.20 percent average rate of inflation was expected over the 1-year period, and so on. An analysis of the inflation expectations in column 3 for March 23, 2007 suggests that at that time a general expectation of slightly increasing inflation existed. Simply stated, the March 23, 2007 yield curve for government of Canada securities was upward-sloping as a result of the expectation that the rate of inflation would increase slightly in the future.

Maturity, t	Yield (R_{F_t}) (1)	Real interest rate, k^* (2)	Inflation expectation, IP_t [(1) − (2)] (3)
3 months	2.91%	2.00%	0.91%
1 year	3.20	2.00	1.20
5 years	4.52	2.00	2.52
30 years	5.56	2.00	3.56

3. Although government of Canada securities have no risk of default or illiquidity, they do suffer from maturity, or interest rate, risk—the risk that interest rates will change in the future and thereby affect longer maturities more than shorter maturities. Therefore the longer the maturity of a federal government (or any other) security, the greater its interest rate risk. The impact of interest-rate changes on bond values is discussed later in the chapter.

Generally, under the expectations hypothesis, an increasing inflation expectation results in an upward-sloping yield curve; a decreasing inflation expectation results in a downward-sloping yield curve; and a stable inflation expectation results in a flat yield curve. Although, as we'll see, other theories exist, the observed strong relationship between inflation and interest rates (see Figure 8.2) supports this widely accepted theory.

liquidity preference theory
Theory suggesting that for any given issuer, long-term yields tend to be higher than short-term yields due to the lower liquidity and higher responsiveness to general interest rate movements of longer-term securities; causes the yield curve to be upward-sloping.

Liquidity Preference Theory The tendency for yield curves to be upward-sloping can be further explained by **liquidity preference theory**. This theory indicates that for a given issuer, yields on long-term securities tend to be higher than yields on short-term securities. This belief is based on two behavioural facts:

1. Investors perceive less risk in short-term securities than in longer-term securities and are therefore willing to accept lower yields on them. Debt securities with longer maturities are more sensitive to changing required returns (yields) in the market. For a given change of yields in the market, the price (value) of long-term debt securities will be more significantly changed (both up and down) than those with shorter maturities. This issue is discussed in more detail in Section 8.3.
2. Borrowers are generally willing to pay a higher rate for long-term than for short-term financing. By locking in funds for a longer period of time, they can eliminate the potential adverse consequences of having to roll over short-term debt at unknown costs to obtain long-term financing.

Investors (lenders) tend to require a premium for tying up funds for longer periods, whereas borrowers are generally willing to pay a premium to obtain longer-term financing. These preferences of lenders and borrowers cause the yield curve to tend to be upward-sloping. Simply stated, longer maturities tend to have higher yields than shorter maturities.

market segmentation theory
Theory suggesting that the market for loans is segmented on the basis of maturity and that the supply of and demand for loans within each segment determine prevailing yields; the slope of the yield curve is determined by the general relationship between the prevailing rates in each segment.

Market Segmentation Theory The **market segmentation theory** suggests that the market for loans is segmented on the basis of maturity and that the supply of and demand for loans within each segment determine prevailing yields. In other words, the equilibrium between suppliers and demanders of short-term funds, such as seasonal business loans, would determine prevailing short-term interest rates, and the equilibrium between suppliers and demanders of long-term funds, such as bonds, would determine prevailing long-term interest rates. The slope of the yield curve would be determined by the general relationship between the prevailing rates in each market segment.

Hint
An upward-sloping yield curve would result if the supply outstrips the demand for short-term loans, thereby resulting in relatively low short-term rates at a time when long-term rates are high because the demand for long-term loans is far above their supply.

Simply stated, if the demand from borrowers for longer-term loans is higher than for shorter-term loans, the cost of the longer-term loans, the interest rate charged, will be higher. This will result in an upward-sloping yield curve. If the demand from investors for longer-term securities were higher than the supply, then prices will rise causing yields to fall. If the demand from investors for shorter-term securities were lower than the supply, then prices will fall causing yields to rise. The combination will result in a flat, and possibly an inverted yield curve.

All three theories of term structure have merit. From them we can conclude that at any time the slope of the yield curve is affected by (1) inflationary expectations, (2) liquidity preferences, and (3) the comparative equilibrium of supply and demand for short- and long-term securities. Upward-sloping yield curves result from higher future inflation expectations, lender preferences for shorter-maturity loans, and greater supply, relative to demand, of short-term versus long-term funds from providers. The opposite behaviours would result in a downward-sloping yield curve. At any point in time, the interaction of these three forces will determine the prevailing slope of the yield curve.

Risk Premiums: Issuer and Issue Characteristics

So far we have considered only default-risk-free government of Canada securities. We now reintroduce the risk premium and assess it in view of risky non-federal government issues. Recall Equation 8.1, restated here:

$$k_j = \underbrace{k^* + IP}_{\substack{\text{risk-free} \\ \text{rate, } R_F}} + \underbrace{RP}_{\substack{\text{risk} \\ \text{premium}}}$$

In words, the required return for security j (k_j) is equal to the risk-free rate, consisting of the real rate of interest (k^*) plus the inflation expectation premium (IP), plus the risk premium (RP). The *risk premium* varies with specific issuer and issue characteristics; it causes similar-maturity securities[4] to have differing nominal rates of interest.

Example Assume that on March 23, 2007, the yields on six classes of long-term debt securities with 10 years to maturity were as shown in column 3:

Issuer	DBRS rating	Yield	Risk premium
Government of Canada	AAA	5.16%	0
Province of New Brunswick	A	5.55	5.55% – 5.16% = 0.39%
Corporate bonds	AAA	6.06	6.06% – 5.16% = 0.90%
Corporate bonds	AA	6.31	6.31% – 5.16% = 1.15%
Corporate bonds	A	6.56	6.56% – 5.16% = 1.40%
Corporate bonds	BBB	8.88	8.88% – 5.16% = 3.72%

Since the time to maturity of all five securities is the same, there is no difference in maturity risk. Different yields must be due to different default risk. Since the government of Canada is the least risky issuer of debt securities in the country, the yield on this security is lowest for any ten-year debt security. This yield is termed the **floor rate.** We can calculate the risk premium of the other securities by subtracting the floor rate, 5.16 percent, from the other yields. The results are provided in the final column.

floor rate
The yield on the debt securities, of any maturity, for the least risky issuer in the country—the government of Canada.

These risk premiums reflect differing levels of default risk. There is essentially no default risk on government of Canada debt securities. For the Province of

4. To provide for the same risk-free rate of return, $k^* + IP$, it is necessary to assume equal maturities. By doing this the inflationary expectations premium, IP, and therefore R_F, will be held constant, and the issuer and issue characteristics premium, RP, becomes the key factor differentiating the yields on various securities.

New Brunswick, more default risk is present, but the risk premium is a relatively modest 39 basis points, or 0.39 percent. Corporate bonds carry more default risk than any government security and this is reflected in the risk premium. The risk premium for AAA corporates is 90 basis points, almost 1 percent, and the premium gradually increases for the AA and A rated corporate bonds. The risk premium explodes to 3.72 percent for the BBB rated bonds. In March 2007, the bond market was very wary of higher-risk bonds and demanded a large premium for assuming the greater risk.

For this example, an alternative method of examining the risk premium is to recognize that the yield on the ten-year government of Canada debt security really consists of two components. Since this security has ten years to maturity, there is maturity risk present. If we knew that on March 23, 2007, the 3-month treasury bill rate was 2.91 percent, then the yields in the above table can be shown to consist of three components: the risk-free rate, a maturity (or time) risk premium, and a default risk premium. This analysis is provided below.

Issuer	Risk-free rate	+	Maturity risk premium	+	Default risk premium	=	Yield
Government of Canada	2.91%	+	2.25%	+	0	=	5.16%
Province of New Brunswick	2.91%	+	2.25%	+	0.39	=	5.55%
Corporate bonds	2.91%	+	2.25%	+	0.90%	=	6.06%
Corporate bonds	2.91%	+	2.25%	+	1.15%	=	6.31%
Corporate bonds	2.91%	+	2.25%	+	1.40%	=	6.56%
Corporate bonds	2.91%	+	2.25%	+	3.72%	=	8.88%

The maturity risk premium of 2.25 percent is based on the difference between the risk-free rate (3-month treasury bill rate) and the yield on the ten-year government of Canada bond (5.16% – 2.91%). This is because there is essentially no default risk on federal government bonds, so the yield is based on the first two components. The risk-free rate and the maturity risk premium are the same for all five securities, since we are dealing with ten-year debt securities. The default risk premium was based on the previous table. This leads to an important result for debt securities. The required return is based on:

$$k_j = R_F + \text{MRP} + \text{DRP} \tag{8.5}$$

The maturity risk premium (MRP) is based on the time to maturity and should be consistent across all debt securities with the same time to maturity. It will also include tax risk. The default risk premium (DRP) consists of all issuer- and issue-related components including the bond rating, liquidity risk, and any contractual provisions in the trust deed. The various components of risk are briefly discussed in Table 8.1. In general, the highest risk premiums, and therefore the highest returns, are to be found in securities issued by firms with a high risk of default and in long-term maturities that are not actively traded, have unfavourable contractual provisions, and have less security.

TABLE 8.1 Issuer- and Issue-Related Risk Components

Maturity risk (also called *interest-rate risk*)	The longer the maturity of a debt issue, the more the value of a security will change in response to a given change in yields. If yields on otherwise similar-risk securities suddenly rise due to a change in the money supply, the prices of long-term bonds will decline by more than the prices of short-term bonds, and vice versa.[a]
Tax risk	The chance that federal or provincial governments will make unfavourable changes in tax laws. The greater the potential impact of a tax law change on the return of a given security, the greater its tax risk. Generally, long-term securities are subject to greater tax risk than those that are closer to their maturity dates. Therefore, this risk is captured in the maturity risk premium.
Default risk	The possibility that the issuer of debt will not pay the contractual interest or principal as scheduled. The greater the uncertainty as to the borrower's ability to meet these payments, the greater the risk premium. High bond ratings reflect low default risk, and low bond ratings reflect high default risk.
Liquidity risk	The ease with which securities can be converted into cash without experiencing a loss in value. Generally, securities actively traded on major exchanges and over the counter have low liquidity risk, and less actively traded securities in a "thin market" have high liquidity risk.
Contractual provisions	Conditions that are often included in a debt agreement or a share issue. Some of these reduce risk, whereas others may increase risk. For example, a provision allowing a bond issuer to retire its bonds prior to their maturity under favourable terms would increase the bond's risk.

[a]A detailed discussion of the effects of interest rates on the price or value of bonds and other fixed-income securities is presented later in this chapter.

Risk and Return

The fact that a positive relationship exists between risk and the required return should be evident. Investors tend to purchase those securities that are expected to provide a return commensurate with the perceived risk. The actual return earned on the security will affect whether investors sell, hold, or buy additional securities. In addition, most investors look to certain types of securities to provide a given range of risk–return behaviours.

risk–return tradeoff
The expectation that for accepting greater risk, investors must be compensated with greater returns.

As illustrated in Chapter 7, a **risk–return tradeoff** exists: investors will require higher returns before accepting greater risk. This concept is again illustrated in Figure 8.4. The various types of financial securities have very different risk profiles, and therefore very different required returns. Higher returns are required for securities with greater risk. The figure should look familiar to readers; it was shown a number of times in Chapter 7. The measure of risk could be the standard deviation or beta. When beta is used, the nondiversifiable risk of a security is measured and the line depicting the relationship between risk and return is the security market line (SML).

Understanding the risk–return tradeoff is imperative not only for financial managers, but also for all managers of a company. There are risks associated with the various financing alternatives available to a company, and also for investments in assets. All expenditures of company funds entail risk. So, in attempting to maximize share price, a company's management must always be aware of the impact of risk and return.

FIGURE 8.4
Risk–Return Tradeoff
Risk–return profile for popular securities

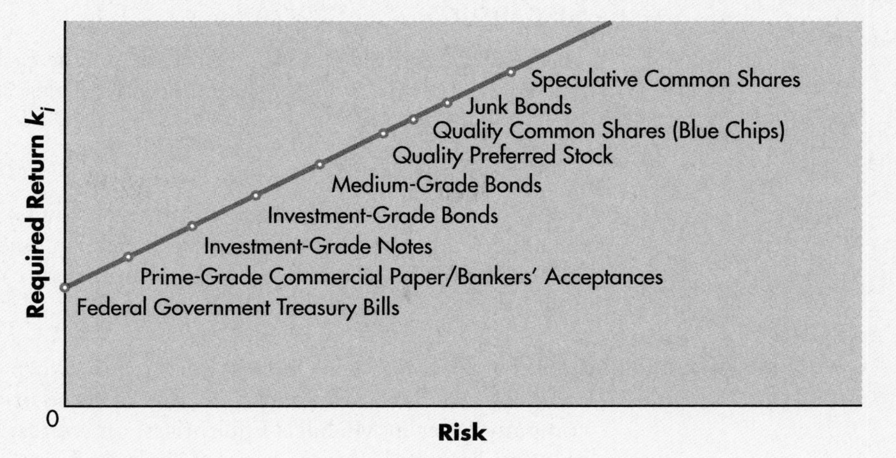

? Review Questions

8–1 What is the *real rate of interest?* Differentiate it from the *nominal rate of interest* for the risk-free asset, a 3-month government of Canada treasury bill. How can the real rate of interest be estimated?

8–2 What is the *term structure of interest rates,* and how does it relate to the *yield curve?* For a given class of similar-risk securities, what does each of the following yield curves reflect about interest rates: (**a**) downward-sloping; (**b**) upward-sloping; and (**c**) flat? Which form historically has been dominant?

8–3 Briefly describe the following theories of the general shape of the yield curve: (**a**) expectations hypothesis; (**b**) liquidity preference theory; and (**c**) market segmentation theory.

8–4 List and briefly describe the potential component risks that are embodied in the risk premium. What is meant by the *risk–return tradeoff?* How should this relationship affect the actions of financial managers?

8.2 Valuation Fundamentals

valuation
The process that links risk and return to determine the value of an asset.

As was noted in Chapter 7, all major financial decisions must be viewed in terms of their estimated risk, required return, and how these impact the value of a productive asset. **Valuation** is the process that links risk and return to determine the value of an asset. It is a relatively simple process that can be applied to *expected* streams of benefits from real assets such as new manufacturing equipment or plants, new products or product line expansions, or new business development, and financial assets such as long-term debt and preferred and commom shares. To determine the value of an asset at a given point in time, the manager uses the time-value-of-money techniques presented in Chapter 6 and the concepts of risk and return developed in Chapter 7.

Key Inputs

The key inputs to the valuation process include cash flows (returns), timing, and the required return, which is based on risk. A description of each follows.

Cash Flows (Returns)

The value of any asset depends on the cash flow(s) it is *expected* to provide over the expected life of the asset. To have value, an asset does not have to provide an annual cash flow; it can provide an intermittent cash flow or even a single cash flow over the complete period.

Example Celia Sargent, financial analyst for Groton Corporation, a diversified holding company, wishes to estimate the value of three of its assets: common shares the company owns in Michaels Enterprises, an interest in an oil well, and an original painting by a well known artist. Her cash flow estimates for each were as follows.

Shares of Michaels Enterprises *Expect* to receive cash dividends of $300 per year indefinitely.

Oil well *Expect* to receive cash flow of $2,000 at the end of 1 year, $4,000 at the end of 2 years, and $10,000 at the end of 4 years, when the well is to be sold.

Original painting *Expect* to be able to sell the painting in 5 years for $85,000.

With these cash flow estimates, Celia has taken the first step toward placing a value on each of these assets.

Timing

In addition to making cash flow estimates, we must know the timing of the cash flows. As is noted in Chapter 6, the point in time a cash flow is received is an important factor in determining the "true" value of the cash flow.[5] For example, Celia expected the cash flows of $2,000, $4,000, and $10,000 for the oil well to occur at the end of years 1, 2, and 4, respectively. In combination, the cash flow and its timing fully define the return expected from the asset.

Required Return (Risk)

Hint
The required rate of return is the result of investors being risk-averse. In order for the risk-averse investor to purchase a given asset, the investor *must have* at least enough return to compensate for the asset's perceived risk.

As is clear from Chapters 5 and 7, and from Section 8.1, the level of risk associated with a given cash flow can significantly affect its value. In general, the greater the risk of (or the less certain) a cash flow, the lower its value. Greater risk can be incorporated into an analysis by using a higher required return or discount rate. In the valuation process, just as in present value calculations, the required return incorporates risk into the analysis: the higher the risk, the greater the required return; the lower the risk, the less the required return.

5. Although cash flows can occur at any time during a year, for computational convenience as well as custom, we will assume they occur at the end of the year unless otherwise noted

Example Let's return to Celia Sargent's task of placing a value on Groton Corporation's original painting and consider two scenarios.

Scenario 1—Certainty A major art gallery has contracted to buy the painting for \$85,000 at the end of 5 years. Because this is considered a certain situation, Celia views this asset as "money in the bank." Therefore, she plans to use the current yield on five-year government of Canada bonds, 9 percent, as the required return when calculating the value of the painting.

Scenario 2—High Risk The value of original paintings by this artist has fluctuated widely over the past 10 years. Although Celia expects to be able to get \$85,000 for the painting, she realizes that its sale price in 5 years could range between \$30,000 and \$140,000. Due to the high uncertainty surrounding the painting's value, Celia believes that a 15 percent required return is appropriate.

These two estimates of the appropriate required return illustrate how this rate captures risk. The often subjective nature of such estimates is also clear.

The Basic Valuation Model

Simply stated, the value of any asset is *the present value of all future cash flows it is expected to provide over its useful life*. The relevant time period is the useful life of the asset, which could be as short as 1 year or as long as infinity. The value of an asset is therefore determined by discounting the expected cash flows back to their present value, using the required return that reflects the asset's risk. Utilizing the present value techniques presented in Chapter 6, we can express the value of any asset at time zero, V_0, as:

$$V_0 = \frac{CF_1}{(1+k)^1} + \frac{CF_2}{(1+k)^2} + \cdots + \frac{CF_n}{(1+k)^n} \quad (8.6)$$

where:

V_0 = value of the asset at time zero
CF_t = cash flow *expected* at the end of year t
k = appropriate required rate of return (discount rate)
n = relevant time period

Using the present value interest factor notation, $PVIF(k\%, n \text{ per})$ from Chapter 6, Equation 8.6 can be rewritten as:

$$V_0 = [CF_1 \times PVIF(k\%, 1 \text{ per})] + [CF_2 \times PVIF(k\%, 2 \text{ per})] + \cdots + [CF_n \times PVIF(k\%, n \text{ per})] \quad (8.7)$$

Substituting the expected cash flows, CF_t, over the relevant time period, n, and the appropriate required return, k, into Equation 8.7, we can determine the value of any asset. A simple example of valuing a project with a ten-year life is provided in Spreadsheet Application 8.1.

Example Celia Sargent, using the appropriate required return and Equation 8.7, calculated the value of each asset. Note that she used a financial calculator for the calculations, and her results are shown in Table 8.2. Michaels Enterprises common shares have a value of \$2,500, the oil well's value is \$9,266.98, and the original painting has a value of \$42,260.03. Note that regardless of the pattern of the expected cash flow from an asset, the basic valuation equation can be used to determine its value.

8.1 SPREADSHEET APPLICATION

Microsoft Excel - Spreadsheet Application 8-1.xls

	A	B	C	D	E
2	**Basic Process Used to Value an Asset**				
3					
4	Required rate of return	10.0%			
5			PV of		
6	**Project Life (in Years)**	**Cash Flow**	**Cash Flow**		**Formulas**
7	1	$1,000	$909	←	=PV($B$4,A7,,-$B7)
8	2	$2,500	$2,066	←	=PV($B$4,A8,,-$B8)
9	3	$6,500	$4,884	←	=PV($B$4,A9,,-$B9)
10	4	$7,800	$5,328		
11	5	$9,600	$5,961		
12	6	$10,500	$5,927		
13	7	$15,600	$8,005		
14	8	$22,100	$10,310		
15	9	$26,800	$11,366		
16	10	$31,900	$12,299		
17					
18	Total PV of Cash Flows		$67,054	←	=SUM(C7:C16)
19					
20					

SA 8-1

Ready NUM

TABLE 8.2 Valuation of Groton Corporation's Assets by Celia Sargent

Asset	Cash flow, CF		Appropriate required return	Valuation
Michaels Enterprises shares	$300/year indefinitely[a]		12%	$V_0 = \$300 \times PVIFa(k\%, \infty)$ $= \$300 \times \frac{1}{0.12} = \underline{\underline{\$2{,}500}}$
Oil well[b]	Year (t)	CF_t	20%	$V_0 = [\$2{,}000 \times PVIF(20\%, 1 \text{ per})]$
	1	$ 2,000		$+ [\$4{,}000 \times PVIF(20\%, 2 \text{ per})]$
	2	4,000		$+ [\$10{,}000 \times PVIF(20\%, 4 \text{ per})]$
	3	0		$= \$1{,}666.67 + \$2{,}777.78$
	4	10,000		$+ \$4{,}822.53$
				$= \underline{\underline{\$9{,}266.98}}$
Original painting[c]	$85,000 at end of year 5		15%	$V_0 = \$85{,}000 \times PVIF(15\%, 5 \text{ per})$ $= \underline{\underline{\$42{,}260.03}}$

[a]This is a perpetuity (infinite-life annuity). Value is calculated using Equation 6.25.

[b]This is a mixed stream of cash flows and therefore requires a number of $PVIF$ calculations, as shown.

[c]This is a lump-sum cash flow and therefore requires a single calculation, as shown.

8.1 **IN PRACTICE**

Valuing a Dream

For many people, owning their own business represents the dream of a lifetime. But how much should this dream cost? One method is to calculate the expected cash flows the business will generate over its useful life and discount these back to time 0 at your required rate of return. The resulting answer is the value of the business based on the present value of the cash flows. Numerous other methods have been devised that may also be useful. Some of these are discussed on the Web.

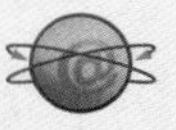

www.businesstown.com/valuing/index.asp

The Businesstown site suggests that the amount to pay for a business ranges from 1 to 10 times current profits depending on: the length of time the business has been established, current market position, competitive pressures, volatility of earnings, value of assets, and level of dependency on management's skills for success.

An extremely well established and steady business with a rock-solid market position, whose continued earnings are not dependent upon a strong management team, may sell for a multiple of 8 to 10 times current earnings. A small personal service business where the new owner will be one of the only workers may sell for a multiple of 1 times current earnings. The Web site also lists a number of valuation techniques that could be used to value a business, including: a multiple of cash flow, book value, liquidation value, a discounted cash flow approach, common sense, and excess earnings methods. All experts agree that when it comes to buying a new business, the key is not to pay too much.

The Web site **www.businessesforsale.com** lists businesses for sale around the world. In November 2006, some of the businesses for sale included a 30-room youth hostel in a Georgian Town House in York, England; a golf course in Saskatchewan; a service station in Victoria, British Columbia; a pub and one-bedroom apartment in Ibiza, Spain; a candy retailer and rental property business in Mahone Bay, Nova Scotia; an IT support company in Manchester, England; an independent golf retailer in Malaga, Spain; a company that designs and manufactures audio surveillance recording systems in California; a funeral home in South Africa that has been operating for 115 years; and a credit reporting service in Orange, California.

For the credit reporting service business, the selling price was $1.7 million. The company's sales revenue for the most recent fiscal year was $1.3 million, and profits were $480,000. The company worked with banks and other lending institutions and consolidated credit reports into a single easy-to-read report. The company was in business for seven years, had between 8 and 12 employees depending on the season, and had "room to grow." When earnings are used to determine a value for a business, earnings before interest, taxes, amortization, and owner's compensation are often used. Given that the selling price was only a little over 3.5 times profits ($1,700,000/$480,000), the selling price seemed quite reasonable. This view is reinforced upon learning that the selling price included $250,000 in accounts receivable and that one of the reasons the current owner was selling was that he was "set for life!"

SOURCES: Value a Business—Sample Valuation Guidelines at **www.businesstown.com**; Valuation Techniques, at **www.businesstown.com**.

? Review Questions

8–5 Define *valuation* and explain why it is important for the financial manager to understand the valuation process.

8–6 Briefly describe the three key inputs to the valuation process. Does the valuation process apply only to assets providing an annual cash flow? Explain.

8–7 Define and specify the general equation for the value of any asset, V_0, in terms of its *expected* cash flow in each year and the appropriate required return.

8.3 Long-Term Debt Valuation

The basic valuation equation can be customized for use in valuing specific financial securities—long-term debt, preferred shares, and common shares. Long-term debt and preferred shares are similar, because they have stated contractual cash flows (interest or dividend). The dividends on common shares, on the other hand, are not known in advance. The principles associated with the valuation of long-term debt are discussed in this section, common shares in the following section, while preferred share valuation principles are covered in Section 8.6.

Long-Term Debt Fundamentals

Hint
A bondholder receives two cash flows from a bond if held to maturity—interest and the bond's face value. For valuation purposes, the interest is an annuity and the face value is a single payment received at a specified future date.

As discussed in Chapter 5, long-term debt is used by business and government to raise large sums of money, typically from a diverse group of lenders. Most long-term debt securities pay interest *semiannually* (every 6 months) at a stated *coupon rate,* have an initial *maturity* of 10 to 30 years, and have a *par,* or *face, value* of $1,000 that must be repaid at maturity.[6] An example will illustrate the terms of a corporate bond.

Example On January 1, 2008, Mills Company, a large defence contractor, issued a 10-year bond with a $1,000 par value and a 10 percent coupon rate that pays interest semiannually. Investors who buy this bond receive the contractual right to two cash flows: (1) $100 annual interest (10% coupon rate × $1,000 par value) with $50 (½ × $100) paid every 6 months and (2) the $1,000 par value at the end of the tenth year.

We will use data for Mills's bond issue to look at basic bond valuation.

6. As discussed in Chapter 5, long-term debt securities can be either bonds or debentures. The term *bond* is often used as a general descriptor of long-term debt, and this convention is used in the remainder of this chapter. Bonds often have features that allow them to be retired by the issuer prior to maturity; these call and conversion features were presented in Chapter 5. For purposes of the current discussion, these features are ignored.

Basic Bond Valuation

The value of a bond is the present value of the payments its issuer is contractually obligated to make, from the current time until it matures. The basic equation for the value, V_0, of a bond is given by Equation 8.8:

$$V_0 = I \times \left[\sum_{t=1}^{n} \frac{1}{(1+k_d)^t}\right] + M \times \left[\frac{1}{(1+k_d)^n}\right] \quad (8.8)$$

where:

V_0 = value of the bond at time zero
I = coupon payment per period in dollars
n = number of periods to maturity
M = par value in dollars
k_d = required rate of return on a bond of similar risk

Since the semiannual coupons are an annuity, and the par value at maturity is a lump sum, this equation can be modified as follows:

$$V_0 = [I \times PVIFa\ (k_d\%,\ n \text{ per})] + [M \times PVIF\ (k_d\%,\ n \text{ per})] \quad (8.9)$$

So the value of the bond is based on the present value of the coupons, plus the present value of the par value at maturity. The value is equal to the present value of the cash flows. Note that in Equations 8.8 and 8.9, V_0 symbolizes the value of the bond. This is the same symbol used in Equations 8.6 and 8.7 for the general valuation formula, and will be the standard symbol used throughout the book for value. In finance, we generally try to calculate the value of an asset at time 0, and we will use that standard notation. The reader should understand the type of asset for which the value is being calculated.

We will calculate the value of a bond using a financial calculator. But first, we need to explain the procedure to use when bonds pay coupons semiannually. To do this, follow a three-step process:

1. Convert the annual coupon payment to semiannual by dividing the annual amount by 2.
2. Convert the number of years to maturity to the number of semiannual periods to maturity by multiplying the number of years by 2.
3. Convert the required return for similar-risk bonds from an annual rate to a semiannual rate by dividing the required return by 2.

We will illustrate this process using an example.

Example ▼ Assume we wish to value the Mills Company bond from the above example on the date of issue using the valuation concepts discussed above. To do so, we require the three variables necessary to calculate value. The first is the cash flows which are the $50 semiannual coupons, the $100 annual coupons divided by 2. The second is the timing which is 20 periods, the ten-year life of the bond multiplied by 2. The third is the discount rate which is the yield on comparable-risk bonds. Since this is the date of issue, the yield will be the coupon rate. The market will only buy this bond from Mills Company if the coupon offered is equivalent to the yield on bonds with the same risk. As explained in Chapter 5, current yields on comparable-risk bonds is the basis for setting the coupon rate. So, in this example, the discount rate is 5 percent, the 10 percent divided by 2. The following time line presents the sequence of cash flows that will be generated over the next 20 periods for this bond.

Graphic depiction of the valuation of Mills Company's 10% coupon rate, 10-year bond with a required return of 10%

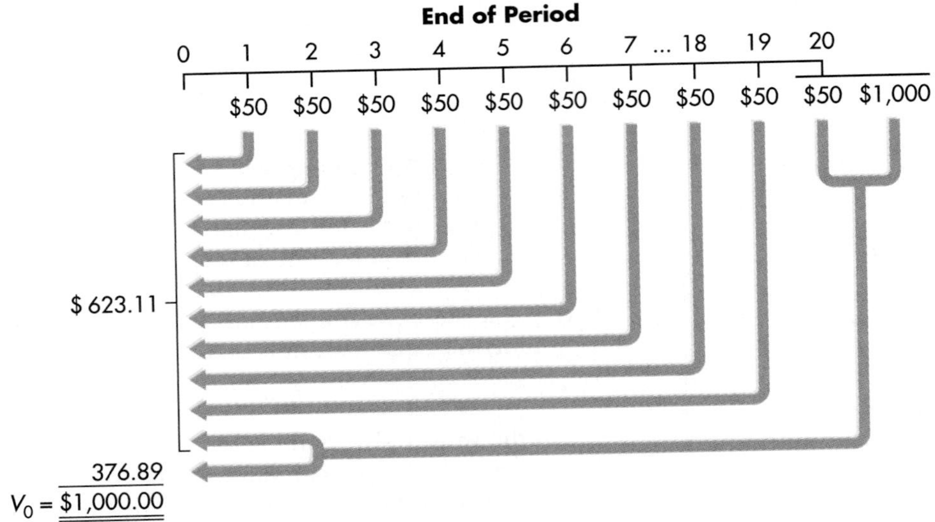

A financial calculator can also be used to calculate the value of the bond. Following the process below will confirm that the bond's value is exactly $1,000.

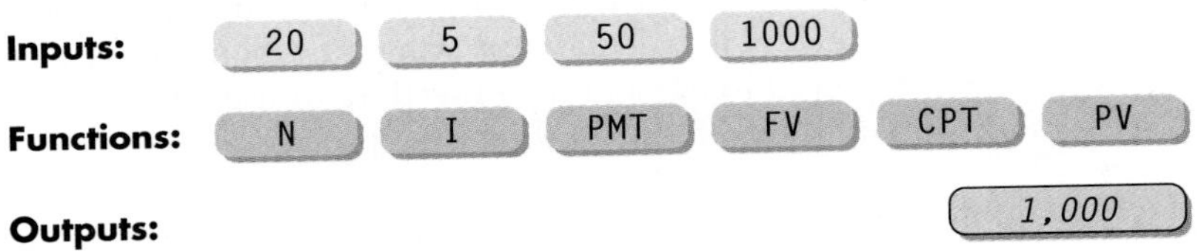

Note that the bond value calculated in the example is equal to its par value. This will always be the case when the required return is equal to the coupon rate.

So the value of the bond is based on the present value of the coupons, plus the present value of the par value at maturity.[7] Given this set of data, the bond is worth $1,000, and would be quoted at 100 in the bond market. This is not surprising, since we are determining the value on the date of issue. Using your financial calculator, you can determine the value of each cash flow separately or in one set of inputs. The above analysis provides the process to determine value in one set of inputs. You should be able to calculate value in total or as two components.

7. Although it may appear inappropriate to use the semiannual discount rate for the maturity value, M, this technique is necessary to find the correct bond value. The analysis that follows confirms the accuracy of this approach for calculating the bond value. When the required return and coupon rate are equal, V_0 equals M.

Bond Value Behaviour

In practice, the value of a bond in the marketplace is rarely equal to its par value. As was seen in the bond quotations in Table 5.8, the closing prices of bonds differ from their par values of 100 (100% of par). Some are valued below par (quoted below 100%), and others are valued above par (quoted above 100%). A variety of forces in the economy as well as the passage of time tend to affect value. Because these external forces are in no way controlled by bond issuers or investors, it is useful to understand the impact that required return and time to maturity have on bond value.

Required Returns and Bond Values

Recall from Chapter 5 that the coupon rate on a bond is set at the time of issue and does not change for the life of the bond. For many bonds, this could be for the term of 20 to 30 years. As discussed in Chapter 5 and in the previous section, the coupon rate is based on the floor rate, the rate on government of Canada bonds with the same time to maturity, plus a premium for risk. The only time the coupon rate and the required rate of return for a bond might be equal, over the full life of the bond, may be the two to three days after the bond is issued.

Once the bond is issued, it begins to trade in the secondary market of the capital market, and it trades based on yield. Since the coupon rate and par value are constant for the term of the debt issue, they will not change regardless of what happens to rates of return in the market. Therefore, when the required return on a bond differs from the bond's coupon rate, the bond's value will differ from its par value. The required return on the bond is likely to differ from the coupon rate because either (1) economic conditions have changed, causing a shift in the current yield on long-term funds, or (2) the firm's risk has changed. Increases in the current yields on long-term funds or in risk will raise the required return; decreases in the current yield or in risk will lower the required return.

Regardless of the exact cause, what is important is the relationship between the required return (the yield on comparable-risk bonds) and the coupon rate. When the required return is greater than the coupon rate, the bond value will be less than the par value. On the other hand, when the required return is less than the coupon rate, the bond value will be greater than the par value. The relationship between the coupon rate and required return (yield) and the par value and market price (value) of a bond is displayed in Figure 8.5. It is also illustrated in the following example.

FIGURE 8.5

Relationship Between Coupon Rates and Required Returns (Yields) and the Par Value and Market Price (Value) of a Bond

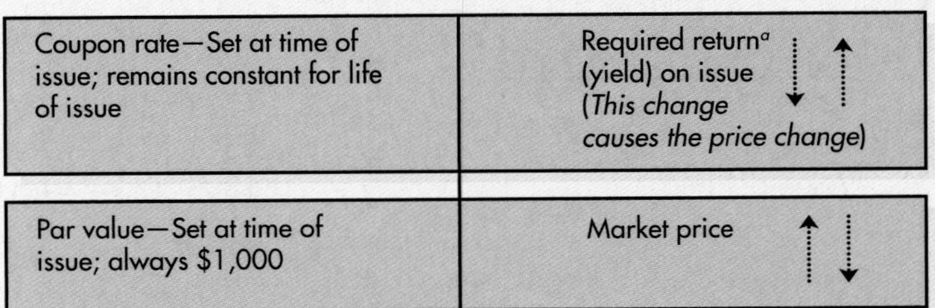

[a] The required return (yield) on a bond may differ from the coupon rate because:
1. interest rates in the market changed since the date of issue, causing yields on long-term debt to change, or
2. the risk of the issuer has changed.

Example For the Mills Company bond, we saw that when the required return equalled the coupon rate, the bond's value equalled its \$1,000 par value. If for the same bond the required return increased to 12 percent one week after the bond was issued, its value calculated using Equation 8.9 and a financial calculator would be:

$$V_0 = [\$50 \times PVIFa\ (6\%, 20 \text{ per})] + [\$1{,}000 \times PVIF\ (6\%, 20 \text{ per})]$$
$$= \$885.30$$

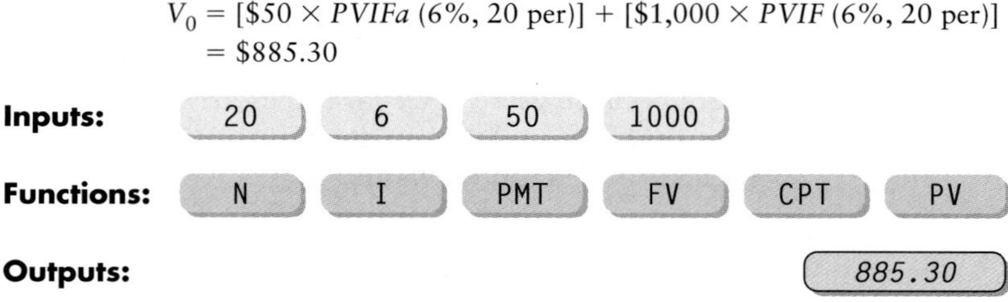

Note that this result is also provided in Spreadsheet Application 8.2.

The bond's value would be \$885.30, and it would be selling in the market for substantially less than its par value. Yields in the market increased and the bond's value fell. If, on the other hand, the required return decreased to 8 percent one week after the bond was issued, its value calculated using Equation 8.9 and a financial calculator would be:

$$V_0 = [\$50 \times PVIFa\ (4\%, 20 \text{ per})] + [\$1{,}000 \times PVIF\ (4\%, 20 \text{ per})]$$
$$= \$1{,}135.90$$

8.2 SPREADSHEET APPLICATION

Microsoft Excel - Spreadsheet Application 8-2.xls

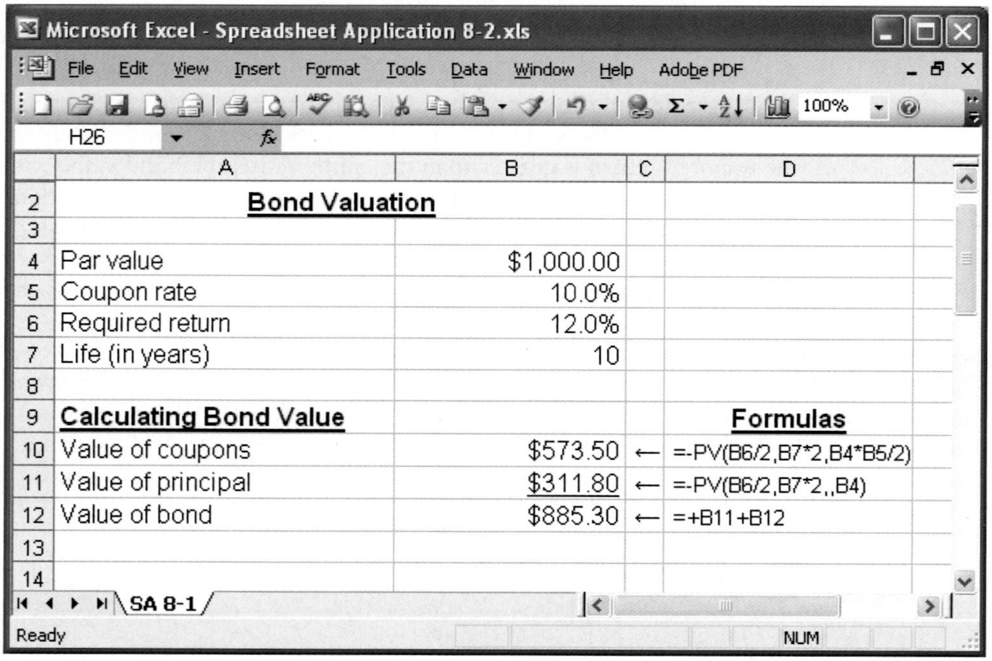

	A	B	C	D
2	**Bond Valuation**			
3				
4	Par value	\$1,000.00		
5	Coupon rate	10.0%		
6	Required return	12.0%		
7	Life (in years)	10		
8				
9	**Calculating Bond Value**			**Formulas**
10	Value of coupons	\$573.50	←	=-PV(B6/2,B7*2,B4*B5/2)
11	Value of principal	\$311.80	←	=-PV(B6/2,B7*2,,B4)
12	Value of bond	\$885.30	←	=+B11+B12
13				
14				

SA 8-1

Inputs:	20	4	50	1000		
Functions:	N	I	PMT	FV	CPT	PV
Outputs:						1,135.90

The bond's value would be $1,135.90, and it would be selling in the market for substantially more than its par value. Yields in the market decreased and the bond's value increased. The results of this and earlier calculations for Mills Company's bond values are summarized in Table 8.3 and graphically depicted in Figure 8.6.

Time to Maturity and Bond Values

As we illustrated in the previous section, the amount of time to maturity also affects the value of bonds. This is maturity risk. Given the discussion, it was clear that the longer the time to maturity, the greater the risk of the bond. How risk is reflected in bond value is dependent on whether required returns are less than or greater than the coupon rate. If required returns are less than the coupon rate, bond values are greater than the par value. But longer-term bonds are worth more than shorter-term bonds. This is the case since the investor in longer-term bonds has taken more risk and has been rewarded with higher values. When required returns are more than the coupon rate, longer-term bonds are worth less than shorter-term bonds. The investor in longer-term bonds has taken more risk and has been penalized with larger decreases in value. An example will help illustrate this.

Example Consider what happens to the Mills Company bond if required returns are 8 percent, 10 percent, or 12 percent. We see the value of the bond in these three cases in Table 8.3. What happens if the required returns remain at these levels for the full term of the bond? For example, what happens if yields are still 8 percent with nine years to maturity, eight years, etc.? The impact is illustrated in Figure 8.7. Note that all features of the bond are the same; only the time to maturity changes.

The impact is clear. As the time to maturity declines, the bond value approaches the par value. Why is that? As the time to maturity declines, the bond will trade very close to par ($1,000), since the company will repay the par value of the bond ($1,000) in a very short period of time. For long-term bonds, the coupons that will be paid have a much greater impact on value. (Of course, when the required return equals the coupon rate, the bond's value will remain at par until it matures.)

What can we learn? When yields in the market for bonds change, the market price changes inversely. Also, the market prices of longer-term bonds are affected much more than shorter-term. Longer-term bonds are riskier, and this risk is reflected in the value when required returns change. The chance that interest rates will change and thereby change the required return and bond value is called **interest-rate risk**. Longer maturities have more interest rate risk than do short maturities. This higher risk will be reflected in bond values when required returns inevitably change in the market.

interest-rate risk
The chance that interest rates will change and thereby change the required return and bond value.

TABLE 8.3 Mills Company Bond: Values at Various Required Returns

Required return, k_d	Bond value, V_0	Status
12%	$ 885.30	Selling for less than par value
10	1,000.00	Selling for par value
8	1,135.90	Selling for more than par value

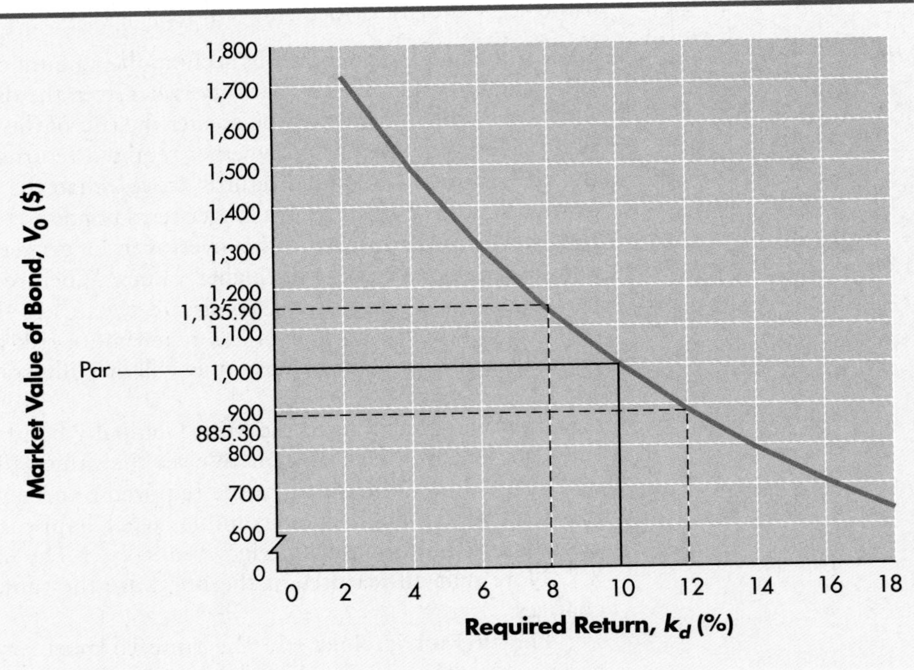

FIGURE 8.6

Required Returns and Bond Values

Mills Company Bond: Bond values at various required returns

Example The effect of changing required returns on bonds of differing maturity can be illustrated by using Mills Company's bond and Figure 8.7. If, as denoted by the dashed line at eight years to maturity, the required return rises from 10 percent to 12 percent, the bond's value decreases from $1,000 to $898.94—a 10.1 percent decrease. If the same change in required return had occurred with only three years to maturity, as denoted by the dashed line, the bond's value would have dropped to just $950.83—a decrease of only 4.9 percent. With eight years to maturity, if required returns decrease from 10 percent to 8 percent, the bond's value increases 11.7 percent. If the same change in required return had occurred with only three years to maturity, the bond's value only increases by 5.2 percent. The shorter the time to maturity, the smaller the impact on bond value caused by a given change in the required return.

FIGURE 8.7

Time to Maturity and Bond Values

Mills Company Bond: Value of bond for different required returns and times to maturity

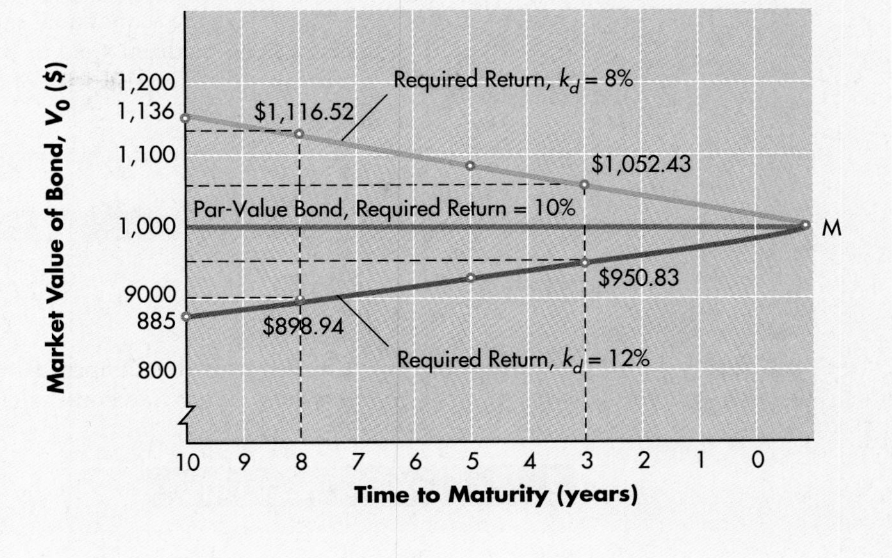

Lenders recognize that interest rate risk exists and, as we have already discussed, prefer to invest their money for shorter time periods due to the lower risk. To encourage investors to lend for longer time periods, borrowers must offer higher returns.

Yield to Maturity (YTM)

yield to maturity (YTM) The rate of return investors earn if they buy a bond at a specific price and hold it until maturity. Assumes that issuer makes all scheduled interest and principal payments as promised.

When investors evaluate and trade bonds, they always consider **yield to maturity (YTM)**, which is the rate of return investors earn if they buy the bond at a specific price and hold it until maturity. The measure assumes, of course, that the issuer makes all scheduled interest and principal payments as promised. The yield to maturity on a bond with a current price equal to its par value (i.e., $V_0 = M$) will always equal the coupon rate. When the bond value differs from par, the yield to maturity will differ from the coupon rate.

Example ▼ Assume the Mills Company bond discussed above has 7.5 years to run to maturity and is quoted in the market for 108.31. This implies that the bond is trading for 108.31 percent of par, or $1,083.10 for each $1,000 of par. Since we have the price, we can calculate the required return, or yield to maturity, by using Equation 8.9 and a financial calculator as follows. Note that in this case all of the variables must be inputted in one step, and then solved for k_d%, the yield on the bond. Since the price of the bond is greater than par, the yield will be less than the coupon rate or, in this case, less than 10 percent.

$$\$1{,}083.10 = [\$50 \times PVIFa\ (k_d\%, 15\text{ per})] + [\$1{,}000 \times PVIF\ (k_d\%, 15\text{ per})]$$

Note: Most calculators require *either* the present value (price) or future value (par value) to be inputted as a negative number to calculate yield to maturity.

The *PV* is negative in this case. Using the inputs shown, you will find that the yield is 4.24 percent. But this is the semiannual rate, so this answer must be multiplied by 2 to calculate the annualized yield of 8.48 percent. So the yield is less than the coupon rate as suggested by the price of the bond.

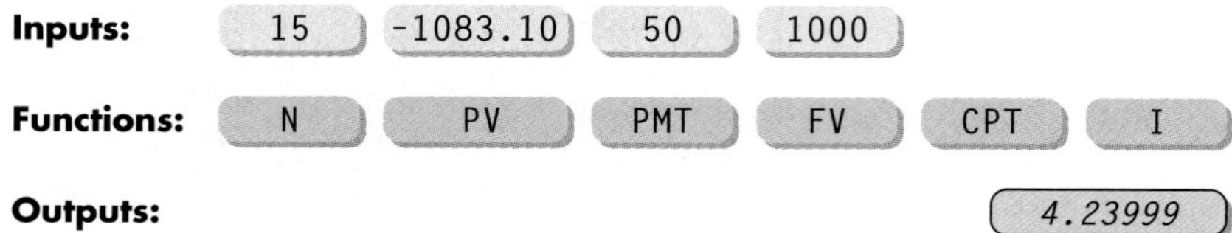

www.calculatorweb.com/calculators/bondcalc.shtml

Note that this result is also provided in Spreadsheet Application 8.3. Also, there are a number of Web sites that provide bond calculators.

? Review Questions

8–8 Describe the basic procedure used to value a bond.

8–9 Under what circumstances will a bond sell for (**a**) its par value? (**b**) above par? (**c**) below par?

8.3 SPREADSHEET APPLICATION

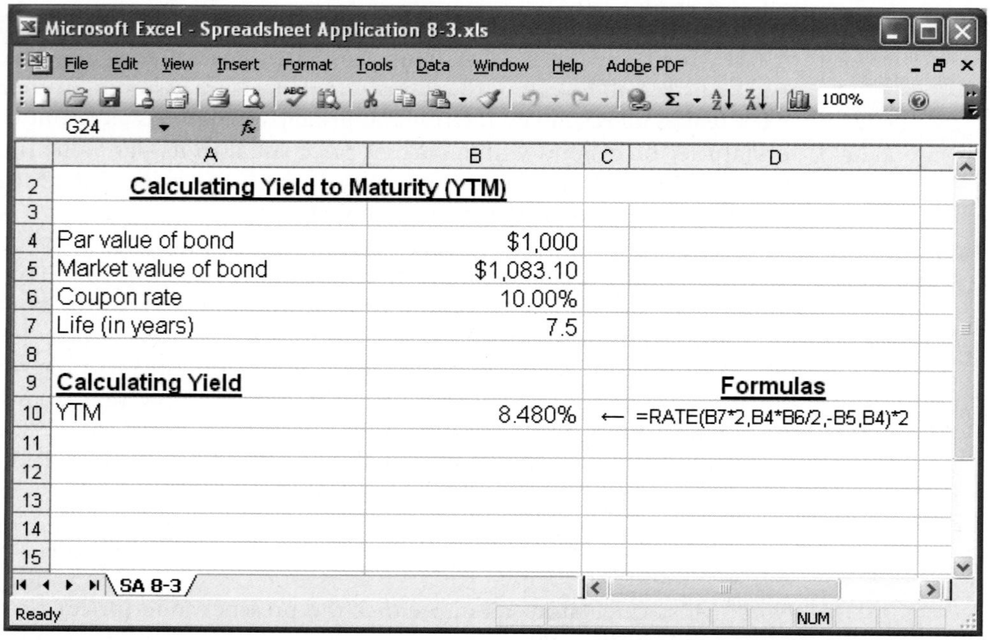

Microsoft Excel - Spreadsheet Application 8-3.xls

	A	B	C	D
2	**Calculating Yield to Maturity (YTM)**			
3				
4	Par value of bond	$1,000		
5	Market value of bond	$1,083.10		
6	Coupon rate	10.00%		
7	Life (in years)	7.5		
8				
9	**Calculating Yield**			**Formulas**
10	YTM	8.480%	←	=RATE(B7*2,B4*B6/2,-B5,B4)*2
11				
12				
13				
14				
15				

SA 8-3

8.2 **IN PRACTICE**

The Value of a Zero

The majority of long-term debt securities outstanding make coupon payments semiannually and repay the par value at maturity. For many investors, this is exactly what they require: a steady stream of known payments. So why would an investor buy a zero-coupon bond, one that makes no regular payments? One reason is their cost. Since zeros only pay the par value at maturity, they sell at a deep discount from the par value. For example, a $1,000 par value, 30-year government of Canada zero-coupon bond might cost $174.11. At maturity, the investor receives $1,000. The difference between the price paid now and the par value received at maturity is the return to the investor, in this case $825.89. What is the annual yield, in percent, that an investor would receive on the zero? Using your financial calculator results in an answer of 6 percent. Note that this answer represents compounding. Each year, over the term of the bond, it is assumed that the interest was paid and was then reinvested in the zero.

This is an important consideration for investors in Canada since the investor must claim the yearly gain in the value of the zero as interest income, even though no cash was actually received. To calculate the amount of interest that is deemed to be received, the zero's value must be calculated at the beginning and end of each year. To determine the values, the formula $M/(1 + K_d)^n$ is used. For the formula, M is the par value, K_d is the required rate of return, and n is the time to maturity. Note that the values can be calculated by using the formula or a financial calculator.

Assume that an investor buys a $1,000 par value zero-coupon bond with a yield of 6.5 percent and 5 years to maturity. Calculate the initial price of the bond. It is $729.88. The total return (interest) received on the bond over the 5 years is $270.12 ($1,000 – $729.88). A table can be easily developed indicating the zero's value at the beginning and end of each year, and the amount of interest that is deemed to be received. This is provided below. Given the high taxes on interest income, as discussed in Section 8.6, most individual investors should hold zero-coupon bonds in tax-sheltered accounts, like registered retirement savings plans (RRSPs).

Year	Beginning value	Ending value	Implicit interest income
1	$729.88	$ 777.32	$ 47.44
2	777.32	827.85	50.53
3	827.85	881.66	53.81
4	881.66	938.97	57.31
5	938.97	1,000.00	61.03
Total			$270.12

8–10 If the required return on a bond differs from its coupon rate and is assumed to be constant until maturity, describe the behaviour of the bond value over the passage of time as the bond moves toward maturity.

8–11 As a risk-averse investor, to protect against the potential impact of rising interest rates on bond value, would you prefer bonds with short or long periods until maturity? Explain why.

8–12 What is meant by a bond's *yield to maturity (YTM)*? Briefly describe how to use a financial calculator for finding YTM.

8.4 Valuation of Common Shares

Common shareholders expect to be rewarded through periodic cash dividends and an increasing—or at least nondeclining—share value. Like current owners, prospective owners and security analysts frequently estimate the firm's value. They purchase the stock when they believe that it is *undervalued*—that its true value is greater than its market price. They sell the stock when they feel that it is *overvalued*—that its market price is greater than its true value.

In this section, we will describe four specific stock valuation techniques. First, though, we will look at the concept of an efficient market, which questions whether the prices of actively traded stocks can differ from their true values.

Market Efficiency[8]

Economically rational buyers and sellers use their assessment of an asset's expected cash flows and its risk to determine its value. To a buyer, the asset's value represents the maximum price that he or she would pay to acquire it; a seller views the asset's value as a minimum sale price. In competitive markets with many active participants, such as the Toronto Stock Exchange, the interactions of many buyers and sellers result in an equilibrium price—the *market value*—for each security. This price reflects the collective actions of buyers and sellers based on all available information. Buyers and sellers are assumed to immediately digest new information as it becomes available, and through their purchase and sale activities to quickly create a new market equilibrium price.

Hint

Be sure to clarify in your own mind the difference between the required return and the expected return. *Required return* is the yearly return an investor requires given the risk of the asset. The expected return is the yearly return an investor expects to receive based on an analysis of the fundamentals of the asset and its ability to generate cash flows in the future.

Market Adjustment to New Information

The process of market adjustment to new information can be viewed in terms of rates of return. From Chapter 7, we know that for a given level of risk, investors require a specified return—the *required return*, k_j—which can be estimated by using beta and CAPM. Note that the equation of the CAPM is simply a different form of Equation 8.2, the basic required rate of return equation, shown earlier in the chapter. This is illustrated below:

$$k_j = R_F + RP \qquad \text{Required rate of return}$$
$$k_j = R_F + [\beta_j \times (k_m - R_F)] \qquad \text{CAPM}$$

The second component of the CAPM is simply the asset risk premium which is based on the market risk premium and the measure of nondiversifiable risk, beta.

8. A great deal of theoretical and empirical research has been performed in the area of market efficiency. For purposes of this discussion, generally accepted beliefs about market efficiency are described rather than the technical aspects of the various forms of market efficiency and their theoretical implications. For a good discussion of the theory and evidence relative to market efficiency, see W. Sean Cleary and Charles P. Jones, *Investments: Analysis and Management* (Toronto: John Wiley & Sons, 2000), Chapter 10.

expected return, $\hat{k}_j$
The yearly return an investor expects to receive based on an analysis of the fundamentals of the asset and its ability to generate cash flows in the future. The expected return on a common share

For common shares, investors regularly estimate the **expected return, $\hat{k}_j$**—the yearly return an investor expects to receive based on an analysis of the fundamentals of the asset and its ability to generate cash flows in the future. The expected return on a common share can be estimated by using a simplified form of Equation 7.1:

$$\hat{k}_j = \frac{\text{expected benefit during upcoming period}}{\text{current price of the common shares}} \tag{8.10}$$

Hint
This relationship between the expected return and the required return can be seen in Equation 8.10, where a decrease in the current share price will result in an increase in the expected return.

Whenever investors find that the expected return is not equal to the required return ($\hat{k}_j \neq k_j$), a market price adjustment will occur. If the expected return is less than the required return ($\hat{k}_j < k_j$), investors will sell the shares, because they do not expect them to earn a return commensurate with their risk. Such action would drive the price down, which (assuming no change in expected benefits) will cause the expected return to rise to the level of the required return. If the expected return were above the required return ($\hat{k}_j > k_j$), investors would buy the shares, driving their price up and the expected return down to the point where it equals the required return.

Example The common shares of Alton Industries (A) are currently selling for $50 per share, and market participants expect them to generate cash flows of $6.50 per share during the coming year. When these values are substituted into Equation 8.10, the expected return, $\hat{k}_A$, on Alton's common shares is:

$$\hat{k}_A = \frac{\$6.50}{\$50.00} = \underline{\underline{13\%}}$$

In addition, the risk-free rate, R_F, is currently 7 percent; the market return, k_m, is 12 percent; and the stock's beta, β_A, is 1.20. When these values are substituted into the CAPM (see above or Equation 7.13), the current required return, k_A, is

$$k_A = 7\% + [1.20 \times (12\% - 7\%)] = 7\% + 6\% = \underline{\underline{13\%}}$$

Because $\hat{k}_A = k_A$, the market price of the common shares is equal to the value of the common shares, and the market is said to be in equilibrium. The stock is fairly priced at $50 per share.

Assume that a press release announces that a major product liability suit has been filed against Alton Industries. As a result, investors immediately adjust their risk assessment upward, raising the firm's beta from 1.20 to 1.40. The new required return, k_A, becomes

$$k_A = 7\% + [1.40 \times (12\% - 7\%)] = 7\% + 7\% = \underline{\underline{14\%}}$$

Now with the higher required return of 14 percent, investors will sell the shares driving the value of Alton's common shares down. This will occur unless the cash flows investors expect to receive increase. Assuming no change in cash flows, the new, higher required return means the value of Alton's common shares will be:

$$V_0 = \frac{\text{expected benefit}}{k_A} = \frac{\$6.50}{14\%} = \$46.43$$

The lower price of \$46.43 means investors now buying the shares are expected to earn a return of 14 percent as follows:

$$\hat{k}_A = \frac{\$6.50}{\$46.43} = \underline{\underline{14\%}}$$

The new price brings the market back into equilibrium, because the expected return now equals the required return.

The Efficient Market Hypothesis

As noted in Chapters 5 and 7, active markets such as the Toronto Stock Exchange are believed to be both operationally and financially efficient. Millions of buy and sell orders on thousands of shares are quickly filled at the best possible price. The markets are made up of many rational investors who react quickly and objectively to new information. The **efficient market hypothesis (EMH),** which is the basic theory describing the behaviour of such a "perfect" market, specifically states:

efficient market hypothesis (EMH)
Theory describing the behaviour of an assumed "perfect" market, which states (1) securities are typically in equilibrium, (2) security prices fully reflect all public information available and react swiftly to new information, and (3) because stocks are fairly priced, investors need not waste time looking for mispriced securities.

1. Securities are typically in equilibrium, meaning that they are fairly priced—their "true" value is equal to their market price, and their expected returns equal their required returns.
2. At any point in time, security prices fully reflect all public information available about the firm and its securities,[9] and these prices react swiftly to new information.
3. Because stocks are fully and fairly priced, investors need not waste their time trying to find and capitalize on mispriced (undervalued or overvalued) securities. In an efficient market there aren't any!

While most academic researchers believe in the EMH, most people who work in the investment industry (practitioners working for investment dealers) and many investors, both individual and institutional, do not believe in the EMH. Many feel that it is worthwhile to search for undervalued or overvalued securities and to trade them to profit from market inefficiencies. Others argue that it is mere luck that would allow market participants to correctly anticipate new information and as a result earn *excess returns*—that is, actual returns greater than required returns. They believe that it is unlikely that market participants can *over the long run* earn excess returns.

Contrary to this belief, some well-known investors such as Warren Buffett of Berkshire Hathaway, Gerald Schwartz of Onex Corporation, and Peter Cundill and Francis Chou (mutual funds managers), *have,* over the long run, consistently earned excess returns on their portfolios. It is unclear whether their performance is the result of their superior ability to anticipate new information or some form of market inefficiency. For evidence of this consistent ability to "beat the market," review the performance of these investors on their Web sites.

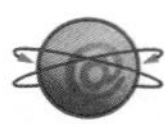

www.berkshirehathaway.com
www.onex.com
www.globefund.com
www.choufunds.com

9. Those market participants who have nonpublic—*inside*—information may have an unfair advantage that permits them to earn an excess return. Since the mid-1980s with the disclosure of the insider-trading activities of a number of well-known financiers and investors, major national attention has been focused on the "problem" of insider trading and its resolution. Clearly, those who trade securities based on inside information have an unfair and illegal advantage. Empirical research has confirmed that those with inside information do indeed have an opportunity to earn an excess return. Here we ignore this possibility, given its illegality and that enhanced surveillance and enforcement by the securities industry and the government have in recent years (it appears) significantly reduced insider trading. We, in effect, assume that all relevant information is public, and therefore the market is efficient.

In this section, it is assumed that the market is efficient. This means that the expected return and required return on an investment are equal. This also means that share prices accurately reflect true value based on risk and return. In other words, we will operate under the assumption that the market price at any point in time is the best estimate of value. We're now ready to look closely at the mechanics of stock valuation.

The Basic Common Share Valuation Equation

Like the value of all productive assets, the value of a common share is equal to the present value of all future cash flows the share is expected to provide. Since the cash flows provided by common shares are dividends, *the value of common shares is equal to the present value of all future dividends the company is expected to pay over an infinite time horizon.*[10] Some may read this and say, "I will not hold the shares forever. At some point I will sell the shares and receive the selling price and, hopefully, a capital gain. Shouldn't this be one of the cash flows considered?"

Well, yes, but consider that the price received when the shares are sold will be based on the dividends received from that point to infinity. So, even though an investor may buy and only hold the shares for three years, the price received when the shares are sold in three years is based on all dividends that will be received from year 4 and on. Therefore, *from a valuation viewpoint, only dividends are relevant.* Redefining terms in the basic valuation model provided as Equation 8.6, we can develop a valuation equation for common shares as follows:

$$V_0 = \frac{D_1}{(1+k_s)^1} + \frac{D_2}{(1+k_s)^2} + \cdots + \frac{D_\infty}{(1+k_s)^\infty} \qquad (8.11)$$

where:

V_0 = value of a company's common shares
D_t = per share dividend expected at the end of year t
k_s = required return on the company's common shares

dividend valuation model (DVM)
The value of common shares is dependent on the present value of the dividends received over an infinite time horizon.

This equation is referred to as the **dividend valuation model (DVM)**: the value of common shares is dependent on the present value of the dividends received. The equation can be simplified somewhat by redefining each year's dividend, D_t, in terms of anticipated growth from the previous year. We will consider three cases here—zero growth in dividends, constant growth in dividends, and variable growth in dividends.

What about the many companies that are not expected to pay dividends in the foreseeable future? In such cases, it could be argued that the value of such companies is based on a distant dividend expected to result from the sale of the company and the liquidation of its assets. However, that may not occur for many years, and estimating this amount is guesswork at best. Instead, numerous other valuation models have been developed that can be used for non-dividend-paying companies. We will consider three such models later in this chapter.

---

10. The need to consider an infinite time horizon is not critical, because a sufficiently long period, say 50 years, will result in about the same present value as an infinite period for moderate-sized required returns. For example, at 15 percent, $1,000 to be received 50 years from now, *PVIF*(15%, 50 per), is worth only about $0.92 today.

Zero Growth

zero-growth model An approach to dividend valuation that assumes a constant, nongrowing dividend stream.

The simplest approach to dividend valuation, the **zero-growth model,** assumes a constant, nongrowing dividend stream. In terms of the notation already introduced:

$$D_0 = D_1 = D_2 = \cdots = D_\infty$$

Letting D_1 represent the dollar amount of the annual dividend, expected in the upcoming year (D_1), Equation 8.11 for zero growth would reduce to:

$$V_0 = D_1 \times \sum_{t=1}^{\infty} \frac{1}{(1+k_s)^t} = \frac{D_1}{k_s} \tag{8.12}$$

The equation shows that with zero growth, the value of a share would equal the present value of a perpetuity of D_1 dollars discounted at a rate k_s.

Example The dividend of Denham Company, an established textile producer, is expected to remain constant at $3 per share indefinitely. If the required return on the company's common shares is 15 percent, the value of the shares is:

$$V_0 = \frac{\$3.00}{0.15} = \$20.00$$

Constant Growth

constant-growth model A widely cited dividend valuation approach that assumes that dividends will grow at a constant rate that is less than the required return.

The most widely cited and used dividend valuation approach, the **constant-growth model,** assumes that dividends will grow at a constant rate, g, that is less than the required return, k_s. The assumption that $k_s > g$ is a necessary mathematical condition for deriving this model. By letting D_0 represent the most recent yearly dividend that was paid, Equation 8.11 can be rewritten as follows:

$$V_0 = \frac{D_0 \times (1+g)^1}{(1+k_s)^1} + \frac{D_0 \times (1+g)^2}{(1+k_s)^2} + \cdots + \frac{D_0 \times (1+g)^\infty}{(1+k_s)^\infty} \tag{8.13}$$

By assuming g is constant, we can simplify Equation 8.13, as follows:[11]

$$V_0 = \frac{D_1}{k_s - g} \tag{8.14}$$

11. For the interested reader, the calculations necessary to derive Equation 8.14 from Equation 8.13 follow. The first step is to multiply each side of Equation 8.13 by $(1 + k_s)/(1 + g)$ and subtract Equation 8.13 from the resulting expression. This yields

$$\frac{V_0 \times (1+k_s)}{1+g} - V_0 = D_0 - \frac{D_0 \times (1+g)^\infty}{(1+k_s)^\infty} \tag{1}$$

Because k_s is assumed to be greater than g, the second term on the right side of Equation 1 should be zero. Thus,

$$V_0 \times \left(\frac{1+k_s}{1+g} - 1\right) = D_0 \tag{2}$$

Equation 2 is simplified as follows:

$$V_0 \times \left[\frac{(1+k_s)-(1+g)}{1+g}\right] = D_0 \tag{3}$$

$$V_0 \times (k_s - g) = D_0 \times (1+g) \tag{4}$$

$$V_0 = \frac{D_1}{k_s - g} \tag{5}$$

Equation 5 is Equation 8.14.

Gordon model
A common name for the *constant-growth model* that is widely cited in dividend valuation.

The constant-growth model in Equation 8.14 is commonly called the **Gordon model.** It is important to recognize the assumptions made by the model. First, it is assumed that the dividends paid will be based on the company's earnings. Second, it is assumed that the rate of growth used in the model applies to both earnings and dividends. This means that the dividend payout ratio will not change over time. While this is likely not a realistic assumption in the short term, in the long-term (the time frame assumed by the model) it is a valid assumption.

Third, the rate of growth will also apply to the company's share price. Therefore, the model assumes that in the long term, earnings, dividends, and share price will all grow at the constant g. Fourth, the rate of growth expected in the future is based on the past growth in these variables. For this to be realistic, the variable and the past period used to estimate growth must be representative of the future. To illustrate the constant growth model, an example will be used.

Example ▼ It is January 3, 2008, and we wish to estimate the value of the common shares of Lamar Company, a small cosmetics company. We know that Lamar paid the following dividends per share (DPS) over the previous six years. It is believed that the growth experienced in DPS over the previous six years is representative of the growth expected in the future.

Year	Dividend per share
2002	$1.00
2003	1.05
2004	1.12
2005	1.20
2006	1.29
2007	1.40

To estimate the value of the shares, we require an estimate for growth. We will base this on the growth in DPS over the six years from 2002 to 2007. Using a financial calculator, in conjunction with the technique described for finding growth rates in Chapter 6, we find that the annual growth rate of dividends equals 7 percent.[12] Based on growth, we can now estimate the dividend to be paid in 2008 (D_1) as follows:

$$\begin{aligned} D_1 &= D_0 \times (1 + g) \\ &= \$1.40\,(1.07) \\ &= \$1.50 \end{aligned}$$

12. For a financial calculation, 1.00 is the *PV*, 1.40 is the *FV*, and *N* is 5. Although six dividends are shown, *they reflect only 5 years of growth*. The number of years of growth can alternatively be found by subtracting the earliest year from the most recent year, i.e., 2007 − 2002 = *5 years of growth*. (Most calculators require *either* the *PV* or *FV* value to be inputted as a negative number to calculate an unknown interest or growth rate. That approach is used here.) Using the inputs shown, you should find the growth rate to be 6.96 percent, which we round to 7 percent.

Inputs:	−1.00	1.40	5	0		
Functions:	PV	FV	N	PMT	CPT	I
Outputs:						6.96

If the required return, k_s, is assumed to be 15 percent, we can substitute these values into Equation 8.14, to determine the value of the common shares as:

$$V_0 = \frac{\$1.50}{0.15 - 0.07} = \frac{\$1.50}{0.08}$$

$$= \$18.75 \text{ per share}$$

Assuming that the values of g, D_1, and k_s, are accurately estimated, the value of Lamar Company's common shares is $18.75 per share.

Note that this result is also provided in Spreadsheet Application 8.4. So, given our estimates, the value of Lamar's common shares is $18.75. If we went to the market where Lamar's common shares are traded and found that the shares were trading for $16.15, what should we do? First, we should question our estimates, since this would imply that the market is not efficient—value is not equal to price. However, if we felt confident in our estimates, we would conclude that Lamar's common shares are undervalued in the market and that we should buy. If we did buy, and our estimates were accurate, then our expected return would be greater than our required return $\hat{k}_s > k_s$.

If instead we went to the market and found that the shares were trading for $21.53, we would conclude that Lamar's common shares are overvalued and that we should not buy the shares. If we did buy, and our estimates were accurate, then our expected return would be less than our required return $\hat{k}_s < k_s$. If we went to the market and found that the shares were trading for $18.75, then we would conclude the market is efficient. If we bought the shares, our expected return would be equal to our required return $\hat{k}_s = k_s$.

If the market is efficient, this allows us to do something interesting with Equation 8.14. As was explained above, if the market is efficient, the value of the common share (V_0) is equal to market price (P_0). Therefore, Equation 8.14 can be manipulated to solve for k_s, investors' required rate of return on common shares as follows:

$$k_s = \frac{D_1}{P_0} + g \tag{8.15}$$

This equation indicates that investors' required return is based on the expected dividend yield (D_1/P_0) plus the expected growth in earnings, dividends, and share price (g). Readers should note that this is an alternative method to the CAPM that can be used to calculate the required return on common shares.

Variable Growth

The zero- and constant-growth common share models do not allow for any shift in expected growth rates in dividends. Because future growth rates might shift up or down due to changing earnings and expectations, it is useful to consider a **variable-growth model** that allows for a change in the dividend growth rate.[13] We will let g_1 be the growth rate in dividends during the initial growth period and g_2 the growth rate for the subsequent growth period. By assuming a single

variable-growth model
A dividend valuation approach that allows for a change in the dividend growth rate.

13. Although more than one change in the growth rate can be incorporated in the model, to simplify the discussion we will consider only a single growth-rate change. The number of variable-growth valuation models is technically unlimited, but concern over all likely shifts in growth is unlikely to yield much more accuracy than a simpler model.

8.4 SPREADSHEET APPLICATION

	A	B	C	D
2	Valuation of Common Shares Using			
3	The Constant Growth DVM			
4				
5	Current dividend (D0)	$1.40		
6	Expected growth in dividends (g)	7.0%		
7	Required return (ks)	15.0%		
8				
9	Calculating Share Value			Formulas
10	Expected dividend (D1)	$1.50	←	=ROUND(B5*(1+B6),2)
11	Difference between ks and g	8.0%	←	=+B7-B6
12	Value of common share	$18.75	←	=+B10/(B7-B6)

shift in growth rates occurs at the end of year N, we can use the following four-step procedure to determine the value of the common shares.

Step 1 Find the value of the cash dividends at the end of *each year*, D_t, during the initial growth period—years 1 through N. This step may require adjusting the most recent dividend that was paid, D_0, using the initial growth rate, g_1, to calculate the dividend amount for each year. Therefore, for the first N years:

$$D_t = D_0 \times (1 + g_1)^t$$

Step 2 Find the present value of the dividends expected during each year of the initial growth period, then sum the present values. By using the notation presented earlier, the total value can be calculated as follows:

$$\sum_{t=1}^{N} (D_t \times PVIF\ (k_s, t \text{ per}))$$

Step 3 Find the value of the shares *at the end of the initial growth period*, $V_N = (D_{N+1})/(k_s - g_2)$, which is the present value of all dividends expected from year $N + 1$ to infinity—assuming a constant dividend growth rate, g_2. This value is found by applying the constant-growth model (presented as Equation 8.14 in the preceding section) to the dividends expected from year $N + 1$ to infinity. The present value of V_N

would represent the value *today* of all dividends that are expected to be received from year $N + 1$ to infinity. This value can be represented by

$$\frac{D_{N+1}}{k_s - g_2} \times PVIF(k_s, N \text{ per})$$

Step 4 Add the present value components found in Steps 2 and 3 to find the value of the shares, V_0, given in Equation 8.16:

$$V_0 = \underbrace{\sum_{t=1}^{N} (D_t \times PVIF\,(k_s, t \text{ per}))}_{\substack{\text{Present value}\\ \text{of dividends}\\ \text{during initial}\\ \text{growth period}}} + \underbrace{\left[\frac{D_{N+1}}{k_s - g_2}\right] \times PVIF\,(k_s, N \text{ per})}_{\substack{\text{Present value of}\\ \text{the common share}\\ \text{price at the}\\ \text{end of the initial}\\ \text{growth period}}} \tag{8.16}$$

The following example illustrates the application of these steps to a variable-growth situation with only one growth rate change.

Example In early January 2009, Todd Bartlett, the finance manager of Warren Industries, a rapidly growing boat manufacturer, was considering whether to repurchase some of their common shares. To make the decision, he wished to estimate the value of the shares using the dividend valuation model. During the 2008 fiscal year, Warren had paid a dividend of $1.50 per share. Todd knew that Warren was about to launch a sailboat with a new design that was expected to generate very high sales for the company. Todd believed that the company's earnings and dividends would increase by 10 percent per year over the next 3 years, 2009, 2010, and 2011 (g_1).

After the three years, the firm's mature product line would result in the growth of earnings and dividends slowing to 5 percent per year for the foreseeable future (g_2). Todd believes investors' required return on the firm's common shares is 15 percent. Todd plans on using this data to estimate the value of Warren's common shares today. To do this, he will use the four-step procedure presented above. He will then make the decision on whether to recommend a share repurchase to the senior management team.

Step 1 The value of the cash dividends in each of the next 3 years is calculated in column 2 of Table 8.4. The 2009, 2010, and 2011 dividends are $1.65, $1.82, and $2, respectively.

Step 2 The present value of the three dividends expected during the 2009 to 2011 initial growth period is calculated in column 3 of Table 8.4. The sum of the present values of the three dividends is $4.13.

Step 3 The value of the shares at the end of the initial growth period, at the end of 2011, can be found by using the constant growth dividend valuation model. Note that after the initial higher growth period, the growth in dividends declines to 5 percent and is expected to remain at that level indefinitely. This implies that we need to calculate the dividend that is expected to be paid next year, 2012, and then use Equation 8.14 to calculate the value of the shares as of the end of 2011, the beginning of 2012. This analysis is provided in Table 8.4. The value of the shares at the end of 2011, based on the expected dividends from 2012 onwards, is \$21. On a present value basis, this is equal to \$13.81.

Step 4 Adding the present value of the initial dividend stream (found in Step 2) to the present value of the shares at the end of the initial growth period (found in Step 3) as specified in Equation 8.16, we have estimated that the value of Warren Industries' common shares at the beginning of 2009 is \$17.94. This analysis is also provided below as a time line.

Calculating the value of Warren Industries' common shares using a time line

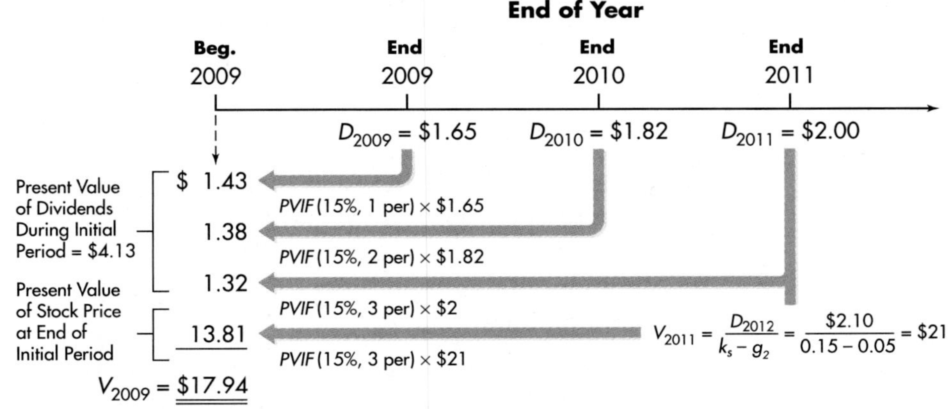

TABLE 8.4 Calculation of Value of Warren Industries' Common Shares

Year	Expected dividend during year*	Present value of dividend
2009	$D_1 = \$1.50 \times (1.10) = \$1.65$	$\$1.65 \times PVIF\ (15\%, 1\ \text{per}) = \$1.43$
2010	$D_2 = \$1.65 \times (1.10) = \$1.82$	$\$1.82 \times PVIF\ (15\%, 2\ \text{per}) = \$1.38$
2011	$D_3 = \$1.82 \times (1.10) = \$2.00$	$\$2.00 \times PVIF\ (15\%, 3\ \text{per}) = \$1.32$
Total present value of the expected dividends during the 3 years		= \$4.13

$^*D_N = D_{N-1} \times (1 + g)$.

Value of the shares at the end of 2011

$$D_{2012} = \$2.00 \times (1.05) = \$2.10$$

$$V_{2011} = \frac{\$2.10}{15\% - 5\%} = \$21.00$$

Present value $= \$21.00 \times PVIF\ (15\%, 3\ \text{per})$ = \$13.81

Value of Warren Industries' common shares, beginning of 2009 = \$17.94

So what should Todd Bartlett, the finance manager of Warren Industries, do? He should check the price of the company's common shares in the market and, if he felt confident in his estimates, recommend the shares be repurchased if they were trading for less than \$17.94. If they were trading for more, the company would not wish to repurchase. ▲

It is important to recognize that the zero-, constant-, and variable-growth valuation models provide useful frameworks for estimating the value of common shares. Clearly, the estimates produced cannot be very precise, given that the forecasts of future growth and discount rates are themselves necessarily approximate. Looked at another way, a great deal of rounding error can be introduced into the share price estimate as a result of the estimates used for both the growth and the discount rate. When applying valuation models, it is therefore advisable to carefully estimate these rates and conservatively round them to the nearest tenth of a percent.

Other Approaches to Common Share Valuation

Many other approaches to common share valuation exist. The more popular approaches include book value, liquidation value, and the price/earnings multiple model.

Book Value

book value per share
The amount per common share that would be received if all of the firm's assets were *sold for their exact book (accounting) value* and the proceeds remaining after paying all liabilities (and preferred shares) were divided among the common shareholders.

Book value per share is simply the amount per common share that would be received if all of the firm's assets were *sold for their exact book (accounting) value* and the proceeds remaining after paying all liabilities (and preferred shares) were divided among the common shareholders. This method lacks sophistication and can be criticized on the basis of its reliance on historical balance sheet data. It ignores the firm's expected earnings potential and generally lacks any true relationship to the firm's value in the marketplace. Let us look at an example.

Example ▼ At the end of the 2008 fiscal year, Lamar Company's balance sheet shows total assets of \$6 million, total liabilities of \$3.9 million, and preferred shares of \$600,000. The company has 100,000 common shares outstanding. Its book value per share therefore would be

$$\frac{\$6{,}000{,}000 - \$3{,}900{,}000 - \$600{,}000}{100{,}000 \text{ shares}} = \frac{\$1{,}500{,}000}{100{,}000 \text{ shares}} = \$15 \text{ per share}$$

Because this value assumes that assets could be sold for their book value, it may not represent the minimum price at which shares are valued in the marketplace. As a matter of fact, although most shares sell above book value, it is not unusual to find shares selling below book value when investors believe either that assets are overvalued or the firm's liabilities are understated. ▲

Liquidation Value

liquidation value per share
The *actual amount* per common share that would be received if all of the firm's assets were *sold for their market value*, liabilities (and preferred shares) were paid, and any remaining money were divided among the common shareholders.

Liquidation value per share is the *actual amount* per common share that would be received if all of the firm's assets were *sold for their market value*, liabilities (and preferred shares) were paid their liquidation amounts, and any remaining money were divided among the common shareholders.[14] This measure is more realistic than book value—because it is based on current market value of the firm's assets—but it still fails to consider the earning power of those assets. An example will illustrate.

Example For Lamar Company, of the $6 million of assets, $2.4 million were current assets, and the remainder fixed. The company believes that they will be able to liquidate the current assets for an average of 75 percent of their book value. For the fixed assets, the liquidation value would be 60 percent. In a liquidation situation, the liabilities could be repaid at an average of 70 percent of their book value, while the preferred shares would be redeemed for 40 percent of their value. The firm's liquidation value per common share therefore would be based on the following:

Current assets:	$2.4 million × 75%	=	$1,800,000	
Fixed assets:	$3.6 million × 60%	=	$2,160,000	
Total proceeds received				$3,960,000
Total liabilities:	$3.9 million × 70%	=	$2,730,000	
Preferred shares:	$600,000 × 40%	=	$ 240,000	
Total payments required		=		$2,970,000
Liquidation value				$ 990,000
Liquidation value per share				$ 9.90

Ignoring liquidation expenses, this amount would be the firm's minimum value.

Price/Earnings (P/E) Multiple Model

price/earnings multiple approach
A technique to estimate the firm's share value; calculated by multiplying the firm's expected earnings per share (EPS) by an appropriate price/earnings (P/E) ratio.

The *price/earnings (P/E) ratio,* introduced in Chapter 3, reflects the amount investors are willing to pay for each dollar of earnings. The average P/E ratio for a company over a representative time period or the average P/E ratio for the firm's industry could be used to estimate the value of the company's common shares. This assumes that investors will continue to value the firm's earnings in the same way as they did in the past, or that the firm is like the average firm in the industry. The **price/earnings multiple approach** is a popular technique to estimate the firm's share value, by multiplying the firm's expected earnings per share (EPS) by an appropriate price/earnings (P/E) ratio as follows:

$$V_0 = E_1 \times M \tag{8.17}$$

where:

E_1 = earnings per share (EPS) for the company for the upcoming year or an average for a number of future periods

M = "appropriate" P/E multiple for the company

14. In the event of liquidation, creditors' claims must be satisfied first, then those of the preferred shareholders. Anything left goes to common shareholders.

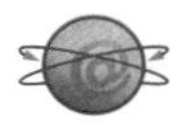

http://today.reuters.com/investing
www.theglobeandmail.com/business
http://finance.yahoo.com

The P/E multiple approach to valuing publicly traded companies is very straightforward given the ease of accessing data on both estimated earnings and historic price-earnings multiples. Such data is available from many sources on the Web. The P/E multiple approach is also useful for valuing private companies. When used for privately owned or closely owned companies, a premium is added to the P/E multiple in order to account for the issue of control. A premium is necessary because the P/E ratio for publicly traded companies implicitly reflects a minority interest in the company. When buying a private company, a control stake is purchased, and control stakes *always* trade at a premium.

In any case, the price/earnings multiple approach is considered superior to the use of book or liquidation values because it considers *expected* earnings.[15] An example will demonstrate the use of price/earnings multiples.

Example For the most recent fiscal year, Lamar Company reported EPS of $2.25. For the next fiscal year, earnings are expected to increase by 12 percent. This expectation is based on an analysis of the firm's historical earnings trend and expected economic and industry conditions. The average price/earnings (P/E) ratio for firms in the same industry is 15.7, and this is considered an appropriate P/E multiple to use to value Lamar. We wish to estimate the value of Lamar's common shares.

First, we require an estimate of the earnings per share (EPS) for the company for the upcoming year. This is equal to $2.52 ($2.25 × 1.12). Multiplying Lamar's expected earnings per share (EPS) of $2.52 by 15.7 gives us a value for the firm's shares of $39.56. This analysis assumes that 15.7 is an appropriate P/E multiple to use for Lamar and that 12 percent is an accurate estimate for growth in EPS. As with all of the common share valuation models, the output (value) is only as good as the inputs (the estimates used to calculate value).

So after the various methods are used to calculate the value of a company's common shares, what are they really worth? That's a tricky question, because there is no one right answer. It is important to recognize that the answer depends on the assumptions made and the techniques used. Professional securities analysts typically use a variety of models and techniques to value shares. For example, an analyst might use the constant-growth model, liquidation value, and price/earnings (P/E) multiples to estimate the value of a company's common shares. If the analyst feels comfortable with his or her estimates, the shares would be valued at no more than the largest estimate.

Of course, should the firm's estimated liquidation value per share exceed its "going concern" value per share, estimated by using one of the valuation models (zero-, constant-, or variable-growth) or the P/E multiple approach, the firm would be viewed as being "worth more dead than alive." In such an event, the firm would lack sufficient earning power to justify its existence and should probably be liquidated.

Hint
From an investor's perspective, the stock in this situation would be an attractive investment only if it could be purchased at a price below its liquidation value—which in an efficient market could never occur.

15. The price/earnings multiple approach to valuation does have a theoretical explanation. If we view 1 divided by the price/earnings ratio, or the *earnings/price ratio*, as the rate at which investors discount the firm's earnings, and if we assume that the projected earnings per share will be earned indefinitely (i.e., no growth in earnings per share), the price/earnings multiple approach can be looked on as a method of finding the present value of a perpetuity of projected earnings per share at a rate equal to the earnings/price ratio. This method is in effect a form of the zero-growth model presented in Equation 8.12.

? Review Questions

8–13 In an *efficient market,* describe the events that occur in response to new information that cause the expected return on common shares to exceed the required return. What happens to the value of the shares?

8–14 What does the *efficient market hypothesis* say about (**a**) securities prices, (**b**) their reaction to new information, and (**c**) investor opportunities to profit?

8–15 Describe, compare, and contrast the following versions of the dividend valuation model: (**a**) zero-growth, (**b**) constant-growth, and (**c**) variable-growth.

8–16 Explain each of the three other approaches to common share valuation: (**a**) book value, (**b**) liquidation value, and (**c**) price/earnings (P/E) multiple model. Which of these is considered the best?

8–17 When using the P/E multiple model to value common shares, why might an inaccurate estimate for value occur?

8.5 Decision Making and Common Share Value

Valuation equations measure the share value at a point in time based on expected return (D_1, g) and risk (k_s) data. Any decisions of the financial manager that affect these variables can cause the value of the firm to change. Figure 8.8 depicts the relationship among financial decisions, return, risk, and share value.

Changes in Expected Cash Flows

Assuming that economic conditions remain stable, any management action that would cause current and prospective common shareholders to change their expectations regarding the cash flows that will be received will impact the estimate of the value of the firm's common shares. In Equation 8.14,[16] we can see that V_0 will increase for any increase in D_1 or g. Any action of the financial manager that will increase the level of expected cash flows without changing risk (the required return) should be undertaken, because it will positively affect owners' wealth.

FIGURE 8.8

Decision Making and Common Share Value
Financial decisions, return, risk, and share value

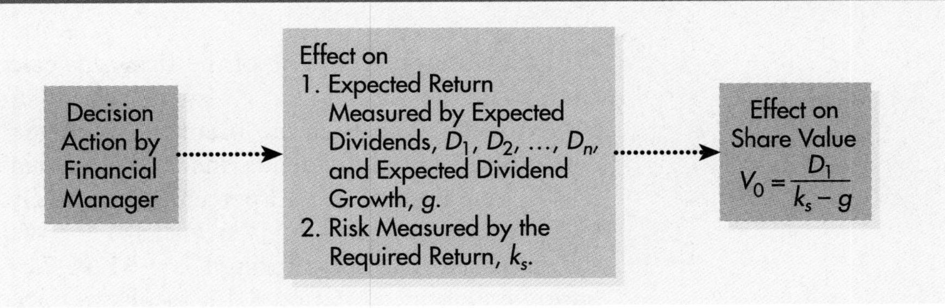

16. To convey the interrelationship among financial decisions, return, risk, and share value, the constant-growth dividend-valuation model is used. Other models—zero-growth or variable-growth—could be used, but the simplicity of exposition using the constant-growth model justifies its use here.

Example Using the constant-growth model, Lamar Company was found to have a share value of \$18.75. On the following day, the firm announced a major technological breakthrough that would revolutionize its industry. Current and prospective shareholders would not be expected to adjust their required return of 15 percent as a result, but they would expect future dividends to increase. Specifically, they would feel that although the dividend next year, D_1, will remain at \$1.50, the expected rate of growth thereafter will increase from 7 to 9 percent. If we substitute $D_1 = \$1.50$, $k_s = 0.15$, and $g = 0.09$ into Equation 8.14, the resulting value equals \$25 (i.e., \$1.50 ÷ [0.15 − 0.09]). The increased value of the common shares, therefore, resulted from the higher expected future dividends reflected in the increase in the growth rate.

The value of the shares would decline if cash flows were projected to decline in the future.

Changes in Risk

As pointed out in Chapter 7, the capital asset pricing model (CAPM) indicates that investors' required return is directly related to nondiversifiable risk, as measured by beta, and as restated as Equation 8.18 below.

$$k_s = R_F + [\beta \times (k_m - R_F)] \tag{8.18}$$

With the risk-free rate, R_F, and the market return, k_m, held constant, the required return, k_s, depends directly on beta. In other words, any action taken by the financial manager that increases risk will also increase the required return. In Equation 8.14, we can see that with all else constant, an increase in the required return, k_s, will reduce share value, V_0. Likewise, a decrease in the required return will increase share value. Thus, any action of the financial manager that increases risk contributes toward a reduction in value, and any action that decreases risk contributes toward an increase in value.

Example Assume that Lamar Company's 15 percent required return resulted from a risk-free rate of 9 percent, a market return of 13 percent, and a beta of 1.50. Substituting into the capital asset pricing model, Equation 8.18, we get a required return, k_s, of 15 percent:

$$k_s = 9\% + [1.50 \times (13\% - 9\%)] = \underline{\underline{15\%}}$$

With this return, the value of the firm was calculated to be \$18.75 in the earlier example.

Now imagine that the financial manager makes a decision that, without changing expected dividends, increases the firm's beta to 1.75. Assuming that R_F and k_m remain at 9 and 13 percent, respectively, the required return will increase to 16 percent (i.e., 9% + [1.75 × (13% − 9%)]) to compensate shareholders for the increased risk. Substituting $D_1 = \$1.50$, $k_s = 0.16$, and $g = 0.07$ into the valuation equation, Equation 8.14, results in a share value of \$16.67 (i.e., \$1.50 ÷ [0.16 − 0.07]). As expected, increasing the required return (without any corresponding increase in cash flows) causes the firm's common share value to decline. Clearly, the financial manager's action was not in the owners' best interest.

Combined Effect

A financial decision rarely affects return and risk independently; most decisions affect both factors. In terms of the measures presented, with an increase in risk (as measured by β) one would expect an increase in return (D_1 or g, or both), assuming that R_F and k_m remain unchanged. The net effect on value depends on the size of the changes in these variables.

Example If we assume that the two changes illustrated for Lamar Company in the preceding examples occur simultaneously as a result of an action of the financial decision maker, key variable values would be $D_1 = \$1.50$, $k_s = 0.16$, and $g = 0.09$. Substituting into the valuation model, we obtain a share price of \$21.43 (i.e., $\$1.50 \div [0.16 - 0.09]$). The net result of the decision, which increased return (g from 7 to 9%) as well as risk (β from 1.50 to 1.75 and therefore k_s from 15 to 16%), is positive: the value of the common shares is expected to increase from \$18.75 to \$21.43. Assuming that the key variables are accurately measured, the decision appears to be in the best interest of the firm's owners, because it increases their wealth.

? Review Questions

8–18 Explain the linkages among financial decisions, return, risk, and stock value. How do the *capital asset pricing model (CAPM)* and the *Gordon model* fit into this basic framework? Explain.

8–19 Assuming that all other variables remain unchanged, what impact would *each* of the following have on the value of the common shares? **(a)** The firm's beta increases. **(b)** The firm's required return decreases. **(c)** The dividend expected next year decreases. **(d)** The rate of growth in dividends is expected to increase. Explain your answers.

LG6

8.6 Valuation of Preferred Shares

As stated earlier, the value of any productive asset, real or financial, is the present value of the cash flows generated over the life of the asset. For preferred shares, there are two cash flows: dividends and the amount received when the preferred share is sold in the future. But, as with common shares, the price received when the preferred share is sold will be based on the dividends received from that point to infinity. So the value of a preferred is based on dividends the preferred will pay for as long as it is outstanding.

So, to value preferred shares, the assumption made is that the preferred share is a perpetuity paying a constant dividend over an infinite period. For many preferred share issues, this is a reasonable assumption.[17] The discount rate used to value the preferred is the required return on preferred shares of comparable risk. Comparable risk would be evaluated by using a preferred share rating. Therefore, to value a preferred share that is rated Pfd-2(low), yields on Pfd-2(low)-rated preferred shares would need to be determined.

17. For a redeemable preferred share, the assumption of a perpetuity may not be valid. In such a case, the value of the redeemable preferred could be determined in exactly the same manner as valuing a bond.

For example, assume a company issues a preferred share with a dividend rate of 4 percent. As years pass, yields in the market increase. If dividend yields on comparable-risk preferred shares never drop below the dividend rate paid on an outstanding preferred share, then there is little reason for the company to redeem the preferred. Unless the share is retractable, preferred shareholders cannot force a company to redeem the shares. Therefore, if a preferred share is not redeemed, it will remain outstanding, essentially becoming a perpetuity. To value a perpetuity, Equation 8.12 is used; the slightly revised equation is provided below:

$$V_0 = \frac{D_1}{k_p} \tag{8.19}$$

where

V_0 = value of a company's preferred shares
D_1 = yearly dividend per preferred share
k_p = required return on the company's preferred shares

Example Telus Corporation has a preferred share issue outstanding with a stated value of \$100 that pays a dividend of 4.375 percent. The preferred was issued in March 1965 and it is redeemable at a 4 percent premium. Telus's preferred shares are rated Pfd-3(high), and required return on these preferred shares is 6.3 percent. This implies that if Telus issued new preferred shares, a 6.3 percent dividend rate would be required. Since the dividend rate on the preferred share outstanding is 4.375 percent, Telus will not redeem this issue and it would be considered a perpetuity. What is the value of the preferred share?

$$V_0 = \frac{\$4.375}{0.063} = \$69.44$$

The preferred share is trading well below its stated value, since required returns in the market have increased to a level above the dividend rate on the preferred share. Therefore, the preferred share will trade for an amount below its stated value and the company will not redeem the issue. The assumption that it will remain outstanding in perpetuity is valid.

Assuming the market for preferred shares is efficient, a very valid assumption for preferred equity, the value of a preferred (V_0) is equal to the market price (P_0). This allows Equation 8.19 to be modified to calculate the required return on preferred shares as follows:

$$k_p = \frac{D_1}{P_0} \tag{8.20}$$

Taxation Issues for Preferred Shares

As discussed in Chapter 5, preferred shares are similar in nature to long-term debt. However, preferred shares are riskier since, unlike debtholders, preferred shareholders do not have the power to put a company into bankruptcy. If preferred shares are riskier, the yield on preferred shares should be higher than on long-term debt. Is this the case?

Example

On May 14, 2007, the Bank of Nova Scotia had a Series 12 preferred share issue outstanding with a stated value of \$25 and an annual dividend of \$1.3125 (or 5.25%). The market price of this preferred was \$24.60. Equation 8.20 can be used to calculate the yield to perpetuity on preferred shares as follows:

$$k_p = \frac{\$1.3125}{\$24.60}$$

$$= 5.34\%$$

On May 14, the yield on 20-year government of Canada debt was 5.55 percent. The yield on the preferred share *is less than* the yield on Canadian government debt.

While this result is based on actual data, it is an illogical outcome for two reasons. First, since preferred shares are riskier than long-term debt, the yield should be higher. Second, the issuer of the preferred share is riskier. The Bank of Nova Scotia is a very secure company and there is little chance of bankruptcy. But all corporations are riskier than the federal government. The federal government is the most secure issuer of financial securities in Canada, so therefore the yield on Government of Canada debt should be lower than the yield on Bank of Nova Scotia preferred shares. The fact that it isn't seems to contradict the risk–return tradeoff.

The explanation for this odd outcome, however, has nothing to do with risk; it is due to how the various types of investment income are taxed in Canada. Interest income is taxed at a much higher rate than income from equity securities (dividends and capital gains). For the most recent tax rates that apply to both income and dividends, visit the Web. Consider Table 8.5, where the taxation of the three types of investment income are considered.

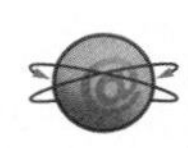

www.taxtips.ca/tax_rates.htm

For the 2006 tax year for middle-income earners, the federal tax rate was 22 percent of taxable income and the provincial rate was 12.3 percent of taxable income. Other information used to calculate taxes is provided in the footnotes to the table. The net impact of the analysis is that interest income attracts \$343 in taxes, providing an after-tax return of \$657. Only \$98.35 in taxes is paid on dividend income, providing an after-tax return of \$901.65, while the tax on capital gains is \$171.50, providing an \$828.50 after-tax return.

The focus of this analysis is on interest and dividends. Note that the difference in the after-tax returns is \$244.65. This indicates that the raw *before-tax yields* on equity and long-term debt securities cannot be compared. A tax-related adjustment termed the **interest equivalent factor** must be used to adjust the before-tax dividend yield on equity securities so it can be compared to the before-tax return on debt securities. The interest equivalent factor is calculated as follows:

interest equivalent factor
A tax-related adjustment that must be made that allows the before-tax dividend yield on equity securities to be compared to the before-tax yield on debt securities.

$$\text{Interest equivalent factor} = \frac{\text{after-tax dividend income}}{\text{after-tax interest income}} \tag{8.21}$$

For the above example, the interest equivalent factor is:

$$\text{Interest equivalent factor} = \frac{\$901.65}{\$657} = 1.37237$$

TABLE 8.5 Taxation of Interest, Dividend, and Capital Gains Income for the 2006 Tax Year

	Interest	Dividend	Capital gains
Income received	$1,000	$ 1,000	$ 1,000
Tax adjustment	0	+ 450[a]	− 500[b]
Taxable income	1,000	1,450	500
Federal tax (22%)[c]	220	319	110
Federal dividend tax credit[a]	—	275	—
Net federal tax payable	220	44	110
Provincial tax (12.3%)[d]	123	178.35	61.50
Provincial dividend tax credit[a]	—	124.00	—
Net provincial tax	123	54.35	61.50
Total taxes payable	343	98.35	171.50
After-tax return	$ 657	$901.65	$828.50

[a] For dividends received from taxable Canadian corporations, an individual must first gross-up (increase) the dividend by 45 percent. The taxable income is 1.45 times the actual amount received. But, to compensate for double-taxation issues, a dividend tax credit is allowed that reduces the effective amount of tax on the dividend. The federal dividend tax credit is 27.5 percent of the actual dividend received, while the average provincial dividend tax credit is 12.4 percent of the actual dividend received.

[b] Only 50 percent of capital gains are taxable, so 50 percent are excluded from income.

[c] For the 2006 tax year, the federal tax rate on taxable income of between $36,378 and $72,756 is 22 percent. Since this tax range is where most middle-income earners are taxed, this rate is used in the example.

[d] Provincial tax rates for middle-income earners for 2006 vary from a low of 9.15 percent in Ontario and British Columbia to a high of 18.02 percent in Newfoundland. The simple average of the provincial tax rates is 12.3 percent and this rate is used in the example.

This factor means that to be in the same *after-tax* position, a middle-income investor receiving $1,000 of dividend income must receive $1,372.37 ($1,000 × 1.37237) of interest income. After taxes, both investors would have the same amount, in this case $901.65. The larger amount of interest income is required due to the differences in taxation. An investor receiving $1,372.37 of interest income will pay a combined tax rate of 34.3 percent, or $470.72. This will leave $901.65 after tax.

Example The Bank of Nova Scotia example presented an illogical outcome. This was due to tax differences. Therefore, to complete the analysis, the 5.34 percent dividend yield on the Bank of Nova Scotia preferred shares cannot be compared to the 5.55 percent yield on 20-year government debt. These yields are in a different scale. The dividend yield must be adjusted for the differences in taxation by multiplying it by the interest equivalent factor. The interest equivalent yield is 7.33 percent (5.34% × 1.37237). The yield on the preferred share is now 1.78 basis points higher than the yield on the Government of Canada debt (7.33% − 5.55%). The risk–return tradeoff now applies.

? Review Questions

8–20 What assumption is made to value preferred shares and what is the equation to determine value? If you knew the amount of the yearly dividend and the current price of a preferred share, rewrite the equation to determine required return (yield).

8–21 What is the interest equivalent factor, why is it calculated, and how is it used?

SUMMARY

LG1 **Describe interest rate fundamentals and the factors that affect required rates of return.** The flow of funds between savers (suppliers) and investors (demanders) is regulated by the interest rate or required return. In a perfect, inflation-free world there would be one cost of money: the real rate of interest. The nominal or actual interest rate is the sum of the risk-free rate, which is the sum of the real rate of interest and the inflationary expectation premium, and a risk premium reflecting issuer and issue characteristics. For any class of similar-risk securities, the term structure of interest rates reflects the relationship between the interest rate, or rate of return, and the time to maturity. Yield curves can be downward-sloping (inverted), upward-sloping (normal), or flat. Three theories—the expectations hypothesis, liquidity preference theory, and market segmentation theory—are cited to explain the general shape of the yield curve. Because investors must be compensated for taking risks, they expect higher returns for greater risk.

LG2 **Describe the key inputs and basic model used in the valuation process.** Key inputs to the valuation process include cash flows (returns), timing, and the required return (risk). The value, or worth, of any asset is equal to the present value of all future cash flows it is *expected* to provide over its expected life. The key variable definitions and the basic valuation formula for any asset are summarized in Table 8.6.

LG3 **Apply the basic valuation model to long-term debt to determine value and yield to maturity (YTM) and describe the impact that changes in required rates of return and time to maturity have on bond values.** The value of a bond is the present value of its coupon payments plus the present value of its par value. The key variable definitions and the basic valuation formula for a bond are summarized in Table 8.6. The discount rate used to determine bond value is the required return, which is the yield on bonds of comparable risk. A bond's value in the market can be less than par, implying yields have increased; can be more than par, implying yields have decreased; or can be par, implying yields have not changed. So, when yields in the market for bonds change, the market price changes inversely. In addition, the market prices of longer-term bonds are affected much more than those of shorter-term bonds. Longer-term bonds are riskier, and this risk is reflected in the value when required returns change. The chance that interest rates will change and thereby change the required return and bond value is called interest rate risk. Longer maturities have more interest rate risk than short maturities. Lenders recognize that interest rate risk exists and prefer to invest their money for shorter time periods due to the lower risk. To encourage investors to lend for longer time periods, borrowers must offer higher returns.

Yield to maturity (YTM) is the rate of return investors earn if they buy a bond at a specific price and hold it until maturity, assuming that the issuer makes all scheduled interest and principal payments as promised.

Understand the concept of market efficiency and four techniques used to determine the value of common shares: (1) the dividend valuation model (DVM), (2) book value, (3) liquidation value, and (4) the price/earnings (P/E) multiple. Market efficiency suggests that there are many rational investors whose quick reactions to new information cause the market value of common shares to adjust upward or downward depending upon whether the expected return is above or below, respectively, the required return for the common share. The efficient market hypothesis suggests that securities are fairly priced, they reflect fully all publicly available information, and investors should therefore not waste time trying to find and capitalize on mispriced securities. The value of a common share is the present value of all future dividends it is expected to provide over an infinite time horizon. Three cases of dividend growth—zero growth, constant growth, and variable growth—can be considered in common share valuation. The key variable definitions and the basic valuation formulas for each of these cases are summarized in Table 8.6. The most widely cited model is the constant-growth model.

Book value per share is the amount per common share that would be received if all of the firm's assets were *sold for their book (accounting) value* and the proceeds remaining after paying all liabilities and preferred shares were divided among the common shareholders.

Liquidation value per share is the *actual amount* per common share that would be received if all of the firm's assets were *sold for their market value,* liabilities and preferred shares were paid their liquidation amounts, and the remaining money were divided among the common shareholders.

The price/earnings (P/E) multiple approach estimates share value by multiplying the firm's expected earnings per share (EPS) by an appropriate price/earnings (P/E) ratio. Of these approaches, P/E multiples are the most popular in practice because, unlike book and liquidation value, they view the firm as a going concern whose value lies in its earning power rather than its asset values.

Understand the relationships among financial decisions, return, risk, and the firm's value. In a stable economy, any action of the financial manager that increases the level of expected cash flows without changing risk should increase share value, and any action that reduces the level of expected cash flows without changing risk should reduce share value. Similarly, any action that increases risk (required return) will reduce share value, and any action that reduces risk will increase share value. In the constant-growth model, returns are measured by next year's dividend (D_1) and its growth rate (g), and risk is measured by the required return (k_s). Because most financial decisions affect both return and risk, an assessment of their combined effect on value must be part of the financial decision-making process.

Discuss valuation concepts and the techniques used to determine the value and required returns on preferred shares. To value preferred shares, the assumption made is that the preferred share is a perpetuity paying a constant dividend over an infinite period. For many preferred share issues, this is a reasonable assumption. The key variable definitions and basic valuation formulas are summarized in Table 8.6. Preferred shares are similar in nature to long-term debt. However, preferred shares are riskier since, unlike debtholders, preferred shareholders do not have the power to put a company into bankruptcy. Therefore, the yield on preferred shares should be higher than on long-term debt. This is not the case, however, when raw before-tax yields are considered. This is due to different taxation of interest and equity investment income. Since dividends are taxed more favourably than interest income, an interest equivalent factor must be used to adjust the dividend yield on equity securities so it can be compared to the before-tax return on debt securities.

TABLE 8.6 Summary of Key Valuation Definitions and Formulas

Variable definitions

k_j = required return on asset j, which could be a bond (k_d), common share (k_s), or preferred share (k_p)

$\hat{k}_j$ = expected return on asset j, which could be a bond ($\hat{k}_d$), common share ($\hat{k}_s$), or preferred share ($\hat{k}_p$)

k^* = real rate of interest

R_F = risk-free rate of return

IP = inflation premium

MRP = maturity risk premium

DRP = default risk premium

V_0 = value of an asset, which could be a bond, common share, or preferred share

P_0 = market price of an asset, which could be a bond, common share, or preferred share

E_1 = earnings per share (EPS) for the company for the upcoming year or an average for a number of future periods

M = "appropriate" P/E multiple for the company

CF_t = cash flow *expected* at the end of year t

I = interest on a bond (either annual or semiannual)

M = par, or face, value of a bond

n = relevant time period, or number of years to maturity

D_0 = most recent per-share dividend

D_t = per-share dividend expected at the end of year t

g = constant rate of growth in dividends

g_1 = initial dividend growth rate (in variable growth model)

g_2 = subsequent dividend growth rate (in variable growth model)

N = last year of initial growth period (in variable growth model)

Valuation formulas

Value of any asset:

$$V_0 = \frac{CF_1}{(1+k)^1} + \frac{CF_2}{(1+k)^2} + \cdots + \frac{CF_n}{(1+k)^n} \quad \text{[Eq. 8.6]}$$

$$= [CF_1 \times PVIF(k\%, 1 \text{ per})] + [CF_2 \times PVIF(k\%, 2 \text{ per})] + \ldots + [CF_n \times PVIF(k\%, n \text{ per})] \quad \text{[Eq. 8.7]}$$

Bond value:

$$V_0 = [I \times PVIFa\ (k_d\%, n \text{ per})] + [M \times PVIF\ (k_d\%, n \text{ per})] \quad \text{[Eq. 8.9]}$$

Expected return (common shares:

$$\hat{k}_j = \frac{\text{expected benefit during upcoming period}}{\text{current price of the common shares}} \quad \text{[Eq. 8.10]}$$

Common share value:

Zero growth: $V_0 = \dfrac{D_1}{k_s}$ (also used to value preferred stock) [Eq. 8.12]

Constant growth: $V_0 = \dfrac{D_1}{k_s - g}$ [Eq. 8.14]

Constant growth extension: $k_s = \dfrac{D_1}{P_0} + g$ [Eq. 8.15]

Variable growth:

$$V_0 = \sum_{t=1}^{N} D_t \times PVIF\ (k_s, t \text{ per}) + \left[\frac{D_{N+1}}{k_s - g_2}\right] \times PVIF\ (k_s, n \text{ per}) \quad \text{[Eq. 8.16]}$$

Price/earnings multiple model: $V_0 = E_1 \times M$ [Eq. 8.17]

Preferred share value: $V_0 = \dfrac{D_1}{K_p}$ [Eq. 8.19]

$k_p = \dfrac{D_1}{P_0}$ [Eq. 8.20]

SELF-TEST PROBLEMS

(Solutions in Appendix B)

ST 8–1 **Bond valuation** Lahey Industries has a bond issue outstanding that has an 8 percent coupon rate. The coupons are paid semiannually. The issue has 12 years remaining to maturity.

a. What is the value of each $1,000 of par value of the bond when the required return is (1) 6 percent, (2) 8 percent, and (3) 10 percent?

b. Indicate for each case in **a** whether the bond is selling for its par value, and why it is or isn't.

ST 8–2 **Yield to maturity** Elliot Enterprises has a bond issue outstanding that has an 11 percent coupon rate. The coupons are paid semiannually. The bond issue has 18 years remaining to maturity, and is now trading in the market for 115.

a. Calculate the bonds' yield to maturity (YTM).

b. Compare the YTM calculated in **a** to the bonds' coupon rate, and explain why there is a difference and how this is reflected in the market price.

ST 8–3 **Common share valuation** In the most recent year, Perry Motors paid a per-share dividend of $1.80 on their common shares. The required return on the common shares is 12 percent. Estimate the value of the common shares under each of the following assumptions.

a. Dividends will not change. Perry will pay a dividend of $1.80 per share to infinity.

b. Dividends are expected to grow at a constant annual rate of 5 percent to infinity.

c. Dividends are expected to grow at an annual rate of 10 percent for each of the next 3 years, followed by a constant annual growth rate of 5 percent in years 4 to infinity.

d. Explain why the share price is different in parts **a**, **b**, and **c** above.

PROBLEMS

8–1 **Interest rate fundamentals: the real rate of return** Carl Foster, a trainee at an investment banking firm, is trying to get an idea of what real rate of return investors are expecting in today's marketplace. He has looked up the rate paid on 3-month government of Canada t-bills and found it to be 5.5 percent. He has decided to use the rate of change in the Consumer Price Index as a proxy for the inflationary expectations of investors. That annualized rate now stands at 2 percent. Based on the information that Carl has collected, what estimate can he make of the real rate of return?

8–2 **Real rate of interest** To estimate the real rate of interest, the economics division of Atlantic Banks has gathered the data summarized in the following table. Because there is a high likelihood that new tax legislation will be passed in the near future, current data as well as data reflecting the likely impact of passage of the legislation on the demand for funds are also included in the table. (*Note:* The proposed legislation will not have any impact on the supply schedule of funds. Assume a perfect world in which inflation is expected to be zero, lenders and borrowers have no liquidity preference, and all outcomes are certain.)

	Currently		With passage of tax legislation
Amount of funds supplied/demanded ($ billion)	**Interest rate required by lenders**	**Interest rate required by borrowers**	**Interest rate required by borrowers**
$ 1	2%	7%	9%
5	3	6	8
10	4	4	7
20	6	3	6
50	7	2	4
100	9	1	3

a. Draw the supply curve and the demand curve for funds using the current data. (*Note:* Unlike Figure 8.1, the functions here will not appear as straight lines.)
b. Using your graph, label and note the real rate of interest using current data.
c. Add to the graph drawn in **a** the new demand curve expected in the event the proposed tax legislation becomes effective.
d. What is the new real rate of interest? Compare and analyze this finding in light of your analysis in **b**.

INTERMEDIATE  8–3 **Real and nominal rates of interest** Zane Perelli currently has $300 that he can spend today on polo shirts costing $75 each. Instead, he could invest the $300 in a risk-free government of Canada security that is expected to earn a 9 percent nominal rate of interest. The consensus forecast of leading economists is a 5 percent rate of inflation over the coming year.
a. How many polo shirts can Zane purchase today?
b. How much money would Zane have at the end of 1 year if he forgoes purchasing the polo shirts today?
c. How much would you expect the polo shirts to cost at the end of 1 year in light of the expected inflation?
d. Use your findings in **b** and **c** to determine how many polo shirts (fractions are OK) Zane could purchase at the end of 1 year. In percentage terms, how many more or fewer polo shirts can Zane buy at the end of 1 year?
e. What is Zane's real rate of return over the year? How does it relate to the percentage change in Zane's buying power found in **d**? Explain.

INTERMEDIATE  8–4 **Yield curve** A firm wishing to evaluate interest rate behaviour has gathered yield data on five government of Canada debt securities, each having a different maturity and all measured at the same point in time. The summarized data follows:

Government of Canada security	Time to maturity	Yield
A	1 year	12.6%
B	10 years	11.2
C	6 months	13.0
D	20 years	11.0
E	5 years	11.4

a. Draw the yield curve associated with the data given.
b. Describe the resulting yield curve in **a**, and explain the general expectations embodied in it.

CHALLENGE 

8–5 Nominal interest rates and yield curves A recent study of inflationary expectations has disclosed that the consensus among economic forecasters yields the following average annual rates of inflation expected over the periods noted. (*Note:* Assume that the risk that future interest rate movements will affect longer maturities more than shorter maturities is zero; that is, there is no *maturity risk.*)

Period	Average annual rate of inflation
3 months	5%
1 year	6
5 years	8
10 years	8.5
20 years	9

a. If the real rate of interest is currently 2.5 percent, find the nominal interest rate on each of the following government of Canada debt issues: 20-year bond, 3-month bill, 1-year bill, and 5-year bond.
b. If the real rate of interest suddenly drops to 2 percent without any change in inflationary expectations, what effect, if any, would this have on your answers in **a**? Explain.
c. Using your findings in **a**, draw a yield curve for government of Canada securities. Describe the general shape and expectations reflected by the curve.
d. What would a follower of the *liquidity preference theory* say about how the preferences of lenders and borrowers tend to affect the shape of the yield curve drawn in item **c**? Illustrate that effect by placing a dotted line on your graph that approximates the yield curve without the effect of liquidity preference.
e. What would a follower of the *market segmentation theory* say about the supply and demand for long-term loans versus the supply and demand for short-term loans given the yield curve constructed for part **c** of this problem?

INTERMEDIATE 

8–6 Nominal and real rates and yield curves A firm wishing to evaluate interest rate behaviour has gathered nominal rate of interest and inflationary expectation data on five government of Canada debt securities, each having a different maturity and each measured at a different point in time during the year just ended. (*Note:* Assume that the risk that future interest rate movements will affect longer maturities more than shorter maturities is zero; that is, there is no *maturity risk*.) These data are summarized in the following table.

Government of Canada security	Point in time	Maturity	Nominal rate of interest	Inflationary expectation
A	Jan. 7	1 year	12.6%	9.5%
B	Mar. 12	10 years	11.2	8.2
C	May 30	6 months	13.0	10.0
D	Aug. 15	20 years	11.0	8.1
E	Dec. 30	5 years	11.4	8.3

a. Using the preceding data, find the real rate of interest at each point in time.
b. Describe the behaviour of the real rate of interest over the year. What forces might be responsible for such behaviour?
c. Draw the yield curve associated with these data, assuming that the nominal rates were measured at the same point in time.
d. Describe the resulting yield curve in **c**, and explain the general expectations embodied in it.

INTERMEDIATE 

8–7 Term structure of interest rates The following yield data for a number of highest quality corporate bonds existed at each of the three points in time noted.

Time to maturity (years)	Yield		
	5 years ago	2 years ago	Today
1	9.1%	14.6%	9.3%
3	9.2	12.8	9.8
5	9.3	12.2	10.9
10	9.5	10.9	12.6
15	9.4	10.7	12.7
20	9.3	10.5	12.9
30	9.4	10.5	13.5

a. On the same set of axes, draw the yield curve at each of the three given times. Label the axes.
b. Label each curve in **a** as to its general shape (inverted, normal, or flat).
c. Describe the general inflationary and interest rate expectation existing at each of the three times.

BASIC 

8–8 Risk-free rate and risk premiums The real rate of interest is currently 3 percent; the inflation expectation and risk premiums for a number of securities follow:

Security	Inflation expectation premium	Risk premium
A	6%	3%
B	9	2
C	8	2
D	5	4
E	11	1

a. Find the risk-free rate of interest, R_F, that is applicable to each security.
b. Although not noted, what factor must be the cause of the differing risk-free rates found in **a**?
c. Find the nominal rates of return for each security.
d. What factor must be causing the risk premium to be different for each security?

INTERMEDIATE  **8–9 Risk premiums** Eleanor Burns is attempting to find the nominal rate of interest for two securities—A and B—issued by different firms at the same point in time. She has gathered the following data:

Characteristic	Security A	Security B
Time to maturity	3 years	15 years
Inflation expectation premium	9.0%	7.0%
Risk premium for:		
Default risk	1.0%	2.0%
Maturity risk	0.5%	1.5%
Liquidity risk	1.0%	1.0%
Other risk	0.5%	1.5%

a. If the real rate of interest is currently 2 percent, find the risk-free rate of interest applicable to each security.
b. Find the total risk premium attributable to each security's issuer and issue characteristics.
c. Calculate the nominal rate of interest for each security. Compare and discuss your findings.

INTERMEDIATE  **8–10 Valuation fundamentals** Imagine that you are trying to evaluate the economics of purchasing an automobile. You expect the car to provide annual after-tax cash benefits of $1,200 per year for five years. You can sell the car for after-tax proceeds of $5,000 at the end of the planned 5-year ownership period. All funds for purchasing the car will be drawn from your savings, which are currently earning 6 percent after taxes.
a. Identify the cash flows, their timing, and the required return applicable to valuing the car.
b. What is the maximum price you would be willing to pay to acquire the car? Explain.

BASIC  **8–11 Valuation of assets** Using the information provided in the following table, find the value of each asset.

Asset	Cash flow: End of year	Cash flow: Amount	Appropriate required return
A	1	$ 5,000	18%
	2	5,000	
	3	5,000	
B	1 through ∞	$ 300	15%
C	1	$ 0	16%
	2	0	
	3	0	
	4	0	
	5	35,000	
D	1 through 5	$ 1,500	12%
	6	8,500	
E	1	$ 2,000	14%
	2	3,000	
	3	5,000	
	4	7,000	
	5	4,000	
	6	1,000	

INTERMEDIATE  **8–12 Asset valuation and risk** Laura Drake wishes to estimate the value of an asset expected to provide cash inflows of $3,000 per year at the end of years 1 through 4 and $15,000 at the end of year 5. Her research indicates that she must earn 10 percent on low-risk assets, 15 percent on average-risk assets, and 22 percent on high-risk assets.

a. What is the most Laura should pay for the asset if it is classified as (1) low risk, (2) average risk, and (3) high risk?

b. If Laura is unable to assess the risk of the asset and wants to be certain she's making a good deal, based on your findings in **a**, what is the most she should pay? Why?

c. All else being the same, what effect does increasing risk have on the value of an asset? Explain in light of your findings in **a**.

BASIC  **8–13 Bond valuation** Complex Systems has a bond issue outstanding that has a 12 percent coupon rate. The coupons are paid semiannually. The bond issue has 16 years remaining to maturity.

a. If bonds of similar risk are currently yielding 10 percent, how much should each $1,000 of par value of the Complex Systems bond sell for today?

b. Describe the *two* possible reasons that similar-risk bonds are currently earning a return below the coupon rate on the Complex Systems bond.

c. If the required return were at 12 percent instead of 10 percent, what would the current value of Complex Systems' bond be? Contrast this finding with your findings in **a** and discuss.

d. If the required return were 15 percent instead of 10 percent, what would the current value of Complex Systems' bonds be? Contrast this finding with your findings in **a** and **c**, and discuss.

BASIC  8–14 **Bond valuation** Calculate the value of each of the bonds shown in the following table, all of which pay interest *semiannually*.

Bond	Par value	Coupon rate	Years to maturity	Required return
A	$1,000	14%	20	12%
B	1,000	8	16	8
C	100	10	8	13
D	500	16	13	18
E	1,000	12	10	10

INTERMEDIATE  8–15 **Bond value and required returns** Midland Utilities has a bond issue outstanding that has an 11 percent coupon rate. The coupons are paid semiannually. The bond issue has 12 years remaining to maturity.

a. Find the value of $1,000 of par value of the bond if the required return is: (1) 7 percent, (2) 9 percent, (3) 11 percent, (4) 13 percent, (5) 15 percent.

b. Plot your findings in **a** on a chart where required return is the x axis and market value of bond is the y axis.

c. Use your findings in **a** and **b** to discuss the relationship between the coupon interest rate on a bond and the required return and the market value of the bond relative to its par value.

d. What two reasons cause the required return to differ from the coupon interest rate?

INTERMEDIATE  8–16 **Bond value and time** Pecos Manufacturing issued a 20-year bond with a 6.6 percent coupon rate, five years ago. The coupons are paid semiannually. The required return is currently 10.2 percent, where the company is certain it will remain until the bond matures in 15 years.

a. Assuming that the required return does remain at 10.2 percent until maturity, find the value of each $1,000 of par value of the bond with (1) 15 years, (2) 12 years, (3) 9 years, (4) 6 years, (5) 3 years, and (6) 1 year to maturity.

b. Plot your findings on a chart where time to maturity is the x axis and market value of bond is the y axis as in Figure 8.7.

c. All else remaining the same, when the required return differs from the coupon rate and is assumed to be constant to maturity, what happens to the bond value as time moves toward maturity? Explain in light of the graph in **b.**

INTERMEDIATE  8–17 **Bond value and time** Lynn Parsons is considering investing in either of two outstanding bonds. The bonds both have $1,000 par values and 11 percent coupon rates and pay *semiannual* interest. Bond A has exactly 5 years to maturity, and bond B has 15 years to maturity.

a. Calculate the value of bond A if the required return is (1) 8 percent, (2) 11 percent, and (3) 14 percent.

b. Calculate the value of bond B if the required return is (1) 8 percent, (2) 11 percent, and (3) 14 percent.

c. From your findings in **a** and **b,** complete the following table, and discuss the relationship between time to maturity and changing required returns.

Required return	Value of bond A	Value of bond B
8%	?	?
11	?	?
14	?	?

d. If Lynn wanted to minimize *interest-rate risk,* which bond should she purchase? Why?

BASIC  8–18 **Yield to maturity** The relationship between a bond's yield to maturity and coupon rate can be used to determine its value. For each of the bonds listed below, state whether the price of the bond will be par, greater than par, or less than par.

Bond	Coupon rate	Yield to maturity	Price
A	6%	10%	
B	8	8	
C	9	7	
D	7	9	
E	12	10	

BASIC  8–19 **Yield to maturity** The Salem Company has a bond issue outstanding that has a 7.9 percent coupon rate. The coupons are paid semiannually. The bond issue has 18.5 years remaining to maturity, and is now trading in the market for 91.15.

a. Calculate the yield to maturity (YTM) for $1,000 of par value.

b. Explain the relationship that exists between the coupon rate and yield to maturity and the par value and market value of a bond.

INTERMEDIATE  8–20 **Yield to maturity** Each of the bonds shown in the following table pays interest *semiannually.*

Bond	Par value	Coupon rate	Years to maturity	Current price
A	$1,000	9%	8	82.0
B	1,000	12	16	100.0
C	500	12	12	56.75
D	1,000	15	10	112.8
E	1,000	5	3	90.16

a. Calculate the yield to maturity (YTM) for each bond.

b. What relationship exists between the coupon rate and yield to maturity and the par value and market value of a bond? Explain.

CHALLENGE  8–21 **Bond valuation and yield to maturity** Mark Goldsmith's broker has shown him two bonds. Each has a maturity of 5 years, a par value of $1,000, and a yield to maturity of 12 percent. Bond A has a coupon rate of 6 percent, bond B a coupon rate of 14 percent, and both are paid semiannually.

a. Calculate the value of each of the bonds.

b. Mark has $20,000 to invest. Based on the price of the bonds, how many of either one could Mark purchase if he were to choose it over the other? (Mark cannot really purchase a fraction of a bond, but for purposes of this question, pretend that he can.)

c. Calculate the yearly interest income of each bond based on its coupon rate and the number of bonds that Mark could buy with his $20,000.

d. Assume that Mark will reinvest the interest payments as they are paid and that his yearly rate of return on the reinvestment is 10 percent. For each bond, calculate the future value of the reinvested coupons plus the value of the par value when the bond matures in 5 years.

e. Why are the two values calculated in **d** different? If Mark were worried that he would earn less than the 12 percent yield to maturity rate on the reinvested interest payments, which of these two bonds would be a better choice?

BASIC LG3 **8–22 Bond valuation** Find the value of a bond maturing in 6 years, with a $1,000 par value and a coupon rate of 10 percent, paid semiannually, if the required return on similar-risk bonds is 14 percent.

BASIC LG3 **8–23 Bond valuation** Calculate the value of each of the bonds shown in the following table, all of which pay interest *semiannually*.

Bond	Par value	Coupon rate	Years to maturity	Required return
A	$1,000	10%	12	8%
B	1,000	12	20	12
C	500	12	5	14
D	1,000	14	10	10
E	100	6	4	14

INTERMEDIATE  **8–24 Bond valuation—Quarterly interest** Calculate the value of a $5,000-par-value bond paying quarterly interest at an annual coupon rate of 10 percent and having 10 years until maturity if the required return on similar-risk bonds is currently 12 percent.

BASIC  **8–25 Common share valuation—Zero growth** Scotto Manufacturing is a mature firm in the machine tool component industry. In the most recent year, the firm paid a common share dividend of $2.40 per share. Due to its long history as well as stable sales and earnings, the firm's management feels that dividends will remain at the current level for the foreseeable future.

a. If the required return on the shares is 12 percent, what will be the value of Scotto's common shares?

b. If the firm's risk as perceived by market participants suddenly increases, causing the required return to rise to 20 percent, what will happen to the value of the common shares?

c. Based on your findings in **a** and **b**, what impact does risk have on value? Explain.

INTERMEDIATE  **8–26 Common share value—Zero growth** Kelsey Drums, Inc., is a well-established supplier of fine percussion instruments to orchestras all over Canada. The company's class A common shares have paid a dividend of $5 per share per year for the last 15 years. Management expects to continue to pay at that rate for the foreseeable future. Sally Talbot purchased 100 shares of Kelsey class A common 10 years ago, at a time when the required rate of return for the shares was 16 percent. She wants to sell her shares today. The current required rate of return for the shares is 12 percent. How much capital gain or loss will she have on her shares?

BASIC  **8–27 Common share value—Constant growth** Use the constant-growth dividend valuation model (Gordon model) to find the value of each of the firms shown in the following table.

Firm	Most recent dividend paid	Dividend growth rate	Required return
A	$1.20	8%	13%
B	4.00	5	15
C	0.65	10	14
D	6.00	8	9
E	2.25	8	20

INTERMEDIATE  **8–28 Common share value—Constant growth** It is early January and McCracken Roofing, Inc., common shares paid a dividend of $1.20 per share last year. The company expects earnings and dividends to grow at a rate of 5 percent per year for the foreseeable future.

a. If McCracken's shares are trading in the market for $28, and this is considered the value of the shares, what is investors' required return on the shares?

b. Now assume that the growth in McCracken's earnings and dividends will be 10 percent. McCracken's shares are trading in the market for $28, and this is considered the value of the shares. What is investors' required return on the shares?

INTERMEDIATE  **8–29 Common share value—Constant growth** It is early January 2009, and Elk County Telephone has paid the dividends shown in the following table over the past 6 years. The implied growth rate is expected to continue well into the future.

Year	Dividend per share
2003	$2.25
2004	2.37
2005	2.46
2006	2.60
2007	2.76
2008	2.87

a. If you can earn 13 percent on similar-risk investments, what is the most you would now pay for Elk's common shares?

b. If you can earn only 10 percent on similar-risk investments, what is the most you would be willing to pay per share?

c. Compare and contrast your findings in **a** and **b**, and discuss the impact of changing risk on share value.

CHALLENGE  8–30 **Common share value—Variable growth** Newman Manufacturing is considering a takeover of Grips Tool. During the year just completed, Grips earned $4.25 per share and paid cash dividends of $2.55 per share. Grips' earnings and dividends are expected to grow at 25 percent per year for the next 3 years, after which they are expected to grow at 10 percent per year to infinity. What is the maximum price per common share Newman should pay for Grips if it has a required return of 15 percent on investments with risk characteristics similar to those of Grips' common shares?

CHALLENGE  8–31 **Common share value—Variable growth** Home Place Hotels, Inc., is entering into a 3-year remodelling and expansion project. The construction will have a limiting effect on earnings during that time but should allow the company to enjoy much improved growth in earnings and dividends when it is complete. Last year, the company paid a dividend of $3.40. It expects zero growth in the next year. In years 2 and 3, 5 percent growth is expected, and in year 4, 15 percent growth. In year 5 and thereafter, growth should be a constant 10 percent per year. What is the maximum price that an investor who requires a return of 14 percent should pay for Home Place Hotels' common shares?

CHALLENGE  8–32 **Common share value—Variable growth** Lawrence Industries' most recent annual dividend was $1.80 per share. The required return on the firm's common shares is 11 percent. Find the market value of Lawrence's shares when:

a. Dividends are expected to grow at 8 percent annually for 3 years followed by a 0 percent constant annual growth rate in years 4 to infinity.

b. Dividends are expected to grow at 8 percent annually for 3 years followed by 5 percent annual growth in years 4 to infinity.

c. Dividends are expected to grow at 8 percent annually for 3 years followed by a 10 percent constant annual growth rate in years 4 to infinity.

CHALLENGE  8–33 **Valuation—All growth models** You are evaluating the potential purchase of a small business currently generating $42,500 of after-tax cash flow. Based on a review of similar-risk investment opportunities, you feel you must earn an 18 percent rate of return on the proposed purchase. Because you are relatively uncertain about future cash flows, you decide to estimate the firm's value using several possible growth rate assumptions for the cash flow.

a. What is the firm's value if cash flows are expected to remain at the current level from now to infinity?

b. What is the firm's value if cash flows are expected to grow at a constant annual rate of 7 percent to infinity?

c. What is the firm's value if cash flows are expected to grow at an annual rate of 12 percent for the first 4 years followed by a constant annual rate of 7 percent in years 5 to infinity?

d. Explain why the company's value is different in parts **a**, **b**, and **c** above.

INTERMEDIATE 

8–34 Book and liquidation value The balance sheet for Gallinas Industries is as follows.

Balance Sheet
Gallinas Industries
December 31, 2008

Assets		**Liabilities and shareholders' equity**	
Cash	$ 40,000	Accounts payable	$ 100,000
Marketable securities	60,000	Line of credit	30,000
Accounts receivable	120,000	Accrued wages	30,000
Inventories	160,000	Total current liabilities	$160,000
Total current assets	$380,000	Long-term debt	$180,000
Land and buildings (net)	$150,000	Preferred shares	$ 80,000
Machinery and equipment	250,000	Common equity	360,000
Total fixed assets (net)	$400,000	Total liabilities and shareholders' equity	$780,000
Total assets	$780,000		

Additional information with respect to the firm is available:

(1) Preferred shares will be redeemed for 50 percent of their stated value.
(2) Accounts receivable and inventories can be liquidated at 90 percent of book value.
(3) The firm has 10,000 common shares outstanding.
(4) All interest and dividends owed are currently paid.
(5) Land and buildings can be liquidated at 130 percent of book value.
(6) Machinery and equipment can be liquidated for 60 percent of book value.
(7) Cash and marketable securities can be liquidated at book value.
(8) Accounts payable and accruals will be repaid at 60 percent of book value.
(9) The line of credit and long-term debt will require a 75 percent payment on the outstanding amounts.

Given this information, answer the following:

a. What is Gallinas Industries' book value per share?
b. What is its liquidation value per share?
c. Compare, contrast, and discuss the values found in **a** and **b**.

BASIC  

8–35 Price/earnings multiple model For each of the firms shown in the following table, use the data given to estimate their common share values employing price/earnings (P/E) multiple model.

Firm	Current EPS	Expected growth in EPS	Appropriate price/earnings multiple
A	$3.11	8.6%	6.2
B	4.56	12.9	10.0
C	1.80	15.6	12.6
D	2.44	7.2	8.9
E	5.19	18.6	15.0

CHALLENGE  **8–36 Calculating value and returns** McCrain Company's common shares are trading in the market for $18.50. Investors require a return of 18 percent on the company's shares. The company's current EPS is $1.40. Earnings are expected to increase by 14.2 percent during the next year. An appropriate price/earnings multiple for the company is thought to be 13.5.

a. Using the price/earnings multiple model, what is the value of McCrain's common shares?

b. If you bought the shares, what is your expected return on the shares?

c. Would you buy the shares? Justify your decision.

d. If the company paid an $0.80 per share dividend during the upcoming year, would this affect your answers in **b** and **c** above?

INTERMEDIATE  **8–37 Management action and stock value** The most recent dividend REH Corporation paid was $3 per share. The company's expected annual rate of dividend growth is 5 percent, and the required return is 15 percent. A variety of proposals are being considered by management to redirect the firm's activities. For each of the following proposed actions, determine the impact on share price and indicate the best alternative.

a. Do nothing, which will leave the key financial variables unchanged.

b. Invest in a new machine that will increase the dividend growth rate to 6 percent and lower the required return to 14 percent.

c. Eliminate an unprofitable product line, which will increase the dividend growth rate to 7 percent and raise the required return to 17 percent.

d. Merge with another firm, which will reduce the growth rate to 4 percent and raise the required return to 16 percent.

e. Acquire a subsidiary operation from another manufacturer. The acquisition should increase the dividend growth rate to 8 percent and increase the required return to 17 percent.

  INTERMEDIATE **8–38 Integrative—Valuation and CAPM formulas** Given the following information for the common shares of Foster Company, calculate its beta.

Current price per common share	$50
Expected dividend per share next year	$ 3
Constant annual dividend growth rate	9%
Risk-free rate of return	7%
Return on market portfolio	10%

 CHALLENGE **8–39 Integrative—Risk and valuation** Giant Enterprises has a beta of 1.20, the risk-free rate of return is currently 10 percent, and the market return is 14 percent. The company anticipates that its future dividends will increase at an annual rate consistent with that experienced over the 2002–2008 period, when the following dividends were paid:

Year	Dividend per share
2002	$1.73
2003	1.80
2004	1.82
2005	1.95
2006	2.10
2007	2.28
2008	2.45

a. Use the capital asset pricing model (CAPM) to determine the required return on Giant Enterprises' common shares.

b. Using the constant-growth model and your finding in **a**, estimate the value of Giant Enterprises' common shares.

c. Explain what effect, if any, a decrease in beta would have on the value of Giant's common shares.

CHALLENGE

8–40 **Integrative—Valuation and CAPM** Hamlin Steel Company wishes to determine the value of Craft Foundry, a firm that it is considering acquiring. Hamlin wishes to use the capital asset pricing model (CAPM) to determine the required return they should use as an input to the constant-growth valuation model. Craft's stock is not publicly traded. After studying the betas of firms similar to Craft that are publicly traded, Hamlin believes that an appropriate beta for Craft's stock would be 1.25. The risk-free rate is currently 9 percent, and the market risk premium is 6.6 percent. Craft's historic dividend per share for each of the past 6 years is shown in the following table. It is believed that the growth experienced over these previous six years is representative of the growth expected in the future.

Year	Dividend per share
2003	$2.45
2004	2.75
2005	2.90
2006	3.15
2007	3.28
2008	3.44

a. Assume it is early January, 2009. Determine the maximum amount Hamlin should pay for each common share of Craft.

b. Discuss the use of the CAPM for estimating the value of common shares, and describe the effect on the resulting value of Craft of the following independent events:

(1) A decrease in its dividend growth rate of 2 percent from that exhibited over the 2003–2008 period.

(2) A decrease in its beta to 1.

INTERMEDIATE  8–41 **Preferred share valuation** Jones Design wishes to estimate the value of its outstanding preferred shares. The preferred issue has an $80 stated value and pays an annual dividend of $6.40 per share. Similar-risk preferred shares are currently yielding 9.3 percent.

a. What is the value of the outstanding preferred shares?

b. If an investor purchases the preferred shares at the value calculated in **a**, how much does she gain or lose per share if she sells the shares when the required return on similar-risk preferreds has risen to 10.5 percent? Explain.

BASIC  8–42 **Preferred share valuation** Southam Ltd. has two issues of $50 stated value preferred shares outstanding. The dividend rate on the first issue is $2.20, and 6.2 percent on the second. Southam is rated Pfd-2 and the required return on preferreds of this risk level is 5.2 percent. Calculate the maximum amount an investor should pay for these preferred shares.

BASIC  8–43 **Preferred share valuation** Spenceley Enterprises has a Series C preferred share issue outstanding which is rated Pfd-2(low). The stated value is $25 and the preferred share pays a dividend of 11 percent. The current price of the preferred is $27.25. Calculate the yield.

CHALLENGE  8–44 **Preferred share valuation** Sandy Inc. has a $25 stated value preferred outstanding which pays a dividend of 8 percent. The current price of the preferred share is $24.10. The company can redeem the preferred in three years at the stated value plus a 2 percent call premium. Calculate the yield an investor would receive assuming:

a. The preferred share was not redeemed.

b. The preferred share was redeemed.

CHALLENGE  8–45 **Interest equivalent factor** Lori Stratton is considering investing in a bond that provides a yield of 8.35 percent or a preferred share with a yield of 7.09 percent. Lori lives in Ontario and at her level of taxable income, the federal tax rate is 29 percent and the provincial tax rate is 15.4 percent.

a. What should Lori do to compare the yields earned on the two investments?

b. What yields would Lori use to make the comparison? To answer this question, use the dividend tax credit rates provided in Table 8.5.

CASE CHAPTER 8

Assessing the Impact of Suarez Manufacturing's Proposed Risky Investment on Its Bond and Common Share Values

See the enclosed Student CD-ROM for cases that help you put theories and concepts from the text into practice.

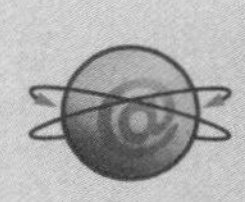

Be sure to visit the Companion Website for this book at **www.pearsoned.ca/gitman** for a wealth of additional learning tools including self-test quizzes, Web exercises, and additional cases.

CHAPTER 9

The Cost of Capital

LEARNING GOALS

LG1 Understand the basic assumptions, concept, and specific sources of capital underlying the cost of capital.

LG2 Determine the cost of long-term debt and the cost of preferred equity.

LG3 Calculate the cost of common equity, recognizing that there are two sources of common equity financing: reinvested profits and the sale of new common shares.

LG4 Find the weighted average cost of capital (WACC) and discuss the alternative weighting schemes.

LG5 Describe the rationale for and procedures used to determine break points and the marginal cost of capital (MCC).

LG6 Explain how the marginal cost of capital (MCC) can be used to make the firm's financing/investment decisions.

9.1 An Overview of the Cost of Capital

The cost of capital is an extremely important financial concept. It acts as a major link between valuation concepts (discussed in Part 3 of this book) and the long-term investment decisions (discussed in Part 5). Cost of capital is based on the concept that lenders and investors require a return when they lend funds to a company, or invest in the equity of a company. This return is a cost to the com-

The Right Cost

If you had a choice of buying three products that were identical in all respects except price, what would you do? Like most people, you would buy the one with the lowest cost. This will result in you maximizing the benefits associated with the product, while minimizing your cost. In addition, you will maximize your wealth. It is the same with companies and their choice of financing and the cost of that financing. The success of any firm depends in large part on the difference between the cost of the firm's funding from various sources and the return earned on investment projects. This chapter illustrates that a company's cost of capital is a function of the costs of the individual sources of financing—long-term debt, preferred equity, and common equity—and the percentages of the individual sources of financing in the company's *optimal* capital structure. The weighted average cost of capital is simply the sum of the individual costs multiplied by the individual weights. The right mix results in the lowest overall cost of capital and the highest value for the company's common shares.

pany. The firm's object is to minimize the overall cost of the funds, which will maximize the market value of the company for the common shareholders.

Cost of capital is, in effect, the "magic number" that is used to decide whether a proposed corporate investment will increase or decrease the firm's stock price. Clearly, only those investment projects whose expected returns are *greater than or equal to* the cost of the funds used to acquire the projects would be recommended. Such projects will result in a company's common shares

LINKING THE DISCIPLINES: Cross-Functional Interactions

- ***Accounting personnel*** need to understand the various sources of capital and how their costs are calculated. They provide the data used to determine the firm's overall cost of capital, such as the book value and historic value data to measure the proportion of the types of capital in its capital structure.
- ***Information systems analysts*** need to understand the various sources of capital and how their costs are calculated in order to develop systems that will estimate the costs of those sources of capital and determine the overall cost of capital.
- ***Management*** must understand cost of capital, as it is the key link between the valuation of financial securities and making investment decisions. Management will use the cost of capital when assessing the acceptability and relative ranking of capital expenditure projects. Management will also decide the firm's target capital structure, which is a vital step in determining the firm's overall cost of capital.
- The ***marketing department*** will be concerned with the overall cost of capital, because acceptance of its proposed projects will depend on whether their expected returns are greater than the cost of capital.
- Personnel in the ***operations department*** need to understand the firm's cost of capital to assess the economic viability of investments in plant and equipment needed to improve or grow the firm's capacity.

increasing in value. Due to its key role in financial decision making, the importance of the cost of capital cannot be overemphasized.

cost of capital
The rate of return that a firm must earn on its investment projects to increase the market value of its common shares.

The **cost of capital** is the rate of return that a firm must earn on its investment projects to increase the market value of its common shares. It can also be thought of as the rate of return required by the market suppliers of capital to attract their funds to the firm. If risk is held constant, projects with a rate of return equal to or above the cost of capital will increase the value of the firm, and projects with a rate of return below the cost of capital will decrease the value of the firm. Since the objective of the firm is to maximize the value of the common shares, a key way to do this is to minimize the company's cost of capital. This concept is also discussed in more detail in Chapter 10.

Basic Assumptions

The cost of capital is a dynamic concept affected by a variety of economic and corporate factors. To isolate the basic structure of the cost of capital, we make some key assumptions relative to risk and taxes:

business risk
The risk to the firm of being unable to cover operating costs.

financial risk
The risk to the firm of being unable to cover required financial obligations (interest, lease payments, preferred share dividends and principal repayments).

1. **Business risk**—the risk to the firm of being unable to cover operating costs—*is assumed to be unchanged.* This assumption means that the firm's acceptance of a given project does not affect its ability to meet operating costs.
2. **Financial risk**—the risk to the firm of being unable to cover required financial obligations (interest, lease payments, preferred share dividends, principal repayments)—*is assumed to be unchanged.* This assumption means that

projects are financed in such a way that the firm's ability to meet required financing costs is unchanged.

3. After-tax costs are considered relevant. In other words, *the cost of capital is measured on an after-tax basis*. This assumption is consistent with the framework used to make decisions regarding investments in assets.

Risk and Financing Costs

Regardless of the type of financing employed, the following equation explains the general relationship between risk and financing costs:

$$k_l = r_l + bp + fp \tag{9.1}$$

where:

k_l = nominal cost of the various types of long-term financing, l
r_l = risk-free cost of the given type of financing, l
bp = business risk premium
fp = financial risk premium

Hint
You can again see the relationship between risk and return. A firm's financing cost will be higher if it has high business and/or financing risks.

Equation 9.1 is merely another form of the nominal interest equation—Equation 8.2 presented in the last chapter—where r_l equals R_F and $bp + fp$ equals RP, the factor for issuer and issue characteristics. It indicates that the cost of each type of capital depends on the risk-free cost of that type of funds, the business risk of the firm, and the financial risk of the firm.[1] We can evaluate the equation in either of two ways:

1. *Time-series comparisons* are made by comparing the firm's cost of each type of financing *over time*. Here the differentiating factor is the risk-free cost of the given type of financing.
2. *Comparisons between firms* are made at a single point in time by comparing a firm's cost of each type of capital with its cost *to another firm*. In this case, the risk-free cost of the given type of financing would remain constant,[2] and the cost differences would be attributable to the differing business and financial risks of each firm.

Example Hobson Company, an Alberta-based meat packer, had a cost of long-term debt 2 years ago of 8 percent. This 8 percent represented a 4 percent risk-free cost of long-term debt, a 2 percent business risk premium, and a 2 percent financial risk premium. Currently, the risk-free cost of long-term debt is 6 percent. How much would you expect the company's cost of long-term debt to be today, assuming that its business and financial risk have remained unchanged? The previous

---

1. Although the relationship between r_l, bp, and fp is presented as linear in Equation 9.1, this is only for simplicity; the actual relationship is likely to be much more complex mathematically. The only definite conclusion that can be drawn is that the cost of a specific type of financing for a firm is somehow functionally related to the risk-free cost of that type of financing adjusted for the firm's business and financial risks [i.e., that $k_l = f(r_l, bp, fp)$].

2. The risk-free cost of each type of financing, r_l, may differ considerably. In other words, at a given point in time, the risk-free cost of long-term debt may be 6% while the risk-free cost of common shares may be 9%. The risk-free cost is expected to be different for each type of financing, l. The risk-free cost of different *maturities* of the same type of debt may differ, because, as discussed in Chapter 8, long-term issues are generally viewed as more risky than short-term issues.

business risk premium of 2 percent and financial risk premium of 2 percent will still prevail, because neither has changed. Adding that 4 percent total risk premium to the 6 percent risk-free cost of long-term debt results in a cost of long-term debt to Hobson Company of 10 percent. In this *time-series comparison,* in which business and financial risk are assumed to be constant, the cost of the long-term funds changes only in response to changes in the risk-free cost of the given type of funds.

Another company, Red Deer Meats, which has a 2 percent business risk premium and a 4 percent financial risk premium, can be used to demonstrate *comparisons between firms.* Although Red Deer and Hobson are both in the meat-packing business (and thus have the same business risk premium of 2%), the cost of long-term debt to Red Deer Meats is currently 12 percent (the 6% risk-free cost plus a 2% business risk premium plus a 4% financial risk premium). This is greater than the 10 percent cost of long-term debt for Hobson. The difference is attributable to the greater financial risk associated with Red Deer. ▲

Cost of Capital: The Basic Concept

marginal cost of financing
The cost of financing today, based on company-specific and financial market data; it is based on an estimate of investors' current required returns.

The cost of capital is estimated at a given point in time. It reflects the expected cost of financing today, based on company-specific and financial market data. This is termed the **marginal cost of financing**—that is, the cost of raising new financing. To determine this value, the company will analyze their own financial securities that may be trading in the financial markets. They will also consider the financial securities of other, similar risk companies. In this manner, they will be able to estimate investors' current required returns. This will be the basis for calculating the company's marginal cost of financial securities.

optimal capital structure (OCS)
The mix of debt and equity financing that results in the lowest possible cost of capital for a company.

The cost of capital is also based on how the company has financed their assets. As discussed in Chapter 3, this is termed the *capital structure.* All firms have an **optimal capital structure (OCS)**, the mix of debt and equity financing that results in the lowest possible cost of capital. This is also the point at which the value of the firm is maximized. This is the ideal mix of financing, and, for cost-of-capital purposes, the way it is assumed the firm raises financing for all projects. The following example illustrates the concept of the optimal capital structure.

Example ▼ Okotoks Oil is attempting to estimate their optimal capital structure. The company has many different financing options using debt and equity capital as provided in Table 9.1. The cost of the debt and equity capital for each of the financing options is also provided. Using the percentage weight and cost of each of the components, we can calculate the firm's cost of capital for each of the financing options. This is provided in Table 9.1 and illustrated in Figure 9.1. If the firm is financed with 100 percent equity, then the cost of equity, and the cost of capital, is 15 percent.

As the firm adds debt to the capital structure, note the impact. The firm is replacing high-cost equity with low-cost debt. As a result, the cost of capital declines. As more debt is added, the cost of both debt and equity begins to increase, due to the increase in company risk. Debt adds financial obligations, and investors will recognize this and rationally demand a higher rate of return. But note that the cost of capital still declines; this continues until the debt ratio reaches about 40 percent. Here, the cost of capital bottoms out at about 13.4

percent. So this is the company's optimal capital structure, meaning the company will attempt to maintain this structure.

This implies that the company must raise all financing in this mix. So the firm will finance all investment projects using 40 percent debt financing, 60 percent equity. But, in reality, this is not practical. Firms raise financing in block amounts. That is, they may use reinvested profits every year, but to supplement this they may use debt financing for three straight years. In the fourth year the firm may sell additional common shares. The impact is that they will move away from the OCS. Is this a problem?

Not really. Note another feature of Table 9.1 and Figure 9.1. The cost of capital remains in the 13.5 percent range when the debt ratio is anywhere between 35 and 55 percent. So, while we assume for cost-of-capital calculation purposes that all financing is raised in the OCS percentages, in reality it does not have to be. As we see in Table 9.1 and Figure 9.1, as long as the debt ratio remains in the fairly broad range of between 35 and 55 percent, the cost of capital is essentially minimized. This analysis is also provided as Spreadsheet Application 9.1.

When cost of capital is minimized, the value of the firm is maximized. To illustrate, assume we have a firm that will generate after-tax cash flows of \$1 million per year indefinitely. This is a perpetuity. As we saw in Chapter 8, the value of an asset is based on the present value of the cash flows that will be generated over the asset's useful life. The discount rate to use is the required rate of return which, for a company, is the cost of capital. If the minimum cost of capital for the firm is 8 percent, the value of the firm using the general equation for a perpetuity is:

$$V = \frac{\$1{,}000{,}000}{8\%} = \$12{,}500{,}000$$

TABLE 9.1 **Cost of Financing and Overall Cost of Capital for Various Capital Structures**

Capital structure		After-tax cost of financing		
Debt	**Equity**	**Debt**	**Equity**	**After-tax cost of capital**
0%	100%	5.2%	15.0%	15.00%
10%	90%	5.2%	15.4%	14.38%
20%	80%	5.4%	16.2%	14.04%
30%	70%	6.0%	17.1%	13.77%
40%	60%	6.6%	18.0%	13.44%
50%	50%	7.5%	19.5%	13.50%
60%	40%	8.9%	21.3%	13.86%
70%	30%	10.8%	23.8%	14.70%
80%	20%	12.8%	27.8%	15.80%
90%	10%	16.5%	31.8%	18.03%
100%	0%	22.0%	36.0%	22.00%

9.1 SPREADSHEET APPLICATION

Microsoft Excel - Spreadsheet Application 9-1.xls

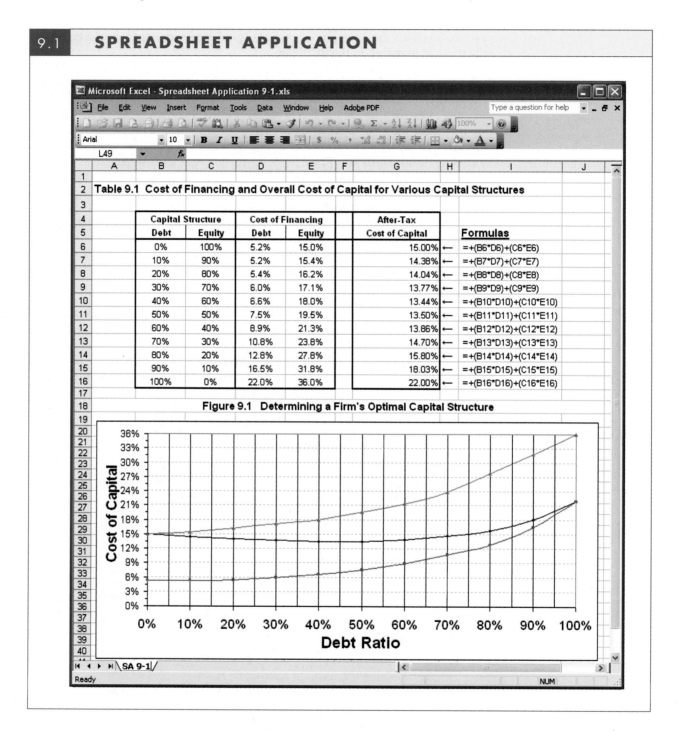

Table 9.1 Cost of Financing and Overall Cost of Capital for Various Capital Structures

Capital Structure		Cost of Financing		After-Tax		
Debt	Equity	Debt	Equity	Cost of Capital		Formulas
0%	100%	5.2%	15.0%	15.00%	←	=+(B6*D6)+(C6*E6)
10%	90%	5.2%	15.4%	14.38%	←	=+(B7*D7)+(C7*E7)
20%	80%	5.4%	16.2%	14.04%	←	=+(B8*D8)+(C8*E8)
30%	70%	6.0%	17.1%	13.77%	←	=+(B9*D9)+(C9*E9)
40%	60%	6.6%	18.0%	13.44%	←	=+(B10*D10)+(C10*E10)
50%	50%	7.5%	19.5%	13.50%	←	=+(B11*D11)+(C11*E11)
60%	40%	8.9%	21.3%	13.86%	←	=+(B12*D12)+(C12*E12)
70%	30%	10.8%	23.8%	14.70%	←	=+(B13*D13)+(C13*E13)
80%	20%	12.8%	27.8%	15.80%	←	=+(B14*D14)+(C14*E14)
90%	10%	16.5%	31.8%	18.03%	←	=+(B15*D15)+(C15*E15)
100%	0%	22.0%	36.0%	22.00%	←	=+(B16*D16)+(C16*E16)

Figure 9.1 Determining a Firm's Optimal Capital Structure

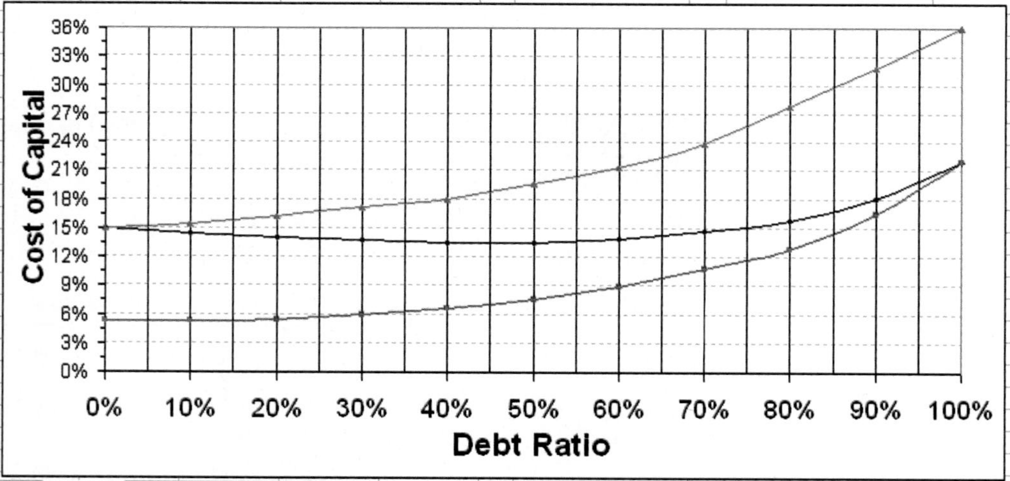

If the firm's cost of capital were 10 percent, the value of the firm would only be $10 million. Therefore, maximizing the firm's cash flow while minimizing risk, thus reducing the firm's cost of capital, is important in terms of maximizing the value of the firm to the owners.

FIGURE 9.1 Determining a Firm's Optimal Capital Structure

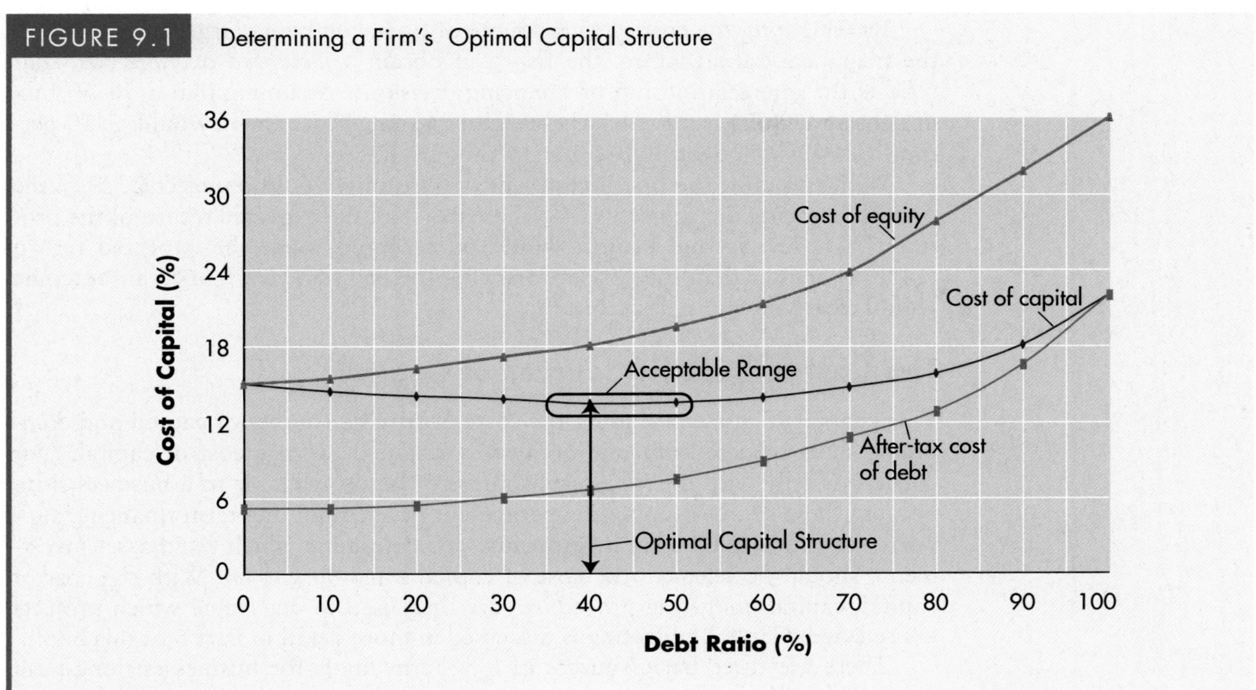

With the OCS and the costs of the individual sources of financing estimated, the company can then evaluate individual investment projects. To do this, the overall cost of capital must be considered, not the cost of the specific sources of funds actually used to finance a given project. The following example illustrates the logic of this process.

Example ▼ A firm has the opportunity to invest in the following project:

Cost = \$100,000
Life = 20 years
Expected return = 7%

To finance the project, the firm could use the lowest-cost source of financing. This is debt with an after-tax cost of 6 percent. Since the company can earn a 7 percent return on the project, it seems to make sense for the company to invest in the project; the cost of the funds is less than the expected return.

Imagine that *1 week later* a new investment opportunity is presented with the same \$100,000 cost, the same life of 20 years, *but* with an expected return of 12 percent. The lowest cost source of financing available is common equity with a cost of 14 percent. In this instance, the firm rejects the opportunity, because the 14 percent financing cost is greater than the 12 percent expected return.

Were the firm's actions in the best interests of its owners? No—it accepted a project yielding a 7 percent return and rejected one with a 12 percent return. Clearly, there should be a better way to make the project selection decision, and there is: The firm can use a combined cost, which over the long run would provide for the best investment decisions.

By weighting the cost of each source of financing by its target proportion in the firm's capital structure, the firm can obtain a *weighted average cost* that reflects the interrelationship of financing decisions. Assuming that a 50–50 mix of debt and equity is targeted, the weighted average cost above would be 10 percent [(0.50 × 6% debt) + (0.50 × 14% equity)].

With this cost, the first investment opportunity would be rejected, since the cost of financing the project (10%) is greater than the expected return of the project (7%). The second project would be accepted, since the expected return (14%) is greater than the cost of financing the project (10%). Such an outcome would clearly be more desirable.

The Cost of Specific Sources of Capital

This chapter focuses on finding the costs of specific sources of capital and combining them to determine and apply the weighted average cost of capital. Our concern is only with the *long-term* sources of funds available to a business firm, because these sources supply the permanent financing. Long-term financing supports the firm's fixed asset investments.[3] To determine which fixed asset investments should be selected, the cost of capital *must be known*. With the cost of capital, capital budgeting procedures are then used to determine which projects are selected. Capital budgeting is discussed in more detail in Part 5 of this book.

There are three basic sources of long-term funds for businesses: long-term debt, preferred equity, and common equity. As discussed in Chapter 5, there are two sources of common equity financing. First, a company sells common shares to investors and the funds raised are obviously a source of financing. Second, an ongoing source of financing is reinvested profits. Assuming a company is profitable and that all of the profits are not paid out as dividends, the reinvested profits are a source of financing. The reinvested profits flow to the balance sheet and appear as retained earnings. The right-hand side of a balance sheet can be used to illustrate these sources:

Balance Sheet		
	Current liabilities	
	Long-term debt	**Sources of long-term funds**
Assets	Shareholders' equity: Preferred shares Common equity: Common shares Retained earnings	

3. The role of both long-term and short-term financing in supporting both fixed and current asset investments is addressed in Chapter 14. Suffice it to say that long-term funds are at minimum used to finance fixed assets.

Note that for the retained earnings account, the source of financing is the current year's contribution to retained earnings, reinvested profits, not the total of retained earnings shown on the balance sheet. Remember, retained earnings are simply the running total of reinvested profits. Retained earnings are used to determine the percentage of common equity in the optimal capital structure, but the current year's reinvested profits are a source of common equity financing.

Although not all firms will use each of these methods of financing, each firm is expected to have funds from some of these sources in its capital structure. The *specific cost* of each source of financing is the *after-tax* cost of obtaining the financing *today*, not the historically based cost reflected by the existing financing on the firm's books. Techniques for determining the specific cost of each source of long-term funds are presented on the following pages.

Although these techniques tend to develop precisely calculated values, the resulting values are at best *rough approximations* because of the numerous assumptions and forecasts that underlie them. Although we round calculated costs to the nearest 0.1 percent throughout this chapter, it is not unusual for practising financial managers to use costs rounded to the nearest 1 percent because the calculated values are merely estimates.

? Review Questions

9–1 What is the *cost of capital?* What role does it play in making long-term investment decisions? Why is use of a weighted average cost rather than the specific cost of a financing source recommended?

9–2 Why are business and financial risk assumed to be unchanged when evaluating the cost of capital? Discuss the implications of these assumptions on the acceptance and financing of new projects.

9–3 Why is the cost of capital most appropriately measured on an after-tax basis?

9–4 What is a company's optimal capital structure? Discuss the process used to estimate the optimal capital structure.

9–5 At a meeting of the senior management team, the operations manager has just said,"Because we are going to finance this project with debt, its expected rate of return must exceed the cost of debt." Do you agree or disagree with the statement? Explain.

9.2 The Cost of Long-Term Debt

cost of long-term debt, k_{dt}
The after-tax cost today of raising long-term funds through borrowing from either financial institutions or investors.

The **cost of long-term debt, k_{dt},** is the after-tax cost today of raising long-term funds through borrowing from either financial institutions or investors. The long-term borrowing could be raised by getting a term loan from a bank or by using bonds or debentures. Consistent with previous chapters, the term *bond* will be used to denote long-term debt. The coupon payments are assumed to be made semiannually.

Net Proceeds

net proceeds
Funds actually received from the sale of a security.

flotation costs
The total costs of issuing and selling a security.

discounts
Reductions in the price of the security that are required to sell this security to investors.

As discussed in Chapter 5, bonds are sold in the primary market of the capital market by using an underwriter (investment dealer). The **net proceeds** from the sale of a bond, or any security, are the funds that are actually received from the sale. There are two types of costs that can be incurred when selling financial securities. Both of these costs reduce the net proceeds from the sale of a security. The first is **flotation costs**—the total costs of issuing and selling a security—which reduce the net proceeds from the sale. These costs apply to all public offerings of securities—debt, preferred shares, and common shares. They include two components: (1) *underwriting costs*—compensation earned by investment bankers for selling the security—and (2) *administrative costs*—issuer expenses such as legal, accounting, printing, and other expenses.

The second cost is **discounts** to the price of the security that are required to sell the security to investors. Discounts from par value generally only apply to long-term debt. Discounts to the current share price apply to the sale of new common shares.

Why might discounts occur? For bonds, a discount might occur due to changes in market yields. Between the time the lead underwriter(s) and the company issuing the bond settle on a coupon rate on the bond issue (as provided in the final prospectus), and the time the bonds are actually sold to investors, a few days can elapse. In that period, yields in the market will fluctuate. For example, assume the coupon rate on an issue of bonds is set at 6.6 percent. After setting this rate, and before the bonds are sold, yields in the market for bonds of comparable risk increase to 6.7 percent.

As a result, investors planning to buy the bonds may change their minds. Why accept a return of 6.6 percent on a new issue when you can buy an existing issue with the same risk and receive a 6.7 percent return? If enough investors think like this, the company will not be able to sell the issue. So to sell, the bond will have to be discounted. The discount might be 1 or 2 percent of the par value, $10 or $20. In such case, each bond will still have a $1,000 par value, but the investors will not pay $1,000, nor will the company receive $1,000. Note that yields in the market might also fall between the time the coupon rate is set and before the bonds are sold. In that case, the bond could be sold for a premium. The premium will offset some or all of the flotation costs.

For preferred shares, similar outcomes are possible; however, selling preferred shares at a discount or premium is quite rare. For common shares, it is usual for the new issues of shares to be sold at a discount to the market price of the shares currently trading on the stock exchange. As discussed in Chapter 5, this is due to investors recognizing the possible dilutive effect of the new share issue.

Example ▼ Duchess Corporation, a major hardware manufacturer, is contemplating selling $10 million worth of 20-year bonds with a 9 percent coupon rate. The coupons are paid semiannually. Because similar-risk bonds are yielding slightly more than 9 percent, the firm must discount each $1,000 of par value of the bonds by $15, selling them for $985 to compensate for the lower coupon rate. In addition, the flotation costs are 2.5 percent of the par value of the bond (2.5% × $1,000), or $25 per bond. The net proceeds to the firm from the sale of each $1,000 of par value are therefore $960 ($985 − $25). ▲

Before-Tax Cost of Debt

The before-tax cost of debt, k_d, for a bond can be obtained in one of three ways—by market quotes, by using a financial calculator, or by approximation.

Using Market Quotes

Hint
From the issuer's perspective, the IRR on a bond's cash flows is its *cost to maturity;* from the investor's perspective, the IRR on a bond's cash flows is its *yield to maturity (YTM)*, as explained in Chapter 8. These two measures are conceptually similar, although their point of view is different.

When the net proceeds from sale of a bond equal its par value, the before-tax cost would just equal the coupon rate. For example, a bond with a 10 percent coupon rate that sells for $1,000 would have a before-tax cost, k_d, of 10 percent.

A market quote will provide the *yield to maturity (YTM)* (see Chapters 5 and 8) on a similar-risk bond.[4] For example, if a similar-risk bond, as measured by the bond rating and time to maturity, is quoted in the market as having a YTM of 9.7 percent, this value can be used as the before-tax cost of debt, k_d.

Calculating the Cost

In the above example, the cost of debt is not calculated, it is provided by the quote. If a cost must be calculated, we will use an approach that is based on the method illustrated in Chapter 8 for yield to maturity. But here, we wish to determine the cost to maturity of the cash flows associated with the debt. The calculation is based on the following equation where we solve for the before-tax cost of debt:

$$N_d = [I \times PVIFa\ (k_d, n \text{ per})] + [M \times PVIF\ (k_d, n \text{ per})] \tag{9.2}$$

where:

N_d = proceeds received from the long-term debt issue
I = semiannual coupon payments in dollars
n = number of periods to maturity
k_d = before-tax cost of debt
M = par value in dollars

From the issuer's point of view, we wish to calculate the cost to maturity (k_d). The value calculated using Equation 9.2 represents the semiannual before-tax percentage cost of the debt.

Example ▼ In the preceding example, the net proceeds for Duchess Corporation from the sale of each $1,000 of par value of the 20-year bond with a 9 percent coupon rate paid semiannually was $960. To determine the annual cost we use Equation 9.2, but the cash flow pattern is the opposite of the pattern from an investor's perspective. It consists of an initial inflow (the net proceeds) followed by a series of annual outlays (the coupon payments). In the final year, when the debt issue is retired, an outlay representing the repayment of the principal also occurs. The cash flows associated with $1,000 of par value Duchess Corporation bonds are as follows:

Period(s)	Cash flow
0	$ 960
1–40	−$ 45
40	−$1,000

4. Generally, the yield to maturity of bonds with a similar bond rating and time to maturity is used. Bond ratings, which are published by independent agencies, were discussed in Chapters 5 and 8.

The initial \$960 inflow is followed by the semiannual outflows of \$45 [(9% coupon rate × \$1,000 par value)/2] over the 20-year life of the bond. In period 40 (end of year 20), an outflow of \$1,000 (the repayment of the principal) occurs. The before-tax cost of debt can be determined by finding the discount rate that equates the present value of the outflows with the initial inflow as follows:

$$\$960 = [\$45 \times PVIFa\ (k_d, 40 \text{ per})] + [\$1{,}000 \times PVIF\ (k, 40 \text{ per})]$$

We can solve this equation by using a financial calculator. Recall from Chapter 8 that we input values for the four variables and then solve for the interest variable, which in this case is the before-tax cost of debt. We must also remember to input the present value (net proceeds) as a negative number as illustrated below:

Inputs:	40	-960	45	1000		
Functions:	N	PV	PMT	FV	CPT	I
Outputs:						4.724

Using the above process, the before-tax cost of the bond issue appears to be 4.724 percent. But recall that this is on a semiannual basis. Multiplying this answer by 2 means the cost to maturity of the bond issue is 9.45 percent.

If you did not have a financial calculator, you could approximate the before-tax cost of debt, k_d, for \$1,000 of par value of a bond issue by using the following equation:

$$k_d = \left[\frac{I + \dfrac{\$1{,}000 - N_d}{n}}{\dfrac{N_d + \$1{,}000}{2}}\right] \times 2 \qquad (9.3)$$

Example Substituting the appropriate values from the Duchess Corporation example into the approximation formula given in Equation 9.3, we get:

$$k_d = \left[\frac{\$45 + \dfrac{\$1{,}000 - \$960}{40}}{\dfrac{\$960 + \$1{,}000}{2}}\right] \times 2 = \left[\frac{\$45 + \$1}{\$980}\right] \times 2$$

$$= \frac{\$46}{\$980} \times 2 = 4.694 \times 2 = \underline{\underline{9.39\%}}$$

This approximate before-tax cost of debt does not differ greatly from the 9.45 percent value determined when using the calculator.

After-Tax Cost of Debt

As indicated earlier, the *specific cost* of financing must be stated on an after-tax basis. Because interest on debt is tax-deductible, it reduces the firm's taxable income. The interest deduction therefore reduces taxes by an amount equal to the product of the deductible interest and the firm's tax rate. In light of this, the after-tax cost of debt, k_{dt}, can be found by multiplying the before-tax cost, k_d, by 1 minus the tax rate, T, as stated in the following equation:

$$k_{dt} = k_d \times (1 - T) \tag{9.4}$$

Example We can demonstrate the after-tax debt cost calculation using the 9.45 percent before-tax debt cost calculated for Duchess Corporation. Assume the company's tax rate is 40 percent. Applying Equation 9.4 results in an after-tax cost of debt of 5.67 percent [9.45% × (1 − 0.40)].

The after-tax cost of long-term debt is less than the cost of any of the alternative forms of long-term financing for two reasons. First, long-term debt is the most secure source of financing, since investors have the power to bankrupt the firm if interest payments are missed. Therefore, investors' required return on this financial security is the lowest. Second, as shown above, interest payments are tax-deductible, lowering the cost even further. Therefore, the cost of debt to a company is the lowest of the three sources of financing.

? Review Questions

9–6 What is meant by the *net proceeds* from the sale of a bond? What costs can be incurred when selling financial securities, and how do they affect a bond's net proceeds?

9–7 Describe how to calculate the before-tax cost of debt. How does this calculation relate to a bond's *cost to maturity*?

9–8 How is the before-tax cost of debt converted into the after-tax cost? Why is the after-tax cost of debt the appropriate cost to use?

LG3

9.3 The Cost of Preferred Equity

Preferred equity represents a special type of ownership interest in the firm. It gives preferred shareholders the right to receive their *stated* dividends before any earnings can be distributed to common shareholders. Because preferred shares are a form of ownership, the proceeds from their sale are expected to be held for an infinite period of time. The key characteristics of preferred shares were described in Chapter 5.

Briefly, preferred shares are sold for their stated value. The main reason investors buy preferred shares is for the dividend. Dividends are stated either as a dollar amount, which is the amount paid each year, or as a percentage rate. If shown as a percent, the rate is a percent of the stated value. For instance, a preferred share with a $50 stated value and an 8 percent dividend would be expected to pay an annual dividend of $4 a share (0.08 × $50 stated value = $4). Before the cost of preferred equity is calculated, any dividends stated as percentages should be converted to annual dollar dividends.

Calculating the Cost of Preferred Equity

cost of preferred equity, k_p
The relationship between the cost of the preferred equity and the amount of funds provided by the preferred share issue; found by dividing the annual dividend, D_t, by the net proceeds from the sale of the preferred share, N_p.

The **cost of preferred equity, k_p,** is the cost of a new issue of preferred shares. Remember, cost of capital is a marginal analysis so we are not concerned with the historic cost of preferred equity, but rather the cost the firm would incur *today* if a new issue of preferred shares were sold to investors. This cost is the ratio of the annual dividend paid on the preferred share divided by the net proceeds per share from the sale of the preferred shares. The net proceeds represent the amount of money to be received minus any flotation costs. Equation 9.5 gives the cost of preferred equity, k_p, in terms of the annual dollar dividend, D_t, and the net proceeds from the sale of the shares, N_p:

$$k_p = \frac{D_t}{N_p} \tag{9.5}$$

Since dividends are paid out of after-tax income, a tax adjustment is not required; the cost of equity securities is already after-tax.

Example If Duchess Corporation decide to raise financing using preferred shares, they plan to sell an issue with a \$25 stated value. Preferred shares with a comparable rating as Duchess are currently yielding 10 percent in the market. This then would be the annual dividend rate the company would have to provide on the issue. Flotation costs are expected to be 5.6 percent of the stated value. To determine the cost of preferred equity to Duchess, use Equation 9.5 as follows:

$$k_p = \frac{\$25 \times 10\%}{\$25 - (\$25 \times 5.6\%)}$$

$$= \frac{\$2.50}{\$25 - \$1.40}$$

$$= \frac{\$2.50}{\$23.60}$$

$$= 10.59\%$$

Note that the dollar amount of the annual dividend is based on the stated value and the dividend rate. The net proceeds are found by subtracting the flotation costs from the stated value. Given the above values, the cost of preferred equity is 10.59 percent. The cost of preferred equity is higher than the cost of long-term debt (5.67%) due to the two reasons discussed earlier: interest is tax-deductible and, from an investor's perspective, debt is less risky than preferred equity.

? Review Question

9–9 How is the cost of preferred equity calculated? Why do we concern ourselves with the net proceeds from the sale of the shares instead of its sale price (stated value)? Why is the cost of preferred equity higher than that of long-term debt?

9.4 The Cost of Common Equity

The *cost of common equity* is the return required on a company's common equity by investors in the financial marketplace. There are two forms of common equity financing: (1) reinvested profits and (2) new issues of common shares. The cost of the two sources of common equity financing is based on the concepts associated with calculating the general cost of common equity. Therefore, first consider the following general discussion concerning the cost of common equity.

Finding the Cost of Common Equity

cost of common equity, k_s
The expected return investors require to hold the common shares of a company.

The **cost of common equity, k_s**, is the return investors require to hold the common shares of a company. As discussed in Chapter 8, there are two techniques used to determine investors' required rate of return on common equity: the constant-growth dividend valuation model (DVM) and the capital asset pricing model (CAPM).

Using the Constant-Growth Dividend Valuation Model (DVM)

constant-growth dividend valuation (Gordon) model
Assumes that the value of a common share equals the present value of all future dividends (assumed to grow at a constant rate) that it is expected to provide over an infinite time horizon.

The **constant-growth dividend valuation model (DVM)**—the **Gordon model**—was presented in Chapter 8. It is based on the widely accepted premise that the value of a common share is equal to the present value of all future dividends (assumed to grow at a constant rate) over an infinite time horizon. The key expression, derived in Chapter 8, is restated below as Equation 9.6:

$$V_0 = \frac{D_1}{k_s - g} \tag{9.6}$$

where:

V_0 = value of a common share
D_1 = per share dividend expected at the end of year 1
k_s = investors' required return on common equity
g = constant rate of growth in dividends

If it were assumed the market is efficient, the value of the common share (V_0) will be equal to the market price of the share (P_0). This means that investors' required and expected returns are equal, $k_s = \hat{k}_s$. If this were the case, Equation 9.6 could be rewritten to solve for the cost of common equity as follows:

$$k_s = \frac{D_1}{P_0} + g \tag{9.7}$$

Equation 9.7 indicates that the cost of common equity can be found by dividing the dividend expected during the upcoming year by the current common share price and adding the expected growth rate. Remember, g represents the expected growth in DPS, EPS, and the price of the common shares. Because common share dividends are paid from *after-tax* income, no tax adjustment is required.

Example ▼ Duchess Corporation wishes to determine its cost of common equity, k_s. The market price, P_0, of its common stock is $50 per share. The dividends per share (DPS) paid on the common shares over the past 6 years (2003–2008) are provided below. It is believed that the growth experienced over these six years is representative of the growth expected in the future.

Year	DPS
2003	$1.19
2004	1.30
2005	1.42
2006	1.55
2007	1.69
2008	1.83

Using a financial calculator, in conjunction with the technique described for finding growth rates in Chapters 6 and 8, we can calculate the annual growth rate of dividends, g. It turns out to be 9 percent (more precisely, it is 8.9885%). To calculate the cost of common equity we need D_1. The DPS expected in 2009 is based on the DPS actually paid in 2008 ($1.83) increased by the expected rate of growth (9%). Therefore, the DPS in 2009 is expected to be:

$$\begin{aligned} D_1 &= D_0\,(1 + g) \\ &= \$1.83\,(1 + 0.09) \\ &= \$1.83\,(1.09) \\ &= \$1.9947 \text{ (rounded up to \$2)} \end{aligned}$$

Substituting $D_1 = \$2$, $P_0 = \$50$, and $g = 9\%$ into Equation 9.7 results in the cost of common equity for Duchess Corporation of:

$$\begin{aligned} k_s &= \frac{\$2}{\$50} + 9\% \\ &= 4\% + 9\% = 13.0\% \end{aligned}$$

The 13.0 percent cost of common equity represents the return required by *existing* common shareholders. If Duchess achieves this return on the common equity financing used for its investment projects in 2009, what happens? If investors purchase the shares now for $50 each, and the company does pay the $2.00 DPS in 2009, investors will receive a 4 percent yield. In addition, investors are expecting growth in share price to be 9 percent. If this is achieved, the shares will increase in value by $4.50 ($50 × 9%), and will close the year at $54.50 per share. Therefore, shareholders will receive their required rate of return. Companies must view the common equity financing that is invested in assets as having a cost. The cost is investors' required return. ▲

Using the Capital Asset Pricing Model (CAPM)

capital asset pricing model (CAPM) Calculates investors' required return on common equity based on the risk-free rate of return plus the asset risk premium.

The **capital asset pricing model (CAPM)** was developed and discussed in Chapter 7. It calculates investors' required return on common equity based on the risk-free rate of return (R_F) plus the asset risk premium (RP). The asset risk premium is based on the market risk premium adjusted for the nondiversifiable risk of the firm as measured by beta, β. This is shown as Equation 9.8. Investors taking more risk, as measured by beta, will be compensated with higher rates of returns. The CAPM also calculates the company's cost of common equity.

$$k_s = R_F + [\beta \times (k_m - R_F)] \tag{9.8}$$

where:

R_F = risk-free rate of return
k_m = market return; return on the market portfolio of assets

Example Duchess Corporation now wishes to calculate its cost of common equity, k_s, by using the capital asset pricing model. The firm's investment advisors and its own analyses indicate that the risk-free rate, R_F, equals 7 percent; the firm's beta, β, equals 1.5; and the market return, k_m, equals 11 percent. By substituting these values into Equation 9.8, the company estimates the cost of common equity, k_s, as follows:

$$k_s = 7.0\% + [1.5 \times (11.0\% - 7.0\%)] = 7.0\% + 6.0\% = \underline{\underline{13.0\%}}$$

The 13.0 percent cost of common stock equity, which is the same as that found by using the constant growth DVM, represents investors' required return on Duchess Corporation's common shares.[5]

Comparing the Constant-Growth DVM and CAPM Techniques

Use of CAPM differs from the constant-growth DVM in that it directly considers the firm's risk, as reflected by beta, in determining the *required* return or cost of common equity. The constant-growth DVM does not look at risk; it uses the market price, P_0, as a reflection of the *expected* risk–return preference of investors in the marketplace. The constant-growth DVM and CAPM techniques for finding k_s are, in a practical sense, theoretically equivalent. But it is difficult to demonstrate that equivalency, due to measurement problems associated with growth, beta, the risk-free rate, and the market return. The use of the constant-growth DVM is often preferred because the data required are more readily available.

Note though that the constant-growth DVM cannot be used for companies that do not pay dividends or for companies that do not have a history of stable dividend payments. The vast majority of companies that trade on the Toronto Stock Exchange fall into one of these two categories. Also, the CAPM has a stronger theoretical foundation than the DVM, though the computational appeal of the constant-growth DVM explains its widespread use. Therefore, those wishing to calculate the cost of common equity (or the equivalent concept of investors' required rate of return) must know and be able to use both of the techniques described above.

The Cost of Reinvested Profits

Reinvested profits are the amount of money remaining after a company pays common share dividends from the earnings available for common shareholders. Recall from Chapter 2 that all earnings remaining after the payment of preferred

5. In reality, it is unusual for the cost of common equity calculated using the two techniques to be equal. The cost of common equity calculated using the DVM is usually different from the cost calculated using the CAPM.

Hint
Using reinvested profits as a major source of financing for capital expenditures does not give away control of the firm and does not dilute present earnings per share, as would occur if new common shares were issued. However, the firm must effectively manage reinvested profits, in order to produce returns that increase future earnings.

share dividends belong to the common shareholders. A company can pay all, or a portion, of these earnings to common shareholders who can then decide how to use the cash. Alternatively, the company could decide to retain all of these earnings for corporate purposes. By retaining the earnings, the company is using common shareholders' funds.

Common shareholders will not provide this money free of charge. Common shareholders expect the company will invest their funds to earn the shareholders' required rate of return. If the company invests the funds and earns, at minimum, shareholders' required return, the price of the common shares will increase. If the company invests the funds and earns less than the shareholders' required return, the common share price may decline or may not increase the required percentage. In either case, shareholders will be disappointed. Reinvested profits are not free. These funds have a cost, which is common shareholders' required rate of return. This is the cost of common equity calculated above. Therefore, the **cost of reinvested profits, k_r,** is equal to the cost of common equity, k_s, as follows:

cost of reinvested profits, k_r
Since reinvested profits are common shareholders' money, these funds have a cost which is the cost of common equity, k_s.

$$k_r = k_s \tag{9.9}$$

It is not necessary to adjust the cost of reinvested profits for flotation costs, because by retaining earnings, the firm "raises" equity capital without incurring these costs.

Example The cost of reinvested profits for Duchess Corporation was actually calculated in the preceding examples: It is equal to the cost of common equity. Thus, k_r equals 13.0 percent. As with preferred equity, a tax adjustment is not required. The cost of equity securities is already after-tax. As we will show in the next section, the cost of reinvested profits is always lower than the cost of a new issue of common shares, due to the absence of flotation costs.

The Cost of New Issues of Common Shares

Our purpose in finding the firm's overall cost of capital is to determine the after-tax cost of *new* funds required for financing projects. Attention must therefore be given to the cost of a new issue of common shares, k_n. As will be explained later, this cost is important only when there are insufficient reinvested profits available to provide the equity portion of the financing required for investment projects.

cost of a new issue of common shares, k_n
The cost of common shares, net of discounts and associated flotation costs.

discounted
Sold at a price below current market price, P_0.

The **cost of a new issue of common shares, k_n,** is determined by calculating the cost of common shares, net of discounts and associated flotation costs. Normally, to sell a new issue, it will have to be **discounted**—sold at a price below the current market price, P_0. Firms underprice new issues for a variety of reasons. First, when the market is in equilibrium (i.e., the demand for shares equals the supply of shares), additional demand for shares can be achieved only at a lower price.

Second, when additional shares are issued, each share's percent of ownership in the firm is diluted, thereby justifying a lower share value. Third, many investors view the issuance of additional shares as a signal that management is selling additional common shares because it believes that the shares are currently overpriced. Therefore, investors will buy shares only at a price below the current market price. Clearly, these and other factors necessitate discounting new offerings of common shares. Flotation costs paid for issuing and selling the new issue will further reduce proceeds.

The cost of new issues can be calculated using the constant-growth DVM expression for the cost of existing common shares, k_s, as a starting point. If we let

N_n represent the net proceeds from the sale of new common shares after subtracting the discount and flotation costs, the cost of the new issue, k_n, can be expressed as follows:[6]

$$k_n = \frac{D_1}{N_n} + g \tag{9.10}$$

The CAPM can also be used to determine the cost of a new issue of common shares. Since the company will be receiving less than the full proceeds from the sale of new common shares, the company will have to generate a higher return on the net proceeds in order to meet investors' required rate of return. This requirement increases the risk associated with the financing raised through the sale of common shares. This increased risk will increase the cost of new common shares, k_n, expressed, for the CAPM, as follows:

$$k_n = R_F + \left[(k_m - R_F) \times \beta \times \frac{P_0}{N_n}\right] \tag{9.11}$$

The net proceeds from sale of new common shares, N_n, is always less than the current market price, P_0. Therefore, for both methods of calculating the cost of common equity, the cost of new issues, k_n, will always be greater than the cost of reinvested profits, k_r. *The cost of new common shares is greater than the cost of any other long-term source of financing.*

Example ▼ For Duchess Corporation, the cost of common equity, k_s, using both the constant-growth DVM and the CAPM, was 13 percent. This is the cost of reinvested profits, k_r.

To determine the cost of *new* common shares, k_n, Duchess Corporation has estimated that new shares can be sold for $48.50. The $1.50 discount to the current price of $50 is necessary due to the dilution of earnings per share that will occur when new common shares are sold. Prospective purchasers of new common shares expect to pay less than the current market price for new common shares. A second cost associated with a new issue is flotation costs of $4 per share that would be paid to issue and sell the new issue. Therefore, the total of the discount and of flotation costs is expected to be $5.50 per share.

Subtracting the $5.50 per share from the current $50 share price, P_0, results in expected net proceeds, N_n, of $44.50 per share ($50 − $5.50). Substituting the appropriate amounts in Equation 9.10 results in a cost of new common shares using the constant-growth DVM as follows:

$$k_n = \frac{\$2}{\$44.50} + 9\%$$

$$= 4.5\% + 9\% = 13.5\%$$

6. An alternative, but computationally less straightforward, form of this equation is

$$k_n = \frac{D_1}{P_0 \times (1 - f)} + g \tag{9.10a}$$

where f represents the *percentage* reduction in current market price expected as a result of discounting and flotation costs. Simply stated, N_n in Equation 9.10 is equivalent to $P_0 \times (1 - f)$ in Equation 9.10a. For convenience, Equation 9.10 is used to define the cost of a new issue of common shares, k_n.

Substituting the appropriate amounts into Equation 9.11 results in a cost of new common shares using the CAPM as follows:

$$k_n = 7\% + \left[(11\% - 7\%) \times 1.5 \times \frac{\$50}{\$44.50}\right]$$
$$= 7\% + 6.7\% = 13.7\%$$

The two techniques yield very similar results, so the average of the two, 13.6 percent, will be used to calculate Duchess Corporation's cost of capital.

Other Techniques to Determine the Cost of Equity

The sections above discussed the two usual methods that are used to estimate the cost of common equity for a firm. However, there are other techniques that can be used. First is the "bond yield plus a premium" approach. Here, the cost of common equity is estimated by adding a risk premium to the firm's cost of long-term debt. Depending on the risk of the company, the premium might be low, say 5 to 8 percent, or quite high. Depending on the risk of the company, premiums of up to three times the cost of long-term debt are possible.

Second, the firm's normalized return on equity (ROE) might be used as a basis for the cost of common equity for the firm. Recall that ROE provides the return common shareholders receive given their investment in the firm. It is calculated as follows:

$$\text{ROE} = \frac{\text{earnings available to common shareholders}}{\text{common equity}}$$

An average of a company's ROE over a normalized operating cycle may provide a good estimate of the company's cost of common equity. If a firm generates an average ROE of 21.3 percent over a ten-year operating cycle, this might be a good approximation of the "true" cost of common equity.

Third, venture capitalists provide equity financing to firms that are viewed as "promising." When venture capitalists provide equity financing, they do so in the expectation that they will receive a significant return on the investment. This is because studies show that of every ten investments made by venture capitalists, three are writeoffs, meaning almost everything invested is lost, four are essentially breakeven propositions, while the final three make large returns to compensate for the other seven. Although it would vary across venture capitalist firms, it is believed that the required return sought by these investors would approach 25 to 45 percent depending on the company. This may be a basis for setting the cost of common equity for a firm. The implication of using this figure is that if venture capitalists seek this rate of return, why wouldn't the other equity investors in the company?

Depending on the situation, one or more of these more subjective techniques might be used together with the more theoretically based techniques discussed earlier. An interesting application of the various methods used to estimate the cost of common equity for regulated Canadian railway companies is available on the Web.

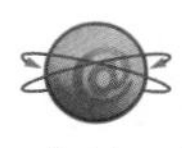

www.cta-otc.gc.ca/rulings-decisions/decisions/2004/R/52-R-2004_e.html

? Review Questions

9–10 How can the cost of common equity be calculated? What are the equations used and what do each of the components of the equations represent?
9–11 Why do reinvested profits have a cost? Why shouldn't a company view reinvested profits as a free, internally generated source of funds?
9–12 Why do new issues of common shares have a different cost than reinvested profits? Is the cost higher or lower, and why?
9–13 Discuss some of the other techniques that can be used to estimate a company's cost of equity.

9.5 The Weighted Average Cost of Capital (WACC)

weighted average cost of capital (WACC), k_a
Reflects the expected cost of funds for the upcoming year; found by weighting the cost of each specific type of capital by its proportion in the firm's capital structure.

Now that we have reviewed methods for calculating the cost of specific sources of financing, we can present techniques for determining the overall cost of capital. As noted earlier, the **weighted average cost of capital (WACC), k_a,** reflects the expected cost of funds for the upcoming year. It is found by weighting the cost of each specific type of capital by its proportion in the firm's optimal capital structure.

Calculating the Weighted Average Cost of Capital (WACC)

The calculation of the weighted average cost of capital (WACC) is performed by multiplying the specific cost of each form of financing by its proportion in the firm's optimal capital structure and summing the weighted values. As an equation, the weighted average cost of capital, k_a, can be specified as follows:

$$k_a = (w_d \times k_{dt}) + (w_p \times k_p) + (w_s \times k_{r \text{ or } n}) \tag{9.12}$$

where:

$$\begin{aligned} w_d &= \text{proportion of long-term debt in capital structure} \\ w_p &= \text{proportion of preferred equity in capital structure} \\ w_s &= \text{proportion of common equity in capital structure} \\ w_d + w_p + w_s &= 1.0 \end{aligned}$$

Three important points should be noted in Equation 9.12:

1. For computational convenience, it is best to convert the weights to decimal form and leave the specific costs in percentage terms.
2. *The sum of weights must equal 1.0.* Simply stated, all capital structure components must be accounted for.
3. The firm's common equity weight, w_s, is multiplied by either the cost of reinvested profits, k_r, or the cost of new common shares, k_n. Which cost is used depends on whether the firm's reinvested profits have been fully used for investment purposes.

Example In earlier examples, we found the costs of the various types of capital for Duchess Corporation to be as follows:

After-tax cost of debt,	k_{dt} = 5.67%, say 5.7%
Cost of preferred equity,	k_p = 10.59%, say 10.6%
Cost of reinvested profits,	k_r = 13.0%
Cost of new common shares,	k_n = 13.6%

We shall assume that Duchess Corporation's optimal capital structure (OCS) is:

Source of capital	OCS weight
Long-term debt	40%
Preferred equity	10
Common equity	50
Total	100%

For the upcoming year, Duchess is expected to generate net income of \$550,000, of which \$300,000 will be reinvested. So, in the initial calculation of cost of capital, the 13 percent cost is used as the cost of common equity. Since reinvested profits are generated internally and have a lower cost than a new issue of common shares, it is *always* assumed that reinvested profits will provide the first wave of common equity financing.

Duchess Corporation's weighted average cost of capital is calculated in Table 9.2. The resulting weighted average cost of capital for Duchess is 9.9 percent. Given the analysis to this point and assuming an unchanged risk level, the firm should accept all projects that will earn a return greater than or equal to 9.9 percent. This is the case, since the cost of the funds used to finance investment projects is 9.9 percent. A project *must* be expected, at least, to return its cost of financing. In essence, the 9.9 percent is Duchess's required return on investment in assets.

Weighting Schemes

For the OCS, weights can be calculated based on *book value* or on *market value* and using *historic* or *target* proportions.

Hint For computational convenience, the financing proportion weights are listed in decimal form in column 1 and the specific costs are shown in percentage terms in column 2.

TABLE 9.2 Calculation of the Weighted Average Cost of Capital for Duchess Corporation

Source of capital	Weight (1)	Cost (2)	Weighted cost [(1) × (2)] (3)
Long-term debt	0.40	5.7%	2.3%
Preferred equity	0.10	10.6	1.1
Common equity	0.50	13.0	6.5
Totals	1.00		9.9%

Weighted average cost of capital = 9.9%

Book Value Versus Market Value

book value weights
Weights that use accounting values to measure the proportion of each type of capital in the firm's financial structure.

market value weights
Weights that use market values to measure the proportion of each type of capital in the firm's financial structure.

Book value weights use accounting values to measure the proportion of each type of capital in the firm's financial structure. **Market value weights** measure the proportion of each type of capital at its market value. Market value weights are appealing, because the market values of securities closely approximate the actual dollars to be received from their sale. Moreover, because the costs of the various types of capital are calculated by using prevailing market prices, it seems reasonable to use market value weights. In addition, the long-term investment cash flows to which the cost of capital is applied are estimated in terms of current as well as future market values. *Market value weights are clearly preferred over book value weights.*

Historic Versus Target

historic weights
Either book or market value weights based on *actual* capital structure proportions.

Historic weights can be either book or market value weights based on *actual* capital structure proportions. For example, past or current book value proportions would constitute a form of historic weighting, as would past or current market

9.1 IN PRACTICE

The Cost of Capital at Brookfield Asset Management

Brookfield Asset Management is a diversified asset manager with holdings in four core businesses: real estate, power generation, timber and infrastructure, and financial services. For the fiscal year ended December 31, 2005, Brookfield had total sales of $5.2 billion, net income after tax of $1.7 billion, and total assets under management of $50 billion. In their annual report, Brookfield provides their cost of capital, discusses in detail the factors affecting the cost of capital, and illustrates why it is important for the company to know and control the cost. The information provided in the annual report is summarized below.

www.brookfield.com

Brookfield is focused on maximizing the value of existing operations by actively managing assets to create operating efficiencies, lower its cost of capital, and enhance cash flows. The company has been successful in decreasing its overall weighted average cost of capital (WACC) in recent years. In 2003, it was decreased to 9.5 percent and it has remained at this level in 2004 and 2005. This assumed a 21 percent return objective for common equity. In other words, Brookfield assumed investors' required return on common equity was 21 percent. On a book value basis, Brookfield's capital structure in 2005 consisted of 42 percent debt, 18.5 percent preferred shares, and 39.5 percent common equity.

The strength of the company's capital structure is that it enables them to achieve a low cost of capital for shareholders and, at the same time, provide the company with the flexibility to react quickly to potential investment opportunities. The objective is to maintain a strong and flexible capitalization structure made up largely of long-term financing and permanent equity. They believe this is the most appropriate method of financing long-term assets. The high quality of the assets and the associated cash flows enable the company to raise long-term financing in a cost-effective way.

▶

(Continued)

Brookfield makes judicious use of debt and preferred equity to enhance returns to common shareholders. The access to a broad range of financing, including preferred equity issued over many years principally in the form of perpetual preferred shares, lowers the company's cost of capital. They arrange their financing to maintain strong investment grade ratings, which lower their cost of borrowing and broaden the company's access to capital. Brookfield also endeavours to minimize liquidity and refinancing risks to the company by issuing long-dated securities and spreading out maturities. They feel that they have a lower WACC than other companies and that this creates a significant strategic and competitive advantage for the company.

Since 2003, Brookfield has been locking in longer-term fixed rates and closing out floating rate swap positions. Despite increased carrying charges, this is expected to provide greater stability and a lower cost of capital over the long term. In 2005, the average cost of term debt was 7 percent with an average term to maturity of 12 years. This was a large increase over the average nine-year term in 2004. In addition, further progress was made in lowering the cost of capital when DBRS upgraded Brookfield's credit ratings to A (low). This broadened the company's access to financial markets, allowing them to prudently leverage common shareholders' equity.

Through the continuous monitoring of the balance between debt and equity financing, the company strives to reduce their WACC on a risk-averse basis, thereby improving common shareholder returns. This seemed to work in 2005. Investors recognized the strength of Brookfield's cash flows and the fact that they were backed by long-term contracts. This led to a 40 percent increase in the company's common share price during the year.

SOURCES: Adapted from information taken from the 2005 annual report of Brookfield Asset Management, available at **www.brookfield.com**.

value proportions. Such a weighting scheme would therefore be based on real—rather than desired—proportions.

target weights
Either book or market value weights based on *optimal* capital structure proportions.

Target weights, which can also be based on either book or market values, reflect the firm's *optimal* capital structure proportions. Firms using target weights establish such proportions on the basis of the "optimal" capital structure they wish to achieve. The development of these proportions and the optimal structure was discussed earlier in the chapter and will be considered again in Chapter 10.

When one considers the somewhat approximate nature of the weighted average cost of capital calculation, the choice of weights may not be critical. However, from a strictly theoretical point of view, the *preferred weighting scheme is target market value proportions,* and these are assumed throughout this chapter.

? Review Question

9–14 What is the *weighted average cost of capital (WACC),* and how is it calculated? Describe the logic underlying the use of *target capital structure weights,* and compare and contrast this approach with the use of *historic weights.*

9.6 The Marginal Cost and Investment Decisions

The firm's weighted average cost of capital is a key input to the investment decision-making process. As demonstrated earlier in the chapter, the firm should accept only those investments for which the expected return is equal to or greater than the weighted average cost of capital. Of course, at any given time, the firm's financing costs and investment returns will be affected by the volume of financing and investment undertaken. The concepts of a *marginal cost of capital* and an *investment opportunities schedule* provide the mechanisms whereby financing and investment decisions can be made simultaneously. In addition, the firm may wish to calculate a single overall cost of capital to make investment decisions, and this process is also discussed in this section.

The Marginal Cost of Capital (MCC)

The weighted average cost of capital may vary at any time depending on the volume of financing the firm plans to raise. *As the volume of financing increases, the costs of the various types of financing will increase, raising the firm's weighted average cost of capital.* Therefore, it is useful to calculate the **marginal cost of capital (MCC)**, which is simply the firm's weighted average cost of capital associated with its *next dollar* of total new financing. This marginal cost is relevant to decisions regarding investment projects.

marginal cost of capital (MCC)
The firm's average cost of capital associated with its *next dollar* of total new financing.

Because the costs of the financing components—debt, preferred equity, and common equity—rise as larger amounts are raised, the MCC is an increasing function of the level of total new financing. Increases in the component financing costs occur because the larger the amount of new financing, the greater the risk to the funds supplier. Funds suppliers require greater returns in the form of interest, dividends, or growth as compensation for the increased risk introduced as larger volumes of *new* financing are undertaken.

Another factor that causes the weighted average cost of capital to increase is that once the amount of reinvested profits used to finance investment projects is exhausted, higher-cost new common share issues must be used to raise the assumed dollar amount of common equity financing. This will result in a higher MCC.

Finding Break Points

To calculate the MCC, we must calculate the **break points,** which reflect the level of new financing at which the cost of one of the financing components rises. The following general equation can be used to find break points:

break point
The level of new financing at which the cost of one of the financing components rises, thereby causing an upward shift in the *marginal cost of capital (MCC).*

$$BP_j = \frac{AF_j}{w_j} \tag{9.13}$$

where:

BP_j = break point for financing source j
AF_j = amount of funds available from financing source j at a given cost
w_j = capital structure weight (historic or target, stated in decimal form) for financing source j

A key assumption of Equation 9.13 is that a company will raise the financing used to fund investment projects in the optimal capital structure percentages. While this assumption is vital for calculating the weighted average cost of capital, it is not necessary for a company actually to do this. This was discussed and illustrated earlier in the chapter. There we saw that as long as Okotoks Oil maintained a debt ratio in the range of between 35 and 55 percent, the cost of capital remained in the 13.5 percent range. So, while we assume financing is raised in the OCS weights, it is not necessary for the company to *actually* do so.

Example When Duchess Corporation exhausts its $300,000 of available reinvested profits with a cost of 13 percent (k_r = 13.0%), it must use the more expensive new common share financing with a cost of 13.6 percent (k_n = 13.6%) to meet its common equity needs. In addition, the firm expects that it can borrow only $400,000 of debt at the 5.6 percent cost; additional debt will have an after-tax cost (k_{dt}) of 8.4 percent. Two break points therefore exist—(1) when the $300,000 of reinvested profits costing 13.0 percent is exhausted and (2) when the $400,000 of long-term debt costing 5.6 percent is exhausted.

The break points can be found by substituting these values and the corresponding capital structure weights given earlier into Equation 9.13. We get:

$$BP_{\text{common equity}} = \frac{\$300{,}000}{0.50} = \$600{,}000$$

$$BP_{\text{long-term debt}} = \frac{\$400{,}000}{0.40} = \$1{,}000{,}000$$

If Duchess raised $600,000 of financing, the assumption made is that it is raised in the optimal capital structure (OCS) weights. So, 40 percent or $240,000 is assumed to come from issuing long-term debt; 10 percent or $60,000 from selling preferred shares; and 50 percent or $300,000 from common equity. The $300,000 of common equity financing is reinvested profits. If Duchess raised one additional dollar of financing beyond $600,000, the assumption is that 40 percent will be long-term debt, 10 percent is preferred shares, and 50 percent is common equity. The 50 percent of common equity must be new common shares since once $600,000 of financing is raised, reinvested profits are exhausted.

At $1,000,000 of financing, the same assumption applies. So, 40 percent or $400,000 is long-term debt, 10 percent or $100,000 is preferred equity, and 50 percent or $500,000 is common equity. For common equity, the first $300,000 is reinvested profits; the other $200,000 is raised from selling new common shares.

If Duchess raises one more dollar of financing beyond $1,000,000, then it is assumed that 40 percent comes from long-term debt, 10 percent from preferred shares, and 50 percent from common equity. The 40 percent of long-term debt will be the higher-cost debt, with an after-tax cost of 8.4 percent. The cost of the 10 percent preferred equity will remain the same, in this case 10.6 percent. The 50 percent of common equity must come from the sale of new shares with a cost of 13.6 percent. These assumptions are reflected when calculating the WACC and MCC.

Calculating the MCC

Once the break points have been determined, the next step is to calculate the weighted average cost of capital over the range of total new financing between break points. First, we find the WACC for a level of total new financing between $1 and the first break point. Next, we find the MCC for a level of total new financing between the first and second break points, and so on. By definition, for each of the ranges of total new financing between break points, certain component capital costs will increase, causing the weighted average cost of capital to increase to a higher level than that over the preceding range.

marginal cost of capital (MCC) schedule
Graph that relates the firm's weighted average cost of capital to the level of total new financing.

Together, these data can be used to prepare the **marginal cost of capital (MCC) schedule,** which is a graph that relates the firm's weighted average cost of capital to the level of total new financing.

Example Table 9.3 summarizes the calculation of the WACC for Duchess Corporation over the three financing ranges created by the two break points—$600,000 and $1,000,000. Comparing the costs in column 3 of the table for each of the three ranges, we can see that the costs in the first range ($1 to $600,000) are those calculated in earlier examples and used in Table 9.2. The second range ($600,001 to $1,000,000) reflects the increase in the common equity cost to 13.6 percent. In the final range (above $1,000,001) the increase in the long-term debt cost to 8.4 percent is introduced.

The weighted average costs of capital (WACC) for the three ranges created by the two break points are summarized in the table shown at the bottom of Figure 9.2. These data describe the marginal cost of capital (MCC), which increases as levels of total new financing increase. Figure 9.2 presents the MCC schedule. Again, it is clear that the MCC is an increasing function of the amount of total new financing raised.

TABLE 9.3 Weighted Average Cost of Capital for Ranges of Total New Financing for Duchess Corporation

Range of total new financing	Source of capital (1)	Weight (2)	Cost (3)	Weighted cost [(2) × (3)] (4)
$1 to $600,000	Debt	0.40	5.7%	2.3%
	Preferred	0.10	10.6	1.1
	Common	0.50	13.0	6.5
		Weighted average cost of capital		9.9%
$600,001 to $1,000,000	Debt	0.40	5.7%	2.3%
	Preferred	0.10	10.6	1.1
	Common	0.50	13.6	6.8
		Weighted average cost of capital		10.2%
$1,000,001 and above	Debt	0.40	8.4%	3.4%
	Preferred	0.10	10.6	1.1
	Common	0.50	13.6	6.8
		Weighted average cost of capital		11.3%

The Investment Opportunities Schedule (IOS)

investment opportunities schedule (IOS) A ranking of investment possibilities from best (highest return) to worst (lowest return).

At any given time, a firm has certain investment opportunities available to it. These opportunities differ with respect to the size of investment and return.[7] The firm's **investment opportunities schedule (IOS)** is a ranking of investment possibilities from best (highest return) to worst (lowest return). As the cumulative amount of money invested in a firm's investment projects increases, the return (IRR) on the projects will decrease; generally, the first project selected will have the highest return, the next project the second-highest, and so on. In other words, the return on investments will *decrease* as the firm accepts additional projects.

Example Duchess Corporation's current investment opportunities schedule (IOS) lists the best (highest return) to the worst (lowest return) investment possibilities in column 1 of Table 9.4. Column 2 of the table shows the initial investment required by each project. Column 3 shows the cumulative total invested funds required to finance all projects better than and including the corresponding investment opportunity. Plotting the expected returns of the projects against the cumulative investment (column 1 against column 3 in Table 9.4) and the MCC for the various financing ranges (as in Figure 9.2) results in the firm's investment opportunities schedule (IOS). A graph of the IOS for Duchess Corporation is given in Figure 9.3. Use of the IOS along with the MCC in decision making is discussed in the following section.

FIGURE 9.2

MCC Schedule

Marginal cost of capital (MCC) schedule for Duchess Corporation

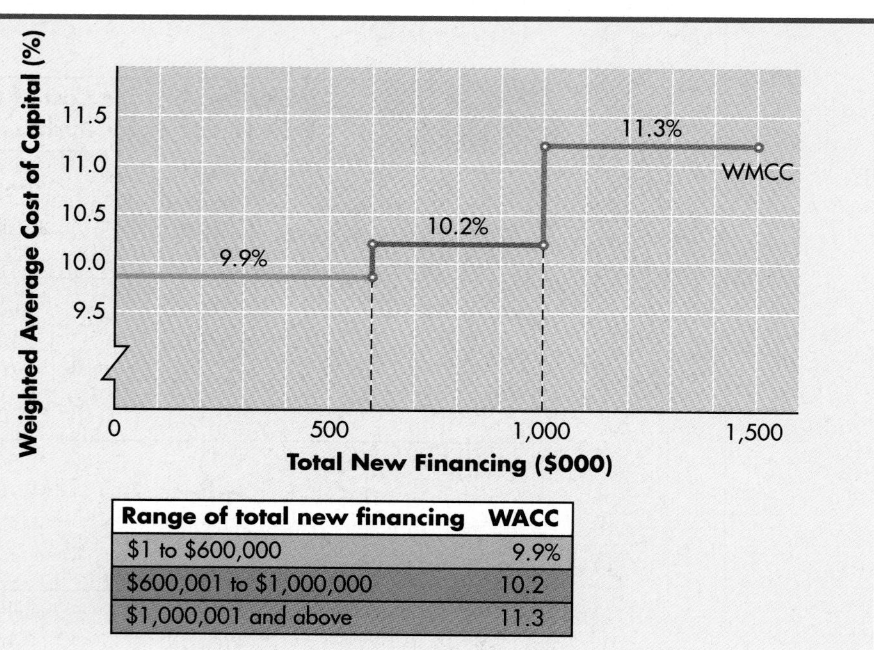

Range of total new financing	WACC
$1 to $600,000	9.9%
$600,001 to $1,000,000	10.2
$1,000,001 and above	11.3

7. Because the calculated weighted average cost of capital does not apply to risk-changing investments, we assume that all opportunities have risk equal to that of the firm. This assumption will be relaxed in Chapter 13.

TABLE 9.4 Investment Opportunities Schedule (IOS) for Duchess Corporation

Investment opportunity	Expected return (IRR) (1)	Initial investment (2)	Cumulative investment[a] (3)
A	15.0%	$100,000	$ 100,000
B	14.5	200,000	300,000
C	14.0	400,000	700,000
D	13.0	100,000	800,000
E	12.0	300,000	1,100,000
F	11.0	200,000	1,300,000
G	10.0	100,000	1,400,000

[a]The cumulative investment represents the total amount invested in projects with higher returns plus the investment required for the given investment opportunity.

Using the MCC and IOS to Make Financing/ Investment Decisions

As long as a project's expected return (internal rate of return) is equal to or greater than the marginal cost of new financing, the firm should accept the project. The return will decrease with the acceptance of more projects, and the weighted marginal cost of capital will increase because greater amounts of financing will be required. The firm would therefore *accept projects up to the point at which the marginal return on its investment equals its marginal cost of capital.* Beyond that point, the investment project's expected return will be less than the cost of capital—the project's required return.

This approach is consistent with the maximization of shareholder wealth. The acceptance of investment projects, beginning with those having the largest positive difference between expected return (IRR) and MCC and declining to the point where the IRR of a project is equal to the MCC, should result in the maximum total value for all investment projects accepted. Such an outcome is completely consistent with the firm's goal of owner wealth maximization. Returning to the Duchess Corporation example, we can demonstrate this procedure.

Example Figure 9.3 shows the Duchess Corporation's MCC schedule and IOS on the same set of axes. By using these two functions in combination, the firm's optimal capital budget ("X" in the figure) is determined. By raising $1.1 million of new financing and investing these funds in projects A, B, C, D, and E, the firm should maximize the wealth of its owners, because these projects result in the maximum total value. Note that the 12.0 percent return on the last dollar invested (in project E) *exceeds* its 11.3 percent weighted average cost; investment in project F is not feasible because its 11.0 percent return is *less than* the 11.3 percent cost of funds available for investment.

Note that at the point at which the IRR equals the weighted average cost of capital, k_a—the optimal capital budget of $1,100,000 at point X in Figure 9.3—

FIGURE 9.3

IOS and MCC Schedules
Using the IOS and MCC to select projects

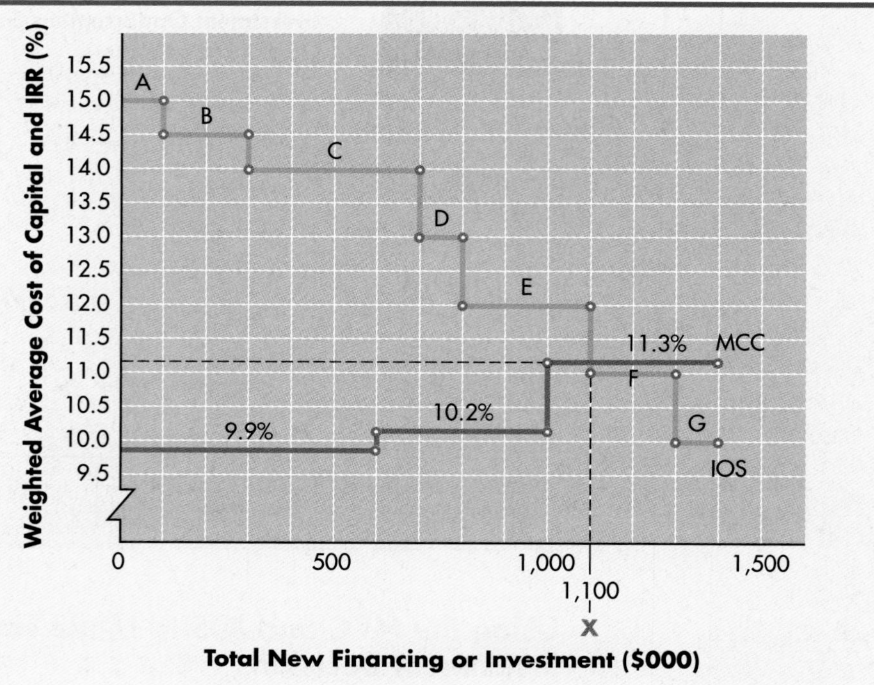

the firm's size, in terms of assets, and its market value will be maximized. In a sense, the size of the firm is determined by the market—the availability of and returns on investment opportunities, and the availability and cost of financing.

Of course, as will be discussed in Chapter 13, all companies will have a limited amount of funds to invest in projects. This situation is referred to as *capital rationing*. Management usually imposes an internal capital expenditure (and therefore financing) budget constraint that is below the optimum capital budget (where expected return = k_a). Suffice it to say that due to capital rationing, a gap frequently exists between the theoretically optimal capital budget and the firm's actual level of financing/investment.

Calculating the Overall Cost of Capital

In the Brookfield Asset Management reading, we saw that the company had a single cost of capital: 9.5 percent. But for Duchess, we have three costs. While this is theoretically correct, it might be more appealing to a company to have a single cost of capital. In addition, reconsider Table 9.4 and Figure 9.3. Here we see that projects F and G were not acceptable. But, if projects F and G were considered first and not last, they would both be acceptable. In other words, if the seven investment opportunities were ranked from lowest to highest return, and put on Figure 9.3 in that order, all would be acceptable.

Therefore, these two issues lead us to present an alternative approach to making the investment decisions: calculate a single overall cost of capital. To do so, reconsider the range of total new financing and the costs shown at the bottom of Figure 9.2. If we weight the range by the total financing raised and multiply this by the cost of capital for that range, we can calculate a single overall cost of capital. We will apply this to Duchess Corporation below.

Example The value of the investment opportunities available to Duchess total \$1.4 million. Given this total possible investment, and the cost of capital and marginal costs of capital provided in Table 9.3, the company's overall cost of capital is:

$$\text{Overall } k_a = \frac{\$600{,}000}{\$1{,}400{,}000}(9.9\%) + \frac{\$400{,}000}{\$1{,}400{,}000}(10.2\%) + \frac{\$400{,}000}{\$1{,}400{,}000}(11.3\%)$$
$$= 4.24\% \quad + 2.91\% \quad + 3.23\%$$
$$= 10.38\%$$

With an overall cost of capital of 10.38 percent, which projects should Duchess select? All but project G. Why? Projects A to F all have expected returns greater than 10.38 percent, while project G's expected return is less. When project G is eliminated as an investment opportunity, we can recalculate the company's overall cost of capital.

$$\text{Overall } k_a = \frac{\$600{,}000}{\$1{,}300{,}000}(9.9\%) + \frac{\$400{,}000}{\$1{,}300{,}000}(10.2\%) + \frac{\$300{,}000}{\$1{,}300{,}000}(11.3\%)$$
$$= 4.57\% \quad + 3.14\% \quad + 2.61\%$$
$$= 10.32\%$$

The company's overall cost of capital is 10.32 percent. The firm will raise \$1.3 million and the overall cost of these funds will be 10.32 percent. The company will proceed with projects A to F requiring total investment of \$1.3 million. All projects are expected to provide a return greater than the cost of financing. As a result, all providers of financing will receive their required returns.

Note that this decision regarding the choice of investment projects differs from the one that used the investment opportunities schedule. Which decision is correct? We will go with the overall cost of capital approach. Using a single cost of capital is intuitively appealing and reflects current practice in the corporate world. Therefore, it is recommended that Duchess Corporation invest in projects A to F.

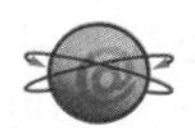

http://pages.stern.nyu.edu/~adamodar/New_Home_Page/datafile/wacc.html

The cost of capital for more than 7,100 real-world companies is provided on the Web.

? Review Questions

9–15 What is the *marginal cost of capital (MCC)*? What does the *MCC schedule* represent? Why does this schedule increase?

9–16 What is the *investment opportunities schedule (IOS)*? Is it typically depicted as an increasing or decreasing function of the level of investment at a given point in time? Why?

9–17 Use a graph to show how the MCC schedule and the IOS can be used to find the level of financing/investment that maximizes owner wealth. Why, on a practical basis, do many firms finance/invest at a level below this optimum?

9–18 Discuss the process of calculating the overall cost of capital for a company. Why is this approach more appealing to use versus the investment opportunities schedule?

SUMMARY

LG1 **Understand the basic assumptions, concept, and specific sources of capital underlying the cost of capital.** The cost of capital is the rate of return that a firm must earn on its investments to maintain its market value and attract needed funds. The specific costs of the basic sources of capital (long-term debt, preferred equity, and common equity) can be calculated individually. Only the cost of debt must be adjusted for taxes. The cost of each is affected by business and financial risks, which are assumed to be unchanged, and by the risk-free cost of the type of financing. All firms have an optimal capital structure (OCS), the mix of debt and equity financing that results in the lowest possible cost of capital. This is also the point where the value of the firm is maximized. This is the ideal mix of financing and, for cost of capital purposes, the way it is assumed the firm raises financing for all projects. But, as long as the capital structure remains in a stated range, the cost of capital remains fairly stable. So, for cost-of-capital purposes, while we assume financing is raised in the OCS weights, it is not necessary for the company to *actually* do so. To capture the interrelatedness of financing, a weighted average cost of capital should be used.

LG2 **Determine the cost of long-term debt and the cost of preferred equity.** The cost of long-term debt is the after-tax cost today of raising long-term funds through borrowing. The cost can be determined by using market quotes for bonds of similar risk as measured by the bond rating and time to maturity. The cost can also be calculated using a financial calculator or it can be approximated. The after-tax cost of debt is the rate used for cost-of-capital purposes. The cost of preferred equity is the stated annual dividend expressed as a percentage of the net proceeds from the sale of preferred shares. The key variable definitions and formulas for the before- and after-tax cost of debt and the cost of preferred equity are given in Table 9.5.

LG3 **Calculate the cost of common equity, recognizing that there are two sources of common equity financing: reinvested profits and the sale of new common shares.** The cost of common equity can be calculated by using the constant-growth dividend valuation model (DVM) or the capital asset pricing model (CAPM). The cost of reinvested profits is equal to the cost of common equity. An adjustment in the cost of common equity to reflect discounting and flotation cost is required to find the cost of new issues of common shares. The key variable definitions and formulas for the cost of common equity, the cost of reinvested profits, and the cost of new issues of common shares are given in Table 9.5. Three other techniques can also be used to estimate the cost of equity: the bond yield plus a premium approach, the firm's normalized return on equity (ROE), or the return required by venture capitalists.

LG4 **Find the weighted average cost of capital (WACC) and discuss the alternative weighting schemes.** The firm's WACC reflects the expected cost of funds for the upcoming year. It can be determined by combining the costs of specific types of capital after weighting each cost using historical book or market value weights, or target book or market value weights. The theoretically preferred approach uses target weights based on market values. The key variable definitions and formula for WACC are given in Table 9.5.

LG5 **Describe the rationale for and procedures used to determine break points and the marginal cost of capital (MCC).** A firm's MCC reflects the fact that as the dollar amount of total new financing increases, the costs of the various types of financing will increase, raising the firm's WACC. Break points, which are found by dividing the amount of funds available from a given financing source by its capital structure weight, represent the level of new financing at which the cost of one of the financing components rises, causing an upward shift in the MCC. The MCC is the firm's WACC associated with its next dollar of new financing. The MCC schedule relates the WACC to each level of total new financing.

LG6 **Explain how the marginal cost of capital (MCC) can be used to make the firm's financing/investment decisions.** The investment opportunities schedule (IOS) presents a ranking of currently available investments from those with the highest returns to those with the lowest returns. It is used in combination with the MCC to find the level of financing/investment that maximizes owners' wealth. With this approach, the firm accepts projects up to the point at which the marginal return on its investment equals its weighted marginal cost of capital.

An alternative approach is to calculate a single overall cost of capital for a company. To do so, we weight each range of financing by the total financing raised and multiply this by the cost of capital for that range.

TABLE 9.5 Summary of Key Definitions and Formulas for Cost of Capital

Variable definitions

AF_j = amount of funds available from financing source j at a given cost

β = beta coefficient or measure of nondiversifiable risk

BP_j = break point for financing source j

D_1 = per share dividend expected at the end of year 1

D_t = annual preferred share dividend (in dollars)

g = constant rate of growth in dividends

I = interest paid on a bond (in dollars)

k_a = weighted average cost of capital

k_d = before-tax cost of debt

k_{dt} = after-tax cost of debt

k_m = return on the market portfolio

k_n = cost of a new issue of common shares

k_p = cost of preferred equity

k_r = cost of reinvested profits

k_s = required return on common equity

n = number of years to the bond's maturity

N_d = net proceeds from the sale of debt (bond)

N_n = net proceeds from the sale of new common shares

N_p = net proceeds from the sale of preferred shares

R_F = risk-free rate of return

T = firm's tax rate

V_0 = value of common shares

w_d = proportion of long-term debt in capital structure

w_j = capital structure proportion (historic or target, stated in decimal form) for financing source j

w_p = proportion of preferred equity in capital structure

w_s = proportion of common equity in capital structure

Cost of capital formulas

Before-tax cost of debt:

$$N_d = [I \times PVIFa\ (k_d, n \text{ per})] + [M \times PVIF\ (k_d, n \text{ per})] \quad \text{[Eq. 9.2]}$$

After-tax cost of debt:

$$k_{dt} = k_d \times (1 - T) \quad \text{[Eq. 9.4]}$$

Cost of preferred equity:

$$k_p = \frac{D_t}{N_p} \quad \text{[Eq. 9.5]}$$

Cost of common equity:

Using constant-growth DVM:

$$k_s = \frac{D_1}{P_0} + g \quad \text{[Eq. 9.7]}$$

Using CAPM:

$$k_s = R_F + [\beta \times (k_m - R_F)] \quad \text{[Eq. 9.8]}$$

Cost of reinvested profits:

$$k_r = k_s \quad \text{[Eq. 9.9]}$$

Cost of new issue of common shares (DVM):

$$k_n = \frac{D_1}{N_n} + g \quad \text{[Eq. 9.10]}$$

Cost of new issue of common shares (CAPM):

$$k_n = R_F + \left[(k_m - R_F) \times \beta \times \frac{P_0}{N_n}\right] \quad \text{[Eq. 9.11]}$$

Weighted average cost of capital (WACC):

$$k_a = (w_d \times k_{dt}) + (w_p \times k_p) + (w_s \times k_{r \text{ or } n}) \quad \text{[Eq. 9.12]}$$

Break point:

$$BP_j = \frac{AF_j}{w_j} \quad \text{[Eq. 9.13]}$$

SELF-TEST PROBLEMS

(Solutions in Appendix B)

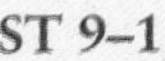

ST 9–1 **Specific costs, WACC, MCC, and overall cost of capital** Humble Manufacturing is interested in measuring its overall cost of capital for the fiscal year that is about to begin. Current investigation has gathered the following data. The firm's tax rate is 40 percent.

Debt The firm can raise sufficient debt for their financing opportunities for the year. The firm is planning to sell 10-year bonds, with a 10 percent coupon rate. The coupons are paid semiannually. To sell the issue, each $1,000 of par value will have to be discounted by $15 per bond. In addition, flotation costs of $35 per bond will also have to be paid.

Preferred equity Humble can sell sufficient preferred shares for their financing opportunities for the year. The shares could have any stated value the company desires. Preferred shares with a comparable risk rating as Humble are currently yielding 11 percent in the market. Flotation costs are expected to be 4 percent of the stated value.

Common equity The firm expects to have $225,000 of reinvested profits available in the coming year. The firm's common shares currently sell for $80 per share. The most recent dividend paid by the firm on the common shares was $5.66 per share. The firm's dividends have been growing at an annual rate of 6 percent, and this rate is expected to continue in the future. The common shares will have to be discounted by $2.50 per share, and flotation costs are expected to amount to $5.50 per share. The firm can sell as many common shares as they require under these terms.

a. Calculate the specific cost of each source of financing. (Round to the nearest 0.1 percent.)

b. The firm's optimal capital structure is provided in the following table.

Source of capital	Weight
Long-term debt	40%
Preferred equity	15
Common equity	45
Total	100%

(1) Calculate the single break point associated with the firm's financial situation. (*Hint:* This point results from using all of the reinvested profits.)

(2) Calculate the weighted average cost of capital for new financing of between $1 and the amount calculated in (1).

(3) Calculate the marginal cost of capital for new financing above the break point calculated in (1).

c. Using the results of **b**, together with the information shown in the following table on the available investment opportunities, determine Humble's overall cost of capital.

Investment opportunity	Expected return	Initial investment
A	11.2%	$100,000
B	9.7	500,000
C	12.9	150,000
D	16.5	200,000
E	11.8	450,000
F	10.1	600,000
G	10.5	300,000

d. Which, if any, of the available investments do you recommend that the firm accept? Explain your answer. How much total new financing is required? What is the cost of this financing? Why is knowing the cost important?

Note: While the solution for this problem is provided in Appendix A, it is also displayed as Spreadsheet Application 9.2 (see next page).

PROBLEMS

BASIC 

9–1 Cost of debt—Risk premiums Mulberry Printing's cost of long-term debt last year was 10 percent. This rate was attributable to a 7 percent risk-free cost of long-term debt, a 2 percent business risk premium, and a 1 percent financial risk premium. The firm currently wishes to obtain a long-term loan.

a. If the firm's business and financial risk are unchanged from the previous period and the risk-free cost of long-term debt is now 8 percent, at what rate would you expect the firm to obtain a long-term loan?

b. If, as a result of borrowing, the firm's financial risk will increase enough to raise the financial risk premium to 3 percent, how much would you expect the firm's borrowing cost to be?

c. One of the firm's competitors has a 1 percent business risk premium and a 2 percent financial risk premium. What is that firm's cost of long-term debt likely to be?

9–2 Concept of cost of capital Wren Manufacturing is in the process of analyzing its investment decision-making procedures. The two projects evaluated by the firm during the past month were projects 263 and 264. The basic variables for each project and the resulting decision actions are summarized in the following table.

Basic variables	Project 263	Project 264
Cost	$64,000	$58,000
Life	15 years	15 years
Expected return (IRR)	8%	15%
Least-cost financing		
Source	Debt	Equity
Cost (after-tax)	7%	16%
Decision		
Action	Accept	Reject
Reason	8% IRR > 7% cost	15% IRR < 16% cost

9.2 SPREADSHEET APPLICATION

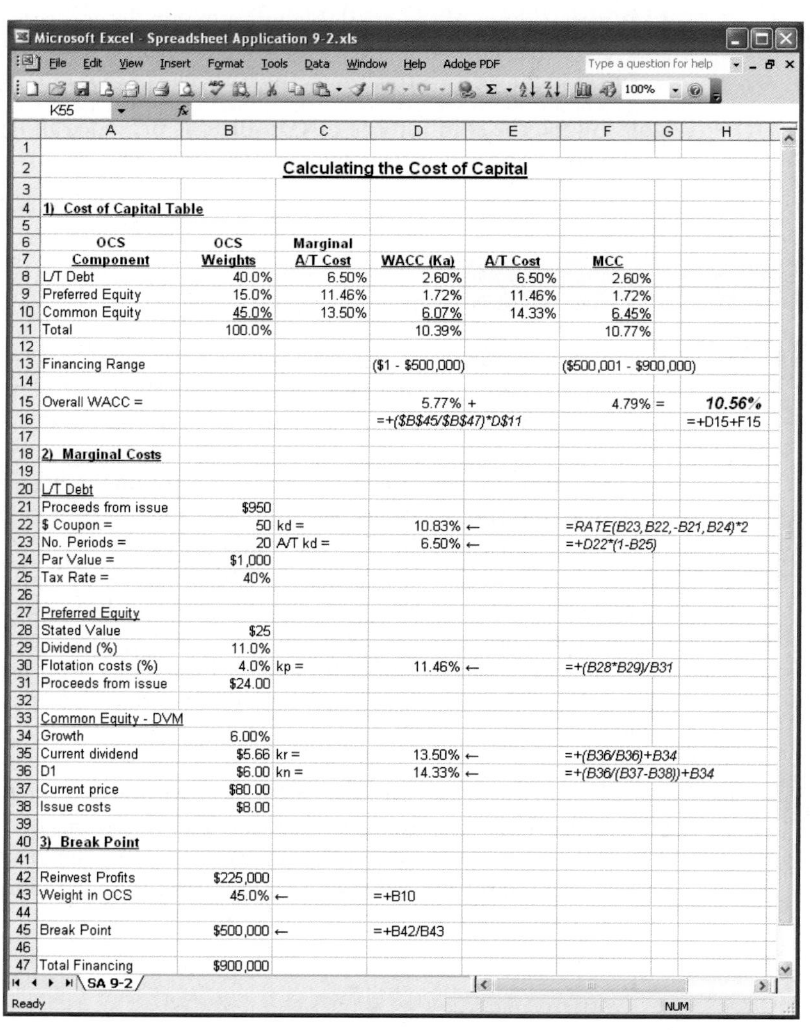

Microsoft Excel - Spreadsheet Application 9-2.xls

	A	B	C	D	E	F	G	H
1								
2			Calculating the Cost of Capital					
3								
4	1) Cost of Capital Table							
5								
6	OCS	OCS	Marginal					
7	Component	Weights	A/T Cost	WACC (Ka)	A/T Cost	MCC		
8	L/T Debt	40.0%	6.50%	2.60%	6.50%	2.60%		
9	Preferred Equity	15.0%	11.46%	1.72%	11.46%	1.72%		
10	Common Equity	45.0%	13.50%	6.07%	14.33%	6.45%		
11	Total	100.0%		10.39%		10.77%		
12								
13	Financing Range			($1 - $500,000)		($500,001 - $900,000)		
14								
15	Overall WACC =			5.77%	+	4.79%	=	10.56%
16				=+($B$45/$B$47)*D$11				=+D15+F15
17								
18	2) Marginal Costs							
19								
20	L/T Debt							
21	Proceeds from issue	$950						
22	$ Coupon =	50	kd =	10.83%	←	=RATE(B23,B22,-B21,B24)*2		
23	No. Periods =	20	A/T kd =	6.50%	←	=+D22*(1-B25)		
24	Par Value =	$1,000						
25	Tax Rate =	40%						
26								
27	Preferred Equity							
28	Stated Value	$25						
29	Dividend (%)	11.0%						
30	Flotation costs (%)	4.0%	kp =	11.46%	←	=+(B28*B29)/B31		
31	Proceeds from issue	$24.00						
32								
33	Common Equity - DVM							
34	Growth	6.00%						
35	Current dividend	$5.66	kr =	13.50%	←	=+(B36/B36)+B34		
36	D1	$6.00	kn =	14.33%	←	=+(B36/(B37-B38))+B34		
37	Current price	$80.00						
38	Issue costs	$8.00						
39								
40	3) Break Point							
41								
42	Reinvest Profits	$225,000						
43	Weight in OCS	45.0%	←	=+B10				
44								
45	Break Point	$500,000	←	=+B42/B43				
46								
47	Total Financing	$900,000						

SA 9-2

a. Evaluate the firm's decision-making procedures, and explain why the acceptance of project 263 and rejection of project 264 may not be in the company's best interest.
b. If the firm's optimal capital structure is 40 percent debt and 60 percent equity, find the weighted average cost using the data in the table.
c. Had the firm used the weighted average cost calculated in **b**, what actions would have been taken relative to projects 263 and 264?
d. Compare and contrast the firm's actions with your findings in **c**. Which decision method seems more appropriate? Explain why. What assumption have you made when answering this question?

  9–3 **Cost of debt** Warren Industries can sell 15-year bonds, with a 12 percent coupon rate. The coupons are paid semiannually. As a result of changing market yields, the bonds can be sold for $1,010 per $1,000 of par value. Flotation costs of $30 per bond will have to be paid. The firm is in the 40 percent tax bracket.
a. Find the net proceeds from sale of the bond, N_d.
b. Show the cash flows from the firm's point of view over the maturity of the bond.
c. Calculate the before-tax and after-tax cost of debt using a financial calculator.
d. Estimate the before-tax and after-tax cost of debt using the *approximation formula*.
e. Compare and contrast the cost of debt calculated in **c** and **d**. Which approach is preferred? Why?

BASIC  9–4 **Cost of debt** For each of the following bonds, calculate the after-tax cost of debt. Assume the coupons are paid semiannually, that the tax rate is 40 percent, and that we are dealing with $1,000 of par value.

Bond	Life	Underwriting fee	Discount (−) or premium (+)	Coupon rate
A	20 years	$20	−$ 5	9%
B	16	4% of par	+ 10	10.4
C	15	3% of par	− 15	6.8
D	25	$15	None	9.3
E	22	2% of par	− 20	5.9

  9–5 **Cost of debt** Gronseth Drywall Systems, Inc., is in discussions with its investment banker regarding the issuance of new bonds. The investment banker has informed the firm that different maturities will carry different coupon rates and sell at different prices. The firm must choose among several alternatives. Calculate the after-tax cost of debt of each of the following alternatives assuming the coupons are paid semiannually, that the tax rate is 40 percent, that we are dealing with $1,000 of par value, and that flotation costs are 3 percent of par.

Alternative	Coupon rate	Time to maturity	Premium or discount
A	9%	16 years	$250
B	7	5	50
C	6	7	par
D	5	10	−75

BASIC LG2

9–6 Cost of preferred equity Taylor Systems has just issued preferred shares. The shares have a 12 percent annual dividend and a $100 stated value and were sold at $97.50 per share. In addition, flotation costs of $2.50 per share must be paid.

a. Calculate the cost of the preferred shares. What is the after-tax cost of the preferred shares?

b. If the firm sells the preferred stock with a 10 percent annual dividend and nets $90 after flotation costs, what is its cost?

BASIC LG2

9–7 Cost of preferred equity Determine the cost for each of the following preferred shares.

Preferred share	Stated value (SV)	Sale price	Flotation cost	Annual dividend
A	$100	$100	6.2% of SV	9.4%
B	50	48	$2.50	8.2%
C	25	25	4% of SV	$2.875
D	10	$10.50	5% of SV	6.75%
E	20	20	5.5% of SV	8.9%

BASIC LG3

9–8 Cost of common equity—CAPM J&M Corporation common shares have a beta, β, of 1.2. The risk-free rate is 6 percent, and the market return is 11 percent.

a. Determine the market risk premium.

b. Determine the risk premium on J&M's common shares.

c. Determine the required return that J&M common shares should provide.

d. Determine J&M's cost of common equity using the CAPM.

INTERMEDIATE 

9–9 Cost of common equity Ross Textiles wishes to estimate the company's cost of common equity. The firm's common shares are currently selling for $57.50. The dividends per share paid for the past 5 years are shown in the following table. It is believed that the growth experienced over these five years is representative of the growth expected in the future. On a sale of new common shares, Ross will have to discount the shares by $1.50, and flotation costs will be 6.5 percent of the selling price.

Year	DPS
2004	$2.11
2005	2.30
2006	2.60
2007	2.92
2008	3.09

a. Determine the growth rate of dividends.
b. Determine the DPS the firm will pay in 2009.
c. Determine the net proceeds, N_n, that the firm will receive from any sale of new common shares. How much are the flotation costs?
d. Using the constant-growth DVM, determine the cost of reinvested profits, k_r.
e. Using the constant-growth DVM, determine the cost of new common shares, k_n.
f. Explain why your answers to parts **d** and **e** are different. In a market where there are no costs of any type to issue securities, what would you expect your answers to be for parts **d** and **e**? Explain.

INTERMEDIATE  9–10 **Cost of reinvested profits versus new common shares—DVM** Using the data for each firm shown in the following table, calculate the cost of reinvested profits and the cost of new common shares using the constant-growth DVM.

Firm	Current market price per share	Dividend growth rate	Current dividend per share	Discount per share	Flotation cost per share
A	$52.00	8%	$2.25	$2.00	5% of selling price
B	20.00	4	1.00	0.50	1.50
C	42.50	6	2.00	1.00	6% of selling price
D	19.00	2	2.10	1.30	1.70

INTERMEDIATE  9–11 **Cost of reinvested profits and new common shares—CAPM** Using the data for each firm shown in the following table, calculate the cost of reinvested profits and new common shares using the CAPM.

Firm	Beta	Current market price per share	Risk-free rate	Market-risk premium	Total of discount and flotation costs
1	0.84	$15.40	3.2%	4.8%	$1.12
2	1.46	9.65	4.1	6.1	0.78
3	1.12	32.10	6.6	5.6	2.94
4	0.61	25.00	2.8	5.8	2.41

 BASIC 9–12 **The effect of tax rate on WACC** Equity Lighting Corp. wishes to explore the effect the corporate tax rate has on its cost of capital. The firm wishes to maintain a capital structure of 30 percent debt, 10 percent preferred equity, and 60 percent common equity. The cost of financing with reinvested profits is 14 percent, the cost of preferred equity financing is 9 percent, and the before-tax cost of debt financing is 11 percent. Calculate the weighted average cost of capital (WACC) given the tax rate assumptions in parts **a** to **c**.

a. Tax rate = 40 percent
b. Tax rate = 35 percent
c. Tax rate = 25 percent
d. Describe the relationship between changes in the rate of taxation and the weighted average cost of capital. Explain the relationship.

  CHALLENGE

9–13 **Calculating marginal costs** Magna Inc. is considering issuing $50 million of debentures for a term of 15 years. The DBRS has a rating of A (low) on Magna's debentures. MayBorder Ltd. has a bond issue outstanding that has 15 years to run to maturity. The bond has a coupon rate of 11 percent, paid semiannually, and is trading in the market for $116.289. The DBRS has a rating of A (low) on MayBorder's bond.

Magna's lead underwriter for the new debt issue knows that the current yield on MayBorder's bond will be the basis for setting the coupon rate on Magna's debt issue. But, since Magna is issuing a debenture while MayBorder's debt issue is a bond, the underwriter feels Magna will have to set a coupon rate that provides a 25-basis-point premium over the yield on the MayBorder's issue. With this coupon rate, the lead underwriter feels that the bonds will sell at a premium of $1,005 per $1,000 of par. The underwriter has also informed Magna that their fee for handling the transaction will be 2 percent of each $1,000 of par sold.

Magna is also considering raising $20 million by selling a new issue of preferred shares. The DBRS has a rating of Pfd-2 (high) on Magna's preferred shares. Petro-Canada's preferred shares are also rated Pfd-2 (high) by DBRS. Petro-Canada has a preferred share outstanding with a $25 stated value and a 7.75 percent dividend rate. The share is trading for $23.75. The current yield on Petro-Canada's preferreds will be the basis for setting the dividend rate on Magna's new issue of $25-stated-value preferreds. Flotation costs associated with a preferred share issue by Magna will be 2.2 percent of the stated value of the preferred share.

Magna's beta is 1.65 and the estimates for the average market return and t-bill rate are expected to be 14 percent and 7.5 percent, respectively. Magna's common shares are currently trading for $20.80 per share. Flotation costs on a sale of common shares will be 5 percent of the market price. In the latest fiscal year, Magna's earnings per share were $1.91 and dividends per share were $0.45. The company has 35 million common shares outstanding. Magna's tax rate is 38 percent.

a. What is the dollar amount of Magna's reinvested profits for the latest fiscal year?

b. What is Magna's cost of long-term debt, preferred equity, reinvested profits, and new common shares for cost-of-capital purposes? (*Note:* You do not have to calculate Magna's cost of capital.)

9–14 **WACC—Book weights** Ridge Tool has on its books the amounts and specific (after-tax) costs shown in the following table for each source of capital.

Source of capital	Book value	Specific cost
Long-term debt	$700,000	5.3%
Preferred equity	50,000	12.0
Common equity	650,000	16.0

a. Calculate the firm's weighted average cost of capital using book value weights.

b. Explain how the firm can use this cost in the investment decision-making process.

INTERMEDIATE  **9–15 WACC—Book weights and market weights** Webster Company has compiled the information shown in the following table.

Source of capital	Book value	Market value	After-tax cost
Long-term debt	$4,000,000	$3,840,000	6.0%
Preferred equity	40,000	60,000	13.0
Common equity	1,060,000	3,000,000	17.0
Total value	$5,100,000	$6,900,000	

a. Calculate the weighted average cost of capital using book value weights.
b. Calculate the weighted average cost of capital using market value weights.
c. Compare the answers obtained in **a** and **b**. Explain the differences.

INTERMEDIATE  **9–16 WACC and target weights** After careful analysis, Dexter Brothers has determined that its optimal capital structure is composed of the sources and target market value weights shown in the following table.

Source of capital	Target market value weight
Long-term debt	30%
Preferred equity	15
Common equity	55
Total	100%

The cost of debt is estimated to be 7.2 percent; the cost of preferred equity is estimated to be 13.5 percent; the cost of reinvested profits is estimated to be 16.0 percent; and the cost of new common shares is estimated to be 18.0 percent. All of these are after-tax rates. Currently, the company's debt represents 25 percent, preferred equity represents 10 percent, and common equity represents 65 percent of total capital based on the market values of the three components. The company expects to have a significant amount of reinvested profits available and does not expect to sell any new common shares.

a. Calculate the weighted average cost of capital based on historic market value weights.
b. Calculate the weighted average cost of capital based on target market value weights.
c. Explain the difference.

  CHALLENGE

9–17 Cost of capital and break point Edna Recording Studios, Inc., reported earnings available for common shareholders of $4,200,000 last year. From that, the company paid a dividend of $1.26 on each of its 1,000,000 common shares outstanding. The capital structure of the company is 40 percent debt, 10 percent preferred equity, and 50 percent common equity. The company's tax rate is 40 percent.

a. If the market price of the common shares is $40 and dividends are expected to grow at a rate of 6 percent a year for the foreseeable future, what is the company's cost of reinvested profits?

b. If flotation costs on new shares of common stock amount to $3.25 per share, what is the company's cost of financing with new common shares?

c. The company can issue preferred shares with a $25 stated value and a $2 dividend. Flotation costs would amount to $3 per share. What is the cost of preferred equity financing?

d. The company can issue 5-year bonds, with an 8.2 percent coupon rate. The coupons are paid semiannually. As a result of changing market yields, the bonds can be sold for $993.50 per $1,000 of par value. Flotation costs of $30 per bond will have to be paid. Calculate the after-tax cost of debt.

e. What is the maximum investment that Edna Recording can make in new projects before it must issue new common shares? Assume for the upcoming fiscal year, reinvested profits will increase by 7.5 percent from the level recorded the previous year.

f. What is the WACC for projects with a required investment of between $1 and the amount calculated in part e?

g. What is the MCC for projects with a required investment above the amount calculated in part e?

INTERMEDIATE

9–18 **Calculating WACC and MCC** A portion of Cognos Inc.'s balance sheet is presented below. During 2008, the company's earnings available to common shareholders were $843,000. The average dividend rate on the company's preferred shares is 11 percent and there are 20,000 shares outstanding. Cognos paid common share dividends of $1.23 per share in 2008. The cost of a new issue of mortgage bonds would be 12 percent. New preferred share financing would cost the company 8.82 percent. The company's cost of reinvested profits is 16 percent, while the cost of new common shares is 16.8 percent. Cognos' tax rate is 40 percent. In 2009, reinvested profits are expected to increase by 20 percent. Cognos plans to invest $5 million in assets during the 2009 fiscal year.

Portion of Balance Sheet
December 31, 2008

Mortgage bonds	$1,487,500
Preferred equity (20,000 shares)	427,000
Common shares (225,000 shares)	315,000
Retained earnings	1,270,500
Total	$3,500,000

a. Calculate Cognos Inc.'s net income after tax, and their reinvested profits in 2008.

b. Calculate the reinvested profits Cognos is expected to generate in 2009.

c. Determine the overall cost of capital the company should use to evaluate the planned asset acquisitions in 2009.

CHALLENGE  9–19 **Calculation of specific costs, WACC, and MCC** Dillon Labs has asked its financial manager to measure the cost of each specific type of capital as well as the weighted average cost of capital. The company's optimal capital structure is 40 percent long-term debt, 10 percent preferred equity, and 50 percent common equity. The firm's tax rate is 40 percent.

Debt The firm can sell a 10-year bond with a 9.8 percent coupon rate. The coupons are paid semiannually. As a result of changing market yields, the bonds can be sold for only $990 per $1,000 of par value. Flotation costs of 3.5 percent of par must be paid.

Preferred equity The company can sell preferred shares for any stated value the company desires. Preferred shares with a comparable risk rating as Dillon are currently yielding 8.5 percent in the market. Flotation costs of 5 percent of the stated value must be paid to their investment bankers.

Common equity The firm's common shares are currently selling for $50 per share. Dillon Labs' dividend payments, which have been approximately 60 percent of earnings per share in each of the past 5 years, are as shown in the following table.

Year	DPS
2004	$2.86
2005	3.15
2006	3.30
2007	3.50
2008	3.75

It is believed that the growth experienced over these five years is representative of the growth expected in the future. On a sale of new common shares, Dillon will have to discount the shares by $2.50, and flotation costs will be $3.00 per share.

a. Calculate the after-tax cost of each source of financing.

b. If earnings available for common shareholders are expected to be $7 million in 2009, what is the break point associated with reinvested profits?

c. Determine the weighted average cost of capital between $1 and the break point calculated in **b.**

d. Determine the weighted average cost of capital for one dollar of additional financing just beyond the break point calculated in **b.**

CHALLENGE  9–20 **Calculation of specific costs, WACC, and MCC** Lang Enterprises is interested in measuring its overall cost of capital. Current investigation has gathered the following data. The firm's tax rate is 40 percent.

Debt The firm can raise debt by selling 20-year bonds with an 8 percent coupon rate. The coupons are paid semiannually. As a result of a significant change in market yields, the bonds can only be sold for $970 per $1,000 of par value. Flotation costs of 3 percent of par must also be paid.

Preferred equity The company will sell preferred shares with a $25 stated value. Preferred shares of comparable risk are currently yielding 8.25 percent in the market. Flotation costs of 4.6 percent of the stated value must be paid.

Common equity The firm's common shares are currently selling for $90 per share. The firm paid a cash dividend of $6.60 per share this year. The firm's dividends have been growing at an annual rate of 6 percent, and this is expected to continue into the future. For a sale of new common shares, the shares would have to be discounted by $3 per share. Flotation costs would be $5 per share. Lang expects to have available $100,000 of reinvested profits in the coming year.

a. Calculate the specific cost of each source of financing. (Round answers to the nearest 0.1%.)
b. The firm's optimal capital structure is shown below. Calculate Lang's weighted average cost of capital. (Round answer to the nearest 0.1%.)

Source of capital	Weight
Long-term debt	30%
Preferred equity	20
Common equity	50
Total	100%

c. Calculate the single break point for Lang Enterprises for the coming year. For what financing range does the cost calculated in **b** apply?
d. Calculate the marginal cost of capital associated with one more dollar of financing above the break point calculated in **c**.
e. If Lang is planning to invest $600,000 in assets during the coming year, what is the company's overall cost of capital?

CHALLENGE

9–21 **WACC, MCC, and IOS** Cartwell Products has compiled the data shown in the following table for the current costs of its three sources of capital—long-term debt, preferred equity, and common equity—for various ranges of new financing.

Source of capital	Range of new financing	After-tax cost
Long-term debt	$1 to $320,000	6%
	$320,001 and above	8
Preferred equity	$1 and above	17%
Common equity	$1 to $200,000	20%
	$200,001 and above	24

The company's optimal capital structure, which is used to calculate the weighted average cost of capital, is shown in the following table.

Source of capital	Weight
Long-term debt	40%
Preferred equity	20
Common equity	40
Total	100%

a. Determine the break points and ranges of new financing associated with each source of capital. At what financing levels will Cartwell's weighted average cost of capital change?

b. Calculate the weighted average cost of capital for each range of total new financing found in **a.** (*Hint:* There are three ranges.)

c. Using the results of **b** along with the following information on the available investment opportunities, draw the firm's marginal cost of capital (MCC) schedule and investment opportunities schedule (IOS).

Investment opportunity	Expected return (IRR)	Initial investment
A	19%	$200,000
B	15	300,000
C	22	100,000
D	14	600,000
E	23	200,000
F	13	100,000
G	21	300,000
H	17	100,000
I	16	400,000

d. Which, if any, of the available investments do you recommend that the firm select? Explain your answer.

e. Now calculate the overall cost of capital for Cartwell Products. Which projects should the firm select? Does your answer differ from your answer to part **d**? If so, explain why.

LG5 LG6 INTERMEDIATE

9–22 WACC, MCC, and IOS Grainger Corp., a supplier of fitness equipment, is trying to decide which proposed projects in its investment opportunities schedule (IOS) it should undertake. The firm's cost of capital schedule and investment opportunities schedule are presented below:

Cost of capital schedule			
Range of new financing	**Source**	**Weight**	**After-tax cost**
$1–$600,000	Debt	0.50	6.3%
	Preferred equity	0.10	12.5
	Common equity	0.40	15.3
$600,001–$1,000,000	Debt	0.50	6.3%
	Preferred equity	0.10	12.5
	Common equity	0.40	16.4
$1,000,001 and above	Debt	0.50	7.8%
	Preferred equity	0.10	12.5
	Common equity	0.40	16.4

Investment opportunities schedule		
Investment opportunity	**Expected return**	**Cost**
Project H	14.5%	$200,000
Project G	13.0	700,000
Project K	12.8	500,000
Project M	11.4	600,000
Project E	10.5	400,000
Project P	11.6	460,000

a. Complete the cost of capital schedule by calculating the WACC and MCC for the various ranges of new financing.
b. Calculate the overall cost of capital for Grainger Corp. Which projects should the firm select? Explain why these projects are acceptable.

CHALLENGE

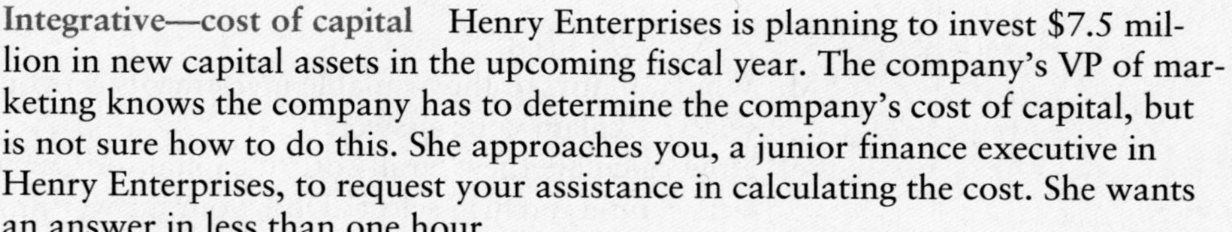
9–23 **Integrative—cost of capital** Henry Enterprises is planning to invest $7.5 million in new capital assets in the upcoming fiscal year. The company's VP of marketing knows the company has to determine the company's cost of capital, but is not sure how to do this. She approaches you, a junior finance executive in Henry Enterprises, to request your assistance in calculating the cost. She wants an answer in less than one hour.

Henry Enterprises has the following capital structure, which is viewed to be optimal:

Long-term debt (14% coupon, due in 15 years)	$25,000,000
Preferred shares (6% dividend, 25,000 shares outstanding)	2,500,000
Common shares (750,000 shares outstanding)	5,000,000
Retained earnings	7,500,000
Total capital	$40,000,000

Other information the marketing VP thought might be useful is provided below:

- The current bank prime rate is 8.0 percent.
- The yield on 3-month government of Canada t-bills is expected to be 7 percent.
- A new issue of long-term debt with a life of 25 years would require a coupon rate of 10 percent. The coupons are paid semiannually. For each $1,000 of par value, the bonds would be sold at a discount of 1.5 percent of par. Flotation costs would be another 1.5 percent of par.
- The current issue of preferred shares has a stated value of $100. A new issue of preferred shares would require a dividend of 8 percent. Flotation costs would be 4 percent of the stated value.
- The rate of return on the market portfolio is expected to average 14 percent over the immediate future.
- Henry Enterprises' beta, whatever that is, is thought to be 1.3.
- For the most recent fiscal year, Henry Enterprises' net income after tax was $2,025,000 and the company paid common share dividends of $1 per share.
- Henry's common shares are currently trading for $25 per share. A new share issue would be sold at a 2 percent discount to the current price and flotation costs would be $1 per share.
- For the upcoming fiscal year, Henry is expecting to grow their reinvested profits by 12 percent over the current year.
- The company's tax rate is 39 percent.

a. Calculate Henry Enterprises' overall cost of capital for the upcoming fiscal year. Explain to the VP of marketing what cost of capital is and how it would be used by the company.

b. Based on the above analysis, the VP of marketing is concerned that the company will reject launching a new product that was recently developed by the marketing department. Since Henry Enterprises can borrow at prime plus 50 basis points, she suggests that this rate be used to evaluate the proposed launch of the new product. Develop a detailed written response to the VP explaining your views on this suggestion.

   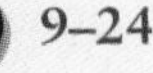

9–24 **Integrative—cost of capital** The following capital structure is taken from Bata Boots Co. balance sheet for the fiscal year ended April 30, 2008. This is considered the firm's optimal capital structure.

Mortgage bonds (due 2023)	$16,000,000
Debentures (due 2009)	12,000,000
Preferred share "A" (dividend 12%)	12,000,000
Preferred share "B" (dividend $1.80)	4,000,000
Common shares (3,600,000 outstanding)	8,000,000
Retained earnings	28,000,000
Total capital	$80,000,000

For the 2009 fiscal year, Bata Boots is evaluating three independent investment opportunities. The first (asset A) costs $9 million and is expected to provide a 14 percent rate of return. The second (asset B) costs $11.5 million and is expected to provide a 16.8 percent rate of return. The third (asset C) costs $17 million and is expected to provide a 13.4 percent rate of return.

The firm's president, Boots Bailey, wonders which of the three investment opportunities the firm should proceed with. He has been informed that determining the firm's after-tax cost of capital is the first step in making this decision. Boots has approached you with the following information to see if you can help him with his problem.

The company's common shares have been trading on the Toronto Stock Exchange for the past 28 years; the current price is $17.50 per share. Earnings per share for the previous ten years is provided below. Boots has suggested that the past ten years is not a representative time period to estimate future growth. Boots expects future growth will be only 75 percent of that experienced over the past ten years.

Year	EPS	Year	EPS
1999	$0.34	2004	$0.85
2000	0.41	2005	1.02
2001	0.50	2006	1.22
2002	0.59	2007	1.46
2003	0.71	2008	1.75

Bata attempts to maintain a common share dividend payout ratio of 40 percent. A recent discussion with their investment bankers, Revell & Co., indicates that if Boots issued additional common shares, the discount to the current price would be 8 percent. In addition, flotation costs would be $2.10 per share.

The company sold their "A" preferred share issue in 1984 and they currently trade for $31.58. The "B" issue of preferreds were sold in 1988 and they currently trade for $18.95. Both preferreds have $25 stated values. Revell & Co. has informed Boots that the flotation costs on a new issue of preferred shares would be 5 percent of the stated value.

The debentures were issued in December 1989, for par, with a coupon rate of 5.5 percent paid semiannually. They are rated BB and quoted at 75.07. Revell & Co. has informed Boots that the market will only purchase a five-year debenture from Bata Boots. Debentures rated BB with five years to maturity are currently trading to yield 11.79 percent. Flotation costs associated with an issue of five-year debentures for Bata would be 2.1 percent of par and the debentures would sell at a discount of 1.2 percent per $1,000 of par value.

The 20-year mortgage bonds were issued five years ago with a coupon rate of 14 percent, paid semiannually. They are now quoted at 118.80 in the market. If Bata issued new 20-year mortgage bonds, the company would have to pay a premium of 29 basis points above the yield on the mortgage bonds currently outstanding. While they would sell for par, flotation costs on the new bonds would be 1.8 percent per $1,000 of par value.

a. Given the above information, calculate Bata Boots' overall cost of capital. Bata's tax rate is 40 percent.

b. Considering the choice of projects given at the beginning of this problem, which project(s) would you recommend Bata Boots accept? Explain.

CASE CHAPTER 9 Making Star Products' Financing/Investment Decision

See the enclosed Student CD-ROM for cases that help you put theories and concepts from the text into practice.

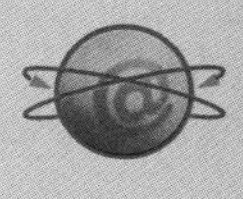

Be sure to visit the Companion Website for this book at **www.pearsoned.ca/gitman** for a wealth of additional learning tools including self-test quizzes, Web exercises, and additional cases.

CHAPTER

10

Leverage and Capital Structure

LEARNING GOALS

LG1 Discuss the role of breakeven analysis, how to determine the operating breakeven point, and the effect of changing costs on the breakeven point.

LG2 Understand operating, financial, and total leverage and the relationships among them.

LG3 Describe the basic types of capital, external assessment of capital structure, and capital structure theory.

LG4 Explain the optimal capital structure using a graphic view of the firm's debt, equity, and weighted average cost of capital functions, and a modified form of the zero-growth valuation model.

LG5 Discuss the graphic presentation, risk considerations, and basic shortcomings of using the EBIT–EPS approach to compare alternative capital structures.

LG6 Review the return and risk of alternative capital structures and their linkage to market value, and other important capital structure considerations.

10.1 Leverage

Leverage is the advantage gained by using a lever. To move a large boulder, the lever might be a smaller rock and a long piece of wood. To lift a car, the lever is a jack. Applying this concept to finance, the boulder (or car) is to maximize the return to the company's owners, which is measured by return on common equity

Jacking Up Owners' Wealth

Remember from your science class that a lever is a simple instrument that gives you more power. Although we think of levers being used principally to lift weights in various situations, the principle of leverage also is demonstrated in instruments such as scissors, nutcrackers, crowbars, and catapults. Leverage in finance involves the use of fixed costs and/or debt financing (the lever) to magnify returns to the company's owners. Leverage is desirable to common shareholders because it produces more earning power per common share. However, the use of leverage in the firm's operating and capital structures has the potential also to increase the firm's risk. This chapter will show that leverage and capital structure are closely related concepts that can be used to minimize the firm's cost of capital and to maximize owners' wealth.

(ROE) or earnings per share (EPS). There are two levers available that can be used to achieve this objective: operating leverage and financial leverage. The benefit of leverage is that it can magnify returns to common shareholders, the owners of the company. The operating structure and capital structure selected by a company significantly affect the value of the company. Increasing leverage increases risk and expected return; decreasing leverage decreases risk and expected return.

LINKING THE DISCIPLINES: Cross-Functional Interactions

- ***Accounting personnel*** need to understand how to calculate and analyze operating and financial leverage and to be familiar with the tax and earnings effects of various capital structures.
- ***Information systems analysts*** will provide the information needed for management to determine the best capital structure for the firm and will design systems to determine the impact changing costs and sales figures will have on the company's breakeven point and operating and financial leverage.
- ***Management*** need to understand leverage so they can control risk and magnify returns for the firm's owners. Management will have to decide how much financial leverage the firm will have. Increasing financial leverage may increase the EPS, but investors may feel that the additional risk is not adequately compensated for by the increased EPS and the stock price will decline.
- The ***marketing department*** uses breakeven analysis in pricing and new product decisions. For example, when setting the price for a new product, marketing must understand that the price selected must cover the direct costs of producing the product, plus provide a return on the capital invested in producing the product.
- Personnel in the ***operations department*** will be concerned with the firm's operating leverage. The actions the firm takes and how it structures its operating costs will have a major impact on the firm's operating leverage. Personnel in this department will also need to understand the impact of fixed and variable operating costs on the firm's breakeven point and its operating leverage, since these costs will have a major impact on the firm's risk and return.

Unlike some causes of risk, management has almost complete control over the risk introduced through the use of leverage. Because of its effect on value, the financial manager must understand how to measure and evaluate leverage, particularly when making capital structure decisions.

The three basic types of leverage can best be defined with reference to the firm's income statement, as shown in the general income statement format in Table 10.1:

1. *Operating leverage* is concerned with the relationship between the firm's sales revenue and its earnings before interest and taxes, or EBIT. (EBIT is a descriptive label for *operating profits*.)
2. *Financial leverage* is concerned with the relationship between the firm's EBIT and its earnings per share (EPS) or return on equity (ROE).
3. *Total leverage* is concerned with the relationship between the firm's sales revenue and EPS and/or ROE.

We will examine the three types of leverage concepts in detail in sections that follow. First, though, we will look at breakeven analysis, which lays the foundation for leverage concepts by demonstrating the effects of fixed costs on the firm's operations.

Breakeven Analysis

breakeven analysis
Indicates the level of operations necessary to cover all operating costs and the profitability associated with various levels of sales.

Breakeven analysis, sometimes called *cost-volume-profit analysis*, is used by the firm (1) to determine the level of operations necessary to cover all operating costs and (2) to evaluate the profitability associated with various levels of sales. The

TABLE 10.1 General Income Statement Format and Types of Leverage

Breakeven and operating leverage	Sales revenue	**Total leverage**
	Less: Cost of goods sold	
	Gross margin	
	Less: Operating expenses	
Financial leverage	Earnings before interest and taxes (EBIT)	
	Less: Interest	
	Earnings before taxes	
	Less: Taxes	
	Net income after taxes (NIAT)	
	Less: Preferred share dividends	
	Earnings available for common shareholders (EAC)	
	Earnings per share (EPS)	

operating breakeven point
The level of sales necessary to cover all *operating costs;* the point at which EBIT = \$0.

firm's **operating breakeven point** is the level of sales necessary to cover all *operating costs.* At that point, earnings before interest and taxes equals \$0.[1]

The first step in finding the operating breakeven point is to separate all operating costs into two categories: fixed and variable operating costs. *Fixed costs* are a function of time, not sales volume, and are typically contractual; rent, for example, is a fixed cost. *Variable costs* vary directly with sales and are a function of volume, not time; direct materials, for example, are a variable cost.

Some costs are semi-variable; they are partly fixed and partly variable. Equipment maintenance is one example. Regardless of production volume, a certain amount of maintenance must be performed on production equipment (a fixed cost). At higher production volumes, more maintenance would have to be performed (a variable cost). In this chapter, it is assumed that all semi-variable costs are separated into their fixed and variable components. Table 10.2 provides examples of the three types of operating expenses.

The Algebraic Approach

Using the following variables, we can recast the operating portion of the firm's income statement given in Table 10.1 into the algebraic representation shown in Table 10.3.

P = sale price per unit
Q = sales quantity in units
FC = fixed operating cost per period
VC = variable operating cost per unit

Rewriting the algebraic calculations in Table 10.3 as a formula for earnings before interest and taxes results in the following:

$$\text{EBIT} = \text{Total sales} - \text{total variable costs} - \text{total fixed costs}$$

1. Occasionally, the breakeven point is calculated so that it represents the point at which *all operating and financial costs* are covered. Our concern in this chapter is not with this method of calculating the breakeven point.

TABLE 10.2 Examples of Fixed, Variable, and Semi-variable Expenses

Fixed	Variable	Semi-variable
Rent	Raw materials	Maintenance
Amortization	Direct (factory) labour	Repairs
Management salaries	Direct factory overhead	Utilities
Property taxes	Sales commissions	
Marketing	Shipping costs	
Research and development		
General and administrative		
Selling		

which in symbols becomes Equation 10.1:

$$\text{EBIT} = (P \times Q) - (VC \times Q) - FC \tag{10.1}$$

Simplifying Equation 10.1 yields

$$\text{EBIT} = Q \times (P - VC) - FC \tag{10.2}$$

As noted above, the operating breakeven point is the level of sales at which all fixed and variable *operating costs* are covered—the level at which EBIT equals \$0. Setting EBIT equal to \$0 and solving Equation 10.2 for Q yields:

$$Q = \frac{FC}{P - VC} \tag{10.3}$$

Since $P - VC$ is the gross margin per unit (GM/unit), Equation 10.3 can be further simplified as follows: [2]

$$Q = \frac{FC}{GM/\text{unit}} \tag{10.4}$$

For Equations 10.3 and 10.4, Q is the company's operating breakeven point in *units*. This method of solving for the operating breakeven point implicitly

TABLE 10.3 Operating Leverage, Costs, and Breakeven Analysis

	Item	Algebraic representation
Operating leverage	Sales revenue	$(P \times Q)$
	Less: Variable operating costs	$-(VC \times Q)$
	Less: Fixed operating costs	$-\ \ FC$
	Earnings before interest and taxes	EBIT

2. In this discussion the difference between the selling price and variable cost per unit is termed *gross margin*. This terminology makes it consistent with the terms used in earlier chapters. An alternative term used by some is *contribution margin per unit*.

assumes that the firm sells a single product, so Q is in number of units. Since many companies sell more than one product, the operating breakeven point is often found in terms of total sales revenue (S). In this case, rather than GM/unit, the gross margin percent ($GM\%$) is used as follows:

$$S = \frac{FC}{GM\%} \tag{10.5}$$

The $GM\%$ can be found on either a per unit or total dollar basis as follows:

Per unit	***Total dollar***
$P - VC = GM/\text{unit}$	$(P \times Q) - (VC \times Q) = Total\ GM$
$GM\% = \frac{GM/\text{unit}}{P}$	$GM\% = \frac{Total\ GM}{P \times Q}$

Therefore, the general formula for breakeven is $FC \div GM$. To calculate the breakeven point in units (Q), GM/unit is used. To calculate the breakeven point in total sales revenue, total dollars (S), $GM\%$ is used.

Example Assume that Cheryl's Posters, a small poster retailer, has fixed operating costs of \$2,500, its sale price per unit (poster) is \$10, and its variable operating cost per unit is \$5. Determine Cheryl's Posters' breakeven point in both units and total sales revenue. Applying Equations 10.4 and 10.5 yields:

$$Q = \frac{\$2{,}500}{\$10 - \$5} = \frac{\$2{,}500}{\$5} = 500 \text{ units}$$

$$S = \frac{\$2{,}500}{\frac{\$10 - \$5}{\$10}} = \frac{\$2{,}500}{\frac{\$5}{\$10}} = \frac{\$2{,}500}{0.50} = \$5{,}000$$

Note that once breakeven in units is calculated, an alternative to calculate breakeven in dollars is to multiply Q by P. For Cheryl's Posters, this would be \$5,000 (500 units × \$10) or \$5,000 as calculated above.

At sales of 500 units (\$5,000), the firm's EBIT should just equal \$0. The firm will have positive EBIT for sales greater than 500 units (\$5,000) and negative EBIT, or a loss, for sales less than 500 units (\$5,000). We can confirm this by substituting values above and below 500 units, along with the other values given, into Equation 10.1.

The Graphic Approach

Figure 10.1 presents in graph form the breakeven analysis of the data in the preceding example. The firm's operating breakeven point is the point at which its *total operating cost*—the sum of its fixed and variable operating costs—equals sales revenue. At this point, EBIT equals \$0. The figure shows that for sales *below* 500 units (\$5,000), total operating cost exceeds sales revenue, and EBIT is less than \$0. For sales *above* the breakeven point of 500 units (\$5,000), sales revenue exceeds total operating cost, and EBIT is greater than \$0.

FIGURE 10.1

Breakeven Analysis

Graphic operating breakeven analysis

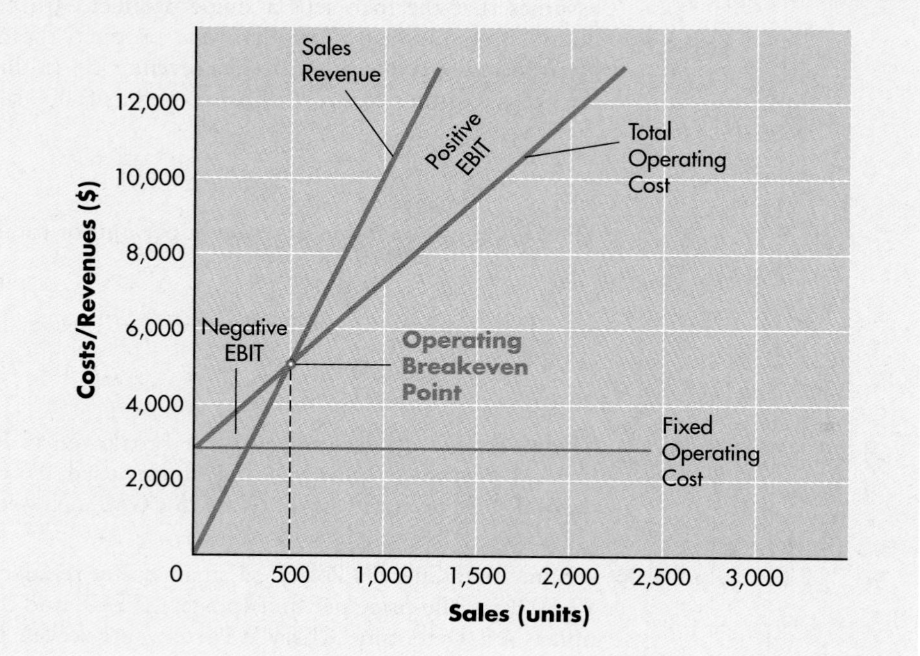

Changing Costs and the Operating Breakeven Point

A firm's operating breakeven point is sensitive to a number of variables: fixed operating cost (*FC*), the sale price per unit (*P*), and the variable operating cost per unit (*VC*). The effects of increases or decreases in these variables can be readily seen by referring to Equation 10.3. The sensitivity of the breakeven point to an *increase* in each of these variables is summarized in Table 10.4. As might be expected, an increase in cost (*FC* or *VC*) tends to increase the operating breakeven point, whereas an increase in the sale price per unit (*P*) will decrease the operating breakeven point.

Example Assume that Cheryl's Posters wishes to evaluate the impact of several options: (1) increasing fixed operating costs to \$3,000, (2) increasing the sale price per unit to \$12.50, (3) increasing the variable operating cost per unit to \$7.50, and (4) simultaneously implementing all three of these changes. Substituting the appropriate data into Equation 10.4 yields the following results:

$$\text{(1) Operating breakeven point} = \frac{\$3{,}000}{\$10 - \$5} = 600 \text{ units}$$

$$\text{(2) Operating breakeven point} = \frac{\$2{,}500}{\$12.50 - \$5} = 333\tfrac{1}{3} \text{ units}$$

$$\text{(3) Operating breakeven point} = \frac{\$2{,}500}{\$10 - \$7.50} = 1{,}000 \text{ units}$$

$$\text{(4) Operating breakeven point} = \frac{\$3{,}000}{\$12.50 - \$7.50} = 600 \text{ units}$$

TABLE 10.4 Sensitivity of Operating Breakeven Point to Increases in Key Breakeven Variables

Increase in variable	Effect on operating breakeven point
Fixed operating cost *(FC)*	Increase
Sale price per unit (*P*)	Decrease
Variable operating cost per unit *(VC)*	Increase

Note: Decreases in each of the variables shown would have the opposite effect from that indicated on the breakeven point.

Comparing the resulting operating breakeven points to the initial value of 500 units, we can see that the cost increases (actions 1 and 3) raise the breakeven point, whereas the revenue increase (action 2) lowers the breakeven point. The combined effect of increasing all three variables (action 4) also results in an increased operating breakeven point. Note that in all four cases, the breakeven point in sales (*S*) is simply the breakeven point in units (*Q*) times the selling price per unit (*P*).

In certain cases, per-unit information may not be available. This might be because the firm sells many products and we do not have access to all required per-unit information. In such cases we can still calculate breakeven, but total dollar amounts, not per-unit amounts, will be used. The total dollar amounts are available on the income statement. On an income statement, variable costs are normally represented by the COGS, the direct costs of production. Fixed costs are normally represented by the operating costs.

Example Broadom Inc.'s income statement for the current fiscal year is provided below. The company wishes to determine their breakeven point in dollars.

Sales	$650,000
Cost of goods sold	338,000
Gross margin	312,000
Operating expenses	
Management salaries	76,500
General and administrative	42,600
Marketing expense	78,200
Amortization	58,300
Total operating expenses	255,600
Operating earnings (EBIT)	56,400
Interest	21,900
Earnings before taxes	34,500
Taxes (20%)	6,900
Net income after taxes	$27,600

To determine the breakeven point in dollars, we need the fixed costs and gross margin percentage. Since we do not have detailed information, just the income statement, fixed costs can be estimated by the total operating costs. These are \$255,600. The gross margin percentage is equal to the gross margin divided by sales. This equals 48 percent (\$312,000/\$650,000). Therefore, the breakeven point in total sales dollars (S) is:

$$S = \frac{\$255,600}{48\%}$$

$$= \$532,500$$

Therefore, to just break even during the year, Broadom Inc. must generate sales of \$532,500. Sales less than this will result in negative operating earnings. Sales of more than this will lead to positive operating earnings, as in the current year.

An analysis such as this is very useful to use with forecasted data, or when the company wishes to estimate their level of operating risk. When the company is operating very close to the breakeven point, the company's operating risk is high. This will be reflected in the leverage calculations as discussed below.

Operating Leverage

operating leverage
The use of *fixed operating costs* to magnify the effects of changes in sales on the firm's earnings before interest and taxes.

Operating leverage results from the existence of *fixed operating costs* in the firm's cost structure. Using the structure presented in Table 10.3, we can define **operating leverage** as the use of *fixed operating costs* to magnify the effects of changes in sales on the firm's earnings before interest and taxes.

Example Using the data for Cheryl's Posters (sale price, P = \$10 per unit; variable operating cost, VC = \$5 per unit; fixed operating cost, FC = \$2,500), Figure 10.2 presents the operating breakeven graph originally shown in Figure 10.1. The additional notations on the graph indicate that as the firm's sales increase from 1,000 to 1,500 units (Q_1 to Q_2), its EBIT increases from \$2,500 to \$5,000 ($EBIT_1$ to $EBIT_2$). In other words, a 50 percent increase in sales (1,000 to 1,500 units) results in a 100 percent increase in EBIT. Table 10.5 includes the data for Figure 10.2 as well as relevant data for a 500-unit sales level. We can illustrate two cases using the 1,000-unit sales level as a reference point:

Case 1 A 50 percent *increase* in sales (from 1,000 to 1,500 units) results in a 100 percent *increase* in earnings before interest and taxes (from \$2,500 to \$5,000).

Case 2 A 50 percent *decrease* in sales (from 1,000 to 500 units) results in a 100 percent *decrease* in earnings before interest and taxes (from \$2,500 to \$0).

From the preceding example, we see that operating leverage works in *both directions*. When a firm has fixed operating costs, operating leverage is present. An increase in sales results in a more-than-proportional increase in EBIT; a decrease in sales results in a more-than-proportional decrease in EBIT.

FIGURE 10.2

Operating Leverage

Breakeven analysis and operating leverage

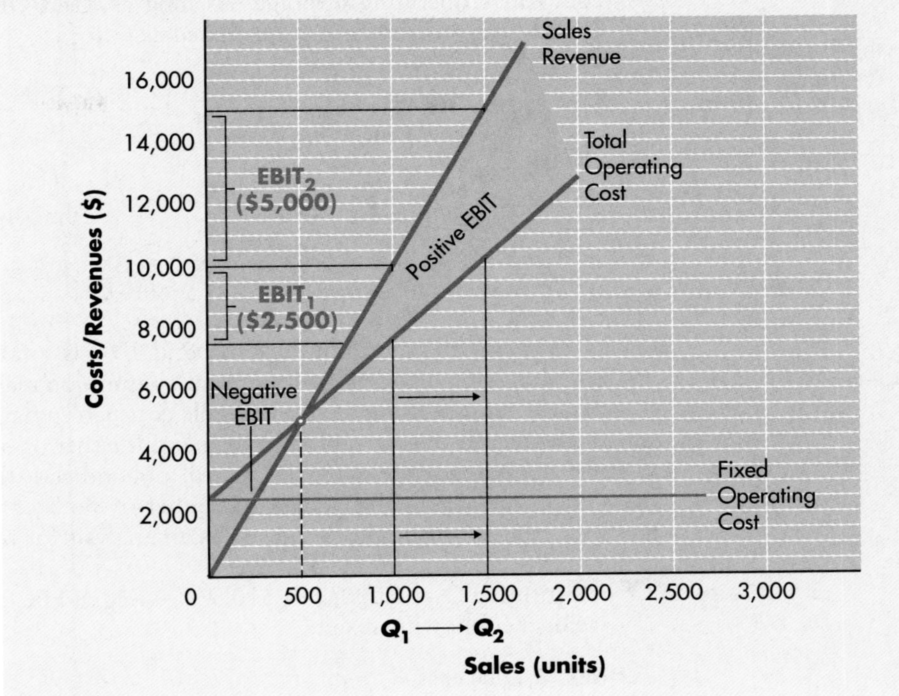

Measuring Operating Leverage: The Degree of Operating Leverage (DOL)

degree of operating leverage (DOL) The numerical measure of the firm's operating leverage.

Whenever the percentage change in EBIT resulting from a given percentage change in sales is greater than the percentage change in sales, operating leverage exists. The **degree of operating leverage (DOL)** is the numerical measure of a

TABLE 10.5 **The EBIT for Various Sales Levels**

	Case 2		Case 1
	−50%		+50%
Sales (in units)	500	1,000	1,500
Sales revenue[a]	$5,000	$10,000	$15,000
Less: Variable operating costs[b]	2,500	5,000	7,500
Less: Fixed operating costs	2,500	2,500	2,500
Earnings before interest and taxes (EBIT)	$ 0	$ 2,500	$ 5,000
	−100%		+100%

[a]Sales revenue = $10/unit × sales in units.

[b]Variable operating costs = $5/unit × sales in units.

company's operating leverage. As long as the DOL is greater than 1, there is operating leverage. DOL is calculated as follows:

$$\text{DOL at base sales level } Q = \frac{(P \times Q) - (Q \times VC)}{(P \times Q) - (Q \times VC) - FC} \tag{10.6}$$

$$= \frac{TR - TVC}{TR - TVC - FC} \tag{10.6a}$$

$$= \frac{GM\$}{EBIT} \tag{10.6b}$$

Note that *TR* is total sales revenue and *TVC* is total variable costs, both at production volume of *Q*.[3] An important assumption made in this analysis is that the variable cost per unit (or the variable cost percentage) and the fixed costs remain unchanged from one period to the next. If either or both of these assumptions do not apply, the calculated DOL will not indicate the correct change in EBIT. Given that it is highly likely that either or both of the costs will change in the long run, DOL should be viewed as an analysis for use in the short term.

Example Substituting $Q = 1{,}000$, $P = \$10$, $VC = \$5$, and $FC = \$2{,}500$ into Equation 10.6 yields the following result:

DOL at 1,000 units =

$$\frac{1{,}000 \times (\$10 - \$5)}{1{,}000 \times (\$10 - \$5) - \$2{,}500} = \frac{\$10{,}000 - \$5{,}000}{\$10{,}000 - \$5{,}000 - \$2{,}500} = \frac{\$5{,}000}{\$2{,}500} = 2.0$$

The use of the formula results in the same value for DOL (2.0) as that found by using Table 10.5. The DOL of 2 means that for every 1 percent change in sales (either up or down), EBIT will change by the DOL, in this case 2 percent (again either up or down). This was highlighted in Table 10.5.

For Case 1, if sales increase by 50 percent, EBIT is expected to increase by 100 percent (50% × 2). For Case 2, if sales decrease by 50 percent, EBIT is expected to decrease by 100 percent (−50% × 2). The higher the DOL, the greater the impact changes in sales have on EBIT. Higher levels of DOL imply greater operating risk.

Fixed Costs and Operating Leverage

Changes in fixed operating costs affect operating leverage significantly. Firms can sometimes incur fixed operating costs rather than variable operating costs and at other times may be able to substitute one type of cost for the other. For example, a firm could modernize its production facilities, replacing variable cost direct labour with fixed cost fixed assets. Technologically advanced equipment results in increased productivity, lower variable costs, and higher fixed costs. Or it could compensate sales representatives with a fixed salary and bonus rather than

3. Because the concept of leverage is *linear,* positive and negative changes of equal magnitude will always result in equal degrees of leverage when the same base sales level is used as a point of reference. This relationship holds for all types of leverage discussed in this chapter.

on a pure percent-of-sales commission basis. The effects of changes in operating costs on operating leverage can best be illustrated by continuing our example.

Example Assume that Cheryl's Posters exchanges a portion of its variable operating costs for fixed operating costs by eliminating sales commissions and increasing sales salaries. This exchange results in a reduction in the variable operating cost per unit from $5 to $4.50 and an increase in the fixed operating costs from $2,500 to $3,000. Table 10.6 presents an analysis like that in Table 10.5, but using new costs. Although the EBIT of $2,500 at the 1,000-unit sales level is the same as before the shift in operating cost structure, Table 10.6 shows that the firm has increased its operating leverage by shifting to greater fixed operating costs.

With the substitution of the appropriate values into Equation 10.6, the degree of operating leverage at the 1,000-unit base level of sales becomes

$$\text{DOL at 1,000 units} = \frac{1{,}000 \times (\$10 - \$4.50)}{1{,}000 \times (\$10 - \$4.50) - \$3{,}000} = \frac{\$5{,}500}{\$2{,}500} = 2.2$$

By comparing this value to the DOL of 2.0 before the shift to more fixed costs, it is clear that the higher the firm's fixed operating costs relative to variable operating costs, the greater the degree of operating leverage. Higher levels of DOL indicate both greater return and risk: greater return if sales increase, greater risk if sales decrease.

Example Broadom Inc.'s DOL can also be calculated using the income statement provided earlier. Here we see that the DOL at the current sales level is:

$$\text{DOL (at sales of \$650,000)} = \frac{\$312{,}000}{\$56{,}400}$$
$$= 5.532$$

TABLE 10.6 Operating Leverage and Increased Fixed Costs

		Case 2		Case 1	
		−50%		+50%	
Sales (in units)	500		1,000		1,500
Sales revenue[a]	$5,000		$10,000		$15,000
Less: Variable operating costs[b]	2,250		4,500		6,750
Less: Fixed operating costs	3,000		3,000		3,000
Earnings before interest and taxes (EBIT)	−$ 250		$ 2,500		$ 5,250
		−110%		+110%	

[a]Sales revenue was calculated as indicated in Table 10.5.
[b]Variable operating costs = $4.50/unit × sales in units.

At the current sales level, if sales change by 10 percent, EBIT is expected to change by 55.32 percent. But, again, this assumes that the variable cost percentage and the fixed costs remain unchanged from one period to the next. If either or both change, the actual impact of sales changes on EBIT would be different than that expected using the calculated DOL.

Note that for Broadom, the DOL is quite high. DOLs in the 1.5 range would be considered very low, about the lowest that could be expected. This can be seen when Equation 10.6b is reconsidered. Very low DOLs mean that gross margin and EBIT would be very similar amounts. This outcome would be highly unlikely, unless the firm has a very high gross margin and/or very low operating expenses. When a company is operating very close to the breakeven point, the company's operating risk is high. This will be reflected in high DOLs.

Financial Leverage

financial leverage
The use of *fixed financial costs* to magnify the effects of changes in earnings before interest and taxes on the firm's earnings per share.

Financial leverage results from the presence of *fixed financial costs* in the firm's income stream. Using the framework in Table 10.1, we can define **financial leverage** as the use of *fixed financial costs* to magnify the effects of changes in earnings before interest and taxes on the firm's earnings per share.[4] The two fixed financial costs that may be found on the firm's income statement are (1) interest on debt and (2) preferred share dividends. These charges must be paid regardless of the amount of EBIT available to pay them.

As noted in Chapter 5, although preferred share dividends can be "passed" (not paid) at the option of the firm's directors, it is generally believed that payment of such dividends is necessary. *This text treats the preferred share dividend as a contractual obligation, not only to be paid as a fixed amount, but also to be paid as scheduled.* Although failure to pay preferred dividends cannot force the firm into bankruptcy, the non-payment sends a message to investors that the company is having extreme financial difficulties. Consequently, when companies fail to pay preferred share dividends, the risk of the company significantly increases, driving down the value of all of the company's financial securities. In reality, most companies that fail to pay preferred share dividends end up going into bankruptcy.

Example Chen Foods, a small Oriental food company, expects EBIT of $10,000 in the current year. The company has $20,000 of debt with a 10 percent interest rate, 600 preferred shares with a stated value of $50 on which they pay an 8 percent dividend, and 1,000 common shares outstanding. The annual interest on the bond issue is $2,000 (10% × $20,000). The annual dividends on the preferred shares are $2,400 ($50 × 8% = $4.00/share × 600 shares). Table 10.7 presents the EPS corresponding to levels of EBIT of $6,000, $10,000, and $14,000, assuming that the firm is in the 40 percent tax bracket. Two situations are shown:

Case 1 A 40% *increase* in EBIT (from $10,000 to $14,000) results in a 100% *increase* in earnings per share (from $2.40 to $4.80).

Case 2 A 40% *decrease* in EBIT (from $10,000 to $6,000) results in a 100% *decrease* in earnings per share (from $2.40 to $0).

---

4. Rather than EPS, return on common equity (ROE) could be used to evaluate financial leverage. When EPS is used to examine financial leverage, the number of common shares must remain unchanged at different levels of EBIT.

10.1 IN PRACTICE

Simulating Operating Leverage

CAE is the world leader in the design and manufacture of civil flight simulators and visual systems used to train airline and business jet pilots, with a global market share exceeding 80 percent. In addition, CAE is number two in the world in the training of commercial aviation pilots, with a global network of more than 20 training centres equipped with more than 100 simulators. The company is a global leader in the design of advanced military training systems for air, land, and sea application and is a prime contractor in the U.S. defence market, the largest in the world. CAE is truly a global corporation with manufacturing operations and training facilities in 19 countries on five continents. For the fiscal year ended December 31, 2006, the company had annual revenues of almost $1.2 billion, of which 90 percent were from worldwide exports.

The year ended December 31, 2006 was a period of transition at CAE as the company moved to establish a solid foundation for shareholder value in the future. As part of a restructuring plan, CAE strengthened its balance sheet and generated sizeable free cash flow. New synergies within its core businesses resulted in cost savings of $14 million, and this is expected to rise to $30 million in fiscal 2008. Future growth is underpinned by a $2.5 billion backlog of orders. CAE is a major provider of integrated training solutions for civilian and military customers engaged in flight, marine, and land-based activities.

Such an operation incurs the bulk of its costs up front, in the design and production of the product (the flight simulator) or in the establishment of the training programs. With CAE's sales coming from these two business lines, the potential for economies of scale to magnify returns is huge. In addition, a key element of CAE's finance strategy is the sale and leaseback of full-flight simulators installed in the company's global network of training centres. This provides CAE with a cost-effective long-term source of fixed cost financing and thus additional operational leverage. As a result, increases in sales lead to large increases in returns as measured by operating earnings (EBIT). The following results for CAE illustrate the benefit of operating leverage for the year ended December 31, 2006:

	2005 fiscal year	2006 fiscal year	% change
Sales revenue (in millions)	$1,085.6	$1,197.7	10.33%
EBIT (in millions)	($53.7)	$102.6	91.06%
DOL	8.82		

In this example, DOL was calculated by dividing the percentage change in EBIT by the percentage change in sales (91.06% ÷ 10.33%). This is an alternative method to calculate DOL when information for two separate periods (like two years) is provided. CAE's use of operating leverage magnified the increase in EBIT in 2006. Every 1 percent increase in sales resulted in a 8.82 percent increase in EBIT. Obviously, operating leverage of this magnitude can be a great benefit. For CAE, it helped swing the company from a small operating profit in 2005, to a much larger operating profit in 2006.

Such a move will also benefit the owners of CAE (the common shareholders). In early January 2003, the price of CAE's common shares on the Toronto Stock Exchange was less than $5.00. By early April, 2007, the stock price has increased to $13.60, an average yearly return of 26.5 percent. CAE's use of operating leverage magnified returns to shareholders. (*Note:* It is important to remember that this example represents only two years of data and that CAE's DOL may change in the future.)

SOURCE: CAE, 2005 and 2006 yearly and quarterly reports, available at **www.cae.com**.

TABLE 10.7 The EPS for Various EBIT Levels[a]

		Case 2		Case 1	
		−40%		+40%	
EBIT	$6,000		$10,000		$14,000
Less: Interest (I)	2,000		2,000		2,000
Earnings before taxes	$4,000		$ 8,000		$12,000
Less: Taxes (T = 0.40)	1,600		3,200		4,800
Net income after taxes (NIAT)	$2,400		$ 4,800		$ 7,200
Less: Preferred share dividends (PD)	2,400		2,400		2,400
Earnings available for common (EAC)	$ 0		$ 2,400		$ 4,800
Earnings per share (EPS)	$\frac{\$0}{1{,}000} = \$0$		$\frac{\$2{,}400}{1{,}000} = \$2.40$		$\frac{\$4{,}800}{1{,}000} = \$4.80$
		−100%		+100%	

[a]As noted in Chapter 2, for accounting and tax purposes, interest is a *tax-deductible expense,* whereas dividends must be paid from after-tax cash flows.

The effect of financial leverage is such that an increase in the firm's EBIT results in a more-than-proportional increase in the firm's earnings per share, whereas a decrease in the firm's EBIT results in a more-than-proportional decrease in EPS.[5]

Measuring Financial Leverage: The Degree of Financial Leverage (DFL)

degree of financial leverage (DFL) The numerical measure of the firm's financial leverage.

The **degree of financial leverage (DFL)** is the numerical measure of the firm's financial leverage. Whenever the percentage change in EPS resulting from a given percentage change in EBIT is greater than the percentage change in EBIT, financial leverage exists. This means that whenever DFL is greater than 1, there is financial leverage.

The DFL is calculated at a base level of EBIT. For Chen Foods in the previous example, the base level of EBIT is $10,000. The following equation is used to calculate DFL where the notation is taken from Table 10.7. Note that in the denominator, the term $(1 - T)$ converts the after-tax preferred share dividend to a before-tax amount for consistency with the other terms in the equation.

$$\text{DFL at base level EBIT} = \frac{\text{EBIT}}{\text{EBIT} - I - \left(\frac{PD}{1-T}\right)} \tag{10.7}$$

5. We have already seen this same effect in Chapter 3, but there we used ROE rather than EPS as the way to demonstrate the impact of financial leverage.

Example Substituting EBIT = \$10,000, I = \$2,000, PD = \$2,400, and the tax rate (T = 0.40) into Equation 10.7 yields the following result:

$$\text{DFL at \$10,000 EBIT} = \frac{\$10{,}000}{\$10{,}000 - \$2{,}000 - \left(\dfrac{\$2{,}400}{1-0.40}\right)}$$

$$= \frac{\$10{,}000}{\$4{,}000} = 2.5$$

Since the DFL at EBIT of \$10,000 is greater than 1, Chen Foods is using financial leverage. The higher the value, the greater the DFL and the greater the impact changing levels of EBIT have on EPS. For Chen Foods, the DFL of 2.5 means that for every 1 percent change in EBIT, EPS will change by 2.5 percent.

For case 1, where EBIT increases by 40 percent, EPS is expected to increase by 100 percent (40% × 2.5). Based on the results provided in Table 10.7, this is exactly what happens. For case 2, where EBIT decreases by 40 percent, EPS is expected to decrease by 100 percent (–40% × 2.5). Again, this is what occurs in Table 10.7. As with DOL, DFL is a measure of risk and returns—returns when EBIT increases, risk when EBIT decreases. The higher the value of DFL, the greater the risk, but also the greater the potential return.

Total Leverage

total leverage
The use of *fixed costs, both operating and financial,* to magnify the effect of changes in sales on the firm's earnings per share.

We also can assess the combined effect of operating and financial leverage on the firm's risk using a framework similar to that used to develop the individual concepts of leverage. This combined effect, or **total leverage,** can be defined as the use of *fixed costs, both operating and financial,* to magnify the effect of changes in sales on the firm's earnings per share. Total leverage can therefore be viewed as the *total impact of the fixed costs* in the firm's operating and financial structure.

Example Cables Inc., a computer cable manufacturer, recorded sales for the month of September of \$100,000. Cost of goods sold (variable costs) are 45 percent of sales, while fixed monthly operating costs are \$30,000. The firm must make interest payments of \$12,000 and preferred share dividend payments of \$4,000 per month. The firm has a tax rate of 20 percent and has 5,000 common shares outstanding. For the month of October, the firm expects sales to increase by 50 percent. The variable expense ratio and all other dollar amounts will not change in October. With this information, the firm can calculate earnings per share (EPS), the breakeven point, and the three measures of leverage for September. This information will then be used to estimate the EBIT and EPS for October.

To complete the analysis, an important assumption that must be made is that the cost structure does not change from one period to the next. Given that we are dealing with months, this assumption is likely valid. However, if the cost structure did change, the calculated values for October would not be correct. Table 10.8 presents the levels of earnings per share associated with the current sales of \$100,000, and the expected sales of \$150,000.

The table illustrates that as a result of a 50 percent increase in sales (from \$100,000 to \$150,000), the firm could expect to experience a 343.75 percent (or \$4.40) increase in earnings per share (from \$1.28 to \$5.68). Although this is not shown in the table, a 50 percent decrease in sales would, conversely, result in a 343.75 percent (or \$4.40) decrease in earnings per share to −\$3.12 per share.

TABLE 10.8 The Total Leverage Effect

		+50%		
Sales revenue	$100,000	$150,000		
Less: Cost of goods sold[a]	45,000	67,500	$\text{DOL} = \dfrac{\$100{,}000 - \$45{,}000}{\$55{,}000 - \$30{,}000}$	
Gross margin	55,000	82,500		
Less: Fixed operating costs	30,000	30,000		
Earnings before interest and taxes (EBIT)	$ 25,000	$ 52,500	= 2.20	
		+110%		DTL = 2.20 × 3.125 = 6.875
Less: Interest	12,000	12,000		
Earnings before taxes	$ 13,000	$ 40,500		
Less: Taxes (20%)	2,600	8,100	$\text{DFL} = \dfrac{\$25{,}000}{13{,}000 - \dfrac{\$4{,}000}{1 - 0.20}}$	
Net income after taxes	$ 10,400	$ 32,400		
Less: Preferred share dividends	4,000	4,000		
Earnings available for common	$ 6,400	$ 28,400	= 3.125	
Earnings per share (EPS)	$\dfrac{\$6{,}400}{5{,}000} = \$1.28$	$\dfrac{\$28{,}400}{5{,}000} = \$5.68$		
		+343.75%		

[a] This is variable operating costs, which is given as 45% of sales.

The linear nature of the leverage relationship accounts for the fact that sales changes of equal magnitude in opposite directions result in EPS changes of equal magnitude in the corresponding direction. At this point, it should be clear that whenever a firm has fixed costs—operating or financial—in its structure, total leverage will exist. This analysis is also provided as Spreadsheet Application 10.1. In addition, some simple models that determine and graph breakeven are freely available on the Web.

www.jaxworks.com/calc6.htm

Measuring the Degree of Total Leverage (DTL)

degree of total leverage (DTL)
The numerical measure of the firm's total leverage.

The **degree of total leverage (DTL)** is the numerical measure of the firm's total leverage. Whenever the percentage change in EPS resulting from a given percentage change in sales is greater than the percentage change in sales, total leverage exists. This means that as long as the DTL is greater than 1, there is total leverage.

The DTL is calculated at a base level of sales. For Cables Inc., the base level is sales of $100,000. Total leverage reflects the *combined impact* of operating and financial leverage on the firm. High operating leverage and high financial leverage will cause total leverage to be high. The opposite will also be true. The relationship between operating leverage and financial leverage is *multiplicative* rather than *additive*. The relationship between the degree of total

10.1 SPREADSHEET APPLICATION

Microsoft Excel - Spreadsheet Application 10-1.xls

Calculating Breakeven and Measures of Leverage

Income Statement	Current Month	Forecast Month		Changes
Sales revenue	$100,000	$150,000	↑	50.00%
Cost of goods sold (45%)	45,000	67,500		
Gross margin	55,000	82,500		
Fixed operating costs	30,000	30,000		
EBIT	25,000	52,500	↑	110.00%
Interest expense	12,000	12,000		
Earnings before taxes	13,000	40,500		
Taxes (20%)	2,600	8,100		
Net income after taxes	$10,400	$32,400		
Preferred share dividends	$4,000	$4,000		
Earnings available for common	$6,400	$28,400		
Earnings per share (EPS)	$1.28	$5.68	↑	343.75%
Gross margin (%)	45.00%	45.00%		
Tax rate	20%	20%		
Outputs				
Breakeven in dollars	$66,666.67	$66,666.67	←	=+B8/B19
Degree of operating leverage (DOL)	2.20		←	=+B7/B9
Degree of financial leverage (DFL)	3.125		←	=+B9/(B11-(B15/(1-$B20)))
Degree of total leverage (DTL)	6.875		←	=+B24*B25

SA 10-1

leverage (DTL) and the degrees of operating leverage (DOL) and financial leverage (DFL) is given by Equation 10.8.

$$\text{DTL} = \text{DOL} \times \text{DFL} \tag{10.8}$$

Example Substituting the values calculated for DOL and DFL, shown on the right-hand side of Table 10.8, into Equation 10.8 yields

$$\text{DTL} = 2.2 \times 3.125 = 6.875$$

The DTL indicates what is expected to happen to EPS given a change in sales. For Cables Inc., the DTL of 6.875 means that for a 1 percent change in sales, EPS is expected to change by 6.875 percent. This 6.875 percent change consists of a 2.2 percent change in EBIT, which leads to a 3.125 percent change in EPS. The total effect is multiplicative. For the example in Table 10.8, the 50 percent increase in sales leads to a 343.75 percent (50% × 6.875) increase in EPS. This total increase consists of two separate items. First, based on a 50 percent increase in sales, EBIT is expected to increase by 110 percent (50% × 2.2). Second, the 110 percent increase in EBIT leads to a 343.75 percent (110% × 3.125) increase in EPS.

What happens if sales decrease 20 percent? EPS is expected to decline by 137.5 percent (–20% × 6.875). This decrease consists of two separate components. First, EBIT is expected to decline 44 percent (–20% × 2.2), to $14,000. Based on the 44 percent decrease in EBIT, EPS is expected to decline 137.5 percent (–44% × 3.125), to −0.48 ($1.28 × [1 − 1.375]). Obviously, the higher the DTL, the greater the potential return (if sales increase) and risk (if sales decrease).

Another method to calculate the degree of total leverage at a given base level of sales, *Q*, is given by Equation 10.9, which uses the same notation presented earlier:

$$\text{DTL at base sales level } Q = \frac{Q \times (P - VC)}{Q \times (P - VC) - FC - I - \left(PD \times \frac{1}{1 - T}\right)} \qquad (10.9)$$

$$= \frac{TR - TVC}{TR - TVC - FC - I - \frac{PD}{1 - T}} \qquad (10.9a)$$

$$= \frac{GM\$}{EBT - \frac{PD}{1 - T}} \qquad (10.9b)$$

Example Substituting the required variables from Table 10.8 into Equation 10.9 yields the following:

$$\text{DTL at \$100,000 sales} = \frac{\$100,000 - \$45,000}{\$100,000 - \$45,000 - \$30,000 - \$12,000 - \frac{\$4,000}{1 - 0.2}}$$

$$= \frac{\$55,000}{\$8,000} = 6.875$$

Clearly, Equation 10.8 provides a much more direct and intuitive method for calculating the DTL.

? Review Questions

10–1 What is meant by the term *leverage*? How do operating leverage, financial leverage, and total leverage relate to the income statement?

10–2 What is the *operating breakeven point*? How do changes in fixed operating costs, the sale price per unit, and the variable operating cost per unit affect it?

10–3 What is *operating leverage*? What causes it? How is the *degree of operating leverage (DOL)* measured?

10–4 What is *financial leverage*? What causes it? How is the *degree of financial leverage (DFL)* measured?

10–5 What is the general relationship among operating leverage, financial leverage, and the total leverage of the firm? Do these types of leverage complement each other? Why or why not?

10.2 The Firm's Capital Structure

Capital structure is one of the most complex areas of financial decision making due to its interrelationship with other financial decision variables.[6] Poor capital structure decisions can result in a high cost of capital, thereby making more investment projects unacceptable. Effective decisions can lower the cost of capital, resulting in more acceptable projects, thereby increasing the value of the firm. This section links together the concepts presented in Chapters 6 through 9 and the discussion of leverage in this chapter.

Types of Capital

Most of the items on the right-hand side of the firm's balance sheet are sources of capital. The following simplified balance sheet illustrates the basic breakdown of total capital into its two components—*debt capital* and *equity capital.*[7]

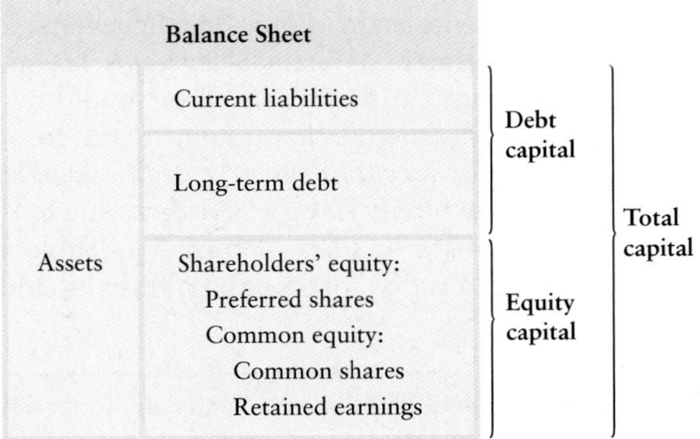

The various types and characteristics of *long-term debt,* a major source of *capital,* were discussed in detail in Chapter 5. In Chapter 9, the cost of debt was found to be less than the cost of other forms of financing. Lenders demand relatively lower returns because they take the least risk of any long-term contributors of capital. Consider: (1) they have a higher priority of claim against any earnings or assets available for payment, (2) they have a far stronger legal claim against the company to make payment than do preferred or common shareholders, and (3) the tax-deductibility of interest payments lowers the debt cost to the firm substantially.

6. Of course, although capital structure is financially important, it, like many business decisions, is generally not as important as the firm's products or services. In a practical sense, a firm can probably more readily increase its value by improving quality and reducing costs rather than by fine-tuning its capital structure.

7. Some of the items on a company's balance sheet are simply accounting items that are not sources of financing. This includes items like deferred taxes, deferred gains, and reserves. These types of items are ignored in our analysis. Sources of financing include items like accounts payable, accruals, line of credit and other short-term loans, long-term debt, preferred equity, and common equity. The items that are sources of financing are the focus of our discussion. Note that at least two of these items, accounts payable and accruals, are no-cost sources of financing. This concept was fully covered in Chapter 4.

Unlike borrowed funds that must be repaid at a specified future date, *equity capital* is expected to remain in the firm for an indefinite period of time. The two basic sources of equity capital are (1) preferred shares and (2) common equity, which includes common shares and retained earnings. As was demonstrated in Chapter 9, common shares are typically the most expensive form of equity, followed by reinvested profits and preferred shares, respectively. Our concern here is the relationship between debt and equity capital. Key differences between these two types of capital, relative to voice in management, claims on income and assets, maturity, and tax treatment, were summarized in Chapter 5. Due to its secondary position relative to debt, suppliers of equity capital take greater risk and therefore must be compensated with higher expected returns than suppliers of debt capital.

Capital Structure of Canadian Companies

Earlier it was shown that *financial leverage* results from the use of fixed-payment financing, such as debt and preferred shares, to magnify return and risk. Leverage ratios, which measure the firm's degree of financial leverage, were presented in Chapter 3. A direct measure of the degree of indebtedness is the *debt ratio*. The higher this ratio, the greater the firm's financial leverage. Measures of the firm's ability to meet fixed payments associated with debt include the *times interest earned ratio* and the *fixed-payment coverage ratio*. These ratios provide indirect information on financial leverage. The smaller these ratios, the less able the firm is to meet payments as they come due. In general, low debt payment ratios are associated with high degrees of financial leverage. The more risk a firm takes, the greater its financial leverage. In theory, the firm should maintain financial leverage consistent with a capital structure that minimizes the cost of capital and maximizes owners' wealth.

An acceptable degree of financial leverage for one industry or line of business can be highly risky in another, due to differing operating characteristics between industries or lines of business. Table 10.9 presents the debt and times interest earned ratios for selected industries and lines of business in Canada for 2004.

TABLE 10.9 Debt Ratios and Times Interest Earned Ratios for Selected Industries for 2004

Industry	Debt ratio	Times interest earned ratio
Total for all industries	73.19%	3.21
Total finance and insurance industries	85.23%	3.97
Total non-financial industries	61.27%	3.00
Primary industries		
Agriculture, forestry, fishing, and hunting	56.41%	2.77
Oil and gas extraction and coal mining	52.92%	3.89
Mining	40.06%	2.54
Utilities	80.82%	1.55
Construction	73.63%	3.40
Manufacturing industries		
Food manufacturing	57.99%	3.36
Alcoholic beverage and tobacco manufacturing	55.57%	3.65
Clothing, textile, and leather manufacturing	62.04%	1.78
Wood product manufacturing	48.65%	3.27

continued

TABLE 10.9 Debt Ratios and Times Interest Earned Ratios for Selected Industries for 2004 (continued)

Industry	Debt ratio	Times interest earned ratio
Printing and related support activities	43.96%	3.18
Petroleum and coal products manufacturing	38.29%	28.70
Chemicals, plastic, and rubber manufacturing	52.05%	4.19
Non-metallic mineral product manufacturing	39.06%	9.43
Primary metal manufacturing	48.33%	3.67
Fabricated metal product manufacturing	56.12%	3.81
Electrical equipment and appliance manufacturing	44.81%	5.16
Computer and electronic product manufacturing	25.75%	3.01
Motor vehicle and trailer manufacturing	65.52%	2.97
Other transportation equipment manufacturing	67.30%	1.70
Furniture and related product manufacturing	58.50%	3.15
Pharmaceutical and medicine manufacturing	46.64%	13.41
Miscellaneous manufacturing	59.72%	3.67
Wholesaler and distributor industries		
Wholesale food, beverage, and tobacco	77.19%	3.33
Petroleum products	72.12%	4.30
Motor vehicle and parts	68.65%	5.62
Building material and supplies	62.96%	7.74
Farm, construction, and industrial machinery and equipment	61.02%	4.12
Computer and communications machinery and equipment	61.54%	5.58
Other wholesaler-distributors	63.71%	5.86
Retailing industries		
Motor vehicle and parts dealers	77.72%	2.17
Furniture, electronics, and appliance stores	76.29%	2.46
Building material and garden equipment and supplies	65.18%	3.52
Food and beverage stores	62.97%	11.53
Gasoline stations	66.77%	1.50
Clothing, department, and general-merchandise stores	60.49%	2.69
Other retail	71.37%	4.30
Service industries		
Air transportation	84.84%	–0.05
Rail, truck, water, and other transportation	60.09%	3.29
Pipelines, warehousing, and transportation support	74.89%	1.48
Publishing industries	57.03%	1.31
Broadcasting, movie, sound, and information services	68.22%	1.78
Telecommunications	61.15%	1.74
Real estate	70.20%	1.53
Automotive, machinery, and equipment rental and leasing	76.77%	1.15
Professional, scientific, and technical services	59.87%	2.70
Administrative and support, and waste management services	66.76%	2.98
Educational, healthcare, and social assistance services	55.89%	5.50
Arts, entertainment, and recreation	71.51%	10.67
Accommodation services	70.33%	1.30
Food and beverage services	84.31%	1.52
Repair, maintenance, and personal services	57.86%	2.94

SOURCE: Statistics Canada, "Financial and Taxation Statistics for Enterprises," Table 180-00031, retrieved from E-Stat, Business Enterprises, Business Finance.

The overall debt ratio for all Canadian industries is 73.2 percent, which seems very high. The reason for this very high ratio is because financial companies like banks and insurance companies are included. These types of companies have very high debt ratios (deposits are liabilities for banks) which artificially increases the overall debt ratio for companies in Canada.

For non-finance companies, the debt ratio is lower, but still high at 61.3 percent. It should be noted that in calculating the debt ratio, a category of debt termed "other liabilities" is included that accounts for about half of the total liabilities. This likely includes some liabilities that do not have a financing cost, so the ratio provided likely overstates the true debt position. The times interest earned (TIE) ratio for the financial industries, at almost 4, is quite high, reflecting the high profitability of this industry. At 3 for the non-financial industries, the ratio indicates that the required interest payments on the debt are well covered. So, while debt is high, the TIE ratio indicates that both major industry sectors adequately cover the required interest payments on the debt.

Table 10.9 also indicates that significant differences in both ratios exist across industries. For 2004, the debt ratio ranges from a low of 25.8 percent for the computer and electronic product manufacturing industry to a high of 84.8 percent for the air transportation industry. For TIE, the ratio ranges from a low of –0.05 for the air transportation industry to a high of 28.7 for the petroleum and coal products manufacturing industry. The TIE ratio for both industries is due to the same factor. In 2004, oil prices were climbing thus reducing the profitability of airline companies while increasing those of the oil companies. This is obvious in the data. In addition, the wide range of outcomes for these ratios indicates significant differences in operation and financial structures. Differences in these ratios are also likely to exist *within* an industry or line of business.

Capital Structures in Other Countries

In general, Canadian and U.S. companies have similar debt ratios, given the high degree of integration between the two countries. Also, companies in both countries have similar capital markets, creditors, and investors. It is not surprising, therefore, that creditors and investors in the two countries seek similar characteristics in the companies they lend to and invest in.

For non–North American companies, particularly in Europe and Japan, different capital market and corporate ownership structures result in different capital structures for corporations. Companies in these countries generally have higher debt ratios than similar companies in North America. This is the case since in these countries, banks are allowed to hold equity investments in corporations, a practice that is very rare in North America. Also, in these countries, corporate ownership is more tightly controlled among fewer large investors. Such a structure reduces agency problems and costs, thus allowing these companies to tolerate higher debt ratios.

Capital Structure Theory

Research suggests that there is an optimal capital structure range. However, *the understanding of capital structure at this point does not provide financial managers with a direct approach to use to determine a firm's optimal capital structure.* Nevertheless, financial theory does provide help in understanding how a firm's chosen financing mix affects the firm's value.

In 1958, Franco Modigliani and Merton H. Miller (commonly known as MM) demonstrated that, assuming perfect markets, the capital structure that a firm chooses does not affect its value. The MM theory of capital structure is discussed in more detail in the Appendix to this chapter. Many researchers, including MM, have examined the effects of less restrictive assumptions on the relationship between capital structure and the firm's value. The result is a theoretical *optimal* capital structure based on balancing the benefits and costs of debt financing.

The major benefit of debt financing is the tax shield, which allows interest payments to be deducted in calculating taxable income. The cost of debt financing results from (1) the increased probability of bankruptcy caused by debt obligations, (2) the *agency costs* of the lender's monitoring the firm's actions, and (3) the costs associated with managers having more information about the firm's prospects than do investors.

Tax Benefits

Allowing firms to deduct interest payments on debt when calculating taxable income reduces the amount of the firm's earnings paid in taxes, thereby making more earnings available for bondholders and shareholders. The deductibility of interest means the cost of debt to the firm is subsidized by taxpayers. Letting k_d equal the before-tax cost of debt and T equal the tax rate, from Chapter 9, we have $k_{dt} = k_d \times (1 - T)$.

Probability of Bankruptcy

The chance that a firm will become bankrupt due to an inability to meet its obligations as they come due depends largely on its level of both business risk and financial risk.

Business Risk In Chapter 9, we defined *business risk* as the risk to the firm of being unable to cover its operating costs. In general, the greater the firm's *operating leverage*—the use of fixed operating costs—the higher its business risk. Although operating leverage is an important factor affecting business risk, two other factors—revenue stability and cost stability—also affect it. *Revenue stability* refers to the relative variability of the firm's sales revenues. Firms with reasonably stable levels of demand and with products that have stable prices have stable revenues. The result is low levels of business risk. Firms with highly volatile product demand and prices have unstable revenues that result in high levels of business risk. *Cost stability* refers to the relative predictability of input prices such as those for labour and materials. The more predictable and stable these input prices are, the lower the business risk; the less predictable and stable they are, the higher the business risk.

Business risk varies among firms, regardless of their lines of business, and is not affected by capital structure decisions. The level of business risk must be taken as a "given." The higher a firm's business risk, the more cautious the firm must be in establishing its capital structure. Firms with high business risk therefore tend toward less highly leveraged capital structures, and firms with low business risk tend toward more highly leveraged capital structures.

For example, Table 10.9 indicates that the mining industry has a debt ratio of about 40 percent. Given the uncertainty of revenues in this industry (since revenues are based on the world price of commodities), it makes sense for this industry to have a lower than average debt ratio. On the other hand, the wholesale food, beverage, and tobacco industry has very secure revenues; therefore the industry can tolerate a higher debt ratio. This is illustrated in Table 10.9, where this industry's debt ratio is 77.2 percent. In the discussion that follows, we will assume that business risk is constant.

Example Cooke Company, a soft drink manufacturer, is preparing to make a capital structure decision. It has obtained estimates of sales and the associated levels of earnings before interest and taxes (EBIT) from its financial analysts, as follows: There is a 25 percent chance that sales will total $400,000, a 50 percent chance that sales will total $600,000, and a 25 percent chance that sales will total $800,000. Fixed operating costs total $200,000, and variable operating costs equal 50 percent of sales. These data are summarized and the resulting EBIT calculated in Table 10.10.

The table shows that there is a 25 percent chance that the EBIT will be $0, a 50 percent chance that it will be $100,000, and a 25 percent chance that it will be $200,000. The financial manager must accept as given these levels of EBIT and their associated probabilities when developing the firm's capital structure. These EBIT data effectively reflect a certain level of business risk that captures the firm's operating leverage, sales revenue variability, and cost predictability.

Hint The cash flows to investors from bonds are less risky than the dividends from preferred shares, which are less risky than dividends from common shares. Only with bonds is the issuer contractually obligated to pay the scheduled interest, and the amounts due to bondholders and preferred shareholders are usually fixed. Therefore, the required return for bonds is generally lower than for preferred shares, which is lower than for common shares.

Financial Risk The firm's capital structure directly affects its *financial risk*, which is the risk to the firm of being unable to cover required financial obligations. The penalty for not meeting financial obligations is bankruptcy. The more fixed cost financing—debt (including financial leases) and preferred shares—a firm has in its capital structure, the greater its financial leverage and risk. Financial risk depends on the capital structure decision made by the management, and that decision is affected by the business risk the firm faces.

The *total risk* of a firm—business and financial risk combined—determines its probability of bankruptcy. Financial risk, its relationship to business risk, and their combined impact can be demonstrated by continuing the Cooke Company example.

Example Cooke Company's current capital structure is as shown:

Current capital structure	
Debt	$ 0
Common equity (25,000 shares at $20)	500,000
Total capital	$500,000

In this example, total capital equals total assets, meaning all capital is costly.

TABLE 10.10 Sales and Associated EBIT Calculations for Cooke Company ($000)

Probability of sales	0.25	0.50	0.25
Sales revenue	$400	$600	$800
Less: Fixed operating costs	200	200	200
Less: Variable operating costs (50% of sales)	200	300	400
Earnings before interest and taxes (EBIT)	$ 0	$100	$200

Hint
As you learned in Chapter 3, the debt ratio is equal to the amount of total debt divided by the total assets. The higher this ratio, the more financial leverage a firm is using.

Common equity is the combination of the proceeds from the sale of common shares and retained earnings. For the purposes of the example, we will assume that the book value of common equity is $20 per share and that at a 100 percent equity ratio (0% debt ratio), Cooke Company has 25,000 common shares outstanding. For the remainder of the Cooke Company example, we will assume the $20 book value per share figure does not change.

Let us assume that the firm is considering seven alternative capital structures. If we measure these structures using the debt ratio, they are associated with ratios of 0, 10, 20, 30, 40, 50, and 60 percent. Assuming (1) the firm has no current liabilities, (2) its capital structure currently contains all equity as shown, and (3) the total amount of capital remains constant at $500,000, the mix of debt and equity associated with the seven debt ratios is shown in Table 10.11. Also shown in the table is the number of common shares outstanding under each alternative.

Associated with each of the debt levels in column 3 of Table 10.11 would be an interest rate that would be expected to increase with increases in financial leverage. The level of debt, the associated interest rate (assumed to apply to *all* debt), and the dollar amount of annual interest associated with each of the alternative capital structures are summarized in Table 10.12. Because both the level of debt and the interest rate increase with increasing financial leverage (debt ratios), the annual interest increases as well.

Table 10.13 uses the levels of EBIT and associated probabilities developed in Table 10.10, the number of common shares found in column 5 of Table 10.11, and the annual interest values calculated in column 3 of Table 10.12 to calculate the earnings per share (EPS) for debt ratios of 0, 30, and 60 percent. A 40 percent tax rate is assumed. Also shown are the resulting expected EPS, the standard deviation of EPS, and the coefficient of variation of EPS associated with each debt ratio.

TABLE 10.11 Capital Structures Associated with Alternative Debt Ratios for Cooke Company

	Capital structure ($000)			
Debt ratio (1)	Total assets[a] (2)	Debt [(1) × (2)] (3)	Equity [(2) − (3)] (4)	Number of common shares outstanding [(4) ÷ $20][b] (5)
0%	$500	$ 0	$500	25,000
10	500	50	450	22,500
20	500	100	400	20,000
30	500	150	350	17,500
40	500	200	300	15,000
50	500	250	250	12,500
60	500	300	200	10,000

[a]Total assets must equal the total capital of $500,000. In this example, it is assumed that all capital is costly.

[b]The $20 value represents the book value per common share as noted earlier.

TABLE 10.12 Level of Debt, Interest Rate, and Dollar Amount of Annual Interest Associated with Cooke Company's Alternative Capital Structures

Debt ratio	Debt ($000) (1)	Interest rate on *all* debt (2)	Interest ($000) [(1) × (2)] (3)
0%	$ 0	0.0%	$ 0.00
10	50	9.0	4.50
20	100	9.5	9.50
30	150	10.0	15.00
40	200	11.0	22.00
50	250	13.5	33.75
60	300	16.5	49.50

TABLE 10.13 Calculation of EPS for Selected Debt Ratios ($000) for Cooke Company

Debt Ratio = 0%

Probability of EBIT	0.25	0.50	0.25
EBIT (Table 10.10)	$ 0.00	$100.00	$200.00
Less: Interest (Table 10.12)	0.00	0.00	0.00
Earnings before taxes	$ 0.00	$100.00	$200.00
Less: Taxes (T = 0.40)	0.00	40.00	80.00
Net income after taxes	$ 0.00	$ 60.00	$120.00
EPS (25,000 shares, Table 10.11)	$ 0.00	$ 2.40	$ 4.80
Expected EPS[a]		$ 2.40	
Standard deviation of EPS[a]		$ 1.70	
Coefficient of variation of EPS[a]		0.71	

Debt Ratio = 30%

Probability of EBIT	0.25	0.50	0.25
EBIT (Table 10.10)	$ 0.00	$100.00	$200.00
Less: Interest (Table 10.12)	15.00	15.00	15.00
Earnings before taxes	($15.00)	$ 85.00	$185.00
Less: Taxes (T = 0.40)	(6.00)[b]	34.00	74.00
Net income after taxes	($ 9.00)	$ 51.00	$111.00
EPS (17,500 shares, Table 10.11)	($ 0.51)	$ 2.91	$ 6.34
Expected EPS[a]		$ 2.91	
Standard deviation of EPS[a]		$ 2.42	
Coefficient of variation of EPS[a]		0.83	

continued

TABLE 10.13 Calculation of EPS for Selected Debt Ratios ($000) for Cooke Company (continued)

Debt Ratio = 60%			
Probability of EBIT	0.25	0.50	0.25
EBIT (Table 10.10)	$ 0.00	$100.00	$200.00
Less: Interest (Table 10.12)	49.50	49.50	49.50
Earnings before taxes	($49.50)	$ 50.50	$150.50
Less: Taxes ($T = 0.40$)	(19.80)[b]	20.20	60.20
Net income after taxes	($29.70)	$ 30.30	$ 90.30
EPS (10,000 shares, Table 10.11)	($ 2.97)	$ 3.03	$ 9.03
Expected EPS[a]		$ 3.03	
Standard deviation of EPS[a]		$ 4.24	
Coefficient of variation of EPS[a]		1.40	

[a]The procedures used to calculate the expected value, standard deviation, and coefficient of variation were presented in Chapter 7.

[b]It is assumed that the firm receives the tax benefit from its loss in the current period.

Table 10.14 summarizes the pertinent data for the seven alternative capital structures. The values shown for 0, 30, and 60 percent debt ratios were developed in Table 10.13, whereas calculations of similar values for the other debt ratios (10, 20, 40, and 50%) are not shown. Because the coefficient of variation measures the risk relative to the expected EPS, it is the preferred risk measure for use in comparing capital structures. As the firm's financial leverage increases, so does its coefficient of variation of EPS. As expected, an increasing level of risk is associated with increased levels of financial leverage.

TABLE 10.14 Expected EPS, Standard Deviation, and Coefficient of Variation for Alternative Capital Structures for Cooke Company

Capital structure debt ratio	Expected EPS (1)	Standard deviation of EPS (2)	Coefficient of variation of EPS [(2) ÷ (1)] (3)
0%	$2.40	1.70	0.71
10	2.55	1.88	0.74
20	2.72	2.13	0.78
30	2.91	2.42	0.83
40	3.12	2.83	0.91
50	3.18	3.39	1.07
60	3.03	4.24	1.40

FIGURE 10.3

Probability Distributions

Probability distributions of EPS for debt ratios of 0 and 60% for Cooke Company

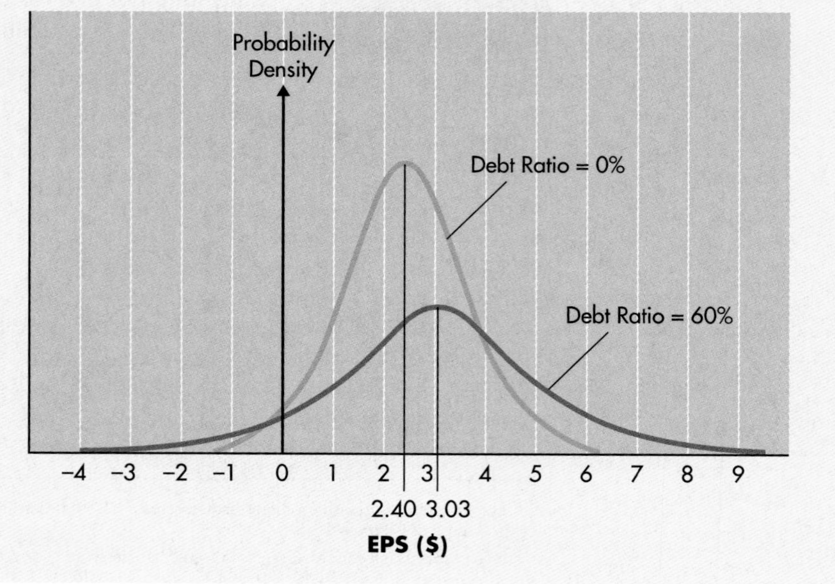

The relative risk of the two extremes of the capital structures evaluated in Table 10.13 (debt ratios = 0% and 60%) can be illustrated by showing the probability distribution of EPS associated with each of them. Figure 10.3 shows these two distributions. The expected level of EPS increases with increasing financial leverage, and so does risk, as reflected in the relative dispersion of each of the distributions. Clearly, the uncertainty of the expected EPS, as well as the chance of experiencing negative EPS, is greater when higher degrees of financial leverage are employed.

Further, the nature of the risk–return tradeoff associated with the seven capital structures under consideration can be clearly observed by plotting the expected EPS and coefficient of variation relative to the debt ratio. Plotting the data from Table 10.14 results in Figure 10.4. The figure shows that as debt is

FIGURE 10.4

Expected EPS and Coefficient of Variation of EPS

Expected EPS and coefficient of variation of EPS for alternative capital structures for Cooke Company

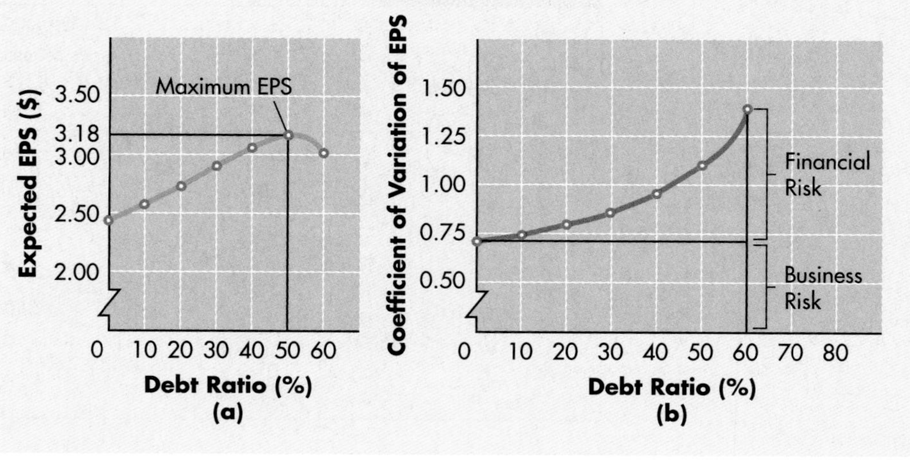

substituted for equity (as the debt ratio increases), the level of EPS rises and then begins to fall (graph *a*). The graph demonstrates that the peak earnings per share occurs at a debt ratio of 50 percent. The decline in earnings per share beyond that ratio results from the fact that the significant increases in interest are not fully offset by the reduction in the number of common shares outstanding.

If we look at the risk behaviour as measured by the coefficient of variation (graph *b*), we can see that risk increases with increasing leverage. A portion of the risk can be attributed to business risk, but that portion changing in response to increasing financial leverage would be attributed to financial risk.

Clearly, a risk–return tradeoff exists relative to the use of financial leverage. How to combine these risk–return factors into a valuation framework will be addressed later in the chapter. The key point to recognize here is that as a firm introduces more leverage into its capital structure, it will experience increases in both the expected level of return and the associated risk.

The Altman Z-Score is a tool that can be used to measure the overall financial health of a business. The Z-Score was developed in 1968 by Dr. Edward I. Altman, a finance professor at New York University.[8] It is a predictive model that combines five financial ratios to determine the likelihood of a company going bankrupt. As a multivariate approach for measuring the financial risk of a company, it is a powerful way to forecast the probability of a company going bankrupt within a two-year period. Studies measuring the effectiveness of the model indicate it accurately predicts bankruptcy 72 to 80 percent of the time.

The Z-Score uses five common business ratios, plus a weighting system designed by Altman, to determine the likelihood of a company going bankrupt. The tool was developed using data for manufacturing firms, but with some modifications it is also effective in determining the chance that service firms will go bankrupt. The general equation for the Z-Score is:

$$Z = \left[\frac{\text{EBIT}}{\text{Total assets}} \times 3.3\right] + \left[\frac{\text{Net sales}}{\text{Total assets}} \times 0.999\right] + \left[\frac{\text{Market value of equity}}{\text{Total liabilities}} \times 0.6\right] + \left[\frac{\text{Working capital}}{\text{Total assets}} \times 1.2\right] + \left[\frac{\text{Retained earnings}}{\text{Total assets}} \times 1.4\right] \quad (10.10)$$

Generally speaking, the higher the score, the lower the chance of bankruptcy. Companies with Z-Scores above 3 are considered healthy and therefore unlikely to enter bankruptcy within two years from the date of the financial data. Scores between 2.7 and 2.99 suggest one should exercise caution. Scores between 1.8 and 2.7 suggest that there is a good chance of the company going bankrupt. Scores below 1.80 suggest the probability of going bankrupt within two years is very high. Models that calculate the Z-Score for a company are freely available on the Web.

www.creditguru.com/CalcAltZ.shtml
www.jaxworks.com/calc2a.htm

8. See "Financial Ratios, Discriminant Analysis and the Prediction of Corporate Bankruptcy," *Journal of Finance*, September 1968, pp. 589–609; *The Z-Score Bankruptcy Model: Past, Present, and Future* (New York: John Wiley & Sons, 1977); or *Corporate Financial Distress and Bankruptcy*, 2nd ed. (New York: John Wiley & Sons, 1993).

Agency Costs Imposed by Lenders

As noted in Chapter 1, the managers of firms typically act as *agents* of the owners (shareholders). The owners give the managers the authority to manage the firm for the owners' benefit. The *agency problem* created by this relationship extends not only to the relationship between owners and managers, but also to the relationship between owners and lenders.

When a lender provides funds to a firm, the interest rate charged is based on the lender's assessment of the firm's risk. The lender–borrower relationship, therefore, depends on the lender's expectations for the firm's subsequent behaviour. The borrowing rates are, in effect, locked in when the loans are negotiated. After obtaining a loan at a certain rate, the firm could increase its risk by investing in risky projects or by incurring additional debt. Such action could weaken the lender's position in terms of its claim on the cash flow of the firm. From another point of view, if these risky investment strategies paid off, the shareholders would benefit. Because payment obligations to the lender remain unchanged, the excess cash flows generated by a positive outcome from the riskier action would enhance the value of the firm to its owners. In other words, if the risky investments pay off, the owners receive all the benefits; but if the risky investments do not pay off, the lenders share in the costs.

Clearly, an incentive exists for the managers acting on behalf of the shareholders to "take advantage" of lenders. To avoid this situation, lenders impose certain monitoring techniques on borrowers, who as a result incur *agency costs*. The most obvious strategy is to deny subsequent loan requests or to increase the cost of future loans to the firm. Because this strategy is an after-the-fact approach, other controls must be included in the loan agreement. Lenders typically protect themselves by including provisions that limit the firm's ability to significantly alter its business and financial risk. These loan provisions tend to centre on issues such as a minimum level of liquidity and coverage, and limitations on asset acquisitions, executive salaries, dividend payments, and future debt.

By including appropriate provisions in the loan agreement, the lender can control the firm's risk and thus be protected from the adverse consequences of this agency problem. Of course, in exchange for incurring agency costs by agreeing to the operating and financial constraints placed on it by the loan provisions, the firm should benefit by obtaining funds at a lower cost.

Hint
Typical loan provisions included in corporate bonds are discussed in Chapter 5.

Asymmetric Information

pecking order
A hierarchy of financing beginning with reinvested profits followed by debt financing and finally external equity financing.

Some recent research has examined the capital structure decisions actually made by companies.[9] There are two views that may explain how the financing (capital structure) decision is made: (1) maintaining a *target capital structure* or (2) following a hierarchy of financing. This hierarchy, called a **pecking order,** begins

9. See, for example, J. Michael Pinegar and Lisa Wilbricht, "What Managers Think of Capital Structure Theory: A Survey," *Financial Management* (Winter 1989), pp. 82–91; R. R. Kamath, "Long-Term Financing Decisions: Views and Practices of Financial Managers of NYSE Firms," *The Financial Review*, 1997, Vol. 32, 350–356; L. Shyam-Sunder and S. Myers, "Testing Static Tradeoff Against Pecking Order Models of Capital Structure," *Journal of Financial Economics*, 1999, Vol. 51, 219–244; and Gishan Dissanaike, Bart M. Lambrecht, and Antonio Saragga-Seabra, "Differentiating Debt Target from Non-target Firms: An Empirical Study on Corporate Capital Structure," University of Cambridge, JIMS Working Paper No. 18, September 2001.

with reinvested profits, followed by debt financing, and finally external equity financing. The surveys of companies indicate that about one-third of firms attempt to implement a target capital structure, while two-thirds follow the pecking order method of financing. Shyam-Sunder and Myers' findings suggest that the pecking order model better explains the debt–equity choice made by companies than the target capital structure model, at least for the mature public firms that they examined.

At first glance, on the basis of financial theory, this choice appears to be inconsistent with wealth maximizing goals. However, Stewart Myers explained how "asymmetric information" could account for the pecking order financing preferences of financial managers.[10] **Asymmetric information** results when managers of a firm have more information about operations and future prospects than do investors. Assuming that managers make decisions with the goal of maximizing the wealth of existing shareholders, then asymmetric information can affect the capital structure decisions that managers make.

asymmetric information
The situation in which managers of a firm have more information about operations and future prospects than do investors.

Suppose, for example, that management has found a valuable investment that will require additional financing. Management believes that the prospects for the firm's future are very good and that the market, as indicated by the firm's current share price, does not fully appreciate the firm's value. In this case, it would be advantageous to current shareholders if management raised the required funds using debt rather than issuing new shares. Using debt to raise funds is frequently viewed as a **signal** that reflects management's view of the firm's share value. Debt financing is a *positive signal* suggesting that management believes that the shares are "undervalued" and therefore a bargain. When the firm's positive future outlook becomes known to the market, the increased value would be fully captured by existing owners, rather than having to be diluted across additional common shares.

signal
A financing action by management that is believed to reflect its view of the firm's common share value; generally, debt financing is viewed as a *positive signal* that management believes that the shares are "undervalued," and a new share issue is viewed as a *negative signal* that management believes that the shares are "overvalued."

If, however, the outlook for the firm is poor, management may believe that the firm's shares are "overvalued." In that case, it would be in the best interest of existing shareholders for the firm to issue new common shares. Therefore investors often interpret the announcement of a share issue as a *negative signal*—bad news concerning the firm's prospects—and the share price declines. This decrease in share value, along with high underwriting costs for share issues (compared to debt issues), makes new common share financing very expensive. When the negative future outlook becomes known to the market, the decreased value would impact both the new and the existing shares.

Because asymmetric information conditions exist from time to time, firms should maintain some reserve borrowing capacity, by keeping debt levels low. This reserve allows the firm to take advantage of good investment opportunities without having to sell common shares at low values or send signals that unduly influence the share price.

The Optimal Capital Structure

So, what *is* an optimal capital structure? To provide some insight into an answer, we will examine some basic financial relationships. It is known that *the value of the*

10. Stewart C. Myers, "The Capital Structure Puzzle," *Journal of Finance* (July 1984), pp. 575–592.

firm is maximized when the cost of capital is minimized. By using a modification of the simple perpetuity, we can define the value of the firm, V, by Equation 10.11:

$$V = \frac{\text{EBIT} \times (1 - T)}{k_a} \tag{10.11}$$

where:

EBIT = earnings before interest and taxes
T = tax rate
k_a = weighted average cost of capital

Clearly, if we assume that EBIT is constant, the value of the firm, V, is maximized by minimizing the weighted average cost of capital, k_a. This concept was also discussed in Chapter 9.

Cost Functions

Figure 10.5(a) plots three cost functions—the after-tax cost of debt, k_{dt}; the cost of equity, k_s; and the weighted average cost of capital, k_a—as a function of financial leverage measured by the debt ratio (debt to total assets). The *cost of debt* remains low due to the tax shield but slowly increases with increasing leverage to compensate lenders for increasing risk. The *cost of equity* is above the cost of debt and increases with increasing financial leverage, but generally increases more rapidly than the cost of debt. The increase in the cost of equity occurs because the shareholders require a higher return as leverage increases, to compensate for the higher degree of financial risk.

FIGURE 10.5

Cost Functions and Value
Capital costs and the optimal capital structure

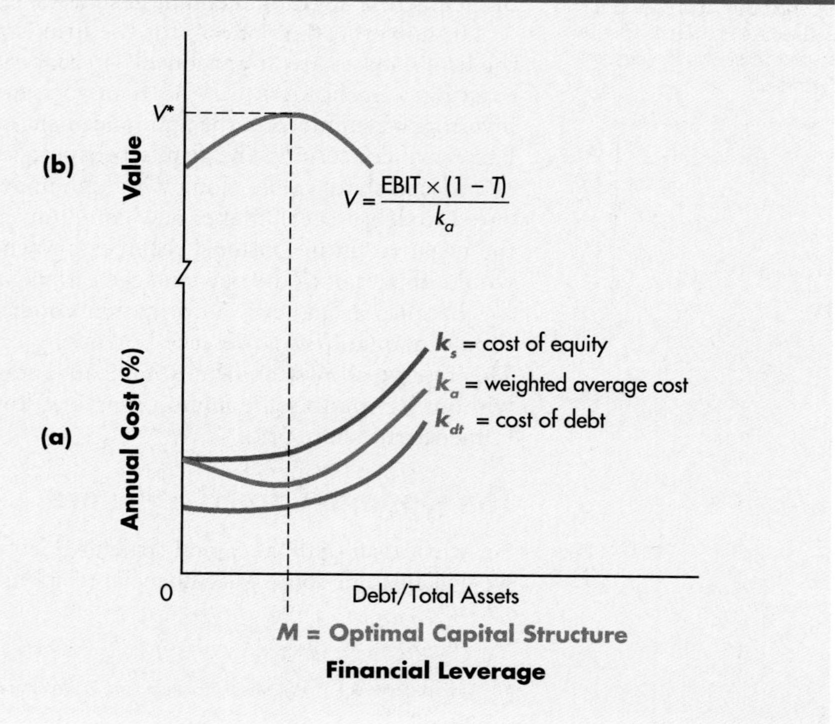

The *weighted average cost of capital, k_a*, results from a weighted average of the firm's debt and equity capital costs. At a debt ratio of zero, the firm is 100 percent equity financed. As debt is substituted for equity and as the debt ratio increases, the weighted average cost of capital declines because the debt cost is less than the equity cost ($k_{dt} < k_s$). As the debt ratio continues to increase, the increased debt and equity costs eventually cause the weighted average cost of capital to rise [after point M in Figure 10.5(a)]. This behaviour results in a U-shaped, or saucer-shaped, weighted average cost of capital function, k_a.

A Graphic View of the Optimal Structure

Because the maximization of value, V, is achieved when the overall cost of capital, k_a, is at a minimum, the **optimal capital structure** is therefore that at which the weighted average cost of capital, k_a, is minimized. In Figure 10.5(a), point M represents the *minimum weighted average cost of capital*—the point of optimal financial leverage and hence of optimal capital structure for the firm.

optimal capital structure
The capital structure at which the weighted average cost of capital is minimized, thereby maximizing the firm's value.

Figure 10.5(b) plots the value of the firm resulting from substitution of k_a in Figure 10.5(a) for various levels of financial leverage into Equation 10.10. As shown in Figure 10.5(b), at the optimal capital structure, point M, the value of the firm is maximized at V^*.

Generally, the lower the firm's weighted average cost of capital, the greater the difference between the return on a project and this cost, and therefore the greater the owners' return. Simply stated, minimizing the weighted average cost of capital allows management to undertake a larger number of profitable projects, thereby further increasing the value of the firm.

As a practical matter, there is no way to calculate the exact optimal capital structure point implied by Figure 10.5. Because it is impossible either to know or remain at the precise optimal capital structure, firms generally try to operate in a range that places them near what they believe to be the optimal capital structure. The fact that a company raises financing in block amounts, rather than in the exact optimal capital structure percentages, causes a company's actual capital structure to vary over time.

For example, for a particular year, a company may raise required financing using reinvested profits. This will change the company's capital structure. The next year the company may raise financing using reinvested profits and new debt financing. Again the capital structure will change. *But*, as long as the debt ratio remains within a range of up to 15 to 20 percent around the optimal point, a firm, in reality, will be viewed to be operating at the optimal capital structure and will minimize their cost of capital. This was clearly shown in the example provided in Chapter 9.

Therefore, in Figure 10.5(a), the k_a curve shows a very gradual change at the minimum point (a gradual U-like shape). This is also shown in Figure 9.1 in Chapter 9. While it is very difficult to determine the exact optimal capital structure point, most firms can calculate an optimal range. For most firms, the optimal range for debt with an obvious cost of financing will be in the range of 35 to 55 percent. At a level below this, the firm will not benefit from financial leverage and may have too high a cost of capital. At levels above, the firm may be increasing risk beyond an acceptable level. But it is important to note that the optimal range for the debt ratio will vary by industry and company.

? Review Questions

10–6 What is a firm's *capital structure*? What ratios assess the degree of financial leverage in a firm's capital structure?

10–7 "In Canada, most companies have the same capital structure and likely the same optimal capital structure." Do you agree with this statement? Discuss.

10–8 What is the major benefit of debt financing? How does it affect the firm's cost of debt?

10–9 Define *business risk,* and discuss the three factors that affect it. What influence does business risk have on the firm's capital structure decisions? Define *financial risk,* and explain its relationship to the firm's capital structure.

10–10 Briefly describe the *agency problem* that exists between owners and lenders. Explain how the firm must incur *agency costs* for the lender to resolve this problem.

10–11 How does *asymmetric information* affect the firm's capital structure decisions? Explain how and why investors may view the firm's financing actions as *signals.*

10–12 Describe the generally accepted theory concerning the behaviour of the cost of debt, the cost of equity, and the weighted average cost of capital as the firm's financial leverage increases from zero. Where is the *optimal capital structure* under this theory? Where is the optimal capital structure in reality? What is the relationship between the optimal capital structure, cost of capital, and the value of the firm?

10.3 The EBIT–EPS Approach to Capital Structure

EBIT–EPS approach
An approach for selecting the capital structure that maximizes earnings per share over the expected range of earnings before interest and taxes.

The **EBIT–EPS approach** to capital structure involves selecting the capital structure that maximizes earnings per share over the expected range of earnings before interest and taxes. Here the main emphasis is on the effects of various capital structures on *owners' returns.* Because one of the key variables affecting the market value of the firm's shares is its earnings, EPS can be conveniently used to analyze alternative capital structures.

Presenting a Financing Plan Graphically

To analyze the effects of a firm's capital structure on the owners' returns, we consider the relationship between earnings before interest and taxes (EBIT) and earnings per share (EPS). A constant level of EBIT—constant *business risk*—is assumed, to isolate the effect on returns of the financing costs associated with alternative capital structures. EPS is used to measure the owners' returns, which are expected to be closely related to share price.[11]

11. The relationship that is expected to exist between EPS and owner wealth is not one of cause and effect. As indicated in Chapter 1, the maximization of profits does not necessarily assure the firm that owners' wealth is also being maximized. Nevertheless, it is expected that the movement of earnings per share will have some effect on owners' wealth, because EPS data constitute one of the few pieces of information investors receive, and they often bid the firm's share price up or down in response to the level of these earnings.

The Data Required

To graph a financing plan, we need to know at least two EBIT–EPS coordinates. The approach for obtaining coordinates can be illustrated by an example.

Example EBIT–EPS coordinates can be found by assuming two EBIT values and calculating the EPS associated with them.[12] Such calculations for three capital structures—debt ratios of 0, 30, and 60 percent—for Cooke Company were presented in Table 10.13. By using the EBIT values of $100,000 and $200,000, the associated EPS values calculated there are summarized in the table within Figure 10.6.

FIGURE 10.6

EBIT–EPS Approach

A comparison of selected capital structures for Cooke Company (data from Table 10.13)

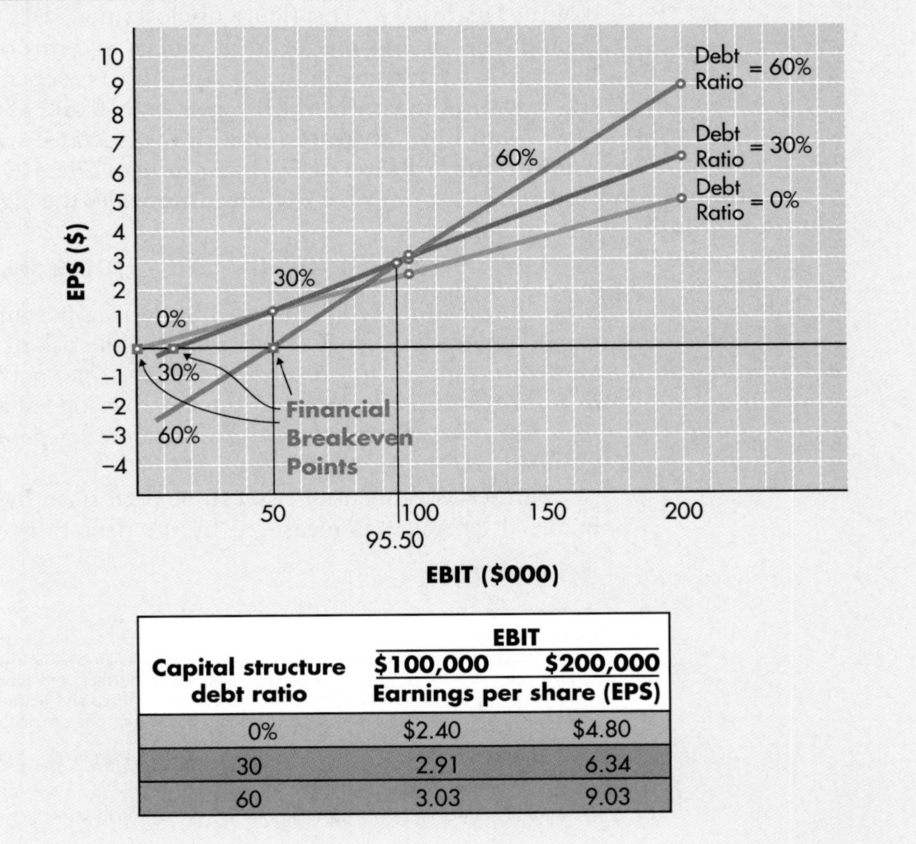

Capital structure debt ratio	EBIT $100,000	EBIT $200,000
	Earnings per share (EPS)	
0%	$2.40	$4.80
30	2.91	6.34
60	3.03	9.03

12. A convenient method for finding one EBIT–EPS coordinate is to calculate the *financial breakeven point*, the level of EBIT for which the firm's EPS just equals $0. It is the level of EBIT needed just to cover all fixed financial costs—annual interest (I) and preferred share dividends (PD). The equation for the financial breakeven point is

$$\text{Financial breakeven point} = I + \frac{PD}{1 - T}$$

where T is the tax rate. It can be seen that when PD = $0, the financial breakeven point is equal to I, the annual interest payment.

Plotting the Data

financial breakeven point
The level of EBIT necessary just to cover all fixed financial costs; the level of EBIT for which EPS = $0.

The Cooke Company data can be plotted on a set of EBIT–EPS axes, as shown in Figure 10.6. The figure shows the level of EPS expected for each level of EBIT. For levels of EBIT below the *x*-axis intercept, a loss (negative EPS) results. Each of the *x*-axis intercepts is a **financial breakeven point,** where EBIT just covers all fixed financial costs (EPS = $0).

Comparing Alternative Capital Structures

We can compare alternative capital structures by graphing financing plans as shown in Figure 10.6. The following example illustrates this procedure.

Example Cooke Company's capital structure alternatives were plotted on the EBIT–EPS axes in Figure 10.6. This figure discloses that over certain ranges of EBIT, each capital structure is superior to the others in terms of maximizing EPS. The zero-leverage capital structure (debt ratio = 0%) is superior to either of the other capital structures for levels of EBIT between $0 and $50,000; between $50,000 and $95,500 of EBIT, the capital structure associated with a debt ratio of 30 percent is preferred. At a level of EBIT in excess of $95,500, the capital structure associated with a debt ratio of 60 percent provides the highest earnings per share.[13]

Considering Risk in EBIT–EPS Analysis

When interpreting EBIT–EPS analysis, it is important to consider the risk of each capital structure alternative. Graphically, the risk of each capital structure can be viewed in light of the *financial breakeven point* (EBIT-axis intercept) and the *degree of financial leverage* reflected in the slope of the capital structure line: *The higher the financial breakeven point and the steeper the slope of the capital structure line, the greater the financial risk.*[14]

Further assessment of risk can be performed by using ratios. With increased financial leverage, as measured by the debt ratio, we expect a corresponding

13. An algebraic technique can be used to find the *indifference points* between the capital structure alternatives. This technique involves expressing each capital structure as an equation stated in terms of earnings per share, setting the equations for two capital structures equal to each other, and solving for the level of EBIT that causes the equations to be equal. By using the notation from footnote 12 and letting *n* equal the number of common shares outstanding, the general equation for the earnings per share from a financing plan is:

$$\text{EPS} = \frac{(1 - T) \times (\text{EBIT} - I) - PD}{n}$$

Comparing Cooke Company's 0 and 30 percent capital structures, we get:

$$\frac{(1 - 0.40) \times (\text{EBIT} - \$0) - \$0}{25} = \frac{(1 - 0.40) \times (\text{EBIT} - \$15) - \$0}{17.50}$$

$$\frac{0.60 \times \text{EBIT}}{25} = \frac{0.60 \times \text{EBIT} - \$9}{17.50}$$

$$10.50 \times \text{EBIT} = 15 \times \text{EBIT} - \$225$$

$$\$225 = 4.50 \times \text{EBIT}$$

$$\text{EBIT} = \$50$$

The calculated value of the indifference point between the 0 and 30 percent capital structures is therefore $50,000, as shown in Figure 10.6.

14. The degree of financial leverage (DFL) is reflected in the slope of the EBIT–EPS function. The steeper the slope, the greater the degree of financial leverage, because the change in EPS (*y* axis) resulting from a given change in EBIT (*x* axis) will increase with increasing slope and will decrease with decreasing slope.

decline in the firm's ability to make scheduled interest payments, as measured by the times interest earned ratio.

Example Reviewing the three capital structures plotted for Cooke Company in Figure 10.6, we can see that as the debt ratio increases, so does the financial risk of each alternative. Both the financial breakeven point and the slope of the capital structure lines increase with increasing debt ratios. If we use the $100,000 EBIT value, the times interest earned ratio (EBIT ÷ interest) for the zero-leverage capital structure is infinity ($100,000 ÷ $0); for the 30 percent debt case, it is 6.67 ($100,000 ÷ $15,000); and for the 60 percent debt case, it is 2.02 ($100,000 ÷ $49,500).

Because lower times interest earned ratios reflect higher risk, these ratios support the earlier conclusion that the risk of the capital structures increases with increasing financial leverage. A capital structure consisting of 60 percent debt is riskier than one with 30 percent, which in turn is riskier than a capital structure with no debt. But returns to the owners are also likely to be lower with a 0 or 30 percent debt ratio.

Basic Shortcoming of EBIT–EPS Analysis

The most important point to recognize when using EBIT–EPS analysis is that this technique tends to concentrate on *maximizing earnings* rather than maximizing owner wealth. The use of an EPS-maximizing approach generally ignores risk. If investors did not require risk premiums (additional returns) as the firm increased the proportion of debt in its capital structure, a strategy involving maximizing EPS would also maximize owner wealth. Because risk premiums increase with increases in financial leverage, the maximization of EPS *does not* ensure owner wealth maximization. To select the best capital structure, both return (EPS) and risk (via the required return, k_s) must be integrated into a valuation framework consistent with the capital structure theory presented earlier.

? Review Question

10–13 Explain the *EBIT–EPS approach* to capital structure. Include in your explanation a graph indicating the *financial breakeven point*; label the axes. Is this approach consistent with maximization of value? Explain.

LG6

10.4 Choosing the Optimal Capital Structure

Creating a wealth maximization framework for use in making capital structure decisions is not easy. Although the two key factors—return and risk—can be used separately to make capital structure decisions, integration of them into a market value context provides the best results. This section describes the procedures for linking the return and risk associated with alternative capital structures to market value to select the best capital structure.

Linkage

To determine its value under alternative capital structures, the firm must find the level of return that must be earned to compensate investors and owners for the risk being incurred. That is, the risk associated with each structure must be linked to the required rate of return. Such a framework is consistent with the overall valuation framework developed in Chapter 8 and applied to capital budgeting decisions in Chapters 12 and 13.

The required return associated with a given level of financial risk can be estimated in a number of ways. Theoretically, the preferred approach would be to first estimate the beta associated with each alternative capital structure and then use the CAPM to calculate the required return, k_s. A more operational approach involves linking the financial risk associated with each capital structure alternative directly to the required return. Such an approach is similar to the CAPM-type approach demonstrated in Chapter 13 for linking risk and required return (RADR). Here it involves estimating the required return associated with each level of financial risk, as measured by a statistic such as the coefficient of variation of EPS. Regardless of the approach used, one would expect that the required return would increase as the financial risk increases.

Example Cooke Company, using the coefficients of variation of EPS associated with each of the seven alternative capital structures as a risk measure, estimated the associated required returns. These are shown in Table 10.15. As expected, the estimated required return, k_s, increases with increasing risk, as measured by the coefficient of variation of EPS.

Estimating Value

The value of the firm associated with alternative capital structures can be estimated by using one of the standard valuation models. If, for simplicity, we assume that all earnings are paid out as dividends, we can use a zero-growth valuation model as developed in Chapter 8. The model is restated here with EPS

TABLE 10.15 Required Returns for Cooke Company's Alternative Capital Structures

Capital structure debt ratio	Coefficient of variation of EPS (from column 3 of Table 10.14) (1)	Estimated cost of capital, k_a (2)
0%	0.71	11.5%
10	0.74	11.7
20	0.78	12.1
30	0.83	12.5
40	0.91	14.0
50	1.07	16.5
60	1.40	19.0

substituted for dividends, because in each year the dividends would equal EPS and the firm's cost of capital used for the required return:

$$V_0 = \frac{\text{EPS}}{k_a} \tag{10.12}$$

By substituting the estimated level of EPS and the associated cost of capital, k_a, into Equation 10.12, we can estimate the per share value of the firm, V_0.

Example Returning again to Cooke Company, we can now estimate the value of its shares under each of the alternative capital structures. Substituting the expected EPS (from column 1 of Table 10.14) and the cost of capital, k_a (from column 2 of Table 10.15), into Equation 10.12 for each of the alternative capital structures, we obtain the share values given in column 3 of Table 10.16. Plotting the resulting share values against the associated debt ratios, as shown in Figure 10.7, clearly illustrates that the maximum share value occurs at the capital structure associated with a debt ratio of 30 percent.

Maximizing Value Versus Maximizing EPS

Throughout this text, the goal of the financial manager has been specified as maximizing owner wealth, not profit. Although there is some relationship between the level of expected profit and value, there is no reason to believe that profit-maximizing strategies necessarily result in wealth maximization. It is therefore the wealth of the owners as reflected in the estimated share value that should serve as the criterion for selecting the best capital structure. A final look at Cooke Company will help to reinforce this point.

Example Further analysis of Figure 10.7 clearly shows that although the firm's profits (EPS) are maximized at a debt ratio of 50 percent, share value is maximized at a 30 percent debt ratio. In this case, the preferred capital structure would be the 30 percent debt ratio. The EPS-maximization approach does not provide a

TABLE 10.16 Calculation of Share Value Estimates Associated with Alternative Capital Structures for Cooke Company

Capital structure debt ratio	Expected EPS (from column 1 of Table 10.14) (1)	Estimated cost of capital, k_a (from column 2 of Table 10.15) (2)	Estimated value per common share [(1) ÷ (2)] (3)
0%	$2.40	0.115	$20.87
10	2.55	0.117	21.79
20	2.72	0.121	22.48
30	2.91	0.125	23.28
40	3.12	0.140	22.29
50	3.18	0.165	19.27
60	3.03	0.190	15.95

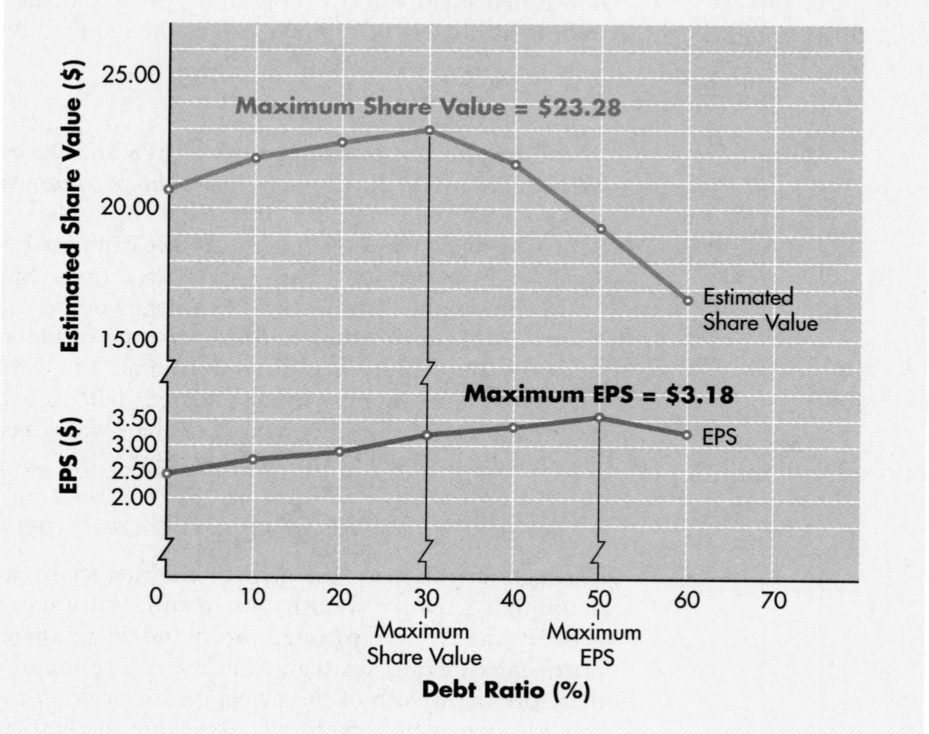

FIGURE 10.7

Estimating Value

Estimated share value and EPS for alternative capital structures for Cooke Company

similar conclusion because it does not consider risk. Therefore, to maximize owner wealth, Cooke Company should employ the capital structure that results in a 30 percent debt ratio. ▲

Some Other Important Considerations

Because there is really no practical way to calculate the optimal capital structure, any quantitative analysis of capital structure must be tempered with other important considerations. Numerous additional factors relative to capital structure decisions could be listed; some of the more important factors, categorized by broad area of concern, are summarized in Table 10.17.

? Review Questions

10–14 Do *maximizing value* and *maximizing EPS* lead to the same conclusion about the optimal capital structure? If not, what is the cause?

10–15 How might a firm go about determining its optimal capital structure? In addition to quantitative considerations, what other important factors should a firm consider when it is making a capital structure decision?

TABLE 10.17 Important Factors to Consider in Making Capital Structure Decisions

Concern	Factor	Description
Business risk	Revenue stability	Firms having stable and predictable revenues can more safely undertake highly levered capital structures than can firms with volatile patterns of sales revenue. Firms with growing sales tend to be in the best position to benefit from added debt because they can reap the positive benefits of leverage, which magnifies the effect of these increases.
	Cash flow	When considering a new capital structure the firm must focus on its ability to generate the necessary cash flows to meet obligations. Cash forecasts reflecting an ability to service debts (and preferred shares) must support any capital structure shift.
Agency costs	Contractual obligations	A firm may be contractually constrained with respect to the type of funds that it can raise. For example, a firm might be prohibited from selling additional debt except when the claims of holders of such debt are made subordinate to the existing debt. Contractual constraints on the sale of additional common shares as well as the ability to distribute dividends might also exist.
	Management preferences	Occasionally, a firm will impose an internal constraint on the use of debt to limit its risk exposure to a level deemed acceptable to management. In other words, due to risk aversion, the firm's management constrains the firm's capital structure at a level that may or may not be the true optimum.
	Control	A management concerned about control may prefer to issue debt rather than (voting) common shares. Under favourable market conditions, a firm that wanted to sell equity could issue *non-voting shares* or make a *preemptive offering* (see Chapter 5), allowing each shareholder to maintain proportionate ownership. Generally, only in closely held firms or firms threatened by takeover does control become a major concern in the capital structure decision.
Asymmetric information	External risk assessment	The firm's ability to raise funds quickly and at favourable rates depends on the external risk assessments of lenders and bond raters. The firm must therefore consider the potential impact of capital structure decisions both on share value and on published financial statements from which lenders and raters tend to assess the firm's risk.
	Timing	At times when interest rates are low, debt financing might be more attractive; when interest rates are high, the sale of common shares may be more appealing. Sometimes both debt and equity capital become unavailable at what would be viewed as reasonable terms. General economic conditions—especially those of the capital market—can thus significantly affect capital structure decisions.

SUMMARY

Discuss the role of breakeven analysis, how to determine the operating breakeven point, and the effect of changing costs on the breakeven point. Breakeven analysis measures the level of sales necessary to cover total operating costs. The operating breakeven point may be calculated by dividing fixed operating costs by the gross margin, the difference between sales and variable costs, on a per unit or percentage basis. Breakeven can be shown in number of units (Q), total sales, or graphically. The operating breakeven point increases with increased fixed and variable operating costs and decreases with an increase in sale price, and vice versa. If the income statement is used to determine breakeven, COGS, the direct costs of production, are considered variable costs. Fixed costs are normally represented by the operating costs.

Understand operating, financial, and total leverage and the relationships among them. Operating leverage is the use of fixed operating costs by the firm to magnify the effects of changes in sales on EBIT. The higher the fixed operating costs, the greater the operating leverage. Financial leverage is the use of fixed financial costs by the firm to magnify the effects of changes in EBIT on EPS. The higher the fixed financial costs—typically, interest on debt and preferred share dividends—the greater the financial leverage. The total leverage of the firm is the use of fixed costs—both operating and financial—to magnify the effects of changes in sales on EPS. Total leverage reflects the combined effect of operating and financial leverage. When using measures of leverage, an assumption made is that the cost structure remains the same from one period to the next. If this is not the case, the calculated measures of leverage will not apply for the future period.

Describe the basic types of capital, external assessment of capital structure, and capital structure theory. The two basic types of capital—debt and equity—that make up a firm's capital structure differ with respect to voice in management, claims on income and assets, maturity, and tax treatment. Capital structure can be externally assessed by using financial ratios—debt ratio, times interest earned ratio, and fixed-payment coverage ratio. The capital structure used varies by industry and companies within the industry; however, in 2004, the average debt ratio for non-financial industries in Canada was 61.3 percent and the times interest earned ratio was 3.0.

Research suggests that there is an optimal capital structure that balances the firm's benefits and costs of debt financing. The major benefit of debt financing is the tax shield. The costs of debt financing include the probability of bankruptcy, caused by business and financial risk; agency costs imposed by lenders; and asymmetric information, which typically causes firms to raise funds in a pecking order of reinvested profits, then debt, and finally external equity financing, to send positive signals to the market and thereby enhance the wealth of shareholders. The Altman Z-Score is a predictive multivariate model that measures the financial risk of a company, and forecasts the probability of a company going bankrupt within a two-year period.

Explain the optimal capital structure using a graphic view of the firm's debt, equity, and weighted average cost of capital functions, and a modified form of the zero-growth valuation model. The zero-growth valuation model can be used to define the firm's value as its after-tax EBIT divided by its weighted average cost of capital. Assuming that EBIT is constant, the value of the firm is maximized by minimizing its weighted average cost of capital (WACC). The optimal capital structure is the one that minimizes the WACC. Graphically, although both debt and equity costs rise with increasing financial leverage, the lower cost of debt causes the WACC to decline and then rise with increasing financial leverage. As a result, the firm's WACC exhibits a U-shape having a minimum value, which defines the optimum capital structure—the one that maximizes owner wealth.

Discuss the graphic presentation, risk considerations, and basic shortcomings of using the EBIT–EPS approach to compare alternative capital structures. The EBIT–EPS approach can be used to evaluate capital structures in light of the returns they provide the firm's owners and their degree of financial risk. Under the EBIT–EPS approach, the preferred capital structure is the one that is expected to provide maximum EPS over the firm's expected range of EBIT. Graphically, this approach reflects risk in terms of the financial breakeven point and the slope of the capital structure line. The major shortcoming of EBIT–EPS analysis is that by ignoring risk, it concentrates on maximizing earnings rather than owners' wealth.

Review the return and risk of alternative capital structures and their linkage to market value, and other important capital structure considerations. The best capital structure can be selected from various alternatives by using a valuation model to link return and risk factors. The preferred capital structure would be the one that results in the highest estimated share value—not the highest profits (EPS). Other important nonquantitative factors, such as revenue stability, cash flow, contractual obligations, management preferences, control, external risk assessment, and timing, must also be considered when making capital structure decisions.

SELF-TEST PROBLEMS (Solutions in Appendix B)

ST 10–1 **Breakeven and all forms of leverage** For the upcoming fiscal year, TOR Inc. expects to be able to produce and sell 100,000 units of product. The product's selling price is \$7.50 per unit. Variable operating costs are \$3 per unit, while fixed operating costs total \$250,000. Annual interest charges are \$80,000, and the firm has 8,000 preferred shares outstanding that pay a \$5 annual dividend. TOR has 20,000 common shares outstanding, and the company's tax rate is 40 percent.

a. At what level of sales in units and sales dollars would the firm breakeven on operations (i.e., EBIT = \$0)?

b. Calculate the firm's earnings per share (EPS) in tabular form at (1) the expected level of sales, and (2) at sales of 120,000 units.

c. Using the expected 100,000 units of sales as a base, calculate the firm's degree of operating leverage (DOL).

d. Using the EBIT associated with the expected 100,000 units of sales as a base, calculate the firm's degree of financial leverage (DFL).

e. Calculate the degree of total leverage (DTL) for TOR Inc. at the expected sales level of 100,000 units. If sales increase 20 percent from that level, determine the dollar and percentage change in EBIT and earnings per share (EPS).

ST 10–2 **EBIT–EPS analysis** Newlin Electronics is considering raising additional financing of \$10,000. It currently has \$50,000 of 12 percent (annual interest) bonds and 10,000 common shares outstanding. The firm can obtain the additional financing through a 12 percent (annual interest) bond issue or the sale of 1,000 common shares. The firm has a 40 percent tax rate.

a. Calculate two EBIT–EPS coordinates for each plan by selecting any two EBIT values and finding their associated EPS.

b. Plot the two financing plans on a set of EBIT–EPS axes.

c. On the basis of your graph in **b**, at what level of EBIT does the bond plan become superior to the stock plan?

  **ST 10–3 Optimal capital structure** Hawaiian Macadamia Nut Company has collected the following data regarding the company's expected earnings per share and cost of capital at various debt ratios.

Debt ratio	Expected earnings per share	Cost of capital, k_a
0%	$3.12	13%
10	3.90	15
20	4.80	16
30	5.44	17
40	5.51	19
50	5.00	20
60	4.40	22

a. Compute the estimated value for each of the firm's common shares for each of the debt ratios using the simplified method described in this chapter (see Equation 10.12).
b. Determine the optimal capital structure based on (1) maximization of expected earnings per share and (2) maximization of share value.
c. Which capital structure do you recommend? Why?

PROBLEMS

BASIC   **10–1 Breakeven point—Algebraic** Kate Rowland wishes to estimate the number of flower arrangements she must sell at $24.95 to break even. She has estimated fixed operating costs of $12,350 per year and variable operating costs of $15.45 per arrangement. How many flower arrangements must Kate sell to break even on operating costs? What will her total sales revenue be at breakeven? Calculate this answer in two different ways.

BASIC   **10–2 Breakeven comparisons—Algebraic** Given the price and cost data shown in the following table for each of the three firms, F, G, and H, answer the following questions.

Firm	F	G	H
Sale price per unit	$ 18.00	$ 21.00	$ 30.00
Variable operating cost per unit	6.75	13.50	12.00
Fixed operating cost	45,000	30,000	90,000

a. What is the operating breakeven point in units and sales dollars for each firm?
b. How would you rank these firms in terms of their risk?

INTERMEDIATE  10–3 **Breakeven point—Algebraic and graphic** Fine Leather Enterprises sells its single product for $129 per unit. The firm's fixed operating costs are $473,000 annually, and its variable operating costs are $86 per unit.

a. Find the firm's operating breakeven point in units and sales dollars.

b. Label the *x* axis "Sales (units)" and the *y* axis "Costs/Revenues ($)," and then graph the firm's sales revenue, total operating cost, and fixed operating cost functions on these axes. In addition, label the operating breakeven point and the areas of loss and profit (EBIT).

INTERMEDIATE  10–4 **Breakeven analysis** Barry Carter is considering opening a record store. He wants to estimate the number of CDs he must sell to break even. The CDs will be sold for $13.98 each, variable operating costs are $10.48 per CD, and annual fixed operating costs are $73,500.

a. Find the operating breakeven point in CDs.

b. Calculate the total operating costs at the breakeven volume found in **a**.

c. If Barry estimates that at a minimum he can sell 2,000 CDs *per month,* should he go into the record business?

d. How much EBIT would Barry realize if he sells the minimum 2,000 CDs per month noted in **c**?

e. Determine the number of units Barry must sell to generate an EBIT of 50 percent of the fixed operating costs.

f. Assuming Barry can sell 2,000 CDs per month, what is the DOL of the operation? What is the implication of your answer?

INTERMEDIATE  10–5 **Breakeven point—Changing costs/revenues** JWG Company publishes *Creative Crosswords.* Last year the book of puzzles sold for $10 with variable operating cost per book of $8 and fixed operating costs of $40,000. How many books must be sold this year to achieve the breakeven point for the stated operating costs, given the following different circumstances?

a. All figures remain the same as last year.

b. Fixed operating costs increase to $44,000; all other figures remain the same.

c. The selling price increases to $10.50; all costs remain the same as last year.

d. Variable operating cost per book increases to $8.50; all other figures remain the same.

e. What conclusions about the operating breakeven point can be drawn from your answers?

INTERMEDIATE  10–6 **Breakeven analysis** Molly Jasper and her sister, Caitlin Peters, got into the novelties business almost by accident. Molly, a talented sculptor, would make little figurines as gifts for friends. Occasionally, she and Caitlin would set up a booth at a crafts fair and sell a few of the figurines along with jewellery that Caitlin made. Little by little, demand for the figurines, now called Mollycaits, grew, and the sisters began to reproduce some of the favourites in resin using molds of the originals. The day came when a buyer for a major department store offered them a contract to produce 1,500 figurines of various designs for $10,000. Molly and Caitlin realized that it was time to get down to business. To make bookkeeping simpler, Molly had priced all of the figurines at $8 each. Variable operating costs amounted to an average of $6 per unit. In order to produce the order, Molly and Caitlin would have to rent industrial facilities for a month, which would cost them $4,000.

a. Calculate Mollycait's operating breakeven point in units and sales dollars on the department store contract.
b. Calculate Mollycait's EBIT on the department store order. Should Molly take the contract?
c. If Molly renegotiates the contract at a price of $10 per unit, what will the EBIT be?
d. If the store refuses to pay more than $8 per unit, but is willing to negotiate quantity, what quantity of figurines would result in an EBIT of $4,000?
e. At this time, Mollycaits come in 15 different varieties. Whereas the average variable cost per unit is $6, the actual cost varies from unit to unit. What recommendation would you have for Molly and Caitlin with regard to pricing and/or the number and type of units that they offer for sale?

INTERMEDIATE 

10–7 **EBIT sensitivity** Stewart Industries sells its finished product for $9 per unit. Its fixed operating costs are $20,000, and the variable operating cost per unit is $5.
a. Calculate the firm's earnings before interest and taxes (EBIT) for sales of 10,000 units.
b. Calculate the firm's EBIT for sales of 8,000 and 12,000 units, respectively.
c. Calculate the percentage changes in sales (from the 10,000-unit base level) and associated percentage changes in EBIT for the shifts in sales indicated in **b**.
d. On the basis of your findings in **c**, comment on the sensitivity of changes in EBIT in response to changes in sales.

INTERMEDIATE 

10–8 **Degree of operating leverage** Grey Products has fixed operating costs of $380,000, variable operating costs per unit of $16, and a selling price of $63.50 per unit.
a. Calculate the operating breakeven point in units.
b. Calculate the firm's EBIT at 9,000, 10,000, and 11,000 units, respectively.
c. By using 10,000 units as a base, what are the percentage changes in units sold and EBIT as sales move from the base to the other sales levels used in **b**?
d. Use the percentages computed in **c** to determine the degree of operating leverage (DOL).
e. Use the formula for degree of operating leverage to determine the DOL at 10,000 units.

INTERMEDIATE 

10–9 **Degree of operating leverage—Graphic** Levin Corporation has fixed operating costs of $72,000, variable operating costs of $6.75 per unit, and a selling price of $9.75 per unit.
a. Calculate the operating breakeven point in units.
b. Compute the degree of operating leverage (DOL) for the following unit sales levels: 25,000, 30,000, 40,000.
c. Graph the DOL figures that you computed in **b** (on the y axis) against sales levels (on the x axis).
d. Compute the degree of operating leverage at 24,000 units; add this point to your graph.
e. What principle is illustrated by your graph and figures?

INTERMEDIATE  **10–10 EPS calculations** Southland Industries has $60,000 of 16 percent (annual interest) bonds outstanding, 1,500 preferred shares paying an annual dividend of $5 per share, and 4,000 common shares outstanding. Assuming that the firm has a 40 percent tax rate, compute earnings per share (EPS) for the following levels of EBIT:

a. $24,600
b. $30,600
c. $35,000

INTERMEDIATE  **10–11 Degree of financial leverage** Northwestern Trust has a current capital structure consisting of $250,000 of 16 percent (annual interest) debt and 2,000 common shares. The firm pays taxes at the rate of 40 percent.

a. Using EBIT values of $80,000 and $120,000, determine the associated earnings per share (EPS).
b. Using $80,000 of EBIT as a base, calculate the degree of financial leverage (DFL).
c. Rework parts **a** and **b** assuming that the firm has $100,000 of 16 percent (annual interest) debt and 3,000 common shares.

  INTERMEDIATE **10–12 DFL and graphic display of financing plans** Wells and Associates has EBIT of $67,500. Interest costs are $22,500, and the firm has 15,000 common shares outstanding. Assume a 40 percent tax rate.

a. Use the degree of financial leverage (DFL) formula to calculate the DFL for the firm.
b. Using a set of EBIT–EPS axes, plot Wells and Associates' financing plan.
c. Assuming that the firm also has 1,000 preferred shares paying a $6 annual dividend per share, what is the DFL?
d. Plot the financing plan including the 1,000 shares of $6 preferred stock on the axes used in **b**.
e. Briefly discuss the graph of the two financing plans.

  INTERMEDIATE **10–13 Integrative—Multiple leverage measures** Play-More Toys produces inflatable beach balls, selling 400,000 balls a year. Each ball produced has a variable operating cost of $0.84 and sells for $1. Fixed operating costs are $28,000. The firm has annual interest charges of $6,000, preferred share dividends of $2,000, and a 40 percent tax rate.

a. Calculate the operating breakeven point in units and dollars.
b. Calculate the degree of operating leverage (DOL) at sales of $400,000. Explain the meaning of your answers.
c. Calculate the degree of financial leverage (DFL) at sales of $400,000. Explain the meaning of your answers.
d. Calculate the degree of total leverage (DTL) at sales of $400,000. Explain the meaning of your answers.

  INTERMEDIATE **10–14 Calculating breakeven and measures of leverage** Evans Enterprises is considering introducing a new product that will sell for $200 per unit. It is possible to produce the product in two ways. The first is capital-intensive. With this method, fixed costs would be $60,000, variable costs $0.80 per unit, and interest expense $12,000. The second method is labour-intensive. With this method, fixed costs would be $12,000, variable costs $1.60 per unit, and interest

expense $4,000. Evans' tax rate is 40 percent and they have 8,000 common shares outstanding.

a. Calculate breakeven in units and in dollars for both production methods, and prove that the breakeven calculated is correct.
b. Calculate the degree of operating leverage for Evans' two cost structures at production of 60,000 units. Discuss the implication of your answers. When using the DOL, what assumption must you make?
c. If Evans could only hope to sell 60,000 units, which cost structure would you recommend they select? Explain.
d. Calculate the degree of financial leverage for the two cost structures at production of 60,000 units. Discuss the implication of your answers.
e. Now assume that the basic cost structures will apply if production increases to 80,000 units. Calculate the degree of operating leverage, degree of financial leverage, and degree of total leverage and discuss the implications of your answers. If Evans could sell 80,000 units, which cost structure would you recommend they select? Explain.
f. At what production volume would Evans Enterprises be indifferent with regard to the cost structure selected?

INTERMEDIATE 

10–15 Integrative—Leverage and risk Firm R has sales of 100,000 units at $2 per unit, variable operating costs of $1.70 per unit, and fixed operating costs of $6,000. Interest is $10,000 per year. Firm W has sales of 100,000 units at $2.50 per unit, variable operating costs of $1 per unit, and fixed operating costs of $62,500. Interest is $17,500 per year. Assume that both firms are in the 40 percent tax bracket.

a. Compute the degree of operating, financial, and total leverage for firm R. Explain the meaning of your answers.
b. Compute the degree of operating, financial, and total leverage for firm W. Explain the meaning of your answers.
c. Compare the relative risks of the two firms.
d. Discuss the principles of leverage illustrated in your answers.

 INTERMEDIATE

10–16 Integrative—Multiple leverage measures and prediction Carolina Fastener, Inc., makes a patented marine bulkhead latch that wholesales for $6. Each latch has variable operating costs of $3.50. Fixed operating costs are $50,000 per year. The firm pays $13,000 interest and $7,000 of preferred share dividends per year. At this point, the firm is selling 30,000 latches a year and is taxed at 40 percent.

a. Calculate Carolina Fastener's operating breakeven point in units and sales dollars.
b. Based on the firm's current sales of 30,000 units per year and its interest and preferred dividend costs, calculate its EBIT and EAC.
c. Calculate the firm's degree of operating leverage (DOL). Explain the answer.
d. Calculate the firm's degree of financial leverage (DFL). Explain the answer.
e. Calculate the firm's degree of total leverage (DTL). Explain the answer.
f. Carolina Fastener has entered into a contract to produce and sell an additional 15,000 latches in the coming year. Use the DOL, DFL, and DTL to predict and calculate the changes in EBIT and EAC. Check your work by a simple calculation of Carolina Fastener's EBIT and EAC using the basic information given.

  INTERMEDIATE

10–17 Calculating breakeven and measures of leverage B&N Corporation's income statement for the current fiscal year is provided below.

Sales	$8,000,000
Cost of goods sold	3,200,000
Gross margin	4,800,000
General and administrative expenses	2,000,000
Amortization	800,000
Operating earnings	2,000,000
Interest (10% interest rate)	280,000
Earnings before taxes	1,720,000
Taxes (40%)	688,000
Net income after taxes	$1,032,000

a. What is the company's breakeven point in dollars?
b. What is their cash breakeven point, the level of sales required to cover all cash operating expenses?
c. What is B&N Corporation's degree of operating leverage, degree of financial leverage, and degree of total leverage at the current level of production? What is the implication of your answers?

  CHALLENGE

10–18 Integrative—Breakeven and leverage measures Maclauchlan Inc. sells a number of products whose average selling price is $7.50. The company is planning to produce 100,000 units of the various items. Forecasted operational costs are as follows:

Amortization	$175,000
Management salaries	110,000
Factory labour	205,000
Marketing expenses (fixed)	72,000
Direct materials	189,000
Maintenance (50% fixed)	36,000
Direct factory overhead	38,000
Rent	90,000
Total	$915,000

a. Is breakeven going to be more or less than 100,000 units? Which costs are fixed and variable? Calculate the total fixed costs and per-unit variable costs. For all remaining questions, assume that the fixed costs remain fixed at all levels of production.
b. What is Maclauchlan Inc.'s EBIT at a production volume of 100,000 units?
c. Calculate Maclauchlan Inc.'s breakeven in units and total dollar sales.
d. Calculate the selling price Maclauchlan must charge just to break even at production volumes of 100,000, 125,000, and 200,000 units.
e. If Maclauchlan wishes to earn an EBIT that is 10 percent of sales, how many units must the company sell?

f. Based on the total fixed costs and per-unit variable costs calculated in part **a**, and assuming these will remain the same, calculate the DOL, DFL, and DTL at a production volume of 220,000 units. Maclauchlan has total assets of $925,000 and the company has 79,000 common shares outstanding. The average interest rate on their outstanding debt is 10 percent. The company's equity ratio is 60 percent and their tax rate is 20 percent. Prove that the DOL, DFL, and DTL calculated are correct.

BASIC  **10–19 Various capital structures** Charter Enterprises currently has $1 million in total assets and is totally equity financed. It is contemplating a change in capital structure. Compute the amount of debt and equity that would be outstanding if the firm were to shift to one of the following debt ratios: 10, 20, 30, 40, 50, 60, and 90 percent. (*Note:* The amount of total assets would not change.) Is there a limit to the debt ratio's value?

CHALLENGE  **10–20 Debt and financial risk** Tower Interiors has made the forecast of sales shown in the following table. Also given is the probability of each level of sales.

Sales	Probability
$200,000	0.20
300,000	0.60
400,000	0.20

The firm has fixed operating costs of $75,000 and variable operating costs equal to 70 percent of the sales level. The company pays $12,000 in interest per period. The tax rate is 40 percent.

a. Compute the earnings before interest and taxes (EBIT) for each level of sales.

b. Compute the earnings per share (EPS) for each level of sales, the expected EPS, the standard deviation of the EPS, and the coefficient of variation of EPS, assuming that there are 10,000 common shares outstanding.

c. Tower has the opportunity to reduce leverage to zero and pay no interest. This will require that the number of shares outstanding be increased to 15,000. Repeat **b** under this assumption.

d. Compare your findings in **b** and **c,** and comment on the effect of the reduction of debt to zero on the firm's financial risk.

INTERMEDIATE  **10–21 Calculating the Altman Z-Score** Use the data in Problem 3–17 in Chapter 3 to calculate the Altman Z-Score for the three years that the required data is available. Assume the book value of equity equals the market value of equity. Comment on the trends in the score over the three years. What does the data suggest regarding the probability of the firm going bankrupt?

INTERMEDIATE  **10–22 Calculating the Altman Z-Score** Use the data in Integrative Case 1, the Track Software case provided on the Student CD-Rom, to calculate the Altman Z-Score for the two years that the required data is available. Assume the book value of equity equals the market value of equity. Comment on the trends in the score over the two years. What does the data suggest regarding the probability of the firm going bankrupt?

INTERMEDIATE 

10–23 EPS and optimal debt ratio Williams Glassware has estimated, at various debt ratios, the expected earnings per share and the standard deviation of the earnings per share as shown in the following table.

Debt ratio	Earnings per share (EPS)	Standard deviation of EPS
0%	$2.30	$1.15
20	3.00	1.80
40	3.50	2.80
60	3.95	3.95
80	3.80	5.53

a. Estimate the optimal debt ratio based on the relationship between earnings per share and the debt ratio. You will probably find it helpful to graph the relationship.

b. Graph the relationship between the coefficient of variation and the debt ratio. Label the areas associated with business risk and financial risk.

INTERMEDIATE 

10–24 EBIT–EPS and capital structure Data-Check is considering two capital structures. The key information is shown in the following table. Assume a 40 percent tax rate.

Source of capital	Structure A	Structure B
Long-term debt	$100,000 at 16% coupon rate	$200,000 at 17% coupon rate
Common equity	4,000 shares	2,000 shares

a. Calculate two EBIT–EPS coordinates for each of the structures by selecting any two EBIT values and finding their associated EPS.

b. Plot the two capital structures on a set of EBIT–EPS axes.

c. Indicate over what EBIT range, if any, each structure is preferred.

d. Discuss the leverage and risk aspects of each structure.

e. If the firm is fairly certain that its EBIT will exceed $75,000, which structure would you recommend? Why?

INTERMEDIATE 

10–25 EBIT–EPS and preferred equity Litho-Print is considering two possible capital structures, A and B, shown in the following table. Assume a 40 percent tax rate.

Source of capital	Structure A	Structure B
Long-term debt	$75,000 at 16% coupon rate	$50,000 at 15% coupon rate
Preferred equity	$10,000 with an 18% annual dividend	$15,000 with an 18% annual dividend
Common equity	8,000 shares	10,000 shares

a. Calculate two EBIT–EPS coordinates for each of the structures by selecting any two EBIT values and finding their associated EPS.

b. Graph the two capital structures on the same set of EBIT–EPS axes.

c. Calculate the financial breakeven points for both structures and calculate the indifference point, the level of EBIT where you would be indifferent between the two structures.
d. Discuss the leverage and risk associated with each of the structures.
e. Over what range of EBIT is each structure preferred?
f. Which structure do you recommend if the firm expects its EBIT to be $35,000? Explain.

INTERMEDIATE

10–26 **Integrative—Optimal capital structure** Medallion Cooling Systems, Inc., has total assets of $10,000,000, EBIT of $2,000,000, and preferred dividends of $200,000, and is taxed at a rate of 40 percent. In an effort to determine the optimal capital structure, the firm has assembled data on the cost of debt, the number of common shares for various levels of indebtedness, and the firm's cost of capital:

Debt ratio	Cost of debt, k_d	Number of common shares	Cost of capital, k_a
0%	0%	200,000	12%
15	8	170,000	13
30	9	140,000	14
45	12	110,000	16
60	15	80,000	20

a. Calculate earnings per share for each of the debt ratios.
b. Use Equation 10.12 and the earnings per share calculated in part a to calculate the value of each of the firm's common shares for each of the debt ratios.
c. Choose the optimal capital structure. Justify your choice.

CHALLENGE

10–27 **Integrative—Optimal capital structure** Nelson Corporation has made the following forecast of sales, with the associated probability of occurrence noted.

Sales	Probability
$200,000	0.20
300,000	0.60
400,000	0.20

The company has fixed operating costs of $100,000 per year, and variable operating costs represent 40 percent of sales. The existing capital structure consists of 25,000 common shares that have a $10 per share book value. No other capital items are outstanding. The marketplace has assigned the following discount rates to risky earnings per share.

Coefficient of variation of EPS	Estimated cost of capital, k_a
0.43	15%
0.47	16
0.51	17
0.56	18
0.60	22
0.64	24

The company is contemplating *shifting its capital structure* by substituting debt in the capital structure for common equity. The three different debt ratios under consideration are shown in the following table, along with an estimate of the corresponding required interest rate on *all* debt.

Debt ratio	Interest rate on *all* debt
20%	10%
40	12
60	14

The tax rate is 40 percent. The market value of the equity for a levered firm can be found by using the simplified method (see Equation 10.12).

a. Calculate the expected earnings per share (EPS), the standard deviation of EPS, and the coefficient of variation of EPS for the three proposed capital structures.

b. Determine the optimal capital structure, assuming (1) maximization of earnings per share and (2) maximization of share value.

c. Construct a graph (similar to Figure 10.7) showing the relationships in **b.** (*Note:* You will probably have to sketch the lines, because you have only three data points.)

CHALLENGE

10–28 **Integrative—Optimal capital structure** The board of directors of Morales Publishing, Inc., has commissioned a capital structure study. The company has total assets of $40,000,000. It has earnings before interest and taxes of $8,000,000 and is taxed at 40 percent.

a. Create a spreadsheet like the one in Table 10.11 showing values of debt and equity as well as the total number of shares, assuming a book value of $25 per share.

% Debt	Total assets	$ Debt	$ Equity	No. of shares @ $25
0%	$40,000,000	$ ____	$ ____	____
10	40,000,000	____	____	____
20	40,000,000	____	____	____
30	40,000,000	____	____	____
40	40,000,000	____	____	____
50	40,000,000	____	____	____
60	40,000,000	____	____	____

b. Given the before-tax cost of debt at various levels of indebtedness, calculate the yearly interest expenses.

% Debt	$ Total debt	Before-tax cost of debt, k_d	$ Interest expense
0%	$ ____	0.0%	$ ____
10	____	7.5	____
20	____	8.0	____
30	____	9.0	____
40	____	11.0	____
50	____	12.5	____
60	____	15.5	____

c. Using EBIT of $8,000,000, a 40 percent tax rate, and information developed in parts **a** and **b**, calculate the most likely earnings per share for the firm at various levels of indebtedness. Mark the level of indebtedness that maximizes EPS.

% Debt	EBIT	Interest expense	EBT	Taxes	Net income	No. of shares	EPS
0%	$8,000,000	____	____	____	____	____	____
10	8,000,000	____	____	____	____	____	____
20	8,000,000	____	____	____	____	____	____
30	8,000,000	____	____	____	____	____	____
40	8,000,000	____	____	____	____	____	____
50	8,000,000	____	____	____	____	____	____
60	8,000,000	____	____	____	____	____	____

d. Using the EPS developed in part **c**, the estimates of the firm's cost of caital, k_a, and Equation 10.12, estimate the value per share at various levels of indebtedness. Mark the level of indebtedness that results in the maximum value per share, V_0.

Debt	EPS	k_a	V_0
0%	___	10.0%	—
10	___	10.3	—
20	___	10.9	—
30	___	11.4	—
40	___	12.6	—
50	___	14.8	—
60	___	17.5	—

e. Prepare a recommendation to the board of directors of Morales Publishing, Inc., that specifies the degree of indebtedness that will accomplish the firm's goal of optimizing shareholder wealth. Use your findings in parts a through d to justify your recommendation.

    CHALLENGE

10–29 **Integrative—Optimal capital structure** Country Textiles, which has fixed operating costs of $300,000 and variable operating costs equal to 40 percent of sales, has made the following three sales estimates, with their probabilities noted.

Sales	Probability
$ 600,000	0.30
900,000	0.40
1,200,000	0.30

The firm wishes to analyze five possible capital structures—0, 15, 30, 45, and 60 percent debt ratios. The firm's total assets of $1 million are assumed to be constant. Its common equity has a book value of $25 per share, and the firm is in the 40 percent tax bracket. The following additional data have been gathered for use in analyzing the five capital structures under consideration.

Debt ratio	Before-tax cost of debt, k_d	Cost of capital, k_a
0%	0.0%	10.0%
15	8.0	10.5
30	10.0	11.6
45	13.0	14.0
60	17.0	20.0

a. Calculate the level of EBIT associated with each of the three levels of sales.

b. Calculate the amount of debt, the amount of equity, and the number of common shares outstanding for each of the capital structures being considered.

c. Calculate the annual interest on the debt under each of the capital structures being considered. (*Note:* The before-tax cost of debt, k_d, is the interest rate applicable to *all* debt associated with the corresponding debt ratio.)

d. Calculate the EPS associated with each of the three levels of EBIT calculated in **a** for each of the five capital structures being considered.

e. Calculate the (1) expected EPS, (2) standard deviation of EPS, and (3) coefficient of variation of EPS for each of the capital structures, using your findings in **d.**

f. Plot the expected EPS and coefficient of variation of EPS against the capital structures (x axis) on separate sets of axes, and comment on the return and risk relative to capital structure.

g. Using the EBIT–EPS data developed in **d,** plot the 0, 30, and 60 percent capital structures on the same set of EBIT-EPS axes, and discuss the ranges over which each is preferred. What is the major problem with the use of this approach?

h. Using the valuation model given in Equation 10.12 and your findings in **e,** estimate the value of each of the firm's common shares for each of the debt ratios.

i. Compare and contrast your findings in **f** and **h.** Which structure is preferred if the goal is to maximize EPS? Which structure is preferred if the goal is to maximize share value? Which capital structure do you recommend? Explain.

CASE CHAPTER 10 Evaluating Tampa Manufacturing's Capital Structure

See the enclosed Student CD-ROM for cases that help you put theories and concepts from the text into practice.

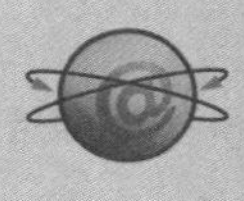

Be sure to visit the Companion Website for this book at **www.pearsoned.ca/gitman** for a wealth of additional learning tools including self-test quizzes, Web exercises, and additional cases.

Appendix to Chapter 10

The Modigliani and Miller Theory of Capital Structure

INTRODUCTION

In 1958, two young financial economists published two groundbreaking academic papers on the capital structure decisions faced by the firm.[15] In these papers, Franco Modigliani and Merton Miller presented the theory that the capital structure selected by a company was irrelevant. Modigliani and Miller (commonly known as MM) suggested that the cost of capital for a corporation is not affected by how the firm raises financing; it doesn't matter if a firm sells common shares or issues debt. While debt is a cheaper form of financing, if a firm issues more debt, equity holders will rationally demand a higher return that exactly offsets the savings from issuing debt. Thus, there is no reduction in the cost of capital, meaning a corporation's value in the stock market is independent of its capital structure. The conclusion: capital structure decisions were irrelevant!

Later in life Miller used the analogy of a pizza to explain the theory that, regardless of how the firm's cash flows were split between debtholders and equity holders, the value of the firm was not changed. He wrote, borrowing from Yogi Berra, "Think of the firm as a gigantic pizza, divided into quarters. If now you cut each quarter in half into eighths, the M&M proposition says you will have more pieces, but not more pizza."[16] Essentially, the MM proposition implies that the choice of the financing instrument is irrelevant in determining the firm's cost of capital and thus firm value. Value depends solely on the risk of the investment, regardless of how it is financed.

15. "The Cost of Capital, Corporation Finance, and the Theory of Investment," *American Economic Review*, June 1958, pp. 261–297; and "The Cost of Capital, Corporation Finance, and the Theory of Investment: Reply," *American Economic Review*, September 1958, pp. 655–659.

16. See www-rcf.usc.edu/~etalley/busorg/MILLER.html or "An Economist for All Seasons," *CFO Magazine*, August 1, 2000, available www.cfo.com/article.cfm/2990948?f=related.

Franco Modigliani won the 1985 Nobel Prize in Economics for this and his other contributions to economic theory. Merton Miller won the 1990 Nobel Prize in Economics, along with Harry Markowitz and William Sharpe, with Miller specifically cited for his "fundamental contributions to the theory of corporate finance."

THE MM THEORY

To develop their model, MM made some important assumptions. They assumed that the capital markets were perfect. Perfect capital markets have the following characteristics: (1) there are no taxes; (2) there are no transaction costs of any type; (3) all investors have access to all information and have identical estimates of a company's earnings; (4) the interest rate is the risk-free rate and all market participants can borrow at this rate; and (5) there are no bankruptcy costs. In such a market the value of a firm is unaffected by its financing. Both the total value of a firm's securities and its cost of capital are independent of its capital structure. In this Appendix, we will provide an illustration of MM's original analysis that provides these results.

Consider two firms that have identical business risks, the same expected level of earnings before interest and taxes (EBIT), and the same amount of total assets. We assume that all business risk is based on the probability distribution of EBIT and that these two firms have identical distributions. The EBIT of the firms is $200,000 and both companies have $2.5 million of assets. Company L has $1 million of 6 percent bonds outstanding, while company E has no debt, but $2.5 million of equity. We wish to determine the market value of L's common shares, and therefore the company's total value.

If there is an advantage to using debt financing, L's total value will be greater than E's. If debt financing increases risk with no offsetting return, L's value will be less than E's. We can solve the problem by examining the consequences of first assuming that adding debt to the capital structure reduces value. Then we can assume that it increases value. If we find that neither assumption is realistic, then total value of the two firms must be the same. In addition, analyzing the situation in this way is consistent with MM's discussion of their theory. Is there more or less pizza depending on how it is cut?

Suppose that the total value of L's financial securities is only $2.2 million, in contrast with E's $2.5 million. Since the debt is worth $1 million, debt financing has reduced L's value by $300,000, meaning the value of the equity is $1.2 million. Consider an investor who wishes to purchase 10 percent of a company with the same risks as E and L. For an investment of $250,000, the investor could purchase 10 percent of E's common shares. The investor also receives the right to 10 percent of E's income. Since there is no interest expense or taxes, the company's EBIT equals its net income. So the investor receives $20,000.

The investor could also invest in L, which has identical risk to E. The investor could purchase 10 percent of L's bonds at a cost of $100,000, which would provide $6,000 interest, and 10 percent of L's common shares at a cost of $120,000 with a right to receive $14,000 of L's net income. The investor's total expected income from L's securities is $20,000, the same as from E's. The probability of receiving this income is identical for the two companies. This is illustrated in Table 10A.1.

TABLE 10A.1 Value of Companies E and L, and Investor's Cost and Income Assuming a 10% Purchase

Financial statement data	Company E	Company L
Operating earnings (EBIT)	$200,000	$200,000
Interest (6% rate)	0	60,000
Earnings before taxes	200,000	140,000
Taxes (0%)	0	0
Net income after taxes	$200,000	$140,000
Total assets	$2,500,000	$2,500,000
Market value		
Debt	$ 0	$1,000,000
Equity	2,500,000	1,200,000
Total value of company	$2,500,000	$2,200,000
Investor buys 10% of financial securities		
Cost	$250,000	$220,000
Expected income		
Bonds	$ 0	$ 6,000
Equity	20,000	14,000
Total income	$20,000	$20,000

But we have a problem. Purchasing the right to 10 percent of L's income only costs the investor $220,000. Obtaining a right to the same $20,000 of expected income from the investment in E's common shares costs $250,000. If you were the investor, which company would you invest in? Obviously, you would prefer to buy L's securities. In a perfect market, identical substitutes cannot sell at different prices. If all investors agree that the level of income generated by the two firms is equal, their securities must sell at prices that provide the same returns.

Either E's common shares must sell for less than $2.5 million, or L's equity and debt must sell for more than $2.2 million. Regardless of which is the case, the total value of L's securities cannot be lower than E's. If they were, all investors would purchase a combination of shares and bonds issued by L rather than purchase any of E's common shares. Therefore, given the assumptions made in this example, the value of a firm using debt financing cannot be lower than what it would be if all equity financing was used.

What about the possibility that L's value will be greater than E's? As above, an investor purchasing 10 percent of E's common shares will pay $250,000 for the right to $20,000 of income. If the market value of L's equity is more than $1.5 million, then to buy $20,000 of L's income will cost more than $250,000. For example, if L's equity was worth $1.8 million, the right to $20,000 of L's income will cost $280,000 [($1 million + $1.8 million) × 10%]. As before, in a perfect market, identical substitutes cannot sell at different prices. Either E's common shares must sell for more than $2.5 million, or L's equity and debt must sell for less than $2.8 million.

So we have just proven MM's theory. The total value of L cannot be greater or less than the total value of E. In a perfect capital market, the values of L and E must be equal and, therefore, a firm's total value (equity plus debt) does not depend on its financial structure. Indeed, it doesn't matter if you slice a 12-inch pizza once or six times, it is still a 12-inch pizza!

IMPACT OF CORPORATE TAXES ON THE CORPORATE STRUCTURE DECISION

In response to comments on their original papers, MM relaxed one of their original set of assumptions. In a new paper, they determined the impact corporate taxes would have on the choice of capital structures.[17] To illustrate MM's analysis, we will return to the companies E and L example from the previous section, with one change—we will now assume that the corporate tax rate is 40 percent. All other assumptions regarding perfect capital markets remain. Instead of considering a purchase of 10 percent of the company, we will now consider the total company. Table 10A.2 provides the analysis.

Now, the total cash flows provided by L are higher than E's. Why? It must be due to the impact of corporate taxes, since that is the only difference between the two examples. The effect is that the interest payments are tax-deducible, and this has provided a benefit to the firm and its investors. Now investors in E are entitled to $120,000 of cash flow, but L's investors receive $144,000 of cash. This will increase the value of company L over company E. The increased value is based on the tax savings associated with the interest payments. As discussed in Chapters 2 and 5, the tax savings are based on the interest payments times the tax rate; in this case $24,000 ($60,000 × 40%).

So the cash flows that company L can pay investors are increased by the tax savings of $24,000. This will also result in the value of company L being higher than that of company E. Given the perfect capital market conditions assumed by MM, this effect will continue until L has a debt ratio of 99.99 percent. The implication of MM's theory is that the value of the firm is maximized when its capital structure contains only debt. The inference of MM's model is that firms should

TABLE 10A.2 Cash Flows of Companies E and L with Corporate Taxes

Financial statement data	Company E	Company L
Operating earnings (EBIT)	$200,000	$200,000
Interest (6% rate)	0	60,000
Earnings before taxes	200,000	140,000
Taxes (40%)	80,000	56,000
Net income after taxes	$120,000	$84,000
Total assets	$2,500,000	$2,500,000
Financing		
Debt	0	$1,000,000
Equity	$2,500,000	$1,500,000
Total financing	$2,500,000	$2,500,000
Cash flow to investors		
To bond holders	$0	$60,000
To equity holders	$120,000	$84,000
Total cash flow	$120,000	$144,000

17. "Corporation Income Taxes and the Cost of Capital: A Correction," *American Economic Review*, June 1963, pp. 433–443.

use as much debt as they possibly can. The benefit of debt financing is the increased cash flow due to the tax-deductibility of interest. In addition, in MM's perfect world, there is no disadvantage of using debt financing.

CONCLUSION

The Modigliani-Miller (MM) theory indicates that if there are no taxes, firms are indifferent concerning the method of financing; the financing decision is irrelevant. But with corporate taxes, firms should maximize the use of debt. Debt is superior to any other financing source. However, the MM model assumes away many factors that can imply that a particular blend of debt and equity financing is best for a given firm.

Existing theoretical models provide only a partial explanation of how corporations are financed in reality. In addition, there are serious difficulties in empirically measuring the impact of leverage on firm value. From Table 10.9 in the chapter, we know that capital structures differ across industries. In addition, in many industries the individual firms have similar capital structures, since business risks are comparable.

It is not clear whether this similarity in financing policies is due to "herding" behaviour, to market conditions that lead to common decisions among firms, or to a correct estimation of the optimal capital structure by managers. The question of optimal capital structure remains an unresolved issue in corporate finance. The MM theories were simply a first but very important step on a path that is still unfolding in finance research.

CHAPTER 11

Dividend Policy

LEARNING GOALS

LG1 Understand cash dividend payment procedures and the role of dividend reinvestment plans.

LG2 Describe the residual theory of dividends and the key arguments with regard to dividend irrelevance and relevance.

LG3 Discuss the key factors involved in formulating a dividend policy.

LG4 Review and evaluate the three basic types of dividend policies.

LG5 Evaluate stock dividends from the accounting, shareholder, and company points of view.

LG6 Explain stock splits and common share repurchases and the firm's motivation for undertaking each of them.

11.1 Dividend Fundamentals

reinvested profits
Earnings not distributed as dividends; a form of *internal* financing.

As we saw in Chapter 8, expected cash dividends are a key cash flow that the owners of a company (the common shareholders) can use to determine the value of the company. They represent a source of cash flow to shareholders and provide information about the firm's current and future performance. Because **reinvested profits**—earnings not distributed as dividends—are a form of *internal*

Paying Dividends

When investors evaluate companies, one of the key features considered is dividends. What are the dividends per share? What is the dividend yield? What has been the growth in dividends? In addition, the tax advantages of dividends will be considered. An overall question associated with dividends is why some companies pay them and others do not. Are dividends relevant to investors and, if so, why? Some view dividends as the cash remaining after all acceptable investment opportunities have been undertaken. The size and pattern of the dividends provide information about the firm's current and future performance. Some shareholders want and expect to receive dividends, whereas others are content to see an increase in stock price without receiving dividends. This chapter addresses the issue of whether dividends matter to shareholders and discusses the key aspects of dividend policy.

financing, the dividend decision can significantly affect the firm's *external* financing requirements, as shown in Chapter 4.

In other words, if the firm requires financing, the larger the cash dividend paid, the greater the amount of financing that must be raised externally through borrowing or through the sale of common or preferred shares. (Remember dividends are paid in cash and indirectly reduce retained earnings through the amount of net income that is reinvested.) To understand the fundamentals of

LINKING THE DISCIPLINES: Cross-Functional Interactions

- ***Accounting personnel*** need to understand the types of dividends and the payment procedures in order to record and report declaration and payment of dividends. They will provide the financial data needed by management to make dividend decisions, provide the board of directors with the current cash balance, and assist in estimating future cash flows.

- ***Information systems analysts*** need to understand types of dividends, the payment procedures, and the financial data that the firm must have to make and implement dividend decisions.

- ***Management*** need to understand types of dividends and dividend policies and the factors that affect dividend policy in order to make appropriate dividend decisions for the firm. Management will provide the background information to help the board establish the best dividend policy. They will need to explain to the board future capital expenditures and financing plans that will affect future dividends. They will also have to understand what the owners of the firm want in terms of distributions from the company.

- The ***marketing department*** needs to understand factors affecting dividend policy because it would prefer a no-dividends policy so that the firm retains its funds for use in new marketing programs or products.

- Personnel in the ***operations department*** need to understand factors affecting dividend policy because it may find that the firm's dividend policy imposes limitations on planned replacement, modernization, or expansion projects.

dividend policy, you first need to understand the procedures for paying cash dividends.

Cash Dividend Payment Procedures

As was discussed in Chapter 5, most publicly traded companies that pay dividends do so quarterly. The payment of cash dividends to shareholders is decided by the firm's board of directors. The directors will meet each quarter to determine whether and in what amount dividends should be paid. The past period's financial performance and future outlook, as well as recent dividends paid, are key inputs to the dividend decision. The payment date of the cash dividend, if one is declared, must also be established.

Once declared, the board and company are legally obligated to make the dividend payment. Note, though, there is no obligation to *declare* a dividend, even in cases where a company has been paying dividends for many years. The payment of dividends is at the total discretion of the board of directors. The quarterly dividend becomes the basis for the annual indicated dividend as reported in the financial press. For example, if the board of directors declared a quarterly common share dividend of \$0.70 per share, the annual dividend indicated is \$2.80 (\$0.70 × 4).

dividend yield
The percentage return an investor holding the common share today would receive based on the most recent quarterly dividend; the indicated yearly dividend divided by the share price.

With the annual indicated dividend, we could determine the **dividend yield** on a share. To do so we require the share price. The dividend yield is the percentage return an investor holding the common share today would receive based on the most recent quarterly dividend. It is the indicated yearly dividend divided by the share price. If, in the above example, the company's share price was $79.10, the dividend yield is 3.54 percent ($2.80/$79.10). An investor buying the share today would receive this return given the expected dividend to be received over the next year.

Amount of Dividends

Whether dividends should be paid and, if so, how large they should be are important decisions that depend primarily on the firm's dividend policy. Many firms pay some cash dividends each period. Most firms have a set policy with respect to the amount of the periodic dividend, but the firm's directors can change this amount at the dividend meeting, based largely on significant increases or decreases in earnings.

Relevant Dates

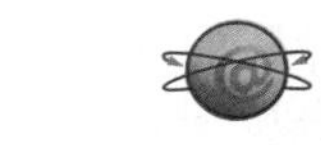

www.globeinvestor.com/v5/content/news

www.newswire.ca

If the directors of the firm declare a dividend, they also indicate the record and payment dates associated with the dividend. Typically, the directors issue a statement indicating their dividend decision, the record date, and the payment date. This statement is generally provided in a press release and then reported in financial newspapers such as the *Globe and Mail*'s Report on Business and the *Financial Post*. These press releases are also available on the Web.

date of record (dividends)
Set by the firm's directors, the date on which all persons whose names are recorded as shareholders receive a declared dividend at a specified future time.

ex dividend
Period beginning two *business days* prior to the date of record during which a stock is sold without the right to receive the current dividend.

Record Date All persons whose names are recorded as shareholders on the **date of record,** which is set by the directors, receive a declared dividend at a specified future time. These shareholders are often referred to as *holders of record.*

Due to the time needed to make bookkeeping entries when shares are traded, the shares begin selling **ex dividend** two *business days* prior to the date of record. Purchasers of shares selling ex dividend do not receive the current dividend. A simple way to determine the first day on which the stock sells ex dividend is to subtract two days from the date of record; if a weekend intervenes, subtract four days. Ignoring general market fluctuations, the stock's price is expected to drop by the amount of the declared dividend on the ex dividend date.

payment date
The actual date on which the firm makes the dividend payment to the holders of record.

Payment Date The payment date is also set by the directors and is generally a few weeks after the record date. The **payment date** is the actual date on which the firm makes the dividend payment to the holders of record. An example will clarify the various dates and the accounting effects.

Example ▼ At the quarterly board of directors' meeting of Rudolf Company held June 10, the directors declared an $0.80-per-share cash dividend for holders of record on Monday, June 30. June 10 is termed the declaration date. The firm has 100,000 common shares outstanding. The payment date for the dividend is August 1. Before the dividend was declared, the key accounts of the firm were as follows:

Cash	$200,000	Dividends payable	$ 0
		Retained earnings	1,000,000

When the dividend was declared by the directors, the expectation is that the common share price would increase by $0.80 per share, since the dividend payment becomes a legal obligation. For accounting purposes, $80,000 of the retained earnings ($0.80 per share × 100,000 shares) would be transferred to the dividends payable account. The key accounts thus become:

Cash	$200,000	Dividends payable	$ 80,000
		Retained earnings	920,000

Rudolf Company's shares will start to trade ex dividend (without the dividend) two *business days* prior to the date of record, which is June 26. This date was found by subtracting four days (because a weekend intervened) from the June 30 date of record. Purchasers of Rudolf's stock on June 25 or earlier received the rights to the dividend; those purchasing the stock on or after June 26 do not. Assuming a stable market, Rudolf's common share price is expected to drop by approximately $0.80 per share when it begins trading ex dividend on June 26. When the August 1 payment date arrives, the firm makes the dividend payment to the holders of record as of June 30. This produces the following balances in the key accounts of the firm:

Cash	$120,000	Dividends payable	$ 0
		Retained earnings	920,000

The net effect of declaring and paying the dividend is to reduce the firm's total assets (and shareholders' equity) by $80,000.

www.newswire.ca/en
www.globeinvestor.com/v5/content/news

Examples of recent dividend declarations are available on the Web.

Dividend Reinvestment Plans

dividend reinvestment plans (DRIPs) Plans that enable shareholders to use dividends received on the firm's shares to acquire additional full or fractional shares at no transaction (brokerage) cost.

Today many firms offer **dividend reinvestment plans (DRIPs),** which enable shareholders to use dividends received on the firm's shares to acquire additional shares—even fractional shares—at no transaction (brokerage) cost. Some companies even allow investors to make their *initial purchases* of the firm's shares directly from the company without going through a stockbroker. Under current tax law, cash dividends received (or the amount invested through a DRIP) are taxed as ordinary income. The taxation of dividends was discussed in Chapter 8, with an example provided in Table 8.5. Recall, for tax purposes, that the dividend is increased by 45 percent but then a dividend tax credit is allowed that greatly reduces the taxes paid on dividends versus on interest income. When the shares acquired through a DRIP are sold, the proceeds in excess of the original purchase price are taxed as a capital gain.

Many companies that offer DRIPs also offer share purchase plans (SPPs) that allow shareholders to make optional cash contributions (OCC), either monthly or quarterly up to some maximum amount, that are then used to purchase additional common shares for the investor. Participation in both DRIPs and SSPs is voluntary; shareholders may or may not choose to enroll in the plans.

The benefit of DRIPs and SSPs for investors is that they regularly (every quarter) acquire additional common shares of the company. Over time, with the compounding effect, a very modest initial holding of common shares can become a very large number of shares. The compounding effect is multiplied as a company increases the dividends paid on common shares. In addition, the company assumes all administrative and brokerage fees associated with the plan. The investor receives a statement outlining their dividend payments, shares purchased, and shares held each quarter. The statement also allows investors to mail to the company OCCs that are then used to purchase common shares on the shareholder's behalf. Some companies that offer DRIPs purchase additional common shares for investors at a 5 percent discount to the market price. This incentive may encourage many of the company's individual shareholders to participate in the DRIP.

The benefit of the DRIP and SPP for the company is that they can raise financing avoiding underpricing and flotation costs associated with a public offering of new common shares. In addition, many companies want individuals as shareholders since they are considered more "loyal" investors and will hold the common shares for long periods of time. Also, individuals who own shares are often loyal users of the company's product or services. The DRIP and SPP act as incentives for individuals to become shareholders.

www.ndir.com/SI/DRPs.shtml
www.bmoinvestorline.com/FAQs/FAQ_DRIP.html

Numerous companies in Canada offer DRIPs and SPPs. Lists of these companies are available on the Web.

? Review Questions

11–1 How do the *declaration date*, *date of record*, and *holders of record* relate to the payment of cash dividends? What does the term *ex dividend* mean?

11–2 What is a *dividend reinvestment plan?* What benefit is available to plan participants? What is a share purchase plan? Why might companies offer these two plans?

LG2

11.2 The Relevance of Dividend Policy

Numerous theories and empirical findings concerning dividend policy have been reported in the financial literature. Although this research provides some interesting insights about dividend policy, capital budgeting and capital structure decisions are generally considered far more important than dividend decisions. In other words, good investment and financing decisions should not be sacrificed for a dividend policy of questionable importance.

A number of key questions have yet to be resolved: Does dividend policy matter? What effect does dividend policy have on share price? Is there a model that can be used to evaluate alternative dividend policies in view of share value? Here we begin by describing the residual theory of dividends, which is used as a backdrop for discussion of the key arguments in support of dividend irrelevance and then those in support of dividend relevance.

The Residual Theory of Dividends

residual theory of dividends
A theory that the dividend paid by a firm should be the amount left over after all acceptable investment opportunities have been undertaken.

One school of thought—the **residual theory of dividends**—suggests that the dividend paid by a firm should be viewed as a *residual*—the amount left over after all acceptable investment opportunities have been undertaken. Using this approach, the firm would treat the dividend decision in three steps as follows:

Step 1 Determine its optimum level of capital expenditures, which would be those investment projects whose expected returns are greater than or equal to the firm's overall cost of capital. This would also be the point where the investment opportunities schedule (IOS) and marginal cost of capital (MCC) schedule intersect or where the expected return on the projects being considered is greater than or equal to the firm's overall cost of capital (see Chapter 9).

Step 2 Using the optimal capital structure proportions (see Chapter 10), estimate the total amount of equity financing needed to support the expenditures generated in Step 1.

Step 3 Because the cost of reinvested profits, k_r, is less than the cost of new common shares, k_n, use reinvested profits to meet the equity requirement determined in Step 2. If reinvested profits are inadequate to meet this need, sell new common shares. If the available reinvested profits are in excess of this need, distribute the surplus amount—the residual—as dividends.

Following this approach, cash dividends are not paid if all of the firm's profits are needed to finance projects. The argument supporting this approach is that it is sound management to be certain that the company has the money it needs to compete effectively and therefore increase share price. This view of dividends tends to suggest that the required return of investors, k_s, is *not* influenced by the firm's dividend policy—a premise that in turn suggests that dividend policy is irrelevant.

FIGURE 11.1

MCC and IOSs

MCC and IOSs for Overbrook Industries

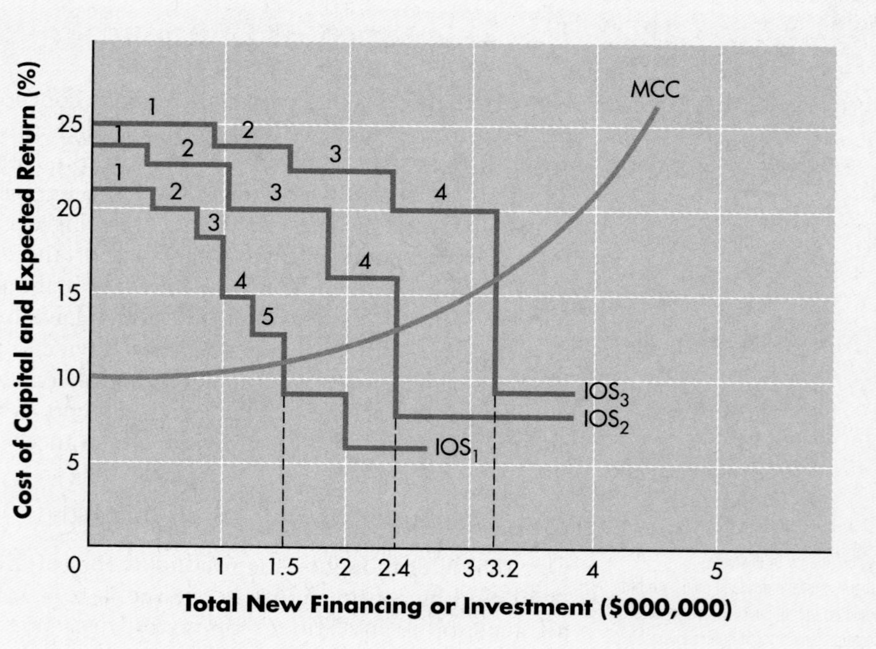

Example ▼ Overbrook Industries has earnings available for common shareholders (EAC) of \$1.8 million that can be retained or paid out in dividends. The firm's optimal capital structure is 30 percent debt and 70 percent equity. Figure 11.1 depicts the firm's marginal cost of capital (MCC) schedule along with three investment opportunities schedules. For each IOS, the level of total new financing required (investment made) is determined by the point of intersection of the IOS and the MCC has been noted.

For IOS_1, the firm will invest in five projects whose expected returns are greater than the cost of capital. These projects will require \$1.5 million of financing. For IOS_2 the firm will invest in four projects whose expected returns are greater than the cost of capital. These projects will require \$2.4 million of financing. For IOS_3 the firm will invest in four projects whose expected returns are greater than the cost of capital. These projects will require \$3.2 million of financing. Although only one IOS will exist in practice, it is useful to look at the possible dividend decisions generated by applying the residual theory in each of the three cases. Table 11.1 summarizes this analysis.

The table shows that if IOS_1 exists, the firm will pay out \$750,000 in dividends, because only \$1,050,000 of the \$1,800,000 of available earnings is needed. A 41.7 percent payout ratio results. For IOS_2, dividends of \$120,000 (a payout ratio of 6.7%) result. Should IOS_3 exist, the firm would pay no dividends (a 0% payout ratio), because its earnings available of \$1,800,000 would be less than the \$2,240,000 of equity needed. In this case, the firm would have to sell new common shares to meet the requirements generated by the intersection of the IOS_3 and the MCC. Depending on which IOS exists, the firm's dividend would in effect be the residual, if any, remaining after providing the equity financing required to fund all acceptable investments. ▲

TABLE 11.1 Applying the Residual Theory of Dividends to Overbrook Industries for Each of Three IOSs (shown in Figure 11.1)

Item	Investment opportunities schedules		
	IOS_1	IOS_2	IOS_3
(1) Investments made/new financing required (Fig. 11.1)	\$1,500,000	\$2,400,000	\$3,200,000
(2) Earnings available (given)	\$1,800,000	\$1,800,000	\$1,800,000
(3) Equity needed [70% × (1)]	1,050,000	1,680,000	2,240,000
(4) Dividends [(2) − (3)]	\$ 750,000	\$ 120,000	0[a]
(5) Dividend payout ratio [(4) ÷ (2)]	41.7%	6.7%	0%

[a]In this case, additional new common shares in the amount of \$440,000 (\$2,240,000 needed−\$1,800,000 available) would have to be sold; no dividends would be paid.

This view of dividends is consistent with Michael Jensen's "free cash flow" theory.[1] Jensen defines "free cash" as a company's operating cash flow in excess of the amount that can be profitably reinvested in the business. Jensen's view is that companies with substantial free cash flow will often destroy company value by investing this money in low- or negative-return projects, particularly the takeovers of other companies. These companies can often add significant value for shareholders by increasing dividends or repurchasing shares. By doing so, this will reduce the opportunity for managers to invest in low-return projects. Companies with limited growth opportunities should pay out their excess cash to shareholders.

Dividend Irrelevance Arguments

The residual theory of dividends implies that if the firm is not expected to earn a return from the investment of its earnings that is in excess of the cost of the funds, it should distribute the earnings by paying dividends to shareholders. This approach suggests that dividends are irrelevant—that they represent an earnings residual rather than an active decision variable that affects the firm's value. Such a view is consistent with the **dividend irrelevance theory** put forth by Merton H. Miller and Franco Modigliani (MM).[2] MM's theory shows that in a perfect world (certainty, no taxes, no transactions costs, and no other market imperfections), the value of the firm is unaffected by the distribution of dividends. They argue that the firm's value is determined solely by the earning power and risk of its assets (investments) and that the manner in which it splits its earnings stream between dividends and internally retained (and reinvested) funds does not affect this value.

dividend irrelevance theory
A theory put forth by Miller and Modigliani that, in a perfect world, the value of a firm is unaffected by the distribution of dividends and is determined solely by the earning power and risk of its assets.

However, studies have shown that large dividend changes affect share price in the same direction—increases in dividends result in increased share price, and decreases in dividends result in decreased share price. In response, MM argue that these effects are attributable not to the dividend itself but rather to the **informational content** of dividends with respect to future earnings. In other words, it is not the preference of shareholders for current dividends (rather than future capital gains) that is responsible for this behaviour. Instead, a change in dividends, up or down, is viewed as a *signal* that management expects future earnings to change in the same direction. An increase in dividends is viewed as a *positive signal* that causes investors to bid up the share price; a decrease in dividends is a *negative signal* that causes a decrease in share price.

informational content
The information provided by the dividends of a firm with respect to future earnings, which causes owners to bid the price of the firm's shares up or down.

MM further argue that a **clientele effect** exists: A firm attracts shareholders whose preferences with respect to the payment and stability of dividends correspond to the payment pattern and stability of the firm itself. Investors desiring stable dividends as a source of income hold the shares of firms that have a stable dividend payout ratio every year. Investors preferring to earn capital gains are more attracted to growing firms that reinvest a large portion of their earnings, resulting in a fairly unstable pattern of dividends or no dividends. Because the shareholders get what they expect, MM argue that the value of their firm's stock is unaffected by dividend policy.

clientele effect
The argument that a firm attracts shareholders whose preferences with respect to the payment and stability of dividends correspond to the payment pattern and stability of the firm itself.

1. "Agency Costs of Free Cash Flow, Corporate Finance, and Takeovers," *American Economic Review*, 1986, pp. 323–339.

2. Merton H. Miller and Franco Modigliani, "Dividend Policy, Growth and the Valuation of Shares," *Journal of Business* 34 (October 1961), pp. 411–433.

In summary, MM and other dividend irrelevance proponents argue that, all else being equal, an investor's required return—and therefore the value of the firm—is unaffected by dividend policy for three reasons:

1. The firm's value is determined solely by the earning power and risk of its assets.
2. If dividends do affect value, they do so solely because of their informational content, which signals management's earnings expectations.
3. A clientele effect exists that causes a firm's shareholders to receive the dividends they expect.

These views of MM with respect to dividend irrelevance are consistent with the residual theory, which focuses on making the best investment decisions to maximize share value. The proponents of dividend irrelevance conclude that because dividends are irrelevant to a firm's value, the firm does not need to have a dividend policy. Although many studies have researched the dividend irrelevance theory, none have been able to fully validate or refute the theory.

Dividend Relevance Arguments

dividend relevance theory
The theory that there is a direct relationship between a firm's dividend policy and its market value.

bird-in-the-hand argument
The belief, in support of *dividend relevance theory,* that current dividend payments ("a bird in the hand") reduce investor uncertainty and result in a higher value for the firm's shares.

The key argument in support of **dividend relevance theory** is attributed to Myron J. Gordon and John Lintner,[3] who suggest that there is, in fact, a direct relationship between the firm's dividend policy and its market value. Fundamental to this proposition is their **bird-in-the-hand argument,** which suggests that investors are generally risk-averse and attach less risk to current dividends than to future dividends or capital gains. Simply stated, "a bird in the hand is worth two in the bush." Current dividend payments are therefore believed to reduce investor uncertainty, causing investors to discount the firm's earnings at a lower rate and, all else being equal, to place a higher value on the firm's common shares. Conversely, if dividends are reduced or not paid, investor uncertainty will increase, raising the required return and lowering the share's value.

Although many other arguments relating to dividend relevance have been put forward, *numerous empirical studies fail to provide conclusive evidence in support of the intuitively appealing dividend relevance argument.* In practice, however, the actions of financial managers and shareholders alike often tend to support the belief that dividend policy does affect share value. Because our concern centres on the day-to-day behaviour of business firms, the remainder of this chapter is consistent with the belief that *dividends are relevant*—that each firm must develop a dividend policy that fulfills the goals of its owners and maximizes their wealth as reflected in the firm's share price.

? Review Questions

11–3 Describe the *residual theory of dividends.* Does following this approach lead to a stable dividend? Is this approach consistent with dividend relevance? Explain.

3. Myron J. Gordon, "Optimal Investment and Financing Policy," *Journal of Finance* 18 (May 1963), pp. 264–272, and John Lintner, "Dividends, Earnings, Leverage, Stock Prices, and the Supply of Capital to Corporations," *Review of Economics and Statistics* 44 (August 1962), pp. 243–269.

11–4 Describe and contrast the basic arguments concerning dividend policy given by: (a) Miller and Modigliani (MM) and (b) Gordon and Lintner.

11.3 Factors Affecting Dividend Policy

dividend policy
The plan to be followed when making the dividend decision.

A company's **dividend policy** represents the plan to be followed when making the dividend decision. Companies should develop plans consistent with their financial goals. Before reviewing some types of dividend policies, we discuss the factors involved in developing a dividend policy. These include legal constraints, contractual constraints, internal constraints, the firm's growth prospects, owner considerations, and market considerations.

Legal Constraints

It is illegal for Canadian companies to pay dividends that would reduce the value of the common share account, the direct financing provided by the owners to the company. Dividends can only be paid from earnings: the current year's and the total of prior year's reinvested profits as reflected in retained earnings. To pay dividends in excess of this amount would mean the company was returning to common shareholders their original investment in the company.

net profits rule
Dividends can only be paid from current and past earnings.

capital impairment rule
Prevents the payment of dividends from the value of common shares on the balance sheet.

insolvency rule
A company cannot pay dividends while insolvent or if the payment of dividends makes the company insolvent.

When paying dividends, three rules must be followed: (1) the **net profits rule** means that dividends can only be paid from current and past earnings; (2) the **capital impairment rule** prevents the payment of dividends from the value of common shares on the balance sheet; (3) the **insolvency rule** indicates a company cannot pay dividends while insolvent or if the payment of dividends makes the company insolvent.[4] Each of these rules has the same effect: to protect creditors. The rules prevent a company from making payments to common shareholders at the expense of creditors.

Example Miller Flour Company, a large grain processor located in Saskatchewan, had net income after tax of $45,000 for the current fiscal year. The company's shareholders' equity account as of the end of the previous fiscal year is presented below:

Miller Flour Company Shareholders' Equity	
Common shares	$300,000
Retained earnings	140,000
Total shareholders' equity	$440,000

What is the maximum amount of dividends that Miller Flour could legally pay? The total of current and past reinvested earnings is $185,000 ($45,000 +

4. Insolvency occurs when liabilities exceed assets or when a company is not able to pay its bills. The second situation generally occurs well before the first.

$140,000), so this is the maximum dividend that the company could pay in the current fiscal year. Paying more would affect the common share account, and this would be illegal. It would reduce the company's ability to meet its obligations to creditors.

Based on this discussion, a company can pay a dividend that is more than current earnings. While this may seem odd, in reality it happens regularly. Consider the case where a company incurs a loss in a year. If the company has a long-standing policy of paying dividends, dividends can be paid even though there are no current profits to pay the dividend from. As long as the company has sufficient retained earnings on the balance sheet, a dividend payment may be made. This also assumes, of course, that the company has sufficient cash to make a dividend payment.

Example If, in the previous example, Miller Company's net income after tax for the current fiscal year was a loss of $20,000, what is the maximum dividend that could be paid? For the current fiscal year, the loss of $20,000 would flow to retained earnings, reducing the balance to $120,000 ($140,000 – $20,000). Therefore, the maximum dividend would be $120,000. In reality, a company would not pay this amount, since it would negatively affect their ability to remain solvent. Legally, however, Miller could pay this amount in dividends.

Contractual Constraints

Often, the firm's ability to pay cash dividends is constrained by restrictive provisions in a loan agreement. Generally, these constraints prohibit the payment of cash dividends until a certain level of earnings has been achieved, or they may limit dividends to a certain dollar amount or percentage of earnings. Constraints on dividends help to protect creditors from losses due to the firm's insolvency. The violation of a contractual constraint is generally grounds for creditors to demand immediate payment of the funds, or to force the firm into bankruptcy, if necessary.

Internal Constraints

The firm's ability to pay cash dividends is generally constrained by the amount of excess cash available rather than the level of retained earnings against which to charge them. Although it is possible for a firm to borrow funds to pay dividends, lenders are generally reluctant to make such loans because they produce no tangible or operating benefits that will help the firm repay the loan. Although a firm may have high earnings, its ability to pay dividends may be constrained by a low level of liquid assets (cash and marketable securities).

Example Miller Flour Company's shareholders' equity account presented earlier indicates that the firm could pay $185,000 in dividends. If the firm has total liquid assets of $50,000 ($20,000 in cash plus marketable securities worth $30,000) and $35,000 of this is needed for operations, the maximum cash dividend the firm can pay is $15,000 ($50,000 – $35,000).

Growth Prospects

Hint
Firms that grow very rapidly, such as high-tech firms, cannot afford to pay dividends. Their shareholders are influenced by the possibility of exceptionally high growth in share price and dividend levels in the future.

The firm's financial requirements are directly related to the anticipated degree of asset expansion. If the firm is in a growth stage, it may need all its funds to finance capital expenditures. Firms exhibiting little or no growth may nevertheless periodically need funds to replace or renew assets.

A firm must evaluate its financial position from the standpoint of profitability and risk to develop insight into its ability to raise capital externally. It must determine not only its ability to raise funds, but also the cost and speed with which financing can be obtained. Generally, a large, mature firm has adequate access to new capital, whereas a rapidly growing firm may not have sufficient funds available to support its numerous acceptable projects. A growth firm is likely to have to depend heavily on internal financing through reinvested profits; it is likely to pay out only a very small percentage of its earnings as dividends. A more stable firm that needs long-term funds only for planned outlays is in a better position to pay out a large proportion of its earnings, particularly if it has ready sources of financing.

Owner Considerations[5]

A company should establish a dividend policy that has a favourable effect on the wealth of the *majority* of owners.

One consideration is the *tax status of a firm's owners.* If a firm has a large percentage of wealthy shareholders who are in a high tax bracket, it may decide to pay out a *lower* percentage of its earnings to allow the owners to delay the payment of taxes until they sell the stock. Of course, when the share is sold, if the proceeds are in excess of the original purchase price, the capital gain will be taxed, possibly at a more favourable rate than the one applied to dividend income. Lower income shareholders, however, who need dividend income, will prefer a *higher* payout of earnings.

A second consideration is the *owners' investment opportunities.* A firm should not retain funds for investment in projects yielding lower returns than the owners could obtain from external investments of equal risk. If it appears that the owners have better opportunities externally, the firm should pay out a higher percentage of its earnings. If the firm's investment opportunities are at least as good as similar-risk external investments, a lower payout would be justifiable.

A final consideration is the *potential dilution of ownership.* If a firm pays out a higher percentage of earnings, new equity capital will have to be raised with common shares, which may result in the dilution of both control and earnings for the existing owners. By paying out a low percentage of its earnings, the firm can minimize such possibility of dilution.

---

5. Theoretically, in an *efficient market,* owner considerations are automatically handled by the pricing mechanism of the market. The logic is as follows. The share price of a firm that pays a dividend that is smaller than required by a large number of owners will decline because the dissatisfied shareholders will sell their shares. The resulting drop in share price will (as explained in Chapter 8) raise the return required by investors, which will cause the firm's MCC to rise. As a result—all else being equal—the value of the projects acceptable to the company will decline and the demand for reinvested profits will fall. This decrease should allow the firm to satisfy shareholders by paying the higher dividends that they demand. In spite of this logic, it is helpful to understand some of the important considerations underlying owner behaviour.

Market Considerations

An awareness of the market's probable response to certain types of policies is helpful in formulating a suitable dividend policy. Shareholders are believed to value a *fixed or increasing level of dividends*, as opposed to a fluctuating pattern of dividends. This belief is supported by the research of John Lintner, who found that corporate managers are averse to changing the dollar amount of dividends in response to changes in earnings, particularly when earnings decline.[6]

Dividends are unlikely to decline, are tied to long-term sustainable earnings, and are smoothed from year to year. In addition, shareholders are believed to value a policy of *continuous dividend payment*. Because regularly paying a fixed or increasing dividend eliminates uncertainty about the frequency and magnitude of dividends, the earnings of the firm are likely to be discounted at a lower rate. This should result in an increase in the market value of the share and therefore increased owners' wealth.

Hint
The risk–return concept also applies to the firm's dividend policy. A firm that lets its dividends fluctuate from period to period will be viewed as risky, and investors will require a higher rate of return, which will increase the firm's cost of capital.

A final market consideration is the *informational content* of dividends. As indicated earlier, shareholders often view the firm's dividend payment as a *signal* relative to its future success. A stable and continuous dividend is a *positive signal* that conveys to the owners that the firm is in good health. If the firm skips a dividend payment in a given period due to a loss or to very low earnings, shareholders are likely to interpret this as a *negative signal*. The nonpayment of the dividend creates uncertainty about the future, and this uncertainty is likely to result in lower share value. Owners and investors generally construe a dividend payment when a loss occurs as an indication that the loss is merely temporary.

? Review Question

11–5 What factors affect dividend policy? Briefly describe each of them.

LG4

11.4 Types of Dividend Policies

A company's dividend policy must be formulated with two basic objectives in mind: to ensure the company has sufficient internal financing to invest in projects, and to maximize the wealth of the firm's owners. These two interrelated objectives must be fulfilled in light of the previously discussed factors that limit the policy alternatives. Three of the more commonly used dividend policies are described in the following sections. A particular firm's cash dividend policy may incorporate elements of each.

dividend payout ratio
Indicates the percentage of each dollar earned that is distributed to the owners in the form of cash; calculated by dividing the firm's cash dividend per share by its earnings per share.

Constant-Payout-Ratio Dividend Policy

One type of dividend policy occasionally adopted by firms is the use of a constant payout ratio. The **dividend payout ratio,** calculated by dividing the firm's cash

6. John Lintner, "Distribution of Income of Corporations Among Dividends, Retained Earnings, and Taxes," *American Economic Review* 46 (May 1956), pp. 97–113.

dividend per share by its earnings per share, indicates the percentage of each dollar earned that is distributed to the owners in the form of cash. With a **constant-payout-ratio dividend policy,** the firm establishes that a certain percentage of earnings is paid to owners in each dividend period.

constant-payout-ratio dividend policy
A dividend policy based on the payment of a certain percentage of earnings to owners in each dividend period.

The problem with this policy is that if the firm's earnings drop or if a loss occurs in a given period, the dividends may be low or even nonexistent. Because dividends are often considered an indicator of the firm's future condition and status, the firm's stock price may thus be adversely affected by this type of policy.

Example Peachtree Industries, a miner of potassium, has a policy of paying out 40 percent of earnings in cash dividends. In periods when a loss occurs, the firm's policy is to pay no cash dividends. Peachtree's earnings per share, dividends per share, and average price per share for the past six years are shown in the following table.

Year	Earnings/share	Dividends/share	Average price/share
2003	$4.50	$1.80	$50.00
2004	$2.00	$0.80	$41.10
2005	−$1.50	$0.00	$29.73
2006	$1.75	$0.70	$36.24
2007	$3.00	$1.20	$45.36
2008	−$0.50	$0.00	$31.86

Dividends increased in 2006 and 2007 and decreased in the other years. Not surprisingly, in years when earnings and dividends decreased, the firm's share price fell. In years when earnings and dividends increased, the stock price increased. Peachtree's sporadic pattern of earnings and dividends makes shareholders uncertain about the company's prospects and, as a result, the company's share price fluctuates widely. Note that the share price never reaches the $50 level of 2003, and that by 2008, when the company again loses money, the shares have lost 36 percent of their value.

Hint
Regulated utilities in low-growth areas can use a constant-payout-ratio dividend policy. Their capital requirements are usually low and their earnings are more certain than most firms.

A constant-payout-ratio dividend policy is only recommended for firms that have a relatively secure revenue source and good cost control, thus ensuring reliable earnings. In reality, companies that follow such a policy try to maintain a dividend payout ratio that falls in a target range, for example, between 40 and 55 percent. This is because so many factors influence earnings that it is impossible to maintain a single-number payout policy. Some examples of Canadian companies that follow such a dividend policy include the six major Canadian chartered banks, and utilities such as Fortis, TransCanada, and Canadian Utilities. The dividend payment history for these companies is available on their Web sites. Note that the dividends paid by these companies increase each year as earnings increase, but a target range is maintained.

www.bmo.com
www.scotiabank.com
www.rbc.com
www.fortisinc.com
www.transcanada.com
www.canadian-utilities.com

Regular Dividend Policy

regular dividend policy
A dividend policy based on the payment of a fixed-dollar dividend in each period.

The **regular dividend policy** is based on the payment of a fixed-dollar dividend in each period. The regular dividend policy provides the owners with generally positive information, thereby minimizing uncertainty. Often, firms using this policy increase the regular dividend once a *proven* increase in earnings has occurred. Under this policy, dividends are almost never decreased.

Example The dividend policy of Woodward Laboratories, a producer of a popular artificial sweetener, is to pay annual dividends of $1 per share until earnings per share have exceeded $4 for three consecutive years. In the fourth year, dividends per share will be increased to $1.50 per share and a new earnings plateau established. The firm does not anticipate decreasing its dividend unless its liquidity is in jeopardy. Woodward's earnings per share, dividends per share, and average price per share for the past 12 years are shown in the following table.

Year	Earnings/share	Dividends/share	Average price/share
1997	$2.85	$1.00	$35.00
1998	$2.70	$1.00	$33.24
1999	$0.50	$1.00	$28.86
2000	$0.75	$1.00	$30.14
2001	$3.00	$1.00	$39.96
2002	$6.00	$1.00	$46.74
2003	$2.00	$1.00	$36.21
2004	$5.00	$1.00	$44.19
2005	$4.20	$1.00	$41.16
2006	$4.60	$1.00	$43.31
2007	$3.90	$1.50	$46.36
2008	$4.50	$1.50	$52.76

Whatever the level of earnings, Woodward Laboratories paid dividends of $1 per share through 2006. In 2007, the dividend was increased to $1.50 per share because earnings in excess of $4 per share had been achieved during the previous three years. In 2007, the firm also had to establish a new earnings plateau for further dividend increases. Woodward Laboratories' average price per share exhibited a stable, increasing behaviour in spite of a somewhat volatile pattern of earnings.

target dividend-payout ratio
A policy under which the firm attempts to pay out a certain percentage of earnings as a stated dollar dividend, which it adjusts toward a target payout as proven earnings increases occur.

Often, a regular dividend policy is built around a **target dividend-payout ratio.** Under this policy, the firm attempts to pay out a certain percentage of earnings, but rather than let dividends fluctuate, it pays a stated dollar dividend and adjusts it toward the target payout as proven earnings increases occur. For instance, Woodward Laboratories appears to have a target payout ratio of around 35 percent. The payout was about 35 percent ($1 ÷ $2.85) when the dividend policy was set in 1997, and when the dividend was raised to $1.50 in 2007, the payout ratio was about 38 percent ($1.50 ÷ $3.90).

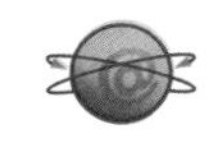

www.transalta.com

A Canadian company that seems to have followed a regular dividend policy is TransAlta Corporation. The company's dividends have been about $1 per share since 1991. The company's dividend payment history is available on their Web site.

Low-Regular-and-Extra Dividend Policy

low-regular-and-extra dividend policy
A dividend policy based on paying a low regular dividend, supplemented by an additional dividend when earnings are higher than normal.

extra dividend
An additional dividend optionally paid by the firm if earnings are higher than normal in a given period.

Some firms establish a **low-regular-and-extra dividend policy,** paying a low regular dividend, supplemented by an additional dividend when earnings are higher than normal in a given period. This additional dividend is called an **extra dividend,** which avoids giving shareholders false expectations that it will be maintained. The use of the "extra" designation is especially common among companies that experience cyclical shifts in earnings.

By establishing a low regular dividend that is paid each period, the firm gives investors the stable income necessary to build confidence in the firm, and the extra dividend permits them to share in the earnings from an especially good period. Firms using this policy must raise the level of the regular dividend once proven increases in earnings have been achieved.

For some companies, the extra dividend may become a regular event, due to the nature of the business. For others, it may only occur on a very sporadic basis. The use of a target dividend-payout ratio in establishing the regular dividend is advisable. A Canadian company that has followed an extra dividend policy is Canadian General Investment. The company pays very low quarterly dividends but then, in most years, pays a year-end special dividend to investors. The company's dividend payment history is available on their Web site. Microsoft has also paid special dividends to shareholders even though the company has been only paying quarterly dividends since 2005, and in very low amounts.

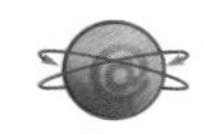

www.mmainvestments.com

? Review Question

11–6 Describe a constant-payout-ratio dividend policy, a regular dividend policy, and a low-regular-and-extra dividend policy. What are the effects of these policies?

11.5 Other Forms of Corporate Distribution

Three other forms of corporate distributions to shareholders are discussed in this section. First, rather than pay cash dividends, a company may pay a dividend in the form of additional common shares, a stock dividend. Second, stock splits are closely related to stock dividends and give the impression of adding value for shareholders. Finally, over the past 20 years, share repurchases have become quite common and these may be viewed as an alternative way to distribute cash to shareholders.

Stock Dividends

stock dividend
The payment to existing owners of a dividend in the form of common shares.

A **stock dividend** is the payment to existing common shareholders of a dividend in the form of common shares. Often, firms pay stock dividends as a replacement for or a supplement to cash dividends. Although stock dividends do not have a real value, shareholders may perceive them to represent something they did not have before and therefore to have value.

Accounting Aspects

In an accounting sense, the payment of a stock dividend is a shifting of funds between capital accounts rather than a use of funds. When a firm declares a stock dividend, the procedures for announcement and distribution are the same as those described earlier for a cash dividend. The accounting entries associated with the payment of stock dividends are illustrated in the following example.

Example The current shareholders' equity on the balance sheet of Garrison Corporation, a distributor of prefabricated cabinets, is shown in the following accounts.

Preferred shares	$ 300,000
Common shares (100,000 shares)	900,000
Retained earnings	800,000
Total shareholders' equity	$2,000,000

If Garrison declares a 10 percent stock dividend, 10,000 (10% × 100,000) new common shares are issued. If the prevailing market price of the common shares is $15, the value of the stock dividend is $150,000 (10,000 shares × $15). This amount is transferred from retained earnings to common shares as follows:

Preferred shares	$ 300,000
Common shares (110,000 shares)	1,050,000
Retained earnings	650,000
Total shareholders' equity	$2,000,000

The firm's total shareholders' equity has not changed; funds have only been *redistributed* among the accounts.

The Shareholder's Viewpoint

It should be recognized that shareholders receiving a stock dividend receive nothing of real value. After the dividend is paid, the per-share values decrease in proportion to the dividend in such a way that the market value of the firm remains unchanged. Each shareholder's proportion of ownership in the firm also remains the same, and *as long as the firm's earnings remain unchanged,* so does his or her share of total earnings. (Clearly, if the firm's earnings and cash dividends increase at the time the stock dividend is issued, an increase in share value is likely to result.) A continuation of the preceding example will clarify this point.

Example Ms. X owned 10,000 common shares of Garrison Corporation, which are trading for $15 per share. The company's most recent earnings were $220,000, and earnings are not expected to change in the near future. Before the stock dividend, Ms. X owned 10 percent (10,000 shares ÷ 100,000 shares) of the firm's common shares. Earnings per share were $2.20 ($220,000 ÷ 100,000 shares). Because Ms. X owned 10,000 shares, her earnings were $22,000 ($2.20 per share × 10,000 shares). After receiving the 10 percent stock dividend, Ms. X has 11,000 shares, which again is 10 percent of the ownership (11,000 shares ÷ 110,000 shares).

The market price of the stock can be expected to drop to $13.64 per share [$15 × (1.00 ÷ 1.10)], which means that the market value of Ms. X's holdings is

$150,000 (11,000 shares × $13.64 per share). This is the same as the initial value of her holdings (10,000 shares × $15 per share). The earnings per share drops to $2 ($220,000 ÷ 110,000 shares), because the same $220,000 in earnings must now be divided among 110,000 shares. Because Ms. X still owns 10 percent of the company, her share of total earnings is still $22,000 ($2 per share × 11,000 shares). Essentially, nothing has changed.

In summary, if the firm's earnings remain constant and total cash dividends do not increase, a stock dividend results in a lower per-share market value for the firm's common shares but the same total value. Since the effect of stock dividends, in reality, is nil for both investors and the company, stock dividends rarely occur in Canada's relatively sophisticated financial markets. Investors recognize that there is no real benefit and as a result, there is no point in a company incurring the expenses associated with a stock dividend.

Stock Splits

stock split
A method commonly used to lower the market price of a firm's common shares by increasing the number of shares belonging to each shareholder.

Although not a type of dividend, *stock splits* have an effect on a firm's share price similar to that of stock dividends. A **stock split** is a method commonly used to lower the market price of a firm's common shares by increasing the number of shares held by each shareholder. There is an inverse impact on the two variables. For example, in a 2-for-1 stock split (abbreviated 2:1), shareholders receive two shares for each share previously held. At the same time, the market price of the firm's common shares is cut in half. There is no impact on the company's capital structure or on the total value of investors' holdings of common shares.

A company will undertake a stock split when they feel their share price is too high and that reducing the price will increase trading activity and make the shares more attractive for individual investors.

It is not unusual for a stock split to cause a slight increase in the market value of the stock. This is attributable to the informational content of stock splits and the fact that *total* dividends paid commonly increase slightly after a split.[7]

Example Delphi Company, a forest products concern, has 200,000 common shares outstanding. Because the shares are selling at a high market price, the firm has declared a 2-for-1 stock split. The total before- and after-split shareholders' equity is shown in the following table.

Before split	
Common shares (200,000 shares)	$4,400,000
Retained earnings	2,000,000
Total shareholders' equity	$6,400,000

continued

7. Eugene F. Fama, Lawrence Fisher, Michael C. Jensen, and Richard Roll, "The Adjustment of Stock Prices to New Information," *International Economic Review* 10 (February 1969), pp. 1–21, found that the stock price increases after the split announcement, and the increase in stock price is maintained if dividends per share are increased but is lost if dividends per share are *not* increased following the split.

After 2-for-1 split	
Common shares (400,000 shares)	$4,400,000
Retained earnings	2,000,000
Total shareholders' equity	$6,400,000

The insignificant effect of the stock split on the firm's books is obvious.

Common shares can be split in any way desired. For example, the most common share split ratio is 2-for-1, but 3-for-1 and 3-for-2 splits are also usual. Stock splits are most common during a bull market, when the prices of common shares are increasing, and rare during bear markets. For example, in Canada between September 2002 and May 2007, the S&P/TSX Composite Index increased from 6,180 points to the 13,700 point level. During this lengthy bull market run, the common shares of many individual companies did even better and, as a result, dozens of companies split their shares. Again, companies do this to keep their share price in a range that is attractive to individual shareholders. In Canada, individual investors seem to like shares to be priced between $20 and $50. As a result many of the stock splits in Canada are 2:1, 3:1, or 4:1.

share consolidation (reverse stock split)
A method used to raise the market price of a firm's stock by exchanging a certain number of outstanding shares for one new share of stock.

Sometimes a **share consolidation (reverse stock split)** is made: a certain number of outstanding shares are exchanged for one new share. For example, in a 1-for-10 split, one new share is exchanged for 10 old shares. Share consolidations are initiated when a company's common shares are selling at a very low price (often less than $1) and a company wishes to raise the price to a higher level. Often investors feel shares trading at very low prices (penny stocks) are "too cheap" and thus low-quality, very high-risk investments.

For example, on December 1, 2006, Nortel Networks implemented a share consolidation of one share for 10 shares (1:10). The consolidation reduced the number of shares outstanding from 4.3 billion to 433 million. The reason for the consolidation was the dramatic decline in the value of the company's common shares that had started in July 2000 when the share price peaked at $124.50. By October 2002, the shares had bottomed out at $0.67. From May 2005, the shares traded in the $2.00 to $3.00 range. The consolidation was meant to raise the company's shares to a level that would attract the interest of institutional investors. Examples of recent stock splits or share consolidations are available on the Web.

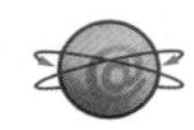

www.newswire.ca/en
www.globeinvestor.com/v5/content/news

Share Repurchases

Share repurchases occur when a company buys and then retires its own shares. These are sometimes referred to as *share buybacks*. Share repurchases should not be confused with the redemption of long-term debt or preferred shares. Companies have the option of redeeming and retiring these other types of securities; there is no redemption provision associated with common shares. Common shares are a permanent source of financing and will remain outstanding for as long as the company operates, unless the company repurchases the shares.

share repurchase
Company purchase of its own common shares from investors in the stock market; the company then retires the shares.

The basics of a **share repurchase** are simple. First, the company receives permission to repurchase shares from the regulating agency that oversees the opera-

11.1 **IN PRACTICE**

Why Companies Split

Typically, companies announce stock splits when their shares reach a point at which investors consider the shares expensive. In Canada, this often occurs when the share price increases to the $50 to $90 range. Dividing a high-priced share into two or three lower-priced shares can increase its marketability by attracting more investors.

"Splits are very important to individual investors, even though you're essentially getting two fives for a 10," suggests a financial analyst. Generally, shares that split have performed very well in the past, so many investors believe splits indicate good performance may continue. There is some evidence that this is indeed true. One study showed that over 15 years, a portfolio of 1,275 stocks that split yielded an average return of 19 percent in the first year after the split and 65 percent over 3 years, compared to returns of 11 and 53 percent, respectively, for a similar group of stocks that did not split. In the short term, share prices tend to rise between the time the split is announced and the date of the split.

Corby Distilleries markets liquor brands such Lamb's rum, Polar Ice vodka, Chivas Regal, Jameson's, Beefeater gin, Mumm champagne, and Jacob's Creek and Wyndham Estate wines. On February 9, 2006, Corby announced healthy earnings, returns, and cash flow, and a 4-for-1 stock split effective February 24, 2006. On February 8, 2006, Corby's shares closed at $76.25. With the announcement on the 9th, the shares closed at $82.00, a 7.5 percent increase. During the next ten trading days to February 23, the share price rose to $85.50, for an overall increase of 12.1 percent. And again, this was all triggered by the February 9 announcement. On February 24, the shares split. The shares closed trading that day at $21.99, or $87.96 on a pre-split basis. By March 16, the shares were trading for $27.90, or $111.60 on a pre-split basis. For investors, this meant the shares increased in value by 46.4 percent since February 8, just 28 trading days later. The shares continued to trade in the mid-to-high twenties and closed 2006 at $27.00.

However, some analysts point out that stocks that split have already risen in price, so the above-average performance simply reflects an increase in the company's growth and earnings. Splits also signal management's confidence that the upward trend will continue. Companies don't want to split a $50 stock into two shares at $25 and then see the price drop. Yet sometimes this occurs for reasons outside the company's control.

RONA is a distributor and retailer of hardware, home renovation, and gardening products. On March 10, 2005, RONA announced a 2-for-1 stock split. The next day, the share price increased $1.50 from $48.50 to $50.00. On March 18, 2005, the stock split took effect, and the shares closed trading at $25.37, or $50.74 on a pre-split basis. Over the six trading days, the share price increased by 4.6 percent. The split seemed to generate a positive result for shareholders. Yet, by April 1, 2005, RONA shares were trading for $23.40 and this downward trend continued with the shares hitting a low of $19.45 on January 26, 2006. As of December 1, 2006, the shares were trading for $21.40, still well below the pre-split price. The company was the victim of the expected downturn in the housing market in Canada.

Financial advisors remind investors that a stock split, by itself, is not a reason to buy a stock. As with any stock purchase, you should evaluate the fundamentals of the company, including key ratios, its price/earnings multiple, profit outlook, and industry factors. In terms of a company's underlying value, a stock split is essentially a nonevent.

SOURCES: Daniel Kadlec, "The Dumb Money," *Time*, February 22, 1999. Annual reports of Corby Distilleries Limited and RONA.

tion of the stock exchange that lists the company's shares. In Canada, this is the Toronto Stock Exchange. Second, the company then buys shares from investors through an investment dealer. The company receives the shares which are then retired; the investor receives cash. Over the past 20 years, there has been a tremendous increase in the volume of share repurchases in both Canada and the United States. The next section discusses the two methods used to repurchase common shares.

Types of Share Repurchases

open-market share repurchases
Company purchases of its own shares on a stock exchange at the market price once approval from the stock exchange is received; termed a *normal course issuer bid* in Canada.

There are two types of share repurchases: open-market offers and fixed-price tender bids. **Open-market share repurchases** are company purchases of its own shares on a stock exchange at the market price. In Canada, these are called *normal course issuer bids*, and companies must gain approval for these bids from the stock exchange. Open-market repurchases must be completed within one year and are restricted to the greater of 10 percent of the public float or 5 percent of the shares outstanding. Companies must report to the exchange the number of shares repurchased on a monthly basis. Open-market repurchases are executed at the market price prevailing at the time of the company's order. Over the year the normal course bid is open, there might be numerous market orders, all at substantially different prices.

fixed-price tender bid
An offer by a company to purchase a certain percentage of its own shares at a stated price that is well above the current market price within a specified time period; termed a *substantial issuer bid*.

Fixed-price tender bids are offers by a company to purchase a certain percentage of its own shares at a stated price within a specified time period. These are termed *substantial issuer bids*. Tender bids are generally for much more than 5 percent of the outstanding shares and are open for, generally, no longer than 20 trading days. A tender bid is at a stated price, which is usually at least 20 percent above the market price prior to the announcement of the offer. Tender bids are used when a company wants either to send a strong message to the market that the company's shares are undervalued, or to defeat a hostile takeover by reducing the number of shares outstanding and rewarding shareholders for not tendering their shares to the takeover offer.

Dutch-auction bid
A variation of the fixed-price tender bid where the company specifies the number of shares it wishes to repurchase and a range of prices at which it will purchase the shares.

In a **Dutch-auction bid**, a variation of the fixed-price tender bid, a company specifies the number of shares it wishes to repurchase and a range of prices at which it will purchase its shares. Shareholders then choose the number of shares they wish to tender to the bid and the lowest price, within the range established by the company, at which they are willing to sell their shares to the company. On the basis of the choices made by tendering shareholders, the company then establishes the lowest price, commonly referred to as the "clearing price," within the range of prices that will result in the company acquiring the maximum number of shares to be purchased under the bid. All shares tendered at or below the clearing price are purchased by the company. Shares tendered above the clearing price are not purchased.

www.newswire.ca/en
www.globeinvestor.com

For an open-market repurchase, the seller does not know the company is the buyer of the shares. With a tender offer, the seller knows the company is buying the shares. Examples of companies launching or announcing the results of share repurchases are available on various Web sites.

Reasons Companies Repurchase Shares

So, why do companies repurchase their own shares? A number of motives have been suggested.

1. Share repurchases reduce the number of common shares outstanding, thereby increasing EPS. Increasing EPS may lead to higher share prices.
2. Repurchases may send a positive signal to the market that the management of the company believes the share price is undervalued.
3. Repurchases may provide price support for a company's common shares if the price has been declining in the market.
4. Share repurchases allow a company to adjust their debt ratio to achieve an optimal capital structure.
5. Stock options have become a significant part of the pay packages of corporate management. To avoid diluting earnings and ownership from the exercise of stock options, a company may repurchase sufficient common shares to offset the exercise of the options.
6. Repurchases act as a defence in the event of an unfriendly takeover offer by reducing the number of publicly traded shares on the market.

Each of these reasons likely applies in some situations when companies repurchase common shares. A seventh reason for share repurchases is the subject of the following section.

Share Repurchases as an Alternative to a Cash Dividend

When common shares are repurchased for retirement, the underlying effect is to distribute cash to the common shareholders who sell their shares to the company. As a result of any repurchase, the participating owners receive cash for their shares. Generally, as long as earnings remain constant, and no additional common shares are issued via other means, the repurchase reduces the number of outstanding shares, raising the earnings per share and therefore the market price per share. In addition, certain owner tax benefits may result.

Only those shareholders who wish to receive cash will participate. Those who do not wish to receive cash (either a dividend or the proceeds from selling) due to tax consequences will hold their shares. The selling shareholders receive cash and any gain on the shares (difference between the selling price and original cost) is a capital gain. In Canada, as was shown in Table 8.5, and Chapter 2, only one-half of a capital gain is taxed. Depending on an investor's tax rate, capital gains may be taxed more favourably than dividend income. Companies may repurchase shares when they feel that some of their shareholders do not wish to receive cash dividends. So, when companies pay dividends or shareholders participate in a repurchase, there is a benefit—shareholders receive cash. How are repurchases a benefit to shareholders who do not participate?

The repurchase of common shares results in a type of *reverse dilution*; earnings per share increase since the number of common shares outstanding is reduced. This *may* result in the market price of the common shares increasing. Thus, a share repurchase may be viewed as an alternative to a cash dividend where both sets of shareholders (participants and non-participants in the repurchase) benefit. The following example will illustrate the logic.

Example Benton Company, a national sportswear chain, has released the following financial data:

Earnings available for common shareholders	$1,000,000
Number of common shares outstanding	400,000
Earnings per share ($1,000,000 ÷ 400,000)	$2.50
Market price per share	$50
Price/earnings (P/E) ratio ($50 ÷ $2.50)	20

The firm is contemplating using $800,000 of its earnings either to pay cash dividends or to repurchase shares. If the firm pays cash dividends, the amount of the dividend would be $2 per share ($800,000 ÷ 400,000 shares). Due to tax consequences, some shareholders may not wish to receive the dividend. Instead, the company could announce a share repurchase, providing cash to those shareholders wishing to sell. With the repurchase announcement, the share price will likely increase due to the reasons discussed earlier. Assuming the price increases to $51, Benton could acquire 15,686 shares ($800,000 ÷ $51). These shares are retired and 384,314 (400,000 – 15,686) shares remain outstanding.

Earnings per share (EPS) rise to $2.60 ($1,000,000 ÷ 384,314). If the shares still sold at 20 times earnings (P/E = 20), applying the *price/earnings multiple approach* presented in Chapter 8, its market price would rise to $52 per share ($2.60 × 20). The net effect is that the selling shareholders receive the certain $51. The holding shareholders may see the value of their shares increase. This example supports the view that share repurchases provide benefits to both sets of shareholders and result in higher share prices.

From an accounting perspective, a share repurchase results in a decline in cash. For the equity accounts, the amount paid by the company is first deducted from the value of common shares. But if this amount is more than the proceeds received when the shares were originally sold, the excess is deducted from retained earnings. This process was fully discussed in Chapter 5.

Recent Research on Corporate Payments to Shareholders

As discussed earlier in the chapter, over 50 years ago in 1956, John Lintner laid the foundation for the modern understanding of dividend policy. Lintner (1956) interviewed managers from 28 companies and found that managers target a long-term payout ratio when determining dividend policy. He also concluded that dividends are more likely to be paid by mature companies; be sticky—that is, tied to long-term sustainable earnings; and be smoothed from year to year.

While dividends are still paid by mature companies, much has changed in corporate Canada in the last 50 years. One of the biggest changes is the large increase in share repurchases. Even 20 years ago, share repurchases were rare. Today, they are the norm in corporate Canada. Of the largest 500 publicly traded companies in Canada, very few *would not* repurchase some of their shares during the year. Many billions of dollars are spent on share repurchases in Canada each year. And this is money that could have been paid as dividends. Smaller companies are less likely to pay dividends or repurchase shares due to cash constraints.

A paper has recently been published that reports on how today's companies determine dividend and repurchase policies.[8] This paper sheds light on managers' motives for making payments to shareholders, and finds that maintaining the amount of dividends paid is on par with investment decisions. In other words, once a firm starts to make dividend payments, they are very hesitant to reduce the payment. The dividend payment is treated the same as investment decisions, meaning regardless of what happens to earnings, the dividend stays. This is consistent with companies following the regular dividend policy discussed earlier in the chapter.

Given this view of dividends, it is not surprising that many managers now favour repurchases, which are viewed as more flexible than dividends. So the expected stability of future earnings affects dividend policy. While dividends are a commitment that firms find very difficult to break, repurchases are made out of the residual cash flow after investment spending. In addition, unlike dividends, repurchases can be used by managers to buy undervalued shares, to increase earnings per share, or to offset the dilutive effect of the exercise of the options provided to managers.

Finally, senior managers now believe that institutional investors, like pension plans and mutual fund managers, are indifferent between dividends and repurchases, and that payout policies have little impact on their investors. In general, the views of corporate managers provide little support for agency, signalling, and clientele hypotheses of payout policy. Tax considerations play a secondary role.

11.2 **IN PRACTICE**

Banking on Shareholder Returns

The Bank of Montreal (BMO), one of the Big 5 Canadian banks and among the 10 largest companies in Canada in terms of market capitalization, has paid dividends to its shareholders since 1829, a period of about 180 years. While some companies reduce or eliminate dividends to save cash, 2006 marked the 15th consecutive year that the BMO increased the dividend paid to common shareholders. In 1992, BMO paid a dividend of $0.53 per share. By 2006, that had grown to $2.26, an average yearly increase of 10.9 percent. During 2006, the company raised dividends twice, and the value of dividends declared rose 22.2 percent from the $1.85 per share paid in 2005. Dividends paid over the 7-year period from 2000 to 2006 increased at an average annual rate of 14.6 percent.

The BMO's dividend policy is to increase dividends in line with long-term trends in earnings per share growth, while retaining sufficient profits to support anticipated business growth, fund strategic investments, and provide continued support for depositors. BMO's policy is to maintain a dividend payout ratio of 45 to 55 percent over time.

Some feel that dividends are "out of style," and a tax-inefficient way of delivering returns to shareholders. This is because dividends are taxed twice, once at

▶

8. A. Brav, J. R. Graham, C. R. Harvey, and R. Michaely, "Payout Policy in the 21st Century," *Journal of Financial Economics* 77 (2005), pp. 483–528.

the corporate level and again when received by investors. People in this camp feel companies should reinvest profits into the business, pay down debt, or repurchase shares. "Increasing share prices, not dividends, attract investors," they would say.

For others, the size and pattern of dividends provide information about a firm's current and future performance. Dividend increases send strong signals to investors that a company is confident of its future financial health. "Management believes that the company has enough cash to invest in its growth, pay higher dividends, and buy back shares," they would say. Over time, companies with long histories of dividend increases have maintained the steady earnings growth required to support higher dividend payouts. In addition, recent tax changes have reduced the taxation of dividends, making them more attractive to shareholders.

Besides dividends, BMO also repurchases shares. In 2006, BMO repurchased 5,919,400 common shares at a cost of $376 million. The share repurchase program offsets the impact of dilution caused by the exercise of management stock options, the company's dividend reinvestment plan, and the conversion of convertible shares. On September 1, 2006, a new one-year normal course issuer bid was announced under which BMO may repurchase for cancellation up to 15 million common shares, representing approximately 3 percent of BMO's public float.

Direct payments, like dividends and share repurchases, seem to matter to shareholders in companies like the Bank of Montreal. For example, over the six years to October 31, 2006, the average return on BMO's common shares was 15.7 percent. Said one analyst, "If a company is willing to pay a dividend, then they must actually have the cash in the till." When it comes to dividend policy, that is important!

SOURCES: Various annual reports and financial reports, Bank of Montreal; Richard Blackwell, "List of Dividend-Paying Firms Shrinking," *The Globe and Mail*, February 11, 2002.

? Review Questions

11–7 What is a *stock dividend*? Why do firms issue stock dividends? Comment on the following statement: "I have a stock that promises to pay a 20 percent stock dividend every year, and therefore it guarantees that I will break even in 5 years."

11–8 What is a *stock split*? What is a *reverse stock split*? Compare a stock split with a stock dividend.

11–9 What is the logic behind *repurchasing shares* to distribute excess cash to the firm's owners?

11–10 What methods can be used to repurchase shares? Why do companies repurchase common shares?

11–11 Discuss managers' current views on how cash should be distributed to shareholders.

SUMMARY

Understand cash dividend payment procedures and the role of dividend reinvestment plans. The cash dividend decision is normally a quarterly decision made by the board of directors that establishes the record date and payment date. Generally, the larger the dividend charged to retained earnings and paid in cash, the greater the amount of financing that must be raised externally. Some firms offer dividend reinvestment plans (DRIPs) that allow shareholders to acquire shares in lieu of cash dividends, sometimes at a 5 percent discount to the market price. DRIPs provide benefits to both shareholders and the company.

Describe the residual theory of dividends and the key arguments with regard to dividend irrelevance and relevance. The residual theory suggests that dividends should be viewed as the earnings left after all acceptable investment opportunities have been undertaken. Dividend irrelevance, which is implied by the residual theory, is argued by Miller and Modigliani using a perfect world wherein information content and clientele effects exist. Gordon and Lintner argue dividend relevance based on the uncertainty-reducing effect of dividends, supported by their bird-in-the-hand argument. Although intuitively appealing, empirical studies fail to provide clear support of dividend relevance. The actions of financial managers and shareholders alike, however, tend to support the belief that dividend policy does affect stock value.

Discuss the key factors involved in formulating a dividend policy. A firm's dividend policy should maximize the wealth of its owners while providing for sufficient financing. Dividend policy is affected by certain legal, contractual, and internal constraints as well as growth prospects, owner considerations, and market considerations. Legal constraints prohibit corporations from paying out as cash dividends any portion of the common share account; dividends must be paid from earnings: the current year's and the total of all past years' reinvested profits. Firms with overdue liabilities or those legally insolvent or bankrupt cannot pay cash dividends. Contractual constraints result from restrictive provisions in the firm's loan agreements. Internal constraints tend to result from a firm's limited excess cash availability. Growth prospects affect the relative importance of retaining earnings rather than paying them out in dividends. The tax status of owners, the owners' investment opportunities, and the potential dilution of ownership are also important considerations. Finally, market considerations relate to shareholders' preference for the continuous payment of fixed or increasing streams of dividends and the perceived informational content of dividends.

Review and evaluate the three basic types of dividend policies. With a constant-payout-ratio dividend policy, the firm pays a fixed percentage of earnings out to the owners each period. With this policy, dividends move up and down with earnings, and no dividend is paid when a loss occurs. In reality, the payout ratio is usually in a range. Under a regular dividend policy, the firm pays a fixed-dollar dividend each period; it increases the amount of dividends only after a proven increase in earnings has occurred. The low-regular-and-extra dividend policy is similar to the regular dividend policy, except that it pays an "extra dividend" in periods when the firm's earnings are higher than normal. In reality, many companies combine the regular and payout ratio dividend policies by attempting to maintain a payout ratio range, while never allowing the dividend to decline.

Evaluate stock dividends from the accounting, shareholder, and company points of view. Occasionally, firms pay stock dividends as a replacement for or supplement to cash dividends. The payment of stock dividends involves a shifting of funds between capital accounts rather than a use of funds. Shareholders receiving stock dividends typically receive nothing of value—the market value of their holdings, their proportion of ownership, and their share of total earnings remain unchanged. Since the effect of stock dividends, in reality, is nil for both investors and the company, stock dividends rarely occur in Canada's relatively sophisticated financial markets.

Explain stock splits and common share repurchases and the firm's motivation for

undertaking each of them. Stock splits are sometimes used to enhance trading activity of a firm's shares by lowering the market price of its shares. A stock split merely involves accounting adjustments—it has no effect on either the firm's cash or its capital structure. Share repurchases can be made in lieu of cash dividend payments to retire outstanding shares and delay the payment of taxes for the shareholders. They involve the actual outflow of cash to reduce the number of outstanding shares and thereby increase earnings per share and the market price per share. Whereas stock repurchases can be viewed as dividend alternatives, stock splits are used to deliberately adjust the market price of shares. Based on recent research, managers report that maintaining the amount of dividends paid is on par with investment decisions. In other words, once a firm starts to make dividend payments, they are very hesitant to reduce the payment. This is consistent with companies following the regular dividend policy discussed in the chapter. Given this view of dividends, it is not surprising that many managers now favour repurchases.

SELF-TEST PROBLEM

(Solution in Appendix B)

ST 11–1 **Share repurchase** The Off-Shore Steel Company has earnings available for common shareholders of $2 million and 500,000 common shares outstanding with a current market price of $60 per share. The firm is currently contemplating paying a $2 per share cash dividend.

a. Calculate the firm's current earnings per share (EPS) and price/earnings (P/E) ratio.

b. If the firm can repurchase common shares at $62 per share, how many shares can be purchased in lieu of making the proposed cash dividend payment?

c. If the firm makes the proposed repurchase, what will happen to EPS? Provide a numeric analysis and explain why this result occurred.

d. If the shares sell for the same P/E ratio as before the repurchase, what will the market price be after repurchase?

e. Compare and contrast the shareholders' position under the dividend and repurchase alternatives.

PROBLEMS

11–1 **Dividend payment procedures** Wood Shoes, at the quarterly dividend meeting, declared a cash dividend of $1.10 per share for holders of record on Monday, July 10. The firm has 300,000 shares of common stock outstanding and has set a payment date of July 31. Prior to the dividend declaration, the firm's key accounts were as follows:

Cash	$500,000	Dividends payable	$ 0
		Retained earnings	2,500,000

a. Show the entries after the meeting adjourned.

b. When is the ex dividend date? What is meant by the term "ex dividend"?

c. After the July 31 payment date, what values would the key accounts have?
d. What effect, if any, will the dividend have on the firm's total assets?
e. Ignoring general market fluctuations, what effect, if any, will the dividend have on the firm's stock price on the day the dividend is declared and on the ex dividend date?

INTERMEDIATE  **11–2 Dividend payment** Kathy Snow wishes to purchase shares of Countdown Computing, Inc. The company's board of directors has declared a cash dividend of $0.80 to be paid to holders of record on Wednesday, May 12.

a. What is the last day that Kathy can purchase the shares (trade date) in order to receive the dividend?
b. What day does this stock begin trading ex dividend?
c. What change, if any, would you expect in the price per share on the day the dividend is declared and on the day the stock begins trading ex dividend?
d. If Kathy held the stock for less than one quarter and then sold it for $39 per share, would she achieve a higher investment return by (1) buying the stock *prior to* the ex dividend date at $35 per share and collecting the $0.80 dividend or (2) buying it *on* the ex dividend date at $34.20 per share but not receiving the dividend?

INTERMEDIATE  **11–3 Residual dividend policy** As president of Young's of Charlottetown, a large clothing chain, you have just received a letter from a major shareholder asking about the company's dividend policy. The shareholder has asked you to estimate the amount of the dividend that you are likely to pay next year. You have not yet collected all the information about the expected dividend payment, but you do know the following:

(1) The company follows a residual dividend policy.
(2) The total capital budget for next year is likely to be one of three amounts, depending on the results of capital budgeting studies that are currently under way. The capital expenditure amounts are $2 million, $3 million, and $4 million.
(3) The forecasted level of reinvested profits next year is $2 million.
(4) The target or optimal capital structure is a debt ratio of 40 percent.

You have decided to respond by sending the shareholder the best information available to you.

a. Describe a *residual dividend policy*.
b. Compute the amount of the dividend (or the amount of new common share financing needed) and the dividend payout ratio for each of the three capital expenditure amounts.
c. Compare, contrast, and discuss the amount of dividends (calculated in **b**) associated with each of the three capital expenditure amounts.

INTERMEDIATE  **11–4 Dividend constraints** The Howe Company's shareholders' equity account is as follows:

Common shares (400,000 shares)	$2,600,000
Retained earnings	1,900,000
Total shareholders' equity	$4,500,000

The earnings available for common shareholders from this period's operations are $100,000, which have been included as part of the $1.9 million in retained earnings.

a. What is the maximum dividend per share that the firm can pay?

b. If the firm has $160,000 in cash, what is the largest per-share dividend it can pay without borrowing?

c. Indicate the accounts and changes, if any, that will result if the firm pays the dividends indicated in **a** and **b**.

d. Indicate the effects of an $80,000 cash dividend on shareholders' equity.

INTERMEDIATE LG3

11–5 Dividend constraints A firm with 25,000 common shares outstanding has $800,000 of common share financing and $40,000 of retained earnings (including the current year's reinvested earnings) on the balance sheet. In the current year, the firm has $29,000 of earnings available for the common shareholders.

a. What is the most the firm can pay in cash dividends to each common shareholder?

b. What effect would a cash dividend of $0.80 per share have on the firm's balance sheet entries?

c. If the firm cannot raise any new funds from external sources, what do you consider the key constraint with respect to the magnitude of the firm's dividend payments? Why?

INTERMEDIATE  LG4

11–6 Low-regular-and-extra dividend policy Bennett Farm Equipment Sales, Inc., is in a highly cyclical business. While the firm has a target payout ratio of 25 percent, its board realizes that strict adherence to that ratio would result in a fluctuating dividend and create uncertainty for the firm's shareholders. Therefore, the firm has declared a regular dividend of $0.125 per share per quarter with extra cash dividends to be paid when earnings justify them. Earnings per share for the last several years are as follows:

Year	EPS
2003	$1.97
2004	2.15
2005	2.80
2006	2.20
2007	3.00
2008	3.40

a. Calculate the payout ratio for each year based on the regular $0.125 quarterly dividend and the cited EPS.

b. Calculate the difference between the regular $0.125 quarterly dividend and a 25 percent payout for each year.

c. Bennett has established a policy of paying an extra dividend of $0.025 per quarter when the difference between the regular dividend and a 25 percent payout amounts to $0.25 or more. The extra dividend will be paid in the following year. Show the regular and extra dividends in those years when an extra dividend would be paid. What would be done with the "extra" in years when an extra dividend is not paid?

d. The firm expects that future earnings per share will continue to cycle but remain above $2.20 per share in most years. What factors should be considered in making a revision to the amount paid as a regular dividend? If the firm revises the regular dividend, what new amount should it pay?

INTERMEDIATE 

11–7 Alternative dividend policies Over the last 10 years, a firm has had the earnings per share shown in the following table.

Year	Earnings per share
1999	$0.25
2000	– 0.50
2001	1.80
2002	1.20
2003	2.40
2004	3.20
2005	2.80
2006	3.20
2007	3.80
2008	4.00

a. If the firm's dividend policy were based on a constant payout ratio of 40 percent for all years with positive earnings and 0 percent otherwise, what would be the quarterly dividend paid each year?

b. If the firm had a quarterly dividend payout of $0.25 per share, increasing by $0.025 per share whenever the quarterly dividend payout fell below 50 percent for two consecutive years, what quarterly dividend would the firm pay each year?

c. If the firm's policy were to pay a quarterly dividend of $0.125 per share except when earnings per share exceed $3, when an extra dividend equal to 80 percent of earnings beyond $3 would be paid, what annual dividend would the firm pay each year?

d. Discuss the pros and cons of each dividend policy described in **a** through **c**.

CHALLENGE 

11–8 Alternative dividend policies Given the earnings per share over the period shown in the following table, determine the quarterly and annual dividend per share under each of the policies set forth in **a** through **d**.

Year	Earnings per share
2001	$0.44
2002	1.00
2003	0.60
2004	1.05
2005	– 0.85
2006	1.20
2007	1.56
2008	1.40

a. Pay out 50 percent of earnings in all years with positive earnings.
b. Pay $0.125 per share and increase to $0.20 per share whenever earnings per share rise above $0.90 per share for two consecutive years.
c. Pay $0.125 per share except when earnings exceed $1 per share, in which case an extra dividend of 60 percent of earnings above $1 per share is paid.
d. Combine policies in **b** and **c.** When the dividend is raised (in **b**), raise the excess dividend base (in c) from $1 to $1.10 per share.
e. Compare and contrast each of the dividend policies described in **a** through **d.**

BASIC LG5

11–9 **Stock dividend—Firm** Columbia Paper has the shareholders' equity account given below. The firm's common shares have a current market price of $30 per share.

Preferred shares	$100,000
Common shares (10,000 shares)	300,000
Retained earnings	100,000
Total shareholders' equity	$500,000

a. Show the effects on Columbia of a 5 percent stock dividend.
b. Show the effects of (1) a 10 percent and (2) a 20 percent stock dividend.
c. In light of your answers to **a** and **b,** discuss the effects of stock dividends on shareholders' equity.

INTERMEDIATE 

11–10 **Cash versus stock dividend** Sudbury Tool has the shareholders' equity account given below. The firm's common shares currently sell for $4 per share.

Preferred shares	$ 100,000
Common shares (400,000 shares)	600,000
Retained earnings	320,000
Total shareholders' equity	$1,020,000

a. Show the effects on the firm of a $0.01, $0.05, $0.10, and $0.20 per-share *cash* dividend.
b. Show the effects on the firm of a 1, 5, 10, and 20 percent *stock* dividend.
c. Compare the effects in **a** and **b.** What are the significant differences in the two methods of paying dividends?

INTERMEDIATE 

11–11 **Stock dividend—Investor** Sarah Warren currently holds 400 shares of Nutri-Foods. The firm has 40,000 shares outstanding. The firm most recently had earnings available for common shareholders of $80,000, and its shares have been selling for $22 per share. The firm intends to retain its earnings and pay a 10 percent stock dividend.
a. How much does the firm currently earn per share?
b. What proportion of the firm does Sarah Warren currently own?
c. What proportion of the firm will Ms. Warren own after the stock dividend? Explain your answer.
d. At what market price would you expect the stock to sell after the stock dividend?
e. Discuss what effect, if any, the payment of stock dividends will have on Ms. Warren's share of the ownership and earnings of Nutri-Foods.

INTERMEDIATE  **11–12 Stock dividend—Investor** Security Data Company has 50,000 common shares outstanding currently selling at $40 per share. The firm most recently had earnings available for common shareholders of $120,000, but it has decided to retain these funds and is considering either a 5 or 10 percent stock dividend in lieu of a cash dividend.

a. Determine the firm's current earnings per share.
b. If Sam Waller currently owns 500 shares, determine his proportion of ownership currently and under each of the proposed stock dividend plans. Explain your findings.
c. Calculate and explain the market price per share under each of the stock dividend plans.
d. For each of the proposed stock dividends, calculate the earnings per share after payment of the stock dividend.
e. What is the value of Sam Waller's holdings under each of the plans? Explain.
f. Should Mr. Waller have any preference with respect to the proposed stock dividends? Why or why not?

INTERMEDIATE  **11–13 Stock split—Firm** Growth Industries' current shareholders' equity account is as follows:

Preferred shares	$ 400,000
Common shares (600,000 shares)	2,000,000
Retained earnings	800,000
Total shareholders' equity	$3,200,000

a. Indicate the change, if any, expected if the firm declares a 2-for-1 stock split.
b. Indicate the change, if any, expected if the firm declares a 1-for-1½ share consolidation.
c. Indicate the change, if any, expected if the firm declares a 3-for-1 stock split.
d. Indicate the change, if any, expected if the firm declares a 6-for-1 stock split.
e. Indicate the change, if any, expected if the firm declares a 1-for-4 share consolidation.

  INTERMEDIATE **11–14 Stock split versus stock dividend—Firm** Mammoth Corporation is considering a 3-for-2 stock split. It currently has the shareholders' equity position shown. The current share price is $120. The most recent period's earnings available for common stock is included in retained earnings.

Preferred shares	$ 1,000,000
Common shares (100,000 shares)	2,000,000
Retained earnings	10,000,000
Total shareholders' equity	$13,000,000

a. What effects on Mammoth would result from the stock split?
b. What change in stock price would you expect to result from the stock split?
c. What is the maximum cash dividend per common share that the firm could pay before and after the stock split?
d. Contrast your answers to **a** through **c** with the circumstances surrounding a 50 percent stock dividend.
e. Explain the differences between stock splits and stock dividends.

  INTERMEDIATE

11–15 Stock dividend versus stock split—Firm The board of Wicker Home Health Care, Inc., is exploring ways to expand the number of shares outstanding in order to reduce the market price per share to a level that the firm considers more appealing to investors. The options under consideration are a 20 percent stock dividend or a 5-for-4 stock split. At the present time, the firm's equity account and other per share information are as follows:

Common shares (100,000 shares)	1,000,000
Retained earnings	700,000
Total shareholders' equity	$1,700,000
Price per share	$30.00
Earnings per share	$3.60
Dividend per share	$1.08

a. Show the effect on the equity accounts and per share data of a 20 percent stock dividend.
b. Show the effect on the equity accounts and per share data of a 5-for-4 stock split.
c. Which option will accomplish Wicker's goal of reducing current stock price while maintaining a stable level of retained earnings?
d. What legal constraints might encourage the firm to choose a split over a stock dividend?

11–16 Share repurchase The following financial data on the Bond Recording Company are available:

Earnings available for common shareholders	$800,000
Number of common shares outstanding	400,000
Earnings per share ($800,000 ÷ 400,000)	$2
Market price per share	$20
Price/earnings (P/E) ratio ($20 ÷ $2)	10

The firm is currently contemplating using $400,000 of its earnings to pay cash dividends or repurchasing shares at the required price.

a. Approximately how many common shares can the firm repurchase using the funds that would have gone to pay the cash dividend? Assume that on the day the share repurchase was announced, the market price per share increased to $21.
b. Calculate EPS after the repurchase. Explain your calculations.
c. If the common shares still sell at 10 times earnings, what will the market price be after the repurchase?
d. Compare and contrast the pre- and post-repurchase earnings per share.
e. Compare and contrast the shareholders' position under the dividend and repurchase alternatives. What are the tax implications under each alternative?

11–17 Share repurchase Harte Textiles, Inc., a maker of custom upholstery fabrics, is concerned about preserving the wealth of its shareholders during a cyclical downturn in the home furnishings business. The company has maintained a constant dividend payout of $2 tied to a target payout ratio of 40 percent.

Management is preparing a share repurchase recommendation to present to the firm's board of directors. The following data have been gathered from the last two years:

	2007	2008
Earnings available for common shareholders	$1,260,000	$1,200,000
Number of shares outstanding	300,000	300,000
Earnings per share	$4.20	$4.00
Market price per share	$23.50	$20.00
Price/earnings ratio	5.6	5.0

a. For 2008, in order to have a $2 per share dividend and meet the 40 percent target payout ratio, how many common shares should the company have outstanding?

b. How many shares would have to be repurchased to have the level of shares outstanding calculated in **a**? If the firm repurchased these shares, what do you expect would happen to the market price per share?

CASE CHAPTER 11 Establishing General Access Company's Dividend Policy and Initial Dividend

See the enclosed Student CD-ROM for cases that help you put theories and concepts from the text into practice.

Be sure to visit the Companion Website for this book at **www.pearsoned.ca/gitman** for a wealth of additional learning tools including self-test quizzes, Web exercises, and additional cases.

CHAPTER 12

Capital Budgeting: Principles and Techniques

LEARNING GOALS

LG1 Discuss the motives for capital expenditures, the steps in the capital budgeting process, the types of capital budgeting projects, approaches to capital budgeting decisions, and cash flow patterns.

LG2 Introduce the process used to analyze capital budgeting projects, discuss the basic cash flow components of projects, and illustrate how projects are evaluated by comparing the value of a project to its cost.

LG3 Describe the relevant cash flows that are considered in capital budgeting; calculate the incremental cost for a project and the change in net working capital; describe the four components of cash inflows—operating income, tax shield from CCA, ITC, and government incentives—and calculate the total cash inflows; and determine the terminal cash flow.

LG4 Describe and illustrate the complete process for calculating the net present value for a capital budgeting project.

LG5 Discuss two other capital budgeting techniques—the payback period and internal rate of return (IRR)—and show how each is calculated.

LG6 Compare the NPV and IRR approaches to capital budgeting, focusing on the conflicting ranking that can occur, and discuss the cross-over rate.

12.1 The Capital Budgeting Decision Process

Long-term investments represent sizable outlays of funds that commit a firm to a course of action. Consequently, the firm needs procedures to analyze and properly select those investments. It must be able to measure relevant cash flows and apply appropriate decision techniques. As time passes, fixed assets may become obsolete or may require an overhaul; at these points, too, financial decisions may be required. As discussed throughout this book, we know that a company's prin-

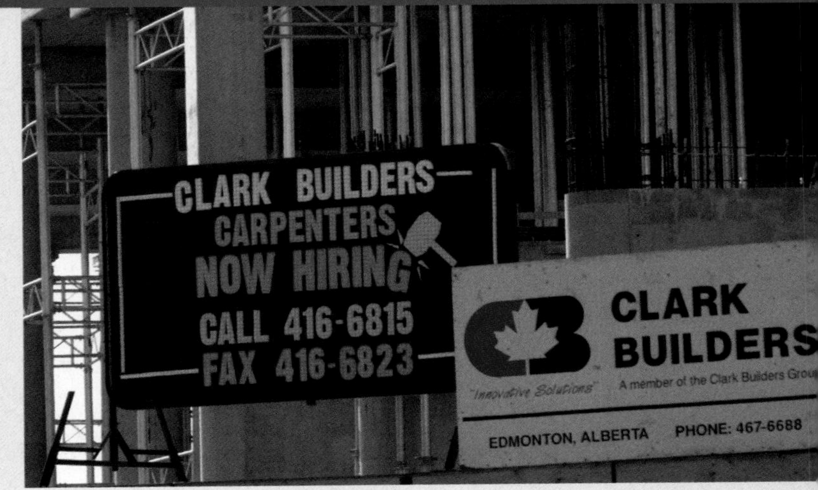

From Dreams to Reality

Every year, with great hope and expectations, businesspeople dream up new plans for expanding, replacing, or renewing the long-term assets they use to run their businesses. These dreams often are the stuff that success is made of, yet they can turn into nightmares for the firm, managers, shareholders, and creditors if they fail to produce the necessary financial returns. Good capital budgeting projects are those that increase the market value of the company. These are the projects that are expected to provide a return that covers the cost of financing the project. Therefore, besides dreams, companies also need some very down-to-earth consideration of the costs of implementing their dreams and the returns they are likely to reap from these expenditures. This process is called *capital budgeting*. It is an important topic in finance and vital for a company if it is to continue to operate and grow. This chapter explains the principles and techniques of capital budgeting so that the dreams that become reality are successes.

cipal financial objective is to maximize the market value of the company's common shares. Making correct capital budgeting decisions is imperative for this to occur.

capital budgeting
The process of evaluating and selecting long-term investment projects that achieve the goal of owner wealth maximization.

Capital budgeting is associated with investments in assets whose returns extend beyond one year. **Capital budgeting** is the process of evaluating and selecting long-term investment projects that achieve the goal of owner wealth maximization. Firms typically make a variety of long-term investments, but the most common for a manufacturing firm is in *fixed assets*, which include property

LINKING THE DISCIPLINES: Cross-Functional Interactions

- ***Accounting personnel*** need to understand the cash flows used in capital budgeting to provide revenue, cost, amortization, and tax data for use in both monitoring existing projects and developing cash flows for proposed projects.
- ***Information systems analysts*** need to understand the capital budgeting process to design decision models that determine the value of existing and proposed projects and to maintain and facilitate the retrieval of cash flow data for projects.
- ***Management*** need to know the principles, concepts, and techniques of capital budgeting to understand the relevance of positive and negative net present value projects. Management must also recognize the cash flows that are relevant when making decisions regarding the replacement of assets, expansions, the introduction of new products, and other major questions.
- The ***marketing department*** is extremely involved in the capital budgeting process. New product proposals and production expansion plans must all go through the capital budgeting process.
- Personnel in the ***operations department*** will submit proposals for the acquisition of new equipment and plants. They will frequently be asked to assist in determining operating cost changes for many capital budgeting proposals.

(land), plant, and equipment. Other examples include building a new factory, developing a new product, entering a new line of business, expanding to another country, buying a company, and R&D or marketing expenditures. These types of investments are often referred to as *earning assets*. They provide the basis for the firm's earnings, cash flows, and overall value.

Capital budgeting (investment) and financing decisions are treated *separately*. That is, in the analysis of projects, it is assumed that the necessary financing is in place and that this financing's overall cost is used to discount the cash flows associated with the project. The discount rate is the company's cost of capital. This issue was the subject of Chapter 9. In Chapters 12 and 13 we concentrate on fixed asset acquisition. We begin by discussing the motives for capital expenditures.

Capital Expenditure Motives

capital expenditure
An outlay of funds by the firm that is expected to produce benefits over a period of time *greater than* one year.

operating expenditure
An outlay of funds by the firm resulting in benefits received *within* one year.

A **capital expenditure** is an outlay of funds by the firm that is expected to produce benefits over a period of time *greater than* one year. An **operating expenditure** is an outlay resulting in benefits received *within* one year. Fixed asset outlays are capital expenditures, but not all capital expenditures are classified as fixed assets. A \$600,000 outlay for a new machine with a usable life of 15 years is a capital expenditure that would appear as a fixed asset on the firm's balance sheet. A \$600,000 outlay for advertising that is expected to produce benefits over a three-year period is also a capital expenditure, but advertising would rarely be shown as a fixed asset.[1] Both actions would be considered capital budgeting pro-

1. Some firms do, in effect, capitalize advertising outlays if there is reason to believe that much of the benefit of the outlay will be received at some future date. The capitalized advertising may appear as a deferred charge such as "deferred advertising expense," which is then amortized over the future. Expenses of this type are often deferred for reporting purposes to increase reported earnings, whereas for tax purposes the entire amount will be expensed to reduce tax liability.

jects since the amounts spent are expected to provide returns over a period of time longer than one year. So the expenditures relating to capital budgeting projects may be expensed or capitalized.

Capital expenditures are made for many reasons. The basic motives for capital expenditures are to expand, replace, or renew fixed assets, or to obtain some other less tangible benefit over a long period. Table 12.1 briefly describes the key motives for making capital expenditures.

Steps in the Process

capital budgeting process
Consists of five distinct but interrelated steps beginning with *proposal generation*, followed by *review and analysis, decision making, implementation, and follow-up.*

The **capital budgeting process** consists of five distinct but interrelated steps. It begins with *proposal generation*, followed by *review and analysis, decision making, implementation*, and *follow-up*. Table 12.2 describes these steps. Each step in the process is important. Review and analysis and decision making—Steps 2 and 3—consume the majority of time and effort in our discussion of the process, however. Because of their fundamental importance, and because in a single university course we have limited time to generate ideas or implement and follow up on projects, primary attention is given to review and analysis and decision making.

Follow-up (Step 5) is an important, but often ignored, step in the process. Monitoring a previous investment is a vital part of capital budgeting. Consider that a firm is making a decision now (at time zero) regarding an asset that will generate returns for years into the future. The estimates of these returns are subject to major error. After making the investment in the capital budgeting project, the firm must monitor the returns to determine if the estimated returns are actually achieved. If not, the initial decision may have been incorrect. If the company does not monitor previous capital budgeting decisions, then the capital budgeting process cannot be improved. If the company makes mistakes, then these mistakes must be acknowledged and changes implemented aimed at ensuring the firm improves the accuracy of the cash flow estimates.

TABLE 12.1 Key Motives for Making Capital Expenditures

Motive	Description
Expansion	The most common motive for a capital expenditure is to expand the level of operations—usually through acquisition of fixed assets. A growing firm often needs to acquire new fixed assets rapidly, such as the purchase of property and plant facilities.
Replacement	As a firm's growth slows and it reaches maturity, most capital expenditures will be made to replace or renew obsolete or worn-out assets. Each time a machine requires a major repair, the outlay for the repair should be compared to the outlay to replace the machine and the benefits of replacement.
Renewal	Renewal, an alternative to replacement, may involve rebuilding, overhauling, or retrofitting an existing fixed asset. For example, an existing drill press could be renewed by replacing its motor and adding a numeric control system, or a physical facility could be renewed by rewiring and adding air conditioning. To improve efficiency, both replacement and renewal of existing machinery may be suitable solutions.
Other purposes	Some capital expenditures do not result in the acquisition or transformation of tangible fixed assets. Instead, they involve a long-term commitment of funds in expectation of a future return. These expenditures include outlays for advertising, research and development, management consulting, and new products. Other capital expenditure proposals—such as the installation of pollution-control and safety devices mandated by the government—are difficult to evaluate because they provide intangible returns rather than clearly measurable cash flows.

TABLE 12.2 Steps in the Capital Budgeting Process

Steps (listed in order)	Description
1. Proposal generation	Proposals for capital expenditures are made at all levels within a business organization. To stimulate a flow of ideas, many firms offer cash rewards for proposals that are ultimately adopted. Capital expenditure proposals typically travel from the originator to a reviewer at a higher level in the organization. Clearly, proposals that require large outlays will be much more carefully scrutinized than less costly ones.
2. Review and analysis	Capital expenditure proposals are formally reviewed (1) to assess their appropriateness in light of the firm's overall objectives and plans and, more important, (2) to evaluate their economic validity. The proposed costs and benefits are estimated and then converted into a series of relevant cash flows. Various capital budgeting techniques are applied to these cash flows to measure the investment merit of the potential outlay. In addition, various aspects of the *risk* associated with the proposal are evaluated. Once the economic analysis is completed, a summary report, often with a recommendation, is submitted to the decision maker(s).
3. Decision making	The actual dollar outlay and the importance of a capital expenditure determine the organizational level at which the expenditure decision is made. Firms typically delegate capital expenditure authority on the basis of certain dollar limits. Generally, the board of directors reserves the right to make final decisions on capital expenditures requiring outlays beyond a certain amount. Inexpensive capital expenditures, such as the purchase of a hammer for $15, are treated as operating outlays not requiring formal analysis.[a] Generally, firms operating under critical time constraints with respect to production often give the plant manager the power to make decisions necessary to keep the production line moving.
4. Implementation	Once a proposal has been approved and funding has been made available,[b] the implementation phase begins. For minor outlays, the expenditure is made and payment is rendered. For major expenditures, greater control is required. Often the expenditures for a single proposal may occur in phases, each outlay requiring the signed approval of company officers.
5. Follow-up	Involves monitoring the results during the operating phase of a project. Comparison of actual costs and benefits with those expected and those of previous projects is vital. When actual outcomes deviate from projected outcomes, action may be required to cut the costs, improve benefits, or possibly terminate the project. Analysis of deviations of actual from forecast values provides data that can be used to improve the capital budgeting process, particularly the accuracy of cash flow estimates.

[a]There is a certain dollar limit beyond which outlays are *capitalized* (i.e., treated as a fixed asset) and *amortized* rather than *expensed.* In accounting, the issue of whether to capitalize or expense an outlay is resolved by using the *principle of materiality,* which suggests that any outlays deemed material (i.e., large) relative to the firm's scale of operations should be capitalized, whereas others should be expensed in the current period.

[b]Capital expenditures are often approved as part of the annual budgeting process, although funding will not be made available until the budget is implemented—frequently as long as 6 months after approval.

Capital Budgeting Terminology

Before developing the concepts, principles, and techniques related to the capital budgeting process, we need to introduce and explain some basic terminology. This section considers four key concepts associated with capital budgeting.

Types of Capital Budgeting Projects

independent projects
Projects whose cash flows are unrelated or independent of one another; the acceptance of one does not eliminate the others from further consideration.

The three most common project types are independent projects, mutually exclusive projects, and replacement projects. **Independent projects** are those whose cash flows are unrelated or independent of one another; the acceptance of one project *does not eliminate* the others from further consideration. If a firm has unlimited funds to invest, all the independent projects that meet its minimum acceptance criterion can be implemented.

For example, a firm with unlimited funds may be faced with three acceptable independent projects: (1) installing air conditioning in the plant, (2) acquiring a small supplier, and (3) purchasing a new computer system. Clearly, the acceptance of any one of these projects does not eliminate the others from further consideration; all three could be undertaken. If the projects were labelled A, B, and C, then the company has eight possible selection alternatives. The company could select project A, or B, or C, or A and B, or A and C, or B and C, or A, B, and C, or none of A, B, or C. For independent projects, the selection of one project has no impact on the decisions regarding the other projects.

mutually exclusive projects
Projects that compete with one another, so that the acceptance of one eliminates the others from further consideration.

Mutually exclusive projects are those that have the same function and therefore compete with one another. The acceptance of one *eliminates* from further consideration all other similar-function projects. For example, a firm in need of increased production capacity might obtain it by: (1) expanding its plant, (2) acquiring another company, or (3) contracting with another company for production. Clearly, the acceptance of one eliminates the need for either of the others. Again, if the projects were labelled A, B, and C, then there are four possible selection alternatives: select project A, or B, or C, or none of the projects.

replacement projects
Projects that involve replacing an existing asset with a new asset.

Another type of mutually exclusive project is a **replacement project.** In this case, a company is considering replacing an existing asset with a new asset. There might be one or ten assets that could be used as the replacement, but, regardless, the firm faces a mutually exclusive decision. If there is a machine that could replace an existing machine, the mutually exclusive decision is to keep the old or replace with the new. If there are three machines, then the decision is similar to that discussed in the previous paragraph.

Unlimited Funds Versus Capital Rationing

unlimited funds
The financial situation in which a firm is able to accept all independent projects that provide an acceptable return.

capital rationing
The financial situation in which a firm has only a fixed number of dollars to allocate among competing capital expenditures.

The availability of funds for capital expenditures affects the firm's decisions. If a firm has **unlimited funds** for investment, making capital budgeting decisions is quite simple: all projects that will provide returns greater than a predetermined level can be accepted.

Typically, though, firms are not in such a situation; they operate instead under **capital rationing.** This means that they have only a fixed number of dollars available for capital expenditures and that numerous projects will compete for these dollars. Therefore the firm must ration its funds by allocating them to projects that will maximize share value. Procedures for dealing with capital rationing are presented in Chapter 13. The discussions that follow in this chapter assume unlimited funds.

Accept/Reject Versus Ranking Approaches

accept/reject approach
The evaluation of capital expenditure proposals to determine whether they meet the firm's minimum acceptance criterion.

Two basic approaches to capital budgeting decisions are available. The **accept/reject approach** involves evaluating capital expenditure proposals to determine whether they meet the firm's minimum acceptance criterion. This approach can be used when the firm has unlimited funds, as a preliminary step when evaluating mutually exclusive projects, or in a situation in which capital must be rationed. In all cases, only acceptable projects should be considered.

ranking approach
The ranking of capital expenditure projects on the basis of some predetermined measure, such as the rate of return.

The second method, the **ranking approach**, involves ranking projects on the basis of some predetermined measure, such as the rate of return. The project with the highest return is ranked first, and the project with the lowest return is ranked last. Only acceptable projects should be ranked. Ranking is useful in selecting the "best" of a group of mutually exclusive projects and in evaluating projects with a view to capital rationing.

Cash Flow Patterns

cash flow pattern
An initial outflow followed by a series of inflows.

Cash flow patterns are the type of cash flows that are expected to be generated by a capital budgeting project. The usual **cash flow pattern** consists of an initial outflow followed by a series of inflows. For example, a firm may spend $10,000 today and as a result expect to receive equal annual cash inflows of $2,000 each year for the next 8 years (an annuity), as depicted on the time line in Figure 12.1.[2] Another type of cash flow pattern is a project that provides unequal annual cash inflows, as depicted in Figure 12.2. As was observed in Chapter 6, time value of money concepts are much simpler to apply when the pattern of cash flows is an annuity. An annuity for ten years involves one time value calculation. For a project with ten unequal cash flows, ten time value calculations are required.

? Review Questions

12–1 What is *capital budgeting*? How do capital expenditures relate to the capital budgeting process? Do all capital expenditures involve fixed assets? Explain.

12–2 What are the key motives for making capital expenditures? Discuss, compare, and contrast them.

12–3 Briefly describe each of the five steps involved in the capital budgeting process.

12–4 Differentiate between each of the following terms: (**a**) independent versus mutually exclusive versus replacement projects; (**b**) unlimited funds versus capital rationing; (**c**) accept/reject versus ranking approaches; (**d**) annuities versus unequal cash flows.

FIGURE 12.1
Cash Flow Pattern for an Annuity
Time line for a project with equal annual cash inflows: an annuity

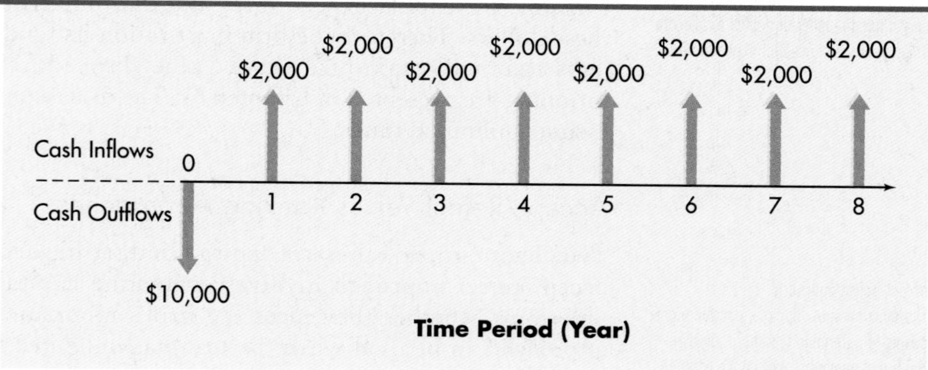

2. Arrows rather than plus or minus signs are frequently used on time lines to distinguish between cash inflows and cash outflows. Upward-pointing arrows represent cash inflows (positive cash flows), and downward-pointing arrows represent cash outflows (negative cash flows).

12.2 Basic Capital Budgeting Process

incremental cash flows
The additional cash flows—outflows or inflows—expected to result from a proposed capital expenditure.

To evaluate capital expenditure alternatives, the firm must determine the relevant cash flows, which are the *incremental cash outflows (the amount invested) and subsequent after-tax inflows*. The **incremental cash flows** represent the *additional* cash flows—outflows or inflows—expected to result from a proposed capital expenditure. As noted in Chapter 2, cash flows, rather than accounting figures, are used because it is the cash flows associated with projects that directly affect the firm's ability to pay expenses, purchase assets, provide returns to investors, and increase firm value.

Basic Cash Flow Components

In its simplest form, the cash flows of any project include three basic components: (1) the incremental cost, (2) operating cash inflows, and (3) the terminal cash flow. All projects—whether for expansion, replacement, renewal, or some other purpose—have the first two components, and most will also have the final component, a terminal cash flow.

incremental cost
The relevant cash outflow required now, at time zero, for a capital budgeting project.

operating cash inflows
The incremental after-tax cash inflows resulting from use of a project during its life.

Figure 12.2 depicts the cash flows for a project on a time line. Each of the cash flow components is labelled. The **incremental cost** is $50,000 for the proposed project. This is the relevant cash outflow required now, at time zero. For some projects, the incremental cost may occur over a number of years. For example, building a new plant may take three years and incremental costs may occur throughout the three years. The **operating cash inflows**, the incremental after-tax cash inflows resulting from use of the project during its life, gradually increase from $4,000 in the first year to $10,000 in its tenth and final year.

These cash inflows are the key benefit associated with investing in a project. The components of the incremental cash inflows include increases in operating

FIGURE 12.2

Cash Flow Components
Time line for major cash flow components

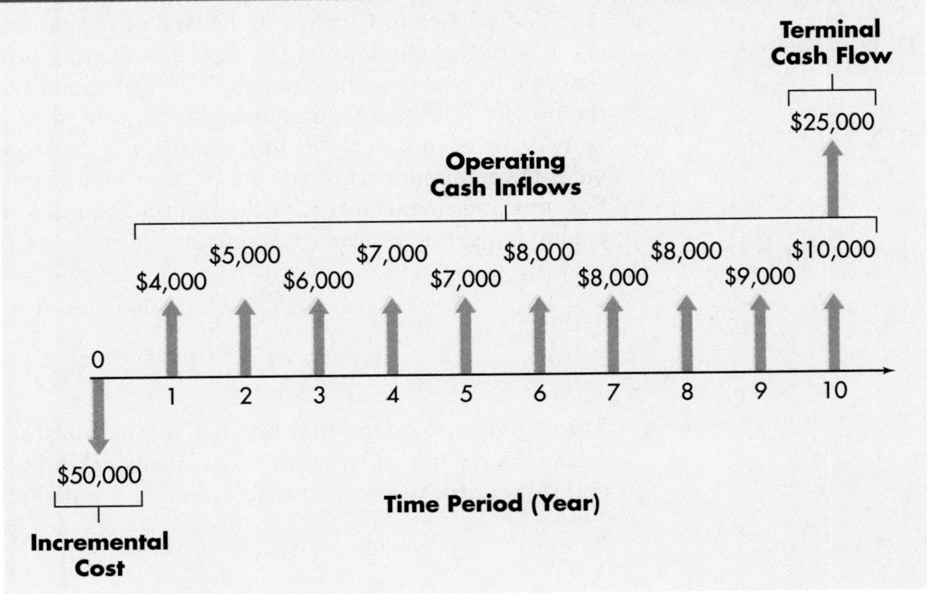

income generated by the investment project and any tax benefits associated with the project. Both of these components are discussed in detail in Section 12.3.

terminal cash flow
The after-tax non-operating cash flow occurring in the final year of a project, usually attributable to liquidation of the pro-

The **terminal cash flow** of \$25,000, received at the end of the project's 10-year life, is the after-tax non-operating cash flow occurring in the final year of the project. It is usually attributable to liquidation of the project. Note that the terminal cash flow does *not* include the \$10,000 operating cash inflow for year 10.

Evaluating Projects

When the relevant cash flows have been determined, an analysis must be completed to evaluate whether a project is acceptable, and to rank projects. A number of techniques are available for performing this analysis. The preferred approaches integrate time value procedures (Chapter 6), risk and return considerations (Chapter 7), and valuation concepts (Chapter 8) to select capital expenditures that are consistent with the firm's goal of maximizing owners' wealth.

sophisticated approaches to capital budgeting
Capital budgeting techniques that integrate time value procedures, risk and return considerations, and valuation concepts to select capital expenditures that are consistent with the firm's goal of maximizing owners' wealth.

The approaches that consider all three concepts are referred to as **sophisticated approaches to capital budgeting**. This section illustrates the capital budgeting process using a simple example. The purpose is to focus on the basic procedures used to estimate the value of an asset to a company, and then the method used to decide whether the company should proceed with the investment in the asset.

The Value of an Investment Project

In Section 8.1 of Chapter 8, we saw that the value of an asset is based on the present value of the cash flows generated by the asset over its useful life. As we saw in Chapter 8, the rate used to discount the cash flows is the return required to compensate for the risk of the asset. What is the required rate of return for capital budgeting projects? The return required is the company's cost of capital. Why? For a capital budgeting project, the company must raise financing to invest in the project. This new financing has an overall cost that, as we saw in Chapter 9, is termed the cost of capital.

As discussed in Chapter 9, the cost of capital reflects the business and financial risk of the company. If the capital budgeting project is in the company's current line of business, the company's cost of capital, by default, reflects the risk of the project. Therefore, discounting the proposed project's cash flows at the company's cost of capital builds into the analysis the requirement that the project provides the minimum required rate of return—the cost of capital. By doing so, the business and financial risk of the project is considered. Therefore, the value of a capital budgeting project to a company at time 0 (V_0) is based on the following:

$$V_0 = \text{Present value of the asset's incremental after-tax cash inflows}$$

$$V_0 = \sum_{t=1}^{n} CF_t\,(1 - T) \times PVIF\,(k_a,\ t \text{ years}) \tag{12.1}$$

This equation indicates that the cash inflow for year t is calculated after-tax, discounted t periods at the firm's cost of capital, and then summed to all previous and subsequent discounted cash inflows for n periods, the life of the project.

Example ▼ McLaughlin Construction is considering purchasing a hydraulic lift that has a cost of $33,000. The lift will have a life of 8 years and is expected to generate extra (incremental) before-tax cash inflows of $7,500 per year. The company's tax rate is 20 percent and their cost of capital is 13 percent. McLaughlin Construction wonders whether they should purchase the new hydraulic lift.

To decide, the first step is to consider the cash flow pattern associated with this project. This can be depicted on a time line like the one shown in Figure 12.1, though for this project, the numbers will change, but the time period is the same. Next, the value of the machine to the company must be determined. The value of the hydraulic lift to McLaughlin Construction is based on the present value of the cash flows the lift will generate over its 8-year life.

The cash flows are $7,500 per year, but this is before-tax. Remember, the cash flow must be considered after-tax, since the company will not see any benefits until it has satisfied the government's tax claims. The after-tax cash flow is $6,000 per year [$7,500 × (1 − 0.20)]. To determine the present value of the cash flows, the discount rate that reflects the risk of the project must be used. For McLaughlin Construction this is 13 percent, the company's cost of capital. Therefore, by applying Equation 12.1, the value of the new hydraulic lift to the company is:

$$V_0 = [\$7{,}500 \times (1 - 0.20)] \times PVIFa\ (13\%, 8\ \text{years})$$

$$= \$6{,}000 \times PVIFa\ (13\%, 8\ \text{years}) = \$28{,}793$$

Using a financial calculator, PMT is $6,000, N is 8, and I is 13 percent. Prior to computing the answer, remember to input 0 in the function not being used, in this case FV. Now press CPT and PV. The answer is $28,793 (ignore the negative sign). The value of the hydraulic lift to McLaughlin Construction is $28,793. This is the present value of the after-tax cash flows for the life of the project, discounted at the company's cost of capital, which reflects the risk of the project for the company. ▲

Comparing Value to Cost

The above analysis calculated the value of the asset to the company today (at time 0). This is the case since the cash flows were discounted. The value can now be compared to the incremental cost of the asset, which is already at time 0. By subtracting the incremental cost of the project (C_0) from the value of the project to the company, the **net present value (NPV)** of the project is determined. This is illustrated below in Equation 12.2.

net present value (NPV)
The difference between the value of the project to the company and the project's incremental cost.

$$NPV = (\text{present value of the after-tax cash inflows}) - (\text{incremental cost})$$

$$NPV = \left[\sum_{t=1}^{n} CF_t\,(1 - T) \times PVIF\,(k_a, t\ \text{years})\right] - C_0 \qquad (12.2)$$

Example ▼ Extending the McLaughlin Construction example, recall that the new hydraulic lift has an incremental cost of $33,000. The value of the lift to the company is $28,793. Therefore, the NPV of the lift is:

$$NPV = \$28{,}793 - \$33{,}000 = -\$4{,}207$$

This analysis indicates that the cost of the asset is greater than the value of the asset to the company. Therefore, the company should not purchase the new hydraulic lift; the benefits associated with the asset are less than the cost of the asset. Negative NPV projects should *never* be accepted.

The NPV of –$4,207 is the loss the company would incur, discounted to time 0, if they proceeded with the investment. This assumes that all of the forecasts used in the analysis were correct. An alternative way of phrasing the loss is to recognize that the discount rate, the cost of capital, is the required return on the project. Since the NPV is negative, the *expected return* on the project (k_j) is less than the required return (k_a). Therefore, McLaughlin Construction should not acquire the new hydraulic lift.

Extending the Analysis

What happens if some of the variables in the above example are changed? Consider the following independent changes:

1. The company's cost of capital is 11 percent.
2. The expected life of the hydraulic lift is 12 years.
3. The present value of the after-tax cash inflows is $33,000.
4. The new hydraulic lift will replace an existing lift. The book value (unamortized value) of the existing lift is $4,609 but it could be sold for $5,000. The old lift accounted for $7,500 of before-tax cash inflows per year, while the new lift will generate $15,000 in before-tax cash inflows.

For each of these cases, a new NPV must be calculated and McLaughlin Construction must make an accept/reject decision regarding the project.

Changing the Cost of Capital

For the first change, the 11 percent is used as the discount rate rather than 13 percent. This change will increase the present value of the after-tax cash inflows since lower discount rates increase present values. The value of the asset to the company increases to $30,877, so:

$$\text{NPV} = \$30,877 - \$33,000 = -\$2,123$$

Even though the value of the lift to the company increases, the cost is still greater, meaning that the firm should not acquire the asset.

Changing the Life

If the hydraulic lift's expected life is 12 years, cash inflows are received for a longer period of time, which increases the value of the lift to McLaughlin Construction. Using the original cost of capital of 13 percent, the value of the asset to the company increases to $35,506.

$$\text{NPV} = \$35,506 - \$33,000 = +\$2,506$$

Now the value of the lift is greater than its cost, implying that the firm should invest in the asset. Note that the +$2,506 is the value of the lift to McLaughlin, over and above the incremental cost on a present value basis, at time 0. The NPV analysis has built in the requirement that the project generates a 13 percent rate of return—McLaughlin's cost of capital. The +$2,506 means that the project has generated a return greater than 13 percent. The expected return for the lift (k_j) is greater than the required return (k_a).

NPV Equals Zero

If the present value of the after-tax cash inflows was $33,000, the NPV is equal to zero; the value of the lift to the company is equal to the cost of the asset.

$$\text{NPV} = \$33{,}000 - \$33{,}000 = \$0$$

An NPV of zero indicates that the lift is expected to provide exactly its required rate of return, in this case exactly 13 percent. The company should acquire the lift; it is expected to generate exactly its required rate of return.

Replace an Existing Asset

The fourth scenario is a replacement project. If McLaughlin acquires the new lift, they do not need the old, so it will be sold. The old lift has a book value of $4,609 but a market value of $5,000. Book value is simply the unamortized value of the asset on the company's books.[3] Market value is what a buyer will pay for the old asset. If the company sells the old lift, the cash inflow is the market value, the amount a potential buyer will pay. The incremental cost (C_0) of the new lift is the $33,000 (purchase price of new) minus $5,000 (proceeds from sale of the old).

The new machine is expected to generate cash inflows of $15,000 per year, but the old machine was already generating cash inflows of $7,500 per year. Therefore, the incremental (extra) cash flow is $7,500 per year. The NPV of the project can be calculated using Equation 12.3, which is a slight variation of Equation 12.2:

$$\text{NPV} = (\text{present value of the incremental after-tax cash inflows}) - (\text{incremental cost})$$

$$\text{NPV} = \left[\sum_{t=1}^{n} ICF_t\,(1 - T) \times PVIF\,(k_a, t \text{ years})\right] - C_0 \qquad (12.3)$$

where: ICF is the incremental cash inflows
C_0 is the incremental cost of the project.

Applying this equation to the information for McLaughlin results in:

$$\begin{aligned}\text{NPV} &= [(\$15{,}000 - \$7{,}500) \times (1 - 0.20) \times PVIFa\,(13\%, 8\text{ per})] - [\$33{,}000 - \$5{,}000]\\ &= \$28{,}793 - \$28{,}000\\ &= +\$793\end{aligned}$$

The value of the new lift is greater than its incremental cost; McLaughlin should replace the existing lift with the new. The project's expected rate of return is greater than the required rate of return.

3. The book value could also be the undepreciated capital cost (UCC) of the asset. Recall from Chapter 2 that the tax version of amortization is termed the capital cost allowance (CCA). For tax purposes, the company must claim CCA and not amortization. So the book value could be the UCC, which we will term the *tax value* of the asset. This issue is considered in more detail in Chapter 13.

? Review Questions

12–5 What is meant by the phrase *incremental cash flows*, and what are the three relevant cash flows considered for capital budgeting projects? When do these three cash flows occur?

12–6 Explain how capital budgeting integrates time value procedures, risk and return considerations, and valuation concepts.

12–7 What is the value of a capital budgeting project to a company based on? What is this value compared to? What is then done?

12–8 Fully explain why a company's cost of capital is important for capital budgeting purposes and how it is used. What is the effect of using the cost of capital to discount the cash flows?

12.3 Calculating Cash Flows

Calculating cash flows, both outflows and inflows, is a critical part of the review and analysis step in the capital budgeting process. This section explains some of the fundamentals associated with calculating cash flows, considers the process of calculating the incremental cost of a project, and illustrates how cash inflows are determined.

Relevant Cash Flows

Developing relevant cash flows is most straightforward in the case of *expansion decisions*. In this case, the incremental cost of operating cash inflows and terminal cash flow are merely the after-tax cash outflow and inflows associated with the proposed outlay.

The development of relevant cash flows for *replacement decisions* is a little more involved; the firm must find the *incremental* cash outflows and inflows that will result from the proposed replacement. The initial investment in this case is the difference between the investment needed to acquire the new asset and the proceeds from the sale of the asset being replaced. The operating cash inflows are the difference between the operating cash inflows from the new asset and those from the old asset. The terminal cash flow is the estimated net proceeds from the sale of the new asset at the end of its useful life. These relationships are shown in Figure 12.3 and an example was provided at the end of Section 12.2.

Actually, all capital budgeting decisions can be viewed as replacement decisions. Expansion decisions are merely replacement decisions in which all cash flows from the old asset are zero. In light of this fact, the following discussions emphasize the more general replacement decisions.

Sunk Costs and Opportunity Costs

When estimating the relevant cash flows associated with a proposed capital expenditure, the firm must distinguish between *sunk costs* and *opportunity costs*. These costs are easy to misinterpret or ignore, particularly when determining a

FIGURE 12.3

Relevant Cash Flows for Replacement Decisions

Calculation of the three components of relevant cash flow for a replacement decision

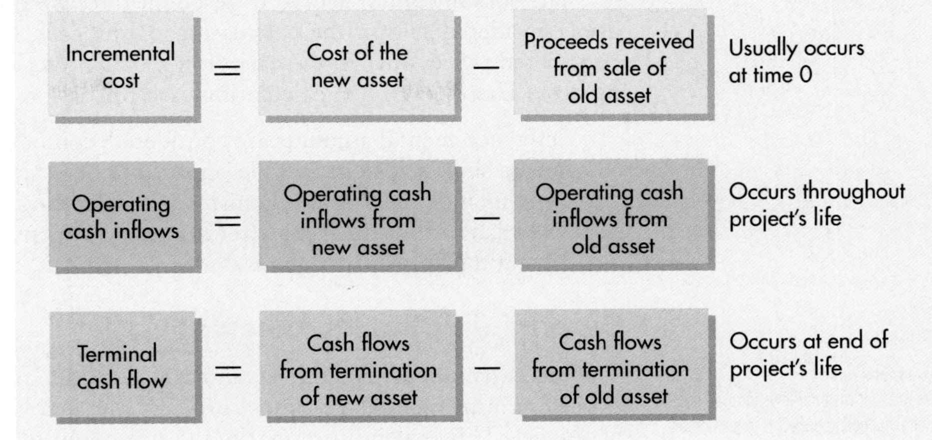

sunk costs
Cash outlays that have already been made (i.e., past outlays) and therefore have no effect on the cash flows relevant to a current decision.

opportunity costs
Cash flows that could be realized from an alternative use of an owned asset.

project's incremental cash flows. **Sunk costs** are cash outlays that have already been made (i.e., past outlays) and therefore are not relevant for the current decision. As a result, *sunk costs should not be included in a project's incremental cash flows.* **Opportunity costs** are cash flows that could be realized from an alternative use of an owned asset. They therefore represent cash flows that will *not be realized* as a result of employing that asset in the proposed project. Because of this, any *opportunity costs should be included as cash outflows when determining a project's incremental cash flows.*

Example Jankow Equipment is considering converting an old warehouse it owns into a new retail store. Two years ago the company paid a consultant $125,000 to study the market potential associated with establishing a retail store at this location. Currently, Jankow rents the old warehouse to a furniture distributor for storage and Jankow receives $3,500 per month in rent.

The $125,000 is a *sunk cost* because it represents a cash outlay that occurred earlier. It doesn't matter if Jankow converts or does not convert the warehouse, the $125,000 is already spent. The cost is not incremental to the project and *would not be included in the analysis.*

The $3,500 per month in rent is an *opportunity cost.* If Jankow converts the warehouse, they lose the opportunity to rent the warehouse. The $3,500 per month *would be included as a cash outlay* in the analysis of the retail store. Note that any expenses incurred in earning the rent would be deducted from the monthly rent, and the net amount taken after tax since rent is taxable income.

Hint
The concepts of sunk and opportunity costs must be fully understood. Funds already spent are irrelevant to future decisions, but if the opportunity to receive cash inflows is lost due to changing the status of an asset, the lost cash inflows are a relevant cost.

Operational and Financial Cash Flows

When calculating cash flows only operational, cash items are considered. Operational cash flows are those that affect the calculation of operating income (EBIT). Non-cash expenses would not be considered. Financing costs like interest, lease payments, principal repayments, and dividends are ignored. This is because, as explained earlier, investment (capital budgeting) and financing decisions are treated separately. For capital budgeting, it is assumed that the financing decisions have already been made and the company has considered all factors that determine their cost of capital.

The cost of capital is used to discount the cash flows. If financing costs were also considered within the calculation of the cash flows, these costs would be considered twice: once in the cash flow calculations and again in the discounting process. Therefore, when calculating cash flows:

1. Only incremental amounts are considered; compare the new asset with the old.
2. Ignore sunk costs but include opportunity costs.
3. Only include operational items; ignore financing costs.
4. The cash inflows must be after tax; the company only receives benefits after paying the appropriate taxes.

Determining the Incremental Cost

incremental cost
The relevant cash outflows incurred if a capital budgeting project is implemented.

The **incremental cost** is the relevant cash outflows incurred if a capital budgeting project is implemented. For most projects, the incremental cost is incurred now, at time 0. This expenditure marks the beginning of the project's life. For some projects, subsequent investments may also be required. These may be expenditures that are capitalized or expensed. Regardless, these are costs of the project that must be recognized and then discounted the appropriate period to time zero.

Example Franklin Freezers is planning to manufacture a new line of products. The company will require a new plant that will take two years to construct. A payment of $750,000 is required now to begin construction. A further payment of $1 million is required at the end of year 1, and a final payment of $1.5 million at the end of year 2. Each of these is a capital expenditure. In addition, Franklin will have to spend $500,000 in each of years 1 and 2 on development costs that will be treated as operating expenditures and expensed. Franklin's tax rate is 30 percent.

Figure 12.4 provides the relevant cash outflows for this new manufacturing plant for Franklin. Note that the cash outflows for the capital expenditures are shown as the stated amounts, while the cash outflows for the development costs are shown after tax. Also, to make the various expenditures comparable, the initial investments for years 1 and 2 must be discounted at Franklin's cost of capital for the appropriate number of years to make them comparable to the time 0 investment. Therefore, $1,350,000 would be discounted one period and $1,850,000 would be discounted two periods, both at the firm's cost of capital. Then, we would have the present value of the five costs at time 0 and the incremental cost of the project can be calculated.

installation cost
Costs incurred to place equipment or machinery into operation.

incremental cost of a new asset
The total of all costs incurred to get an asset to the point of being able to produce cash inflows for the company, less the proceeds from the sale of the asset being replaced.

The incremental cost also includes **installation costs** incurred to place equipment or machinery into operation. The **incremental cost of a new asset** is the total of all costs incurred to get an asset to the point of being able to produce cash inflows for the company, less the proceeds from the sale of the asset being replaced.[4] Occasionally, the asset being replaced may have no value. It may actually cost the company money to dispose of an old asset.

4. Depending on the selling price of the old asset, there may be tax implications of the sale. These are considered in Chapter 13.

FIGURE 12.4

Incremental Cost for Franklin Freezers' New Plant

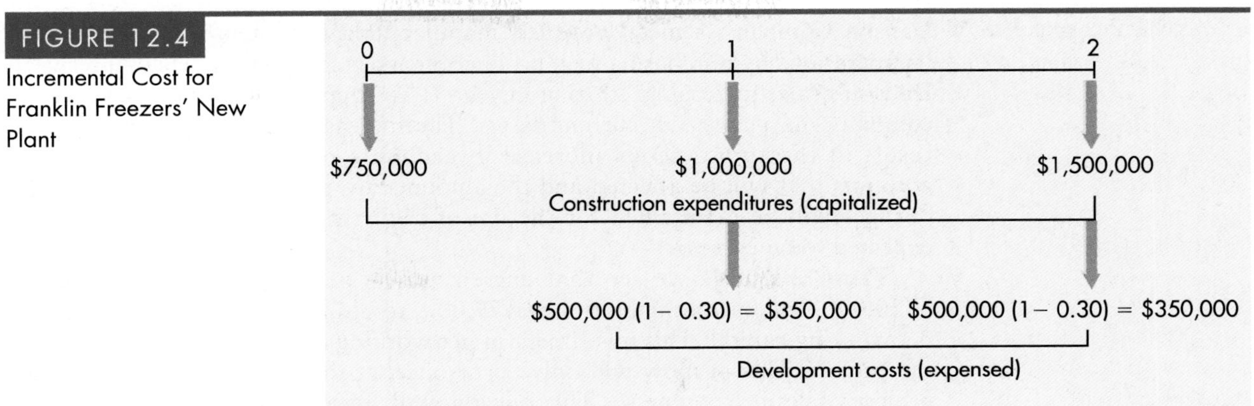

Change in Net Working Capital[5]

Net working capital, as noted in Chapter 3, is the amount by which a firm's current assets exceed its current liabilities. As shown in Chapter 4, if a company invests in assets that increase sales, levels of cash, accounts receivable, inventories, accounts payable, and accruals will also increase. As was noted in Chapters 2 and 4, increases in current assets are *uses of cash* (investments). Increases in current liabilities are *sources of cash* (provide financing). As long as the increased sales associated with the project continue, the increased investment in current assets (cash, accounts receivable, and inventories) and increased current liability financing (accounts payable and accruals) would also continue.

change in net working capital
The difference between the change in current assets and current liabilities associated with an investment project.

The difference between the change in current assets and the change in current liabilities is the **change in net working capital.** Generally, current assets increase by more than current liabilities, resulting in increased net working capital, which would be treated as an initial outflow. This outflow is assumed to occur at the beginning of the year the project's sales start. If the incremental sales for a project are expected to begin in year 1, the investment in working capital is assumed to be made at the beginning of year 1, which is time 0 (now).[6] If the change in net working capital were negative, it would be shown as an initial inflow. The change in net working capital—whether an increase or a decrease—*is not taxable*, because it merely involves a net buildup (or reduction) of net current assets.

When the sales associated with the project stop, there is no longer a need for the investment in working capital. The working capital investment was made to support the increased sales. If there are no sales, there is no need for the investment. Therefore, at the end of the project's life, the working capital investment will be recovered. The net impact of the working capital investment is that it is an opportunity cost of the project for the life of the asset. The cost is based on the life of the project and the firm's cost of capital.

5. Occasionally, this cash outflow is intentionally ignored to enhance the attractiveness of a proposed investment and thereby improve its likelihood of acceptance. Similar intentional omissions and/or overly optimistic estimates are sometimes made to enhance project acceptance. The presence of formal review and analysis procedures should help the firm to ensure that capital budgeting cash flow estimates are realistic and unbiased and that the "best" projects—those making the maximum contribution to owner wealth—are accepted.

6. In practice, the change in net working capital will frequently occur over a period of months, as the project is implemented.

Example Danson Company, a metal products manufacturer, is contemplating expanding its operations by purchasing new production assets. The new assets will result in Danson's sales increasing, starting in year 1. To support the increasing sales, the company must invest in current assets. The increasing current assets will also result in the spontaneous increase in accounts payable and accruals. The accounts that will be affected and the amounts are provided in Table 12.3. The changes will be maintained for the life of the new production assets which is expected to be 20 years.

From the table we see that current assets are expected to increase by \$220,000, and current liabilities by \$79,000, resulting in a \$141,000 increase in net working capital. This investment in net working capital is a cash outflow for the project. This outflow will only occur once, at the beginning of the year the project's sales start (time 0). This outflow will support the increase in sales for the full life of the project. At the end of year 20, the need for the additional working capital will no longer exist, since the sales associated with the new production assets will stop. This means Danson will recover the additional working capital at that time. They will have to finance the \$141,000 increase in net working capital for the 20 years.

Note that in the above example, taxes are not considered. Why is there no tax impact associated with changes in net working capital? By reviewing Table 12.3, we can see that the change in net working capital is essentially an investment in assets. We have already seen that an investment in fixed assets is capitalized and then expensed over time. The tax impact is reflected in the tax shield on CCA.

But investments in current assets are not capitalized, since they are essentially short-term investments. When a company acquires more inventory, that particular set of inventory is sold a short time later. When a company incurs more accounts receivable, those particular receivables are collected a short time later. When a company holds more cash, that particular amount of cash is spent a short time later. When a company incurs more accounts payable (accruals), those particular payables (accruals) are paid a short time later. For net working capital, each individual action has only a short-term impact on the balance sheet.

Furthermore, changes in net working capital accounts impact sales, cost of goods sold, and other expenses. Changes in inventory and accounts receivable

TABLE 12.3 Calculation of Change in Net Working Capital for Danson Company

Current asset liability	Change in balance	
Cash	+ \$ 40,000	
Accounts receivable	+ 100,000	
Inventories	+ 80,000	
(1) Current assets		+ \$220,000
Accounts payable	+ \$ 47,000	
Accruals	+ 32,000	
(2) Current liabilities		+ 79,000
Change in net working capital [(1) − (2)]		+ \$141,000

are captured in sales. Changes in accounts payable, accruals, and cash are captured in cost of goods sold and other expenses. The tax impact of changes in net working capital are captured on the income statement. Therefore, for these two reasons, there is no direct tax impact of changes in net working capital items for capital budgeting purposes.

Determining the Cash Inflows

As was mentioned earlier, the underlying reason a company invests in a capital project is for the cash inflows the project is expected to generate over its useful life. There are four major components of these cash inflows. Each is discussed below.

Incremental After-Tax Operating Income

operating income
The principal reason a company considers investing in a fixed asset; operating income may increase because sales increase, costs decrease, or both occur.

Obviously, the principal reason a company considers investing in a fixed asset is the expected increase in operating income. **Operating income** may increase because operating sales increase, operating costs decrease, or both occur. Here the focus is on cash operating sales and costs; non-cash costs are considered in the next section. The following process is used to calculate incremental after-tax operating income:

	Incremental sales
less:	Incremental direct costs (COGS)
	Incremental gross margin
less:	Incremental general operating costs
	Incremental operating income
less:	Taxes
	Incremental after-tax operating income

Many investment projects result in both operating sales and costs increasing. This is because when sales increase, costs to produce and sell the product or service will be incurred. For some projects you may only be provided information about operating costs in total and not the two components. In that case, rather than the direct and general categories, just a single expense would be used.

Example ▼ A company is planning to invest in a project that will result in sales increasing by $440,000 for each year of the project's life. The direct costs of producing the product are 42 percent. The firm will also incur additional selling and administrative expenses of $96,500. The firm's tax rate is 22 percent. The process used to calculate the incremental after-tax operating income is provided below:

Incremental sales	$440,000
less: Incremental direct costs (42%)	184,800
Incremental gross margin	255,200
less: Incremental general operating costs	96,500
Incremental operating income	158,700
less: Taxes (20%)	31,740
Incremental after-tax operating income	$126,960

For each year of its life, this project is expected to generate incremental after-tax operating income of $126,960. This is the principal reason the firm would invest in the asset. ▲

Some fixed assets do not generate sales. Instead, there is a cost to operate the asset. Newer, more efficient versions of the asset may result in operating costs declining. This will result in operating income increasing.

Example The operating costs for a piece of equipment are $698,000 per year. A more efficient version of the equipment is available and costs only $258,000 per year to operate. To determine the incremental operating income, the process provided above is used, with a focus on the difference between the new and old equipment. The tax rate is 22 percent.

	Current equipment	New equipment	Incremental
Sales	$ 0	$ 0	$ 0
less: Operating costs	698,000	258,000	– 440,000
Operating income	–$698,000	–$258,000	+$440,000
less: Taxes (22%)	153,560	56,760	96,800
After-tax operating income	–$544,440	–$201,240	+$343,200

When comparing projects that either increase sales or decrease costs, it should be noted that cost decreases are more valuable than sales increases. This is the case since with sales increases, operating costs must be deducted. Cost decreases fall straight to operating income. This is clear when the incremental after-tax operating incomes for the two examples above are compared. In the first case, sales increased by $440,000, and the incremental after-tax operating income is $126,960. In the second case, operating costs declined by $440,000 and the incremental after-tax operating income is $343,200.

Some assets lead to both sales increasing and costs decreasing. This often occurs if production equipment is very old.

Example Spenceley Automotive is a small manufacturer of specialized car parts. Their current production equipment is 18 years old but could last for many years. Their production is limited to $650,000 of sales per year. Total cash operating costs are 65 percent of sales. Newer, much more efficient and high capacity production equipment is available. With it, Spenceley could produce and sell $1,000,000 of product per year while total cash operating costs would be 41 percent of sales. Spenceley's tax rate is 34 percent. In this example, with both sales increasing and costs declining, the incremental after-tax operating income soars, significantly enhancing the viability of the project, as shown in the following schedule:

	Current equipment	New equipment	Incremental
Sales	$650,000	$1,000,000	+$350,000
less: Operating costs	422,500	410,000	– 12,500
Operating income	$227,500	$ 590,000	+$362,500
less: Taxes (34%)	77,350	200,600	+ 123,250
After-tax operating income	$150,150	$ 389,400	+$239,250

Capital Cost Allowance (CCA)

In the above discussion, it was stated that when calculating incremental operating income, non-cash expenses were excluded. In this section, we consider non-cash expenses, with the most visible one being amortization. As discussed in Chapter 2, amortization is the systematic expensing of a portion of the cost of a fixed asset against sales. Expenditures on fixed assets are not expensed; rather they are capitalized and the expenditure is written off over time via the amortization expense. This yearly expense allocates the cost of the asset over its useful life and recognizes that the asset has declined in value. The amortization expense may be used for financial reporting purposes; however, for tax purposes, the Canada Revenue Agency (CRA) requires companies to use the capital cost allowance.

capital cost allowance (CCA)
The tax version of amortization, a non-cash expense that increases cash flow.

As discussed in Chapter 2, the **capital cost allowance (CCA)** is simply the tax version of amortization. When calculating the cash flows for capital budgeting projects, CCA is used since this is the actual amount claimed by the company when filing taxes. CCA is a benefit since it is deducted from income when calculating taxable income, *but*, as a non-cash expense, it reduces taxes but no cash has actually been paid. CCA reduces net income but increases cash flow. This concept is illustrated in Chapter 2 and again below.

CCA rates
Rates set by the Canada Revenue Agency (CRA) that are used to calculate the CCA on an asset class; the rates range from 4 to 100 percent.

undepreciated capital cost (UCC)
The undepreciated value of an asset or asset class that is the basis for the amount of CCA that is claimed; also referred to as the *tax value of an asset.*

The CRA has allocated all assets into various asset classes. All assets in the same class are considered in total for CCA calculation purposes. Table 2.6 in Chapter 2 provided some examples of asset classes, the applicable CCA rate, and examples of assets that are included in the class. The **CCA rates** range from 4 percent to 100 percent. The dollar amount of CCA that can be charged in any year is based on the **undepreciated capital cost (UCC)** in the asset class multiplied by the CCA rate. CCA is generally calculated based on the declining balance of the UCC. The UCC is the undepreciated value of an asset or asset class on which CCA is charged; also referred to as the tax value of an asset.

Example Tiger Beer acquires a new computer system costing $100,000. This is a Class 10 asset with a CCA rate of 30 percent. The dollar amount of CCA that can be claimed for the first four years is:

Year	UCC, beginning of year	CCA	UCC, end of year[a]
1	$100,000	$15,000[b]	$85,000
2	$ 85,000	$25,500	$59,500
3	$ 59,500	$17,850	$41,650
4	$ 41,650	$12,495	$29,155

[a]The undepreciated capital cost (UCC) is the asset's tax value.

[b]Note that in the year an asset is acquired, only one-half of the allowable CCA can be deducted. This is termed the *half-year rule*. So, for this example, 15%, half of the 30% CCA rate is used as the CAA rate for Year 1.

The benefit of CCA is the tax saving associated with the firm claiming the non-cash expense. This tax saving is termed a tax shield. It is calculated using Equation 12.4 as follows:

$$\text{Tax shield} = \text{CCA} \times \text{tax rate} \tag{12.4}$$

In the Tiger Beer example above, if the company's tax rate were 40 percent, the tax shields associated with CCA for the first two years are:

$$\text{Tax shield (Year 1)} = \$15{,}000 \times 40\% = \$6{,}000$$
$$\text{Tax shield (Year 2)} = \$25{,}500 \times 40\% = \$10{,}200$$

tax shields
The tax savings the firm will experience from being able to claim the CCA on the asset.

The **tax shields** are the tax savings the firm will experience from being able to claim the CCA on the asset. It is a benefit since the firm can claim the expense, but not actually spend any cash. The benefit is the tax saved from claiming the expense. The impact is that the firm's cash flow will increase by the calculated amount.

Putting the First Two Components of Cash Inflows Together

The two sections above provided background material required to be able to calculate cash inflows. Based on this discussion, we are ready to calculate the total cash inflows for a project. To do this, however, we need to expand the process beyond operating income to include the benefit of the tax shield on CCA. The revised process is provided in Table 12.4.

TABLE 12.4 Process Used to Calculate Cash Inflows

	Incremental sales
less:	Incremental operating costs
	Incremental operating income
less:	Taxes
	Incremental after-tax operating income
plus:	Tax shield from CCA
	Incremental after-tax cash inflow

Example Branch Inc. is trying to determine whether they should purchase a new machine costing $52,000. The machine is a Class 8 asset with a CCA rate of 20 percent. The asset will result in sales increasing by $60,000 and operating costs increasing by $25,000 per year. Branch's tax rate is 40 percent. Branch wishes to determine the incremental after-tax cash flows for this project for the first three years of its life. To calculate the incremental after-tax cash flows from the project, the tax shield from CCA is required. So the starting point is to complete the CCA table generating the tax shield for each of the first three years. Spreadsheet Application 12.1 provides a template for calculating tax shields, and their present values. Note that more years can be easily added to the template.

Year	UCC, beginning of year	CCA	UCC, end of year	Tax shield
1	$52,000	$5,200[a]	$46,800	$2,080
2	$46,800	$9,360	$37,440	$3,744
3	$37,440	$7,488	$29,952	$2,995

[a]Half-year rule, so use 10%.

Now the cash inflows are calculated using the process provided in Table 12.4. The results are presented in Table 12.5.

12.1 SPREADSHEET APPLICATION

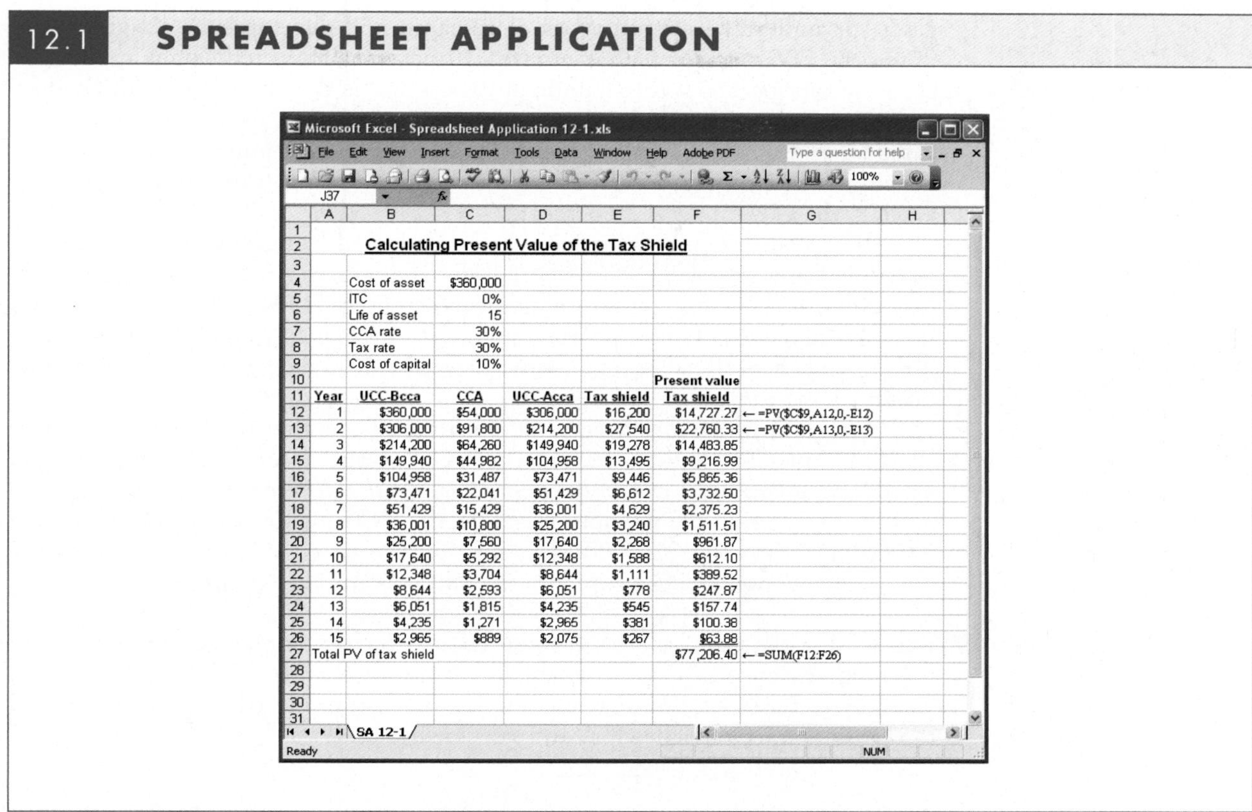

Calculating Present Value of the Tax Shield

Cost of asset	$360,000
ITC	0%
Life of asset	15
CCA rate	30%
Tax rate	30%
Cost of capital	10%

Year	UCC-Bcca	CCA	UCC-Acca	Tax shield	Present value Tax shield	
1	$360,000	$54,000	$306,000	$16,200	$14,727.27	← =PV($C$9,A12,0,-E12)
2	$306,000	$91,800	$214,200	$27,540	$22,760.33	← =PV($C$9,A13,0,-E13)
3	$214,200	$64,260	$149,940	$19,278	$14,483.85	
4	$149,940	$44,982	$104,958	$13,495	$9,216.99	
5	$104,958	$31,487	$73,471	$9,446	$5,865.36	
6	$73,471	$22,041	$51,429	$6,612	$3,732.50	
7	$51,429	$15,429	$36,001	$4,629	$2,375.23	
8	$36,001	$10,800	$25,200	$3,240	$1,511.51	
9	$25,200	$7,560	$17,640	$2,268	$961.87	
10	$17,640	$5,292	$12,348	$1,588	$612.10	
11	$12,348	$3,704	$8,644	$1,111	$389.52	
12	$8,644	$2,593	$6,051	$778	$247.87	
13	$6,051	$1,815	$4,235	$545	$157.74	
14	$4,235	$1,271	$2,965	$381	$100.38	
15	$2,965	$889	$2,075	$267	$63.88	
Total PV of tax shield					$77,206.40	← =SUM(F12:F26)

Remaining Components of Cash Inflows

To complete the discussion of the calculation of cash inflows, the remaining two components of the cash inflows must be considered. These are considered in the following sections.

Investment Tax Credit (ITC)

investment tax credit (ITC)
An incentive for businesses in various regions of the country to purchase certain types of fixed assets or undertake certain types of research and development activities; results in a reduction in federal taxes payable.

As discussed in Chapter 2, the **investment tax credit** (**ITC**) is an incentive for businesses in various regions of the country to purchase certain types of fixed

TABLE 12.5 Cash Inflows for the Project

	Year 1	Year 2	Year 3
Incremental sales	$60,000	$60,000	$60,000
less: Incremental operating cost	25,000	25,000	25,000
Incremental operating income	35,000	35,000	35,000
less: Tax (40%)	14,000	14,000	14,000
Incremental after-tax operating income	21,000	21,000	21,000
plus: Tax shield from CCA	2,080	3,744	2,995
Incremental after-tax cash inflow	$23,080	$24,744	$23,995

assets or undertake certain types of research and development activities. For 2006, the ITC rate for real assets was 10 percent. This credit only applied for corporations located in the Atlantic provinces and in the Gaspé region of Quebec. For Canadian-controlled private corporations (CCPC) located throughout Canada, an ITC of 35 percent was allowed on the first $2 million of research and development expenditures. For expenditures above $2 million and for non-CCPCs, the ITC rate was 20 percent.

The dollar amount of the ITC can be deducted from *federal taxes payable.* The dollar amount of the ITC is based on the amount of the qualifying expenditure times the ITC rate. So assuming the expenditure is $100,000 and it qualifies for a 20 percent ITC, the dollar amount of the ITC is $20,000 ($100,000 × 20%). This is a direct benefit of the project and is recognized as a cash flow occurring in year 1.

One minor drawback associated with the ITC is that the dollar amount of the ITC must be deducted from the UCC of the asset for CCA purposes. Therefore, *a company can only claim CCA on the difference between the UCC and the ITC.* So, in the previous example, the UCC for CCA purposes would be $100,000 minus the $20,000 ITC, making the UCC $80,000. The company would then compute CCA based on the $80,000 and the CCA rate.

Example Recalculate the cash inflows for the Branch Inc. example, assuming the new machine costing $52,000 qualified for a 10 percent ITC. The ITC is $5,200. Therefore, the UCC for the machine at the beginning of year 1 is $46,800 ($52,000 − $5,200). The CCA and tax shields are:

Year	UCC, beginning of year	CCA	UCC, end of year	Tax shield
1	$46,800	$4,680	$42,120	$1,872
2	$42,120	$8,424	$33,696	$3,370
3	$33,696	$6,739	$26,957	$2,696

When calculating the cash inflows there are two changes. First, the tax shield from CCA changes in each of the three years. Second, the ITC is a separate component of the cash flows. The results are presented in Table 12.6.

TABLE 12.6 Cash Inflows for the Project with ITC Included

	Year 1	Year 2	Year 3
Incremental sales	$60,000	$60,000	$60,000
less: Incremental operating cost	25,000	25,000	25,000
Incremental operating income	35,000	35,000	35,000
less: Tax (40%)	14,000	14,000	14,000
Incremental after-tax operating income	21,000	21,000	21,000
plus: Tax shield from CCA	1,872	3,370	2,696
plus: ITC	5,200		
Incremental after-tax cash inflow	28,072	24,370	$23,696

12.2 SPREADSHEET APPLICATION

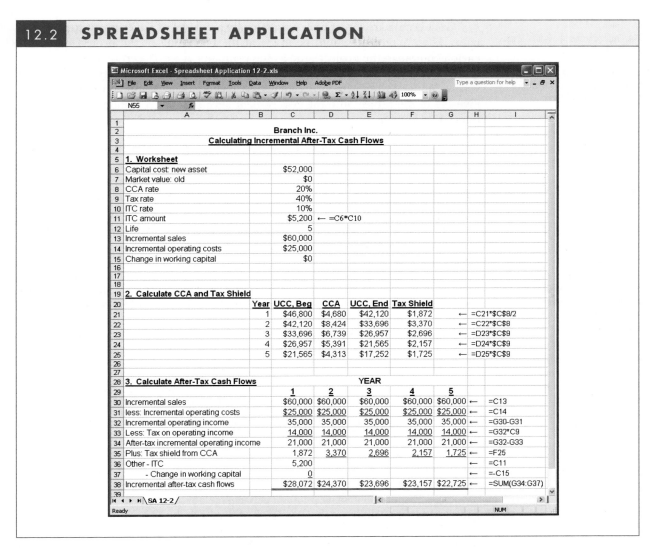

Microsoft Excel - Spreadsheet Application 12-2.xls

Branch Inc.

Calculating Incremental After-Tax Cash Flows

1. Worksheet

Capital cost new asset	$52,000	
Market value: old	$0	
CCA rate	20%	
Tax rate	40%	
ITC rate	10%	
ITC amount	$5,200	← =C6*C10
Life	5	
Incremental sales	$60,000	
Incremental operating costs	$25,000	
Change in working capital	$0	

2. Calculate CCA and Tax Shield

Year	UCC, Beg	CCA	UCC, End	Tax Shield		
1	$46,800	$4,680	$42,120	$1,872	←	=C21*$C$8/2
2	$42,120	$8,424	$33,696	$3,370	←	=C22*$C$8
3	$33,696	$6,739	$26,957	$2,696	←	=D23*$C$9
4	$26,957	$5,391	$21,565	$2,157	←	=D24*$C$9
5	$21,565	$4,313	$17,252	$1,725	←	=D25*$C$9

3. Calculate After-Tax Cash Flows

	YEAR						
	1	2	3	4	5		
Incremental sales	$60,000	$60,000	$60,000	$60,000	$60,000	←	=C13
less: Incremental operating costs	$25,000	$25,000	$25,000	$25,000	$25,000	←	=C14
Incremental operating income	35,000	35,000	35,000	35,000	35,000	←	=G30-G31
Less: Tax on operating income	14,000	14,000	14,000	14,000	14,000	←	=G32*C9
After-tax incremental operating income	21,000	21,000	21,000	21,000	21,000	←	=G32-G33
Plus: Tax shield from CCA	1,872	3,370	2,696	2,157	1,725	←	=F25
Other - ITC	5,200					←	=C11
- Change in working capital	0					←	=-C15
Incremental after-tax cash flows	$28,072	$24,370	$23,696	$23,157	$22,725	←	=SUM(G34:G37)

SA 12-2

Comparing the cash flows in the two examples indicates that the benefit of the ITC in the first year more than compensates for the minor loss of tax shield in the subsequent year. The assumption made for the ITC is that it is received when the company's tax return is filed, which is assumed to be at the end of the fiscal year.

The process used to calculate the yearly cash flows is also provided as Spreadsheet Application 12.2. The SSA allows for additional variables to be added to the analysis.

Government Incentives

The federal government and all provincial governments provide incentives for business to expand operations or to locate a business in a particular location. Since these types of business decisions are capital budgeting projects, the incentives must be included when calculating the cash inflows for a project. Government incentives include cash grants, interest rate buydowns, wage subsidies, rent subsidies, and tax breaks.

cash grants
Direct cash payments by any level of government to the company.

interest rate buydowns
Government payments of interest on a loan on behalf of a company.

Cash grants are direct cash payments by any level of government to the company. These payments could be made at the beginning of the project and/or at various points in the project's life as the company achieves certain predetermined targets. **Interest rate buydowns** are associated with loans a company negotiates with a lender in order to proceed with a project. The money borrowed is then invested in the project and the government agrees to pay a certain amount of the interest on the loan.

Example Jameson Box Company is considering expanding their plant. This will result in the company hiring an additional 120 employees. The cost of the expansion is $7 million. The provincial government indicates that to enhance the feasibility of the project, the government will pay the first 5 percent of interest on a loan of up to $5 million. A condition of the buydown is that Jameson must negotiate the loan with a major chartered bank and the total amount of the loan must be invested in the expansion project.

wage and rent subsidies
Payment made by the government to the company's employees or landlord to reduce the effective cost of proceeding with a project.

tax breaks
Reductions in the property taxes or reductions in income taxes the company would have to pay on the profits generated on an operation.

Wage and rent subsidies are payments made by the government to the company's employees or landlord to reduce the effective cost of proceeding with a project. **Tax breaks** may be reductions in property taxes paid by the company on the land and building where the company locates, or reductions in income taxes the company would have to pay on the profits generated on an operation. Many governments around the world have created "tax-free zones" where all types of taxes are eliminated for a period of time for companies that locate in these areas.

Differences Between Cash Inflows and Profitability

This section discusses and illustrates the fundamentals of calculating cash inflows. It is important to remember that the focus of capital budgeting is on cash flows, not profits. Therefore while, in some respects, the process used to calculate both cash inflows and profitability appears similar, there is a major difference. Consider the following example.

Example Fadeon Inc. is evaluating the purchase of a new lathe. The lathe is expected to generate sales of $125,000 per year and incur operating costs of $78,000. CCA on the lathe in year 1 will be $22,000. Fadeon's tax rate is 30 percent. The profit the lathe will generate in year 1 is provided below:

Sales	$125,000
less: Cash operating costs	78,000
Operating income	47,000
less: CCA	22,000
Incremental income before taxes	25,000
less: Taxes (30%)	7,500
Incremental income after taxes	17,500
plus: CCA	22,000
Incremental after-tax cash inflow	$ 39,500

To adjust the above for cash flows, one alternative is to recognize that CCA, a non-cash expense, was deducted from operating income. To calculate cash inflows, CCA should be added back to the bottom line in the above analysis, as was illustrated in Chapter 2 for the Statement of Cash Flows, and as is done above. An alternative is to use the process that was discussed earlier and is provided below.

Sales	$125,000
less: Cash operating costs	78,000
Operating income	47,000
less: Taxes (30%)	14,100
Incremental after-tax operating income	32,900
plus: tax shield from CCA[a]	6,600
Incremental after-tax cash inflow	$ 39,500

[a]As was shown earlier, a non-cash expense results in tax savings equal to non-cash expense × T. For the above, $22,000 × 30% = $6,600.

Note the major difference between the profitability and the cash flow of the asset. The reason for the difference is the non-cash expense, CCA. While the profit on the project in year 1 is only $17,500, the cash inflow is over double at $39,500. This type of difference will always exist when CCA is a significant amount. Readers should understand why there is a difference between profits and cash inflows and be able to calculate cash inflows using both of the above approaches.

Terminal Cash Flows

All investment projects have a finite life. Fixed assets eventually wear out and become obsolete, at which time the project is terminated and the assets liquidated. This may generate terminal cash flows. The proceeds from the sale of the asset are termed the **salvage value**. This is the amount the company receives from the sale of the asset, *less any removal or clean-up costs incurred.* In some cases there may not be any salvage value or there may be a cost associated with terminating a project. The environmental costs of returning a property to its original condition can be very high for some types of projects.

salvage value
The amount received when a project is terminated and an asset is sold.

A second terminal cash flow is associated with the net working capital investment made at the beginning of the project's life. At termination, the sales associated with the project cease, as does the need for the net working capital. Therefore, at termination, the originally invested **net working capital will be recovered.** As with the original working capital investment, there are no tax consequences of the recapture, since this is an internal reduction of current assets and liabilities.

net working capital recovered
With the termination of a project, the sales associated with the project cease, and the company will recover the originally invested net working capital.

? Review Questions

12–9 Discuss the differences between the relevant cash flows for an expansion versus a replacement project.

12–10 Distinguish between (**a**) sunk costs and opportunity costs, and (**b**) operational and financial cash flows. Which are included and which are ignored for capital budgeting purposes, and why?

12–11 What is the incremental cost of a capital budgeting project, and what type of costs are considered?

12–12 What is the change in net working capital and why, and how is it considered when evaluating an investment project? Consider both the beginning and end of a project's life.

12–13 There are four major components of cash inflows for capital budgeting projects. List and fully describe each of these.

12–14 Explain each of the following terms: (**a**) CCA; (**b**) asset class; (**c**) UCC; (**d**) tax shield; (**e**) tax value; (**f**) ITC; (**g**) government incentives.

12–15 What is the process used to calculate cash inflows for investment projects?

12.4 Splitting Cash Flows: The Complete Net Present Value Approach

In the previous section, the various components of the incremental cost and cash inflows for a capital budgeting project were discussed. The various components of the inflows are calculated and added to determine the incremental after-tax cash inflow for each year of a project's life. An understanding of cash flows is vital to an understanding of capital budgeting; however, for calculation purposes there are some issues with this approach. The two major issues are discussed next.

Issues with Calculating Cash Inflows Each Year

The first issue is associated with calculating cash inflows for projects with very long lives. In Section 12.3, the process for calculating the tax shield from CCA was discussed. This is a key component of cash inflows. Note, however, that the CCA changes each year, since the dollar amount is based on the declining balance of UCC and a stated percentage rate (the CCA rate). Therefore, for projects with long expected lives, say 25 years, 50 different calculations must be made, just to determine the tax shield. The tax shield must then be added to the after-tax operating income and any other cash inflow components to determine the incremental after-tax cash inflow each year. The cash inflows each year would then have to be discounted back to time 0 for the appropriate number of years at the company's cost of capital. Obviously, this would be a very time-consuming process if done with just a calculator. A computer spreadsheet would greatly speed the process, but even then it is a challenge to structure the analysis.

The second issue is also associated with the tax shield. Since the calculation of CCA is based on the declining balance of UCC, the UCC never reaches zero. As long as there is UCC in the asset class, CCA can be charged on the asset and there is a benefit associated with the project. For example, if a company constructs a new plant (a Class 1 asset with a 4% CCA rate) at a cost of $5 million, the plant may be expected to have a useful life of 50 years. The implication is that CCA and tax shields will have to be calculated for 50 years. But even after 50 years, there is still $662,959 of UCC remaining on the plant.[7]

In other words, in order to determine the total benefit of the tax shield from CCA for the plant, the CCA and tax shield will have to be calculated for well

7. The equation used to calculate this amount was provided in Chapter 2, Equation 2.4.

over 50 years, and each year's tax shield discounted back to time 0. Again, while not mathematically complicated, it is very time-consuming and not the most pleasant way to spend 30 minutes! Also, after analyzing one or two projects, most students would very quickly tire of capital budgeting. But, thankfully, there is a way around this time-consuming process. The present value of the total tax shield on an asset can be calculated by using Equation 12.5 as follows:

$$\text{PV of tax shield from CCA} = C_0 \left[\frac{d \times T}{d + k_a}\right]\left[\frac{1 + k_a/2}{1 + k_a}\right] \quad (12.5)$$

where:

C_0 = incremental amount of UCC resulting from an asset acquisition
d = CCA rate for the asset
T = company's tax rate
k_a = company's cost of capital

Note that the final component of the equation accounts for the half-year rule. It is important to recognize that the tax shield formula assumes the asset being acquired is held forever, or until it has zero market value. If this assumption is not valid, the analysis must be modified. This is discussed in a few pages.

Example For the plant in the earlier discussion, what is the total present value of the tax shield? The incremental amount of UCC is the construction cost of \$5,000,000. If we assume the company's tax rate is 32 percent, and their cost of capital is 10 percent, the present value of the tax shield is \$436,364, calculated as follows:

$$\text{PV of tax shield} = \$5{,}000{,}000 \left[\frac{0.04 \times 0.32}{0.04 + 0.10}\right]\left[\frac{1 + (0.10/2)}{1 + 0.10}\right] = \$436{,}364$$

Note that for a replacement project, the UCC would be reduced by the proceeds received from the sale of the old asset. Also, the UCC would be reduced if the project qualified for an ITC.

Example Now assume that the new plant replaces an existing plant that is sold for scrap, raising \$300,000 after clean-up costs. Also, the new building will qualify for a 10 percent ITC. The present value of the total tax shield is based on the incremental amount of UCC added to asset Class 1. By liquidating the existing building and receiving \$300,000, the company will have to subtract that amount from the UCC of Class 1. The new building will add \$5,000,000, so the incremental amount of UCC is \$4,700,000. The new building also qualifies for a 10 percent ITC; therefore, the company will receive an ITC of \$500,000 (\$5,000,000 × 10%). Since the company can only claim CCA on the difference between the UCC and the ITC, C_0, the incremental amount being added to the asset class is \$4,200,000 (\$5,000,000 − \$300,000 − \$500,000). The present value of the total tax shield on the building is \$366,545, calculated as follows:

$$\text{PV of tax shield} = \$4{,}200{,}000 \left[\frac{0.04 \times 0.32}{0.04 + 0.10}\right]\left[\frac{1 + (0.10/2)}{1 + 0.10}\right] = \$366{,}545$$

Implication of the Analysis

If it is more straightforward to calculate the present value of the total tax shield from CCA using a simple equation, it seems reasonable to calculate the present value of each of the remaining cash inflows separately as well. In other words, the individual components of the cash inflows are considered separate items, the present value of each calculated, and then the present values added together to determine the value of the project to the company. The value is then compared to the incremental cost of the project, the NPV calculated, and a decision made regarding the project, as was presented in Section 12.2. This process is illustrated using an example.

Example ▼ Gekkos Toys operates a machine that was purchased five years ago for $510,000 and that now has a tax value (UCC) of $104,083. The machine is a Class 43 asset with a CCA rate of 30 percent. The current market value of the machine is $100,000. The machine is expected to last 10 more years, at which time it will have no value. A much more efficient version of the machine is now available at a cost of $460,000. The new machine has an expected life of 10 years, at which point it would have no market value. The company's operations manager is wondering whether to replace the current machine with the newer efficient model.

It costs Gekkos $95,000 per year to operate the current machine, but due to improved efficiencies, the operating costs for the new machine would fall to $32,000 per year. The new machine is also a Class 43 asset. The company's tax rate is 40 percent and their cost of capital is 10 percent. Should Gekkos replace the existing machine with the new model?

To answer this question, the NPV of the proposed project must be calculated. To calculate the NPV, the incremental cost and the value of the project to Gekkos must be calculated. If Gekkos Toys buys the new machine, they will pay $460,000. *But*, if they buy the new machine, they will sell the old, raising $100,000. Since we are evaluating a replacement project, we assume the old machine will be sold. The incremental cost of the new machine is $360,000 ($460,000 − $100,000).

The value of the project to Gekkos is, as we already know, based on the present value of the cash inflows the project will generate. For the new machine, there are two components of the cash inflows: the incremental after-tax operating income and the tax shield from the CCA based on the incremental amount of UCC added to the asset class. As discussed above, rather than determine the yearly cash inflows, the two components of the incremental after-tax cash flows will be split. The present values of these two items will be analyzed and calculated separately, and added together to determine the present value of the incremental after-tax cash inflows.

The first component of the cash inflows is the incremental operating income which, in this case, is based on the decreased operating costs. The old machine cost $95,000 per year to operate. The new machine costs $32,000 per year, a cost savings of $63,000 per year. This is the incremental operating income. Multiply this amount by (1 – tax rate). The incremental after-tax operating income is $37,800. Note that Gekkos will receive this after-tax saving each year for the 10-year life of the new machine. The $37,800 income is an annuity for 10 periods. Therefore, to calculate the present value of the incremental after-tax income using a financial calculator, $37,800 is the PMT, 10 percent is I (the discount rate), and N is 10. Compute the present value and the answer is $232,265. This is the incremental after-tax operating income. This is shown below as an equation in stages:

$$\begin{aligned}\text{Present value of incremental after-tax operating income} &= (\$95{,}000 - \$32{,}000) = \$63{,}000 \times (1 - 0.40)\\ &= \$37{,}800 \times PVIFa(10\%, 10 \text{ years})\\ &= \$232{,}265\end{aligned}$$

The second component of the cash inflows is the present value of the tax shield from CCA. What amount should be used to calculate the tax shield? Recall from Chapter 2 that when an asset is sold and another purchased, the CCA that can be claimed is based on the net additions to the class. This is the difference between the cost of the asset acquired during the year and the lesser of the original cost or proceeds of the asset disposed of during the year. In this case that is $360,000 ($460,000 – $100,000).

The tax shield from CCA is then based on this additional amount of UCC. But, some may wonder, why is the tax shield on the $104,083 of UCC that is currently in the asset class not also claimed? That amount will be in the asset class *regardless* of whether Gekkos replaces or doesn't replace the asset. The $104,083 is not incremental to the project, so it can be safely ignored.

Now, we can use Equation 12.5 to determine the total present value of the tax shield. The incremental amount of UCC on which to base the tax shield is $360,000, the incremental cost of the asset. The tax shield for the new machine is:

$$\text{PV of tax shield} = \$360{,}000\left[\frac{0.30 \times 0.40}{0.30 + 0.10}\right]\left[\frac{1 + (0.10/2)}{1 + 0.10}\right] = \$103{,}091$$

The present value of the tax shield is $103,091. You now have the PV of the two components of the cash inflows for the project. These are summed to determine the value of the new machine to Gekkos. This value is $335,356 ($232,265 + $103,091). The NPV of the new machine is:

$$\begin{aligned}\text{NPV} &= (\$232{,}265 + \$103{,}091) - \$360{,}000\\ &= -\$24{,}644\end{aligned}$$

The value of the new machine to Gekkos is less than the incremental cost of the machine; the machine's NPV is −$24,644. A negative NPV indicates Gekkos should not replace the existing machine: The asset is not expected to generate its required rate of return. Remember, the NPV process builds into the analysis the requirement that the asset provide a return of, at least, its cost of capital. The negative NPV indicates the project does not generate the required return of 10 percent.

Extending the Analysis to Include Other Components

Section 12.3 indicates that numerous other cash flow components can be associated with a capital budgeting project. This section considers some additional items.

Salvage Value

As discussed in Section 12.3, salvage value is the proceeds the company receives from the sale of an asset at the end of its useful life. If the salvage is associated with the asset that is being replaced, it is considered at time 0 and is used to calculate the incremental cost of the asset. If the salvage is associated with the asset that is being acquired, it is considered at the time the asset is no longer useful, and is a cash inflow at that time. How does the salvage of the asset being acquired impact the analysis?

Example In the original discussion of the new machine that Gekkos Toys was considering acquiring, it was stated that the new machine was expected to have no salvage value at the end of its 10-year life. Upon further investigation, it is discovered that the machine will actually have a salvage value of $108,000 at the end of its 10-year life. Now, should Gekkos replace the existing machine with the new model?

There are two impacts of salvage on the analysis. First, the salvage value is a benefit of the project; it is a cash inflow. At the end of year 10, Gekkos will sell this asset, raising $108,000. Since the inflow occurs in the future, it must be discounted at the cost of capital for the appropriate time period using Equation 12.6:

$$S_0 = S_n \times PVIF\,(k_a, n \text{ years}) \tag{12.6}$$

where:

S_0 is the present value of the salvage at time 0
S_n is the salvage value of the asset at the end of year n.

Applying this to Gekkos results in the present value of the salvage of:

$$\begin{aligned} S_0 &= \$108{,}000 \times PVIF\,(10\%, 10 \text{ years}) \\ &= \$41{,}639 \end{aligned}$$

The second impact of salvage is that a portion of the previously calculated tax shield is lost. Recall that when using the tax shield formula, the assumption made is that the asset being acquired is held forever, or until it has zero market value.

As it turns out, this is not the case for the new machine Gekkos is evaluating. Gekkos will use the new machine for 10 years, at which time it will be worth an estimated $108,000, or $41,639 today. Therefore, Gekkos loses some of the previously calculated tax shield. The amount lost is based on the present value of the salvage, and is calculated using Equation 12.7:

$$\text{PV of tax shield lost} = S_0 \left[\frac{d \times T}{d + k_a}\right] \tag{12.7}$$

Notice that in Equation 12.7, the latter part of the tax shield equation, Equation 12.5, is not used since the half-year rule no longer applies. At the time salvage is realized, year 1 has passed. Applying the equation to the new machine Gekkos is considering results in:

$$\begin{aligned} \text{PV of tax shield lost} &= \$41{,}639 \left[\frac{0.30 \times 0.40}{0.30 + 0.10}\right] \\ &= \$12{,}492 \end{aligned}$$

TABLE 12.7 NPV Analysis for the New Machine

Present value of incremental after-tax operating income	$232,265
PV of tax shield from the incremental CCA	103,091
PV of salvage	41,639
PV of tax shield lost due to salvage	–12,492
Value of new machine	$364,503
Incremental cost of machine	360,000
NPV	$ 4,503

So the tax shield lost is $12,492 and is a cash outflow. Now there are four components of the cash flows generated by the new machine and the value of the machine to Gekkos is based on the sum of these four amounts. The NPV of the new machine is based on the analysis presented in Table 12.7.

In this case the combination of these four cash flows equals $364,503. Therefore, the value of the asset is greater than the incremental cost of the asset, implying that the project has a net present value of $4,503. Remember, this *doesn't* mean that the project generates a return of $4,503. It does mean that the project generates a rate of return greater than the cost of capital, which is the required rate of return. In this example, the expected rate of return will be greater than 10 percent, so Gekkos Toys should replace the existing machine with the new machine. ▲

Another example, illustrating the complete process used to determine the NPV of a project, is provided below.

Example ▼ The Wright Company is contemplating developing and marketing a new, technologically superior product, Zapp, for the spectrum radio systems market. It will take two years to develop the product. The initial costs of developing and marketing Zapp are estimated to be $1,800,000. Of this total cost, $1,350,000 will be spent immediately on a new plant. This amount will be capitalized in CCA Class 18, which has a CCA rate of 20 percent. As well, of the $1,350,000 cost, $625,000 qualifies for a 10 percent ITC. The remainder of the project's total cost will be spent on marketing Zapp prior to the product's launch in order to raise awareness. These outlays will be expensed and will be spent equally in years 1 and 2.

The marketing department estimates that sales of Zapp of $650,000 per year will begin two years after the initial $1,350,000 investment. This sales level will last for ten years, when sales will increase to $875,000 per year for the final 15 years. The direct costs of the system are expected to be 24 percent of sales. Other incremental operating costs will be $185,000 per year. These expenses will not change over the life of the project. The new product will also require an investment of $250,000 in net working capital due to the increasing sales. The salvage value of the project is expected to be $500,000 at the end of the 25 years of sales.

To encourage the production of this product on Prince Edward Island, the provincial government has indicated they are willing to provide a non-taxable cash grant of $350,000, $200,000 payable when the company begins spending on the project and $150,000 one year later. Wright Company's cost of capital is 15 percent, and their marginal tax rate is 29 percent. Should Wright Company develop and market Zapp?

NPV of Zapp:

− Incremental Cost (C_0)		=	−\$1,350,000
+ PV of ITC			
$625,000 (10%) = $62,500 × *PVIF* (15%, 1 *per*)		=	\$ 54,348
− PV of marketing expense			
$225,000 (1 − 0.29) × *PVIFa* (15%, 2 *per*)		=	−\$ 259,707
− PV of additional working capital			
$250,000 × PVIF (15%, 2 *per*)		=	−\$ 189,036
+ PV of cash grant			
$200,000 + [$150,000 × *PVIF* (15%, 1 *per*)]		=	\$ 330,435
+ PV of incremental after-tax operating income			
[($650,000 × (1 − 0.24)) − $185,000]			
= $309,000 × (1 − 0.29) × *PVIFa* (15%, 10 *per*)			
= $1,101,068 × *PVIF* (15%, 2 *per*)	= $832,565		
[($875,000 × (1 − 0.24)) − $185,000]			
= $480,000 × (1 − 0.29) × *PVIFa* (15%, 15 *per*)			
= $1,992,784 × *PVIF* (15%, 12 *per*)	= $372,466		
PV of incremental after-tax operating income		=	\$1,205,031
+ PV of tax shield from incremental CCA			
$(\$1{,}350{,}000 - \$62{,}500)\left[\dfrac{0.20 \times 0.29}{0.20 + 0.15}\right]\dfrac{1.075}{1.15}$		=	\$ 199,443
+ PV of salvage on asset			
$500,000 × *PVIF* (15%, 27 *per*)		=	\$ 11,485
− PV of tax shield lost due to salvage on asset			
$\$11{,}485 \times \left[\dfrac{0.20 \times 0.29}{0.35}\right]$		=	−\$ 1,903
+ Recover working capital			
$250,000 × *PVIF* (15%, 27 *per*)		=	+\$ 5,742
NPV		**=**	**+\$ 5,837**

Note that each of the cash flows is discounted at 15 percent for the appropriate time period. Readers are encouraged to draw a time line for this project and put the appropriate cash flows on the line to see that the numeric analysis provided above matches the time line analysis of the various expected cash flows. The overall result is a very small positive NPV. Does this result mean that the Wright Company will only make $5,837 on a multi-million dollar project? No, the positive NPV means that the project's expected return is greater than the required rate of return of 15 percent. Therefore, Wright Company should proceed with the Zapp project. The process used to calculate the NPV for this project is also provided as Spreadsheet Application 12.3.

12.3 SPREADSHEET APPLICATION

Microsoft Excel - Spreadsheet Application 12-3.xls

	A	B	C	D
1				
2	**Calculating Net Present Value of an Investment Project**			
3				
4	**Variables**			
5	Incremental cost	$1,350,000		
6	Incremental cost expensed	$225,000		
7	ITC ($ amount)	$62,500		
8	Additional working capital	$250,000		
9	Sales	$650,000	$875,000	
10	Direct production costs	$156,000	$210,000	
11	Other operating costs	$185,000	$185,000	
12	Incremental operating income	$309,000	$480,000	
13	Salvage	$500,000		
14	Tax rate	29%		
15	CCA rate	20%		
16	Cost of capital	15%		
17				
18	**NPV Analysis**			
19	- Incremental cost		-$1,350,000	← =-B5
20				
21	+ PV ITC equipment		$54,348	← =PV(B16,1,0,-B7)
22				
23	- Incremental cost expensed			
24	Year 1: $225,000 x (1 - 0.29) x PVIF (15%, 1 per)	-$138,913		← =PV(B16,1,0,(B6*(1-B14)))
25	Year 2: $225,000 x (1 - 0.29) x PVIF (15%, 2 per)	-$120,794	-$259,707	
26				
27	- PV of additional working capital			
28	$250,000 x PVIF (15%, 1 per)		-$189,036	← =PV($B$16,2,0,B$8)
29				
30	+ Cash grant			
31	Year 0: $200,000	$200,000		
32	Year 1: $150,000 x PVIF (15%, 1 per)	$130,435	$330,435	← =PV($B$16,1,0,-150000)
33				
34	+ PV of incremental after-tax operating income			
35	Years 3 to 12	$1,101,068	$832,565	← =PV($B$16,10,-B12*(1-$B$14))
36	Years 13 to 27	$1,992,784	$372,466	← =PV($B$16,12,0,-B36)
37	PV of incremental after-tax operating income		$1,205,031	
38				
39	+ PV of tax shield from CCA		$199,443	← =((B5-B7)*((B15*B14)/(B15+$B$16))*((1+B16/2)/(1+B16)))
40				
41	+ Salvage value of equipment		$11,485	← =PV($B$16,27,0,-B13)
42				
43	- PV of tax shield loss		-$1,903	← =-C42*(B15*B14)/(B15+$B$16)
44				
45	+ PV of recovery of working capital		$5,742	← =PV($B$16,27,0,-B$8)
46				
47	**NPV**		**$5,837**	← =SUM(C19:C46)-C37

SA 12-3

12.1 IN PRACTICE

Positive NPV on the Horizon

Before undertaking any major project, extensive research, planning, and analysis must be conducted to determine the viability of the proposed project. The project details, such as resource availability, the required initial investment and ongoing expenditures, the expected benefits, and the feasibility of the project must be carefully examined. Canadian Natural Resources Limited, one of the largest independent crude oil and natural gas producers in the world, is an example of a company that takes the planning process seriously. The execution of the company's Horizon Oil Sands Project comes as the result of carefully following the capital budgeting process.

Before senior management approved the project, four years and over $400 million were spent to understand what they wanted to build and how they wanted to build it. This investment was well worth the effort, as it helped to achieve something that is very difficult for mega-projects such as Horizon—cost certainty. For example, 68 percent of construction costs were tendered under fixed price bids, a first in the oil sands industry. Canadian Natural extensively evaluated their options before determining the technology to be used in mining the oil sands. The decision was made to manage the project in segments and contracts to ensure a phased, measured approach to development.

The result of this structured planning is a three-phase implementation strategy over a seven-year period from 2005 to 2012. This phased, orderly development improves control of a project of this magnitude and allows for level growth and opportunities for infrastructure supply to keep up with demand. The Horizon Project is located 70 kilometres north of Fort McMurray, Alberta, where Canadian Natural owns and operates leases covering 46,500 hectares through lease arrangements with the Province of Alberta. The project will utilize open pit mining methods to extract the more than 6 billion barrels of oil sands that the lease contains.

The first phase of the project will see production of 110,000 barrels of synthetic crude oil per day in the second half of 2008. The second phase of production, expected to take place in 2010, will see an increase in production of 45,000 barrels of synthetic crude oil per day. The third and final phase of development, expected to take place in 2012, will bring total production to 232,000 barrels per day. By 2017, the company expects to see the total output of crude oil double to 500,000 barrels per day.

A project of this magnitude will certainly have an equally large price tag attached. Indeed, the project's annual operating budget is $740 million and the total capital investment in the project is expected to be $10.8 billion. Cash outflows were $1.3 billion in 2005, and are expected to be $2.6 billion in 2006 and $2.9 billion in 2007 and 2008 combined. But the expected benefits of the project far exceed the cost. The Horizon Project is expected to realize economic benefits of about $24 billion for Alberta and Canada over the project's 40-year life span. The Horizon Project is also producing benefits for the labour market, with 2,400 permanent employees expected to be hired by 2011 and as many as 6,000 jobs created during construction peaks in 2006 and 2007.

With the Horizon Project, Canadian Natural focused on minimizing risk to ensure greater advantages. For example, the project is based on technology that is already in use in existing plants, minimizing risk in phase 1. In addition, the company has reduced risk by extensive drilling activity. The result is a well-designed plan that has been optimized to support oil extraction and processing. These factors and more have contributed to the success of the Horizon Project. Once up and running, Horizon will only require sustaining capital of $1.22 per barrel at a time when oil prices are in the $60 per barrel range. Significant free cash flow will be generated.

Clearly, the Horizon Oil Sands Project will add value to Canadian Natural and their shareholders. The project is under way and on schedule. This was not a result of luck, but of a careful, well-structured plan. The phased, orderly development of this tremendous resource will ensure Horizon generates a return that will more than compensate for the cost of the funds invested. And such an outcome is the whole point of the capital budgeting process.

SOURCE: Canadian Natural Resources Limited, 2005 annual report.

? Review Questions

12–16 What are the two issues associated with calculating cash inflows in total for each year of a project's life? How are these issues resolved?

12–17 What is the formula for calculating the tax shield from CCA? What does this formula do? What does this formula assume?

12–18 What process is used to calculate the NPV of an investment project when the incremental cash flows are split into their separate components?

12–19 What impact does salvage value have on the analysis of an investment project?

12.5 Other Capital Budgeting Techniques

NPV is one technique used to evaluate capital budgeting projects. The *payback period* and *internal rate of return (IRR)* are two other common approaches that are often used.[8] This section discusses and illustrates these two approaches and compares them to the NPV approach. (For a discussion of the capital budgeting techniques that are actually used by companies, read the paper at the Web site provided.)

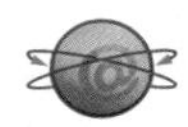

http://faculty.fuqua.duke.edu/~jgraham/website/SurveyJACF.pdf

SRL Metals is a small metal fabricator located in northern Newfoundland. The company is contemplating two investment projects. Both have an initial cost of $25,000 and both have expected lives of five years. Table 12.8 provides the cash flow patterns for these two projects. Note that all components of the cash inflows are considered, including the full value of the tax shield. A simplified example is used in order to focus the discussion on the two techniques. The remainder of this section covers the two other capital budgeting techniques and compares them to the NPV method.

Payback Period

payback period
The length of time in years it takes for a project's yearly incremental after-tax cash inflows to recover the incremental cost of the project.

The **payback period** is the length of time in years it takes for a project's yearly incremental after-tax cash inflows to recover the incremental cost of the project. In the case of an *annuity*, the payback period can be found by dividing the incremental cost by the annual cash inflow. When the cash inflows are different amounts each year (a *mixed stream*), the yearly cash inflows must be accumulated until the initial investment is recovered. Although popular, the payback period is generally viewed as an *unsophisticated capital budgeting technique*, because it does *not* explicitly consider the time value of money by discounting cash flows to find present value.

8. Two other closely related techniques that are sometimes used to evaluate capital budgeting projects are the *average (or accounting) rate of return (ARR)* and the *profitability index (PI)*. The ARR is an unsophisticated technique that is calculated by dividing a project's average profits after taxes by its average investment. Because it fails to consider cash flows and the time value of money, it is ignored here. The PI, sometimes called the *benefit–cost ratio*, is calculated by dividing the project's net present value by its incremental cost. This technique, which does consider the time value of money, is sometimes used as a starting point in the selection of projects under capital rationing. It is discussed more fully in Chapter 13.

TABLE 12.8 Cash Flow Patterns for Two Investment Projects

	Year	Project A	Project B
Incremental cost		$25,000	$25,000
Cash inflows[a]:	1	$12,500	$ 4,000
	2	12,500	5,000
	3	4,000	6,500
	4	800	12,500
	5	500	12,500

[a]All components of the cash inflows are included.

When the payback period is used to make accept/reject decisions, the decision criteria are:

1. For independent projects, if the payback period is *less than* the maximum acceptable payback period, *accept* the project. If the payback period is *greater than* the maximum acceptable payback period, *reject* the project.
2. For mutually exclusive projects, the project with the lower payback period is ranked first (if the period is less than the maximum acceptable value).

The length of the maximum acceptable payback period is determined by management. This value is set *subjectively*, based on a number of factors including, but not limited to, the type of project (expansion, replacement, renewal, etc.), the perceived risk of the project, and the perceived relationship between the payback period and share value. It is simply a value that management feels will, on average, result in good—that is, value-creating—investment decisions. This value will vary from company to company.

Example We can calculate the payback period for the two projects SRL Metals is evaluating. For both projects, the cash inflows must recoup the $25,000 incremental cost. For project A, the first year's cash inflow is $12,500, which is half of the cost. Year 2's cash inflow is also $12,500 and the sum of these two amounts fully recovers the initial investment. So, project A's payback period is 2 years.

For project B, the first year's cash flow of $4,000 recovers a very small portion of the incremental cost. In year 2, $5,000 is recovered, so the cumulative cash inflows are $9,000 ($4,000 + $5,000). For year 3, $6,500 is recovered, so the cumulative cash inflows are $15,500 ($9,000 + $6,500). In year 4, the cash inflow is $12,500, so the cumulative amount is $28,000 ($15,500 + $12,500). The payback period is less than 4 years, but more than 3. To recover the $25,000 cost of the project, $9,500 ($15,500 + $9,500 = $25,000) of year 4's cash inflow is required. This is 76 percent ($9,500 ÷ $12,500) of year 4's cash inflow. Therefore the payback period for project B is 3.76 years (3 years plus 76% of year 4).

If SRL's maximum acceptable payback period were 4 years and the projects were independent, both projects would be acceptable. If the projects were mutually exclusive, project A would be selected since it has the shorter payback period.

Hint
In all three of the decision methods presented in this text, the relevant data are *after-tax cash inflows*. The only relevance of accounting profits is to help determine the incremental after-tax operating income.

Hint
The payback period indicates to firms taking on projects of high risk how quickly they can recover their investment. In addition, it tells firms with limited sources of capital how quickly the funds invested in a given project will become available for future projects.

The payback period is widely used in reality due to its computational simplicity and its intuitive appeal. By considering cash flows rather than accounting profits, it measures how quickly the firm recovers its initial investment. Because it can be viewed as a measure of *risk exposure*, many firms use the payback period as a decision criterion or as a supplement to sophisticated decision techniques. The longer the firm must wait to recover its invested funds, the greater the possibility of unforeseen negative events occurring. Therefore, the shorter the payback period, the lower the firm's exposure to such risk.

Problems with the Payback Period

There are three *major* problems with the payback period as a method of evaluating capital budgeting projects. First, the payback period ignores cash flows that occur after the payback period. When the payback period for project A was calculated, we stopped the analysis at the end of year 2. The problem is that the cash inflows for project A after year 2 decline significantly; total cash inflows over the remaining three years are only $5,300. For project B, the cash inflows in years 3, 4, and 5 total $31,500. By not considering all of the data, we are not fully analyzing the project.

Second, the payback period fails to consider explicitly the time value of money. By simply cumulating cash flows over time, a cash inflow in year 1 is treated the same as a cash inflow in year 4. This is clearly an inappropriate way to analyze a project.[9]

Example To illustrate this, the NPVs of projects A and B are calculated in Table 12.9. SRL's cost of capital is 10 percent so this is the discount rate used to calculate the value of the two projects to SRL Metals. The NPV analysis clearly indicates that by ignoring time value considerations, SRL would make an incorrect decision by ranking project A ahead of B. Clearly project B creates more value for shareholders; its expected return is greater than project A's. While both projects are acceptable (since both have positive NPVs), B is superior to A.

Third, the maximum payback period set by management is merely a subjectively determined number. By using it, a project cannot be evaluated in light of the wealth maximization goal because the method is not based on discounted cash flows. It is not known if the project adds to the firm's value. Instead, the appropriate payback period is simply the maximum acceptable period of time over which management decides that a project's cash flows must equal the initial investment.

fish-and-bait test
A description for the payback period; it concentrates on recovering the bait (the incremental cost), paying no attention to the size of the fish (the present value of all cash inflows).

In conclusion, the payback period technique could be described as the **fish-and-bait test:** It concentrates on recovering the bait (the incremental cost), paying no attention to the size of the fish (the present value of all cash inflows). It is a measure of a project's liquidity and capital recovery, rather than the project's ability to generate positive cash flow and increase company value.

9. To consider differences in timing *explicitly* in applying the payback method, the *present value payback period* is sometimes used. It is found by first calculating the present value of the cash inflows at the appropriate discount rate and then finding the payback period by using the present value of the cash inflows.

TABLE 12.9 Calculation of NPVs for Two Investment Projects

	Cash inflow		Present value of cash inflow[a]	
Year	Project A	Project B	Project A	Project B
1	$12,500	$ 4,000	$11,364	$ 3,636
2	$12,500	$ 5,000	10,331	4,132
3	$ 4,000	$ 6,500	3,005	4,884
4	$ 800	$12,500	546	8,538
5	$ 500	$12,500	310	7,762
Present value of cash inflows			$25,556	$28,952
Less: Initial cost			25,000	25,000
NPV			$ 556	$ 3,952

[a]This is calculated by discounting each of the yearly cash inflows for the appropriate time period at 10%. When using a financial calculator, the cash inflow is the FV, the appropriate year is N, and 10%, SRL's cost of capital, is I. The PV is computed after inputting 0 into PMT.

Internal Rate of Return (IRR)

internal rate of return (IRR)
The discount rate that equates the present value of the cash inflows with the incremental cost of a capital budgeting project; the discount rate that makes the NPV of a project equal to 0.

The **internal rate of return (IRR)** of a capital budgeting project is the discount rate that equates the present value of the cash inflows with the incremental cost of the project. In other words, the IRR is the discount rate that makes the NPV of a project equal to 0. The IRR is the expected return of the project. The IRR method is considered a sophisticated capital budgeting technique that has wide appeal in practice. The reason for its wide appeal is that it reduces a capital budgeting project to a single, easily understood number: a percentage return.

A difficulty with IRR is that it is time-consuming to calculate by hand. Without a financial calculator or computer spreadsheet, the IRR for a project must be calculated by trial and error. For simple capital budgeting problems, a financial calculator can be used; but for complex problems, a computer spreadsheet is used to calculate the IRR. The equation for IRR is easily extended from Equation 12.3, the calculation of the NPV for a project, as provided in Equation 12.8:

$$NPV = 0 = \left[\sum_{t=1}^{n} CF_t\,(1 - T) \times PVIF\,(k_a, t \text{ years})\right] - C_0 \tag{12.8}$$

If the IRR for a project is greater than or equal to the company's cost of capital, then the project should be accepted since the NPV of the project will be greater than or equal to 0. If the IRR for a project is less than the company's cost of capital, the project's NPV will be less than 0 and the project is clearly unacceptable.

Calculating the IRR

For a basic capital budgeting project, like those discussed for SRL Metals, the calculation of IRR is not difficult, just time consuming, since a trial-and-error approach must be used. This section considers the process used to calculate IRR. We will start by considering a project where the cash inflows are an annuity.

Example ▼ Reconsider the McLaughlin Construction example from Section 12.2. In this example, the company was considering purchasing a new hydraulic lift with a cost of $33,000, a life of 8 years, and incremental after-tax cash inflows of $6,000 per year. To calculate the IRR for this project using a financial calculator, 6,000 is the PMT, 8 is N, the PV is 33,000. Input 0 in FV and compute (CPT) I. For some calculators, the PV may have to be input as a negative number. In this case, I is 9.17 percent; this is the IRR for the project. To verify it, determine the value of the project to McLaughlin assuming the company's cost of capital was 9.17 percent. The value is $33,000, meaning the NPV is zero. Therefore, the IRR is 9.17 percent. ▲

When the cash inflows are different amounts each year (a mixed stream), as for the two projects being evaluated by SRL Metals, a different approach to calculating the IRR must be used. This is the NPV profile approach. A **NPV profile** is a table and/or graph that shows the NPV for a project at various discount rates. To illustrate this approach, consider the following example.

NPV profile
A table and/or graph that shows the NPV for a project at various discount rates.

Example ▼ We want to calculate the IRR for the two projects being considered by SRL Metals. NPV profiles for the two projects are developed by simply discounting the cash inflows for each of the years at a stated discount rate and determining the NPVs. The outcome of this process for 6 discount rates is provided in Table 12.10.

The data in Table 12.10 can be used to develop NPV profiles on a graph. Figure 12.5 provides the NPV profiles for projects A and B for SRL Metals. While the table does not determine the exact IRRs, it can narrow the range. For Project A, based on the NPV, it is clear the IRR is between 10 percent and 12 percent, but closer to 12 percent. (This is why NPVs are not provided for the 14 percent and 16 percent discount rates.) If, for example, 11.5 percent is used as a discount rate, an NPV of –$41 results. Since this is very close to 0, it would be reasonable to conclude that the IRR is a little less than 11.5 percent, say about 11.4 percent. The exact answer is 11.39 percent.

TABLE 12.10 NPV Profile for Two Investment Projects[a]

Discount rate (%)	NPV Project A	NPV Project B
0	$5,300	$15,500
5	2,748	9,037
10	556	3,952
12	–235	2,221
14	—	637
16	—	–817

[a]To determine the NPVs, the cash inflows for the two projects are discounted at the stated rate for the appropriate period, summed, and then subtracted from the incremental cost. At a 0% discount rate, cash flows over time are equivalent, so the cash inflows are simply added and the incremental cost subtracted to calculate NPV.

FIGURE 12.5

Net Present Value Profiles for Projects A and B

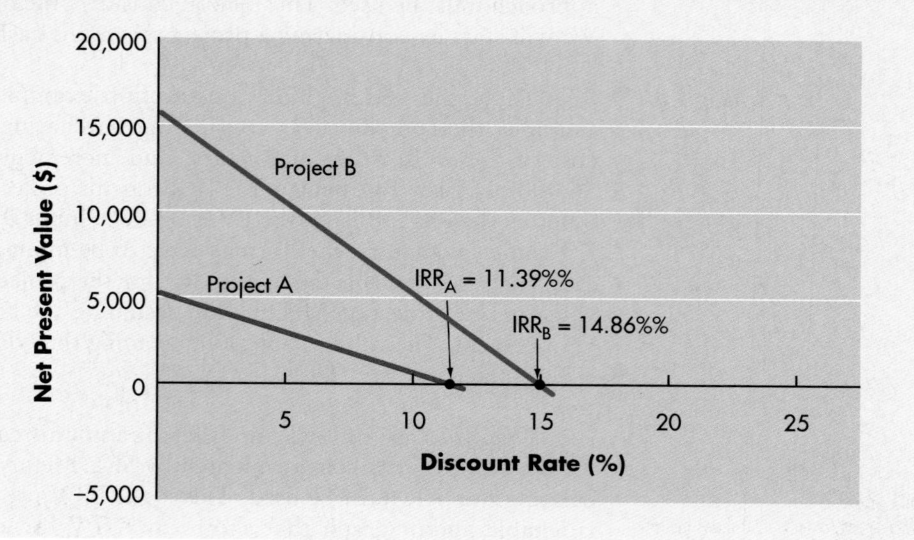

For project B, the IRR is between 14 percent and 16 percent and based on the NPVs, close to 15 percent. At 15 percent, the NPV is $106, so the IRR is slightly less than 15 percent, say 14.8 percent. The exact IRR is 14.86 percent.[10] A graph drawn to scale, like Figure 12.5, would also allow the analyst to narrow down the correct IRR.

For SRL Metals, we have analyzed the two investment projects using three techniques. The results are summarized below:

	Project A	Project B
Payback period	2 years	3.76 years
NPV (@10%)	$556	$3,952
IRR	11.39%	14.86%

What should SRL Metals do? First, given the major problems associated with the payback period technique, the result indicating that project A is superior to B should be ignored. The two sophisticated approaches, NPV and IRR, both give the same result: project B is superior to project A. Project B has a much larger NPV and IRR. This is clearly seen in Figure 12.5. If the projects are mutually exclusive, B is ranked first. If the projects are independent, both are acceptable. Both generate a return greater than SRL's cost of capital, as is clear when the values for NPV and IRR are considered.

10. Most financial calculators are preprogrammed to calculate IRRs for these simple types of capital budgeting projects through the cash flow (CF) function. The yearly cash inflows are inputted into the calculator, the incremental cost in the PV function (as a negative number), and the IRR computed. To ease the process of determining IRRs, learn how to make full use of your calculator.

? Review Questions

12–20 What is the payback period and how is it calculated? Why is it used by companies?

12–21 List and discuss the weaknesses of the payback period.

12–22 What is the internal rate of return of an investment project? How is it calculated?

12–23 How is the IRR used to determine whether a project is acceptable? Why is this approach used?

12–24 Compare the process used to calculate the IRR for a project where the cash inflows are the same amount each year to one where the inflows differ from year to year.

12–25 Do the NPV and IRR approaches always provide the same accept/reject decision for a project? Why is this the case?

12.6 Comparing the NPV and IRR Techniques

Even though both NPV and IRR are sophisticated capital budgeting techniques and will *always* generate the same accept/reject decisions for projects, differences in their underlying assumptions can cause them to *rank* projects differently. In other words, for independent projects, both techniques will always result in the same decisions. Different decisions can result, however, for mutually exclusive projects. This section illustrates the difference, explains why different rankings can occur, and considers which of the two approaches, NPV or IRR, is better to use.

Example For SRL Metals, based on the previous section, it is very clear that if the projects are independent, both projects A and B are acceptable to the company. If the projects are mutually exclusive, project B is clearly superior to A. Project B's NPV is much higher, as is the expected return, its IRR. Now assume that SRL has the opportunity to invest in a third project, project C. The cash flows associated with this project are provided in Table 12.11.

Projects B and C are mutually exclusive projects so they must be ranked. The payback period, NPV, and IRR for project B are already known; they must be calculated for project C. (We will calculate the payback period for practice.) The payback period for C is 1.5 years ($21,250 + $3,750), noting that half

TABLE 12.11 Cash Flow Pattern for Project C

	Year	Project C
Incremental cost		$25,000
Cash inflows:	1	$21,250
	2	7,500
	3	3,000
	4	500
	5	500

TABLE 12.12 NPV Profile for Project C[a]

Discount Rate (%)	Project C
0	$7,750
5	5,435
10	3,422
15	1,656
20	95
21	–196

[a]To determine the NPVs, the cash inflows for the two projects are discounted at the stated rate for the appropriate period, summed, and then subtracted from the incremental cost.

($3,750 ÷ 7,500) of year 2's cash inflow is needed. To calculate the IRR for project C, the NPV profile presented in Table 12.12 for project C is used.

Note that the IRR is between 20 percent and 21 percent but closer to 20 percent, say 20.3 percent. The exact IRR is 20.32 percent. Figure 12.6 provides the NPV profiles for both projects B and C. Note that in the process of developing the NPV profile, the NPV of project C was also calculated. What do the various capital budgeting techniques suggest about the two projects? The results are summarized below.

	Project B	Project C
Payback period	3.76 years	1.5 years
NPV (@ 10%)	$3,952	$3,422
IRR	14.86%	20.32%

Based on NPV, project B is superior to C; based on IRR the reverse holds. What should SRL Metals do? To answer this question, we will consider why different rankings can occur.

Reason for Different Ranking

conflicting rankings
Conflicts in the ranking of projects using the NPV and IRR techniques resulting from differences in the magnitude and timing of cash inflows.

Conflicting rankings using the NPV and IRR techniques result from differences in the magnitude and timing of cash inflows. Projects with very large cash inflows in the early years of a project's life tend to result in high IRRs. The IRR for projects with low cash inflows in the early years and high cash inflows in the later years tend to generate lower IRRs.

The underlying reason for this is the assumption that the two techniques make concerning the reinvestment of a project's cash inflows. The NPV method assumes the project's cash inflows are reinvested at the cost of capital. IRR assumes the cash inflows are reinvested at the IRR. IRR is a *compounded rate of return*, meaning the technique assumes the yearly cash inflows can be reinvested at the IRR and the return compounds over time. In other words, for project C, the

FIGURE 12.6

Net Present Value Profile with Cross-Over Rate

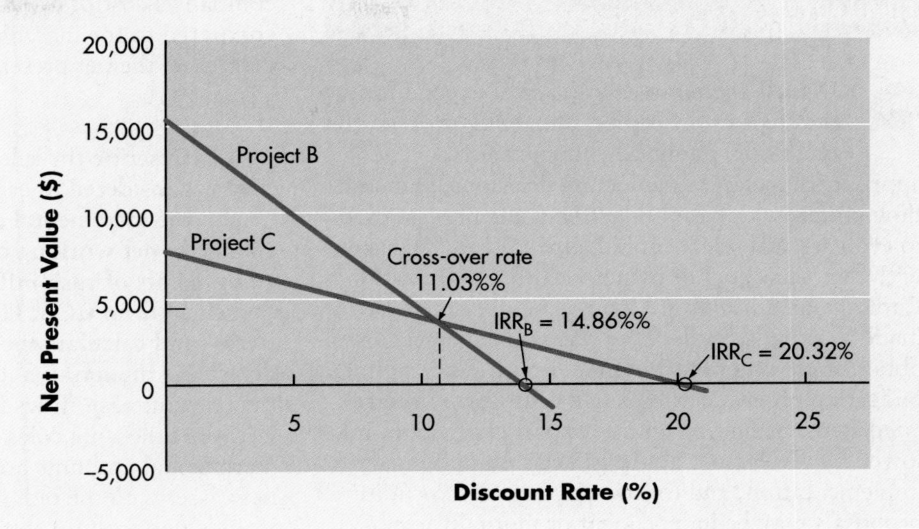

IRR method assumes that the $21,250 cash inflow received in year 1 is reinvested by the company to earn a 20.32 percent return. This is an unrealistic assumption for high IRR projects, especially for SRL Metals, given that the company's cost of capital is less than half at 10 percent. If the company cannot reinvest the $21,250 at 20.32 percent, then the true IRR on the project will be much lower.

Since the NPV technique makes a much safer and more realistic reinvestment rate assumption, that the cash inflows will be reinvested at the cost of capital, the NPV technique is preferred to the IRR.

Cross-Over Rate

cross-over rate
The discount rate where NPV profiles intersect, meaning the NPVs of the two projects are equal, and where the ranking decision for the projects changes.

Another way to compare the NPV and IRR methods is through the use of the **cross-over rate.** Referring again to Figure 12.6, note that the NPV profiles for projects B and C intersect. The intersection point occurs at a discount rate of 11.03 percent, and then the lines quickly diverge in both directions. At the intersection point, the NPVs of the two projects are equal at $3,040 and, therefore, a company would be indifferent to the two projects. Also, at this point the ranking decisions for the projects change. If SRL Metal's cost of capital is less than 11.03 percent, project B is preferred. This is clearly seen in the figure, with the NPV profile of project B being above C when the discount rate is less than 11.03 percent. If the cost of capital is greater than 11.03 percent, project C is preferred. Again, note that the NPV profile for C is above B's in Figure 12.6. For SRL Metals, the cost of capital is 10 percent; therefore project B is ranked ahead of C.

? Review Questions

12–26 For mutually exclusive projects, do the NPV and IRR techniques provide the same ranking? Explain.

12–27 What is the cross-over point and why is it important when ranking projects?

SUMMARY

Discuss the motives for capital expenditures, the steps in the capital budgeting process, the types of capital budgeting projects, approaches to capital budgeting decisions, and cash flow patterns. Capital budgeting is the process used to evaluate and select capital expenditures consistent with the firm's goal of owner wealth maximization. Capital expenditures are long-term investments made to expand, replace, or renew fixed assets or to obtain some other less tangible benefit. The capital budgeting process contains five distinct but interrelated steps, beginning with proposal generation, followed by review and analysis, decision making, implementation, and follow-up. Capital expenditure proposals may be independent or mutually exclusive. Typically, firms have only limited funds for capital investments and must ration funds among carefully selected projects. To make investment decisions when proposals are mutually exclusive or when capital must be rationed, projects must be ranked; otherwise, accept/reject decisions must be made. Cash flow patterns consist of an initial outflow followed by a series of inflows; the inflows can be annuities, different amounts each year (mixed streams), or a combination of the two.

Introduce the process used to analyze capital budgeting projects, discuss the basic cash flow components of projects, and illustrate how projects are evaluated by comparing the value of a project to its cost. To evaluate capital budgeting projects, the firm must determine the relevant cash flows, which are the incremental cash outflows (the amount invested) and subsequent after-tax inflows. The cash flows of any project can include three basic components: (1) the incremental cost, (2) operating cash inflows, and (3) the terminal cash flow. To evaluate projects, the preferred approaches integrate time value procedures, risk and return considerations, and valuation concepts to select capital expenditures that are consistent with the firm's goal of maximizing owners' wealth. The value of an asset is based on the present value of the cash flows generated by the asset over its useful life. The discount rate used is the return required on the asset that compensates for the risk of the project. For capital budgeting, this is the company's cost of capital. The value of the asset is compared to the incremental cost of the asset to determine the net present value (NPV) of the project.

Describe the relevant cash flows that are considered in capital budgeting; calculate the incremental cost for a project and the change in net working capital; describe the four components of cash inflows—operating income, tax shield from CCA, ITC, and government incentives—and calculate the total cash inflows; and determine the terminal cash flow. When calculating the relevant cash flows for a capital budgeting project, the following rules must be obeyed: (1) only incremental amounts are considered—compare the new asset with the old; (2) ignore sunk costs but include opportunity costs; (3) only include operational items—ignore financing costs; and (4) the cash inflows must be after tax—the company only receives benefits after paying the appropriate taxes. The incremental cost of a project generally occurs at time 0 and marks the beginning of the project's life. For some projects, subsequent investments may also be required and these may be capitalized or expensed. Projects that result in sales increasing may also require the investment of working capital—the difference between increases in current assets and current liabilities. There are four major components of the cash inflows: (1) Incremental after-tax operating income, the principal reason a company considers investing in a fixed asset which may result from sales increasing, operating costs decreasing, or both. (2) The tax shield on capital cost allowance (CCA). Since expenditures on fixed assets are capitalized, the expenditure is written off over time by charging CCA. CCA is a benefit since it is deducted from income when calculating taxable income, *but*, as a non-cash expense, it reduces taxes but no cash has actually been used. The benefit of CCA is the tax saving associated with the firm claiming the non-cash expense, which is the tax shield. (3) The investment tax credit (ITC), an incentive for businesses in various regions of the country to make certain expenditures that result in a reduction in federal taxes payable. (4) Government incentives. These four items are the total cash inflows. The terminal cash flow is the combination of the salvage value of the asset and the recapture of working capital.

LG4 **Describe and illustrate the complete process for calculating the net present value for a capital budgeting project.** When calculating cash inflows for individual years, there are two issues. First, since CCA changes each year of a project's life, the tax shield changes. For projects with very long lives, say 25 years, 50 different calculations must be made just to determine the tax shield. The tax shield must then be added to the other cash inflow components and the incremental after-tax cash inflows for each year would then have to be discounted back to time 0. This would be a very time-consuming process. Second, since the UCC never reaches zero, the full value of the tax shield cannot be totally calculated when determining yearly cash inflows. Therefore, Equation 12.5 in the chapter is used to calculate the total present value of the tax shield. The implication is that the individual components of the cash inflows are considered separate items, the present value of each calculated, and then the present values added together to determine the value of the project to the company. The value is then compared to the incremental cost, the NPV calculated, and a decision made regarding the project. The components include the incremental cost, the four components of the inflows, and the terminal value of the project.

LG5 **Discuss two other capital budgeting techniques—the payback period and internal rate of return (IRR)—and show how each is calculated.** NPV is one technique used to evaluate capital budgeting projects. The *payback period* and *internal rate of return (IRR)* are two other common approaches that are often used. The payback period is the length of time in years it takes for a project's yearly incremental after-tax cash inflows to recover the incremental cost of the project. A maximum acceptable payback period is subjectively set by a company to evaluate projects. The payback period is widely used in reality due to its computational simplicity and its intuitive appeal, but there are three problems with this technique. First, the payback period ignores cash flows that occur after the payback period. Second, the payback period fails to explicitly consider the time value of money. Third, the maximum payback period set by management is merely a subjectively determined number. The internal rate of return (IRR) of a capital budgeting project is the discount rate that equates the present value of the cash inflows with the incremental cost of the project; it is the expected return of a project. The IRR is the discount rate that makes the NPV of a project equal to 0. The IRR is calculated by developing an NPV profile for a project. The NPV and IRR techniques will always result in the same accept/reject decision for independent projects.

Compare the NPV and IRR approaches to capital budgeting, focusing on the conflicting ranking that can occur, and discuss the cross-over rate. Even though both NPV and IRR are sophisticated capital budgeting techniques and will always generate the same accept/reject decisions for projects, differences in their underlying assumptions can cause them to rank mutually exclusive projects differently. Conflicting rankings are due to differences in the magnitude and timing of cash inflows. Projects with very large cash inflows in the early years tend to result in high IRRs. This is because the IRR method assumes the cash inflows are reinvested at the IRR, and the return compounds over time. The NPV method assumes cash inflows are reinvested at the cost of capital. Since the NPV technique makes a much safer and realistic reinvestment rate assumption, the NPV technique is preferred to IRR. The cross-over rate is the discount rate where NPV profiles intersect, meaning the NPVs of the two projects are equal, and where the ranking decision for the projects changes.

SELF-TEST PROBLEMS (Solutions in Appendix B)

ST 12–1 Determining cash inflows and calculating NPV Laidlaw Inc. is evaluating the acquisition of a new piece of equipment that will cost $280,000 to purchase. Installation will cost an additional $20,000. The equipment will have a life of five years, and is a Class 10 asset which has a CCA rate of 30 percent. The new equipment qualifies for an investment tax credit of 10 percent. The new equipment will replace an existing machine that has a remaining useful life of five years but could be sold today for $50,000. The undepreciated capital cost of the existing machine is $34,532. The new machine will result in changes to sales and costs for the five years of the asset's life as shown below. With the increasing sales, current assets are expected to increase by $40,000. In addition, accounts payable will increase by $15,000. At the end of five years, the new equipment is expected to have a salvage value of $35,000. The firm's tax rate is 40 percent and their cost of capital is 18 percent.

Year	Increase in revenue	Change in costs
1	$ 85,000	–$15,000
2	105,000	–5,000
3	115,000	+15,000
4	95,000	+25,000
5	95,000	+35,000

a. Calculate the yearly incremental after-tax cash inflows associated with this machine for the five years of its useful life.
b. If you were required to compute the NPV for this piece of equipment, how would your analysis differ from the process used to solve part **a**? Why would you approach the problem in this manner?
c. Compute the NPV for this piece of equipment. Should Laidlaw purchase this new piece of equipment? Explain.

ST 12–2 All techniques with NPV profile—Mutually exclusive projects Fitch Industries is evaluating two equal-risk, mutually exclusive capital budgeting projects—M and N. The relevant cash flows for each project are shown in the following table. The firm's cost of capital is 14 percent.

	Project M	Project N
Incremental cost	$28,500	$27,000
Year (t)	Cash inflows (CF_t)	
1	$10,000	$11,000
2	10,000	10,000
3	10,000	9,000
4	10,000	8,000

a. Calculate each project's payback period.
b. Calculate the net present value (NPV) for each project.
c. Calculate the internal rate of return (IRR) for each project using NPV profiles.
d. Draw the net present value profiles for each project on the same set of axes, and explain the circumstances under which a conflict in rankings might exist.
e. Summarize the preferences dictated by each measure calculated above, and indicate which project you would recommend. Explain why.

PROBLEMS

BASIC LG2 **12–1** **NPV** Calculate the net present value (NPV) for the following 20-year projects. Comment on the acceptability of each. Assume that the firm has cost of capital of 14 percent.

a. Incremental cost is $10,000; cash inflows are $2,000 per year.
b. Incremental cost is $25,000; cash inflows are $3,000 per year.
c. Incremental cost is $30,000; cash inflows are $5,000 per year.

BASIC LG2 **12–2** **NPV for varying costs of capital** Dane Cosmetics is evaluating a new fragrance-mixing machine. The machine's cost is $24,000 and will generate after-tax cash inflows of $5,000 per year for 8 years. For each of the costs of capital listed, (1) calculate the net present value (NPV), (2) indicate whether to accept or reject the machine, and (3) explain your decision.

a. The cost of capital is 10 percent.
b. The cost of capital is 12 percent.
c. The cost of capital is 14 percent.

BASIC LG2 **12–3** **Net present value—Independent projects** Using a 14 percent cost of capital, calculate the net present value for each of the independent projects shown in the following table and indicate whether or not each is acceptable.

	Project A	Project B	Project C	Project D	Project E
Incremental cost (C_0)	$26,000	$500,000	$170,000	$950,000	$80,000
Year (t)	Total cash inflows (CF_t)				
1	$4,000	$100,000	$20,000	$230,000	$ 0
2	4,000	120,000	19,000	230,000	0
3	4,000	140,000	18,000	230,000	0
4	4,000	160,000	17,000	230,000	20,000
5	4,000	180,000	16,000	230,000	30,000
6	4,000	200,000	15,000	230,000	0
7	4,000		14,000	230,000	50,000
8	4,000		13,000	230,000	60,000
9	4,000		12,000		70,000
10	4,000		11,000		

BASIC  12–4 **NPV, with rankings** Botany Bay, Inc., a maker of ship supplies, is considering four projects. Because of past financial problems, the company has a high cost of capital at 15 percent. Which of these projects would be acceptable under those cost circumstances?

	Project A	Project B	Project C	Project D
Incremental cost	$50,000	$100,000	$80,000	$180,000
Year (t)	Cash inflows (CF_t)			
1	$20,000	$35,000	$20,000	$100,000
2	20,000	50,000	40,000	80,000
3	20,000	50,000	60,000	60,000

a. Calculate the NPV of each project using a cost of capital of 15 percent.
b. Rank acceptable projects by NPV.
c. At what approximate cost of capital would all of the projects be acceptable?

INTERMEDIATE  12–5 **Basic capital budgeting process and minimum acceptable NPV** Musoka Hobbycats is evaluating an investment project with an incremental cost of $92,000 and an expected life of 10 years. The incremental sales are expected to be $38,000 per year and the company's operating costs are 48 percent of sales. These are the only benefits of the project. Musoka's cost of capital is 14 percent and the company tax rate is 20 percent.
a. Determine the NPV for this project.
b. For this project to be acceptable,
i. What would the expected life of the project have to be?
ii. What would the incremental cost of the project have to be?
iii. What would the incremental after-tax operating income have to be?
iv. What would the incremental before-tax operating income have to be?
v. What would the incremental sales have to be?
vi. What would Musoka's cost of capital have to be? Explain each of your answers, indicating why the project is acceptable.

INTERMEDIATE  12–6 **NPV** Simes Innovations, Inc., is negotiating to purchase exclusive rights to manufacture and market a solar-powered toy car. To acquire the rights, the car's inventor has given Simes the choice of making either a one-time payment of $1,875,000 today or a series of 5 year-end payments of $481,250. In either case the payments would be treated as an operating expense. Simes' tax rate is 20 percent, while their cost of capital is 9 percent.
a. Which payment option should the company choose?
b. What yearly payment would make the two offers identical?
c. Would your answer to part **a** be different if the yearly payments were made at the beginning of each year? Show your work.
d. If Simes acquires the rights to the car, the new project will result in incremental before-tax cash inflows of $312,500 per year for 15 years. Will this factor change the firm's decision as to how to acquire the rights to the car? Explain?

BASIC

12–7 Incremental cost Cushing Corporation is considering the purchase of a new grading machine to replace the existing one. The existing machine was purchased 3 years ago at an installed cost of $20,000. The existing machine is expected to have a useful life of at least 5 more years. The new machine costs $35,000 and requires $5,000 in installation costs. The existing machine can currently be sold for $13,500 without incurring any removal or cleanup costs. Both assets have a CCA rate of 20 percent. Calculate the UCC of the existing asset and the incremental cost associated with the proposed purchase of a new grading machine.

INTERMEDIATE

12–8 Incremental operating cash inflows Strong Tool Company has been considering replacing an existing lathe that could be used for 5 more years. The UCC of the lathe is $974 while its current market value is $10,000. The new lathe will cost $70,000, will have a 5-year life, and has a CCA rate of 15 percent. The firm estimates that the operating revenues and expenses for the new and the old lathes will be as shown in the following table. The firm's tax rate is 40 percent.

	New lathe		Old lathe	
Year	Sales	Operating expenses	Sales	Operating expenses
1	$60,000	$30,000	$35,000	$20,000
2	70,000	30,000	38,000	20,000
3	75,000	30,000	42,000	23,000
4	80,000	30,000	45,000	25,000
5	82,000	30,000	50,000	30,000

a. Calculate the CCA that can be claimed on the new lathe for its 5-year life.
b. Calculate the incremental operating cash inflows resulting from the proposed lathe replacement.
c. Depict on a time line the incremental operating cash inflows calculated in **b.**
d. Calculate the value of the new lathe using the cash inflows calculated in **b.** The firm's cost of capital is 10 percent. Should the firm replace the lathe?
e. What is wrong with the analysis completed in part **d**?

BASIC

12–9 Relevant cash flow pattern fundamentals For each of the following projects, determine the *relevant cash flows,* classify the cash flow pattern, and depict the cash flows on a time line.

a. A project with an incremental cost of $120,000 that generates annual operating cash inflows of $25,000 for the next 18 years.
b. A new machine having an installed cost of $85,000. Sale of the old machine will yield $30,000 after removal costs. Operating cash inflows generated by the replacement will exceed the operating cash inflows of the old machine by $20,000 in each year of a 6-year period. At the end of year 6, sale of the new machine will yield $20,000, which is $10,000 greater than the proceeds expected from the old machine had it been retained and sold at the end of year 6.
c. An asset with an incremental cost of $2 million that will yield annual operating cash inflows of $300,000 for each of the next 10 years. Operating cash outlays will be $20,000 for each year except year 6, when an overhaul

requiring an additional cash outlay of $500,000 will be required. The asset's market value at the end of year 10 is expected to be $75,000.

BASIC

12–10 **Expansion versus replacement cash flows** Edison Systems has estimated the after-tax operating cash inflows over the 5-year lives for two projects, A and B, which are summarized in the following table.

	Project A	Project B
Incremental cost	$40,000	$12,000
Year	**After-tax cash inflows**	
1	$10,000	$ 6,000
2	12,000	6,000
3	14,000	6,000
4	16,000	6,000
5	10,000	6,000

a. If the projects were independent, which should the company select assuming the firm's cost of capital is 10 percent? Explain.
b. If project A were actually a *replacement* for project B and if the $12,000 cost shown for B was the cash inflow expected from selling it, what would be the relevant incremental cost and after-tax cash inflows for this replacement decision?

BASIC

12–11 **Change in net working capital calculation** Samuels Manufacturing is considering the purchase of a new machine to replace one they feel is obsolete. The firm has total current assets of $920,000 and total current liabilities of $640,000. As a result of the proposed replacement, the following *changes* are anticipated in the levels of the current asset and current liability accounts noted.

Account	Change
Accruals	+ $ 40,000
Marketable securities	0
Inventories	− 10,000
Accounts payable	+ 90,000
Line of credit	+ 45,000
Accounts receivable	+ 150,000
Cash	+ 15,000

a. Using the information given, calculate the change, if any, in net working capital that is expected to result from the proposed replacement action.
b. Explain why a change in these current accounts would be relevant in determining the initial investment for the proposed capital expenditure.
c. Would the change in net working capital enter into any of the other cash flow components comprising the relevant cash flows for the project? Explain.

  BASIC

12–12 Calculating incremental cost Vastine Medical, Inc., is considering replacing its existing computer system which was purchased 2 years ago for a cost of $350,000. The system can be sold today for $200,000. The system is a Class 10 asset with a CCA rate of 30 percent. A new computer system will cost $500,000 to purchase and install. Replacement of the computer system would not involve any change in net working capital.

a. Calculate the book value (UCC) of the existing computer system.

b. Calculate the incremental cost associated with the replacement project.

   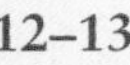  INTERMEDIATE

12–13 Integrative—Complete investment decision Wells Printing is considering the purchase of a new printing press. The total installed cost of the press is $2.2 million. This outlay would be partially offset by the sale of an existing press. The old press cost $2.1 million 10 years ago, and can be sold currently for $1.2 million. As a result of the new press, sales in each of the next 5 years are expected to increase by $1.6 million, while operating costs are 50 percent of sales. The new press will not affect the firm's net working capital requirements. The CCA rate on the press is 15 percent. The firm's tax rate is 40 percent. Wells Printing's cost of capital is 11 percent.

a. Determine the incremental cost of the new press.

b. Determine the incremental after-tax operating income and the tax shield on the new press for the 5-year life of the new press.

c. Determine the payback period of the new press.

d. Determine the net present value (NPV) and the internal rate of return (IRR) for the new press.

e. Make a recommendation to accept or reject the new press, and justify your answer.

12–14 Basic terminology A firm is considering the following three separate situations.

Situation A Build either a small office building or a retail store on a parcel of land located in a high-traffic area. The office building will cost $620,000 and is expected to provide before-tax cash inflows of $90,000 per year for 20 years. The retail store is expected to cost $500,000 and to provide a growing stream of before-tax cash inflows over its 20-year life. The initial operating cash inflow is $50,000 and will increase by 5 percent each year.

Situation B Replace a machine with a new one costing $60,000 and providing operating cash inflows of $15,000 per year for the first 5 years. The current value of the old machine is $10,000. At the end of year 5, a machine overhaul costing $20,000 is required. After it is completed, expected operating cash inflows are $10,000 in year 6; $7,000 in year 7; $4,000 in year 8; and $1,000 in year 9, at the end of which the machine will be scrapped for $10,000.

Situation C Invest in any combination of the four machines whose relevant cash flows are given in the following table. The firm has $500,000 budgeted to fund these machines, all of which are known to be acceptable. The cost for each machine is $250,000.

Year	Operating cash inflows			
	Machine 1	Machine 2	Machine 3	Machine 4
1	$ 50,000	$70,000	$65,000	$90,000
2	70,000	70,000	65,000	80,000
3	90,000	70,000	90,000	70,000
4	−30,000	70,000	90,000	60,000
5	150,000	70,000	−20,000	50,000

For each situation or project, indicate

a. Whether the *situation* is independent or mutually exclusive.

b. Whether the availability of funds is unlimited or if capital rationing exists.

c. Whether accept–reject or ranking decisions are required.

d. Whether each *project's* cash flow pattern is an annuity or a mixed stream.

e. Now assume that the firm's tax rate is 20 percent and for Situation A, the firm's cost of capital is 10 percent. For the office building project, calculate the payback period, NPV, and IRR. For the convenience store, calculate the present value of the after-tax cash inflows for the first 5 years of the project's life. If you were asked to calculate the NPV and IRR of this project, what would be the easiest way to do this?

f. Assume for Situation B that the cash inflows are after-tax. The firm's cost of capital for this project is 10 percent. Calculate the NPV for Situation B.

g. For Situation C, assume the cash inflows are after-tax and the company's cost of capital is 10 percent. Determine the payback period, NPV, and IRR for each machine. Develop NPV profiles for all four machines.

i. If the four machines were independent projects, which should be selected?

ii. If the four machines were independent, but the company had $1 million of funds available, which machines should be selected? Explain.

iii. If the machines were mutually exclusive, which machine should be selected? Explain the reason for your answer.

BASIC

12–15 Payback and NPV Neil Corporation has three projects under consideration. The cash flows for each of them are shown in the following table. The firm has a 16 percent cost of capital.

	Project A	Project B	Project C
Incremental cost	$40,000	$40,000	$40,000
Year (t)	Cash inflows (CF_t)		
1	$13,000	$ 7,000	$19,000
2	13,000	10,000	16,000
3	13,000	13,000	13,000
4	13,000	16,000	10,000
5	13,000	19,000	7,000

a. Calculate each project's payback period. Which project is preferred according to this method?

b. Calculate each project's net present value (NPV). Which project is preferred according to this method?
c. Comment on your findings in **a** and **b**, and recommend the best project. Explain your recommendation.

INTERMEDIATE

12–16 **All techniques, conflicting rankings** Nicholson Roofing Materials, Inc., is considering two mutually exclusive projects, each with an incremental cost of $150,000. The company's board of directors has set a 4-year payback requirement and the company's cost of capital is 9 percent. The cash inflows associated with the two projects are as follows:

	Cash inflows (CF_t)	
Year	Project A	Project B
1	$45,000	$75,000
2	45,000	60,000
3	45,000	30,000
4	45,000	30,000
5	45,000	30,000
6	45,000	30,000

a. Calculate the payback period for each project.
b. Calculate the NPV of each project.
c. Calculate the IRR of each project. Develop an NPV profile.
d. Rank the projects using each of the techniques. Make and justify a recommendation.

BASIC

12–17 **Payback, NPV, and IRR** Rieger International is attempting to evaluate the feasibility of investing $95,000 in a piece of equipment having a 5-year life. The firm has estimated the *cash inflows* associated with the proposal as shown in the following table. The firm has a 12 percent cost of capital.

Year (t)	Cash inflows (CF_t)
1	$20,000
2	25,000
3	30,000
4	35,000
5	40,000

a. Calculate the payback period for the proposed investment.
b. Calculate the net present value (NPV) for the proposed investment.
c. Calculate the internal rate of return (IRR) for the proposed investment using an NPV profile.
d. Evaluate the acceptability of the proposed investment using NPV and IRR. What recommendation would you make relative to implementation of the project? Why?

BASIC

12–18 **All techniques** Pound Industries is attempting to select the best of three mutually exclusive projects. The incremental cost and after-tax cash inflows associated with each project are shown in the following table.

Cash flows	Project A	Project B	Project C
Incremental cost	$60,000	$100,000	$110,000
Cash inflows (*CF*), years 1–5	$20,000	$ 31,500	$ 32,500

a. Calculate the payback period for each project.
b. Calculate the net present value (NPV) of each project, assuming that the firm has a cost of capital equal to 13 percent.
c. Calculate the internal rate of return (IRR) for each project using an NPV profile.
d. Summarize the preferences dictated by each measure, and indicate which project you would recommend. Explain why.

BASIC

12–19 **All techniques** Projects A and B are equal-risk alternatives for expanding the firm's capacity. The firm's cost of capital is 13 percent. The after-tax cash inflows for each project are shown in the following table.

	Project A	Project B
Incremental cost	$80,000	$50,000
Year (t)	After-tax cash inflows (CF_t)	
1	$15,000	$15,000
2	20,000	15,000
3	25,000	15,000
4	30,000	15,000
5	35,000	15,000

a. Calculate each project's payback period.
b. Calculate the net present value (NPV) for each project.
c. Calculate the internal rate of return (IRR) for each project using an NPV profile.
d. Summarize the preferences dictated by each measure, and indicate which project you would recommend. Explain why.

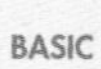 

BASIC

12–20 **Calculating operating income** Vegan Foods has a choice of two projects. Project A will result in sales increasing by $100,000. Project B will result in operating costs decreasing by $100,000. Operating costs are 35 percent of sales and the company's tax rate is 25 percent. Which project generates higher incremental after-tax operating income? Explain why this is the case.

INTERMEDIATE 

12–21 **Sunk costs and opportunity costs** Masters Golf Products, Inc., spent 3 years and $1,000,000 to develop its new line of club heads to replace a line that is becoming obsolete. In order to begin manufacturing the new line, the company will have to invest $1,800,000 in new equipment. The new clubs are expected to generate an increase in operating cash inflows of $750,000 per year for the next

10 years. The company has determined that the existing line could be sold to a competitor for $250,000. In addition, rather than developing the new golf club line itself, Masters could sell the rights to the line for $400,000.

a. How should the $1,000,000 in development costs be classified?

b. How should the $250,000 sale price for the existing line be classified?

c. How should the $400,000 selling price for the rights to the new line be treated?

d. Depict all of the known relevant cash flows on a time line.

BASIC LG3 **12–22** **CCA** A firm is evaluating the acquisition of an asset that costs $64,000 and requires $4,000 in installation costs. If this is a class 43 asset, determine the CCA the firm can claim for each of the first 5 years.

BASIC LG3 **12–23** **Calculating CCA and tax shield** Asto Company just purchased a class 17 asset at a cost of $175,000. Asto Company's tax rate is 26 percent.

a. Calculate the amount of CCA Asto could claim for the first 4 years of the asset's life. (See Chapter 2 for CCA rates for the various asset classes.)

b. How much tax shield would the company receive each year?

c. Explain what is meant by the term tax shield and why it is treated as a cash inflow for capital budgeting purposes.

INTERMEDIATE LG3 **12–24** **Calculating CCA, ITC, and tax shield** For Asto Company in the above question, assume the class 17 asset being purchased at a cost of $175,000 is replacing another class 17 asset. The current asset has a book value of $33,426, but it could be sold for $22,000. The new asset qualifies for an ITC of 10 percent. For capital budgeting purposes, answer the following questions:

a. What is the incremental cost of the new asset?

b. What is the incremental amount of UCC that will be added to the class 17 asset class?

c. Calculate the amount of CCA and the tax shield from the CCA for the first four years of the asset's life.

INTERMEDIATE LG3 **12–25** **Determining operating cash flows** Scenic Tours, Inc., located in Moncton, New Brunswick, is a provider of bus tours throughout the New England area. The corporation is considering replacing 10 of its older buses. The existing buses were purchased 4 years ago at a total cost of $2,700,000. The new buses would have larger passenger capacity and better fuel efficiency as well as lower maintenance costs. The total cost for 10 new buses is $3,000,000. Currently the old buses could be sold for $1,100,000. The CCA rate on the buses is 30 percent and Scenic Tours tax rate is 40 percent. The following table presents sales and operating expenses for the new and old buses for their 6-year operational lives.

a. Use all of the information given to calculate the incremental after-tax cash inflows for the proposed purchase of new buses for 6 years.

b. Should Scenic Tours replace the existing buses with the new buses, assuming the firm's cost of capital is 9 percent? Explain.

	Year					
	1	2	3	4	5	6
With the proposed new buses						
Sales	$1,850,000	$1,850,000	$1,830,000	$1,825,000	$1,815,000	$1,800,000
−Expenses	460,000	460,000	468,000	472,000	485,000	500,000
With the present buses						
Sales	$1,800,000	$1,800,000	$1,790,000	$1,785,000	$1,775,000	$1,750,000
−Expenses	500,000	510,000	520,000	520,000	530,000	535,000

INTERMEDIATE  12–26 **Comparing cash flows and profitability** Radeon Corp. is considering replacing an existing piece of production equipment. The current equipment generates sales of $1,500,000 per year, while operating costs are $1,050,000. Sales for the new production equipment will total $1,900,000 with costs of $1,100,000. The CCA on the old equipment is $35,000 but will be $175,000 on the new. The company's tax rate is 30 percent. Calculate the incremental profitability and cash inflows on the new production equipment for the first year of its life.

INTERMEDIATE  12–27 **Sunk costs and opportunity costs** Covol Industries is developing the relevant cash flows associated with the proposed replacement of an existing machine tool with a new technologically advanced one. Given the following costs related to the proposed project, explain whether each would be treated as a *sunk cost* or an *opportunity cost* in developing the relevant cash flows associated with the proposed replacement decision.

a. Covol would be able to use the same tooling on the new machine tool as it had used on the old one. The original cost of the machine tools was $105,000. The tools now have a book value (UCC) of $32,509, and a market value of $22,000.

b. Covol would be able to use its existing computer system to develop programs for operating the new machine tool. The old machine tool did not require these programs. Although the firm's computer has excess capacity available, the capacity could be leased to another firm for an annual fee of $17,000.

c. Covol would have to obtain additional floor space to accommodate the larger new machine tool. The space that would be used is currently being leased to another company for $10,000 per year.

d. Covol would use a small storage facility to store the increased output of the new machine tool. The storage facility was built by Covol at a cost of $120,000 three years earlier. Because of its unique configuration and location, it is currently of no use to either Covol or any other firm.

e. Covol would have to retain an existing overhead crane, which it had planned to sell for its $180,000 market value. Although the crane was not needed with the old machine tool, it would be used to position raw materials on the new machine tool.

BASIC

12–28 **NPV and IRR** Benson Designs has prepared the following estimates for a long-term project it is considering. The initial cost is $18,250, and the project is expected to yield after-tax cash inflows of $4,000 per year for 7 years. The firm has a 10 percent cost of capital.

a. Determine the net present value (NPV) for the project.
b. Determine the internal rate of return (IRR) for the project.
c. Would you recommend that the firm accept or reject the project? Explain your answer.

CHALLENGE

12–29 Marcus Tube, a manufacturer of high-quality aluminum tubing, has maintained stable sales and profits over the past 10 years. Although the market for aluminum tubing has been expanding by 3 percent per year, Marcus has been unsuccessful in sharing this growth. To increase its sales, the firm is considering an aggressive marketing campaign that centres on regularly running ads in all relevant trade journals and exhibiting products at all major regional and national trade shows.

The campaign will begin immediately and will require a tax-deductible expenditure of $300,000 per year over each of the next five years. Sales are currently $20 million per year and if the proposed marketing campaign is not initiated, sales are expected to remain at this level for the foreseeable future. With the marketing campaign, sales are expected to rise to the levels shown in the following table for each of the next five years. To maintain sales at the year-5 level for the following ten years (year 6 to year 15), an ongoing yearly marketing expenditure of $100,000 will be required.

Cost of goods sold is expected to remain at 80 percent of sales; general and administrative expense (exclusive of any marketing campaign outlays) is expected to remain at 10 percent of sales; and annual amortization expense is expected to remain at $500,000. With sales increasing, Marcus Tube will be required to invest additional funds in working capital. The yearly investment in net working capital will be 10 percent of the increase in yearly sales. Marcus Tube's tax rate is 40 percent, and their cost of capital is 12 percent.

a. Should Marcus Tube proceed with the proposed marketing campaign? Explain.

Sales Forecast
Marcus Tube

Year	Sales
1	$20,500,000
2	21,000,000
3	21,500,000
4	22,500,000
5	23,500,000

   CHALLENGE

12–30 **Integrative—Investment decision** Holliday Manufacturing is considering replacing an existing machine. The new machine costs $1.2 million and requires installation costs of $150,000. The existing machine is 2 years old, cost $800,000 new, and has a book value (UCC) of $367,962. The current market value of the machine is $185,000. The machine could be used for 5 more years, when it would be worth $50,000. Over its 5-year life, the new machine should reduce operating costs by $350,000 per year. The CCA rate on the machine is 30 percent. The new machine could be sold for $250,000, net of removal and cleanup costs, at the end of 5 years. An increased investment in net working capital of $25,000 will be needed to support operations if the new machine is acquired. The firm has a 9 percent cost of capital and a 40 percent tax rate.

a. Determine the net present value (NPV) of the proposal.

b. Determine the internal rate of return (IRR) of the proposal.

c. Make a recommendation to accept or reject the replacement proposal, and justify your answer.

d. What is the highest cost of capital the firm could have and still accept the proposal? Explain.

12–31 **Tax value** Find the tax value (UCC) for each of the assets shown in the following table, assuming that the maximum amount of CCA was claimed each year.

Asset	Installed cost	Asset class	CCA rate	Elapsed time since purchase
A	$ 950,000	1	4%	15 years
B	40,000	6	10	4
C	96,000	8	20	6
D	350,000	10	30	1
E	1,500,000	16	40	9

CHALLENGE 

12–32 **Integrative—Determining NPV** Irvin Enterprises has been evaluating an investment project that will use a warehouse the company currently owns but is not using. This project will require an immediate capital expenditure of $1 million for required equipment. The unused warehouse will require very little work in order for the equipment to be put into operation. Irvin has no other intended use for the warehouse but the company has been renting the warehouse for $70,000 a year.

For the project, Irvin will also use equipment that was purchased a year ago for $525,000, but which has yet to be used. The equipment is highly technical and Irvin has no other use for it. Over the year of ownership the equipment has significantly declined in value. If Irvin were to sell the equipment, the most they would receive is $300,000. The equipment has yet to have any CCA charged against the original purchase price.

The incremental operating income for the project is expected to be $355,000 a year for 6 years, at which time it will increase to $425,000 a year for another 6 years. At the end of the project's life, all of the equipment used for the project is expected to have a market value of only $110,000. With sales increasing, the company will be required to invest an additional $160,000 in current assets. Accounts payable and accruals are also expected to increase by a total of $60,000. The CCA rate on all of the equipment is 30 percent. Irvin's tax rate is 39 percent and their cost of capital is 14 percent.

a. Should Irvin proceed with the new project?

b. If Irvin's cost of capital was not constant over the life of the project, how could this be handled within your analysis?

INTERMEDIATE  12–33 **Integrative—Determining NPV** Lombard Company is contemplating the purchase of a new high-speed widget grinder to replace the existing grinder. The existing grinder was purchased 2 years ago at an installed cost of $60,000. The existing grinder could be used for 5 more years. The new grinder costs $105,000 and requires $5,000 in installation costs; it has a 5-year life. The existing grinder can currently be sold for $70,000 but removal and cleanup costs will total $42,000.

To support the increased business resulting from purchase of the new grinder, accounts receivable would increase by $40,000, inventories by $30,000, and accounts payable by $58,000. At the end of 5 years, the existing grinder is expected to have a market value of zero; the new grinder would be sold to net $29,000 after removal and cleanup costs. Grinders are considered a Class 8 asset with a CCA rate of 20 percent. Lombard's tax rate is 40 percent and cost of capital is 12 percent. The estimated operating income over the 5 years for both the new and existing grinder are shown in the following table.

	Operating income before taxes	
Year	New grinder	Existing grinder
1	$43,000	$26,000
2	43,000	24,000
3	43,000	22,000
4	43,000	20,000
5	43,000	18,000

Should Lombard replace the existing grinder? Explain.

CHALLENGE  12–34 **Integrative—Determining NPV** Liam Henby, a financial analyst working for Delta Company, has developed an excellent investment proposal that his boss, the VP of Finance, wishes him to analyze. The VP also wants Liam to recommend whether the company should proceed with the project. The VP will take this recommendation to the company's CEO. Liam has approached you to help him complete the task.

The project involves the production of components for the wireless communication business and requires a two-year development period. The project requires the immediate purchase of land costing $600,000. A specialized building will be constructed over the next year with payment of $1.1 million due in exactly one year. Testing will begin at this point, and after a year the machinery required to produce the components will be purchased at a cost of $175,000. Payment is due at the end of the second year.

Sales will begin in the third year and, as is usual, sales and expenses will be deemed to be received at the end of each year. For each year of the 10-year life of the project, sales are expected to be $900,000 while operating expenses will be $325,000. These are the averages of the estimates obtained from the marketing staff and the production department. In addition, to support the increased sales, the firm will have to invest $250,000 in current assets, while payables and accruals are expected to increase by a total of $80,000.

After ten years of sales, the project will be terminated. Proceeds from the sale of the building are expected to be $500,000, but Delta Company will be required to spend $200,000 to complete an environmental cleanup. In addition, it will cost $75,000 to have the building moved off the site. The machinery will have a scrap value of $50,000. The land on which the building sat is expected to appreciate in value at an average rate of 9 percent per year. The CCA rate on the building is 4 percent and is 30 percent on the machinery. Delta Company's cost of capital is 15 percent and the company's tax rate is 40 percent. Note that only one-half of capital gains are taxable.

Analyze this project for Liam Henby and develop the recommendation that Liam should present to the VP of finance. Be sure to provide a complete rationale for your recommendation.

CHALLENGE  12–35 **Integrative—Determining NPV** The Alberta Development Corporation (ADC) is investigating whether they should replace an existing piece of machinery with a technically superior product. The current machine is used to process heavy oil extract and costs $800,000 per year to operate. Its current tax value (UCC) is $125,156 and it could conceivably last an additional 20 years with minimal repairs.

Two machines are currently available that meet the specifications set out by ADC's engineers: Machine X costs $500,000, Machine Y $850,000. Both are expected to have lives of 20 years. The cost of operating Machine X is estimated to be $740,000 per year, while Machine Y is expected to cost $690,000 per year to operate over its economic life.

If the current machine is traded in on Machine X, ADC will receive $50,000 for it. If it is traded in on Machine Y, ADC will receive $75,000. These machines are Class 8 assets with a CCA rate of 20 percent. Machine X is anticipated to have a salvage value of $20,000 and Machine Y a salvage value of $75,000 at the end of their respective lives. ADC's marginal rate of tax is 40 percent and their cost of capital is 14 percent.

a. Which machine would you recommend the company purchase? Explain.

b. Assuming that both machines qualify for a 10 percent ITC, how would this change your analysis?

c. If the current machine could no longer be operated, would this change your decision? Explain.

CHALLENGE  12–36 **Integrative—Determining NPV** MFC Ltd. is considering introducing a new product. It will take two years to develop the new product at a total cost of $1,100,000. Of this amount, $850,000 will be spent immediately and capitalized in a CCA class that has a CCA rate of 15 percent. This expenditure qualifies for a scientific research investment tax credit (ITC) of 35 percent. The remainder of the project's total cost will be spent on a marketing campaign in year 3 of the project's life.

After the 2-year development period, sales of the new product will begin in Year 3. The marketing department estimates that sales will be $480,000 per year. The new product will then be produced and sold for 15 years. The direct costs of the product are expected to be 30 percent of sales. Yearly marketing expenses will be $100,000 per year. To support the product's sales, the firm will have to invest $175,000 in current assets, while payables and accruals are expected to increase by a total of $65,000. At the end of the project's life, the salvage value of the assets purchased is expected to be $150,000.

The company is located in northern Ontario, and to encourage the company's expansion, the provincial government has indicated they are willing to provide a non-taxable property tax rebate of $40,000 per year for the life of the project. MFC's cost of capital is 12 percent, while their tax rate is 22 percent. Should MFC develop and market the new product?

INTERMEDIATE

12–37 Integrative—Determining NPV Atlantic Drydock, located in Georgetown, Prince Edward Island, is considering replacing an existing hoist with one of two newer, more efficient pieces of equipment. The existing hoist is 3 years old, cost $32,000, and has a remaining usable life of 5 years. Hoist A, one of the two possible replacement hoists, costs $40,000 to purchase and $8,000 to install. The other hoist, B, costs $54,000 to purchase and $6,000 to install. Both hoists have 5-year lives and are Class 7 assets with CCA rates of 15 percent. The hoists will qualify for a 10 percent ITC.

Increased investments in net working capital will accompany the decision to acquire hoist A or hoist B. Purchase of hoist A would result in a $4,000 increase in net working capital; hoist B would result in a $6,000 increase in net working capital. The projected operating income with each alternative hoist and the existing hoist are given in the following table.

	Operating income before taxes		
Year	With hoist A	With hoist B	With existing hoist
1	$21,000	$22,000	$14,000
2	21,000	24,000	14,000
3	21,000	26,000	14,000
4	21,000	26,000	14,000
5	21,000	26,000	14,000

The existing hoist can currently be sold for $18,000. At the end of 5 years, the existing hoist could be sold to net $1,000. Hoists A and B could be sold to net $12,000 and $20,000, respectively, at the end of their 5-year lives. The firm's cost of capital is 14 percent and their tax rate is 26 percent.

a. Should Atlantic Drydock replace the existing hoist? If so, which hoist do you recommend, A or B? Why?

BASIC LG5 **12–38** **Payback period** Jordan Enterprises is considering a capital expenditure that requires an initial investment of $42,000 and returns after-tax cash inflows of $7,000 per year for 10 years. The firm has a maximum acceptable payback period of 8 years.

a. Determine the payback period for this project.
b. Should the company accept the project? Why or why not?

BASIC LG5 **12–39** **Calculating IRR** Wagner Plows is evaluating the investment in a new computer system with an expected cost of $20,000. The project has a 3-year life and is expected to generate the following after-tax cash inflows:

Year	Cash inflow
1	$11,000
2	9,000
3	5,800

a. Calculate the payback period for this project.
b. Using an NPV profile, determine the IRR for this project. Provide both a table and a graph. Provide your answer to the nearest tenth of a decimal point. If the firm's cost of capital was 12.6 percent, should Wagner invest in the project? Explain.

BASIC LG5 **12–40** **Payback comparisons** Nova Products is considering investing in two new assets and must decide what they should do. To make the decision, the company plans to use the payback period as a capital budgeting technique. Nova Products has a 5-year maximum acceptable payback period. The first asset's incremental cost is $14,000. The asset is expected to generate after-tax cash inflows of $3,000 for each of the 7 years of the asset's life. The second asset's incremental cost is $21,000 and will provide after-tax cash inflows of $4,000 per year for each of its 20 years of life.

a. Determine the payback period for each asset.
b. If the assets were independent, what should Nova do? If the assets were mutually exclusive, what should Nova do?
c. If you were also told the company's cost of capital was 12 percent, what would you do with this information? Illustrate and discuss.
d. Does this problem illustrate any of the criticisms of the payback period as a method of evaluating capital budgeting projects? Discuss.

INTERMEDIATE LG5 **12–41** **Payback period and NPV** Shell Camping Gear, Inc., is considering two mutually exclusive projects. Each has an incremental cost of $100,000. John Shell, president of the company, has set a maximum payback period of 4 years. The after-tax cash inflows associated with each project are as follows:

Year	After-tax cash inflows (CF_t) Project A	Project B
1	$10,000	$40,000
2	20,000	30,000
3	30,000	20,000
4	40,000	10,000
5	20,000	20,000

a. Determine the payback period of each project. Which should be selected and why?
b. Determine the NPV of each project assuming the firm's cost of capital is 9 percent. Which project should be selected?
c. Based on your answers above, comment on the payback period as a capital budgeting technique.

INTERMEDIATE LG5 12–42 **IRR—Mutually exclusive projects** Bell Manufacturing is attempting to choose the better of two mutually exclusive projects for expanding the firm's warehouse capacity. The relevant cash flows for the projects are shown in the following table. The firm's cost of capital is 13 percent.

	Project X	Project Y
Incremental cost	$500,000	$325,000
Year (t)	After-tax cash inflows (CF_t)	
1	$100,000	$140,000
2	120,000	120,000
3	150,000	95,000
4	190,000	70,000
5	250,000	50,000

a. Calculate the payback period, IRR, and NPV for the two projects. For each capital budgeting technique, which project is preferred? Which project would you recommend the company select? Explain your answer.

BASIC LG5 12–43 **IRR** Oak Enterprises is evaluating a project that will cost $61,450. The project is expected to provide after-tax cash inflows of $10,000 per year over its ten year life. Oak's cost of capital is 15 percent.
a. Determine the IRR of this project. Is it an acceptable project? Explain.
b. Assuming that the cash inflows continue to be $10,000 per year, how many *additional years* would the cash flows have to continue to make the project acceptable?
c. With the given life, cost, and cost of capital, what minimum annual cash inflow does the firm require for this project to be acceptable?

INTERMEDIATE 

LG5 12–44 **Internal rate of return** For each of the projects shown in the following table, calculate the internal rate of return (IRR) using NPV profiles. In order for all of these projects to be acceptable to a company, in what range would the company's cost of capital have to fall? Explain.

	Project A	Project B	Project C	Project D
Incremental cost	$90,000	$490,000	$20,000	$240,000
Year (t)	After-tax cash inflows (CF_t)			
1	$20,000	$150,000	$7,500	$120,000
2	25,000	150,000	7,500	100,000
3	30,000	150,000	7,500	80,000
4	35,000	150,000	7,500	60,000
5	40,000	—	7,500	—

INTERMEDIATE

12–45 **Calculating cash flows** Alden Ltd. is evaluating the purchase of a new machine with a cost of $200,000 and a useful life of 4 years. The new machine will replace an existing machine that still functions and has a market value of $45,000 and book value (UCC) of $25,915. The new machine qualifies for an investment tax credit (ITC) of 10 percent. The CCA rate on these machines is 25 percent. The company's tax rate is 40 percent.

Alden now sells 200,000 units of product each year at a price of $6 per unit. Variable costs of production are $3.50 per unit. If the new machine is purchased, production and sales will increase by 15,000 units per year. In addition, variable production costs will decrease by $0.10/unit. The net investment in working capital will increase by $0.16 per $1 of increased sales.

a. Calculate the relevant cash inflows for the new machine for the 4 years of its expected life.

BASIC

12–46 **Calculating NPV** Roger's Motors can immediately invest in two projects that they believe will help them increase car sales. Project A is a new, very tasteful advertising campaign designed by the firm of James and Associates. The advertising campaign will cost $18,000 to design and $50,000 to implement. These amounts will be paid to start the project and will be tax-deductible expenses. The effects of the campaign are expected to last for two years and result in 150 extra cars being sold in year 1 and 75 in year 2.

Project B is a three-week employee training seminar offered by the human relations firm of Collins and Associates. The seminar cost will be paid to start the project and will be a tax-deductible expense. Collins and Associates contend that they can turn Roger's Motors salesmen into "selling machines." The salesman training seminar will cost $50,000 to design and implement, and Collins and Associates have suggested that its effects on salesman performance will be felt for a minimum of 3 years. They contend that each salesman (Roger's has nine) will sell an additional 10 cars per year during each of the next 3 years.

The average selling price for a vehicle sold by Roger's is $14,425, while the costs incurred in acquiring and selling the car amount to $12,905. Roger's required return on investments is 14 percent and their tax rate is 40 percent.

a. Would these two projects be considered capital budgeting projects? Explain why or why not.

b. If the projects were independent, which should be selected? Why?

c. If the projects were mutually exclusive, which should be selected? Why?

INTERMEDIATE

12–47 **Replacement project** Dimples Baby Products is considering replacing a machine used in manufacturing its product "Vegey Goo," a smooth, creamy vegetable pablum for infants. The new machine will cost $200,000 and has an expected life of 10 years. At the end of this period, the machine will have a salvage value of $20,000. The tax value of the old machine is $952 while its market value is $25,000. The CCA rate on the machines is 20 percent.

The demand for "Vegey Goo" is relatively stable with sales of about 400,000 bottles per year. The product's selling price is $1.25/bottle. The new machine's increased efficiency would decrease production costs by $0.10 per bottle produced. In addition, the new machine qualifies for a 10 percent ITC. The company is in the 40 percent tax bracket and has a 10 percent cost of capital.

a. Should Dimples Baby Products replace the current machine?

INTERMEDIATE

12–48 **Calculating NPV** Pepe Ski Shop is contemplating replacing its equipment for designing custom foot beds into the linings of downhill ski boots to provide a "custom" fit. The machine currently in use was purchased eight years ago for $16,000, there is no UCC in the asset class, and the asset has a current market value of $4,200. Pepe is considering two mutually exclusive alternatives:

Alternative 1 A similar but larger capacity machine that costs $39,500 and has a CCA rate of 15 percent. Pepe estimates that this machine will increase annual revenues by $15,000 and increase annual direct expenses by $5,500 over its estimated 15-year life. To support the increased sales, Pepe will have to invest $12,000 in current assets, primarily more expensive foot beds. At the end of the 15 years, the salvage value on this machine is expected to be $2,000.

Alternative 2 The latest in custom foot bed technology: a high-pressure machine capable of forming a new ultra-light foot bed with exceptional insulation characteristics and high resistance to breakdown. The cost of the required equipment is $60,000, and the CCA rate is 25 percent. The equipment and type of foot bed are relatively untested in either production or extended use, but since ultra-light foot beds represent the frontier in ski boot technology, Pepe anticipates that cachet-conscious skiers will pay a premium for this process. As a result, he estimates that this process will provide an increase in annual revenues of $24,000 and an increase in annual direct expenses of $10,000 over the equipment's 15-year life. To support the increased sales, Pepe will have to invest $18,000 in net current assets. The equipment is expected to have zero salvage value at the end of 15 years.

Pepe estimates his cost of capital at 10 percent and has a marginal tax rate of 40 percent. Since Pepe is located in New Brunswick, both alternatives qualify for an investment tax credit of 10 percent.

a. What should Pepe do? He has offered you a new pair of foot beds if you can help him make the decision.

INTERMEDIATE

12-49 **Calculating NPV** Bo Humphries, chief financial officer of Clark Upholstery Company, expects the firm's *after-tax operating income* for the next 5 years to be as shown in the following table.

Year	After-tax operating income
1	$100,000
2	150,000
3	200,000
4	250,000
5	320,000

This income would be generated using Clark's only depreciable asset. Bo is beginning to develop the information needed to analyze whether to renew or replace this asset, a machine that originally cost $230,000 but could now be sold for $20,000. The tax value (UCC) of the machine is $66,293. Bo estimates that at the end of 5 years, the existing machine could be sold for $2,000. The following information is available for Bo to use to determine which of the two alternatives he should recommend to the company's board of directors.

Alternative 1 Renew the existing machine at a total cost of $290,000. The renewed machine would have a 5-year life. The CCA rate for the machine is 20 percent. Renewing the machine would result in the following projected sales and operating expenses for Clark Upholstery:

Year	Sales	Operating expenses
1	$1,000,000	$801,500
2	1,175,000	884,200
3	1,300,000	918,100
4	1,425,000	943,100
5	1,550,000	968,100

Since the renewed machine would result in increasing sales, an increased investment of $15,000 in net working capital would be required. At the end of 5 years, the renewed machine could be sold to net $8,000.

Alternative 2 Replace the existing machine with a new machine costing $370,000 and requiring installation costs of $50,000. The new machine would have a 5-year life. The total installed cost of the new machine qualifies for a 10 percent ITC and has a CCA rate of 20 percent. The firm's projected sales and operating expenses if it acquires the machine would be as follows:

Year	Sales	Operating expenses
1	$1,000,000	$764,500
2	1,175,000	839,800
3	1,300,000	914,900
4	1,425,000	989,900
5	1,550,000	998,900

With the new machine, the company would have to change suppliers and would be forced to pay accounts payable in a more timely manner. As a result, the new machine would result in an increased investment of $42,000 in net working capital. At the end of 5 years, the new machine could be sold to net $25,000. Clark Upholstery's cost of capital is 13 percent and the company tax rate is 25 percent.

a. Should the company replace the existing machine and, if so, which of the two alternatives should Bo recommend to Clark's board of directors?

CHALLENGE

12–50 **Calculating NPV and interest rate buydown** DCK Company is evaluating a project with an incremental cost of $500,000. Installation costs are $60,000. The incremental operating income is expected to be $80,000 per year over the project's 15-year life. The CCA rate for the asset is 25 percent. The salvage of the asset is expected to be $90,000. DCK Company's tax rate is 21 percent while their cost of capital is 12 percent.

a. Should the company acquire the asset?

b. Now assume that the company's borrowing rate is 12 percent. If the company proceeds with the project, the provincial government will provide an interest rate buydown of 9 percent on a loan of up to $300,000. The term of the loan is 15 years. This is an interest-only loan, meaning that the principal is repaid at the end of the borrowing period, in this case 15 years. So each year the company pays only interest; the principal borrowed is repaid once the loan matures. What is the impact of the interest rate buydown on the NPV of the project? *Hint:* What is the present value of the after-tax cost of a loan of $300,000 at a borrowing rate of 12 percent? Then consider: What is the present value of the after-tax cost of a loan of $300,000 at a borrowing rate of 12 percent, when you only have to pay 3 percent rather than 12 percent?

CHALLENGE

12–51 **Comprehensive** Masters Golf Products, Inc., spent three years and $1,000,000 to develop a new line of club heads to replace a existing line that is becoming obsolete. This expenditure was treated as a tax-deductible expense. In order to begin manufacturing the new club heads, the company will have to invest $1,800,000 in new equipment. The investment will occur in one year's time, when the company will stop manufacturing the current line of club heads and sales of the old line cease. Sales of the new line of club heads will begin at that time. The CCA rate on the new equipment is 20 percent, and it will qualify for a 15 percent ITC.

In addition, Masters will have to spend an additional $400,000 on R&D in year 1 and $300,000 in year 2. R&D is a tax-deductible expense in the year of the expenditure. The provincial government has indicated they will provide a non-taxable cash grant of $200,000 now and $100,000 at the end of years 1 and 2, if Masters Golf Products proceeds with the project.

The new golf club head line will generate sales for 20 years, at which time the head line will be scrapped. The following sales increases are expected once sales begin.

Year	Sales increase
1	$250,000
2	400,000
3	450,000
4	480,000
5	500,000
6–20	550,000

Masters' direct costs of production will be 34 percent. Other operating costs will total $76,000 per year, while the interest on the new golf heads will be $56,000 per year. To support the increased sales associated with the new line, additional working capital of $125,000 will be required. The company has determined that the equipment used to manufacture the existing line will be sold for $250,000. The sale will occur when the company stops manufacturing the current line in one year's time.

At the end of the project's 20-year life, the production equipment used to manufacture the new line of club heads will be worth $275,000. It will cost $75,000 to dismantle and move the equipment. Masters Golf's cost of capital is 12.5 percent and their tax rate is 32 percent.

a. Should the company manufacture the new line of golf heads? Explain your answer.

CASE CHAPTER 12 Should Diagnostic Chemicals Proceed with the Development of the DNA-Based Genetic Testing Instrument?

See the enclosed Student CD-ROM for cases that help you put theories and concepts from the text into practice.

Be sure to visit the Companion Website for this book at **www.pearsoned.ca/gitman** for a wealth of additional learning tools including self-test quizzes, Web exercises, and additional cases.

Appendix to Chapter 12

Economic Value Added—Another Way to Measure Value

A complete understanding of economic value added (EVA) involves more than knowing how to calculate EVA. It is important to know and understand how and why it was developed, what it is used for, how it can be increased, how it compares to NPV, and how it can be implemented within a firm. These topics, and more, are discussed below. The successful implementation of the EVA concept requires not only that a firm know how to calculate its economic value added but also that it understand and incorporate EVA into all of its management systems.

HISTORY OF EVA

The concept of economic value added is rooted in economic theory. It evolved from the work of two Nobel Prize–winning financial economists, Merton H. Miller and Franco Modigliani. In their academic papers, written between 1958 and 1961, these economists argued that economic income was the source of value creation in the firm. In their work, Miller and Modigliani provided information about economic income and value creation in the firm, but they did not advance a technique to measure it.[11]

It was not until many years later that such a measure was developed. The measure, known as *economic value added*, was formulated by G. Bennett Stewart III, a senior partner at New York consulting firm Stern Stewart & Co. In their financial consulting work, Stern Stewart emphasized cash flow and the *net present value of future cash flows*, a term coined by Joel Stern in 1972.[12] It was this latter financial concept that Stern Stewart used to measure changes in a company's economic income, but they believed there were two problems with this method. First, the projected cash flows are discounted to today's value rather

---

11. See "Dividend Policy, Growth, and the Valuation of Shares," *Journal of Business*, October 1961, pp. 411–433 and "The Cost of Capital, Corporation Finance and the Theory of Investment," *American Economic Review*, June 1958, pp. 261–297.

12. As reported on page 17 in Joel M. Stern and John S. Shiely (with Irwin Ross), *The EVA Challenge: Implementing Value-Added Change in an Organization* (New York: John Wiley and Sons, 2001).

than providing a historic year-to-year measure. Second, it is impossible to accurately predict the expected future cash flows.

To fill the perceived gap, Bennett Stewart began working on a way to measure economic income. Stewart followed developments in Modigliani and Miller's seminal papers on valuation and dividend policy. After stripping away the complicated mathematics, economic value added stared back at him. The concept of economic value added, or EVA, as a performance measurement tool, was introduced in 1989, has since been trademarked by Stern Stewart, and is the focus of the company's consulting work.

www.sternstewart.com

The development of EVA was motivated by two issues affecting companies. The first was the separation of ownership and control of publicly traded corporations. This results in an agency problem that may require actions to ensure management acts in the best interests of the owners of the company—the shareholders. EVA, with its focus on the maximization of shareholder wealth, can be used to deal with the agency problem by aligning the interests of managers with those of the shareholders. Decision making and incentive plans based on EVA help to keep managers focused on the ultimate goal of the company: the maximization of shareholder wealth.

The second issue was the widespread acceptance of accounting measures to determine corporate value, a purpose for which they were never intended. The importance of cash to a firm has long been recognized, yet the accounting measures of a firm's success, net income, earnings per share, and return on equity do not consider the cash flow of the firm and its ability to create wealth. A firm does not create wealth until it generates a return greater than its cost of capital—the cost of both debt and equity. Accounting measures do not consider the cost of equity and thus are not a true measure of a firm's success. A firm can be very profitable yet still destroy wealth by generating a return less than its cost of capital. EVA eliminates accounting distortions and shows a true picture of the firm's success and its ability to create wealth by including the total cost of capital in the calculation.

EVA DEFINED

EVA is a performance measure that focuses on economic profit rather than accounting profit. It allows for a look beyond headline earnings, and concentrates on free cash flow as a way to measure the value of a company. EVA captures a firm's true economic profit by recognizing that the capital used by a firm has a cost. This cost, called the *cost of capital* or *capital charge*, includes the cost of both debt and equity. EVA, over a given time period, is defined as the difference between a company's net operating profit after tax and the total cost of invested capital.

EVA is based on three concepts. The first is that cash flows are the best indicators of performance. Accounting distortions must therefore be corrected when calculating EVA. As a result, the accrual-based operating profit (EBIT) is translated into a cash-based EBIT. Second, some expenses are really investments and should be capitalized on the balance sheet. The calculation of EVA therefore involves the reclassification of some current expenses as balance sheet items. The combination of items 1 and 2, on an after-tax basis, is net operating profit after tax (NOPAT). Third, the capital invested in the business is not free and this cost must be accounted for. The EVA calculation therefore deducts a charge for the invested capital. As discussed in Chapter 9, this cost is the firm's weighted average cost of capital (WACC). A more detailed discussion of the inputs required in the EVA calculation is presented below. Using each of the above inputs, the EVA of a company can be determined as follows:

$$\text{EVA} = \text{NOPAT} - (\text{dollar amount of invested capital} \times \text{WACC\%}) \qquad (12.1\text{A})$$

A positive EVA means the company has created value above the minimum required rate of return, whereas a negative EVA means the company has fallen short of the minimum required rate of return and has thus destroyed wealth. An EVA of zero means the company is generating a return equal to the investors' required rate of return. This is acceptable, but a high positive EVA is always preferred as this is a sign of a very effective management team.

THE INPUTS REQUIRED

As discussed above, three inputs are required to calculate EVA: net operating profits after tax (NOPAT), the total invested capital, and the firm's weighted average cost of capital. While the inputs seem to be straightforward, their final determination can be quite time-consuming.

Net Operating Profit After Tax (NOPAT)

To calculate a firm's NOPAT, the starting point is the firm's earnings before interest and taxes (EBIT). If only earnings before taxes (EBT) is shown on the income statement, the company's interest expense must be added back to determine EBIT. A series of adjustments are then made to eliminate accounting distortions. If EBIT were used, the economic profit would be underestimated for two reasons. First, accounting is accrual-oriented, but EVA is cash-based. So, accrual accounting is converted to cash accounting. Often this can be done following the process covered in Chapter 2. Second, accounting rules treat many items as current expenses. But, from a shareholder's perspective, these items are assets and should be on the balance sheet. So some expenses are reclassified as investments. These capitalizing adjustments will increase both the operating profit and the invested capital.

In total, over 160 accounting "problems" have been identified that must be corrected when calculating net operating profit. For most companies using EVA, fewer than 15 adjustments are necessary. With the net operating profit determined, taxes must be subtracted to calculate the after-tax amount. But the tax rate to be used is not the rate used for book purposes, but rather the rate used when filing taxes with the government. So the overall objective of the process of calculating NOPAT is to eliminate the accounting distortions associated with the income statement.

Some examples of areas where adjustments to the income statement and balance sheets are required are for accounts such as research and development (R&D), inventory costing, amortization, bad debt reserves, operating leases, goodwill, and unusual items such as restructuring charges. For example, GAAP requires companies to expense research and development outlays even though these expenditures are investments in future products or processes. In contrast, EVA capitalizes R&D spending and amortizes it over an appropriate period.

Similar adjustments are made to the balance sheet to get a more accurate accounting of the total capital invested in an enterprise in order to assess the proper capital charge.

Total Invested Capital

There are three steps involved in the calculation of a firm's invested capital. The first step is to determine the book value of invested capital from the balance sheet. This consists of all liabilities and equity that have a cost of financing. Next, adjustments are made to match the changes that occurred in the calculation of NOPAT. Third, adjustments are made to recognize off-balance-sheet sources of funds. These last two steps involve matching the adjustments made to NOPAT with changes in balance sheet accounts. For example, in calculating NOPAT, research and development expenses are capitalized and added to the operating earnings. This capitalized research and development investment must also be added to the balance sheet and the amount of the investment will therefore be included in the cost of invested capital.

Weighted Average Cost of Capital (WACC)

The cost of capital (Stern Stewart refers to this as a *capital charge*) is included because the company must generate a return to the providers of capital, for the use of their capital. As discussed in Chapters 8 and 9, the capital the firm uses is not provided for free; it has a cost, and this cost is the provider's required rate of return. The capital charge includes the cost of interest-bearing liabilities and the cost of funds provided by preferred and common shareholders. Common equity is the most expensive form of financing. The cost is equal to the shareholders' required rate of return, or the minimum return shareholders could receive by investing in securities of similar risk. The calculation of a firm's cost of capital was discussed in detail in Chapter 9 and will not be included here.

By putting the three variables together, a company's EVA can be calculated using the formula discussed earlier. Since EVA is so important to managers and investors, it is essential that managers know how to increase the EVA of the company. For any company, a higher EVA is always better than a lower EVA. There are four ways to increase EVA:

1. Increase earnings and cash flow.
2. Reduce the dollar amount of capital employed. This can be accomplished by disposing of unnecessary or underutilized capital assets and/or through better management of working capital.
3. Lower the cost of the individual sources of financing used. This can be achieved by reducing the perceived risk of the company.
4. Allocate more capital to high-returning projects and reduce capital to low-returning activities—high EVA growth often comes from this factor alone.

USES OF EVA

EVA has many uses within a firm. As previously discussed, it provides an accurate portrayal of a firm's financial situation and its ability, or inability, to create wealth for shareholders. It also ensures that managers are working in the best interests of the shareholders, and it encourages decision makers to think about economic profits when they are evaluating new business opportunities. Other important uses of EVA include setting organizational goals, measuring performance, determining bonuses, communicating financial information to shareholders and investors, motivating managers, and for capital budgeting and corporate valuation purposes.

EVA is not only a tool managers can use to evaluate company performance, but also a popular tool employed by investors to determine the value of a company. As a performance measurement tool, EVA has two important advantages for investors. The first is that it ignores noise and emotion in the marketplace and focuses solely on whether a company is creating or destroying wealth. Second, EVA is a reliable continuous-improvement measure of performance: more EVA is always better than less, which cannot be said of some other measures. EVA has only been used as an investment tool for a short period of time, but it has proven to be a good valuation tool. A number of studies have been conducted to assess the ability of EVA to predict stock price behaviour. Most studies have concluded that EVA has superior predictive power.[13]

COMPARING EVA AND NPV

EVA shares some important similarities with net present value (NPV), another value measurement tool. First, both EVA and NPV recognize that equity has a cost to the firm and include the firm's cost of capital in the valuation analysis. EVA uses the company's cost of capital to determine the total cost of the funds invested during a given time period. NPV uses the company's cost of capital as the rate used to discount the expected cash flows back to present value.

Second, both approaches recognize the importance of the after-tax cash flows in determining value. The calculation of EVA requires that accounting adjustments be made to translate the financial statements from accrual accounting to cash-based accounting. For the NPV technique, the expected future cash flows are used in the calculation, not the net income.

Third, the conclusions drawn from the results of the calculation are similar. A positive value for EVA and NPV means the company is generating a return greater than the investors' required rate of return. As prominent management consultant and researcher Peter Drucker has written: "Until a business returns a profit that is greater than its cost of capital, it operates at a loss. Never mind that it pays taxes as if it had a genuine profit. The enterprise still returns less to the economy than it devours in resources. Until then it does not create wealth; it destroys it." Both EVA and NPV recognize that when managers employ capital they must pay for it. Businesses must view capital as an expense of doing business, just like any other expense.

A negative value for EVA and NPV is not desirable; it means the company is generating a return that is less than investors' required rate of return. A value of zero is acceptable under both approaches; it means the company is generating a return exactly equal to investors' required rate of return. Under both approaches, a higher outcome is more favourable.

---

13. For examples, see Brian A. Schofield, "EVAluating Stocks," *Canadian Investment Review*, Spring 2000; Jeffrey M. Bacidore, John A. Boquist, Todd T. Milbourn, and Anjan V. Thakor, "The Search for the Best Financial Performance Measure," *Financial Analysts Journal*, May/June 1997, pp. 11–20; and Gary C. Biddle, Robert M. Bowen, and James S. Wallace, "Evidence on EVA," *Journal of Applied Corporate Finance*, Summer 1999.

Despite the similarities, there are some important differences between NPV and EVA. One difference involves the application of the technique. While both EVA and NPV are valuation tools, EVA is most commonly used to determine whether in a given year the company added value for the providers of financing. Therefore, it relies on historical data. EVA is most commonly used as a backward-looking valuation tool. It uses actual data from a company's financial statements to determine whether the company created extra value for the providers of financing, in particular the common shareholders. In addition, EVA can be calculated every year and compared to previous years to determine if the company is continually creating value for shareholders.

In contrast, the NPV technique is future-oriented. After-tax cash flows are estimated into the future, and value is calculated on the basis of these and the firm's cost of capital. NPV can be used for a single project (asset), or for the company as a whole. When used for a single project, the estimated value of the project is compared to the cost of the project, and the NPV determined. For the company as a whole, the value of the company can be calculated and compared to the company's current market value (if the company is publicly traded) or to the asking price for the company (if it were for sale). The difference between the estimated value and the current value (actual or asking) is the NPV of the company. A positive NPV means that the estimated value is greater than the current value. If this were the case, it would be an opportune time to purchase all or a portion of the company.

So, while EVA and NPV can be used for valuation purposes, the focus is very different. EVA uses historical data, focuses on the firm as a whole, and indicates what happened in the past. The expectation is that for firms where EVA is negative, corrective actions will be taken. In contrast, NPV is future-oriented and can be used to value individual projects (assets) or the firm as a whole. The technique requires estimates of future cash flows that are used to calculate value now. Since these are only estimates, they are very subjective. Two analysts could reach two very different, but equally justifiable, conclusions even if they start with the same information.

IMPLEMENTATION OF EVA

To implement an EVA-based management and incentive compensation system, Stern Stewart recommends companies follow a process based on the "4 M's." These are:

- *Measurement:* The first step in the EVA implementation process is developing the EVA measure using the three required inputs. Adjustments to the financial statements must be made to convert them from an accounting framework to an economic framework. The necessary adjustments can vary from industry to industry and even company to company, but the overall goal of the EVA measure remains the same—to better capture the economic performance of the measured unit.
- *Management:* The management phase of the implementation process involves utilizing EVA to bring about better decision making throughout the organization. This involves the development of decision tools to help improve the analysis of business issues, and to ensure the documentation, the project approval, and the decision-making processes are consistent throughout the organization.

- *Motivation:* An important part of the EVA implementation process is the creation of incentives that are directly linked to the creation of shareholder wealth. With an EVA-based incentive plan, managers are rewarded only if they create shareholder value through continuous improvements in operating performance.
- *Mindset:* A significant amount of time and effort is spent on training and communication to shift the employee mindset to one of value creation. The key staff of the company learn about EVA concepts and corporate finance topics to create a foundation for better understanding. The EVA philosophy and its successful application are continually communicated to help keep everyone focused on these ideas.

The implementation of an EVA management system is a complex process that involves acceptance and compliance by everyone in the organization. EVA needs to be adopted, not simply calculated. It must be made the centre of a comprehensive financial management system that includes all the policies, procedures, measures, and methods companies use to guide and control their operations and strategy. The EVA mindset must permeate the whole business, including how overall financial goals are set, how the goals are communicated inside the organization and to the investment community, and how decision makers evaluate opportunities to build the business and invest capital. Everyone in the organization must accept and adopt the EVA-based management system and all employees must be included in the implementation process and receive proper training.

Due to its complexity, an EVA management system cannot be implemented overnight. For a company with sales under $250 million, implementation generally takes four to five months. For companies with up to $1 billion in sales, it might take six to nine months, and for a larger company a couple of years.

EXAMPLES OF COMPANIES THAT USE EVA

www.diageo.com

Since it was first introduced, EVA has been adopted by over 300 companies around the world, and it has proved to be beneficial. London-based Diageo PLC, the company that owns brands such as Guinness, Johnnie Walker, Smirnoff, Captain Morgan, and Cuervo, reaped the benefits of using EVA when it used the tool to determine which of its liquor brands generated the best returns. The analysis determined that because of the time required for storage and care, aged Scotch didn't generate as much value as vodka, which could be sold within weeks of being distilled. Based on the EVA analysis, management began to emphasize vodka production and sales.

Some examples of Canadian companies using EVA include Alcan Aluminum, Domtar Inc., Grand & Toy, Robin Hood Multifoods, Cogeco Inc., Long Manufacturing, and Philips Environmental. In their 2005 annual report, Alcan stated:

> The company's governing objective is to maximize value. Achieving this in today's fast-paced and highly competitive global economy requires that we identify and pursue the highest value opportunities available to us. Striving for value energizes and empowers us to rethink how we do things at Alcan. By providing a strategic framework for all decision-making with a systematic approach, we aim to generate value and earn more than the cost of our capital in every business. Delivering a

www.alcan.com

positive return on capital employed (ROCE) in excess of our cost of capital represents a very important objective for Alcan. Value impact is the decisive factor for all capital and resource allocation. Our rigorous fact-based approach helps us uncover new opportunities to create value and to identify and cease activities that do not. It keeps all of us focused on making the right decisions to improve our cash flow and generate sustainable value for our shareholders.

Domtar is also a believer in the EVA approach. As the company states in their 2005 annual report, in addition to using return on equity as an important financial metric, Domtar also uses EVA to ensure that its decision-making processes are aligned with the objective of increasing shareholder value. EVA is used at Domtar to measure performance and to evaluate investment decisions. Domtar's EVA for 2005 was negative $487 million. The 2005 results were negatively impacted by the continued strengthening of the Canadian dollar and higher costs, especially for purchased fibre, chemicals, energy, and freight. This was only partially offset by higher U.S. dollar selling prices for most of its products. In late 2005, Domtar announced a series of targeted measures aimed at returning the company to profitability. Domtar remains committed to creating long-term shareholder value and will continue to exercise financial discipline, especially with respect to capital management.

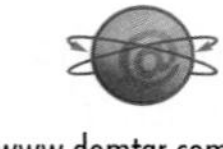
www.domtar.com

PROBLEMS

BASIC **12–1A** **Calculating EVA** Pristine Pottery Inc. is in the process of implementing an EVA-based performance measurement system. The company recorded net operating earnings before taxes of $137,600 for the 2008 fiscal year. Its costly sources of financing totalled $812,300 at year-end. Pristine Pottery has a tax rate of 22 percent and a cost of capital of 12 percent. Using an EVA analysis, determine the value created (or destroyed) by Pristine Pottery during the 2008 fiscal year.

INTERMEDIATE **12–2A** **Calculating EVA** For the 2008 fiscal year, Biomedics Inc. reported earnings before taxes of $112,455. This included an interest expense of $16,400 and a research and development expense of $120,000. Although the R&D expenditure was made in 2008, it is expected that the expense will generate benefits to the firm for 4 years. Financing for the R&D expenditure will be split equally between long-term debt and common equity. Information about the company's costly sources of financing, before any required adjustments, is shown below:

Source	Amount	Cost
Short-term debt	$ 80,000	5.2%
Long-term debt	125,000	7.1%
Preferred equity	75,000	9.2%
Common equity	248,370	15%

a. Given the information provided, what adjustments should be made to the firm's earnings before taxes and total invested capital if the firm were to use an EVA analysis to measure performance?
b. What is Biomedics' adjusted net operating profit after taxes (NOPAT) and total invested capital? Biomedics' tax rate is 22 percent.
c. Calculate Biomedics' adjusted weighted average cost of capital.
d. Calculate and evaluate Biomedics' EVA.

CHALLENGE 12–3A **Calculating EVA** Ranger Enterprising is in the process of implementing an EVA management system. Ranger's VP of Finance wishes to calculate the company's EVA for the last three fiscal years. He has collected the following information:

	2006	2007	2008
Net income	$120,685	$104,730	$78,880
Interest expense	15,700	17,100	22,050
Tax rate	20.2%	18.5%	18.5%
Accounting adjustments to the income statement	47,212	44,948	39,862
Adjusted amount of costly short-term debt	140,000	160,000	195,000
Adjusted amount of costly long-term debt	150,000	165,000	215,000
Adjusted amount of common equity	348,430	432,860	515,890
After-tax cost of short-term debt	6%	6.2%	6.3%
After-tax cost of long-term debt	7.2%	7.3%	7.4%
Cost of common equity	18%	19.2%	20.6%

a. From the above information, determine Ranger's EVA for the three years.
b. Evaluate the company's financial performance over these three years. Has it improved or gotten worse? Why?
c. How could the company improve their performance in the future?
d. If in 2008 the company reduced their assets by $120,000 and this was equally split among the three sources of financing, how would this have impacted EVA in 2008?

CHAPTER 13

Dealing with Project Risk and Other Topics in Capital Budgeting

LEARNING GOALS

LG1 Understand the importance of explicitly recognizing risk in the analysis of capital budgeting projects.

LG2 Discuss breakeven cash flow, sensitivity and scenario analysis, and simulation as behavioural approaches for dealing with risk, and the unique risks facing multinational companies.

LG3 Describe the two basic risk-adjustment techniques in terms of NPV and the procedures for applying the certainty equivalent (CE) approach.

LG4 Review the use of risk-adjusted discount rates (RADRs), portfolio effects, and the practical aspects of RADRs relative to CEs.

LG5 Consider the impact closing an asset class has on the evaluation of a capital budgeting project, and describe the process used to evaluate mutually exclusive projects with unequal lives by calculating their annualized net present value (ANPV).

LG6 Explain the role of real options and the objective of, and basic approaches to, project selection under capital rationing.

13.1 Introduction to Risk in Capital Budgeting

The capital budgeting techniques introduced in Chapter 12 were applied in an environment where we assumed the risk of the investment project being evaluated was the same as the company's overall risk. Therefore, the cash flows developed using the techniques presented in Chapter 12 were discounted at the company's

Getting a Handle on Risk

Every year, millions of visitors pour into casinos or play video lottery terminals, or play the lotteries offered by the federal and provincial governments. All these players are looking for big—or even modest—returns on their gambling dollars. Two key features of gambling, of course, are uncertainty and hope—the uncertainty of when, if ever, there will be a payoff, and the ongoing hope that it will come with the next quarter, or dollar, or twenty "invested." Although most business investments are not gambles, a similar uncertainty does exist. Managers do all they can to ensure the outcomes of their investments, but despite their best planning and analysis, risk remains because of events outside the company's immediate control. In the previous chapter, we considered capital budgeting projects that had the same level of risk as the overall company. In this chapter, we turn to the issue of how projects with levels of risk different from the overall company are evaluated. We show how risk is incorporated into capital budgeting decisions.

cost of capital, the discount rate that reflects the current business and financial risk of the company. In other words, in Chapter 12, all projects, independent or mutually exclusive, were assumed to be equally risky, and the acceptance and implementation of a project would not change the overall risk of the company. While in reality these types of similar-risk projects are quite common, they are not the only kind of capital budgeting project a company must review and analyze, and for which the appropriate accept/reject or ranking decision must be made.

LINKING THE DISCIPLINES: Cross-Functional Interactions

- ***Accounting personnel*** need to understand the risk caused by the variability of cash flows, how to compare projects with unequal lives, and how to measure project returns when capital is being rationed.
- ***Information systems analysts*** will be a key part of the capital expenditure analysis process. They will design the systems to help complete the sensitivity and scenario analysis and the simulation approach.
- ***Management*** need to understand behavioural approaches for dealing with risk in capital budgeting decisions, how to risk-adjust discount rates, how to refine capital budgeting techniques when projects have unequal lives or when capital is rationed, and how to recognize real options embedded in capital projects.
- The ***marketing department*** will be very involved in developing the projected cash flows for the analysis of capital expenditure proposals. They will provide the revenue estimates for the various proposals.
- Personnel in the ***operations department*** will prepare the cost estimates for many of the capital expenditure proposals. These employees are closest to the operations and know how changes will affect their costs.

Sometimes a project will be in a different line of business from the firm's current line, or the project's cash flows will have a different level of risk from the company's. The acceptance of such a project will impact the firm's overall risk, though often in a minor way. In this chapter, we assume that the projects being evaluated have different risk characteristics from the overall company. This implies the company cannot analyze the project in exactly the same manner as presented in Chapter 12. The assumption of equal-risk projects is relaxed in order to focus on how a different level of risk is incorporated in the capital budgeting decision process.

Source of Risk

risk
The chance that the inputs into the analysis of an investment project will prove to be wrong.

For capital budgeting, **risk** refers to the chance that the inputs used in the analysis of an investment project will prove to be wrong. The key inputs are, of course, the various components of the cash flows and the discount rate. If either the estimates for the cash flows or the cost of capital is seriously in error, then the capital budgeting decision made *may* be incorrect. If the cash inflows are overestimated and/or the cost of capital underestimated, then decisions that prove to be very costly for the firm and the shareholders can result. Either occurrence is an example of the adage **GIGO (garbage in, garbage out)**. Poor forecasts result in poor decisions, *no matter how thorough the analysis of the numbers.*

GIGO (garbage in, garbage out)
If cash inflows are overestimated and/or the cost of capital underestimated, then decisions that prove to be very costly for the firm and the shareholders can result; poor forecasts can result in poor capital budgeting decisions.

For an investment project, when we say that the cash inflow for a particular year is expected to be $1,000, we are really saying that based on the range of possible cash inflows and the probability of these cash inflows occurring, we expect the cash inflow to be $1,000. Expected cash inflow estimates are, of course, subject to error. The wider the range of possible inflows, the greater the risk of the expected inflow. Projects with very low positive net present values (NPVs) and a broad range of expected cash inflows are more risky than projects with high NPVs and a narrow range of expected cash inflows.

When analyzing projects, it is useful to consider that for any given firm, positive NPV projects are limited, in some cases very rare. For every positive NPV investment project, it is useful and highly recommended that the personnel involved in the analysis reconsider all aspects of the project to ensure that forecasting errors have not occurred. Take a step back and consider what makes the project attractive. Companies must always remember that other people's money is being invested. It might be useful to build into the capital budgeting process a healthy skepticism of positive NPV projects. Companies that do this tend to explicitly recognize and deal with risk and, as a result, tend to make fewer capital budgeting decisions that destroy company and shareholder wealth.

To illustrate risk concepts, we will assume Bennett Company is analyzing two mutually exclusive projects: A and B. Project A has an incremental cost of $42,000; project B, $45,000. Both projects are expected to have five-year lives and the relevant cash inflows are presented in Table 13.1. Note that the cash inflows include all benefits including incremental operating income, tax shield from CCA, and salvage. Part B of the table indicates that by using Bennett Company's cost of capital of 10 percent, project A should be selected since project A's NPV is greater than B's: the expected return from A is greater than B. The cash flows for the two projects are depicted on time lines in Figure 13.1, as is the calculation of the NPV for the two projects. This analysis should be straightforward if Chapter 12 has been completed.

The project evaluation presented in Figure 13.1 assumes the two projects have the same risk as the company. In the following two sections, we use the basic risk concepts presented in Chapter 7 to demonstrate both behavioural and quantitative approaches for explicitly recognizing risk in the analysis of capital budgeting projects.

TABLE 13.1 Relevant Cash Flows and NPVs for Bennett Company's Projects

	Project A	Project B
A. Relevant Cash Flows		
Incremental cost	**$42,000**	**$45,000**
Year	**Operating after-tax cash inflows**	
1	$14,000	$28,000
2	14,000	12,000
3	14,000	10,000
4	14,000	10,000
5	14,000	10,000
B. Decision Technique		
NPV @ 10% cost of capital[a]	$11,071	$10,924

[a]From Figure 13.1, calculated using a financial calculator.

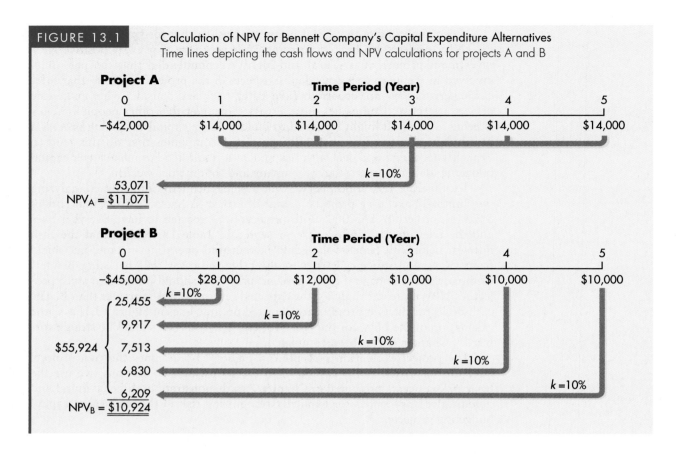

FIGURE 13.1 Calculation of NPV for Bennett Company's Capital Expenditure Alternatives
Time lines depicting the cash flows and NPV calculations for projects A and B

? Review Questions

13–1 In Chapter 12, what assumption was made concerning the risk of capital budgeting projects? What happens if this assumption doesn't hold? How can the acceptance of a project change the overall risk of a company? Provide an example.

13–2 For capital budgeting, what is meant by the term "risk"? What are the sources of risk?

13–3 What is meant by the phrase "garbage in, garbage out" when applied to capital budgeting? What concept does the phrase reflect?

13.2 Behavioural Approaches for Dealing with Risk

Behavioural approaches can be used to get a "feel" for the level of project risk, whereas *quantitative approaches* allow explicit adjustment of projects for risk. Here we present a few behavioural approaches for dealing with risk in capital budgeting: risk and cash inflows, sensitivity analysis and scenario analysis, and simulation. In addition, some international risk considerations are discussed. We consider quantitative approaches in a later section.

Risk and Cash Inflows

forecasting risk
The possibility that the estimated cash flows are wrong (either too high or low) and, as a result, a wrong decision is made.

One of the major components of risk for a project is the projected cash flows. Recognize that many projects have very long expected lives and that forecasting error is a real concern. **Forecasting risk** is the possibility that the estimated cash flows are wrong (either too high or low) and, as a result, a wrong decision is made. It is reasonable to assume that cash flow forecasts for six plus years into the future are subject to more forecasting error than forecasts for one to five years into the future. But the NPV analysis implicitly recognizes this through the present value interest factor. Consider that the present value of an expected cash inflow of $1,000 in one year's time, assuming a 12 percent discount rate, is $892.86. The present value of the same $1,000 expected in 10 years' time is only $321.97. So the NPV process implicitly recognizes that the more distant the expected cash inflow, the higher the risk.

For cash flows, risk is associated almost entirely with the cash inflows. The incremental cost of the project is known with virtual certainty, since the cash flow occurs now, at time 0. For most capital budgeting projects, the firm will know the cost of the asset and, if a replacement project, the salvage value of the asset being replaced. If the incremental cost is spread out over a number of years, much of this cost will be contracted at the time of the decision. So there is very little—virtually no—risk associated with the incremental cost. If this is the case, then there is little risk associated with any investment tax credit (ITC) or the tax shield from CCA.[1]

Risk is associated with the principal reason a company considers investing in a capital budgeting project: the expected increase in operating income. This increase is associated with the expected level of sales, the cost of raw materials, labour costs, factory overhead, selling and administrative expenses, and all other cash costs that will be affected by the project. The overall expected level of operating income is associated with the interaction of these underlying variables. The other components of the cash flows that are subject to risk include the change in net working capital (since this is based on uncertain sales) and the salvage value of the asset at the end of its useful life. On a present value basis, however, both of these variables are minor: the key component of the cash flows that is subject to significant risk is the incremental operating income.

Therefore, to assess the risk of a proposed capital expenditure, the focus is on the operating income component of the cash inflows. The firm must determine the probability that the operating income will be large enough so that the project is acceptable.

Example ▼ Treadwell Tire Company, a tire retailer with a 10 percent cost of capital (k_a), is considering investing in either of two mutually exclusive projects A or B, each requiring a $10,000 initial investment and expected to provide equal annual incremental after-tax operating incomes (the only relevant cash inflow) over their 15-year lives. For either project to be acceptable, according to the net present value technique, its NPV must be equal to or greater than zero. If we let *CF* equal

1. The risk of the tax shield from CCA is associated with the certainty of the discount rate (considered later in the chapter) and the firm's tax rate. Tax rate changes are *entirely* outside the firm's control; therefore, the firm must use the tax rate currently in effect in the analysis of a project. If the tax rate changes in the future, this will affect the tax shield, and other variables, but this is entirely unpredictable. It is a political risk that cannot be controlled or evaluated.

the annual after-tax cash inflow and C_0 equal the incremental cost, the following condition must be met for projects with annuity cash inflows, such as A and B, to be acceptable:

$$NPV = [CF \times PVIFa\,(k_a, n \text{ years})] - C_0 = \$0 \tag{13.1}$$

breakeven cash inflow
The minimum level of after-tax cash inflow necessary for a project to be acceptable; that is, NPV $\geq$ \$0.

By substituting k_a = 10%, n = 15 years, and C_0 = \$10,000, we can find the **breakeven cash inflow**—the minimum level of after-tax cash inflow necessary for Treadwell's projects to be acceptable:

$$[CF \times PVIFa\,(10\%, 15 \text{ years})] - \$10{,}000 \geq \$0$$
$$CF \times (7.60608) \geq \$10{,}000$$
$$CF \geq \frac{\$10{,}000}{7.60608} \geq \underline{\underline{\$1{,}315}}$$

Note that a financial calculator was used to solve this problem where the \$10,000 is the PV, I is 10 percent, and N is 15. Input 0 as the FV and compute (CPT) PMT. The result indicates that for the projects to be acceptable to Treadwell Tire, they must have incremental after-tax operating incomes (cash inflows) of at least \$1,315 per year.[2]

Given this breakeven level of cash inflows, the risk of each project could be assessed by determining the probability that the project's cash inflows will equal or exceed this breakeven level. The various statistical techniques that would determine that probability are covered in Chapter 7, Section 7.2. For now, we can simply assume that such a statistical analysis results in the following:

Probability of $CF_A \geq \$1{,}315 \rightarrow 100\%$
Probability of $CF_B \geq \$1{,}315 \rightarrow 65\%$

Because project A is certain (100% probability) to have a positive net present value, whereas there is only a 65 percent chance that project B will have a positive NPV, project A is less risky than project B. Of course, the potential level of returns associated with each project must be evaluated in view of the firm's risk preference before the preferred project is selected.

The example clearly identifies risk as it relates to the chance that a project is acceptable, but it does not address the issue of cash flow variability. Even though project B has a greater chance of loss than project A, it might result in higher potential NPVs. Recall from Chapters 7 and 8 that it is the *combination* of risk and return that determines value. Similarly, the worth of a capital expenditure and its impact on the firm's value must be viewed in light of both risk and return. The analyst must therefore consider the *variability* of cash inflows and NPVs to assess project risk and return fully.

Sensitivity and Scenario Analysis

sensitivity analysis
A behavioural approach that uses a number of possible values for a given variable to assess its impact on a firm's return.

Two approaches for dealing with project risk to capture the variability of cash inflows and NPVs are sensitivity analysis and scenario analysis. **Sensitivity analysis**, as noted in Chapter 7, is a behavioural approach that uses a number of

2. Note that for the remainder of this chapter, the generic term "cash inflow" will be used. Remember, however, that it is the operating income component that makes cash inflows risky.

possible values for a given variable, such as cash inflows, to assess its impact on the firm's return, measured here by NPV. This technique is often useful in getting a feel for the variability of return in response to changes in a key variable. In capital budgeting, one of the most common sensitivity approaches is to estimate the NPVs associated with pessimistic (worst), most likely (expected), and optimistic (best) cash inflow estimates. The *range* can be determined by subtracting the pessimistic-outcome NPV from the optimistic-outcome NPV.

Example Continuing with Treadwell Tire Company, assume that the financial manager made pessimistic, most likely, and optimistic estimates of the cash inflows for each project. The cash inflow estimates and resulting NPVs in each case are summarized in Table 13.2. Comparing the ranges of cash inflows ($1,000 for project A and $4,000 for B) and, more important, the ranges of NPVs ($7,606 for project A and $30,424 for B) makes it clear that project A is less risky than project B. Given that both projects have the same most likely NPV of $5,212, the assumed risk-averse decision maker may take project A because it has less risk and no possibility of loss. The deciding factor will be the probabilities attached to each of the possible outcomes. If there is only a 10 percent probability of the pessimistic outcome occurring and a 40 percent probability of the optimistic outcome occurring for the two projects, then the decision may swing in favour of project B.

scenario analysis
A behavioural approach that evaluates the impact on return of simultaneous changes in a number of variables.

Scenario analysis, which is a behavioural approach similar to sensitivity analysis but broader in scope, is used to evaluate the impact of various circumstances on the firm's return. Rather than isolating the effect of a change in a single variable, scenario analysis evaluates the impact of simultaneous changes in a number of variables, such as the various components of the cash inflows, the

TABLE 13.2 Sensitivity Analysis of the Two Treadwell Projects

	Project A	Project B
Incremental cost	**$10,000**	**$10,000**
	Annual after-tax cash inflows	
Outcome		
Pessimistic	$1,500	$ 0
Most likely	2,000	2,000
Optimistic	2,500	4,000
Range	$1,000	$4,000
	Net present values[a]	
Outcome		
Pessimistic	$1,409	−$10,000
Most likely	5,212	5,212
Optimistic	9,015	20,424
Range	$7,606	$30,424

[a]These values were calculated by using the corresponding annual cash inflows, the 10% cost of capital, and a 15-year life.

cash outflows, and the cost of capital. For example, the firm might evaluate the impact of both high inflation (scenario 1) and low inflation (scenario 2) on a project's NPV. Or it might consider the impact of different marketing campaigns, selling prices, production processes, or operating or financial structures on cash inflows, outflows, cost of capital, and NPVs. Each scenario will affect the firm's cash inflows, cash outflows, and cost of capital, thereby resulting in different levels of NPV. The decision maker can use these NPV estimates to roughly assess the risk involved with respect to the level of inflation. The widespread availability of computer-based spreadsheet programs (such as Excel and Quattro Pro) has greatly enhanced the use of both scenario and sensitivity analyses.

Simulation

simulation
A statistically based behavioural approach that applies predetermined probability distributions and random numbers to estimate risky outcomes.

Simulation is a statistically based behavioural approach that applies predetermined probability distributions and random numbers to estimate risky outcomes. By tying the various cash flow components together in a mathematical model and repeating the process numerous times, the financial manager can develop a probability distribution of project returns. Figure 13.2 presents a flowchart of the simulation of the net present value of a project. The process of generating random numbers and using the probability distributions for cash inflows and outflows allows the financial manager to determine values for each of these variables. Substituting these values into the mathematical model results in an NPV. By repeating this process perhaps a thousand times, a probability distribution of net present values is created.

Although only gross cash inflows and outflows are simulated in Figure 13.2, more sophisticated simulations using individual inflow and outflow components,

FIGURE 13.2
NPV Simulation
Flowchart of a net present value simulation

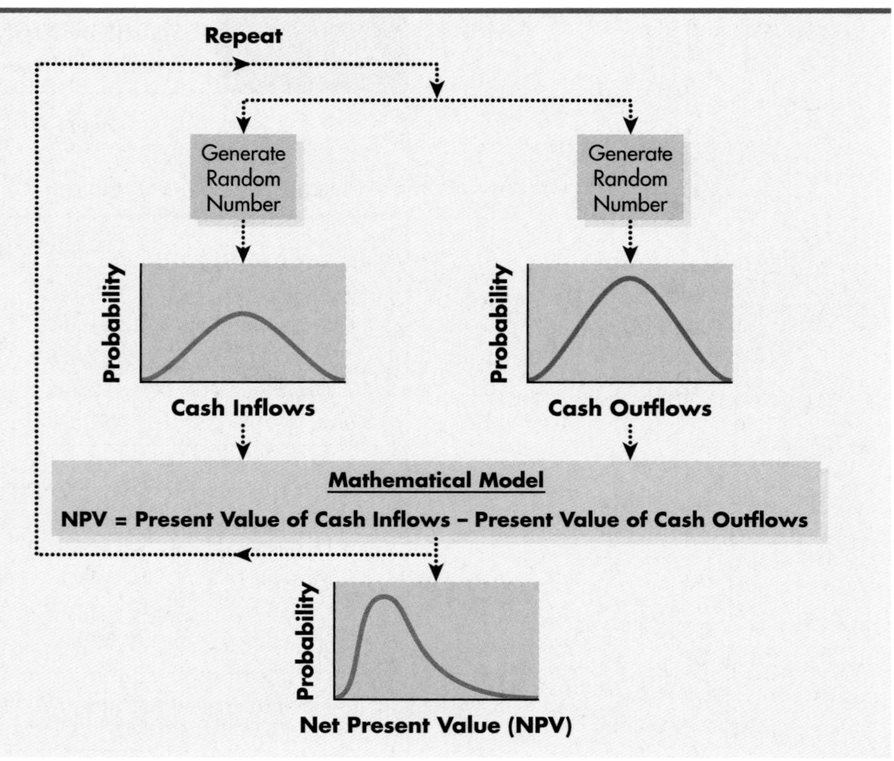

Hint
These behavioural approaches may seem a bit imprecise to one who has not used them. But repeated use and an "after the fact" review of previous analyses improve the accuracy of the users.

such as sales volume, sales price, raw material cost, labour cost, selling and administrative expenses, and so on, are quite common. From the distribution of returns, regardless of how they are measured (NPV or IRR), the decision maker can determine not only the expected value of the return but also the probability of achieving or surpassing a given return. The use of computers has made the simulation approach feasible. The output of simulation provides an excellent basis for decision making, because it allows the decision maker to view a continuum of risk–return tradeoffs rather than a single-point estimate.

Monte Carlo is one type of simulation that randomly generates values for uncertain variables over and over to simulate what might actually occur in reality. This is done using an appropriate probability distribution for the uncertain variable. The usual assumption is that the variable is normally distributed, but other types of distributions (log-normal, chi-square, gamma, exponential) could also be assumed. As many scenarios as the user wishes to evaluate can be modelled; the only limit is the computing power available. This allows the user to determine the NPV of a project using thousands of different estimates for each of the variables considered.

International Risk Considerations

Although the basic techniques of capital budgeting are the same for purely domestic firms as for multinational companies (MNCs), firms that operate in several countries face risks that are unique to the international arena. Two types of risk are particularly important: exchange rate risk and political risk—including, in the extreme, the risk that assets in foreign countries will be seized by the host government.

exchange rate risk
The danger that an unexpected change in the exchange rate between the dollar and the currency in which a project's cash flows are denominated can reduce the market value of that project's cash flow.

Exchange rate risk reflects the danger that an unexpected change in the exchange rate between the Canadian dollar and the currency in which a project's cash flows are denominated can reduce the market value of that project's cash flow. Although a project's incremental cost can usually be predicted with some certainty, the dollar value of future cash inflows can be dramatically altered if the local currency depreciates against the dollar. In the short term, specific cash flows can be hedged by using financial instruments such as currency futures and options. Long-term exchange rate risk can best be minimized by financing the project, in whole or in part, in local currency.

Political risk is much harder to protect against. Once a foreign project is accepted, the foreign government can block the return of profits back to Canada, seize the firm's assets, or otherwise interfere with a project's operation. The inability to manage political risk after the fact makes it even more important that managers account for political risks before making an investment. They can do so either by adjusting a project's expected cash inflows to account for the probability of political interference or by using risk-adjusted discount rates (discussed later in this chapter) in the capital budgeting decision-making process. In general, it is much better to subjectively adjust individual project cash flows for political risk than to use a blanket adjustment for all projects.

In addition to unique risks that MNCs must face, several other special issues are relevant only for international capital budgeting. One of these special issues is tax law differences between Canada and the country where the project is located. Often, one of the reasons a company locates a project in another country is lower taxes. Because only after-tax cash flows are relevant for capital budgeting, financial managers must carefully account for taxes paid to foreign governments on profits earned within their borders. They must also assess the impact of these tax payments on the parent company's Canadian tax liability, because full or partial credit is generally allowed for foreign tax payments. This issue is discussed in Chapter 19.

A second special issue is transfer pricing. Much of the international trade involving MNCs is, in reality, simply the shipment of goods and services from one of a parent company's wholly owned subsidiaries to another subsidiary located abroad. The parent company therefore has great discretion in setting the **transfer prices,** the prices that subsidiaries charge each other for the goods and services traded between them. The widespread use of transfer pricing in international trade makes capital budgeting in MNCs very difficult unless the transfer prices accurately reflect actual costs and incremental cash flows.

transfer prices
Prices that subsidiaries charge each other for the goods and services traded between them.

A third special issue in international capital budgeting is that MNCs often must approach international capital projects from a strategic point of view, rather than from a strictly financial perspective. For example, an MNC may feel compelled to invest in a country to ensure continued access, even if the project itself may not have a positive net present value. This motivation was important for Japanese automakers who set up assembly plants in Canada in the 1980s. For much the same reason, U.S. investment in Europe surged during the years before the market integration of the European Community in 1992. MNCs often will invest in production facilities in the home country of major rivals to deny these competitors an uncontested home market. Finally, MNCs may feel compelled to invest in certain industries or countries to achieve a broad corporate objective such as completing a product line or diversifying raw material sources, even when the project's cash flows may not be sufficiently profitable.

? Review Questions

13–4 When the various cash flow components associated with a project are considered, which are risky and which have no or very little risk? Explain why this is the case. How is forecasting risk already reflected in cash flows that occur well in the future?

13–5 How can determination of the *breakeven cash inflow* be used to gauge project risk? Explain.

13–6 Briefly describe, compare, and explain how each of the following behavioural approaches can be used to deal with project risk: (**a**) sensitivity analysis; (**b**) scenario analysis; and (**c**) simulation.

13–7 Briefly define and explain how each of the following items that are unique to multinational companies affect their capital budgeting decisions: (**a**) exchange rate risk; (**b**) political risk; (**c**) tax law differences; (**d**) transfer pricing; and (**e**) strategic rather than financial viewpoint.

13.3 Risk-Adjustment Techniques

The approaches for dealing with risk that have been presented so far allow the financial manager to get a "feel" for project risk. Unfortunately, they do not provide a quantitative basis for evaluating risky projects. We will now illustrate the two major risk-adjustment techniques using the net present value (NPV) decision method.[3] The NPV decision rule of accepting only those projects with NPVs

3. The IRR could just as well have been used, but because NPV is theoretically preferable, it is used instead.

greater than or equal to \$0 will continue to hold. The basic equation for NPV, first presented in Equation 12.3, is restated below:

$$\text{NPV} = \left[\sum_{t=1}^{n} CF_t(1-T) \times PVIF(k_a, t \text{ years})\right] - C_0 \tag{13.2}$$

where:

CF_t = incremental cash inflow in year t
C_0 = incremental cost
k_a = cost of capital or discount rate (in percent)
n = life of project (in years)

Close examination of Equation 13.2 reveals that since the incremental cost (C_0) occurs, or is contracted, at time zero, it is known with certainty. Therefore, a project's risk is embodied in the present value of its cash inflows:

$$\sum_{t=1}^{n} CF_t(1-T) \times PVIF(k_a, t \text{ years}) \tag{13.3}$$

This means that there are two ways to adjust the present value of cash inflows for risk: (1) the cash inflows, CF_t, can be adjusted or (2) the discount rate, k_a, can be adjusted. Here we describe and compare two techniques—the cash inflow adjustment process, using *certainty equivalents,* and the discount rate adjustment process, using *risk-adjusted discount rates.* In addition, we consider the portfolio effects of project analysis as well as the practical aspects of certainty equivalents and risk-adjusted discount rates.

Certainty Equivalents (CEs)

certainty equivalents (CEs)
Risk-adjustment factors that represent the percent of estimated cash inflow that investors would be satisfied to receive *for certain* rather than the cash inflows that are possible for each year.

One of the most direct and theoretically preferred approaches for risk adjustment is the use of **certainty equivalents (CEs),** which represent the percent of estimated cash inflow that investors would be satisfied to receive *for certain* rather than the cash inflows that are *possible* for each year. Equation 13.4 presents the basic expression for NPV when certainty equivalents are used for risk adjustment:

$$\text{NPV} = \left[\sum_{t=1}^{n} (\alpha_t \times CF_t) \times PVIFa(R_F, t \text{ years})\right] - C_0 \tag{13.4}$$

where:

α_t = certainty equivalent factor in year t ($0 \le \alpha_t \le 1$)
CF_t = relevant incremental cash inflow in year t
R_F = risk-free rate of return

risk-free rate, R_F
The rate of return that one would earn on a virtually riskless investment such as a short-term Government of Canada treasury bill.

The equation shows that a project's incremental cash inflows for each year t are first adjusted for risk by converting the expected cash inflows to certain amounts, $\alpha_t \times CF_t$. These certain cash inflows are, in effect, equivalent to "cash in hand," but not at time zero. The second part of the calculation adjusts the certain cash inflows for the time value of money by discounting them at the risk-free rate, R_F. The **risk-free rate, R_F,** is the rate of return that one would earn on a virtually riskless investment such as a short-term Government of Canada treasury bill. This was discussed in Chapter 5. It is used to discount the certain cash inflows and should not be confused with a risk-adjusted discount rate. (If a risk-adjusted rate were used, the risk would in effect be counted twice.) Although the process described here of converting risky cash inflows to certain cash inflows is somewhat subjective, the technique is theoretically sound.

Example Bennett Company wishes to consider risk in the analysis of two projects, A and B. The relevant cash flows for these projects were presented in part A of Table 13.1, and the NPVs, assuming that the projects had equivalent risks, were presented in part B. Ignoring risk differences and using net present value, calculated using the firm's 10 percent cost of capital, project A was preferred over project B, because its NPV of $11,071 was greater than B's NPV of $10,914.

Now let's assume, however, that on further analysis the firm found that project A was actually more risky than project B. To consider the differing risks, the firm estimated the certainty equivalent factors for each project's cash inflows for each year. Column 2 of Table 13.3 shows the estimated values for projects A and B, respectively. Multiplying the risky cash inflows, in column 1, by the corresponding certainty equivalent factors, in column 2, gives the certain cash inflows for projects A and B shown in column 3.

Upon investigation, Bennett's management estimated the prevailing risk-free rate of return, R_F, to be 6 percent. Using that rate to discount the certain cash inflows for each of the projects results in the net present values of $4,544 for project A and $10,152 for B, as shown at the bottom of column 4. Note that as a result of the risk adjustment, project B is now preferred. The usefulness of the certainty equivalent approach for risk adjustment should be quite clear. The only difficulty lies in the need to make subjective estimates of the certainty equivalent factors.

Risk-Adjusted Discount Rates (RADRs)

A popular approach for risk adjustment involves the use of *risk-adjusted discount rates (RADRs)*. Instead of adjusting the cash inflows for risk, as the certainty equivalent approach does, this approach adjusts the discount rate.[4] Equation 13.2 is used with one minor adjustment: the discount rate is k_j, the risk-adjusted discount rate, rather than k_a, the company's cost of capital, as noted in Equation 13.5.

$$\text{NPV} = \left[\sum_{t=1}^{n} CF_t\,(1 - T) \times PVIF\,(k_j,\ t \text{ years})\right] - C_0 \qquad (13.5)$$

risk-adjusted discount rate (RADR)
The rate of return that must be earned on a given project to compensate for the risk of the project.

The **risk-adjusted discount rate (RADR)** is the rate of return that must be earned on a given project to compensate for the risk of the project and ensure that the providers of financing receive a rate of return commensurate with the project's risk. This rate will compensate the providers of both debt and equity capital with their required rate of return. As a consequence, the firm's common share price will increase. The higher the risk of a project, the higher the RADR and therefore the lower the net present value for a given stream of cash inflows. Because the logic underlying the use of RADRs is closely linked to the capital asset pricing model (CAPM) developed in Chapter 7, here we review CAPM, discuss its use in finding RADRs, and describe the application of RADRs.

4. The risk-adjusted discount rate approach can be applied in using the internal rate of return as well as the net present value. The IRR of the project must be greater than or equal to the risk-adjusted discount rate. In using NPV, the projected cash inflows are merely discounted at the risk-adjusted discount rate.

TABLE 13.3 **Analysis of Bennett Company's Projects A and B Using Certainty Equivalents**

Project A

Year (t)	Cash inflows (1)	Certainty equivalent factors[a] (2)	Certain cash inflows [(1) × (2)] (3)	Present value[b] (4)
1	$14,000	0.90	$12,600	$11,887
2	14,000	0.90	12,600	11,214
3	14,000	0.80	11,200	9,404
4	14,000	0.70	9,800	7,763
5	14,000	0.60	8,400	6,277
		Present value of cash inflows		$46,545
		−Incremental cost		42,000
		Net present value (NPV)		$ 4,545

Project B

Year (t)	Cash inflows (1)	Certainty equivalent factors[a] (2)	Certain cash inflows [(1) × (2)] (3)	Present value[b] (4)
1	$28,000	1.00	$28,000	$26,415
2	12,000	0.90	10,800	9,612
3	10,000	0.90	9,000	7,557
4	10,000	0.80	8,000	6,337
5	10,000	0.70	7,000	5,231
		Present value of cash inflows		$55,152
		− Incremental cost		45,000
		Net present value (NPV)		$10,152

Note: The relevant cash flows for these projects were presented in Table 13.1, and the analysis of the projects using NPV and assuming equal risk was presented in Figure 13.1.

[a] These values were estimated by management; they reflect the risk that managers perceive in the cash inflows.

[b] Calculated by determining the present value of each of the certain cash inflows using the 6 percent discount rate and the appropriate number of years. The certain cash flow is a future value.

Review of CAPM

In Chapter 7, the *capital asset pricing model (CAPM)* was used to link the *relevant* risk and return for all assets traded in *efficient markets*. In the development of the CAPM, the *total risk* of an asset was defined as

$$\text{Total risk} = \text{nondiversifiable risk} + \text{diversifiable risk} \quad (13.6)$$

For assets traded in an efficient market, the *diversifiable risk,* which results from uncontrollable or random events, can be eliminated through diversification. The relevant risk is therefore the *nondiversifiable risk*—the risk for which owners of these assets are rewarded. Nondiversifiable risk for securities is commonly measured by using *beta,* which is an index of the degree of movement of an asset's return in response to a change in the market return.

Using beta, β_j, to measure the relevant risk of any asset j, the CAPM is

$$k_j = R_F + [\beta_j \times (k_m - R_F)] \qquad (13.7)$$

where:

k_j = required return on asset j
R_F = risk-free rate of return
β_j = beta coefficient for asset j
k_m = return on the market portfolio of assets

In Chapter 7, we demonstrated that the required return on any asset could be determined by substituting values of R_F, β_j, and k_m into the CAPM—Equation 13.7. Any security that is expected to earn a return that is equal to or greater than its required return would be acceptable, and those that are expected to earn less than the required return would be rejected.

Using CAPM to Find RADRs

If we assume for a moment that real corporate assets such as property, plant, and equipment are traded in efficient markets, the CAPM could be redefined as noted in Equation 13.8:

$$k_{\text{project } j} = R_F + [\beta_{\text{project } j} \times (k_m - R_F)] \qquad (13.8)$$

The *security market line* (SML)—the graphic depiction of the CAPM—is shown Figure 13.3. Any project having an expected return (IRR) falling on or above the SML would be acceptable, because its IRR would equal or exceed the required return, k_{project}. Any project with an IRR below k_{project} would be rejected. In terms of NPV, any project falling above the SML would have a positive NPV, and any project falling below the SML would have a negative NPV.[5]

Example Two projects, L and R, are shown in Figure 13.3. Project L has a beta, β_L, and generates an expected return of IRR_L. The required return for a project with risk β_L is k_L. Because project L generates a return greater than that required ($\text{IRR}_L > k_L$), project L would be acceptable. Project L would have a positive NPV when its cash inflows are discounted at its required return, k_L. Project R, on the other hand, generates an IRR below that required for its risk, β_R ($\text{IRR}_R < k_R$). This project would have a negative NPV when its cash inflows are discounted at its required return, k_R. Project R should be rejected.[6]

5. As noted earlier, whenever the IRR is above the cost of capital or required return (IRR > k_j), the NPV is positive, and whenever the IRR is below the cost of capital or required return (IRR < k_j), the NPV is negative. Because by definition the IRR is the discount rate that causes NPV to equal zero and the IRR and NPV always agree on accept–reject decisions, the relationship noted in Figure 13.3 logically follows.

FIGURE 13.3

CAPM and SML

CAPM and SML in capital budgeting decision making

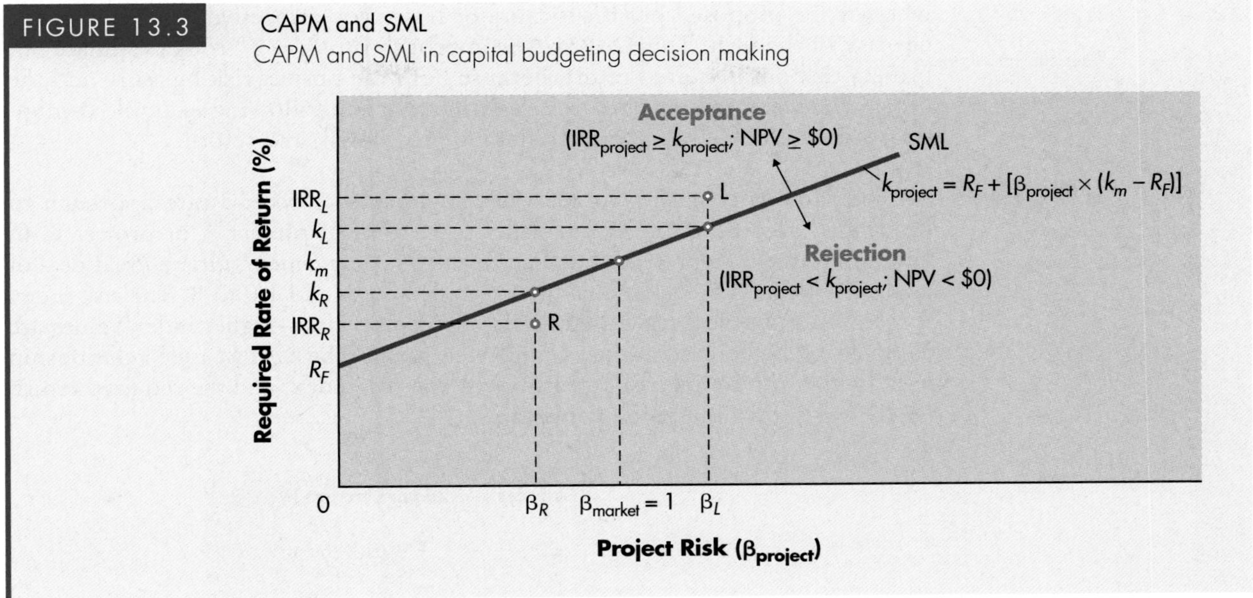

Applying RADRs

Because the CAPM is based upon an assumed efficient market, which does *not* exist for real corporate assets such as property, plant, and equipment, the CAPM is not directly applicable in making capital budgeting decisions. Attention is therefore typically devoted to assessing the *total risk* of a project and using it to determine the risk-adjusted discount rate (RADR), which can be used in Equation 13.5 to find the NPV.

In order for the firm not to damage its market value, it must use the correct discount rate when evaluating a project. If a firm discounts a risky project's cash inflows at too low a rate and incorrectly accepts the project, the firm's market price may drop as investors recognize that the firm has invested in a negative NPV project and has become more risky. On the other hand, if the firm discounts a project's cash inflows at too high a rate and incorrectly rejects acceptable projects, it will not grow as it should. Eventually, the firm's market price may drop because investors, believing that the firm is being overly conservative, will sell their stock, putting downward pressure on the firm's market value.

Unfortunately, there is no formal mechanism for linking total project risk to the level of required return. As a result, most firms subjectively determine the RADR by adjusting their existing required return up or down depending on

6. If there were a third project with a beta of 1 and an IRR (expected return) of k_m, what should be done? In this case the project's required return is equal to the expected return (IRR = k). The intersection of the risk (beta) and the RADR for the project would be on the SML. This means that the project would have an NPV equal to 0, and therefore should be accepted.

whether the proposed project is more or less risky, respectively, than the average risk of the firm. This CAPM-type approach provides a "rough estimate" of project risk and required return because both the project risk measure and the linkage between risk and return are estimates. The following example demonstrates this CAPM-type approach linking project risk and return.

Example Bennett Company wishes to use the risk-adjusted discount rate approach to determine, according to NPV, whether to implement project A or project B. In addition to the data presented earlier, Bennett's management, after a great deal of analysis, assigned a "risk index" of 1.6 to project A and 1.0 to B. The risk index is merely a numerical scale used to classify project risk—higher index values are assigned to higher-risk projects, and vice versa. The CAPM-type relationship used by the firm to link risk, measured by the risk index, and the required return (RADR) is shown in the following table.

	Risk index	Required return (RADR)
	0.0	6% (risk-free rate, R_F)
	0.2	7
	0.4	8
	0.6	9
	0.8	10
Project B→	1.0	11
	1.2	12
	1.4	13
Project A→	1.6	14
	1.8	16
	2.0	18

Note that this table can be easily converted to a graph like Figure 13.3. The one major change for the new graph is that rather than beta being the measure of risk on the x axis, the risk measure is the risk index. Figure 13.4 presents this data in graphical format.

Because project A is riskier than project B (index of 1.6 for A versus 1.0 for B), its RADR of 14 percent is greater than B's RADR of 11 percent. The net present value of each project, using its RADR, is calculated in Figure 13.5. The results clearly show that project B is preferable, because its risk-adjusted NPV of $9,798 is greater than the $6,063 risk-adjusted NPV for project A. This is the same conclusion that resulted from using certainty equivalents in the example on page 738. As noted by the NPVs in part B of Table 13.1, when the discount rates are not adjusted for risk, project A would be preferred to project B.

The usefulness of risk-adjusted discount rates should now be clear. The real difficulty of this approach lies in estimating project risk and linking it to the required return (RADR).

FIGURE 13.4

Risk Index

Use of the risk index in capital budgeting decision making

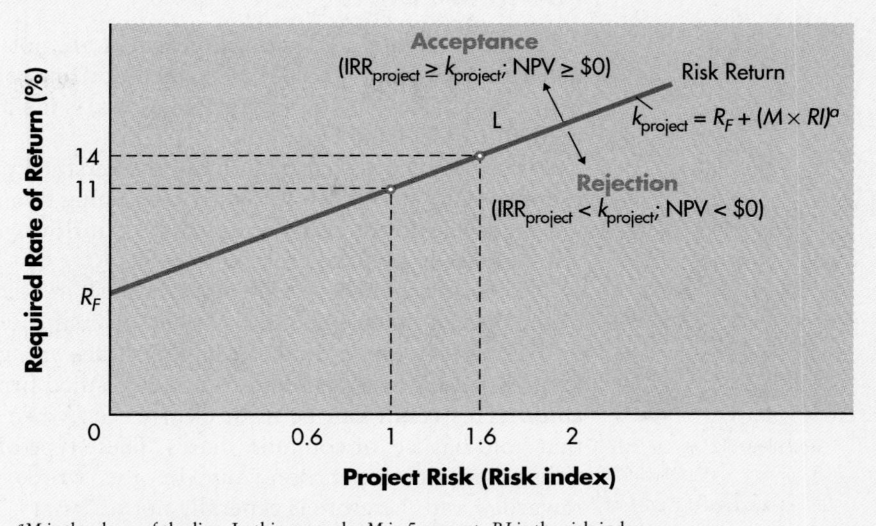

[a] M is the slope of the line. In this example, M is 5 percent. RI is the risk index.

FIGURE 13.5

Calculation of NPVs for Bennett Company's Capital Expenditure Alternatives Using RADRs

Time lines depicting the cash flows and NPV calculations using RADRs for projects A and B

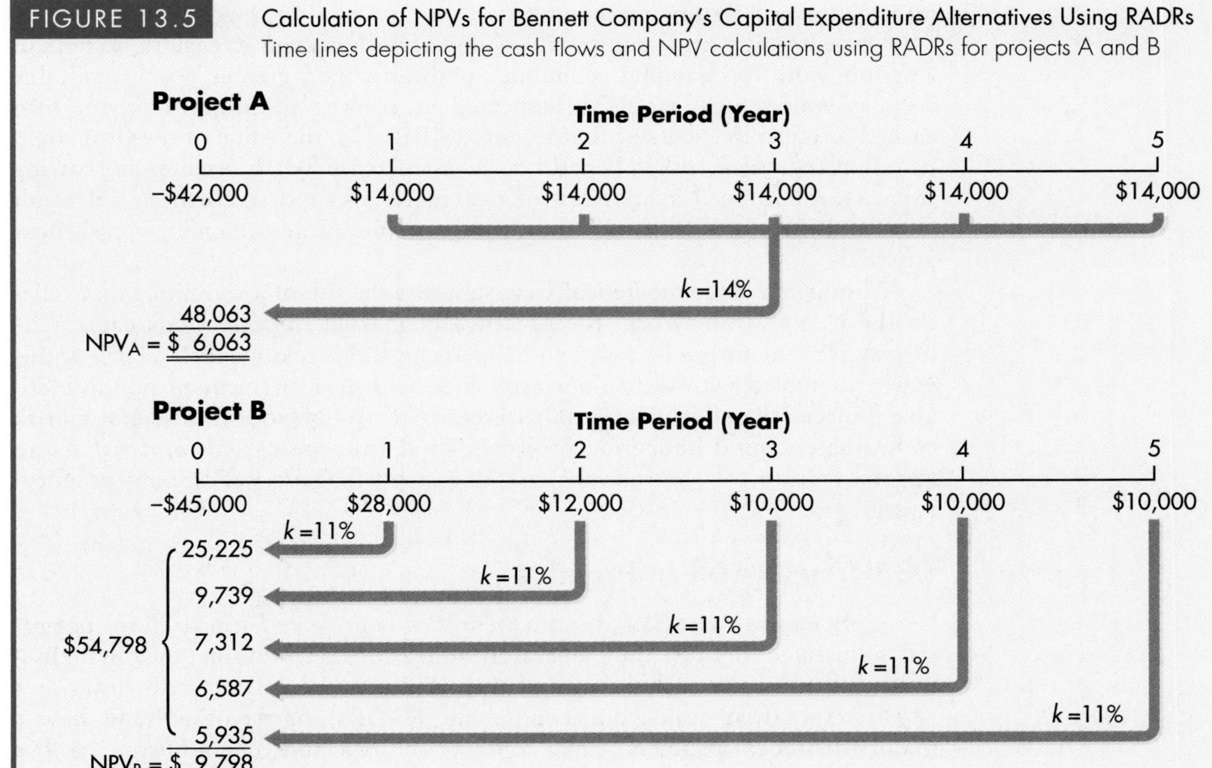

NOTE: When we use the risk indexes of 1.6 and 1 for projects A and B, respectively, a risk-adjusted discount rate (RADR) of 14 percent results for project A and a RADR of 11 percent results for project B.

Portfolio Effects

As noted in Chapter 7, because investors are not rewarded for taking diversifiable risk, they should hold a diversified portfolio of securities. Because a business firm can be viewed as a portfolio of assets, is it similarly important that the firm maintain a diversified portfolio of assets?

It seems logical that by holding a diversified portfolio the firm could reduce the variability of its cash flows. By combining two projects with negatively correlated cash inflows, the combined cash inflow variability—and therefore the risk—could be reduced.

Are firms rewarded for diversifying risk in this fashion? If they are, the value of the firm could be enhanced through diversification into other lines of business. Surprisingly, not only do the common shares of highly diversified publicly traded firms not trade at a premium to nondiversified firms, they usually trade at a *discount*. This result can be most clearly seen when focusing on closed-end funds that hold baskets of common shares. These type of funds almost always trade at a discount to their net asset value. In other words, diversification is not normally rewarded and therefore is generally not necessary.

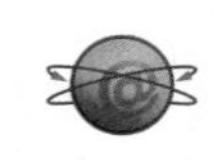

www.site-by-site.com/usa/cef/cef_profiles.htm
www.closed-endfunds.com

Why are firms not rewarded for diversifying? Because investors themselves can diversify by holding securities in a variety of firms; they do not need the firm to do it for them. And investors can diversify more readily—they can make transactions more easily and at a lower cost because of the greater availability of information and trading mechanisms.

Of course, if a firm acquires a new line of business and its cash flows tend to respond more to changing economic conditions (i.e., greater nondiversifiable risk), greater returns would be expected. If, for the additional risk, the firm earned a return in excess of that required (IRR > k), the value of the firm could be enhanced. Also, other benefits such as increased cash, greater borrowing capacity, guaranteed availability of raw materials, and so forth, could result from and therefore justify diversification, in spite of any immediate cash flow impact.

Although a strict theoretical view supports the use of a technique that relies on the CAPM framework, the presence of market imperfections causes the market for real corporate assets to be inefficient. The relative inefficiency of this market, coupled with difficulties associated with measurement of nondiversifiable project risk and its relationship to return, tends to favour the use of total risk to evaluate capital budgeting projects. Therefore, the use of *total risk* as an approximation for the relevant risk does tend to have widespread practical appeal.

CE Versus RADR in Practice

Certainty equivalents (CEs) are the *theoretically preferred* approach for project risk adjustment because they separately adjust for risk and time; they first eliminate risk from the cash flows and then discount the certain cash flows at a risk-free rate. Risk-adjusted discount rates (RADRs), on the other hand, have a major theoretical problem: They combine the risk and time adjustments in a single discount-rate adjustment. Because of the basic mathematics of compounding and discounting, the RADR approach therefore implicitly assumes that risk is an increasing function of time. Rather than demonstrate this

13.1 **IN PRACTICE**

What Happens When Risk Is Not Correctly Recognized?

The word "risk" comes from the early Italian word *risicare*, which means "to dare." During the frantic run-up in the high-tech sector in the 1997 to 2000 period, many companies took the idea of *risicare* to a new level. They dared with the takeovers of companies in the high-tech sector, and shareholders paid a heavy price when the sector nosedived in the punishing bear market of 2001–2002. Daring to dream about new opportunities—new business ideas—is what capital budgeting is all about. To dare is to create growth and wealth for the company and the common shareholders.

But sometimes, the dream becomes a nightmare because the risk of the investment project hasn't been well evaluated and considered. The shareholders of numerous companies that purchased other companies, a classic and very costly type of risky capital budgeting project, can attest to the damage that can be done if the risks of takeovers are not correctly evaluated. For example, recent research reports that acquiring firm shareholders lost $120 per $1,000 spent on takeovers for a total loss of $240 billion during the stock market bubble of 1998 to 2001. The major destruction of shareholder wealth was due to the overestimation of expected cash flows.

In September 2000, Quebecor Inc. and the Caisse de dépôt et placement du Québec purchased Groupe Vidéotron Ltée, a Quebec-based cable television provider. Quebecor Inc. is one of the largest communications companies in the world, operating in eight lines of business. Vidéotron is the largest cable operator in Quebec and the third-largest in Canada, and a provider of Internet and telephony services. Quebecor also owns companies in numerous other media-related businesses. The Caisse de dépôt manages Quebec's public pension funds.

The two organizations teamed together to acquire Vidéotron, paying $45 per share, or $3,300 per subscriber, for a total cost of $5.7 billion. To finance the deal, Quebecor and the Caisse used $3 billion of debt and $2.7 billion from the sale of common shares. The offer provided Vidéotron's shareholders with a 35.6 percent premium on the pre-offer price of the shares. The winning bid was, as one person knowledgeable about the takeover stated, "far too high" and was motivated to defeat Rogers Communications' initial $4.9 billion bid for the company.

As it turned out, the above comment proved to be true. By 2003, Quebecor and the Caisse wrote off over $4 billion, or 70 percent, of the purchase price due to the declining value of the investment. Quebecor's share price declined from $36 in October 2000 to $17 by the summer of 2001. It is clear that the amount paid by Quebecor and the Caisse greatly exceeded Vidéotron's true value. The capital budgeting process used to justify the initial transaction was badly flawed.

This example illustrates the great damage that can be done to the company and to shareholders if risk is not explicitly recognized or not recognized correctly when analyzing investment projects. In the example, either the expected cash inflows should have been reduced and/or the discount rate used to evaluate the takeover increased. If either or both of these corrections had been made more often, perhaps many of the takeovers that destroyed shareholder value in the tech sector would not have been undertaken.

SOURCES: Robert Gibbens, "Caisse, Quebecor May Take Vidéotron Hit," *National Post*, October 12, 2002, FP3; Mathew Ingram, "More to Quebecor Suit Than Meets the Eye," *The Globe and Mail*, September 20, 2002; S. B. Moeller, F. P. Schlingemann, and R. M. Stulz, "Wealth Destruction on a Massive Scale? A Study of Acquiring-Firm Returns in the Recent Merger Wave," *Journal of Finance* 60 (2005), pp. 757–782; Andrew Wahl, "CEO on Top: A Stacked Share Structure and Buddy-Buddy Directors," *Canadian Business*, August 19, 2002, p. 41.

implicit assumption, suffice it to say that *CEs are theoretically superior to RADRs.*

However, because of the complexity of developing CEs, *RADRs are more often used in practice.* Their popularity stems from two facts: (1) they are consistent with the general disposition of financial decision makers toward rates of return[7] and (2) they are easily estimated and applied. The first reason is clearly a matter of personal preference, but the second is based on the computational convenience and well developed procedures involved in the use of RADRs. In practice, risk is often subjectively categorized rather than related to a continuum of RADRs associated with each level of risk, as was illustrated in the preceding example.

Hint

The use of risk classes is consistent with the concept that risk-averse investors require a greater return for greater risks. In order to increase shareholders' wealth, risky projects must earn greater returns in order to warrant acceptance.

Firms often establish a number of *risk classes,* with a RADR assigned to each. Each project is then subjectively placed in the appropriate risk class, and the corresponding RADR is used to evaluate it. This is sometimes done on a division-by-division basis, each division having its own set of risk classes and associated RADRs similar to those in Table 13.4. The use of *divisional costs of capital* and associated risk classes allows the large multidivisional firm to incorporate differing levels of divisional risk into the capital budgeting process and still recognize differences in the levels of individual project risk.

Example Assume that the management of Bennett Company decided to use a more subjective but also more practical RADR approach to analyze projects. Each project would be placed in one of four risk classes according to its perceived risk. The classes are ranged from I for the lowest-risk projects to IV for the highest-risk projects. Associated with each class was a RADR that was appropriate to the level of risk of projects in the class. A brief description of each class, along with the associated RADR, is given in Table 13.4. It shows that lower-risk projects tend to involve routine replacement or renewal activities, whereas higher-risk projects involve expansion, often into new or unfamiliar activities.

The financial manager of Bennett has assigned project A to Class III and project B to Class II. The cash flows for project A would therefore be evaluated by using a 14 percent RADR, and project B's would be evaluated by using a 10 percent RADR.[8] The net present value of project A at 14 percent was calculated in Figure 13.5 to be \$6,063, and the NPV for project B at a 10 percent RADR was shown in Table 13.1 to be \$10,924. Clearly, with RADRs based on the use of risk classes, project B is preferred over project A. As noted earlier, this result is contrary to the preferences shown in Table 13.1, where no attention was given to the differing risk of projects A and B.

7. Recall that although NPV was the theoretically preferred evaluation technique, IRR was more popular in actual business practice due to the general preference of businesspeople for rates of return rather than pure dollar returns. The preference for RADRs over CEs is therefore consistent with the preference for IRR over NPV.

8. Note that the 10% RADR for project B using the risk classes in Table 13.4 differs from the 11% RADR used when the risk index of the project was considered. This difference is attributable to the less precise nature of the use of risk classes.

TABLE 13.4 Bennett Company's Risk Classes and RADRs

Risk class	Description	Risk-adjusted discount rate, RADR
I	*Below-average risk:* Projects with low risk. Typically involve routine replacement without renewal of existing activities.	8%
II	*Average risk:* Projects similar to those currently implemented. Typically involve replacement or renewal of existing activities.	10%[a]
III	*Above-average risk:* Projects with higher-than-normal, but not excessive, risk. Typically involve expansion of existing or similar activities.	14%
IV	*Highest risk:* Projects with very high risk. Typically involve expansion into new or unfamiliar activities.	20%

[a]This RADR is actually the firm's cost of capital, which was discussed and illustrated in Chapters 9 and 12. It represents the firm's required return on its existing portfolio of projects, which is assumed unchanged with acceptance of the "average risk" project.

? Review Questions

13–8 Explain the concept of *certainty equivalents (CEs)*. How are they used in the risk-adjustment process?

13–9 Describe the logic as well as the basic procedures involved in using *risk-adjusted discount rates (RADRs)*. How does this approach relate to the *capital asset pricing model*? Explain.

13–10 Explain why a firm whose stock is actively traded in the securities markets need not concern itself with diversification. In spite of this emphasis on non-diversifiable risk, how is the risk of capital budgeting projects frequently measured? Why?

13–11 Compare and contrast CEs and RADRs from both a theoretical and a practical point of view. In practice, how are risk classes often used to apply RADRs? Explain.

13.4 Capital Budgeting Refinements

Refinements must often be made in the analysis of capital budgeting projects to accommodate special circumstances. These adjustments permit the relaxation of certain simplifying assumptions presented earlier. Four areas in which special forms of analysis are frequently needed are: (1) calculation of the NPV of an asset where the asset class will be closed at the end of the asset's life, (2) comparison of mutually exclusive projects having unequal lives, (3) recognition of real options, and (4) capital rationing caused by a binding budget constraint.

Closing an Asset Class

Up to this point in capital budgeting, we have assumed that the company will continue to operate with assets in the CCA asset class at the end of the project's life. But what happens if the asset being evaluated is the only asset in the class? As we saw in Chapter 2, in such a case the sale of the only asset in the class will affect the calculation of the tax shield lost and will also trigger either a recapture or a terminal loss. This will occur because the undepreciated capital cost (UCC) of the asset at the end of its useful life (its tax value) will almost certainly not be the asset's fair market value.

If the asset's tax value is greater than its market value at the end of its useful life, a terminal loss will be the result. Since a terminal loss is deductible for tax purposes, in the NPV analysis this will be a benefit. The benefit will be the present value of the tax savings due to the terminal loss (terminal loss × tax rate). If the asset's tax value is less than its market value at the end of its useful life, a recapture will occur. Since a recapture is considered income for tax purposes, this will be a cost. The cost will be the present value of the additional tax owing on the recapture (recapture × tax rate). At this time, you may wish to review the material concerning this topic in Chapter 2.

Example Bennett Company has a third capital budgeting project that must be considered. The incremental cost of the asset is $396,000, and it will result in incremental operating income of $90,000 per year for the eight-year life of the project. The CCA rate on the asset is 25 percent, and it is expected to have a salvage value of $65,000 at the end of its life. The company's tax rate is 22 percent and this is considered a risk class III asset. Therefore, we see from Table 13.4 that the RADR used to evaluate this asset is 14 percent. If the standard assumptions are made, the NPV will be calculated in the regular fashion and the result would be an NPV of $1,638. Therefore, Bennett Company should invest in the asset, as its expected return is greater than the RADR.

Now, if it is assumed that this is the only asset in the class, what will happen when it is sold at the end of its useful life? First, we will assume that the asset is sold at the beginning of year 9, so the CCA for the asset's final year of life (year 8) will be claimed. Next, we must calculate the tax value of the asset at the beginning of year 9. We can calculate the tax value of the asset at this time by using Equation 2.4 in Chapter 2, which is provided below as Equation 13.9, where d is the CCA rate:

$$\text{UCC (tax value)}_{\text{Beg Yr } N} = \text{UCC} \times (1 - d/2) \times (1 - d)^{N-2} \tag{13.9}$$

For the Bennett Company example, we must calculate the tax value as of the beginning of year 9:

$$\begin{aligned}\text{UCC (tax value)}_{\text{Beg Yr 9}} &= \$396{,}000 \times (1 - 0.25/2) \times (1 - 0.25)^{9-2} \\ &= \$396{,}000 \times 0.875 \times 0.133483887 \\ &= \$46{,}252\end{aligned}$$

So the tax value of the asset is less than its salvage value. As discussed in Chapter 2, there are two impacts of closing out the asset class. First, the tax shield lost on the asset will be affected. Recall that the tax shield is lost, since we are not satisfying the assumption that the asset will be held until it has a zero value. In the case where the asset class is closed, the tax shield lost is based on the tax value of the asset, not the market value. (This is the only time this is done.) In addition, there will be a recapture or terminal loss. By using the same process as provided in Chapter 2, we see:

UCC_{BS}	\$46,252	
Asset sold:		
Original cost	\$396,000	No capital gain
Proceeds	\$65,000	
UCC_{AS}	–\$18,748	Recapture

By the beginning of year 9, Bennett Company would have claimed \$349,748 (\$396,000 – \$46,252) of CCA on the asset. But, given the fair market value, the company should have claimed \$331,000 (\$396,000 – \$65,000) of CCA. This implies that the company claimed "too much" CCA and, as of the beginning of year 9, has recaptured previously deducted CCA. The recaptured amount is \$18,748. So, when the asset class is closed out, the expected salvage value is split into two parts: tax shield lost and a recapture (or terminal loss). In this case, the impact of the \$65,000 salvage value is split between tax shield lost (based on \$46,252) and a recapture (\$18,748) that is income for tax purposes. Based on this discussion, the NPV of the asset for Bennett Company is provided in Table 13.5.

The impact of closing out the asset class at the end of the project's life is to reduce the NPV of the asset; however, the NPV is still positive, so Bennett Company should acquire the asset.

TABLE 13.5 **Bennett Company: Net Present Value When the Asset Class Is Closed**

– Incremental cost	=	–\$396,000
+ PV of incremental after-tax operating income		
\$90,000 × (1 – 0.22) = \$70,200 × *PVIFa* (14%, 8 per)	=	+\$325,648
+ Present value of tax shield from CCA		
$\$396{,}000 \times \left[\frac{0.25 \times 0.22}{0.25 + 0.14}\right] \times \frac{1.07}{1.14}$	=	+ \$52,417
+ Present value of salvage		
\$65,000 × *PVIF* (14%, 8 per)	=	+\$22,786
– Present value of tax shield lost due to UCC[a]		
$\$46{,}252 \times PVIF\ (14\%, 8\ \text{per}) \times \left[\frac{0.25 \times 0.22}{0.25 + 0.14}\right]$	=	– \$2,287
– Present value of the tax on recapture[a]		
\$18,748 × (0.22) × *PVIF* (14%, 8 per)	=	– \$1,446
NPV of the asset	=	+ \$1,118

[a] When the asset class is expected to be closed at the end of the asset's life, the impact of the salvage value on the analysis is split into two parts: tax shield lost and a recapture (or terminal loss). The tax shield lost is based on the tax value of the asset, not the market value.

Comparing Projects with Unequal Lives

The financial manager must often select the best of a group of projects that have unequal lives. If the projects are independent, their different lives are unimportant when deciding which to accept: all those whose NPV ≥ 0 should be selected. But, when projects that have unequal lives are mutually exclusive, the impact of differing lives must be considered because the projects do not provide service over comparable time periods. This is especially important when continuing service is needed from the project under consideration. The discussions that follow assume that the mutually exclusive projects with unequal lives that are being compared *are ongoing*. If they were not, the project with the highest NPV would be selected.

The Problem

A simple example will demonstrate the basic problem of noncomparability caused by the need to select the best of a group of mutually exclusive projects with differing lives.

Example The AT Company, a regional cable-television company, is evaluating two projects, X and Y. The relevant cash flows for each project are given in the following table. The applicable discount rate to use in evaluating these equally risky projects is 10 percent.

	Project X	Project Y
Incremental cost	$70,000	$85,000
Year	Cash inflows	
1	$28,000	$35,000
2	33,000	30,000
3	38,000	25,000
4	—	20,000
5	—	15,000
6	—	10,000

The net present value of each project at the 10 percent cost of capital using a financial calculator is:

$$NPV_X = \$81,277 - \$70,000 = \underline{\underline{\$11,277}}$$

$$NPV_Y = \$104,013 - \$85,000 = \underline{\underline{\$19,013}}$$

If the projects are independent, we can see that both projects are acceptable (both NPVs are greater than zero). On the other hand, if the projects are mutually exclusive, their differing lives must be considered. At this point in the analysis, the projects are not comparable since they have different lives: project Y provides 3 more years of service than project X.

The above analysis is incomplete if the projects are mutually exclusive (which will be our assumption throughout the remaining discussions). To compare these mutually exclusive projects with unequal lives correctly, the differing lives must be considered in the analysis; an incorrect decision could result from simply using the above-calculated NPVs to select the best project. Although a number of approaches are available for dealing with unequal lives, here we present the most efficient technique—the annualized net present value (ANPV) approach.

Annualized Net Present Value (ANPV) Approach

annualized net present value (ANPV) approach
An approach to evaluating unequal-lived projects that converts the net present value of unequal-lived, mutually exclusive projects into an equivalent annual amount (in NPV terms).

The **annualized net present value (ANPV) approach** converts the net present value of projects with unequal lives into an equivalent annual amount (in NPV terms) that can be used to select the best project.[9] This net-present-value-based approach can be applied to unequal-lived, mutually exclusive projects by using the following steps:

Step 1 Calculate the net present value of each mutually exclusive project j, NPV_j, over its life, n_j, using the appropriate discount rate, k_j.

Step 2 Divide the net present value of each project having a positive NPV by the present value interest factor for an annuity at the given discount rate and the project's life to get the annualized net present value for each project j, $ANPV_j$, as shown below:

$$ANPV_j = \frac{NPV_j}{PVIFa\ (k_j, n_j\ per)} \tag{13.10}$$

Step 3 Select the project having the highest ANPV.

Example By using the AT Company data presented earlier for projects X and Y, the three-step ANPV approach can be applied as follows:

Step 1 The net present values of projects X and Y discounted at 10 percent—as calculated in the preceding example for a single purchase of each asset—are

$$NPV_X = \$11{,}277$$
$$NPV_Y = \$19{,}013$$

Step 2 Calculate the annualized net present value for each project by applying Equation 13.10 to the NPVs and using a financial calculator:

$$ANPV_X = \frac{\$11{,}277}{PVIFa\ (10\%, 3\ yrs)} = \underline{\underline{\$4{,}535}}$$

$$ANPV_Y = \frac{\$19{,}013}{PVIFa\ (10\%, 6\ yrs)} = \underline{\underline{\$4{,}366}}$$

(*Note:* To make the calculation using a financial calculator, the NPV is the PV, I is 10 percent, and N is the life of the project. Input 0 in FV and compute PMT.)

9. The theory underlying this as well as other approaches for comparing projects with unequal lives assumes that each project can be repeated in the future for the same incremental cost and that each will provide the same expected future cash inflows. Although changing technology and inflation will affect the incremental cost and expected cash inflows, the lack of specific attention to them does not detract from the usefulness of this technique.

Step 3 Reviewing the ANPVs calculated in Step 2, we can see that project X would be preferred over project Y. Given that projects X and Y are mutually exclusive, project X would be the recommended project because it provides the higher annualized net present value.

The process used to calculate the annual net present value is also provided as Spreadsheet Application 13.1. Note that the spreadsheet is easily modified to add additional years of cash inflows.

Recognizing Real Options

real options
Opportunities that are embedded in capital projects that enable managers to alter their cash flows and risk in a way that affects project acceptability (NPV). Also called *strategic options.*

The procedures described in Chapter 12 and thus far in this chapter suggest that to make capital budgeting decisions, we must (1) estimate relevant cash flows, (2) apply an appropriate decision technique such as NPV or IRR to those cash flows, and (3) recognize and adjust the decision technique for project risk. Although this traditional procedure is believed to yield good decisions, a more *strategic approach* to these decisions has emerged in recent years. This more modern view considers any **real options**—opportunities that are embedded in capital projects ("real," rather than financial, asset investments) that enable

13.1 SPREADSHEET APPLICATION

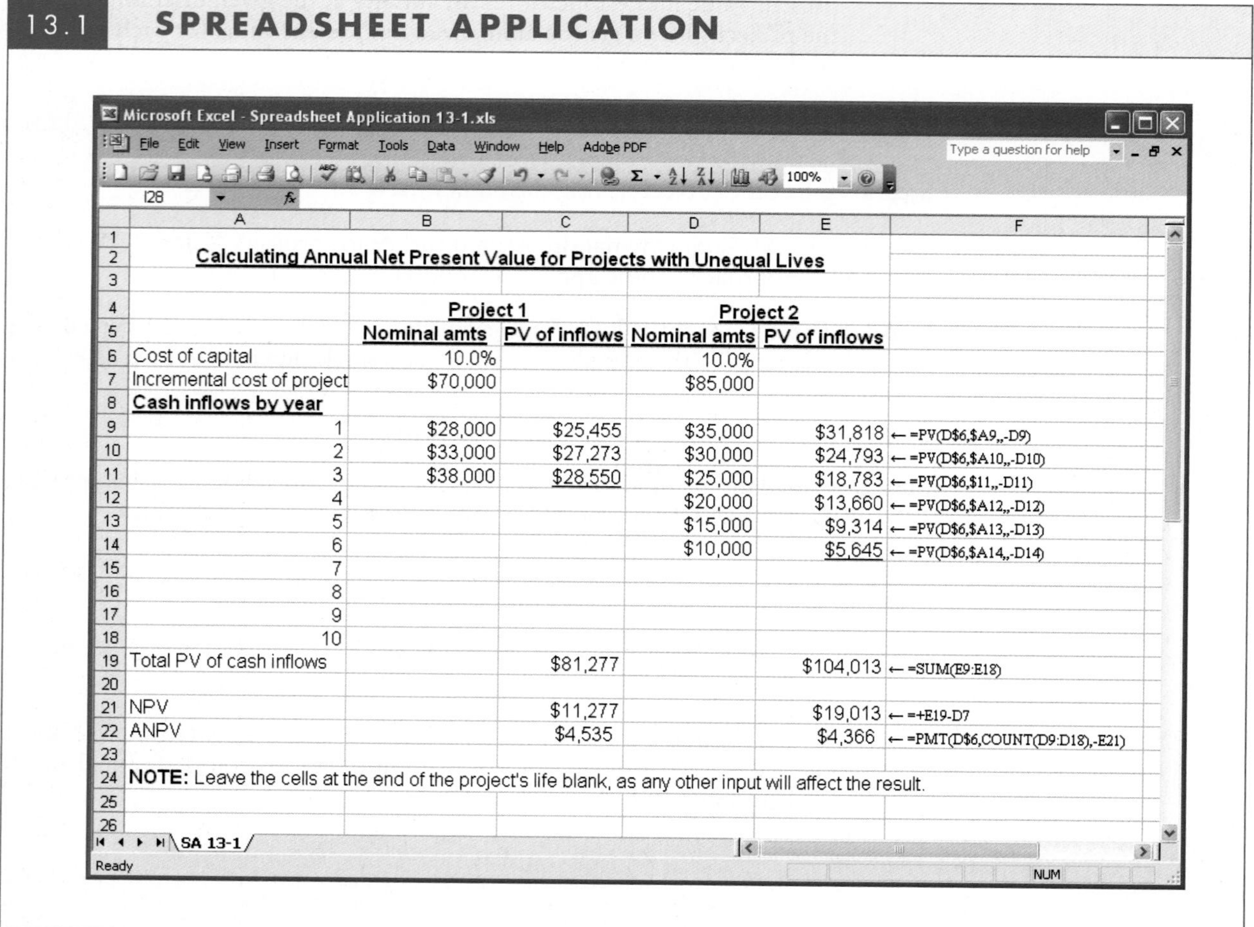

Calculating Annual Net Present Value for Projects with Unequal Lives

	Project 1		Project 2		
	Nominal amts	PV of inflows	Nominal amts	PV of inflows	
Cost of capital	10.0%		10.0%		
Incremental cost of project	$70,000		$85,000		
Cash inflows by year					
1	$28,000	$25,455	$35,000	$31,818	← =PV(D$6,$A9,,-D9)
2	$33,000	$27,273	$30,000	$24,793	← =PV(D$6,$A10,,-D10)
3	$38,000	$28,550	$25,000	$18,783	← =PV(D$6,$11,,-D11)
4			$20,000	$13,660	← =PV(D$6,$A12,,-D12)
5			$15,000	$9,314	← =PV(D$6,$A13,,-D13)
6			$10,000	$5,645	← =PV(D$6,$A14,,-D14)
7					
8					
9					
10					
Total PV of cash inflows		$81,277		$104,013	← =SUM(E9:E18)
NPV		$11,277		$19,013	← =+E19-D7
ANPV		$4,535		$4,366	← =PMT(D$6,COUNT(D9:D18),-E21)

NOTE: Leave the cells at the end of the project's life blank, as any other input will affect the result.

managers to alter their cash flows and risk in a way that affects project acceptability (NPV). Because these opportunities are more likely to exist in, and be more important to, large "strategic" capital budgeting projects, they are sometimes called *strategic options*.

Some of the more common types of real options—abandonment, flexibility, growth, and timing—are briefly described in Table 13.6. It should be clear from their descriptions that each of these types of options could be embedded in a capital budgeting decision and that explicit recognition of them would probably alter the cash flow and risk of a project and change its NPV.

By explicitly recognizing these options when making capital budgeting decisions, managers can make improved, more strategic decisions that consider in advance the economic impact of certain contingent actions on project cash flow and risk. The explicit recognition of real options embedded in capital budgeting projects will cause the project's *strategic* NPV to differ from its *traditional* NPV as indicated by Equation 13.11.

$$NPV_{strategic} = NPV_{traditional} + \text{value of real options} \tag{13.11}$$

TABLE 13.6 Major Types of Real Options

Option type	Description
Abandonment option	The option to abandon or terminate a project prior to the end of its planned life. This option allows management to avoid or minimize losses on projects that turn bad. Explicitly recognizing the abandonment option when evaluating a project often increases its NPV.
Flexibility option	The option to incorporate flexibility into the firm's operations, particularly production. It generally includes the opportunity to design the production process to accept multiple inputs, use flexible production technology to create a variety of outputs by reconfiguring the same plant and equipment, and purchase and retain excess capacity in capital-intensive industries subject to wide swings in output demand and long lead time in building new capacity from scratch. Recognition of this option embedded in a capital expenditure should increase the NPV of the project.
Growth option	The option to develop follow-on projects, expand markets, expand or retool plants, and so on, that would not be possible without implementation of the project that is being evaluated. If a project being considered has the measurable potential to open new doors if successful, then recognition of the cash flows from such opportunities should be included in the initial decision process. Growth opportunities embedded in a project often increase the NPV of the project in which they are embedded.
Timing option	The option to determine when various actions with respect to a given project are taken. This option recognizes the firm's opportunity to delay acceptance of a project for one or more periods, to accelerate or slow the process of implementing a project in response to new information, or to shut down a project temporarily in response to changing product market conditions or competition. As in the case of the other types of options, the explicit recognition of timing opportunities can improve the NPV of a project that fails to recognize this option in an investment decision.

Example Assume that a strategic analysis of Bennett Company's projects A and B (see cash flows and NPVs in Table 13.1) finds no real options embedded in project A and two real options embedded in project B. The two real options in project B are as follows: (1) the project would have, during the first two years, some downtime that would result in unused production capacity that could be used to perform contract manufacturing for another firm and (2) the project's computerized control system could, with some modification, control two other machines, thereby reducing labour cost, without affecting operation of the new project.

Bennett's management estimated the NPV of the contract manufacturing over the 2 years following implementation of project B to be \$1,500 and the NPV of the computer control sharing to be \$2,000. Management felt there was a 60 percent chance that the contract manufacturing option would be exercised and only a 30 percent chance that the computer control sharing option would be exercised. The combined value of these two real options would be the sum of their expected values.

$$\text{Value of real options for project B} = (0.60 \times \$1{,}500) + (0.30 \times \$2{,}000)$$
$$= \$900 + \$600 = \$1{,}500$$

Substituting the \$1,500 real options value along with the traditional NPV of \$10,924 for project B (from Table 13.1) into Equation 13.10, we get the strategic NPV for project B.

$$\text{NPV}_{\text{strategic}} = \$10{,}924 + \$1{,}500 = \$12{,}424$$

Bennett Company's project B therefore has a strategic NPV of \$12,424, which is above its traditional NPV and now exceeds project A's NPV of \$11,071. Clearly, recognition of project B's real options improved its NPV (from \$10,924 to \$12,424) and causes it to be preferred over project A (NPV of \$12,424 for B > NPV of \$11,071 for A), which has no real options embedded in it.

It is important to realize that the recognition of attractive real options when determining NPV could cause an otherwise unacceptable project ($\text{NPV}_{\text{traditional}} < \$0$) to become acceptable ($\text{NPV}_{\text{strategic}} \geq \$0$). The failure to recognize the value of real options could therefore cause management to reject projects that are acceptable. Although doing so requires more strategic thinking and analysis, it is important for the financial manager to identify and incorporate real options in the NPV process. The procedures for doing this efficiently are emerging, and the use of the strategic NPV that incorporates real options is expected to become more commonplace in the future.

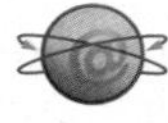

www.puc-rio.br/marco.ind/ro-links.html

http://pages.stern.nyu.edu/~adamodar/pdfiles/papers/realopt.pdf

Numerous sites are now available on the Web that discuss and illustrate real options.

Capital Rationing

Firms commonly operate under *capital rationing*—they have more acceptable independent projects than they can fund. *In theory,* capital rationing should not exist. Firms should accept all projects that have positive NPVs (or IRRs ≥ the cost of capital). However, *in practice,* most firms operate under capital rationing. Generally, firms attempt to isolate and select the best acceptable projects subject to a capital expenditure budget set by management. Research has found that management internally imposes capital expenditure constraints to avoid what it

Hint
Since everyone in the firm knows that long-term funds are rationed and they want a portion of them, there is intense competition for those funds—which increases the need for the firm to be objective and proficient in its analysis. Knowing how to use the techniques discussed in this chapter to justify your needs will help you get your share of the available long-term funds.

deems to be "excessive" levels of new financing, particularly debt. Although failing to fund all acceptable independent projects is theoretically inconsistent with the goal of owner-wealth maximization, here we discuss capital rationing procedures because they are widely used in practice.

The objective of *capital rationing* is to select the group of projects that provides the *highest overall net present value* and does not require more dollars than are budgeted. As a prerequisite to capital rationing, the best of any mutually exclusive projects must be chosen and placed in the group of independent projects. Two basic approaches to project selection under capital rationing are discussed here.

internal rate of return approach
An approach to capital rationing that involves graphing project IRRs in descending order against the total dollar investment, to determine the group of acceptable projects.

investment opportunities schedule (IOS)
The graph that plots project IRRs in descending order against total dollar investment.

Internal Rate of Return Approach

The **internal rate of return approach** involves graphing project IRRs in descending order against the total dollar investment. This graph, which was discussed in more detail in Chapter 9, is called the **investment opportunities schedule (IOS)**. By drawing the cost of capital line and then imposing a budget constraint, the financial manager can determine the group of acceptable projects. The problem with this technique is that it does not guarantee the maximum dollar return to the firm. It merely provides a satisfactory solution to capital rationing problems.

Example

Tate Company, a fast-growing plastics company, is confronted with six projects competing for its fixed budget of $250,000. The incremental cost and IRR for each project are as follows:

Project	Incremental cost	IRR
A	$ 80,000	12%
B	70,000	20
C	100,000	16
D	40,000	8
E	60,000	15
F	110,000	11

The firm has a cost of capital of 10 percent. Figure 13.6 presents the IOS resulting from ranking the six projects in descending order based on IRRs. According to the schedule, only projects B, C, and E should be accepted. Together they will absorb $230,000 of the $250,000 budget. Projects A and F are acceptable but cannot be chosen because of the budget constraint. Project D is not worthy of consideration, because its IRR is less than the firm's 10 percent cost of capital.

The drawback of this approach is that there is no guarantee that the acceptance of projects B, C, and E will maximize the total NPV of the invested funds, and therefore owners' wealth.

Profitability Index Approach

profitability index
The project's NPV divided by its incremental cost; used to determine the group of projects with the highest overall present value.

The profitability index approach is based on the net present value method. The **profitability index** is the project's NPV divided by its incremental cost. The objective is to determine the group of projects that will maximize the NPV of the

FIGURE 13.6

Investment Opportunities Schedule

Investment opportunities schedule (IOS) for Tate Company projects

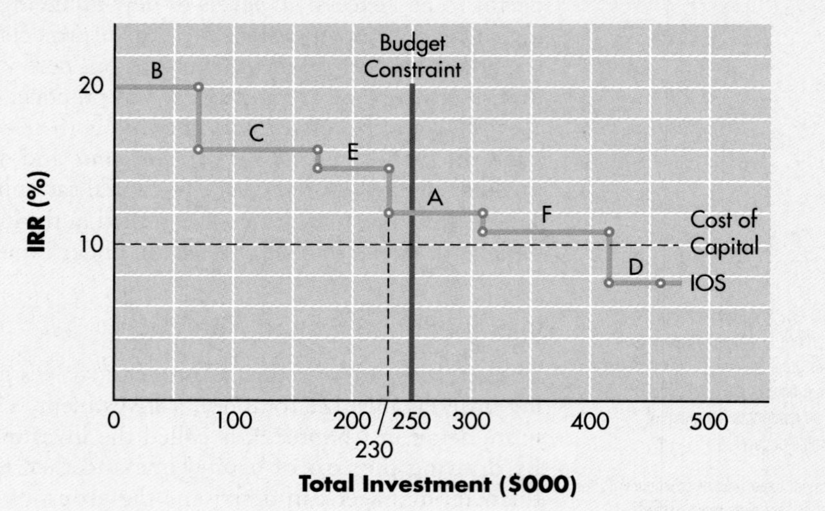

invested funds and owners' wealth. It is implemented by ranking projects on the basis of NPV, then calculating each project's profitability index to determine the combination of projects with the highest overall net present value. This is the same as maximizing net present value where the entire budget is viewed as the total incremental cost. Any portion of the firm's budget that is not used does not increase the firm's value. The unused money might be used by the firm in ways that do not increase the wealth of the owners.

Example Table 13.7 ranks the group of projects described in the preceding example on the basis of the profitability index, as shown in the final column of the table. The incremental cost, present value of the cash inflows, and NPVs for each of the projects are also included in the table. By ranking on the profitability index, we get the same results as before. Projects B, C, and E have the highest profitability indexes. Together they cost $230,000, and yield an NPV of $106,000. Is this the best set of projects to select?

TABLE 13.7 Rankings for Tate Company Projects

Project	Incremental cost	Present value of inflows at 10%	NPV	Profitability index
B	$ 70,000	$112,000	$42,000	0.60
C	100,000	145,000	45,000	0.45
E	60,000	79,000	19,000	0.32
A	80,000	100,000	20,000	0.25
F	110,000	126,500	16,500	0.15
D	40,000	36,000	−4,000	N/A

Consider that if projects B, C, and A were implemented, the total budget of $250,000 would be used, and the NPV of these projects would be $107,000. This is $1,000 greater than the return expected from selecting the projects on the basis of the profitability index. Implementing B, C, and A is preferable, because this group of projects maximizes the present value for the given budget. The firm's objective is to use the full budget available to generate the highest present value of inflows. Assuming that any unused portion of the budget generates, at best, the firm's cost of capital, the total NPV for projects B, C, and E is $106,000. For projects B, C, and A the total NPV is $107,000. This is the selection that maximizes NPV, and is the preferred choice.

? Review Questions

13–12 Explain why a mere comparison of the NPVs of unequal-lived, ongoing, mutually exclusive projects is inappropriate. Describe the *annualized net present value (ANPV)* approach for comparing unequal-lived, mutually exclusive projects.

13–13 What are real options? What are some major types of real options?

13–14 What is the difference between the *strategic* NPV and the *traditional* NPV? Do they always result in the same accept/reject decisions?

13–15 What is *capital rationing?* In theory, should capital rationing exist? Why does it frequently occur in practice?

13–16 Compare and contrast the *internal rate of return approach* and the *profitability index approach* to capital rationing. Which is better? Why?

SUMMARY

Understand the importance of explicitly recognizing risk in the analysis of capital budgeting projects. Capital budgeting projects can have risk characteristics that are different from the overall firm. These projects must be analyzed in a different manner from projects with the same risk as the firm. Risk refers to the chance that the inputs into the analysis of an investment project will prove to be wrong. The key inputs that are subject to risk are the cash flows and the discount rate. If either of these estimates is incorrect, very costly mistakes can be made. So it is important to incorporate risk considerations in capital budgeting. Various behavioural and quantitative approaches are available for explicitly recognizing risk in the analysis of capital budgeting projects. The acceptance of a project with a level of risk different from the firm impacts the firm's overall risk.

Discuss breakeven cash flow, sensitivity and scenario analysis, and simulation as behavioural approaches for dealing with risk, and the unique risks facing multinational companies. Risk in capital budgeting is concerned with either the chance that a project will prove unacceptable or, more formally, the degree of variability of cash flows. Finding the breakeven cash inflow and assessing the probability that it will be realized make up one behavioural approach that is used to assess the chance of success. Sensitivity analysis and scenario analysis are also behavioural approaches for dealing with project risk to capture the variability of cash inflows and NPVs. Simulation is a statistically based approach that results in a probability distribution of project returns. It usually requires a computer and allows the decision maker to understand the risk–return tradeoffs involved in a proposed investment. Although the basic capital budgeting techniques are the same for purely domestic and multinational companies, firms that operate in several countries must also deal with both exchange rate and political risks, tax law differences, transfer pricing, and strategic rather than strict financial issues.

Describe the two basic risk-adjustment techniques in terms of NPV and the procedures for applying the certainty equivalent (CE) approach. The risk of a project whose initial investment is known with certainty is embodied in the present value of its cash inflows, using NPV. The procedure used to calculate this present value provides two opportunities for quantitative risk adjustment: either the cash inflows or the discount rate can be adjusted for risk. The cash inflow adjustment is called certainty equivalents (CEs) and the discount rate adjustment is called risk-adjusted discount rates (RADRs). CEs are used to adjust the risky cash inflows to certain amounts, which are discounted at a risk-free rate to find the NPV. Although the process of converting risky to certain cash inflows is subjective, the use of CEs is theoretically sound.

Review the use of risk-adjusted discount rates (RADRs), portfolio effects, and the practical aspects of RADRs relative to CEs. The RADR technique includes a market-based adjustment of the discount rate used to calculate NPV. The RADR is closely linked to CAPM, but because real corporate assets are generally not traded in an efficient market, the CAPM cannot be applied directly to capital budgeting. Instead, firms develop some CAPM-type relationship to link a project's risk to its required return, which is used as the discount rate. Often, for convenience, firms will rely on total risk as an approximation for relevant risk when estimating required project returns. RADRs are commonly used in business practice because decision makers prefer rates of return and find them easier to estimate and apply, although CEs are the theoretically superior risk-adjustment technique.

Consider the impact closing an asset class has on the evaluation of a capital budgeting project, and describe the process used to evaluate mutually exclusive projects with unequal lives by calculating their annualized net present value (ANPV). For capital budgeting, if the asset being evaluated is the only asset in the class, the sale of the asset at the end of its useful life will both affect the calculation of the tax shield lost and trigger either a recapture or a terminal loss. This will occur because the undepreciated capital cost (UCC) of the asset at the end of its useful life (its tax value) will almost certainly not be the asset's fair market value. The problem of comparing mutually exclusive projects with unequal lives is that the projects do not provide service over comparable time periods. The annualized net present value (ANPV) approach is the most efficient method of comparing ongoing mutually exclusive projects having unequal usable lives. It converts the NPVs of unequal-lived projects into an equivalent annual amount—its ANPV—by dividing each project's NPV by the present value interest factor for an annuity at the given cost of capital and project life. The project with the highest ANPV is best.

Explain the role of real options and the objective of, and basic approaches to, project selection under capital rationing. Real options are opportunities that are embedded in investment projects that allow managers to alter the cash flows and risk in a way that affects a project's NPV. By explicitly recognizing real options, a project's strategic NPV can be calculated. Some of the more common types of real options are abandonment, flexibility, growth, and timing options. The strategic NPV explicitly recognizes the value of real options and thereby improves the quality of the capital budgeting decision. Capital rationing exists when firms have more acceptable independent projects than they can fund. Although, in theory, capital rationing should not exist, in practice it commonly occurs. Its objective is to select from all acceptable projects the group that provides the highest overall net present value and does not require more dollars than are budgeted. The two basic approaches for choosing projects under capital rationing are the internal rate of return approach and the profitability index. The goal of the exercise is to use the full capital budget available while maximizing the dollar amount of NPV.

SELF-TEST PROBLEM (Solution in Appendix B)

ST 13–1 **Certainty equivalents and risk-adjusted discount rates** The CAPM-type relationship linking a risk index to the required return (RADR) and the certainty equivalent factors applicable to CBA Company's mutually exclusive projects A and B follow:

Risk index	Required return (RADR)
0.0 (risk-free rate, R_F)	7.0%
0.2	8.0
0.4	9.0
0.6	10.0
0.8	11.0
1.0	12.0
1.2	13.0
1.4	14.0
1.6	15.0
1.8	16.0
2.0	17.0

	Certainty equivalent factors (α_t)	
Year (t)	Project A	Project B
0	1.00	1.00
1	0.95	0.90
2	0.90	0.85
3	0.90	0.70

The firm is considering two mutually exclusive projects, A and B. Project data are shown in the following table.

	Project A	Project B
Incremental cost (C_0)	$15,000	$20,000
Project life	3 years	3 years
Annual after-tax cash inflow	$ 7,000	$10,000
Risk index	0.4	1.8

a. Ignoring any differences in risk and assuming that the firm's cost of capital is 10 percent, calculate the net present value (NPV) of each project.
b. Using the data concerning certainty equivalents, which of the two projects should the company select? Explain.
c. Using the data concerning the risk-adjusted discount rates, which of the two projects should the company select? Explain.
d. Discuss your findings in **a**, **b**, and **c**.

PROBLEMS

  **13–1 Recognizing risk** Caradine Corp., a media services firm with net income of $3,200,000 last year, is considering several projects.

Project	Initial investment	Details
A	$ 35,000	Replace existing office furnishings.
B	500,000	Purchase digital film-editing equipment for use with several existing accounts.
C	450,000	Develop proposal to bid for a $2,000,000 per year 10-year contract with a potential new client.
D	685,000	Purchase the exclusive rights to market a quality educational television program in syndication to local markets, a part of the firm's existing business activities.

The media services business is cyclical and highly competitive. The board of directors has asked you, as chief financial officer, to:

a. Evaluate the risk of each proposed project and rank it "low," "medium," or "high."

b. Comment on why you chose each ranking. What makes the project risky?

 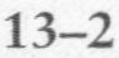 **13–2 Breakeven cash flows** Etsitty Arts, Inc., a leading producer of fine cast silver jewellery, is considering the purchase of new casting equipment that will allow it to expand the product line into award plaques. The incremental cost of the equipment is $35,000. The company expects that the equipment will produce steady income throughout its 12-year life.

a. If Etsitty requires a 14 percent return on its investment, what minimum yearly cash inflow would be necessary for the company to go forward with this project?

b. How would the minimum yearly cash inflow change if the company required a 10 percent return on its investment?

INTERMEDIATE  **13–3 Breakeven cash inflows and risk** Pueblo Enterprises is considering investing in either of two mutually exclusive projects of equal risk. Project X's cost is $30,200, project Y's $40,250. Both projects have 5-year lives. Project X's inflows are $10,000 per year; project Y's are $15,000. The firm's cost of capital is 15 percent.

a. Find the NPV for each project. Are the projects acceptable?

b. Find the *breakeven cash inflow* for each project.

c. The firm has estimated the probabilities of achieving various ranges of cash inflow for the two projects, as shown in the following table. What is the probability that each project will achieve at least its breakeven cash inflow found in **b**?

Range of cash inflow	Probability of achieving cash inflow in given range	
	Project X	Project Y
$0 to $5,000	0%	10%
$5,000 to $7,000	5	15
$7,000 to $9,000	10	20
$9,000 to $12,000	50	20
$12,000 to $15,000	15	20
$15,000 to $20,000	15	15
Above $20,000	5	0

d. Which project is more risky? Which project has the potentially higher NPV? Discuss the risk–return tradeoffs of the two projects.
e. If the firm wished to minimize the chance of accepting a negative NPV project, which project would you recommend? Which would you recommend if the goal, instead, was achieving the higher NPV?

BASIC  **13–4 Basic sensitivity analysis** Murdock Paints is in the process of evaluating two mutually exclusive additions to their processing capacity. The firm's financial analysts have developed pessimistic, most likely, and optimistic estimates of the annual cash inflows associated with each project. These estimates are shown in the following table.

	Project A	Project B
Incremental cost (C_0)	$8,000	$8,000
Outcome	Annual cash inflows (*CF*)	
Pessimistic	$ 200	$ 900
Most likely	1,000	1,000
Optimistic	1,800	1,100

a. Determine the *range* of annual cash inflows for each of the two projects.
b. Assume that the firm' s cost of capital is 10 percent and that both projects have 20-year lives. Construct a table similar to that above for the NPVs for each project. Include the *range* of NPVs for each project.
c. Do **a** and **b** provide consistent views of the two projects? Explain.
d. Which project do you recommend? Why?

BASIC  **13–5 Sensitivity analysis** James Secretarial Services is considering the purchase of one of two new personal computers, P and Q. Both are expected to provide benefits over a 10-year period, and each has a cost of $3,000. The firm uses a 10 percent cost of capital. Management has constructed the following table of estimates of probabilities and annual cash inflows for pessimistic, most likely, and optimistic results.

	Computer P	Computer Q
Outcome	Annual cash inflows (CF)	
Pessimistic	$ 500	$ 400
Most likely	750	750
Optimistic	1,000	1,200

a. Determine the *range* of annual cash inflows for each of the two computers.
b. Construct a table similar to that above for the NPVs associated with each outcome for both computers.
c. Find the *range* of NPVs, and subjectively compare the risk of each computer.

INTERMEDIATE  13–6 **Simulation** Ogden Corporation has compiled the following information on a capital expenditure proposal:
(1) The projected cash *inflows* are normally distributed with a mean of $36,000 and a standard deviation of $9,000.
(2) The projected cash *outflows* are normally distributed with a mean of $30,000 and a standard deviation of $6,000.
(3) The firm has an 11 percent cost of capital.
(4) The probability distributions of cash inflows and cash outflows are not expected to change over the project's 10-year life.
a. Describe how the preceding data can be used to develop a simulation model for finding the net present value of the project.
b. Discuss the advantages of using a simulation to evaluate the proposed project.

INTERMEDIATE  13–7 **Certainty equivalents** Allison Industries has constructed the following table that gives expected cash inflows and certainty equivalent factors for these cash inflows. These measures are for a new machine with a 5-year life that has an incremental cost of $95,000. The firm has a 15 percent cost of capital, and the risk-free rate is 10 percent.

Year (t)	Cash inflows (CF_t)	Certainty equivalent factors (α_t)
1	$35,000	1.0
2	35,000	0.8
3	35,000	0.6
4	35,000	0.6
5	35,000	0.2

a. What is the net present value for the machine (unadjusted for risk)?
b. What is the certainty equivalent net present value for the machine?
c. Should the firm accept the project? Explain.
d. Management has some doubts about the estimate of the certainty equivalent factor for year 5. There is some evidence that it may not be any lower than that for year 4. What impact might this have on the decision you recommended in c? Explain.

INTERMEDIATE  **13–8** **Certainty equivalents** Kent Manufacturing is considering investing in either of two mutually exclusive projects, C or D. The firm has a 14 percent cost of capital, and the risk-free rate is currently 9 percent. The incremental cost, expected cash inflows, and certainty equivalent factors associated for each of the projects are shown in the following table.

	Project C		Project D	
Incremental cost	**$40,000**		**$56,000**	
Year (t)	**Cash inflows (CF_t)**	**Certainty equivalent factors (α_t)**	**Cash inflows (CF_t)**	**Certainty equivalent factors (α_t)**
1	$20,000	0.90	$20,000	0.95
2	16,000	0.80	25,000	0.90
3	12,000	0.60	15,000	0.85
4	10,000	0.50	20,000	0.80
5	10,000	0.40	10,000	0.80

a. Find the net present value (unadjusted for risk) for each project. Which is preferred using this measure?
b. Find the certainty equivalent net present value for each project. Which is preferred using this risk-adjustment technique?
c. Compare and discuss your findings in **a** and **b.** Which, if either, of the projects do you recommend that the firm accept? Explain.

INTERMEDIATE  **13–9** **Risk-adjusted discount rates** Country Wallpapers is considering investing in one of three mutually exclusive projects, E, F, and G. The firm's cost of capital, k_a, is 15 percent, and the risk-free rate, R_F, is 10 percent. The firm has gathered the following basic cash flow and risk index data for each project.

	Project (j)		
	E	F	G
Incremental cost	**$15,000**	**$11,000**	**$19,000**
Year (t)		**Cash inflows (CF_t)**	
1	$ 6,000	$ 6,000	$ 4,000
2	6,000	4,000	6,000
3	6,000	5,000	8,000
4	6,000	2,000	12,000
Risk index (RI_j)	1.80	1.00	0.60

a. Find the net present value (NPV) of each project using the firm's cost of capital. Which project is preferred in this situation?
b. The firm uses the following equation to determine the risk-adjusted discount rate, RADR_j, for each project j:

$$\text{RADR}_j = R_F + [5\% \times RI_j]$$

where:

R_F = risk-free rate of return

RI_j = risk index for project j

Substitute each project's risk index into this equation to determine its RADR.

c. Use the RADR for each project to determine its risk-adjusted NPV. Which project is preferable in this situation?

d. Compare and discuss your findings in **a** and **c.** Which project do you recommend that the firm accept?

INTERMEDIATE

13–10 **Certainty equivalents and risk-adjusted discount rates** After a careful evaluation of investment alternatives and opportunities, Masters School Supplies has developed a CAPM-type relationship linking a risk index to the required return (RADR) as shown in the following table.

Risk index	Required return (RADR)
0.0	7.0% (risk-free rate, R_F)
0.2	8.0
0.4	9.0
0.6	10.0
0.8	11.0
1.0	12.0
1.2	13.0
1.4	14.0
1.6	15.0
1.8	16.0
2.0	17.0

The firm is considering two mutually exclusive projects, A and B. The following are the data the firm has been able to gather about the projects:

	Project A	Project B
Incremental cost	$20,000	$30,000
Project life	5 years	5 years
Annual cash inflow (*CF*)	$ 7,000	$10,000
Risk index	0.2	1.4

	Certainty equivalent factors (α_t)	
Year (t)	Project A	Project B
0	1.00	1.00
1	0.95	0.90
2	0.90	0.80
3	0.90	0.70
4	0.85	0.70
Greater than 4	0.80	0.60

All the firm's cash inflows have already been adjusted for taxes.

a. Evaluate the projects using *certainty equivalents*.
b. Evaluate the projects using *risk-adjusted discount rates*.
c. Discuss your findings in **a** and **b**, and explain why the two approaches are alternative techniques for considering risk in capital budgeting.

INTERMEDIATE  13–11 **Risk-adjusted rates of return and certainty equivalents** Centennial Catering, Inc., is considering two mutually exclusive investments. The company wishes to use two different evaluation methods—certainty equivalents and risk-adjusted rate of return—in its analysis. Centennial's cost of capital is 12 percent and the current risk-free rate of return is 7 percent. Cash flows associated with the two projects are as follows:

	Project X	Project Y
Incremental cost	$70,000	$78,000
Year (t)	**Cash inflows (CF_t)**	
1	$30,000	$22,000
2	30,000	32,000
3	30,000	38,000
4	30,000	46,000

a. Use a certainty equivalent approach to calculate the net present value of each project given the following certainty equivalent factors:

Year	Project X	Project Y
1	0.85	0.95
2	0.90	0.90
3	0.95	0.85
4	0.95	0.80

b. Use a risk-adjusted rate of return approach to calculate the net present value of each project given that project X has a risk index of 1.20 and project Y has a risk index of 1.40. Use the following equation to calculate the required project return for each:

$$k_j = R_F + [RI \times (k_a - R_F)]$$

c. Explain why the results of the two approaches may differ from one another. Which project would you choose? Justify your choice.

INTERMEDIATE  13–12 **Risk classes and RADR** Moses Manufacturing is attempting to select the best of three mutually exclusive projects, X, Y, and Z. Though all the projects have 5-year lives, they possess differing degrees of risk. Project X is in Class V, the highest-risk class; project Y is in Class II, the below-average-risk class; and project Z is in Class III, the average-risk class. The basic cash flow data for each project and the risk classes and risk-adjusted discount rates (RADRs) used by the firm are shown in the following tables.

	Project X	Project Y	Project Z
Incremental cost	$180,000	$235,000	$310,000
Year (t)	Cash inflows (CF_t)		
1	$80,000	$50,000	$90,000
2	70,000	60,000	90,000
3	60,000	70,000	90,000
4	60,000	80,000	90,000
5	60,000	90,000	90,000

Risk Classes and RADRs		
Risk class	Description	Risk-adjusted discount rate (RADR)
I	Lowest risk	10%
II	Below-average risk	13
III	Average risk	15
IV	Above-average risk	19
V	Highest risk	22

a. Find the risk-adjusted NPV for each project.
b. Which project, if any, would you recommend that the firm undertake?

INTERMEDIATE

13–13 **Graphing risk, determining equation for the line, calculating NPV** Preston Lumber has recently calculated the following relationship between the risk index and the required rate of return:

Risk index	Required rate of return
0.0	6%
0.4	8
0.8	10
1.2	12
1.6	14
2.0	16

The firm is evaluating the following mutually exclusive projects which both have 4-year lives and incremental costs of $4,000. The annual cash inflows under three operating environments are provided below. All components of the cash inflows are included.

	Project A		Project B	
	Annual cash inflows	Probability	Annual cash inflows	Probability
Pessimistic	$–2,000	0.25	$–100	0.20
Most likely	2,000	0.50	1,600	0.50
Optimistic	6,000	0.25	3,000	0.30

a. Graph the relationship between risk and return as suggested by the above data. Be sure to label the axis and indicate the area of risk premium. What is the equation for this line?
b. Calculate the expected cash inflows for both projects.
c. The risk index for project A is 1.4 but only 0.60 for project B. Use the equation determined in **a** to determine the appropriate risk-adjusted discount rate Preston should use to evaluate each project.
d. Which project do you recommend the company select and why?

CHALLENGE

13–14 **Integrative—Determining NPV** Mead Computing is considering entering a new line of business: either the SAT or the TAT software market. The annual incremental before-tax operating incomes associated with a range of outcomes and the probabilities of the outcomes occurring are presented below:

	SAT		TAT	
Outcome	Incremental operating income	Probability	Incremental operating income	Probability
Optimistic	$24,000	15%	$42,000	10%
Most likely	18,500	60	29,000	70
Pessimistic	11,750	25	3,000	20

Both projects require that Mead acquire additional fixed assets. The cost for SAT is $42,150 while TAT's cost is $56,150. Due to increasing sales, SAT will require that Mead invest an additional $12,500 in net working capital while TAT will require an additional $14,000 investment in net working capital. The assets for both projects are Class 8 with a CCA rate of 20 percent. The two projects are expected to have five-year lives, when SAT's market value will be $1,000. TAT's market value will be $10,000. Mead Computing's tax rate is 40 percent. Based on the risk indexes for the two projects, Mead Company's CFO has determined that the risk-adjusted discount rate is 13.7 percent for SAT and 16.2 percent for TAT.

a. Calculate the expected operating income for both the SAT and the TAT project.
b. Which project would you recommend the company accept: (i) if the projects were independent; (ii) if the projects were mutually exclusive? Explain the reasons for your answers.
c. Now assume that at the end of both projects' useful lives, the asset classes will be closed. What impact does this have on your answers to part **b**?
d. Now assume that TAT will have a life of 8 years. What impact does this have on your answers to part **b**? For this part, assume the asset classes are not closed.

CHALLENGE

13–15 **Integrative—Determining NPV** The Tuna Company is contemplating introducing a new product, Zape, either on a limited scale in New Brunswick or on a broader scale throughout the Maritime provinces. The incremental cost will be \$150,000 if Zape is launched only in New Brunswick but \$500,000 if a full Maritime provinces launch is undertaken. Both projects qualify for a 10 percent ITC. The assets acquired for the projects are similar and have a CCA rate of 15 percent. Both projects are expected to have productive lives of 15 years. The salvage values are expected to be \$43,000 and \$122,000 for the New Brunswick and Maritime projects, respectively.

The company's management has estimated that the expected incremental before-tax operating income associated with Zape will be \$58,000 for the New Brunswick launch but will be \$150,000 for the Maritime province-wide launch. Both projects will require increased investments in net working capital. For the New Brunswick project it will total \$40,000 but a more substantial \$125,000 will be required for the Maritime province project. Tuna Company's marginal tax rate is 40 percent. A consultant hired by Tuna Company has suggested that due to different risk profiles, the two projects should be evaluated at different discount rates. The consultant has suggested that 11.5 percent is an appropriate RADR for the New Brunswick launch but due to greater risk, a 13.3 percent RADR should be used for the Maritime province-wide launch.

a. Should Zape be introduced? If so, which is better, only in New Brunswick or throughout the Maritimes?

b. If the SML were used to determine project selection, what additional information is needed? Explain each component.

c. Now assume that at the end of both projects' useful lives, the asset classes will be closed. What impact does this have on your answer to part **a**?

d. Now assume that the Maritime project will have a life of 20 years. What impact does this have on your answers to part **a**? For this part, assume the asset classes are not closed.

INTERMEDIATE 

13–16 **Unequal lives** Evans Industries wishes to select the best of three possible machines, each expected to fulfill the firm's ongoing need for additional aluminum-extrusion capacity. The three machines—A, B, and C—are equally risky. The firm plans to use a 12 percent cost of capital to evaluate each of them. The incremental costs and annual cash inflows over the life of each of the machines are shown in the following table.

	Machine A	Machine B	Machine C
Incremental cost	\$92,000	\$65,000	\$100,500
Year (t)	**Cash inflows (CF_t)**		
1	\$12,000	\$10,000	\$30,000
2	12,000	20,000	30,000
3	12,000	30,000	30,000
4	12,000	40,000	30,000
5	12,000	—	30,000
6	12,000	—	—

a. Calculate the NPV for each machine over its life. Rank the machines in descending order based on NPV.

b. Use the *annualized net present value (ANPV)* approach to evaluate and rank the machines in descending order based on the ANPV.

c. Discuss your findings in **a** and **b**. Which machine would you recommend that the firm acquire? Why?

INTERMEDIATE 

13–17 **Unequal lives** Portland Products is considering the purchase of one of three mutually exclusive projects for increasing production efficiency. The firm plans to use a 14 percent cost of capital to evaluate these equal-risk projects. The costs and annual cash inflows over the life of each project are shown in the following table.

	Project X	Project Y	Project Z
Incremental cost	$78,000	$52,000	$66,000
Year (t)		Cash inflows (CF_t)	
1	$17,000	$28,000	$15,000
2	25,000	38,000	15,000
3	33,000	—	15,000
4	41,000	—	15,000
5	—	—	15,000
6	—	—	15,000
7	—	—	15,000
8	—	—	15,000

a. Calculate the NPV for each project over its life. Rank the projects in descending order based on NPV.

b. Use the *annualized net present value (ANPV)* approach to evaluate and rank the projects in descending order based on the ANPV.

c. Discuss your findings in **a** and **b**. Which project would you recommend that the firm purchase? Why?

INTERMEDIATE 

13–18 **Unequal lives** JBL Co. can design a new product sampling system, but management must choose among three alternative courses of action: (1) Complete the design and then sell it outright to another corporation with payment over 2 years. (2) License the design to another manufacturer for a period of 5 years, its likely product life. (3) Manufacture and market the system itself. The company has a cost of capital of 12 percent. Cash flows associated with each alternative are as follows:

Alternative	Sell	License	Manufacture
Cost	$200,000	$200,000	$450,000
Year (t)	Cash inflows (CF_t)		
1	$200,000	$250,000	$200,000
2	250,000	100,000	250,000
3		80,000	200,000
4		60,000	200,000
5		40,000	200,000
6			200,000

a. Calculate the net present value of each alternative and rank the alternatives according to NPV.
b. Calculate the *annualized net present value (ANPV)* of each alternative and rank them accordingly.
c. Which project should be selected? Why? Why is ANPV preferred over NPV when ranking projects with unequal lives?

13–19 Real options and the strategic NPV Jenny Rene, the CFO of Asor Products, Inc., has just completed an evaluation of a proposed capital expenditure for equipment that would expand the firm's manufacturing capacity. Using the traditional NPV methodology, she found the project unacceptable because

$$NPV_{traditional} = -\$1,700$$

Before recommending rejection of the proposed project, she has decided to assess whether there might be real options embedded in the firm's cash flows. Her evaluation uncovered the following three options.

Option 1: Abandonment—The project could be abandoned at the end of 3 years, resulting in an addition to NPV of $1,200.

Option 2: Expansion—If the projected outcomes occurred, an opportunity to expand the firm's product offerings further would occur at the end of 4 years. Exercise of this option is estimated to add $3,000 to the project's NPV.

Option 3: Delay—Certain phases of the proposed project could be delayed if market and competitive conditions caused the firm's forecast revenues to develop more slowly than planned. Such a delay in implementation at that point has an NPV of $10,000.

Rene estimated that there was a 25 percent chance that the abandonment option would need to be exercised, a 30 percent chance that the expansion option would be exercised, and only a 10 percent chance that the implementation of certain phases of the project would have to be delayed.

a. Use the information provided to calculate the strategic NPV, $NPV_{strategic}$, for Asor Products' proposed equipment expenditure.
b. Judging on the basis of your findings in part **a**, what action should Rene recommend to management with regard to the proposed equipment expenditures?
c. In general, how does this problem demonstrate the importance of considering real options when making capital budgeting decisions?

INTERMEDIATE 

13–20 Capital rationing Valley Corporation is attempting to select the best of a group of independent projects competing for the firm's fixed capital budget of $4.5 million. The firm recognizes that any unused portion of this budget will earn, at best, its 15 percent cost of capital. The firm has summarized the key data to be used in selecting the best group of projects in the following table.

Project	Incremental cost	IRR	Present value of inflows at 15%
A	$5,000,000	17%	$5,400,000
B	800,000	18	1,100,000
C	2,000,000	19	2,300,000
D	1,500,000	16	1,600,000
E	800,000	22	900,000
F	2,500,000	23	3,000,000
G	1,200,000	20	1,300,000

a. Use the *internal rate of return (IRR) approach* to select the best group of projects.
b. Use the *profitability index approach* to select the best group of projects.
c. Which projects should the firm implement? Why?

INTERMEDIATE 

13–21 Capital rationing A firm with a 13 percent cost of capital must select the optimal group of projects from those shown in the following table, given its capital budget of $1 million.

Project	Incremental cost	NPV at 13% cost of capital
A	$300,000	$ 84,000
B	200,000	10,000
C	100,000	25,000
D	900,000	90,000
E	500,000	70,000
F	100,000	50,000
G	800,000	160,000

a. Select the optimal group of projects, keeping in mind that unused funds will earn, at most, the firm's cost of capital.

CASE CHAPTER 13 Evaluating Cherone Equipment's Risky Plans for Increasing Its Production Capacity

See the enclosed Student CD-ROM for cases that help you put theories and concepts from the text into practice.

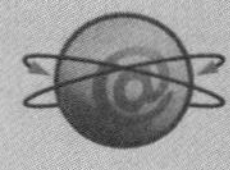

Be sure to visit the Companion Website for this book at **www.pearsoned.ca/gitman** for a wealth of additional learning tools including self-test quizzes, Web exercises, and additional cases.

CHAPTER 14

Working Capital and the Management of Current Assets

LEARNING GOALS

LG1 Understand why the active management of working capital is important, the concept of net working capital, and the related tradeoff between profitability and risk.

LG2 Describe the cash conversion cycle, the required financing that is implied in the calculation, and three strategies that firms may follow to finance this investment in net working capital.

LG3 Discuss inventory management: differing views, common techniques, and international concerns.

LG4 Explain the credit selection process and the quantitative procedure for evaluating changes in credit standards.

LG5 Review the procedures for quantitatively considering cash discount changes, other aspects of credit terms, and credit monitoring.

LG6 Understand the management of receipts and disbursements, including float, speeding up collections, slowing payments, cash concentration, zero-balance accounts, and investing in marketable securities.

14.1 Working Capital Fundamentals

The firm's balance sheet provides information about the structure of its investments on the one hand and the structure of its financing sources on the other. The structures chosen should consistently lead to the maximization of the value of the owners' investment in the firm.

Accelerating the Flow

Managing current assets and financing the investment in current assets is a vital task for most businesses. This is particularly the case for small businesses and for retailers who have proportionally much larger investments in current assets than large or manufacturing-oriented businesses. The amount of cash to hold, accounts receivable policy and management, and decisions regarding inventory are daily issues for financial managers. So too are decisions regarding how the investment in these current assets is financed. Deciding on the mix of financing that should be used is an ongoing concern. Making correct working capital decisions is vital for a firm to remain solvent and for firm value to increase. But managing a business's current assets and securing appropriate financing are complex tasks. In this chapter, we look at techniques and strategies for managing working capital—current assets and liabilities. We first discuss the fundamentals of net working capital and then demonstrate the cash conversion cycle. The balance of the chapter considers the management of inventory, accounts receivable, and receipts and disbursements in the context of the cash conversion cycle.

Important components of the firm's structure include the level of investment in current assets and the use of current liability financing. Figure 14.1 provides a breakdown of the assets and liabilities for non-financial Canadian corporations for the first quarter of 2006. To put these percentages in perspective, total assets for these non-financial corporations were $2.42 trillion. For the assets, it is interesting to note that the percentages for the three main assets, current, investments,

LINKING THE DISCIPLINES: Cross-Functional Interactions

- *Accounting personnel* need to understand the cash conversion cycle and the management of inventory, accounts receivable, and the cash receipts and disbursements. They will also do the aging of accounts receivable and will be helpful in making the determination of whether the credit standards of the firm should be changed.
- *Information systems analysts* need to understand the cash conversion cycle and the management of inventory, accounts receivable, and the cash receipts and disbursements to design systems that facilitate effective short-term financial management.
- *Management* need to understand working capital to decide how much to invest in each current asset and how to finance the investment in the current assets.
- The *marketing department* need to understand credit selection and monitoring, because sales will be affected by the availability of credit to purchasers. In addition, sales will be greatly affected by inventory management.
- Personnel in the *operations department* will need to understand the cash conversion cycle, because they will be responsible for reducing the cycle through the efficient management of production, inventory, and costs.

and net fixed assets, are all roughly the same. While much attention is paid to the management of fixed assets, it is obvious from this figure that the management of the current assets and investment accounts are also vital.

Of the total assets, current assets were $681.8 billion, or 28.2 percent of total assets. Of the current assets, accounts receivable was the largest at $293.1 billion (43% of total current assets), inventory was next at $239 billion (35.1% of total current assets), while cash was $149.7 billion (21.9% of total current assets). These are very large numbers and explain why working capital management is important.

FIGURE 14.1

Quarterly Balance Sheet for Non-financial Canadian Companies, 2006

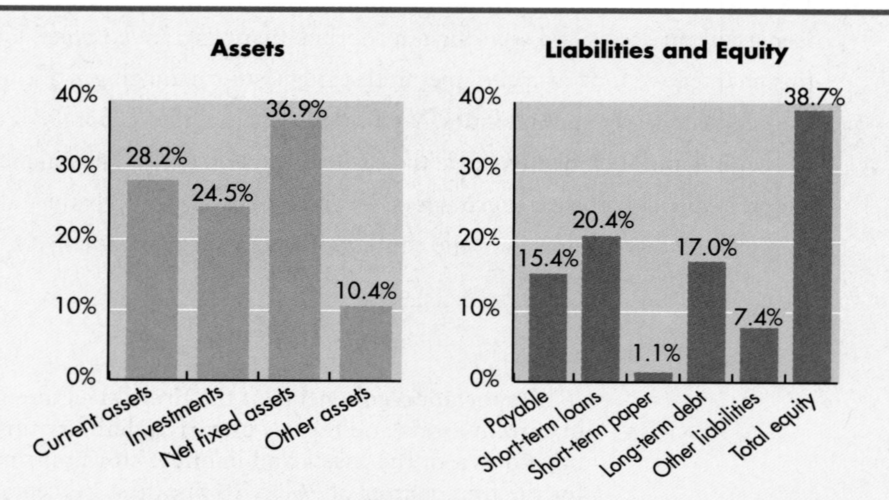

SOURCE: "Quarterly Balance Sheet for Non-financial Canadian Companies," adapted from the Statistics Canada CANSIM II database cansim2.statcan.ca/cgi-win/CNSMCGI.EXE, table 187-0001.

Turning to the liabilities and equity part of the figure, current liabilities are a surprisingly high portion of total liabilities and equity. Accounts payable and accruals are 15.4 percent of the total and a similar amount is long-term debt. Short-term loans and short-term paper combined are 21.5 percent and are a larger percentage of the total than is long-term debt. Total current liabilities, at 36.9 percent of total liabilities and equity, are about the same percentage as equity. Given these real statistics, it is clear that current liabilities are a large and important source of financing for Canadian corporations. It is also surprising to see that current liabilities are much larger than current assets. This may be explained by two factors.

First, is the classification system used in collecting the data. The investments account likely has a significant amount of short-term items that would increase the current asset percentage. Second, referring back to Figure 8.2, we can see that short-term interest rates declined dramatically during the 1990s, and remained very low through the 2000s. Corporations would see this trend, and many likely switched some of their borrowing from the long-term to the short-term markets.

short-term financial management or **working capital management** Management of current assets and current liabilities.

Given these statistics, it should not be surprising to learn that **short-term financial management**—managing current assets and current liabilities—is one of the financial manager's most important and time-consuming activities. A study of 1,000 companies found that more than one-third of financial management time is spent managing current assets and about one-fourth of financial management time is spent managing current liabilities.[1] This finding is understandable given that decisions in these two areas must be made on a daily basis. In contrast, investment decisions for fixed assets or longer term investments are often made only a few times per year and, while clearly major decisions, likely consume less total time.

The goal of short-term financial management is to manage each of the firm's current assets (inventory, accounts receivable, cash, and marketable securities) and current liabilities (accounts payable, accruals, and short-term loans) to achieve a balance between profitability and risk that contributes positively to the firm's value. Too large an investment in current assets can reduce profitability, whereas too little investment increases liquidity risk: the risk of not being able to repay debts as they come due. Too little current liability financing can reduce profitability, whereas too much increases liquidity risk. These situations generally lead to a reduction in the value of the firm.

For all companies, there is an optimal level of current assets and optimal amount of current liabilities. In reality, as with all things optimal, the difficulty is trying to determine these "ideal" amounts. In this chapter, we first use net working capital to consider the basic relationship between current assets and current liabilities and then use the cash conversion cycle to consider the key aspects of current asset management. In the following chapter, we consider current liability management.

Net Working Capital

Short-term financial management is also referred to as **working capital management.** The two terms are used interchangeably in the book. As previously discussed, current assets represent the portion of investment that circulates from

1. Lawrence J. Gitman and Charles E. Maxwell, "Financial Activities of Major U.S. Firms: Survey and Analysis of Fortune's 1000," *Financial Management*, Winter 1985, pp. 57–65.

one form to another in the ordinary conduct of business. This idea embraces the recurring transition from cash to inventories to receivables and back to cash. As cash substitutes, *marketable securities* are considered part of working capital.

Current liabilities represent the firm's short-term financing, because they include all debts of the firm that come due (must be paid) in 1 year or less. These debts usually include amounts owed to suppliers (accounts payable), employees and governments (accruals), and banks (short-term loans like a line of credit), among others.

net working capital
The difference between the firm's current assets and its current liabilities; can be positive or negative.

As noted in Chapters 2 and 12, **net working capital** is commonly defined as the difference between the firm's current assets and its current liabilities. When the current assets exceed the current liabilities, the firm has *positive net working capital.* When current assets are less than current liabilities, the firm has *negative net working capital.* The first situation is the more usual one.

Hint
Stated differently, some portion of current assets is usually held to provide liquidity in case it is unexpectedly needed.

The conversion of current assets from inventory to receivables to cash provides the source of cash used to pay the current liabilities. The cash outlays for current liabilities are relatively predictable. When an obligation is incurred, the firm generally knows when the corresponding payment will be due. What is difficult to predict are the cash inflows—the conversion of the current assets to more liquid forms. The more predictable its cash inflows, the less net working capital a firm needs. Because most firms are unable to match cash inflows to outflows with certainty, current assets that more than cover outflows for current liabilities are usually necessary. In general, the greater the margin by which a firm's current assets cover its current liabilities, the better able it will be to pay its bills as they come due.

The Tradeoff Between Profitability and Risk

profitability
The relationship between revenues and costs generated by using the firm's assets—both current and fixed—in productive activities.

risk (of technical insolvency)
The probability that a firm will be unable to pay its bills as they come due.

technically insolvent
Describes a firm that is unable to pay its bills as they come due.

A tradeoff exists between a firm's profitability and its risk. **Profitability,** in this context, is the relationship between revenues and costs generated by using the firm's assets—both current and fixed—in productive activities. A firm's profits can be increased by (1) increasing revenues or (2) decreasing costs. **Risk,** in the context of short-term financial management, is the probability that a firm will be unable to pay its bills as they come due. A firm that cannot pay its bills as they come due is said to be **technically insolvent.** It is generally assumed that the greater the firm's net working capital, the lower its risk. In other words, the more net working capital, the more liquid the firm and therefore the lower its risk of becoming technically insolvent. Using these definitions of profitability and risk, we can demonstrate the tradeoff between them by considering changes in current assets and current liabilities separately.

Changes in Current Assets

How does changing the level of a firm's current assets affect its risk/return tradeoff? To answer, we will consider the ratio of current assets to total assets. This ratio indicates the *percentage of total assets* that is current. For purposes of illustration, we will assume that the amount of total assets remains unchanged.[2] The effects of an increase or decrease in this ratio on both profitability and risk are summarized in the upper portion of Table 14.1. When the

2. In order to isolate the effect of changing asset and financing mixes on the firm's profitability and risk, we assume the level of total assets to be *constant* in this and the following discussion.

TABLE 14.1 Effects of Changing Ratios on Profits and Risk

Ratio	Change in ratio	Effect on profit	Effect on risk
Current assets / Total assets	Increase	Decrease	Decrease
	Decrease	Increase	Increase
Current liabilities / Total assets	Increase	Increase	Increase
	Decrease	Decrease	Decrease

ratio increases—that is, when current assets increase—profitability decreases. Why? Because current assets are less profitable than fixed assets. Fixed assets are more profitable because they add more value to the product than that provided by current assets. Without fixed assets, the firm could not produce the product.

Risk, however, decreases as the ratio of current assets to total assets increases. The increase in current assets increases net working capital, thereby reducing the risk of technical insolvency. In addition, as you go down the asset side of the balance sheet, the risk associated with the assets increases: investment in cash and marketable securities is less risky than investment in accounts receivable, inventories, and fixed assets. Accounts receivable investment is less risky than investment in inventories and fixed assets. Investment in inventories is less risky than investment in fixed assets. The nearer an asset is to cash, the more liquid, and therefore the less risky, it is. The opposite effects on profit and risk result from a decrease in the ratio of current assets to total assets.

Hint
Receivables are more liquid than inventory; they are one step away from cash. Inventory is two steps away; it must first be sold, then converted to a receivable before it becomes cash.

Changes in Current Liabilities

Changing the level of a firm's current liabilities also affects its risk–return tradeoff. This can be demonstrated by using the ratio of current liabilities to total assets. This ratio indicates the percentage of total assets that have been financed with current liabilities. Again, assuming that total assets remain unchanged, the effects on both profitability and risk of an increase or decrease in the ratio are summarized in the lower portion of Table 14.1. When the ratio increases, return (profitability) increases. Why? Because the firm uses more of the less expensive current liability financing and less long-term financing.

Current liabilities are less expensive because only short-term loans have a direct cost. The other current liabilities, especially accounts payable, do not have an interest cost (assuming the company pays them within the credit period). From Figure 14.1, it can be seen that accounts payable and accruals, the no-cost sources of financing, are a large component of total current liabilities. However, when the ratio of current liabilities to total assets increases, the risk of technical insolvency also increases, because the increase in current liabilities in turn decreases net working capital. The opposite effects on profit and risk result from a decrease in the ratio of current liabilities to total assets.

? Review Questions

14–1 Why is *short-term financial management* one of the most important and time-consuming activities of the financial manager? What is *net working capital*?

14–2 What is the relationship between the predictability of a firm's cash inflows and its required level of net working capital? How are net working capital, liquidity, and *risk of technical insolvency* related?

14–3 Why does an increase in the ratio of current to total assets decrease both profits and risk as measured by net working capital? How do changes in the ratio of current liabilities to total assets affect profitability and risk?

14.2 The Cash Conversion Cycle

Central to short-term financial management is an understanding of the firm's cash conversion cycle.[3] This cycle frames discussion of the management of the firm's current assets in this chapter and that of the management of current liabilities in Chapter 15. Here, we demonstrate the calculation and application of the cash conversion cycle. Before doing so, however, we introduce the concept of investing in net working capital using an example.

Example Assume a firm starts a new fiscal year with $0 amount of cash, inventory, accounts receivable, and accounts payable. During January, the company purchases $400,000 of materials on credit. The company also incurs $250,000 of labour expense that they pay for in cash by the end of the month. During the month, the company produces finished products that can be sold for $1,300,000 (twice the cost of production). In January they sell $335,000 of the product for cash and $445,000 on credit. No collections of the credit sales are made by month-end. On January 30, the company makes a $60,000 payment to their supplier for the materials purchased. Determine the values of each of the accounts as of the end of January. What is the implication?

	Start of year	End of January
Cash	$0	$ 25,000
Inventory	$0	$260,000
Accounts receivable	$0	$445,000
Accounts payable	$0	$340,000

The firm's mark-up is 100% of the production costs. During January, they sold 60 percent of production, so inventory is 40 percent of the costs incurred, or $260,000. So, at the end of January, the firm has $730,000 invested in current assets (a required investment), offset by $340,000 in accounts payable. Thus, by the end of January, the firm requires $390,000 of financing. Holding cash, inventory, and receivables requires financing. This is partially offset by the financing received from suppliers. Note that increasing payables is a spontaneous source of financing; it occurs when the firm buys the materials needed to produce inventory.

3. The conceptual model that is used in this section to demonstrate basic short-term financial management strategies was developed by Lawrence J. Gitman in "Estimating Corporate Liquidity Requirements: A Simplified Approach," *The Financial Review,* 1974, pp. 79–88, and refined and operationalized by Lawrence J. Gitman and Kanwal S. Sachdeva in "A Framework for Estimating and Analyzing the Required Working Capital Investment," *Review of Business and Economic Research*, Spring 1982, pp. 35–44.

Calculating the Cash Conversion Cycle

operating cycle (OC)
The time from the beginning of the production process to the collection of cash from the sale of the finished product.

Hint
A firm can lower its working capital if it can speed up its operating cycle. For example, if a firm accepts credit cards, it will receive cash sooner after the sale is transacted than if it has to wait until the customer pays its accounts receivable.

cash conversion cycle (CCC)
The amount of time a firm's resources are tied up; calculated by subtracting the average payment period from the operating cycle.

A firm's **operating cycle** (OC) is the time from the beginning of the production process to collection of cash from the sale of the finished product. The operating cycle encompasses two major short-term asset categories: inventory and accounts receivable. It is measured in elapsed time by summing the *average age of inventory (AAI)* and the *average collection period (ACP)*.

$$OC = AAI + ACP \tag{14.1}$$

However, the process of producing and selling a product also includes the purchase of production inputs (raw materials) on account, which results in accounts payable. Accounts payable reduce the number of days a firm's resources are tied up in the operating cycle. The time it takes to pay the accounts payable, measured in days, is the *average payment period (APP)*. The operating cycle less the average payment period is referred to as the **cash conversion cycle (CCC)**. It represents the amount of time the firm's resources are tied up. The formula for the cash conversion cycle is

$$CCC = OC - APP \tag{14.2}$$

Substituting the relationship in Equation 14.1 into Equation 14.2, we can see that the cash conversion cycle has three main components, as shown in Equation 14.3: (1) average age of the inventory, (2) average collection period, and (3) average payment period.

$$CCC = AAI + ACP - APP \tag{14.3}$$

Clearly, if a firm changes any of these time periods, it changes the amount of funds tied up in the day-to-day operation of the firm.

Example MAX Company, a producer of paper dinnerware, has annual credit sales of \$10 million, a cost of goods sold of 75 percent of sales, and purchases that are 65 percent of cost of goods sold. MAX has an average age of inventory (AAI) of 60 days, an average collection period (ACP) of 40 days, and an average payment period (APP) of 35 days. Thus the cash conversion cycle for MAX is 65 days (60 + 40 − 35). Figure 14.2 presents MAX Company's operating cycle and cash conversion cycle as a time line.

The funds MAX must invest in this cash conversion cycle (based on a 365-day year) are provided below. Note the implication. This analysis means that for an average day during the year, MAX Company must secure financing of \$1,861,301 to support the 65-day net investment that must be made in inventory and receivables. Short- and/or long-term sources of financing will be used.

Inventory = [(\$10,000,000 × 0.75) ÷ 365] × 60 days	=	\$1,232,877
+ Accounts receivable = (\$10,000,000 ÷ 365) × 40 days	=	+\$1,095,890
− Accounts payable = [(\$10,000,000 × 0.75 × 0.65) ÷ 365] × 35 days	=	−\$ 467,466
Net funds invested in the CCC (inventory and receivables)		\$1,861,301

Note that the basic process used to calculate these amounts is based on the ratios used to calculate AAI, ACP, and APP that were discussed in Chapter 3. Total inventory is based on daily inventory times AAI. Accounts receivable are

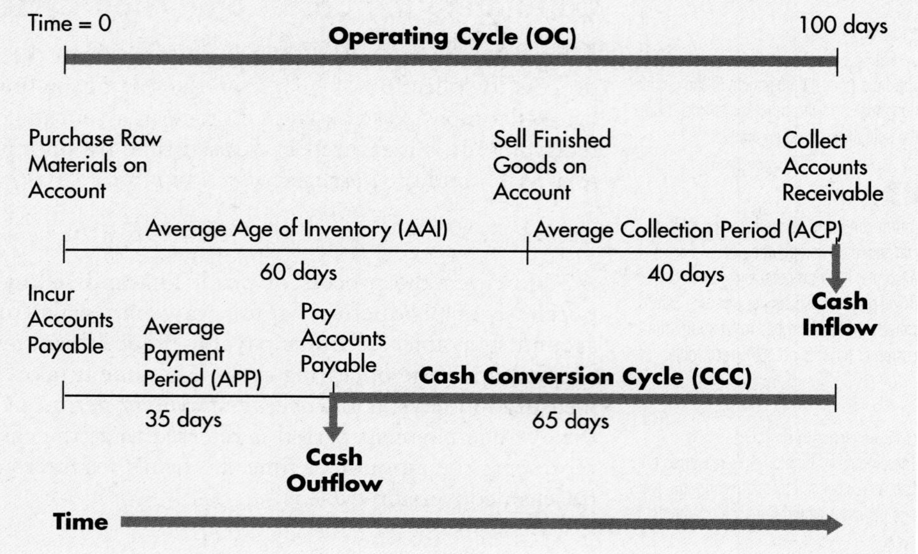

FIGURE 14.2
Time Line for MAX Company's Cash Conversion Cycle
MAX Company's operating cycle is 100 days, and its cash conversion cycle is 65 days

based on daily credit sales times ACP. Accounts payable are based on daily credit purchases times APP.

Changes in any of the time periods will change the resources tied up in operations. For example, if MAX could reduce the average collection period on its accounts receivable by 5 days, it would shorten the cash conversion cycle by 5 days and thus reduce the amount MAX must invest in operations. For MAX, a 5-day reduction in the average collection period would reduce the resources invested in the cash conversion cycle by \$136,986 [(\$10,000,000 ÷ 365) × 5] or 7.4 percent.

The process used to calculate the annual net investment in the CCC and to calculate the CCC is provided as Spreadsheet Application 14.1. Note that the spreadsheet is easily modified.

Funding Net Working Capital (Cash Conversion Cycle)

We can use the cash conversion cycle as a basis for discussing how the firm funds its required investment in net working capital. We first differentiate between permanent and seasonal financing needs and then describe three strategies for financing the required investment.

Permanent Versus Seasonal Financing

If a firm's sales and all other accounts are the same amount each day, then its investment in net working capital (CCC) will never vary—it will be the same each day. This means that there will be a permanent amount of current assets on the balance sheet that must be financed. The firm requires **permanent financing** of this same amount.

permanent financing
Financing required to fund a permanent amount of current assets on the balance sheet.

14.1 SPREADSHEET APPLICATION

Microsoft Excel - Spreadsheet Application 14-1.xls

File Edit View Insert Format Tools Data Window Help Adobe PDF

J51

	A	B	C	D
1				
2	**Calculating the CCC or the Net Funds Invested in the CCC**			
3				
4	**Calculating Net Funds Invested in CCC - MAX Company**			
5	Credit sales	$10,000,000		
6	COGS (% of sales)	75.0%		
7	Purchases (% of COGS)	65.0%		
8	Average age of inventory (days)	60.0		
9	Average collection period (days)	40.0		
10	Average payment period (days)	35.0		
11	Cost of funds invested in current assets	10.6%		
12				
13	**Outputs**			**Formulas**
14	Operating cycle (in days) - OC	100	←	=+B8+B9
15	Cash conversion cycle (in days) - CCC	65	←	=+B14-B10
16	Amount invested in inventory	$1,232,877	←	=+((B5*B6)/365)*B8
17	Amount invested in receivables	$1,095,890	←	=+(B5/365)*B9
18	Level of payables	$467,466	←	=+((B5*B6*B7)/365)*B10
19	Net funds invested in CCC	$1,861,301	←	=+B16+B17-B18
20				
21	Cost of funds invested	$197,298	←	=+B19*B11
22				
23				
24	**Calculating CCC - Assumed Numbers**			
25	Credit sales	$6,537,129		
26	COGS (% of sales)	61.1%		
27	Purchases (% of COGS)	48.1%		
28	Inventory	$911,004		
29	Accounts receivable	$986,382		
30	Accounts payable	$409,304		
31	Cost of funds invested in current assets	10.6%		
32				
33	**Outputs**			
34	Average age of inventory (in days)	83.3	←	=+B28/((B25*B26)/365)
35	Average collection period (in days)	55.1	←	=+B29/(B25/365)
36	Average payment period (in days)	77.8	←	=+B30/((B25*B26*B27)/365)
37				
38	Operating cycle (in days) - OC	138.3	←	=+B34+B35
39	Cash conversion cycle (in days) - CCC	60.6	←	=+B38-B36
40				
41	Cost of funds invested	$157,737	←	=+(B28+B29-B30)*B31
42				

SA 14-1

Ready NUM

Example Nicholson Company's business is very stable and sales are roughly the same amount every day of the year. In addition, the company's costs, AAI, ACP, and APP are very stable throughout the year. As a result, inventory, accounts receivable, and accounts payable are $1,250,000, $750,000, and $425,000, respectively, every day of the year. In addition, Nicholson's goal is to hold $125,000 of cash and marketable securities. Therefore, Nicholson has a permanent investment in current assets of $2,125,000 ($125,000 + $1,250,000 + $750,000). The company must finance this investment. One source of financing will be the permanent accounts payable of $425,000. Therefore, the company must secure additional permanent financing of $1,700,000 for each day of the year.

The above example is not realistic. No firm will have a constant level of sales, costs, and assets. These accounts are all cyclical. This means that the investment in net working capital (CCC) will vary—it will be a different amount each day due to this seasonal variation in current assets. But, if a balance sheet were developed every day of the year, there would always be an amount of current assets. The minimum amount during the year is permanent current assets. The difference between any particular day and the permanent amount is seasonal current assets. Both components of assets must be financed, and one option is **seasonal financing** that will vary with the seasonal current assets.

seasonal financing
Financing required for the seasonal amount of current assets on the balance sheet.

Example Semper Pump Company, which produces bicycle pumps, has a very seasonal pattern of sales, expenses, and asset investments. Semper's sales are driven by the large peak in summertime purchases of bicycle pumps. Semper begins the 2008 fiscal year with $482,000 of current assets. In mid-February, Semper's current assets bottom out at $285,000. Inventories then start to build to May, when sales start to ramp up and receivables are incurred.

The peak occurs in early July, when large amounts of both inventory and receivables are on the balance sheet. Together with increasing cash, current assets peak at $950,000. As inventory sells and receivables are collected, current assets decline to $550,000 in late August. Another mini-peak occurs in mid-October at $690,000 due to Christmas sales. Current assets then decline and close the 2008 fiscal year at $508,000.

Accordingly, for 2008, Semper requires permanent financing of $285,000 for its permanent level of current assets, and seasonal financing requirements of $665,000 ($950,000 − $285,000) for the seasonal peak. Figure 14.3 depicts these needs over time. Note that Semper only requires total financing of $950,000 for short periods during the year. For the overall year, current assets average $572,230 (this is based on information not provided).

Financing the Investment in Current Assets

In the previous section we saw that the investment in current assets will consist of a permanent and seasonal component. To invest in current assets we need financing. A company with high inventory and/or receivables must also secure more financing and vice versa. Management of inventory and receivables is vital for all firms, but especially those that are smaller and those that sell manufactured products on credit. How to finance the investment in the current assets is an important component of working capital policy. We have three choices.

FIGURE 14.3

Semper Pump Company's Total Financing Required: Permanent and Seasonal Needs

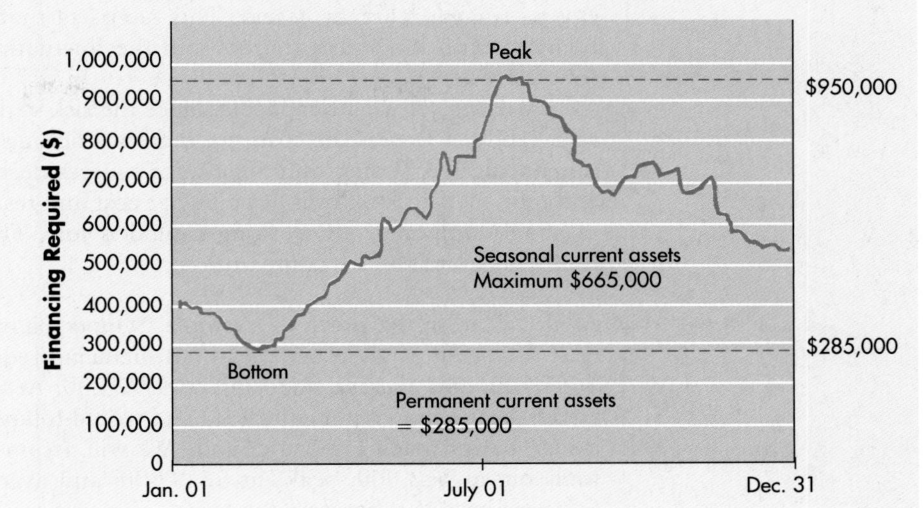

First, we could use only current liabilities. As discussed in the previous sections, the first source of financing is accounts payable and accruals. These spontaneous, no-cost sources that adjust with sales are always assumed to be the first choice for financing. If additional financing is required, the other major short-term source is short-term debt, like a line of credit. This is an attractive source, since, as we discussed in Chapter 8, short-term funds are typically less expensive than long-term funds. This is because the yield curve is typically upward-sloping. So, by using current liabilities, we lower the cost of financing.

However, using only short-term financing exposes the firm to three types of risk. First, liquidity risk increases, since the firm's current liabilities rise to a very high level. Second, with this approach, the firm may not be able to obtain all of the financing needed. Once short-term debt matures, the firm must renegotiate with the loan provider, and there is no guarantee that the provider will provide the necessary financing. This is termed **refinancing risk**. Third, as discussed in Chapter 8, the company also incurs interest rate risk, the risk that interest rates may increase. This is an issue because the interest rate on short-term loans is based on the prime rate, and prime will fluctuate. It is an **aggressive financing strategy**; it reduces costs, but increases the three forms of risk.

refinancing risk
The risk that the firm may not be able to obtain all of the financing needed once short-term debt matures.

aggressive financing strategy
Use only current liabilities to finance the investment in the current assets; it reduces costs, but increases the three forms of risk.

The second choice to finance the investment in current assets is to use long-term financing like long-term debt or equity. Long-term funds allow the firm to lock in its cost of funds over a long period of time and thus avoid refinancing and interest-rate risk. Also, long-term financing ensures that the required funds are available to the firm when needed. This **conservative financing strategy** reduces risk, but since the cost of long-term financing is much higher than short-term, it increases the cost. It will also result in large amounts of surplus cash when the seasonal component of current assets is low.

conservative financing strategy
Use of long-term financing (long-term debt or equity) to finance the investment in current assets.

The third choice to finance the investment in current assets is to use a combination of financing sources: use short-term debt to finance the seasonal current assets and long-term sources to finance the permanent current assets. This is termed the **matching strategy** which is based on the matching principle. The principle says that a company should finance long-term assets with long-term financing

matching strategy
Use short-term debt to finance the seasonal current assets and long-term sources to finance the permanent current assets.

and short-term assets with short-term financing. This is usually the optimal strategy to finance current assets. This suggests that the permanent amount is financed with long-term sources and the fluctuating amounts with short-term sources.

By doing so, we attempt to balance the risk–return tradeoff. Using only current liabilities lowers the cost, but increases liquidity risk, interest rate risk, and refinancing risk. Using only long-term sources decreases liquidity, interest rate, and refinancing risk. But it has a higher cost and results in surplus cash when the seasonal component of working capital is low. This combination reduces the return generated by the company.

Example ▼ As discussed in the previous example, Semper Pump Company requires permanent financing of \$285,000, seasonal financing requirements of a maximum of \$665,000, and average financing of \$572,230. Accounts payables and accruals could also be shown in Figure 14.3 and would follow a similar pattern as current assets, but at much lower amounts. We will assume that the total amount bottoms out at \$62,000, peaks at \$278,000, and averages \$155,290 for the year. Semper's cost of short-term funds is 6.25 percent, while the overall cost of long-term funds is 11.8 percent. The company can earn 4 percent on the investment of any surplus cash. The following table provides the data.

	Peak	**Average**	**Permanent**
Total current assets	\$950,000	\$572,230	\$285,000
Payables and accruals	\$278,000	\$155,290	\$ 62,000
Financing required	\$672,000	\$416,940	\$223,000

Using this data, we can calculate the cost of an aggressive, conservative, and matching strategy of financing the investment in current assets. With the aggressive strategy, only current liabilities are used to finance the investment in the current assets. So, on average, \$572,230 of financing is required, with \$155,290 provided by no-cost payables and accruals. The difference of \$416,940 is financed with short-term funds costing 6.25 percent. So the cost of following this strategy is \$26,058.75 (\$416,940 × 6.25%).

With the conservative strategy, long-term financing is used to finance the investment in current assets. So Semper will have to arrange for a maximum amount of financing of \$672,000. This will cost \$79,296 (\$672,000 × 11.8%). But, with this policy, surplus cash balances will be created when seasonal needs decline, and these can be invested. In Figure 14.3, this surplus will be the difference between the peak need of \$672,000 and the average need of \$416,940, or \$255,060. This amount of surplus will generate a return of \$10,202.40 (\$255,060 × 4%). So the overall cost of the conservative policy is \$69,093.60 (\$79,296 − \$10,202.40).

With the matching strategy, short-term financing is used to finance the seasonal current assets, with long-term sources to finance the permanent current assets. So the cost of financing the permanent current assets of \$223,000 is \$26,314 (\$223,000 × 11.8%). The average seasonal financing required is \$193,940 (\$416,940 − \$223,000). The cost to finance this average amount of seasonal current assets is \$12,121.25 (\$193,940 × 6.25%). The total cost of the matching strategy is \$38,435.25.

It is clear from these calculations that for Semper the aggressive strategy is the least expensive. However, Semper has substantial peak-season current asset needs and the company must have adequate funding available to finance these and ensure ongoing operations. The aggressive strategy involves much greater liquidity risk. In addition, the heavy reliance on short-term financing makes it riskier because of interest rate swings and possible difficulties in obtaining needed short-term financing quickly when seasonal peaks occur.

The conservative strategy avoids these risks through the locked-in cost of long-term financing, but is much more costly. The matching strategy is the middle alternative. It minimizes costs and risks. It seems clear that it is the best approach. But it all comes down to management's disposition toward risk and the strength of its banking relationships.

Strategies for Managing the Cash Conversion Cycle

A positive cash conversion cycle, as we saw for MAX Company in the earlier example, means the firm must use short-term loans (such as bank loans) to support its operating assets. Loans carry an explicit cost, so the firm benefits by minimizing their use in supporting operating assets. Minimizing the dollar amount of costly short-term financing should be a financial goal for the firm. This goal can be achieved by implementing each of the following operating strategies:

1. *Turn over inventory as quickly as possible* without stockouts that result in lost sales (minimize AAI).
2. *Collect accounts receivable as quickly as possible* without losing sales from high-pressure collection techniques (minimize ACP).
3. *Pay accounts payable as slowly as possible* without damaging the firm's credit rating (maximize APP).
4. *Manage float*, the time it takes to handle and deposit payments, so that it is minimized for payments received from customers but maximized for payments made to suppliers.

Techniques for implementing these four strategies are the focus of the remainder of this chapter and the following chapter.

? Review Questions

14–4 What is the difference between the firm's *operating cycle* and its *cash conversion cycle*?

14–5 Why is it helpful to divide the financing needs of a seasonal business into permanent and seasonal requirements when developing a strategy?

14–6 What are the benefits, costs, and risks of an aggressive, conservative, and matching financing strategy? Under which strategy is the borrowing often in excess of the actual need?

14–7 Why is it important for a firm to minimize the length of its cash conversion cycle? What strategies can a firm follow to minimize the CCC?

14.1 **IN PRACTICE**

Using the Net to Reduce Working Capital Requirements

Dell Computer has long been recognized for its pioneering supply-chain and e-commerce strategies. The direct-to-customer PC company knows how to use technology to manage all aspects of its business, from back-office systems to online ordering. By integrating its various systems, the company continues to provide quality products at low costs, as well as excellent customer service. Its customer relationship management software tracks which computers its customers order. Feeding those data to the production planning systems tells manufacturing what components it needs to fill the orders, and supply chain programs send parts forecasts to vendors. Dell requires key suppliers to be linked over the Web so that the process moves forward automatically, keeping Dell's costs, receivables, and inventories very low. As well, the company actively manages their payables to delay payment as long as possible, thereby generating financing for the company.

Dell's direct business model allows the company to maintain an innovative asset management system. The result is amazing working capital management. For the fiscal year ended February 3, 2006, Dell's average age of inventory (AAI) was 4 days, their average collection period (ACP) was 29 days, and their average payment period (APP) was 77 days, meaning the company's cash conversion cycle (CCC) was a *negative* 44 days. Cash and cash equivalents totalled $9.1 billion, while cash flow from operations was $4.8 billion. With these funds, Dell invested in highly liquid, secure marketable securities of various maturities. Dell has a highly structured investment program that seeks to maximize returns while minimizing risk. The company is capable of minimizing inventory risk while collecting amounts due from customers before paying vendors, thus generating cash flows from operations that exceed net income. This is driven mainly by high profitability, and the impressive cash conversion cycle.

This was not always the case. For the fiscal year ended February 1, 1996, Dell's average age of inventory (AAI) was 31 days, their average collection period (ACP) was 42 days, and their average payment period (APP) was 33 days, meaning the company's cash conversion cycle (CCC) was 40 days. As a result, cash was required to finance the net investment in current assets. For 1996, this amounted to $195 million. While this would be considered very good in some industries, for a leading-edge technology company it was much too high. So Dell's CFO made liquidity re-engineering a company-wide priority. In just ten years, the results have been impressive.

Supply chain software is becoming essential for most companies. It brings together and automates a company's order taking, purchasing, inventory management, and payment processes. A well-designed system shortens product cycle times by helping to anticipate demand, finding suppliers to provide materials on time, and identifying the least costly delivery method and routing.

SOURCES: Dell, various annual reports, available at **www.dell.com**; Brian Milligan, "Supply Chain Software Moves to the Web," *Purchasing*, April 6, 2000.

14.3 Inventory Management

The first component of the cash conversion cycle is the average age of inventory. The objective for managing inventory, as noted above, is to turn over inventory as quickly as possible without losing sales from stockouts. The financial manager tends to act as an advisor or "watchdog" in matters concerning inventory; he or she does not have direct control over inventory but does provide input to the inventory management process.

Differing Viewpoints About Inventory Level

Differing viewpoints about appropriate inventory levels commonly exist among a firm's finance, marketing, manufacturing, and purchasing managers. Each views inventory levels in light of his or her own objectives. The *financial manager's* general disposition toward inventory levels is to keep them low, to ensure that the firm's money is not being unwisely invested in excess resources. The *marketing manager*, on the other hand, would like to have large inventories of the firm's finished products. This would ensure that all orders could be filled quickly, eliminating the need for back orders due to stockouts.

The *manufacturing manager's* major responsibility is to implement the production plan so that it results in the desired amount of finished goods of acceptable quality at a low cost. In fulfilling this role, the manufacturing manager would keep raw materials inventories high to avoid production delays. He or she also would favour large production runs for the sake of lower unit production costs, which would result in high finished goods inventories.

The *purchasing manager* is concerned solely with the raw materials inventories. He or she must have on hand, in the correct quantities at the desired times and at a favourable price, whatever raw materials are required by production. Without proper control, in order to get quantity discounts or in anticipation of rising prices or a shortage of certain materials, the purchasing manager may purchase larger quantities of resources than are actually needed at the time.

Common Techniques for Managing Inventory

Numerous techniques are available for effectively managing the firm's inventory. Here we briefly consider four commonly used techniques.

The ABC System

ABC inventory system
Inventory management technique that divides inventory into three groups—A, B, and C—in descending order of importance and level of monitoring, on the basis of the dollar investment in each.

A firm using the **ABC inventory system** divides its inventory into three groups: A, B, and C. This system is based on the 20/80 concept that seems to apply to many multi-product firms. This concept suggests that 20 percent of the firm's products account for 80 percent of the firm's sales, and therefore 80 percent of the investment in inventory. The products within this 20 percent are classified as A items and are actively managed. The B group consists of items that account for the next largest investment in inventory. The C group consists of a large number of items that require a relatively small investment.

The inventory group of each item determines the item's level of monitoring. The A group items receive the most intense monitoring because of the high dollar investment. Typically, A group items are tracked on a perpetual inventory system that allows daily verification of each item's inventory level. B group items are frequently controlled through periodic, perhaps weekly, checking of their levels. C group items are monitored with unsophisticated techniques, such as the **two-bin method**. With the two-bin method, the item is stored in two bins. As an item is needed, inventory is removed from the first bin. When that bin is empty, an order is placed to refill the first bin while inventory is drawn from the second bin. The second bin is used until empty, and so on.

two-bin method
Unsophisticated inventory-monitoring technique that is typically applied to C group items and involves reordering inventory when one of two bins is empty.

The large dollar investment in A and B group items suggests the need for a better method of inventory management than the ABC system. The EOQ model, discussed next, is an appropriate model for the management of A and B group items.

The Economic Order Quantity (EOQ) Model

economic order quantity (EOQ) model
Inventory management technique for determining an item's optimal order size, which is the size that minimizes the total of its order costs and carrying costs.

order costs
The fixed costs of placing, receiving, and handling an inventory order.

carrying costs
The variable costs per unit of holding an item in inventory for a specific period of time.

One of the most common techniques for determining the optimal order size for inventory items is the **economic order quantity (EOQ) model.** The EOQ model considers various costs of inventory and then determines what order size minimizes total inventory cost.

EOQ assumes that the relevant costs of inventory can be divided into *order costs* and *carrying costs*. (The model excludes the actual cost of the inventory item.) Each of them has certain key components and characteristics. **Order costs** include the fixed costs of placing and receiving orders: the cost of writing a purchase order, of processing the resulting paperwork, of receiving an order and checking it against the invoice, and of handling the inventory. Order costs are stated in dollars per order. **Carrying costs** are the variable costs per unit of holding an item in inventory for a specific period of time. Carrying costs include storage costs, insurance costs, the costs of deterioration and obsolescence, and the opportunity or financial cost of having funds invested in inventory. These costs are stated in dollars per unit per period.

Order costs decrease as the size of the order increases. Carrying costs, however, increase with increases in the order size. The EOQ model analyzes the tradeoff between order costs and carrying costs to determine the *order quantity that minimizes the total inventory cost.*

Mathematical Development of EOQ A formula can be developed for determining the firm's EOQ for a given inventory item, where

S = usage in units per period
O = order cost per order
C = carrying cost per unit per period
Q = order quantity in units

The first step is to derive the cost functions for order cost and carrying cost. The order cost can be expressed as the product of the cost per order and the number of orders. Because the number of orders equals the usage during the period divided by the order quantity (S/Q), the order cost can be expressed as follows:

$$\text{Order cost} = O \times S/Q \tag{14.4}$$

The carrying cost is defined as the cost of carrying a unit per period multiplied by the firm's average inventory. The average inventory is the order quantity divided by 2 ($Q/2$), because inventory is assumed to be depleted at a constant rate. Thus carrying cost can be expressed as follows:

$$\text{Carrying cost} = C \times Q/2 \tag{14.5}$$

total cost of inventory
The sum of order costs and carrying costs of inventory.

The firm's **total cost of inventory** is found by summing the order cost and the carrying cost. Thus the total cost function is

$$\text{Total cost} = (O \times S/Q) + (C \times Q/2) \tag{14.6}$$

Hint
The EOQ calculation helps management minimize the total cost of inventory. Lowering order costs will cause an increase in carrying costs and may increase total cost. Likewise, a decrease in total cost may result from reduced carrying costs. The goal, facilitated by using the EOQ calculation, is to lower total cost.

Because the EOQ is defined as the order quantity that minimizes the total cost function, we must solve the minimum of the total cost function for the EOQ. The resulting equation is

$$\text{EOQ} = \sqrt{\frac{2 \times S \times O}{C}} \tag{14.7}$$

Although the EOQ model has weaknesses, it is certainly better than subjective decision making. Despite the fact that the use of the EOQ model is outside the control of the financial manager, the financial manager must be aware of its utility and must provide certain inputs, specifically with respect to inventory carrying costs.

reorder point
The point at which to reorder inventory, expressed as days of lead time × daily usage.

Reorder Point Once the firm has determined its economic order quantity, it must determine when to place an order. The **reorder point** reflects the firm's daily usage of the inventory item and the number of days needed to place and receive an order. Assuming that inventory is used at a constant rate, the formula for the reorder point is

$$\text{Reorder point} = \text{days of lead time} \times \text{daily usage} \tag{14.8}$$

safety stock
Extra inventory that is held to prevent stockouts of important items.

For example, if a firm knows that it takes 3 days to place and receive an order, and if it uses 15 units per day of the inventory item, then the reorder point is 45 units of inventory (3 days × 15 units/day). Thus, as soon as the item's inventory level falls to the reorder point (45 units, in this case), an order will be placed at the item's EOQ. If the estimates of lead time and daily usage are correct, then the order will arrive exactly as the inventory level reaches zero. However, lead times and usage rates are not precise, so most firms hold **safety stock** (extra inventory) to prevent stockouts of important items.

Example MAX Company has an A group inventory item that is vital to the production process. This item costs \$524, and MAX uses 1,100 units of the item per year. MAX wants to determine its optimal order strategy for the item. To calculate the EOQ, we need the following inputs:

$$\text{Order cost per order} = \$150$$
$$\text{Carrying cost per unit per year} = \$50$$

Substituting into Equation 14.7, we get

$$\text{EOQ} = \sqrt{\frac{2 \times 1{,}100 \times \$150}{\$50}} \approx 81 \text{ units}$$

The reorder point for MAX depends on the number of days MAX operates per year. Assuming that MAX operates 250 days per year and uses 1,100 units of this item per year, its daily usage is 4.4 units (1,100 ÷ 250). If its lead time is 2 days and MAX wants to maintain a safety stock of 4 units, the reorder point for this item is 12.8 units [(2 × 4.4) + 4]. However, orders are made only in whole units, so the order is placed when the inventory falls to 13 units.

The firm's goal for inventory is to turn it over as quickly as possible without stockouts. Inventory turnover is best calculated by dividing cost of goods sold by average inventory. The EOQ model determines the optimal order size and, indirectly, through the assumption of constant usage, the average inventory. Thus the EOQ model determines the firm's optimal inventory turnover rate, given the firm's specific costs of inventory.

Just-in-Time (JIT) System

just-in-time (JIT) system
Inventory management technique that minimizes inventory investment by having materials arrive at exactly the time they are needed for production.

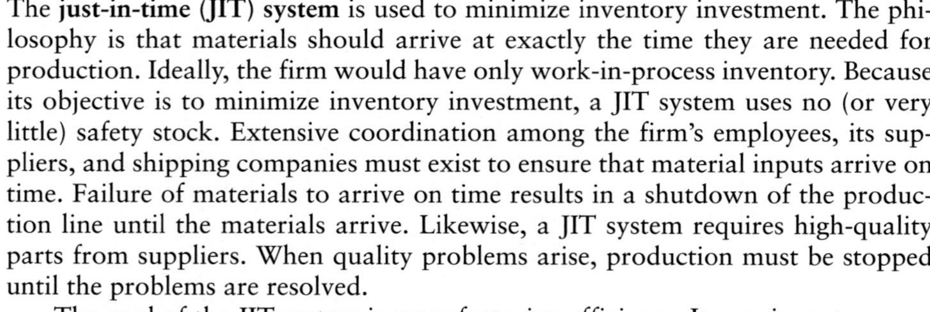

The **just-in-time (JIT) system** is used to minimize inventory investment. The philosophy is that materials should arrive at exactly the time they are needed for production. Ideally, the firm would have only work-in-process inventory. Because its objective is to minimize inventory investment, a JIT system uses no (or very little) safety stock. Extensive coordination among the firm's employees, its suppliers, and shipping companies must exist to ensure that material inputs arrive on time. Failure of materials to arrive on time results in a shutdown of the production line until the materials arrive. Likewise, a JIT system requires high-quality parts from suppliers. When quality problems arise, production must be stopped until the problems are resolved.

The goal of the JIT system is manufacturing efficiency. It uses inventory as a tool for attaining efficiency by emphasizing quality of the materials used and their timely delivery. When JIT is working properly, it forces process inefficiencies to surface. For additional readings on the JIT system, see the many stories available on the Web.

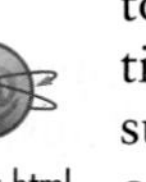

www.bola.biz/jit/index.html

Materials Requirement Planning (MRP) System

materials requirement planning (MRP) system
Inventory management technique that applies EOQ concepts and a computer to compare production needs to available inventory balances and determine when orders should be placed for various items on a product's bill of materials.

Many companies use a **materials requirement planning (MRP) system** to determine what materials to order and when to order them. MRP applies EOQ concepts to determine how much to order. By means of a computer, it simulates each product's bill of materials, inventory status, and manufacturing process. The *bill of materials* is simply a list of all the parts and materials that go into making the finished product. For a given production plan, the computer simulates materials requirements by comparing production needs to available inventory balances. On the basis of the time it takes for a product that is in process to move through the various production stages and the lead time required to get materials, the MRP system determines when orders should be placed for the various items on the bill of materials.

The advantage of the MRP system is that it forces the firm to consider its inventory needs more carefully. The objective is to lower the firm's inventory investment without impairing production. If the firm's opportunity cost of capital for investments of equal risk is 15 percent, every dollar of investment released from inventory increases before-tax profits by $0.15.

International Inventory Management

International inventory management is typically much more complicated for exporters in general, and for multinational companies in particular, than for purely domestic companies. The production and manufacturing economies of scale that might be expected from selling products globally may prove elusive if products must be tailored for individual local markets, as very frequently happens, or if actual production of goods takes place in factories around the world. When raw materials, intermediate goods, or finished products must be transported long distances—particularly by ocean shipping—there will inevitably be more delays, confusion, damage, theft, and other difficulties to overcome than occur in a one-country operation. The international inventory manager therefore puts a premium on flexibility. He or she is usually less concerned about ordering the economically optimal quantity of inventory than about making sure that sufficient quantities of inventory are delivered where they are needed, when they are needed, and in a condition to be used as planned.

? Review Questions

14–8 What are likely to be the viewpoints of each of the following managers about the levels of the various types of inventory: finance, marketing, manufacturing, and purchasing? Why is inventory an investment?

14–9 Briefly describe each of the following techniques for managing inventory: ABC system, economic order quantity (EOQ) model, just-in-time (JIT) system, and materials requirement planning (MRP) system.

14–10 What factors make managing inventory more difficult for exporters and multinational companies?

14.4 Accounts Receivable Management

Hint
Some small businesses resolve these problems by selling their accounts receivable to a third party at a discount. Though expensive, this strategy overcomes the problem of not having adequate personnel. It also creates a buffer between the small business and those customers who need a little prodding to stay current.

The second component of the cash conversion cycle is the average collection period: the average length of time (in days) that it takes to collect the cash from a credit sale. The average collection period has two parts. The first part is the time from the sale until the customer mails the payment. The second part is the time from when the payment is mailed until the firm has the collected funds in its bank account. The first part of the average collection period involves managing the credit available to the firm's customers, and the second part involves collecting and processing payments. This section of the chapter discusses the firm's accounts receivable credit management.

The objective for managing accounts receivable is to collect accounts receivable as quickly as possible without losing sales from high-pressure collection techniques. Accomplishing this goal encompasses three topics: (1) credit selection and standards, (2) credit terms, and (3) credit monitoring.

Credit Selection and Standards

credit standards
The firm's minimum requirements for extending credit to a customer.

Credit selection involves application of techniques for determining which customers should receive credit. This process involves evaluating the customer's creditworthiness and comparing it to the firm's **credit standards**, its minimum requirements for extending credit to a customer.

The Four C's of Credit

four C's of credit
The four key dimensions—character, capacity, capital, and conditions—used by credit analysts to provide a framework for in-depth credit analysis.

One popular credit selection technique is the **four C's of credit**, which provides a framework for the in-depth credit analysis. Because of the time and expense involved, this credit selection method is used for large-dollar credit requests. The four C's are:

1. *Character:* The applicant's record of meeting past obligations.
2. *Capacity:* The applicant's ability to repay the requested credit, as judged in terms of financial statement analysis focused on cash flows available to repay debt obligations.
3. *Capital:* The applicant's total assets and net worth (value of common equity). The greater the assets, the more potential security that exists for the credit. Also, growing assets suggests a growing, successful business. High net worth indicates past financial success and a commitment by the shareholders to the company. Net worth can provide a cushion for creditors in times of economic downturns.
4. *Conditions:* Current general and industry-specific economic conditions, and any unique conditions surrounding a specific transaction.

Hint

Computers are widely used to aid in the credit decision process. Data on each customer's payment patterns are maintained and can be called forth to evaluate requests for renewed or additional credit.

Analysis via the four C's of credit does not yield a specific accept/reject decision, so its use requires an analyst experienced in reviewing and granting credit requests. Application of this framework tends to ensure that the firm's credit customers will pay, without being pressured, within the stated credit terms.

Evaluating Credit Applicants

While the four C's of credit are a good framework for analyzing credit applications, information on which to base the analysis is required. One potential source of the information is the applicant. As part of the application process, a company may require that the applicant complete forms providing financial and credit information and references. The application process may also request that the credit applicant provide financial statements for the past few years. They will allow the company to analyze a potential customer's financial position using ratio analysis. The key ratios to focus on for short-term trade credit are liquidity and activity ratios.

A potential problem with this approach to gathering information is that some applicants may not wish to give their financial statements to a supplier. Obviously, very sensitive data is provided in the statements and many managers would not want to divulge this information to suppliers. In this case, a second source of information is required. One such source is D&B (the old Dun & Bradstreet). D&B has developed an extensive database of financial and rating information on millions of Canadian companies. D&B provides numerous types of reports that allow businesses to assess and manage the risk of doing business with a customer. One report that D&B provides is "D&B Industry Norms and Key Business Ratios." This report was discussed in Chapter 3.

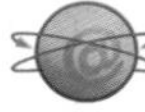

http://dnb.ca/creditandrisk/businessinforeport.html

A second report for analyzing risk is the "D&B Business Information Report." This report provides basic company and historical information, financial information, and the company's payment history. It also provides an important rating: the D&B Composite Credit Rating, which gives an indication of creditworthiness. Part A of Table 14.2 provides a rating scale for the D&B Composite Credit Rating. The D&B Rating (e.g., 4A3) is divided into two parts. The financial strength code (4A) indicates the amount of the subject's tangible net worth (i.e., the shareholders' funds less any intangible assets). The second number (3) reflects the company's level of risk and is an overall evaluation of creditworthiness.

A third report provided by D&B is the Payment Profile Report. This report provides a business summary including key financial data, a summary of the

TABLE 14.2 D&B Credit Rating Scales

Part A: Key to D&B composite credit rating

	Composite credit appraisal[b]			
Estimated financial strength[a]	High	Good	Fair	Limited
5A: $50,000,000 and over	1	2	3	4
4A: $10,000,000 to $49,999,999	1	2	3	4
3A: $1,000,000 to $9,999,999	1	2	3	4
2A: $750,000 to $999,999	1	2	3	4
1A: $500,000 to $749,999	1	2	3	4
BA: $300,000 to $499,999	1	2	3	4
BB: $200,000 to $299,999	1	2	3	4
CB: $125,000 to $199,999	1	2	3	4
CC: $75,000 to $124,999	1	2	3	4
DC: $50,000 to $74,999	1	2	3	4
DD: $35,000 to $49,999	1	2	3	4
EE: $20,000 to $34,999	1	2	3	4
FF: $10,000 to $19,999	1	2	3	4
GG: $5,000 to $9,999	1	2	3	4
HH: up to $4,999	1	2	3	4

[a]The estimated financial strength is based on tangible net worth.

[b]The credit appraisal is based on payment history, the company's financial position, management history, and other general quantitative and qualitative factors.

Part B: Key to Payment Index[a]

Score	Payment[b]
100	Anticipate
90	Discount
80	Prompt
70	Slow to 15
60	Slow to 22
50	Slow to 30
40	Slow to 60
30	Slow to 90
20	Slow to 120
UN	Unavailable

[a]The score is based on the combined individual payment experience of a business, indicating its current payment situation. The higher the score, the more timely the payment history.

[b]*Anticipate* means the customer paid before the invoice was received. *Discount* means the customer paid within the discount period. *Prompt* means the customer paid within the credit terms. *Slow* means the customer paid within the stated number of days after the credit period.

SOURCE: D&B; see http://dnb.ca/creditandrisk/businessinforeport.html and http://dnb.ca/creditandrisk/payprofrep.html. Reprinted with permission. © 2006 The D&B Companies of Canada Ltd. www.dnb.ca.

company's bill payment history over the last two years, and the company's *payment index* rating. This rating is an overall summary measure of the company's bill payment pattern; the higher the score, the better the credit. One feature in the report that is particularly useful is a graph comparing the company's payment index to the industry median and the upper and lower 25 percent in the industry. This report will provide all of the information needed to evaluate most credit applicants. Part B of Table 14.2 provides a rating scale for the payment index rating.

http://dnb.ca/creditandrisk/payprofrep.html

There is a wealth of information available concerning potential credit customers. To avoid making credit-granting mistakes, it is important companies access as much information as necessary so bad decisions are not made. The amount of information to collect is based on the potential size of the account. The higher the sales that may be made to a potential customer, the greater the cost of a credit-granting mistake, and therefore the more detailed the information that should be collected and analyzed.

Credit Scoring

credit scoring
A credit selection method commonly used with high-volume/small-dollar credit requests; relies on a credit score determined by applying statistically derived weights to a credit applicant's scores on key financial and credit characteristics.

Credit scoring is a method of credit selection that is commonly used with high-volume/small-dollar credit requests. It applies statistically derived weights for key financial and credit characteristics to predict whether a credit applicant will pay the requested credit in a timely fashion. Simply stated, the procedure results in a score that measures the applicant's overall credit strength, and the score is used to make the accept/reject decision for granting the applicant credit. Credit scoring is most commonly used by large credit card operations, such as those of banks, oil companies, and department stores. The purpose of credit scoring is to make a relatively informed credit decision quickly and inexpensively, recognizing that the cost of a single bad scoring decision is small. However, if bad debts from scoring decisions increase, then the scoring system must be re-evaluated. For a demonstration of credit scoring, including use of a spreadsheet for that purpose, see the book's Web site.

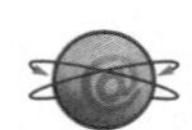

www.pearsoned.ca/gitman

Managing International Credit

Credit management is difficult enough for managers of purely domestic companies, and these tasks become much more complex for companies that operate internationally. This is partly because (as we have seen before) international operations typically expose a firm to *exchange rate risk*. It is also due to the dangers and delays involved in shipping goods long distances and in having to cross at least two international borders.

Exports of finished goods are usually priced in the currency of the importer's local market; most commodities, on the other hand, are priced in U.S. dollars. Therefore, a Canadian company that sells a product in Japan, for example, would have to price that product in Japanese yen and extend credit to a Japanese wholesaler in the local currency (yen). If the yen depreciates against the dollar before the Canadian exporter collects on its accounts receivable, the Canadian company experiences an exchange rate loss; the yen collected are worth fewer dollars than expected at the time the sale was made. Of course, the dollar could just as easily depreciate against the yen, yielding an exchange rate gain to the Canadian exporter. Most companies fear the loss more than they welcome the gain. This issue is discussed more fully in Chapter 19.

For a major currency such as the Japanese yen, the exporter can *hedge* against this risk by using the currency futures, forwards, or options markets, but it is costly to do so, particularly for relatively small amounts. If the exporter is selling to a customer in a developing country, there will probably be no effective instrument available for protecting against exchange rate risk at any price. This risk may be further magnified because credit standards may be much lower (and acceptable collection techniques much different) in developing countries than in North America.

Although it may seem tempting just "not to bother" with exporting, especially for smaller companies, Canada is a trading country and cannot concede export markets to foreign competitors. In 2006, Canadian businesses exported over $530 billion of products to about 200 countries. Exports accounted for 42 percent of Canada's gross domestic product (GDP) versus only 26 percent in 1990. In terms of the percentage of GDP, Canada exports about four times as much as the United States or Japan and is, by far, the biggest exporter in the G7. Canadian companies are active participants in export markets, particularly to the United States. These export sales, if carefully monitored and (where possible) effectively hedged against exchange rate risk, often prove to be very profitable.

This is especially the case where sales are made to the United States, priced in U.S. dollars. It is often the case that U.S. sales are sold at the same price as Canadian sales, but quoted in U.S. dollars. For example, a supplier may quote a Canadian customer a price of $10 per unit. This would be in Canadian dollars. A U.S. customer would receive the same $10 quote, but in this case, it would be in U.S. dollars. Given that a U.S. dollar has been worth, on average, about $1.35 Canadian between 1990 and 2006, U.S. sales in U.S. dollars are usually much more profitable for Canadian exporters than are equivalent Canadian sales.

Credit Terms

credit terms
The terms of sale for customers who have been extended credit by the firm.

cash discount
A percentage deduction from the purchase price; available to credit customers that pay their accounts within a specified time.

The second component of accounts receivable management is credit terms. **Credit terms** are the terms of sale for customers who have been extended credit by the firm. Terms of *net 30* mean the customer has 30 days from the beginning of the credit period (the *date of invoice*) to pay the full invoice amount. Some firms offer **cash discounts**, percentage deductions from the purchase price for paying within a specified time. For example, terms of *2/10 net 30* mean the customer can take a 2 percent discount from the invoice amount if the payment is made within 10 days of the beginning of the credit period, or can pay the full amount of the invoice within 30 days.

A firm's regular credit terms are strongly influenced by the firm's business. For example, a firm selling perishable items will have very short credit terms, because its items have little long-term collateral value; a firm in a seasonal business may tailor its terms to fit the industry cycles. A firm wants its regular credit terms to conform to its industry's standards. If its terms are more restrictive than its competitors', it will lose business; if its terms are less restrictive than its competitors', it will attract poor-quality customers that probably could not pay under the standard industry terms.

The bottom line is that a firm should compete on the basis of quality and price of its product and service offerings, but offering customers different credit terms may provide the firm with a competitive advantage. A firm may also wish to only sell to a select group of customers through unique or very restrictive credit terms. In addition, individual customers may be offered "special" terms that reflect the risk of the account.

Cash Discount

Including a cash discount in the credit terms is a popular way to achieve the goal of speeding up collections without putting pressure on customers. The cash discount provides an incentive for customers to pay sooner. By speeding collections, the discount decreases the firm's investment in accounts receivable (which is the objective), but it also decreases the proceeds received from the sale. Additionally, initiating a cash discount should reduce bad debts because customers who take the discount pay the account. The discount should also increase sales volume because the lower price should increase demand. Accordingly, firms that consider offering a cash discount must perform a benefit–cost analysis to determine whether extending a cash discount is profitable.

Cash Discount Period

cash discount period
The number of days after the beginning of the credit period during which the cash discount is available.

The **cash discount period**, the number of days after the beginning of the credit period during which the cash discount is available, can be changed by the financial manager. The net effect of changes in this period is difficult to analyze because of the nature of the forces involved. For example, if a firm were to increase its cash discount period by 10 days (e.g., changing its credit terms from 2/10 net 30 to 2/20 net 30), the following changes would be expected to occur:

1. Sales would increase, positively affecting the firm's cash flow.
2. Bad debt expenses would decrease, also positively affecting cash flow.
3. As customers accounting for more of the sales take the discount, cash flow will decrease.

The difficulty for the financial manager lies in assessing what impact an increase in the cash discount period would have on the firm's investment in accounts receivable. This investment will decrease because of non-discount takers now paying earlier. However, the investment in accounts receivable will increase for two reasons: (1) discount takers will still get the discount but will pay later and (2) new customers attracted by the new policy will result in new accounts receivable. If the firm were to decrease the cash discount period, the effects would be the opposite of those just described.

Credit Period

credit period
The number of days after the beginning of the credit period until full payment of the account is due.

Changes in the **credit period**, the number of days after the beginning of the credit period until full payment of the account is due, also affect a firm's profitability. For example, increasing a firm's credit period from net 30 days to net 45 days should increase sales, positively affecting cash flow. But the investment in both accounts receivable and bad debt expenses would also increase, negatively affecting cash flow. The increased investment in accounts receivable would result from both more sales and generally slower payment, on average, as a result of the longer credit period. The increase in bad debt expenses results from the fact that the longer the credit period, the more time available for a firm to fail, making it unable to pay its accounts payable. A decrease in the length of the credit period is likely to have the opposite effects.

Changing Credit Standards or Terms

The firm sometimes will contemplate changing its credit standards or terms in order to improve its returns and create greater value for its owners. To demonstrate, consider the impact on the firm's cash flow if credit standards or terms are relaxed.

Hint
Relaxing the credit standards and/or credit terms will increase the risk of the firm, but it may also increase the return to the firm. Bad debts and the average collection period will both increase with more lenient credit standards and/or credit terms, but overall cash flow may increase.

Variable affected by relaxation	Direction of change	Impact on cash flow
Sales volume	Increase	Positive
Investment in accounts receivable	Increase	Negative
Bad debt expenses	Increase	Negative
Cash discounts	Increase	Negative

If credit standards or terms were tightened, the opposite impacts would be expected.

Example Dodd Tool, a manufacturer of lathe tools, is currently selling a product for \$10 per unit. Sales (all on credit) for last year were 60,000 units. The variable cost per unit is \$6. The firm's total fixed costs are \$120,000.

The firm is currently contemplating a *relaxation of credit terms* that is expected to result in the following: a 5 percent increase in unit sales to 63,000 units, an increase in the average collection period from 30 days (its current level) to 45 days, and an increase in bad debt expenses from 1 percent of sales (the current level) to 2 percent. The firm's cost of investing in assets (their cost of capital) is 15 percent.

To determine whether to relax its credit terms, Dodd Tool must calculate the additional gross margin earned on the increasing sales, the cost of the increased investment in accounts receivable, and the increased bad debts.

Additional Gross Margin on Sales Because fixed costs are "sunk" and thereby unaffected by a change in the sales level, the only cost relevant to a change in sales is variable costs. Sales are expected to increase by 5 percent, or 3,000 units. The gross margin per unit will equal the difference between the sale price per unit (\$10) and the variable cost per unit (\$6). The gross margin per unit therefore will be \$4. The total additional gross margin from sales will be \$12,000 (3,000 units × \$4 per unit).

Cost of the Increased Investment in Accounts Receivable The cost of the increased investment in receivables is based on the change in the amounts invested in receivables if the credit terms are changed. The average investment in receivables is calculated using the same process discussed earlier in the chapter and in Chapter 3:

$$\begin{array}{c}\text{Average investment}\\ \text{in accounts receivable}\end{array} = \frac{\text{Credit sales}}{\text{365 days}} \times \text{ACP (in days)} \qquad (14.9)$$

As before, if credit sales are not specified, total sales are used in equation 14.9. For Dodd, credit sales are given, so the investments in receivables for the two plans are:

$$\text{Under current terms: } \frac{60{,}000 \text{ units} \times \$10}{365 \text{ days}} \times 30 \text{ days} = \$49{,}315$$

$$\text{Under proposed terms: } \frac{63{,}000 \text{ units} \times \$10}{365 \text{ days}} \times 45 \text{ days} = \$77{,}671$$

The cost of the increased investment in accounts receivable is:

Average investment under proposed terms	$77,671
− Average investment under current terms	49,315
Increased investment in accounts receivable	$28,356
× Required return on investment	15%
Cost of increased investment in receivables	$ 4,253

The $4,253 is a cost, since this is the cost of the additional funds that will be invested in the asset account. We know from earlier in this chapter, and from Chapters 8, 9, 12, and 13, that when a firm invests in an asset, the funds invested are not free—they come with a cost. For Dodd Tool, the cost is 15 percent.

Increased Bad Debts The increased bad debts is found by taking the difference between the level of bad debts before and after the proposed relaxation of credit terms as follows.

Bad debts for proposed terms: (2% × $630,000) =	$12,600
Bad debts for current terms: (1% × $600,000) =	6,000
Increased bad debts	$ 6,600

The difference between the two amounts is the cost of bad debts, since this is the cash the company will lose when a customer does not pay for its purchases. ▲

The results and key calculations relating to Dodd Tool's decision whether to relax its credit terms are summarized in Table 14.3. The impact of the proposed change in credit terms is an increase in cash flow of $1,147. Therefore, the firm should make the change.

The procedures described here for evaluating a proposed change in credit terms are used to evaluate all proposed changes in the management of accounts receivable. If Dodd Tool had been contemplating tightening its credit standards, for example, the cost would have been a reduction in the gross margin from sales, and the return would have been from reductions in the cost of the investment in accounts receivable and reduced bad debts.

Another example of the analysis that should be completed is provided below. Here we focus on the impact of offering credit terms that include a cash discount.

Example ▼ MAX Company has an average collection period of 40 days. In accordance with the firm's credit terms of net 30, this period consists of the 35 days until the customers place their payments in the mail (not everyone pays within 30 days) and the 5 days to receive, process, and collect payments once they are mailed. MAX is considering initiating a cash discount by changing its credit terms from net 30 to 2/10 net 30. The firm expects this change to reduce the average collection period to 22 days.

TABLE 14.3 The Effects on Dodd Tool of a Relaxation of Credit Terms

Additional gross margin on sales		
[3,000 units × ($10 − $6)]		$12,000
Cost of increased investment in accounts receivable		
Average investment under proposed terms:		
$\frac{\$630{,}000}{365} \times 45$	$77,671	
Average investment under current terms:		
$\frac{\$600{,}000}{365} \times 30$	49,315	
Increased investment in receivables	$28,356	
Cost of increased investment in receivables		($ 4,253)
Increased bad debts		
Bad debts for proposed terms (2% × $630,000)	$12,600	
Bad debts for current terms (1% × $600,000)	6,000	
Increase in bad debts		($ 6,600)
Net increase in cash flow		**$ 1,147**

As noted earlier in the EOQ example, MAX has a product with current sales of 1,100 units. Each finished product produced requires 1 unit of a raw material that costs $524 per unit, and incurs another $1,381 of variable cost in the production process. The product sells for $3,000 on terms of net 30.

If the new credit terms were offered, MAX estimates that sales of the product will increase by 50 units, from 1,100 to 1,150 per year. In addition, customers accounting for 80 percent of the sales will take the discount. The bad debt expense percentage is currently 2.6 percent of sales. While this percentage is not expected to change, it will only apply to the sales on which the discount is not taken. MAX's cost of capital is 14 percent. Should MAX offer the proposed cash discount?

Table 14.4 provides an analysis similar to that shown in the example above. Here we see that the proposed cash discount will generate an increase in cash flow of $88,928. Obviously, MAX should initiate the proposed cash discount.

Credit Monitoring

The third and final component a firm should consider in its accounts receivable management is credit monitoring. **Credit monitoring** is an ongoing review of the firm's accounts receivable to determine whether customers are paying according to the stated credit terms. If they are not paying in a timely manner, credit monitoring will alert the firm to the problem. Slow payments are costly to a firm because they lengthen the average collection period and thus increase a firm's investment in accounts receivable. Two frequently cited techniques for credit monitoring are average collection period and aging of accounts receivable. In addition, a number of popular collection techniques are used by firms.

credit monitoring
The ongoing review of a firm's accounts receivable to determine whether customers are paying according to the stated credit terms.

TABLE 14.4 Analysis of Initiating a Cash Discount for MAX Company

Additional gross margin on sales		
50 units × [\$3,000 – (\$524 + \$1,381)]		\$54,750
Savings from reduced investment in accounts receivable		
Investment with current terms		
$\frac{\$3,300,000}{365} \times 40$ days	\$361,644	
Investment with proposed terms		
$\frac{\$3,450,000}{365} \times 22$ days	\$207,945	
Reduced investment in receivables	\$153,699	
Benefit of the reduced investment (\$153,699 × 14%)		\$21,518
Reduction in bad debts		
Current terms (\$3,300,000 × 2.6%)	\$85,800	
New terms (\$3,450,000 × 20% × 2.6%)	\$17,940	
Savings in bad debts		\$67,860
Cost of discount		
(\$3,450,000 × 80% × 2%)		(\$55,200)
Net increase in cash flow		\$88,928

Average Collection Period

The *average collection period* is the second component of the cash conversion cycle. As noted in Chapter 3, it is the average number of days that credit sales are outstanding. The average collection period has two components: (1) the time from sale until the customer places the payment in the mail and (2) the time to receive, process, and collect the payment once it has been mailed by the customer. The formula for finding the average collection period is

$$\text{Average collection period} = \frac{\text{accounts receivable}}{\text{average credit sales per day}} \tag{14.10}$$

Again, total sales are used if credit sales are not specified. The average collection period tells the firm, on average, when its customers pay their accounts.

Knowing its average collection period enables the firm to determine whether there is a general problem with accounts receivable. For example, a firm that has credit terms of net 30 would expect its average collection period (minus receipt, processing, and collection time) to equal about 30 days. If the actual collection period is significantly greater than 30 days, the firm has reason to review its credit operations. If the firm's average collection period is increasing over time, it has cause for concern about its accounts receivable management. A first step in analyzing an accounts receivable problem is to "age" the accounts receivable. By this process the firm can determine whether the problem exists in its accounts receivable in general or is attributable to a few specific accounts.

Aging of Accounts Receivable

aging of accounts receivable
A credit-monitoring technique that uses a schedule indicating the percentages of the total accounts receivable balance that have been outstanding for specified periods of time.

The **aging of accounts receivable** segments the firm's accounts receivable on the basis of the time outstanding. The breakdown of the accounts is typically made on a month-to-month basis, going back at least six months. The result is a schedule indicating the percentages of the total accounts receivable balance that have been outstanding for specified periods of time. Its purpose is to enable the firm to pinpoint collection problems.

If a firm with terms of net 30 has an average collection period of 50 days, the firm will want to age its accounts receivable. If the majority of accounts are less than three months old, then the firm has a general collection problem and should review its accounts receivable operations. If the aging shows that most accounts are collected in about 35 days and a few accounts are way past due, then the firm should analyze and pursue collection of those specified past-due accounts.

Example Assume that O'Hare Tools extends credit terms of net 30 to its customers. The firm's balance sheet for the most recent fiscal year shows $200,000 of accounts receivable. An evaluation of those accounts receivable results in the following breakdown:

	Days outstanding					
	1–31	32–61	62–92	93–122	123–153	
Month of sale	December	November	October	September	August	Total
Accounts receivable	$60,000	$40,000	$66,000	$26,000	$8,000	$200,000
Percentage of total	30%	20%	33%	13%	4%	100%

Because O'Hare Tools gives its customers 30 days to pay their accounts, December receivables are considered current. All of these sales are within the credit terms. (This is not quite true, since sales made on December 1 should have been collected on December 31. While this is not a major issue, the days outstanding row accounts for the number of days in each of the months.) November receivables are between 32 and 61 days outstanding, and are thus between 2 and 31 days overdue. October receivables still unpaid are between 62 and 92 days outstanding, and are thus between 32 and 62 days overdue, and so on.

The table shows that 30 percent of the firm's receivables are current, 20 percent are 1 month late, 33 percent are 2 months late, 13 percent are 3 months late, and 4 percent are more than 3 months late. Although payment seems generally slow, a noticeable irregularity in these data is the high percentage represented by October receivables. This indicates that some problem may have occurred in October. Investigation may find that the problem can be attributed to the hiring of a new credit manager, the acceptance of a new account that has made a large credit purchase it has not yet paid for, or ineffective collection policy. When such a discrepancy is found, the analyst should determine its cause.

The aging schedule data allows the analyst to estimate the average number of days that sales are outstanding. This is done by using the average number of days the monthly accounts have been outstanding. For example, as shown on the aging schedule, the October receivables have been outstanding for between

62 and 92 days. On average, the sales made in October were made on the middle day of October, or on October 15.5.

This implies that, on average, the October sales have been outstanding for 15.5 days in October, 30 days in November, and 31 days in December, or a total of 76.5 days (31 + 30 + 15.5 days). This is an average of 46.5 days overdue, which is a problem. All of the aging schedule data can be used to determine the overall average number of days sales are outstanding (Overall DSO) as follows:

$$\begin{aligned}\text{Overall DSO} &= (30\% \times 15.5 \text{ days}) + (20\% \times 46 \text{ days}) + (33\% \times 76.5 \text{ days}) + (13\% \\ &\quad \times 107 \text{ days}) + (4\% \times 137.5 \text{ days}) \\ &= 4.7 \text{ days} + 9.2 \text{ days} + 25.2 \text{ days} + 13.9 \text{ days} + 5.5 \text{ days} \\ &= 58.5 \text{ days}\end{aligned}$$

Now it is easy to confirm that there is a problem with the collection of accounts receivable. The overall average number of days that sales are outstanding is almost twice the firm's credit terms of net 30. O'Hare Tools has a receivable collection problem, a credit standards and selection problem (they are making mistakes in whom they grant credit to), or a combination of the two. Regardless, it is clear from the analysis of the aging schedule that the management of accounts receivable must improve. ▲

Popular Collection Techniques

A number of collection techniques, ranging from letters to legal action, are employed. As an account becomes more and more overdue, the collection effort becomes more personal and more intense. In Table 14.5 the popular collection techniques are listed, and briefly described, in the order typically followed in the collection process.

? Review Questions

14–11 What is the role of the *four C's of credit* in the credit selection activity? How does a firm evaluate a company based on the four C's? What are the usual sources of the required information?

14–12 Explain why *credit scoring* is typically applied to consumer credit decisions rather than to mercantile credit decisions.

14–13 What are the basic tradeoffs in a *tightening* of credit standards?

14–14 Why are the risks involved in international credit management more complex than those associated with purely domestic credit sales?

14–15 Why do a firm's regular credit terms typically conform to those of its industry?

14–16 Why should a firm actively monitor the accounts receivable of its credit customers? How do the techniques of *average collection period* and *aging of accounts receivable* work?

TABLE 14.5 Popular Collection Techniques

Technique[a]	Brief description
Letters	After a certain number of days, the firm sends a polite letter reminding the customer of the overdue account. If the account is not paid within a certain period after this letter has been sent, a second, more demanding letter is sent.
Telephone calls	If letters prove unsuccessful, a telephone call may be made to the customer to request immediate payment. If the customer has a reasonable excuse, arrangements may be made to extend the payment period. A call from the seller's attorney may be used.
Personal visits	This technique is much more common at the consumer credit level, but it may also be effectively employed by industrial suppliers. Sending a local salesperson or a collection person to confront the customer can be very effective. Payment may be made on the spot.
Collection agencies	A firm can turn uncollectible accounts over to a collection agency or an attorney for collection. The fees for this service are typically quite high; the firm may receive less than 50 cents on the dollar from accounts collected in this way.
Legal action	Legal action is the most stringent step, an alternative to the use of a collection agency. Not only is direct legal action expensive, but it may force the debtor into bankruptcy without guaranteeing the ultimate receipt of the overdue amount.

[a]Techniques are listed in the order in which they are typically followed in the collection process.

14.5 Management of Receipts and Disbursements

Hint
The financial manager of a small business must have a very strong relationship with a commercial banker. Because the small firm cannot afford to hire someone strictly as a manager of receipts and disbursements, the financial manager, who is probably a generalist, needs to rely on the expertise of the commercial banker for the firm's most cost-effective means of managing cash.

As discussed in the previous section, the average collection period (the second component of the cash conversion cycle) has two parts: (1) the time from sale until the customer mails the payment and (2) the receipt, processing, and collection time. The third component of the cash conversion cycle, the average payment period, also has two parts: (1) the time from purchase of goods on account until the firm mails its payment and (2) the receipt, processing, and collection time required by the firm's suppliers. The receipt, processing, and collection time for the firm, both from its customers and to its suppliers, is the focus of receipts and disbursements management.

Float

float
Funds that have been sent by the payer but are not yet usable funds to the payee.

Float refers to funds that have been sent by the payer but are not yet usable funds to the payee. Float is important in the cash conversion cycle because its presence lengthens both the firm's average collection period and its average payment period. However, the goal of the firm should be to shorten its average collection period and lengthen its average payment period. Both can be accomplished by managing float.

Float has three component parts:

mail float
The time delay between when payment is placed in the mail and when it is received.

processing float
The time between receipt of a payment and its deposit into the firm's account.

clearing float
The time between deposit of a payment and when spendable funds become available to the firm.

1. **Mail float** is the time delay between when payment is placed in the mail and when it is received.
2. **Processing float** is the time between receipt of the payment and its deposit into the firm's account.
3. **Clearing float** is the time between deposit of the payment and when spendable funds become available to the firm. This component of float is attributable to the time required for a cheque to clear the banking system.

Some popular techniques for managing the component parts of float to speed up collections and slow down payments are described below.[4]

Hint
One method of accelerating the collection of accounts receivable is to let someone else do the financing for you, such as by using bank credit cards or selling accounts receivable to a third party at a discount. Another method is to change the credit terms: increase the cash discount and shorten the required payment period.

Speeding Up Collections

Speeding up collections reduces customer collection float time and thus reduces the firm's average collection period, which reduces the investment the firm must make in its cash conversion cycle. In our earlier examples, MAX Company had annual sales of $10 million and 5 days of total collection float (receipt, processing, and collection time). If MAX can reduce its float time to 2 days, it will reduce its investment in the cash conversion cycle by $82,192 ([$10,000,000 ÷ 365 days] × 3 days).

lockbox system
A collection procedure in which customers mail payments to a post office box that is emptied regularly by the firm's bank, which processes the payments and deposits them in the firm's account. This system speeds up collection time by reducing processing time as well as mail and clearing time.

A popular technique for speeding up collection is a lockbox system. A **lockbox system** works as follows: instead of mailing payments to the company, customers mail payments to a post office box. The firm's bank empties the post office box regularly, processes each payment, and deposits the payments in the firm's account. Deposit slips, along with payment enclosures, are sent (or transmitted electronically) to the firm by the bank so that the firm can properly credit customers' accounts. Lockboxes are geographically dispersed to match the location of the firm's customers. A lockbox system affects all three components of float.

Lockboxes reduce mail time and often clearing time by being near the firm's customers. Lockboxes reduce processing time to nearly zero, because the bank deposits payments before the firm processes them. Obviously, a lockbox system reduces collection float time, but not without a cost; therefore, a firm must perform an economic analysis to determine whether to implement a lockbox system.

Lockbox systems are commonly used by large firms whose customers are geographically dispersed. However, a firm does not have to be large to benefit from a lockbox. Smaller firms can also benefit from a lockbox system. The benefit to small firms often comes primarily from transferring the processing of payments to the bank.

Slowing Down Payments

controlled disbursing
The strategic use of mailing points and bank accounts to lengthen mail float and clearing float, respectively.

Float is also a component of the firm's average payment period. In this case, the float is in the favour of the firm. The firm may benefit by increasing all three of the components of its *payment float*. One popular technique for increasing payment float is **controlled disbursing**, which involves the strategic use of mailing

4. Float, the delay in processing payments, is slowly becoming a thing of the past for many companies. As electronic banking becomes more common among companies, payments are now being made through electronic connections between banks and companies. Now, with the click of a mouse, funds are transferred from the bank account of the paying company and deposited to the bank account of the payee. Float is reduced to nanoseconds!

points and bank accounts to lengthen mail float and clearing float, respectively. This approach should be used carefully, though, because longer payment periods may strain supplier relations.

Hint
Data on clearing time among banks located in various cities can be developed by the firm itself. It also can be obtained from a major bank's cash management service department or purchased from a firm that sells such information.

In summary, a reasonable overall policy for float management is (1) to collect payments as quickly as possible, because once the payment is in the mail, the funds belong to the firm, and (2) to delay making payment to suppliers, because once the payment is mailed, the funds belong to the supplier.

Cash Concentration

cash concentration
The process used by the firm to bring lockbox and other deposits together into one bank, often called the *concentration bank*.

Cash concentration is the process used by the firm to bring lockbox and other deposits together into one bank, often called the *concentration bank*. Cash concentration has three main advantages. First, it creates a large pool of funds for use in making short-term cash investments. Because there is a fixed-cost component in the transaction cost associated with such investments, investing a single pool of funds reduces the firm's transaction costs. The larger investment pool also allows the firm to choose from a greater variety of short-term investment vehicles. Second, concentrating the firm's cash in one account improves the tracking and internal control of the firm's cash. Third, having one concentration bank enables the firm to implement payment strategies that reduce idle cash balances.

There are a variety of mechanisms for transferring cash from the lockbox bank and other collecting banks to the concentration bank. One mechanism is a **depository transfer cheque (DTC)**, which is an unsigned cheque drawn on one of the firm's bank accounts and deposited in another. For cash concentration, a DTC is drawn on each lockbox or other collecting bank account and deposited in the concentration bank account. Once the DTC has cleared the bank on which it is drawn (which may take several days), the transfer of funds is completed. Most firms currently provide deposit information by telephone to the concentration bank, which then prepares and deposits into its account the DTC drawn on the lockbox or other collecting bank account.

depository transfer cheque (DTC)
An unsigned cheque drawn on one of a firm's bank accounts and deposited in another.

A second mechanism is an **ACH (automated clearinghouse) transfer**, which is a preauthorized electronic withdrawal from the payer's account. A computerized clearing facility (called the *automated clearinghouse*, or *ACH*) makes a paperless transfer of funds between the payer and payee banks. An ACH settles accounts among participating banks. Individual accounts are settled by respective bank balance adjustments. ACH transfers clear in one day. For cash concentrations, an ACH transfer is made from each lockbox or other collecting bank to the concentration bank. An ACH transfer can be thought of as an electronic DTC, but because the ACH transfer clears in one day, it provides benefits over a DTC; however, both banks in the ACH transfer must be members of the clearinghouse.

ACH (automated clearinghouse) transfer
Preauthorized electronic withdrawal from the payer's account and deposit into the payee's account via a settlement among banks by the automated clearinghouse, or ACH.

A third cash concentration mechanism is a **wire transfer**. A wire transfer is an electronic communication that, via bookkeeping entries, removes funds from the payer's bank and deposits them in the payee's bank. Wire transfers can eliminate mail and clearing float and may reduce processing float as well. For cash concentration, the firm moves funds using a wire transfer from each lockbox or other collecting account to its concentration account. Wire transfers are a substitute for DTC and ACH transfers, but they are more expensive.

wire transfer
An electronic communication that, via bookkeeping entries, removes funds from the payer's bank and deposits them in the payee's bank.

It is clear that the firm must balance the costs and benefits of concentrating cash to determine the type and timing of transfers from its lockbox and other collecting accounts to its concentration account. The transfer mechanism selected should be the one that is most profitable. (The profit per period of any transfer mechanism equals earnings on the increased availability of funds minus the cost of the transfer system.)

Zero-Balance Accounts

zero-balance account (ZBA)
A disbursement account that always has an end-of-day balance of zero because the firm deposits money to cover cheques drawn on the account only as they are presented for payment each day.

Zero-balance accounts (ZBAs) are disbursement accounts that always have an end-of-day balance of zero. The purpose is to eliminate non-earning cash balances in corporate chequing accounts. A ZBA works well as a disbursement account under a cash concentration system.

ZBAs work as follows: Once all of a given day's cheques are presented for payment from the firm's ZBA, the bank notifies the firm of the total amount of cheques, and the firm transfers funds into the account to cover the amount of that day's cheques. This leaves an end-of-day balance of $0 (zero dollars). The ZBA enables the firm to keep all of its operating cash in an interest-earning account, thereby eliminating idle cash balances. Thus a firm that used a ZBA in conjunction with a cash concentration system would need two accounts. The firm would concentrate its cash from the lockboxes and other collecting banks into an interest-earning account and would write cheques against its ZBA. The firm would cover the exact dollar amount of cheques presented against the ZBA with transfers from the interest-earning account, leaving the end-of-day balance in the ZBA at $0.

A ZBA is a disbursement management tool. As we discussed earlier, the firm would prefer to maximize its payment float. However, some cash managers feel that actively attempting to increase float time on payment is unethical. A ZBA enables the firm to maximize the use of float on each cheque without altering the float time of payments to its suppliers. Keeping all the firm's cash in an interest-earning account enables the firm to maximize earnings on its cash balances by capturing the full float time on each cheque it writes.

Investing in Marketable Securities

Marketable securities are short-term, interest-earning money market instruments that can easily be converted into cash.[5] Marketable securities are classified as part of the firm's liquid assets. The firm uses them to earn a return on temporarily idle funds. To be truly marketable, a security must have (1) a ready market in order to minimize the amount of time required to convert it into cash and (2) safety of principal, which means that it experiences little or no loss in value over time.

www.bankofcanada.ca/en/rates/interest-look.html

www.canada.com/nationalpost/financialpost/fpmarketdata/index.html

The securities that are most commonly held as part of the firm's marketable-securities portfolio are treasury bills issued by the federal government; certificates of deposit (CDs) issued by chartered banks or trust companies; and various securities issued by corporations. These securities include commercial paper, finance company paper, bankers' acceptances, forward rate agreements, and Euro-deposits. Each of these securities were discussed in Chapter 5. In December 2006, the Bank of Canada rate was 4.5 percent, while yields on one-month t-bills were about 4.1 percent. Current yields on all marketable securities are available on a number of Web sites.

5. As explained in Chapter 5, the *money market* results from a financial relationship between the suppliers and demanders of short-term funds, that is, marketable securities.

? Review Questions

14–17 What is *float* and what are its three components? Why might the concept of managing float soon be obsolete?

14–18 What are the firm's objectives with regard to collection float and to payment float?

14–19 What are the three main advantages of cash concentration?

14–20 What are three mechanisms of cash concentration? What is the objective of using a zero-balance account (ZBA) in a cash concentration system?

14–21 What two characteristics make a security marketable? Why are the yields on non-government marketable securities generally higher than the yields on government issues with similar maturities?

SUMMARY

LG1 **Understand why the active management of working capital is important, the concept of net working capital, and the related tradeoff between profitability and risk.** Short-term financial management is focused on managing each of the firm's current assets (inventory, accounts receivable, cash, and marketable securities) and current liabilities (accounts payable, accruals, and short-term debt) in a manner that positively contributes to the firm's value. Net working capital is the difference between current assets and current liabilities. Profitability is the relationship between revenues and costs. Risk, in the context of short-term financial decisions, is the probability that a firm will become technically insolvent—unable to pay its bills as they come due. Assuming a constant level of total assets, the higher a firm's ratio of current assets to total assets, the less profitable the firm, and the less risky it is. The converse is also true. With constant total assets, the higher a firm's ratio of current liabilities to total assets, the more profitable and the more risky the firm is. The converse of this statement is also true.

Describe the cash conversion cycle, the required financing that is implied in the calculation, and three strategies that firms may follow to finance this investment in net working capital. The cash conversion cycle represents the amount of time a firm's resources are tied up. It has three components: (1) average age of inventory, (2) average collection period, and (3) average payment period. The length of the cash conversion cycle determines the amount of time resources are tied up in the firm's day-to-day operations. To finance the investment in current assets, we assume that accounts payable and accruals is the first source of financing. For the remainder of the financing, a firm could use an aggressive financing strategy (only current liabilities), a conservative financing strategy (only long-term financing), or a matching strategy (short-term financing for seasonal current assets, long-term sources for permanent current assets). The choice depends on management's disposition toward risk and the strength of the firm's banking relationships. To minimize its reliance on negotiated liabilities, the financial manager seeks to (1) turn over inventory as quickly as possible, (2) collect accounts receivable as quickly as possible, (3) pay accounts payable as slowly as possible, and (4) manage mail, processing, and clearing time. Use of these strategies should shorten the cash conversion cycle.

LG3 **Discuss inventory management: differing views, common techniques, and international concerns.** The viewpoints of marketing, manufacturing, and purchasing managers about the appropriate levels of inventory tend to cause higher inventories than those deemed appropriate by the financial manager. Four commonly used techniques for effectively managing inventory to keep its level low are (1) the ABC system, (2) the economic order quantity (EOQ) model, (3) the just-in-time (JIT) system, and (4) the materials requirement planning (MRP) system. International inventory managers place greater emphasis on making sure that sufficient quantities of inventory are delivered where they are needed, when they are needed, and in the right condition, than on ordering the economically optimal quantities.

LG4 **Explain the credit selection process and the quantitative procedure for evaluating changes in credit standards.** Credit selection and standards are concerned with applying techniques for determining which customers' creditworthiness is consistent with the firm's credit standards. Two popular credit selection techniques are the four C's of credit and credit scoring. To evaluate credit applicants, information to base the analysis on is required. One potential source of the information is the applicant. Another is agencies, such as D&B, that collect financial and rating information on millions of Canadian companies that can then be used to evaluate the risk of credit applicants. Changes in credit standards and terms can be financially evaluated by assessing the effects of a proposed change on gross margin, the cost of accounts receivable investment, bad debt costs, and the cost of discounts.

LG5 **Review the procedures for quantitatively considering cash discount changes, other aspects of credit terms, and credit monitoring.** Changes in credit terms (particularly the initiation of, or a change in, the cash discount) can be quantified in a way similar to that for changes in credit standards. Changes in the cash discount period can also be evaluated using similar methods. Credit monitoring, the ongoing review of customer payment of accounts receivable, frequently involves use of the average collection period and the aging of accounts receivable. A number of popular collection techniques are used by firms.

Understand the management of receipts and disbursements, including float, speeding up collections, slowing payments, cash concentration, zero-balance accounts, and investing in marketable securities. Float refers to funds that have been sent by the payer but are not yet usable funds to the payee. The components of float are mail time, processing time, and clearing time. Float occurs in both the average collection period and the average payment period. One technique for speeding up collections to reduce collection float is a lockbox system. A popular technique for slowing payments to increase payment float is controlled disbursing, which involves strategic use of mailing points and bank accounts. The goal for managing operating cash is to balance the opportunity cost of non-earning balances against the transaction cost of temporary investments. Firms commonly use depository transfer cheques (DTCs), ACH transfers, and wire transfers to transfer lockbox receipts to their concentration banks quickly. Zero-balance accounts (ZBAs) can be used to eliminate non-earning cash balances in corporate chequing accounts. Marketable securities are short-term, interest-earning, money market instruments used by the firm to earn a return on temporarily idle funds. They may be government or non-government issues.

SELF-TEST PROBLEMS

(Solutions in Appendix B)

ST 14–1 **Cash conversion cycle** Hurkin Manufacturing Company pays accounts payable on the tenth day after purchase. The average collection period is 30 days, and the average age of inventory is 40 days. The firm is considering a plan that would stretch its amounts payable by 20 days. The firm's credit purchases are $8,762,319 per year. If the cost to the firm of investing in assets is 12 percent, what annual savings can it realize by this plan? There is no discount for the early payment of accounts payable.

ST 14–2 **EOQ analysis** Thompson Paint Company uses 60,000 gallons of pigment per year. The cost of ordering pigment is $200 per order, and the cost of carrying the pigment in inventory is $1 per gallon per year. The firm uses pigment at a constant rate every day throughout the year.

a. Calculate the EOQ.

b. Determine the total cost of the plan based on **a**.

c. Assuming that it takes 20 days to receive an order once it has been placed, determine the reorder point in terms of gallons of pigment.

ST 14–3 **Relaxing credit standards** Regency Rug Repair Company is trying to decide whether it should relax its credit standards. The firm repairs 72,000 rugs per year at an average price of $32 each. Bad debt expenses are 1 percent of sales, the average collection period is 40 days, and the variable cost per unit is $28. Regency expects that if it does relax its credit standards, the average collection period will increase to 48 days and that bad debts will increase to 1.5 percent of sales. Sales will increase by 4,000 repairs per year. The firm also expects to save $15,000 per year in collection expenses. If the firm's cost of capital is 14 percent, what recommendation would you give the firm? Provide a complete analysis to justify your answer.

PROBLEMS

14–1 **Cash conversion cycle** American Products is concerned about managing cash efficiently. On the average, inventories have an age of 90 days, and accounts receivable are collected in 60 days. Accounts payable are paid approximately 30 days after they arise. Credit sales are $30 million per year, cost of goods sold is 42 percent of sales, and credit purchases are $9,622,159 per year.

a. Calculate the firm's operating cycle.

b. Calculate the firm's cash conversion cycle.

c. Calculate the amount of financing needed to support the firm's cash conversion cycle.

d. Discuss how management might be able to reduce the cash conversion cycle.

14–2 **Changing cash conversion cycle** Camp Manufacturing turns over its inventory 8 times each year, has an average payment period of 35 days, and has an average collection period of 60 days. The firm's credit sales are $852,360 per year, cost of goods sold is 36.5 percent of sales, and credit purchases are 46.2 percent of cost of goods sold.

a. Calculate the firm's operating and cash conversion cycles.

b. Calculate the amount of financing needed to support the firm's operating cycle. How will the firm finance a portion of this investment? Provide exact dollar amounts and actual or possible sources.

c. If the firm were able to favourably change the average age of inventory by 15.2 days, and the firm's cost of capital was 14 percent, what would be the impact on cash flows?

INTERMEDIATE 

14–3 **Cash conversion cycle** Harris & Company has an inventory turnover of 12 times each year, an average collection period of 45 days, and an average payment period of 40 days. The firm's credit sales are $5,512,079 per year, cost of goods sold is $2,023,792, and credit purchases are 46.2 percent of cost of goods sold.

a. Calculate the firm's operating cycle and cash conversion cycle.

b. Calculate the amount of costly financing required to support the firm's cash conversion cycle.

c. If the firm's average collection period were increased by 10 days without any change in its average payment period (APP), how would this affect its cash conversion cycle and costly financing need?

BASIC 

14–4 **Changes in cash conversion cycles** A firm is concerned about their working capital management. They are considering five plans that will impact the AAI, ACP, and APP. The expected changes for the plans are provided in the following table. Which plan would you favour? Explain.

	Change		
Plan	Average age of inventory	Average collection period	Average payment period
A	+30 days	+20 days	+5 days
B	+20 days	−10 days	+15 days
C	−10 days	0 days	−5 days
D	−15 days	+15 days	+10 days
E	+5 days	−10 days	+15 days

INTERMEDIATE 

14–5 **Multiple changes in cash conversion cycle** Garrett Industries turns over its inventory 6 times each year; it has an average collection period of 45 days and an average payment period of 30 days. The firm's credit sales are $11.4 million per year, cost of goods sold is 33.4 percent of sales, and credit purchases are $2,221,535 per year.

a. Calculate the firm's cash conversion cycle and the amount of financing needed to support its cash conversion cycle.

b. Find the firm's cash conversion cycle and financing required if it makes the following changes simultaneously: shortens the average age of inventory by 5 days, speeds up the collection of accounts receivable by an average of 10 days, extends the average payment period by 10 days.

c. If the firm's cost of capital is 13 percent, by how much could it increase its annual cash flow as a result of the changes in part **b**?

d. If the annual cost of achieving the cash flow in part **c** is $35,000, what action would you recommend to the firm? Why?

CHALLENGE 

14–6 **Changing the cash conversion cycle** Aspen Jeans' average payment period is 46.7 days, average collection period 41.3 days, and average age of inventory 51.6 days. The firm's credit sales are $15,124,350 per year, cost of goods sold is $10,193,812, and credit purchases are 54.1 percent of cost of goods sold. Aspen has been offered a large contract to produce private-label jeans for a large retailer. Without the contract, little will change with the company's operation. With the contract, Aspen's sales will increase by 20 percent, the gross margin will fall by 2.3 percent, and credit purchases will increase to 55.3 percent of cost of goods sold.

In addition, since the large retailer works on a JIT inventory system, Aspen will be asked to carry more inventory, so the company's average age of inventory will increase to 58.9 days. In addition, the retailer will take longer to pay, so Aspen's collection period will increase to 56.3 days. Since the retailer is very particular regarding the material used in the clothing they will purchase from Aspen, Aspen will have to maintain an excellent relationship with one supplier. This will result in the company's average payment period declining to 40.3 days. No other changes will occur. Aspen's firm's cost of capital is 14.8 percent.

a. Should Aspen accept the contract from the large retailer? Provide a complete financial analysis.

INTERMEDIATE 

14–7 **Financing strategy** Dynabase Tool has forecast the difference between its current assets and the total of accounts payable and accruals for each month in the coming year as shown in the following table.

Month	Amount	Month	Amount
January	$2,000,000	July	$12,800,000
February	2,200,000	August	14,000,000
March	2,400,000	September	9,000,000
April	4,000,000	October	5,000,000
May	6,000,000	November	4,000,000
June	9,000,000	December	3,200,000

a. What do the above monthly forecasts imply about the firm's need for financing for the coming year? Split the monthly financing requirements into (1) a *permanent* component and (2) a *seasonal* component, and find the monthly averages for all of the variables.

b. How would the firm finance the required investment in net current assets if it were to follow: (1) an aggressive strategy? (2) a conservative strategy? (3) a matching strategy?

c. Assuming that short-term funds cost 12 percent annually and that the cost of long-term funds is 17 percent annually, use your answers above to calculate the total costs of the three financing strategies.

d. Discuss the risk–return tradeoffs associated with the three financing strategies.

CHALLENGE 

14–8 **Financing strategy** Benitez Industrial Services Corp.'s cost of short-term funds is 7 percent while the cost of long-term funds is 12 percent. The company can invest surplus cash in marketable securities providing a yield of 3.6 percent. A forecast of the company's current assets and the total of accounts payable and accruals for each month of the coming year is as follows.

Month	Current assets	Payables and accruals	Month	Current assets	Payables and accruals
January	$ 8,900,000	$2,300,000	July	$10,500,000	$3,850,000
February	8,500,000	2,450,000	August	10,000,000	3,800,000
March	8,700,000	2,720,000	September	9,600,000	3,140,000
April	9,200,000	3,050,000	October	9,400,000	2,980,000
May	9,800,000	3,400,000	November	9,000,000	2,640,000
June	10,300,000	4,200,000	December	9,000,000	2,410,000

a. What do the above monthly forecasts imply about the firm's need for financing for the coming year? Split the monthly financing requirements into permanent and seasonal components. Calculate the monthly averages for all of the above variables.

b. Calculate the yearly cost if the firm finances the required investment in net current assets using: (1) an aggressive strategy; (2) a conservative strategy; (3) a matching strategy.

c. Discuss the risks associated with each of the three financing strategies. Based on your results above, explain why virtually no firm should follow an aggressive financing strategy.

INTERMEDIATE 

14–9 **Financing strategy** Marbell International has forecast its seasonal costly financing needs for the next year as shown in the table below. Assuming that the firm's permanent amount of net current assets is $4 million, calculate the total annual financing costs using an *aggressive strategy* and those using a *conservative strategy.* Recommend one of the strategies under each of the following conditions:

a. Short-term funds cost 9 percent annually, and long-term funds cost 15 percent annually.

b. Short-term funds cost 10 percent annually, and long-term funds cost 13 percent annually.

c. Both short-term and long-term funds cost 11 percent annually.

d. Calculate the cost of the matching strategy using each of the sets of costs provided above. Now which financing strategy do you recommend the firm use?

Month	Seasonal requirement	Month	Seasonal requirement
January	$ 0	July	$700,000
February	300,000	August	400,000
March	500,000	September	0
April	900,000	October	200,000
May	1,200,000	November	700,000
June	1,000,000	December	300,000

CHALLENGE  14–10 **Financing strategy** On average, Lear Inc. holds $800,000 of net current assets (current assets less accounts payable and accruals). Of the $800,000, $350,000 is considered permanent current assets. In addition, the firm has invested $600,000 in net fixed assets. Lear is investigating two methods of financing this investment in assets.

Plan 1 calls for Lear to finance all fixed assets and half the permanent current assets with long-term financing. To finance these assets, Lear will use 40 percent long-term debt and 60 percent common equity. The cost of the long-term debt is 11.8 percent. The remaining current assets would be financed with a line of credit at a cost of prime plus 150 basis points. Prime is 4.5 percent.

Plan 2 calls for Lear to finance all fixed assets, all permanent current assets, and half of the seasonal current assets with 40 percent long-term debt and 60 percent common equity. The cost of the long-term debt is 10 percent. The remaining seasonal current assets would be financed with a line of credit at a cost of prime plus 50 basis points. Prime is 4.5 percent.

For both plans, Lear's sales will be $1,250,000 and earnings before interest and taxes (EBIT) will be 20 percent of sales. Lear's tax rate is 30 percent.

a. Calculate Lear's debt ratio, net income after tax (NIAT), and return on equity (ROE) under both financing plans.

b. Comment on the benefits and drawbacks of each plan. In your discussion, be sure to discuss why the cost of debt for the first financing plan is higher than for the second.

c. As a financial consultant to Lear, which financing plan would you recommend and why?

BASIC LG3 14–11 **EOQ analysis** Tiger Corporation purchases 1,200,000 units per year of one component. The fixed cost per order is $25. The annual carrying cost of the item is 27 percent of its $2 cost.

a. Determine the EOQ.

b. What happens to the EOQ if (1) order costs are $0? (2) carrying costs are $0? What do your answers illustrate about the EOQ model? Discuss.

INTERMEDIATE  14–12 **EOQ, reorder point, and safety stock** Alexis Company uses 800 units of a product per year on a continuous basis. Ordering costs are $50 per order, and its carrying cost is $2 per unit per year. It takes 5 days to receive a shipment after an order is placed, and the firm wishes to hold 10 days' usage in inventory as a safety stock.

a. Calculate the EOQ.

b. Determine the average level of inventory.

c. Determine the reorder point.

d. Indicate which of the following variables change if the firm does not hold the safety stock: (1) order cost, (2) carrying cost, (3) total inventory cost, (4) reorder point, (5) economic order quantity. Explain.

INTERMEDIATE  **14–13 Inventory—The ABC system** Newton, Inc., has 16 different items in its inventory. The average number of units held in inventory and the average unit cost for each item are listed in the following table. The firm wishes to introduce the ABC system of inventory management. Suggest a breakdown of the items into classifications of A, B, and C. Justify your selection and point out items that could be considered borderline cases.

Item	Average number of units in inventory	Average cost per unit
1	1,800	$ 0.54
2	1,000	8.20
3	100	6.00
4	250	1.20
5	8	94.50
6	400	3.00
7	80	45.00
8	1,600	1.45
9	600	0.95
10	3,000	0.18
11	900	15.00
12	65	1.35
13	2,200	4.75
14	1,800	1.30
15	60	18.00
16	200	17.50

INTERMEDIATE  **14–14 Graphic EOQ analysis** Knoll Manufacturing uses 10,000 units of raw material per year on a continuous basis. Placing and processing an order for additional inventory costs $200 per order. The firm estimates the cost of carrying one unit in inventory at $0.25 per year.

a. What are the annual order costs, carrying costs, and total costs of inventory if the firm orders in quantities of 1,000; 2,000; 3,000; 4,000; 5,000; 6,000; and 7,000 units?

b. Graph the order cost, carrying cost, and total cost (y axis) relative to order quantity (x axis). Label the EOQ.

c. On the basis of your graph, in what quantity would you order? Is this consistent with the EOQ equation? Explain why or why not.

INTERMEDIATE  **14–15 Credit scoring** Clemens Department Store uses credit scoring to evaluate retail credit applications. The financial and credit characteristics considered and weights indicating their relative importance in the credit decision are given in the table that follows. The firm's credit standards are to accept all applicants with credit scores of 80 or more, to extend limited credit on a probationary basis to applicants with scores of greater than 70 and less than 80, and to reject all applicants with scores below 70.

Financial and credit characteristics	Predetermined weight
Credit references	0.25
Education	0.15
Home ownership	0.10
Income range	0.10
Payment history	0.30
Years on job	0.10

The firm wishes to process three applications that were recently received and scored by one of its credit analysts. The scores for each of the applicants on each of the financial and credit characteristics are summarized in the following table:

	Applicant		
Financial and credit characteristics	A	B Score (0 to 100)	C
Credit references	60	90	80
Education	70	70	80
Home ownership	100	90	60
Income range	75	80	80
Payment history	60	85	70
Years on job	50	60	90

a. Use the data presented to find the credit score for each of the applicants.
b. Recommend the appropriate action for each of the three applicants.

BASIC LG4 **14–16 Accounts receivable and costs** Randolph Company's annual credit sales are $1 million per year and the firm makes sales 365 days per year. The company's average collection period is 45 days.
a. What is the firm's average daily credit sales?
b. What is the average daily *investment* in accounts receivable?
c. If the firm's cost of capital is 12 percent, what is the cost of the investment in accounts receivable?

INTERMEDIATE  **14–17 Changing accounts receivable policy** Tara's Textiles currently has credit sales of $360 million per year and an average collection period of 60 days. Assume that the price of Tara's products is $60 per unit and that the variable costs are $55 per unit. The firm is considering changing its accounts receivable policy, resulting in a 20 percent increase in sales and a 20 percent increase in the average collection period. No change in bad debts is expected. The firm's cost of capital is 14 percent.
a. Should the firm implement the proposed change? What other information would be helpful in your analysis?

BASIC   14–18 **Changing accounts receivable standards** A firm is considering a relaxation of its credit standards that would increase bad debts from 2 percent to 4 percent of sales. Sales are currently 50,000 units, the selling price is $20 per unit, and the variable cost per unit is $15. As a result of the proposed change, sales are forecast to increase to 60,000 units. Should the firm implement the proposed plan?

INTERMEDIATE  14–19 **Relaxation of credit standards** Lewis Enterprises is considering relaxing its credit standards to increase its currently sagging sales. As a result of the proposed relaxation, sales are expected to increase by 10 percent from 10,000 to 11,000 units during the coming year; the average collection period is expected to increase from 45 days to 60 days; and bad debts are expected to increase from 1 percent to 3 percent of sales. The sale price per unit is $40, and the variable cost per unit is $31. The firm's cost of capital is 25 percent. Evaluate the proposed change, and make a recommendation to the firm.

INTERMEDIATE  14–20 **Initiating a cash discount** Gardner Company currently makes all sales on credit and offers no cash discount. The firm is considering offering a 2 percent cash discount for payment within 15 days. The firm's current average collection period is 60 days, sales are 40,000 units, selling price is $45 per unit, and variable cost per unit is $36. The firm expects that the change in credit terms will result in an increase in sales to 42,000 units, that 70 percent of the sales will take the discount, and that the overall average collection period will fall to 30 days. If the firm's cost of capital is 25 percent, should the proposed discount be offered?

INTERMEDIATE  14–21 **Shortening the credit period** A firm is contemplating *shortening* its credit period from net 40 to net 30 days and believes that as a result of this change, its average collection period will decline from 45 days to 36 days. Bad-debt expenses are expected to decrease from 1.5 percent to 1 percent of sales. The firm is currently selling 12,000 units but believes that as a result of the proposed change, sales will decline to 10,000 units. The sale price per unit is $56, and the variable cost per unit is $45. The firm's required return on assets is 25 percent. Evaluate this plan, and make a recommendation to the firm.

INTERMEDIATE  14–22 **Changing credit terms** Parker Tool is considering changing their credit terms from net 30 to net 60. Currently, the average collection period is 43.2 days. With the new terms, the average collection period will increase to 81.8 days. The firm's sales are $750,000, while variable costs are $425,000. The change in credit terms is expected to result in sales increasing to $850,000. In addition, with the more lenient credit terms, the cost of evaluating credit applicants will increase by $15,000. Bad-debt expenses will increase from 1 percent to 2 percent of sales. The firm's cost of capital is 20 percent. Due to previous decisions relating to cost control, variable costs are expected to decline to 52 percent of sales. Do you recommend Parker Tool change their credit terms? Provide a financial analysis.

CHALLENGE  14–23 **Changing credit terms** The Imperial Socket Company based in Moncton has a subsidiary located in Toronto. At present, the subsidiary offers its customers terms of 2/10 net 30. The Toronto operation has been under pressure to extend the terms granted to its customers in order to meet the competition's credit terms. After an appraisal of the situation, the company believes that the demand for its product is not very sensitive to price. A proposal by the manager heading the operation in Toronto states that the selling price for the product could be increased by 11 percent if terms of 1/30 net 90 were offered. The number of units sold and costs of production would not be affected by this change.

Currently, 40 percent of customers take the discount. The average collection period (ACP) on the remainder of the sales is 36 days. If the new credit terms were offered, only 25 percent of customers will take the discount. The ACP on the remainder of sales will increase to 105 days. Sales now average $150,000 per month. Past experience has shown that 1.5 percent of credit sales on which the discount is not taken are written off as bad debts. This is expected to increase to 3.2 percent if the new terms are offered. The firm's cost of capital is 20 percent.

a. Should Imperial Socket introduce the proposal suggested by the manager? Provide a complete analysis.

b. Now assume that the company's policy is to write off accounts receivable as bad debts once they have been on the books for 200 days. In this case, the average collection periods in the above discussion only relate to the accounts that are collected. How does this affect the analysis? Will it change your original decision? Provide a numeric analysis.

INTERMEDIATE  14–24 **Aging accounts receivable** Burnham Services' accounts receivable totalled $874,000 on August 31, 2008. A breakdown of these outstanding accounts on the basis of the month in which the credit sale was initially made follows. The firm extends credit terms of net 30 to its credit customers.

Month of credit sale	Accounts receivable
August	$320,000
July	250,000
June	81,000
May	195,000
April or before	28,000
Total (August 31, 2008)	$874,000

a. Prepare an aging schedule for Burnham Services' August 31 accounts receivable balance.

b. Use your aging schedule to estimate the firm's overall average number of days that sales are outstanding (overall DSO).

c. Using your findings in **a** and **b**, evaluate the firm's credit and collection activities.

d. What are some probable causes of the situation discussed in **c**?

  **14–25 Inventory investment** Paterson Products is considering leasing a computerized inventory control system to reduce its average inventories. The annual cost of the system is $46,000. It is expected that with the system the firm's average inventory will decline by 50 percent from its current level of $980,000. The level of stockouts is expected to be unaffected by this system. The firm's cost of capital is 20 percent.

a. What will happen to the firm's level of inventory if the proposed computerized inventory control system is installed? What is the benefit of the change?

b. Should the firm lease the computerized inventory control system? Explain.

 **14–26 Float** Simon Corporation has daily cash receipts of $65,000. A recent analysis of its collections indicated that customers' payments were in the mail an average of 2.5 days. Once received, it takes, on average, 1.5 days to process the payments. After payments are deposited, it takes an average of 3 days for these receipts to clear the banking system.

a. How much collection float (in days and dollars) does the firm currently have?

b. If the firm's cost of investing in assets is 11 percent, would it be economically advisable for the firm to pay an annual fee of $16,500 to reduce collection float by 3 days? Explain.

 **14–27 Lockbox system** Eagle Industries feels that a lockbox system can shorten its average collection period by 3 days. Credit sales are $3,240,000 per year, billed on a continuous basis. The firm's cost of capital is 15 percent. The cost of the lockbox system is $9,000 per year.

a. What amount of cash will be made available for other uses under the lockbox system?

b. What net benefit (cost) will the firm realize if it adopts the lockbox system? Should it adopt the proposed lockbox system?

 **14–28 Zero-balance account** Union Company is considering setting up a zero-balance account. The firm currently maintains an average balance of $420,000 in its disbursement account. As compensation to the bank for maintaining the zero-balance account, the firm will have to pay a monthly fee of $1,000 and maintain a $300,000 non-interest-earning deposit in the bank. The firm currently has no other deposits in the bank. Evaluate the proposed zero-balance account, and make a recommendation to the firm, assuming that it has a 12 percent cost of capital.

CASE CHAPTER 14 Assessing Roche Publishing Company's Capital Management

See the enclosed Student CD-ROM for cases that help you put theories and concepts from the text into practice.

Be sure to visit the Companion Website for this book at **www.pearsoned.ca/gitman** for a wealth of additional learning tools including self-test quizzes, Web exercises, and additional cases.

CHAPTER 15

Management of Current Liabilities

LEARNING GOALS

LG1 Review the concept of spontaneous liabilities, the key components of a firm's credit terms, and the procedures for analyzing them.

LG2 Understand the impact that stretching accounts payable has on the cash conversion cycle, explore the cost of not taking discounts, and consider the benefit of accruals.

LG3 Describe the basic types of unsecured sources of short-term financing, and the interest rates on these loans.

LG4 Discuss the basic features of corporate paper and the key aspects of international short-term loans.

LG5 Explain the characteristics of secured short-term loans and the use of accounts receivable as short-term-loan collateral.

LG6 Describe the various ways in which inventory can be used as short-term-loan collateral.

15.1 Spontaneous Liabilities

spontaneous liabilities
Financing that arises from the normal course of business; the two major short-term sources of such liabilities are accounts payable and accruals.

Spontaneous liabilities arise from the normal course of business. As discussed a number of times in this book, the two major spontaneous sources of short-term financing are accounts payable and accruals. As the firm's sales increase, accounts payable increase in response to the increased purchases necessary to produce higher sales. Also in response to increasing sales, the firm's accruals

Seasonal Rates

In the last chapter we discussed the factors influencing a company's investment in current assets. We also saw that the investment in current assets must be financed. The amount of financing required will vary with sales. A firm anticipating a seasonal increase in sales will have to build up inventories prior to the expected increase. As the inventory is sold, accounts receivable will increase. Thus, increased financing will be required around the seasonal increase in sales. When a seasonal decrease in sales occurs, inventories will be depleted before the temporary sales decline, and accounts receivable will decrease in the period following. Thus, financing needs will decline. Various strategies exist for financing current assets. We assume that accounts payable and accruals, the spontaneous, no-cost sources of financing, are always the first choice for financing. If additional financing is required, short-term debt, like a line of credit, can be used to finance a temporary buildup of inventory and accounts receivable. Long-term financing is also a possibility. In this chapter, we will explain various financing methods and how these can be used to the firm's advantage.

increase as wages rise due to greater labour requirements and taxes rise on the firm's increased earnings. There is normally no explicit cost attached to either of these current liabilities, although they do have certain implicit costs. In addition, both are forms of **unsecured short-term financing**—short-term financing obtained without pledging specific assets as collateral. The firm should take advantage of these "no-cost" sources of unsecured short-term financing whenever possible.

unsecured short-term financing
Short-term financing obtained without pledging specific assets as collateral.

LINKING THE DISCIPLINES: Cross-Functional Interactions

- ***Accounting personnel*** need to understand the various types of short-term loans that they will be required to record and report. They will also be responsible for analyzing supplier credit terms to decide whether the firm should take or give up cash discounts.
- ***Information systems analysts*** need to understand what data the firm will need to process accounts payable, track accruals, and meet bank loans and other short-term debt obligations in a timely manner.
- ***Management*** need to know the sources of short-term loans and understand their availability and costs for use as a short-term source of financing.
- The ***marketing department*** needs to understand how accounts receivable and inventory can be used as loan collateral, because the procedures the firm uses to secure short-term loans with such collateral can affect customer relationships.
- Personnel in the ***operations department*** need to understand the use of accounts payable as a form of short-term financing and the effect the stretching of payables has on relationships with suppliers.

Accounts Payable Management

Hint
Your account payable is your supplier's account receivable. A payable always has an offsetting receivable. Chapter 14 highlighted the key strategies and considerations involved in extending credit to customers.

Accounts payable are the major source of unsecured short-term financing for business firms. As we saw in Figure 14.1 in the last chapter, accounts payable and accruals for the average non-financial company in Canada are 15.4 percent of total liabilities and equity, and are equivalent to long-term debt on the average company's balance sheet. Accounts payable result from transactions in which merchandise is purchased but cash is not paid, and no formal loan agreement is signed that shows the purchaser's liability to the seller.

The purchaser in effect agrees to pay the supplier the amount required in accordance with the credit terms normally stated on the supplier's invoice. Accounts payable are the classic example of an unsecured loan, and this is accepted practice in many industries. It is also how many companies finance the investment required in their own current assets. This is particularly the case for smaller firms and for retailers. The discussion of accounts payable here is presented from the viewpoint of the purchaser.

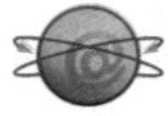

www.theaccountspayablenetwork.com

Role in the Cash Conversion Cycle

The average payment period is the final component of the *cash conversion cycle* introduced in Chapter 14. The average payment period has two parts: (1) the time from the purchase of raw materials until the firm mails the payment and (2) payment float time (the time it takes after the firm mails its payment until the supplier has withdrawn spendable funds from the firm's account). In the preceding chapter, we discussed issues related to payment float time. Here we discuss the management by the firm of the time that elapses between its purchase of raw materials and its mailing payment to the supplier. This activity is **accounts payable management.**

accounts payable management
Management by the firm of the time that elapses between its purchase of raw materials and its mailing payment to the supplier.

The firm's goal is to pay as slowly as possible without damaging its credit rating. This means that accounts should be paid on the last day possible, given the supplier's stated credit terms. For example, if the terms are net 30, then the account should be paid 30 days from the *beginning of the credit period*, which is typically the *date of the invoice*. This allows for the maximum use of an interest-free loan from the supplier and will not damage the firm's credit rating (because the account is paid within the stated credit terms).

Example In the demonstration of the cash conversion cycle (CCC) in Chapter 14, MAX Company had an average payment period of 35 days (consisting of 30 days until payment was mailed and 5 days of payment float), which resulted in average accounts payable of $467,466 (see page 779). Thus the daily accounts payable generated by MAX was $13,356 ($467,466/35). (This can also be calculated by dividing credit purchases by 365. For MAX Company this was $4,875,000/365.)

If MAX were to mail its payments in 35 days instead of 30, its accounts payable would increase by $66,780 ($13,356 × 5). As a result, MAX's cash conversion cycle would decrease by 5 days, and the firm would reduce its net investment in the CCC (receivables and inventory) by $66,780. Clearly, if this action did not damage MAX's credit rating, it would be in the company's best interest.

Analyzing Credit Terms

The credit terms that a firm is offered by its suppliers enable it to delay payments for its purchases. Because the supplier's cost of having its money tied up in merchandise after it is sold is probably reflected in the purchase price, the purchaser is already indirectly paying for this benefit. The purchaser should therefore carefully analyze credit terms to determine the best trade credit strategy. If a firm is extended credit terms that include a cash discount, it has two options—to take the cash discount or to give it up.

Taking the Cash Discount If a firm intends to take a cash discount, it should pay on the last day of the discount period. There is no direct cost associated with taking a cash discount, but note the indirect cost—the cost of paying prior to the end of the full credit period. For the purposes of our discussion, we will assume the indirect cost is very low and thus can be safely ignored.

Example Lawrence Industries, operator of a small chain of video stores, purchased $1,000 worth of merchandise on April 30 from a supplier extending terms of 2/10, net 30. If the firm takes the cash discount, it must pay $980 [$1,000 − (0.02 × $1,000)] by May 10, thereby saving $20—note that the cost is $20, over 20 days. In other words, with the discount, the firm is given the option of making $20 on a $980 investment, over 20 days. What rate of return is implied by this? What is the cost of not taking this option? Here we have two questions, with the same answer.

cost of giving up a cash discount
The rate of interest implied by delaying payment of an account payable for an additional number of days.

Giving Up the Cash Discount If the firm chooses to give up the cash discount, it should pay on the final day of the credit period. There is an implicit cost associated with giving up a cash discount. The **cost of giving up a cash discount** is the rate of interest implied by delaying payment of the accounts payable for the additional number of days between the discount period and the total credit period. Note that there is no direct cost of not taking the discount, as with a loan. The cost is an opportunity cost. In other words, what rate of return would the company have to earn on the funds in order to be indifferent to taking or not taking the discount? This can be illustrated by a simple example. The example assumes that payment will be made on the last possible day (either the final day of the cash discount period or the final day of the credit period).

Example In the preceding example, we saw that Lawrence Industries could take the cash discount on its April 30 purchase by paying $980 on May 10. If Lawrence gives up the cash discount, payment should be made on May 30. To keep its money for an extra 20 days, the firm will give up an opportunity to pay $980 for its $1,000 purchase. In other words, it will cost the firm $20 to delay payment for 20 days. Figure 15.1 shows the payment options that are open to the company. The annual percentage cost of giving up the cash discount can be calculated using Equation 15.1:

$$\text{Cost of giving up cash discount} = \frac{CD}{100\% - CD} \times \frac{365}{CP\text{–}DP} \qquad (15.1)$$

where:

CD = stated cash discount in percentage terms
CP = full credit period
DP = discount period

Substituting the values for CD (2%), CP (30 days), DP (10 days) into Equation 15.1 results in an annualized cost of giving up the cash discount of:

$$\text{Cost of giving up discount} = \frac{2\%}{100\% - 2\%} \times \frac{365}{30 - 10}$$

$$= \frac{2\%}{98\%} \times \frac{365}{20} = 37.24\%$$

So, for Lawrence, the cost of not taking the discount is 37.24 percent on an annual basis.[1] Note that this is not a risky return; it is guaranteed. The implication is that to be indifferent to taking or not taking the discount, Lawrence would have to earn a guaranteed 37.24 percent rate of return on an alternative investment. Unless the firm has an incredible array of investment opportunities, the decision to take the discount seems clear.

Using the Cost of Giving Up a Cash Discount in Decision Making In the previous example, we saw one way to interpret the cost of giving up a discount. There is another way to determine whether it is advisable to take a cash discount. Financial managers must remember that taking cash discounts may represent an important source of additional profitability.

---

1. This example assumes that Lawrence Industries gives up only one discount during the year, which costs it 2.04 percent (i.e., 2% ÷ 98%) for 20 days or 37.24 percent when annualized. However, if Lawrence Industries *continually* gives up the 2 percent cash discounts, the effect of compounding will cause the annualized cost to rise to 44.59 percent:

Annualized cost when discounts are *continually* given up

$$= \left(1 + \frac{CD}{100\% - CD}\right)^{365/N} - 1 \qquad (15.1a)$$

$$= \left(1 + \frac{2\%}{100\% - 2\%}\right)^{365/20} - 1 = \underline{\underline{44.59\%}}$$

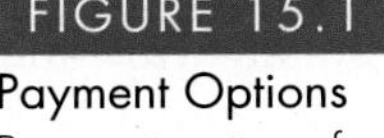

FIGURE 15.1

Payment Options
Payment options for Lawrence Industries

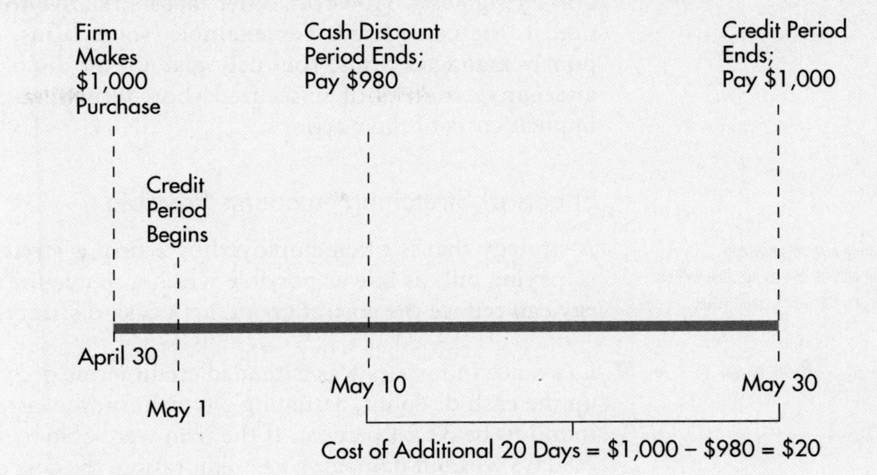

Example Mason Products, a large building-supply company, has four possible suppliers, each offering different credit terms. Otherwise, their products and services are identical. Table 15.1 presents the credit terms offered by suppliers A, B, C, and D and the cost of giving up the cash discounts in each transaction. The cost of giving up the cash discount from supplier A is 37.24 percent; from supplier B, 8.19 percent; from supplier C, 22.58 percent; and from supplier D, 30.42 percent.

If the firm needs short-term funds, which it can borrow from its bank at an interest rate of 13 percent, and if each of the suppliers is viewed *separately,* which (if any) of the suppliers' cash discounts will the firm give up? For supplier A, Mason should take the cash discount, because the cost of giving it up is 37.24 percent. Mason could borrow the funds it requires from its bank at 13 percent interest, and take the discount. The cost of the loan is much less than the opportunity cost of not taking the discount (the implicit benefit of taking the discount).

With supplier B, the firm would do better to give up the cash discount, because the cost of this action is less than the cost of borrowing money from the bank (8.19% versus 13%). For both suppliers C and D, the firm should take the cash discount, because in both cases the cost of giving up the discount is greater than the 13 percent cost of borrowing from the bank.

This example shows that the cost of giving up a cash discount is relevant when one is evaluating a single supplier's credit terms in light of certain *bank*

TABLE 15.1 Cash Discounts and Associated Costs for Mason Products

Supplier	Credit terms	Cost of giving up a cash discount
A	2/10, net 30	37.24%
B	1/10, net 55	8.19%
C	3/20, net 70	22.58%
D	4/10, net 60	30.42%

borrowing costs. However, other factors relative to payment strategies may also need to be considered. For example, some firms, particularly small firms and poorly managed firms, routinely give up *all* discounts because they either lack alternative sources of unsecured short-term financing or fail to recognize the implicit costs of their actions.

Effects of Stretching Accounts Payable

stretching accounts payable
Paying bills as late as possible without damaging the firm's credit rating.

A strategy that is often employed by a firm is **stretching accounts payable**—that is, paying bills as late as possible without damaging its credit rating. Such a strategy can reduce the cost of giving up a cash discount.

Example Lawrence Industries was extended credit terms of 2/10, net 30. The cost of giving up the cash discount, assuming payment on the last day of the credit period, was found to be 37.24 percent. If the firm were able to stretch its account payable to 70 days without damaging its credit rating, the cost of giving up the cash discount would be only 12.41 percent $(2\%/98\%) \times [365 \div (70 - 10)]$. Stretching accounts payable reduces the implicit cost of giving up a cash discount.

www.nysscpa.org/cpajournal/2006/306/essentials/p38.htm
www.cfoselections.com/ccsengine/newsdeskdetail/id.9

Although stretching accounts payable may be financially attractive, it raises an important ethical issue: it means the firm violates the agreement it entered into with its supplier when it purchased merchandise. Clearly, a supplier would not look kindly on a customer who regularly and purposely postponed paying for purchases. While it doesn't make it right, stretching accounts payable is a common business practice.

Accruals

accruals
Liabilities for services received for which payment has yet to be made and for which an invoice has not been received.

The second spontaneous source of short-term business financing is accruals. **Accruals** are liabilities for services received for which payment has yet to be made and for which an invoice has not been received. The most common items accrued by a firm are wages and taxes. Because taxes are payments to the government, their accrual cannot be manipulated by the firm. However, the accrual of wages can be manipulated to some extent. This is accomplished by delaying payment of wages, thereby receiving an interest-free loan from employees who are paid sometime after they have performed the work. The pay period for employees who earn an hourly rate is often governed by union regulations or by provincial law. However, in other cases, the frequency of payment is at the discretion of the company's management.

Example Tenney Company, a large janitorial service company, currently pays its employees at the end of each work week. The weekly payroll totals \$400,000. If the firm were to extend the pay period so as to pay its employees every 2 weeks throughout a year, the employees would in effect be lending the firm \$400,000 every second week, for a year. The accruals would occur every second week (in week 1, 3, etc.). Accruals are a free source of financing, and would replace financing from costly sources. If the firm's cost of capital was 10 percent, the annual savings from the accruals would be \$40,000 (\$400,000 × 10%). But since the accruals only occur every second week, the true savings will be half that, or \$20,000 per year. On a weekly basis, the savings are \$769.23, every second week.

? Review Questions

15–1 What are the two major sources of spontaneous short-term financing for a firm? How do their balances behave relative to the firm's sales?

15–2 Is there a cost associated with *taking a cash discount*? Is there any cost associated with *giving up a cash discount*? How do short-term borrowing costs affect the cash discount decision?

15–3 What is "stretching accounts payable"? What effect does this action have on the cost of giving up a cash discount?

15.2 Unsecured Sources of Short-Term Loans

Businesses obtain unsecured short-term loans from two major sources. The first is banks, which include the Canadian chartered banks, but also trust companies, credit unions, caisses populaires, and finance companies. We will use the generic term "banks" to refer to all of these financial institutions. The second is commercial paper and bankers' acceptances, money market securities, which were briefly discussed in Chapter 5. We will refer to these as *corporate paper*. Unlike the spontaneous sources of unsecured short-term financing, bank loans and corporate paper are negotiated and result from actions taken by the firm's financial manager. Bank loans are more popular because they are available to firms of all sizes; corporate paper is available only to large firms. In addition, international loans can be used to finance international transactions.

Bank Loans

short-term, self-liquidating loan
An unsecured short-term loan in which the use to which the borrowed money is put provides the mechanism through which the loan is repaid.

Banks are a major source of unsecured short-term loans to businesses. The major type of loan made by banks to businesses is the **short-term, self-liquidating loan.** These loans are intended merely to carry the firm through seasonal peaks in financing needs that are due primarily to buildups of inventory and accounts receivable. As inventories and receivables are converted into cash, the funds needed to retire these loans are generated. In other words, the use to which the borrowed money is put provides the mechanism through which the loan is repaid—hence the term *self-liquidating*. Banks lend unsecured, short-term funds in three basic ways: through single-payment notes, lines of credit, and revolving credit agreements. Before we look at these types of loans, we consider loan interest rates.

Loan Interest Rates

prime rate of interest (prime rate)
The lowest rate of interest charged by leading banks on business loans to their most secure business borrowers.

The interest rate on a bank loan can be a fixed or a floating rate, typically based on the prime rate of interest. The **prime rate of interest (prime rate)** is the lowest rate of interest charged by leading banks on business loans to their most secure business borrowers. The prime rate is based on the Bank of Canada rate, the rate the Bank of Canada uses to control inflation and the value of the Canadian dollar in relation to other currencies. The bank rate was discussed in Chapter 5.

Actual or expected changes in the Bank of Canada rate trigger changes in the prime rate and all other interest rates in the economy. The difference between the

Bank of Canada rate and the prime rate is based on the supply-and-demand relationships for short-term funds.[2] Banks generally determine the rate to be charged to various borrowers by adding a premium to the prime rate to adjust it for the borrower's "riskiness." The premium may be as small as 0.10 percent (10 basis points) or as high as 5 percent to 6 percent (500 to 600 basis points). For most unsecured loans, the premium is usually less than 3 percent.[3]

fixed rate loan
A loan with a rate of interest that is determined at a set increment above the prime rate at which it remains fixed until maturity.

floating rate loan
A loan with a rate of interest initially set at a stated premium above the prime rate and allowed to "float," or vary, as the prime rate varies until maturity.

Fixed and Floating Rate Loans Loans can have either fixed or floating interest rates. On a **fixed rate loan,** the rate of interest is determined at a set increment above the prime rate on the date of the loan and remains unvarying at that fixed rate until maturity. On a **floating rate loan,** the increment above the prime rate is initially established, and the rate of interest is allowed to "float," or vary, *as the prime rate varies* until maturity. Generally, the increment above the prime rate will be *lower* on a floating rate loan than on a fixed rate loan of equivalent risk, because the lender bears less risk with a floating rate loan. As a result of the volatile nature of the prime rate during recent years, today *most short-term business loans are floating rate loans.*

Method of Computing Interest Once the *nominal (or stated) annual rate* is established, the method of computing interest is determined. Interest can be paid either when a loan matures or in advance. If interest is paid *at maturity,* the *effective (or true) annual rate*—the actual rate of interest paid—for an assumed 1-year period[4] is equal to:

$$\frac{\text{Interest}}{\text{Amount borrowed}} \tag{15.2}$$

Many short-term bank loans to businesses require the interest payment at maturity. As discussed in Chapter 6, these are interest-only loans.

discount loans
Loans on which interest is paid in advance by being deducted from the amount borrowed.

When interest is paid *in advance,* it is deducted from the loan so that the borrower actually receives less money than is requested. Loans on which interest is paid in advance are called **discount loans.** The *effective annual rate for a discount loan,* assuming a 1-year period, is calculated as

$$\frac{\text{Interest}}{\text{Amount borrowed} - \text{interest}} \tag{15.3}$$

Paying interest in advance raises the effective annual rate above the stated annual rate.

Example ▼ Wooster Company, a manufacturer of athletic apparel, wants to borrow $10,000 at a stated annual rate of 10 percent interest for 1 year. If the interest on the loan is paid at maturity, the firm will pay $1,000 (0.10 × $10,000) for the use of the

2. Since 1980, the prime rate has varied from a record high of 22.75 percent (August 1981) to a low of 3.75 percent (January 2002 through to mid-April 2002). Since 1996, prime has fluctuated from a high of 7.5 percent to a low of 3.75 percent. In December 2006, the prime rate was 6 percent.

3. Some, generally very large, firms can borrow from their banks at an interest rate slightly below the prime rate. This typically occurs when the borrowing firm either maintains high deposit balances at the bank over time or agrees to pay an upfront fee to "buy down" the interest rate. Below-prime-rate loans are clearly the exception rather than the rule.

4. Effective annual rates (EARs) for loans with maturities of less than 1 year can be found by using the technique presented in Chapter 6 for finding EARs when interest is compounded more frequently than annually. See Equation 6.10.

$10,000 for the year. Substituting into Equation 15.2 reveals that the effective annual rate is therefore the stated rate of 10 percent:

$$\frac{\$1{,}000}{\$10{,}000} = 10.0\%$$

If the money is borrowed at the same *stated* annual rate for 1 year but interest is paid in advance, the firm still pays $1,000 in interest, but it receives only $9,000 ($10,000 − $1,000). Thus, the effective annual rate in this case is

$$\frac{\$1{,}000}{\$10{,}000 - \$1{,}000} = \frac{\$1{,}000}{\$9{,}000} = 11.1\%$$

Paying interest in advance thus makes the effective annual rate (11.1%) greater than the stated annual rate (10.0%).

Single-Payment Notes

single-payment note
A short-term, one-time loan made to a borrower who needs funds for a specific purpose for a short period.

A **single-payment note** can be obtained from a commercial bank by a creditworthy business borrower. This type of loan is usually a one-time loan made to a borrower who needs funds for a specific purpose for a short period. The resulting instrument is a *note,* signed by the borrower, that states the terms of the loan, including the length of the loan and the interest rate. This type of short-term note generally has a maturity of 30 days to one year. The interest charged is usually tied in some way to the prime rate of interest.

Example Gordon Manufacturing, a producer of rotary mower blades, recently borrowed $100,000 from each of two banks—bank A and bank B. The loans were incurred on the same day, when the prime rate of interest was 9 percent. Each loan involved a 90-day note with interest to be paid at the end of 90 days. The interest rate was set at 1.5 percent above the prime rate on bank A's *fixed rate note.* Over the 90-day period, the rate of interest on this note will remain at 10.5 percent (9% prime rate + 1.5% increment) regardless of fluctuations in the prime rate. The total interest cost on this loan is $2,589 [$100,000 × (10.5% × 90/365)]. The effective 90-day rate on this loan is 2.589 percent ($2,589/$100,000).

Assuming that the loan from bank A is rolled over each 90 days throughout the year under the same terms and circumstances, and that the interest is not paid but simply accumulated with the note, the effective annual cost of the note is found by using Equation 6.10. Since the cost of the loan is 2.589 percent for 90 days, it is necessary to compound this cost for four periods (the four renewals) and then subtract 1 as follows:

$$\begin{aligned}\text{Effective annual rate} &= (1 + 0.02589)^4 - 1\\ &= 1.10765 - 1 = 0.10765\\ &= \underline{\underline{10.77\%}}\end{aligned}$$

The effective annual rate of interest on the fixed-rate, 90-day note is 10.77 percent.

Bank B set the interest rate at 1 percent above the prime rate on its *floating rate note.* The rate charged over the 90 days will vary directly with the prime rate. Initially, the rate will be 10 percent (9% + 1%), but when the prime rate changes, so will the rate of interest on the note. For instance, if after 30 days the prime rate rises to 9.5 percent, and after another 30 days it drops to 9.25 percent, the firm would be paying 0.822 percent for the first 30 days (10% × 30/365), 0.863 percent for the next 30 days (10.5% × 30/365), and 0.842 percent for the last 30 days (10.25% × 30/365). Its total interest cost would be $2,527 [$100,000 × (0.822% + 0.863% + 0.842%)], resulting in an effective 90-day rate of 2.527 percent ($2,527/$100,000).

Again, assuming the loan is rolled over each 90 days throughout the year under the same terms and circumstances, its effective *annual* rate is 10.5 percent:

$$\begin{aligned}\text{Effective annual rate} &= (1 + 0.02527)^4 - 1 \\ &= 1.10498 - 1 = 0.1050 \\ &= \underline{\underline{10.50\%}}\end{aligned}$$

Clearly, in this case the floating rate loan would have been less expensive than the fixed rate loan due to its generally lower effective annual rate, although this analysis is based on an unknown variable—the prime rate in the future.

Lines of Credit

line of credit
An agreement between a commercial bank and a business specifying the amount of unsecured short-term borrowing the bank will make available to the firm over a given period of time.

A **line of credit** is an agreement between a commercial bank and a business specifying the amount of unsecured short-term borrowing the bank will make available to the firm over a given period of time. It is similar to the agreement under which issuers of bank credit cards, such as MasterCard and Visa, extend preapproved credit to cardholders. A line-of-credit agreement is typically made for a period of 1 year and often places certain constraints on the borrower. It is *not a guaranteed loan* but indicates that if the bank has sufficient funds available, it will allow the borrower to owe it *up to* a certain amount of money. The amount of a line of credit is *the maximum amount the firm can borrow from the bank* at any point in time.

When applying for a line of credit, the borrower may be required to submit such documents as its cash budget, its pro forma income statement and balance sheet, and its recent actual financial statements. If the bank finds the customer acceptable, the line of credit will be extended. The major attraction of a line of credit from a company's perspective is that it provides access to a predetermined maximum amount of funds, when the firm desires. It allows the firm to finance temporary cash shortages, or temporary increases in accounts receivable and/or inventory, without seeking a loan from a bank each time. For most companies, a line of credit is an operational and financial necessity. The major attraction of a line of credit from the bank's point of view is that it eliminates the need to examine the creditworthiness of a customer each time it borrows money.

Interest Rates The interest rate on a line of credit is normally stated as a floating rate—the *prime rate plus a premium*. If the prime rate changes, the interest rate charged on new *as well as outstanding* borrowing automatically changes. The amount a borrower is charged in excess of the prime rate depends on its creditworthiness. The more creditworthy the borrower, the lower the premium (interest increment) above prime, and vice versa.

operating-change restrictions
Contractual restrictions that a bank may impose on a firm's financial condition or operations as part of a line-of-credit agreement.

Operating-Change Restrictions In a line-of-credit agreement, a bank may impose **operating-change restrictions**, which give it the right to revoke the line if any major changes occur in the firm's financial condition or operations. The firm is usually required to submit up-to-date, and preferably audited, financial statements for periodic review. In addition, the bank typically needs to be informed of shifts in key managerial personnel or in the firm's operations before changes take place. Such changes may affect the future success and debt-paying ability of the firm and thus could alter its credit status. If the bank does not agree with the proposed changes and the firm makes them anyway, the bank has the right to revoke the line of credit.

compensating balance
A required chequing account balance equal to a certain percentage of the amount borrowed from a bank under a line-of-credit or revolving credit agreement.

Compensating Balances To ensure that the borrower will be a good customer, many short-term unsecured bank loans—single-payment notes and lines of credit—often require the borrower to maintain, in a chequing account, a **compensating balance** equal to a certain percentage of the amount borrowed. Compensating balances of up to 20 percent may be required. A compensating balance not only forces the borrower to be a good customer of the bank but may also raise the interest cost to the borrower.

Example

Hint
Sometimes the compensating balance is stated as a percentage of the amount of the line of credit. In other cases, it is linked to both the amount borrowed and the amount of the line of credit.

Estrada Graphics, a graphic design firm, has borrowed $1 million under a line-of-credit agreement. It must pay a stated interest rate of 10 percent and maintain, in its non-interest-paying chequing account, a compensating balance equal to 20 percent of the amount borrowed, or $200,000. Thus it actually receives the use of only $800,000. To use that amount for a year, the firm pays interest of $100,000 (0.10 × $1,000,000). The effective annual rate on the funds is therefore 12.5 percent ($100,000 ÷ $800,000), 2.5 percent more than the stated rate of 10 percent.

If the firm normally maintains a balance of $200,000 or more in its chequing account, the effective annual rate equals the stated annual rate of 10 percent because none of the $1 million borrowed is needed to satisfy the compensating balance requirement. If the firm normally maintains a $100,000 balance in its chequing account, only an additional $100,000 will have to be tied up, leaving it with $900,000 of usable funds. The effective annual rate in this case would be 11.1 percent ($100,000 ÷ $900,000). Thus a compensating balance raises the cost of borrowing *only if* it is larger than the firm's normal cash balance.

annual cleanup
The requirement that for a certain number of days during the year borrowers under a line of credit carry a zero loan balance (i.e., owe the bank nothing).

Annual Cleanups To ensure that money lent under a line-of-credit agreement is actually being used to finance seasonal needs, many banks require an **annual cleanup.** This means that the borrower must have a loan balance of zero—that is, owe the bank nothing—for a certain number of days during the year. Insisting that the borrower carry a zero loan balance for a certain period ensures that short-term loans do not turn into long-term loans.

All the characteristics of a line-of-credit agreement are negotiable to some extent. Today, banks bid competitively to attract well-known, secure firms. A prospective borrower should attempt to negotiate a line of credit with the most favourable interest rate, for an optimal amount of funds, and with a minimum of restrictions. Borrowers today frequently pay fees to lenders instead of maintaining deposit balances as compensation for loans and other services. The lender attempts to get a good return with maximum safety. Negotiations should produce a line of credit that is suitable to both borrower and lender.

Revolving Credit Agreements

revolving credit agreement
A line of credit guaranteed to a borrower by a commercial bank regardless of the scarcity of money.

commitment fee
The fee that is normally charged on a *revolving credit agreement*; it often applies to the average unused balance of the borrower's credit line.

A **revolving credit agreement** is nothing more than a *guaranteed line of credit.* It is guaranteed in the sense that the commercial bank assures the borrower that a specified amount of funds will be made available regardless of the scarcity of money. The interest rate and other requirements are similar to those for a line of credit. It is not uncommon for a revolving credit agreement to be for a period greater than 1 year.[5] Because the bank guarantees the availability of funds, a **commitment fee** is normally charged on a revolving credit agreement.[6] This fee often applies to the average unused balance of the credit line. It is normally about 0.5 percent of the *average unused portion* of the funds.

Example REH Company, a major real estate developer, has a $2 million revolving credit agreement with its bank. Its average borrowing under the agreement for the past year was $1.5 million. The bank charges a commitment fee of 0.5 percent. Because the average unused portion of the committed funds was $500,000 ($2 million − $1.5 million), the commitment fee for the year was $2,500 (0.005 × $500,000). Of course, REH also had to pay interest on the actual $1.5 million borrowed under the agreement. Assuming that $160,000 interest was paid on the $1.5 million borrowed, the effective cost of the agreement is 10.83 percent [($160,000 + $2,500)/$1,500,000]. Although more expensive than a line of credit, a revolving credit agreement can be less risky from the borrower's viewpoint, because the availability of funds is guaranteed.

Corporate Paper

corporate paper
A form of financing consisting of short-term, unsecured promissory notes issued by firms with a high credit standing.

Corporate paper is a form of financing that consists of short-term, unsecured promissory notes issued by firms with a high credit standing. The usual types of corporate paper are commercial paper and bankers' acceptances, two securities that trade in the money market and that are a short-term financing source only available to very large, usually publicly traded corporations. These securities were discussed in Chapter 5. Generally, only quite large firms of unquestionable financial soundness are able to issue corporate paper. Most corporate paper has maturities ranging from 30 to 90 days. Although there is no set denomination, it is generally issued in multiples of $1,000,000 or more. A large portion of the corporate paper today is issued by finance companies. Manufacturing firms account for a smaller portion of this type of financing. Businesses with surplus cash purchase corporate paper, which they hold as marketable securities. This means the surplus cash provides a return while still maintaining the company's liquidity.

5. A revolving credit agreement may be classified as a form of *intermediate-term financing,* defined as having a maturity of 1 to 7 years. In this text, the intermediate-term financing classification is not used; only short-term and long-term classifications are made. Because many revolving credit agreements are for more than 1 year, they can be classified as a form of long-term financing; however, they are discussed here because of their similarity to line-of-credit agreements.

6. Some banks not only require payment of the commitment fee, but also require the borrower to maintain, in addition to a compensating balance against actual borrowings, a compensating balance of 10 percent or so against the unused portion of the commitment.

15.1 **IN PRACTICE**

Financing Footwear

You won't see "Bennett Footwear Group" on any of the shoes in your closet, but you may own some of its shoe brands, which include Franco Sarto, Danelle, and Zodiac. Bennett designs, imports, and distributes women's and children's footwear and also markets its footwear through private-label programs with many key customers. The company, founded in 1961 as Bennett Importing, merged in 1998 with two other footwear companies, positioning the combined enterprise to serve a wide range of footwear markets. The company imports shoes from Italy, Brazil, China, and Portugal. Today, Bennett's customers include value-oriented retailers such as Payless ShoeSource and Wal-Mart, as well as many boutiques and even online shoe stores.

Although the merger created economies of scale and better market penetration, it also brought Bennett a complex financial structure with too much debt. Bennett also needed funds to grow its business quickly in three areas: (1) to take advantage of the increasing popularity of the Franco Sarto brand, (2) to branch out into men's shoes and accessories, and (3) to expand its private-label products for mass merchandisers.

To deal with its financing problems, Bennett approached CIT Group. CIT Group is a leading source of factoring, financing, and leasing capital and an advisor for companies in more than 30 industries. CIT manages about $50 billion in assets across a diversified portfolio. The company, founded in 1908, operates in Canada and the United States. It is a leading lender to companies in the apparel and footwear industry.

Bennett and CIT Group worked together to develop a sound program to restructure the company's debt, provide growth capital, and improve liquidity. CIT's industry knowledge and its experience lending to similar companies helped it arrive at a fair value for the inventory and accounts receivable that would serve as loan collateral (security). CIT provided Bennett with a $20 million revolving line of credit secured by inventory, accounts receivable, and trade names, as well as a $6 million 3-year term loan.

This financing allowed Bennett to replace debt provided by a former lender and retire $11.5 million of short-term notes. The CIT loans also provided abundant liquidity for Bennett to continue to pursue its aggressive expansion plans for Franco Sarto. With the new line of credit, Bennett had the funds to clean up its balance sheet and keep growing by expanding the popular Franco Sarto line of footwear.

SOURCE: Case study—Bennett Footwear Group, available at **www.citcommercialfinance.com/commcms/articles_outlooks CmF/dsp_articles_bennPge.htm**; Bennett Footwear Group company overview, available at **www.brownshoe.com.**

Interest on Corporate Paper

Corporate paper is sold at a discount from its *par,* or *face, value.* The dollar amount of interest paid by the issuer of corporate paper is determined by the return required by the lender and the length of time to maturity. The actual interest earned by the purchaser is determined by certain calculations, illustrated by the following example.

Example ▼ Bertram Corporation, a large shipbuilder, has just issued $1 million worth of corporate paper that has a 90-day maturity and sells for $980,000. At the end of 90 days, the purchaser of this paper will receive $1 million for its $980,000 investment. The interest paid on the financing is therefore \$20,000 on a principal of \$980,000. The effective 90-day rate on the paper is 2.04 percent (\$20,000/\$980,000). To determine the effective annual cost (or rate of return), Equation 15.4 is used, where V_0 is the par value of the discounted security, P is the amount paid, i is the annual yield, and n is the number of days to maturity:

$$V_0 = P \times \left[1 + \frac{i \times n}{365}\right] \tag{15.4}$$

Based on this equation, the effective annual cost of Bertram Corporation's corporate paper is:

$$\$1{,}000{,}000 = \$980{,}000 \times \left[1 + \frac{i \times 90}{365}\right]$$

$$\$1{,}000{,}000 = \$980{,}000 + \frac{\$980{,}000 \times i \times 90}{365}$$

$$\$20{,}000 = 241{,}643.8356i$$

$$i = 0.082766 \text{ or } 8.277\%$$

An interesting characteristic of corporate paper is that its interest cost is *normally* 1.5 to 3 percent below the prime rate. In other words, firms are able to raise funds more cheaply by selling corporate paper than by borrowing from a commercial bank. The reason is that many suppliers of short-term funds do not have the option, as banks do, of making low-risk business loans at the prime rate. They can invest safely only in marketable securities such as Government of Canada treasury bills and corporate paper. The yields on these marketable securities on December 15, 2006, when the prime rate of interest was 6 percent, were about 4.17 percent for 3-month t-bills and about 4.33 percent for 3-month corporate paper. Recent rates are available on the Web.

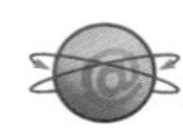

www.bankofcanada.ca/en/rates/monmrt.html

Although the stated interest cost of borrowing through the sale of corporate paper is normally lower than the prime rate, the *overall cost* of corporate paper may not be less than that of a bank loan. Additional costs include the fees paid by most issuers to obtain the bank line of credit used to back the paper, fees paid to obtain third-party ratings used to make the paper more salable, and flotation costs. In addition, even if it is slightly more expensive to borrow from a commercial bank, it may at times be advisable to do so to establish a good working relationship with a bank. This strategy ensures that when money is tight, funds can be obtained promptly and at a reasonable interest rate.

Hint

Corporate paper is directly placed with investors by the issuer or is sold by dealers in corporate paper. Most of it is purchased by other businesses and financial institutions.

International Loans

In some ways, arranging short-term financing for international trade is no different from financing purely domestic operations. In both cases, producers must finance production and inventory and then continue to finance accounts receivable before collecting any cash payments from sales. In other ways, however, the short-term financing of international sales and purchases is fundamentally different from that of strictly domestic trade.

International Transactions

The important difference between international and domestic transactions is that payments are often made or received in a foreign currency. Not only must a Canadian company pay the costs of doing business in the foreign exchange market, but it also is exposed to *exchange rate risk*. A Canadian-based company that exports goods and has accounts receivable denominated in a foreign currency faces the risk that the Canadian dollar will appreciate in value relative to the foreign currency. The risk to a Canadian importer with foreign-currency-denominated accounts payable is that the dollar will depreciate. Although *exchange rate risk* can often be *hedged* by using currency forward, futures, or options markets, doing so is costly and is not possible for all foreign currencies.

Typical international transactions are large in size and have long maturity dates. Therefore, companies that are involved in international trade generally have to finance larger dollar amounts for longer time periods than companies that operate domestically. Furthermore, because foreign companies may be deemed more risky, some financial institutions are reluctant to lend to Canadian exporters or importers, particularly smaller firms.

Financing International Trade

letter of credit
A letter written by a company's bank to the company's foreign supplier, stating that the bank guarantees payment of an invoiced amount if all the underlying agreements are met.

Several specialized techniques have evolved for financing international trade. Perhaps the most important financing vehicle is the **letter of credit,** a letter written by a company's bank to the company's foreign supplier, stating that the bank guarantees payment of an invoiced amount if all the underlying agreements are met. The letter of credit essentially substitutes the bank's reputation and creditworthiness for that of its commercial customer. A Canadian exporter is more willing to sell goods to a foreign buyer if the transaction is covered by a letter of credit issued by a well-known bank in the buyer's home country.

Firms that do business in foreign countries on an ongoing basis often finance their operations, at least in part, in the local market. A company that has an assembly plant in Mexico, for example, might choose to finance its purchases of Mexican goods and services with peso funds borrowed from a Mexican bank. This not only minimizes exchange rate risk, but also improves the company's business ties to the host community. Multinational companies, however, sometimes finance their international transactions through dollar-denominated loans from international banks. The *Eurocurrency loan markets* allow creditworthy borrowers to obtain financing on very attractive terms.

Transactions Between Subsidiaries

Much international trade involves transactions between corporate subsidiaries. A Canadian company might, for example, manufacture one part in an Asian plant and another part in the United States, assemble the product in Brazil, and sell it in Europe. The shipment of goods back and forth between subsidiaries creates accounts receivable and accounts payable, but the parent company has considerable discretion about how and when payments are made. In particular, the parent can minimize foreign exchange fees and other transaction costs by "netting" what affiliates owe each other and paying only the net amount due, rather than having both subsidiaries pay each other the gross amounts due.

? Review Questions

15–4 How is the *prime rate of interest* relevant to the cost of short-term bank borrowing? What is a *floating rate loan*?

15–5 How does the *effective annual rate* differ between a loan requiring interest payments *at maturity* and another, similar loan requiring interest *in advance*?

15–6 What are the basic terms and characteristics of a *single-payment note*? How is the *effective annual rate* on such a note found?

15–7 What is a *line of credit*? Describe each of the following features that are often included in these agreements: (**a**) operating change restrictions; (**b**) compensating balance; and (**c**) annual cleanup.

15–8 What is a *revolving credit agreement*? How does this arrangement differ from the line-of-credit agreement? What is a *commitment fee*?

15–9 How is *corporate paper* used to raise short-term funds? Who can issue corporate paper? Who buys corporate paper?

15–10 What is the important difference between international and domestic transactions? How is a *letter of credit* used in financing international trade transactions? How is "netting" used in transactions between subsidiaries?

15.3 Secured Sources of Short-Term Loans

secured short-term financing
Short-term financing (loans) that has specific assets pledged as collateral.

security agreement
The agreement between the borrower and the lender that specifies the collateral held against a secured loan.

When a firm has exhausted its sources of unsecured short-term financing, it may be able to obtain additional short-term loans on a secured basis. **Secured short-term financing** has specific assets pledged as collateral. The *collateral* commonly takes the form of an asset, such as accounts receivable or inventory. The lender obtains a security interest in the collateral through the execution of a **security agreement** with the borrower that specifies the collateral held against the loan. In addition, the terms of the loan against which the security is held form part of the security agreement. They specify the conditions required for the security interest to be removed, along with the interest rate on the loan, repayment dates, and other loan provisions.

Characteristics of Secured Short-Term Loans

Although many people believe that holding collateral as security reduces the risk of a loan, lenders do not usually view loans in this way. Lenders recognize that holding collateral can reduce losses if the borrower defaults, but *the presence of collateral has no impact on the risk of default.* A lender requires collateral to ensure recovery of some portion of the loan in the event of default. What the lender wants above all, however, is to be repaid as scheduled. In general, lenders prefer to make less risky loans at lower rates of interest than to be in a position in which they must liquidate collateral.

Collateral and Terms

Lenders of secured short-term funds prefer collateral that has a duration closely matched to the term of the loan. Current assets—accounts receivable and inventories—are the most desirable short-term loan collateral, because they can normally be converted into cash much sooner than fixed assets. Thus, the short-term lender of secured funds generally accepts only liquid current assets as collateral.

percentage advance
The percentage of the book value of the collateral that constitutes the principal of a secured loan.

Typically, the lender determines the desirable **percentage advance** to make against the collateral. This percentage advance constitutes the principal of the secured loan and is normally between 30 and 100 percent of the book value of the collateral. It varies according to the type and liquidity of collateral.

Hint
Remember that firms typically borrow on a secured basis only after exhausting less costly, unsecured sources of short-term funds.

The interest rate that is charged on secured short-term loans is typically lower than on unsecured short-term loans. For example, the interest rate on a secured line of credit is usually lower than on an unsecured line of credit. The security (collateral) pledged ensures that the company is able to repay all or a very high percentage of the amount borrowed so the bank is willing to lend money at a lower interest rate. The lower rate is usually indicated by a lower premium added to the prime rate. For some types of secured loans, however, a higher rate of interest may be charged. This is often due to the high risk associated with the borrower or with the collateral pledged.

When inventory and accounts receivable are used as collateral for a secured loan, like a line of credit, the rules of thumb allowed by most banks are 50 percent of the value of the inventory available and 75 percent of the value of accounts receivable. This gives the lender plenty of excess security in the case of default. There are two reasons for the much lower percentage allowed for inventory versus accounts receivable. First, as discussed in Chapter 14, inventory is two steps removed from cash and therefore less liquid. Second, inventory is subject to obsolescence, spoilage, and theft and is therefore a less desirable collateral.

Institutions Extending Secured Short-Term Loans

The primary sources of secured short-term loans to businesses are commercial banks and finance companies. Both institutions deal in short-term loans secured primarily by accounts receivable and inventory. The operations of these institutions were described in Chapter 5.

Only when its unsecured and secured short-term borrowing power from the commercial bank is exhausted will a borrower turn to a finance company for additional secured borrowing. Because the finance company generally ends up with higher-risk borrowers, its interest charges on secured short-term loans are usually higher than those of commercial banks.

The Use of Accounts Receivable as Collateral

www.cit.com

http://strategis.ic.gc.ca/sc_mangb/stepstogrowth/engdoc/step2/tacl-2-3b.php

Two commonly used means of obtaining short-term financing with accounts receivable are *pledging accounts receivable* and *factoring accounts receivable*. Actually, only a pledge of accounts receivable creates a secured short-term loan; factoring really entails the *sale* of accounts receivable at a discount. Although factoring is not actually a form of secured short-term borrowing, it does involve the use of accounts receivable to obtain needed short-term funds. More information about using accounts receivable as collateral is available on the Web.

Pledging Accounts Receivable

pledge of accounts receivable
The use of a firm's accounts receivable as security, or collateral, to obtain a short-term loan.

A **pledge of accounts receivable** is often used to secure a short-term loan. Because accounts receivable are normally quite liquid, they are an attractive form of short-term loan collateral.

The Pledging Process When a firm requests a loan against accounts receivable, the lender first evaluates the firm's accounts receivable to determine their desirability as collateral. The lender makes a list of the acceptable accounts, along with the billing dates and amounts. If the borrowing firm requests a loan for a fixed amount, the lender needs to select only enough accounts to secure the funds requested. If the borrower wants the maximum loan available, the lender evaluates all the accounts to select the maximum amount of acceptable collateral.

After selecting the acceptable accounts, the lender normally adjusts the dollar value of these accounts for expected returns on sales and other allowances. If a customer whose account has been pledged returns merchandise or receives some type of allowance, such as a cash discount for early payment, the amount of the collateral is automatically reduced. For protection from such occurrences, the lender normally reduces the value of the acceptable collateral by a fixed percentage.

lien
A publicly disclosed legal claim on collateral.

Next, the percentage to be advanced against the collateral must be determined. The lender evaluates the quality of the acceptable receivables and the expected cost of their liquidation. This percentage represents the principal of the loan and typically ranges between 50 and 90 percent of the face value of acceptable accounts receivable. To protect its interest in the collateral, the lender files a **lien,** which is a publicly disclosed legal claim on the collateral. For an example of the complete pledging process, see the book's Web site.

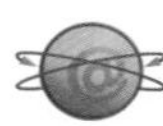

www.pearsoned.ca/gitman

non-notification basis
The basis on which a borrower, having pledged an account receivable, continues to collect the account payments without notifying the account customer.

notification basis
The basis on which an account customer whose account has been pledged (or factored) is notified to remit payment directly to the lender (or factor).

Notification Pledges of accounts receivable are normally made on a **non-notification basis,** meaning that a customer whose account has been pledged as collateral is not notified. Under the non-notification arrangement, the borrower still collects the pledged account receivable, and the lender trusts the borrower to remit these payments as they are received. If a pledge of accounts receivable is made on a **notification basis,** the customer is notified to remit payment directly to the lender.

Pledging Cost The stated cost of a pledge of accounts receivable is normally 2 to 5 percent above the prime rate. In addition to the stated interest rate, a service charge of up to 3 percent may be levied by the lender to cover its administrative costs. Clearly, pledges of accounts receivable are a high-cost source of short-term financing.

Factoring Accounts Receivable

factoring accounts receivable
The outright sale of accounts receivable at a discount to a factor or other financial institution.

factor
A financial institution that specializes in purchasing accounts receivable from businesses.

Factoring accounts receivable involves selling them outright, at a discount, to a financial institution. A **factor** is a financial institution that specializes in purchasing accounts receivable from businesses. Some commercial banks and finance companies also factor accounts receivable. Although not the same as obtaining a short-term loan, factoring accounts receivable is similar to borrowing with accounts receivable as collateral.

Factoring Agreement A factoring agreement normally states the exact conditions and procedures for the purchase of an account. The factor, like a lender against a pledge of accounts receivable, chooses accounts for purchase, selecting only those that appear to be acceptable credit risks. Where factoring is to be on a continuing basis, the factor will actually make the firm's credit decisions, because this will guarantee the acceptability of accounts.[7] Factoring is normally done on a *notification basis,* and the factor receives payment of the account directly from the customer. In addition, most sales of accounts receivable to a factor are made on a **non-recourse basis.** This means that the factor agrees to accept all credit risks. Thus, if a purchased account turns out to be uncollectible, the factor must absorb the loss.

non-recourse basis
The basis on which accounts receivable are sold to a factor with the understanding that the factor accepts all credit risks on the purchased accounts.

Typically, the factor is not required to pay the firm until the account is collected or until the last day of the credit period, whichever occurs first. The factor sets up an account similar to a bank deposit account for each customer. As payment is received or as due dates arrive, the factor deposits money into the seller's account, from which the seller is free to make withdrawals as needed.

In many cases, if the firm leaves the money in the account, a *surplus* will exist on which the factor will pay interest. In other instances, the factor may make *advances* to the firm against uncollected accounts that are not yet due. These advances represent a negative balance in the firm's account, on which interest is charged.

Factoring Cost Factoring costs include commissions, interest levied on advances, and interest earned on surpluses. The factor deposits in the firm's account the book value of the collected or due accounts purchased by the factor, less the commissions. The commissions are typically stated as a 1 to 3 percent discount from the book value of factored accounts receivable. The *interest levied on advances* is generally 2 to 4 percent above the prime rate. It is levied on the actual amount advanced. The *interest paid on surpluses* is generally between 0.2 and 0.5 percent per month. An example of the factoring process is included on the book's Web site.

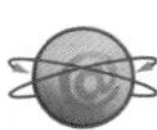

www.pearsoned.ca/gitman

Although its costs may seem high, factoring has certain advantages that make it attractive to many firms. One is the ability it gives the firm to *turn accounts receivable immediately into cash* without having to worry about repayment. Another advantage of factoring is that it ensures a *known pattern of cash flows.* In addition, if factoring is undertaken on a continuing basis, the firm *can eliminate its credit and collection departments.* More information about factoring is available at the Web sites of the many companies that provide this service.

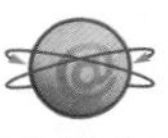

www.affacturage.ca/english/faq.htm
http://www.edc.ca/english/financing_factoring.htm

The Use of Inventory as Collateral

Inventory is generally second to accounts receivable in desirability as short-term loan collateral. Inventory normally has a market value that is greater than its book value, which is used to establish its value as collateral. A lender whose loan is secured with inventory will probably be able to sell that inventory for at least book value if the borrower defaults on its obligations.

7. The use of credit cards such as MasterCard and Visa by consumers has some similarity to factoring, because the vendor that accepts the card is reimbursed at a discount for purchases made with the card. The difference between factoring and credit cards is that cards are nothing more than a line of credit extended by the issuer, which charges the vendors a fee for accepting the cards. In factoring, the factor does not analyze credit until after the sale has been made; in many cases (except when factoring is done on a continuing basis), the initial credit decision is the responsibility of the vendor, not the factor who purchases the account.

15.2 IN PRACTICE

Securitization of Accounts Receivable

Traditionally, corporations raise funds by using either debt or equity capital. The debt could be short-term, like a line of credit or corporate paper, or long-term, like long-term bank loans, bonds and debentures, or mortgages. During the 1980s, securitization started to be used as a method of raising financing. Sometimes referred to as structured financing, this method is now widely used in Canada. Structured financing typically involves converting an income-producing asset to cash, thus providing a source of financing for the company.

Securitization is often used with accounts receivable. This technique takes accounts receivable off the company's balance sheet while generating cash for the company. Financing is raised without issuing either debt or equity. Therefore, securitization can raise financing without affecting the company's capital structure, thus preserving the company's borrowing capacity. In addition, unlike the pledging or factoring of accounts receivable, the financing raised through securitization has a very low cost and can be raised at fixed or floating interest rates.

As an example, Aliant Telecom, a telecommunications company serving all of Atlantic Canada, initiated a five-year securitization agreement in December 2001. The agreement was renewed in December 2006. This $150-million accounts receivable securitization agreement is with the Bank of Nova Scotia. To raise financing, Aliant sells accounts receivable to a securitization trust on a revolving basis. As at December 31, 2005, Aliant had received net cash proceeds of $120 million on the sale of accounts receivable to the trust. Aliant is required to provide security, in the form of additional accounts receivable over and above the cash proceeds received, which are held and owned by the trust. This security amounted to $39.5 million at December 31, 2005. The company continues to service these accounts receivable and collect the amounts owing, but the trust ranks ahead of the company in case of default.

Under the agreement the trust reinvests the amounts collected by buying additional interest in Aliant's accounts receivable until the agreement expires. The administration fees on the agreement are $3.5 million, while the overall cost of funds in 2005 was a very attractive 2.98 percent. This was up from an even lower 2.62 percent in 2004. The bad debts ratio on the securitized accounts receivable was 1.04 percent in 2005, up from 0.96 percent in 2004. The average collection period on the receivables was 45 days.

In Canada, the methods used to raise financing are constantly changing as new techniques are developed by financial intermediaries. These new methods can have a number of advantages over the traditional ways of raising funds. The securitization of receivables is a popular and rapidly growing way of raising inexpensive short-term financing.

SOURCES: Aliant Inc., 2002–2005 annual reports.

The most important characteristic of inventory being evaluated as loan collateral is *marketability,* which must be considered in light of its physical properties. A warehouse of *perishable* items, such as fresh peaches, may be quite marketable, but if the cost of storing and selling the peaches is high, they may not be desirable collateral. *Specialized items,* such as fibre-optic cable, are not desirable collateral either, because finding a buyer for them could be difficult. When evaluating inventory as possible loan collateral, the lender looks for items with very stable market prices that have ready markets and that lack undesirable physical properties.

Floating Inventory Liens

floating inventory lien
A secured short-term loan against inventory under which the lender's claim is on the borrower's inventory in general.

A lender may be willing to secure a loan under a **floating inventory lien,** which is a claim on inventory in general. This arrangement is most attractive when the firm has a stable level of inventory that consists of a diversified group of relatively inexpensive merchandise. Inventories of items such as auto tires, screws and bolts, and shoes are candidates for floating-lien loans. Because it is difficult for a lender to verify the presence of the inventory, the lender will generally advance less than 50 percent of the book value of the average inventory. The interest charge on a floating lien is 3 to 5 percent above the prime rate. Commercial banks often require floating liens as extra security on what would otherwise be an unsecured loan. Floating-lien inventory loans may also be available from finance companies. An example of a floating lien is included on the book's Web site.

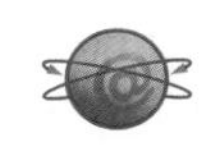

www.pearsoned.ca/gitman

Trust Receipt Inventory Loans

trust receipt inventory loan
A secured short-term loan against inventory under which the lender advances 80 to 100 percent of the cost of the borrower's relatively expensive inventory items in exchange for the borrower's promise to repay the lender, with accrued interest, immediately after the sale of each item of collateral.

A **trust receipt inventory loan** often can be made against relatively expensive automotive, consumer durable, and industrial goods that can be identified by serial number. Under this agreement, the borrower keeps the inventory and the lender may advance 80 to 100 percent of its cost. The lender files a *lien* on all the items financed. The borrower is free to sell the merchandise but is trusted to remit the amount lent, along with accrued interest, to the lender immediately after the sale. The lender then releases the lien on the item. The lender makes periodic checks of the borrower's inventory to make sure that the required amount of collateral remains in the hands of the borrower. The interest charge to the borrower is normally 2 percent or more above the prime rate.

Trust receipt loans are often made by manufacturers' wholly owned financing subsidiaries, known as *captive finance companies,* to their customers. Captive finance companies are especially popular in industries that manufacture consumer durable goods, because they provide the manufacturer with a useful sales tool. For example, General Motors Acceptance Corporation (GMAC), the financing subsidiary of General Motors, grants these types of loans to its dealers. Trust receipt loans are also available through commercial banks and finance companies.

Warehouse Receipt Loans

warehouse receipt loan
A secured short-term loan against inventory under which the lender receives control of the pledged inventory collateral, which is stored by a designated warehousing company on the lender's behalf.

A **warehouse receipt loan** is an arrangement whereby the lender, who may be a commercial bank or finance company, receives control of the pledged inventory collateral, which is stored by a designated agent on the lender's behalf. After selecting acceptable collateral, the lender hires a warehousing company to act as its agent and take possession of the inventory.

Two types of warehousing arrangements are possible. A *terminal warehouse* is a central warehouse that is used to store the merchandise of various customers. The lender normally uses such a warehouse when the inventory is easily transported and can be delivered to the warehouse relatively inexpensively. Under a *field warehouse* arrangement, the lender hires a field warehousing company to set up a warehouse on the borrower's premises or to lease part of the borrower's warehouse to store the pledged collateral. Regardless of which type of warehouse is used, the warehousing company places a guard over the inventory. Only on written approval of the lender can any portion of the secured inventory be released by the warehousing company.

The actual lending agreement specifically states the requirements for the release of inventory. As in the case of other secured loans, the lender accepts only collateral that is believed to be readily marketable and advances only a portion—generally 75 to 90 percent—of the collateral's value. The specific costs of warehouse receipt loans are generally higher than those of any other secured lending arrangements due to the need to hire and pay a warehousing company to guard and supervise the collateral. The basic interest charged on warehouse receipt loans is higher than that charged on unsecured loans, generally ranging from 3 to 5 percent above the prime rate. In addition to the interest charge, the borrower must absorb the costs of warehousing by paying the warehouse fee, which is generally between 1 and 3 percent of the amount of the loan. The borrower is normally also required to pay the insurance costs on the warehoused merchandise. An example of the procedures and costs of a warehouse receipt loan is included on the book's Web site.

www.pearsoned.ca/gitman

? Review Questions

15–11 Are secured short-term loans viewed as more risky or less risky than unsecured short-term loans? Why?

15–12 In general, what interest rates and fees are levied on secured short-term loans? Why are these rates generally *higher* than the rates on unsecured short-term loans?

15–13 Describe and compare the basic features of the following methods of using *accounts receivable* to obtain short-term financing: (**a**) pledging accounts receivable and (**b**) factoring accounts receivable. Be sure to mention the institutions that offer each of them.

15–14 For the following methods of using *inventory* as short-term loan collateral, describe the basic features of each, and compare their use: (**a**) floating lien; (**b**) trust receipt loan; and (**c**) warehouse receipt loan.

SUMMARY

LG1 **Review the concept of spontaneous liabilities, the key components of a firm's credit terms, and the procedures for analyzing them.** The major spontaneous source of short-term financing is accounts payable, which are the primary source of short-term funds. Accounts payable result from credit purchases of merchandise. The key features of this form of financing are summarized in part I of Table 15.2. Credit terms may differ with respect to the credit period, cash discount, cash discount period, and beginning of the credit period. The cost of giving up cash discounts is a factor in deciding whether to take or give up a cash discount. Cash discounts should be given up only when a firm in need of short-term funds must pay an interest rate on borrowing that is greater than the cost of giving up the cash discount.

LG2 **Understand the impact that stretching accounts payable has on the cash conversion cycle, explore the cost of not taking discounts, and consider the benefit of accruals.** Stretching accounts payable can lower the cost of giving up a cash discount. This is because the firm can keep its money longer if it gives up the discount. Accruals, which result primarily from wage and tax obligations, are virtually free. The key features of this spontaneous liability are summarized in part I of Table 15.2.

LG3 **Describe the basic types of unsecured sources of short-term financing, and the interest rates on these loans.** Banks are the major source of unsecured short-term loans to businesses. The interest rates on these loans are based on the prime rate of interest plus a risk premium and may be fixed or floating. Loans should be evaluated by using the effective annual rate. This rate is calculated differently, depending on whether interest is paid when the loan matures or in advance. Bank loans may take the form of a single-payment note, a line of credit, or a revolving credit agreement. The key features of the various types of bank loans are summarized in part I of Table 15.2.

Discuss the basic features of corporate paper and the key aspects of international short-term loans. Corporate paper is an unsecured IOU issued by firms with a high credit standing. The key features of corporate paper are summarized in part II of Table 15.2. International sales and purchases expose firms to exchange rate risk. They are larger and of longer maturity than typical transactions, and can be financed using a letter of credit, by borrowing in the local market, or through dollar-denominated loans from international banks. On transactions between subsidiaries, "netting" can be used to minimize foreign exchange fees and other transaction costs.

Explain the characteristics of secured short-term loans and the use of accounts receivable as short-term-loan collateral. Secured short-term loans are those for which the lender requires collateral—typically, current assets such as accounts receivable or inventory. Only a percentage of the book value of acceptable collateral is advanced by the lender. These loans are more expensive than unsecured loans; collateral does not lower the risk of default, and increased administrative costs result. Both commercial banks and finance companies make secured short-term loans. Both pledging, which is the use of accounts receivable as loan collateral, and factoring, which is the outright sale of accounts receivable at a discount, involve the use of accounts receivable to obtain needed short-term funds. The key features of loans using accounts receivable as collateral are summarized in part III of Table 15.2.

Describe the various ways in which inventory can be used as short-term-loan collateral. Inventory can be used as short-term-loan collateral under a floating lien, a trust receipt arrangement, or a warehouse receipt loan. The key features of loans using inventory as collateral are summarized in part III of Table 15.2.

TABLE 15.2 Summary of Key Features of Common Sources of Short-Term Financing

Type of short-term financing	Source	Cost or conditions	Characteristics
I. Spontaneous sources of short-term financing			
Accounts payable	Suppliers of merchandise	No stated cost except when a cash discount is offered for early payment.	Credit extended on open account for 1 to 120 days. The largest source of short-term financing.
Accruals	Employees and government	Free.	Result because wages (employees) and taxes (government) are paid at discrete points in time after the service has been rendered. Hard to manipulate this source of financing.
II. Unsecured sources of short-term loans			
Bank sources			
(1) Single-payment notes	Commercial banks	Prime plus 0% to 4% risk premium—fixed or floating rate.	A single-payment loan used to meet a funds shortage expected to last only a short period of time.
(2) Lines of credit	Commercial banks	Prime plus 0% to 4% risk premium—fixed or floating rate. Often must maintain a compensating balance and clean up the line annually.	A prearranged borrowing limit under which funds, if available, will be lent to allow the borrower to meet seasonal needs.
(3) Revolving credit agreements	Commercial banks	Prime plus 0% to 4% risk premium—fixed or floating rate. Often must maintain 10% to 20% compensating balance and pay a commitment fee of approximately 0.5% of the average unused balance.	A line-of-credit agreement under which the availability of funds is guaranteed. Often for a period greater than one year.
Corporate paper	Business firms—both nonfinancial and financial	Generally 1.5% to 3% below the prime rate of interest.	An unsecured short-term promissory note issued by the most financially sound firms.
III. Secured sources of short-term loans			
Accounts receivable collateral			
(1) Pledging	Commercial banks and finance companies	2% to 5% above prime plus up to 3% in fees. Advance 50% to 90% of collateral value.	Selected accounts receivable are used as collateral. The borrower is trusted to remit to the lender on collection of pledged accounts. Done on a non-notification basis.
(2) Factoring	Factors, commercial banks, and finance companies	1% to 3% discount from face value of factored accounts. Interest of 2% to 4% above prime levied on advances. Interest between 0.2% and 0.5% per month earned on surplus balances left with factor.	Selected accounts are sold—generally without recourse—at a discount. All credit risks go with the accounts. Factor will lend (make advances) against uncollected accounts that are not yet due. Factor will also pay interest on surplus balances. Typically done on a notification basis.

(continued)

TABLE 15.2 continued

Type of short-term financing	Source	Cost or conditions	Characteristics
Inventory collateral			
(1) Floating liens	Commercial banks and finance companies	3% to 5% above prime. Advance less than 50% of collateral value.	A loan against inventory in general. Made when firm has stable inventory of a variety of inexpensive items.
(2) Trust receipts	Manufacturers' captive financing subsidiaries, commercial banks, and finance companies	2% or more above prime. Advance 80% to 100% of cost of collateral.	Loan against relatively expensive automotive, consumer durable, and industrial goods that can be identified by serial number. Collateral remains in possession of borrower, who is trusted to remit proceeds to lender upon its sale.
(3) Warehouse receipts	Commercial banks and finance companies	3% to 5% above prime plus a 1% to 3% warehouse fee. Advance 75% to 90% of collateral value.	Inventory used as collateral is placed under control of the lender either through a terminal warehouse or through a field warehouse. A third party—a warehousing company—guards the inventory for the lender. Inventory is released only on written approval of the lender.

SELF-TEST PROBLEM

Solution in Appendix B

ST 15–1 **Cash discount decisions** The credit terms for each of three suppliers are shown in the following table.

Supplier	Credit terms
X	1/10, net 55
Y	2/10, net 30
Z	2/20, net 60

a. Determine the cost of giving up the cash discount from each supplier.

b. Assuming that the firm needs short-term financing, recommend whether it would be better to give up the cash discount or take the discount and borrow from a bank at 15 percent annual interest. Evaluate each supplier separately using your findings in part **a**.

c. Assume the firm could stretch the final due date on the accounts payable from supplier Z by 20 days. What impact would this have on your answer in part **b**?

PROBLEMS

BASIC  **15–1 Payment dates** Determine when a firm must make payment for purchases invoiced November 25 under each of the following credit terms.

a. net 30
b. net 15
c. net 45
d. net 50

BASIC  **15–2 Cost of giving up cash discounts** Determine the cost of giving up cash discounts under each of the following terms of sale.

a. 2/10, net 30
b. 1/10, net 30
c. 2/10, net 45
d. 3/10, net 45
e. 1/10, net 60
f. 3/10, net 30
g. 4/10, net 180

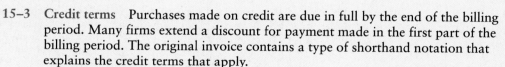

BASIC  **15–3 Credit terms** Purchases made on credit are due in full by the end of the billing period. Many firms extend a discount for payment made in the first part of the billing period. The original invoice contains a type of shorthand notation that explains the credit terms that apply.

a. Write the shorthand expression of credit terms for each of the following.

Cash discount	Cash discount period	Credit period
1%	15 days	45 days
2	10	30
2	7	28
1	10	60

b. For each of the sets of credit terms in **a**, determine the date when the discounted payment is due for invoices dated March 12.
c. For each of the set of credit terms, calculate the cost of giving up the cash discount.
d. If the firm's cost of short-term financing is 8 percent, what would you recommend the firm do regarding the discounts available?

BASIC  **15–4 Cash discount versus loan** Erica Stone works in an accounts payable department. She has attempted to convince her boss to take the discount on the 3/10, net 45 credit terms most suppliers offer, but her boss argues that giving up the 3 percent discount is less costly than a short-term loan at 14 percent. Prove who is right.

  BASIC

15–5 Cash discount decisions Prairie Manufacturing has four possible suppliers, all of whom offer different credit terms. Except for the differences in credit terms, their products and services are virtually identical. The credit terms offered by each supplier are shown in the following table.

Supplier	Credit terms
J	1/10, net 30
K	2/20, net 80
L	1/20, net 60
M	3/10, net 55

a. Calculate the cost of giving up the cash discount from each supplier.

b. If the firm needs short-term funds, which are currently available from its commercial bank at 16 percent, and if each of the suppliers is viewed *separately,* which, if any, of the suppliers' cash discounts should the firm give up? Explain why.

c. What impact, if any, would the fact that the firm could stretch its accounts payable (net period only) by 30 days from supplier M have on your answer in part **b** relative to this supplier?

INTERMEDIATE 

15–6 Changing payment cycle Upon accepting the position of chief executive officer and chairperson of Reeves Machinery, Frank Cheney changed the firm's weekly payday from Monday afternoon to the following Friday afternoon. The firm's weekly payroll was $10 million, and the cost of short-term funds was 13 percent. If the effect of this change was to delay cheque clearing by three days, what *annual* savings, if any, were realized?

15–7 Spontaneous sources of funds, accruals When Tallman Haberdashery, Inc., merged with Meyers Men's Suits, Inc., Tallman's employees were switched from a weekly to a biweekly pay period. Tallman's weekly payroll amounted to $750,000. The cost of funds for the combined firms is 11 percent. What annual savings, if any, are realized by the change of pay period?

15–8 Cost of bank loan Data Back-Up Systems has obtained a $10,000, 90-day bank loan at an annual interest rate of 15 percent, payable at maturity.

a. How much interest (in dollars) will the firm pay on the 90-day loan?

b. Find the effective 90-day rate on the loan.

c. Annualize your finding in part **b** to find the effective annual rate for this loan, assuming that it is rolled over each 90 days throughout the year under the same terms and circumstances and that the interest is not paid but simply accumulated with the loan.

15–9 Effective annual rate A company borrowed $100,000 for one-year at 10 percent interest, requiring a compensating balance equal to 20 percent of the face value of the loan. Determine the effective annual cost of this loan if the firm has a $0 balance in its chequing account.

INTERMEDIATE  15–10 **Compensating balances and effective annual rates** Lincoln Industries has a $2 million line of credit at The Imperial Bank that requires it to pay 11 percent interest on its borrowing and maintain a compensating balance equal to 15 percent of the amount borrowed. Last year, the firm borrowed, on average, $800,000 from the line of credit. Calculate the effective annual dollar and percentage cost of the firm's borrowing in each of the following circumstances:

a. The firm normally maintains no balance in their chequing account at The Imperial Bank.
b. The firm normally maintains a $70,000 balance in their chequing account at The Imperial Bank.
c. The firm normally maintains a $150,000 balance in their chequing account at The Imperial Bank.
d. What explains the differences in your findings in parts **a, b,** and **c**?

INTERMEDIATE  15–11 **Compensating balance versus discount loan** Weathers Catering Supply, Inc., requires $150,000 of financing for 6 months. The Eastern Bank has offered to loan the necessary funds at a 9 percent annual rate subject to a 10 percent compensating balance. The Western Bank has offered to lend the funds at a 9 percent annual rate with discount-loan terms. The principal of both loans would be payable at maturity as a single sum. The firm's policy is to have a $0 balance in their chequing account.

a. Calculate the effective annual cost of each loan. Which bank should the company select?
b. What could Weathers do that would reduce the effective annual rate on the the Eastern Bank loan?

INTERMEDIATE  15–12 **Integrative—Comparison of loan terms** Cumberland Furniture wishes to establish a prearranged borrowing agreement with its bank. The bank's terms for a line of credit are 3.30 percent over the prime rate, and each year the borrowing must be reduced to zero for a 30-day period. For an equivalent revolving credit agreement, the rate is 2.80 percent over prime with a commitment fee of 0.50 percent on the average unused balance. With both loans, the required compensating balance is equal to 20 percent of the amount borrowed. The prime rate is currently 8 percent. Both agreements have $4 million borrowing limits. The firm expects that they will require, on average, $2 million to finance their investment in net working capital during the year.

a. What is the effective annual cost (both dollar and percent) of using the line of credit to finance the required investment?
b. What is the effective annual cost (both dollar and percent) of using the revolving credit agreement to finance the required investment?
c. Which arrangement would you recommend for the borrower? Why?

INTERMEDIATE  15–13 **Cost of corporate paper** Fan Corporation just sold an issue of 90-day corporate paper with a face value of $1 million. The firm received proceeds of $978,000.

a. What is the effective annual percentage cost to Fan Corporation of the corporate paper?
b. If the investment banker selling the issue for Fan charged a brokerage fee of $9,612, what happens to the effective annual percentage cost of the issue?

CHALLENGE  **15–14 Corporate paper** Morgan Group is using the money market to raise short-term financing. The corporation wishes to issue corporate paper with a face value of $50,000,000. The paper will be sold for $49,351,565 and will mature in 90 days, at which time the investor will receive the face value.

a. What is the dollar and percentage cost of the corporate paper to Morgan?

b. If the investment banker selling the issue for Morgan charged an issue fee of 5.5 basis points of the face value of the issue, what will be the percentage cost of the corporate paper to Morgan?

c. If Morgan Group wishes to reduce the cost of the paper to 4.95 percent, at what price will they need to sell the corporate paper? What will be the company's dollar cost? Note that the issue fee will not apply.

d. If the corporate paper had a maturity of 30 days, what would happen to the proceeds received by Morgan? Calculations are not required, just an explanation.

INTERMEDIATE  **15–15 Accounts receivable as collateral** Kentville City Castings (KCC) is attempting to obtain the maximum loan possible using accounts receivable as collateral. The firm's credit terms are net 30. The following table provides credit information for KCC's 12 credit customers. Here we see the size and average age of the most recent credit purchase outstanding, and each customer's historic average payment period.

Customer	Account receivable	Average age of account	Historic average payment period of customer
A	$37,000	45 days	30 days
B	42,000	25	50
C	15,000	40	60
D	8,000	30	35
E	50,000	31	40
F	12,000	28	30
G	24,000	30	70
H	46,000	29	40
I	3,000	30	65
J	22,000	25	35
K	62,000	35	45
L	80,000	60	70

a. The bank will accept all accounts that are outstanding for less than 45 days as long as the customer's historic average payment period is 45 days or less. Which accounts will the bank accept? What is the total dollar amount of accounts receivable available as collateral?

b. In addition to the conditions in part **a**, the bank reduces the amount they will lend by 5 percent due to returns and allowances. Also, the bank will lend only 80 percent of the acceptable collateral (after adjusting for returns and allowances). What level of funds would be made available through this lending source?

INTERMEDIATE  **15–16 Accounts receivable as collateral** Springer Products wishes to borrow $80,000 from a local bank using its accounts receivable to secure the loan. The bank's policy is to accept as collateral any accounts that are normally paid within 15 days of the end of the credit period, as long as the average age of the account is not more than five days longer than the customer's average payment period. Information on the size and average age of the most recent credit purchase outstanding, and each customer's historic average payment period for Springer's credit customers, is provided below. The company extends credit terms of net 30 days.

Customer	Account receivable	Average age of account	Historic average payment period of customer
A	$20,000	10 days	40 days
B	6,000	40	35
C	22,000	62	50
D	11,000	68	65
E	2,000	14	30
F	12,000	38	50
G	27,000	55	60
H	19,000	20	35

a. Calculate the dollar amount of acceptable accounts receivable collateral held by Springer Products.
b. The bank reduces the amount of the allowable loan by 10 percent for returns and allowances. What is the level of acceptable collateral under this condition?
c. The bank will advance 75 percent against the firm's acceptable collateral (after adjusting for returns and allowances). What amount can Springer borrow against these accounts?
d. What is the implication of your answer in part c for Springer?

  CHALLENGE **15–17 Accounts receivable as collateral, cost of borrowing** Maximum Bank has analyzed the accounts receivable of Scientific Software, Inc. The bank has chosen eight accounts totalling $134,000 that it will accept as collateral. The bank's terms include a lending rate set at prime + 3 percent and a 2 percent commission charge. The prime rate currently is 8.5 percent.
a. The bank will adjust the accounts by 10 percent for returns and allowances. It then will lend up to 85 percent of the adjusted acceptable collateral. What is the maximum amount that the bank will lend to Scientific Software?
b. What is Scientific Software's effective annual rate of interest if it borrows $100,000 for 12 months? For 6 months? For 3 months? (Assume that the prime rate remains at 8.5 percent during the life of the loan.)

INTERMEDIATE  **15–18 Factoring** Blair Finance factors the accounts of the Holder Company. All eight factored accounts are shown in the table below, with the amount factored, the date due, and the status as of May 30. Indicate the amounts Blair should have remitted to Holder as of May 30 and the dates of those remittances. Assume that the factor's commission of 2 percent is deducted as part of determining the amount of the remittance.

Account	Amount	Date due	Status on May 30
A	$200,000	May 30	Collected May 15
B	90,000	May 30	Uncollected
C	110,000	May 30	Uncollected
D	85,000	June 15	Collected May 30
E	120,000	May 30	Collected May 27
F	180,000	June 15	Collected May 30
G	90,000	May 15	Uncollected
H	30,000	June 30	Collected May 30

CHALLENGE

15–19 **Inventory financing** Raymond Manufacturing faces a liquidity crisis—it requires a loan of $100,000 for 30 days. The firm's accounts receivable are quite low, but its inventory is considered liquid and reasonably good collateral. The book value of the inventory is $300,000, of which $120,000 is finished goods. The company has three options to raise the required financing.

(1) The Nation Bank will make a $100,000 *trust receipt* loan against the finished goods inventory. The annual interest rate on the loan is 12 percent on the outstanding loan balance plus a 0.25 percent administration fee levied against the $100,000 initial loan amount. Because the loan will be liquidated as inventory is sold, the average amount outstanding over the 30 days is expected to be $75,000.

(2) The Bank of PEI will lend $100,000 against a *floating lien* on the book value of inventory for the 30-day period at an annual interest rate of 13 percent.

(3) Citizens' Bank and Trust will loan $100,000 against a *warehouse receipt* on the finished goods inventory and charge 15 percent annual interest on the outstanding loan balance. A 0.5 percent warehousing fee will be levied against the average amount borrowed. Because the loan will be liquidated as inventory is sold, the average loan balance outstanding is expected to be $60,000 over the 30 days.

a. Calculate the dollar cost of each of the proposed plans for obtaining an initial loan amount of $100,000.

b. Which plan do you recommend? Why?

c. Now assmume that 10 days ago Raymond Manufacturing made a purchase of $100,000 for which it had been given credit terms of 2/10, net 30. Raymond can borrow the required amount of money from one of the banks and take the discount. Assume the company will repay the full amount borrowed in 20 days. Should they borrow the money and, if so, from which bank? Provide a complete financial analysis including the net impact, in dollars, of the arrangement.

CASE CHAPTER 15 Selecting Kanton Company's Financing Strategy and Unsecured Short-Term Borrowing Arrangement

See the enclosed Student CD-ROM for cases that help you put theories and concepts from the text into practice.

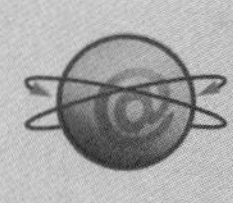

Be sure to visit the Companion Website for this book at **www.pearsoned.ca/gitman** for a wealth of additional learning tools including self-test quizzes, Web exercises, and additional cases.

CHAPTER 16

Lease Financing: Concepts and Techniques

LEARNING GOALS

LG1 Review the concept that the value of an asset is in its use, not its ownership, and introduce information regarding leasing and the leasing industry in Canada.

LG2 Describe and differentiate between operating and financial leases, introduce the different types of financial leases, and explain other conditions included in lease agreements.

LG3 Explain how leases are disclosed on a company's financial statements, and exhibit how leasing and purchasing an asset have similar impacts on a firm's financial position.

LG4 Discuss the cash flows and the discount rate used to evaluate whether an asset should be leased or purchased, and illustrate the process used to answer the lease-or-purchase question.

LG5 Introduce the method used to calculate the net present value of leasing, show how other variables can affect the lease-or-purchase question, and discuss the advantages and disadvantages of leasing.

LG6 Examine leasing from the lessor's perspective, focusing on how leasing can benefit both the lessee and the lessor due to differing discount and tax rates, and illustrate the process lessors use to calculate the minimum and maximum lease payment that they could charge on a lease.

16.1 Fundamentals of Leasing

Chapter 12 explored how a company should analyze the acquisition of fixed assets. In that chapter, we saw that the value of an asset was in its use, not in how it was financed. In fact, Chapter 12 specifically indicated that financing

It's the Lease We Can Do

For most businesses, it happens on a regular basis. The decision has been made to acquire a new asset that will improve productivity or help grow sales. But, another key question to answer at that point is: How should the asset be acquired? For many this seems to be an odd question, since the obvious answer is to buy the asset. Isn't that what companies do, buy assets? Well, not always! An alternative approach is to lease assets. With this approach, the firm gains use of the asset, but not the ownership. Some might be thinking, is that legal? It is, as long as the firm makes the required lease payments. Answering the lease-or-purchase question is a vital part of the asset acquisition process for a firm. Is the cost of the required lease payments less than the cost of purchasing the asset? This chapter explains the principles and techniques of lease financing, an alternative method of financing the acquisition of fixed assets.

costs are ignored when calculating the cash flows associated with capital budgeting projects. Chapter 12 also indicated that the company's cost of capital is used to discount the cash flows. The cost of capital is based on the firm's overall optimal capital structure and the marginal costs of these financing sources. The

LINKING THE DISCIPLINES: Cross-Functional Interactions

- *Accounting personnel* provide important data and tax information to help answer the question of whether assets should be leased or purchased. This analysis is important to both the purchasing and selling functions of the firm. Accounting personnel are required to record and report leasing arrangements because a complete understanding of these arrangements and the disclosure process is imperative.
- *Information systems analysts* must understand the types of leasing arrangements in order to design systems that will track data used to make lease-or-purchase decisions and to design applications that quickly, easily, and accurately analyze the decision based on given inputs.
- *Management* must understand when and why it may make better sense to lease assets rather than to purchase them so that they make decisions that provide the greatest benefit to the firm.
- The ***marketing department*** will have to determine whether to sell or lease the firm's products and recognize leasing as a way of financing a new project proposal. Marketing personnel must also understand the analysis used to make the lease-or-purchase decision so that they have an understanding of the prepurchase decision process of their prospective customers.
- Personnel in the ***operations department*** help make the decision regarding the assets to be acquired, and must understand the role of leasing in financing new equipment. They also must be aware of the maintenance obligations that may be associated with new equipment.

actual cash costs of the financing used to acquire an individual asset could be safely ignored.

By discounting the relevant cash flows at the firm's cost of capital, the decision to acquire an asset can be made. This process allows the financial analyst to calculate the net present value of the asset. If the present value of the cash flows are greater than or equal to the incremental cost of the asset, then the asset should be acquired. This would be the case since the project's net present value would be greater than or equal to zero ($0). Recall that how the asset would be acquired was never considered. Usually, the assumption made is that the asset will be purchased, and the firm will own the asset.

But note: the value of an asset is in its use, its ability to generate cash flows, not in its ownership. A firm doesn't have to own the asset to derive benefits from the asset; the firm has to use the asset. The use of the asset, not its ownership, results in the incremental cash flows being generated. The purpose of this chapter is to determine how firms should acquire the use of their assets. For companies, there are two ways to acquire the use of an asset: purchase the asset, and then own and use it, or lease the asset and then use it. This chapter discusses and illustrates how the acquisition decision should be made.

leasing
The process by which a firm can obtain the use of fixed assets for which it must make a series of contractual, periodic, tax-deductible payments.

lessee
Has physical control of and uses the assets under a lease contract; makes the lease payments.

lessor
The owner of an asset being leased; receives the lease payments.

Leasing Terminology

Leasing allows a firm to obtain the use of fixed assets for which it must make a series of contractual, periodic, tax-deductible payments. The **lessee** has physical control of and uses the asset under the lease contract; they must make the lease payments. The **lessor** is the owner of the asset and retains all rights of ownership; they receive the lease payments. More leasing terminology is available on the Web.

www.ilc1.com/gloss.htm

We begin this section of the chapter by reviewing general information about leasing in Canada.

Information on Leasing in Canada

Leasing is a source of financing for a company that can be either short-term or long-term. Often, the length of this source of financing is directly tied to the life of the asset leased. If the leased asset has an expected life of 20 years, the length of the lease, and thus the source of financing, may be 20 years. In this regard, leasing is like long-term debt financing. As we saw in Chapter 5, the term of a long-term loan is generally tied to the life of the asset purchased. But some leases are short-term in nature and will not be for the full expected life of the asset. If so, the lease may be viewed as short- or intermediate-term financing.

Leasing, as a form of financing, has become increasingly popular since World War II. A surprising array of companies now lease many of the assets they use. These companies range from small retail stores or manufacturers, to franchise operations, to airlines, to banks, to oil and gas companies, to hotels. There are very few industries, both service and manufacturing, in which leasing is *not* used as a form of financing.

There are numerous reasons why leasing has grown so popular, but the overriding explanation is the large increase in the number of leasing companies that offer the service (including the Big Five Canadian banks). As a result, a large amount of low-cost capital has flowed into the industry resulting in financially attractive leasing deals being offered to companies. In a free-enterprise economy, as more competition enters an industry, the quality, price, and service offered to customers usually improves. This seems to have occurred in the leasing market in Canada, and in part it explains the large increase in the use of this source of financing.

www.cfla-acfl.ca

The Canadian Finance and Leasing Association (CFLA) represents the leasing industry. As of the summer of 2006, there were 235 members active in the industry. CFLA members range from large multinationals to national and smaller regional domestic companies, crossing the financial services spectrum from manufacturers' finance companies and independent leasing companies to banks, insurance companies, and suppliers. About 60 percent of the industry's customers are small and medium-sized enterprises (SME).

The leasing industry is the second-largest provider of debt financing in Canada, after the traditional lenders (banks and credit unions). In 1997, the value of assets leased in Canada was $50 billion. By 2004, the value had doubled to $103 billion. Of this, $56.4 billion was for businesses to acquire equipment and vehicles. The remainder are vehicle leases to consumers, a topic that is not discussed in this chapter. According to Statistics Canada, business spending on machinery and equipment averages at least $100 billion yearly. Between 20 percent and 25 percent of annual new business investment in machinery, equipment, and commercial vehicles is financed by the leasing industry, a tremendous increase from the 5 percent level recorded in the mid-1980s.

As with debt, the lessee uses the asset as security for the lease contract. Since the lessor retains legal ownership of the asset for the full lease period, this allows the lessee to qualify for lease financing on the basis of its ability to generate cash flow rather than on a net worth or asset-based lending formula typically used by traditional lenders. On average, equipment lessors accept about 66 percent of the applications for lease financing; this is below the mid-70s percent level reported in the late 1990s.

The services of the leasing industry are complementary to traditional banking and other financial lending in providing incremental capital that increases the pool of available credit in Canada, and provide a vital competitive alternative in the financial services sector. Funding for this industry comes from commercial markets, notably from pension funds, insurance companies, and banks. In addition, manufacturing and servicing companies have become lessors in order to leverage their own equity base.

www.easy-lease.com/public/leasing/leasing_buy_loan.asp

? Review Questions

16–1 What is leasing? What is the difference between a lessee and a lessor?
16–2 Explain why leasing has grown so popular in Canada.
16–3 What is the governing body of the leasing industry in Canada? What type of companies are members?

16.2 Types and Conditions of Leases

The two basic types of leases that are available to a business are *operating* and *financial leases* (the latter being called *capital leases* by accountants). An important point to note is that leases are not conditional sales agreements. With a lease, the lessor retains title to the asset; the lessor owns but does not use the asset. The lessee uses but does not own the asset. A **conditional sales agreement** is really just another way to finance the purchase of an asset with debt. With these sales agreements, the debt financing is provided to the purchaser by the asset vendor. The purchaser then makes periodic installment loan payments over a stated time period. Each payment consists of both interest and principal. In such cases, the purchaser is not a lessee, but the owner of the asset. Conditional sales agreements are not leases and are not the subject of this chapter.

conditional sales agreement
A way to finance the purchase of an asset with the debt financing provided to the purchaser by the asset vendor.

Operating Leases

An **operating lease** is a contractual arrangement in which the lessor allows the lessee use of an asset in return for stated periodic payments. Assets acquired through operating leases have useful lives that are longer than the term of the lease. Usually, however, the asset becomes less efficient and technologically obsolete if leased for a long time period. Computer systems are prime examples of assets whose relative efficiency is expected to diminish over time as the technology changes. An operating lease is therefore a common arrangement for obtaining such systems, as well as for other relatively short-lived assets such as automobiles and office equipment. Generally, the total payments made by the lessee to the lessor are less than the initial cost of the leased asset.

operating lease
A cancellable contractual arrangement in which the lessor allows the lessee use of an asset in return for stated periodic payments; generally, the term of the lease is less than the life of the asset, and the total payments over the term of the lease are less than the lessor's initial cost of the leased asset.

With an operating lease, the lessee acquires the use of an asset on a periodic basis for a set number of periods. The periodic basis could be days, weeks, or months. The set number of periods might be weeks, months, or years. For example, a specialized computer system might be leased by a company on a daily basis for six weeks; the lease rate would be quoted on a daily basis. Or a specialized printing press might be leased on a weekly basis for six months; the lease rate would be quoted on a weekly basis. Or a vehicle might be leased on a monthly basis for three years; the lease rate would be quoted on a monthly basis. All three are examples of operating leases. In general, it is unusual for operating leases to be for longer than four years.

cancellable
An option on an operating lease that allows the lessee to stop making lease payments and return the asset to the lessor.

A key characteristic of an operating lease is that it is generally **cancellable** at the option of the lessee. If the lease is cancelled, the lessee will stop making the lease payments and return the asset to the lessor. In such cases, the lessee is required to pay the lessor a penalty charge as compensation. If an operating lease is held to maturity, the lessee will return the asset to the lessor, who may then lease it again or sell the asset. Normally, the asset still has a positive market value at the end of the lease. In some instances, the lease contract will give the lessee the opportunity to purchase the leased asset for the fair market value.

With an operating lease, the party responsible for maintenance, insurance, and taxes is subject to negotiation. The lessor may agree to pay these (adjusting the required lease payment accordingly). In such cases, the lease is termed a *service* or *maintenance operating lease*. Or the lessee may feel they can get a better deal on these variables (excluding taxes) and agree to insure and maintain the asset. Since the lessee is responsible for returning the asset to the lessor in usable form, it can make sense for the lessee to assume responsibility for these costs.

Financial (or Capital) Leases

financial (or capital) lease
A non-cancellable contractual arrangement for major fixed assets requiring the lessee to make periodic payments to the lessor; generally, the term of the lease is the life of the asset, and the total payments over the term of the lease are greater than the lessor's initial cost of the leased asset.

Financial (or capital) leases are very different from operating leases. First, financial leases are commonly used for leasing major fixed assets like land, buildings, large pieces of equipment, and whole manufacturing facilities. Examples of equipment that are often leased are: railway cars, aircraft, point-of-sale cash registers, telecommunications and broadcasting equipment, hotel and restaurant equipment, agricultural equipment, office buildings, buses, ski lifts, and grooming machines. Numerous types of assets are leased by companies. Second, financial leases are much longer-term than operating leases. They are usually for all or most of the expected life of the asset.

Third, with a financial lease, the total payments over the lease period are greater than the lessor's initial cost of the leased asset. In other words, the lessor receives more than the asset's purchase price and earns its required return on the investment. Fourth, financial leases are non-cancellable and obligate the lessee to make payments for the use of an asset over the contracted and predetermined period of time. The non-cancellable feature of the financial lease makes it similar to certain types of long-term debt. The lease payment becomes a fixed, tax-deductible expenditure that must be paid at predefined dates. As with debt, failure to make the contractual lease payments can result in bankruptcy for the lessee.

Finally, with financial leases, the lessee is almost always responsible for the taxes, maintenance, and insurance on the asset. The lease contract would specifically state that the latter two payments are a required condition of the lease. To be considered a financial (or capital) lease, the Canadian Institute of Chartered Accountants (CICA) regulation 3065 (Leases) requires that the contract arrangement must transfer a significant portion of the benefits and risks of ownership to the lessee at the inception of the lease. This would be deemed to have occurred when one or more of the following conditions are present:

1. The lease transfers ownership of the asset to the lessee by the end of the lease term.
2. The lessee has an option to purchase the property at a "bargain price" when the lease expires.
3. The lease term is equal to 75 percent or more of the estimated economic life of the property.
4. At the beginning of the lease, the present value of the lease payments is equal to 90 percent or more of the fair market value of the leased property.[1]

If one or more of these features is present, then, for accounting purposes, the arrangement is a capital lease, otherwise it is an operating lease. This chapter emphasizes financial leases because they result in inescapable long-term financial commitments by the firm.

Types of Financial (or Capital) Leases

There are three types of financial (or capital) leases. These are different long-term leasing arrangements that may be negotiated between a lessor and lessee. Historically, lessees have approached lessors to arrange for a lease but recently, as the market has become more competitive, lessors have begun to approach prospective companies to see if they might be interested in acquiring new assets through a financial lease. The type of leasing arrangement used depends largely on the desires of the prospective lessee.

Direct Lease

direct lease
A lease under which a lessor purchases assets that are then leased to a given lessee.

A **direct lease** results when a lessor purchases assets that are then leased to the lessee. The lessee usually negotiates the price and delivery terms with the manufacturer, and then the lessor pays the manufacturer that amount. At the same time, the lessor and lessee sign the previously negotiated lease agreement. The asset is delivered to, and then used by, the lessee. The lessee did not previously own the assets that it is leasing. These are also termed *true leases* or *tax leases*.[2]

Sale-Leaseback Arrangement

sale-leaseback arrangement
A lease where a lessee sells assets they already own to the lessor and, at the same time, commits to leasing them back.

In a **sale-leaseback arrangement**, the lessee sells assets they already own to the lessor and, at the same time, commits to leasing them back. This technique is normally initiated by a firm that needs funds for operations. By selling an existing asset to a lessor and then leasing it back, the lessee receives cash for the asset immediately, while obligating itself to make fixed periodic payments for the use of the leased asset.

These types of leasing arrangements are very popular for companies experiencing cash flow problems. But note that the long-term fundamental position of

1. The way to calculate the present value of the lease payments is similar to the process discussed in Section 16.3 for determining the capitalized value of a lease.

2. Accountants term these *direct financing leases*. Sometimes the manufacturer of the asset is also the lessor. This arrangement is termed a *sales-type lease*.

the firm has not changed. The firm has simply swapped higher longer-term cash balances for higher short-term cash balances. Airline companies were major users of these types of leases after many experienced financial problems in 2001 and 2002. The airlines received needed cash up front, but were then locked into non-cancellable long-term lease obligations. It is interesting that now, very few airline companies actually own the airplanes they fly. Most were either leased outright—often through the airplane manufacturer—or were sold to lessors and then leased back.

Leveraged Lease

leveraged lease
A lease under which the lessor acts as an equity participant, supplying only about 20 percent of the cost of the asset, while a lender supplies the balance.

Leasing arrangements that include one or more third-party lenders are leveraged leases. Under a **leveraged lease**, the lessor acts as an equity participant, supplying only about 20 percent of the cost of the asset, with a lender supplying the balance. Leveraged leases have become especially popular in structuring leases of very expensive assets.

Other Conditions Included in Lease Agreements

maintenance clauses
Provisions normally included in a lease that require one of the parties to maintain the assets and to make insurance and tax payments.

renewal option
Grants the lessee the right to re-lease the asset at the expiration of the lease contract.

purchase option
Allows the lessee to purchase the leased asset at maturity for a pre-specified price, generally the asset's fair market value.

As discussed earlier, a lease agreement normally specifies whether the lessee is responsible for maintenance and insurance of the leased assets. Operating leases can include **maintenance clauses** requiring the lessor to maintain the assets and to make insurance and tax payments. Financial leases almost always include clauses that require the lessee to pay maintenance and all other costs.

Operating leases can include a **renewal option** that grants the lessee the right to re-lease the assets at the expiration of the lease contract. This is possible because the term of an operating lease is generally shorter than the usable life of the leased assets. This option is usually not included in financial leases, since their terms are generally for the life of the asset. A **purchase option** allows the lessee to purchase the leased asset at maturity, typically for a pre-specified price. As will be seen, the pre-specified price is generally, but not always, an estimate of what the asset's fair market value will be at the end of the lease period. This option is frequently included in both operating and financial leases.

The lessor can be one of a number of parties. In operating leases, the lessor is likely to be the manufacturer's leasing subsidiary. Examples include the finance company subsidiaries of all automotive manufacturers (as offered through car dealerships), or of computer and office equipment manufacturers. Financial leases are frequently handled by the leasing subsidiaries of large financial institutions such as commercial banks, life insurance companies, trust companies, and pension plans. In addition, many manufacturers of major pieces of equipment have finance company subsidiaries that arrange leases. Finally, there are many independent leasing companies in Canada that negotiate both operating and financial leases.

www.ilc1.com/guide.htm

? Review Questions

16–4 Explain the difference between a lease and a conditional sales agreement.

16–5 Define, compare, and contrast operating leases and financial (or capital) leases.

16–6 To be considered a financial (or capital) lease for accounting purposes, what features must the contract arrangement include?
16–7 How is a financial lease similar to long-term debt?
16–8 List and describe the three types of financial (or capital) leases.
16–9 What is the primary reason a firm would enter into a sale-leaseback agreement?
16–10 What are renewal options, and why wouldn't this option normally be included in a financial lease?

16.3 Accounting For Leases

As we have seen in earlier chapters in the book, lease payments are a deductible expense for tax purposes, but only if the tax authorities, the Canada Revenue Agency (CRA), agree that the contractual arrangement is a lease. If the asset arrangement is viewed by the CRA as a conditional sales agreement disguised as a lease, the periodic payments would be deemed installment loan payments and disallowed as a deduction. Taxes would then be assessed as if the asset had been purchased on the date of the "lease" agreement.

The CRA may rule that an apparent "lease" arrangement is not a lease, but a conditional sales agreement, if the lessee provides a description of the arrangement that is not reflective of its true legal form. In such a case, the CRA could use the general anti-avoidance rule and claim the arrangement results in the misuse or abuse of the provisions in the *Income Tax Act*.[3] Since it is very easy to correctly structure contracts, there is no reason why the CRA should ever rule a leasing arrangement is really a conditional sales agreement. So lease payments are deductible from income—but does leasing assets impact the lessee's balance sheet? To determine whether it should, let's consider an example.

Example ▼ Dooley Tools' current simplified balance sheet is shown in Panel A in Table 16.1. Dooley is planning to expand by acquiring new equipment at a cost of $100,000. A capital budgeting analysis has been completed and the net present value of the new equipment is $32,614. Clearly, this new equipment should be acquired. But should the equipment be purchased or leased? If a financial lease were used, and Dooley did not have to report the lease on the balance sheet, the company's balance sheet does not change. They still have a very attractive financial position with a debt ratio of only 24 percent.[4]

If instead Dooley purchased the equipment using a long-term loan as financing, their balance sheet would change as shown in Panel B of Table 16.1. Now, the balance sheet has been impacted: assets have increased by 40 percent and debt by 167 percent, while the debt ratio has increased to 45.7 percent. So the

3. At one time the CRA had much greater power when evaluating lease arrangements and could rule that a lease was a conditional sales agreement. This might occur if, at any time in the leasing period, the lessee was required to buy the asset, if the lessee automatically received ownership of the asset, or if the lessee had the option to buy the asset for a "bargain price." This changed on June 14, 2001, due to a successful court challenge of the CRA conditions.

4. Anyone analyzing the firm's income statement would probably realize that an asset is being leased (since the expense is present). But the actual details of the amount and term of the lease would not be provided.

TABLE 16.1 Balance Sheets for Dooley Tools

Panel A: Initial Balance Sheet

		Debt	$ 60,000
		Equity	190,000
Total assets	$250,000	Total debt and equity	$250,000

Panel B: Balance Sheet After Purchase

Previous assets	$250,000	Debt	$160,000
New equipment	100,000	Equity	190,000
Total assets	$350,000	Total debt and equity	$350,000

company's financial position has been greatly altered. But would there really be any difference in the firm's financial position if they leased rather than purchased the asset?

Not at all! When purchasing the asset, Dooley has acquired the long-term use of the asset, and has incurred a long-term obligation (the interest and principal) that must be repaid in order for the firm to continue to enjoy the use of the asset. The lease has resulted in exactly the same situation—the long-term use of the asset with a long-term obligation (the lease payments) that must be paid. Therefore, if the asset is leased, the initial balance sheet (Panel A) does not correctly reflect the company's financial position. In reality, the company has a higher level of assets and liabilities than is reflected on the balance sheet in Panel A.

off-balance-sheet financing
Financing that does not have to be shown on the balance sheet, but only reported in the notes to the financial statements.

If Dooley did not have to report the lease on the balance sheet, as in the example above, the lease would be considered **off-balance-sheet financing.** This is financing that only has to be reported in the notes to the financial statements, not on the balance sheet itself. While this type of financial reporting is still allowed in some European countries, since 1979 the practice is not permitted in Canada. In 1979, also with previously discussed regulation 3065, the CICA ruled that all financial (capital) leases must be explicitly disclosed on the firm's balance sheet. Because of the regulation, for the contractual arrangement to be considered a financial (capital) lease, one of the four conditions discussed earlier in the chapter must be present.

www.investopedia.com/articles/stocks/04/102004.asp

capitalized lease
As required by Canadian accounting regulations, a financial (capital) lease that has the present value of the payments included as an asset and as an offsetting liability on the firm's balance sheet.

If one of the four conditions is present, the capitalized value of the lease must be shown on the firm's balance sheet. This is termed a **capitalized lease,** and it means that the present value of the lease payments must be shown as an asset and as an offsetting liability on the firm's balance sheet. To capitalize the lease, two variables are required: the lease payments and a discount rate. The lease payments are obviously available. The discount rate to use is the lower of two rates: either the lessee's borrowing rate or the lessor's implied discount rate. This is the discount rate that makes the present value of the minimum lease payments plus the present value of the expected salvage value equal to the original cost of the asset. In no case may the capitalized value of the lease exceed the original cost of the asset.

Example Lawrence Company, a manufacturer of water purifiers, has just leased an asset for 10 years with required payments of $15,000 per year, with the first payment due when the lease contract is signed. The original cost of the asset is $128,500 and it has an expected life of 10 years. To determine the capitalized value of the lease, the present value of the lease payments over the life of the lease must be calculated. Lawrence's borrowing rate is 7.7 percent, while the lessor's implied discount rate is 6.75 percent. The appropriate rate to discount the lease payments is the lower of the two rates, so in this case 6.75 percent. The capitalized (present) value of the lease is $113,776 {$15,000 + [$15,000 × *PVIFa* (6.75%, 9 years)]}.[5]

The lease is considered a financial lease for accounting purposes, since conditions 3 and 4 of the four CICA conditions are present. The capitalized value of $113,776 would be shown as an asset and a corresponding liability on the firm's balance sheet. This will provide an accurate reflection of the firm's true financial position. The capitalized value of the lease liability on the balance sheet declines each year as lease payments are made and deducted for income statement and tax purposes.

Because the consequences of missing a financial lease payment are the same as those of missing an interest or principal payment on debt, a financial analyst must view the lease as a long-term financial commitment of the lessee. The inclusion of each financial (capital) lease as an asset and corresponding liability (i.e., long-term debt) provides for a balance sheet that more accurately reflects the firm's financial status.

Example So, reflecting back on the Dooley Tools example, the lease arrangement should have been reflected on the balance sheet as shown in Table 16.2. Here we assume that the capitalized value of the lease is $100,000. Since leasing is similar to debt, this balance sheet truly reflects the financial position of the company and, as under the purchase and borrowing example, Dooley's true debt ratio is 45.7 percent.

So unlike Panel A where it was up to the analyst evaluating the company's financial position to find the leasing arrangement in the notes, under CICA regulations the lease must be directly disclosed on the balance sheet. This means that

TABLE 16.2 Balance Sheet for Dooley Tools with the Lease Reported

Balance Sheet After Lease

Previous assets	$250,000	Debt	$ 60,000
Asset under lease	100,000	Obligations under lease	100,000
		Equity	190,000
Total assets	$350,000	Total debt and equity	$350,000

5. Since the lease payments are made at the beginning of the year, the capitalized value is calculated using an annuity due. More discussion of annuities due is provided in Section 16.4.

the users of financial statements (investors, suppliers, bankers, employees, and other users) can rely on the statements to disclose this material obligation. The impact of this disclosure is that it directly affects the firm's financial position, financial ratios, and ability to obtain future financing.

Finally, it is important to note that operating leases do not need to be shown on the balance sheet. This is because operating leases do not normally meet any of the four conditions that the CICA uses to judge whether a leasing arrangement needs to be capitalized and disclosed directly on the financial statements. But operating leases must still be disclosed in the notes to the financial statements.

? Review Questions

16–11 Under what condition might the CRA rule that a lease arrangement is a conditional sales agreement?
16–12 Explain why leasing affects a firm's financial position in the same way that purchasing an asset does.
16–13 What is meant by the phrase "capitalizing a lease"?
16–14 Why are leases capitalized? How are leases capitalized?
16–15 Do operating leases need to be capitalized? Explain.

16.4 The Lease-or-Purchase Question

lease-or-purchase question
The question facing firms looking to acquire new fixed assets: whether to lease the assets or to purchase them using borrowed funds.

Firms contemplating the acquisition of new fixed assets commonly confront the question, should we **lease or purchase** the assets? To access the financing needed to acquire assets, a firm has four alternatives:

1. Borrow the funds required and purchase the assets.
2. Sell common shares to raise the funds required and purchase the assets.
3. Purchase the assets using available liquid resources (which might come from reinvested profits).
4. Lease the assets.

Alternatives 1, 2, and 3 are all considered equivalent forms of financing, and thus are analyzed similarly. At first glance, this statement seems odd given that these three forms of financing are very different. But recall the issues discussed in Chapters 9 and 12 relating to cost of capital and capital budgeting. There we saw that the firm is assumed to raise all financing in the optimal capital structure to finance asset acquisitions, *regardless of how the firm actually finances the assets acquired*. This was done in order to treat all asset acquisitions the same. A similar logic is used in this chapter. For reasons to be discussed shortly, here we are going to assume that alternatives 2 and 3 are equivalent to alternative 1: borrow the funds required to purchase the assets. Therefore, we only need to compare alternatives 1 and 4 to answer the question of whether to lease or purchase assets.

As discussed earlier, the lease-or-purchase question is directly associated with the capital budgeting concepts discussed in Chapter 12. In that chapter we used the net present value (NPV) technique to determine whether an asset should be acquired. If the NPV of the asset was greater than or equal to 0, the asset was expected to generate at least its required rate of return, the firm's cost of capital, and therefore should be acquired.

The analysis of the lease-or-purchase question picks up at that point. Here we consider that the value of an asset is in its use, not in its ownership. If an NPV analysis indicates that an asset should be acquired, then the next question is: Should the asset be purchased or leased? So, for this analysis, we shall assume that the decision to acquire the asset has been made; what we are considering is the method of acquisition.

Cash Flows and Discount Rate Issues

To evaluate whether an asset should be leased or purchased, three variables must be estimated: the cash flows associated with the alternatives, the time period to use in the analysis, and the discount rate. The cash flows that should be considered are:

1. The cost of the asset
2. The yearly lease payments
3. The tax savings on the yearly lease payments
4. The tax shield from the capital cost allowances that will be claimed on the asset
5. The salvage value of the asset at the end of the lease period[6]
6. The tax shield from CCA lost due to salvage
7. Any investment tax credits available on the asset
8. Taxes, maintenance, and insurance, if applicable
9. Other cash flows, depending on the negotiated lease arrangement

Also note the cash flows that are *not* included in the analysis. These are the incremental operating income associated with the asset and, for a replacement, the salvage value of the asset being replaced. These cash flows are not considered in the analysis of the lease-or-purchase question, since they are the same regardless of whether the company leases or purchases the asset. If the company buys the asset, these cash flows are received; if they lease, they are also received. As will be discussed shortly, whether the nine cash flows listed above are a cash inflow or outflow depends on whether the firm leases or purchases the asset.

For costs such as the maintenance and insurance of the asset, their treatment in the analysis is decided by the party responsible for making the payment. If the lessee makes the payments, these costs are ignored, since the amounts would be the same regardless of whether the company purchases or leases the asset. Since these types of cash flows are not incremental to the analysis, they can be safely ignored. If, however, the lessor makes one or both of the payments, these costs would be included in the quoted lease payment. Therefore, to treat both options equally, these costs must also be included in the analysis of the purchase option.

The time period to use is the term of the lease. Financial leases are generally for all or most of the expected life of the asset. Regardless, even if they were not,

6. By including the expected salvage value of the asset at the end of the lease term in the analysis, any purchase option in the lease agreement can be ignored. This is because the salvage value used in the analysis is the estimate of the fair market value of the asset at the end of the lease. Therefore, using the salvage value means the purchase option for the fair market value of the asset can be ignored.

by including the salvage value in the analysis, the value of the asset at the expiration of the lease is captured in the analysis. This approach means that the lease and purchase alternatives have the same lives, the term of the lease. Thus, any cash flows after the lease period are not relevant to the decision.

The discount rate to use to evaluate the lease-or-purchase question is also a vital part of the analysis. If the company leases, consider the situation. The firm is committed to a series of fixed payments, the lease payments must be made before any income accrues to the common shareholders, and if the lease payments are not made, the lessor can reclaim the asset. The obligations associated with a lease are the same as for long-term debt. Both types of financing affect the company's financial risks in the same manner.

Therefore, leasing should be viewed as a substitute for long-term debt. The characteristics and accounting treatment for leasing, as discussed earlier in the chapter, fully support this claim. As such, the interest rate the company would have to pay to borrow the funds required to purchase the asset is the basis for the discount rate used to evaluate the lease-or-purchase question. But since interest payments are tax-deductible, it is the firm's after-tax cost of long-term debt that is used.

Analyzing the Lease-or-Purchase Question

To illustrate the technique used to analyze the lease-or-purchase question, a problem will be used. The objective is to compare the present value of the cost of purchasing and owning the asset to the present value of the cost of leasing and using the asset. Again, the focus is on costs. The key benefit, the operating income, associated with the asset is ignored for the reasons discussed earlier. The option with the lower cost is the preferred choice.[7]

Example ▼ After a thorough capital budgeting analysis, Roberts Company, a small machine shop, has decided to acquire a new machine tool that has a cost of \$56,000, including all taxes, delivery, and installation charges. The machine tool is expected to have a useful life of ten years, after which time it is expected to have a fair market value of \$8,000. The company could buy the machine tool or arrange for a lease with Canadian Equipment Leasing (CEL). CEL indicates that they will lease the machine tool to Roberts for a ten-year period. The required lease payment is \$7,300 per year, with the first lease payment due when the lease agreement is signed. All taxes are included in the quoted payment.

The subsequent nine payments are due on the anniversary date of the lease. At the end of the lease agreement, in ten years, Roberts could purchase the machine from CEL for its fair market value. The machine tool has a CCA rate of 30 percent. Roberts Company could borrow the \$56,000 needed to purchase the machine tool at a rate of 10 percent. The company's tax rate is 40 percent. Roberts Company is required to maintain and insure the asset. Should Roberts Company buy or lease the new machine tool?

The initial question to consider here is: If Roberts enters into an agreement with CEL, will the CRA view this arrangement as a lease or a purchase? This is

7. An alternative approach is to calculate the NPV of the lease. If the NPV of the lease (NPV_L) is positive, then the company should lease the asset; if negative, buy the asset. This approach is illustrated in Section 16.5.

clearly a lease. The CRA could not use the general anti-avoidance rule and claim the arrangement results in the misuse or abuse of the provisions in the *Income Tax Act*.

The next question is: If Roberts does lease the asset, will it be considered a financial (capital) lease for accounting purposes? Referring to the four CICA conditions discussed earlier, it is clear that the CEL offer is a financial lease based on conditions 3 and 4. The lease term is for the full expected life of the asset and, as will be shown shortly, on a present value basis, the lease payments are equal to more than 90 percent of the cost of the machine tool. There is no question, this arrangement is a financial lease.

The final question to consider is: What should Roberts Company do, lease or purchase the new machine tool? If the company purchases the machine tool, what cash flows should be considered? The company will have to pay the $56,000 to the manufacturer, and will then be the owner of the asset. As the owner, the company is entitled to claim the CCA and will receive the market value of the asset at the end of its useful life. In addition, they will lose some of the previously calculated tax shield. Recall from Chapter 12 that the present value of the tax shield calculation assumes that the asset is held until it has a zero market value. If this is not the case, some of the previously calculated tax shield is lost.

www.dscp.ca/pdf/dscp-news-feb2004.pdf

To account for the time value issues associated with the question, what discount rate should be used in the analysis? As discussed earlier, leasing an asset is equivalent to using a long-term loan to purchase the asset. Therefore, the company's after-tax borrowing rate should be used. But which borrowing rate? Certainly not a short-term rate, since leasing is a long-term commitment. The ideal borrowing rate to use is the rate the company would have to pay on a loan with a term similar to that of the lease. If this were not available, the company's long-term borrowing rate would be used. Since interest payments are deductible for tax purposes, the true cost is the after-tax borrowing rate calculated as follows:

$$\text{After-tax borrowing rate} = \text{before-tax borrowing rate} \times (1 - \text{tax rate})$$

For Roberts Company, this equals:

$$\begin{aligned}\text{After-tax borrowing rate} &= 10\%(1 - 0.40)\\ &= 6\%\end{aligned}$$

The present value of the cost of purchasing the machine tool is provided in Table 16.3.

Note that in the above analysis, the cost items are positive while inflows are negatives. This is done because we are calculating the *cost* of purchasing. For most other types of analyses that we complete in finance, benefits are positive and costs negative. But again, we are considering the cost of the alternative, so the usual analysis is reversed.

Now consider the leasing alternative. If the company leases the machine tool, what cash flows should be considered? The only cost is the lease payments which, as was discussed earlier, are fully deductible for tax purposes. So it seems that the yearly after-tax cost of leasing would be calculated as follows:

$$\text{Yearly lease payments} \times (1 - \text{tax rate}) = \text{yearly after-tax lease payments}$$

So for Roberts Company the yearly after-tax lease payment would be: $7,300 × (1 − 0.40) = $4,380. The present value of the cost of leasing would be

TABLE 16.3 Roberts Company: The Present Value of the Cost of Purchasing the Machine Tool

+ Incremental cost	=	+$56,000
− Present value of tax shield from CCA[a]		
$\$56{,}000 \times \left[\frac{0.30 \times 0.40}{0.30 + 0.06}\right] \times \frac{1.03}{1.06}$	=	−$18,138
− Present value of salvage		
$8,000 × *PVIF* (6%, 10 per)	=	−$ 4,467
+ Present value of tax shield lost due to salvage[a]		
$\$4{,}467 \times \left[\frac{0.30 \times 0.40}{0.30 + 0.06}\right]$	=	+$ 1,489
Present value of the cost of purchasing the asset	=	$34,884

[a]See Chapter 12 for a discussion of the process used to calculate the present value of the tax shield and the present value of the tax shield lost due to salvage.

calculated by recognizing that the yearly after-tax lease payments are an annuity, the discount rate is the after-tax cost of debt, and the number of periods is the term of the lease.

But there is a problem with this analysis. The lease payments are due at the beginning of the year. The first lease payment is due when the lease agreement between the lessor and the lessee is signed. This is at time 0. But the tax savings associated with the lease payments are received only when the company files their taxes. The usual assumption made in this situation is that the company receives the tax savings one year after they make the payment, at the end of the year. So we have the situation depicted in Figure 16.1, where LP is the lease payment and TS-LP is the tax savings associated with the relevant lease payment.

FIGURE 16.1
The Cash Flows Associated with Leasing

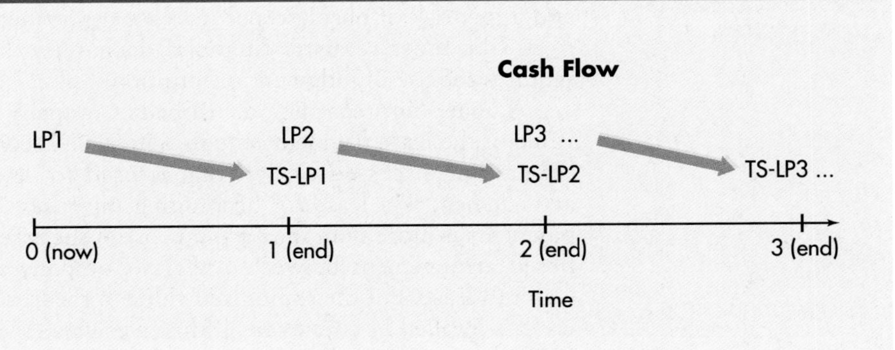

TABLE 16.4 **Roberts Company: The Present Value of the Cost of Leasing the Machine Tool**

+ Present value of the lease payments[a]		
$7,300 + [$7,300 × *PVIFa* (6%, 9 years)] =		
$7,300 + $49,652	=	+$56,952
− Present value of the tax shield on the lease payments		
$7,300 × (0.40) × *PVIFa* (6%, 10 years) =		
$2,920 × *PVIFa* (6%, 10 years)	=	−$21,491
Present value of the cost of leasing	=	$35,461[b]

[a]As discussed, this is an annuity due. See Chapter 6 for a refresher on calculating the present value of an annuity due. If the cash outflow associated with the lease payment and the cash inflow associated with the tax savings from the lease payment occur at the same time, the single calculations shown earlier could be used.

[b]Again, in this analysis, the cash outflow is treated as a positive and the cash inflow a negative, since we are calculating the cost of leasing.

There is a one-year lag between the lease payment and the tax shield on the lease payment. The lease payments are an annuity due, the tax savings on the lease payments an ordinary annuity. Therefore, the present value of the cost of leasing the machine tool is provided in Table 16.4.

The present value of the cost of leasing is greater than the present value of the cost of purchasing. It will cost more to lease than purchase. The difference in the two costs, on a present value basis, is $577. Clearly, it makes more financial sense for Roberts Company to purchase the machine tool. This is the best alternative to acquire the use of this valuable asset.

As will be discussed in more detail in Section 16.6, the lower cost of one alternative over the other results from factors such as the differing tax brackets of the lessor and lessee, differing tax treatments of the cash flows associated with leasing and purchasing, and differing risks and borrowing costs for the lessor and lessee. Therefore, when considering whether to lease or purchase an asset, a firm will find that inexpensive borrowing opportunities, high required lessor returns, and a low risk of obsolescence increase the attractiveness of purchasing. In addition, like most realistic financial decisions, the lease-or-purchase decision requires the use of judgment or intuition.

A final point regarding the Roberts Company example. Note that the present value of the lease payments equals $56,952. Reconsider condition 4 of the CICA regulation, discussed earlier, that is used to determine whether a contractual arrangement is a lease for accounting purposes. The present value of the lease payments is more than the original cost of the asset. As indicated earlier, the proposed arrangement between Roberts Company and CEL is clearly a financial (capital) lease. But the capitalized value of the lease would be calculated using the lessor's implied discount rate, if this rate were less than 6 percent. If not, the capitalized value on the balance sheet would be capped at $56,000.

16.1 **IN PRACTICE**

Leasing: The New Way to Acquire Assets?

Many businesses, large and small, are opting to lease rather than purchase and finance equipment. As previously discussed, the leasing industry in Canada is large and rapidly growing. When opening a new business, an owner may choose to lease the equipment and the big-ticket items. When expanding, it may be more attractive to arrange a lease through a leasing company rather than try to negotiate a long-term loan with a bank. When buying an expensive, specialized piece of equipment, the manufacturer may have their own leasing subsidiary that offers favourable terms to the acquiring company, thus presenting an attractive alternative to issuing long-term debt in the capital market.

While determining which machine will generate the best productivity improvement or additional sales can be difficult, finding the best way to pay for it is at least as important to the bottom line. Is leasing or buying the best way to finance equipment for expansion? While there is no universal answer to that question, it's important to avoid jumping into a deal without considering what each strategy can bring to your business. Ownership gives you clear title to the asset when it's paid, and CCA is available at rates that are likely to be faster than the decline in the value of the new equipment over the years. The primary disadvantage of borrowing for new equipment is that the additional leverage can crimp your bottom line, especially if accelerated CCA leaves the asset with a much lower value on the books than the residual amount still owing.

Leasing takes care of many of these problems, since borrowing is not required. The leasing company owns the equipment, with payments often structured to provide a reasonable buyout at the end of the lease period. And leases preserve cash flow, since they are tax-deductible. But a firm's ability to negotiate a lease rate with a leasing company, as with a loan from a bank, depends on the ability to demonstrate that the business is a low-risk proposition. In-house leasing programs offered by equipment manufacturers and distributors, however, are often better tuned to the needs of lessees and can add options such as an early "out" if the business is trading up.

Manufacturing companies are among the largest users of equipment lease financing, although service firms such as restaurants, hotels, ski resorts, and microbreweries find it attractive as well. Leasing is particularly appealing to small companies, because their bankers may have tight credit standards on more traditional financing alternatives. When credit markets are tight, small business owners find leasing an attractive alternative since they do not have to buy equipment, which frees up cash for other purposes. In addition to preserving cash, small business owners like being able to leave maintenance to the lessor who owns the equipment.

According to an Equipment Leasing Association survey, the top reasons why small and medium-sized businesses choose to lease rather than buy equipment are to preserve cash flow (cited by 35%), to lock in financing costs (17%), convenience and flexibility of leasing (13%), tax advantages (13%), inclusion of maintenance costs (13%), and ability to afford state-of-the-art technology (9%). With a lease, the company's payments are set at the beginning of the lease term for the life of the lease, so the company is not affected by changes in interest rates. Companies may be able to structure variable payment terms as well, to accommodate seasonal cash flow patterns, and they may also be able to upgrade equipment during the lease term.

Before jumping into lease financing, however, a company must carefully consider all of the factors—the purchase price, the CCA rate, the market value of the asset at the end of the lease, the down payment required, the monthly payments, the responsibilities for maintenance, and insurance for the lease—and they must know their tax rate and the cost of borrowing funds for the long term. Then they should calculate the net present value (NPV) of the lease to determine if leasing or purchasing is the better choice.

SOURCES: Canadian Finance and Leasing Association, 2004–2005 annual report, available at www.cfla-acfl.ca; Mark Henricks, "To Say the Leased," *Entrepreneur*, February 2002; "Report Sees the Future of the Equipment Leasing and Financing Industry," *Business Wire*, April 5, 2001; Jim Anderton, "Financing Finesse: Financing for New Equipment Doesn't Have to Be Nerve-Wracking If You're Prepared," *Service Station & Garage Management* 33(9) (September 2003).

? Review Questions

16–16 In analyzing the lease-or-purchase question, why are borrowing funds, selling shares, and using available liquid resources considered equivalent forms of financing?
16–17 Describe the process involved in analyzing the lease-or-purchase question. How are capital budgeting methods applied in this process?
16–18 In analyzing the lease-or-purchase question, which cash flows are included and which are not, and why?
16–19 What are the three questions to consider when analyzing the lease-or-purchase question?
16–20 What cash flows are included in calculating the present value of the cost of purchasing? In calculating the present value of the cost of leasing?
16–21 What discount rate is used when analyzing the lease-or-purchase question? Why is this rate used?
16–22 What issue is associated with the lease payments and the tax shield from the lease payments in the analysis? What is done to deal with this problem?

16.5 Extending the Analysis of the Lease-or-Purchase Question

There is another approach that can be used to make the lease-or-purchase decision, and a number of other cash flows that might be considered in the analysis. This section considers six additional items. In addition, we shall consider the commonly cited advantages and disadvantages of leasing from the lessee's perspective.

Discount Rate to Use for Salvage

Note that in the original analysis, the rate used to discount all of the cash flows was the after-tax cost of debt. As explained, this was because leasing is a substitute for debt and all cash flows are known with certainty. But does this comment apply to all of the cash flows? Consider the list back on page 864. The comment does apply to the purchase price, investment tax credit, tax shield from CCA, lease payments and taxes, maintenance, and insurance. Each of these cash flows is known with certainty; there is no risk of them changing. Which ones are not certain?

The cash flow that is estimated is the salvage value. In the Roberts Company example, the assumption was that the machine tool would be worth $8,000 at the end of its useful life. If after ten years it turns out that it is actually worth this amount, it makes sense to purchase. But what happens if after ten years the tool is actually only worth $1,000? Then, the original decision to purchase may have been wrong.

If the tool is only worth $1,000, the present value of the salvage falls to $558, and the present value of the tax shield lost due to salvage to $186. Now, the present value of the cost of purchasing is $37,490 and the net present value of the lease is +$2,029. The machine tool should have been leased; if it had been purchased, the wrong decision was made.

This analysis illustrates that there is risk associated with the estimate of the salvage value. To reflect this risk, as we saw in Chapters 7 and 13, it makes good financial sense to use a higher rate to discount this risky cash flow. But what rate should be used? Recall from Chapters 9 and 12 that the cost of capital reflects the overall risk of the company. Since salvage is a risky item, it seems reasonable that the lessee's cost of capital should be used to discount the salvage. It might also be argued that another discount rate could be used, but that would be an arbitrary decision. There are good theoretical and practical reasons for using the cost of capital for this purpose.

A follow-up issue is what discount rate should be used in calculating the present value of the tax shield lost due to salvage. Consider that the risk of the salvage has been reflected in the present value of the salvage calculation; there is no need to consider it again. Therefore, the lessee's after-tax cost of debt can still be used for the calculation.

Example For the Roberts Company example, assume the company's cost of capital is 12 percent. The impact the higher discount rate has on the purchase alternative is shown in Table 16.5.

Now the cost of purchasing is greater than the $35,461 cost of leasing; the difference between the two costs on a present value basis is $684 in favour of leasing. Clearly, using a higher discount rate to reflect the greater risk associated with the estimated salvage can have a significant impact on the decision of whether to lease or purchase an asset.

From this point on we will assume that the lessee's cost of capital will be used to discount the estimated salvage value.

Calculating the NPV of the Lease

Rather than calculating the present value of the cost of purchasing and leasing separately, the net present value of the leasing alternative can be considered in a

TABLE 16.5 Roberts Company: The Present Value of the Cost of Purchasing the Machine Tool with the Cost of Capital Used for Salvage

+ Incremental cost	=	+$56,000
− Present value of tax shield from CCA		
$\$56{,}000 \times \left[\frac{0.30 \times 0.40}{0.30 + 0.06}\right] \times \frac{1.03}{1.06}$	=	−$18,138
− Present value of salvage		
$8,000 × *PVIF* (12%, 10 per)	=	−$ 2,576
+ Present value of tax shield lost due to salvage		
$\$2{,}576 \times \left[\frac{0.30 \times 0.40}{0.30 + 0.06}\right]$	=	+$ 859
Present value of the cost of purchasing the asset	=	$36,145

single analysis. This is equivalent to the NPV process discussed in Chapter 12. To calculate the net present value of the lease (NPV_L), consider how each of the cash flows would be treated if the company leased the asset. If the company leases the asset, they do not have to pay the purchase price, but, since they are not the owners, they do not receive the tax shield on the CCA or the salvage. Also, they do not lose the tax shield due to the salvage. The company will have to make the lease payments (an annuity due), but will receive the tax shield on the lease payments (an ordinary annuity). Combining these various components, and using the correct signs, Table 16.6 calculates the NPV of the lease for Roberts Company.

The NPV of the lease is positive, +$684, meaning Roberts Company should lease and not purchase the new machine tool. Notice that this is exactly the same result calculated in the analysis in the previous section. This is because the net present value of the lease process simply compares the present value of the cost of purchasing and leasing in a single analysis. The two methods will always result in the same answer and decision, since exactly the same cash flows are considered.

Some instructors or students may wish to use this alternative approach when analyzing the lease-or-purchase question as it is consistent with the net present value approach used in capital budgeting. Also note that instead of calculating the net present value of the lease, we could have calculated the net present value of the purchase (NPV_P) by simply reversing the signs of each of the cash flows. If this were done, the NPV of purchasing would be −$684.

TABLE 16.6 Roberts Company: The Net Present Value of the Lease of the Machine Tool

NPV_L =	Incremental cost	=	+$56,000
	− Present value of tax shield from CCA		
	$\$56{,}000 \times \left[\frac{0.30 \times 0.40}{0.30 + 0.06}\right] \times \frac{1.03}{1.06}$	=	−$18,138
	− Present value of salvage		
	$8,000 × *PVIF* (12%, 10 per)	=	−$ 2,576
	+ Present value of tax shield lost due to salvage[a]		
	$\$2{,}576 \times \left[\frac{0.30 \times 0.40}{0.30 + 0.06}\right]$	=	+$ 859
	− Present value of the lease payments		
	$7,300 + [$7,300 × *PVIFa* (6%, 9 years)] =		
	$7,300 + $49,652	=	−$56,952
	+ Present value of the tax shield on the lease payments		
	$7,300 × (0.40) × *PVIFa* (6%, 10 years) =		
	$2,920 × *PVIFa* (6%, 10 years)	=	+$21,491
NPV_L		=	+$ 684

Investment Tax Credit

As discussed in Chapter 12, the investment tax credit (ITC) is an incentive for businesses in the Atlantic provinces and in the Gaspé region of Quebec to purchase fixed assets such as buildings, machinery, and equipment. The ITC rate for assets used in manufacturing and processing, mining, oil and gas, logging, farming, or fishing is 10 percent. This rate is applied to the total cost of the qualifying expenditure to determine the dollar amount of ITC.

The benefit of the ITC is that the full amount can be deducted from federal taxes payable. A minor drawback with the ITC is that the dollar amount of ITC must be deducted from the undepreciated capital cost (UCC) of the asset for CCA purposes. Therefore, a company can only claim CCA on the difference between the UCC and the ITC. The owner of the asset is entitled to the ITC so, in the lease-or-purchase analysis, the ITC is reflected as a benefit in the purchase alternative. If a company leases an asset that qualifies for the ITC, the lessor receives the ITC.

Example ▼ For the Roberts Company example, assume Roberts is located in Nova Scotia and that the company is a manufacturer. If so, then the machine tool purchased qualifies for a 10 percent ITC. The impact the ITC has on the purchase alternative is shown in Table 16.7.

Now the cost of purchasing is much less than the cost of leasing. The net present value of the lease is a very significant −\$2,786. Clearly, when assets purchased by companies qualify for the ITC, the decision is skewed toward purchasing, unless the lessor reduces the lease payment in recognition of the ITC. ▲

TABLE 16.7 Roberts Company: The Present Value of the Cost of Purchasing the Machine Tool with the ITC Included

+ Incremental cost	=	+\$56,000
− Present value of ITC		
\$56,000 (10%) × *PVIF* (6%, 1 year)	=	−\$ 5,283
− Present value of tax shield from CCA		
$(\$56{,}000 - \$5{,}600) \times \left[\dfrac{0.30 \times 0.40}{0.30 + 0.06}\right] \times \dfrac{1.03}{1.06}$	=	−\$16,325
− Present value of salvage		
\$8,000 × *PVIF* (12%, 10 per)	=	−\$ 2,576
+ Present value of tax shield lost due to salvage		
$\$2{,}576 \times \left[\dfrac{0.30 \times 0.40}{0.30 + 0.06}\right]$	=	+\$ 859
Present value of the cost of purchasing the asset	=	\$32,675

Lease Rate Includes Maintenance and Insurance

For some leases, the lessor may wish to maintain and insure the asset. This may be the case for very specialized types of equipment where the lessee may not have the staff available to service the equipment, or where insurance is difficult to negotiate. If this were the situation, how would this be treated in the analysis of the lease-or-purchase decision?

Example Assume that for the Roberts Company example, the $7,300 lease payment included the maintenance and insurance on the machine tool. Then, to correctly analyze the lease and purchase options, the cost of these two items must be factored into the analysis of the purchase alternative. Since these two costs are included in the cost of the lease, they must also be included in the cost of purchasing. Assume that Roberts' operations manager estimates that the cost to maintain the machine tool would be, on average, $280 per year while the extra insurance cost would be $80 per year. Since insurance payments are made at the beginning of the year, but maintenance is performed during the year (on average at the end of the year), and that these are both tax-deductible expenses, the present value of the costs is:

After-tax maintenance cost:	$280 (1 − 0.40) × *PVIFa* (6%, 10 years)	=	$1,237
+ Cost of the insurance:	$80 + $80 × *PVIFa* (6%, 9 years)	=	+$ 624
− Tax savings on insurance:	$80 (0.40) × *PVIFa* (6%, 10 years)	=	−$ 236
Total present value of the after-tax costs		=	$1,625

This amount is added to the previously calculated cost of purchasing of $36,145 (see Table 16.5, so the cost of purchasing the machine tool is $37,770 ($36,145 + $1,625). This is greater than the $35,461 cost of leasing; the net present value of the lease is +$2,309. Now, it is clearly better for Roberts Company to lease the machine tool.

Damage Deposit

Some leases require the lessee to pay a damage deposit to the lessor. This is a form of insurance for the lessor in case the lessee damages or does not correctly maintain the equipment. The damage deposit is made when the lease is initially signed (time 0), and returned at the end of the lease assuming the asset is returned in acceptable condition. The damage deposit is not tax-deductible when it is paid, since it is not an expense. But, if the lessor keeps the deposit at the end of the lease, it would become an expense for the lessee.

Example Assume that for the Roberts Company example, CEL required a $2,000 damage deposit on the date the lease contract was signed. Roberts has every intention to adequately maintain the machine tool, so they expect to receive the $2,000 back at the end of the ten-year lease period. The damage deposit is associated with the leasing alternative, so the cost of leasing ($35,461) is affected as follows:

Damage deposit	−$ 2,000
Return damage deposit: $2,000 × *PVIF* (6%, 10 per)	$ 1,117
Present value of the cost of the damage deposit	$ 883

Essentially, the cost of the damage deposit is the lost opportunity of being able to use the $2,000 for the ten-year term of the lease. This concept is very similar to the cost of net working capital that we saw in capital budgeting. Now the cost of leasing is $36,344 ($35,461 + $883), which is greater than the $36,145 cost of purchasing, so the net present value of the lease is −$199. This alters the initial decision; now purchasing the machine tool is the better alternative.

Recapture and Terminal Loss

To this point, the analysis of the lease-or-purchase question assumes that the company evaluating the lease continues to operate with assets in the CCA asset class at the end of the lease. But what happens if that is the only asset in the class? As we saw in Chapters 2 and 12, in such a case the sale of the only asset in the class will affect the calculation of the tax shield lost, and it will trigger either a recapture or a terminal loss. This will occur because the undepreciated capital cost (UCC) of the asset at the end of its useful life (its tax value) will almost certainly not be the asset's fair market value.

If the asset's tax value is greater than its market value at the end of its useful life, we have a terminal loss. Since a terminal loss is deductible for tax purposes, in the lease-or-purchase analysis, this will be a benefit of purchasing. The benefit will be the present value of the tax shield on the terminal loss (terminal loss × tax rate). If the asset's tax value is less than its market value at the end of its useful life, we have a recapture. Since a recapture is considered income for tax purposes, in the lease-or-purchase analysis, this will be a cost of purchasing. The cost will be the present value of the additional tax owing on the recapture (recapture × tax rate). At this time, you may wish to review the material concerning this topic in Chapter 2.

Example For the Roberts Company example, we have seen that the CCA rate on the $56,000 asset is 30 percent, and that the expected fair market value of the asset at the end of its ten-year life is $8,000. If it is assumed that this is the only asset in the class, what will happen when it is sold at the end of year 10?[8] To answer this, first we have to calculate the tax value of the asset at the end of year 10. We can calculate the tax value of the machine tool at this time by using Equation 2.4 in Chapter 2, which is provided below as Equation 16.1, where d is the CCA rate:

$$\text{UCC (tax value)}_{\text{Beg Yr } N} = \text{UCC} \times (1 - d/2) \times (1 - d)^{N-2} \qquad (16.1)$$

For Roberts Company, we must calculate the tax value as of the beginning of year 10 (before the CCA for year 10 was claimed).

$$\begin{aligned}\text{UCC (tax value)}_{\text{Beg Yr 10}} &= \$56{,}000 \times (1 - 0.30/2) \times (1 - 0.30)^{10-2}\\ &= \$56{,}000 \times 0.85 \times 0.05764801\\ &= \$2{,}744.05 = \$2{,}744 \text{ (rounded)}\end{aligned}$$

So the tax value of the machine tool, before CCA is claimed in year 10, is $2,744, while its fair market value is expected to be $8,000. To determine the impact of closing out the asset class, we will use the same process we discussed in

8. Here we are assuming that the CCA for the final year will not be claimed since the asset will be sold at the end of year 10. The CCA for year 10 will be reflected in the recapture or terminal loss.

Chapters 2 and 12. First, the tax shield lost on the asset will be affected. Recall that the tax shield is lost, since we are not satisfying the assumption that the asset will be held until it has a zero value. In the case where the asset class is being closed out, the tax shield lost is based on the tax value of the asset, not the market value. (This is the only time this is done.) In addition, there will be a recapture or terminal loss. By using the same process as provided in Chapter 2 we see:

UCC_{BS}	\$2,744	
Asset sold		
Original cost	\$56,000	No capital gain
Proceeds	\$8,000	
UCC_{AS}	–\$5,256	Recapture

By the end of year 10, Roberts Company would have claimed \$53,256 (\$56,000 – \$2,744) of CCA on the machine tool. But, given the fair market value, the company should have claimed \$48,000 (\$56,000 – \$8,000) of CCA. This implies that the company claimed "too much" CCA and, as of the end of year 10, has recaptured previously deducted CCA. The recaptured amount is \$5,256 (\$8,000 – \$2,744). So, when the asset class is closed out, the expected salvage value is split into two parts: tax shield lost and a recapture (or terminal loss). In this case, the impact of the \$8,000 salvage value is split between tax shield lost (based on \$2,744) and a recapture (\$5,256) that is income for tax purposes. The impact is that the cost of purchasing the asset for Roberts Company will increase as shown in Table 16.8.

TABLE 16.8 Roberts Company: The Present Value of the Cost of Purchasing the Machine Tool Assuming the Asset Class Is Closed

+ Incremental cost	=	+\$56,000
– Present value of tax shield from CCA		
$\$56{,}000 \times \left[\dfrac{0.30 \times 0.40}{0.30 + 0.06}\right] \times \dfrac{1.03}{1.06}$	=	–\$18,138
– Present value of salvage		
\$8,000 × *PVIF* (12%, 10 per)	=	–\$ 2,576
+ Present value of tax shield lost due to UCC[a]		
$\$2{,}744 \times PVIF\,(6\%, 10\text{ per}) \times \left[\dfrac{0.30 \times 0.40}{0.30 + 0.06}\right]$	=	+\$ 511
+ Present value of the tax on recapture[a]		
\$5,256 × (0.40) × *PVIF* (6%, 10 per)	=	+\$ 1,174
Present value of the cost of purchasing the asset	=	\$36,971

[a] When the asset class is expected to be closed at the end of the asset's life, the impact of the salvage value on the analysis is split into two parts: tax shield lost and a recapture (or terminal loss). The tax shield lost is based on the tax value of the asset, not the market value. It could be argued that the tax shield lost due to the UCC and the tax on recapture should be discounted with the firm's cost of capital. We will continue to use the after-tax cost of debt.

Now the \$36,971 cost of purchasing is significantly greater than the \$35,461 cost of leasing; the NPV of the lease is +\$1,510. Clearly, whether the asset class will continue to hold assets can have an impact on the decision of whether to lease or purchase an asset.

Spreadsheet Application 16.1 provides a template that can be used to calculate the cost of purchasing and leasing an asset, and the NPV of the lease.

16.1 SPREADSHEET APPLICATION

Microsoft Excel - Spreadsheet Application 16-1.xls

	A	B	C	D
1				
2	**Should a Company Lease or Purchase an Asset?**			
3				
4	**Variable**	**Value**		
5	Capital cost	\$265,000		
6	ITC rate (if applicable)	0.00%		
7	Lease payment	\$31,978		
8	CCA rate	25.00%		
9	Salvage value	\$13,000		
10	Length of lease (years)	15		
11	Borrowing rate	8.80%		
12	Cost of capital	13.20%		
13	Tax rate	35.00%		
14	After-tax borrowing rate	5.72%		
15				
16				
17	**Present Value of the Cost of Purchasing**			**Formulas**
18	Cost of asset	\$265,000	←	=B\$5
19	Present value of ITC	\$0	←	=PV(B\$14,1,0,(+B\$5*B\$6))
20	Tax shield on CCA	-\$73,438	←	=-B\$5*(1-B\$6)*(B\$8*B\$13)/(B\$8+B\$14)*(1+(0.5*B\$14))/(1+B\$14)
21	Present value of salvage	-\$2,024	←	=PV(B\$12,B\$10,0,B\$9)
22	Tax shield lost due to salvage	\$577	←	=-B\$21*B\$8*B\$13/(B\$8+B\$14)
23	Present value of the cost of purchasing	\$190,114	←	=SUM(B18:B22)
24				
25	**Present Value of the Cost of Leasing**			
26	Present value of lease payments	\$334,435	←	=PV(B\$14,B\$10,-B\$7,0,1)
27	Tax shield on lease payments	-\$110,719	←	=PV(B\$14,B\$10,(B\$7*B\$13))
28	Present value of the cost of leasing	\$223,716	←	=SUM(B26:B27)
29				
30	***Solution: The cost of purchasing is less,***			***ıase.***
31				
32	**Net Present Value of Lease**			
33	Cost of asset	\$265,000	←	=B\$5
34	Present value of ITC	\$0	←	=PV(B\$14,1,0,(+B\$5*B\$6))
35	Tax shield on CCA	-\$73,438	←	=-B\$5*(1-B\$6)*(B\$8*B\$13)/(B\$8+B\$14)*(1+(0.5*B\$14))/(1+B\$14)
36	Present value of salvage	-\$2,024	←	=PV(B\$12,B\$10,0,B\$9)
37	Tax shield lost due to salvage	\$577	←	=-B\$21*B\$8*B\$13/(B\$8+B\$14)
38	Present value of lease payments	-\$334,435	←	=PV(B\$14,B10,B7,0,1)
39	Tax shield on lease payments	\$110,719	←	=PV(B14,B10,(-B7*B13))
40	NPV of lease	-\$33,602	←	=SUM(B33:B39)
41				
42	***Solution: The NPV of the lease is negative, therefore purchase.***			
43				

SA 16-1

Ready NUM

Advantages and Disadvantages of Leasing

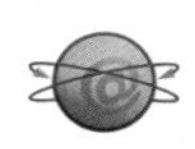

www.chooseleasing.org
www.allbusiness.com/articles/StartingBusiness/2540-25-1792.html

Leasing has a number of commonly cited advantages and disadvantages that should be considered when making a lease-or-purchase decision. It is not unusual for a number of them to apply in a given situation. More information regarding the advantages and disadvantages of leasing is available on the Web.

Advantages

There are nine commonly cited advantages of leasing as follows:

1. The total cost of leasing may be less than the total cost of owning due to differences in taxation and costs of financing. Lessors with high tax rates and low costs of financing may offer lease rates that are cheaper than the cost of buying for companies with low tax rates and high costs of financing. Often, this is the main reason small firms lease assets.
2. In a lease arrangement, the lessee may avoid the cost of obsolescence. This can occur if the lessor fails to accurately anticipate obsolescence and estimates a higher fair market value for the asset than is actually received. If this occurs, the lease payment charged will be too low. In essence, the lessor assumes the risk of the salvage value and this is an advantage for the lessee. This is especially true in the case of leases that have relatively short lives.
3. Leasing usually has fewer restrictive covenants than long-term debt. As was discussed in Chapter 5, long-term loan agreements often require the borrower to maintain certain minimum ratio or working capital positions, may prohibit the sale of assets, may restrict the payment of dividends, may constrain subsequent borrowing, or may contain numerous other conditions. Lease agreements do not usually have as many restrictive conditions imposed regarding the operation of the company.
4. In the case of low-cost assets that are frequently acquired, leasing—especially operating leases—may provide the firm with needed financing flexibility. That is, the firm does not have to arrange for small amounts of financing on a regular basis in order to acquire these assets.
5. A related advantage is that some firms, particularly small ones, find it difficult to raise debt financing due to risk concerns or the conditions imposed by other debt financing. These may not be major concerns for a lease if the lessor feels the company can generate the cash flows necessary to service the lease.
6. Sale-leaseback arrangements may permit the firm to increase its liquidity by converting an existing asset into cash, which can then be used as working capital. This can be advantageous for a firm short of working capital or in a liquidity bind. But, as discussed earlier, the firm is simply swapping higher long-term cash balances for higher short-term cash balances.
7. Leasing allows the lessee, in effect, to amortize land, which is not allowed if the land were purchased. A company leasing a plant or office space is essentially paying for the use of the land as part of the lease payment. If the leased asset was owned by the lessee, CCA could only be claimed on the actual building, not the land. By deducting the total lease payment as an expense for tax purposes, the effect is the same as if the firm had purchased the land and then claimed CCA on it. But since land often increases in value over

time, by leasing land the lessee may lose the opportunity for a capital gain on the purchase of the land.

8. Leasing provides 100 percent financing. Most loan agreements for the purchase of fixed assets require the borrower to pay a portion of the purchase price as a down payment. As a result, the borrower is able to borrow, at most, 90 to 95 percent of the purchase price of the asset. But, since leases require the first payment in advance, less than 100 percent of the cost of the asset is actually secured.
9. As we saw in Chapter 5, a company will often pledge the asset purchased with the loan as security for the loan. In addition, the lender may require additional security. This can be provided as a floating charge on all assets that allows the lender to claim all assets necessary to recoup the remaining principal on the loan in case the company defaults. With a lease, the leased asset is the only security pledged.

Disadvantages

There are four commonly cited disadvantages of leasing as follows:

1. With a financial lease, if the leased asset becomes obsolete, the lessee must still make lease payments over the remaining term of the lease. This is true even if the asset is unusable.
2. Unlike a loan, a lease does not have a stated interest cost. Thus, the lessor may use a high rate of return to calculate the required lease payment. If so, the lessee may be better off borrowing to purchase the asset. In this situation, the lessee should be able to estimate the lessor's rate of return since all the dollar amounts used in setting the lease payment will be known.
3. At the end of the term of the lease agreement, the salvage value of an asset, if any, is realized by the lessor. If the lessee purchases the asset, they will receive the salvage value. Of course, the impact of the expected salvage value should be reflected in lower lease payments, if the lessor used an accurate estimate for the salvage value in the initial analysis.
4. With a lease, the lessee is generally prohibited from making improvements on the leased asset without the approval of the lessor. If the asset was owned outright, this difficulty would not arise. Of course, lessors generally encourage leasehold improvements when they are expected to enhance the asset's salvage value.

? Review Questions

16–23 Describe the NPV approach to analyzing the lease-or-purchase question. What is the benefit of using this approach?

16–24 If the asset being evaluated qualifies for an investment tax credit, how does this impact the lease-or-purchase analysis?

16–25 What is unique about the treatment of the salvage value in the lease-or-purchase analysis?

16–26 If the quoted lease rate includes maintenance and insurance costs, how does this impact the lease-or-purchase analysis?

16–27 How is a damage deposit included in the analysis of the lease-or-purchase question? How is the cost of the damage deposit similar to the cost of net working capital in the capital budgeting analysis?

16–28 Discuss how closing out the asset class at the end of the lease term impacts the lease-or-purchase analysis.

16–29 Why might the total cost of leasing be less than the total cost of purchasing and owning?

16–30 List and discuss the commonly cited advantages and disadvantages that should be considered when making the lease-or-purchase decision.

16.6 Leasing from the Lessor's Perspective

As we saw in the original Roberts Company example, the cost of leasing the asset was higher than the cost of purchasing; the net present value of the lease (NPV_L) was negative. This implies that the lessee would lose financially from the lease, and the lessor benefit. In other words, the NPV of the lease from the lessor's perspective would be positive. This makes perfect sense. The lessor is going to set a lease rate that results in the leasing arrangement being beneficial to the company.

To illustrate, reconsider the Roberts Company example. When Canadian Equipment Leasing (CEL) set the lease rate of $7,300 per year for ten years, that would have been done in the expectation that the company would financially benefit from the arrangement. Table 16.9 provides an NPV of the lease analysis from CEL's perspective.[9] Here we assume that CEL has the same discount rate and tax rate as Roberts Company. As a result, the analysis is almost identical to the initial one completed for Roberts shown on pages 866–868. The cash flows associated with leasing from the lessor's perspective are the same as the lessee's, only the signs of the cash flows differ—they are opposite. As a result, the NPV of the lease analysis for CEL is $577, the opposite of what it was for the Roberts Company example.[10]

So it appears we have a paradox. If the lessor always benefits on a lease deal, doesn't the lessee always lose? If the lessee benefited, wouldn't the lessor lose? And, if this is the case, why would leasing occur at all, since it seems to be a zero-sum game? But, as we have already seen, billions of dollars of new leases are negotiated every year in Canada; leasing is a huge business. Since businesses do not freely enter into contracts on which they *know* they will lose money, somehow both parties must benefit from leasing. So there must be a resolution to the paradox.

Reconsider the above example. Here we assumed that both the lessor and lessee have the same tax and discount rate. In such circumstances, leasing is a zero-sum game—one party will win, one will lose—and leasing would not occur. But since a great deal of leasing does occur, the reason it occurs must be because of differences in tax and/or discount rates between lessees and lessors. These issues are discussed below.

www.gfl.ca/en/fournisseur.html

9. When we analyze the lease from the lessor's perspective, we will use the NPV of the lease process due to the types of analyses that we will be completing. This will become clear as we proceed.

10. In addition, note that when the lessor and lessee have the same discount and tax rates, the NPV of the lease from the lessor's perspective is the same as the NPV of purchasing from the lessee's perspective.

TABLE 16.9 The Net Present Value of the Roberts Company Lease from CEL's Perspective

NPV_L	= − Incremental cost	=	−\$56,000
	+ Present value of tax shield from CCA[a]		
	$\$56{,}000 \times \left[\dfrac{0.30 \times 0.40}{0.30 + 0.06}\right] \times \dfrac{1.03}{1.06}$	=	+\$18,138
	+ Present value of salvage		
	\$8,000 × *PVIF* (6%, 10 per)	=	+\$ 4,467
	− Present value of tax shield lost due to salvage		
	$\$4{,}467 \times \left[\dfrac{0.30 \times 0.40}{0.30 + 0.06}\right]$	=	−\$ 1,489
	+ Present value of the lease payments		
	\$7,300 + [\$7,300 × *PVIFa* (6%, 9 years)] =		
	\$7,300 + \$49,652	=	+\$56,952
	− Present value of tax shield on the lease payments		
	\$7,300 × (0.40) × *PVIFa* (6%, 10 years) =		
	\$2,920 × PVIFa (6%, 10 years)	=	−\$21,491
NPV_L		=	+\$ 577

[a]The Canada Revenue Agency (CRA) rules governing lease arrangement also affect the use of the CCA deduction by lessors. As we saw earlier, the CRA can rule that a lease contract is not a lease. If a lease arrangement truly exists, however, CRA regulations only allow the lessor to use the CCA deduction to reduce leasing income. CCA cannot be used to reduce other types of income earned by the lessor. Normally, this is not a major issue for lessors.

Discount Rates

As we have already seen, to analyze a lease from the lessee's perspective, the after-tax cost of debt is used. This is because leasing is simply a substitute for debt. For the lessor, however, leasing is their business. Purchasing and leasing assets is what they do, so the lease analysis is a capital budgeting analysis. Therefore, the lessor would have to use their cost of capital when setting lease rates. As we saw in Chapter 9, a company's after-tax cost of debt is lower than their cost of capital (assuming equity financing is used). If so, then wouldn't the lease rate charged by the lessor always be so high as to make the NPV of the lease for the lessee always negative?

That would seem to be the case but, as with financial institutions, leasing companies have capital structures that are usually heavily weighted to debt. In addition, they are low-risk companies, so their before-tax cost of debt is low. Also, as will be discussed next, these companies have high tax rates. So their after-tax cost of debt is very low. Finally, the small portion of equity used in the capital structure doesn't have a high cost, since the risk of the leasing company is not high. Therefore, it is very likely that the lessor's cost of capital will be lower than the lessee's after-tax cost of debt. This is particularly the case if the lessee is a small company. Small companies are riskier with higher borrowing rates, low tax rates, and thus higher after-tax costs of debt.

With different discount rates, both the lessor and lessee can financially benefit from a lease.

Tax Rates

Since lessors are often an arm of large financial or manufacturing institutions, their tax rates are usually quite high. This means the tax shield benefits from CCA are very valuable to the lessor. If the lessee has a lower tax rate, the tax shield is less valuable. In addition, since CCA is an accelerated tax deduction, more of the deduction is received earlier in the asset's life. Combine the larger, earlier cash flows with a low discount rate, and the tax shield becomes very valuable on a present value basis. This combination will result in the tax shield on CCA being more valuable for the lessor, meaning that the lessor can charge a lower lease payment.

Example ▼ A company with a 20 percent tax rate is planning to acquire a $50,000 asset that has a 30 percent CCA rate. They may purchase or lease the asset. Their cost of borrowing is 8 percent. The prospective lessor has a 45 percent tax rate and a 6.4 percent cost of capital. What is the value of the tax shield on the CCA to the prospective lessee and lessor?

Present value of tax shield from CCA for lessee:

$$\$50{,}000 \times \left[\frac{0.30 \times 0.20}{0.30 + 0.064}\right] \times \frac{1.032}{1.064} = +\$7{,}994$$

Present value of tax shield from CCA for lessor:

$$\$50{,}000 \times \left[\frac{0.30 \times 0.45}{0.30 + 0.064}\right] \times \frac{1.032}{1.064} = +\$17{,}986$$

Note that the discount rates used for the lessor and lessee in this example are the same. Even though, as discussed above, this will seldom be the case in reality, we have done this so we can focus on the impact the tax rate has on the benefit of the tax shield. The example clearly illustrates that the tax shield is much more valuable to the lessor than the lessee due to the tax differences. The tax shield is 125 percent more valuable, *which is also the difference in the tax rates*. In addition, if the lessor's cost of capital was 5 percent, not 6.4 percent, the present value of the tax shield increases even further to $18,827. The combination of the two rate differences will have the effect of allowing the lessor to reduce the quoted lease payment. ▲

Calculating the Lease Payment

To calculate the lease payment the lessor will charge, we will use the NPV of the lease approach. We do this because this is a capital budgeting analysis for the lessor; thus, the minimum lease payment that could be charged is the amount that makes the NPV of the lease equal to zero. With this payment, the lessor will receive a return that exactly covers their cost of capital.

Example ▼ Maritime Airlines (MAL) has approached Royal Dominion Bank Leasing (RDBL), the leasing arm of the Royal Dominion Bank, with a leasing proposal. MAL, a small privately owned airline company, wishes to purchase three new aircraft to modernize their small fleet. The cost of each airplane is $3.2 million, and the planes have expected lives of 25 years. The financial lease will be for the same time period. Aircraft are a Class 9 asset, and have a CCA rate of 25 percent. The aircraft are expected to be worth $600,000 each as scrap at the end of their useful lives.

If MAL purchased the planes, they could borrow the required funds at a rate of 8 percent. Their cost of capital is 12.9 percent and their tax rate is 20 percent. RDBL is financed with 90 percent long-term debt with a cost of 6.67 percent, and 10 percent common equity with a cost of 17 percent. Their tax rate is 45 percent. To determine the lease payment to charge, RDBL must first calculate their cost of capital. We will use the same process as in Chapter 9. Note that the after-tax cost of the long-term debt is 3.67 percent (6.67 × (1 − 0.45)). The process is provided below. RDBL's cost of capital is 5.0 percent.

Source of financing	Percent of financing	After-tax cost	WACC
Long-term debt	90%	3.67%	3.30%
Common equity	10%	17.00%	1.70%
			5.00%

With the lessor's cost of capital, we can now calculate the minimum lease payment to charge, RDBL will set the NPV of the cash flows associated with leasing to zero to solve for the lease payment. This analysis is provided in Table 16.10.[11] If the lessor leases the asset to the lessee, the lessor must purchase the aircraft from the manufacturer; this is a cash outflow. As the owner of the aircraft, the lessor receives the present values of the tax shield and salvage (cash inflows) but loses the tax shield lost due to salvage (outflow). The lessor receives the lease payments (an annuity due) but must pay tax on these (an ordinary annuity).

Note that for the analysis we know the answer; to determine the minimum lease payment to charge, the NPV of the lease is zero ($0). Therefore, we can calculate the minimum lease payment the lessor can charge for the asset. To do this we determine the *PVIFa* factors using our financial calculators. Input a payment of 1, and the relevant number of periods and discount rates and compute the PV. This will result in the time value factors shown in the table. Now, solving for L in the above example, the minimum lease payment RDBL should charge MAL for each plane is:

$$\begin{aligned} NPV_L &= 0 = -\$1{,}917{,}832 + 14.79864179L - \$6.342275055L \\ &= -\$1{,}917{,}832 + 8.45636674L \end{aligned}$$

Now solve for L by moving the known amount across the equal sign, which changes the sign, and then solve for the unknown, the lease payments, as follows:

$$\begin{aligned} NPV_L &= 0 + \$1{,}917{,}832 = 8.45636674L \\ L &= \frac{\$1{,}917{,}832}{8.45636674} \\ L &= \$226{,}791 \end{aligned}$$

So, to receive exactly a 5 percent return on the leasing contract, RDBL would charge MAL a lease payment of $226,791 per plane per year for 25 years.

11. Note that the analysis uses only one plane. The calculated lease payment will then be multiplied by three, for the three planes, to calculate the total yearly lease payments required. The purchase price for all three planes could have been used in the analysis.

TABLE 16.10 Calculating the Minimum Lease Payment RDBL Could Charge

$NPV_L = -$ Incremental cost	=	−\$3,200,000
+ Present value of tax shield from CCA		
$\$3{,}200{,}000 \times \left[\frac{0.25 \times 0.45}{0.25 + 0.05}\right] \times \frac{1.025}{1.05}$	=	+\$1,171,429
+ Present value of salvage		
\$600,000 × *PVIF* (5%, 25 per)	=	+\$177,182
− Present value of tax shield lost due to salvage		
$\$177{,}182 \times \left[\frac{0.25 \times 0.45}{0.25 + 0.05}\right]$	=	−\$66,443
+ Present value of the lease payments		
\$*L* + [\$*L* × *PVIFa* (5%, 24 years)] =		
\$*L* + \$13.79864179*L*	=	+\$14.79864179*L*
− Present value of the taxes paid on the lease payments		
\$*L* × (0.45) × *PVIFa* (5%, 25 years) =		
\$*L* × (0.45) × 14.09394457	=	−\$6.342275055*L*
NPV_L	=	\$0

Lessee's Evaluation of the Lease Proposal

If \$226,791 were the quoted lease payment, should MAL lease the aircraft from RDBL? Recall that MAL's borrowing rate if they were to purchase the airplanes is 8 percent, their cost of capital is 12.9 percent, and their tax rate is 20 percent. Therefore, their after-tax borrowing rate, the discount rate for many of the cash flows, is 6.4 percent. Now, to answer this question, determine the present value of the cost of leasing and purchasing the aircraft (or determine the NPV of the lease). This analysis is provided in Table 16.11.

Clearly MAL should lease the aircraft. The cost of leasing is much less than purchasing; the NPV of the lease is \$269,060.

Implication of the Analysis

Based on the above realistic example, both the lessee and the lessor benefit from the leasing arrangement. As discussed earlier, this is because the discount and tax rates differ for the two parties. In such cases, both can benefit from leasing. This example clearly illustrates why leasing is such a popular method to finance the acquisition of fixed assets, particularly for companies with high borrowing rates or low tax rates.

Therefore, at a lease rate of \$226,791 per year, both MAL and RDBL benefit from the lease arrangement. But RDBL may wish to charge a lease payment where the NPV of the lease, from their perspective, is greater than zero. How much more could RDBL charge MAL before MAL would be indifferent to leasing or purchasing? This is the point where, from MAL's perspective, the cost of leasing is the same as the cost

TABLE 16.11 **Maritime Airlines: The Present Value of the Cost of Purchasing and Leasing Based on the Quoted Lease Rate from RDBL**

Present value of the cost of purchasing the airplanes		
+ Incremental cost	=	+$3,200,000
− Present value of tax shield from CCA		
$\$3,200,000 \times \left[\frac{0.25 \times 0.20}{0.25 + 0.064}\right] \times \frac{1.032}{1.064}$	=	−$494,229
− Present value of salvage		
$600,000 × *PVIF* (12.9%, 25 per)	=	−$28,894
+ Present value of tax shield lost due to salvage		
$\$28,894 \times \left[\frac{0.25 \times 0.20}{0.25 + 0.064}\right]$	=	+$4,601
Present value of the cost of purchasing the airplanes	=	$2,681,478
Present value of the cost of leasing the airplanes		
+ Present value of the lease payments		
$226,791 + [$226,791 × *PVIFa* (6.4%, 24 years)] = $226,791 + $2,744,057	=	$2,970,848
− Present value of the tax shield on the lease payments		
$226,791 × (0.20) × *PVIFa* (6.4%, 25 years) = $45,358 × *PVIFa* (6.4%, 25 years)	=	− $ 558,430
Present value of the cost of leasing the airplanes	=	$2,412,418

of purchasing. This is where the NPV of the lease is zero. Table 16.12 illustrates the process used to calculate this maximum lease payment MAL would pay.

By following the same process as before, we can solve for L and determine that the maximum lease payment MAL could pay would be:

$$\text{NPV}_L = 0 = \$2{,}681{,}478 - 10.63718641L$$

$$L = \frac{\$2{,}681{,}478}{10.63718641}$$

$$L = \$252{,}085$$

If the lease payment is $226,971, RDBL receives exactly their required return of 5 percent, and leasing is preferred to purchasing for MAL. If the lease payment is $252,085, RDBL would receive more than a 5 percent return, and MAL is indifferent to leasing or purchasing; the costs are exactly the same.

So, as long as the lease payment is at least $226,791 but less than $252,085, both parties benefit from leasing. From RDBL's perspective, this means there is room to negotiate the actual payment to charge MAL. In reality, RDBL would have a very good idea of MAL's borrowing rate and would likely initially quote a lease payment closer to $252,085 than to $226,791. In this way, RDBL would receive more of the benefits associated with the different discount and tax rates that exist between the two parties.

TABLE 16.12 Calculating the Maximum Lease Payment Maritime Airlines Could Pay

NPV_L = + Incremental cost	=	+\$3,200,000
− Present value of tax shield from CCA		
$\$3{,}200{,}000 \times \left[\frac{0.25 \times 0.20}{0.25 + 0.064}\right] \times \frac{1.032}{1.064}$	=	−\$ 494,229
− Present value of salvage		
\$600,000 × *PVIF* (12.9%, 25 per)	=	−\$ 28,894
+ Present value of tax shield lost due to salvage		
$\$28{,}894 \times \left[\frac{0.25 \times 0.20}{0.25 + 0.064}\right]$	=	+\$ 4,601
− Present value of the lease payments		
\$*L* + [\$*L* × *PVIFa* (6.4%, 24 years)] =		
\$*L* + \$12.09949808*L*	=	−\$13.09949808*L*
+ Present value of the tax shield on the lease payments		
\$*L* × (0.20) × *PVIFa* (6.4%, 25 years) =		
\$*L* × (0.20) × 12.31155835	=	+\$ 2.46231167*L*
NPV_L	=	\$0

Extending the Analysis

As with analyzing the lease from the lessee's perspective, additional variables could also be considered when analyzing the lease from the lessor's perspective. What impact would adding other variables to the analysis have on the lease payment the lessor would charge? The impact is outlined below:

Variable	Impact on lease payment charged by lessor
Maintenance and insurance included	Increase lease payment
Damage deposit charged	No impact
Asset qualifies for ITC	Decrease lease payment
Only asset in class	Normally increase lease payment

For example, since MAL is located in Nova Scotia, assume that the aircraft qualify for a 10 percent investment tax credit. How does this impact the previous analysis? Since the owner of the asset receives the ITC, RDBL will be able to reduce their federal taxes by the dollar amount of the ITC, in this case, \$320,000 (\$3.2 million × 10 percent) per plane, or \$960,000 in total. Given the large size of the company, and the high tax rate, RDBL will be able to use all of the ITC in the year the aircraft are purchased. As such, this will significantly reduce the lease payment that could be charged, as provided in Table 16.13. Using the same process as before, we solve for *L*.

$$NPV_L \text{ (with ITC)} = 0 = -\$1{,}730{,}213 + 8.45636674L$$

$$L = \frac{\$1{,}730{,}213}{8.45636674}$$

$$L = \$204{,}605$$

TABLE 16.13 Calculating the Minimum Lease Payment RDBL Could Charge with ITC Included

NPV_L = − Incremental cost	=	−\$3,200,000
+ Present value of the ITC		
\$320,000 × *PVIF* (5%, 1 per)	=	+\$304,762
+ Present value of tax shield from CCA		
$(\$3{,}200{,}000 - \$320{,}000) \times \left[\frac{0.25 \times 0.45}{0.25 + 0.05}\right] \times \frac{1.025}{1.05}$	=	+\$1,054,286
+ Present value of salvage		
\$600,000 × *PVIF* (5%, 25 per)	=	+\$177,182
− Present value of tax shield lost due to salvage		
$\$177{,}182 \times \left[\frac{0.25 \times 0.45}{0.25 + 0.05}\right]$	=	−\$66,443
+ Present value of the lease payments		
\$*L* + [\$*L* × *PVIFa* (5%, 24 years)] =		
\$*L* + \$13.79864179*L*	=	+\$14.79864179*L*
− Present value of the taxes paid on the lease payments		
\$*L* × (0.45) × *PVIFa* (5%, 25 years) =		
\$*L* × (0.45) × 14.09394457	=	− \$6.342275055*L*
NPV_L	=	\$0

The calculated lease payment is \$22,186 less than the previously calculated lease payment of \$226,791. The fact that RDBL is able to use all of the ITC in the year the aircraft are purchased is important and helps explain why assets that qualify for ITC are leased. If the acquiring firm has insufficient federal taxes to use all of the ITC in the year the asset is acquired, the unused amount can be used in future years. But the present value of the benefit will be reduced. To maximize this benefit, it makes sense to use it as quickly as possible. Transferring ownership of the asset to the lessor, thus transferring the ITC, allows this to happen and benefits both the lessor (reduces taxes) and lessee (reduces lease payment).

Spreadsheet Application 16.2 provides a template that can be used to calculate the minimum lease payment a lessor could charge to lease an asset.

? Review Questions

16–31 If potential lessors and lessees had the same tax and discount rates, what would happen?

16–32 Explain the reasons why both the lessee and the lessor can benefit from a leasing arrangement.

16–33 Do you agree with the statement "Leasing is a zero-sum game"? Discuss.

16–34 Why is the lessor's cost of capital often lower than the lessee's after-tax cost of borrowing?

16–35 Why is the tax shield from CCA often more valuable for the lessor? What impact can this have on the lease payment the lessor charges?

16–36 Describe the process to determine the minimum lease payment the lessor could charge.

16–37 What does the minimum lease payment the lessor could charge represent?

16–38 Explain, in detail, how the inclusion of maintenance and insurance costs would impact the lease payment charged by the lessor.

16.2 SPREADSHEET APPLICATION

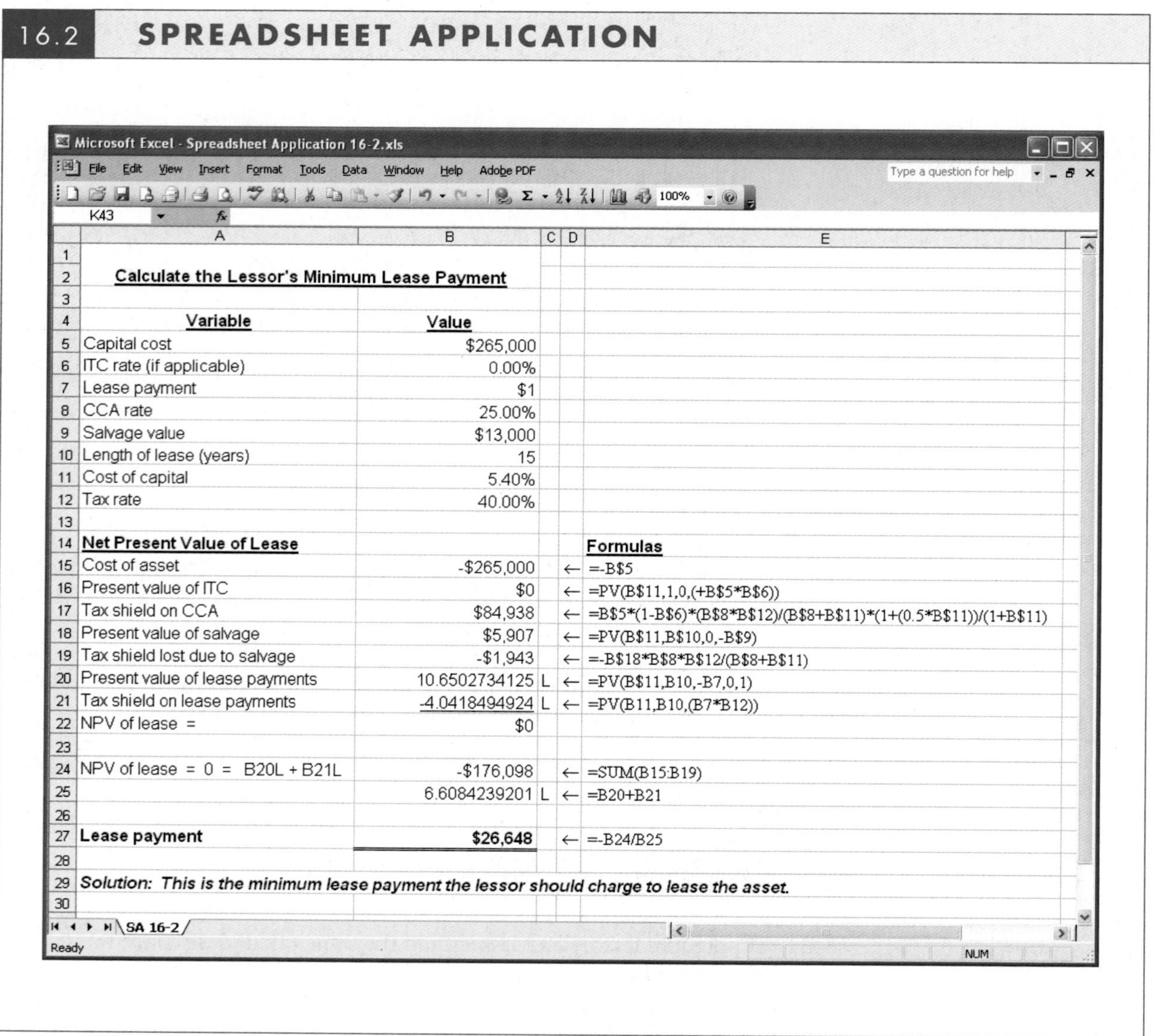

Microsoft Excel - Spreadsheet Application 16-2.xls

	A	B	C	D	E
1					
2	**Calculate the Lessor's Minimum Lease Payment**				
3					
4	**Variable**	**Value**			
5	Capital cost	$265,000			
6	ITC rate (if applicable)	0.00%			
7	Lease payment	$1			
8	CCA rate	25.00%			
9	Salvage value	$13,000			
10	Length of lease (years)	15			
11	Cost of capital	5.40%			
12	Tax rate	40.00%			
13					
14	**Net Present Value of Lease**				**Formulas**
15	Cost of asset	-$265,000		←	=-B$5
16	Present value of ITC	$0		←	=PV(B$11,1,0,(+B$5*B$6))
17	Tax shield on CCA	$84,938		←	=B$5*(1-B$6)*(B$8*B$12)/(B$8+B$11)*(1+(0.5*B$11))/(1+B$11)
18	Present value of salvage	$5,907		←	=PV(B$11,B$10,0,-B$9)
19	Tax shield lost due to salvage	-$1,943		←	=-B$18*B$8*B$12/(B$8+B$11)
20	Present value of lease payments	10.6502734125	L	←	=PV(B$11,B10,-B7,0,1)
21	Tax shield on lease payments	-4.0418494924	L	←	=PV(B11,B10,(B7*B12))
22	NPV of lease =	$0			
23					
24	NPV of lease = 0 = B20L + B21L	-$176,098		←	=SUM(B15:B19)
25		6.6084239201	L	←	=B20+B21
26					
27	**Lease payment**	**$26,648**		←	=-B24/B25
28					
29	***Solution: This is the minimum lease payment the lessor should charge to lease the asset.***				
30					

SUMMARY

Review the concept that the value of an asset is in its use, not its ownership, and introduce information regarding leasing and the leasing industry in Canada. The value of an asset is in its use, not in its ownership. There are two ways to acquire the use of an asset: buy or lease it. Leasing is a source of financing that allows a firm to obtain the use of fixed assets in exchange for a series of contractual, periodic, tax-deductible payments. The lessee uses the asset and makes lease payments to the lessor, the owner of the asset. The leasing industry, which is represented by the Canadian Financing and Leasing Association, is the second-largest provider of debt financing in Canada. The services of the leasing industry are complementary to those of traditional financial institutions by providing incremental capital that increases the pool of available credit in Canada. They are a vital competitive alternative in the financial service sector. Funding for this industry comes from pension funds, insurance companies, banks, and manufacturing and servicing companies.

Describe and differentiate between operating and financial leases, introduce the different types of financial leases, and explain other conditions included in lease agreements. There are two basic types of leases available to businesses. Operating leases are generally five or fewer years in term, cancellable, and renewable, and they provide for maintenance by the lessor. Financial leases are longer-term, non-cancellable, and not renewable, and they require the lessee to maintain the asset. CICA regulations provide specific guidelines for defining a financial lease. A lessor can obtain assets to be leased through a direct lease, a sale-leaseback arrangement, or a leveraged lease. Leases can include several conditions, including maintenance clauses and purchase and renewal options. Lessors might be any one of a number of parties, including leasing subsidiaries of large financial institutions and manufacturers, or independent companies.

Explain how leases are disclosed on a company's financial statements, and exhibit how leasing and purchasing an asset have similar impacts on a firm's financial position. Lease payments are an expense and must be accounted for on a firm's financial statements. They are tax-deductible, but only if the CRA agrees the contract is a lease and not a conditional sales agreement. Accounting standards establish detailed guidelines to be used in capitalizing and disclosing leases. CICA regulations require firms to show financial leases as assets and corresponding liabilities on their balance sheets; operating leases must be shown in footnotes to the financial statements. The capitalized value of the lease on the balance sheet declines as lease payments are made and deducted for tax purposes. As with purchasing assets, leasing assets can have a major impact on a firm's financial situation. The firm acquires the long-term use of the asset with a long-term obligation that must be paid. A lease is viewed as a long-term financial commitment of the lessee, because the consequences of missing a financial lease payment are the same as those of missing an interest or principal payment on debt.

Discuss the cash flows and the discount rate used to evaluate whether an asset should be leased or purchased, and illustrate the process used to answer the lease-or-purchase question. A firm has four alternatives to acquire an asset: it can obtain financing in three ways to purchase the asset or it can lease the asset. The important decision facing firms is whether to lease the assets or purchase them using borrowed funds. The lease-or-purchase question can be evaluated by calculating the after-tax cash outflows associated with the leasing and purchasing alternatives. The cash flows associated with the alternatives, the time period to use in the analysis, and the discount rate are the three important variables that must be estimated to complete the analysis. Since leasing is viewed as a substitute for long-term debt, the after-tax interest rate the company would have to pay to borrow the funds to purchase the asset is used as the discount rate. The focus of the analysis is on costs, so the option with the lower cost is the preferred choice. In the analysis, cost items are positive while inflows are negative, since it is the cost being calculated.

Introduce the method used to calculate the net present value of leasing, show how other variables can affect the lease-or-purchase question, and discuss the advantages and disadvantages of leasing. A net present value approach can also be used to analyze the lease-or-purchase question. This approach simplifies the decision into a single analysis. The NPV of the lease considers how the cash flows would be treated if the company leased the asset. A negative value means the firm should purchase the asset rather than lease it. The cost of capital is used to discount the salvage value due to the risk associated with the salvage value. A number of commonly cited advantages and disadvantages should be considered when making the lease-or-purchase decision.

LG6 **Examine leasing from the lessor's perspective, focusing on how leasing can benefit both the lessee and the lessor due to differing discount and tax rates, and illustrate the process lessors use to calculate the minimum and maximum lease payment that they could charge on a lease.** In a leasing agreement the lessor is going to set a lease rate that is beneficial to the company, but this does not mean the lessee always loses. Both the lessor and the lessee can benefit from a leasing arrangement. The lessee and the lessor have different discount and tax rates, which allows both parties to benefit from leasing. Lessors use their cost of capital and since most leasing companies are heavily weighted to debt and have high tax rates, the lessor will often have a cost of capital that is lower than the lessee's after-tax cost of debt. The lessor can calculate the minimum lease payment it must charge to cover its cost of capital. In a similar way, the lessee can calculate the maximum lease payment it can pay.

SELF-TEST PROBLEMS

(Solutions in Appendix B)

ST 16–1 **Lease or purchase** Nelson Company is deciding whether it should purchase or lease a new heavy-duty air compressor that has an expected life of eight years. Nelson could purchase a new air compressor for $86,000. This quote includes all taxes and delivery. Alternatively, the compressor can be leased for eight years for $17,400 per year, with the first payment due when the lease contract is signed. The lessor's implied discount rate on the lease is 13.5 percent. The CCA rate on the compressor is 30 percent. The lease includes maintenance costs estimated at $2,000 per year. The salvage value of the compressor is estimated to be $4,000 at the end of its useful life. The company's borrowing rate is 15 percent, their cost of capital is 15.5 percent, and their marginal tax rate is 25 percent.

a. How would the Canada Revenue Agency (CRA) determine whether the proposed arrangement is a lease?
b. Would the proposed arrangement be considered a financial lease? Explain.
c. In your analysis of the alternatives, should the maintenance costs be considered, and if so, how?
d. What is the present value of the cost of purchasing the new air compressor?
e. What is the present value of the cost of leasing the new air compressor?
f. What is the NPV of the leasing option?
g. What should Nelson Company do, lease or purchase the air compressor?
h. What do your results imply about the lessor's tax rate and/or required rate of return on the lease? (*Note:* An exact numeric answer is not required; just provide a range.)
i. Now assume that the new air compressor is the only asset in its asset class. How will this affect the decision to lease or purchase the asset?

  **ST 16–2** **Calculating lease payments** Bayview Industrial manufactures heavy equipment for use in all kinds of marine applications. ClearWater Inc., a local boat builder, has approached Bayview regarding the acquisition of a new, high-capacity hydraulic lift. The selling price of the lift is $247,000, and this includes all taxes. Delivery and installation will cost another $18,000 and must be paid by the purchaser. The lift is a Class 39 asset with a CCA rate of 25 percent and a useful life of 15 years. The market value of the lift at the end of its useful life is expected to be $13,000.

ClearWater is also interested in evaluating the option of leasing the new lift from Bayview Industrial's leasing subsidiary. Bayview's leasing policy is to determine the minimum yearly lease payment they could charge, then add a 20 percent premium to the calculated amount to allow for "unaccounted risk factors." The first lease payment is due when the contract is signed. Bayview Industrial's tax rate is 40 percent and their cost of capital is 5.4 percent.

a. Determine the minimum yearly lease payment Bayview Industrial could charge for the new lift. What lease rate will Bayview actually charge ClearWater to lease the lift?

b. Should ClearWater purchase or lease the lift? If ClearWater Inc. purchases the lift, they could borrow the required funds at a rate of 8.8 percent. Their cost of capital is 13.2 percent and their tax rate is 35 percent.

c. What is the maximum yearly amount ClearWater would be willing to pay to lease the lift?

PROBLEMS

  **16–1** **Capitalized lease values** Calculate the capitalized value of each of the following capital leases using the information provided in the following table. Assume that the first lease payment is due when a contract is signed.

Asset	Cost of asset	Annual lease payment	Lease term	Lessee's borrowing rate	Lessor's implied discount rate
A	$1,200,000	$140,000	12 years	10.2%	11%
B	700,000	120,000	8 years	13.2	12
C	75,000	9,000	18 years	14	11.6
D	40,000	16,000	3 years	9.3	8.2
E	400,000	47,000	20 years	11.9	12.1

BASIC  **16–2** **Cost of leases** Given the lease payments and terms shown in the following table, determine the present value of the after-tax cost of the lease for each firm. Assume that the first lease payment is due when the contract is signed.

Firm	Annual lease payment	Lease term	Tax rate	Borrowing rate
A	$100,000	4 years	30%	8%
B	80,000	14 years	22	10
C	150,000	8 years	45	6
D	60,000	25 years	18	11
E	20,000	10 years	36	7.2

BASIC  **16–3 Accounting for leases** The balance sheet for Samson & Son Restorations is shown below. The company is considering leasing an asset using a financial lease. The lease will require payments of $6,500 per year for 8 years with the first payment to be made upon the signing of the lease contract. Samson & Son has a tax rate of 40 percent and a borrowing rate of 7 percent. The lessor's implied discount rate on the lease is 7.45 percent. The cost of the asset is $48,300. Assuming Samson & Son enters into the leasing arrangement, develop the company's balance sheet on day 1 of the lease agreement.

Samson & Son Restorations
Balance Sheet
Before Lease

		Liabilities	$160,000
		Equity	250,000
Total assets	$410,000	Total liabilities and equity	$410,000

CHALLENGE  **16–4 Accounting for leases** Sigma Inc.'s balance sheet for the December 31, 2008, fiscal year is shown below. On June 30, 2009, Sigma plans to enter into a leasing contract in which it will agree to lease a piece of equipment for 10 years with lease payments of $12,000 per year with the first payment to be made at the time of the agreement. Of the cash needed to make the lease payments, 35 percent will be debt while 65 percent will be reinvested profits. Sigma's borrowing and tax rates are 7.9 percent and 30 percent, respectively. Sigma can purchase the equipment for $91,000. The equipment has a useful life of 13 years. The lessor's implied discount rate is 7.3 percent.

Sigma Inc.
Balance Sheet
as of December 31, 2008

		Liabilities	$360,000
		Equity	260,000
Total assets	$620,000	Total liabilities and equity	$620,000

a. What was Sigma Inc.'s debt ratio as of December 31, 2008?
b. Should Sigma capitalize the lease on their 2009 balance sheet? Explain why or why not.
c. If the lease were capitalized, what would the capitalized value be as soon as the company agrees to the lease arrangement on June 30, 2009?
d. Now develop Sigma's balance sheet as of December 31, 2009. Assume no other changes occurred in the company's assets, liabilities, or equity.
e. Based on your answer to part **d**, what is Sigma's debt ratio at the end of 2009? Comment on the change.
f. What will the capitalized value of the lease be on the December 31, 2011, balance sheet?

INTERMEDIATE

16–5 Capitalizing leases Information on five leasing arrangements is presented below. Determine which of the leasing arrangements are considered leases and need to be capitalized on a firm's balance sheet. Comment on what condition(s) makes each arrangement a financial lease. What is the capitalized value of each of the leases? Assume the first lease payment is due when the contract is signed.

	Lease 1	Lease 2	Lease 3	Lease 4	Lease 5
Cost of asset	$80,000	$94,300	$154,000	$475,000	$62,000
Borrowing rate	6.5%	10.8%	5.0%	7.25%	12.4%
Lease payments	$9,000	$12,750	$21,700	$38,500	$10,800
Term of lease	10 years	8 years	8 years	16 years	6 years
Estimated life of asset	15 years	12 years	14 years	20 years	8 years
Lessor's implied discount rate	6.8%	10.2%	6.1%	4.5%	11.1%
Estimated fair market value of asset at end of lease	$8,000	$7,000	$11,000	$14,000	$4,500
Purchase option at end of lease	$10,500	$7,000	$1,000	$14,000	$5,800

BASIC 

16–6 Valuing tax shields Dino's Delivery is considering the lease of a new delivery van from Auto Shop Leasing, the leasing subsidiary of a large vehicle manufacturer. The van has a cost of $52,000 and a CCA rate of 20 percent. The van is expected to have a useful life of 8 years, at which time it will have a salvage value of $6,800.

a. Determine the value of the tax shield from CCA for both companies. Dino's has a borrowing rate of 12 percent and a cost of capital of 10.7 percent. Auto Shop Leasing has a borrowing rate of 8 percent and a cost of capital of 4.5 percent. Both companies have a tax rate of 35 percent.

b. Repeat the calculation in part **a** but with the following adjustments: Dino's has a tax rate of 25 percent, and Auto Shop has a cost of capital of 9 percent and a tax rate of 45 percent.

c. Comment on the values calculated in part **a** and in part **b**. Which has the bigger impact on the difference between the tax shields, the discount rate or the tax rate? Explain why.

BASIC 

16–7 Impact of ITC on leases Southside Farms has just completed a lease-or-purchase analysis on a new machine. The net present value of the lease was $23,560. Now, Southside Farms has realized that if they purchase the machine, the company will receive an ITC of 10 percent. The machine has a cost of $427,500 and a CCA rate of 30 percent. Southside Farms has an after-tax borrowing rate of 7.3 percent, a cost of capital of 12.6 percent, and a tax rate of 35 percent. What impact, if any, will the ITC have on the decision to lease?

BASIC 

16–8 Lease or purchase Doyle Farm Supply, a manufacturer of farm equipment, has offered your company the opportunity to lease or purchase a piece of machinery that has a useful life of 5 years. The asset sells for $40,000 and has a CCA rate of 20 percent. The machinery is expected to have a salvage value of $4,500 at the end of its useful life. At your option, Doyle Farm Supply will guarantee a 5-year bank loan at an interest rate of 10 percent, the best rate available, to cover the purchase price. Alternatively, Doyle will lease the asset to your company for 5 years. The yearly lease payments will be $10,200, with the first payment due when the lease contract is signed.

a. Having decided to acquire this piece of equipment, what would you recommend regarding the machinery: should it be purchased or leased? Your company's cost of capital is 12 percent while the tax rate is 20 percent.

b. If instead of making yearly payments you could make monthly lease payments of $850 per month, would this change your recommendation in **a**? Explain.

INTERMEDIATE 

16–9 **Lease or purchase** Emery Bat and Ball has made the decision to acquire a new lathe, which will replace an existing lathe. The company can purchase or lease the lathe. The existing lathe is currently worth $40,000, while the new lathe will cost $300,000. The new lathe will result in cost savings of $66,500 per year. The new lathe qualifies for a 10 percent ITC and will have a salvage value of $35,000 at the end of its useful life.

The CCA rate for lathes is 30 percent and the new lathe is expected to have a life of 12 years. For a 12-year lease, the lease payment would be $40,000 per year with the first payment due when the lease contract is signed. Emery's cost of capital is 11 percent, tax rate 40 percent, while their cost of raising long-term debt is expected to be 8 percent. Should the company lease or purchase the new lathe?

  INTERMEDIATE

16–10 **Lease or purchase** A government agency that pays no taxes is evaluating whether to lease or purchase an asset. The agency can borrow the full purchase price of the asset at an interest rate of 5 percent. The loan would be for a term of 5 years and the payments would be $12,050 per year, payable at the end of the year. Lease payments would be $11,000 per year, with the first payment due when the lease contract is signed. The CCA rate on the asset is 20 percent. Both the loan and lease would run for the 5-year expected life of the asset. The salvage value of the asset is expected to be $2,000. Given the uncertainty inherent in this estimate, the discount rate applicable to the salvage value is 14 percent.

a. Using the information provided, what is the purchase price of the asset?

b. Which alternative would you recommend to the government agency, lease or purchase the asset?

c. What would the salvage value have to be before you would reverse your decision above?

CHALLENGE 

16–11 **Lease or purchase** Shaw Company Ltd. wishes to expand their manufacturing operation by acquiring a $500,000 stamping machine. The CCA rate on the machine is 50 percent and the machine is expected to have a 15-year life. McGuigan Machines, the manufacturer, has offered to lease the machine to Shaw Company. The sales manager of McGuigan Machines indicates to Shaw that since the leasing subsidiary of McGuigan can borrow funds at a very low rate, it is possible for them to offer Shaw an attractive lease rate to secure the machine. For a 15-year lease, the rate would be $50,000 per year, with the first payment due when the lease contract is signed.

Alternatively, Shaw could borrow the $500,000 for 15 years at 10 percent; this would require annual debt repayments of $65,737. At the end of 15 years, the machine could be sold for $20,000. The stamping machine qualifies for an investment tax credit of 10 percent of the cost of the asset. Shaw's cost of capital is 12.6 percent, while their tax rate is 30 percent. Since the new stamping machine would result in the creation of four new jobs, Shaw has approached the provincial government regarding financial assistance for the acquisition of the stamping machine. The province has offered a cash grant of $40,000, payable when the machine is acquired, but the grant will be paid only if Shaw purchases the machine.

It has been suggested to Shaw's finance manager that, since the lease rate is over $15,000 per year less than the cost of borrowing the funds required to acquire the stamping machine, Shaw should lease. What would you recommend to Shaw's finance manager: should they lease or purchase the stamping machine? To answer the question, calculate the NPV of the lease.

INTERMEDIATE

16–12 **Lease or purchase** Foreign Fuels Ltd. is faced with the decision of whether to purchase or to lease a new extractor vehicle. The extractor vehicle can be purchased for $5,750,000 and it is expected to be operational for 8 years. The extractor vehicle has a CCA rate of 30 percent. Canadian Equipment Leasing has agreed to lease the new extractor vehicle to Foreign Fuels for 8 years for $850,000 per year, with the first payment due when the lease contract is signed. The lease rate includes maintenance and service. The extractor is expected to have a salvage value of $600,000 at the end of the 8 years. If the extractor is owned, Foreign Fuels' operations manager feels maintenance expenses would be $80,000 a year. If Foreign Fuels were to borrow from a financial institution for a term of 8 years, the borrowing rate would be 9 percent. Foreign Fuels has a 40 percent tax rate and a cost of capital of 12 percent.

a. Should Foreign Fuels buy or lease the extractor?

b. Now assume the extractor vehicle is the only asset in its class. Calculate the tax value of the asset at the end of its useful life, and determine the impact that closing out the asset class has on the decision to purchase or lease the extractor vehicle.

INTERMEDIATE

16–13 **Lease or purchase** Sand Castle Inc., a distributor of sand and soil for construction companies, is considering the purchase of a new dump truck at a cost of $82,000. The new dump truck will replace an older model that has a tax value of $12,000 and that could be sold for $8,300. Both trucks have CCA rates of 30 percent. The new truck has an expected life of 15 years, when it will have a salvage value of $8,000. The operating cost of the new truck is expected to be $11,800 per year. Sand Castle also has the option of leasing the dump truck. The lease payments would be $7,500 per year for the life of the asset, with the first payment due when the lease contract is signed. Sand Castle has a borrowing rate of 7 percent and a cost of capital of 12.4 percent.

a. Assuming Sand Castle has a tax rate of 40 percent, use the NPV approach to determine if Sand Castle should purchase or lease the new dump truck.

b. Repeat the process assuming Sand Castle's tax rate is 45 percent. What should Sand Castle do?

c. Explain the impact, if any, the change in the tax rate has on the lease-or-purchase decision.

BASIC

16–14 **Calculating lease payments and lease or purchase** The Clarkton Company produces an industrial machine that has an expected life of 5 years. Clarkton is willing to sell the machines for $30,000, or to lease them for an amount that provides a return to Clarkton of 6 percent. The machines qualify for a CCA rate of 25 percent and will have a salvage value of $4,000. The company's tax rate is 40 percent. The first lease payment is due when the contract is signed.

The Stockton Machine Shop is contemplating acquiring a machine like those manufactured by Clarkton. The machine will produce net benefits of $10,000 per year. Stockton can buy or lease the machine from Clarkton. Stockton's cost of debt is 10 percent, cost of capital 12 percent, and tax rate 40 percent.

a. Why would Clarkton use a return of 6 percent when calculating their lease rate?

b. What is the minimum lease rate Clarkton Company would charge for the machines?

c. If Clarkton Company charged the amount calculated in part **b,** should Stockton Machine Shop lease or purchase the new machine?

d. If Clarkton required a return of 9 percent rather than 6 percent on the lease, what would happen to the minimum lease rate the company could charge? What is the new lease rate?

e. If Clarkton charges this new lease rate, would it alter Stockton's decision?

INTERMEDIATE LG6 16–15 **Calculating lease payments** Finley Company just purchased a new piece of machinery for $160,000 on behalf of a company that has agreed to lease the machinery. The problem is, Finley is not sure how much they should charge the lessee for the machinery. The machine qualifies for a 10 percent ITC and has a CCA rate of 30 percent. The machine is expected to have a useful life of 12 years, at which time it will have a scrap value of $9,300. The first lease payment is due when the contract is signed

a. If Finley's tax rate and cost of capital are 40 percent and 8.7 percent, respectively, what is the minimum lease payment that Finley should charge?

b. What would the minimum lease payment be if the machine did not qualify for the ITC?

CHALLENGE  16–16 **Lease or purchase** Due to improving technology, Greenwood Logistics Co. must acquire a new computer system to better track customer data. While a very important investment, the new computer system is only expected to have a useful life of 5 years. The computer system can be purchased for $86,000 or it can be leased for $15,000 per year for 5 years, with the first payment due when the lease contract is signed. The company's existing computer system, which was bought 6 years ago for $73,000, will be sold for its current market value of $6,990. The new computer system is expected to result in incremental after-tax operating income of $27,000 per year, 10 percent more than the existing computer system.

At the end of the 5 years, the computer system will have a salvage value of $7,800. Due to the advanced technology of the computer system, the lessor has agreed to include a maintenance clause to cover the yearly maintenance expenses which are expected to be $1,400. Greenwood must pay the insurance cost of $840 per year. If Greenwood purchases the computer system, it will receive an investment tax credit of 20 percent and will be able to borrow the required funds at a rate of 8 percent. The computer system is a Class 10 asset with a CCA rate of 30 percent. Greenwood's cost of capital and tax rate are 11.4 percent and 35 percent, respectively.

a. Using the NPV approach, determine whether Greenwood should purchase or lease the computer system.

b. At what lease payment would Greenwood be indifferent between leasing and purchasing the computer system?
c. Now assume the new computer system is the only asset in its class. Determine the impact the sale of the computer system at the end of its useful life will have on the analysis. Use the original lease payment in the analysis.

CHALLENGE

16–17 **Integrative—Calculating lease payments and lease or purchase** J&M Leasing, the leasing subsidiary of Jenkins Manufacturing Ltd., has approached D'Angelo Fabrications Inc. regarding the acquisition of a new welding machine. D'Angelo had previously expressed an interest in purchasing the machine, but the CFO of the company is very hesitant to purchase given their very high borrowing rate of 15 percent. As a result, J&M Leasing is planning to make a leasing proposal to D'Angelo Fabrications.

The welding machine has a cost of $315,000 and qualifies for an ITC of 15 percent. It is a Class 43 asset with a CCA rate of 30 percent and an expected useful life of 12 years, at which time it will have a salvage value of $3,000. The CFO of D'Angelo expects the machine to generate an increase in after-tax operating income of $48,000 per year. D'Angelo's cost of capital is 13 percent and their tax rate is 25 percent. Due to the technical sophistication of the machine, J&M Leasing includes maintenance and insurance costs in the lease payments. Given the large number of machines J&M leases, these costs are $1,100 and $800 per year, respectively. The first lease payment is due when the lease contract is signed.

D'Angelo's plant manager has studied the new machines and believes that if the company had to maintain the welding machine, the cost would be $1,750 per year. Insurance would cost $950 per year. J&M Leasing requires a damage deposit of $6,000 for the machine. D'Angelo expects that this will be fully returned at the end of the leasing period.

a. If J&M Leasing has a cost of capital of 8.6 percent, a borrowing rate of 10.8 percent, and a tax rate of 45 percent, what is the minimum lease payment the company could charge D'Angelo for the welding machine?
b. If the lease payment did not include the maintenance and insurance expenses, what impact would this have on the minimum lease payment J&M Leasing would charge?
c. If J&M Leasing charges the lease payment calculated in part **a**, would D'Angelo prefer to purchase or lease the machine?
d. Now suppose J&M Leasing actually charges a 15 percent premium on its minimum required payment to account for risk factors. Will D'Angelo prefer to purchase or lease the machine?
e. Suppose D'Angelo does not take proper care of the machinery and J&M Leasing withholds the damage deposit because the machine is not in "acceptable condition" at the end of the leasing period. What impact does this have on the D'Angelo decision if J&M charges the lease payment calculated in part **d**?

INTERMEDIATE

16–18 **Calculating lease payments and lease or purchase** Circuit Town, an electronics company, is considering leasing one of the products it manufactures, in addition to selling it to customers. The product, which sells for $17,900, has an economic life of 7 years and a CCA rate of 20 percent. Circuit Town's after-tax cost of debt is 7.5 percent and the company has a tax rate of 30 percent. The first lease payment is due when the lease contract is signed.

a. To earn 13 percent, what annual lease payment must Circuit Town require?
b. If the product has a salvage value of $3,200 at the end of 7 years, what annual lease payment will be required?
c. Sound Bytes Inc. has approached Circuit Town regarding the lease of the product. Circuit Town will charge a lease rate 20 percent greater than that calculated in part **b**. Sound Bytes has no other assets in the same asset class. Using the information above, determine the cost of purchasing and the cost of leasing the product assuming Sound Bytes has an after-tax borrowing rate of 7 percent, a cost of capital of 10 percent, and a tax rate of 40 percent.

INTERMEDIATE  16–19 **Calculating lease payments** A business friend has offered to sell you his truck for $10,000; he will then lease the truck back from you. The lease calls for annual lease payments over 4 years, with the first due when the lease contract is signed. It is expected that the truck will have no salvage value at the end of the 4 years. CCA can be claimed at a rate of 20 percent. Your tax rate is 40 percent, and you want to achieve an effective after-tax return on your capital of 12 percent per year.

a. If you were to enter into this arrangement, what lease rate would you charge your business friend?
b. Assume that you will finance $6,000 of the acquisition price of the truck by borrowing at a rate of 15 percent. Given the lease payments calculated in part **a**, what percentage rate of return would you then achieve on your remaining equity investment of $4,000?
c. Would your answer in part **a** change if the lease payments were monthly, payable at the beginning of each month? Explain and provide calculations.

CASE CHAPTER 16 Rashid Company: Acquiring a Chemical Waste Disposal System

See the enclosed Student CD-ROM for cases that help you put theories and concepts from the text into practice.

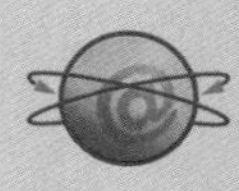

Be sure to visit the Companion Website for this book at **www.pearsoned.ca/gitman** for a wealth of additional learning tools including self-test quizzes, Web exercises, and additional cases.

CHAPTER

17

Corporate Securities, Derivatives, and Swaps

LEARNING GOALS

- LG1 Introduce the concept of hybrid and derivative securities and swap instruments, and how they are used by a corporation.
- LG2 Describe the basic types and general features of convertible securities, and demonstrate the procedures for determining the straight bond value, conversion (or share) value, and market value of a convertible bond.
- LG3 Explain the basic characteristics of warrants, the implied price of an attached warrant, and the values of warrants.
- LG4 Define and discuss options and the terminology and features of options, and identify the six variables affecting the pricing of options.
- LG5 Explain option trading and option quotes, illustrate the payoff to option trading, and discuss how companies use options.
- LG6 Discuss the general features of swaps and illustrate how they can be of benefit to both parties that are involved in the transaction.

17.1 An Overview of Derivatives and Swaps

Chapter 5 described the characteristics of the key securities issued by corporations to raise long-term financing: long-term debt, preferred shares, and common shares. In their simplest form, bonds are pure debt and common shares are pure equity. Preferred shares, on the other hand, are a form of equity that promises to pay fixed periodic dividends that are similar to the fixed contractual interest payments on bonds.

Deriving Value

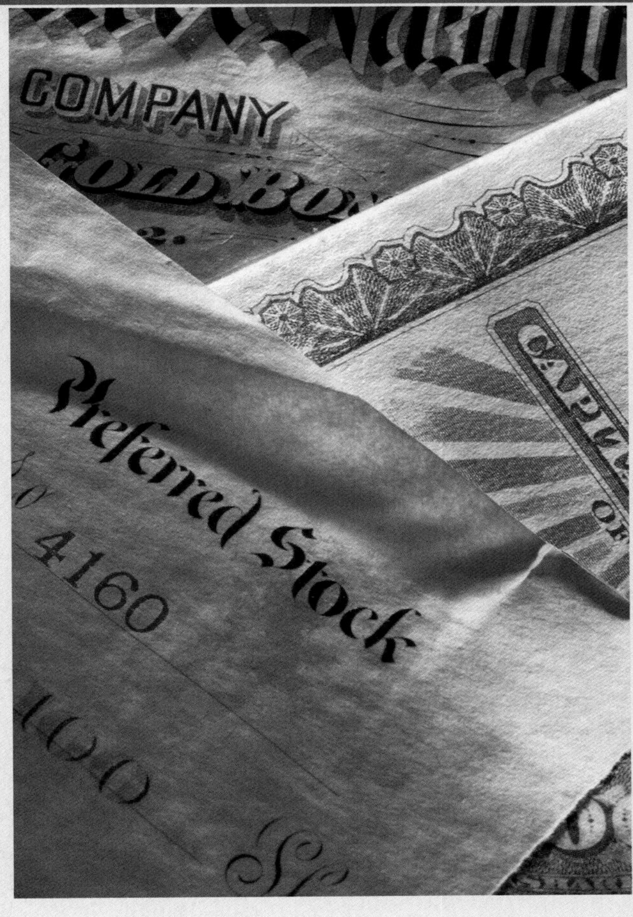

In Chapter 5, we saw that corporations can raise financing using debt and equity securities. But, to broaden the firm's capital structure and entice investors to purchase securities, firms sometimes issue convertibles. With these securities, investors can receive a coupon or dividend payment, yet still participate in any price increase in the company's common shares. These convertibles *derive* their value from the value of the common shares. Swaps are ways for both companies involved in the transaction to benefit from lower interest rates. Swaps have become a huge component of trading in the financial markets. Options are traded on, and derive their value from, a company's common shares. They are a way investors can trade on the expected change in value of a firm's common shares. In addition, a firm can use options on interest rates or commodities to hedge their own risk. Derivatives are a large and growing part of the financial markets, and an important component of corporate finance.

hybrid security
A form of debt or equity financing that possesses characteristics of *both* debt and equity financing.

derivative security
A security that is neither debt nor equity but derives its value from an underlying asset that is often another security; called *derivative* for short.

Because they blend the characteristics of *both* debt (issued at a stated value, rated for default, traded on basis of yield, and makes fixed payments to holders) and equity (pay dividends, a permanent source of financing, holders cannot force bankruptcy), preferred shares are considered a **hybrid security.** Another popular hybrid form of financing is convertible securities. A convertible security starts life as either debt or preferred equity, but becomes a predetermined number of common shares at a specified time in the future.

In addition to hybrid securities, this chapter focuses on two popular **derivative securities**—securities that are neither debt nor equity. Derivatives derive their

LINKING THE DISCIPLINES: Cross-Functional Interactions

- *Accounting personnel* need to understand the general features of convertible securities, warrants, swaps, and options that they will be required to record and report.
- *Information systems analysts* will design systems that provide timely information that can be used to monitor and track the market behaviour of the firm's outstanding securities.
- *Management* must understand how convertible securities and warrants work and the impact interest rate and currency swaps would have on the firm to help decide when the firm would benefit from their use.
- The *marketing department* needs to understand how hybrid securities such as convertible securities and derivatives such as warrants can be used to raise funds for new projects.
- Personnel in the *operations department* need to understand how hybrid securities and derivatives can be used to raise funds to finance new equipment and production capabilities.

value from an underlying asset that is often another security. The two derivatives that we will discuss are warrants and options. Warrants are created by a corporation as part of an issue of financial securities. Warrants act as an added incentive for investors to purchase the issue. Options are created by investors as an alternative to investing in the underlying financial security, most often common shares, on which the derivative's value is based. Options can also be used to hedge the risk of an investor's holding of financial securities. In addition, stock options are created by companies and then granted to employees (most often senior management) as part of an incentive plan.

Based on the descriptions above, it is clear that convertible securities are a type of derivative. Since a convertible bond or preferred share is convertible into a stated number of common shares, part of the value of the convertible security is *derived* from the value of the company's common shares. A convertible security could be considered a derivative.

Finally, in the chapter, we discuss swaps. These are financial instruments that allow two parties to exchange, or swap, cash flows in a mutually beneficial way. Generally speaking, swaps are used by firms that desire a type of interest rate structure, either in their own or in another currency, that another firm can provide less expensively. There are many kinds of swaps and the swap market worldwide is very large even though the evolution of swaps only began in 1981. In this chapter we will discuss the concept of swaps and introduce interest rate and currency swaps.

? Review Question

17–1 Differentiate among a *hybrid security*, a *derivative security*, and a *swap*. What are some examples of these securities?

17.2 Convertible Securities

conversion feature
An option that is included as part of a long-term debt or a preferred share issue that allows its holder to change the security into a stated number of common shares.

A **conversion feature** is an option that is included as part of a long-term debt or a preferred share issue that allows the holder to change the security into a stated number of common shares. The conversion feature typically enhances the marketability of an issue.

Types of Convertible Securities

Corporate bonds and preferred shares may be convertible into common shares. The most common type of convertible security is the bond. Convertibles normally have an accompanying *call feature.* This feature permits the issuer to retire or encourage conversion of outstanding convertibles when appropriate.

Convertible Bonds

convertible bond
A bond that can be changed into a specified number of common shares.

straight bond
A bond that is nonconvertible, having no conversion feature.

A **convertible bond** can be changed into a specified number of common shares. It is almost always a *debenture*—an unsecured bond—with a call feature. Because the conversion feature provides the purchaser with the possibility of becoming a shareholder on favourable terms, convertible bonds are generally a less expensive form of financing than similar-risk nonconvertible or **straight bonds.** The conversion feature adds a degree of speculation to a bond issue, although the issue still maintains its value as a bond.

Convertible Preferred Shares

convertible preferred shares
Preferred shares that can be changed into a specified number of common shares.

straight preferred shares
Preferred shares that have no conversion feature.

Convertible preferred shares can be changed into a specified number of common shares. They can normally be sold with a lower stated dividend than similar-risk nonconvertible or **straight preferred shares.** The reason is that the convertible preferred holder is assured of the fixed dividend payment associated with a preferred share and also may receive the appreciation resulting from increases in the market price of the underlying common shares. Convertible preferred shares behave much like convertible bonds. The following discussions will concentrate on the more popular convertible bonds.

General Features of Convertibles

Convertible securities are almost always convertible any time during the life of the security. Occasionally, conversion is permitted only for a limited number of years, say, for 5 or 10 years after issuance of the convertible.

Conversion Ratio

conversion ratio
The ratio at which a convertible security can be exchanged for common shares.

conversion price
The per-share price that is effectively paid for common shares as the result of conversion of a convertible security.

The **conversion ratio** is the ratio at which a convertible security can be exchanged for common shares. The conversion ratio can be stated in two ways.

1. Sometimes the conversion ratio is stated in terms of a given number of common shares. To find the **conversion price,** which is the per-share price that is effectively paid for common shares as the result of conversion, the par

value (not the market value) of the convertible security must be divided by the conversion ratio.

Example Western Wear Company, a manufacturer of denim products, has a convertible bond outstanding. Each $1,000 of par value is convertible into 25 common shares. The bond's conversion ratio is 25 shares. The conversion price for the bond is $40 per share ($1,000 ÷ 25).

2. Sometimes, instead of the conversion ratio, the conversion price is given. The conversion ratio can be obtained by dividing the *par value* of the convertible by the conversion price.

Example Mosher Company, a franchiser of seafood restaurants, has a 20-year convertible bond outstanding. Each $1,000 of par value of the bond is convertible into common shares at a price of $50 per share. The conversion ratio is 20 shares ($1,000 ÷ $50).

The conversion ratio of a convertible security is set at the time of issue. The ratio will always result in a conversion price per share that is above the current market price per share. If the prospective purchasers do not expect the company's market price to ever reach the conversion price, they will not purchase the convertible, opting instead for a straight security or another company's convertible issue.

Example Chargers Ltd. is planning to issue $250 million of preferred shares with a $100 stated value. Therefore, the company will issue 2.5 million preferred shares. Each share will be convertible into five common shares, meaning the conversion price is $20 ($100 ÷ 5). At the time of the issue, the firm's shares will be trading for less than $20, say $16 per share. This implies that the common share price will have to increase by more than 25 percent before conversion becomes viable.

Conversion (or Share) Value

conversion (or share) value
The value of a convertible security measured in terms of the market price of the common shares into which it can be converted.

The **conversion (or share) value** is the value of the convertible measured in terms of the market price of the common shares into which it can be converted. The conversion value can be found simply by multiplying the conversion ratio by the current market price of the firm's common shares.

Example McNamara Industries, a petroleum processor, has a convertible bond issue outstanding. Each $1,000 of par value of the bond is convertible into 16 common shares, meaning the conversion price is $62.50 ($1,000 ÷ 16). Because the current market price of the common shares is $65 per share, the conversion value is $1,040 (16 × $65). Because the conversion value is above the bond value of $1,000, conversion is a viable option for the owner of the convertible security.

In the Chargers Ltd. example above, the conversion value of the preferred share is $80 (5 × $16 per share). Obviously, at this time, conversion is not a viable option. The common share price will have to increase by just over 25 percent, at which point conversion begins to become viable.

Effect on Earnings

contingent securities
Convertibles, warrants, and stock options. Their presence affects the reporting of a firm's earnings per share (EPS).

basic EPS
Earnings per share (EPS) calculated without regard to any contingent securities.

diluted EPS
Earnings per share (EPS) calculated under the assumption that all contingent securities that would have dilutive effects are converted into common shares.

The presence of **contingent securities,** which include convertibles as well as warrants (described later in this chapter) and stock options (described in Chapter 1 and later in this chapter), affects the reporting of the firm's earnings per share (EPS). Firms with contingent securities that if converted or exercised would dilute (i.e., lower) earnings per share are required to report earnings in two ways—*basic EPS* and *diluted EPS.*

Basic EPS is calculated without regard to any contingent securities. It is found by dividing earnings available for common shareholders by the number of common shares outstanding. This is the standard method of calculating EPS that has been used throughout this textbook.

Diluted EPS is calculated under the assumption that all contingent securities that would have dilutive effects are converted into common shares. It is found by adjusting basic EPS for the impact of converting all convertibles and exercising all warrants and options that would have dilutive effects on the firm's earnings. This approach treats as common shares *all* contingent securities.

Diluted EPS is calculated by dividing earnings available for common shareholders (adjusted for interest and preferred share dividends that would *not* be paid given assumed conversion of *all* outstanding contingent securities that would have dilutive effects) by the number of common shares that would be outstanding if *all* contingent securities that would have dilutive effects are converted and exercised. Rather than demonstrate these accounting calculations, suffice it to say that firms with outstanding convertibles, warrants, and/or stock options must report basic and diluted EPS on their income statements.

Financing with Convertibles

Using convertible securities to raise long-term funds can help the firm achieve its cost of capital and capital structure goals. There also are a number of more specific motives and considerations involved in evaluating convertible financing.

Motives for Convertible Financing

Convertibles can be used for a variety of reasons. One popular motive is their use as a form of *deferred common share financing.* When a convertible security is issued, both issuer and purchaser expect the security to be converted into common shares at some future point. Because the security is first sold with a conversion price above the current market price of the firm's shares, conversion is initially not attractive. The issuer of a convertible could alternatively sell common shares, but only at or below their current market price. By selling the convertible, the issuer in effect makes a *deferred sale* of common shares. As the market price of the firm's common shares rises to a higher level, conversion may occur. By deferring the issuance of new common shares until the market price of the shares has increased, fewer shares will have to be issued, thereby decreasing the dilution of both ownership and earnings.

Hint
Convertible securities are advantageous to both the issuer and the holder. The issuer does not have to give up immediate control as it would have to if it were issuing common shares. The holder of a convertible security has the possibility of a future speculative gain.

Another motive for convertible financing is its *use as a "sweetener" for financing.* Because the purchaser of the convertible is given the opportunity to become a common shareholder and share in the firm's future success, *convertibles can be normally sold with lower interest rates than nonconvertibles.* Therefore, from the firm's viewpoint, including a conversion feature reduces the coupon rate on the debt. The purchaser of the issue sacrifices a portion of interest return for the potential opportunity to become a common shareholder. Another important motive for issuing convertibles is that, generally speaking, *convertible securities can be issued with far fewer restrictive covenants than nonconvertibles.* Because many investors view convertibles as equity, the covenant issue is not important to them.

A final motive for using convertibles is to *raise cheap funds temporarily.* By using convertible bonds, the firm can temporarily raise debt, which is typically less expensive than common shares, to finance projects. Once such projects are on line, the firm may wish to shift its capital structure to a less highly levered position. A conversion feature gives the issuer the opportunity, through actions of convertible holders, to shift its capital structure at a future point in time.

Other Considerations

When the price of the firm's common shares rises above the conversion price, the market price of the convertible security will normally rise to a level above its conversion value. When this happens, many convertible holders will not convert, because they already have the market price benefit obtainable from conversion and can still receive fixed periodic interest payments. Because of this behaviour, virtually all convertible securities have a *call feature* that enables the issuer to encourage or *"force" conversion.* The call price of the security generally exceeds the security's par value by a stated premium. Although the issuer must pay a premium for calling a security, the call privilege is generally not exercised until the conversion value of the security is 10 to 20 percent *above the call price.* This type of premium above the call price helps to assure the issuer that the holders of the convertible will convert it when the call is made, instead of accepting the call price.

overhanging issue
A convertible security that cannot be forced into conversion by using the call feature.

Unfortunately, there are instances when the market price of a security does not reach a level sufficient to stimulate the conversion of associated convertibles. A convertible security that cannot be forced into conversion by using the call feature is called an **overhanging issue.** An overhanging issue can be quite detrimental to a firm. If the firm were to call the issue, the bondholders would accept the call price rather than convert the bonds. In this case, the firm not only would have to pay the call premium, but would require additional financing to pay off the bonds at their par value. If the firm raised these funds through the sale of equity, a large number of shares would have to be issued due to their low market price. This, in turn, could result in the dilution of existing ownership. The firm could use debt or preferred shares to finance the call, but this use would leave the firm's capital structure no less levered than before the call.

Determining the Value of a Convertible Bond

The key characteristic of convertible securities that enhances their marketability is their ability to minimize the possibility of a loss while providing a possibility of capital gains. Here we discuss the three values of a convertible bond: (1) the straight bond value, (2) the conversion value, and (3) the market value.

Straight Bond Value

straight bond value
The price at which a convertible bond would sell in the market without the conversion feature.

The **straight bond value** of a convertible bond is the price at which it would sell in the market without the conversion feature. This value is found by determining the value of a nonconvertible bond with similar payments and time to maturity issued by a firm with the same risk. The straight bond value is typically the *floor,* or minimum, price at which the convertible bond would be traded. The straight bond value equals the present value of the bond's coupon and principal payments discounted at the interest rate the firm would have to pay on a nonconvertible bond. This process was fully considered in Chapter 8.

Example Duncan Company, a discount store chain, sold a 20-year convertible debenture three years ago. The coupon rate on the debenture is 6.5 percent, with the coupons paid semiannually. The current yield on convertible debentures of similar risk and time to maturity is 8 percent. The value of each $1,000 of par value of the debenture is calculated using Equation 8.9, as was illustrated in Chapter 8, and provided below:

$$V_0 = [I \times PVIFa\ (k_d\%, n \text{ per})] + [M \times PVIF\ (k_d\%, n \text{ per})] \quad (17.1)$$

In this case, $32.50 is the semiannual coupon payment, there are 17 years or 34 periods to run to maturity, the discount rate is 4 percent, the semiannual yield on comparable risk securities, and the par value to be received at maturity is $1,000. Inputting these values into a financial calculator results in the following value:

$$V_0 = [\$32.50 \times PVIFa\ (4\%, 34 \text{ per})] + [\$1{,}000 \times PVIF\ (4\%, 34 \text{ per})]$$

$$V_0 = \$861.92$$

The value of the convertible debenture will be less than each $1,000 of par value since yields have increased since the time of the issue. The calculated value is $861.92. This is the minimum price at which the convertible bond is expected to sell. When the market price of the company's common shares is below the conversion price, the bond is expected to trade at this price.

Conversion (or Share) Value

Recall that the *conversion (or share) value* of a convertible security is the value of the convertible measured in terms of the market price of the common shares into which the security can be converted. When the market price of the common shares exceeds the conversion price, the conversion (or share) value exceeds the par value. An example will clarify the point.

Example Duncan Company's convertible bond described above is convertible at $50 per share. Each bond can be converted into 20 shares, because each bond has a $1,000 par value. The conversion values of the bond when the shares are selling at $30, $40, $50, $60, $70, and $80 per share are shown in the following table.

Market price of stock	Conversion value
$30	$ 600
40	800
50 (conversion price)	1,000 (par value)
60	1,200
70	1,400
80	1,600

When the market price of the common stock exceeds the $50 conversion price, the conversion value exceeds the $1,000 par value. Because the straight bond value (calculated in the preceding example) is $861.92, the bond will, in a stable environment, never sell for less than this amount, regardless of how low its conversion value is. If the market price per share were $30, the bond would still sell for $861.92—not $600—because its value as a bond would dominate. If the common share price were $60, the bond would sell for more than $1,200, assuming there is still time remaining before conversion. This is the case since the market will price the possibility that the share price will increase beyond $60.

Market Value

market premium
The amount by which the market value exceeds the straight or conversion value of a convertible security.

The market value of a convertible is likely to be greater than its straight value or its conversion value. The amount by which the market value exceeds its straight or conversion value is called the **market premium.** The general relationship of the straight bond value, conversion value, market value, and market premium for Duncan Company's convertible bond is shown in Figure 17.1.

The straight bond value acts as a floor for the security's value up to the point X, where the price of the common shares is high enough to cause the conversion value to exceed the straight bond value.[1] The market premium is attributed to the fact that the convertible gives investors a chance to experience attractive capital gains from increases in the share price while taking less risk.

In other words, part of the market value of a convertible (the market premium) is derived from the value of the underlying common shares. As was mentioned in Section 17.1, a convertible security is, in part, a derivative security.

The floor (straight bond value) provides protection against losses resulting from a decline in the share price caused by falling profits or other factors. The market premium tends to be greatest when the straight bond value and conversion (or share) value are within 10 to 15 percent of one another. Investors are willing to pay a higher market premium at this point since modest increases in the price of the common shares will lead to conversion becoming viable or a more attractive option. The derivative component of the convertible's value is greatest at point X.

1. Note that as yields for bonds of comparable risk vary, so too will the floor price (the straight bond value). For example, for the Duncan Company bond, if 3 more years elapse and yields on bonds of comparable risk are now 6 percent, the straight bond value will be $1,046.91 and this will act as the floor price, regardless of what has happened to the market price of Duncan's common shares.

FIGURE 17.1

Values and Market Premium
The values and market premium for Duncan Company's convertible bond

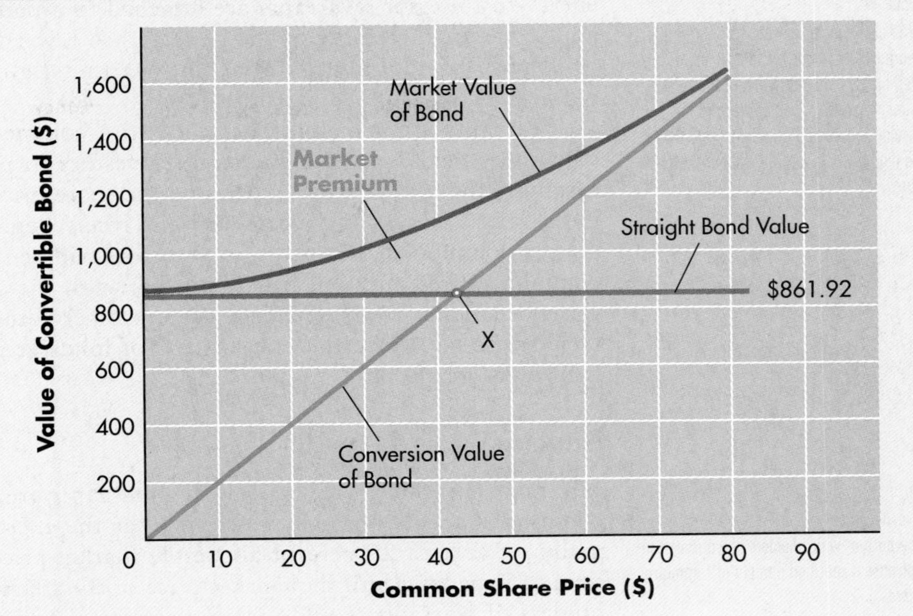

? Review Questions

17–2 What is the *conversion feature*? What is a *conversion ratio*? How do convertibles and other *contingent securities* affect EPS? Briefly describe the motives for convertible financing.

17–3 When the market price of the stock rises above the conversion price, why may a convertible security *not* be converted? How can the *call feature* be used to force conversion in this situation? What is an *overhanging issue*?

17–4 Define the *straight bond value, conversion (or share) value, market value,* and *market premium* associated with a convertible bond, and describe the general relationships among them.

17.3 Warrants

warrant
An instrument that gives its holder the right to purchase a certain number of common shares at a specified price within a certain period of time.

Warrants are similar to share *rights,* which were briefly described in Chapter 5. A **warrant** gives the holder the right to purchase a certain number of common shares at a specified price within a certain period of time. Holders of warrants earn no income from them until the warrants are exercised or sold. Warrants also bear some similarity to convertibles in that they provide for the injection of additional equity capital into the firm at some future date.

Basic Characteristics

Warrants can be attached to an issue of any of the three types of financial securities: long-term debt, preferred shares, or common shares. Warrants are "sweet-

Hint
One of the major reasons for attaching a warrant to an issue, or for offering a convertible, is that with either of these features the investor will not require the issuing firm to pay an interest rate that is as high as for a security without these features.

eners" to the issue. Warrants are attached to a debt or preferred share issue to add to the marketability of the issue and to lower the required coupon or dividend rate. In addition, by attaching warrants, a company may avoid certain restrictive covenants on a debt issue.

Warrants are sometimes attached to a common share issue of higher risk companies. The warrants encourage investors to purchase the issue and then, assuming the company does well and the share price increases, more fully share in the future success of the company and receive higher returns. If the price of the issuer's common shares increases, investors will benefit from the purchase of the common shares and will benefit further with the warrants. When a firm first raises financing from outside investors or creditors, warrants are sometimes included to allow the earlier providers of funds greater potential to profit from their investment.

Exercise Price

exercise price
The price at which holders of warrants can purchase a specified number of common shares.

The price at which holders of warrants can purchase a specified number of common shares is normally referred to as the **exercise price.** This price is normally set at least 20 percent above the market price of the firm's shares at the time of issuance. Until the market price of the shares exceeds the exercise price, holders of warrants would not exercise them, because they could purchase the stock more inexpensively in the marketplace.

Warrants normally have a life of no more than 5 years, although some have longer lives. Although, unlike convertible securities, warrants cannot be called, their limited life results in holders exercising them when the market price of the common shares is above the exercise price of the warrant.

Warrant Trading

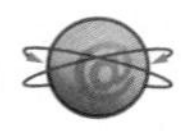

www.canada.com/nationalpost/financialpost/fpmarketdata/index.html

A warrant is *detachable* from the security with which it was sold. This means that the security holder may sell the warrant without selling the security to which it is attached. Many detachable warrants are listed and actively traded on the Toronto Stock Exchange (TSX). Warrants often provide investors with better opportunities for large percentage gains (with increased risk) than the underlying common stock. A current list of warrants trading on the TSX is available on the Web.

Comparison of Warrants to Rights and Convertibles

The similarity between a warrant and a right should be clear. Both result in new equity capital, although the warrant provides for *deferred* equity financing. The life of a right is typically not more than four weeks; a warrant is generally exercisable for a period of years. Rights are issued at a subscription price below the prevailing market price of the stock when issued; warrants have an exercise price at least 20 percent above the prevailing market price.

Warrants and convertibles also have similarities. The exercise of a warrant shifts the firm's capital structure to a less highly levered position because new common shares are issued without any change in debt. If a convertible bond were converted, the reduction in leverage would be even more pronounced, because common shares would be issued in exchange for a reduction in debt. In addition, the exercise of a warrant provides an influx of new capital; with convertibles, the new capital is raised when the securities are originally issued rather than when converted. The influx of new equity capital resulting from the exercise of a warrant does not occur until the firm has achieved a certain degree of success that is reflected in an increased price for its stock. In this instance, the firm conveniently obtains needed funds.

The Implied Price of an Attached Warrant

implied price of a warrant
The price effectively paid for each warrant attached to a bond.

When attached to a bond, the **implied price of a warrant**—the price that is effectively paid for each attached warrant—can be found by first using Equation 17.2:

$$\text{Implied price of } \textit{all} \text{ warrants} = \text{price of bond with warrants attached} - \text{straight bond value} \tag{17.2}$$

The straight bond value is found in a fashion similar to that used in valuing convertible bonds. Dividing the implied price of *all* warrants by the number of warrants attached to each bond results in the implied price of *each* warrant.

Example Martin Marine Products, a manufacturer of marine drive shafts and propellers, issued a 20-year bond with a 10.5 percent coupon rate paid semiannually. Each $1,000 of par value of the bond has 15 warrants attached that can be used to purchase the firm's common shares. The bonds were initially sold for their $1,000 par value. When issued, similar-risk straight bonds without warrants with 20 years to maturity were trading to yield 11.5 percent. The straight value of the bond is based on the present value of its payments discounted at the 11.5 percent yield on similar-risk straight bonds. This is equal to $922.34.

Substituting the $1,000 price of the bond with warrants attached and the $922.34 straight bond value into Equation 17.2, we get an implied price of *all* warrants of $77.66:

$$\text{Implied price of } \textit{all} \text{ warrants} = \$1{,}000 - \$922.34 = \underline{\underline{\$77.66}}$$

Dividing the implied price of *all* warrants by the number of warrants attached to each bond—15 in this case—we find the implied price of *each* warrant:

$$\text{Implied price of } \textit{each} \text{ warrant} = \frac{\$77.66}{15} = \underline{\underline{\$5.18}}$$

Therefore, by purchasing Martin Marine Products' bond with warrants attached for $1,000, one is effectively paying $5.18 for each warrant.

The implied price of each warrant is meaningful only when compared to the specific features of the warrant—the number of shares that can be purchased and the specified exercise price. These features can be analyzed in light of the prevailing common share price to estimate the true *market value* of each warrant. Clearly, if the implied price is above the estimated market value, the price of the bond with warrants attached may be too high. If the implied price is below the estimated market value, the bond may be quite attractive. Firms must therefore price their bonds with warrants attached in a way that causes the implied price of its warrants to fall slightly below their estimated market value. Such an approach allows the firm to more easily sell the bonds with a lower coupon rate than would apply to straight debt, thereby reducing its debt service costs.

The Value of Warrants

warrant premium The difference between the actual market value and theoretical value of a warrant.

Like a convertible security, a warrant has both a market and an intrinsic value. The difference between these values, or the **warrant premium,** depends largely on investor expectations and the ability of investors to get more leverage from the warrants than from the underlying stock.

Intrinsic Value of a Warrant

intrinsic value The positive difference between the current market price of a firm's common shares and the exercise price of the warrant.

The **intrinsic value** of a warrant is the positive difference between the current market price of a firm's common shares and the exercise price of the warrant. Equation 17.3 provides the equation.

$$IV_W = \frac{P_0 - E}{N} \tag{17.3}$$

where:

IV_W = intrinsic value of a warrant
P_0 = current market price of the common shares
E = exercise price of the warrant
N = number of warrants needed to purchase one common share

The use of Equation 17.3 can be illustrated by the following example.

Example Dustin Electronics, a major producer of transistors, has outstanding warrants that are exercisable at $40 per share and entitle holders to purchase one common share. The warrants were initially attached to a bond issue to sweeten the bond. The common shares of the firm are currently selling for $45 per share. Substituting P_0 = $45, E = $40, and N = 1 into Equation 17.3 yields a theoretical warrant value of $5 [($45 − $40)/1]. Therefore, the intrinsic value of Dustin's warrants is $5.

If Dustin Electronics' common shares were trading for $38 per share, the intrinsic value of the warrant would be 0. When Equation 17.3 is used, the answer is −$2 ($38 − $40). But a warrant cannot have a negative intrinsic value. In this case, Dustin Electronics' warrant would have no intrinsic value.

Market Value of a Warrant

The market value of a warrant is always above the intrinsic value of the warrant, except at the point of expiry. As the expiry date of a warrant gets nearer, the market value of the warrant declines and approaches its intrinsic value so the difference between the two values is reduced to 0. Also, when the market value of a warrant is very high (the market price of a common share is well above the exercise price of the warrant), the market value of a warrant approaches the intrinsic value. This occurs since investors will try to reduce the risk of large losses on the warrant. Also, as warrant prices increase, the ability to leverage higher percentage returns from investing in warrants disappears.

The general relationship between the intrinsic and market values of Dustin Electronics' warrants is presented graphically in Figure 17.2. The market value of warrants generally exceeds the intrinsic value by the greatest amount when the market price of the common shares is close to the warrant exercise price per share. In addition, the amount of time until expiration also affects the market value of the warrant. Generally speaking, the more distant the expiration date, the greater the gap between a warrant's market value and its intrinsic value.

Warrant Premium

The *warrant premium*, or amount by which the market value of Dustin Electronics' warrants exceeds the intrinsic value of these warrants, is also shown in Figure 17.2. This premium results from a combination of positive investor expectations, time to warrant expiry, and the ability of the investor with a fixed sum to invest to obtain much larger potential returns (and risk) by trading in warrants rather than the underlying common shares. The warrant premium is sometimes termed the time value of the warrant. The warrant premium (WP) is equal to:

$$WP = V_W - IV_W \qquad (17.4)$$

where V_W is the market value of the warrant.

Example Stan Buyer has $2,880, which he is interested in investing in Dustin Electronics. The firm's stock is currently selling for $45 per share, and its warrants are selling for $8 per warrant. Each warrant entitles the holder to purchase one of Dustin's common shares at $40 per share. Because the stock is selling for $45 per share, the intrinsic value, calculated in the preceding example, is $5 per warrant. The warrant premium of $3 ($8 − $5) results from positive investor expectations, time to expiry, and leverage opportunities.

FIGURE 17.2

Values and Warrant Premium

The values and warrant premium for Dustin Electronics' stock purchase warrants

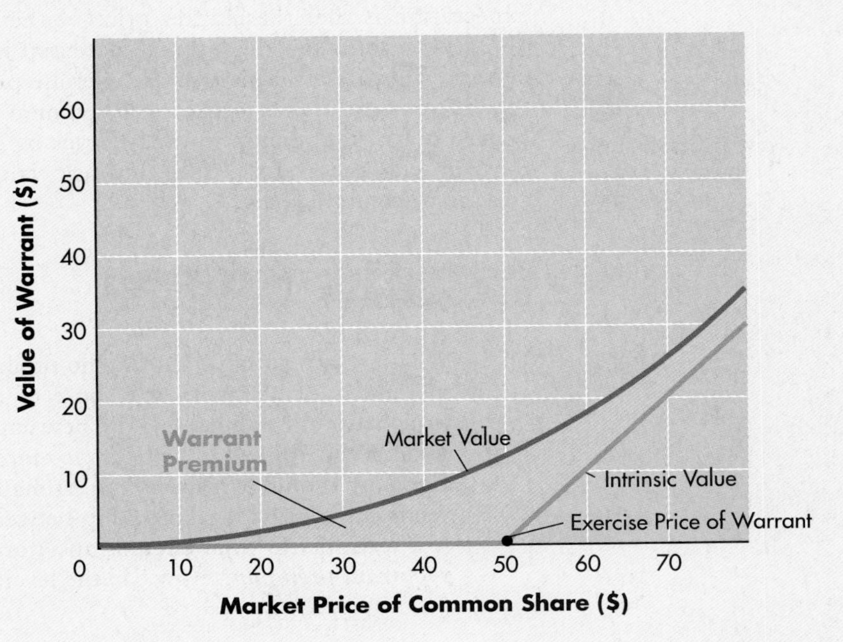

Stan Buyer could invest his $2,880 in either of two ways: He could purchase 64 common shares at $45 per share, or 360 warrants at $8 per warrant, ignoring brokerage fees. If Mr. Buyer purchases the shares and the price rises to $48, his gain is $192 ($3 × 64 shares), or 6.67 percent ($192 ÷ $2,880) on the initial investment. If instead he purchases the warrants and Dustin Electronics' common share price increases to $48, then the warrant will increase by at least $3. If the warrant price were to increase to $12 per warrant, the warrant's intrinsic value would be $8 per share while the premium has increased to $4. Mr. Buyer's gain is $4 per warrant or $1,440 ($4 × 360 warrants) in total. On a percentage basis, the gain is 50 percent ($1,440 ÷ $2,880).

The greater leverage associated with trading warrants should be clear from the example. Of course, because leverage works both ways, it results in greater risk. If the market price of the common shares fell by $3, the loss on the common share investment would be $192. The market price of the warrant may fall to $4 (a $2 intrinsic value and $2 warrant premium), meaning Mr. Buyer would lose $1,440, or half his investment. Clearly, investing in warrants is more risky than investing in the underlying stock. The leverage of a warrant can be calculated by using Equation 17.5:

$$\text{Leverage} = \frac{P_0}{V_W} \tag{17.5}$$

where: P_0 = current market price of the common shares
V_W = current market value of the warrant

Generally, the higher the measure of leverage, the greater the leverage effect. In the example above, the leverage potential is 5.625 ($45 ÷ $8). This means that if the price of Dustin Electronic's common shares increases by 10 percent, the expectation is that the market price of the warrant will increase by at least 56.25 percent. When the leverage potential is extremely high, investors should beware. This often means that the exercise price of the warrant is much higher than the current market price of the common shares. In such a case, the warrant is deep out of the money and may never be exercised. Market quotes for warrants provide the exercise price, intrinsic value, warrant premium (time value), and the warrant's leverage.

www.canada.com/nationalpost/financialpost/fpmarketdata/index.html

? Review Questions

17–5 What are *warrants*? What are the similarities and key differences between the effects of warrants and those of convertibles on the firm's capital structure and its ability to raise new capital?

17–6 What is the *implied price of a warrant*? How is it estimated? To be effective, how should it relate to the estimated *market value* of a warrant?

17–7 What is the general relationship between the intrinsic and market values of a warrant? In what circumstances are these values quite close? What is a *warrant premium*? How can the leverage of a warrant be calculated?

17.4 Option Features and Pricing

option
An instrument that provides its holder with an opportunity to purchase or sell a specified asset at a stated price on or before a set *expiration date.*

In the most general sense, an **option** can be viewed as an instrument that provides its holder with an opportunity to purchase or sell a specified asset at a stated price on or before a set *expiration date*. Options are a popular type of *derivative security* with a long history of use. Ancient Romans, Grecians, and Phoenicians traded options against outgoing cargoes from their local seaports. When used in relation to financial securities, options are a contract between two parties where the holder of the option has the right, but not the obligation, to buy some underlying asset. Providing rights without obligations has financial value which may be sold. Since options derive their value from another asset, they are called derivative assets.

Our discussion of options centres on options on common shares. The development of organized options exchanges has created markets in which to trade these financial securities. Four basic forms of derivative securities are rights, warrants, convertibles, and options. Rights were discussed in Chapter 5, while warrants and convertibles were described in the preceding sections. In this section, the many features of options are discussed.

Option Basics and Terminology

call option
A security that provides the holder the right to purchase the common shares of a specific company, on or before a specified future date, at a stated price.

put option
A security that provides the holder the right to sell the common shares of a specific company, on or before a specified future date, at a stated price.

The two basic types of options are calls and puts. A **call option** is a security that provides the holder the right to *purchase* the common shares of a specific company, on or before a specified future date, at a stated price. A **put option** is a security that provides the holder the right to *sell* the common shares of a specific company, on or before a specified future date, at a stated price. Options usually have initial lives of one to nine months, although there are longer-term options available that have lives as long as three years. A standardized feature of options on common shares is that they are always for 100 shares. One call option contract gives the holder the right to buy 100 of the underlying company's common shares. One put option contract gives the holder the right to sell 100 of the underlying company's common shares.

The focus of the above descriptions of options is on common shares. Note, however, that options are a derivative security and are available on many types of real and financial assets. For example, options are available on currencies, long-term debt, stock market indexes, and commodities such as wheat, cotton, cattle, orange juice, crude oil, and natural gas. While it is important to note that there are additional types of options, in this section we concentrate our discussion on options on common shares.

option writer
Creates an option contract for sale to option buyers.

strike (exercise) price
The stated price at which the holder of the option can exercise the option.

Table 17.1 summarizes the positions of both the buyer and the seller of call and put options. Options are used by investors as a way of speculating on the price of a company's common shares, or as a way of reducing (hedging) the risk of an investor's holdings of common shares. The buyer of the option is said to be "long" the option or "going long." The seller of an option is termed the **option writer**. The writer creates the option contract in anticipation that another investor will purchase it. The writer is said to be "short" the option or "going short."

The **strike price** is the stated price at which the holder of the option can exercise the option. Exercising an option can be done at any time prior to the option's expiration date. The strike price is sometimes referred to as the **exercise** price. For a call option, the holder can buy the shares at the strike price. For a put

TABLE 17.1 Positions of the Buyer and Seller of a Call and Put Option

Call option	
Buyer	Pay a premium for *the right to buy* a given quantity of the underlying financial security at the strike price on or before the expiration date.
Seller	Receive premium and incur *the obligation to sell* a given quantity of the underlying financial security at the strike price on or before the expiration date.
Put option	
Buyer	Pay a premium for *the right to sell* a given quantity of the underlying financial security at the strike price on or before the expiration date.
Seller	Receive the premium and incur *the obligation to buy* a given quantity of the underlying financial security at the strike price on or before the expiration date.

option, the holder can sell the shares at the strike price. The strike price is generally set at or near the prevailing market price of the common shares at the time the option is created, depending on market demand. For example, if a firm's shares are currently selling for $30 per share, a call option created today would likely have a strike price in the $25 to $40 range. The various strike prices set for a particular company's options may differ by as little as $0.50 or as much as $5. The lower the price of the underlying company's common shares, the smaller the difference in the strike prices on the options.

option premium
The price paid by the buyer of an option contract, and the amount received by the seller; it is quoted on a per-share basis.

To purchase an option, a specified price per share must be paid. This is termed the *option premium*. The **option premium** is the price paid by the buyer of an option contract, and the amount received by the seller. The premium is quoted on a per-share basis (e.g., $1.20) and since the standard option contract is for 100 shares, the cost of a single option contract is the per-share premium multiplied by 100 (e.g., $1.20 × 100 = $120).

expiration date
The last day on which the option can be exercised; this is the third Friday of the month of the option contract.

The **expiration date** for options on common shares is the last day on which the option can be exercised. Options stop trading at the market close on the third Friday of the month of the option contract. Options actually expire on Saturday. This difference of one day is a technical issue that allows time for the option exchange to reconcile option trading. At the close of trading on the Friday, the option becomes worthless. Investors holding option contracts that have value must take action prior to the market close on Friday to receive the value. If an investor does not take action before the expiration date, any value the option contract may have is permanently lost.[2] In other words, the purchaser of an option must sell the same option prior to expiry to close her position. The seller of an option must buy the same option prior to expiry to close his position. "Same option" means an option with the same month of expiry and strike price.

Example It is September 6 and Wing Enterprise's common shares are trading for $30 per share. There is a December call option contract available for Wing Enterprise with a strike price of $30. The premium on the option is $2.50, or $250 for one contract. This call option contract will expire at the close of trading on the

2. In practice, if the option has value, the option exchange on which the option trades will automatically exercise the option at maturity.

third Friday of December. You purchase this contract, which will be known as a *Dec 30 call*.

If on the third Friday of December Wing Enterprise's common shares were trading for $36 per share, then your call option will be worth at least $6.00 per share. To capture the $6-per-share value of the option, you must sell a Dec 30 call on Wing prior to the market close. By doing so, you will make $3.50 per share ($6− $2.50) or $350 on one contract. You bought a Dec 30 call for $2.50 and sold a Dec 30 call for $6. You made $350, and your position in the Dec 30 call option on Wing Enterprise's common shares is now closed.

Other Features of Options

Hint
Options are created by investors. The firm has nothing to do with the creation of these securities. Warrants and convertibles are created by companies to raise financing.

To fully understand options, several other features should also be considered. Four of these are discussed in the following sections.

American and European Options

American option
An option contract that may be exercised at any time up to the expiration date.

European option
An option contract that may be exercised only on the expiration date.

Calls and puts are the two types of options available. Another way to categorize options is by when the option may be exercised. An **American option** may be exercised at any time up to the expiration date. A **European option** may be exercised only on the expiration date. All options on the common shares of individual companies are American options. Options on stock market indexes (like the S&P/TSX Index), currencies, and commodities are European options.

Long-Term Equity AnticiPation Security (LEAPS)

Long-Term Equity AnticiPation Security (LEAPS)
A long-term call or put option, on either common shares or stock market indexes, with expiration dates that are at least 1 year and up to 2.5 to 3 years in the future.

Another form of option is a **Long-term Equity AnticiPation Security (LEAPS)**. LEAPS are long-term options on either common shares or stock market indexes. Like options, LEAPS may be calls or puts. LEAPS are identical to standard options except LEAPS have expiration dates that are at least 1 year, and up to 2.5 to 3 years, in the future. Because of their longer lives, the premium on LEAPS with a stated strike price is much higher than on traditional options with the same strike price.

With their longer lives, LEAPS are often compared to warrants. LEAPS are American-style options, and their strike prices usually range around 25 percent above or below the price of the underlying common shares when the LEAPS are first offered by the options exchange. LEAPS were created by the Chicago Board Options Exchange (CBOE), and the term is a registered trademark of the organization. Visit their Web site for more details about options in general, and LEAPS in particular.

http://cboe.com

Rights Versus Obligation

A key distinction between the buyer and seller of an option can be seen by reviewing Table 17.1. Note that the purchaser of an option has the right to buy or sell the underlying financial security, not an obligation to do so. On the other hand, the seller of an option has the obligation to sell or buy the underlying financial security, if the holder of the option exercises her option. To avoid this obligation, the seller of an option can buy the same option and essentially cancel his position in the option.

Example On May 15, Crystal MacLean sold five July 25 call options on Morse Electronic's common shares. At the time, Morse Electronic's common shares were trading for $24. The premium on the option contract was $1.90 per share. Therefore, on this transaction, Crystal earned $950 ($1.90/share × 100 shares × 5 contracts). It is now the third Friday in July and the option contract will stop trading at the market close. Morse Electronic's common share price is $27.50. If Crystal maintains her current option position, what will happen?

Today, the holder of the call option that Crystal wrote will exercise the call option. The owner will exercise the option since he can buy the shares from the seller of the option contract at a price of $25 per share at a time when the shares are trading for $27.50 in the stock market. The holder of the call makes $2.50 per share. Since the owner of the call exercises the option, Crystal (the writer) has the obligation to sell the shares. If Crystal does not own the shares, she will have to buy the shares for $27.50 in the market, and then sell the shares to the option holder for $25.

On this series of transactions, Crystal will lose $2.50 per share (plus all of the commissions on the trades). She received the option premium of $1.90 per share when she sold the contract, so her net loss is $0.60 per share or $300 on the five contracts (again, plus commissions). To avoid buying and then selling the underlying common shares, Crystal could buy five call option contracts any time up to the time the options expire. In this example, that is at the close of trading today. If Crystal did this, then the option contract would be trading for about $2.50. When she buys the five contracts, she will close her position in the July 25 call option contract on Morse Electronic's common shares. She will still end up losing $0.60 per share, but will avoid the time and expense of buying and then selling the underlying common shares of the company.

Zero-Sum Trade

zero-sum trade
Profit made by purchasers of options comes at the expense of sellers; profit made by sellers of options comes at the expense of purchasers.

Another characteristic of option trading is that it is a **zero-sum trade**. This means that any profit made comes at the expense of the other party to the option contract. In other words, profit made by purchasers of options comes at the expense of sellers. Profit made by sellers of options comes at the expense of purchasers. The purchaser's (seller's) profit is the seller's (purchaser's) loss.

Example Pierre has just purchased an April 50 call option paying a premium of $2.50. The following table illustrates Pierre's (the buyer's) and the seller's position at the option's expiry date, assuming different common share prices at that time. Note that Pierre's profits on the option purchase come at the expense of the option seller; Pierre's losses are the seller's profits. (This analysis excludes commissions. The impact of commissions will be to increase the losses and reduce the profits.)

Share price at expiration	Options contract value (per share)	Pierre's total profit (loss) on option purchase[a]	Seller's total profit (loss) on option sale[a]
$48	$0	–$250	+$250
$50	$0	–$250	+$250
$51	$1	–$150	+$150
$55	$5	+$250	–$250
$60	$10	+$750	–$750

[a]This column is the difference between the option contract's value at expiration, as shown in column 2, and the premium paid by Pierre ($2.50 per share) multiplied by 100 shares (one contract). When the value in column 2 is less than $2.50, Pierre loses money and the seller profits. When the value in column 2 is greater than $2.50, Pierre profits and the seller loses.

This characteristic of options sets them apart from other types of financial securities. Consider common shares, for example. Assume Abraham buys 500 common shares of Abbas Trading Company for $14 per share. He holds the shares until the price reaches $20 and then sells the shares. Abraham makes $6 per share, or a total profit of $3,000 on the trade.

If Kylah buys the shares from Abraham (recall that this transaction would be completed on behalf of buyers and sellers by an investment dealer, a stock broker, on a stock exchange) and holds them until the share price reaches $25 per share, she will make $5 per share, or $2,500 on the 500 shares. Kylah's $2,500 profit on the transaction did not come at Abraham's expense. Abraham made money on the purchase of Abbas Trading Company's common shares; so too did Kylah. For common shares, a buyer's (seller's) profit does not come at the seller's (buyer's) expense—it is not a zero-sum trade. Since common shares, in aggregate, increase in value over time (see Figure 7.5 in Chapter 7), all buyers can be winners, assuming they buy and sell at opportune times.

The Pricing of Options

Now that we have a solid understanding of options, we can discuss how options are priced. In other words, how is the value of an option determined? The value of an option, at any point in time, is represented by the premium. The premium for an option is based on the following six variables:

1. The current market price of the common shares
2. The strike (exercise) price
3. The time to expiry
4. The volatility of the common share price
5. Interest rate levels, and
6. The dividends expected over the life of the option.

Each of these variables is discussed below.

Market and Strike Prices

in the money (call) When the current price of a company's common shares (P) is greater than the call option's strike price (S); $P > S$.

intrinsic value (option) The minimum amount an option is worth; this value can never be less than zero.

at the money When the current price of a company's common shares (P) is equal to the call option's strike price (S); $P = S$.

out of the money (call) When the current price of a company's common shares (P) is less than the call option's strike price (S); $P < S$.

Let P represent the current price of a company's common shares. Let S represent the strike price of a call option on the common shares. When $P > S$, the common share is trading for more than the option's strike price, and the premium on the option will be at least the value of $P - S$. This option is said to be **in the money,** in which case the option will have positive intrinsic value. An option's **intrinsic value** is the minimum amount the option is worth due to a positive difference between the share and strike price. The intrinsic value can never be less than zero; the value of an option can never be negative.

If $P = S$, the common share price is the same as the option's strike price. This option is said to be **at the money,** in which case the option will have zero intrinsic value. If $P < S$, the common share price is less than the strike price. This call option is said to be **out of the money,** in which case the option will have zero intrinsic value. Again, the intrinsic value of an option can never be less than zero.

Example

Frank is planning to buy a call option on Perelli Tire's common shares. Perelli's common shares are trading for \$22. Frank is evaluating three different call option contracts. The first has a strike price of \$20, the second \$22, the third \$25. The first call option has an intrinsic value of \$2 (\$22 − \$20) and is an *in the money* option. The second call option has no intrinsic value (\$22 − \$22) and is an *at the money* option. The third is an *out of the money* option and it seems to have −\$3 intrinsic value (\$22 − \$25). But since options can never have negative values, the intrinsic value would be zero.

out of the money (put) When the current price of a company's common shares (P) is greater than the put option's strike price (S); $P > S$.

in the money (put) When the current price of a company's common shares (P) is less than the put option's strike price (S); $P < S$.

For a put option, the relationships described above are reversed. For a put option, when $P > S$, we have an **out of the money** option and when $P < S$, we have an **in the money** option.

Example

Now assume that Frank from the above example is planning to purchase a put option on Perelli Tire's common shares. He is considering the same three strike prices. Now, the first put option is *out of the money* (\$20 − \$22) with zero intrinsic value. The second option is *at the money* with zero intrinsic value. The third is an *in the money* option with an intrinsic value of \$3 (\$25 − \$22). Frank can sell Perelli Tire's common shares for \$25 when they are trading for \$22.

Time to Expiry

time value of an option (TV) The difference between the premium (V) and the intrinsic value (IV) of an option; all options have some time value up to their point of expiration.

As we have seen above, an option may have an intrinsic value of zero or, if the option is in the money, an intrinsic value greater than zero. The premium (value) of an option will be greater than the intrinsic value except at the point of expiry. The difference between the premium (V) and the intrinsic value (IV) is the **time value (TV)** of an option, as follows:

$$TV = V - IV \tag{17.6}$$

All options will have some time value up to their point of expiration. In other words, the time value of an option decays over time; an option is a wasting asset. The longer the time to expiration, the higher the premium and time value. The time value of a call option is also a function of the degree of market optimism concerning the underlying security. The more optimistic the market is about the security, the higher the time value of a call. The reverse holds for a put. The more pessimistic the market is about the security, the higher the time value of a put. Finally, time value varies with the price of the underlying common shares. The time value of lower priced shares is generally much higher, on a percentage basis, than the time value for higher priced shares. This is most obviously seen when considering at the money options.

Example ▼ The common shares of Norbel Network are trading for \$6. The premium on Norbel's Jan 6 call option is \$0.70. This is an example of an at the money option. Therefore, all of the premium is time value. The time value is 11.67 percent of the share price (\$0.70 ÷ \$6.00). The common shares of EnTana Corp are trading for \$50. The premium on EnTana's Jan 50 call option is \$2. Again, this is an at the money option and the premium is all time value. In dollar terms, the time value on the EnTana option is much greater. But, as a percent of the underlying share price, the time value is only 4 percent (\$2.00 ÷ \$50). ▲

Volatility of the Common Share Price

It is clear that the relationship between the price of the common shares and the strike price of the option, and the time to expiry, are key variables affecting the value of an option. An often overlooked variable that has a major impact on the premium is the volatility of the price of the underlying common shares. Common shares that have very volatile prices will have much higher premiums.

Example ▼ The common shares of company A and B are both priced at \$20. Over the previous five-week trading period, company A's share price varied between \$14 and \$26. In the same period, company B's share price varied between \$18 and \$22. If we examined options with the same strike price and time to expiration for these two companies, the premium on company A's put and call options would be much higher than company B's. Why? Given the past volatility of company A's share price, a whole range of options on company A's common shares are more likely to become in the money at some point in the immediate future. Therefore, company A's options will have higher premiums than company B's. ▲

Interest Rate Levels

As with many topics in finance, the interest rate we are concerned with here is the risk-free rate of return. Since the strike price for options is associated with a transaction that will occur in the future, we must recognize time value issues by discounting the strike price for the remaining life of the option. If a call option is exercised, it will occur in the future. Therefore, when interest rates are high, the present value of the strike price will be lower. A lower strike price results in a higher premium on a call option. For a put option the reverse holds. Higher interest rates reduce the premium on a put option.

Example ▼ Assume we are trying to value a call option that is in the money. We are focusing on the impact that changes in the risk-free rate will have on the option premium. Combining the first, second, and fifth variables affecting the value of an option results in the following equation that is used to determine the value of an option:

$$V_0 = P_0 - \frac{S}{(1 + r)^t} \tag{17.7}$$

where:

V_0 = value of the option now (at time 0)
P_0 = current share price
S = strike price of the option
r = risk-free interest rate
t = time to the option's expiration expressed as a fraction of a year

Assume that the current share price is \$25, the strike price for the option is \$20, the risk-free rate is 5 percent, and the time to expiry is six months. Without considering time value issues, the value of the option appears to be \$5 (\$25 − \$20). But, using the above formula, the value of the option is :

$$V_0 = \$25 - \frac{\$20}{(1.05)^{0.5}}$$
$$= \$25 - 19.52 = \$5.48$$

The value of the option is greater than \$5 since the option will not be exercised for six months, thereby reducing the time value of the strike price. If the risk-free rate were to increase to 10 percent, what happens to the value of the option? The value of the option increases to:

$$V_0 = \$25 - \frac{\$20}{(1.10)^{0.5}}$$
$$= \$25 - 19.07 = \$5.93$$

A similar type of analysis could be completed for a put option, and it would show declining option premiums as the risk-free rate increases. Note that the appendix to this chapter discusses a much more elaborate option pricing formula. This is the famous Black-Scholes option pricing model. Readers interested in options may find the appendix a valuable resource that will help in understanding how options are actually valued.

Expected Dividends

If an investor is buying a call option instead of the underlying common shares, then by doing so he will not receive any dividends the firm pays on the common shares over the life of the option. This will reduce the premium on the option. In addition, when the common shares start trading ex dividend, the common share price tends to fall by the amount of the dividend. (This was discussed in Chapter 11.) Therefore, for companies that pay dividends, the premiums on their call options tend to be lower than comparable companies that do not pay dividends, while the premiums on their put options tend to be higher.

Summary of the Impact of the Six Variables

Table 17.2 provides a summary of the impact that changes in the six variables have on the option premium for both call and put options. A positive sign

TABLE 17.2 The Six Variables That Determine Option Values and the Impact a Change in the Variable Will Have on Premiums

Variable	Direction of change	Impact on premium: Call option	Impact on premium: Put option
Common share price	↑	+	−
Strike (exercise) price	↑	−	+
Time to expiry	↑	+	+
Volatility of share price	↑	+	+
Interest rate	↑	+	−
Cash dividends	↑	−	+

indicates that an increase in the variable will increase the premium. A negative sign suggests the opposite. This table assumes all other variables remain the same.

So increasing the strike price will reduce the value of a call, but increase the value of a put. This analysis assumes all other variables remain the same.

? Review Questions

17–8 What is an option? Define call and put options. Discuss the relevant positions of buyers and sellers of calls and puts.

17–9 Describe each of the following concepts: option writer, strike price, number of shares associated with an option contract, option premium, expiration date, American and European options, and LEAPS.

17–10 Discuss the distinction between a right and an obligation regarding call and put options.

17–11 In relation to option trading, what is meant by the term *zero-sum trade*? Provide an example.

17–12 List and briefly discuss the six variables that influence the premium (value) of an option.

17.5 Option Trading

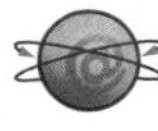

www.m-x.ca

Canadian Derivatives Clearing Corporation (CDCC)
The agency that regulates the trading of options in Canada.

In Canada in 2007, options were traded on the common shares of 123 companies listed on the Toronto Stock Exchange (TSX), on seven stock market indexes, and on the value of the U.S. dollar. The trading of all derivative securities, however, occurs on the Montréal Exchange. All aspects of option trading are regulated, as is the trading of all financial securities. In Canada, the regulatory agency is the **Canadian Derivatives Clearing Corporation** (CDCC). While options are created by an option writer, all of the standardized features of options that were discussed above are set by the CDCC. This includes the setting of the months of

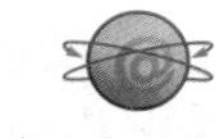
http://cdcc.ca/accueil_en.php

expiry and strike prices, the fact that options stop trading at the close of trading on the third Friday of their month of expiry, and that all options on common shares are for 100 shares.

The CDCC also acts as the issuer, clearinghouse, and guarantor of all option contracts traded on the Montréal Exchange. The role of the clearinghouse is to guarantee the financial obligation of every contract it clears. This is achieved by the clearinghouse acting as the buyer for every seller, and the seller for every buyer. Therefore, an investor buying or selling an option contract has made a deal not to the party on the other side of the transaction, but to the clearinghouse. In other words, the CDCC guarantees that the terms of the option contract will be satisfied. It is the CDCC that ensures that the buyer of a put option will be able to sell common shares at the strike price. If the writer of an option should renege, the CDCC steps in to ensure the terms of the option contract are met.

All option contracts are issued, guaranteed, and cleared by the CDCC. This ensures that the option market is orderly, stable, and dependable, and functions in an efficient manner. The Web sites of the Montréal Exchange and the Canadian Derivatives Clearing Corporation provide more information on option trading in Canada.

Option Trading Volumes in Canada

In Canada, the option market is considered very thin: that is, volumes are quite low. For example, on the Montréal Exchange in early 2007, options were traded on the common shares of 123 companies, on seven stock market indexes, and on the U.S. dollar. Average trading volume was about 52,900 contracts per trading day. As a comparison, on the Chicago Board Options Exchange (CBOE) in early 2007, options were traded on the common shares of over 1,900 companies, and numerous stock market indexes. Average trading volume was about 2,700,000 contracts per day. On the most active option contracts traded on the CBOE, average daily volume is over 85,000 contracts. While the CBOE is the largest options exchange in the United States, it only accounts for about 31 percent of all option trading. Obviously, the Canadian option market is tiny in comparison to the U.S. markets, and can be said to be still in the process of developing. Current trading volume statistics on option trading in Canada and on the CBOE are available at the exchanges' Web sites.

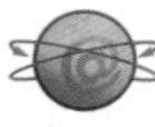
www.m-x.ca/nego_liste_en.php
http://cboe.com/data

Option Quotes

As with money and capital market securities, quotes on options contracts are widely available from investment dealers, on the Web, and are published in the financial press. Figure 17.3 is an excerpt from the December 18, 2006 issue of *The Globe and Mail* providing quotations on the options contracts that traded on various Canadian companies. The data reflects trading that occurred on December 15, 2006, the third Friday in December, the date that all December 2006 options expired.

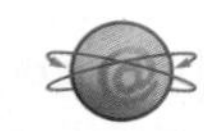
www.canada.com/nationalpost/financialpost/fpmarketcdata/index.html

In the top left-hand side of the figure, a list of the five companies whose options were the most actively traded for the day is provided. Investors traded almost 11,000 contracts of EnCana Corp, a large natural gas producer. This was 70 percent more contracts than the next most active company. The remainder of

FIGURE 17.3 Select Option Quotes for Trading on December 15, 2006

EQUITY OPTIONS

Trading in Canadian equity options on the Montreal Exchange. P is a put.

FIVE MOST ACTIVE

	Volume	Op Int
EnCana Crp	10807	70861
CIBC	6323	80009
Bank of NS	5544	63781
Petro Cda	5400	36776
Cameco	4641	30685

TRADES

stock series		bid	close ask	tot vol last	vol	tot o.i. op int
ATI Tech			**21.75**	**53**		**4358**
Jan07	16.00	8.50	8.65	8.65	1	98
	22.00p	0.35	0.45	0.35	10	78
	28.00	0.35	0.40	0.45	15	75
Apr07	24.00	2.95	3.00	3.20	2	149
	26.00	2.05	2.15	2.25	25	79
ATS Autom			**11.70**	**4**		**468**
May07	10.00	2.40	2.65	2.35	2	2
	12.00	1.35	1.60	1.35	2	17
Abitibi-Cons			**2.65**	**394**		**21581**
Dec06	3.00p	0.25	0.35	0.35	30	100
Mar07	3.00	0.20	0.30	0.25	33	2765
	3.00p	0.45	0.55	0.45	30	116
Jun07	2.00p	0.08	0.10	0.08	100	310
	3.00	0.35	0.45	0.45	151	8913
	3.00p	0.55	0.60	0.60	50	1633
Agnico			**47.20**	**1033**		**7256**
Dec06	46.00	1.20	1.30	1.25	127	203
	46.00p		0.09	0.03	85	295
	48.00p	0.75	0.90	0.60	87	58
	50.00		0.09	0.10	60	257
Jan07	38.00	9.40	9.50	9.55	60	0
	40.00	7.55	7.70	7.55	68	11
	46.00	3.15	3.30	3.10	40	20
	50.00	1.40	1.55	1.55	120	191
	52.00	0.85	1.00	1.10	99	219
	54.00	0.50	0.65	0.90	50	20
Alcan			**57.50**	**1196**		**44090**
Dec06	50.00	7.45	7.55	7.25	30	638
	56.00	1.45	1.60	1.65	61	614
	58.00	0.02	0.09	0.25	96	384
	58.00p	0.45	0.60	0.55	184	389
Jan07	50.00	7.80	7.95	7.80	51	852
	56.00	2.85	3.00	2.70	49	1316
	56.00p	1.15	1.25	1.20	100	1578
	58.00	1.70	1.85	1.75	50	1734
	62.00	0.45	0.60	0.50	120	678
	64.00	0.20	0.35	0.35	112	834
Algoma S			**32.60**	**7**		**444**
Apr07	36.00	1.50	1.70	1.45	7	17
Axcan Pha			**16.49**	**5**		**154**
Dec06	16.00	0.35	0.60	0.40	5	15
BCE Inc			**29.91**	**407**		**55722**
Dec06	26.00	3.90	4.05	3.90	8	8
	30.00		0.05	0.05	11	163
	30.00p	0.03	0.10	0.04	20	184
Jan07	28.00p	0.05	0.10	0.10	200	806
	30.00	0.65	0.75	0.70	20	2594
	30.00p	0.60	0.70	0.60	75	879
Ballard Pow			**7.27**	**104**		**5237**
Dec06	6.00	1.35	1.45	1.35	50	50
	7.00	0.35	0.45	0.30	5	422
	9.00p	1.55	1.65	1.55	9	86
Jan07	8.00	0.15	0.25	0.25	40	747
Bank Montrl			**69.10**	**989**		**50108**
Dec06	70.00p	0.85	1.00	0.90	62	335
Jan07	68.00	1.85	1.90	1.70	40	1106
	68.00p	0.50	0.60	0.60	65	559
	70.00p	1.40	1.50	1.40	197	875
Bank of NS			**52.58**	**5544**		**63781**
Dec06	46.00	6.40	6.55	6.60	604	594
	48.00	4.40	4.55	4.55	150	210
	50.00	2.40	2.55	2.45	722	1169
	52.00	0.40	0.55	0.55	464	1463
	52.00p		0.04	0.02	33	2270
	54.00p	1.45	1.60	1.40	60	57
Jan07	30.00	22.45	22.55	22.70	50	170
	46.00	6.45	6.60	6.60	51	657
	48.00	4.45	4.60	4.60	440	1576
	50.00	2.50	2.65	2.55	538	2808
	52.00	0.95	1.05	0.95	542	4519
	54.00	0.20	0.25	0.25	95	2985
	54.00p	1.95	2.10	1.90	50	207
Barrick			**35.12**	**1061**		**54912**
Dec06	34.00	1.10	1.25	1.30	278	967
	36.00p	0.75	0.90	0.90	86	91
Jan07	32.50p	0.20	0.25	0.30	25	1272
	34.00	1.80	1.90	1.80	102	1590
	35.00	1.20	1.30	1.15	44	2351
	36.00	0.75	0.85	0.80	98	3098
Bema Gl			**5.74**	**70**		**2653**
Dec06	5.00	0.75	0.85	0.85	60	225
	6.00p	0.15	0.25	0.09	10	220
Biovail			**23.65**	**509**		**5676**
Dec06	20.00	3.60	3.75	3.65	28	406
	24.00p	0.25	0.30	0.30	100	94
Jan07	22.00p	0.55	0.65	0.80	45	63
	24.00	0.75	0.90	0.80	58	122
Bombardi			**3.70**	**790**		**80255**
Dec06	3.50	0.20	0.25	0.20	150	222
	4.00p	0.25	0.30	0.20	55	60
Jan07	3.50	0.30	0.35	0.35	40	2376
	4.00	0.08	0.10	0.09	160	9409
	4.00p	0.30	0.35	0.30	50	3989
Brookfiel			**55.31**	**487**		**5224**
Dec06	48.00	7.25	7.60	8.15	30	204
	52.00	3.45	3.55	3.75	5	553
Jan07	58.00	0.35	0.55	0.50	4	122
CAE Inc			**10.67**	**184**		**7016**
Dec06	10.00	0.60	0.70	0.60	104	404
Mar07	12.00p	1.45	1.55	1.45	10	27
Jun07	10.00	1.35	1.45	1.45	20	382
	12.00	0.45	0.55	0.50	50	267
Cameco			**45.70**	**4641**		**30685**
Dec06	36.00	9.65	9.80	9.70	70	125
	40.00	5.65	5.85	5.85	76	1774
	42.00	3.70	3.85	3.85	50	1007
	44.00	1.65	1.85	1.65	358	477
	46.00		0.10	0.05	123	338
	46.00p	0.20	0.35	0.20	320	288
Jan07	40.00	6.00	6.15	6.15	50	373
	40.00p	0.20	0.30	0.30	85	612
	42.00	4.25	4.45	4.45	90	638
	42.00p	0.45	0.55	0.40	140	228
	44.00	2.75	3.00	2.95	368	1651
	46.00	1.65	1.80	1.80	145	2348
	48.00	0.90	1.05	0.95	1991	592
CIBC			**98.25**	**6323**		**80009**
Dec06	80.00	18.05	18.30	18.30	41	56
	85.00	13.05	13.30	13.30	109	192
	90.00	8.05	8.30	8.40	362	6379
	95.00	3.05	3.30	3.25	350	1798
Jan07	78.00	20.10	20.40	20.20	23	281
	80.00	18.10	18.40	18.30	101	562
	85.00	13.10	13.35	13.25	86	2149
	90.00	8.10	8.35	8.25	247	10135
	90.00p	0.09	0.15	0.09	20	512
	95.00	3.45	3.65	3.50	196	1475
	95.00p	0.65	0.75	0.75	32	425
	100.00	0.80	0.90	0.85	87	319
CN Rail			**51.55**	**904**		**16771**
Dec06	44.00	7.80	7.95	7.85	80	110
	48.00	3.80	4.00	3.85	73	623
	50.00	1.80	2.00	2.05	73	591
	52.00	0.05	0.10	0.10	136	910
	54.00p	2.05	2.20	2.00	37	298
	56.00p	4.05	4.20	3.90	40	40
Jan07	54.00p	2.35	2.50	2.30	40	45
Cdn Naturl			**60.38**	**2140**		**36986**
Dec06	58.00	2.65	2.80	2.90	30	436
	60.00	0.65	0.80	0.65	436	1594
	60.00p	0.02	0.10	0.07	246	257
	62.00	0.01	0.03	0.03	259	1068
	62.00p	1.30	1.45	1.20	155	302
	64.00p	3.30	3.45	3.20	130	115
Jan07	54.00	7.20	7.35	7.45	40	593
	56.00	5.55	5.65	5.80	87	652
	58.00	4.05	4.15	4.30	52	400
	58.00p	1.15	1.30	1.30	30	417
	62.00	1.85	1.90	1.85	34	822
	62.00p	2.90	3.05	2.80	80	281
	64.00	1.05	1.20	1.15	38	1482
Cdn Oi			**33.00**	**534**		**12885**
Dec06	30.00	2.65	2.95	2.70	43	1042
	32.00	0.65	1.00	1.15	20	231
Jan07	30.00	3.00	3.25	3.20	45	816
	32.00	1.55	1.85	1.75	100	662
	32.00p	0.70	0.95	0.75	110	277
	34.00	0.65	0.90	0.75	33	555
	38.00	0.07	0.35	0.25	50	560
CP Railway			**63.11**	**201**		**5565**
Dec06	62.00	1.00	1.20	1.15	18	76
	64.00p	0.85	1.00	1.00	82	97
Jan07	60.00	3.60	3.80	3.70	2	333
	60.00p	0.45	0.60	0.50	10	13
	64.00p	1.90	2.10	1.90	82	15
Cdn Tire			**74.57**	**52**		**1343**
Dec06	74.00	0.30	0.65	0.15	25	31
	74.00p		0.10	0.10	5	5
Jan07	76.00	1.00	1.20	0.95	19	71
Celestica			**9.33**	**185**		**11347**
Dec06	9.00	0.25	0.40	0.30	10	33
	10.00p	0.65	0.75	0.70	3	162
	11.00p	1.60	1.75	1.70	35	264
Jan07	10.00	0.15	0.20	0.20	50	521
	10.00p	0.75	0.85	0.80	10	220
Cognos			**48.80**	**114**		**3307**
Dec06	46.00	2.35	2.80	2.75	10	179
	48.00	0.40	0.80	0.70	22	83
Jan07	46.00	4.15	4.40	4.25	13	38
	46.00p	1.45	1.60	1.85	55	55
	48.00	3.00	3.20	3.10	10	437
Cott Corp			**16.30**	**10**		**876**
Dec06	14.00	2.15	2.30	2.10	10	10
Domtar			**9.72**	**234**		**1227**
Dec06	8.00	1.65	1.80	1.65	20	40
	9.00	0.65	0.80	0.60	10	10
Jan07	9.00	0.85	0.95	0.95	10	71
	10.00	0.25	0.35	0.25	50	33
EnCana Crp			**57.09**	**10807**		**70861**
Dec06	56.00	1.75	1.80	2.00	80	40
	58.00		0.02	0.02	3161	1757
	58.00p	0.25	0.30	0.20	546	343
	60.00		0.01	0.05	250	1217
	60.00p	2.25	2.30	2.10	222	309
	62.00p	4.25	4.30	4.05	229	327
Jan07	54.00	4.55	4.65	4.85	114	806
	56.00	3.10	3.20	3.30	321	1391
	56.00p	1.10	1.20	1.10	198	1211
	58.00	1.95	2.05	2.00	742	1900
	58.00p	1.95	2.05	1.95	561	1405
	60.00	1.10	1.20	1.20	1601	5117
	60.00p	3.10	3.20	2.95	332	473
	62.00	0.55	0.65	0.65	326	2018
Enbridge			**39.87**	**89**		**10911**
Dec06	36.00	3.90	4.05	4.50	15	65
	40.00p		0.10	0.10	10	45
Jan07	38.00	2.20	2.35	2.45	13	1169
	40.00	0.75	0.90	0.90	23	428
Apr07	42.00	0.70	0.85	0.75	3	2407
	44.00	0.25	0.40	0.30	25	83
Enerplus			**54.14**	**23**		**4244**
Jan07	60.00		0.50	0.50	4	108
	66.00	0.10	0.40	0.50	8	212
Apr07	56.00	1.65	2.05	1.65	11	300
Ensign Energy			**19.97**	**32**		**2848**
Jan07	20.00	0.70	0.85	0.80	5	90
Apr07	18.00p	0.75	0.90	0.70	20	114
Jul07	24.00	0.75	0.95	0.80	7	7
Finning			**47.49**	**59**		**2347**
Dec06	42.00	5.70	5.95	5.55	3	37
	46.00	1.70	1.95	1.85	20	60
Jan07	46.00	2.40	2.65	2.40	20	1150
Jun07	48.00	3.35	3.60	3.05	2	0
	50.00	2.45	2.70	2.65	14	0
Goldcorp			**32.10**	**2971**		**42957**
Dec06	28.00	4.25	4.35	4.25	156	319
	30.00	2.25	2.40	2.30	176	782
	32.00	0.30	0.40	0.30	370	1199
	32.00p		0.10	0.03	482	359
	34.00p	1.65	1.75	1.75	68	408
Jan07	30.00p	0.60	0.65	0.60	53	2990
	32.00	1.70	1.80	1.75	250	1474
	32.00p	1.30	1.40	1.40	88	390
	34.00	0.90	1.00	0.95	291	4404
	36.00	0.45	0.50	0.50	98	1176
	38.00	0.20	0.25	0.25	57	797
Grt Wst			**33.88**	**93**		**1384**
Dec06	34.00		0.15	0.30	50	50
Apr07	36.00	0.50	0.60	0.50	43	219
Hudbay			**22.53**	**868**		**8702**
Dec06	22.00	0.50	0.65	0.55	76	455
Jan07	22.00	1.90	2.05	2.05	70	610
	22.00p	1.25	1.40	1.30	20	105
	24.00	1.10	1.25	1.10	143	143
	26.00	0.55	0.70	0.55	103	313
Husky Enr			**78.10**	**555**		**15760**
Dec06	78.00	0.05	0.25	0.10	215	223
	78.00p	0.01	0.09	0.04	59	70
	80.00p	1.85	2.05	2.10	55	85
Jan07	76.00	3.70	3.85	3.90	9	202
	80.00	1.55	1.70	1.65	13	429
	80.00p	3.20	3.40	3.20	10	24
	82.00	0.90	1.05	1.15	30	1145
IShares Cdn			**28.55**	**49**		**4501**
Dec06	29.00p	0.40	0.60	0.35	36	76
Jan07	28.00	0.90	1.05	0.95	3	0
	29.00	0.45	0.55	0.65	10	66
IShr TSX 60			**74.57**	**2459**		**49193**
Dec06	63.00	11.40	11.65	12.10	87	97
	63.00p		0.09	0.01	87	292
	67.00	7.50	7.65	8.40	80	635
	72.00	2.50	2.65	2.65	50	183
	73.00	1.50	1.65	1.75	106	293
	74.00	0.50	0.65	1.25	40	63
	75.00p	0.40	0.55	0.35	210	210
Jan07	72.00	2.75	2.90	3.25	40	71
	74.00p	0.85	1.05	1.00	40	227
	75.00	0.80	0.95	1.05	61	2612
	75.00p	1.35	1.55	1.45	527	155
	76.00	0.40	0.60	0.45	117	12
IShares Cdn			**83.50**	**1115**		**34355**
Dec06	80.00	3.45	3.65	3.85	20	90
	82.00	1.45	1.65	1.75	143	194
	84.00p	0.45	0.55	0.30	130	76
	85.00		0.09	0.15	30	278
Jan07	77.00	6.50	6.85	6.60	25	8
	82.00p	1.55	1.80	1.70	105	284
	83.00p	2.00	2.25	1.95	30	0
	84.00	1.75	1.90	1.75	50	115
	85.00	1.30	1.50	1.35	40	69
IShares Cdn			**53.68**	**130**		**36526**
Dec06	51.00	2.55	2.75	2.95	7	131
	53.00	0.55	0.75	0.60	26	264
	54.00p	0.20	0.45	0.25	16	32
Jan07	53.00	0.95	1.15	1.00	10	1164
	54.00	0.40	0.60	0.50	24	25
	55.00	0.15	0.25	0.30	15	0
IShr TSX Cp Go			**80.10**	**570**		**12650**
Dec06	65.00	14.90	15.20	17.00	28	117
	79.00	0.95	1.25	1.30	29	112
	80.00	0.10	0.25	0.25	92	145
	81.00p	0.90	1.05	1.00	51	30
Jan07	79.00	3.50	3.75	3.60	55	73
	80.00	3.00	3.20	3.20	33	112
	88.00	0.55	0.75	1.05	20	7
IShares Cdn			**8.00**	**45**		**2682**
Dec06	8.00	0.03	0.09	0.04	20	98
Jan07	10.00p	1.90	2.05	1.90	5	5
Jun07	8.00	0.65	0.75	0.65	20	41
Iamgold			**10.01**	**136**		**8384**
Dec06	10.00		0.25	0.10	30	351
Jan07	10.00	0.45	0.55	0.55	10	0
Feb07	10.00p	0.55	0.75	0.60	5	206
	11.00p	1.15	1.35	1.15	5	130
Imperial Oil			**43.17**	**269**		**13350**
Dec06	36.00	7.35	7.55	7.35	20	20
	40.00	3.35	3.55	4.20	33	105
	42.00	1.35	1.55	1.60	26	261
	42.00p		0.09	0.09	22	66
	44.00		0.09	0.20	62	244
Jan07	44.00	1.15	1.30	1.35	10	118
	44.00p	1.55	1.65	1.30	10	27
	46.00p	2.85	3.00	2.70	20	20
Inco			**85.77**	**4**		**4431**
Jan07	60.00	25.60	27.85	27.80	4	162
Industrial Alli			**36.25**	**10**		**1689**
Mar07	38.00	0.90	1.00	1.20	10	3
Ipsco			**112.12**	**601**		**2449**
Dec06	95.00	16.90	17.20	17.05	155	58
	110.00	1.90	2.10	2.05	131	73
	110.00p		0.10	0.20	10	68

SOURCE: *The Globe and Mail*, December 18, 2006.

the figure provides quotes for all the option contracts that traded on December 15. To explain the quotes, consider the information provided for CIBC. On the first line is the company name, the closing price for the company's common shares on December 15 ($98.25), the volume of options contracts that traded that day (6,323), and the total open interest of option contracts on CIBC (80,009).

open interest
The number of open option contracts at a given time; it indicates the number of open positions that exist for a particular option contract or for all option contracts for a company.

The **open interest** is the number of open option contracts at a given time. The open interest increases (an open interest is created) when trader A opens a new position by buying an option from a trader who did not previously hold a position in that option. When trader A closes out her position by selling the option, the open interest either remains the same or goes down by 1. If A sells to someone who did not have a position in that option contract, the open interest does not change. If A sells to someone who had earlier sold the option, the open interest decreases by one. Essentially, the open interest indicates the number of open positions that exist for a particular option contract or for all option contracts for a company.

Example Consider the following transactions in the June 25 call option contract for RIN Ltd.:

- On May 1, trader A buys an option from trader B. This creates a trading volume of 1 and leaves an open interest of 1 in the contract.
- On May 2, trader C buys 5 options from trader D, creating a trading volume of 5 and increasing the open interest by 5.
- On May 3, trader A sells an option to trader D. This closes A's position and reduces D's position by 1, thereby reducing the open interest by 1. Trading volume is 1. Trader D still has an open interest of 4.
- On May 4, trader E buys 5 options from trader C. This transaction closes trader C's position in the June 25 call option. But trader E simply replaces C, and therefore the open interest does not change; trading volume is 5.

The following table highlights these transactions and the impact on open interest:

Date	Trading activity	Open interest
May 1	A buys 1 option and B sells 1 option contract	1
May 2	C buys 5 options and D sells 5 option contracts	6
May 3	A sells the 1 option and D buys 1 option contract	5
May 4	E buys 5 options from C who sells 5 option contracts	5

The remaining items shown in Figure 17.3 are the quotes on the various option contracts that traded by month and year of the option expiry. For example, for CIBC, the first set of quotes is for the options expiring in December. The first item shown is the strike price for the contract. If this is followed by a "p," the option is a put. Next come the bid, ask, and last price for the contract, followed by the option volume that day and the open interest on the contract. For the December 2006 options, note that the premium is the difference between the closing share price and the strike price. These options have no time value. Why? Because the quote is for the day the option expires.

For example, the last trading price for the Dec 95.00 call option was \$3.25. This is the difference between the closing share price and the strike price (\$98.25 – \$95.00). The closing quote on the Dec 36.00 put option for Barrick was \$0.90. This is the difference between the strike price and the closing share price (\$36.00 – \$35.12). The same effect can be seen for all three Celestica Dec option contracts, and for most of the options with a Dec expiry.

The open interest for CIBC's Dec 95.00 call was 1,798 contracts. This means that the holders of these contracts will exercise the options and buy 179,800 common shares (1,798 contracts × 100 shares) of CIBC from the option writers for \$95 per share. Depending on the option premium the option writers received when they sold the contracts, the writers may have made or lost money on the contracts.

The concept of intrinsic value and time value can be illustrated by reviewing these quotes. The Dec 30.00 call on BCE Inc. has essentially no intrinsic value or time value; there was no bid and the last trade was for $0.05. The Jan 07 30.00 call on BCE Inc. also has no intrinsic value. But the closing premium was $0.70; this is almost all time value. Options with a longer time to expiry will have more time value. This could be seen if quotes for LEAPS were provided. Unfortunately, no quotes for LEAPS are provided in Figure 17.3. Readers are encouraged to look up quotes for LEAPS to see the substantial premium option buyers are willing to pay for time. Most of the earlier-discussed characteristics and features of options can also be seen in these option quotes.

The Payoff to Option Trading

Investors purchasing call options do so with the expectation that the market price of the underlying common share will rise by more than enough to cover the cost of the option (the option premium), thereby allowing the purchaser of the call to profit.

Example It is September 1 and Wing Enterprise's common shares are currently trading for $30. Cindy Peters believes the shares are undervalued. To benefit from her view, Cindy could buy 100 of Wing's common shares paying $30 per share. Excluding commissions, this transaction would cost Cindy $3,000 ($30 × 100 shares). Alternatively, Cindy could purchase a call option contract on Wing Enterprise's common shares. If Cindy feels that Wing's common shares will increase in price over the next three months, she could buy a December call option. She must then decide on a strike price.

For a common share trading for $30, there may be options available with strike prices ranging from $25 to $40. Wendy decides to buy one Dec 30 call option on Wing Enterprise's common shares. This means Cindy has the option to buy 100 common shares of Wing Enterprise at a price of $30 any time between now and the third Friday in December. The option premium is $2.50 per share; Cindy will pay the writer of the option contract $250 (she would also pay commissions). Note that the current market price and the strike price are the same: $30. This is an *at the money* option; the intrinsic value of this option is 0. But the option has value, due to time. The company's common shares *could* increase between September and the third Friday in December.

For Cindy to break even on this transaction, Wing's common shares must increase to $32.50 per share by the expiry date. If Wing's share price increased to $35 by October 31, then the option will be worth at least $5 per share. The $5 is the difference between the current share price and the strike price ($35 − $30). But there is still time left to the date of expiry. If this time value is assumed to be $2.50 per share, then the option would be trading for $7.50 per share.

To close her position in the options on Wing Enterprise, Cindy would write a Dec 30 call option on Wing and sell it for the option price of $7.50 per share. Cindy would receive $750 ($7.50 × 100 shares). Her gain is $500 ($750 − $250) on a $250 investment or 200 percent ($500 ÷ $250). If she had purchased the shares, Cindy would have made $500 [($35 – $30) × 100 shares], a 16.67 percent return ($500 ÷ $3,000) on her invested money. The very high potential return, on a modest level of investment, illustrates the very high leverage associated with options, and explains the attraction of option trading.

Note, though, that there is also a very high degree of risk with option trading. If, in the above example, Wing's common shares traded between $27.50 and $30.75 in the period between September and December, and closed trading at $29.75 on the third Friday of December, Cindy would have likely held her position, hoping for the expected increase in share price. As such, she would have ended up losing her $250 investment. Options have high potential returns, but high risks as well. This, of course, is to be expected given the risk–return tradeoff that has been considered many times in this book.

The payoff to call options can also be shown in a diagram. Figure 17.4 provides payoff profiles for the buyer and seller of call options on Wing Enterprise's common shares from the previous example. Note that these figures simply illustrate the intrinsic value of the option. Therefore, they illustrate the option payoffs on the option's expiry date. Part A of the figure shows the option buyer's payoff profile. For the call option on Wing's common shares, if the share price is $30 or less, the buyer loses the full premium. In this example, the loss is $2.50 per share. As the share price increases to $32.50, the loss declines. The breakeven point on this option is a share price of $32.50, the sum of the strike price and the premium. As the share price rises beyond $32.50, the buyer profits. Theoretically, the potential profit is unlimited since the share price can keep increasing. So, for the buyer of a call option, the maximum possible loss is the premium paid, in this case $2.50 per share. But there is a *potential* for an unlimited profit.[3]

The opposite situation applies to the writer of the call. This can be seen in Part B of the figure. The writer receives the $2.50 per share, which is the maximum possible profit he can make. The writer's breakeven point on the sale is a share price of $32.50. As the share price rises past $32.50, the writer incurs a loss on the sale.

Put options are purchased in the expectation that the share price of a given security will *decline* over the life of the option. Investors gain from put options when the price of the underlying common shares declines by more than the option premium. The logic underlying the purchase of puts is exactly the opposite of that underlying the purchase of call options.

Example ▼ Assume that Don Kelly bought a six-month put option on Dante United's common shares at a strike price of $40. Don purchased the put option with the expectation that the company's share price would drop due to the introduction of a new product line by Dante's chief competitor. The premium on the option was $3.25. By paying $325, Don is assured that he can sell 100 shares of Dante at $40 per share at any time during the next six months. The share price must drop by $3.25 per share to $36.75 by the expiry date to cover the cost of the option (ignoring any brokerage fees).

If, on the option's expiry date, Dante's common shares were trading for $30 per share, the intrinsic value of the option is $10 per share. Note that Don's profit on this option contract is $675 [($10 − $3.25) × 100 shares]. Remember, though: if the share price dropped to $30 a few weeks before the option expired, the option would be trading for more than its $10 per share intrinsic value due to time value, and Don's return would be greater.

3. In reality, the potential profit is limited. Given the short-term nature of options, common share prices will only rise a certain amount during the life of an option.

FIGURE 17.4

Payoff Profiles for Call Options as of Their Date of Expiration

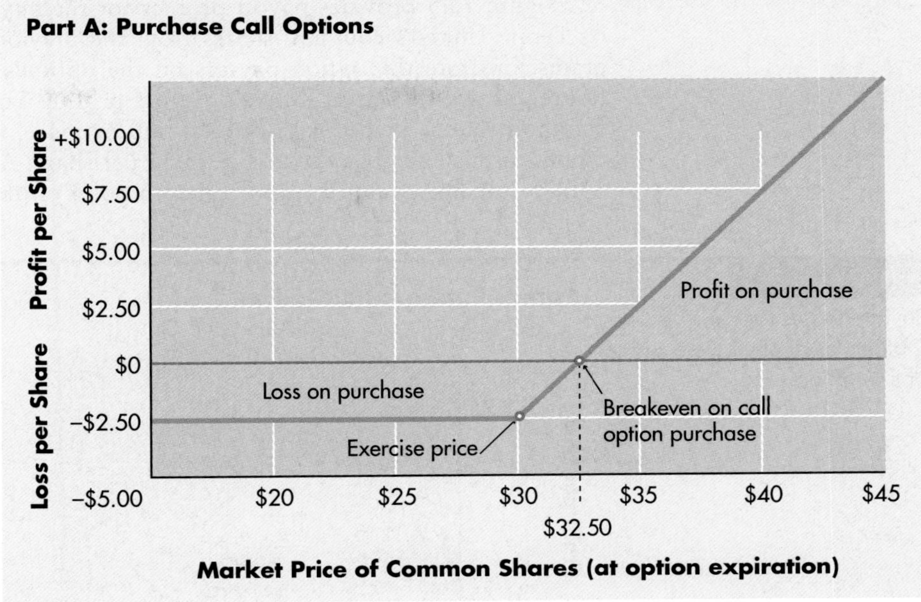

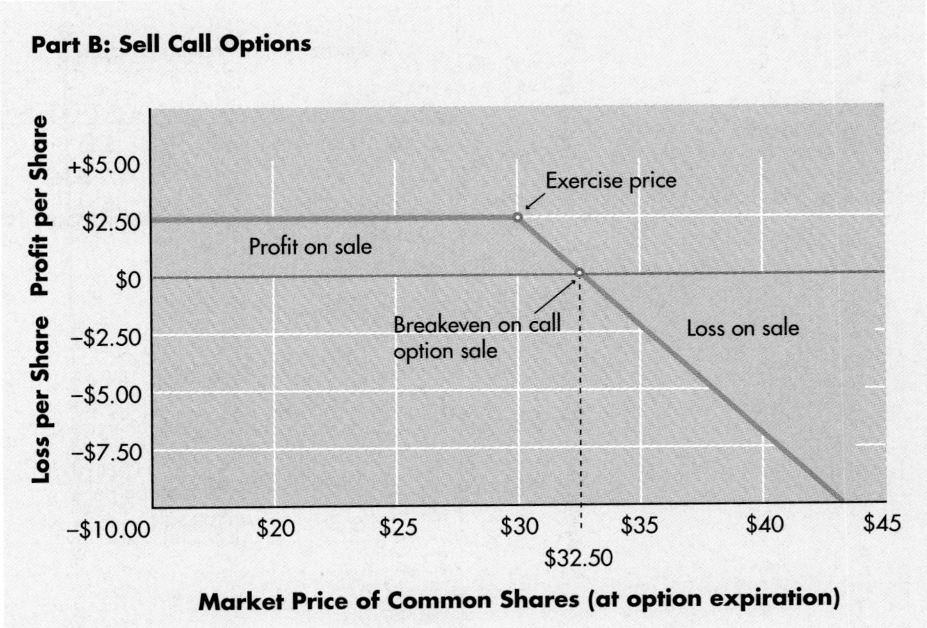

Because the return would be earned on a $325 investment, this again illustrates the high potential leverage associated with the trading of options. Of course, had the price of Dante's common shares risen above $40 per share, Don would have lost the $325, because there would have been no reason to exercise the option. If the share price falls to between $36.75 and $40 per share by the expiry date, Don will close his option position to reduce his loss to an amount less than $325.

Figure 17.5 provides payoff profiles for the buyer and seller of put options on Dante United's common shares from the previous example. Again, the diagrams illustrate the option payoffs on the option's expiry date. Part A of the figure shows the option buyer's payoff profile. For a put option on Dante's common shares, if the share price is $40 or more, the buyer loses the full premium. In this example, the loss is $3.25 per share. As the share price declines to $36.75, the loss declines. The breakeven point on this option is a share price of

FIGURE 17.5

Payoff Profiles for Put Options as of Their Date of Expiration

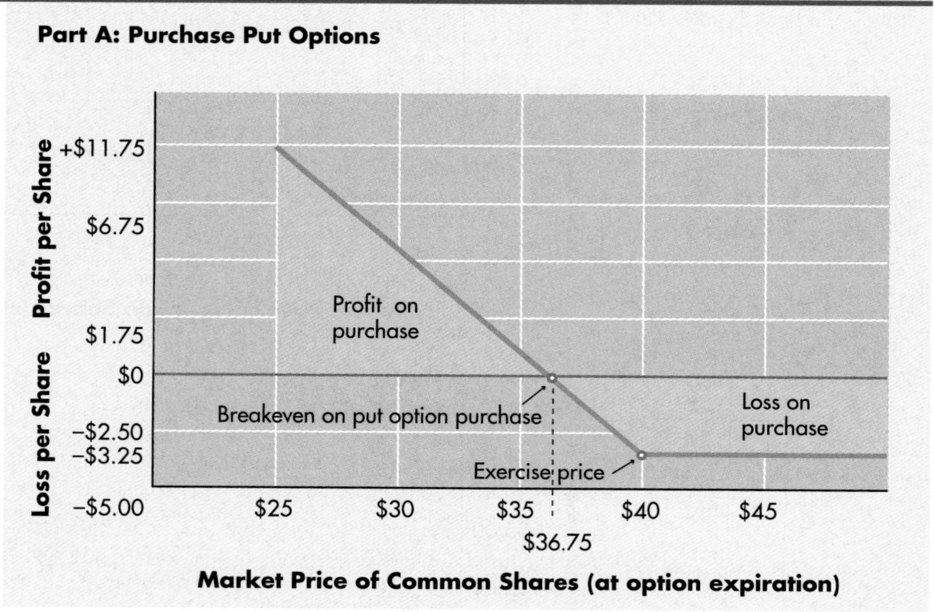

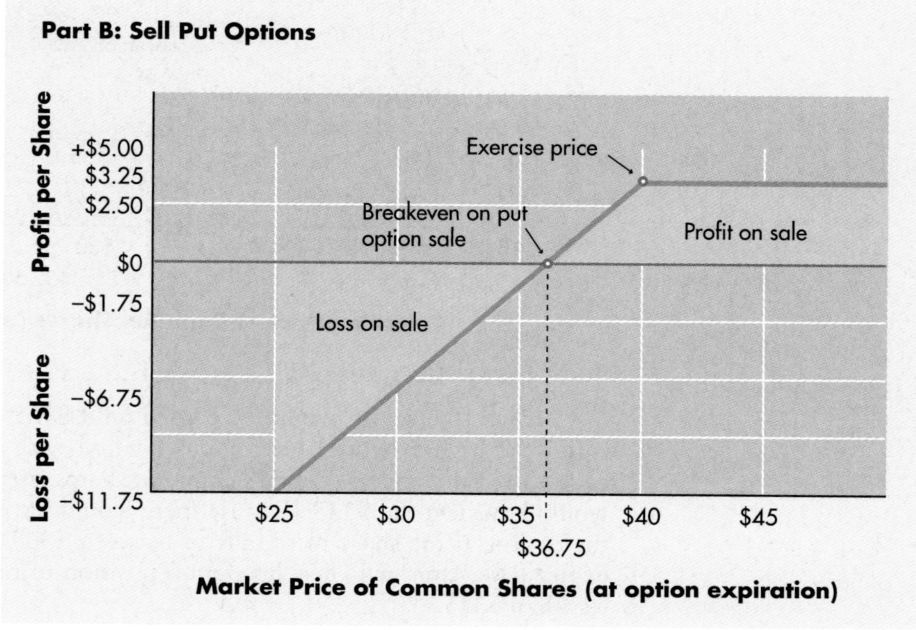

$36.75, the difference between the strike price and the premium. As the share price declines below $36.75, the buyer profits. Theoretically, the potential profit is the difference between the strike price and the premium since the share price can only fall to zero. So, for the buyer of a put option, the maximum possible loss is the premium paid, in this case $3.25 per share. The *potential* profit in this example is $36.75.

The opposite situation applies to the writer of the put. This can be seen in Part B of the figure. The writer receives the $3.25 per share, which is the maximum possible profit he can make. The writer's breakeven point on the sale is a share price of $36.75. As the share price declines below $36.75, the writer incurs a loss on the sale.

Purchasers of put options commonly own the shares of the underlying company, and wish to protect a profit that they have realized since the initial purchase of the shares. Buying a put allows the owner of the shares to lock in a gain, since it enables her to sell the shares at a known price during the life of the option. The option strategy is known as a protective put.

The Use of Options by Companies: Exchange-Traded Options

From a company's perspective, there are two types of options. Exchange-traded options are the type that were discussed above. These options are created by investors and are traded on the options exchange under the CDCC regulations. With exchange-traded options, no new financing is raised by the company. Rather, investors are simply trading financial securities that derive their value from the company's common shares traded on the stock market.

Institutional investors, whose job it is to invest and manage the savings of individuals, may use options as part of their investment activities to earn a return or to protect or lock in returns already earned on securities. The presence of options trading on a firm's shares may lead to increased trading activity, but the financial manager has no direct control over this. Option traders have neither any say in the firm's management nor any voting rights; only shareholders are given these privileges. While extremely popular investment vehicles, exchange-traded options play no direct role in the fund-raising activities of the financial manager. They are not a source of financing to the firm.

While not directly used in fund raising, options are still used by many corporations as a way to reduce risk. In the previous sections, we discussed equity options, options on common shares and stock market indexes. But options also trade on currencies, interest rates, and commodities. These **future options** are used by companies who wish to protect a particular position in a currency, a commodity like lumber, corn, cotton, rice, sugar, or gold, or on the level of interest rates in Canada or another country. This is widely done in reality as a way to protect, or hedge a position in one of these areas.

future options
Options that trade on currencies, interest rates, and commodities like lumber, corn, cotton, rice, sugar, or gold, or on the level of interest rates in Canada or another country, that are used by companies who wish to protect a position in one of these areas.

Example ▼ Leves Company is a manufacturer of cotton clothing. For such a company, maintaining control of the direct costs of production is vital so ensuring a supply of the basic raw material at a stable price is key. Assume that it is October and cotton is trading for $0.55 per pound, but there was some fear that prices may increase in the short term. To ensure stable prices, the company could lock in a long-term supply agreement with a producer, if one was available.

Alternatively, Leves could use an option contract. For example, the company might purchase a March call option for 50,000 pounds of cotton at a strike price of $0.55 per pound, for a premium of 2.18¢ per pound. By buying this option, Leves guarantees that the most they will have to pay for cotton is $0.5718 per pound. If cotton falls in price, there is no requirement that Leves Company exercise the option, so they can benefit from the falling price. The option contract guarantees a maximum price for the needed cotton, at a reasonable premium.

Leves Company is also considering taking a $10 million variable rate loan. Again, there is a fear that interest rates may increase over this period. Interest rate options allow a company to manage its interest rate exposure by providing "insurance" against adverse market moves while still being able to benefit from favourable market moves. The option premium is paid for that protection. In this case, Leves may purchase an option that protects against rising interest rates on variable-rate loans by "capping" the maximum interest rate that must be paid. A premium is paid to establish an interest rate cap on the loan. If market rates rise above the cap, the option compensates the borrower for the difference between the cap rate and the higher market rate. If interest rates fall, the company benefits. This type of option allows a company to budget with the highest borrowing rate known, while still allowing for the company to benefit from falling interest rates.

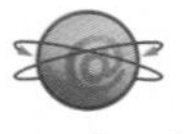

www.canada.com/nationalpost/financialpost/fpmarketdata/index.html

Current market quotes for options on currencies, interest rates, and commodities are available on the Web.

The Use of Options by Companies: Managerial Options

managerial stock options
Options created by the company and granted to senior managers as part of their compensation package; they are often used by publicly traded companies as a way of dealing with the agency issue.

The second type of option is **managerial stock options**. These are options created by the company and granted to senior managers as part of their compensation package. Stock options are often used by publicly traded companies as a way of dealing with the agency issue that was discussed in Chapter 1. Like exchange-traded options, managerial stock options have a stated strike price and expiration date. But the expiration date is measured in years, not months. Many managerial stock options have expiration dates that are seven to ten years in the future. The strike price is generally equal to the common share price on the date the options are granted. Often, managerial stock options may only be exercised after the common shares have increased a stated percentage over the strike price.

In addition, the manager receiving the option does not pay a premium for the option. Rather, if the option is exercised, the manager pays the company the strike price and then receives the stated number of common shares. The manager may then sell the shares on the stock market at the current market price. Managerial stock options raise financing for the company, but not as much as is suggested by the market price of the common shares on the date they are exercised. The options also raise money for the managers. Consider that managers would not exercise their options unless the current market price of the common shares is greater than the strike price of the options.

Example On November 10, 2008, AlumCorp granted 650,000 managerial stock options to the senior managers of the company. The strike price of the options was $38.80, the market price of the common shares on the date the options were granted. The expiration date was 10 years from the date the options were

17.1 IN PRACTICE

Backdating for Managers

If you thought going back in time was only possible in the entertainment industry, think again. It is being done in the corporate world, via a practice termed *backdating*, and many senior managers at publicly traded firms are benefiting. Backdating is the practice of putting a date on a document that is earlier than the actual date the document was created. Some corporations are engaging in this practice for the stock options granted to executives. For most managerial stock options, the exercise price is, at minimum, the market price of the shares on the date the options were granted. So if a company is going to issue options to executives today, the current share price should be the exercise price.

But, if the company's common shares have substantially increased in price over the previous six months, the company could claim to have issued the stock options six months ago when the stock price was lower. This backdating means the lower price that was in effect six months ago becomes the exercise price for the stock options. Obviously, the executives will greatly benefit, as the options are worth much more than they should be in reality. The backdating has inflated the value of the options, and the executives have benefited at the expense of shareholders.

Such manipulation leads one to ask: Is this practice legal? Backdating is actually not illegal provided that four conditions are met: (1) no documents are forged, (2) backdating is clearly communicated to shareholders, (3) backdating is properly reflected in earnings, and (4) backdating is properly reflected in taxes. Since these conditions are rarely met, backdating can be considered a questionable practice. A company that admits to backdating and does not meet these conditions must restate their earnings for the time period involved.

Questionable stock option granting practices have put Waterloo-based Research in Motion Ltd. (RIM), the maker of the ubiquitous BlackBerry, under suspicion of backdating. On September 28, 2006, the company announced a voluntary review of its stock option granting practices. The company said that it had been determined that "GAAP accounting errors were made around the administration of certain historical stock options granted from fiscal 1998 to present." As a result, the company must review over 650,000 documents and restate its earnings. The restatements are expected to see earnings reduced by more than $45 million since 1997.

RIM has suggested that its stock option practices are similar to the option backdating used by hundreds of U.S. companies. An unidentified shareholder has demanded that the company broaden its investigation into the granting of stock options and "should enquire into various forms of manipulation and not be limited to technical errors relating to accounting for historical option grants." The shareholder has also demanded that the audit committee, whose four members have received over $75,000 a year in each of the past three years, not be involved in the investigation.

The allegations did not affect RIM's share price, which reached an all-time high on December 19, 2006. In addition, on December 7, the company's co-CEOs were allowed to exercise stock options despite the investigation. In total, the 745,000 options could be converted into about $115.5 million in RIM stock.

SOURCES: Eric Lie, "Backdating of Executive Stock Option Grants," available at **www.biz.uiowa.edu/faculty/elie/backdating.htm**; Janet McFarland, "RIM Stock Option Review Slowed by Paper Chase," *The Globe and Mail*, December 18, 2006, available at **www.globeinvestor.com/servlet/story/RTGAM.20061218.wrim1218/GIStory**; Theresa Tedesco and Peter Koven, "Push to Widen RIM Options Inquiry," *The National Post*, December 2, 2006, available at **www.canada.com/nationalpost/financialpost/story.html?id=5b0c97ad-f4e7-4803-9178-49eecb130fcf**; Wojtek Dabrowski, "RIM Co-CEOs Allowed to Exercise Stock Options," *The National Post*, December 7, 2006, available at **www.canada.com/nationalpost/financialpost/story.html?id=3f41eebb-9fca-46af-a7d3-e94af92eeca2**.

granted. Managers were only allowed to exercise the options after a three-month holding period. One-third of the options could be exercised when the market price of the shares had increased by 20 percent over the strike price. Two-thirds of the options could be exercised when the market price of the shares had increased by 40 percent over the strike price. All options could be exercised when the market price of the shares had increased by 60 percent over the strike price.

It is now July 22, 2013 and the market price of AlumCorp's common shares is $68.80. The common shares have increased by 77.3 percent, so all of the options that were granted in 2008 are exercisable. If the managers exercise the options, what happens? The managers pay AlumCorp $25,220,000 (650,000 shares × $38.80). AlumCorp raises financing and new common shares are created. The managers can then take the shares and sell them on the stock market. This will generate proceeds of $44,720,000 (650,000 shares × $68.80). The difference of $19,500,000 belongs to the senior managers. This is based on the $30 increase in the value of the shares from the date the options were granted. The company's shares have increased in value benefitting shareholders who owned the shares on November 10, 2008. The senior managers have also benefitted.

? Review Questions

17–13 Discuss the size of the option markets in both Canada and the United States, using the Chicago Board Options Exchange (CBOE) for the U.S. market. Collect recent trading statistics for both markets.

17–14 Discuss the role of the Canadian Derivatives Clearing Corporation regarding option trading in Canada.

17–15 Using Figure 17.3, find examples of in-, at-, and out-of-the-money call and put options. Repeat the exercise using current option quotes taken from a newspaper or from one of the Web sites provided within the chapter. How many option contracts traded in a recent day?

17–16 Regarding options, what is meant by the term *open interest*?

17–17 Explain the payoff to trading call and put options for both the buyer and seller. Provide examples. Explain why an investor would buy a call option versus buying the underlying common shares of the company.

17–18 Other than exchange-traded options, what other types of options are available that a company might use? Why and how would these options be used?

17–19 Compare and contrast exchange-traded options and managerial stock options. How are each used in the fund-raising activities of the firm?

17.6 Swap Contracts[4]

counterparties
The companies that participate in a swap.

Swaps are financial instruments that allow parties to exchange cash flows in a way that benefits both parties engaged in the transaction. For swaps, parties are called **counterparties**, and that term will be used throughout our discussion.

4. We thank Tony Sauer, a sessional lecturer in the School of Business at the University of Prince Edward Island, for his contributions to this section of the chapter.

As an example of swap, assume that Party A can buy cheese for $8.00 per pound, $1.00 less than the price paid by Party B. But B can buy crackers for $0.25 less per pound than A. If A and B both want cheese and crackers, they can swap cheese and crackers in such a way that benefits both. This is the concept of a swap, but rather than dealing in cheese and crackers, the swap market deals in interest rates and currencies.

There are many kinds of swaps and the swap market worldwide is very large, even though the evolution of swaps only began in 1981. Today global swap markets are measured in the many trillions of dollars, and their growth continues as new and innovative types of swaps are created on a regular basis.

The swap market developed because a corporation may be able to borrow at a very attractive rate in one market, but be required to pay a higher rate in another market. This may occur due to lenders in the two markets having different perceptions of the risk of the company. If another company faced the opposite problem, the two companies could counter-match their relative advantages, and both could benefit through a swap.

Interest-Rate Swaps

Interest-rate swaps are financial instruments that allow two counterparties to exchange interest-rate payments to each other. By specifying a dollar amount of a loan (the **notional amount**), type of interest rate (fixed or floating), and start and maturity dates, the two counterparties can determine the amount and timing of the payments they need to make to each other. The oldest and probably still the most common type of interest rate swap is called the *vanilla swap*.

notional amount
The dollar amount of the loan that is subject to a swap.

The "vanilla" swap gets its name from the simplicity of its structure. A **vanilla swap** allows for nothing more than the simple exchange of fixed for floating interest-rate payments. Two counterparties may want to enter into such an arrangement to hedge or offset risk that exists on their balance sheets, to benefit from a borrowing advantage that either or both counterparties may have in a particular debt market, and, for some participants such as hedge funds, to utilize a low-cost/high-leverage method of establishing a trading position in a particular market.

vanilla swap
Allows for the simple exchange of fixed for floating interest rate payments; used as a way to hedge or offset risk that exists on their balance sheets, or to benefit from a comparative borrowing advantage.

Hedging with Interest-Rate Swaps

One of the more common reasons for counterparties to enter into a swap would be to hedge a portion of their balance sheet that may be at risk to adverse moves in interest rates. For example, consider a company that wishes to secure long-term debt financing to improve liquidity and reduce refinancing risk. The company may wish to issue a 25-year bond to meet these two goals.

If the company did, the bond would appear on their balance sheet as a long-term liability. After the date of issue of the bond, interest rates will fluctuate. This means that the value of the liability will change over time. If the issuer did not have any fixed assets to offset the fluctuations in the value of the liability, the company may find itself in a position of financial risk. If the business had large volumes of short-term cash flows from accounts receivable, it would be able to enter into a vanilla swap to hedge, or remove the liability risk from their balance sheet. By receiving a fixed rate of interest from another counterparty for the term of their bond liability and paying them the floating rate they will have removed the risk to their balance sheet of adverse interest-rate moves.

FIGURE 17.6
A Vanilla Swap

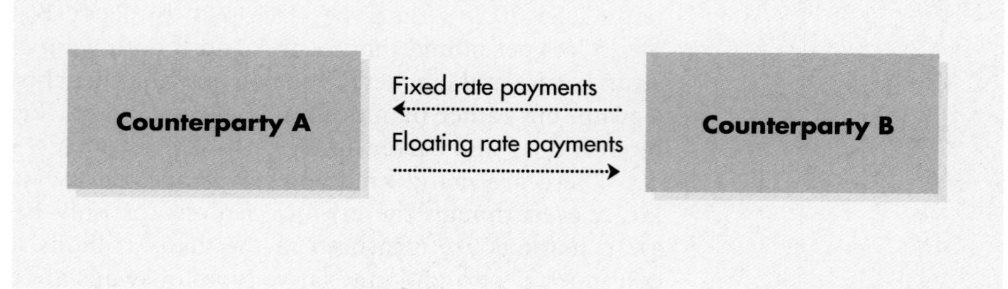

After entering into the swap in Figure 17.6, counterparty A (the bond issuer) will be left with a long-term liability (the bond) and a long-term asset (the fixed rate half of the swap) on its balance sheet which will have offsetting changes in value when interest rates fluctuate. It will also have a short-term liability (the floating rate half of the swap) that will reset periodically, typically every 1 or 3 months, on its balance sheet as a result of entering into the swap. This will be offset by the receivables that are a current asset on the balance sheet.

Counterparty A is now in a position where it is indifferent to interest-rate movements, short-term or long-term, because the revaluation of its assets and liabilities will be offsetting (they are hedged). Counterparty B would be motivated to enter into the swap because their line of business generates current liabilities and long-term assets that they need to offset to fully hedge the position.

Counterparties A and B do not need to know of each other in order for this transaction to occur. As with most financial transactions, financial institutions act as intermediaries on behalf of both companies in the swap market. The financial institution is termed the **swap dealer**. Often, the financial institution would act for both A and B.

swap dealer
The financial institution, usually a bank, that acts as an intermediary on behalf of the companies engaged in the swap.

The swap dealer will make a small profit from this arrangement by adding "spreads" to the fixed rates. For example, the dealer receives a fixed rate of 10 percent from counterparty B but pays a fixed rate of only 9.98 percent to counterparty A. The swap dealer will then match the floating rates received from A and paid to B. The dealer will make a profit of 2 basis points on the notional amount. This may seem small, but remember the dollar amounts of the swap deals are large, normally in multiples of $25 million, and the competition in the swap market fierce. This reduces the opportunity for large spreads. All of the large Canadian banks act as swap dealers.

The fixed rates quoted for swaps are dependent on many factors, but term to maturity and the default risk of the counterparties involved are the main ones. In Figure 17.7, the dealer will determine the fixed rate it is willing to pay and to receive on a daily basis, and even make adjustments within the day when underlying interest rates move and publish these rates to its client base. Fixed swap rates consist of the sum of an underlying government bond or risk-free rate plus a swap spread, and have a term structure similar to the current yield curve. An example of a swap term structure is provided below.

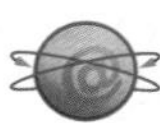

www.tdcommercialbanking.com/foreignx/solutions/risk_swaps.jsp

FIGURE 17.7 A Vanilla Swap Involving a Financial Intermediary

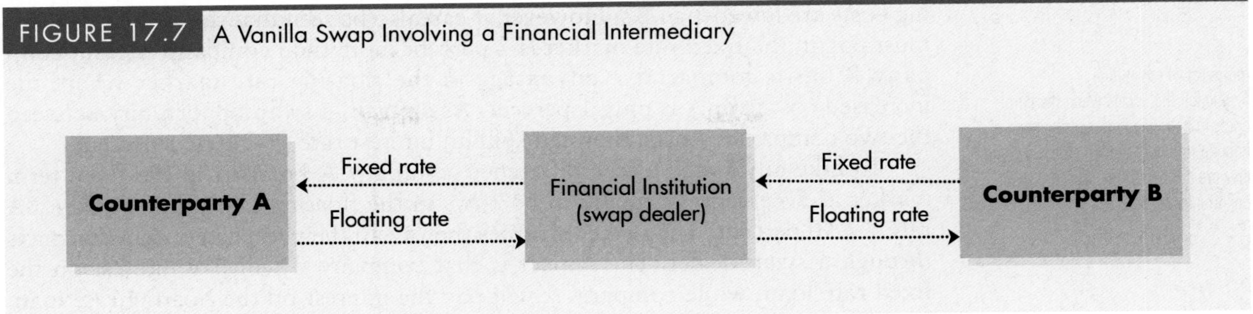

In Table 17.3, rates vary depending on the term to maturity. Also, the swap dealer will embed the creditworthiness of its counterparties into the swap spread. Less creditworthy counterparties will be required to pay higher swap spreads, and thus higher all-in swap rates. More secure clients will be charged lower swap spreads, and thus lower all-in fixed swap rates.

Comparative Advantage of Interest-Rate Swaps

Two companies wish to borrow money. Company A wishes to borrow in the floating rate market, company B in the fixed rate market. The two companies are offered the following borrowing rates where the "BA rate" is the current yield on three-month bankers' acceptances:

	Fixed rate	Floating rate
Company A	5.00%	BA rate + 0.50%
Company B	7.00%	BA rate + 1.50%

Both could simply borrow in the respective markets and raise the required amount of money. But let's consider the information available. Company A is clearly more creditworthy than B, as both its fixed and its floating rate borrow-

TABLE 17.3 **Example of Swap Rates for Various Terms to Maturity**

Term to maturity	Yield on government bond	Swap spread	All-in swap rate
2 years	8.00%	0.20%	8.20%
3 years	8.25	0.22	8.47
4 years	8.50	0.25	8.75
5 years	8.75	0.27	9.02
7 years	9.00	0.30	9.30
10 years	9.25	0.35	9.60
15 years	9.50	0.40	9.90
20 years	9.75	0.50	10.25
30 years	10.00	0.60	10.60

ing costs are lower than B's. However, it can also be seen that the rate company B must pay in the fixed rate market is 2 percent more than company A's. But company B has a **comparative advantage** in the floating rate market where the increased cost over A is only 1 percent. As a result, a swap opportunity between the two companies exists; they can split an interest rate saving of 1 percent.

comparative advantage
A situation that exists when the differences in borrowing rates in the fixed and floating rate debt markets for two companies are not equal; the reason a swap opportunity exists.

To take advantage of the difference, company A borrows in the fixed term market at 5 percent. Company B borrows in the floating rate market at the BA rate + 1.50 percent. The two companies then swap their respective debt contracts through a swap dealer. The impact is that company B will pay interest on the fixed rate loan, while company A will pay the interest on the floating rate loan. This is shown in Figure 17.8.

Company B makes the interest payments on the fixed rate loan to A. Company B pays A 6 percent, but A only has to pay the bank 5 percent, so company A makes 1 percent on the fixed rate half of the swap. At the same time, company A pays B the BA + 1.00 percent, 0.50 percent more than the rate they could actually borrow at. The net effect is that company A saves 0.50 percent on its floating rate borrowing cost.

Turning to company B, we can see that they also benefit from the swap. Company B pays A 6 percent on the fixed rate part of the loan, saving 1 percent on their fixed rate borrowing cost. On the floating rate loan, company A pays B 0.5 percent less than B's actual cost of the loan. The net impact is that company B saves 0.50 percent on its fixed rate borrowing cost.

Both companies benefit from the swap arrangement. In the above example, the companies have split the 1 percent difference in their comparative borrowing rates. In reality, the benefit to both will be slightly less than 0.50 percent, since the financial institution arranging the swap will make a few basis points on the deal.

Currency Swaps

currency swap
Occurs when counterparties exchange fixed or floating interest rate payments in one currency for fixed or floating interest rate payments in another currency; in addition, the notional amount of a currency swap is exchanged.

Another common type of swap is the currency swap. A **currency swap** involves two counterparties exchanging fixed or floating interest rate payments in one currency for fixed or floating interest rate payments in another currency. In addition to the exchange of interest rates, the notional amount of a currency swap is also exchanged at both the inception of the swap and at maturity. This feature distinguishes currency swaps from interest-rate swaps, which involve no

FIGURE 17.8 Interest Rate Swap with Comparative Borrowing Advantage

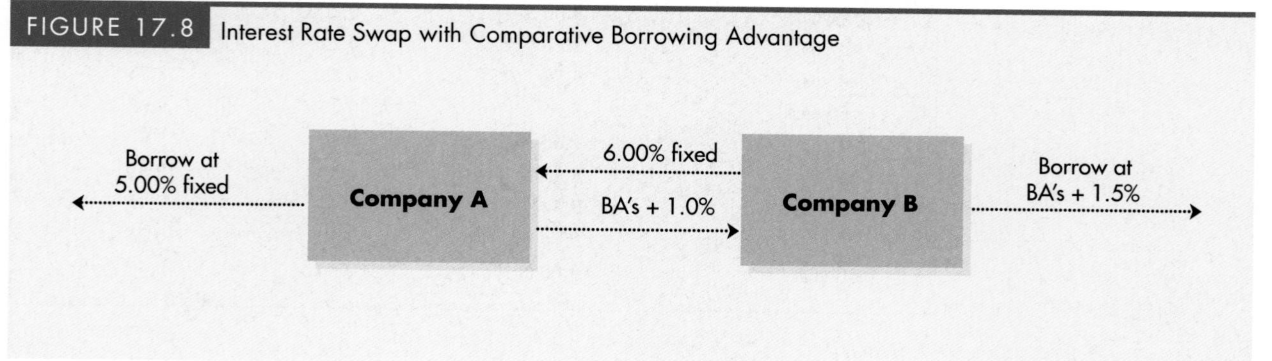

exchange of principal. An interest-rate swap transacted for $100 million does not involve the payment of the $100 million. Rather, only the fixed and floating rate payments calculated based on a principal are exchanged. An example is a good way to illustrate a typical currency swap.

Example Let's say that company A is well known in Canada but not so well known in the United States, and that the opposite is true for company B. Such a situation may lead to a schedule of borrowing costs as follows. The problem is that company A wishes to borrow in U.S. dollars, while company B wishes to borrow in Canadian dollars.

	Fixed rate	Floating rate
Company A	5.00% in C$	3-month US$ floating rate + 2%
Company B	6.00% in C$	3-month US$ floating rate + 1%

In this example, company A has a comparative advantage in Canadian fixed rate markets, whereas company B has a comparative advantage in US$ floating rate markets. If the Canadian-dollar foreign exchange rate were C$1.10 = US$1, the following swap contract would be mutually beneficial to both companies.

Company A borrows C$110,000,000 in the Canadian market at 5 percent and exchanges it for US$100,000,000 with company B. A's net cost is the U.S. floating rate + 1%, which is 1 percent better than it could do on its own in the U.S. market. Company B borrows US$100,000,000 in the U.S. market and exchanges it for C$110,000,000 with company A. B's net cost is a C$ fixed rate of 5 percent, 1 percent better than it could do on its own in the Canadian market.

Currency swaps can be structured in many different ways. Counterparties can exchange fixed for fixed payments, floating for floating, or fixed for floating (as illustrated above), and in numerous different currency pairs. As in the other examples, a swap dealer will facilitate the deal between two counterparties and earn a small spread for the risk of either counterparty forfeiting on their payment obligations under the terms of the swap.

Also, dealers will sometimes "warehouse" deals for a variety of reasons. For instance, company A above might need to transact at a different time than company B. The dealer will often transact with A today knowing that they will be able to transact with B at some later date, or identify a company like B at some point in the future to fulfill their needs. This period can be as short as a day or as

FIGURE 17.9

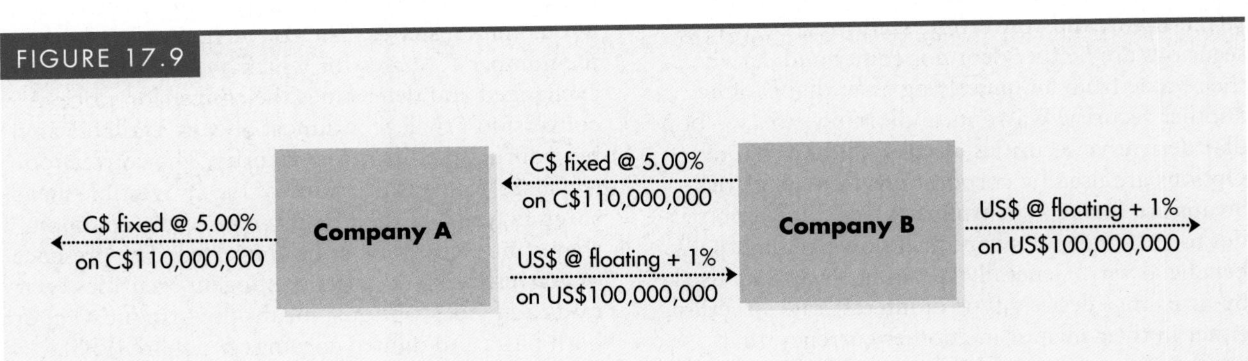

long as months. During this time the dealer bears the risk of markets moving in an adverse fashion; however, most are sophisticated enough to hedge their risk exposures in the interim. In some cases the intermediary will intentionally bear this risk, because they believe markets will move in their favour. In such an instance the dealer has established a "trading" position and is speculating on the future movement of markets.

www.riskglossary.com/link/interest_rate_swap.htm
www.prwebdirect.com/releases/2006/10/prweb455494.htm

The swap market is huge and rapidly growing given the benefits it can provide corporations. More information on the swap market is available on the Web.

? Review Questions

17–20 What is the basic concept of a swap?
17–21 How can an interest-rate swap be used to hedge a portion of a company's balance sheet that may be at risk based on adverse moves in interest rates?
17–22 What is the role of the swap dealer?
17–23 Explain the cash flows in Figure 17.8 and how both company A and company B benefit from the swap arrangement.
17–24 Discuss how currency swaps differ from interest-rate swaps. Why would a company use a currency swap rather than an interest-rate swap?

SUMMARY

LG1 **Introduce the concept of hybrid and derivative securities and swap instruments, and how they are used by a corporation.** Hybrid securities are forms of debt or equity financing that possess characteristics of both debt and equity financing. Two popular hybrid securities are preferred shares and convertible securities. Derivative securities are neither debt nor equity and derive their value from an underlying asset that is often another security. Warrants and options are two popular derivative securities discussed in the chapter. Options are used by corporations to manage risk. Swaps are financial instruments that allow two parties to exchange, or swap, cash flows in a mutually beneficial way. Generally speaking, swaps are used by firms that desire a type of interest-rate structure, either in their own or in another currency, that another firm can provide less expensively.

LG2 **Describe the basic types and general features of convertible securities, and demonstrate the procedures for determining the straight bond value, conversion (or share) value, and market value of a convertible bond.** Corporate bonds and preferred shares may both be convertible into common shares. The conversion ratio indicates the number of shares for which a convertible can be exchanged and determines the conversion price. A conversion privilege is almost always available anytime during the life of the security. The conversion (or share) value is the value of the convertible measured in terms of the market price of the common shares into which it can be converted. The presence of convertibles and other contingent securities (warrants and stock options) means the firm must report both basic and diluted earnings per share (EPS). Convertibles are used to obtain deferred common share financing, to "sweeten" bond issues, to minimize restrictive covenants, and to raise cheap funds temporarily. The call feature is sometimes used to encourage or "force" conversion; occasionally, an overhanging issue results. The straight bond value of a convertible is the price at which it would sell in the market without the conversion feature. It typically represents the minimum (floor) value at which a convertible bond trades. The conversion value of the convertible is found by multiplying the conversion ratio by the current market price of the underlying common shares. The market value of a convertible generally exceeds both its straight and conversion values, thus resulting in a market premium. The premium, which is largest when the straight and conversion values are nearly equal, is due to the attractive gains potential from the common shares and the risk protection provided by the straight value of the convertible.

LG3 **Explain the basic characteristics of warrants, the implied price of an attached warrant, and the values of warrants.** Warrants allow their holders to purchase a certain number of common shares at the specified exercise price. Warrants are often attached to debt issues as "sweeteners," generally have limited lives, are detachable, and may be listed and traded on securities exchanges. Warrants are similar to share rights, except that the life of a warrant is generally longer than that of a right, and the exercise price of a warrant is initially set above the underlying share's current market price. Warrants are similar to convertibles, but exercising them has a less pronounced effect on the firm's leverage and brings in new funds. The implied price of an attached warrant can be found by dividing the difference between the bond price with warrants attached and the straight bond value by the number of warrants attached to each bond. The market value of a warrant usually exceeds its intrinsic value, creating a warrant premium. The premium results from positive investor expectations and the ability of investors to get more leverage from trading warrants than from trading the underlying common shares.

LG4 **Define and discuss options and the terminology and features of options, and identify the six variables affecting the pricing of options.** An option provides its holder with an opportunity to buy or sell a specified asset at a stated price on or before a set expiration date. Call options allow the holder to purchase common shares of a specific company at a stated price; a put allows the holder to sell common shares at a stated price. The stated price is termed the *strike price*. A standardized feature of exchange-traded options on common shares is that they are always for 100 shares. The option premium is the price paid by the buyer of an option and the amount received by the seller; it is quoted on a per-share basis. The premium (value) of an option is based on the six variables: the current market price of the common shares, the strike (exercise) price, the time to expiry, the volatility of the common share price, interest-rate levels, and the dividend history of the company.

LG5 **Explain option trading and option quotes, illustrate the payoff to option trading, and discuss how companies use options.** In Canada, option trading is regulated by the Canadian Derivatives Clearing Corporation, which acts as the issuer, clearinghouse, and guarantor of all option contracts. Investors purchasing call options do so in the expectation that the market price of the underlying common share will rise more than enough to cover the cost of the option (the premium), thereby allowing the purchaser of the call to profit. Put options are purchased in the expectation that the share price of a given security will decline over the life of the option. Investors gain from put options when the price of the underlying common shares declines by more than the option premium. Investors trade options because of the tremendous leverage associated with even small movements in share prices. Exchange-traded options are created by investors. The firm has nothing to do with these securities and no financing is raised. But companies use the option market to hedge risk by limiting the damage that price or interest rate changes could cause. Managerial stock options are options created by the company and granted to senior managers as part of their compensation package. When exercised, these options raise money for the company and also for the managers.

Discuss the general features of swaps and illustrate how they can be of benefit to both parties that are involved in the transaction. Swaps are financial instruments that allow parties to exchange cash flows in a way that benefits both parties engaged in the transaction. Interest-rate swaps are financial instruments that allow two companies to exchange interest-rate payments to each other. By specifying a dollar amount of a loan (the notional amount), type of interest rate (fixed or floating), and start and maturity dates, the two companies can determine the amount and timing of the payments they need to make to each other. The oldest and probably still the most common type of interest rate swap is called the "vanilla" swap. This is nothing more than the simple exchange of fixed for floating interest-rate payments. Two counterparties might want to enter into such an arrangement to hedge or offset risk that exists on their balance sheets, or to take advantage of comparative advantages that either or both companies may have in a particular debt market. Another common type of swap is the currency swap. Here two companies exchange fixed or floating interest-rate payments in one currency for fixed or floating interest-rate payments in another.

SELF-TEST PROBLEMS

(Solutions in Appendix B)

ST 17–1 **Finding convertible bond values** Mountain Mining Company has an outstanding issue of convertible bonds with a $1,000 par value. These bonds are convertible into 40 shares of common stock. They have an 11 percent annual coupon interest rate paid semiannually and mature in 25 years. The current yield on a straight bond of similar risk is currently 13 percent.

a. Calculate the *straight bond value* of the bond.

b. Calculate the *conversion (or share) values* of the bond when the market price of the common shares is $20, $25, $28, $35, and $50 per share.

c. For each of the share prices given in **b**, at what price would you expect the bond to sell? Why?

ST 17–2 **Option pricing and payoffs** On August 6, 2008, McGuigan Tools' common shares closed trading at $25.00 per share. The following four option contracts on McGuigan Tools' common shares were traded. The closing quotes were:

Oct	25	1.80
Oct	27.50	0.45
Nov	27.50p	3.90
Jan09	25	3.15

a. Which of the above contracts are in the money, at the money, and out of the money? Explain.

b. Use the above quotes to illustrate the intrinsic value and time value of options.

c. Assume that on August 6, 2008, you purchased four of the Nov 27.50p option contracts at the closing quote. Excluding commissions, what was the cost of this trade? Explain how you would make money on the purchase of this option.

d. If on the third Friday of November, McGuigan Tools' common shares closed trading at $21.20, what should the closing premium be on the Nov 27.50p option contract?

e. Assume the Nov 27.50p contract closed trading on the third Friday of November at the premium stated in part **d**. To benefit from your purchase in part **c**, what did you have to do prior to the market close on the third Friday of November? Assuming you did this, what is your payoff on your purchase of the four Nov 27.50p option contracts? Provide the per-share, total dollar, and percentage return. What is the seller's payoff (assuming the seller holds his position to the option's expiration)?

f. Assume that on August 6, 2008, you purchased two of the Jan 09 25 option contracts at the closing quote. Excluding commissions, what was the cost of this trade? How would you make money on the purchase? If on the third Friday of January 2009, McGuigan Tools' common shares closed trading at $25.00, what should the closing premium be on the Jan 09 25 option contract? What is your payoff to this option trade? Provide the per-share, total dollar, and percentage return. What is the seller's payoff (assuming the seller holds her position to the option's expiration)?

PROBLEMS

BASIC 

17–1 Conversion price Calculate the conversion price for each of the following convertible bonds:

a. A $1,000-par-value bond that is convertible into 20 common shares.
b. A $500-par-value bond that is convertible into 25 common shares.
c. A $1,000-par-value bond that is convertible into 50 common shares.

BASIC 

17–2 Conversion ratio What is the conversion ratio for each of the following bonds?

a. A $1,000-par-value bond that is convertible into common shares at $43.75 per share.
b. A $1,000-par-value bond that is convertible into common shares at $25 per share.
c. A $600-par-value bond that is convertible into common shares at $30 per share.

BASIC 

17–3 Conversion (or share) value What is the conversion (or share) value of each of the following convertible bonds?

a. A $1,000-par-value bond that is convertible into 25 common shares. The common shares are currently selling at $50 per share.
b. A $1,000-par-value bond that is convertible into 12.5 common shares. The common shares are currently selling at $42 per share.
c. A $1,000-par-value bond that is convertible into 100 common shares. The common shares are currently selling at $10.50 per share.

BASIC 

17–4 Conversion (or share) value Find the conversion (or share) value for each of the convertible bonds described in the following table.

Convertible	Conversion ratio	Current market price of common shares
A	25	$42.25
B	16	50.00
C	20	44.00
D	5	19.50

BASIC 

17–5 Straight bond value Calculate the straight bond value for each of the bonds shown in the following table.

Bond	Par value	Coupon rate (paid semiannually)	Yield on equal-risk straight bond	Years to maturity
A	$1,000	10%	14%	20
B	800	12	15	14
C	1,000	13	16	30
D	1,000	14	17	25

INTERMEDIATE 

17–6 Determining values—Convertible bond Eastern Clock Company has an outstanding issue of convertible bonds with a $1,000 par value. These bonds are convertible into 50 common shares. They have a 10 percent coupon rate paid semiannually and a 20-year maturity. The current yield on straight bonds of similar risk is currently 12 percent.

a. Calculate the *straight bond value* of the bond.

b. Calculate the *conversion (or share) values* of the bond when the market price of the common shares is $15, $20, $23, $30, and $45 per share.

c. For each of the share prices given in **b**, at what price would you expect the bond to sell? Why?

d. What is the least you would expect the bond to sell for, regardless of the price behaviour of the common shares?

INTERMEDIATE 

17–7 Determining values—Convertible bond Craig's Cake Company has an outstanding issue of 15-year convertible bonds with a $1,000 par value. These bonds are convertible into 80 common shares. They have a 13 percent coupon rate paid semiannually. The current yield on straight bonds of similar risk is 16 percent.

a. Calculate the *straight bond value* of this bond.

b. Calculate the *conversion (or share) values* of the bond when the market price is $9, $12, $13, $15, and $20 per common share.

c. For each of the common share prices given in **b**, at what price would you expect the bond to sell? Why?

d. Graph the straight value and conversion value of the bond for each common share price given. Plot the per-common-share prices on the x axis and the bond values on the y axis. Use this graph to indicate the minimum market value of the bond associated with each common stock price.

INTERMEDIATE LG3

17–8 Implied prices of attached warrants Calculate the implied price of *each* warrant for each of the bonds shown in the following table.

Bond	Price of bond with warrants attached	Par value	Coupon rate (paid semiannually)	Yield on equal-risk straight bond	Years to maturity	Number of warrants attached to bond
A	$1,000	$1,000	12%	13%	15	10
B	1,100	1,000	9.5	12	10	30
C	500	500	10	11	20	5
D	1,000	1,000	11	12	20	20

INTERMEDIATE 

17–9 Evaluation of the implied price of an attached warrant Dinoo Mathur wishes to determine whether the $1,000 price asked for Stanco Manufacturing's bond is fair in light of the intrinsic value of the attached warrants. The $1,000-par, 30-year, 11.5 percent coupon-rate bond pays semiannual interest and has 10 warrants attached for purchase of common shares. The intrinsic value of each warrant is $12.50. The current yield on an equal-risk straight bond is 13 percent.

a. Find the straight value of Stanco Manufacturing's bond.
b. Calculate the implied price of *all* warrants attached to Stanco's bond.
c. Calculate the implied price of *each* warrant attached to Stanco's bond.
d. Compare the implied price for each warrant calculated in **c** to its intrinsic value. On the basis of this comparison, what recommendation would you give Dinoo with respect to the fairness of Stanco's bond price? Explain.

CHALLENGE 

17–10 Warrant values Kent Hotels has warrants that allow the purchase of three common shares at $50 per share. The common share price and the market value of the warrant associated with that price are shown in the following table.

Common share price per share	Market value of warrant
$42	$ 2
46	8
48	9
54	18
58	28
62	38
66	48

a. For each of the common share prices given, calculate the intrinsic warrant value.
b. Graph the intrinsic and market values of the warrant on a set of per-share common share price (*x* axis)–warrant value (*y* axis) axes.
c. If the warrant value is $12 when the market price of the common shares is $50, does this contradict or support the graph you have constructed? Explain.
d. Specify the area of *warrant premium*. Why does this premium exist?
e. If the expiration date of the warrants is quite close, would you expect your graph to look different? Explain.

CHALLENGE 

17–11 Common share versus warrant investment Susan Michaels is evaluating the Burton Tool Company's common shares and warrants to choose the better investment. The firm's shares are currently selling for $50 per share; its warrants to purchase three common shares at $45 per share are selling for $20. Ignoring transactions costs, Ms. Michaels has $8,000 to invest. She is quite optimistic with respect to Burton because she has certain "inside information" about the firm's prospects with respect to a large government contract.

a. How many common shares and how many warrants can Ms. Michaels purchase?

b. Suppose Ms. Michaels purchased the common shares, held them for 1 year, then sold them for $60 per share. What total gain would she realize, ignoring brokerage fees and taxes?

c. Suppose Ms. Michaels purchased warrants and held them for 1 year and the market price of the shares increased to $60 per share. What would be her total gain if the market value of warrants increased to $45 and she sold the warrants (ignoring brokerage fees and taxes)?

d. What benefit, if any, do the warrants provide? Are there any differences in the risk of these two alternative investments? Explain.

CHALLENGE  17–12 **Common share versus warrant investment** Tom Baldwin can invest $6,300 in the common shares or the warrants of Lexington Life Insurance. The common shares are currently selling for $30 per share. Its warrants, which provide for the purchase of two shares of common stock at $28 per share, are currently selling for $7. The shares are expected to rise to a market price of $32 within the next year, so the expected intrinsic value of a warrant over the next year is $8. The expiration date of the warrant is 1 year from the present.

a. If Mr. Baldwin purchases the common shares, holds them for 1 year, and then sells them for $32, what is his total gain? (Ignore brokerage fees and taxes.)

b. If Mr. Baldwin purchases the warrants and converts them to common shares in 1 year, what is his total gain if the market price of common shares is actually $32? (Ignore brokerage fees and taxes.)

c. Repeat **a** and **b** assuming that the market price of the common shares in 1 year is (1) $30 and (2) $28.

d. Discuss the two alternatives and the tradeoffs associated with them.

INTERMEDIATE  17–13 **Leverage on warrants** Disco Ltd. and Hiphop Inc. have each issued warrants.

Company	Market price of common shares	Market price of warrant
Disco	$30	$25
Hiphop	$20	$ 2

a. Calculate the leverage on each of the warrants. Which of the warrants have the greatest leverage? Why would Disco's warrant price be so much higher than Hiphop's?

b. What do these measures mean in terms of the market's expectations about the share price?

c. What is the risk associated with a warrant with high leverage?

INTERMEDIATE  17–14 **Options profits and losses** For each of the exchange-traded option contracts shown in the following table, use the underlying share price at expiration and other information to determine the amount of profit or loss an investor would have had, ignoring brokerage fees.

Option	Type of option	Cost of option	Strike price	Common share price at expiration
A	Call	$200	$50	$55
B	Call	350	42	45
C	Put	500	60	50
D	Put	300	35	40
E	Call	450	28	26

BASIC  

17–15 Reading option quotes Use the option quotes provided in Figure 17.3 on page 925 to answer the following:

a. What was the closing price of Alcan's common shares?

b. What was the open interest on Bombardier's option contracts?

c. How many Barrick option contracts were traded?

d. What is the exercise price on the Jan07 Biovail puts that had a closing premium of $0.80?

  INTERMEDIATE

17–16 Call option Carol Krebs is considering buying 100 shares of Sooner Products, Inc., at $62 per share. Because she has read that the firm will likely soon receive certain large orders from abroad, she expects the price of Sooner to increase to $70 per share. As an alternative, Carol is considering purchasing one call option contract of Sooner at a strike price of $60. The 90-day option will cost $600. Ignore any brokerage fees or dividends.

a. On a per-share basis, what is the premium on the option? What are the intrinsic value and time value of the option? Provide both on a per-share basis.

b. What will Carol's profit be on the share transaction if its price does rise to $70 and she sells? Provide both a total dollar and a percentage return.

c. Assume that in 60 days, the price of Sooner's common shares increases to $70 per share. Carol wishes to close her option position by selling a call option. If the time value of the option is reduced by $1 per share, how much will Carol earn on the option transaction? Provide both a total dollar and percentage return.

d. At what price must the common shares of Sooner Products be trading for on the expiry date of the option contract for Carol to break even on the option transaction?

e. Compare, contrast, and discuss the relative profit and risk from the common share and the option transactions.

  INTERMEDIATE

17–17 Put option Ed Martin, the pension fund manager for Stark Corporation, is considering purchasing one put option contract in anticipation of a price decline in the common shares of Carlisle Inc. The option contract has a strike price of $45 and can be purchased for $380. The option will expire in 90 days. Carlisle's common shares currently trade for $46 per share.

a. On a per-share basis, what is the premium on the option? What are the intrinsic value and time value of the option? Provide both on a per-share basis.

b. Ignoring any brokerage fees or dividends, what profit or loss will Ed make if he buys the option, and Carlisle Inc.'s common shares close trading on the expiry date of the option at $46, $44, $40, and $35?
c. What would happen if the price of Carlisle's common shares slowly rose from its initial $46 level to $55 at the end of 90 days? What would happen to the premium on the option?
d. In light of your findings, discuss the potential risks and returns from using put options to attempt to profit from an anticipated decline in share price.

CHALLENGE

17–18 Determining option values On May 21, 2008, the common shares of Infogold closed trading at $15 per share. The closing quotes for the following option contracts on Infogold are available:

Jun	13.50	2.45
Aug	17	0.70
Aug	17p	3.00
Nov	15	1.72
Dec	18p	4.05

a. For each of the above options, develop a table providing: (1) the option premium; (2) a statement indicating whether the option is in the money, at the money, or out of the money; (3) the intrinsic value of the option; and (4) the time value of the option.
b. Assume that on May 21, 2008, you purchased three of the Dec 18p option contracts at the closing price. Excluding commissions, what was the cost of this trade? What would be your profit/loss if the market price of the common shares on the date of expiry of the options was (i) $14? (ii) $20? Provide an answer in dollars and percent.
c. If on the third Thursday of August, the share price of Infogold closed trading at $11, what would the holder of the Aug 17 and Aug 17p option contracts do?
d. Assume that on May 21, 2008, you purchased two of the Nov 15 option contracts at the closing price. What was the cost of the trade, excluding commissions? What would your profit/loss be if on the option's expiry date the closing price of the common shares was (i) $14.75? (ii) $18.75? Provide an answer in dollars and percent.
e. Assume the risk-free rate used to determine the premiums for the Aug 17 and Aug 17p was 5 percent. How would the premiums for these options be affected if the risk-free rate had been (i) 3 percent? (ii) 7 percent? What impact do changes in interest rates have on the premiums for calls and puts?

INTERMEDIATE

17–19 Determining option values What impact will the following events have on the option premium?
a. The market price of the share rises and the investor holds puts.
b. The market price of the share rises and the investor holds calls.
c. The market price of the share falls and the investor holds puts.
d. The market price of the share falls and the investor holds calls.
e. The time to expiry shortens and the investor holds puts.
f. The time to expiry shortens and the investor holds calls.
g. The market anticipates a decline in the market price and the investor holds puts.
h. Interest rates have fallen and the investor holds puts.

i. Interest rates have risen and the investor holds calls that expire in 6 months.
j. The market price of the share is very volatile and the investor holds calls.
k. Common shares begin to pay dividends and the investor holds calls.

INTERMEDIATE  17–20 **Impact of interest rate and time on premium price**

a. Calculate the current value of the following call options, assuming the market price of the common shares is $30 and the strike price of the option is $25.

Risk-free rate (%)	Time to expiry (months)
4	3
4	6
7	3
7	6

b. What impact did changes in the interest rate and time to expiry have on the present value of the option? Explain the reason for the change.

CHALLENGE  17–21 **Interest-rate swap** Dayton Co. wishes to borrow $70 million to finance an expansion. The company can borrow at a fixed rate of 5.4 percent or at a floating rate of BA + 0.5 percent. The BA rate is the current yield on three-month bankers' acceptances. Dayton Co. prefers to finance its expansion with a floating interest rate. Jameson Oil also wishes to borrow $70 million to finance the purchase of assets. Jameson can borrow at a fixed rate of 6.7 percent or a floating rate of BA + 0.5 percent. The company has a heavy investment in fixed assets and so would like to borrow at a fixed rate.

a. Would an interest rate swap be mutually beneficial to the counterparties? Explain why or why not.
b. If Dayton offered Jameson a fixed rate of 6.5 percent in exchange for BA flat, should the swap be completed? Explain. If the swap were completed, what would be the impact for each company on: (1) the interest rate paid on the loan and (2) the dollar amount of interest paid in each year of the loan?
c. If Dayton offered Jameson a fixed rate of 6 percent in exchange for BA + 0.60 percent, should the swap be completed? Explain. If the swap were completed, what would be the impact for each company on: (1) the interest rate paid on the loan and (2) the dollar amount of interest paid in each year of the loan?
d. To be fair to both companies, how should the swap be structured?

CHALLENGE  17–22 **Interest-rate swap** Hefty Discounters wishes to raise $50 million in the debt market to open ten new stores in eastern Canada. Hefty can borrow at a fixed rate of 9.5 percent or a floating rate of BA + 0.5 percent, where the BA rate is the current yield on three-month bankers' acceptances. Remington Industries is also looking to borrow $50 million to expand its operations overseas. The bank has quoted Remington a fixed interest rate of 11 percent or a floating rate of BA + 0.8 percent. Due to the nature of their businesses, Hefty prefers to borrow at a floating rate while Remington prefers to borrow at a fixed rate.

a. Explain why an interest-rate swap would be beneficial for both companies.
b. The swap dealer will charge a spread of 6 basis points on the fixed rate. How much will the swap dealer make each year the swap arrangement is outstanding?

c. If Hefty offers Remington a fixed rate of 10 percent in exchange for a floating rate of BA + 0.20 percent, should the swap be completed? Explain. If the swap were completed, what would be the impact for each company on: (1) the interest rate paid on the loan, and (2) the dollar amount of interest paid in each year of the loan?

d. To be fair to both companies, how should the swap be structured?

CHALLENGE  **17–23 Interest-rate swap** Perry Corporation and D. F. Forestry Ltd. need to obtain financing to fund investments in infrastructure and equipment. Perry Corporation is a diversified conglomerate with holdings in various successful businesses around the world. They are an AA rated company. Currently, the company can borrow funds at either a fixed rate of 4.75 percent or at a floating rate of BA flat. D. F. Forestry Ltd. is a relatively new company with fluctuating sales and assets. It can borrow funds at either a fixed rate of 7.9 percent or at a floating rate of BA + 1.2 percent.

a. Is there an opportunity for both Perry Corporation and D. F. Forestry Ltd. to benefit from an interest-rate swap? Explain why.

b. Suppose you are a representative of a bank that acts as a swap dealer, and you have been given the borrowing rate information for Perry Corporation and D. F. Forestry Ltd. How would you structure an interest-rate swap that would benefit both firms?

c. If the deal is for $100 million and the bank's spread is 5 basis points, how much money would the bank make in each year of the deal?

CASE CHAPTER 17 Rashid Company: Financing the Purchase of the Chemical-Waste-Disposal System

See the enclosed Student CD-ROM for cases that help you put theories and concepts from the text into practice.

Be sure to visit the Companion Website for this book at **www.pearsoned.ca/gitman** for a wealth of additional learning tools including self-test quizzes, Web exercises, and additional cases.

Appendix to Chapter 17

The Black-Scholes Option Valuation Model

In 1973, Fischer Black and Canadian-born and educated Myron Scholes published a research paper that outlined an analytic model that would determine the fair market value for European-type call options on non-dividend-paying firms.[4] Since its publication, the Black-Scholes Option Valuation Model has earned a position as one of the most widely accepted and used financial models.

Today, thousands of traders and investors use the model to value options on markets around the world. In fact, calculators are available with the Black-Scholes model preprogrammed. The research was so influential that in 1997 Myron Scholes was awarded the Nobel Prize in economics due in large part to this 1973 paper. (Fischer Black, who would have shared the prestigious award, died in 1995.) In this appendix, we discuss the well-known option pricing model, a formula that is widely used by both academics and practitioners. By making certain assumptions, Black and Scholes proved that the current price of a call option equals:

$$V_0 = [P_0 \times N(d_1)] - \left[\frac{S}{e^{rt}} \times N(d_2)\right] \tag{17.A1}$$

where:

V_0 = value of the option now (at time 0)
P_0 = current price of the common shares
S = strike price of the option
e = the base of natural logarithms, which equals 2.718282
r = continuously compounded annual risk-free interest rate
t = time to the option's expiration expressed as a fraction of a year

$N(d_1)$ and $N(d_2)$ are the values of the cumulative normal distribution at points d_1 and d_2. These functions indicate the probability of observing a value equal to or less than d_1 and d_2; where d_1 and d_2 equal:

$$d_1 = \frac{\ln(P_0/S) + (r + 0.5\sigma^2)t}{\sigma \times \sqrt{t}} \tag{17.A2}$$

$$d_2 = d_1 - [\sigma \times \sqrt{t}]$$

where:

$\ln(P_0/S)$ = the natural logarithm of (P_0/S)
σ = the expected standard deviation of the annual rate of return on the underlying common shares

4. "The Pricing of Options and Corporate Liabilities," *Journal of Political Economy* 81(3) (1973), pp. 637–654.

Readers should note that five of the six variables that determine option premiums, as discussed in Table 17.2, are used in the model. Dividends are not considered, since the model was developed for non-dividend-paying shares.[5] Determining the values of these variables for use in the model is very straightforward for four of the five variables. The current share price, strike price, and time to the option's expiration are easily observed. For the model, the risk-free interest rate used is supposed to be the constant rate expected during the option holding period. This is not known with certainty, but since most options are short-term in nature, the current yield on government of Canada t-bills with the same maturity as the life of the option is most often used in the model.

The standard deviation of the annual rate of return on the underlying common shares considers the expected volatility of the share price during the holding period. This is the most problematic variable to estimate for the model. The usual procedure used is to base the expected volatility on the volatility recorded in the past. Therefore, the standard deviation of the price of the underlying common shares is calculated using the procedures discussed in Chapter 7; this becomes the estimate used in the Black-Scholes model.

While the model may seem complex, it is easy to understand if we assume that the $N(d)$ terms are the adjusted probabilities of the option expiring in the money. They will always be between 0 and 1. Divide the model into two parts. The first part derives the value of the common shares, adjusted for the remaining variables used in the model. The second part of the model is based on the strike price of the call on the expiration date, adjusted for the remaining variables used in the model. The fair value of the call option is then calculated by taking the difference between these two parts.

As the probability of the option finishing in the money approaches 1, both $N(d)$ terms will be close to 1. In such case, the Black-Scholes model becomes Equation 17.7, discussed in the main body of the chapter. There we saw that the option's value is the time-value-adjusted intrinsic value. As the probability of the option finishing out of the money approaches 1, both $N(d)$ terms will be close to 0. In such case, the Black-Scholes model indicates that the option is worthless.

To illustrate the model, assume we are trying to determine the correct value of a call option on the common shares of Gracy Products. The strike price of the option is \$25, the current market price is \$22.75, and the option expires in six months (0.50 year). The risk-free rate of return is 4.5 percent, and the standard deviation of returns on the company's common shares is 28 percent. What is the most we should pay for this call option on Gracy Products' common shares? To calculate the value, first solve for d_1 by substituting the above values into the relevant equation as follows:

$$d_1 = \frac{\ln(\$22.75/\$25) + [0.045 + 0.5(0.28)^2]0.5}{0.28 \times \sqrt{0.50}}$$

$$= \frac{-0.09431068 + 0.0421}{0.1979899}$$

$$= -0.26$$

Now find d_2:

$$d_2 = -0.26 - (0.28 \times \sqrt{0.50})$$
$$= -0.46$$

5. Since many companies pay dividends, this might seem to be a serious limitation of the model. Recall that dividends reduce the premiums on call options. A common way of adjusting the model for this situation is to subtract the discounted value of the expected future dividend from the common share price used in the model.

TABLE 17.1A **Values of $N(d_1)$ and $N(d_2)$ for Selected Values of d_1 and d_2 for Use in the Black-Scholes Option Valuation Model**

d	*N(d)*	*d*	*N(d)*	*d*	*N(d)*	*d*	*N(d)*	*d*	*N(d)*	*d*	*N(d)*
–3.00	.0013	–1.58	.0571	–0.76	.2236	0.06	.5239	0.86	.8051	1.66	.9515
–2.95	.0016	–1.56	.0594	–0.74	.2297	0.08	.5319	0.88	.8106	1.68	.9535
–2.90	.0019	–1.54	.0618	–0.72	.2358	0.10	.5398	0.90	.8159	1.70	.9554
–2.85	.0022	–1.52	.0643	–0.70	.2420	0.12	.5478	0.92	.8212	1.72	.9573
–2.80	.0026	–1.50	.0668	–0.68	.2483	0.14	.5557	0.94	.8264	1.74	.9591
–2.75	.0030	–1.48	.0694	–0.66	.2546	0.16	.5636	0.96	.8315	1.76	.9608
–2.70	.0035	–1.46	.0721	–0.64	.2611	0.18	.5714	0.98	.8365	1.78	.9625
–2.65	.0040	–1.44	.0749	–0.62	.2676	0.20	.5793	1.00	.8414	1.80	.9641
–2.60	.0047	–1.42	.0778	–0.60	.2743	0.22	.5871	1.02	.8461	1.82	.9656
–2.55	.0054	–1.40	.0808	–0.58	.2810	0.24	.5948	1.04	.8508	1.84	.9671
–2.50	.0062	–1.38	.0838	–0.56	.2877	0.26	.6026	1.06	.8554	1.86	.9686
–2.45	.0071	–1.36	.0869	–0.54	.2946	0.28	.6103	1.08	.8599	1.88	.9699
–2.40	.0082	–1.34	.0901	–0.52	.3015	**0.30**	**.6179**	1.10	.8643	1.90	.9713
–2.35	.0094	–1.32	.0934	–0.50	.3085	0.32	.6255	1.12	.8686	1.92	.9726
–2.30	.0107	–1.30	.0968	–0.48	.3156	0.34	.6331	1.14	.8729	1.94	.9738
–2.25	.0122	–1.28	.1003	**–0.46**	**.3228**	0.36	.6406	1.16	.8770	1.96	.9750
–2.20	.0139	–1.26	.1038	–0.44	.3300	0.38	.6480	1.18	.8810	1.98	.9761
–2.15	.0158	–1.24	.1075	–0.42	.3373	0.40	.6554	1.20	.8849	2.00	.9772
–2.10	.0179	–1.22	.1112	–0.40	.3446	0.42	.6628	1.22	.8888	2.05	.9798
–2.05	.0202	–1.20	.1151	–0.38	.3520	0.44	.6700	1.24	.8925	2.10	.9821
–2.00	.0228	–1.18	.1190	–0.36	.3594	0.46	.6773	1.26	.8962	2.15	.9842
–1.98	.0239	–1.16	.1230	–0.34	.3669	0.48	.6844	1.28	.8997	2.20	.9861
–1.96	.0250	–1.14	.1271	–0.32	.3745	0.50	.6915	1.30	.9032	2.25	.9878
–1.94	.0262	–1.12	.1314	–0.30	.3821	0.52	.6985	1.32	.9066	2.30	.9893
–1.92	.0274	–1.10	.1357	–0.28	.3897	0.54	.7054	1.34	.9099	2.35	.9906
–1.90	.0287	–1.08	.1401	**–0.26**	**.3974**	0.56	.7123	1.36	.9131	2.40	.9918
–1.88	.0301	–1.06	.1446	–0.24	.4052	0.58	.7191	1.38	.9162	2.45	.9929
–1.86	.0314	–1.04	.1492	–0.22	.4129	0.60	.7258	1.40	.9192	2.50	.9938
–1.84	.0329	–1.02	.1539	–0.20	.4207	0.62	.7324	1.42	.9222	2.55	.9946
–1.82	.0344	–1.00	.1587	–0.18	.4286	0.64	.7389	1.44	.9251	2.60	.9953
–1.80	.0359	–0.98	.1635	–0.16	.4365	0.66	.7454	1.46	.9279	2.65	.9960
–1.78	.0375	–0.96	.1685	–0.14	.4443	0.68	.7518	1.48	.9306	2.70	.9965
–1.76	.0392	–0.94	.1736	–0.12	.4523	0.70	.7580	1.50	.9332	2.75	.9970
–1.74	.0409	–0.92	.1788	–0.10	.4602	0.72	.7642	1.52	.9357	2.80	.9974
–1.72	.0427	–0.90	.1841	–0.08	.4681	0.74	.7704	1.54	.9382	2.85	.9978
–1.70	.0446	–0.88	.1894	–0.06	.4761	0.76	.7764	1.56	.9406	2.90	.9981
–1.68	.0465	–0.86	.1949	–0.04	.4841	0.78	.7823	1.58	.9429	2.95	.9984
–1.66	.0485	–0.84	.2005	–0.02	.4920	0.80	.7882	1.60	.9452	3.00	.9986
–1.64	.0505	–0.82	.2061	0.00	.5000	0.82	.7939	1.62	.9474	3.05	.9989
–1.62	.0526	–0.80	.2119	0.02	.5080	0.84	.7996	1.64	.9495		
–1.60	.0548	–0.78	.2177	0.04	.5160						

NOTE: For example, if d_1 is 0.30, then $N(d_1)$ is 0.6179. Based on a cumulative normal distribution, the probability of observing a value of d_1 equal to or less than 0.30 is 61.79%.

Now find $N(d_1)$ and $N(d_2)$. These are based on the values of a normal distribution that are provided in all basic statistics textbooks. Table 17.1A provides a table of *N(d)* values depending on the value of *d*. The table reveals that:

$$N(d_1) = 0.3974$$
$$N(d_2) = 0.3228$$

Finally, we are in the position to calculate the value of the call option:

$$\begin{aligned} V_0 &= [P_0 \times N(d_1)] - \left[\frac{S}{e^{rt}} \times N(d_2)\right] \\ &= [\$22.75 \times 0.3974] - \left[\frac{\$25}{e^{(0.045)(0.5)}} \times 0.3228\right] \\ &= \$9.04 - [24.44 \times 0.3228] \\ &= \$9.04 - \$7.89 \\ &= \$1.15 \end{aligned}$$

According to the Black-Scholes option valuation model, the correct value for this call option is \$1.15. If the current price of the option in the market is greater than \$1.15, the option is overvalued; if less than \$1.15, the option is undervalued. Note, however, that one of the five variables used in the model is an estimate. It may be that the market is setting the value for the option using a different value for the standard deviation of returns on the company's common shares. If so, the current market price of the option may be correct. As with all models, the output provided is only as good as the inputs used.

The Black-Scholes option pricing model can be solved using the formula approach provided above. In addition, Spreadsheet Application 17.A1 can be

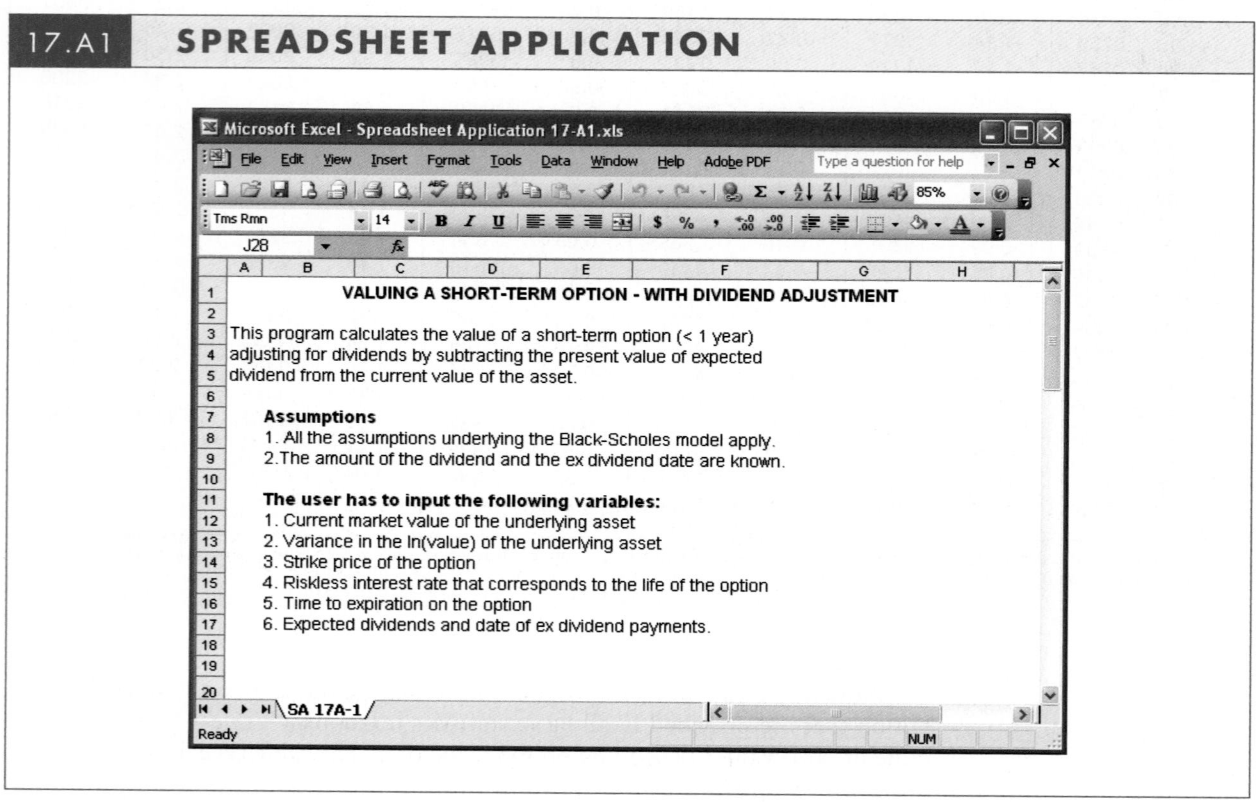

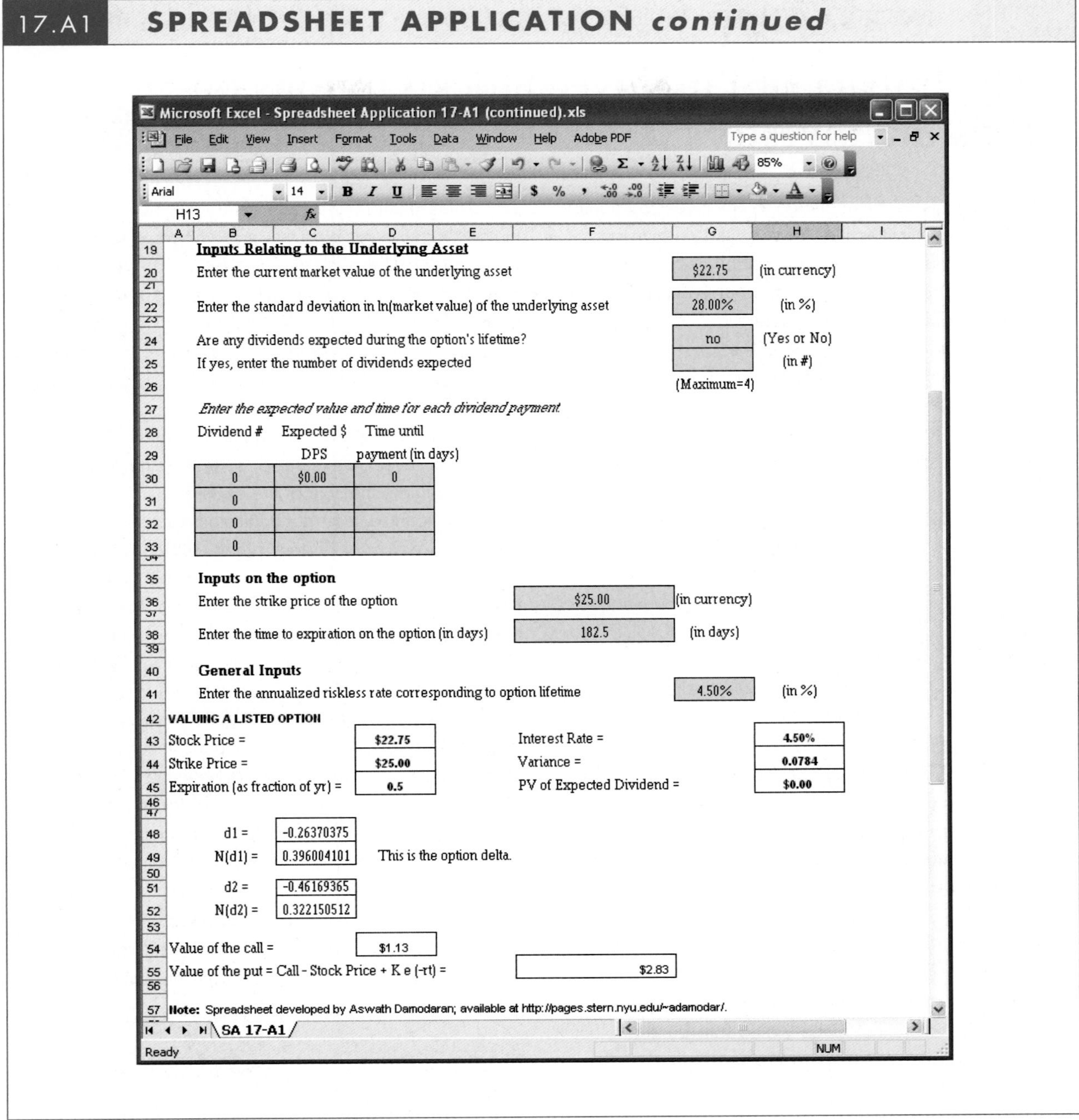

17.A1 SPREADSHEET APPLICATION *continued*

Microsoft Excel - Spreadsheet Application 17-A1 (continued).xls

Inputs Relating to the Underlying Asset

Enter the current market value of the underlying asset	$22.75	(in currency)
Enter the standard deviation in ln(market value) of the underlying asset	28.00%	(in %)
Are any dividends expected during the option's lifetime?	no	(Yes or No)
If yes, enter the number of dividends expected		(in #)
	(Maximum=4)	

Enter the expected value and time for each dividend payment

Dividend #	Expected $ DPS	Time until payment (in days)
0	$0.00	0
0		
0		
0		

Inputs on the option

Enter the strike price of the option	$25.00	(in currency)
Enter the time to expiration on the option (in days)	182.5	(in days)

General Inputs

Enter the annualized riskless rate corresponding to option lifetime	4.50%	(in %)

VALUING A LISTED OPTION

Stock Price =	$22.75	Interest Rate =	4.50%
Strike Price =	$25.00	Variance =	0.0784
Expiration (as fraction of yr) =	0.5	PV of Expected Dividend =	$0.00

d1 =	-0.26370375	
N(d1) =	0.396004101	This is the option delta.
d2 =	-0.46169365	
N(d2) =	0.322150512	

Value of the call = $1.13

Value of the put = Call - Stock Price + K e (-rt) = $2.83

Note: Spreadsheet developed by Aswath Damodaran; available at http://pages.stern.nyu.edu/~adamodar/.

SA 17-A1

www.hoadley.net/options/optiongraphs.aspx?divs=Y

http://bradley.bradley.edu/~arr/bsm/model.html

used to solve for the value of a call option. Note that this application includes dividends within the model, a process that was discussed in footnote 5. In addition, there are many Web sites that can be used to solve for option value. Many of these sites include much more detail than can be provided in a spreadsheet. These Web-based versions of the option pricing model are well worth reviewing.

17.A1 IN PRACTICE

The Impact of Employee Stock Options on Existing Investors

Stock options are often offered to employees by startup, high-tech companies that have limited cash resources, to attract talented employees. Established corporations give stock options to executives to make them feel they have as much at stake as shareholders. However, the use of stock options as an incentive for superior performance and the reporting of stock options in the financial statements have come under question.

Stock options, when exercised, dilute other shareholders' earnings. Let's say all of the employees of a company were given options to buy 500,000 common shares at $2 a share. If the share price increased to, say, $8 a share, the employees could exercise their option at $2 and then sell the 500,000 shares on the open market for $4,000,000. The employees would gain $6 a share, a total gain of $3,000,000. The 500,000 shares the employees received would increase the number of shares outstanding. The company's earnings would then be spread over an increased number of shares. As well, who "paid" for the $3,000,000 the employees made? Is there an expense associated with this transaction?

Further, argue some investors, executives have the power to strongly influence stock price in the short run, which some executives might be tempted to do if they intended to exercise their stock options. The market price of the stock would rise; the executive would exercise the options and sell the shares. By the time the market realized that the positive news was exaggerated or overstated, the share price would fall, but the executive would already have reaped the profit.

The transparency of earnings is the key issue. As one observer suggested: "Financial statements are one of the few indicators you have of the health of the company. You shouldn't have to be a forensic accountant to figure out all the obtuse ways earnings could be stated. The impact of stock options on earnings should be stated...."

Some counterargue that there is no accurate method to put a value on the unexercised options. The usual method, the Black-Scholes option valuation model, incorporates probabilities and is approximate. It does not account for changing exercise prices, a common practice for companies that have experienced a long period of declining share prices. Nor does it account for the lack of a liquid market for the options. Further, a company does not know if and when the options will ever be exercised, so there is no accurate way to estimate the size of the expense.

"The formula may be particularly problematic for companies with volatile stock prices, such as high-tech, emerging growth companies. For example, one company has found that the 'value' of its employee stock options could swing by more than $350 million—roughly 50 percent—by subtly changing just two variables in the Black-Scholes equation: volatility by 15 percent and the average life of an option by just one year." These proponents assert that providing the number of stock options and the exercise value in the footnotes is the most accurate method of stating the option values.

Supporters of the Black-Scholes model argue that many aspects of accounting are based on estimates, and it is the widespread acceptance of the Black-Scholes model in pricing options that strengthens its relevance as a reasonable estimate of the expense of stock options on a company's income statement.

SOURCES: "Navigating Through 'The Perfect Storm': Safeguards to Restore Investor Confidence: Report of the Standing Senate Committee on Banking, Trade and Commerce," June 2003, available at **www.conferenceboard.ca/GCSR/links/pdfs/Senate_Comm_Report_Jun03.pdf**; Derek Strocher, "Financial Management: Options to Expense" *CGA Magazine* May/June 2003, **www.cga-canada.org/eng/magazine/may-jun03/stock_options_e.htm**, accessed December 1, 2003; "Stock Options," available at **www.bus.iastate.edu/cjeffrey/598/Stock_Options_2003.ppt**, slide 57.

PROBLEMS

17–1A Using the same information from the Gracy Products example discussed above, determine the impact the following independent changes in the assumption have on the value of the option, as calculated using the Black-Scholes option valuation model:

a. The current market price is \$25, not \$22.75.

b. The risk-free rate is 10 percent, not 4.5 percent.

c. The standard deviation of returns on the company's common shares is 47 percent, not 28 percent.

17–2A Discuss how changes in these variables affect the value of an option considering your answers above.

CHAPTER 18

Mergers and Acquisitions, and Business Failure

LEARNING GOALS

- LG1 Understand the fundamentals of mergers and acquisitions including basic terminology, motives for merging, types of mergers, and leveraged buyouts (LBOs).
- LG2 Demonstrate the procedures used to analyze mergers, value the target company, calculate the synergy of the merger, and determine the merger's net present value.
- LG3 Discuss the methods a firm can use to pay for an acquisition, and illustrate the impact of using common shares as a method to pay for a merger.
- LG4 Describe the pooling and purchase methods of accounting for mergers and acquisitions and discuss the concept of goodwill.
- LG5 Discuss the merger negotiation process, the role of holding companies, and international mergers.
- LG6 Understand the types and major causes of business failure and explain the two legislative acts governing reorganization and bankruptcy in Canada.

18.1 Merger and Acquisition Fundamentals

Companies sometimes use mergers and acquisitions to expand externally by acquiring control of other firms. Whereas the overriding objective for a merger should be to increase the value of the firm's common shares, a number of more immediate motivations such as diversification, tax considerations, and increasing owner liquidity frequently exist. Sometimes mergers are pursued to acquire needed assets rather than the going concern. Here we discuss the fundamentals of

'Till Death or Mismanagement Do Us Part

Mergers and acquisitions (M&A) and corporate restructuring are a big part of the corporate finance world. Every day, investment bankers arrange M&A transactions, which bring separate companies together to form larger ones. When they're not creating big companies from smaller ones, corporate finance deals do the reverse and break up companies through spinoffs, carve-outs, or tracking stocks. Not surprisingly, these actions make the news. Deals can be worth hundreds of millions, or even billions, of dollars. They can dictate the fortunes of the companies involved for years to come. For a CEO, leading an M&A can represent the highlight of a whole career. And no wonder we hear about so many of these transactions; they happen all the time. Next time you read a newspaper's business section, the odds are good that at least one headline will announce some kind of M&A transaction. But why do companies want to buy or merge with others? Also, should the owners of a company, the common shareholders, cheer or weep when it is announced that the company has bought another company—or has been bought by one? This chapter looks at the topic of mergers and acquisitions. It also considers business failure—what occurs when mergers and other corporate activities are not successful.

mergers and acquisitions: the terminology, motives, and types of mergers including leveraged buyouts (LBOs). In the following sections, we will review the procedures used to analyze and negotiate mergers and acquisitions, describe the methods of accounting for mergers, and discuss the ways companies can pay for acquisitions.

In the broadest sense, activities involving expansion or contraction of a firm's operations or changes in its asset or financial (ownership) structure are called **corporate restructuring.** The topics addressed in this chapter—mergers and acquisitions, and business failure—are two of the most common forms of corporate

corporate restructuring
The activities involving expansion or contraction of a firm's operations or changes in its asset or financial (ownership) structure.

LINKING THE DISCIPLINES: Cross-Functional Interactions

- ***Accounting personnel*** will assist in the financial evaluation of potential mergers, acquisitions, and divestitures. They will provide the important information about the tax effects of the proposed actions. Accounting personnel must also understand bankruptcy procedures, because they will play a large part in any reorganization or liquidation.
- ***Information systems analysts*** need to understand what data need to be tracked in case of mergers, leveraged buyouts, divestitures of assets, or bankruptcy, to develop systems needed to realize these organizational changes.
- ***Management*** need to understand the motives for mergers and how to fend off takeover attempts. Mergers and acquisitions are important to management not only because of their effects on the firm but also because of their effects on managers' jobs. Managers will have more responsibilities and may have to manage a business in which they have little or no experience. They are also concerned about the compatibility of the merging company's corporate culture.
- The ***marketing department*** will be very involved in the analysis of potential mergers and acquisitions that may enable the firm to grow and diversify and require changes in the firm's marketing organization, plans, and goals. The firm's mix of product and service offerings can be significantly altered by these actions. Personnel assignments might also be at issue after the merger has been consummated.
- Personnel in the ***operations department*** will be concerned with mergers and divestitures because ongoing operations will be significantly affected by these organizational changes. Business failure may also result in a reorganization of the firm to provide adequate financing for ongoing operations.

restructuring. But there are many others which are beyond the scope of this text.[1] Here, we define some basic terminology associated with mergers and acquisitions. Other terms are introduced and defined as needed in subsequent sections.

The Terminology of Mergers and Acquisitions

The term *mergers and acquisitions* is frequently used to describe the combination of total companies or parts of companies. There are three forms of business combinations: mergers, consolidations, and acquisitions of assets. In all business combinations, there are two parties to the transaction: the *acquiring* company and the *acquired* company. The acquiring company is referred to as the **bidding company (bidder)**. This is the company that is making the offer to acquire all or part of another company. The acquired company is referred to as the **target company**. This is the company that is the subject of the bidding company's interest. The target firm may or may not be acquired—it depends on the negotiations following the initial announcement of the acquisition.

bidding company (bidder)
The acquiring company; the company making an offer to acquire all or part of another company.

target company
The acquired company; the company that is the subject of the bidding company's interest.

Generally, the bidder identifies and evaluates the target company, and then negotiates the acquisition with the target company's management and board of

1. For comprehensive coverage of the many aspects of corporate restructuring, see J. Fred Weston, Mark L. Mitchell, and J. Harold Mulherin, *Takeovers, Restructuring, and Corporate Governance,* 4th ed. (Englewood Cliffs, NJ: Prentice Hall, 2004).

directors. The board acts on behalf of the owners, the common shareholders. Occasionally, the management and board of a company may initiate its own acquisition by seeking out a friendly bidder. This sometimes occurs when another company has attempted an unfriendly acquisition of the target. This issue is discussed in more detail in Section 18.5.

merger
A bidding company acquires and completely absorbs the target company; the bidder maintains its name and identity after the merger.

consolidation
Two firms are combined but neither maintain their name, identity, or existence; a completely new company is created.

A **merger** occurs when the bidder acquires and completely absorbs the target. The bidder, which is usually the larger of the two firms involved in the transaction, maintains its name and identity after the merger. The assets and liabilities of the target are merged with the bidder's. The identity of the target company may also be maintained in the merged company, but often it is lost. With a **consolidation**, two firms are combined but neither maintain their name, identity, or existence; a completely new company is created. As with a merger, the assets and liabilities of the two consolidated firms are combined.

tender offer (merger)
A public offer by the bidder to acquire all of the common shares of the target company at a stated price.

Since the common shares signify ownership of the company, a merger or consolidation requires the bidder to acquire all of the common shares of the target. By acquiring all of the common shares, the bidder can then merge the target's operation with their own to achieve higher sales, lower costs, higher cash flows, and a higher market value. To acquire the common shares of the target, the bidder may make a tender offer to the common shareholders of the target company. A **tender offer** is a public offer by the bidder to acquire all of the common shares of the target company at a stated price. The payment that is made to the target company's shareholders may be cash, common shares of the merged company, or a combination of the two (some cash, some shares). Tender offers are always contingent on the bidder acquiring a stated minimum percent of the target's common shares. If this percent is not obtained, the tender offer may be withdrawn.

acquisition of assets
The bidder acquires all or some of the assets of the target, with the purchased assets moving to the bidder while the target retains its liabilities and other contingent claims or unsettled lawsuits.

With the **acquisition of assets,** the bidder acquires all or some of the assets of the target. Under this form of business combination, the assets that are purchased move to the bidder company. The target retains their liabilities and other contingent claims or unsettled lawsuits. With the proceeds received from the bidder, the target would be expected to pay off the liabilities that are associated with the assets that were sold. If only some of the target's assets were sold, the target firm could continue to operate. If all assets were sold, it would be expected that the target would pay off all liabilities, pay a liquidating dividend to shareholders, and cease to operate or exist. The corporation would effectively die.

holding company
A corporation that has voting control of one or more other corporations.

subsidiaries
The companies controlled by a holding company.

A **holding company** is a corporation that has voting control of one or more other corporations. Having control in large, widely held companies generally requires ownership of between 10 and 20 percent of the outstanding common shares. The companies controlled by a holding company are normally referred to as its **subsidiaries.** Full control of a subsidiary is typically obtained by purchasing 50 percent plus 1 of the common shares of the company. A holding company's position in a subsidiary may range from 10 percent to 100 percent. For widely held publicly traded companies, effective control can be achieved by holding as little as 10 percent to 20 percent of the outstanding common shares of a company.

Holding companies acquire all or a portion of a target company but do not merge or consolidate the target with the parent company. The subsidiary continues to exist on its own. This is the case even if the holding company acquires 100 percent of a subsidiary's common shares and has full control.

M&A activity
The practitioner term used in the financial press for mergers and acquisitions; it refers to all types of mergers, acquisitions, and consolidations.

In the financial press and in practice, mergers and acquisitions are referred to as **M&A activity**. In this chapter, M&A will refer to all types of mergers, acquisitions, and consolidations.

Friendly Versus Hostile Takeovers

Mergers can occur on either a friendly or a hostile basis. Typically, after identifying the target company, the bidder initiates discussions. If the target management and board of directors is receptive to the bidder's proposal, it may endorse the merger and recommend shareholder approval. If shareholders approve the merger, the transaction is typically consummated either through a cash purchase of shares by the bidder, through an exchange of the bidder's common shares for the target firm's shares, or a combination of the two. This type of negotiated transaction is known as a **friendly merger.** The vast majority of mergers are friendly.

friendly merger
A merger transaction endorsed by the target firm's management and board, approved by its shareholders, and easily consummated.

If, on the other hand, the target's management and board do not support the proposed takeover, it can fight the bidder's actions. In this case, the bidder can attempt to gain control of the firm by buying sufficient shares of the target firm in the marketplace. This is typically accomplished by using *tender offers,* which, as noted above, are formal offers to purchase a given number of common shares at a specified price. This type of unfriendly transaction is commonly referred to as a **hostile takeover.** Clearly, hostile takeovers are more difficult to consummate because the target firm's management and board act to deter rather than facilitate the acquisition. Regardless, hostile takeovers are sometimes successful.

hostile takeover
A merger transaction not supported by the target firm's management and board, forcing the bidding company to try to gain control of the firm by buying common shares on the stock market.

When they are successful, the usual beneficiary is the common shareholders who often see the value of their shares increase significantly from the pre-takeover price. In hostile takeovers, it is not uncommon to see the bidding company increase their offer price three or more times. A hostile takeover that started with a bidding price of $30 per common share could end up with a bid price of $50 or more per share. In such a case, the common shareholders experience tremendous benefit.

Motives for Merging

Firms merge to fulfill certain objectives. The overriding goal for merging is the maximization of shareholders' wealth as reflected in the value (price) of the bidding firm's common shares. Following the merger, the value of the bidding firm's common shares should increase, indicating that the motives for the merger were realized. A merger may be motivated for strategic or financial reasons. More specific motives for mergers include growth or diversification, synergy, fund raising, increased managerial skill or technology, tax considerations, increased ownership liquidity, and defence against takeover. Mergers should only be pursued when they are believed to be consistent with the wealth maximization of the company's common share price.

Strategic Mergers

strategic merger
A merger transaction undertaken to achieve economies of scale.

Strategic mergers seek to achieve various economies of scale by eliminating redundant functions, increasing market share, improving raw material sourcing and finished product distribution, and so on.[2] In these mergers, the expectation is that the operations of the bidding and target firms can be combined to achieve economies and thereby cause the performance of the merged firm to exceed that of the premerged firms.

The mergers of Daimler-Benz and Chrysler (both auto manufacturers) and Air Canada and Canadian Airlines are two examples of strategic mergers. Note, though, that neither merger was entirely successful. In both cases, the merged company struggled, and in the case of Air Canada actually entered bankruptcy protection. An interesting variation of the strategic merger involves the purchase of specific product lines (rather than the whole company) for strategic reasons.

Financial Mergers

financial merger
A merger transaction undertaken with the goal of restructuring the target company to improve its cash flow and unlock its hidden value.

Financial mergers are undertaken with the goal of restructuring the target company to improve its cash flow and unlock hidden value. These mergers involve the acquisition of the target firm by a bidder, which may be another company, a group of investors, or even the firm's existing management. The objective of the bidder is to drastically cut costs and sell off certain unproductive or noncompatible assets in order to increase the firm's cash flow. The increased cash flow is used to service the sizeable debt that is typically incurred to finance these transactions. Financial mergers are based not on the firm's ability to achieve economies of scale but on the bidder's belief that through restructuring, the firm's hidden value can be unlocked.

The ready availability of *junk bond* financing throughout the 1980s fuelled the financial merger mania during that period. Two prominent examples of financial mergers that are still discussed are the takeover of RJR Nabisco by Kohlberg Kravis Roberts (KKR) and Campeau Corporation's (real estate) acquisition of Allied Stores and Federated Department Stores. With the collapse of the junk bond market in the early 1990s, the bankruptcy filings of a number of prominent financial mergers of the 1980s, and the rising stock market of the later 1990s, financial mergers lost their lustre. As a result, the strategic merger, which does not rely as heavily on debt, tends to dominate today.

Growth or Diversification

Companies that desire rapid growth in *size* or *market share* or diversification in *the range of their products* may find that a merger can be used to fulfill this objective. Instead of going through the time-consuming process of internal growth or diversification, the firm may achieve the same objective in a short period of time by merging with an existing firm. Such a strategy is often less costly than the alternative of developing the necessary production capacity. If a firm that wants to expand operations can find a suitable going concern, it may avoid many of the risks associated with the design, manufacture, and sale of

2. A somewhat similar nonmerger arrangement is the *strategic alliance,* typically an agreement between a large company with established products and channels of distribution and an emerging technology company with a promising research and development program in areas of interest to the larger company. In exchange for its financial support, the larger, established company obtains a stake in the technology being developed by the emerging company. Today, strategic alliances are commonplace in the biotechnology, information technology, and software industries.

additional or new products. Moreover, when a firm expands or extends its product line by acquiring another firm, it also removes a potential competitor.[3]

Synergy

Hint
Synergy is said to be present when a whole is greater than the sum of the parts—when "1 + 1 = 3."

The *synergy* of mergers is the economies of scale resulting from the merged firms' lower overhead. These economies of scale from lowering the combined overhead increase earnings to a level greater than the sum of the earnings of each of the independent firms. Synergy is most obvious when firms merge with other firms in the same line of business, because many redundant functions and employees may be eliminated. Staff functions, such as purchasing and sales, are probably most greatly affected by this type of combination.

Fund Raising

Firms sometimes combine to enhance their fund-raising ability. A firm may be unable to obtain outside financing for its own expansion but able to obtain funds for a business combination. A firm may combine with another that has high liquid assets and low levels of liabilities. The acquisition of this type of "cash-rich" company immediately increases the firm's borrowing power by decreasing its financial leverage. This should allow funds to be raised externally at lower cost.

Increased Managerial Skill or Technology

Occasionally, a firm will have good potential that it finds itself unable to develop fully because of deficiencies in certain areas of management or an absence of needed product or production technology. If the firm cannot hire the management or develop the technology it needs, it might combine with a compatible firm that has the needed managerial personnel or technical expertise. This was one of the motivating factors for much of the M&A activity that occurred in the technology industry during the latter half of the 1990s. Of course, any merger should contribute to the maximization of owners' wealth.

Tax Considerations

tax loss carryforward
In a merger, the tax loss of one of the firms that can be applied against the future income of the merged firm over the shorter of either seven years or until the total tax loss has been fully recovered.

Tax considerations can be a key motive for merging. In such a case, the tax benefit generally stems from the fact that one of the firms has a **tax loss carryforward.** This means that the company's tax loss can be applied against the future income of the merged firm over the shorter of either seven years or until the total tax loss has been fully recovered. Two situations could actually exist. A company with a tax loss could acquire a profitable company to utilize its own tax loss. In this case, the bidding firm's loss would be used to offset the taxable income of the acquired firm. The combined firm would pay lower total taxes.

A tax loss may also be useful when a profitable firm acquires a firm that has such a loss. In either situation, however, the merger must be justified not only on the basis of the tax benefits but also on grounds consistent with the goal of shareholder wealth maximization. Moreover, the tax benefits described can be used only in mergers—not in the formation of holding companies—because only in the case of mergers are operating results reported on a consolidated basis for income tax purposes. An example will clarify the use of the tax loss carryforward.

---

3. Certain legal constraints on growth exist—especially when the elimination of competition is expected. Federal laws and regulations restrict business combinations that eliminate competition, particularly when the resulting enterprise would be a monopoly. In Canada, this issue is governed by the *Federal Competition Act.*

Example Bergen Company, a wheel bearing manufacturer, has a total of $450,000 in tax loss carryforwards resulting from operating tax losses of $150,000 a year in each of the past 3 years. To use these losses and to diversify its operations, Hudson Company, a molder of plastics, has acquired Bergen through a merger. Hudson expects to have *earnings before taxes* of $300,000 per year. We assume that the Bergen portion of the merged firm just breaks even, and that Hudson is in the 40 percent tax bracket. The total taxes paid by the two firms and their after-tax earnings without and with the merger are as shown in Table 18.1.

With the merger, total tax payments are $180,000 over the three years. Without the merger, total tax payments are $360,000. The merger results in tax savings of $180,000. Over the three years, total net income after tax is $180,000 higher with the merger: $720,000 versus $540,000. The tax saving associated with the tax loss carryforward could also be calculated as follows: $450,000 × 0.40 = $180,000. The merged firm is able to deduct the tax loss over the shorter of either seven years or until the total tax loss has been fully recovered. In this example, the shorter is at the end of year 2.

Increased Ownership Liquidity

The merger of two small firms or a small and a larger firm may provide the owners of the small firm(s) with greater liquidity. This is due to the higher float associated with the common shares of larger firms. For many small firms, a relatively low number of common shares is actively traded on the stock exchange on which the common shares are listed. This is termed a "thin" market for the shares. Shareholders in such firms may find it difficult to trade a large number of shares at the current market price.

If a small company merges with a larger company, the smaller company's shareholders will receive common shares that are more actively traded and thus more easily liquidated. Also, owning shares for which market price quotations are readily available provides owners with a better sense of the value of their

TABLE 18.1 Total Taxes and After-Tax Earnings for Hudson Company Without and With Merger

	Year			Total for 3 years
	1	2	3	
Total taxes and after-tax earnings without merger				
(1) Earnings before taxes	$300,000	$300,000	$300,000	$900,000
(2) Taxes [0.40 × (1)]	120,000	120,000	120,000	360,000
(3) Net income after tax [(1) −(2)]	$180,000	$180,000	$180,000	$540,000
Total taxes and after-tax earnings with merger				
(4) Earnings before losses	$300,000	$300,000	$300,000	$900,000
(5) Tax loss carryforward	300,000	150,000	0	450,000
(6) Earnings before taxes [(4) − (5)]	$ 0	$150,000	$300,000	$450,000
(7) Taxes [0.40 × (6)]	0	60,000	120,000	180,000
(8) Net income after tax [(4) − (7)]	$300,000	$240,000	$180,000	$720,000

holdings. The improved liquidity of ownership obtainable through a merger with an acceptable firm may have considerable appeal to a small, closely held firm.

Defence Against Takeover

Hint
An unfriendly takeover refers to the fact that top management and the board of directors of the target do not want to become a part of another firm. In some cases, many of the common shareholders do not feel the same about the impending takeover.

Occasionally, when a firm becomes the target of an unfriendly takeover, it will as a defence acquire another company. Such a strategy typically works like this: the original target firm takes on additional debt to finance its defensive acquisition; because of the debt load, the target firm becomes too highly levered financially to be of any further interest to its suitor.

To be effective, a defensive takeover must create greater value for shareholders than they would have realized had the firm been merged with its suitor. Clearly, while the use of a merger as a takeover defence that results in the target taking on a large amount of debt may effectively deter the original takeover, it can also result in subsequent financial difficulty and possibly failure for the original takeover target. An example of this in Canada was Air Canada's defence against a hostile takeover offer made by Onex Corporation in 1999. To defend against Onex's takeover, Air Canada repurchased their own shares (see Chapter 11) using debt financing. In addition, the company also acquired their main competitor, Canadian Airlines. As a consequence, Air Canada's debt load soared and the company subsequently experienced major financial difficulties, culminating in a filing for bankruptcy protection in 2003.

Types of Mergers

Hint
A merger undertaken to obtain the synergy benefit is usually a horizontal merger. Diversification can be either a vertical or congeneric merger. The other benefits of merging can be achieved by any one of the four types of mergers.

The four types of mergers are the (1) horizontal merger, (2) vertical merger, (3) congeneric merger, and (4) conglomerate merger. A **horizontal merger** results when two firms *in the same line of business* are merged. An example would be the merger of two machine-tool manufacturers. This form of merger results in the expansion of a firm's operations in a given product line and at the same time eliminates a competitor.

horizontal merger
A merger of two firms in the *same line of business.*

A **vertical merger** occurs when a firm acquires *a supplier or a customer.* For example, the merger of a machine-tool manufacturer with its supplier of castings would be a vertical merger. The economic benefit of a vertical merger stems from the firm's increased control over the acquisition of raw materials or the distribution of finished goods.

vertical merger
A merger in which a firm acquires a *supplier or a customer.*

A **congeneric merger** is achieved by acquiring a firm that is *in the same general industry* but neither in the same line of business nor a supplier or customer. An example is the merger of a machine-tool manufacturer with the manufacturer of industrial conveyor systems. The benefit of a congeneric merger is the resulting ability to use the same sales and distribution channels to reach customers of both businesses.

congeneric merger
A merger in which one firm acquires another firm that is *in the same general industry* but neither in the same line of business nor a supplier or customer.

A **conglomerate merger** involves the combination of firms in *unrelated businesses.* The merger of a machine-tool manufacturer with a chain of fast-food restaurants would be an example of this kind of merger. The key benefit of the conglomerate merger is its ability to *reduce risk* by merging firms with different seasonal or cyclical patterns of sales and earnings.[4]

conglomerate merger
A merger combining firms in *unrelated businesses.*

---

4. A discussion of the key concepts underlying the portfolio approach to the diversification of risk was presented in Chapter 7. In the theoretical literature, some questions exist relating to whether diversification by the firm is a proper motive consistent with shareholder wealth maximization. Many researchers argue that by buying common shares in different firms, investors can obtain the same benefits as they would realize from owning common shares in the merged firm. It appears that other benefits need to be available to justify mergers.

Leveraged Buyouts (LBOs)

leveraged buyout (LBO)
An acquisition technique involving the use of a large amount of debt to purchase a firm; an example of a *financial merger.*

Hint
The bidders in LBOs are other firms or groups of investors that frequently include key members of the firm's existing management.

A popular technique that was widely used during the 1980s to make acquisitions was the **leveraged buyout (LBO)**, which involves the use of a large amount of debt to purchase a firm. LBOs are a clear-cut example of a *financial merger* undertaken to create a high-debt private corporation with improved cash flow and value. Typically, in an LBO, 90 percent or more of the purchase price is financed with debt. A large part of the borrowing is secured by the target firm's assets, and the lenders, because of the high risk, take a portion of the firm's equity. *Junk bonds* have been routinely used to raise the large amounts of debt needed to finance LBO transactions. Of course, the bidders in an LBO expect to use the improved cash flow to service the large amount of junk bond and other debt incurred in the buyout.

An attractive candidate for acquisition through leveraged buyout should possess three basic attributes:

1. It must have a good position in its industry with a solid profit history and reasonable expectations of growth.
2. It should have a relatively low level of debt, a high level of liquid current assets, and a high level of "bankable" assets that can be used as loan collateral.
3. It must have stable and predictable cash flows that are adequate to meet interest and principal payments on the debt and provide adequate working capital.

With many LBOs, the target's senior management and the board often view the takeover as hostile. This is the case since the bidder must eliminate many employees to generate the cash flow necessary to service the high debt load. As well, when devising the takeover offer, the bidder is expecting to generate large increases in cash flow through better management of the company. If the bidder feels that the current management of the target is not achieving the full potential of the company, the bidder would not want to keep these managers employed when the takeover is completed.

Many LBOs did not live up to original expectations. The largest ever was the late-1988, $24.5 billion buyout of RJR Nabisco by KKR, mentioned earlier. In 1991, RJR was taken public and the firm continued to struggle under the heavy debt of the LBO for a few years before improving its debt position and credit rating. Campeau Corporation's buyouts of Allied Stores and Federated Department Stores resulted in its later filing for bankruptcy protection, from which reorganized companies later emerged. In recent years, other highly publicized LBOs have defaulted on the high yield debt incurred to finance the buyout. Although the LBO remains a viable financing technique under the right circumstances, its use is greatly diminished from the frenzied pace of the 1980s. Whereas the LBOs of the 1980s were used, often indiscriminately, for hostile takeovers, today LBOs are often used to finance management buyouts.

A recent Canadian example of a LBO was BCE Inc.'s $3 billion sale of its phone directories service. In September 2002, BCE sold the Yellow Pages Group to New York–based buyout specialist Kohlberg Kravis Roberts (KKR, again) and the Ontario Teachers' Pension Plan for $3 billion. The Yellow Pages Group is the dominant phone book producer in Ontario and Quebec with a 93 percent market share. It publishes 19 million copies of 235 phone directories. In the LBO, the acquiring group provided $900 million in equity; the remaining

$2.1 billion was debt financing. This turned out to be a very successful LBO with the equity partners receiving a very high return on the investment. By December 2003, the equity partners had made a 200 percent return on their equity investment by selling a portion of the business to the public.

? Review Questions

18–1 Define and differentiate each of the following sets of terms: (**a**) mergers, consolidations, and holding companies; (**b**) bidding versus target company; (**c**) friendly versus hostile mergers; and (**d**) strategic versus financial mergers.

18–2 Briefly describe each of the following motives for merging: (**a**) growth or diversification, (**b**) synergy, (**c**) fund raising, (**d**) increased managerial skill or technology, (**e**) tax considerations, (**f**) increased ownership liquidity, and (**g**) defence against takeover.

18–3 Briefly describe each of the following types of mergers: (**a**) horizontal, (**b**) vertical, (**c**) congeneric, and (**d**) conglomerate.

18–4 What is a *leveraged buyout (LBO)*? What are the three key attributes of an attractive candidate for acquisition using an LBO?

18.2 Analyzing Mergers

We now turn to the procedures that are used to analyze mergers. The first step in any M&A is for the bidding company to uncover a potential target. From the bidder's perspective, there must be at least one underlying motive for the acquisition. In this section of the chapter, we explain how a bidder would value the target company to determine the maximum price to pay for the company. We then consider a situation where a target is acquired for some of its assets.

Valuation Issues with Mergers

Once the bidding company isolates a target company that it wishes to acquire, it must estimate the value of the target. This value would be used, together with a proposed way to pay for the acquisition, to negotiate the transaction. The negotiation could lead to a friendly or hostile takeover. Some takeovers start friendly and become hostile; others are hostile from the beginning. The success of the takeover is dependent on the bidder's negotiation skill and the reactions of the target's management, board, and shareholders.

A takeover is a valuation problem. The value of the target to the bidding company must be calculated. As such, the valuation concepts presented in Chapter 8 would be used. As well, since in a takeover the bidder is acquiring a real asset (the target company) that will generate returns for many years into the future, the techniques presented in Chapters 12 and 13 relating to the analysis of capital budgeting projects are also used. The process employed to determine the value of a target company and to decide whether the acquisition is financially viable is presented below.

Valuing the Target Company

Assume Bidder Company (B) is planning to acquire Target Company (T). As explained above, this is an example of a capital budgeting project. The investment of funds (the acquisition of T) will produce benefits over a period of time greater than one year (the incremental after-tax cash flows T will provide for B). Bidder Company should only acquire Target if the net present value (NPV) of the project from Bidder's point of view is greater than or equal to zero.

If the NPV is equal to zero, then B receives the minimum required return on the investment in T, their cost of capital. If the NPV is greater than zero, B receives a rate of return greater than their cost of capital. Therefore, if TV_{BT} represents the true value of the merged firm, B should acquire T only if:

$$TV_{BT} \geq V_B + P_T \tag{18.1}$$

where:

V_B = the value of Bidder Company prior to the merger
P_T = the amount B pays for T

Note that P_T *is not* the value of T as indicated in the stock market. T's current market value (V_T) is based on the market price of the company's common shares multiplied by the number of common shares outstanding.[5] The amount B will pay for T will be more than T's current market value since in a takeover, a premium to the current market price is almost always paid ($P_T > V_T$). For a merger to make financial sense, T must be worth more to B than T is currently worth in the market. As well, P_T must be at most the true value of T to B (V_{T^B}). In present value terms T must be worth at least the amount B will pay for T. If T is not worth at least P_T, then the merger does not make financial sense.

synergy The extra value created by merging two firms, B and T; the amount by which the value of T to B (V_{T^B}) exceeds the amount that B pays for T (P_T).

From B's perspective, if T is worth more than P_T, the extra value is referred to as **synergy**, the extra value created by combining the two firms, B and T. Synergy would not be valued in the market price of the two firms when they are separate entities. The value of synergy is represented by S_{BT} and is based on:

$$S_{BT} = TV_{BT} - (V_B + P_T) \tag{18.2}$$

Therefore, the true value of Target Company to Bidder Company (V_{T^B}) is:

$$V_{T^B} = P_T + S_{BT} \tag{18.3}$$

Note that S_{BT} is only available if the two firms merge, if the merger cost to B (P_T) does not consume all of S_{BT}, and if the perceived synergies are actually realized. In the past, many mergers have not been successful from a financial perspective because the price paid by the bidder has been too high, or the expected benefits (the expected synergy) of the merger were overestimated or never really existed. In such a case, it could be said that the bidding company made a poor capital budgeting decision. An example of this is discussed in the In Practice box in Chapter 13. As mentioned above, to value the target company, present values must be used. Therefore, V_{T^B} could be considered the NPV of the merger. In this application of capital budgeting, the NPV of the merger would have to be greater than zero in order for synergy to be created.

5. Note that this discussion assumes that both Bidder Company and Target Company are financed totally with common equity.

Example Time Varner, a major media company, is considering acquiring AOLI, a major Internet service and content provider. Time Varner's senior managers and board believe this strategic merger will allow the company to distribute its media content to AOLI's current customer base. This will increase sales and reduce costs. The total value of Time Varner's common shares on the stock market is \$140 million. The total value of AOLI's common shares is \$50 million.[6]

Time Varner's advisors believe that by offering AOLI's shareholders \$60 million for all shares, AOLI's management and the board will recommend the merger offer be accepted by the shareholders. In this case, the value of the bidder company prior to the merger (V_B) is \$140 million. The value of the target (V_T) is \$50 million, but the price of the target (P_T) will be 20 percent more or \$60 million. Time Varner is paying a 20 percent premium to the current market price.

Time Varner's management team believes that major synergies will be created by combining the two companies. After running hundreds of simulations and carefully analyzing the sensitivity of the results, Time Varner feels confident that the following per-year incremental after-tax cash inflows will be realized when the two firms are merged:

Years 1 to 3	\$ 6,000,000
Years 4 to 10	\$10,000,000
Years 11 to 25	\$12,000,000
Years 26 to 50	\$16,000,000

Time Varner's current cost of capital is 12.2 percent. But, since the acquisition will increase the company's level of risk, the CFO recommends that a cost of capital of 13 percent be used to analyze the acquisition of AOLI. In order for the merger to create synergy, the true value of the merged firm (TV_{BT}) must be greater than \$200 million (the value of the bidder company prior to the merger, \$140 million, and the amount the bidder is paying for the target, \$60 million). The total value of AOLI to Time Varner ($V_{T\wedge B}$) is based on the present value of the incremental after-tax cash inflows the merger will generate over the 50-year study period. This is provided in Table 18.2.

TABLE 18.2 The Value of AOLI to Time Varner

$V_{T\wedge B}$ = \$6,000,000 × *PVIFa* (13%, 3 per)	=	\$14,166,916
+ \$10,000,000 × *PVIFa* (13%, 7 per) × *PVIF* (13%, 3 per)[a]	=	\$30,650,909
+ \$12,000,000 × *PVIFa* (13%, 15 per) × *PVIF* (13%, 10 per)[a]	=	\$22,844,898
+ \$16,000,000 × *PVIFa* (13%, 25 per) × *PVIF* (13%, 25 per)[a]	=	\$ 5,524,106
Total value of AOLI to Time Varner ($V_{T\wedge B}$)	=	\$73,186,829

[a] For the second, third, and fourth values, two calculations are made. The first determines the present value of the annuity to the beginning of the year in which the cash flows start. For the second series of cash inflows, that would be to the beginning of year 4. The second calculation discounts this future value to time 0, the present. For the second series of cash inflows that would be for three years, since the beginning of year 4 is the same as the end of year 3. A similar process is used for the third and fourth series of

6. In this example, we assume that both Time Varner and AOLI are financed totally with common equity. Later in the section, we consider a firm that is financed with both common equity and debt.

The value of AOLI to Time Varner is \$73,186,829. Therefore, the value of the synergy from the merger is:

$$\begin{aligned} S_{BT} &= V_{T \wedge B} - P_T \\ &= \$73{,}186{,}829 - \$60{,}000{,}000 \\ &= \$13{,}186{,}829 \end{aligned}$$

So, the total value of the merged firm (TV_{BT}) is:

$$\begin{aligned} TV_{BT} &= V_B + P_T + S_{BT} \\ &= \$140{,}000{,}000 + \$60{,}000{,}000 + \$13{,}186{,}829 \\ &= \$213{,}186{,}829 \end{aligned}$$

The value of Time Varner prior to the merger was \$140,000,000, and Time Varner paid \$60,000,000 for AOLI, a total of \$200,000,000. Since the total value of the merged firm (TV_{BT}), \$213,186,829, is greater than the \$200,000,000, the merger makes financial sense. Time Varner should proceed with the acquisition. An alternative way to view this is to consider the merger from a capital budgeting perspective. The cost of the acquisition was \$60,000,000. The value of the acquisition to Time Varner is \$73,186,829. The NPV of the acquisition to Time Varner is \$13,186,829 (\$73,186,829 − \$60,000,000). The merger is a positive NPV project and should proceed. ▲

In the above example, Time Varner could have paid about \$13,186,000 more than the \$60,000,000 that was actually paid and the merger still would have been an acceptable capital budgeting project. However, the NPV of the project would have been zero; no synergy would have been created. The goal of any merger is to get more than the sum of the parts. For Time Varner and AOLI, the combination created a significant amount of synergy that would accrue to the merged firm's common shareholders. In this merger, 1 and 1 added up to more than 2!

Acquisition of a Target's Assets

Occasionally, a firm is acquired not for its income-earning potential but as a collection of assets (generally fixed assets) that the bidding company wants. The price paid for this type of acquisition depends largely on which assets are being acquired; consideration must also be given to the value of any tax losses. To determine whether the purchase of assets is financially justified, the bidder must estimate the value of the target assets.

Example ▼ Clark Company, a major manufacturer of electrical transformers, is interested in acquiring certain fixed assets of Noble Company, an industrial electronics company. Noble, which has tax loss carryforwards from losses over the past 5 years, is interested in selling out, but it wishes to sell out entirely, not just get rid of certain fixed assets. A condensed balance sheet for Noble Company follows.

Balance Sheet
Noble Company

Assets		Liabilities and shareholders' equity	
Cash	$ 2,000	Total liabilities	$ 80,000
Marketable securities	0	Shareholders' equity	120,000
Accounts receivable	8,000	Total liabilities and shareholders' equity	$200,000
Inventories	10,000		
Machine A	10,000		
Machine B	30,000		
Machine C	25,000		
Land and buildings	115,000		
Total assets	$200,000		

Clark Company wants only machines B and C and the land and buildings. However, it has made some inquiries and has arranged to sell the accounts receivable, inventories, and machine A for $23,000. Together with the $2,000 in cash, Clark will receive $25,000 for the assets they do not require. Since Noble Company has been losing money over the past five years, Clark has negotiated a very good deal for the company with Noble's managers and board. Clark will buy the company for $20,000. Noble's common shareholders will receive $20,000 for their shares, a significant reduction from their value on the balance sheet. Again, this is likely due to the five years of losses.

Since Noble has $80,000 of liabilities that Clark also assumes responsibility for, the true cost of the acquisition is $100,000 ($20,000 + $80,000). But, the actual cash outlay required of Clark after liquidating the unneeded assets will be $75,000 [($80,000 + $20,000) − $25,000]. In other words, to obtain the use of the desired assets (machines B and C and the land and buildings) and the benefits of Noble's tax losses, the cost to Clark is $75,000.

Noble Company's assets are expected to have a life of ten years. The *after-tax cash inflows* and applicable tax losses that are expected to result from the new assets are $14,000 per year for the first 5 years and $12,000 per year for the

TABLE 18.3 The Value of Noble Company's Assets to Clark Company

$V_{T\wedge B}$ = $14,000 × *PVIFa* (11%, 5 per)	=	$51,743
+ $12,000 × *PVIFa* (11%, 5 per) × *PVIF* (11%, 5 per)[a]	=	$26,320
Value of Noble's assets to Clark ($V_{T\wedge B}$)	=	$78,063
Cost of Noble's assets to Clark		75,000
Net present value		$ 3,063

[a] Here, two time value calculations are required. The first determines the present value of the annuity to the beginning of the year in which the cash flows start. In this case that would be to the beginning of year 6. The second calculation discounts this future value to time 0, the present. In this case that would be for five years, since the beginning of year 6 is the same as the end of year 5.

following 5 years. The desirability of this asset acquisition can be determined by calculating the net present value of this outlay using Clark Company's 11 percent cost of capital, as shown in Table 18.3. *Because the net present value of $3,063 is greater than zero, Clark's value should be increased by acquiring Noble Company's assets.* The acquisition creates synergy.

? Review Questions

18–5 Describe the process a bidding company should use to value a target company.

18–6 What is synergy, and how is the value of synergy associated with a merger calculated? How is the concept of synergy related to valuation concepts (from Chapter 8) and capital budgeting (from Chapters 12 and 13)?

18.3 Paying for the Acquisition

With a potential target uncovered and the value of the target calculated, the bidder must determine how to pay for the acquisition. In valuing the takeover, a total purchase price was calculated. This amount is divided by the number of common shares outstanding, and a per-share value is calculated. Both the per-share and total dollar cost of the acquisition are widely quoted in the financial press. The per-share amount could be paid to the common shareholders of the target in one of three ways:

1. The first is to pay cash. About 36 percent of acquisitions are paid for with cash. Each shareholder receives the per-share dollar amount for each share held.
2. The second is for the target company's shareholder to receive common shares of the "new" merged company in exchange for their shares of the target company. About 41 percent of acquisitions are completed this way.
3. The third method is a combination of the two: some cash, some shares. About 23 percent of acquisitions are financed this way.

In this section, we illustrate how common shares can be used to pay for a target.

Acquisitions Financed by Exchanging Common Shares

common share exchange
An acquisition method in which the bidding firm exchanges its common shares for the common shares of the target company according to a predetermined ratio.

With a **common share exchange** transaction, the acquisition is paid for by exchanging shares. The bidding firm exchanges its common shares for the common shares of the target company according to a predetermined ratio. The *ratio of exchange* of shares is determined in the merger negotiations. This ratio affects the various financial yardsticks that are used by existing and prospective shareholders to value the merged firm's shares. With the demise of LBOs, the use of share exchanges to finance mergers has grown in popularity during recent years. This is the case since no cash is involved, only common shares.

Ratio of Exchange

With a share exchange, the firms must determine the number of the bidding firm's common shares to exchange for each share of the target firm. The bidding company must have a sufficient number of authorized common shares available to complete the transaction. As discussed in Chapter 5, when a company is incorporated, it is authorized to issue a specified number of common shares. To exceed this level, the company must amend its *articles of incorporation*. As discussed earlier, the bidding firm generally offers more for each share of the target company than the current market price of the target company's common shares. The actual **ratio of exchange** is the amount *paid* per share of the target company divided by the market price per share of the bidding firm. It is calculated in this manner because the bidding firm pays the target firm in shares, which have a value equal to the bidding firm's market price.

ratio of exchange
The amount paid per share of the target company divided by the market price per share of the bidding firm.

Example Grand Company, a leather products concern whose common shares are currently trading for $80 per share, is interested in acquiring Small Company, a producer of belts. Small's common shares are currently selling for $75 per share, but in the merger negotiations, Grand has found it necessary to offer Small $110 per share. Because Grand does not have sufficient financial resources to purchase the firm for cash and it does not wish to raise these funds, Small has agreed to accept Grand's common shares in exchange for its shares. As stated, Grand's shares currently trade for $80 per share, and it must pay $110 per share for Small. Therefore, the ratio of exchange is 1.375 ($110 ÷ $80). This means that Grand Company must exchange 1.375 of its common shares for each common share of Small Company.

Effect on Earnings per Share

Although cash flows and value are the primary focus of mergers, it is useful to consider the effect a proposed merger may have on earnings per share (EPS). Ordinarily, the resulting earnings per share differ from the premerger earnings per share for both the bidding firm and the target firm. The resulting EPS depends largely on the ratio of exchange and the premerger earnings per share of each firm. It is best to view the initial and long-run effects of the ratio of exchange on earnings per share separately.

Initial Effect When the ratio of exchange is equal to 1 and both the bidding firm and the target firm have the same premerger earnings per share, the merged firm's earnings per share will initially remain constant. In this rare instance, both the bidding and target firms would also have equal price/earnings (P/E) ratios. In actuality, the earnings per share of the merged firm are generally above the premerger earnings per share of one firm and below the premerger earnings per share of the other, after the necessary adjustment has been made for the ratio of exchange.

Example As seen in the preceding example, Grand Company is contemplating acquiring Small Company by swapping 1.375 of its common shares for each share of Small. The current financial data related to the earnings and market price for each of these companies are given in Table 18.4.

TABLE 18.4 Grand Company's and Small Company's Financial Data

Item	Grand Company	Small Company
(1) Earnings available for common shareholders	$500,000	$100,000
(2) Number of common shares outstanding	125,000	20,000
(3) Earnings per share [(1) ÷ (2)]	$4	$5
(4) Market price per share	$80	$75
(5) Price/earnings (P/E) ratio [(4) ÷ (3)]	20	15

To complete the merger and retire Small Company's 20,000 common shares outstanding, Grand will have to issue 27,500 common shares (1.375 × 20,000 shares). Once the merger is completed, Grand will have 152,500 (125,000 + 27,500) common shares outstanding. If the earnings of each of the firms remain constant, the merged company will be expected to have earnings available for the common shareholders of $600,000 ($500,000 + $100,000). The earnings per share of the merged company therefore should equal approximately $3.93 ($600,000 ÷ 152,500 shares).

It would appear at first that Small Company's shareholders have sustained a decrease in per-share earnings from $5 to $3.93, but because each of Small Company's original common shares is equivalent to 1.375 shares of the merged company, the equivalent earnings per share are actually $5.40 ($3.93 × 1.375). In other words, as a result of the merger, Grand Company's original shareholders experience a decrease in earnings per share from $4 to $3.93 to the benefit of Small Company's shareholders, whose earnings per share increase from $5 to $5.40. These results are summarized in Table 18.5.

Hint
If the bidding company were to pay less than the current value per dollar of earnings to acquire each dollar of earnings (P/E paid < P/E of bidding company), the opposite effects would result.

The postmerger earnings per share for owners of the bidding and target companies can be explained by comparing the price/earnings ratio paid by the bidding company with its initial P/E ratio. This relationship is summarized in Table 18.6. By paying more than its current value per dollar of earnings to

TABLE 18.5 Summary of the Effects on Earnings per Share of a Merger Between Grand Company and Small Company at $110 per Share

	Earnings per share	
Shareholders	Before merger	After merger
Grand Company	$4.00	$3.93[a]
Small Company	5.00	5.40[b]

[a] $\dfrac{\$500{,}000 + \$100{,}000}{125{,}000 + (1.375 \times 20{,}000)} = \$3.93.$

[b] $3.93 × 1.375 = $5.40.

TABLE 18.6 Effect of Price/Earnings (P/E) Ratios on Earnings per Share (EPS)

	Effect on EPS	
Relationship between P/E paid and P/E of bidding company	Bidding company	Target company
P/E paid > P/E of bidding company	Decrease	Increase
P/E paid = P/E of bidding company	Constant	Constant
P/E paid < P/E of bidding company	Increase	Decrease

acquire each dollar of earnings (P/E paid > P/E of bidding company), the bidding firm transfers the claim on a portion of its premerger earnings to the owners of the target firm. Therefore, on a postmerger basis *the target firm's EPS increases, and the bidding firm's EPS decreases.* Note that this outcome will occur when the P/E ratio paid for the target is higher than the bidder's P/E ratio prior to the merger. The P/E ratios associated with the Grand–Small merger demonstrate the effect of the merger on EPS.

Example Grand Company's P/E ratio is 20, and the P/E ratio paid for Small Company's earnings was 22 ($110 ÷ $5). Because the P/E paid for Small Company was greater than the P/E for Grand Company (22 versus 20), the effect of the merger was to decrease the EPS for original holders of shares in Grand Company (from $4 to $3.93) and to increase the effective EPS of original holders of shares in Small Company (from $5 to $5.40).

Long-Run Effect The long-run effect of a merger on the earnings per share of the merged company depends largely on whether the earnings of the merged firm grow. Often, although a decrease in the per-share earnings of the bidding firm is expected initially, the long-run effects of the merger on earnings per share can be quite favourable. Because firms generally expect growth in earnings, the key factor enabling the bidding company to experience higher future EPS than it would have without the merger is that the earnings attributable to the target company's assets grow at a faster rate than those resulting from the bidding company's premerger assets. An example will clarify this point.

Example In 2008, Grand Company acquired Small Company by swapping 1.375 of its common shares for each share of Small Company. Other key financial data and the effects of this exchange ratio were discussed in preceding examples. The total earnings of Grand Company were expected to grow at an annual rate of 3 percent without the merger; Small Company's earnings were expected to grow at a 7 percent annual rate without the merger. The same growth rates are expected to apply to the component earnings streams with the merger.[7] The table in Figure 18.1 shows the future effects on EPS for Grand Company without and with the proposed Small Company merger, based on these growth rates.

7. Frequently, because of synergy, the combined earnings stream is greater than the sum of the individual earnings streams. This possibility is ignored here.

The table indicates that the earnings per share without the merger will be greater than the EPS with the merger for 2008 through 2010. After 2010, however, the EPS will be higher than they would have been without the merger as a result of the faster earnings growth rate of Small Company (7% versus 3%). Although a few years are required for this difference in the growth rate of earnings to pay off, in the future Grand Company will receive an earnings benefit as a result of merging with Small Company at a 1.375 ratio of exchange. The long-run earnings advantage of the merger is clearly depicted in Figure 18.1.[8]

Effect on Market Price per Share

The market price per share does not necessarily remain constant after the acquisition of one firm by another. Adjustments occur in the marketplace in response to changes in expected earnings, the dilution of ownership, changes in risk, and

FIGURE 18.1

Future EPS

Future EPS without and with the Grand–Small merger

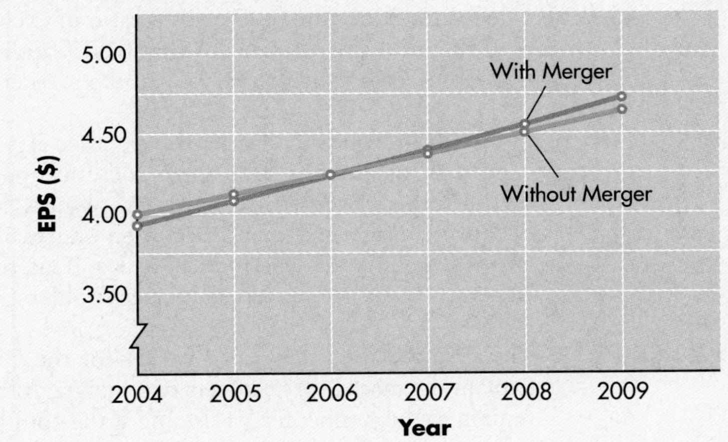

	Without Merger		With Merger	
Year	Total earnings[a]	Earnings per share[b]	Total earnings[c]	Earnings per share[d]
2008	$500,000	$4.00	$600,000	$3.93
2009	515,000	4.12	622,000	4.08
2010	530,450	4.24	644,940	4.23
2011	546,364	4.37	668,868	4.39
2012	562,755	4.50	693,835	4.55
2013	579,638	4.64	719,893	4.72

[a]Based on a 3% annual growth rate.
[b]Based on 125,000 common shares outstanding.
[c]Based on a 3% annual growth in Grand Company's earnings and a 7% annual growth in Small Company's earnings.
[d]Based on 152,500 common shares outstanding [125,000 shares + (1.375 × 20,000 shares)].

8. To discover properly whether the merger is beneficial, the earnings estimates under each alternative would have to be made over a long period of time, say, 50 years, and then converted to cash flows and discounted at the appropriate rate. The alternative with the higher present value would be preferred. For simplicity, only the basic intuitive view of the long-run effect is presented here.

ratio of exchange in market price
Indicates the market price per share of the acquiring firm paid for each dollar of market price per share of the target firm.

certain other operating and financial changes. By using the ratio of exchange, a **ratio of exchange in market price** can be calculated. It indicates the market price per share of the acquiring firm *paid* for each dollar of market price per share of the target firm. This ratio, the *MPR*, is defined by Equation 18.4:

$$MPR = \frac{MP_{\text{bidding}} \times RE}{MP_{\text{target}}} \tag{18.4}$$

where:

MPR = market price ratio of exchange
MP_{bidding} = market price per share of the bidding firm
MP_{target} = market price per share of the target firm
RE = ratio of exchange

Example The market price of Grand Company's common shares was $80, and that of Small Company's was $75. The ratio of exchange was 1.375. Substituting these values into Equation 18.4 yields a ratio of exchange in market price of 1.47 [($80 × 1.375) ÷ $75]. This means that $1.47 of the market price of Grand Company is given in exchange for every $1 of the market price of Small Company.

The ratio of exchange in market price is normally greater than 1, which indicates that to acquire a firm, the bidder must pay a premium over the market price of the target. Even so, the original owners of the bidding firm may still gain because the merged firm's common shares may sell at a price/earnings ratio above the individual premerger ratios. This results from the improved risk and return relationship perceived by shareholders and other investors.

Example The financial data developed earlier for the Grand–Small merger can be used to explain the market price effects of a merger. If the earnings of the merged company remain at the premerger levels, and if the common shares of the merged company sell at an assumed multiple of 21 times earnings, the values in Table 18.7 can be expected. Although Grand Company's earnings per share decline from $4 to $3.93 (refer to Table 18.5), the market price of its shares will increase from $80 to $82.53 as a result of the merger.

Although the behaviour exhibited in this example is not unusual, the financial manager must recognize that only with proper management of the merged enterprise can its market value be improved. If the merged firm cannot achieve

TABLE 18.7 Postmerger Market Price of Grand Company Using a P/E Ratio of 21

Item	Merged company
(1) Earnings available for common shareholders	$600,000
(2) Number of common shares outstanding	152,500
(3) Earnings per share [(1) ÷ (2)]	$3.93
(4) Price/earnings (P/E) ratio	21
(5) Expected market price per share [(3) × (4)]	$82.53

sufficiently high earnings in view of its risk, there is no guarantee that its market price will reach the forecast value. Nevertheless, a policy of buying and merging firms with low P/Es can produce favourable results for the owners of the bidding firm. Acquisitions are especially attractive when the bidding firm's share price is high, because fewer shares must be exchanged to acquire a given firm.

? Review Questions

18–7 What are the three methods a bidding firm could use to pay for the acquisition of a target company?

18–8 When a bidding company pays for a target company by exchanging common shares, what is the ratio of exchange? What impact does the share exchange have on the earnings per share of the merged firm? What role does the price/earnings ratio play in the analysis? Explain.

18.4 Accounting for Mergers and Acquisitions

Once a merger is finalized, the accounting for the transaction must be completed. In this section, we consider the methods that can be used and illustrate one of the methods with an example. We also discuss the concept of *goodwill*—a term that was very prominent with the hundreds of mergers that occurred in the technology sector during the latter half of the 1990s.

Methods of Accounting for Mergers

pooling method
The balance sheets of the two firms are added together (pooled) with the merged firm's balance sheet being a combination of the bidding and target company's balance sheets.

purchase method
The bidding firm determines the fair market value of the target firm's assets and these values are reflected in the merged company's balance sheet.

net fair market value
The market value of the assets acquired, less the amount of the acquired firm's debt.

When a firm is acquired and merged, there are two ways of accounting for the transaction on the merged firm's balance sheet: the pooling of interest method and the purchase method. With the **pooling method**, the balance sheets of the two firms are simply added together (pooled). The merged firm's balance sheet is simply the combination of the bidding and target company's balance sheets. Under the **purchase method,** the bidding firm must determine the fair market value of each of the target firm's assets. These values are then reflected in the merged company's balance sheet. Since July 1, 2001, companies in both Canada and the United States are no longer allowed to use the pooling method of accounting for M&As. Therefore, for the merged firm's balance sheet, the purchase method of accounting must be used. For the merged firm's income statement all sales and expenses are pooled; there is no choice.

In many acquisitions, the price paid for the target in the M&A is greater than the net fair market value of the assets acquired. The **net fair market value** of an acquisition is the market value of the assets acquired, less the amount of the acquired firm's debt as shown on the balance sheet. In an M&A, the bidding company acquires the target's assets; it also acquires their liabilities. The difference between the two values is the net fair market value of the assets acquired. If the amount paid for the target is greater than the net fair market value, then an intangible asset termed goodwill is created.

Goodwill

Goodwill
The difference between the amount the bidder paid for the target and the estimated net fair market value of the assets acquired; it must be greater than zero.

Goodwill is the difference between the amount the bidder paid for the target, and the estimated net fair market value of the assets acquired. Goodwill must be greater than zero; it is not possible to have negative goodwill. In other words, if the net fair market value of the assets acquired was greater than the purchase price, the implication is that negative goodwill would result. This is not possible, so the total market value of the assets is revised down to equal the amount paid for the target.

At one time, the accounting treatment of goodwill required that it be amortized over a period no longer than 20 years. As such, it would be gradually charged against revenues on the income statement. Since 2001, a non-amortization approach to goodwill has been adopted for use both in Canada and the United States. Under this method, goodwill is reviewed for impairment. If in the year of review, the value of goodwill on the balance sheet is more than its fair market value, the difference is expensed against revenues on that year's income statement. Impairment reviews are required only when events occur that suggest that the value of goodwill has declined. It is believed that this approach provides investors with better information about the economic value of goodwill and its impact on a company's profits.

As stated earlier, in Canada companies must use the purchase method of accounting for mergers and acquisitions. To illustrate the method, consider the following example.

Example ▼ Evans Manufacturing has just acquired Wagner Technology, paying $305,000 for the firm. To finance the acquisition, Evans will use $100,000 of cash and issue long-term debt to raise the remainder of the purchase price. The two companies' balance sheets on the day prior to the acquisition are provided in Table 18.8. Evans Manufacturing has carefully evaluated each of Wagner Technology's assets and liabilities and has determined their fair market values as follows:

Cash	No adjustment
Accounts receivable	$177,000
Inventory	$191,000
Net fixed assets	$385,000
Accounts payable	No adjustment
Line of credit	No adjustment
Long-term debt	No adjustment

On the day prior to the merger, the book value of Wagner Technology's assets was $896,000. The net book value of the company (net of liabilities) was $274,000 ($896,000 – $325,000 – $297,000). The fair market value of Wagner Technology's assets was $790,000. The net fair market value of the assets was $168,000 ($790,000 – $325,000 – $297,000). Evans Manufacturing paid $305,000 for a company whose assets had a net fair market value of $168,000. Therefore, goodwill of $137,000 ($305,000 – $168,000) results.

Following the acquisition, the balance sheet of the merged firm is as shown in Table 18.9. Note that the cash account of the merged company declines by $100,000. This reflects the payment made for the acquisition. Long-term debt increases by $205,000, reflecting the use of debt to finance a portion of the acquisition. The difference between the amount paid for Wagner and the net fair market value of the company's assets acquired is goodwill. In this case, it equals $137,000. ▲

TABLE 18.8 **Balance Sheets for Evans (Bidder) and Wagner (Target): Day Prior to Merger**

Evans Manufacturing Balance Sheet day prior to acquisition		Wagner Technology Balance Sheet day prior to acquisition	
Assets		**Assets**	
Cash	$ 277,000	Cash	$ 37,000
Accounts receivable	452,000	Accounts receivable	193,000
Inventory	487,000	Inventory	223,000
Total current assets	1,216,000	Total current assets	453,000
Net fixed assets	1,134,000	Net fixed assets	443,000
Total assets	$2,350,000	Total assets	$896,000
Liabilities and shareholders' equity		**Liabilities and shareholders' equity**	
Accounts payable	$ 403,000	Accounts payable	$145,000
Line of credit	290,000	Line of credit	180,000
Total current liabilities	693,000	Total current liabilities	325,000
Long-term debt	897,000	Long-term debt	297,000
Common shares	279,000	Common shares	125,000
Retained earnings	481,000	Retained earnings	149,000
Total liabilities and shareholders' equity	$2,350,000	Total liabilities and shareholders' equity	$896,000

TABLE 18.9 **Balance Sheet for the Merged Company (Evans) Following the Merger**

Evans Manufacturing Balance Sheet following the acquisition of Wagner Technology	
Assets	
Cash ($277,000 − $100,000 + $37,000)	$ 214,000
Accounts receivable ($452,000 + $177,000)	629,000
Inventory ($487,000 + $191,000)	678,000
Total current assets	1,521,000
Net fixed assets ($1,134,000 + $385,000)	1,519,000
Goodwill	137,000
Total assets	$3,177,000
Liabilities and shareholders' equity	
Accounts payable ($403,000 + $145,000)	$ 548,000
Line of credit ($290,000 + $180,000)	470,000
Total current liabilities	1,018,000
Long-term debt ($897,000 + $205,000 + $297,000)	1,399,000
Common shares	279,000
Retained earnings	481,000
Total liabilities and shareholders' equity	$3,177,000

? Review Question

18–9 Discuss the two methods that can be used to account for a merger transaction. What is goodwill, how is it created, and how is it charged against a firm's revenues?

18.5 Merger Negotiations and Holding Companies

We now turn our attention to the process used to negotiate mergers. In most mergers, particularly where publicly traded companies are involved, investment dealers, law firms, and chartered accounting firms are all closely involved in the process. Larger mergers take months to plan and the deal, once finalized, can take three to six months to close. The fees involved for larger mergers can range into the hundreds of millions of dollars. For investment dealers, M&A activity is one of the largest, and most profitable, components of their revenues. Later in this section, we review the major advantages and disadvantages of holding companies.

The Merger Negotiation Process

investment bankers
Financial intermediaries hired by bidding companies in mergers to find suitable target companies and assist in negotiations.

Mergers are often handled by **investment bankers**—financial intermediaries hired by bidding companies to find suitable target companies and assist in negotiations. Once a target company is selected, the investment banker negotiates with its management or investment banker. Likewise, when management wishes to sell the firm or an operating unit of the firm, it will hire an investment banker to seek out potential buyers.

If attempts to negotiate with the management of the target company break down, the bidding firm, often with the aid of its investment banker, can make a direct appeal to shareholders by using *tender offers*. The investment banker is typically compensated with a fixed fee, a commission tied to the transaction price, or a combination of fees and commissions.

Management Negotiations

To initiate negotiations, the bidding firm must make an offer either in cash or based on an exchange of common shares with a specified ratio of exchange. The target company then reviews the offer and, in light of alternative offers, accepts or rejects the terms presented. A desirable merger candidate often receives more than a single offer. Normally, certain nonfinancial issues must be resolved relating to the existing management, product-line policies, financing policies, and the independence of the target firm. The key factor should be the per-share price offered in cash or reflected in the ratio of exchange. Sometimes negotiations will break down.

Tender Offers

When merger negotiations break down, a tender offer may then be used to negotiate a "hostile takeover" directly with the firm's common shareholders. As noted earlier, a *tender offer* is a formal offer to purchase a firm's common shares at a

18.1 **IN PRACTICE**

Going for the Gold

In mid-2006, there was much speculation in the gold industry of new consolidations and acquisitions as companies strove to become the largest gold miner. In the gold sector, acquisitions are viewed as a necessity to ensure future growth, the strategy being to buy the company that has gold reserves. It is sometimes cheaper to buy companies that have gold reserves rather than go out and discover your own gold. This was the strategy behind Goldcorp's acquisition of Glamis Gold Ltd., a purchase that was expected to incite a wave of merger activity in the gold sector. In early 2006, Glamis Gold acquired Penasquito, a gold and silver project in Mexico. Goldcorp CEO Ian Tefler was also interested in the project and the reserves that have been found there. To get them, he was willing to pay $8.6 billion to buy Glamis, a price that many analysts say is too much.

More importantly, Goldcorp's shareholders had expressed their opposition to the proposed deal. Rob McEwen, the former CEO of Goldcorp, felt that the purchase of Glamis Gold Ltd. was dilutive for Goldcorp shareholders, did not provide an immediate bump for earnings or cash flow, and devoted too much of Goldcorp's financial resources to risky development projects. With the takeover, Tefler did admit that cash flow per share would fall about 20 percent in the first year. This was not a concern, however, because he believed that Goldcorp's cash flows would increase in the future due to increased reserves. After the deal was announced, Goldcorp shares fell $3.22 to close at $30.55. The same day, Glamis shares gained $7.68 to close at $50.70.

In addition, some Goldcorp shareholders were upset because they did not get a say in the deal. The deal was subject to approval by *Glamis* shareholders. Glamis shareholders received 1.69 Goldcorp shares for every share of Glamis they owned. The offer valued Glamis at $51.49 a share based on Goldcorp's close on Wednesday, August 30, 2006, representing a 33 percent premium to the closing share price. The $8.6 billion purchase price was 30 times Glamis' cash flow.

On the other hand, there were those that did like the deal. Said one portfolio manager, "It creates a company on par with Barrick and Newmont. It will have lower production costs [than either Barrick and Newmont], a better growth profile, and I think this company will be very well positioned." With the acquisition, Goldcorp would be the world's third-largest gold miner, with a value of $21.3 billion.

Despite the concerns of some shareholders, the deal was signed. On October 26, 2006, Glamis shareholders approved it, with an overwhelming 98.6 percent in favour. The acquisition was completed on November 3. Following that, the company released its third-quarter earnings, which were lower than expected. In response to the poorer performance, Tefler once again reminded investors to look to the future. "In the short term, the earnings per share will be less in the new Goldcorp than they would have been in the old Goldcorp. But that lasts, depending on your metal prices, for three to four years, and then after that it will be higher. [That is the] choice you have when you make these types of acquisitions—what you are willing to sacrifice in the present for a stronger future—and that was the decision we made with Glamis."

As with most acquisitions, there is no doubt the future of Goldcorp will be watched closely by analysts and investors to see how this controversial acquisition pans out.

SOURCES: Andy Hoffman, "Now, Every Miner Is in Play," *The Globe and Mail*, September 1, 2006, pp. B1, B4; Eric Reguly, "Hefty Price May Take the Glamour out of Goldcorp's Glamis Play," *The Globe and Mail*, September 1, 2006, p. B4; Wendy Stueck, "Goldcorp-Glamis Deal Faces Tough Sell with Investors," *The Globe and Mail*, September 1, 2006, pp. B1, B4; Goldcorp news releases available at **www.globeinvestor.com**.

specified price. The offer is made to all the shareholders at a premium above the market price. The shareholders are advised of a tender offer through announcements in financial newspapers and through direct communications from the bidding firm. Sometimes a tender offer is made to add pressure to existing merger negotiations. In other cases, the tender offer may be made without warning as an attempt at an abrupt corporate takeover.

Fighting Hostile Takeovers

If the management of a target firm does not favour a merger or considers the price offered in a proposed merger too low, it is likely to take defensive actions to ward off the *hostile takeover.* Such actions are generally developed with the assistance of investment bankers and lawyers who help the firm develop and employ effective **takeover defences.** There are obvious strategies such as informing shareholders of the alleged damaging effects of a takeover, acquiring another company (discussed earlier in the chapter), or attempting to sue the bidding firm on antitrust or other grounds. In addition, many other defences exist (some with colourful names)—white knight, poison pills, greenmail, leveraged recapitalization, golden parachutes, and shark repellents.

takeover defences
Strategies for fighting hostile takeovers.

white knight
A takeover defence in which the target firm finds a bidder more to its liking than the initial hostile bidder and prompts the two to compete to take over the firm.

The **white knight** strategy involves the target firm finding a more suitable bidder (the "white knight") and prompting it to compete with the initial hostile bidder to take over the firm. The basic premise of this strategy is that if being taken over is nearly certain, the target firm ought to attempt to be taken over by the firm that is deemed most acceptable to its management. **Poison pills** typically involve the creation of securities that give their holders certain rights that become effective when a takeover is attempted. The "pill" allows the shareholders to receive special voting rights or securities that make the firm less desirable to the hostile bidder. **Greenmail** is a strategy by which the target firm repurchases through private negotiation a large block of its common shares at a premium from one or more shareholders to end a hostile takeover attempt by those shareholders. Clearly, greenmail is a form of corporate blackmail by the holders of a large block of shares.

poison pill
A takeover defence in which a firm issues securities that give their holders certain rights that become effective when a takeover is attempted; these rights make the target firm less desirable to a hostile bidder.

greenmail
A takeover defence under which a target firm repurchases through private negotiation a large block of its common shares at a premium from one or more shareholders to end a hostile takeover attempt by those shareholders.

Another hostile takeover defence involves the use of a **leveraged recapitalization,** which is a strategy involving the payment of a large debt-financed cash dividend to current common shareholders. This strategy significantly increases the firm's financial leverage, thereby deterring the takeover attempt. In addition, as a further deterrent the recapitalization is often structured to increase the equity and control of the existing management. **Golden parachutes** are provisions in the employment contracts of key executives that provide them with sizeable compensation if the firm is taken over. Golden parachutes deter hostile takeovers to the extent that the cash outflows required by these contracts are large enough to make the takeover unattractive to the bidder. Another defence is use of **shark repellents,** which are antitakeover amendments to the corporate charter that constrain the firm's ability to transfer managerial control of the firm as a result of a merger. Although this defence might entrench existing management, many firms have had these amendments ratified by shareholders.

leveraged recapitalization
A takeover defence in which the target firm pays a large debt-financed cash dividend, increasing the firm's financial leverage and deterring the takeover attempt.

golden parachutes
Provisions in the employment contracts of key executives that provide them with sizeable compensation if the firm is taken over; deters hostile takeovers to the extent that the cash outflows required are large enough to make the takeover unattractive.

shark repellents
Antitakeover amendments to a corporate charter that constrain the firm's ability to transfer managerial control of the firm as a result of a merger.

Because takeover defences tend to insulate management from shareholders, the potential for litigation is great when these strategies are employed. Lawsuits are sometimes filed against management by dissident shareholders. In addition, governments may intervene when a proposed takeover is deemed to be in violation of federal or provincial regulations, or when politicians feel a proposed merger may not be in the public's best interest. In Canada, hostile takeovers are quite rare but, when one is announced, it is not unusual for both federal and provincial politicians as well as the courts to get involved in the takeover process.

Holding Companies

As defined earlier, a *holding company* is a corporation that has voting control of one or more other corporations. The holding company may need to own only a small percentage of the outstanding shares to have this voting control. In the case of companies with a relatively small number of shareholders, as much as 30 to 40 percent of the stock may be required. In the case of firms with a widely dispersed ownership, 10 to 20 percent of the shares may be sufficient to gain voting control. A holding company that wants to obtain voting control of a firm may use direct market purchases or tender offers to acquire needed shares. In Canada, holding companies have been a very popular way for bidding companies to acquire a partial or total ownership interest in a target. A few of the better-known holding companies in Canada include BCE Inc., Brookfield Asset Management, Onex Corporation, and Power Corporation.

Advantages of Holding Companies

The primary advantage of holding companies is the *leverage effect* that permits the firm to control a large amount of assets with a relatively small dollar investment. In other words, the owners of a holding company can *control* significantly larger amounts of assets than they could *acquire* through mergers.

Example Carr Company, a holding company, currently holds voting control of two subsidiaries—company X and company Y. The balance sheets for Carr and its two subsidiaries are presented in Table 18.10. Carr owns 16 2/3 percent ($10 ÷ $60) of company X and 20 percent ($14 ÷ $70) of company Y. These holdings are sufficient for voting control.

The owners of Carr Company's $12 worth of equity have control over $260 worth of assets (company X's $100 and company Y's $160). Thus, the owners' equity represents only about 4.6 percent ($12 ÷ $260) of the total assets controlled. From the discussions of ratio analysis, leverage, and capital structure in Chapters 3 and 10, you should recognize that this is quite a high degree of leverage. If an individual shareholder or even another holding company owns $3 of Carr Company's common shares, which is assumed to be sufficient for its control, it will in actuality control the whole $260 of assets. The investment itself in this case would represent only 1.15 percent ($3 ÷ $260) of the assets controlled.

The high leverage obtained through a holding company arrangement greatly magnifies earnings and losses for the holding company. Quite often, a **pyramiding** of holding companies occurs when one holding company controls other holding companies, thereby causing an even greater magnification of earnings and losses. The greater the leverage, the greater the risk involved. The risk–return tradeoff is a key consideration in the holding company decision.

pyramiding
An arrangement among holding companies wherein one holding company controls other holding companies, thereby causing an even greater magnification of earnings and losses.

TABLE 18.10 Balance Sheets for Carr Company and Its Subsidiaries

Assets		Liabilities and shareholders' equity	
Carr Company			
Common share holdings		Long-term debt	$ 6
Company X	$10	Preferred equity	6
Company Y	14	Common equity	12
Total	$24	Total	$24
Company X			
Current assets	$ 30	Current liabilities	$ 15
Fixed assets	70	Long-term debt	25
Total	$100	Common equity	60
		Total	$100
Company Y			
Current assets	$ 20	Current liabilities	$ 10
Fixed assets	140	Long-term debt	60
Total	$160	Preferred equity	20
		Common equity	70
		Total	$160

Another commonly cited advantage of holding companies is the *risk protection* resulting from the fact that the failure of one of the companies (such as Y in the preceding example) does not result in the failure of the entire holding company. Because each subsidiary is a separate corporation, the failure of one company should cost the holding company, at maximum, no more than its investment in that subsidiary. Other advantages include the fact that *lawsuits or legal actions* against a subsidiary will not threaten the remaining companies, and it is *generally easy to gain control* of a firm, because shareholder or management approval is not generally necessary.

Disadvantages of Holding Companies

A major disadvantage of holding companies is the *increased risk* resulting from the leverage effect. When general economic conditions are unfavourable, a loss by one subsidiary may be magnified. For example, if subsidiary company X in Table 18.10 experiences a loss, its inability to pay dividends to Carr Company could result in Carr Company's inability to meet its scheduled payments.

The fact that holding companies are *difficult to analyze* is another disadvantage. Security analysts and investors typically have difficulty understanding holding companies because of their complexity. As a result, these firms tend to sell at low multiples of earnings (P/Es), and the shareholder value of holding companies may suffer.

A final disadvantage of holding companies is the generally *high cost of administration* resulting from maintaining each subsidiary company as a separate entity. A merger, on the other hand, would likely result in certain administrative economies of scale. The need for coordination and communication between the holding company and its subsidiaries may further elevate these costs.

International Mergers

M&As are popular around the world, with the friendly merger being the dominant form. Only in the United States are hostile takeovers evident in large numbers, and even there the number of hostile takeovers has significantly declined since the boom period in the 1980s. One of the reasons for the popularity of M&As around the world is the growing emphasis on creating shareholder value. In addition, the internationalization of the capital markets has created more opportunities for firms to secure the funds necessary to finance acquisitions (see Chapter 5). This combination has resulted in a growing number of M&As around the world.

Table 18.11 provides a breakdown of the number of M&As and their dollar value for 2002 and 2005 in various regions around the world. While 2002 was a good year with almost 25,000 deals announced with a total value of $1,230,584,000,000, or over US$1.2 trillion, 2005 was a blockbuster year, the third-best ever. In 2005, worldwide announced M&A volume soared to over $2.7 trillion, based on the 32,568 deals announced. That marked a 38.4 percent increase from 2004's total of $2 trillion, the best year for M&A since 2000. Based on the data, the average M&A in 2005 was for about $83 million.

The increased activity in 2005 was due to the increased demand for energy assets, easy access to capital, and a record amount of private equity fund raising.

TABLE 18.11 The Number and Value of Announced Mergers and Acquisitions Around the World, 2002 and 2005

	2002		2005	
Country/area lion)	Number of deals	Value (in $US million)	Number of deals	Value (in $US mil
Canada	1,585	57,653.2	1,493	107,417.8
United States	6,833	457,918.8	9,045	1,131,292.2
Western Europe	7,836	460,185.0	8,952	936,428.1
Japan	1,431	47,877.5	2,552	167,573.1
Asia/Pacific	5,098	133,113.4	8,258	214,503.4
Rest of world	2,210	73,836.1	2,268	146,060.2
Worldwide total	24,993	1,230,584.0	32,568	2,703,274.8

SOURCE: Thomson Financial "Europe Outperforms U.S.: Worldwide M&A Value for Announced Deals Falls from 2001," news release, Thomson Financial, December 31, 2002; and *Mergers & Acquisitions Review*, Thomson Financial, Fourth Quarter 2005, available at **www.thomson.com/pdf/financial/league_table/ma/4Q2005/4Q05_MA_Legal_Advisory.pdf.**

Merger activity in the United States was likewise buoyant in 2005 as volume rose 33.3 percent to more than $1.1 trillion from 2004's announced total of $848.7 billion. The recent results marked the first time U.S. M&A proceeds exceeded the trillion-dollar mark since 2000. The average M&A in the United States in 2005 was for about $125 million.

In Canada in 2005, while the number of deals announced declined from 2002, their value almost doubled to about US$107.4 billion. From the table it is clear that Canada is a small player in the worldwide M&A activity, accounting for only about 4 percent of the value of all mergers. In contrast, the United States is the dominant country in terms of M&A activity. But, as a region, western Europe is very comparable in terms of the dollar value of announced mergers in both 2002 and 2005. One of the reasons for the substantial level of M&A activity in Europe was the 1999 decision to adopt the Euro as the common currency in much of the European continent. It is also interesting to note that the Asia/Pacific region was comparable to the United States and western Europe in terms of number of deals, but was a minor player in terms of value.

Increased M&A activity in Europe is also due, in part, to nationally focused companies wishing to achieve economies of scale in manufacturing. In addition, M&As may allow these firms to move towards international product development strategies, and develop distribution networks across the continent. They are also driven by the need to compete with U.S. companies, which have been operating in Europe for decades.

Large European-based companies will probably prove to be even more formidable competitors as more European countries adopt the Euro and as more trading blocs around the world are created and develop. An active M&A market for European corporate equity will further evolve as European companies come to rely more on public capital markets for financing, and as the market for common shares becomes more truly European in character, rather than French or British or German.

? Review Questions

18–10 What role do *investment bankers* often play in the merger negotiation process? What is a *tender offer?* When and how is it used?

18–11 Briefly describe each of the following *takeover defences* against a hostile merger: (**a**) white knight, (**b**) poison pill, (**c**) greenmail, (**d**) leveraged recapitalization, (**e**) golden parachutes, and (**f**) shark repellents.

18–12 What are the key advantages and disadvantages cited for holding companies? What is *pyramiding* and what are its consequences?

18.6 Business Failure

A business failure is an unfortunate circumstance. Although the majority of firms that fail do so within the first year or two of life, other firms grow, mature, and fail much later. The failure of a business can be viewed in a number of ways and can result from one or more causes.

Types of Business Failure

A firm may fail because its *returns are negative or low.* A firm that consistently reports low earnings or losses will experience a decline in market value. A firm that fails to earn a return that is equal to or greater than its cost of capital can be viewed as having failed to achieve its objective of maximizing shareholder wealth. Negative or low returns, unless remedied, are likely to result eventually in one of the following more serious types of failure.

technical insolvency
Business failure that occurs when a firm is unable to pay its liabilities as they come due.

asset insolvency
A type of failure that occurs when the company's liabilities exceed the market value of the company's assets, meaning the company cannot satisfy the claims of creditors.

A second type of failure, **technical insolvency,** occurs when a firm is unable to pay its liabilities as they come due. When a firm is technically insolvent, its assets are still greater than its liabilities, but it is confronted with a *liquidity crisis.* If some of its assets can be converted into cash within a reasonable period, the company may be able to escape complete failure.

A third type of failure is **asset insolvency**. This occurs when the company's liabilities exceed the market value of the company's assets, meaning the company has negative shareholders' equity. In such a case, the company cannot satisfy the claims of creditors. This often occurs following a period in which the company experiences major losses. Negative net income after tax flows through to the retained earnings account on the balance sheet. If the losses are large enough, negative shareholders' equity can result. In such situations, the firm must borrow money to continue to operate, meaning liabilities also increase. The combination results in asset insolvency.

bankruptcy
A legal state resulting in proceedings that can result in the reorganization of a company, or its liquidation.

These two forms of insolvency *can* lead to bankruptcy. **Bankruptcy** is a legal state resulting in proceedings that can lead to the reorganization of a company, or its liquidation. In bankruptcy, some or all of a firm's assets are transferred to the firm's creditors.

Major Causes of Business Failure

The primary cause of business failure is *mismanagement,* which accounts for more than 50 percent of all cases. Numerous specific managerial faults can cause the firm to fail. Overexpansion, unsound financial actions, a poor marketing plan, an ineffective sales force, and high production costs can all singly or in combination cause failure. For example, *unsound financial actions* include faulty capital budgeting decisions (based on unrealistic sales and cost forecasts, failure to identify all relevant cash flows, an incorrect cost of capital, or failure to assess risk properly), poor financial evaluation of the firm's strategic plans prior to making financial commitments, inadequate or nonexistent cash flow planning, and failure to control receivables, inventories, and payables. Because all major corporate decisions are eventually measured in terms of dollars, financial managers will play a key role in avoiding or causing a business failure. It is their duty to monitor the firm's financial pulse.

Two classic examples where the actions of financial managers caused their firm's failures occurred in 2001 and 2002. Late in 2001, Enron Corporation, a Houston-based energy trader, filed for bankruptcy. At the time, Enron listed $63.4 billion in assets; this was the largest bankruptcy in history. In July 2002, WorldCom's bankruptcy filing became the largest in history. WorldCom's assets at the time totalled $107 billion. In both cases, the actions of the company's chief financial officer (CFO) and other members of the finance department contributed to the failures of the firms.

The CFO of Enron had established off-balance-sheet partnerships that were intended to hide debt and expenses, inflate profits, and enrich top management. WorldCom's CFO was accused of fraud, conspiracy, and filing false statements. This was associated with the inaccurate accounting of about $4 billion in routine operating expenses, leading to inflated profits. Criminal charges were filed against the senior managers of both firms. In addition, Arthur Andersen, the former auditor of both companies, was convicted of obstruction of justice and subsequently went out of business.

Economic activity—especially economic downturns—can contribute to the failure of a firm.[9] If the economy goes into a recession, sales may decrease abruptly, leaving the firm with high costs and insufficient revenues to cover them. In addition, rapid rises in interest rates just prior to a recession can further contribute to cash flow problems and make it more difficult for the firm to obtain and maintain needed financing. During the early 1990s, a number of major business failures including Olympia & York (real estate) resulted from overexpansion and the recessionary economy.

A final cause of business failure is *corporate maturity.* Firms, like individuals, do not have infinite lives. Like a product, a firm goes through the stages of birth, growth, maturity, and eventual decline. The firm's management should attempt to prolong the growth stage through research, improved productivity, new products, and mergers. Once the firm has matured and has begun to decline, it should seek to be acquired by another firm or liquidate before it fails. Effective management planning should help the firm to postpone decline and ultimate failure.

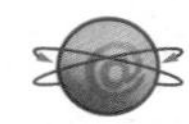

www.creditguru.com/CalcAltZ.shtml
www.jaxworks.com/calcpage.htm

As discussed in Chapter 10, the Altman Z-Score is a tool that can be used to measure the overall financial health of a business and determine the likelihood of a company going bankrupt. It is a multivariate approach for measuring the financial risk of a company, and a powerful diagnostic tool that forecasts the probability of a company going bankrupt. You may wish to review the material concerning the Z-Score from Chapter 10. Models that calculate the Score for a company are freely available on the Web.

Voluntary Settlements

voluntary settlement
An arrangement between a technically insolvent or bankrupt firm and its creditors enabling it to bypass many of the costs involved in legal bankruptcy proceedings.

When a firm becomes technically insolvent or bankrupt, it may arrange with its creditors a **voluntary settlement,** which enables it to bypass many of the costs involved in legal bankruptcy proceedings. The settlement is normally initiated by the debtor firm, because such an arrangement may enable it to continue to exist or to be liquidated in a manner that gives the owners the greatest chance of recovering part of their investment. The debtor arranges a meeting between itself and all its creditors. At the meeting, a committee of creditors is selected to analyze the debtor's situation and recommend a plan of action.

The recommendations of the committee are discussed with both the debtor and the creditors, and a plan for sustaining or liquidating the firm is drawn up.

9. The success of some firms runs countercyclical to economic activity, and other firms are unaffected by economic activity. For example, the auto repair business is likely to grow during a recession, because people are less likely to buy new cars and therefore need more repairs on their unwarranteed older cars. The sale of boats and other luxury items may decline during a recession, whereas sales of staple items such as electricity are likely to be unaffected. In terms of beta—the measure of nondiversifiable risk developed in Chapter 7—a low-beta stock would be associated with a firm whose behaviour is generally countercyclical to economic activity.

Normally, the rationale for sustaining a firm is that it is reasonable to believe that the firm's recovery is feasible. By sustaining the firm, the creditor can continue to receive business from it.

After the situation of the firm has been investigated by the creditor committee, however, the only acceptable course of action may be liquidation of the firm. Liquidation can be carried out in two ways—privately or through the legal procedures provided by bankruptcy law. If the debtor firm is willing to accept liquidation, legal procedures may not be required. Generally, the avoidance of litigation enables the creditors to obtain *quicker* and *higher* settlements. However, all the creditors must agree to a private liquidation for it to be feasible. The objective of the voluntary liquidation process is to recover as much per dollar owed as possible. Under voluntary liquidation, common stockholders (the firm's true owners) cannot receive any funds until the claims of all other parties have been satisfied.

The Process Leading to Reorganization or Bankruptcy

If a voluntary settlement for a failed firm cannot be agreed upon, the firm can use the provisions of one of the two legislative acts governing reorganization and bankruptcy in Canada: the *Companies' Creditors Arrangement Act* or the *Bankruptcy and Insolvency Act*. The following sections discuss each of these federal statutes.

Companies' Creditors Arrangement Act (CCAA)

Companies' Creditors Arrangement Act (CCAA)
Allows a company in financial difficulty to resist its creditors and to negotiate with them in an attempt to avoid bankruptcy and carry on its business as a going concern.

The ***Companies' Creditors Arrangement Act*** **(CCAA)** allows a company in financial difficulty to resist its creditors and to negotiate with them in an attempt to avoid bankruptcy and carry on its business as a going concern. Before being able to use the provisions of the CCAA, the company must be insolvent. This is defined as not being able to pay its bills as they come due, or having a fair market value for its assets that is less than its liabilities. The CCAA is a relatively simple piece of legislation that provides significant flexibility so the distressed company and its creditors can resolve the financial problems.

An application under the CCAA is usually initiated by the debtor company seeking protection. To apply for protection under the CCAA, the debtor company must acknowledge that it is insolvent and it must have debts that exceed $5 million. Essentially, CCAA legislation provides the insolvent company protection from creditors and allows the insolvent company to continue to operate while negotiations between the company and its creditors occur. The purpose of the CCAA is to allow an insolvent company to remain in business and avoid being liquidated.

The CCAA was first passed by Parliament in 1933, during the Great Depression, to allow the creditors of an insolvent company to receive a portion of what they were owed. The CCAA is the Canadian version of Chapter 11 of the U.S. Bankruptcy Code. The CCAA differs significantly from Chapter 11 in the sense that it contains very little statutory guidance on the technical requirements of a solution to the debt problem. Since 1980, it has become the statute most often used in larger corporate restructurings, largely because of its flexibility. It is simple legislation without a lot of rules and, at the same time, it gives the court a great deal of discretion in granting orders to solve practical problems encountered in complex cases.

By using the CCAA, a company experiencing financial difficulties can restructure under court protection. The purpose of the restructuring is to develop a Plan of Arrangement. A **Plan of Arrangement** allows the debtor company to survive, provides repayment to both the secured and unsecured creditors who have extended credit to the business, and may include payments to both preferred and common shareholders. For **secured creditors**, specific assets are pledged as collateral for the loan that was extended and, in liquidation, the creditors receive the proceeds from the sale of those assets. If the proceeds are insufficient to meet the loan, the secured creditors may become **unsecured creditors** for the unrecovered amount. These and all other unsecured creditors equally divide any funds remaining after all higher ranking claims have been satisfied.

Plan of Arrangement
A creditor- and court-approved plan that allows the debtor company to survive, provides repayment to both the secured and unsecured creditors who have extended credit to the business, and may include payments to both preferred and common shareholders.

secured creditors
Creditors who have specific assets pledged as collateral for the loan and in the liquidation of the failed firm receive proceeds from the sale of those assets.

unsecured creditors
Creditors who have a general claim against all of the firm's assets other than those specifically pledged as collateral.

Once the plan is developed, it must be presented to creditors who then vote on it. The secured and unsecured creditors vote separately. If a simple majority of creditors representing two-thirds of the dollar amount of debt vote to accept the plan, then it is implemented and the firm restructures. Once accepted by creditors and approved by the court, it is binding on all of the creditors. To ensure that the plan is approved, it is imperative for the debtor company to foster positive relationships with all classes of creditors by involving all in the CCAA process.

The plan should result in a "win/win" situation for both the company and the creditors. In the plan, the creditors are asked to give up the right to the money they are owed in exchange for an offer by the company to pay a stated number of cents on each dollar owed over time. The amount paid would range from $0.01 to $1. Secured creditors would receive the most per $1 owed, followed by unsecured creditors. If the preferred and common shareholders were included in the plan, they would receive the least. For example, if secured creditors received $0.76 per $1 owed, unsecured creditors may receive $0.22, preferred shareholders $0.07, and common shareholders $0.01. Sometimes the company may be able to repay all of what it owes, but it is granted a period of time, six months or a year, in which it makes no payments.

Hint
Some firms, particularly those in the airline industry, have used the provisions of the CCAA to modify lease and labour contracts on the basis that to force the firm to continue to meet the terms of the contracts would force the firm into bankruptcy.

In some cases, creditors agree to convert their debt into common shares. In others, creditors receive some shares and some cash. In others, it is all cash that is paid out over time. With a successful plan, the company wins because it survives. The creditors win because they retain a customer and also because they get some of their money, whereas in a bankruptcy they would likely receive very little. The shareholders win because the firm has the possibility of returning to profitability.

Bankruptcy and Insolvency Act (BIA)

Bankruptcy and Insolvency Act
A more recent and regulated solution to insolvency that clearly specifies the procedures and time line that must be followed by the debtor and creditors in a reorganization.

The ***Bankruptcy and Insolvency Act*** is a more recent and more regulated solution to insolvency. The BIA clearly specifies the procedures and a time line that must be followed by the debtor and creditors in a reorganization. The BIA regulations are much more restrictive than under the CCAA. The BIA is used by both individuals and businesses. Companies with less than $5 million of debt must use the BIA to deal with their insolvency. Companies with over $5 million of debt can use either the BIA or the CCAA. The objective of both acts is to have the company survive. To do this, a plan must be developed. Under the BIA, the plan is called a corporate proposal. Under the provisions of the BIA, corporate proposals afford a struggling organization protection from creditors and provide the breathing space needed to devise a plan of recovery. The process and deadlines for the BIA are clearly stated in the act. The following steps are required:

- File a notice of intention to file a corporate proposal
- File a cash flow statement
- File the corporate proposal
- Hold the meeting of creditors
- Apply to the court for approval

Filing a notice of intention to file a proposal has the following immediate advantages for a company under siege by its creditors:

- It stops all legal actions undertaken by creditors.
- It gives the company time to approach the creditors, explain the company's financial situation, and ask for their support.
- If a secured creditor has given notice to the company that they wish to seize an asset that is securing a loan, the filing prevents the secured creditor from taking the asset.

Within 5 days of the filing of the notice of intention, all creditors must be notified of the filing. Within 10 days, a cash flow statement must be filed, and within 30 days the proposal itself must be filed. If these procedures are not followed, then the company is considered to be bankrupt. The **proposal** is simply a suggested agreement between the company and the company's creditors regarding repayment of the company's debts. The company develops and distributes the proposal to the company's creditors, asking them to accept a compromise on the money they are owed in order to give the business an opportunity to survive.

proposal
A suggested agreement between the company and the company's creditors regarding repayment of the company's debts.

The proposal must include provisions to pay employee source deductions and outstanding wages immediately after court approval of the proposal. In the proposal, a schedule must be included showing the amount the creditors would receive in a bankruptcy compared with what they would receive under the proposal. The proposal creates a "do or die" situation, placing the fate of the company in the hands of the creditors.

The meeting of creditors is held approximately three weeks after the company files the proposal. At the meeting, the creditors vote on whether to accept or reject the proposal. Accordingly, when developing a proposal, the debtor must consider the interests of all creditors and how the proposal may affect the voting. As with the CCAA, a simple majority of each class of creditor representing two-thirds of the dollar amount of debt must vote to accept the proposal. The court will approve the proposal as long as it is clear that it would provide more money to the creditors than a bankruptcy would.

To establish the amount offered to the creditors, a company must consider what is the most it could afford to pay, over a reasonable time, while still making it worthwhile for the managers and owners to save the company. If the proposal is rejected, then the company will be immediately put into bankruptcy. The company will then be liquidated. If the terms of the proposal are not honoured, creditors may apply to the court for the proposal to be annulled and the company placed into bankruptcy.

The Incidence of Business Failure in Canada

The BIA is more restrictive than the CCAA in terms of the Court's discretion in deciding the terms of the corporate restructuring. As a result, most major restructurings proceed under the provisions of the CCAA. Table 18.12 shows the number of business bankruptcies and the number of proposals (Plans of Arrangement) filed in Canada over the period 1993 to 2005. Note that over the 13 years the number of bankruptcies declined by about 38 percent. The number of proposals, on the other hand, exploded. The number of proposals filed and approved by creditors and the courts increased by an average of 18.1 percent *per year*.

In addition, the total number of business bankruptcies and proposals has been very stable since 2001. This is likely due to the very good economic conditions that existed in Canada during this period. The latest statistics on business bankruptcies and proposals are available on the Web site of the Office of the Superintendent of Bankruptcy (OSB).

http://strategis.ic.gc.ca/epic/internet/inbsf-osb.nsf/en/h_br01011e.html

Table 18.13 provides detailed data regarding the bankruptcies and proposals that occurred in Canada in 2002 and 2005. In the table, note the deficiency, the difference between the assets and liabilities for both the bankruptcies and proposals. In 2005 for the total bankruptcies, liabilities exceeded assets by a factor of 3.72 to 1. In other words, for the bankruptcies reported in 2005, for every $1.00 of assets, the bankrupt firm had $3.72 of liabilities. In contrast, for the proposals, liabilities exceeded assets by a factor of "only" 2.01 to 1. In other words, for the proposals that were accepted in 2005, for every $1.00 of assets, the bankrupt firm had $2.01 of liabilities.

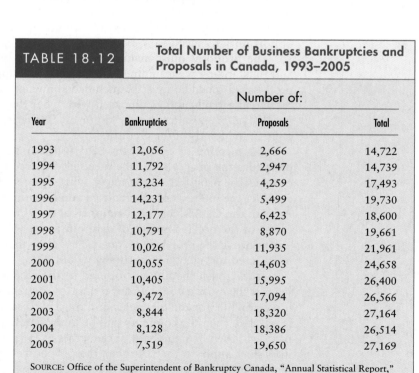

TABLE 18.12 Total Number of Business Bankruptcies and Proposals in Canada, 1993–2005

	Number of:		
Year	Bankruptcies	Proposals	Total
1993	12,056	2,666	14,722
1994	11,792	2,947	14,739
1995	13,234	4,259	17,493
1996	14,231	5,499	19,730
1997	12,177	6,423	18,600
1998	10,791	8,870	19,661
1999	10,026	11,935	21,961
2000	10,055	14,603	24,658
2001	10,405	15,995	26,400
2002	9,472	17,094	26,566
2003	8,844	18,320	27,164
2004	8,128	18,386	26,514
2005	7,519	19,650	27,169

SOURCE: Office of the Superintendent of Bankruptcy Canada, "Annual Statistical Report," available at **http://osb-bsf.gc.ca**.

TABLE 18.13 Detailed Data Regarding Business Bankruptcies Reported and Proposals Filed in Canada, 2002 and 2005

Total Business Bankruptcies Reported

	2002				2005			
Region	Number of bankruptcies	Total assets	Total liabilities	Total deficiency	Number of bankruptcies	Total assets	Total liabilities	Total deficiency
Atlantic	667	$ 66,414,188	$ 362,248,473	$ 295,834,285	577	$ 25,555,391	$ 106,780,306	$ 81,224,915
Quebec	2,221	224,548,726	689,880,260	465,331,534	1,711	178,290,168	815,746,084	637,455,916
Ontario	2,883	529,871,649	4,395,422,854	3,865,551,205	2,716	313,559,357	1,221,196,457	907,637,100
Saskatchewan/ Manitoba/Territories	597	71,287,621	361,022,981	289,735,360	535	60,300,925	143,048,575	82,747,649
Alberta	1,997	261,873,566	545,680,255	283,806,689	1,194	145,929,336	291,100,331	145,170,996
British Columbia	1,107	128,972,420	1,654,723,586	1,525,751,166	786	78,538,775	406,819,439	328,280,664
Total in Canada	9,472	$1,282,968,170	$8,008,978,409	$6,726,010,239	7,519	$802,173,952	$2,984,691,192	$2,182,517,240

Total Proposals Filed

	2002				2005			
Region	Number of proposals	Total assets	Total liabilities	Total deficiency	Number of bankruptcies	Total assets	Total liabilities	Total deficiency
Atlantic	591	$ 42,951,834	$ 98,113,638	$ 55,161,804	826	$ 31,086,633	$ 125,219,146	$ 94,132,513
Quebec	4,445	479,736,229	1,283,777,118	804,040,889	4,424	449,563,199	970,946,999	521,383,800
Ontario	7,987	707,870,598	1,031,586,529	323,715,931	9,962	802,447,722	1,626,565,372	824,117,650
Saskatchewan/ Manitoba/Territories	1,169	79,558,398	217,749,206	138,190,808	1,466	119,454,463	137,420,607	17,966,144
Alberta	1,512	148,345,560	190,071,184	41,725,624	1,551	138,216,653	199,771,558	61,554,905
British Columbia	1,390	235,350,403	406,484,859	171,134,456	1,421	131,044,667	301,358,895	170,314,229
Total in Canada	17,094	$1,693,813,022	$3,227,782,534	$1,533,969,512	19,650	$1,671,813,337	$3,361,282,578	$1,689,469,241

SOURCES: Office of the Superintendent of Bankruptcy Canada, annual statistical reports for the 2002 and 2005 calendar years, available at **http://osb-bsf.gc.ca.**

18.2 **IN PRACTICE**

Who Loses and Gains in a Bankruptcy?

On April 1, 2003, when Air Canada could not raise cash to pay debts that were due, it sought creditor protection under the *Companies' Creditors Arrangement Act* (CCAA). Under this act, Air Canada was given time to restructure in an effort to keep the company operating as a going concern.

Air Canada laid off thousands of employees and got salary concessions from the unions representing the remaining employees. Air Canada also fell in arrears in contributions to the employees' pension fund. Still, as is the case with Air Canada's President Robert Milton, senior executives are often promised multi-million-dollar payouts if they agree to stay on through the restructuring period. Robert Milton was promised $21 million in Air Canada shares if he stayed in the job for four years.

Under the CCAA protection, no interest would accumulate on any of the outstanding secured and unsecured debt. Companies that had borrowed to buy goods and services to resell to Air Canada could not get their goods back and would not be compensated for the interest costs they incurred. Creditors would have been due an estimated monthly $21,000,000 in interest charges if Air Canada had not been under CCAA protection.

Some of the creditors wanted to stop doing business with Air Canada, but were under court order to continue. For example, Global Payments was ordered by Mr. Justice J. Farley of the Superior Court of Justice of Ontario to continue providing the credit card processing services it provided to Air Canada, subject to the parties negotiating reasonable protection for its fees for providing such services.

For some, a company in crisis represents a potential opportunity. The firm's debt or equity can be bought at a discount and then, possibly, resold at a higher price when (and if) the company comes out of bankruptcy protection. Owning the distressed company's financial securities makes the investor a stakeholder and an influencer in the company's future.

Cerberus Capital Management LP, a U.S. investment management company, bought more than $100 million in Air Canada debt and then got a seat on the Unsecured Creditor's Committee. *The Globe and Mail* reported that Cerberus was building a position in Air Canada debt in an effort to acquire a controlling equity position in the company. By September 2003, Cerberus was one of two investors selected by Air Canada to enter into "detailed negotiations" for an equity investment. Air Canada estimated that unsecured bondholders, such as Cerberus, would receive 40 to 65 percent of the new equity, while existing shareholders would see their ownership position in the company severely diluted.

For some creditors, their main concern was ensuring that Air Canada survived so they could do business in the future. Cara Operations, a caterer for Air Canada, wrote down $15.4 million in May 2003, which covered the entire receivable balance it was owed by Air Canada. Cara continued to provide service to Air Canada, which did pay its bills on services provided after filing for creditor protection. "However, should Air Canada not be successful in its restructuring efforts as currently contemplated, [Cara] could be further exposed," a Cara spokesperson said to CBC.

SOURCES: **www.globeandmail.com/servlet/story/RTGAM.20031116.wbonus1116/BNStory/Business**, viewed December 11, 2003; **www.achorizons.ca/en/issues/2003/CCAA/Restructuring%20Bulletin/rest_9.htm**; **http://ctv2.theglobeandmail.com/servlet/story/LAC.20030802.RAIRC/business/Business/Business/&id=LAC_20030802_RAIRC**; **www.cbc.ca/storyview/CBC/2003/09/26/aircan260903**; **www.cbc.ca/storyview/CBC/2003/05/29/cara_030529**.

It seems that the difference between a firm being able to negotiate with its creditors and file an acceptable proposal and its being declared bankrupt is closely related to the firm's total deficiency. Logically, the larger the deficiency, the higher the probability that a firm will not be able to develop a proposal acceptable to creditors and the court. Also, the lower the deficiency, the more realistic it is that the debtor company could implement a proposal that would allow the company to survive.

? Review Questions

18–13 What are the three types of business failure? What is the difference between *technical insolvency* and *bankruptcy*? What is asset insolvency? What are the major causes of business failure?

18–14 Discuss the concept of voluntary insolvency.

18–15 In Canada, there are two federal statutes governing the reorganization and bankruptcy of companies. What is the overriding objective of both methods of dealing with the insolvency of a company? Given the statistics provided in Table 18.12, is the objective being realized? Discuss.

18–16 What is a Plan of Arrangement? What is a corporate proposal? How are they related? How are they different?

SUMMARY

LG1 **Understand the fundamentals of mergers and acquisitions including basic terminology, motives for merging, types of mergers, and leveraged buyouts (LBOs).** Mergers result from the combining of firms. Typically, the bidding company pursues merger with the target company, on either a friendly or a hostile basis. Mergers are undertaken either for strategic reasons to achieve economies of scale or for financial reasons to restructure the firm to improve its cash flow. The overriding goal of merging is maximization of owners' wealth (share price). Other specific merger motives include growth or diversification, synergy, fund raising, increased managerial skill or technology, tax considerations, increased ownership liquidity, and defence against takeover. The four basic types of mergers are horizontal (the merger of two firms in the same line of business); vertical (acquisition of a supplier or customer); congeneric (acquisition of a firm in the same general industry but neither in the same business nor a supplier or customer); and conglomerate (merger between unrelated businesses). Leveraged buyouts (LBOs) involve use of a large amount of debt to purchase a firm. LBOs are generally used to finance management buyouts.

Demonstrate the procedures used to analyze mergers, value the target company, calculate the synergy of the merger, and determine the merger's net present value. The first step in any M&A is for the bidding company to uncover a potential target. Once the bidding company isolates a target company, it must estimate the value of the target. To do this, valuation and capital budgeting concepts must be used. A bidding company should only acquire a target if the net present value (NPV) of the project from the bidder's point of view is greater than or equal to zero. If the target is worth more than the price the bidder will pay, then synergy is created. Synergy is the extra value created by combining the two firms. When it is created, the NPV of the acquisition is positive and it should proceed.

Discuss the methods a firm can use to pay for an acquisition, and illustrate the impact of using common shares as a method to pay for a merger. A bidding firm can pay for the acquisition in one of three ways: by paying cash, by exchanging the target company's common shares for common shares of the "new" merged company, or by a combination of the two: some cash, some shares. When an exchange of common shares is used, a ratio of exchange must be established to measure the amount paid per share of the target company relative to the per-share market price of the bidding firm. The resulting relationship between the price/earnings (P/E) ratio paid by the bidding firm and its initial P/E affects the merged firm's earnings per share (EPS) and market price. If the P/E paid is greater than the P/E of the acquiring company, the EPS of the acquiring company decreases and the EPS of the target company increases.

Describe the pooling and purchase methods of accounting for mergers and acquisitions and discuss the concept of goodwill. When a firm is acquired and merged, the transaction can be accounted for using the pooling or purchase methods. With the pooling method, the balance sheets of the two firms are simply added together (pooled). Under the purchase method, the bidding firm must determine the fair market value of each of the target firm's assets. These values are then reflected in the merged company's balance sheet. In Canada, the purchase method of accounting must be used. For the merged firm's income statement all sales and expenses are pooled; there is no choice. When the price paid for the target is greater than the net fair market value of the assets acquired, an intangible asset termed goodwill is created. Goodwill is charged against revenues on the income statement only when the value of goodwill on the balance sheet is more than its fair market value.

Discuss the merger negotiation process, the role of holding companies, and international mergers. Investment bankers are commonly hired by the bidder to find a suitable target company and assist in negotiations. A merger can be negotiated with the target firm's management and board or, in the case of a hostile merger, directly with the firm's shareholders by using tender offers. When the management of the target firm does not favour the merger, it can employ various takeover defences—a white knight, poison pills, greenmail, leveraged recapitalization, golden parachutes, and shark repellents. A holding company can be created by one firm gaining control of other companies, often by owning as little as 10 to 20 percent of their stock. The chief advantages of holding companies are the leverage effect, risk protection, tax benefits, protection against lawsuits, and the ease of gaining control of a subsidiary. Disadvantages include increased risk due to the magnification of losses, difficulty of analysis, and the high cost of administration. M&As are popular around the world due to the growing emphasis on creating shareholder value. Also, the internationalization of the capital markets has created more opportunities for firms to secure the funds necessary to finance acquisitions.

Understand the types and major causes of business failure and explain the two legislative acts governing reorganization and bankruptcy in Canada. A firm may fail because it has negative or low returns, because it is technically insolvent, or due to asset insolvency. The two forms of insolvency *can* lead to bankruptcy, which is a legal state resulting in proceedings that can lead to the reorganization of a company or its liquidation. In bankruptcy, some or all of a firm's assets are transferred to the firm's creditors. The major causes of business failure are mismanagement, downturns in economic activity, and corporate maturity. Voluntary settlements are initiated by the debtor and can result in sustaining or liquidating the firm. If a voluntary settlement for a failed firm cannot be agreed upon, the firm can use the provisions of one of the two legislative acts governing reorganization and bankruptcy in Canada. The purpose of both Acts is to avoid bankruptcy, if at all possible, and to allow an insolvent company to remain in business and avoid being liquidated. The *Companies' Creditors Arrangement Act* (CCAA) allows a company in financial difficulty to negotiate with its creditors and to develop a restructuring plan termed a Plan of Arrangement. This allows the debtor company to survive, and provides repayment to the company's secured and unsecured creditors.

The *Bankruptcy and Insolvency Act* (BIA) is a more recent and regulated solution to insolvency that clearly specifies the procedures and time line that must be followed by the debtor and creditors in a reorganization. The BIA must be used by companies with less than $5 million of debt, and may be used by other companies. Under the BIA, a company must develop a corporate proposal. The proposal is simply a suggested agreement between the company and the company's creditors regarding repayment of the company's debts. As with the CCAA, the proposal must be approved by both the company's creditors and the court.

SELF-TEST PROBLEMS

(Solutions in Appendix B)

ST 18–1 **Cash acquisition decision** Luxe Foods is contemplating acquisition of Valley Canning Company for a cash price of $180,000. Luxe currently has a very high debt load (high financial leverage) and thus high risk. As a result, the cost of both debt and equity financing for Luxe is quite high, resulting in a cost of capital of 14 percent. If Luxe acquires Valley Canning, the company's debt load will decline, thus reducing risk. Consequently, the firm's cost of capital will decline to 11 percent. The acquisition of Valley Canning is expected to increase Luxe's after-tax cash inflows by $20,000 per year for the first 3 years and by $30,000 per year for the following 12 years.

a. Determine whether the proposed cash acquisition is desirable. Explain your answer.

b. Now assume that Luxe Foods plans to finance the acquisition of Valley Canning using the same capital structure currently in use. The company's risk will remain the same. Would this alter your recommendation in **a**? Support your answer with a financial analysis.

ST 18–2 **Expected EPS—Merger decision** At the end of 2008, Lake Industries had 80,000 shares of common stock outstanding and had earnings available for common shareholders of $160,000. At the end of 2008, Butler Company had 10,000 common shares of common stock outstanding and had $20,000 of earnings available for common shareholders. Lake's earnings are expected to grow at an annual rate of 5 percent, and Butler's growth rate in earnings should be 10 percent per year.

a. Calculate earnings per share (EPS) for Lake Industries for the next 5 years from 2009 to 2013, assuming that there is no merger.

b. Calculate the next 5 years' earnings per share (EPS) for Lake if it acquires Butler using 1.1 of its common shares to acquire each Butler common share.

c. Compare your findings in **a** and **b**, and explain why the merger looks attractive when viewed over the long run.

PROBLEMS

INTERMEDIATE

18–1 **Tax effects of acquisition** Connors Shoe Company is contemplating the acquisition of Salinas Boots, a firm that has shown large operating tax losses over the past few years. As a result of the acquisition, Connors believes that the total pretax profits of the merger will not change from their present level for 15 years. The tax loss carryforward of Salinas is $800,000, and Connors projects annual earnings before taxes to be $280,000 per year for each of the next 15 years. The firm is in the 40 percent tax bracket.

a. If Connors does not make the acquisition, what are the company's tax liability and earnings after taxes each year over the next 15 years?
b. If the acquisition is made, what are the company's tax liability and earnings after taxes each year over the next 15 years?
c. If Salinas can be acquired for $350,000 in cash, should Connors make the acquisition, based on tax considerations? (Ignore present value.)

INTERMEDIATE

18–2 **Tax effects of acquisition** Trapani Tool Company is evaluating the acquisition of Sussman Casting. Sussman has a tax loss carryforward of $1.8 million. Trapani can purchase Sussman for $2.1 million. It can sell the assets for $1.6 million—their book value. Trapani expects earnings before taxes in the 5 years after the merger to be as shown in the following table. Trapani is in the 40 percent tax bracket.

Year	Earnings before taxes
1	$150,000
2	400,000
3	450,000
4	600,000
5	600,000

a. Calculate the firm's tax payments and earnings after taxes for each of the next 5 years *without* the merger.
b. Calculate the firm's tax payments and earnings after taxes for each of the next 5 years *with* the merger.
c. What are the total benefits associated with the tax losses from the merger? (Ignore present value.)
d. Discuss whether you would recommend the proposed merger. Support your decision with figures.

CHALLENGE

18–3 **Tax benefits and price** Hahn Textiles has a tax loss carryforward of $800,000. Two firms are interested in acquiring Hahn for the tax loss advantage. Reilly Investment Group has expected earnings before taxes of $200,000 per year for each of the next 7 years and a cost of capital of 15 percent. Webster Industries has expected earnings before taxes for the next 7 years as shown in the following table. Webster has a cost of capital of 15 percent. Both firms' tax rates are 40 percent.

Webster Industries	
Year	Earnings before taxes
1	$ 80,000
2	120,000
3	200,000
4	300,000
5	400,000
6	400,000
7	500,000

a. What is the tax advantage of the merger each year for Reilly?
b. What is the tax advantage of the merger each year for Webster?
c. What is the maximum cash price each interested firm would be willing to pay for Hahn Textiles?
d. Use your answers in **a** through **c** to explain why a target company can have different values to different potential acquiring firms.

CHALLENGE  18–4 **Asset acquisition decision** Zarin Printing Company is considering the acquisition of Freiman Press at a cash price of $60,000. Freiman Press has liabilities of $90,000. Freiman has a large press that Zarin needs; the remaining assets would be sold to net $65,000. As a result of acquiring the press, Zarin would experience an increase in after-tax cash inflow of $20,000 per year over the next 10 years. The firm has a 14 percent cost of capital.
a. What is the effective or net cost of the large press?
b. If this is the only way Zarin can obtain the large press, should the firm go ahead with the merger? Explain your answer.
c. If the firm could purchase a better-quality press at a price of $120,000 that would generate $26,000 annual after-tax cash inflow for 10 years, which alternative would you recommend? Explain your answer.

CHALLENGE  18–5 **Cash acquisition decision** Benson Oil is being considered for acquisition by Dodd Oil. The combination, Dodd believes, would increase its after-tax cash inflows by $25,000 for each of the next 5 years and $50,000 for each of the following 5 years. Benson has high financial leverage, and Dodd can expect its cost of capital to increase from 12 to 15 percent if the merger is undertaken. The cash price of Benson is $125,000.
a. Would you recommend the merger?
b. Would you recommend the merger if Dodd could use the $125,000 to purchase equipment returning after-tax cash inflows of $40,000 per year for each of the next 10 years?
c. If the cost of capital does not change with the merger, would your decision in **b** be different? Explain.

INTERMEDIATE  18–6 **Ratio of exchange and EPS** Marla's Cafe is attempting to acquire the Victory Club. Certain financial data on these corporations are summarized in the following table. Assume Marla's Cafe has sufficient authorized but unissued shares to carry out the proposed merger.

Item	Marla's Cafe	Victory Club
Earnings available for common shareholders	$20,000	$8,000
Number of common shares outstanding	20,000	4,000
Market price per share	$12	$24

a. If the ratio of exchange is 1.8, what will be the earnings per share (EPS) based on the original shares of each firm?
b. Repeat a if the ratio of exchange is 2.0.
c. Repeat a if the ratio of exchange is 2.2.
d. Discuss the principle illustrated by your answers to a through c.

CHALLENGE  18–7 **EPS and merger terms** Cleveland Corporation is interested in acquiring Lewis Tool Company by swapping 0.4 share of its common shares for each of Lewis' common shares. Certain financial data on these companies are given in the following table. Assume Cleveland has sufficient authorized but unissued shares to carry out the proposed merger.

Item	Cleveland Corporation	Lewis Tool
Earnings available for common shareholders	$200,000	$50,000
Number of common shares outstanding	50,000	20,000
Earnings per share (EPS)	$4.00	$2.50
Market price per share	$50.00	$15.00
Price/earnings (P/E) ratio	12.5	6

a. How many new common shares will Cleveland have to issue to make the proposed merger?
b. If the earnings for each firm remain unchanged, what will the postmerger earnings per share be?
c. How much, effectively, has been earned on behalf of each of the original shares of Lewis stock?
d. How much, effectively, has been earned on behalf of each of the original shares of Cleveland Corporation's stock?

BASIC  18–8 **Ratio of exchange** Calculate the ratio of exchange (1) of shares and (2) in market price for each of the cases shown in the following table. What does each ratio signify? Explain.

	Current market price per share		
Case	Acquiring company	Target company	Price per share offered
A	$50	$25	$ 30.00
B	80	80	100.00
C	40	60	70.00
D	50	10	12.50
E	25	20	25.00

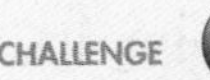

CHALLENGE LG3 **18–9 Expected EPS—Merger decision** Graham & Sons wishes to evaluate a proposed merger with RCN Group. Graham had earnings in 2004 of $200,000, has 100,000 common shares outstanding, and expects earnings to grow at an annual rate of 7 percent. RCN had earnings of $800,000 in 2004, has 200,000 common shares outstanding, and expects its earnings to grow at 3 percent per year.

a. Calculate the expected earnings per share (EPS) for Graham & Sons for each of the next 5 years *without* the merger.

b. What would Graham's common shareholders earn in each of the next 5 years on each of their Graham shares swapped for RCN shares at a ratio of (1) 0.6 and (2) 0.8 shares of RCN for one share of Graham?

c. Graph the premerger and postmerger EPS figures developed in **a** and **b** on a set of year (x axis)–EPS (y axis) axes.

d. If you were the financial manager for Graham & Sons, which would you recommend from **b**, (1) or (2)? Explain your answer.

CHALLENGE LG3 **18–10 EPS and postmerger price** Data for Henry Company and Mayer Services are given in the following table. Henry Company is considering merging with Mayer by swapping 1.25 of its common shares for each share of Mayer stock. Henry Company expects its common shares will trade at the same price/earnings (P/E) multiple after the merger as before merging.

Item	Henry Company	Mayer Services
Earnings available for common shareholders	$225,000	$50,000
Number of of common shares outstanding	90,000	15,000
Market price per share	$45	$50

a. Calculate the ratio of exchange in market price.

b. Calculate the earnings per share (EPS) and price/earnings (P/E) ratio for each company.

c. Calculate the price/earnings (P/E) ratio used to purchase Mayer Services.

d. Calculate the postmerger earnings per share (EPS) for Henry Company.

e. Calculate the expected market price per share of the merged firm. Discuss this result in light of your findings in **a.**

CHALLENGE LG5 **18–11 Holding company** Scully Corporation holds common shares in company A and company B. Simplified balance sheets for the companies are presented in the table that follows.

a. What percentage of the total assets controlled by Scully Corporation does its common equity represent?

b. If another company owns 15 percent of Scully Corporation's common shares and, by virtue of this fact, has voting control, what percentage of the total assets controlled does the outside company's equity represent?

c. How does a holding company effectively provide a great deal of control for a small dollar investment?

d. Answer **a** and **b** in light of the following additional facts.

(1) Company A's fixed assets consist of $20,000 of common shares in company C. This provides voting control.
(2) Company C, which has total assets of $400,000, has voting control of company D, which has $50,000 of total assets.
(3) Company B's fixed assets consist of $60,000 of common shares in both company E and company F. In both cases, this gives it voting control. Companies E and F have total assets of $300,000 and $400,000, respectively.

Assets		Liabilities and stockholders' equity	
Scully Corporation			
Holdings of common shares		Long-term debt	$ 40,000
Company A	$ 40,000	Preferred equity	25,000
Company B	60,000	Common equity	35,000
Total	$100,000	Total	$100,000
Company A			
Current assets	$100,000	Current liabilities	$100,000
Fixed assets	400,000	Long-term debt	200,000
Total	$500,000	Common equity	200,000
		Total	$500,000
Company B			
Current assets	$180,000	Current liabilities	$100,000
Fixed assets	720,000	Long-term debt	500,000
Total	$900,000	Common equity	300,000
		Total	$900,000

INTERMEDIATE  18–12 **Accounting for mergers** Assume that companies A and B from the previous problem are completely independent. Company B has made an offer to acquire company A. The two companies will then merge. The premerger balance sheets for the two companies are provided in the previous problem. Company B's offer of $450,000 to acquire company A has been accepted. The market value of company A's current assets is $80,000. The market value of the fixed assets is $550,000. The fixed assets include land that has increased in value. Using the purchase method of accounting, develop the postmerger balance sheet for the merged firm. Is goodwill created? Why or why not?

INTERMEDIATE  18–13 **Purchase method of accounting for a merger** Easy Rise has decided to expand its operation through the purchase of Best Bagels. Easy Rise has made an offer of $1,100,000, which the company will finance through a combination of $400,000 cash and a new loan of $700,000. The board is concerned about the high level of accounts receivable for each company. Reg Doe has evaluated Best Bagel's balance sheet and concludes some items have to be restated to reflect their fair market value as follows:

Accounts receivable	$ 400,000
Net fixed assets	$1,000,000

Easy Rise Manufacturing
Balance Sheet (day prior to merger)

Assets	
Cash	$ 700,000
Accounts receivable	800,000
Inventory	100,000
Total current assets	1,600,000
Net fixed assets	3,000,000
Total assets	$4,600,000
Liabilities and shareholders' equity	
Accounts payable	$ 200,000
Line of credit	300,000
Total current liabilities	500,000
Long-term debt	700,000
Common shares	300,000
Retained earnings	3,100,000
Total liabilities and shareholders' equity	$4,600,000

Best Bagels
Balance Sheet (day prior to acquisition)

Assets	
Cash	$ 105,000
Accounts receivable	500,000
Inventory	50,000
Total current assets	$ 655,000
Net fixed assets	1,300,000
Total assets	$1,955,000
Liabilities and shareholders' equity	
Accounts payable	$ 200,000
Line of credit	400,000
Total current liabilities	600,000
Long-term debt	297,000
Common shares	125,000
Retained earnings	933,000
Total liabilities and shareholders' equity	$1,955,000

a. What is the value of goodwill after the merger?

b. Develop a postmerger balance sheet for Easy Rise. What are the total assets for the merged company?

CHALLENGE  **18–14 Reviewing goodwill for impairment** InfoWorld bought three emerging high-tech companies in 2006, adding $5,000,000 in goodwill to its balance sheet. The goodwill was attributed as follows:

Softcore	$3,000,000
Celltech	$1,200,000
Omnikey	800,000

The market for Softcore collapsed in 2007 as a competitor went to market with a better product at a lower price. There is little hope that InfoWorld will be able to generate sales from Softcore for the foreseeable future. The Celltech product line was performing as expected. Sales in the Omnikey product line were 15 percent below forecast sales.

Infoworld had a tax rate of 40 percent and a net income after tax of $2,000,000 in 2007 or earnings per share of $1. However, the firm's auditor would not state the financial statements met Generally Accepted Accounting Principles until the income statement was revised to reflect a review of goodwill for impairment.

a. What is meant by a review of goodwill for impairment and why did the auditor insist on changes?
b. Evaluate each of the acquisitions for impairment of goodwill.
c. Recalculate InfoWorld's net income after tax to reflect your review of goodwill for impairment. Justify your decisions. What will be the revised earnings per share?

INTERMEDIATE  **18–15 Bankruptcy protection** One morning, Robin Serge, Chief Financial Officer of Food Service Inc., was shocked to hear that two of its major customers might be declaring bankruptcy. Company A owes FSI $500,000, and Robin has been told the company owes a total of $10,000,000. Company A has pledged equipment as collateral for its debt to FSI. Company B owes FSI $400,000, all of which is unsecured debt. Company B owes creditors a total of $3,000,000.

a. Can company A and company B seek protection from bankruptcy from
(i) the *Companies' Creditors Arrangement Act* (CCAA)?
(ii) the *Bankruptcy and Insolvency Act*?
(iii) a voluntary settlement?
b. Is FSI guaranteed to receive the secured $500,000 loan? Can it receive any of its unsecured loan to company B?
c. What role, if any, can FSI play in protection under the *Companies' Creditors Arrangement Act* (CCAA) or the *Bankruptcy and Insolvency Act*?

CASE CHAPTER 18 Deciding Whether to Acquire or Liquidate Procras Corporation

See the enclosed Student CD-ROM for cases that help you put theories and concepts from the text into practice.

Be sure to visit the Companion Website for this book at **www.pearsoned.ca/gitman** for a wealth of additional learning tools including self-test quizzes, Web exercises, and additional cases.

CHAPTER 19

International Corporate Finance

LEARNING GOALS

- LG1 Understand the major factors influencing the financial operations of multinational companies (MNCs).
- LG2 Describe the key differences between purely domestic and international financial statements: the consolidation of financial statements and the translation of individual accounts.
- LG3 Discuss exchange rate risk and political risk, and explain how MNCs manage them.
- LG4 Describe foreign direct investment, investment cash flows and decisions, the factors that influence MNCs' capital structure, and the international debt and equity instruments that are available to MNCs.
- LG5 Explain the use of the Eurocurrency market in short-term borrowing and investing (lending) and the basics of cash, credit, and inventory management in international operations.
- LG6 Discuss the growth of and special factors relating to international mergers and joint ventures.

19.1 The Multinational Company and Its Environment

multinational companies (MNCs)
Firms that have international assets and operations in foreign markets and draw part of their total revenue and profits from such markets.

In recent years, as world markets have become significantly more interdependent, international finance has become an increasingly important element in the management of **multinational companies (MNCs).** These firms, which might be based anywhere in the world, have international assets and operations in foreign markets and draw part of their total revenue and profits from such markets. The principles of managerial finance presented in this text are applicable to the man-

"Goodbye—Let Us Know When You Get There"

In the year 1271, at the age of 17, Marco Polo left Venice, Italy. Travelling by ship across the Mediterranean and then by camel across Asia, he reached Cathay—China—more than three years later. Able to speak four languages and having much knowledge of the world from his travels, Polo was warmly received. It was an incredible journey of discovery and it resulted in the opening of trading lanes to the vast, exotic countries of Asia. By the time he returned home 24 years later, Polo had logged about 24,000 kilometres. Today, it is not uncommon for businesspeople to travel that distance in a little over a day. Modern transportation and communication systems have been like steroids (without the risks) in promoting the growth of global business opportunities. This chapter will demonstrate how the principles of corporate finance presented in this book can be applied in the international setting.

Hint

One of the reasons that firms have operations in foreign markets is the portfolio concept that was discussed in Chapter 7. Just as it is not wise for the individual investor to put all of his or her investment into the common shares of one firm, it is not wise for a firm to invest in only one market. By having operations in many markets, firms can smooth out some of the cyclical changes that occur in each market.

agement of MNCs. However, certain factors unique to the international setting tend to complicate the financial management of multinational companies. A simple comparison between a domestic Canadian firm (firm A) and a Canadian-based MNC (firm B), as illustrated in Table 19.1, indicates the influence of some of the international factors on MNCs' operations.

In the present international environment, multinationals face a variety of laws and restrictions when operating in different countries. The legal and economic complexities existing in this environment are significantly different from those a domestic firm would face. Here we take a brief look at the newly emerg-

LINKING THE DISCIPLINES: Cross-Functional Interactions

- ***Accounting personnel*** need to understand the tax rules for multinational companies, how to prepare consolidated financial statements for subsidiary companies, and how to account for international items in financial statements.
- ***Information systems analysts*** for firms that undertake foreign operations will need to design systems that track investments and operations in other currencies and their fluctuations against the domestic currency.
- ***Management*** need to understand both the risks and opportunities involved in international operations, the possible role of international financial markets in raising capital, and the basic hedging strategies that multinational companies can use to protect themselves against exchange rate risk.
- The ***marketing department*** need to understand the potential for expanding into international markets and the ways of doing so and how products and services may need to be altered to meet the needs of customers in other countries.
- Personnel in the ***operations department*** need to understand the benefits and costs of moving operations offshore and/or buying equipment, parts, and inventory in foreign markets.

ing trading blocs in North America, western Europe, South America, and throughout the Americas; GAAT; legal forms of business organization; taxation of MNCs; and financial markets.

Free Trade Areas and Trading Blocs

The development of trading blocs results in economic growth for all countries involved. Trade leads to job creation, combats poverty, and strengthens

TABLE 19.1 International Factors and Their Influence on MNCs' Operations

Factor	Firm A (domestic)	Firm B (MNC)
Foreign ownership	All assets owned by domestic entities	Portions of equity of foreign investments owned by foreign partners, thus affecting foreign decision making and profits
Multinational capital markets	All debt and equity structures based on the domestic capital market	Opportunities and challenges arise from the existence of different capital markets where debt and equity can be issued
Multinational accounting	All consolidation of financial statements based on one currency	The existence of different currencies and of specific translation rules influences the consolidation of financial statements into one currency
Foreign exchange risks	All operations in one currency	Fluctuations in foreign exchange markets can affect foreign revenues and profits as well as the overall value of the firm

economies. With closed borders, every country suffers; this lesson was learned in the Great Depression of the 1930s. Trade is important, not only for wealthy countries like Canada, but also for poorer countries including many in Central and South America, as well as Africa and Asia. The countries that often benefit the most from free trade are poorer countries as their goods can enter richer countries' markets tariff-free. As such, they often have a price advantage over the products produced in the home country.

During the 1990s and into the 21st century, an important feature of trade in the world has been the emergence of regional free trade agreements. According to the World Trade Organization, in 2006 there are more than 250 regional free trade agreements in force in the world. A list of these is available from the WTO. This is a sharp departure from the multilateral trade discussion talks, as represented by the Doha Round of discussions, that began in 1999. The purpose of the Doha Round was to lower trade barriers around the world to permit free trade between countries. As of early 2007, the talks were still stalled over a divide between the European Union, the United States, and the major developing countries.

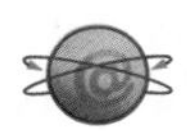

www.wto.org/english/tratop_e/region_e/region_e.htm

This protracted series of talks has led to the surge in regional free trade agreements. These regional trade agreements have become so widespread that all but one WTO member, Mongolia, are now part of one or more of them. It is estimated that more than half of world trade is now conducted under regional trade agreements. Two of the better examples of these regional free trade agreements are those centred in the Americas and western Europe. In 1988, Canada and the United States negotiated essentially unrestricted trade between their countries. This free trade zone was extended to include Mexico in late 1992, when the **North American Free Trade Agreement (NAFTA)** was signed by the prime minister of Canada and the presidents of the United States and Mexico. The agreement will soon include Chile, and may eventually include all countries in the Americas. This will be discussed in more detail later in this section.

North American Free Trade Agreement (NAFTA)
The treaty establishing free trade and open markets among Canada, Mexico, and the United States.

NAFTA simply mirrors underlying economic reality. The United States is Canada's largest trading partner, and vice versa, while Mexico is the United States' third largest trading partner (after Japan). The volume of trade among the three countries is huge. For example, in 2006, Canada's two-way trade in goods and services (imports and exports) was over $1 trillion, or about $2.8 billion *per day*. Of this, about 68 percent of Canada's imports come from the United States, while about 85 percent of Canada's exports go to the U.S. Two-way trade with the United States amounted to about $2.2 billion *per day*, or about 78 percent of Canada's total trade in goods and services. Canada's daily trade with all other countries in the world totals about $600 million per day. Exports of goods and services account for 41 percent of Canada's gross domestic product (GDP).

In 2005, Canada's trade surplus (the excess of exports over imports) was $52 billion, the fourth-highest level ever recorded. The decline from the record level of $64 billion in 2001 was due to the increasing value of the Canadian dollar between 2002 and 2006. Based on these statistics, it is obvious that trade is vital for Canada, the economy, and the workforce. Canada has an obvious interest in ensuring current free trade agreements work and in negotiating additional agreements with other countries throughout the world.

European Union (EU)
A significant economic force currently made up of 25 nations that permit free trade within the union.

The second major free trade zone that exists in the world is in Europe. The **European Union,** or **EU,** has been in existence since 1956. It has a current membership of 25 nations. With a total population estimated at more than 460 million (compared to the population of Canada and the United States of about 340 million) and an overall gross domestic product that is similar to that of the United States, the EU is a significant global economic force. Via a series of major economic, monetary, financial, and legal provisions set forth by the member countries during the 1980s, the countries of western Europe opened a new era of free trade within the union when intraregional tariff barriers fell at the end of 1992. This transformation is commonly called the **European Open Market.**

European Open Market
The transformation of the European Union into a single market at year-end 1992.

Although the EU has managed to reach agreement on most of these provisions, debates continue on certain other aspects (some key), including those related to automobile production and imports, monetary union, taxes, and workers' rights. As a result of the Maastricht Treaty of 1991, 11 of the 15 EU nations (at the time) adopted a single currency, the **Euro,** as a continent-wide medium of exchange beginning January 1, 1999. Beginning January 1, 2002, 12 of the 15 EU nations switched to a single set of Euro bills and coins, causing the national currencies of all 12 countries participating in **monetary union** to suddenly disappear.

Euro
A single currency adopted on January 1, 1999, by 12 of the 15 EU nations, who switched to a single set of Euro bills and coins on January 1, 2002.

monetary union
The official melding of the national currencies of the EU nations into one currency, the *Euro*, on January 1, 2002.

At the same time that the European Union implemented monetary union (which also involved creating a new European Central Bank), the EU had to deal with a wave of new applicants from eastern Europe and the Mediterranean region. The rapidly emerging new community of Europe offers both challenges and opportunities to a variety of players, including multinational firms. Canadian MNCs today face heightened levels of competition when operating inside the EU. As more of the existing restrictions and regulations are eliminated, huge European MNCs will be created that will be fierce competitors for Canadian (and American) multinationals.

The third major trading bloc that arose during the 1990s is the **Mercosur Group** of countries in South America. Beginning in 1991, the nations of Brazil, Argentina, Paraguay, and Uruguay began removing tariffs and other barriers to intraregional trade. The second stage of Mercosur's development began at the end of 1994, and involved the development of a customs union to impose a common tariff on external trade while enforcing uniform and lower tariffs on intragroup trade. The Mercosur countries represent well over half of total Latin America GDP and, to date, the agreement has been even more successful than its founders had imagined.

Mercosur Group
A major South American trading bloc that includes countries that account for more than half of total Latin American GDP.

While NAFTA and the Mercosur agreement will continue, given the huge volume of trade involved, their long-term fate may depend on negotiations that began in 2001 in Quebec City concerning an Americas-wide free trade agreement. The Quebec meeting was followed, in late 2002, by a meeting in Ecuador attended by representatives from 34 countries in the Americas (North, Central, and South America).

The purpose of the Ecuador meeting was to outline a time frame to establish the **Free Trade Area of the Americas (FTAA).** This trading bloc would be an extension of the NAFTA and of the Mercosur Group and would create a free trade area from the Arctic to Cape Horn, the tip of South America. First, though, issues from tariffs on imports to subsidies to business had to be discussed to ensure open borders and a free flow of goods and services between member countries. As of early 2007, negotiations to create this mammoth free trade zone are ongoing. For an update, see the FTAA Web site.

Free Trade Area of the Americas
A trading bloc that would extend the NAFTA and the Mercosur Group to create a free trade zone from the Arctic to Cape Horn.

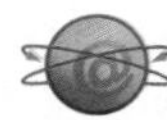

www.ftaa-alca.org/alca_e.asp

Obviously, the outcome of these negotiations, as well as the reality of the current free trade zones in place around the world, loom large in the plans of any MNC that wishes to access the markets in these areas. Canadian MNCs can benefit from the formation of free trade zones, but only if they are prepared. They must offer a desirable mix of products to a collection of varied consumers and be ready to take advantage of a variety of currencies as well as financial markets and instruments (such as the Euroequities discussed later in this chapter). They must staff their operations with the appropriate combination of local and foreign personnel and, when necessary, enter into joint ventures and strategic alliances.

General Agreement on Tariffs and Trade (GATT)

Although it may seem that the world is splitting into a handful of trading blocs, this is less of a danger than it may appear to be, because many international treaties are in force that guarantee relatively open access to at least the largest economies. The most important such treaty is the **General Agreement on Tariffs and Trade (GATT).** Canada is a signatory to the most recent version of this treaty, which has governed world trade throughout most of the postwar era. The current agreement extends free trading rules to broad areas of economic activity—such as agriculture, financial services, and intellectual property rights—that had not previously been covered by international treaty and were thus effectively off limits to foreign competition.

General Agreement on Tariffs and Trade (GATT)
A treaty that has governed world trade throughout most of the postwar era; it extends free trading rules to broad areas of economic activity and is policed by the *World Trade Organization (WTO).*

World Trade Organization (WTO)
International body that polices world trading practices and mediates disputes between member countries.

The 1994 GATT treaty also established a new international body, the **World Trade Organization (WTO)**, to police world trading practices and to mediate disputes between member countries. The WTO began operating in January 1995 and seems to be functioning effectively. In December 2001, the final important nation—the People's Republic of China—was, after years of controversy, granted membership. Now that China's status is resolved, there is an improved chance for stability in world trading patterns, in spite of the stunning collapse of several East Asian economies that began in July 1997. With its recent admittance to the WTO, the long-term economic prognosis for China and the formerly dynamic East Asian markets is much improved.

Legal Forms of Business Organization

foreign subsidiary
An incorporated business established by an MNC that is completely separate from the parent.

branch
A business run by an MNC that is operated directly within a foreign country without incorporating; it is not separate from the parent, but part of the same entity.

foreign affiliate
A foreign corporation in which the MNC owns at least 10 percent of the common shares.

joint venture
A partnership under which the participants have contractually agreed to contribute specified amounts of money and expertise in exchange for stated proportions of ownership and profit.

An MNC can set up a number of different types of operations in a foreign country. First, if an MNC incorporates a business in a foreign country, it is termed a foreign subsidiary. This **foreign subsidiary** is a legal entity that is completely separate from the parent. Second, if an MNC operates directly within a foreign country without incorporating, the foreign operation is a branch. A **branch** is not separate from the parent; it is part of the same entity. Third, an MNC can establish an operation that is partly owned by the MNC. This could be a foreign affiliate, partnership, or joint venture. A **foreign affiliate** is a foreign corporation in which the MNC owns *at least* 10 percent of the common shares. So, note—*a foreign subsidiary is a foreign affiliate.*

To operate in many foreign countries, it is often essential to enter into joint-venture business agreements with private investors or with government-based agencies of the host country. A **joint venture** is a partnership under which the participants have contractually agreed to contribute specified amounts of money and expertise in exchange for stated proportions of ownership and profit. Joint ventures are common in most of the less developed nations.

The governments of numerous countries, such as Brazil, Colombia, Mexico, and Venezuela in Latin America as well as Indonesia, Malaysia, the Philippines, and Thailand in East Asia, have in recent years instituted new laws and regulations governing MNCs. The basic rule introduced by most of these nations requires that the majority ownership of MNCs' joint-venture projects be held by domestically based investors. In other regions of the world, MNCs will face new challenges and opportunities, particularly in terms of ownership requirements and mergers.

The existence of joint-venture laws and restrictions has implications for the operation of foreign-based subsidiaries. First, majority foreign ownership may result in a substantial degree of management and control by host country participants; this in turn can influence day-to-day operations to the detriment of the managerial policies and procedures that are normally pursued by MNCs. Second, foreign ownership may result in disagreements among the partners as to the exact distribution of profits and the portion to be allocated for reinvestment. Third, operating in foreign countries, especially on a joint-venture basis, can involve problems regarding the remittance of profits. In the past, the governments of Argentina, Brazil, Nigeria, Malaysia, and Thailand, among others, have imposed ceilings not only on the repatriation (return) of capital by MNCs, but also on profit remittances by these firms back to the parent companies. These governments usually cite the shortage of foreign exchange as the motivating factor. Fourth, from a "positive" point of view, it can be argued that MNCs operating in many of the less developed countries benefit from joint-venture agreements, given the potential risks stemming from political instability in the host countries. This issue will be addressed in detail in subsequent discussions.

Taxes

Multinational companies, unlike domestic firms, have financial obligations in foreign countries. One of their basic responsibilities is international taxation—a complex issue because national governments follow a variety of tax policies. The following is a simplified discussion of a *very* complex issue. The very detailed particulars of international corporate taxation are well beyond the scope of this book. Interested readers should consult an international taxation book or the relevant publications provided by chartered accounting firms. In general, from the point of view of a Canadian-based MNC, two major factors must be considered concerning taxation issues.

Taxable Income and Tax Rules[1]

To determine the total taxes to be paid by an MNC, the level of taxable income must be calculated. This can be a complex task. In determining taxable income, it is important to note that every corporation is a resident of at least one country. Most developed countries tax their residents on their worldwide income and tax non-residents on the income earned within the country. Therefore, an MNC

---

1. We thank Don Wagner of the School of Business at the University of Prince Edward Island for providing us with many of the details in this section.

based in Canada with a foreign operation may find itself subject to tax *on the same income* both in Canada and in the country where the foreign operation is located. When the same income is taxed twice it is called **double taxation.**

double taxation
A situation wherein the same income is taxed in two separate countries; to reduce double taxation, many countries have negotiated tax treaties that override domestic law.

In order to reduce double taxation, many countries have negotiated tax treaties that override domestic law. These treaties place limitations on one country's right to tax residents of the other country. One important limitation is that a company doing business in another country is not subject to tax in that other country unless the company has a *permanent establishment* in that country. Thus, a company can export into a particular country without being subject to income taxes in that country, provided the company does not set up an office or fixed place of business in the country.

In addition to taxing business income, most countries impose withholding taxes on certain types of payments out of the country. Payments subject to withholding taxes include dividends, interest, royalties, and management fees. The tax rate that applies depends on the country involved, but tends to be in the 5 to 15 percent range. Since tax treaties normally do not eliminate withholding taxes altogether, double taxation can still occur.

Consider that the income earned by a foreign operation is first taxed as business income. If interest or dividends are then paid to the parent MNC, a withholding tax may apply. In the MNC's home country, the total payment made by the foreign operation is deemed to be income and may be subject to tax. In essence, the foreign subsidiary's earnings may end up being taxed *three times*. To alleviate this burden of excess taxation, most countries offer foreign tax credits. These allow MNCs credit for the taxes paid on income earned in foreign countries and then repatriated to the MNC's home country. Foreign tax credits reduce or eliminate double (or triple) taxation.

The rules, however, are different for dividends received from *foreign affiliates* (foreign corporations in which the MNC owns at least 10 percent of the common shares). Income from an *active business* earned by a foreign affiliate in a *treaty country* (a country with which Canada has a tax treaty) is *exempt* from Canadian tax.

Example ▼ Conor Controls is a Canada-based MNC that manufactures heavy machinery. The company has a foreign subsidiary that was financed with equity, in a country with which Canada has a tax treaty. The subsidiary has earnings of $100,000 before local taxes. This is deemed to be active business income. All of the after-tax funds can be paid to the parent as dividends. The applicable taxes consist of a 35 percent foreign income tax rate, and dividend withholding tax of 10 percent.

Subsidiary income before local taxes	$100,000
Foreign income tax at 35%	− 35,000
Dividend declared	$ 65,000
Foreign dividend withholding tax at 10%	− 6,500
Cash dividend payment received by Conor Controls	$ 58,500

While the foreign country has taxed the income and the dividend payment (using a withholding tax), in Canada the dividend income is totally tax exempt. This is the case since the dividend meets the criteria for tax exemption in Canada. The foreign company is an affiliate, operating in a treaty country, and the income was earned by an active business. The total tax burden on Conor Controls' foreign subsidiary would be 35 percent, *if the earnings were not repa-*

triated. Earnings that are repatriated as dividends are subject to a total tax burden of 41.5 percent [35% business income tax + (65% dividend × 10% dividend withholding tax)].

In the above example, it was assumed that the MNC financed the foreign operation with common equity and was the owner of all or a portion (at least 10%) of the operation. It is also possible for the MNC to finance the foreign operation with debt. This often occurs with joint ventures. When debt financing is used, interest payments may make it possible to reduce the foreign operation's taxable income to zero. When the interest payment is made by the foreign operation to the parent, a withholding tax may apply. The parent company must then declare the interest payment as income in Canada, taxes calculated, and the withholding tax claimed as a tax credit. The following example illustrates these concepts.

Example Assume Conor Controls' foreign operation was financed with debt rather than equity. The operation's earnings before interest and taxes (EBIT) are $100,000. The foreign operation owes Conor Controls $100,000 of interest. A 10 percent withholding tax applies to interest payments and the Canadian tax rate is 34 percent. The total situation is shown below:

Foreign operations EBIT	$100,000
Interest payment to Conor Controls	$100,000
Taxable income	$ 0
Foreign income tax	$ 0
Withholding tax on interest payment at 10%	$ 10,000
Conor Controls' deemed interest income	$100,000
Canadian taxes at 34%	$ 34,000
Less: Foreign tax credit	$ 10,000
Canadian taxes due	$ 24,000
Total taxes paid	$ 34,000

The effective tax rate on the $100,000 of income earned by Conor Controls' foreign operation is 34 percent, the same rate as if Conor Controls earned the income in Canada. This is a lower tax rate than would be applied if the foreign operation had paid a dividend to Conor Controls.

As is clear from the above discussion and examples, the decision of whether to finance a foreign operation using debt or equity financing is based on the tax rates in the country where the foreign operation is based and in the home country. In countries with very low tax rates, MNCs are more likely to finance a foreign operation with equity since more income will be available for payment as a dividend, which is then exempt from tax (assuming the income is from an active business and it is earned in a treaty country). In countries with high tax rates, debt will likely be the preferred financing method.

The preceding examples clearly demonstrate that the existence of bilateral tax treaties and the subsequent application of tax rules can significantly enhance the overall net funds available to MNCs from their worldwide earnings. Consequently, in an increasingly complex and competitive international financial environment, international taxation is one of the variables that multinational corporations should fully utilize to their advantage.

When an MNC needs a tax rate to make business decisions for the foreign operation, the rate to be used depends on how and whether the MNC repatriates income to the home country. If the MNC finances with debt and pays foreign income as interest in the year it is generated, the home country tax rate will likely apply. For Conor Controls, this rate would be 34 percent. If the MNC finances with equity and pays foreign income as dividends in the year it is generated, then the tax rate used is based on both the income tax and withholding tax. For Conor Controls, this rate would be 41.5 percent. If dividends will not be paid for a long time, the 35 percent tax rate would be the appropriate rate to use.

Financial Markets

Euromarket
The international financial market that provides for borrowing and lending currencies outside their country of origin.

During the last two decades the **Euromarket**—which provides for borrowing and lending currencies outside their country of origin—has grown rapidly. The Euromarket provides multinational companies with an "external" opportunity to borrow or lend funds, with the additional feature of less government regulation.

Growth of the Euromarket

The Euromarket has grown so large for several reasons. First, beginning in the early 1960s, the Russians wanted to maintain their dollar earnings outside the legal jurisdiction of the United States, mainly because of the Cold War. Second, the consistently large U.S. balance-of-payments deficits helped to "scatter" dollars around the world. Third, the existence of specific regulations and controls on dollar deposits in the United States, including interest rate ceilings imposed by the government, helped to send such deposits to places outside the United States.

These and other factors have combined and contributed to the creation of an "external" capital market. Its size cannot be accurately determined, mainly because of its lack of regulation and control. Several sources that periodically estimate its size are the Bank for International Settlements (BIS), Morgan Guaranty Trust, the World Bank, and the Organisation for Economic Co-operation and Development (OECD). Today the overall size of the Euromarket is well above $4.0 trillion *net* international lending.

offshore centres
Certain cities or states (including London, Singapore, Bahrain, Nassau, Hong Kong, and Luxembourg) that have achieved prominence as major centres for Euromarket business.

One aspect of the Euromarket is the so-called **offshore centres.** Certain cities or states around the world—including London, Singapore, Bahrain, Nassau, Hong Kong, and Luxembourg—are considered major offshore centres for Euromarket business. The availability of communication and transportation facilities, along with the importance of language, costs, time zones, taxes, and local banking regulations, are among the main reasons for the prominence of these centres.

In recent years, a variety of new financial instruments has appeared in the international financial markets. One is interest rate and currency swaps. Another is various combinations of forward and options contracts on different currencies. A third is new types of bonds and notes—along with an international version of commercial paper—with flexible characteristics in terms of currency, maturity, and interest rate. More details will be provided in subsequent discussions.

Major Participants

The Euromarket is still dominated by the U.S. dollar. However, activities in other major currencies, including the Swiss franc, Japanese yen, British pound sterling, Canadian dollar, and (increasingly) the Euro, have in recent years grown much faster than those denominated in the U.S. currency. Similarly, although U.S. financial institutions continue to play a significant role in the global markets, financial giants from Japan and Europe have become major participants in Euromarkets. Canadian financial institutions would be considered minor players.

Following the oil price increases by the Organization of the Petroleum Exporting Countries (OPEC) in 1973–1974 and 1979–1980, massive amounts of dollars were placed in various Euromarket financial centres. International banks, in turn, began lending to different groups of borrowers. At the end of 1994, for example, a group of Latin American countries had total borrowings outstanding of about $437 billion. Also, many of the top corporations in the "Tiger economies" of East Asia had huge amounts of foreign currency-denominated bank debt outstanding when these countries slid into financial crisis in the summer of 1997.

Although developing countries have become a major borrowing group in recent years, the industrialized nations also continue to borrow actively in international markets. Included in the latter group's borrowings are the funds obtained by multinational companies. The multinationals use the Euromarket to raise additional funds as well as to invest excess cash. Both Eurocurrency and Eurobond markets are extensively used by MNCs.

? Review Questions

19–1 What are the three important international trading blocs? What is the European Union and what is its single new unit of currency? What potential trading bloc is emerging? What is GATT?

19–2 What is a *joint venture*? Why is it often essential to use this arrangement? What effect do joint-venture laws and restrictions have on the operation of foreign-based subsidiaries?

19–3 From the point of view of a Canadian-based MNC, what key tax factors need to be considered?

19–4 Discuss the major reasons for the growth of the Euromarket. What is an *offshore centre*? Name the major participants in the Euromarket.

19.2 Financial Statements

Several features differentiate internationally based reports from domestically oriented financial statements. Among these are the issues of consolidation and translation of individual accounts.

Consolidation

At the present time, Canadian accounting rules require the consolidation of financial statements of subsidiaries according to the percentage of ownership by the parent company. Table 19.2 illustrates this point. As indicated, the regula-

TABLE 19.2 Canadian Rules for Consolidation of Financial Statements

Beneficial ownership by parent in subsidiary	Consolidation for financial reporting purposes
0 – < 20%	Deemed a portfolio investment; recognize dividends as received
20 – < 50%	Deemed to be "significant influence," pro rata inclusions of profits and losses
50 – 100%	Full consolidation[a]

[a]Consolidation may be avoided in the case of some majority-owned foreign operations if the parent can convince its auditors that it does not have control of the subsidiaries or if there are substantial restrictions on the repatriation of cash.

SOURCE: Based on Section 3050, "Long-Term Investments," and Section 1590, "Requirements for Consolidation," of the *CICA Handbook*. Refer to any advanced accounting textbook for greater detail.

tions range from a one-line income-item reporting of dividends to a pro rata inclusion of profits and losses to a full disclosure in the balance sheet and income statement.

Translation of Individual Accounts

Unlike domestic items in the financial statements, international items require translation back into Canadian dollars. Since 1983, all financial statements of Canadian MNCs have had to conform to Section 1650, "Foreign Currency Translation," of the *CICA Handbook*. Under the **Section 1650** regulations, foreign operations must be classified as either integrated or self-sustaining. The choice is made by the MNC and is meant to achieve the overall objective of translation, which is to express financial statements of the foreign operation in Canadian dollars in a manner which best reflects the reporting enterprise's exposure to exchange rate changes.

Section 1650
The CICA regulation requiring Canadian companies to convert the financial statements of foreign subsidiaries into Canadian dollars for inclusion in the parent company's consolidated financial statements.

An **integrated foreign subsidiary** is one that is financially or operationally *interdependent* with the parent company. In this case, the parent company's exposure to exchange rate risk due to the foreign operation's activities is the same as if the parent company had undertaken the operation. For integrated foreign operations, the temporal method of translation of financial statements should be used. The **temporal method** takes all transactions that were measured in a foreign currency and translates them into Canadian dollars using the exchange rate in effect on the date of the original transaction. In effect, the temporal method results in financial statements that are identical to those that would have been produced if the parent company had entered into the same transactions incurred by the foreign operation. Under this method, any exchange rate gains and losses are included in the calculation of net income, and will appear on the income statement.

integrated foreign subsidiary
An operation that is financially or operationally *interdependent* with the parent company.

temporal method
The foreign exchange translation method takes all transactions engaged in by the foreign subsidiary and converts them into Canadian dollars using the exchange rate in effect on the date of the original transaction.

A **self-sustaining foreign subsidiary** is one that is financially and operationally *independent* of the parent company. In such a case, the parent's exposure to exchange rate risk is limited to the parent's net investment in the subsidiary. Exchange rate changes associated with the subsidiary's operation will have no

self-sustaining foreign subsidiary
An operation that is financially and operationally *independent* of the parent company.

direct impact on the immediate or short-term cash flows of the parent. As such, the **current rate method** is used to translate the foreign subsidiary's financial statements into Canadian dollars. Under the current rate method, all financial transactions are measured in the currency of the country where the foreign operation is based. Consolidation then occurs by converting all balance sheet accounts at the exchange rate in effect at the close of the fiscal year and all income statement accounts at the average exchange rate for the fiscal year.

current rate method
All financial transactions are measured in the currency of the foreign operations and consolidation occurs by converting all balance sheet accounts at the exchange rate in effect at the close of the fiscal year and all income statement accounts at the average exchange rate for the fiscal year.

Since the exchange rate gains and losses associated with a self-sustaining foreign subsidiary have no direct effect on the activities of the parent, these should not be reflected in the parent's income statement. Instead, they are reported as a separate component of the parent's shareholders' equity. This account is termed the cumulative translation adjustment or foreign currency translation adjustment, and appears on the balance sheet of all Canadian companies with self-sustaining foreign subsidiaries.

? Review Question

19–5 State the rules for consolidation of foreign subsidiaries. Under Section 1650 of the *CICA Handbook,* what are the translation rules for financial statement accounts?

19.3 Risk

The concept of risk clearly applies to international investments as well as to purely domestic ones. However, MNCs must take into account additional factors, including both exchange rate and political risks.

Exchange Rate Risks

Because multinational companies operate in many different foreign markets, portions of these firms' revenues and costs are based on foreign currencies. To understand the **exchange rate risk** caused by varying exchange rates between two currencies, we examine the relationships that exist among various currencies, the causes of exchange rate changes, and the impact of currency fluctuations.

exchange rate risk
The risk caused by varying exchange rates between two currencies.

Relationships Among Currencies

Since the mid-1970s, the major currencies of the world have had a *floating*—as opposed to a *fixed*—relationship with respect to the U.S. dollar and to one another. Among the currencies regarded as being major (or "hard") currencies are the British pound sterling (£), the European Union Euro (€), the Japanese yen (¥), the Canadian dollar (C$), and, of course, the U.S. dollar (US$).

foreign exchange rate
The value of two currencies with respect to each other.

The value of two currencies with respect to each other, or their **foreign exchange rate,** is expressed as follows:

US$1 = C$1.1524
C$1 = US$0.8678

Since the U.S. dollar has served as the principal currency of international finance for nearly 60 years, the usual exchange rate quotation in international markets is given as C$1.1524/US$, where the unit of account is the Canadian dollar (C$) and the unit of currency being priced is one U.S. dollar. In this case, it takes 1.1524 Canadian dollars to buy 1 U.S. dollar. Note that the U.S. dollar is the currency that is actually being priced in terms of the Canadian funds needed to buy 1 U.S. dollar. Expressing the exchange rate as US$0.8678/C$ indicates the U.S. dollar price for a Canadian dollar. The Canadian dollar is priced in U.S. funds.

floating relationship
The fluctuating relationship of the values of two currencies with respect to each other.

fixed (or semifixed) relationship
The constant (or relatively constant) relationship of a currency to one of the major currencies, a combination (basket) of major currencies, or some type of international foreign exchange standard.

spot exchange rate
The rate of exchange between two currencies on any given day.

forward exchange rate
The rate of exchange between two currencies at some specified future date.

For the major currencies, the existence of a **floating relationship** means that the value of any two currencies with respect to each other is allowed to fluctuate on a daily basis. On the other hand, many of the nonmajor currencies of the world try to maintain a **fixed (or semifixed) relationship** with respect to one of the major currencies, a combination of major currencies, or some type of international foreign exchange standard.

On any given day, the relationship between any two of the major currencies will contain two sets of figures. One reflects the **spot exchange rate**—the rate on that day. The other indicates the **forward exchange rate**—the rate at some specified future date. The foreign exchange rates given in Figure 19.1 illustrate these concepts. For instance, the figure shows that on Tuesday, December 19, 2006, the spot rate for the British pound was C$2.2679/£ (or £0.4409/C$, as usually stated), and the forward (future) rate was C$2.2183/£ (£0.4508/C$) for 1-year delivery.

In other words, on December 19, 2006, one could execute a contract to take delivery of British pounds in 1 year at a lower dollar price of C$2.2183/£. Note that forward rates for major currencies are also available for 1-month, 3-month, 6-month, and 1-year to 5-year contracts. For all such contracts, the agreements and signatures are completed on a particular day, but the actual exchange of currencies (say dollars and British pounds) between buyers and sellers will take place on the future date (say, 1 month later).

Figure 19.1 also illustrates the differences between floating and fixed currencies. All the major currencies previously mentioned have spot and forward rates with respect to the Canadian dollar and with each other. Moreover, a comparison of the exchange rates prevailing on December 19, 2006, versus those the previous day, week, or four weeks, indicates that the major currencies' (e.g., U.S. dollar and Japanese yen) exchange rates float in relation to the Canadian dollar; the rates change on a constant basis.

Other currencies, however, such as the Malaysian ringgit and the Saudi Arabian riyal, are controlled by these contries' governments and do not fluctuate on a daily basis with respect to other currencies. These countries have fixed exchange rates. Some other countries have pegged their exchange rates to the U.S. dollar. For example, the Bahamas and Panama have pegged their exchange rates to the U.S. dollar. In these countries, even though they have their own currencies, U.S. dollars widely circulate.

A final point to note is the concept of changes in the value of a currency with respect to the Canadian dollar or another currency. For the floating currencies, changes in the value of foreign exchange rates are called *appreciation* or *depreciation*. For example, Figure 19.1 shows that the value of the Canadian dollar (C$) appreciated against the Mexican peso (MP) from MP9.3388/C$ on December 18 to MP9.4005/C$ on December 19. One C$ bought slightly more MP.

FIGURE 19.1 **Exchange Rates (Tuesday, December 19, 2006)**
Spot and forward exchange rate quotations

Foreign Exchange on 1006.12.19

Per US$	Latest	Previous day	Week ago	4 Weeks ago	% Change on day	% Change in week	% Change in 4 weeks
Canada $	1.1524	1.1574	1.1521	1.1459	−0.4	nil	+0.6
Euro*	1.139	1.3103	1.328	1.2846	+0.7	−0.7	+2.7
Japan yen	118.15	118.11	116.79	117.88	nil	+1.2	+0.2
UK pound*	1.9688	1.9485	1.9707	1.899	+1.0	−0.1	+3.7
Swiss franc	1.2144	1.2222	1.1998	1.2409	−0.6	+1.2	−2.1
Australia $*	0.7836	0.7802	0.7864	0.7715	+0.4	−0.4	+1.6
Mexico peso	10.838	10.815	10.8385	10.9575	+0.2	nil	−1.1
Hong Kong	7.775	7.7739	7.7713	7.7864	nil	nil	−0.1
Singapore $	1.5416	1.5479	1.5393	1.5585	−0.4	+0.1	−1.1
China renminbi	7.8208	7.82	7.83	7.8683	nil	−0.1	−0.6
India rupee	44.60	44.64	44.69	44.78	−0.1	−0.2	−0.4
Russia rouble	26.302	26.3865	26.2255	26.6305	−0.3	+0.3	−1.2
Brazil real	2.1575	2.1502	2.151	2.1626	+0.3	+0.3	−0.2

Per C$	Latest	Previous day	Week ago	4 Weeks ago	% Change on day	% Change in week	% Change in 4 weeks
US $	0.8678	0.864	0.868	0.8727	+0.4	nil	−0.6
Euro*	1.5194	1.5159	1.5295	1.4715	+0.2	−0.7	+3.3
Japan yen	102.48	102.00	101.35	102.84	+0.5	+1.1	−0.4
UK pound*	2.2679	2.2542	2.2697	2.1755	+0.6	−0.1	+4.2
Swiss franc	1.0534	1.0554	1.0411	1.0825	−0.2	+1.2	−2.7
Australia $*	0.9026	0.9026	0.9056	0.8836	Nil	−0.3	+2.2
Mexico peso	9.4005	9.3388	9.4046	9.5589	+0.7	nil	−1.7
Hong Kong	6.7447	6.7133	6.7441	6.7932	+0.5	nil	−0.7
Singapore $	1.3369	1.3367	1.3354	1.3596	nil	+0.1	−1.7
China renminbi	6.7865	6.7565	6.7966	6.8665	+0.4	−0.1	−1.2
India rupee	38.70	38.57	38.79	39.08	+0.3	−0.2	−1.0
Russia rouble	22.8237	22.8013	22.764	23.2466	+0.1	+0.3	−1.8
Brazil real	1.8722	1.858	1.8672	1.8876	+0.8	+0.3	−0.8

*Inverted.

Currency Cross Rates on 2006.12.19

	C$	US$	Euro	Yen ¥	£	Sw. fr.	A$
C$	—	1.1524	1.5194	0.0098	2.2679	0.9493	0.9035
US$	0.8678	—	1.3190	0.0085	1.9688	0.8235	0.7836
Euro	0.6582	0.7582	—	0.6416	1.4923	0.6242	0.5939
Yen ¥	102.48	118.15	155.79	—	232.54	97.26	92.54
£	0.4409	0.5079	0.6698	0.4298	—	0.4181	0.3979
Sw. fr.	1.0534	1.2144	1.6013	1.0276	2.3902	—	0.9512
A$	1.1068	1.2762	1.6826	1.0798	2.5115	1.0504	—
Gold	718.94	623.70	472.82	73696	316.76	757.55	795.74

Forward Exchange on 2006.12.19

Per US$	Spot	1 month	3 month	6 month	1 year	2 year	3 year	4 year	5 year
C$	1.1524	1.1519	1.1511	1.1488	1.1434	1.1341	1.1266	1.1244	1.1229
Euro	1.3190	1.3195	1.3216	1.3258	1.3361	1.3563	1.3741	1.3898	1.4093
Yen ¥	118.15	118.13	118.12	118.11	118.09	118.05	118.02	117.98	117.95
£	1.9688	1.9652	1.9589	1.9512	1.9397	1.9255	1.9174	1.9069	1.9040

Per C$	Spot	1 month	3 month	6 month	1 year	2 year	3 year	4 year	5 year
US$	0.8678	0.8681	0.8688	0.8705	0.8746	0.8818	0.8876	0.8909	0.8906
Euro	1.5194	1.5202	1.5215	1.5227	1.5227	1.5382	1.5481	1.5599	1.5825
Yen ¥	102.48	102.28	101.87	101.29	100.02	97.18	94.39	91.51	88.55
£	2.2679	2.2637	2.2549	2.2417	2.2183	2.1847	2.1617	2.1421	2.1397

SOURCE: *National Post.* Available at **www.canada.com/nationalpost/financialpost/fpmarketdata/currency.html**

But, over the four weeks to December 19, the C$ depreciated against the MP by 1.7 percent. On December 19, C$1 bought 9.4005 MP, less than the 9.5589 MP received four weeks earlier. It is also correct to say that over the four weeks the peso appreciated against the dollar, from C$0.1046/MP to C$0.1064/MP by December 19, 2006. It took more cents to buy one peso on December 19 than it did four weeks earlier.

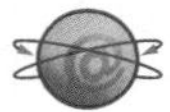

www.canada.com/nationalpost/financialpost/fpmarketdata/currency.html

www.xe.com/ucc

For the fixed currencies, changes in values are called official *revaluation* or *devaluation,* but these terms have the same meanings as appreciation and depreciation, respectively. Current exchange rates are available on the Web at numerous sites.

What Causes Exchange Rates to Change?

Although several economic and political factors influence foreign exchange rate movements, by far the most important explanation for long-term changes in exchange rates is a differing inflation rate between two countries. Countries that experience high inflation rates will see their currencies decline in value (depreciate) relative to the currencies of countries with lower inflation rates.

Example

Assume that the current exchange rate between Canada and the new nation of Farland is 2 Farland Guineas (FG) per Canadian dollar, FG 2.00/C$, which is also equal to C$0.50/FG. This exchange rate means that a basket of goods worth $100 in Canada sells for $100 × FG 2/C$ = FG 200 in Farland, and vice versa (goods worth FG 200 in Farland sell for $100 in Canada).

Now assume that inflation is running at a 25 percent annual rate in Farland but at only a 2 percent annual rate in Canada. In one year, the same basket of goods will sell for 1.25 × FG 200 = FG 250 in Farland, and for 1.02 × $100 = $102 in Canada. These relative prices imply that in 1 year FG 250 will be worth $102, so the exchange rate in 1 year should change to FG 250/$102 = FG 2.45/C$, or C$0.41/FG. In other words, the Farland Guinea will depreciate from FG 2/C$ to FG 2.45/C$, while the dollar will appreciate from C$0.50/FG to C$0.41/FG.

Hint

A firm that borrows money in a developing nation faces the possibility of a double penalty due to inflation. Since many of the loans have floating interest rates, inflation will increase the interest rate on the loan as well as affect the exchange rate of the currencies.

This simple example can also predict what the level of interest rates will be in the two countries. In order to be enticed to save money, an investor must be offered a return that exceeds the country's inflation rate—otherwise there would be no reason to forgo the pleasure of spending money (consuming) today because inflation would make that money less valuable 1 year from now. Let's assume that this *real rate of interest* is 3 percent per year in both Farland and Canada. Using Equation 8.1 (from Chapter 8), we can now reason that the *nominal rate of interest*—quoted market rate, not adjusted for risk—will be approximately equal to the real rate plus the inflation rate in each country, or 3 + 25 = 28 percent in Farland and 3 + 2 = 5 percent in Canada.[2]

---

2. This is an approximation of the true relationship, which is actually multiplicative. The correct formula says that 1 plus the nominal rate of interest, k, is equal to the product of 1 plus the real rate of interest, k^*, and 1 plus the inflation rate, IP; that is, $(1 + k) = (1 + k^*) \times (1 + IP)$. This means that the nominal interest rates for Farland and Canada should be 28.75 percent and 5.06 percent, respectively.

Impact of Currency Fluctuations

Multinational companies face exchange rate risks under both floating and fixed arrangements. The case of floating currencies can be used to illustrate these risks. Returning to the Canadian dollar–British pound relationship, we note that the forces of international supply and demand, as well as economic and political elements, help to shape both the spot and forward rates between these two currencies. Because the MNC cannot control much (or most) of these "outside" elements, the company faces potential changes in exchange rates. These changes can in turn affect the MNC's revenues, costs, and profits as measured in Canadian dollars. For fixed rate currencies, official revaluation or devaluation, like the changes brought about by the market in the case of floating currencies, can affect the MNC's operations and its dollar-based financial position.

Example MNC, Inc., a multinational manufacturer of dental drills based in Canada, has a subsidiary in Great Britain that at the end of 2008 had the financial statements shown in Table 19.3. The figures for the balance sheet and income statement are given in the local currency, British pounds (£). Using the foreign exchange rate of £0.40/C$ for December 31, 2008, MNC has translated the statements into

TABLE 19.3 Financial Statements for MNC, Inc.'s British Subsidiary

Translation of balance sheet			
	12/31/08		12/31/09
Assets	£	C$[a]	C$[b]
Cash	8	20	16
Inventory	60	150	120
Plant and equipment (net)	32	80	64
Total	100	250	200
Liabilities and shareholders' equity			
Debt	48	120	96
Paid-in capital	40	100	80
Retained earnings	12	30	24
Total	100	250	200
Translation of income statement			
Sales	600	1,500	1,200
Cost of goods sold	550	1,375	1,100
Operating profits	50	125	100

[a]Foreign exchange rate: C$1.00 = £0.40, or £1 = C$2.50.

[b]Foreign exchange rate: C$1.00 = £0.50, or £1 = $2.00.

NOTE: This example is simplified to show how the balance sheet and income statement are subject to foreign exchange rate fluctuations. For the applicable rules on the translation of foreign accounts, review the discussion of international financial statements presented earlier.

Canadian dollars. For simplicity, it is assumed that all the local (the pound) figures are expected to remain the same during 2009. As a result, as of January 1, 2009, the subsidiary expects to show the same British pound figures on 12/31/09 as on 12/31/08. However, because of the decline in the value of the British pound relative to the dollar, from £0.40/C$ to £0.50/C$, the translated dollar values of the items on the balance sheet, along with the dollar profit value on 12/31/09, are lower than those of the previous year. The changes are solely due to fluctuations in the foreign exchange rate. ▲

There are additional complexities attached to each individual account in the financial statements. For instance, it is important whether a subsidiary's debt is all in the local currency, all in Canadian dollars, or in several currencies. Moreover, it is important which currency (or currencies) the revenues and costs are denominated in. The risks shown so far relate to what is called the **accounting exposure.** In other words, foreign exchange rate fluctuations affect individual accounts in the financial statements.

accounting exposure
The risk resulting from the effects of changes in foreign exchange rates on the translated value of a firm's financial statement accounts denominated in a given foreign currency.

economic exposure
The risk resulting from the effects of changes in foreign exchange rates on the firm's value.

A different, and perhaps more important, risk element concerns **economic exposure,** which is the potential impact of foreign exchange rate fluctuations on the firm's value. Given that all future revenues and thus net profits can be subject to foreign exchange rate changes, it is obvious that the *present value* of the net profits derived from foreign operations will have, as a part of its total diversifiable risk, an element reflecting appreciation (revaluation) or depreciation (devaluation) of various currencies with respect to the Canadian dollar.

What can the management of MNCs do about these risks? The actions will depend on the attitude of the management toward risk. This attitude, in turn, translates into how aggressively management wants to hedge (i.e., protect against) the company's undesirable positions and exposures. The money markets, the forward (futures) markets, and the foreign currency options markets can be used—either individually or in combination—to hedge foreign exchange exposures. Further details on certain hedging strategies are described later.

Political Risks

political risk
The potential discontinuity or seizure of an MNC's operations in a host country due to the host's implementation of specific rules and regulations.

Another important risk facing MNCs is political risk. **Political risk** refers to the implementation by a host government of specific rules and regulations that can result in the discontinuity or seizure of the operations of a foreign company. Political risk is usually manifested in the form of nationalization, expropriation, or confiscation. In general, the assets and operations of a foreign firm are taken over by the host government, usually without proper (or any) compensation.

macro political risk
The subjection of all foreign firms to political risk (takeover) by a host country because of political change, revolution, or the adoption of new policies.

micro political risk
The subjection of an individual firm, a specific industry, or companies from a particular foreign country to political risk (takeover) by a host country.

Political risk has two basic paths: *macro* and *micro*. **Macro political risk** means that because of political change, revolution, or the adoption of new policies by a host government, *all* foreign firms in the country will be subjected to political risk. In other words, no individual country or firm is treated differently; all assets and operations of foreign firms are taken over wholesale. An example of macro political risk occurred after communist regimes came to power in Russia in 1917, China in 1949, and Cuba in 1959–1960. **Micro political risk,** on the other hand, refers to the case in which an individual firm, a specific industry, or companies from a particular foreign country are subjected to takeover. Examples include the nationalization by a majority of the oil-exporting countries of the assets of the international oil companies in their territories.

19.1 **IN PRACTICE**

Evaluating International Risk Using the O-Factor

Expanding internationally can generate additional revenues from new markets as well as more sources of labour and financing. Financial managers know, however, that doing business overseas is fraught with many types of risk, including exchange rate, political, regulatory, and business environment risks. To help companies decide where to invest and what return on investment to expect, PricewaterhouseCoopers developed its Opacity Index. This analytical model identifies specific incremental borrowing costs related to five key *opacity factors*: legal protections for business, macroeonomic policies, corporate reporting, corruption, and government regulations. *Opacity* refers here to the lack of "clear, accurate, formal, and widely accepted practices."

A country's opacity factor (O-factor) is a composite measure of how these five factors affect the cost of capital and the obstacles to foreign direct investment in a country. The scale ranges from 0 to 150. A lower O-factor means a country is a better location for foreign direct investment. A high O-factor indicates that it is more expensive to operate and raise funds in that country—in effect, that there is a surtax on foreign direct investment (FDI).

What countries are the best places to do business, judging on basis of the Opacity Index? The first Opacity Index, released in early 2001, ranks Singapore first, with the lowest opacity factor (29). And the facts bear this out: Singapore has no tax on FDI. The United States and Chile are next, both with O-factors of 36. The U.K. is a close fourth with a marginally higher O-factor of 38. At the opposite end of the scale are South Korea (73), Turkey (74), Indonesia (75), Russia (84), and China (87).

The O-factor is used to determine two ratings. The first is the tax equivalent rating, which shows the effect of opacity when viewed as if it imposes a hidden tax. For example, Thailand, with an O-factor of 67, has a tax equivalent rating of 30. This indicates that the lack of opacity in that country is equivalent to levying an additional 30 percent corporate income tax. China's tax equivalent rating is a startling 46. The second rating is the risk premium that indicates the increased cost of borrowing in countries due to opacity. Countries with high O-factors have higher interest rates on long-term debt. For example, Thailand's risk premium is 801, indicating international lenders require an extra 8.01 percent on a debt issue in the country. China's rating of 1,316 implies a premium of 13.16 percent.

Making foreign direct investment decisions is risky. A starting point for managers may be to review the Opacity Index when evaluating the merits of investing in a particular country. In addition to the overall O-factor, managers can look at individual scores for each of the five areas. The methodology used to calculate the Opacity Index has been modified, and the clear leader is now Finland. Since the 1980s, Finland has emphasized the creation of strong institutions, regulatory structures, and laws. Corruption there is almost nonexistent. The result? Finland now has one of the most vibrant economies in the world, ranked at the top of the 2003–2004 World Economic Forum's Competitiveness Index. In second place are three other European countries: the United Kingdom, Denmark, and Sweden. The most recent ranking of countries on the Opacity Index is available on the Web.

http://opacityindex.com/opacity_index.pdf

SOURCES: Jennifer Caplan, "Why Singapore Is Less Risky Than the U.S.," **CFO.com**, February 14, 2001; Opacity Index Web site, **www.opacityindex.com**.

Although political risk can take place in any country—including advanced economies like Canada—the political instability of the Third World generally makes the positions of multinational companies most vulnerable there. At the same time, some of the countries in this group have the most promising markets for the goods and services being offered by MNCs. The main question, therefore, is how to engage in operations and foreign investment in such countries and yet avoid or minimize the potential political risk.

Table 19.4 shows some of the approaches that MNCs may be able to adopt to cope with political risk. The negative approaches are generally used by firms in extractive industries such as oil and gas and mining. The external approaches are also of limited use. The best policies MNCs can follow are the positive approaches, which have both economic and political aspects.

In recent years, MNCs have been relying on a variety of complex forecasting techniques whereby "international experts," using available historical data, predict the chances for political instability in a host country and the potential effects on MNC operations. Events in Afghanistan, Pakistan, Indonesia, and India, among others, however, point up the limited use of such techniques and tend to reinforce the usefulness of the positive approaches.

national entry control systems Comprehensive rules, regulations, and incentives introduced by host governments to regulate inflows of *foreign direct investments* from MNCs and at the same time extract more benefits from their presence.

A final point relates to the introduction by most host governments in the last two decades of comprehensive sets of rules, regulations, and incentives. Known as **national entry control systems,** they are aimed at regulating inflows of *foreign direct investments* involving MNCs. They are designed to extract more benefits from MNCs' presence by regulating flows of a variety of factors—local ownership, level of exportation, use of local inputs, number of local managers, internal geographic location, level of local borrowing, and the percentages of profits to be

TABLE 19.4 Approaches for Coping with Political Risks

Positive approaches		Negative approaches
Prior negotiation of controls and operating contracts	Direct	Licence or patent restrictions under international agreements
Prior agreement for sale		Control of external raw materials
Joint venture with government or local private sector		
Use of locals in management	Indirect	
Joint venture with local banks		Control of transportation to (external) markets
Equity participation by middle class		Control of downstream processing
Local sourcing		Control of external markets
Local retail outlets		

External approaches to minimize loss
International insurance or investment guarantees
Thinly capitalized firms:
Local financing
External financing secured only by the local operation

SOURCE: Rita M. Rodriguez and E. Eugene Carter, *International Financial Management,* 3rd ed. (Englewood Cliffs, NJ: Prentice Hall, 1984), p. 512.

remitted and of capital to be repatriated back to parent firms. Host countries expect that as MNCs comply with these regulations, the potential for acts of political risk will decline, thus benefiting MNCs as well.

? Review Questions

19–6 Define *spot* and *forward exchange rates*. Define and compare *accounting exposures* and *economic exposures* to exchange rate fluctuations.

19–7 Explain how differing inflation rates between two countries affect their exchange rates over the long term.

19–8 Discuss *macro* and *micro political risk*. Describe some techniques for dealing with political risk.

19.4 Long-Term Investment and Financing Decisions

Important long-term aspects of international managerial finance include foreign direct investment, investment cash flows and decisions, capital structure, long-term debt, and equity capital. Here we consider the international dimensions of these topics.

Foreign Direct Investment

foreign direct investment (FDI)
The transfer by a multinational firm of capital, managerial, and technical assets from its home country to a host country.

Foreign direct investment (FDI) is the transfer by a multinational firm of capital, managerial, and technical assets from its home country to a host country. The equity participation on the part of an MNC can be 100 percent (resulting in a wholly owned foreign subsidiary) or less (leading to a joint-venture project with foreign participants). In contrast to short-term, foreign portfolio investments undertaken by individuals and companies (such as internationally diversified mutual funds), FDI involves equity participation, managerial control, and day-to-day operational activities on the part of MNCs. Therefore, FDI projects will be subjected not only to business, financial, inflation, and exchange rate risks (as would foreign portfolio investments), but also to the additional element of political risk.

For several decades, U.S.-based MNCs dominated the international scene in terms of both the *flow* and the *stock* of FDI. The total FDI stock of U.S.-based MNCs, for instance, increased from $7.7 billion in 1929 to over $1,245 billion at the end of 2000.

FDI in Canada historically exceeded Canadian corporate FDI abroad. For example, in 1990, FDI in Canada was $130.9 billion while Canadian FDI abroad was $98.4 billion, an FDI surplus of $32.5 billion. By 1999, the figures were $252.6 billion and $290.7 billion, an FDI deficit of $38.1 billion. This swing in FDI balances occurred since 1996, the last year Canada experienced a positive difference in FDI.

The deficit peaked in 2002 at $78.7 billion. In 2005, FDI in Canada and abroad both hit record highs of $415.6 billion and $465.1 billion. Between 1990 and 2005, the rate of growth of FDI in Canada was 8.0 percent per year. For Canadian FDI abroad, the growth rate was 10.9 percent per year. For various reasons, Canadian companies invested more abroad than foreign companies invested in Canada.

The dollar amount of FDI is impressive when compared to U.S. FDI. In 2000, Canadian FDI abroad was $356.5 billion, which is about 28 percent of the level recorded by the United States. Given that the Canadian economy is less than 10 percent of the size of the U.S. economy, the level of Canadian FDI abroad is surprisingly high. This, again, shows that the focus of Canadian companies is external, with both trade and FDI data being much higher, on a relative basis, when compared to our larger neighbour to the south.

The largest source of FDI in Canada was the United States, which accounted for 67 percent of the total. The energy and minerals industries attracted the largest portion of the FDI, with these sectors accounting for 21 percent of the total FDI by the end of 2001. The EU's share of FDI in Canada stood at 24 percent of total FDI. The primary destination of Canadian FDI abroad was the United States, accounting for 51 percent of the total by the end of 2001. The finance and insurance sector accounted for 38 percent of the FDI abroad, up sharply from 1992 when it stood at 28 percent.

Investment Cash Flows and Decisions

Measuring the amount invested in a foreign project, its resulting cash flows, and the associated risk is difficult. The returns and NPVs of such investments can significantly vary from the subsidiary's and parent's points of view. Therefore, several factors that are unique to the international setting need to be examined when making long-term investment decisions.

First, elements relating to a parent company's *investment* in a subsidiary and the concept of taxes must be considered. For example, in the case of manufacturing investments, questions may arise as to the value of the equipment a parent may contribute to the subsidiary. Is the value based on the market conditions in the parent country or the local host economy? In general, the market value in the host country is the relevant "price."

! Hint

The discount rates used by the parent and subsidiary to calculate the NPV will also be different. The parent company has to add in a risk factor based on the possibility of exchange rates changing and the risk of not being able to get the cash out of the foreign country.

The existence of different taxes—as pointed out earlier—can complicate measurement of the *cash flows* to be received by the parent because different definitions of taxable income can arise. There are still other complications when it comes to measuring the actual cash flows. From a parent firm's viewpoint, the cash flows are those that are repatriated from the subsidiary. In some countries, however, such cash flows may be totally or partially blocked. Obviously, depending on the life of the project in the host country, the returns and NPVs associated with such projects can vary significantly from the subsidiary's and the parent's point of view. For instance, for a project of only 5 years' duration, if all yearly cash flows are blocked by the host government, the subsidiary may show a "normal" or even superior return and NPV, although the parent may show no return at all. On the other hand, for a project of longer life, even if cash flows are blocked for the first few years, the remaining years' cash flows can contribute toward the parent's returns and NPV.

Finally, there is the issue of *risk* attached to international cash flows. The three basic types of risk categories are (1) business and financial risks, (2) inflation and exchange rate risks, and (3) political risks. The first category relates to the type of industry the subsidiary is in as well as its financial structure. More details on financial risks are presented later. As for the other two categories, we have already discussed the risks of having investments, profits, and assets/liabilities in different currencies and the potential impacts of political risks.

The presence of the three types of risks will influence the discount rate to be used when evaluating international cash flows. The basic rule is this: The local cost of equity capital (applicable to the local business and financial environments within which a subsidiary operates) is the starting discount rate. To this rate, the risks stemming from exchange rate and political factors would be added; and from it, benefits reflecting the parent's lower capital costs would be subtracted.

Capital Structure

Both theory and empirical evidence indicate that the capital structures of multinational companies differ from those of purely domestic firms. Furthermore, differences are also observed among the capital structures of MNCs domiciled in various countries. Several factors tend to influence the capital structures of MNCs.

International Capital Markets

MNCs, unlike smaller-size domestic firms, have access to the Euromarket (discussed earlier) and the variety of financial instruments available there. Because of their access to the international bond and equity markets, MNCs may have lower long-term financing costs, which result in differences between the capital structures of MNCs and those of purely domestic companies. Similarly, MNCs based in different countries and regions may have access to different currencies and markets, resulting in variances in capital structures for these multinationals.

International Diversification

It is well established that MNCs, in contrast to domestic firms, can achieve further risk reduction in their cash flows by diversifying internationally. International diversification may lead to varying degrees of debt versus equity. Empirically, the evidence on debt ratios is mixed. Some studies have found MNCs' debt proportions to be higher than those of domestic firms. Other studies have concluded the opposite, citing imperfections in certain foreign markets, political risk factors, and complexities in the international financial environment that cause higher agency costs of debt for MNCs.

Country Factors

A number of studies have concluded that certain factors unique to each host country can cause differences in capital structures. These factors include legal, tax, political, social, and financial aspects, as well as the overall relationship between the public and private sectors. Owing to these factors, differences have been found not only among MNCs based in various countries, but also among the foreign subsidiaries of an MNC as well. However, because no one capital structure is ideal for all MNCs, each multinational has to consider a set of global and domestic factors when deciding on the appropriate capital structure for both the overall corporation and its subsidiaries.

Long-Term Debt

As noted earlier, multinational companies have access to a variety of international financial instruments. International bonds are among the most widely used, so we will begin by focusing on them. Next, we discuss the role of international financial institutions in underwriting such instruments. Finally, we consider the use of various techniques by MNCs to change the structure of their long-term debt.

International Bonds

international bond
A bond that is initially sold outside the country of the borrower and often distributed in several countries.

foreign bond
An *international bond* that is sold primarily in the country of the currency of the issue.

Eurobond
An *international bond* that is sold primarily in countries other than the country of the currency in which the issue is denominated.

In general, an **international bond** is one that is initially sold outside the country of the borrower and often distributed in several countries. It is denominated in one of the "hard" currencies like the U.S. or Canadian dollars, Euro, British pound, or Japanese yen. When a bond is sold primarily in the country of the currency of the issue, it is called a **foreign bond.** For example, an MNC based in Germany might float a foreign bond issue in the British capital market underwritten by a British syndicate and denominated in British pounds. When an international bond is sold primarily in countries other than the country of the currency in which the issue is denominated, it is called a **Eurobond.** Thus, a Canadian MNC might float a Eurobond in several European capital markets, underwritten by an international syndicate and denominated in U.S. dollars.

The U.S. dollar and the Euro continue to be the most frequently used currencies for Eurobond issues, with the Euro rapidly increasing in popularity relative to the U.S. dollar. In the foreign bond category, the U.S. dollar and the Euro are major choices. Low interest rates, the general stability of the currency, and the overall efficiency of the European Union's capital markets are among the primary reasons for the growing popularity of the Euro.

Eurobonds are much more widely used than foreign bonds. These instruments are heavily used, especially in relation to Eurocurrency loans in recent years, by major market participants, particularly corporations. In recent years, many more Canadian companies have been using international bonds to raise financing. The so-called *equity-linked Eurobonds* (i.e., Eurobonds convertible to equity) have found strong demand among Euromarket participants. It is expected that more of these innovative types of instruments will emerge on the international scene in the coming years.

A final point concerns the levels of interest rates in international markets. In the case of foreign bonds, interest rates are usually directly correlated with the domestic rates prevailing in the respective countries. For Eurobonds, several interest rates may be influential. For instance, for a Eurodollar bond, the interest rate will reflect several different rates, most notably the U.S. long-term rate, the Eurodollar rate, and long-term rates in other countries.

The Role of International Financial Institutions

For *foreign bonds,* the underwriting institutions are those that handle bond issues in the respective countries in which such bonds are issued. For *Eurobonds,* a number of financial institutions in the United States, Canada, western Europe, and Japan form international underwriting syndicates. The underwriting costs for Eurobonds are comparable to those for major bond flotations for major companies in the Canadian domestic market. Although U.S. institutions used to dominate the Eurobond scene, recent economic and financial strengths exhibited by some western European (especially U.K. and German) financial firms have led to an erosion of that dominance. Since 1986, a number of European firms have shared with U.S. firms the top positions in terms of acting as lead underwriters of Eurobond issues. However, U.S. investment banks continue to dominate most other international security issuance markets—such as international equity, medium-term note, syndicated loan, and commercial paper markets. U.S. corporations account for well over half of the worldwide securities issues made each year.

To raise funds through international bond issues, many MNCs establish their own financial subsidiaries. Some MNCs, for example, have created subsidiaries in the United States and western Europe, especially in Luxembourg. Such subsidiaries can be used to raise large amounts of funds in "one move," the funds being redistributed wherever MNCs need them. (Special tax rules applicable to such subsidiaries also make them desirable to MNCs.)

Changing the Structure of Debt

As will be more fully explained later, MNCs can use *hedging strategies* to change the structure/characteristics of their long-term assets and liabilities. For instance, multinationals can utilize *interest-rate swaps* to obtain a desired stream of interest payments (e.g., fixed rate) in exchange for another (e.g., floating rate). With *currency swaps,* they can exchange an asset/liability denominated in one currency (e.g., the Canadian dollar) for another (e.g., the U.S. dollar). The use of these tools allows MNCs to gain access to a broader set of markets, currencies, and maturities, thus leading to both cost savings and a means of restructuring the existing assets/liabilities. There has been significant growth in such use during the last few years, and this trend is expected to continue. Recall that swaps were discussed in Chapter 17.

Equity Capital

Here we look at how multinational companies can raise equity capital abroad. They can sell their shares in international capital markets, or they can use joint ventures, which are sometimes required by the host country.

Equity Issues and Markets

One means of raising equity funds for MNCs is to have the parent's stock distributed internationally and owned by investors of different nationalities. In the 1980s, the world's equity markets became more "internationalized." In other words, although distinct *national* stock markets (such as Toronto, New York, London, and Tokyo) continue to exist and grow, an *international* stock market has also emerged on the global financial scene.

Euroequity market
The capital market around the world that deals in international equity issues; London has become *the* centre of Euroequity activity.

In recent years, the terms **Euroequity market** and "Euroequities" have become widely known. Although a number of capital markets—including New York, Tokyo, Frankfurt, and Zurich—play major roles as hosts to international equity issues, London has become *the* centre of Euroequity activity. In recent years, government sales of state-owned firms to private investors, referred to as *share-issue privatizations,* have accounted for over half of the total volume of Euroequity issues.

With the full financial integration of the European Union, some European stock exchanges continue to compete with each other. Others have called for more cooperation in forming a single market capable of competing with the New York and Tokyo exchanges. From the multinationals' perspective, the most desirable outcome would be to have uniform international rules and regulations with respect to all the major national stock exchanges. Such uniformity would allow MNCs unrestricted access to an international equity market parallelling the international currency and bond markets.

Joint Ventures

The basic aspects of foreign ownership of international operations were discussed earlier. Worth emphasizing here is that certain laws and regulations enacted by a number of host countries require MNCs to maintain less than 50 percent ownership in their subsidiaries in those countries. For an MNC, for example, establishing foreign subsidiaries in the form of joint ventures means that a certain portion of the firm's total international equity stock is (indirectly) held by foreign owners.

In establishing a foreign subsidiary, an MNC may wish to use as little equity and as much debt as possible, with the debt coming from local sources in the host country or the MNC itself. Each of these actions can be supported. The use of local debt can be a good protective measure to lessen the potential impacts of political risk. Because local sources are involved in the capital structure of a subsidiary, there may be fewer threats from local authorities in the event of changes in government or the imposing of new regulations on foreign business.

In support of the other action—having *more MNC-based debt* in a subsidiary's capital structure—many host governments are less restrictive toward intra-MNC interest payments than toward intra-MNC dividend remittances. The parent firm therefore may be in a better position if it has more MNC-based debt than equity in the capital structure of its subsidiaries.

? Review Questions

19–9 Indicate how NPV can differ depending on whether it is measured from the parent MNC's point of view or from that of the foreign subsidiary when cash flows may be blocked by local authorities.

19–10 Briefly discuss some of the international factors that cause the capital structures of MNCs to differ from those of purely domestic firms.

19–11 Describe the difference between *foreign bonds* and *Eurobonds*. Explain how each is sold, and discuss the determinant(s) of their interest rates.

19–12 What are the long-run advantages of having more *local* debt and less MNC-based equity in the capital structure of a foreign subsidiary?

LG5 19.5 Short-Term Financial Decisions

In international operations, the usual domestic sources of short-term financing, along with other sources, are available to MNCs. Included are accounts payable, accruals, bank and nonbank sources in each subsidiary's local environment, and the Euromarket. Our emphasis here is on the "foreign" sources.

The local economic market is a basic source of both short- and long-term financing for a subsidiary of a multinational company. Moreover, the subsidiary's borrowing and lending status, relative to a local firm in the same economy, can be superior, because the subsidiary can rely on the potential backing and guarantee of its parent MNC. One drawback, however, is that most local markets and local currencies are regulated by local authorities. A subsidiary may ultimately choose to turn to the Euromarket and take advantage of borrowing and investing in an unregulated financial forum.

The Euromarket offers nondomestic long-term financing opportunities through Eurobonds. Short-term financing opportunities are available in **Eurocurrency markets.** The forces of supply and demand are among the main factors determining exchange rates in Eurocurrency markets. Each currency's normal interest rate is influenced by economic policies pursued by the respective "home" government. For example, the interest rates offered in the Euromarket on the U.S. dollar are greatly affected by the prime rate inside the United States, and the dollar's exchange rates with other major currencies are influenced by the supply and demand forces in such markets (and in response to interest rates).

Eurocurrency markets
The portion of the Euromarket that provides short-term, foreign-currency financing to subsidiaries of MNCs.

nominal interest rate
In the international context, the stated interest rate charged on financing when only the MNC parent's currency is involved.

effective interest rate
In the international context, the rate equal to the nominal rate plus (or minus) any forecast appreciation (or depreciation) of a foreign currency relative to the currency of the MNC parent.

Unlike borrowing in the domestic markets, where only one currency and a **nominal interest rate** is involved, financing activities in the Euromarket can involve several currencies and both nominal and effective interest rates. **Effective interest rates** are equal to nominal rates plus (or minus) any forecast appreciation (or depreciation) of a foreign currency relative to the currency of the MNC parent. An example will illustrate the issues involved.

Example A multinational plastics company, International Molding, has subsidiaries in Switzerland (local currency, Swiss franc, Sf) and Japan (local currency, Japanese yen, ¥). On the basis of each subsidiary's forecast operations, the short-term financial needs (in equivalent Canadian dollars) are as follows:

Switzerland: $80 million excess cash to be invested (lent)
Japan: $60 million funds to be raised (borrowed)

On the basis of all the available information, the parent firm has provided each subsidiary with the figures given in the table below for exchange rates and interest rates. (The figures for the effective rates shown are derived by adding the forecast percentage changes to the nominal rates.)

	Currency		
Item	**C$**	**Sf**	**¥**
Spot exchange rates		Sf 1.58/C$	¥125.92/C$
Forecast % change		+1.0%	−2.5%
Interest rates			
Nominal			
Euromarket	4.6%	6.2%	8.5%
Domestic	4.0	5.5	9.0
Effective			
Euromarket	4.6%	7.2%	6.0%
Domestic	4.0	6.5	6.5

From the MNC's point of view, the effective rates of interest, which take into account each currency's forecast percentage change (appreciation or depreciation) relative to the Canadian dollar, are the main considerations in investment and borrowing decisions. (It is assumed here that because of local regulations, a subsidiary is *not* permitted to use the domestic market of *any other* subsidiary.) The relevant question is, where should funds be invested and borrowed?

For investment purposes, the highest available rate of interest is the effective rate for the Swiss franc in the Euromarket. Therefore, the Swiss subsidiary should invest the $80 million in Swiss francs in the Euromarket. To raise funds, the cheapest source *open* to the Japanese subsidiary is the 4.6 percent in the C$ Euromarket. The subsidiary should therefore raise the $60 million in Canadian dollars. These two transactions will result in the most revenues and least costs, respectively.

Several points should be made with respect to the preceding example. First of all, this is a simplified case of the actual workings of the Eurocurrency markets. The example ignores taxes, intersubsidiary investing and borrowing, and periods longer or shorter than a year. Nevertheless, it shows how the existence of many currencies can provide both challenges and opportunities for MNCs. Second, the focus has been solely on accounting values; of greater importance would be the impact of these actions on market value. Third, it is important to note the following details about the figures presented. The forecast percentage change data are those normally supplied by the MNC's international financial managers. Management may, instead, want a *range of forecasts,* from the most likely to the least likely. In addition, the company's management is likely to take a specific position in terms of its response to any remaining exchange rate exposures. If any action is to be taken, certain amounts of one or more currencies will be borrowed and then invested in other currencies in the hope of realizing potential gains to offset potential losses associated with the exposures.

Cash Management

In its international cash management, a multinational firm can respond to exchange rate risks by protecting (hedging) its undesirable cash and marketable securities exposures or by certain adjustments in its operations. The former approach is more applicable in responding to *accounting exposures,* the latter to *economic exposures.* Each of these two approaches is examined here.

Hedging Strategies

hedging strategies
Techniques used to offset or protect against risk; in the international context, these include borrowing or lending in different currencies, undertaking contracts in the forward, futures, and/or options markets, and also swapping assets/liabilities with other parties.

Hedging strategies are techniques used to offset or protect against risk. In international cash management, these strategies include actions such as borrowing or lending in different currencies; undertaking contracts in the forward, futures, and/or options markets; and swapping assets/liabilities with other parties. Table 19.5 briefly outlines some of the major hedging tools available to MNCs. By far the most commonly used technique is to hedge with a forward contract.

To demonstrate how you can use a forward contract to hedge exchange rate risk, assume you are a financial manager for Bombardier Inc., which has just booked a sale of three airplanes worth $100,000,000 to Swiss International Air Lines. The sale is denominated in Swiss francs (international sales are generally

TABLE 19.5 **Exchange Rate Risk Hedging Tools**

Tool	Description	Impact on risk
Borrowing or lending	Borrowing or lending in different currencies to take advantage of interest rate differentials and foreign exchange appreciation/depreciation; can be either on a certainty basis with "up-front" costs or speculative.	Can be used to offset exposures in existing assets/liabilities and in expected revenues/expenses.
Forward contract	"Tailor-made" contracts representing an *obligation* to buy/sell, with the amount, rate, and maturity agreed upon between the two parties; has little up-front cost.	Can eliminate downside risk but locks out any upside potential.
Futures contract	Standardized contracts offered on organized exchanges; same basic tool as a forward contract, but less flexible because of standardization; more flexibility because of secondary market access; has some up-front cost/fee.	Can also eliminate downside risk, plus position can be nullified, creating possible upside potential.
Options	Tailor-made or standardized contracts providing the *right* to buy or to sell an amount of the currency, at a particular price, during a specified time period; has up-front cost (premium).	Can eliminate downside risk and retain unlimited upside potential.
Interest rate swap	Allows the trading of one interest rate stream (e.g., on a fixed-rate Canadian dollar instrument) for another (e.g., on a floating rate Canadian dollar instrument); fee to be paid to the intermediary.	Permits firms to change the interest rate structure of their assets/ liabilities and achieves cost savings due to broader market access.
Currency swap	Two parties exchange principal amounts of two different currencies initially; they pay each other's interest payments, then reverse principal amounts at a preagreed exchange rate at maturity; more complex than interest-rate swaps.	All the features of interest-rate swaps, plus it allows firms to change the currency structure of their assets/ liabilities.
Hybrids	A variety of combinations of some of the preceding tools; may be quite costly and/or speculative.	Can create, with the right combination, a perfect hedge against certain exchange rate exposures.

NOTE: The participants in these activities include MNCs, financial institutions, and brokers. The organized exchanges include Amsterdam, Chicago, London, New York, Philadelphia, and Zurich, among others. Although most of these tools can be utilized for short-term exposure management, some, such as swaps, are more appropriate for long-term hedging strategies.

denominated in the customer's currency), and the current spot exchange rate is Sf 1.4175/$ (or, equivalently, $0.7055/Sf). Therefore, you have priced this airplane sale at Sf 141,750,000. If delivery were to occur today, there would be no foreign exchange risk. However, delivery and payment will not occur for 90 days. If this transaction is not hedged, Bombardier will be exposed to significant risk of loss if the Swiss franc depreciates over the next 3 months.

Let us say that between now and the delivery date, the dollar value of the Swiss franc changes from $0.7055/Sf to $0.6061/Sf. Upon delivery of the airplanes, the agreed-upon Sf 141,750,000 will then be worth only $85,914,675 (Sf 141,750,000 × $0.6061/Sf), rather than the $100,000,000 you originally planned for—a foreign exchange loss of over $14 million. If, instead of remaining unhedged, you had sold the Sf 141,750,000 forward 3 months earlier at the 90-day forward rate of $0.7119/Sf offered to you by your bank, you could have locked in a net dollar sale price of $100,911,825 (Sf 141,750,000 × $0.7119/Sf).

Of course, if you remained unhedged, and the Swiss franc appreciated, your firm would have experienced a foreign exchange profit for the firm—but most MNCs prefer to make profits through sales of goods and services rather than by speculating on the direction of exchange rates.

Adjustments in Operations

In responding to exchange rate fluctuations, MNCs can give some protection to international cash flows through appropriate adjustments in assets and liabilities. Two routes are available to a multinational company. The first centres on the operating relationships that a subsidiary of an MNC maintains with *other* firms—*third parties*. Depending on management's expectation of a local currency's position, adjustments in operations would involve the reduction of liabilities if the currency is appreciating or the reduction of financial assets if it is depreciating.

For example, if a Canadian-based MNC with a subsidiary in Mexico expects the Mexican currency to *appreciate* in value relative to the Canadian dollar, local customers' accounts receivable would be *increased* and accounts payable would be reduced if at all possible. Because the dollar is the currency in which the MNC parent will have to prepare consolidated financial statements, the net result in this case would be to favourably increase the Mexican subsidiary's resources in local currency. If the Mexican currency were instead expected to *depreciate,* the local customers' accounts receivable would be *reduced* and accounts payable would be increased, thereby reducing the Mexican subsidiary's resources in the local currency.

The second route focuses on the operating relationship a subsidiary has with its parent or with other subsidiaries within the same MNC. In dealing with exchange rate risks, a subsidiary can rely on *intra-MNC accounts.* Specifically, undesirable exchange rate exposures can be corrected to the extent that the subsidiary can take the following steps:

1. In appreciation-prone countries, intra-MNC accounts receivable are collected as soon as possible, and payment of intra-MNC accounts payable is delayed as long as possible.
2. In depreciation-prone countries, intra-MNC accounts receivable are collected as late as possible, and intra-MNC accounts payable are paid as soon as possible.

This technique is known as "leading and lagging," or simply as "leads and lags."

Example ▼ Assume that a Canadian-based parent company, Canadian Motors (CM), both buys parts from and sells parts to its wholly owned Mexican subsidiary, Tijuana Motors (TM). Assume further that CM has accounts payable of \$10,000,000 that it is scheduled to pay TM in 30 days and, in turn, has accounts receivable of (Mexican peso) MP 75,900,000 due from TM within 30 days. Because today's exchange rate is MP 7.59/C\$, the accounts receivable are also worth \$10,000,000. Therefore, parent and subsidiary owe each other equal amounts (though in different currencies), and both are payable in 30 days, but because TM is a wholly owned subsidiary of CM, the parent has complete discretion over the timing of these payments.

If CM believes that the Mexican peso will depreciate from MP 7.59/C$ to, say, MP 9.00/C$ during the next 30 days, the combined companies can profit by collecting the weak currency (MP) debt immediately, but delaying payment of the strong currency (C$) debt for the full 30 days allowed. If parent and subsidiary do this, and the peso depreciates as predicted, the net result is that the MP 75,900,000 payment from TM to CM is made immediately and is safely converted into $10,000,000 at today's exchange rate, while the delayed $10,000,000 payment from CM to TM will be worth MP 90,000,000 (MP 9.00/C$ × $10,000,000). Thus, the Mexican subsidiary will experience a foreign exchange trading profit of MP 14,100,000 (MP 90,000,000 – MP 75,900,000), whereas the Canadian parent receives the full amount ($10 million) due from TM and therefore is unharmed.

As this example suggests, the manipulation of an MNC's consolidated intracompany accounts by one subsidiary generally benefits one subsidiary (or the parent) while leaving the other subsidiary (or the parent) unharmed. The exact degree and direction of the actual manipulations, however, may depend on the tax status of each country. The MNC obviously would want to have the exchange rate losses in the country with the higher tax rate. Finally, changes in intra-MNC accounts can also be subject to restrictions and regulations put forward by the respective host countries of various subsidiaries.

Credit and Inventory Management

Multinational firms based in different countries compete for the same global export markets. Therefore, it is essential that they offer attractive credit terms to potential customers. Increasingly, however, the maturity and saturation of developed markets is forcing MNCs to maintain and increase revenues by exporting and selling a higher percentage of their output to developing countries. Given the risks associated with the latter group of buyers, as partly evidenced by their lack of a major (hard) currency, the MNC must use a variety of tools to protect such revenues. In addition to the use of hedging and various asset and liability adjustments (described earlier), MNCs should seek the backing of their respective governments in both identifying target markets and extending credit.

Multinationals based in Canada, a number of western European nations, and Japan currently benefit from extensive involvement of government agencies that provide them with the needed service and financial support. In Canada, Export Development Canada (EDC), a Crown corporation, has a mandate to promote and support Canadian exports around the world. The In Practice reading that follows concerns the operation of EDC.

In terms of inventory management, MNCs must consider a number of factors related to both economics and politics. In addition to maintaining the appropriate level of inventory in various locations around the world, a multinational firm is compelled to deal with exchange rate fluctuations, tariffs, nontariff barriers, integration schemes such as the EU, and other rules and regulations. Politically, inventories could be subjected to wars, expropriations, blockages, and other forms of government intervention.

19.2 **IN PRACTICE**

Developing Export Opportunities

Export Development Canada (EDC) is a Canadian Crown corporation. It operates according to commercial principles at arm's length from government, but reports to Parliament. EDC, which has been operating since 1944, is a type of financial institution devoted exclusively to providing trade finance services to support Canadian exporters and investors in 200 markets around the world. Many of these are developing markets that offer a wealth of opportunity for Canadian exporters and investors, but also involve greater risk. EDC helps business assess the long-term potential and manage the increased complexity and risk involved in exporting to these markets. In 2001, EDC supported $45.4 billion in export sales and investments. Without EDC, many of these deals would not have been possible. Nearly 90 percent of EDC's customers are small companies which develop business leads while EDC provides administration and risk management support, such as collections and cash management.

EDC provides Canadian exporters with financing, insurance, and bonding services as well as foreign market expertise to encourage foreign companies to "buy Canadian." Export financing is provided to buyers of Canadian capital goods and services. With export financing in place, an exporter can offer international buyers flexible financing and payment options resulting in a competitive advantage. Financing can be provided as a direct loan, line of credit, or equity investment. Direct loans are a financing arrangement between EDC and a buyer, or a borrower on behalf of a buyer, for a predetermined transaction. Loans usually involve large transactions with long repayment terms. With a line of credit, EDC lends money to foreign purchasers of Canadian goods and services. With the equity program, EDC invests equity in either the Canadian company or a foreign subsidiary of the company.

EDC also provides various types of insurance for exporters. Accounts receivable insurance protects one of the largest assets on many companies' balance sheet. EDC guarantees payment for up to 90 percent of the value of receivables. This insurance protects the exporter if a foreign buyer defaults on payment due to insolvency, the blockage of funds, the refusal of goods by the buyer, or war. Political risk insurance protects an exporter's investments abroad, covering up to 90 percent of the loss. The types of political risk protected include not being able to convert local earnings into hard currencies or get hard currency out of a country, expropriation of assets, or political violence that destroys or shuts down a business.

EDC's business practices were called into question in 2002, when a past chairperson of EDC revealed that $10.7 billion of EDC's total loan portfolio (loans made to foreign companies to buy Canadian goods) of $21 billion was tied up in customers of just two Canadian companies: Nortel Networks and Bombardier. Such a large exposure to just two industries was viewed to be a very dangerous practice. During 2001 and 2002, Nortel was forced to write off billions in financing they provided to customers, and banks around the world have had to write off billions in loans to telecommunications companies. EDC's shareholders' equity totals $2 billion, but it has also set aside $4.1 billion to cover bad loans. Given that EDC's exposure to Nortel's customers was at least $4 billion, it is possible that much of this amount will have to be used to cover these "single-name exposures."

SOURCES: EDC's Trade Finance Services, available at **www.edc.ca/index.htm**; Derek DeCloet, "EDC's Pain Could Soon Be Yours," *National Post*, October 18, 2002, p. FPl; and Ian Jack, "EDC's Exposure to Nortel, Bombardier Draws Fire," *National Post*, October 19, 2002, p. FP1.

? Review Questions

19–13 What is the *Eurocurrency market*? What are the main factors determining foreign exchange rates in that market? Differentiate between the *nominal interest rate* and *effective interest rate* in this market.

19–14 Discuss the steps to be followed in adjusting a subsidiary's accounts relative to third parties when that subsidiary's local currency is expected to *appreciate* in value in relation to the currency of the parent MNC.

19–15 Outline the changes to be undertaken in *intra-MNC accounts* if a subsidiary's currency is expected to *depreciate* in value relative to the currency of the parent MNC.

19.6 Mergers and Joint Ventures

The motives for domestic mergers—growth or diversification, synergy, fund raising, increased managerial skill or technology, tax considerations, increased ownership liquidity, and defence against takeover—are all applicable to MNCs' international mergers and joint ventures. Several additional points should also be made.

First, international mergers and joint ventures, especially those involving U.S. firms acquiring Canadian firms, Canadian firms acquiring U.S. firms, and European firms acquiring assets in the United States, increased significantly beginning in the 1980s. MNCs based in western Europe, Japan, and North America are numerous. Moreover, a fast-growing group of MNCs has emerged in the past two decades, based in the so-called newly industrializing countries (which include, among others, Brazil, Argentina, Mexico, Hong Kong, Singapore, South Korea, Taiwan, India, and Pakistan).

Even though many of these companies were hit very hard by the economic problems arising in Asia after July 1997 and following the collapse of the Russian economy in August 1998, top firms from the region have been able to survive and even prosper. Additionally, many Western companies have taken advantage of these economies' weakness to buy into companies that were previously off limits to foreign investors. This has added further to the number and value of international mergers.

Foreign direct investments in North America, the economic engine of the world, have also significantly increased recently. Most of the foreign direct investment is generated between the three North American countries—Canada, the United States, and Mexico—but also comes from six other major countries: Britain, France, the Netherlands, Japan, Switzerland, and Germany. The heaviest investments are concentrated in manufacturing, followed by the petroleum and trade/service sectors. Another trend is the current increase in the number of joint ventures between companies based in Japan and firms domiciled elsewhere in the industrialized world, especially U.S.-based MNCs. Although Japanese authorities continue their discussions and debates with other governments regarding Japan's international trade surpluses as well as perceived trade barriers, mergers and joint ventures continue to take place. In the eyes of some corporate executives, such business ventures are viewed as a "ticket into the Japanese market" as well as a way to curb a potentially tough competitor.

Developing countries, too, have been attracting foreign direct investments in many industries. Meanwhile, during the last two decades, a number of these nations have adopted specific policies and regulations aimed at controlling the inflows of foreign investments, a major provision being the 49 percent ownership limitation applied to MNCs. Of course, international competition among MNCs has benefited some developing countries in their attempts to extract concessions from the multinationals. However, an increasing number of such nations have shown greater flexibility in recent dealings with MNCs, as MNCs have become more reluctant to form joint ventures under the stated conditions. Furthermore, it is likely that as more developing countries recognize the need for foreign capital and technology, they will show even greater flexibility in their agreements with MNCs.

A final point relates to the existence of international holding companies. Places such as Liechtenstein and Panama have long been considered promising spots for forming holding companies because of their favourable legal, corporate, and tax environments. International holding companies control many business entities in the form of subsidiaries, branches, joint ventures, and other agreements. For international legal (especially tax-related) reasons, as well as anonymity, such holding companies have become increasingly popular in recent years.

? Review Question

19–16 What are some of the major reasons for the rapid expansion in international mergers and joint ventures of firms?

SUMMARY

LG1 **Understand the major factors influencing the financial operations of multinational companies (MNCs).** Four important trading blocs in the Americas and Europe have emerged over the last 15 years: NAFTA (Canada, the United States, Mexico); the European Union (EU); the Mercosur Group in South America; and the FTAA. The EU is becoming even more competitive as it achieves monetary union and most of its members use the euro as a single currency. Free trade among the largest economic powers is governed by the General Agreement on Tariffs and Trade (GATT) and is policed by the World Trade Organization (WTO).

Setting up operations in foreign countries can entail special problems due to the legal form of business organization chosen, the degree of ownership allowed by the host country, and possible restrictions and regulations on the return of capital and profits. Taxation of multinational companies is a complex issue because of the existence of varying tax rates, differing definitions of taxable income, measurement differences, and tax treaties.

The existence and expansion of dollars held outside the United States have contributed to the development of a major international financial market, the Euromarket. The large international banks, developing and industrialized nations, and multinational companies participate as borrowers and lenders in this market.

LG2 **Describe the key differences between purely domestic and international financial statements: the consolidation of financial statements and the translation of individual accounts.** Regulations that apply to international operations complicate the preparation of foreign-based financial statements. Canadian accounting rules require the consolidation of financial statements of subsidiaries according to the percentage of ownership by the parent in the subsidiary. Individual accounts of subsidiaries must be translated back into Canadian dollars using the procedures outlined in Section 1650 of the *CICA Handbook*. Regulations also require that only certain transactional gains or losses from international operations be included in the Canadian parent's income statement.

LG3 **Discuss exchange rate risk and political risk, and explain how MNCs manage them.** Economic exposure from exchange rate risk results from the existence of different currencies and the potential impact they can have on the value of foreign operations. Long-term changes in foreign exchange rates result primarily from differing inflation rates in the two countries. The money markets, the forward (futures) markets, and the foreign currency options markets can be used to hedge foreign exchange exposure. Political risks stem mainly from political instability and from the associated implications for the assets and operations of MNCs. MNCs can employ negative, external, and positive approaches to cope with political risk.

LG4 **Describe foreign direct investment, investment cash flows and decisions, the factors that influence MNCs' capital structure, and the international debt and equity instruments that are available to MNCs.** Foreign direct investment (FDI) involves an MNC's transfer of capital, managerial, and technical assets from its home country to the host country. The investment cash flows of FDIs are subject to a variety of factors, including taxes in host countries, regulations that may block the return (repatriation) of MNCs' cash flow, the usual business and financial risks, risks stemming from inflation and from currency and political actions by host governments, and the application of a local cost of capital.

The capital structures of MNCs differ from those of purely domestic firms because of the MNCs' access to the Euromarket and the financial instruments it offers; the ability to reduce risk in their cash flows through international diversification; and the impact of legal, tax, political, social, and financial factors unique to each host country. MNCs can raise long-term debt through the issuance of international bonds in various currencies. Foreign bonds are sold primarily in the country of the currency of issue; Eurobonds are sold primarily in countries other than the country of the currency in which the issue is denominated. MNCs can raise equity through the sale of their shares in the international capital markets or through joint ventures. In establishing foreign subsidiaries, it may be more advantageous to issue debt than MNC-owned equity.

LG5 **Explain the use of the Eurocurrency market in short-term borrowing and investing (lending) and the basics of cash, credit, and inventory management in international operations.** Eurocurrency markets allow multinationals to invest (lend) and raise (borrow) short-term funds in a variety of currencies and to protect themselves against exchange rate risk exposures. Effective interest rates, which take into account each currency's forecast percentage change relative to the MNC parent's currency, are the main items considered by an MNC in making investment and borrowing decisions. The MNC invests in the currency with the highest effective rate and borrows in the currency with the lowest effective rate. MNCs must offer competitive credit terms and maintain adequate inventories to provide timely delivery to foreign buyers. Obtaining the backing of foreign governments is helpful to the MNC in effectively managing credit and inventory.

LG6 **Discuss the growth of and special factors relating to international mergers and joint ventures.** International mergers and joint ventures, including international holding companies, increased significantly in the last decade. Special factors affecting these mergers include economic and trade conditions and various regulations imposed on MNCs by host countries.

SELF-TEST PROBLEM

(Solution in Appendix B)

ST 19–1 Tax credits A Canadian-based MNC has a foreign subsidiary that has earnings before interest and local taxes of $150,000. All of the subsidiary's after-tax funds are to be available to be paid to the parent company. The applicable taxes consist of a 32 percent foreign income tax rate, a foreign payment withholding tax rate of 8 percent, and a Canadian tax rate of 34 percent. Calculate the net funds available to the parent MNC if:

a. The foreign subsidiary earns active business income, is in a treaty country, pays no interest, and returns all after-tax funds to the parent MNC through dividends.

b. The foreign subsidiary makes a $150,000 interest payment to the Canadian MNC.

c. Should the foreign operation be financed with debt or equity capital?

PROBLEMS

19–1 Tax credits A Canadian-based MNC has a foreign subsidiary that earns $250,000 before local taxes, with all the after-tax funds to be available to be paid to the parent. The applicable taxes consist of a 33 percent foreign income tax rate, a foreign payment withholding tax rate of 9 percent, and a Canadian tax rate of 34 percent.

a. Calculate the net funds available to the parent MNC if:

(1) The foreign subsidiary earns active business income, is in a treaty country, pays no interest, and returns all after-tax funds to the parent MNC through dividends;

(2) The foreign subsidiary makes a $150,000 interest payment to the Canadian MNC.

b. Should the foreign operation be financed with debt or equity capital?

19–2 Translation of financial statements A Canadian-based MNC has a subsidiary in France (local currency, Euro). The balance sheet and income statement of the subsidiary follow. On December 31, 2008, the exchange rate is Euro 1.50/C$. Assume that the local (Euro) figures for the statements remain the same on December 31, 2009. Calculate the Canadian dollar–translated figures for the two ending time periods, assuming that between December 31, 2008 and 2009 the Euro has appreciated against the Canadian dollar by 6 percent.

Translation of income statement			
	12/31/08		12/31/09
	Euro	C$	C$
Sales	3,000		
Cost of goods sold	2,750	______	______
Operating profits	250	______	______

Translation of balance sheet			
Cash	40		
Inventory	300		
Plant and equipment (net)	160	______	______
Total	500	______	______
Liabilities and shareholders' equity			
Debt	240		
Paid-in capital	200		
Retained earnings	60	______	______
Total	500	______	______

CHALLENGE  19–3 **Euromarket investment and fund raising** A Canadian-based multinational company has two subsidiaries, one in Mexico (local currency, Mexican peso, MP) and one in Japan (local currency, yen, ¥). Forecasts of business operations indicate the following short-term financing position for each subsidiary (in equivalent Canadian dollars):

Mexico: $80 million excess cash to be invested (lent)
Japan: $60 million funds to be raised (borrowed)

The management gathered the following data:

	Currency		
Item	C$	MP	¥
Spot exchange rates		MP 9.18/C$	¥126.7/C$
Forecast % change		+1.5%	+1.0%
Interest rates			
Nominal			
Euromarket	5.0%	6.5%	6.2%
Domestic	4.5	6.1	5.7
Effective			
Euromarket			
Domestic			

Determine the *effective* interest rates for all three currencies in both the Euromarket and the domestic market; then indicate where the funds should be invested and raised. (*Note:* Assume that because of local regulations, a subsidiary is *not* permitted to use the domestic market of *any other* subsidiary.)

CASE CHAPTER 19

Assessing a Direct Investment in Chile by Canadian Computer Corporation

See the enclosed Student CD-ROM for cases that help you put theories and concepts from the text into practice.

Be sure to visit the Companion Website for this book at **www.pearsoned.ca/gitman** for a wealth of additional learning tools including self-test quizzes, Web exercises, and additional cases.

Appendix A

Financial Tables

TABLE A-1 Future Value Interest Factors for One Dollar Compounded at k Percent for n Periods:

$$FVIF\ (k\%, n \text{ per}) = (1 + k)^n$$

TABLE A-2 Future Value Interest Factors for a One-Dollar Annuity Compounded at k Percent for n Periods:

$$FVIFa\ (k\%, n \text{ per}) = \left[\frac{(1 + k)^n - 1}{k}\right]$$

TABLE A-3 Present Value Interest Factors for One Dollar Discounted at k Percent for n Periods:

$$PVIF\ (k\%, n \text{ per}) = \frac{1}{(1 + k)^n}$$

TABLE A-4 Present Value Interest Factors for a One-Dollar Annuity Discounted at k Percent for n Periods:

$$PVIFa\ (k\%, n \text{ per}) = \left[\frac{1 - \dfrac{1}{(1 + k)^n}}{k}\right]$$

TABLE A-1 Future Value Interest Factors for One Dollar Compounded at k Percent for n Periods: $FVIF\ (k\%, n\ \text{per}) = (1 + k)^n$

Period	1%	2%	3%	4%	5%	6%	7%	8%	9%	10%	11%	12%	13%	14%	15%	16%	17%	18%	19%	20%
1	1.010	1.020	1.030	1.040	1.050	1.060	1.070	1.080	1.090	1.100	1.110	1.120	1.130	1.140	1.150	1.160	1.170	1.180	1.190	1.200
2	1.020	1.040	1.061	1.082	1.102	1.124	1.145	1.166	1.188	1.210	1.232	1.254	1.277	1.300	1.322	1.346	1.369	1.392	1.416	1.440
3	1.030	1.061	1.093	1.125	1.158	1.191	1.225	1.260	1.295	1.331	1.368	1.405	1.443	1.482	1.521	1.561	1.602	1.643	1.685	1.728
4	1.041	1.082	1.126	1.170	1.216	1.262	1.311	1.360	1.412	1.464	1.518	1.574	1.630	1.689	1.749	1.811	1.874	1.939	2.005	2.074
5	1.051	1.104	1.159	1.217	1.276	1.338	1.403	1.469	1.539	1.611	1.685	1.762	1.842	1.925	2.011	2.100	2.192	2.288	2.386	2.488
6	1.062	1.126	1.194	1.265	1.340	1.419	1.501	1.587	1.677	1.772	1.870	1.974	2.082	2.195	2.313	2.436	2.565	2.700	2.840	2.986
7	1.072	1.149	1.230	1.316	1.407	1.504	1.606	1.714	1.828	1.949	2.076	2.211	2.353	2.502	2.660	2.826	3.001	3.185	3.379	3.583
8	1.083	1.172	1.267	1.369	1.477	1.594	1.718	1.851	1.993	2.144	2.305	2.476	2.658	2.853	3.059	3.278	3.511	3.759	4.021	4.300
9	1.094	1.195	1.305	1.423	1.551	1.689	1.838	1.999	2.172	2.358	2.558	2.773	3.004	3.252	3.518	3.803	4.108	4.435	4.785	5.160
10	1.105	1.219	1.344	1.480	1.629	1.791	1.967	2.159	2.367	2.594	2.839	3.106	3.395	3.707	4.046	4.411	4.807	5.234	5.695	6.192
11	1.116	1.243	1.384	1.539	1.710	1.898	2.105	2.332	2.580	2.853	3.152	3.479	3.836	4.226	4.652	5.117	5.624	6.176	6.777	7.430
12	1.127	1.268	1.426	1.601	1.796	2.012	2.252	2.518	2.813	3.138	3.498	3.896	4.334	4.818	5.350	5.936	6.580	7.288	8.064	8.916
13	1.138	1.294	1.469	1.665	1.886	2.133	2.410	2.720	3.066	3.452	3.883	4.363	4.898	5.492	6.153	6.886	7.699	8.599	9.596	10.699
14	1.149	1.319	1.513	1.732	1.980	2.261	2.579	2.937	3.342	3.797	4.310	4.887	5.535	6.261	7.076	7.987	9.007	10.147	11.420	12.839
15	1.161	1.346	1.558	1.801	2.079	2.397	2.759	3.172	3.642	4.177	4.785	5.474	6.254	7.138	8.137	9.265	10.539	11.974	13.589	15.407
16	1.173	1.373	1.605	1.873	2.183	2.540	2.952	3.426	3.970	4.595	5.311	6.130	7.067	8.137	9.358	10.748	12.330	14.129	16.171	18.488
17	1.184	1.400	1.653	1.948	2.292	2.693	3.159	3.700	4.328	5.054	5.895	6.866	7.986	9.276	10.761	12.468	14.426	16.672	19.244	22.186
18	1.196	1.428	1.702	2.026	2.407	2.854	3.380	3.996	4.717	5.560	6.543	7.690	9.024	10.575	12.375	14.462	16.879	19.673	22.900	26.623
19	1.208	1.457	1.753	2.107	2.527	3.026	3.616	4.316	5.142	6.116	7.263	8.613	10.197	12.055	14.232	16.776	19.748	23.214	27.251	31.948
20	1.220	1.486	1.806	2.191	2.653	3.207	3.870	4.661	5.604	6.727	8.062	9.646	11.523	13.743	16.366	19.461	23.105	27.393	32.429	38.337
21	1.232	1.516	1.860	2.279	2.786	3.399	4.140	5.034	6.109	7.400	8.949	10.804	13.021	15.667	18.821	22.574	27.033	32.323	38.591	46.005
22	1.245	1.546	1.916	2.370	2.925	3.603	4.430	5.436	6.658	8.140	9.933	12.100	14.713	17.861	21.644	26.186	31.629	38.141	45.923	55.205
23	1.257	1.577	1.974	2.465	3.071	3.820	4.740	5.871	7.258	8.954	11.026	13.552	16.626	20.361	24.891	30.376	37.005	45.007	54.648	66.247
24	1.270	1.608	2.033	2.563	3.225	4.049	5.072	6.341	7.911	9.850	12.239	15.178	18.788	23.212	28.625	35.236	43.296	53.108	65.031	79.496
25	1.282	1.641	2.094	2.666	3.386	4.292	5.427	6.848	8.623	10.834	13.585	17.000	21.230	26.461	32.918	40.874	50.656	62.667	77.387	95.395
30	1.348	1.811	2.427	3.243	4.322	5.743	7.612	10.062	13.267	17.449	22.892	29.960	39.115	50.949	66.210	85.849	111.061	143.367	184.672	237.373
35	1.417	2.000	2.814	3.946	5.516	7.686	10.676	14.785	20.413	28.102	38.574	52.799	72.066	98.097	133.172	180.311	243.495	327.988	440.691	590.657
40	1.489	2.208	3.262	4.801	7.040	10.285	14.974	21.724	31.408	45.258	64.999	93.049	132.776	188.876	267.856	378.715	533.846	750.353	1051.642	1469.740
45	1.565	2.438	3.781	5.841	8.985	13.764	21.002	31.920	48.325	72.888	109.527	163.985	244.629	363.662	538.752	795.429	1170.425	1716.619	2509.583	3657.176
50	1.645	2.691	4.384	7.106	11.467	18.419	29.456	46.900	74.354	117.386	184.559	288.996	450.711	700.197	1083.619	1670.669	2566.080	3927.189	5988.730	9100.191

USING THE CALCULATOR TO COMPUTE THE FUTURE VALUE OF A SINGLE AMOUNT

Before you begin: Make sure your calculator is set for *one payment per year* and that you are in the end mode for calculations. Also, for any problem where you are only using three time value functions, be sure to put a zero in the time value function that is not being used. An alternative is to clear the memory of the calculator before beginning a time value calculation.

SAMPLE PROBLEM

You place $800 in a savings account at 6 percent compounded annually. What is your account balance at the end of 5 years?

Hewlett-Packard HP 12C, 17 BII, and 19 BII[a]

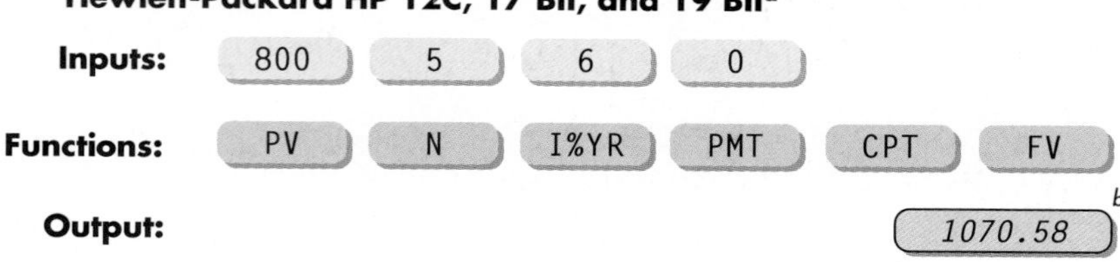

[a]For the 12C, you would use the n key instead of the N key, and the i key instead of the I%YR key.
[b]If a minus sign precedes the output, it should be ignored.

TABLE A-1 (Continued)

Period	21%	22%	23%	24%	25%	26%	27%	28%	29%	30%	31%	32%	33%	34%	35%	40%	45%	50%
1	1.210	1.220	1.230	1.240	1.250	1.260	1.270	1.280	1.290	1.300	1.310	1.320	1.330	1.340	1.350	1.400	1.450	1.500
2	1.464	1.488	1.513	1.538	1.562	1.588	1.613	1.638	1.664	1.690	1.716	1.742	1.769	1.796	1.822	1.960	2.102	2.250
3	1.772	1.816	1.861	1.907	1.953	2.000	2.048	2.097	2.147	2.197	2.248	2.300	2.353	2.406	2.460	2.744	3.049	3.375
4	2.144	2.215	2.289	2.364	2.441	2.520	2.601	2.684	2.769	2.856	2.945	3.036	3.129	3.224	3.321	3.842	4.421	5.063
5	2.594	2.703	2.815	2.932	3.052	3.176	3.304	3.436	3.572	3.713	3.858	4.007	4.162	4.320	4.484	5.378	6.410	7.594
6	3.138	3.297	3.463	3.635	3.815	4.001	4.196	4.398	4.608	4.827	5.054	5.290	5.535	5.789	6.053	7.530	9.294	11.391
7	3.797	4.023	4.259	4.508	4.768	5.042	5.329	5.629	5.945	6.275	6.621	6.983	7.361	7.758	8.172	10.541	13.476	17.086
8	4.595	4.908	5.239	5.589	5.960	6.353	6.767	7.206	7.669	8.157	8.673	9.217	9.791	10.395	11.032	14.758	19.541	25.629
9	5.560	5.987	6.444	6.931	7.451	8.004	8.595	9.223	9.893	10.604	11.362	12.166	13.022	13.930	14.894	20.661	28.334	38.443
10	6.727	7.305	7.926	8.594	9.313	10.086	10.915	11.806	12.761	13.786	14.884	16.060	17.319	18.666	20.106	28.925	41.085	57.665
11	8.140	8.912	9.749	10.657	11.642	12.708	13.862	15.112	16.462	17.921	19.498	21.199	23.034	25.012	27.144	40.495	59.573	86.498
12	9.850	10.872	11.991	13.215	14.552	16.012	17.605	19.343	21.236	23.298	25.542	27.982	30.635	33.516	36.644	56.694	86.380	129.746
13	11.918	13.264	14.749	16.386	18.190	20.175	22.359	24.759	27.395	30.287	33.460	36.937	40.745	44.912	49.469	79.371	125.251	194.620
14	14.421	16.182	18.141	20.319	22.737	25.420	28.395	31.691	35.339	39.373	43.832	48.756	54.190	60.181	66.784	111.119	181.614	291.929
15	17.449	19.742	22.314	25.195	28.422	32.030	36.062	40.565	45.587	51.185	57.420	64.358	72.073	80.643	90.158	155.567	263.341	437.894
16	21.113	24.085	27.446	31.242	35.527	40.357	45.799	51.923	58.808	66.541	75.220	84.953	95.857	108.061	121.713	217.793	381.844	656.841
17	25.547	29.384	33.758	38.740	44.409	50.850	58.165	66.461	75.862	86.503	98.539	112.138	127.490	144.802	164.312	304.911	553.674	985.261
18	30.912	35.848	41.523	48.038	55.511	64.071	73.869	85.070	97.862	112.454	129.086	148.022	169.561	194.035	221.822	426.875	802.826	1477.892
19	37.404	43.735	51.073	59.567	69.389	80.730	93.813	108.890	126.242	146.190	169.102	195.389	225.517	260.006	299.459	597.625	1164.098	2216.838
20	45.258	53.357	62.820	73.863	86.736	101.720	119.143	139.379	162.852	190.047	221.523	257.913	299.937	348.408	404.270	836.674	1687.942	3325.257
21	54.762	65.095	77.268	91.591	108.420	128.167	151.312	178.405	210.079	247.061	290.196	340.446	398.916	466.867	545.764	1171.343	2447.515	4987.883
22	66.262	79.416	95.040	113.572	135.525	161.490	192.165	228.358	271.002	321.178	380.156	449.388	530.558	625.601	736.781	1639.878	3548.896	7481.824
23	80.178	96.887	116.899	140.829	169.407	203.477	244.050	292.298	349.592	417.531	498.004	593.192	705.642	838.305	994.653	2295.829	5145.898	11222.738
24	97.015	118.203	143.786	174.628	211.758	256.381	309.943	374.141	450.974	542.791	652.385	783.013	938.504	1123.328	1342.781	3214.158	7461.547	16834.109
25	117.388	144.207	176.857	216.539	264.698	323.040	393.628	478.901	581.756	705.627	854.623	1033.577	1248.210	1505.258	1812.754	4499.816	10819.242	25251.164
30	304.471	389.748	497.904	634.810	807.793	1025.904	1300.477	1645.488	2078.208	2619.936	3297.081	4142.008	5194.516	6503.285	8128.426	24201.043	69348.375	191751.000
35	789.716	1053.370	1401.749	1861.020	2465.189	3258.053	4296.547	5653.840	7423.988	9727.598	12719.918	16598.906	21617.363	28096.695	36448.051	130158.687	*	*
40	2048.309	2846.941	3946.340	5455.797	7523.156	10346.879	14195.051	19426.418	26520.723	36117.754	49072.621	66519.313	89962.188	121388.437	163433.875	700022.688	*	*
45	5312.758	7694.418	11110.121	15994.316	22958.844	32859.457	46897.973	66748.500	94739.937	134102.187	*	*	*	*	*	*	*	*
50	13779.844	20795.680	31278.301	46889.207	70064.812	104354.562	154942.687	229345.875	338440.000	497910.125	*	*	*	*	*	*	*	*

*Not shown due to space limitations.

Texas Instruments BA-35, BAII, BAII Plus[c]

Inputs:	800	5	6	0		
Functions:	PV	N	%i	PMT	CPT	FV
Output:						1070.58[d]

[c]For the Texas Instruments BAII, you would use the 2nd key instead of the CPT key; for the Texas Instruments BAII Plus, you would use the I/Y key instead of the %i key.

[d]If a minus sign precedes the output, it should be ignored.

TABLE A-2 **Future Value Interest Factors for a One-Dollar Annuity Compounded at k Percent for n Periods:** $FVIFa\,(k\%, n\text{ per}) = \left[\frac{(1+k)^n - 1}{k}\right]$

Period	1%	2%	3%	4%	5%	6%	7%	8%	9%	10%	11%	12%	13%	14%	15%	16%	17%	18%	19%	20%
1	1.000	1.000	1.000	1.000	1.000	1.000	1.000	1.000	1.000	1.000	1.000	1.000	1.000	1.000	1.000	1.000	1.000	1.000	1.000	1.000
2	2.010	2.020	2.030	2.040	2.050	2.060	2.070	2.080	2.090	2.100	2.110	2.120	2.130	2.140	2.150	2.160	2.170	2.180	2.190	2.200
3	3.030	3.060	3.091	3.122	3.152	3.184	3.215	3.246	3.278	3.310	3.342	3.374	3.407	3.440	3.472	3.506	3.539	3.572	3.606	3.640
4	4.060	4.122	4.184	4.246	4.310	4.375	4.440	4.506	4.573	4.641	4.710	4.779	4.850	4.921	4.993	5.066	5.141	5.215	5.291	5.368
5	5.101	5.204	5.309	5.416	5.526	5.637	5.751	5.867	5.985	6.105	6.228	6.353	6.480	6.610	6.742	6.877	7.014	7.154	7.297	7.442
6	6.152	6.308	6.468	6.633	6.802	6.975	7.153	7.336	7.523	7.716	7.913	8.115	8.323	8.535	8.754	8.977	9.207	9.442	9.683	9.930
7	7.214	7.434	7.662	7.898	8.142	8.394	8.654	8.923	9.200	9.487	9.783	10.089	10.405	10.730	11.067	11.414	11.772	12.141	12.523	12.916
8	8.286	8.583	8.892	9.214	9.549	9.897	10.260	10.637	11.028	11.436	11.859	12.300	12.757	13.233	13.727	14.240	14.773	15.327	15.902	16.499
9	9.368	9.755	10.159	10.583	11.027	11.491	11.978	12.488	13.021	13.579	14.164	14.776	15.416	16.085	16.786	17.518	18.285	19.086	19.923	20.799
10	10.462	10.950	11.464	12.006	12.578	13.181	13.816	14.487	15.193	15.937	16.722	17.549	18.420	19.337	20.304	21.321	22.393	23.521	24.709	25.959
11	11.567	12.169	12.808	13.486	14.207	14.972	15.784	16.645	17.560	18.531	19.561	20.655	21.814	23.044	24.349	25.733	27.200	28.755	30.403	32.150
12	12.682	13.412	14.192	15.026	15.917	16.870	17.888	18.977	20.141	21.384	22.713	24.133	25.650	27.271	29.001	30.850	32.824	34.931	37.180	39.580
13	13.809	14.680	15.618	16.627	17.713	18.882	20.141	21.495	22.953	24.523	26.211	28.029	29.984	32.088	34.352	36.786	39.404	42.218	45.244	48.496
14	14.947	15.974	17.086	18.292	19.598	21.015	22.550	24.215	26.019	27.975	30.095	32.392	34.882	37.581	40.504	43.672	47.102	50.818	54.841	59.196
15	16.097	17.293	18.599	20.023	21.578	23.276	25.129	27.152	29.361	31.772	34.405	37.280	40.417	43.842	47.580	51.659	56.109	60.965	66.260	72.035
16	17.258	18.639	20.157	21.824	23.657	25.672	27.888	30.324	33.003	35.949	39.190	42.753	46.671	50.980	55.717	60.925	66.648	72.938	79.850	87.442
17	18.430	20.012	21.761	23.697	25.840	28.213	30.840	33.750	36.973	40.544	44.500	48.883	53.738	59.117	65.075	71.673	78.978	87.067	96.021	105.930
18	19.614	21.412	23.414	25.645	28.132	30.905	33.999	37.450	41.301	45.599	50.396	55.749	61.724	68.393	75.836	84.140	93.404	103.739	115.265	128.116
19	20.811	22.840	25.117	27.671	30.539	33.760	37.379	41.446	46.018	51.158	56.939	63.439	70.748	78.968	88.211	98.603	110.283	123.412	138.165	154.739
20	22.019	24.297	26.870	29.778	33.066	36.785	40.995	45.762	51.159	57.274	64.202	72.052	80.946	91.024	102.443	115.379	130.031	146.626	165.417	186.687
21	23.239	25.783	28.676	31.969	35.719	39.992	44.865	50.422	56.764	64.002	72.264	81.698	92.468	104.767	118.809	134.840	153.136	174.019	197.846	225.024
22	24.471	27.299	30.536	34.248	38.505	43.392	49.005	55.456	62.872	71.402	81.213	92.502	105.489	120.434	137.630	157.414	180.169	206.342	236.436	271.028
23	25.716	28.845	32.452	36.618	41.430	46.995	53.435	60.893	69.531	79.542	91.147	104.602	120.203	138.295	159.274	183.600	211.798	244.483	282.359	326.234
24	26.973	30.421	34.426	39.082	44.501	50.815	58.176	66.764	76.789	88.496	102.173	118.154	136.829	158.656	184.166	213.976	248.803	289.490	337.007	392.480
25	28.243	32.030	36.459	41.645	47.726	54.864	63.248	73.105	84.699	98.346	114.412	133.333	155.616	181.867	212.790	249.212	292.099	342.598	402.038	471.976
30	34.784	40.567	47.575	56.084	66.438	79.057	94.459	113.282	136.305	164.491	199.018	241.330	293.192	356.778	434.738	530.306	647.423	790.932	966.698	1181.865
35	41.659	49.994	60.461	73.651	90.318	111.432	138.234	172.314	215.705	271.018	341.583	431.658	546.663	693.552	881.152	1120.699	1426.448	1816.607	2314.173	2948.294
40	48.885	60.401	75.400	95.024	120.797	154.758	199.630	259.052	337.872	442.580	581.812	767.080	1013.667	1341.979	1779.048	2360.724	3134.412	4163.094	5529.711	7343.715
45	56.479	71.891	92.718	121.027	159.695	212.737	285.741	386.497	525.840	718.881	986.613	1358.208	1874.086	2590.464	3585.031	4965.191	6879.008	9531.258	13203.105	18280.914
50	64.461	84.577	112.794	152.664	209.341	290.325	406.516	573.756	815.051	1163.865	1668.723	2399.975	3459.344	4994.301	7217.488	10435.449	15088.805	21812.273	31514.492	45496.094

USING THE CALCULATOR TO COMPUTE THE FUTURE VALUE OF AN ANNUITY

Before you begin: Make sure your calculator is set for *one payment per year* and that you are in the end mode for calculations. Also, for any problem where you are only using three time value functions, be sure to put a zero in the time value function that is not being used. An alternative is to clear the memory of the calculator before beginning a time value calculation.

SAMPLE PROBLEM

You want to know what the future value will be at the end of 5 years if you place 5 end-of-year deposits of $1,000 in an account paying 7 percent annually. What is your account balance at the end of 5 years?

Hewlett-Packard HP 12C, 17 BII, and 19 BII[a]

Inputs: 1000 | 5 | 7 | 0

Functions: PMT | N | I%YR | PV | CPT | FV

Output: 5750.74[b]

[a]For the 12C, you would use the n key instead of the N key, and the i key instead of the I%YR key.

[b]If a minus sign precedes the output, it should be ignored.

TABLE A-2 (Continued)

Period	21%	22%	23%	24%	25%	26%	27%	28%	29%	30%	31%	32%	33%	34%	35%	40%	45%	50%
1	1.000	1.000	1.000	1.000	1.000	1.000	1.000	1.000	1.000	1.000	1.000	1.000	1.000	1.000	1.000	1.000	1.000	1.000
2	2.210	2.220	2.230	2.240	2.250	2.260	2.270	2.280	2.290	2.300	2.310	2.320	2.330	2.340	2.350	2.400	2.450	2.500
3	3.674	3.708	3.743	3.778	3.813	3.848	3.883	3.918	3.954	3.990	4.026	4.062	4.099	4.136	4.172	4.360	4.552	4.750
4	5.446	5.524	5.604	5.684	5.766	5.848	5.931	6.016	6.101	6.187	6.274	6.362	6.452	6.542	6.633	7.104	7.601	8.125
5	7.589	7.740	7.893	8.048	8.207	8.368	8.533	8.700	8.870	9.043	9.219	9.398	9.581	9.766	9.954	10.946	12.022	13.188
6	10.183	10.442	10.708	10.980	11.259	11.544	11.837	12.136	12.442	12.756	13.077	13.406	13.742	14.086	14.438	16.324	18.431	20.781
7	13.321	13.740	14.171	14.615	15.073	15.546	16.032	16.534	17.051	17.583	18.131	18.696	19.277	19.876	20.492	23.853	27.725	32.172
8	17.119	17.762	18.430	19.123	19.842	20.588	21.361	22.163	22.995	23.858	24.752	25.678	26.638	27.633	28.664	34.395	41.202	49.258
9	21.714	22.670	23.669	24.712	25.802	26.940	28.129	29.369	30.664	32.015	33.425	34.895	36.429	38.028	39.696	49.152	60.743	74.887
10	27.274	28.657	30.113	31.643	33.253	34.945	36.723	38.592	40.556	42.619	44.786	47.062	49.451	51.958	54.590	69.813	89.077	113.330
11	34.001	35.962	38.039	40.238	42.566	45.030	47.639	50.398	53.318	56.405	59.670	63.121	66.769	70.624	74.696	98.739	130.161	170.995
12	42.141	44.873	47.787	50.895	54.208	57.738	61.501	65.510	69.780	74.326	79.167	84.320	89.803	95.636	101.840	139.234	189.734	257.493
13	51.991	55.745	59.778	64.109	68.760	73.750	79.106	84.853	91.016	97.624	104.709	112.302	120.438	129.152	138.484	195.928	276.114	387.239
14	63.909	69.009	74.528	80.496	86.949	93.925	101.465	109.611	118.411	127.912	138.169	149.239	161.183	174.063	187.953	275.299	401.365	581.858
15	78.330	85.191	92.669	100.815	109.687	119.346	129.860	141.302	153.750	167.285	182.001	197.996	215.373	234.245	254.737	386.418	582.980	873.788
16	95.779	104.933	114.983	126.010	138.109	151.375	165.922	181.867	199.337	218.470	239.421	262.354	287.446	314.888	344.895	541.985	846.321	1311.681
17	116.892	129.019	142.428	157.252	173.636	191.733	211.721	233.790	258.145	285.011	314.642	347.307	383.303	422.949	466.608	759.778	1228.165	1968.522
18	142.439	158.403	176.187	195.993	218.045	242.583	269.885	300.250	334.006	371.514	413.180	459.445	510.792	567.751	630.920	1064.689	1781.838	2953.783
19	173.351	194.251	217.710	244.031	273.556	306.654	343.754	385.321	431.868	483.968	542.266	607.467	680.354	761.786	852.741	1491.563	2584.665	4431.672
20	210.755	237.986	268.783	303.598	342.945	387.384	437.568	494.210	558.110	630.157	711.368	802.856	905.870	1021.792	1152.200	2089.188	3748.763	6648.508
21	256.013	291.343	331.603	377.461	429.681	489.104	556.710	633.589	720.962	820.204	932.891	1060.769	1205.807	1370.201	1556.470	2925.862	5436.703	9973.762
22	310.775	356.438	408.871	469.052	538.101	617.270	708.022	811.993	931.040	1067.265	1223.087	1401.215	1604.724	1837.068	2102.234	4097.203	7884.215	14961.645
23	377.038	435.854	503.911	582.624	673.626	778.760	900.187	1040.351	1202.042	1388.443	1603.243	1850.603	2135.282	2462.669	2839.014	5737.078	11433.109	22443.469
24	457.215	532.741	620.810	723.453	843.032	982.237	1144.237	1332.649	1551.634	1805.975	2101.247	2443.795	2840.924	3300.974	3833.667	8032.906	16579.008	33666.207
25	554.230	650.944	764.596	898.082	1054.791	1238.617	1454.180	1706.790	2002.608	2348.765	2753.631	3226.808	3779.428	4424.301	5176.445	11247.062	24040.555	50500.316
30	1445.111	1767.044	2160.459	2640.881	3227.172	3941.953	4812.891	5873.172	7162.785	8729.805	10632.543	12940.672	15737.945	19124.434	23221.258	60500.207	154105.313	383500.000
35	3755.814	4783.520	6090.227	7750.094	9856.746	12527.160	15909.480	20188.742	25596.512	32422.090	41028.887	51868.563	65504.199	82634.625	104134.500	325394.688	*	*
40	9749.141	12936.141	17153.691	22728.367	30088.621	39791.957	52570.707	69376.562	91447.375	120389.375	*	*	*	*	*	*	*	*
45	25294.223	34970.230	48300.660	66638.937	91831.312	126378.937	173692.875	238384.312	326686.375	447005.062	*	*	*	*	*	*	*	*

*Not shown due to space limitations.

Texas Instruments BA-35, BAII, BAII Plus[c]

Inputs: 1000 | 5 | 7 | 0

Functions: PMT | N | %i | PV | CPT | FV

Output: 5750.74[d]

[c]For the Texas Instruments BAII, you would use the 2nd key instead of the CPT key; for the Texas Instruments BAII Plus, you would use the I/Y key instead of the %i key.

[d]If a minus sign precedes the output, it should be ignored.

TABLE A-3 Present Value Interest Factors for One Dollar Discounted at *k* Percent for *n* Periods:

$$PVIF\ (k\%,\ n\ \text{per}) = \frac{1}{(1+k)^n}$$

Period	1%	2%	3%	4%	5%	6%	7%	8%	9%	10%	11%	12%	13%	14%	15%	16%	17%	18%	19%	20%
1	.990	.980	.971	.962	.952	.943	.935	.926	.917	.909	.901	.893	.885	.877	.870	.862	.855	.847	.840	.833
2	.980	.961	.943	.925	.907	.890	.873	.857	.842	.826	.812	.797	.783	.769	.756	.743	.731	.718	.706	.694
3	.971	.942	.915	.889	.864	.840	.816	.794	.772	.751	.731	.712	.693	.675	.658	.641	.624	.609	.593	.579
4	.961	.924	.888	.855	.823	.792	.763	.735	.708	.683	.659	.636	.613	.592	.572	.552	.534	.516	.499	.482
5	.951	.906	.863	.822	.784	.747	.713	.681	.650	.621	.593	.567	.543	.519	.497	.476	.456	.437	.419	.402
6	.942	.888	.837	.790	.746	.705	.666	.630	.596	.564	.535	.507	.480	.456	.432	.410	.390	.370	.352	.335
7	.933	.871	.813	.760	.711	.665	.623	.583	.547	.513	.482	.452	.425	.400	.376	.354	.333	.314	.296	.279
8	.923	.853	.789	.731	.677	.627	.582	.540	.502	.467	.434	.404	.376	.351	.327	.305	.285	.266	.249	.233
9	.914	.837	.766	.703	.645	.592	.544	.500	.460	.424	.391	.361	.333	.308	.284	.263	.243	.225	.209	.194
10	.905	.820	.744	.676	.614	.558	.508	.463	.422	.386	.352	.322	.295	.270	.247	.227	.208	.191	.176	.162
11	.896	.804	.722	.650	.585	.527	.475	.429	.388	.350	.317	.287	.261	.237	.215	.195	.178	.162	.148	.135
12	.887	.789	.701	.625	.557	.497	.444	.397	.356	.319	.286	.257	.231	.208	.187	.168	.152	.137	.124	.112
13	.879	.773	.681	.601	.530	.469	.415	.368	.326	.290	.258	.229	.204	.182	.163	.145	.130	.116	.104	.093
14	.870	.758	.661	.577	.505	.442	.388	.340	.299	.263	.232	.205	.181	.160	.141	.125	.111	.099	.088	.078
15	.861	.743	.642	.555	.481	.417	.362	.315	.275	.239	.209	.183	.160	.140	.123	.108	.095	.084	.074	.065
16	.853	.728	.623	.534	.458	.394	.339	.292	.252	.218	.188	.163	.141	.123	.107	.093	.081	.071	.062	.054
17	.844	.714	.605	.513	.436	.371	.317	.270	.231	.198	.170	.146	.125	.108	.093	.080	.069	.060	.052	.045
18	.836	.700	.587	.494	.416	.350	.296	.250	.212	.180	.153	.130	.111	.095	.081	.069	.059	.051	.044	.038
19	.828	.686	.570	.475	.396	.331	.277	.232	.194	.164	.138	.116	.098	.083	.070	.060	.051	.043	.037	.031
20	.820	.673	.554	.456	.377	.312	.258	.215	.178	.149	.124	.104	.087	.073	.061	.051	.043	.037	.031	.026
21	.811	.660	.538	.439	.359	.294	.242	.199	.164	.135	.112	.093	.077	.064	.053	.044	.037	.031	.026	.022
22	.803	.647	.522	.422	.342	.278	.226	.184	.150	.123	.101	.083	.068	.056	.046	.038	.032	.026	.022	.018
23	.795	.634	.507	.406	.326	.262	.211	.170	.138	.112	.091	.074	.060	.049	.040	.033	.027	.022	.018	.015
24	.788	.622	.492	.390	.310	.247	.197	.158	.126	.102	.082	.066	.053	.043	.035	.028	.023	.019	.015	.013
25	.780	.610	.478	.375	.295	.233	.184	.146	.116	.092	.074	.059	.047	.038	.030	.024	.020	.016	.013	.010
30	.742	.552	.412	.308	.231	.174	.131	.099	.075	.057	.044	.033	.026	.020	.015	.012	.009	.007	.005	.004
35	.706	.500	.355	.253	.181	.130	.094	.068	.049	.036	.026	.019	.014	.010	.008	.006	.004	.003	.002	.002
40	.672	.453	.307	.208	.142	.097	.067	.046	.032	.022	.015	.011	.008	.005	.004	.003	.002	.001	.001	.001
45	.639	.410	.264	.171	.111	.073	.048	.031	.021	.014	.009	.006	.004	.003	.002	.001	.001	.001	*	*
50	.608	.372	.228	.141	.087	.054	.034	.021	.013	.009	.005	.003	.002	.001	.001	.001	*	*	*	*

**PVIF* is zero to three decimal places.

USING THE CALCULATOR TO COMPUTE THE PRESENT VALUE OF A SINGLE AMOUNT

Before you begin: Make sure your calculator is set for *one payment per year* and that you are in the End mode for calculations. Also, for any problem where you are only using three time value functions, be sure to put a zero in the time value function that is not being used. An alternative is to clear the memory of the calculator before beginning a time value calculation.

SAMPLE PROBLEM

You want to know the present value of $1,700 to be received at the end of 8 years, assuming an 8 percent discount rate.

Hewlett-Packard HP 12C, 17 BII, and 19 BII[a]

Inputs:	1700	8	8	0		
Functions:	FV	N	I%YR	PMT	CPT	PV
Output:						918.46[b]

[a]For the 12C, you would use the n key instead of the N key, and the i key instead of the I%YR key.

[b]The minus sign that precedes the output should be ignored.